The Pub Guide 2004

Welcome to the 2004 edition of the AA Pub Guide, fully updated with essential information on nearly 2500 pubs and inns across England, Scotland, Wales, the Channel Islands and, new for 2004, the Isle of Man. We have sought out pubs that are attractive, interesting or in a good location, but above all ones that provide good food and drink in a convivial atmosphere.

Produced by AA Publishing
Directory compiled by AA Hotel Services Department
Directory generated by the AA Establishment Database, Information Research, AA Hotel Services

Advertisement Sales: advertisingsales@theAA.com

Editorial: lifestyleguides@theAA.com

Maps prepared by the Cartography Department of
The Automobile Association
Maps © Automobile Association
Developments Limited 2003

Ordnance Survey® This product includes mapping data licensed from Ordnance Survey® with the permission of the Controller of Her Majesty's Stationery Office.
© Crown copyright 2004
All rights reserved. Licence number 399221

A CIP catalogue record for this book is available from the British Library.

Published by AA Publishing, which is a trading name of Automobile Association Developments Limited whose registered office is Millstream, Maidenhead Road, Windsor, Berkshire, SL4 5GD

Registered number 1878835.

ISBN 0 7495 37558

A02231

Design by Kingswood Graphics, Theale Road, Burghfield, Berkshire RG30 3TP

Editors: Jo Sturges & Denise Laing

Editorial Contributors: Philip Bryant, Nick Channer, David Foster, Julia Hynard, Denise Laing, Philip Round and Jenny White

Cover photograph: The Half Moon Inn, Kirdford

Title page photograph: George III Hotel, Penmaenpool

*Hand*PICKED

*Terms and Conditions

This offer is valid for new bookings taken between 1st October 2003 and 30th September 2004. Bookings are subject to availability and standard Classic Break terms and conditions apply (available in the Classic Breaks brochure). All bookings to be made via Central Reservations on 0845 458 0901 quoting AA-CV1. The number of rooms available at this special AA rate is limited and this offer cannot be used in conjunction with any promotion and excludes Christmas, New Year, Easter, Bank Holidays and major sporting events. This discount is only valid for a two night break booked on a dinner, bed and breakfast basis where two adults share a standard room.

Contents

Welcome to the AA Pub Guide 2004

We aim to bring you the country's best pubs, selected for their atmosphere, great food and good beer. Ours is the only major pub guide to feature colour photographs, and to highlight the 'Pick of the Pubs', uncovering Britain's finest hostelries. Updated every year, this year you will find lots of old favourites as well as plenty of new destinations, including the Isle of Man, for eating and drinking and great places to stay across Britain.

Who's in the Guide?

We make our selection by seeking out pubs that are worth making a detour for - 'destination' pubs - with publicans exhibiting real enthusiasm for their trade and offering a good selection of well-kept drinks and fine food. Pubs make no payment for their inclusion in our guide. They are included entirely at our discretion.

That Special Place

We look for pubs that offer something special: pubs where the time-honoured values of a convivial environment for conversation while supping or eating have not been forgotten. They may be attractive, interesting, unusual or in a good location. Some may be very much a local pub or they may draw customers from further afield, while others may be included because they are in an exceptional place. Interesting towns and villages, eccentric or historic buildings, and rare settings can all be found within this guide.

Tempting Food

We are looking for menus that show a commitment to home cooking, making good use of local produce wherever possible, and offering an appetising range of freshly-prepared dishes. Pubs presenting well-executed traditional dishes like ploughman's or pies, or those offering innovative bar or restaurant food, are all in the running. In keeping with recent trends in pub food, we are keen to include those where particular emphasis is placed on imaginative modern dishes and those specialising in fresh fish.

Pick of the Pubs & Full Page Entries

Some of the pubs included in the guide are particularly special, and we have highlighted these as Pick of the Pubs. For 2004 over 550 pubs have been selected by the personal knowledge of our editorial team, our AA inspectors, and suggestions from our readers. These pubs have a coloured panel and a more detailed description. From these, about 80 have chosen to enhance their entry in the 2004 Guide with two photographs as part of a full-page entry.

Tell us what you think

We welcome your feedback about the pubs included and about the guide itself. We are also delighted to receive suggestions about good pubs you have visited and loved. Reader Report forms appear at the very back of the book, so please write in or e-mail us at lifestyleguides@theAA.com to help us improve future editions. The pubs also feature on the AA internet site, **www.theAA.com**, along with our inspected restaurants, hotels and bed & breakfast accommodation.

AA PUB OF THE YEAR AWARD
for England, Scotland and Wales

Selected with the help of our AA inspectors we have chosen three worthy winners for this prestigious award.

The winners stand out for being great all-round pubs or inns, combining a great pub atmosphere, a warm welcome from friendly efficient hosts and staff with excellent food, well-kept beers and comfortable accommodation. We expect enthusiasm and a high standard of management from hands-on owners.

Pictures of the winning pubs appear on the opening page for each country section in the guide.

PUB OF THE YEAR FOR ENGLAND
The Blue Ball
Triscombe, Somerset
see entry on page 424

PUB OF THE YEAR FOR SCOTLAND
The Plockton Hotel
Plockton, Highlands
see entry on page 593

PUB OF THE YEAR FOR WALES
Pendre Inn
Cilgerran, Pembrokeshire
see entry on page 625

Where Everybody Knows Your Name

Everybody likes visiting pubs, even really famous celebrities, and it is amazing how many of our historical figures can be found in them too. On page 11 Julia Hynard looks at the many pubs where you can see live celebrities or walk in the shoes of dead ones, or find yourself in a scene you would recognise from a film.

Beer Festivals

For 2004 we have added a list of beer festivals as so many of our readers are enthusiastic about them. This enthusiasm is shared by publicans and micro-brewers, with increasing numbers running their own festivals. The list is on pages 18 and 19 so you can plan your visits to the pubs mentioned.

New Walks for 2004

As a popular feature of our guide book we have yet again included about 40 Pub Walks to try. Not too challenging - between 3 and 6 miles in length - perfect for building up a healthy appetite or working off a filling meal.

Walk directions and details are supplied by the pubs featured in these pages. There is a complete list of all the walks on page 645 in the index section at the back of the book.

How to use the Guide

① — NICEPLACE — Map 01 TG22 — **②**

④ — **The Fox Inn** ⊛♦♦♦ 🕙 ♀ **NEW** — **③**
Sand-next-the-Sea SD23 1NL
⑤ — ☎ 01114 71144444 📄 01114 71133333 **email:** foxypub.co.uk
Dir: *From A4 to Hambleton, then R on to B161 to Wartham.*
Timeless 14th-century village pub within easy reach of the
coast. Unspoilt bars, real ale from the cask, and hearty
English cooking using fresh local ingredients. Typical
dishes include game pie, cheese baked crab, ham and
lentil soup, chicken and rabbit pie and, for pudding,
golden syrup sponge. B&B in adjoining cottage.
⑥ — **OPEN:** 11.30-2.30, 6-11, closed 25 Dec **BAR MEALS:** Lunch — **⑦**
⑧ — served all week 12-2,Dinner served Fri & Sat 6.30-8.30. Av main
course £6.80. **RESTAURANT:** Dinner Thu-Sat 7-10.30
⑨ — **BREWERY/COMPANY:** Free House. 🍺: Greene King IPA, — **⑩**
Woodfordes Wherry, guest beers. ♀**10 FACILITIES:** Children's — **⑪**
licence; family area;. Garden, outdoor eating.
⑫ — **NOTES:** Parking 10 No credit cards.
ROOMS: 5 bedrooms 1 en suite. From s £24 d £42 — **⑬**

① **Guide Order**
Pubs are listed alphabetically
by name (ignoring The)
under their village or town.
Towns and villages are listed
alphabetically within their
county (a county map
appears at the back of the
guide). The guide has entries
for England, Channel Islands,
Isle of Man, Scotland and
Wales in that order.

Some village pubs prefer to be
initially located under the
nearest town, in which case
the village name is included in
the address and directions.

Pick of the Pubs
Over 550 of the best pubs in
Britain have been selected by
the editor and inspectors and
highlighted. They have longer,
more detailed descriptions and
a tinted background. Around
80 have a full page entry and
two photographs.

② **Map Reference**
The map reference number
denotes the map page number
in the atlas section at the back
of the book and (except for
London maps) the National
Grid reference. London
references help locate their
position on the Central London
and Greater London maps.

③ **Symbols**
See Symbols in the column on
page 7.

④ **Address and Postcode**
This gives the street name
plus the postcode. If necessary
the name of the village is
included (see 1 above). This
may be up to five miles from
the named Location.

☎ Telephone number

📄 Fax number

email: Wherever possible
we have included
an email address

⑤ **Directions**
Directions are given only
when they have been supplied
by the proprietor.

⑥ **OPEN** indicates the hours and
dates when the establishment
is open and closed.

⑦ **BAR MEALS** indicates the
times and days when
proprietors tell us bar food
can be ordered and the
average price of a main
course as supplied by the
proprietor. Please be aware
that last orders could vary by
up to 30 minutes.

⑧ **RESTAURANT** indicates the
times and days when
proprietors tell us food can be
ordered from the restaurant.
The average cost of a 3-course
à la carte meal and a 3- or 4-
course fixed-price menu are

shown as supplied by the proprietor. Last orders may be approximately 30 minutes before the times stated.

⑨ FREE HOUSE indicates that the pub is independently owned and run. The COMPANY name indicates the name of the Brewery to which the pub is tied or the Company who owns it.

⑩ ◖ The beer tankard symbol indicates the principal beers sold by the pub. Up to five cask or hand-pulled beers served by each pub are listed. Many pubs have a much greater selection, with several guest beers each week.

⑬ ROOMS Only accommodation that has been inspected by The AA, RAC, VisitBritain, VisitScotland or the Welsh Tourist Board is included. AA stars and diamonds are shown at the beginning of an entry. Small stars or diamonds appearing under ROOMS indicates that the accommodation has been inspected by one of the other organisations.

The number of bedrooms and the number of en suite bedrooms are listed. Accommodation prices indicate the minimum single and double room prices per night. Breakfast is generally included in the price, but guests should check when making a reservation.

Circumstances and prices may vary during the currency of the Guide so please check when booking.

♀ The wine glass symbol followed by a number indicates the number of wines sold by the glass.

⑪ FACILITIES This section includes information on children (i.e. if a pub welcomes children, has a children's licence etc), and gardens (e.g. outdoor eating, barbecue area). We also indicate where dogs are welcome.

⑫ NOTES Information on parking and credit cards.

Credit Cards Not Taken
As so many establishments take one or more of the major credit cards only those taking no cards are indicated.

Symbols

◉ Rosettes
The AA's food award.
Explanation on page 9

★ Stars
The rating for Hotel accommodation.
Explanation on page 8

👜 Restaurants with Rooms
Category of inspected accommodation (see page 8)

♦ Diamonds
The rating for Bed and Breakfast accommodation.
Explanation on page 8

🐟 In conjunction with the Seafish Industry Authority, we include a symbol to indicate that a pub serves a minimum of four main course dishes with sea fish as the main ingredient.

♀ Indicates the number of wines available by the glass

◖ Denotes the principle beers sold.

NEW Pubs appearing in the guide for the first time in 2004

London Congestion Charging Scheme

From 17th February 2003 Transport for London (TfL) introduced a congestion charging scheme for most vehicles being used in a designated zone in Central London (roughly all the roads inside the Inner Ring Road and marked on the London maps in this guide).

The charge is an area licence – vehicles used in the central London area must be registered. You pay £5 for the day (zone operates 7am-6.30pm weekdays) and can cross into and out of the zone as much as you want within the day. If your journey takes you into the charging

zone you must either pre-pay the £5 charge or pay it before 10pm that day. Between 10pm and midnight the charge increases to £10 to encourage prompt payment.

The system's controlled using a database of registered car registration numbers and a network of numberplate-reading cameras around and in the zone. At midnight each day all paid accounts are deleted from the system. Any vehicle recorded as having been in the zone during charging hours but with an unpaid account must pay a penalty charge.

Payment can be made at any time

via the call centre 0845 900 1234

via the congestion charging website www.cclondon.com

at paystations, selected petrol stations and retailers displaying the PayPoint logo

For further details on London Congestion Charges see the AA website **www.TheAA.com**. The AA produces a Central Congestion Charging Zone Map obtainable from bookshops or from the AA Travel Bookshop on 01256 491524.

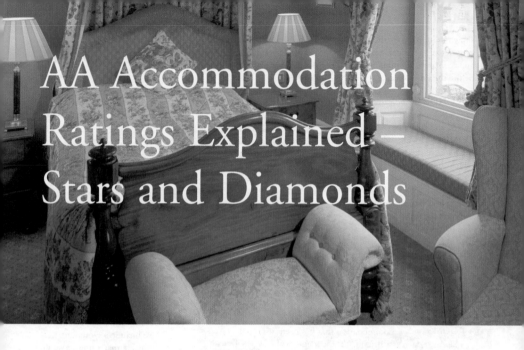

AA Accommodation Ratings Explained – Stars and Diamonds

Where the following AA ratings appear under 'Rooms' in the guide, the establishment has been inspected under nationally recognised Classification schemes. These ratings ensure that your accommodation meets the AA's highest standards of cleanliness with the emphasis on professionalism, proper booking procedures and a prompt and efficient service.

AA Star Classification ★

If you stay in a one-star hotel you should expect a relatively informal yet competent style of service and an adequate range of facilities, including a television in the lounge or bedroom and a reasonable choice of hot and cold dishes. The majority of bedrooms are en suite with a bath or shower room always available.

A two-star hotel is run by smartly and professionally presented management and offers at least one restaurant or dining room for breakfast and dinner, while a three-star hotel includes direct dial telephones, a wide selection of drinks in the bar and last orders for dinner no earlier than 8pm.

A four-star hotel is characterised by uniformed, well-trained staff with additional services, a night porter and a serious approach to cuisine. Finally, and most luxurious of all, is the five-star hotel offering many extra facilities, attentive staff, top quality rooms and a full concierge service. A wide selection of drink, including cocktails, is available in the bar and the impressive menu reflects and complements the hotel's own style of cooking.

The AA's Top 200 Hotels in Britain and Ireland are identified by red stars. These stand out as the very best and range from large luxury destination hotels to snug country inns. To find further details see the AA's internet site at www.theAA.com

AA Diamond Awards ♦

The AA's Diamond Awards cover bed and breakfast establishments only, reflecting guest accommodation at five grades of quality, with one diamond indicating the simplest and five diamonds the upper end of the scale. The criteria for eligibility is guest care and quality rather than the choice of extra facilities.

Establishments are vetted by a team of qualified inspectors to ensure that the accommodation, food and hospitality meet the AA's own exacting standards.

Guests should receive a prompt professional check in and check out, comfortable accommodation equipped to modern standards, regularly changed bedding and towels, a sufficient hot water supply at all times, good well-prepared meals and a full English or continental breakfast.

Restaurants with Rooms 🏠

A Restaurant with Rooms is usually a local (or national) destination for eating out which also offers accommodation, albeit on a smaller scale. Most have 12 bedrooms or less, and public areas may be limited to the restaurant itself. No star or diamond rating is shown in the guide but bedrooms reflect at least the level of quality normally associated with a two star hotel. A red symbol indicates a restaurant with rooms that is amongst the AA's top 200 hotels in Britain and Ireland.

How the AA assesses restaurants for Rosette Awards

Our Philosophy

The team of inspectors assessing for The Restaurant Guide are passionate about good food. They are not looking for restaurants to fail, they are hoping that they will succeed. Nothing brings them greater pleasure than to find a restaurant offering really good cooking at whatever level. Although the Rosette levels are significant in indicating the relative merits of the cooking they are not the whole picture. Many of their own favourite restaurants are to be found at the one and two Rosette levels. They have a belief in honest, intelligent cooking and when they are inspecting, they will have these basic principles in mind:

1. Good cooking is only possible with good quality ingredients, so the chef's first aim should be to acquire and bring out the best in those raw materials.

2. The best ingredients are attained by seeking out fresh, seasonal and in many cases, local produce.

3. Classic dishes and combinations are timeless for the very good reason that they work and the best cooking is underpinned by these principles. Innovation can add excitement and an extra dimension to dishes but it needs to be introduced with intelligence and

understanding. Innovation for its own sake rarely succeeds.

4. Over-complicated dishes with a surfeit of elements are much less likely to succeed.

Excellent local restaurants serving food prepared with care, understanding and skill, using good quality ingredients. These restaurants that stand out in their local area. The same expectations apply to hotel restaurants where guests should be able to eat in with confidence and a sense of anticipation. Around 50% of restaurants with rosettes.

The best local restaurants, which aim for and achieve higher standards, better consistency and where a greater precision is apparent in the cooking. There will be obvious attention to the selection of quality ingredients. Around 40% of restaurants with rosettes.

Outstanding restaurants that demand recognition well beyond their local area. The cooking will be underpinned by the selection and sympathetic treatment of the highest quality ingredients. Timing,

seasoning and the judgement of flavour combinations will be consistently excellent, supported by other elements such as intelligent service and a well-chosen wine list. Around 150 restaurants (less than 10% of those with rosettes).

Amongst the very best restaurants in the British Isles where the cooking demands national recognition. These restaurants will exhibit intense ambition, a passion for excellence, superb technical skills and remarkable consistency. They will combine appreciation of culinary traditions with a passionate desire for further exploration and improvement. Around a dozen restaurants with four rosettes.

The finest restaurants in the British Isles, where the cooking stands comparison with the best in the world. These restaurants will have highly individual voices, exhibit breathtaking culinary skills and set the standards to which others aspire. Around half a dozen restaurants with five rosettes.

How can I get away without the hassle of finding a place to stay?

Booking a place to stay can be a time-consuming process. You choose a place you like, only to find it's fully booked. That means going back to the drawing board again. Why not ask us to find the place that best suits your needs? No fuss, no worries and no booking fee.

Whatever your preference, we have the place for you. From a rustic farm cottage to a smart city centre hotel - we have them all. Choose from around 8,000 quality rated hotels and B&Bs in Great Britain and Ireland.

Just AAsk.

Hotel Booking Service
www.theAA.com

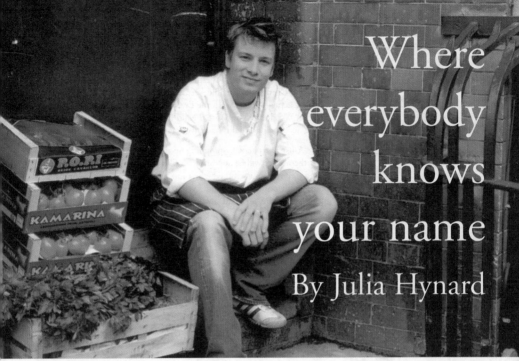

Where everybody knows your name

By Julia Hynard

Celebrated pubs and pub celebrities

The pub 'where everybody knows your name' can have wearisome connotations for those constantly in the public eye, so don't expect any revelations from us on where Liam and Nicole call in for a pint - after all, this is the Pub Guide, and if anyone knows the value of a quiet drink ... That being said, many landlords have been happy to drop a name or two and some we are delighted to share.

Major celebrity hangouts are generally more Hampstead than Hackney, but that's not to say that the capital has the monopoly. In fact some of the most out-of-the-way pubs in the most beautiful parts of the British Isles are total celebrity magnets.

The role call of show business personalities at the Feathers Hotel, Ledbury or the Hare Arms, Stow Bardolph would grace an awards ceremony, but as the landlord of Ye Olde White Bear, London NW3 says, 'Our customers range from dustmen to Hollywood stars and all are treated the same - with courtesy'.

The Red Lion at Burnsall welcomed the film crew of The Calendar Girls (the story of the Rylstone WI nude calendar) and hosted the end of location party. Manchester's Dukes 92 has entertained the cast of Cold Feet and Coronation Street; the Greyhound Inn, Staple Fitzpaine caters for the Tabasco-loving tastes of the Animal Hospital crew, and The Friar's Head at Akebar has in turn welcomed the production team of All Creatures Great and Small and the cast of Heartbeat (who certainly get around), while cast members of EastEnders turn up all over the country.

The Nags Head at Little Hadham, Hertfordshire has its fair share of celebrity visitors, but landlord Kevin Robinson gleefully recalls a time when Fairport Convention lived in the village and held a free concert on Brick Hill - that was the day the pub ran out of beer!

Diners at Glasgow's Ubiquitous Chip range from Mick Jagger to the late Nina Simone, but it was Delia Smith who fell in love with the Caledonian oatmeal ice cream.

Apparently Gary Barlow played keyboard at the Boot Inn, Tarpoley in his early days, and the Cricketers at Clavering played a formative role in the career of celebrity chef Jamie Oliver. We are told that young Jamie started work in their kitchen at the age of eight - and his parents are still running the place!

The War-Bill-in-Tun Inn, Warbleton, was the Beatles' watering hole in the 60s, and Old House Inn at Llangynwyd, near Maesteg was a regular rendezvous of Richard Burton and Elizabeth Taylor in the 70s, while the New Inn, Tresco (Scilly Isles) was a favourite of Harold Wilson's. More recently Tony Blair has entertained French Prime Minister Chirac at The County, Aycliffe Village, in the PM's own Sedgefield constituency.

On location

The most important factor in attracting a celebrity clientele would seem to be location. Somewhere not too far from every major theatrical venue there is a bar where thirsty thespians get together, like the Fire Station, London SE1, close to the Old Vic; the Everyman Bistro, Liverpool, which is actually underneath the Everyman Theatre; and The Red Lion, London W5, located opposite the old Ealing Studios and known as 'Stage Six' (Ealing Studios have five stages).

If the A-list aren't actually propping up the bar the chances are that the pubs themselves will be appearing on film. The Tan Hill Inn at Keld is proud to proclaim itself the highest inn in Great Britain but is probably more familiar as the pub in the Everest Double Glazing ad. Here are a few more stars of the large and smaller screen:

Film credits

Black Lion Hotel, Walsingham	*Waterlands*
Blue Lion, East Witton	*Heartbeat*
Castle Inn, Chiddingstone	*Room with a View, Wicked Lady, Wind in the Willows, Elizabeth R and The Life of Hogarth (filmed in village)*
Earl Arms, Heydon	*Love on a Branch Line, Monty Python, Hitler's Britain and Uprising*
George Inn, Lacock	*Pride and Prejudice, Moll Flanders and Harry Potter (filmed in village)*
Golden Galleon, Exceat	*Great Expectations*
Grenadier, London SW1	*Around the World in 80 Days*
Kings Arms, Amersham	*Four Weddings and a Funeral*
Kings Head Hotel, Masham	*Heartbeat*
Lord Nelson, Brightwell Baldwin	*Midsomer Murders*
Market Porter, London SE1	*Entrapment, Lock Stock and Two Smoking Barrels, American Girls, The Bill and Only Fools and Horses*
Phelips Arms, Montacute	*Sense and Sensibility*
Queens Head Inn, Tirril	*If Only*
Red Lion, London W1	*Spy Game*
Ship Inn, Elie	*The Winter Guest*
Stag & Huntsman Inn, Hambleden	*Band of Brothers, My Uncle Silas and Daniel Deronda (filmed in village)*
Strines Inn, Bradfield Dale	*Heartlands*
Volunteer Inn, Chipping Campden	*Crush*

It should also be noted that three devoted regulars at the White Hart, Oldham were the inspiration for Compo, Clegg and Blamire in the BBC's Last of the Summer Wine.

Literary licence

Enduring fame, the kind that lasts through centuries, marks great achievement, often in the literary world, and as far as pubs go it has to be said that Charles Dickens and Robert Burns got about a bit. More than a dozen pubs in the Guide have been visited by Charles Dickens, and several appear in his books, like the Grapes, London E14, which he used as a model for the 'Six Jolly Fellowship Porters' in *Our Mutual Friend*.

The Black Bull in Moffat was frequented by the Scottish Bard Robert Burns, and it was here that he etched onto a window the famous 'Epigram to a scrimpit nature'. The etched window was later lost (apparently to the Tsar of Russia) though the pub now has a replica in its place. Rabbie drank at the Kirkton Inn, Dalrymple (if he knew his father wasn't in), and was a customer of the Auldgirth Inn, Auldgirth, when he lived at Ellisland Farm, which was owned by Patrick Miller, the creator of the world's first steamboat which was launched in nearby Dalswinton Loch in 1788.

Wilkie Collins reputedly met his mistress in the Fishermans Return, Winterton-on-Sea; J R R Tolkein was a regular at the Shireburn

Facing Page: The George Hotel, Dolgellau, Gwynedd. A location for Casualty and Blind Date, as well as accommodation for the cast and crew of medieval movie First Knight. The visitors book has also been signed by Victorian poet, Gerard Manley Hopkins.

Arms, Clitheroe and the Pheasant Inn, Brill, and Thomas Hardy used to call in at The Anchor in Chideock when visiting friends a couple of doors up. The George Inn at Hubberholme was a favourite haunt of J B Priestly and his ashes are scattered in the local churchyard. R D Blackmore wrote part of *Lorna Doone* at The Crown Hotel, Exford, and another bit at the Rising Sun at Lynmouth. The Bloomsbury Group hung out at the Lamb, London WC1, and the Talbot in Frome is the original home of the nursery rhyme 'Little Jack Horner'.

Many famous people have passed through the portals of the Black Bull, Coniston, including John Ruskin, Turner, Coleridge and de Quincey (on his way to visit Wordsworth). In the early 1800s the Queens Head at Tirril belonged to the Wordsworth family and deeds signed by William Wordsworth are displayed in the bar.

So, dear reader, wherever it is you take a drink, the chances are you're not too far from some celebrity's footsteps. And as you frown on some recalcitrant smoker at the bar, you might muse on the precedent set by Sir Walter Raleigh when he first lit his pipe in the Dolphin Tavern, Penzance in 1586.

Above: A young Charles Dickens

Seafood
- the perfect choice

Whether you're looking for a light and exotic dish or a hearty but healthy meal – seafood is the perfect choice when eating out. You can have it poached, barbecued, fried, stir-fried, baked or steamed, but seafood also tastes great when lightly grilled with a squeeze of lemon.

With up to 100 different species of seafood available in the UK, seafood is a versatile and healthy option, with dishes to suit everyone's taste. From Cullen Skink to Tuna Nicoise or steamed mussels with garlic and white wine, you can find a wide range of succulent and tasty fish and shellfish meals in pubs around Great Britain. So go on, try something new next time you are in a pub and surprise yourself with how wonderful seafood can be.

Good Seafood Served Here

Keen to help you find all the best seafood pub meals, the Sea Fish Industry Authority (Seafish) works with the **AA Pub Guide** to help distinguish the very best sea food pubs in the country. This guide provides you with details of around 800 British pubs that serve excellent seafood dishes. Finding them is easy: your nearest pub is marked with the fish symbol that stands for 'Good Seafood Served Here'. We have also chosen overall winners for England, Scotland and Wales, all of which are highlighted in this guide. Look out for the pubs with a light blue background.

Seafood is delicious and offers oceans of choice when eating out!

Sea Fish Industry Authority, 18 Logie Mill, Logie Green Road, Edinburgh EH7 4HG
Tel: 0131 558 3331 Fax: 0131 558 1442
E-mail: marketing@seafish.co.uk Website: www.seafish.co.uk

Serving the seafood industry

AA Seafood Pubs of the Year

Seafish, the Sea Fish Industry Authority exists to promote the use of seafood throughout the UK. With over 60 different species available from UK waters and many more from abroad, seafood is a healthy option that offers a great diversity of flavours and textures. For the 2004 guide we have sought out some of the pubs that make the most of seafood on their menus and produce the finest fish and shellfish dishes in the country.

England

A great dining pub and hotel, where this stylish modern restaurant is well worth discovering within the 16th-century building

The Hoste Arms

Burnham Market, Norfolk

(see page 324 for full entry)

Scotland

A contemporary stained glass window leaves no doubt about the theme of this specialist restaurant, set in a Highland fishing village

Plockton Inn & Seafood Restaurant

Plockton, Highland

(see page 594 for full entry)

Wales

Seafood doesn't come much fresher than in this display in the upmarket Caesars Arms restaurant, located just 10 miles from the Welsh capital

Caesars Arms

Creigiau, Cardiff

(see page 606 for full entry)

Beer Festivals

Beer festivals are an established part of both the serious beer drinker's life, and many pubs' calendars. Literally hundreds of them are held every year throughout the country. They range from large traditional gatherings that attract a wide following for sometimes several days of unselfconscious consumption of unique or unusual ales, to local or impromptu but none the less enthusiastic celebrations of the hop.

We have listed just a small selection of beer festivals here, many sponsored by CAMRA. The dates are likely to change from year to year, though the months generally remain the same. For up-to-date information, please check directly with the pub or look on the CAMRA website at www.camra.org.uk. We would love to hear from our readers about their favourite beer festivals. E-mail us at lifestyleguides@theAA.com., so that we can include your favourite venue in the 2005 Pub Guide.

JANUARY

Cambridge Winter Ale Festival,
Anglia Polytechnic, off East Road, Cambridge

14th Bent & Bongs Beer Bash (Atherton Beer festival),
Formby Hall, High St, Atherton, Manchester

FEBRUARY

14th Battersea Beer Festival,
Battersea Grand Hall, Lavender Hill, London SW11

Derby Winter Beer Festival,
Assembly Rooms, Market Place, Derby

FEBRUARY/MARCH

Bradford Beer Festival, Victoria Hall, Saltaire, W Yorks

Bristol Beer festival, Council House, College Green, Bristol

MARCH

Leeds Beer Festival,
Pudsey Civic Hall, Dawsons Corner, Pudsey, W Yorks

Hitchin Beer Festival, Town Hall, Hitchin, Herts

Walsall Beer Festival, Town Hall, Leicester St,
Walsall, W Midlands

East Anglian Beer Festival,
Corn Exchange, Bury St Edmunds, Suffolk

6th Fife Beer Festival The Rothes Hall, Glenrothes, Fife

MAY

The Golden Heart, Birdlip, Glos

The Hoop, Stock, Essex

31st Cambridge Beer Festival, Jesus Green, Cambridge

10th Reading Beer Festival, Kings Meadow, Reading, Berks

Stourbridge Beer Festival, Town Hall, Stourbridge, W Midlands

Newark Beer Festival, Riverside Park, Newark on Trent, Notts

JUNE

The Hill House, Happisburgh, Norfolk

The Victoria, Lincoln, Lincs

JULY

30th Kent Beer Festival,
Cowshed, Merton Farm, Merton Lane, Canterbury, Kent

28th Cotswold Beer Festival,
Postlip Hall, nr Winchcombe, Glos

6th Devizes Beer Festival, The Wharf, Devizes, Wilts

27th Derby Beer Festival,
Assembly Rooms, Market Place, Derby

8th Southampton Beer Festival, Guildhall,
West Marlands Road, Southampton, Hants

8th Southdowns Beer & Cider Festival, The Old Corn and Hop Exchange,
Lewes Town Hall, Lewes, E. Sussex

AUGUST

Great British Beer Festival, Olympia, London

Angel Inn, Larling, Norfolk

The Flower Pots Inn, Cheriton, Hants

Peterborough Beer Festival,
River Embankment, Peterborough, Cambs

The Surrey Oaks, Newdigate, Surrey

AA Pub Of The Year for England

The Blue Ball, Triscombe, Somerset

ENGLAND

England

ENGLAND

BEDFORDSHIRE

BEDFORD
Map 12 TL04

The Three Tuns
57 Main Rd, Biddenham MK40 4BD ☎ 01234 354847

A thatched village pub with a large garden, play area and dovecote. It has a friendly atmosphere, and is popular for its wide-ranging bar menu. Choose from sandwiches and snacks or popular main courses like burgers, seafood platter, and steaks with fries. There's also a range of home-made dishes such as the steak and kidney pie, curry of the day, seafood platter, steak in red wine, and peppered pork. Children's meals are also available.
OPEN: 11-2.30 6-11 (Sun 12-3, 7-10.30) **BAR MEALS:** L served all week 12-2 D served Mon-Sat 6-9 Av main course £7
RESTAURANT: L served all week 12-2 D served Mon-Sat 6-9
BREWERY/COMPANY: Greene King 🍺: Greene King IPA, Abbot Ale. **FACILITIES:** Children welcome Garden: Enclosed garden with patio, old mortuary Dogs allowed Water **NOTES:** Parking 20

BROOM
Map 12 TL14

The Cock 🍽️
23 High St SG18 9NA ☎ 01767 314411 📠 314284
Dir: Off B658 SW of Biggleswade
The 17th-century Cock is known as 'The Pub with no Bar', unspoilt to this day with its intimate, quarry-tiled rooms with latched doors and panelled walls. Real ales are served straight from casks racked by the cellar steps. A straightforward pub grub menu includes beef burgers, jacket potatoes, omelettes, ploughman's, sandwiches, jumbo sausage, scampi, and lasagne. Try the giant Yorkshire puddings with various fillings.
OPEN: 12-3 6-11 (Sat 12-4, Sun 12-4) **BAR MEALS:** L served all week 12-2.30 D served Mon-Sat 7-9 Av main course £5.50
RESTAURANT: L served all week 12-2.30 D served Mon-Sat 7-9.30 Av 3 course à la carte £12 **BREWERY/COMPANY:** Greene King 🍺: Greene King Abbot Ale, IPA & Ruddles County.
FACILITIES: Children welcome Garden: 12 Tables on Patio Dogs allowed **NOTES:** Parking 30

EATON BRAY
Map 11 SP92

The White Horse 🍽️ 🍷
Market Square LU6 2DG ☎ 01525 220231 📠 01525 222485
Dir: Take A5 N of Dunstable then A5050, 1m turn L & follow signs
The White Horse is a haven for those who love traditional English inns and good food. It has oak beams and horse brasses inside and a large garden with a children's play area outside. Snacks are available at lunchtime; there is children's

menu, plus a good choice for vegetarians. Chef's specials and other dishes change with the seasons.

OPEN: 11.30-3 6.30-11 (Sun 12-3, 7-10.30) Rest:1 Jan-Easter closed eve
BAR MEALS: L served all week 12-2.15 D served all week 7-9.30 Av main course £11 **RESTAURANT:** L served all week 12-2.15 D served all week 7.30-9.30 Av 3 course à la carte £20
BREWERY/COMPANY: Punch Taverns 🍺: Greene King IPA, Shepherd Neame Spitfire bitter, Carlsberg-Tetley Tetley's. 🍷: 7
FACILITIES: Garden: Lrg secluded garden at rear **NOTES:** Parking 40

KEYSOE
Map 12 TL06

Pick of the Pubs

The Chequers 🍽️
Pertenhall Rd, Brook End MK44 2HR
☎ 01234 708678 📠 01234 708678
e-mail: Chequers.keysoe@tesco.net
Dir: On B660 N of Bedford
In a quiet village, a 15th-century inn characterised by original beams and an open stone fireplace. Take a ridge-top walk for fine views of Graffham Water in anticipation of a warm welcome, good real ale and some fine pub food. Food served in the bar includes chicken curry, fried scampi, steak in a grain mustard cream sauce, chicken breast stuffed with Stilton in a chive sauce, or salads, sandwiches and ploughman's. Good wine list. A play area in the garden, overlooked by a rear terrace, is an added summer attraction.
OPEN: 11.30-2.30 6.30-11 **BAR MEALS:** L served Wed-Mon 12-2 D served Wed-Mon 7-9.45 **BREWERY/COMPANY:** Free House 🍺: Hook Norton Best, Fuller's London Pride.
FACILITIES: Children welcome Garden **NOTES:** Parking 50

LINSLADE
Map 11 SP92

The Globe Inn 🍽️ 🍷
Globe Ln, Old Linslade LU7 2TA
☎ 01525 373338 📠 01525 850551
Dir: A5 S to Dunstable, follow signs to Leighton Buzzard (A4146)
Licensed in 1830 as an official beer shop, this charming, family-friendly whitewashed pub stands by the Grand Union Canal, close to the River Ouzel. It was originally frequented by navvies digging the canal. Rumoured to be the pub where the nearby Great Train Robbery was planned in 1963. Character bars and a good range of ales enhance the interior. Expect tuna steak, red snapper, chef's own pies, garlic salmon, and steaks among the interesting main courses. Under new management.
OPEN: 11-3 (Jan-Feb 12-3, 6-11, Summer 11-11) 6-11 (Sun 12-10.30)
BAR MEALS: L served all week 12-9 D served all week 12-9 Av main

continued

continued

course £7.95 **RESTAURANT:** L served all week 12-3 D served all week 6-9 **BREWERY/COMPANY:** Greene King 🍺: Greene King Abbott Ale, Old Speckled Hen, IPA & Ruddles County Ale, Hook Norton. 👤: 16 **FACILITIES:** Children welcome Garden: Lrg, seats approx 200. Dogs allowed Water **NOTES:** Parking 150

MILTON BRYAN
Map 11 SP93

The Red Lion
Toddington Rd, South End MK17 9HS ☎ 01525 210044
Nestling in a pretty village close to Woburn Abbey, this attractive, brick-built pub is festooned with colourful hanging baskets in the summer. Relaxing, neatly maintained interior, with beams, rugs on wooden floors, and well-kept ales. Wide-ranging menu offering grills, casseroles and pies, along with paella, whole plaice, and nursery puddings.
OPEN: 11.30-3 6-11 **BAR MEALS:** L served all week 12-2.30 D served all week 7-9.30 Av main course £9 **RESTAURANT:** L served all week 12-2.30 D served all week 7-9.30 Av 3 course à la carte £20 **BREWERY/COMPANY:** Free House 🍺: Greene King IPA & Old Speckled Hen, Abbot Ale, plus Guest beers. **FACILITIES:** Children welcome lunchtime only Garden **NOTES:** Parking 40

NORTHILL
Map 12 TL14

The Crown 🐾 👤
2 Ickwell Rd SG18 9AA ☎ 01767 627337 📠 01767 627279
Dir: Telephone for directions
New owners are settling in at this delightful 16th-century pub, in its three-acre garden between Northill church and the village duck pond. This is a popular area with walkers, and the Shuttleworth Collection of vintage aircraft at the Old Warden Air Museum is just down the road. Freshly prepared meals include lasagne, cottage pie, and salmon supreme, as well as main course salads and chargrilled steaks.
OPEN: 11.30-3 (Summer all day Sat-Sun) 6-11.30 Closed: 25 Dec (eve) **BAR MEALS:** L served all week 12-2.30 D served Mon-Sat 7-9.30 Av main course £8.20 **RESTAURANT:** L served all week 12-2.30 D served all week 7-9.30 Av 3 course à la carte £22 **BREWERY/COMPANY:** Greene King 🍺: Greene King IPA, Abbot Ale, plus Guest ales. 👤: 7 **FACILITIES:** Children welcome Garden: Very large safe garden Dogs allowed Water **NOTES:** Parking 30

ODELL
Map 11 SP95

The Bell 👤
Horsefair Ln MK43 7AU ☎ 01234 720254
Dir: Telephone for directions
A Grade II listed 16th-century thatched pub operated by the same management for nearly twenty years. Within, it contains five small inter-linked eating areas all served from a single long bar, while outside is a patio and aviary next to a spacious garden that leads down to the River Ouse. It maintains a high standard of fresh home-made dishes complemented by fine real ales and a good selection of wines. A sample from the menu includes omelette with two fillings, garlicky chicken Kiev, breaded cod fillet and chips, braised lamb shanks, tandoori chicken, or steak and kidney pie. Other options include the specials board, sandwiches, and jacket potatoes.
OPEN: 11-2.30 6-11 (Sun 12-2.30, 7-10.30) **BAR MEALS:** L served all week 12-2 D served Mon-Sat 7-9.30 Av main course £8 **BREWERY/COMPANY:** Greene King 🍺: Greene King IPA, Abbot Ale & Ruddles County & seasonal beers. 👤: 14 **FACILITIES:** Children welcome Garden: Large garden with patio for 40 **NOTES:** Parking 14

OLD WARDEN
Map 12 TL14

Hare and Hounds 🐾 👤
SG18 9HQ ☎ 01767 627225 📠 01767 627209
Two log fires and four separate eating areas suggest that this lovely old pub takes the comfort and well-being of its customers very seriously. Set in a picturesque village near the Shuttleworth collection of old aircraft and cars, it has recently been renovated while the building's natural charm has been kept. Fresh fish including monkfish, sea bass, mussels and scallops are popular in summer, while traditional roasts and local game are also regulars on the menu.
OPEN: 12-3 6-11 **BAR MEALS:** L served Tue-Sun 12-2 D served Tue-Sat 6.30-9.30 Av main course £10 **RESTAURANT:** L served Tue-Sun 12-2 D served Tue-Sat 6.30-9.30 **BREWERY/COMPANY:** Charles Wells 🍺: Wells Bomdardier Premium & Eagle IPA, Adnams. 👤: 8 **FACILITIES:** Garden: Lawns **NOTES:** Parking 35

RADWELL
Map 11 TL05

The Swan Inn 👤
Felmersham Rd MK43 7HS ☎ 01234 781351
Dir: Off A6 N of Bedford
Stone and thatched listed pub in a quiet country setting overlooking the River Ouse. The large garden to the rear is ideal for families. Menu may include salmon fillet, turkey Roquefort, seafood risotto, beef casserole, crayfish or red snapper.
OPEN: 11-11 **BAR MEALS:** L 12-10 D served all week Av main course £6 **RESTAURANT:** L served Tue-Sun 12-2 D served Tue-Sat 6.30-10.00 Av 3 course à la carte £25 Av 3 course fixed price £12.95 **BREWERY/COMPANY:** Charles Wells 🍺: Wells Eagle & Bombardier. **FACILITIES:** Children welcome Garden: Food served outside **NOTES:** Parking 25

SHEFFORD
Map 12 TL13

Pick of the Pubs

The Black Horse 👤
Ireland SG17 5QL ☎ 01462 811398 📠 01462 817238
Dir: Telephone for directions
Set in a beautiful garden of an acre and surrounded by fields and woodland, this pretty inn is covered in flowers outside in summer, and brightly lit inside. Old beams prop up the ceilings and the large brick fireplace, and engender a cosy atmosphere helped by well-spaced tables separated off into cosy sitting areas. Large glass doors open onto the landscaped gardens, where seating is provided amongst the many attractive plants and shrubs. The memorable food attracts a devoted following, and an extensive wine list ensures that there is something to match every dish. Lunchtime sees a selection of imaginative light meals like fennel and almond risotto, leek and halloumi tartlet, and warm salad of duck. In the evening the tempo increases, with calves' liver and black pudding, bison with juniper berry jus, and large battered haddock fillet with hand-cut chips and mushy peas. Puddings are another high point: Grand Marnier soufflé, and poached pear in red wine and cloves are just two examples.
OPEN: 11.30-3 6-11 (Sun 12-6) **BAR MEALS:** L served Mon-Sun 12-2.30 D served Mon-Sat 6.30-10 Av main course £8.95 **RESTAURANT:** L served Mon-Sun 12-2.30 D served Mon-Sat 6.30-10 Av 3 course à la carte £20.50 Av 3 course fixed price £22.95 🍺: Green King IPA, London Pride, Old Speckled Hen, Stella Artois. 👤: 10 **FACILITIES:** Children welcome Garden: Landscaped 1 acre garden, seating available Dogs allowed Water & Toys **NOTES:** Parking 30

England

SILSOE   Map 12 TL03

The Old George Hotel
High St MK45 4EP ☎ 01525 860218 ⬚ 01525 860218
The former ale house, in the heart of the village, for the
workers of the Wrest estate. Many original features survive to
lend atmosphere to the locals' bar, spacious dining room and
simply-appointed bedrooms. Nearby places of interest include
Woburn Abbey and Wrest Park itself. Conventional bar meals
use breads, meat and vegetables from local sources, but
meals in the dining room are more adventurous: fruits de mer
platters, pheasant jardinière and beef Wellington. Jazz nights
and an organist every Sunday.
OPEN: open all day **BAR MEALS:** L served all week 12-2.30 D
served Mon-Sat 7-9.30 Av main course £6 **RESTAURANT:** L served
all week 12-2.30 D served Mon-Sat 7-9.30 Av 3 course à la carte £20
Av 5 course fixed price £11.95 **BREWERY/COMPANY:** Greene King
◗: Greene King Old Speckled Hen & IPA. **FACILITIES:** Children
welcome Garden: Food served outdoors Dogs allowed by prior
arrangement **NOTES:** Parking 40

STANBRIDGE   Map 11 SP92

Pick of the Pubs

The Five Bells ♀
Station Rd LU7 9JF ☎ 01525 210224 ⬚ 01525 211164
e-mail: fivebells@traditionalfreehouses.com
Dir: Off A505 E of Leighton Buzzard
A stylish and relaxing setting for a drink or a meal is offered
by this white-painted 400-year-old village inn, which has
been delightfully renovated and revived. The bar features lots
of bare wood as well as comfortable armchairs and polished,
rug-strewn floors. The modern decor extends to the bright,
airy 75-cover dining room. There's also a spacious garden
with patio and lawns. New hosts Emma Moffitt and Andrew
Mackenzie offer bar meals, set menus and a carte choice for
diners. The bar menu typically includes dishes such as
smoked chicken, sun-dried tomato and pine nut salad;
battered fish, chips and mushy peas; baked courgettes
stuffed with goat's cheese and mint with a mixed salad; rib
eye steak with fries; and chicken, ham, leek and mushroom
pie. From the pudding menu, look out for chocolate and
orange torte and raspberry crème brûlée - and be tempted!
OPEN: 12-3 5-11 **BAR MEALS:** L served all week 12-2.30 D
served all week 7-9 Av main course £7.50 **RESTAURANT:** L
served all week 12-2.30 D served all week 7-9 Av 3 course à la
carte £20 Av 3 course fixed price £15
BREWERY/COMPANY: ◗: Interbrew Bass, Wadworth 6X,
Hook Norton Best Bitter, Well's Bombardier. ♀: 8
FACILITIES: Children welcome Garden: Lrg, traditional garden.
Patio area **NOTES:** Parking 100

TURVEY   Map 11 SP95

The Three Cranes ♀
High St Loop MK43 8EP ☎ 01234 881305 ⬚ 01234 881305
Dir: Through Olney, R at rdbt onto A428, then R towards Bedford
Ivy-clad, stone-built inn dating from the 17th-century, in a pretty
village setting next to the church. A typical menu offers oven-
baked salmon fillet, steak, mushroom and ale pie, medallions of
chicken breast, lasagne, whole baked seabass, and a choice of
steaks. Sandwiches, ploughman's, jacket potatoes, and salad
bowls also available. Refer to blackboard for today's specials.
OPEN: 11-3 (Sun 12-3, 7-10.30) 6-11 (open all day in summer)

BAR MEALS: L served all week 12-2.30 D served all week 6.30-9 Av
main course £8.95 **RESTAURANT:** L served all week 12-2.30 D
served all week 6.30-9 Av 3 course à la carte £15
BREWERY/COMPANY: Greene King ◗: Greene King IPA, Abbot
Ale plus 3 Guest ales. **FACILITIES:** Children welcome Garden: Food
served outside Dogs allowed **NOTES:** Parking 12

BERKSHIRE

ALDERMASTON   Map 05 SU56

The Hinds Head ♀
Wasing Ln RG7 4LX ☎ 0118 9712194 ⬚ 0118 9712194
e-mail: aldermaston@hindshead.freeserve.co.uk
*Dir: A4 towards Newbury, then L on A340 towards Basingstoke, 2m to
village*
With its distinctive clock and belltower, this 17th-century inn
still has the village lock-up which was last used in 1865. The
old brewery (last used in 1921) was recently refurbished to
provide a new restaurant. Typical dishes are pan-fried breast
of chicken with a fricassee of chorizo sausage, smoked bacon
and mushroom, grilled salmon on bubble and squeak glazed
with a Béarnaise sauce, or shoulder of lamb on mustard mash
with rosemary and garlic jus.
OPEN: 11-11 **BAR MEALS:** L served all week 12-2 D served all
week 6-9.30 Av main course £10 **RESTAURANT:** L served all week
12-2 D served all week 6-9.30 Av 3 course à la carte £20
BREWERY/COMPANY: Gales ◗: Gales Best, HSB & Guest ale.
FACILITIES: Garden: Food served outside **NOTES:** Parking 50

ALDWORTH   Map 05 SU57

Pick of the Pubs

The Bell Inn
RG8 9SE ☎ 01635 578272
Dir: Just off B4009 (Newbury-Streatley rd)
One of the few truly unspoiled country pubs where
customers could be forgiven for thinking they have
stepped back in time to a quieter age without piped music,
mobile phones and games machines. Once inside, you'll
see that the interior of this 14th-century, cruck-built inn is
fascinating. Among its most striking features are a glass-
panelled hatch and a shiny ochre ceiling. The landlady's
great-grandmother installed the triple beer engine in 1902,
and the one-handed grandfather clock has been sitting in
the tap room for 300 years. The Bell has been family-run
for five generations, and the present owners have no plans
to change it. Plain, simple but appetising food includes hot
crusty rolls with ample fillings. Ploughman's lunches and a
range of hot and cold puddings are also available. Handy
for the Ridgeway Trail which runs nearby.
OPEN: 11-3 6-11 Closed: Dec 25 **BAR MEALS:** L served Tue-
Sun 11-2.50 D served Tue-Sun 6-10.50
BREWERY/COMPANY: Free House ◗: Arkell's Kingsdown,
3B, West Berkshire Old Tyler & Maggs Magnificent Mild, Guest
Beer. **FACILITIES:** Children welcome Garden: Peaceful, old
fashioned Dogs allowed **NOTES:** Parking 12 **NOTES:** No
credit cards

See Pub Walk on page 25

**Pubs offering a good choice of
fish on their menu**

continued

The Bell

A spectacular walk offering stunning views over spacious downland country towards the Thames Valley. The Ridgeway, possibly Britain's oldest road, is seen in the distance and the whole area conveys a sense of space and isolation - perfect for a country stroll.

From the Bell cross the road and pass the former village shop and post office. Avoid the turning to the downs and keep ahead down the lane to Aldworth Church. From the main entrance, with a 1,000-year-old yew on your left, go through a little gate and turn right at the track.

Pass a footpath and continue on the concrete byway, keeping to the right of farm outbuildings. Cut between fields and, as you approach the road, look to your right for a glimpse of the church. Turn left at the lane and pass a track on the right with a view of Bower Farm. Continue on the lane and look for a footpath on the right at Starveall Barn.

Take the path, cross two stiles and keep along the right edge of the field. A curtain of woodland is seen ahead, with the Ridgeway running this side of it. Make for the bottom right-hand corner of the field, turn right and follow the track. When it bends right, swing left to join a byway and keep a fence on the left.

As you approach a farm, swing left, avoiding a gate and stile, and walk across the field with

THE BELL, ALDWORTH
RG8 9SE

☎ 01635 578272

Directions: Just off B4009 (Newbury-Streatley rd)
Truly unspoilt country pub, cruck built and dating from 14th century. Simple, appetising food, and good puddings.
Open: 11-3 6-11 (Closed Mon, ex BH)
Bar Meals: 11-2.50 6-10.50
Notes: Children welcome. Peaceful garden. Parking.
(See page 24 for full entry)

trees on the right. Pass through a gate and keep right after a few paces at the next junction. Avoid a path on the right, pass a sycamore tree and ignore a track on the left. Take the next footpath on the right and cross several fields to reach the rear of the Bell. Follow the shaded path alongside the pub and turn right at the road.

DISTANCE: 3 1/4 miles/5.3km
MAP: OS Explorer 158 & 170
TERRAIN: Farmland and downland on the southern slopes of the Thames Valley
PATHS: Tracks and field paths
GRADIENT: Level or gently undulating ground. No steep hills

Walk submitted and checked by
Nick Channer

ASCOT
Map 06 SU96

The Thatched Tavern ☺ ♀
Cheapside Rd SL5 7QG ☎ 01344 620874 📠 01344 623043
Dir: *Follow signs for Ascot Racecourse drive through Ascot 1st L (Cheapside) drive 1.5m and pub is on the L*

Just a mile from the racecourse, a 500-year-old building of original beams, flagstone floors and very low ceilings. In summer the sheltered garden makes a fine spot to enjoy real ales and varied choice of food. In the same safe hands for over ten years, the kitchen produces a range of traditional English food and international dishes. In the bar are home-made soup or anchovy Caesar salad. A la carte there may be fragrant Thai chicken soup and Barbary duck breast with egg noodles and blackcurrant coulis.
OPEN: 12-3.30 (Fri-Sun Open all day) 5.30-11 **BAR MEALS:** L served all week 12-2.30 D served all week 7-10 Av main course £7.95 **RESTAURANT:** L served all week 12-3 D served all week 7-10 Av 3 course à la carte £24 **BREWERY/COMPANY:** ◀: Fuller's London Pride, Scottish Courage, IPA. **FACILITIES:** Children welcome Garden: Food served outside, patio Dogs allowed Water **NOTES:** Parking 30

ASHMORE GREEN
Map 05 SU56

The Sun in the Wood ☺ ♀
Stoney Ln RG18 9HF ☎ 01635 42377 📠 01635 528392
e-mail: suninthewood@aol.com
Dir: *A34 Robin Hood rndbt, L to Shaw, at mini rndbt R then 7th L into Stoney Lane, 1.5m, pub on L*
Standing in the shadow of tall trees, this popular, extensively refurbished pub occupies a delightful woodland setting and yet is only a stone's throw from the centre of Newbury. Stone floors, plenty of wood panelling and various prints by Renoir and Monet add to the appeal. The extensive choice includes beef and vegetable stew with dumplings, wild mushroom and tomato lasagne, and grilled tuna fillet with a creamy curry sauce.
OPEN: 12-2.30 6-11 **BAR MEALS:** L served Tue-Sun 12-2 D served Tue-Sat 6.30-9.30 **RESTAURANT:** L served Tue-Sun 12-2 D served Tue-Sat 6.30-9.30 **BREWERY/COMPANY:** Wadworth
◀: Wadworth 6X & Henrys Origional IPA, Badger Tanglefoot. ♀: 9
FACILITIES: Children welcome Garden: Lovely country garden among national woodland **NOTES:** Parking 60

BINFIELD
Map 05 SU87

Stag & Hounds ♀
Forest Rd RH12 4HA ☎ 01344 483553
Historic old pub, with a collection of sporting prints and a restaurant. Low beams, log fires, front terrace and a legend about Elizabeth I and some Morris dancers. There's a large enclosed garden, and decent bar food, with Friday night being fish night.

OPEN: 11.30 -11 **BAR MEALS:** L served all week 12-3 D served all week 6-10 Av main course £7.50 **BREWERY/COMPANY:** Eldridge Pope ◀: Courage Best, Bombadier. ♀: 8 **FACILITIES:** Garden: Large enclosed, 40 tables Dogs allowed Water **NOTES:** Parking 90

BOXFORD
Map 05 SU47

The Bell at Boxford ☺ ♀
Lambourn Rd RG20 8DD ☎ 01488 608721 📠 01488 608749
e-mail: paullavis@lycos.co.uk
Dir: *A338 toward Wantage, R onto B4000, take 3rd L to Boxford*

A mock Tudor country pub at the heart of the glorious Lambourn Valley, renowned for its picturesque downland scenery. The 22-mile Lambourn Valley Way runs through the village. Relax in the cosy bar with its choice of real ales and peruse the impressive wine list (champagne by the glass!) and the bistro-style blackboard menus. Dishes include Boxford steak, game pie, curries, lobster thermidore, tiger prawns, and calamari. Heated terraces for alfresco dining.
OPEN: 11-3 6-11 (Sat 6.30-11, Sun 7-10.30) **BAR MEALS:** L served all week 12-2 D served all week 7-10 Av main course £8 **RESTAURANT:** L served all week 12-2 D served all week 7-10 Av 3 course à la carte £23 Av 2 course fixed price £11.95 **BREWERY/COMPANY:** Free House ◀: Morrells Oxford, Badger Tanglefoot, Interbrew Bass, Scottish Courage Courage Best. ♀: 60 **FACILITIES:** Children welcome Garden: Heated terraces, holds approx 80 people Dogs allowed **NOTES:** Parking 36

BURCHETT'S GREEN
Map 05 SU88

Pick of the Pubs

The Crown ☺
SL6 6QZ ☎ 01628 822844
Dir: *From M4 take A404(M), then 3rd exit*
In the middle of a small hamlet and overlooking the village green, this popular local stands amid a large rose garden, enhanced by handsome garden furniture. Nearby Ashley Hill Woods are a haven for naturalists and walkers, who often stop by for a pint of real ale. Inside, the whitewashed walls and low-beamed ceilings create a welcoming atmosphere, particularly in the intimate dining room, whose tables are decorated with vases and fresh flowers. Do not expect to pop in for a quick snack, as everything is cooked to order from the freshest available ingredients. Tempting main dishes on a short, daily menu may be large grilled Dover sole, calves' liver with bacon and creamed potatoes, monkfish, roast duck with black cherry and brandy sauce, or warm chicken salad with bacon and avocado. Reservations are advised from Friday to Sunday to be sure of a table.
OPEN: 12-3 6-11 **BAR MEALS:** L served all week 12-2.30 D served all week 6.30-10 Av main course £10 **RESTAURANT:** L

continued

continued

served all week 12-2.30 D served all week 6.30-10 Av 3 course à la carte £25 **BREWERY/COMPANY:** Greene King 🍺: Greene King IPA, Ruddles Best. **FACILITIES:** Children welcome Children's licence Garden: Large rose garden overlooking village green **NOTES:** Parking 30

CHADDLEWORTH Map 05 SU47

The Ibex
Main St RG20 7ER ☎ 01488 638311
Dir: *A338 towards Wantage, through Great Shefford then R, then 2nd L, pub is on R in village*
Frequented by the horse-racing fraternity, with many famous stables close by, this Grade II listed building was originally a bakery and then an off-licence before finally becoming a pub. A range of steaks, spare ribs, curries, home-made pies, jacket potatoes, sandwiches and ploughman's are always available, plus dishes such as chicken breast in Stilton and onion sauce, faggots with mashed potatoes, pork fillet in Dijon sauce, and black pudding with bacon, onion and mushrooms.
OPEN: 11.30-2.30 6-11 **BAR MEALS:** L served all week 12-2 D served Mon-Sat 6.30-9.30 **RESTAURANT:** L served all week 12-2 D served Mon-Sat 7-9.30 **BREWERY/COMPANY:** Greene King 🍺: Greene King, Ruddles Best. **FACILITIES:** Children welcome Garden Dogs allowed manager's discretion **NOTES:** Parking 40

CHIEVELEY Map 05 SU47

The Crab at Chieveley 🛏 ⚲
North Heath, Wantage Rd RG20 8UE ☎ 01635 248236 248770 📠 01635 248506
Dir: *Off B4494 N of Newbury*
Until last year, this attractive thatched property was the Blue Boar Inn, apparently because Cromwell's troops left a porcine statue here before the Battle of Newbury. The new name derives from the new owners' previous pub in North Yorkshire, the Crab & Lobster, which specialised in award-winning seafood, and this is the plan here too. Still undergoing major redevelopment at press date.
OPEN: 11-3 6-11 (Sun 12-3, 7-10.30) **BAR MEALS:** L served all week 12-2.30 D served all week 6-10.00 Av main course £12 **RESTAURANT:** L served all week 12-2.30 D served all week 6-10.00 Av 3 course à la carte £25 Av 3 course fixed price £16 **BREWERY/COMPANY:** Free House 🍺: Wadworth 6X, Fullers London Pride, Boddingtons, West Berkshire. ⚲: 14 **FACILITIES:** Children welcome Garden: Seating for 70 with BBQ & Marquee Dogs allowed **NOTES:** Parking 60

COOKHAM Map 06 SU88

Pick of the Pubs

Bel and The Dragon 🛏 ⚲
High St SL6 9SQ ☎ 01628 521263 📠 01628 851008
e-mail: cookham@belandthedragon.co.uk
Dir: *Telephone for directions*
The Cookham Bel and the Dragon (one of three establishments sharing the same name and philosophy) is situated on Cookham's picturesque high street. One of the oldest licensed houses in England, it's built of wattle and daub with a trendy rustic interior featuring wooden tables, bold coloured walls, a real fire and stripped floors. There's a strong emphasis on food here, with a lengthy menu

continued

featuring many dishes that can be ordered as starters or main courses. Begin with the likes of lamb shish kebab with smoked chilli jam, roasted pepper and lemongrass soup or crayfish, shrimp, mango and papaya tian. Follow with slow-roasted lamb shank on a herb mashed potato with rosemary and citrus jus, Thai marinated duck breast with sautéed sweet peppers and chilli jus, or chargrilled rib eye with blue cheese and peppercorn sauce.
OPEN: 11.30-11 (Sun 12-10.30) Rest:25-26 Dec Closed in the evening **BAR MEALS:** L served all week 12-2.30 D served all week 7-10 Av main course £12 **RESTAURANT:** L served all week 12-2.30 D served all week 7-10 Av 3 course à la carte £25 **BREWERY/COMPANY:** Free House 🍺: Brakspear, Marstons Pedigree. ⚲: 10 **FACILITIES:** Children welcome Garden: Pond, terrace & garden Dogs allowed

COOKHAM DEAN Map 05 SU88

Pick of the Pubs

Chequers Inn Brasserie 🛏 ⚲
Dean Ln SL6 9BQ ☎ 01628 481232 📠 01628 481237
e-mail: info@chequers-inn.com
Dir: *From A4094 in Cookham High St take R fork after r'way bridge into Dean Lane. Pub in 1m*
Historic pub with oak beams and open fire, tucked away in one of the prettiest villages in the Thames Valley. The writer Kenneth Grahame, who wrote 'The Wind in the Willows,' spent his childhood here. Striking Victorian and Edwardian villas around the green set the tone, whilst the surrounding wooded hills and dales have earned Cookham Dean the description of a miniature Switzerland. No wonder Grahame returned here to live. Today, the Chequers offers carefully-chosen wines and ales, as well as a daily-changing blackboard menu. Select something from the appetising lunchtime menu: perhaps grilled New Zealand mussels with garlic and herbs, followed by salmon and prawn fishcake, grilled pork loin steak with fondant potato, sage and roast pear jus, or Thai red chicken curry with boiled rice.
OPEN: 11-3 5.30-11 Closed: Dec 25 **BAR MEALS:** L served all week 12-2.30 D served all week 6-9.30 Av main course £12 **BREWERY/COMPANY:** Free House 🍺: Wadworth 6X, Greene King Morland Original, Ruddles County, Stella Artois. ⚲: 7 **FACILITIES:** Children welcome Children's licence Garden: Small lawned area with benches and parasols Dogs allowed Water **NOTES:** Parking 50

Pick of the Pubs

Uncle Tom's Cabin 🛏
Hills Ln SL6 9NT ☎ 01628 483339
Dir: *A4 towards Maidenhead, over bridge, R on to Cookham High St, through town, over r'way, past Whyteladies Ln, pub on L*
Locals' pub in the cosy cottage style, set in beautiful Berkshire countryside within walking distance of the Thames. It is surrounded by lovely walks in all directions - one of the most visited parts of the Thames Valley. Though the pub was renovated in the late 1980s, it retains its 17th-century charm and a relaxing atmosphere throughout a series of little rooms. There is also a lovely big garden at the rear, set on a hill with shade provided by mature fruit trees. In many ways it is everyone's idea of the perfect country pub. The well-kept beers include

continued

England

COOKHAM DEAN continued

Benskins and Fullers, along with Addlestone cider. A good range of dishes is prepared from fresh ingredients. Fishy options might be fresh cod, seafood crêpes, and cod and prawn Creole. Other favourite main courses range through burgers, beef and ale pie, lamb shank, ribs and Cajun chicken.

Uncle Tom's Cabin

OPEN: 11-3 5.30-11 (Sun 7-11) **BAR MEALS:** L served Tues-Sun 12-2 D served Mon-Sat 7.30-10 Av main course £6.50 **RESTAURANT:** L served all week 12-2 D served all week 7.30-10 **BREWERY/COMPANY:** Carlsberg Tetley ☜: Fuller's London Pride, Brakspeare & Guest ales. **FACILITIES:** Children welcome Garden: Food served outside Dogs allowed Water, biscuits **NOTES:** Parking 28

CRAZIES HILL   Map 05 SU78

Pick of the Pubs

The Horns ♀
RG10 8LY ☎ 0118 9401416 ▤ 0118 9404849
Dir: Off A321 NE of Wargrave
Set beside a narrow lane in a small hamlet, this whitewashed timbered cottage started life in Tudor times as a hunting lodge to which a barn (now the dining area) was added some 200 years ago. Sympathetically refurbished by Brakspear's Brewery, it remains a delightful country pub that has three interconnecting rooms complete with old pine tables, exposed beams, open fires, rugby memorabilia, and a peaceful atmosphere free of music and electronic games. Dishes listed on the daily-changing blackboard menus may include sweet pepper, tomato and asparagus pasta bake, chargrilled sirloin slices in mushroom and red wine gravy, or whole oven-baked seabass with tomato, garlic and basil sauce. Fresh filled baguettes and home-made desserts are also available.
OPEN: 11.30-2.30 (Sun 12-6, 7-10.30) 6-11 Closed: 25-26 Dec Rest:Sun closed eve Oct -Mar **BAR MEALS:** L served all week 12-2 D served Mon-Sat 7-9.30 **RESTAURANT:** L served all week 12-2 D served Mon-Sat 7-9.30 Av 3 course à la carte £18.20 **BREWERY/COMPANY:** Brakspear ☜: Brakspear Bitter. **FACILITIES:** Children welcome Garden Dogs allowed garden only, please ask staff **NOTES:** Parking 45

♀ 7   Number of wines by the glass

CURRIDGE   Map 05 SU47

The Bunk Traditional Inn ☜ ♀
RG18 9DS ☎ 01635 200400 ▤ 01635 200336
Dir: M4 J13/A34 N towards Oxford then 1st slip rd then R for 1m. R at T-jnct, 1st R signposted Curridge

Smart and stylish inn dating back about 150 years, with beams, brasses and a log fire in the attractive bar. Informal, friendly atmosphere, pleasant surroundings and good quality menu. Home-cooked dishes include Pad Thai, corned beef hash, prime Scottish sirloin steak, sea bass fillet on fresh spinach with white wine and cream sauce, calves' liver with bacon and bubble and squeak, and tiger prawns with garlic and chilli. Plenty of peaceful woodland walks on the doorstep.
OPEN: 11-11 **BAR MEALS:** L served all week 12-2.30 D served all week 7-10 Av main course £11 **RESTAURANT:** 12-2.30 7-10 **BREWERY/COMPANY:** Free House ☜: Arkells 3B, Wadworth 6X, Fuller's London Pride. **FACILITIES:** Children welcome Garden Dogs allowed **NOTES:** Parking 38

EAST GARSTON   Map 05 SU37

The Queens Arms ♦♦♦ ♀
Newbury Rd RG17 7ET ☎ 01488 648757 ▤ 01488 648642
e-mail: queensarms@barbox.net
A charming 19th-century village inn enjoying a close association with the racing world of the Lambourn Valley. Jockeys, trainers and punters fill its bar and restaurant on Newbury race days, and the food lives up to expectations. Deep-fried brie wedge, chicken fajitas marinated in beer, and lemon tart with passion fruit coulis are typical. A large terrace and garden are ideal for summer, and an adventure playground appeals to children.
BAR MEALS: L served all week D served all week Av main course £8.50 **RESTAURANT:** L served all week 7-11 D served all week 7-11 Av 3 course à la carte £15 **BREWERY/COMPANY:** Free House ☜: Fuller's London Pride. ♀: 12 **FACILITIES:** Children welcome Children's licence Garden: Lrg garden, terrace, BBQ area Dogs allowed **NOTES:** Parking 40 **ROOMS:** 14 bedrooms 14 en suite 4 family rooms s£40 d£60

EAST ILSLEY   Map 05 SU48

The Crown & Horns ♀
RG20 7LH ☎ 01635 281205 & 281545 ▤ 01635 281660
Dir: Telephone for directions
This extended 18th-century pub, just five miles from the M4, might be familiar to you as the Dog & Gun in the old BBC TV serial 'Trainer'. The collection of around 160 whiskies from all over the world is an attraction, as is the comprehensive menu, ranging through sandwiches, speciality pies and a vegetarian selection. A house speciality is chicken breast filled with black pudding and finished with sherry cream sauce.

continued on page 30

The Swan

A pleasant, easy walk exploring the dramatic landscape of Berkshire's remote south-west corner.

Turn left out of the Swan car park, pass a seat on the green and keep right at the junction. Pass a turning on the left for Combe Gibbet and Upper Inkpen and turn left at the 30-mile speed limit sign to join a footpath.

Cross a stile and follow the fence to the next stile which lies hidden beneath trees in the field corner. Emerge from the undergrowth and you'll see Inkpen church ahead. Make for the gate across the field, join the road opposite Church Farm House, turn left for a few paces and then right to visit the church. Parts of St Michael of All Angels date from the mid-13th century and the lychgate was built in memory of a former rector here. The

church remains in view for much of this gentle ramble, nestling comfortably at the foot of the hills.

Return to Church Farm House and walk down the lane to the next junction. Turn left towards Shalbourne and Ham and follow the road out of the village. At the speed sign, look over to the left for a very good view of the church. Pass a path on the left and make for Drove Cottage. Turn right here and follow the track. Turn right further on and pass a galvanised gate on the left.

The path becomes enclosed by trees and bushes now and begins to climb steadily. Continue between thick vegetation and through delightful tunnels of trees

♦♦♦♦
THE SWAN, HUNGERFORD
Craven Road, Lower Green, Inkpen
RG17 9DX

☎ 01488 668326

Dir: S down Hungerford High St, L to common, R on common, pub 3m. Heavily-beamed 17th-century inn close to the Wayfarers Walk, a wonderful area to explore on foot. The much extended area is homely with open fires and photographic prints. Owned by local organic beef farmers, who cook with organic supplies.
Open: 12-2.30 7-11 All day summer weekends
Bar Meals: 12-2.30 7-9.30
Notes: Children welcome, changing room, swing. Garden, terrace. Parking. (See page 31 for full entry)

before the path descends gently to a junction. Turn right and follow a sheltered path, looking for a waymarked turning on the left. Take the path and follow it to a stile on the right. Cross it to a small field and follow the boundary to the road. Turn right and return to the Swan.

DISTANCE: 2 miles/3.2km
MAP: OS Explorer 158
TERRAIN: Downland, farmland and light woodland close to the Hampshire border
PATHS: Quiet roads, field paths, sheltered drove tracks
GRADIENT: Gentle climbing

Walk submitted and checked by Nick Channer

EAST ILSLEY continued

OPEN: 11-11 **BAR MEALS:** L served all week 11.45-2.30 D served all week 6-10 Av main course £7 **RESTAURANT:** L served all week 11.45-2.30 D served all week 6-10 Av 3 course à la carte £20 **BREWERY/COMPANY:** Free House ◖: Brakspear, Old Hookey, Old Peculier, Caledonian & Cornish Original. **FACILITIES:** Children welcome Garden: Paved courtyard area Dogs allowed **NOTES:** Parking 35

The Swan

RG20 7LF ☎ 01635 281238 ▤ 01635 281791
e-mail: theswan@east-ilsley.demon.co.uk
Dir: 5m N of J13 on A34. 18m S of Oxford on A34
16th-century coaching inn nestling in a peaceful downland village close to the long-distance Ridgeway national trail. Enclosed terraced gardens ideal for a drink or lunch. Traditional pub fare includes a selection of pies and cod and chips.
OPEN: 11-2.30 6-11 (Sun 12-3, 7-10.30) Closed: Dec 25 Rest:Dec 26, Jan 1 closed evenings **BAR MEALS:** L served all week 12-2 D served all week 6-10 **BREWERY/COMPANY:** Greene King ◖: Greene King, Abbot Ale & IPA. **FACILITIES:** Children welcome Garden Dogs allowed **NOTES:** Parking 40

FRILSHAM
Map 05 SU57

Pick of the Pubs

The Pot Kiln

RG18 0XX ☎ 01635 201366
Dir: A34 towards Oxford, 1st L to Chieveley, then 1st R to Hermitage. 2nd L onto B4009, 2nd R to Yattendon, R on sharp L bend, on for 1m
Hard to find the first time, but once found, never forgotten. Walkers, cyclists and real ale enthusiasts all keep returning down the dusty track to this 400-year-old brick pub. In many respects it can hardly have changed for absolutely ages. Even the views from its peaceful garden across open meadows and woodland seem timeless. There used to be brick kilns around here, of course, but the outbuildings you see today house the West Berkshire Brewery, run separately from the pub, but which it supplies with monthly guest ales, and with its Brick Kiln Bitter on an exclusive basis. Delightfully old fashioned interior with lobby bar, simple wooden furnishings and warming open fires. Looked after for 23 years by the Gent family, who bill their free house as 'a pub which serves food', not 'a restaurant which serves beer'. So, the food is good and plain, and includes filled rolls, lamb rogan josh, steak and kidney pudding, and pan-fried salmon fishcakes.
OPEN: 12-3 (Tues 6.30-11 only) 6.30-11 Closed: 25 Dec Rest:26 Dec Closed eve **BAR MEALS:** L served Wed-Mon 12-2 D served Wed-Mon 7-9.30 Av main course £7.50
BREWERY/COMPANY: Free House ◖: West Berkshire Brick Kiln, Morlands Original, Arkells 3B, West Berkshire Guest Ales each month. **FACILITIES:** Garden: Large grassed area, picnic benches Dogs allowed Water **NOTES:** Parking 30 No credit cards

For a list of pubs with AA Inspected
Accommodation Awards
♦   see pages 646-651   ★

GREAT SHEFFORD
Map 05 SU37

The Swan Inn 🛏 ♀

Newbury Rd RG17 7DS ☎ 01488 648271
e-mail: cptaylor29@aol.com
Dir: 1.5m north of M4 J14 on A338
Early 19th-century coaching inn situated in the village of Great Shefford in the Lambourn Valley, with river views from both the restaurant and patio. The interior is traditional in style with log-burning fires and a handwritten menu displayed on the blackboard. Favourite dishes include lamb shoulder, spicy cod, tuna penne and chicken Chicago. The Swan is ideal for walkers, with its own circular walk beginning and ending at the pub.
OPEN: 11-3 (Sun 12-3, 7-10.30) 6-11 **BAR MEALS:** L served all week 12-2 D served all week 6-9.30 Av main course £9.50
RESTAURANT: L served all week 12-2.30 D served all week 6.30-9.30 **BREWERY/COMPANY:** Eldridge Pope ◖: Scottish Courage Courage Best, Wadworth 6X plus Guest Ales. ♀: 8
FACILITIES: Children welcome Garden: Patio, food served outside Dogs allowed **NOTES:** Parking 25

HARE HATCH
Map 05 SU87

The Queen Victoria ♀

The Holt RG10 9TA ☎ 0118 9402477
Dir: On A4 between Reading & Maidenhead
A country cottage-style pub dating back over 300 years, handily placed between Reading and Maidenhead. It offers excellent draught beers, good quality pub food and an interesting choice of wines. The blackboard specialities are supported by the likes of cheese and spicy beef tortillas, Chinese-style chicken, pepper and onion kebab, and prawn curry Madras.
OPEN: 11-3 5.30-11 (Sun 12-10.30) Closed: Dec 25-26 **BAR MEALS:** L served all week 12-2.30 D served all week 6-10 Av main course £7 **BREWERY/COMPANY:** Brakspear ◖: Brakspear Bitter & Special. ♀: 11 **FACILITIES:** Children welcome Garden Dogs allowed Water **NOTES:** Parking 20

HUNGERFORD
Map 05 SU36

Pick of the Pubs

The Swan Inn ♦♦♦♦ 🛏

Craven Rd, Lower Green, Inkpen RG17 9DX
☎ 01488 668326 ▤ 01488 668306
e-mail: enquiries@theswaninn-organics.co.uk
See Pub Walk on page 29
See Pick of the Pubs opposite

HURLEY
Map 05 SU88

The Rising Sun ♀

High St SL6 5LT ☎ 01628 824274
Dir: Off the A4130 from Maidenhead
Traditional style pub and restaurant with black beams and a real log fire. Fresh fish and chips on Friday
OPEN: 11.30-3 5.30-11 (Sun 12-10.30, Sat 3-7) **BAR MEALS:** L served all week 12-2 D served Tue-Sun 7-9.30 Av main course £7 **RESTAURANT:** L served Sun only 12-2 D served Tue-Sun 7-9.30 Av 3 course à la carte £20 **BREWERY/COMPANY:** Whitbread ◖: Brakspear, Fullers London Pride. **FACILITIES:** Garden: BBQ Dogs allowed **NOTES:** Parking 10

Open: 12-2.30, 7-11
(all day weekends in summer)
Bar Meals: L served all week 12-2.30,
D served all week 7-9.30.
Av cost main course £8
RESTAURANT: L served Wed-Sun 12-2.30,
D served Wed-Sat 7-9.30.
Av cost 3 course £25
BREWERY/COMPANY:
Free House.
🍺: Butts Traditional, Hook Norton Mild
& Bitter, Caledonian Golden Promise.
FACILITIES: Children welcome. Garden.
NOTES: Parking 50
ROOMS: 10 en suite from s£40 d£75
See Pub Walk on page 29

The Swan Inn

This heavily-beamed 17th-century inn stands mid-way between Newbury and Hungerford and is close to the historic Wayfarers Walk path. Close by are Combe Gibbet and Walbury Hill, the highest points in this part of the south of England, and a wonderful area for exploring on foot.

◆◆◆◆ 🐑

Craven Road, Lower Green, Inkpen,
Hungerford, RG17 9DX
☎ 01488 668326📠 01488 668306
✉ enquiries@theswaninn-
  organics.co.uk
Dir: S down Hungerford High St, L to
common, R on common, pub 3m.

The frontage of terracing with its picnic tables and summer parasols is a natural draw, while the much-extended interior remains true to the pub's original character. Exposed beams, open fires and old photographic prints of the village and surrounding countryside are to be found within, giving the inn a cosy and homely atmosphere.

Unusual stained glass panels on several interior doors are worth closer inspection while sampling a pint of Hook Norton or the local Butts ale. The inn is owned by local organic beef farmers Bernard and Mary Harris, so organically-produced supplies take pride of place on both the bar and restaurant menus, including beef from their own farm. Attached to the Swan is their farm shop where home-cured bacon, gammons and a range of country sausages make a visit doubly worth-while. The pub has a varied menu including rump steak, beef Stroganoff, leek and bacon au gratin, Stilton pasta, cottage

pie and cod in beer batter. Home-made desserts like blackberry and apple crumble are another speciality. In the restaurant, typical choices might include a gravadlax starter, followed by tournedos Rossini, pan-fried fillet of turbot, or a half shoulder of lamb roasted with rosemary and garlic in a red wine jus. Vegetarians are well provided for, with choices such as Mozzarella, tomatoes and olives wrapped in puff pastry, oven roasted and served with a wild mushroom sauce. The wine list is exclusively organic and contains two champagnes and 25 wines from seven countries.

England

HURST
Map 05 SU77

The Green Man 🍴 ⵠ
Hinton Rd RG10 0BP ☎ 0118 934 2599 📠 0118 934 2939
e-mail: info@thegreenman.uk.com
Dir: off the A321 next to Hurst Cricket Club
The success of this admirable pub revolves around the dedicated father and son partnership. Low ceilings, open fires and bric-a-brac feature, and good beers are served in an atmosphere conducive to conversation. Food choices range from children's dishes, through light bites to main courses of grilled sea bass with fresh herbs, marinated lamb steak with garlic and basil, and pan-fried chicken with Parmesan sauce. The large garden has a heated patio and a low-level play area.
OPEN: 11-3 (Sun 12-3, 7-10.30) 5.30-11 Rest:Sun 6-10.30 (May-Sep)
BAR MEALS: L served all week 12-2.30 D served all week 6.30-9.30
RESTAURANT: L served all week 12-2.30 D served all week 6.30-9.30 **BREWERY/COMPANY:** Brakspear 🍺: Brakspear Bitter, Special & Seasonal Ales. ⵠ: 7 **FACILITIES:** Garden: Large garden with heated patio area **NOTES:** Parking 40

KINTBURY
Map 05 SU36

Pick of the Pubs

The Dundas Arms
53 Station Rd RG17 9UT ☎ 01488 658263 📠 01488 658568
e-mail: info@dundasarms.co.uk
Dir: M4 J13 take A34 to Newbury, then A4 to Hungerford, L to Kintbury. Pub 1m next to canal and by railway station

Just outside the front door of this historic inn runs the 87-mile Kennet & Avon Canal which, having been derelict for about 40 years, is now one of the south's most popular waterways - ideal for walking, fishing and studying wildlife. The pub is on one of the loveliest stretches of the canal so take a stroll along the towpath before heading for the pub, named after the first chairman of the canal company. Both a well-established village local (the landlord has been around for 36 years!) and a country pub/restaurant of distinction, the Dundas Arms offers an interesting selection of blackboard specials. Dishes on offer might include fried calves' liver with bubble and squeak, Cumberland sausages and mash, grilled rib eye steak, baked cod with chips and peas, or grilled tuna. Good wine list by bottle.
OPEN: 11-2.30 6-11 (Closed Sun evening) Closed: 25 & 31Dec
BAR MEALS: L served Mon-Sat 12-2 D served Tue-Sat 7-9 Av main course £9.50 **RESTAURANT:** D served Tue-Sat 7-9 Av 3 course à la carte £25 **BREWERY/COMPANY:** Free House
🍺: Ringwood Best, Butts Barbus Barbus, Greene King Morland Origional, West Berkshire Good Old Boy. **FACILITIES:** Children welcome Garden: Riverside patio **NOTES:** Parking 70

KNOWL HILL
Map 05 SU87

Pick of the Pubs

Bird In Hand Country Inn 🍴 ⵠ
Bath Rd RG10 9UP
☎ 01628 826622 & 822781 📠 01628 826748
e-mail: info@birdinhand.co.uk
Dir: On A4, 5m W of Maidenhead, 7m E of Reading

A fascinating old inn that has remained in the same family for three generations. Dating back to the 14th century, its features include a main bar whose oak panelling came from a Scottish castle, and the adjoining farriers, now The Forge Bar, where George III stopped in the late 1700s. He granted a royal charter to the landlord in gratitude for the hospitality shown him. This tradition of warm welcome and friendly service lives on to this day. Bar snacks are available, whilst a more serious restaurant menu offers an appealing mix of modern and classic dishes. A meal could include baked goats' cheese tarte Tatin with pesto dressing, followed by medallions of pork fillet layered with aubergine in an apple and cider sauce. Residents beware of the phantom coach and horses that can be heard at night in the inn's oldest part!
OPEN: 11-3 (Sun 12-4) 6-11 (Sun 7-10:30) **BAR MEALS:** L served all week 12-2.30 D served all week 6.30-10 Av main course £7.50 **RESTAURANT:** L served all week 12-2.30 D served all week 7-10 Av 3 course à la carte £25 Av 3 course fixed price £18.50 **BREWERY/COMPANY:** Free House
🍺: Brakspear Bitter, Fuller's London Pride. ⵠ: 12
FACILITIES: Children welcome Garden: Garden next to patio with fountain Dogs allowed **NOTES:** Parking 86
ROOMS: 15 bedrooms 15 en suite 1 family rooms s£60 d£80 (★★★)

LAMBOURN
Map 05 SU37

The Hare & Hounds 🍴
Ermin St RG17 7SD ☎ 01488 71386 📠 01488 72329
Dir: On B4000 at Lambourn Woodlands. From motorway: Junction 14 or 15.
Notable for its individual decor and good food, this 17th-century coaching inn in the beautiful Lambourn Valley is a favourite with the horseracing fraternity. Dishes on offer include salmon and cod fishcakes, Aberdeen Angus steaks, pan-fried pollock steak on a bed of julienne vegetables, rösti of carrots, parsnips and potato served with a rocket salad, and hot green Thai curry.
OPEN: 12-3.30 6-11 (closed Sun evenings) Rest:Sunday closed eve
BAR MEALS: L served all week 12-2 D served Mon-Sat 7-9.30 Av

continued

main course £10 **RESTAURANT:** L served all week 12-2 D served Mon-Sat 7-9.30 Av 3 course à la carte £23 Av 3 course fixed price £25 **BREWERY/COMPANY:** Free House ◖ Wadworth 6X, Interbrew Flowers IPA & Boddingtons. **FACILITIES:** Children welcome Garden: Food served outdoors Dogs allowed Water **NOTES:** Parking 35

LITTLEWICK GREEN
Map 05 SU87

The Cricketers ◆◆◆ ♀
Coronation Rd SL6 3RA ☎ 01628 822888 ▤ 01628 822888
e-mail: thecricketers.demon.co.uk
Dir: 5m W of Maidenhead on A4 toward Reading. From M4 J8/9 take A404(M) to A4 junction
Standing in the shadow of a lovely walnut tree and overlooking the vast village cricket ground spread out opposite, this late-19th-century inn has an intriguing clocking-in clock inside, possibly once owned by the Great Western Railway. The village has been a location for the 'Midsomer Murders' TV series, and was once the home of composer Ivor Novello. A simple menu offers the likes of game casserole, moules marinieres, mushroom Stroganoff, and lamb shanks.

OPEN: 11-11 **BAR MEALS:** L served all week 12-2 D served Mon-Sat 7-9 Av main course £6.95 **BREWERY/COMPANY:** Free House ◖ King & Barnes Sussex Bitter, Badger Best Bitter, Tanglefoot. ♀: 7 **FACILITIES:** Children welcome **NOTES:** Parking 15 **ROOMS:** 3 bedrooms 3 en suite 1 family rooms s£55 d£60

MAIDENHEAD
Map 06 SU88

The Belgian Arms
Holyport SL6 2JR ☎ 01628 634468
Dir: 0.75m from Maidenhead
Before the First World War this picturesque pub was known as The Eagle, and the sign depicted a Prussian eagle. German prisoners of war detained at a nearby camp would stop and salute the eagle on their daily exercises, and so the pub's name was changed to that part of the world where the fiercest fighting was taking place - Belgium. A selection of dishes from the menu might include lasagne, ham and eggs, fish and chips and home-made burgers.
OPEN: 11-3 5.30-11 (Sat 12-3, 6-11 Sun 12-3, 7-10.30) Rest:Dec 25 Closed eve **BAR MEALS:** L served all week 12-2 D served Mon-Sat 6.30-9.30 Av main course £6.95 **BREWERY/COMPANY:** Brakspear ◖ Brakspear Best, Brakspear Special, Fosters, Stella Artois. **FACILITIES:** Children welcome Garden: Large lawned area, overlooks village pond Dogs allowed **NOTES:** Parking 45

> Most of the pubs in this guide book
> pride themselves on the quality of their food.
> This may take a little time to prepare.

MARSH BENHAM
Map 05 SU46

Pick of the Pubs

The Red House ◉ ♀
RG20 8LY ☎ 01635 582017 ▤ 01635 581621
Dir: 5m from Hungerford, 3m from Newbury & 400yds off the A4

Formerly known as The Water Rat, this handsome brick-and-thatch pub on the Kennet and Avon Canal is deep in 'Wind in the Willows' country. However, with its name change came a new, and contemporary style of inn-keeping. An interesting à la carte (modern British with a French accent) or a set-price bistro menu are offered. Served in starter or main dish sizes is a wild mushroom tart with poached egg and hollandaise sauce, and from a choice of seven main courses, the carte has pan-fried fillet of sea bass with egg noodles, fennel flan and sauce vierge, or roasted rack of Welsh lamb with artichokes, baby onions, lardons and a white truffle sauce. Classic desserts include pear belle Helene or warm bread and butter pudding. The canal-side patio - a great suntrap - is an ideal spot in which to down a pint of ale or enjoy a meal in fine weather.
OPEN: 11.30-3 6-11 **BAR MEALS:** L served Mon-Sun 12-2.15 D served Tue-Sat 7-10 Av main course £15 **RESTAURANT:** L served Mon-Sun 12-2.15 D served Tue-Sat 7-10 Av 3 course à la carte £27 **BREWERY/COMPANY:** Free House ◖ Fuller's London Pride, Greene King Ruddles County Ale. **FACILITIES:** Children welcome Garden **NOTES:** Parking 40

NEWBURY
Map 05 SU46

The Blackbird Inn
Bagnor RG20 8AQ ☎ 01635 40638
A quaint and unpretentious country pub close to Virginia Water and handy for the Watermill Theatre, whose actors are frequent customers. A large landscaped garden with children's adventure playground and a heated patio for adults are very popular. New owners have created a pleasant atmosphere, and serve quick bites along with lasagne, pan-fried liver and bacon, vegetable curry, and chicken tikka Masala, as well as good real ales.
OPEN: 12-11 (March, Mon-Sat, 12-3, 5.30-11) (March, Sun 12-4) Rest:March Closed Sunday Evening **BAR MEALS:** L served all week 12-2 D served all week 6-9 Av main course £6 **RESTAURANT:** L served all week 12-2 D served all week 12-2 ◖ Jesters, Fosters, Good Old Boy, Stella Artois. **FACILITIES:** Children welcome Garden: Large garden with covered and heated patio Dogs allowed **NOTES:** Parking 30

The White Hart Inn
Kintbury Rd, Hamstead Marshall RG20 0HW
☎ 01488 658201 ▪ 01488 657192
e-mail: info@thewhitehart-inn.co.uk
Dir: A4, 2m after Speen, L at x-roads, cross railway & canal, L at jnct, R at next jnct, inn 300yds on R

A 16th-century coaching inn where tenants of the nearby Craven estate came to pay their rent. Decorating the specials board are unusual chalk drawings, a charming feature in the bar. Examples of the enterprising Italian-based blackboard specials and restaurant menu include scallops wrapped in bacon and sage, wild mushroom stuffed ravioli, meatballs stuffed with Mozzarella, rabbit casserole, and pan-fried calves' liver with onions, sage and red wine. The pudding menu also has a delicious Italian tone.

OPEN: 12-2.30 6-11 (closed Sun) Closed: 25-26 Dec, 1 Jan, 2 weeks in summer **BAR MEALS:** L served Mon-Sat 12-2 D served Mon-Sat 6.30-9 Av main course £10.50 **RESTAURANT:** L served Mon-Sat 12-2 D served Mon-Sat 6.30-9 Av 3 course à la carte £16.50 **BREWERY/COMPANY:** Free House 🍺: Wadworth 6X, Hook Norton Best. **FACILITIES:** Garden: Walled garden with lawn and patio **NOTES:** Parking 30 **ROOMS:** 6 bedrooms 6 en suite 2 family rooms (♦♦♦♦) no children overnight

Pick of the Pubs

The Yew Tree Inn 🛏 ♀
Hollington Cross, Andover Rd, Highclere RG20 9SE
☎ 01635 253360 ▪ 01635 255035
Dir: A34 toward Southampton, 2nd exit bypass Highclere, onto A343 at rdbt, thru village, pub on R

Oak-framed inn of local brick and tile, dating back some 350 years and set in rolling countryside close to Highclere Castle. Scrubbed pine tables, low beams and an inglenook fireplace characterise the main bar, while a rambling series of interconnected rooms make up the restaurant area, where log fires and candlelit tables make for an inviting atmosphere. An imaginative menu and daily blackboard specials are served throughout the inn along with a range of fine wines and traditional beers. Representing the fish dishes might be roasted whole Test Valley trout with thyme, lemon and garlic, or whole sea bass stuffed with julienne of vegetables. You can also expect the likes of slow-roasted lamb on parsnip mash and red wine jus, or pork stuffed with sage, pistachio and sausage.
OPEN: 10-11 **BAR MEALS:** L served all week 12-10 D served all week Av main course £9 **RESTAURANT:** L served all week 12-3 D served all week 6.30-10 Av 3 course à la carte £20 Av 3 course fixed price £25 **BREWERY/COMPANY:** Free House 🍺: Guest beers. **FACILITIES:** Children welcome Garden: patio/terrace, food served outdoors Dogs allowed **NOTES:** Parking 40

Fox & Hounds 🛏
RG20 7JN ☎ 01635 248252
Dir: 3 miles from Jct 13 M4, A34 to Oxford

Next to the village cricket ground, these old buildings were converted into a pub some 100 years ago. At the edge of a pretty village dotted with thatched cottages with stunning views over the Berkshire Downs. The main bar has comfy leather sofas and a double aspect log burner that faces both bar and games room. Popular home-made bar food include basket meals, while in the dining room try speciality sausages in onion gravy, Punjabi butter chicken curry, and salmon fillet with black pepper sauce.

OPEN: 11.30-3 6.30-11 (weekdays open 5.30) Rest:Mon-Fri Closed lunchtimes **BAR MEALS:** L served Sat-Sun 12-2 D served Tue-Sun 6.30-9 Av main course £7.25 **RESTAURANT:** L served Sat-Sun 11.30-2 D served Tue-Sun 6.30-10 Av 3 course à la carte £12 🍺: Wadworth 6X, West Berkshire Good Old Boy, Worthingtons.
FACILITIES: Children welcome Garden: Food served outside Dogs allowed Water **NOTES:** Parking 40

Fishermans Cottage 🛏 ♀
224 Kennet Side RG1 3DW ☎ 0118 9571553 ▪ 0118 9571553
Dir: L from Kings Rd into Orts Rd then Canal Way

With its frontage on the Kennet and Avon Canal, and easy accessibility from the tow path and barge moorings at Blake's Lock, this listed building is a significant summer draw for outdoor types. A bar shaped like a canal barge, and a conservatory extension are attractions, along with quick and easy meals including all-day breakfast and burgers. Children's meals are served, with typical popular pub dishes. Monthly music nights.
OPEN: 11.30-3 5.30-11 (Fri-Sun & summer 11.30-11)
BAR MEALS: L served all week 12-2.30 D served all week 6-9 Av main course £5.50 **BREWERY/COMPANY:** Fullers 🍺: Fuller's London Pride & ESB. **FACILITIES:** Children welcome Garden Dogs allowed Water **NOTES:** Parking 10

See Pub Walk on opposite page

Fishermans Cottage

Discover Reading's hidden delights on this fascinating trail which includes scenic riverbanks, quiet canal towpaths, public gardens and ancient abbey ruins - all of which provide the walker with access to an historic corner of the town.

From the front of the pub turn right and walk along the towpath to Blakes Lock. Pass under the railway to reach Kennet Mouth and ahead of you now is the Thames. Cross the Kennet over Horseshoe Bridge and follow the southern bank of the Thames upstream alongside King's Meadow. Continue to Caversham Lock and swing left as you approach Reading Bridge. Turn right at the next junction to a roundabout and then turn left towards the town centre.

Veer left at the next roundabout, cross over at the lights and walk along the pavement, keeping the Forbury Gardens on your right. Enter the gardens and take the left-hand fork towards the statue of a lion. Make for the corner and pass through the old flint arch. The remains of the abbey can be seen on the left. Turn left by the river and walk along Chestnut Walk beside the memorial to Oscar Wilde who was imprisoned in Reading Gaol between 1895 and 1897.

At Blakes Bridge follow the towpath beneath the road and on the right is the Prudential building, once part of the Huntley and Palmer biscuit works. The river here played an

FISHERMANS COTTAGE, READING
24 Kennet Side RG1 3DW
☎ 0118 9571553
Directions: L from King's Rd into Orts Rd then Canal Way
Fronting onto the Kennet & Avon Canal, and handy for tow path walkers and bargees. Quick and easy meals swerved in bar and conservatory, including children's favourites
Open: 11.30-3 5.30-11 (Fri-Sun & Summer 11.30-11)
Bar Meals: 12-2.30 6-9
Notes: Children welcome (Wendy house) & dogs. Garden. Parking. (See page 34 for full entry)

important part in the factory's success, carrying the cargo downstream to London's docks.

Follow the towpath to the next bridge and turn right. Turn left at the next junction and pass one of the surviving Huntley and Palmer buildings. Cross the canal and take the steps down to the towpath. Walk ahead and return to the pub.

DISTANCE: 2 miles/3.2km
MAP: OS Explorer 159
TERRAIN: Urban
PATHS: Streets, tarmac paths, canal and river towpath
GRADIENT: No hills

Walk submitted and checked by Nick Channer

READING continued

The New Inn
Chalkhouse Green Rd, Kidmore End RG4 9AU
☎ 0118 9723115 & 9724733 📠 0118 9724733

It's not unusual to see horses tethered outside this 16th-century inn, whose lovely garden and good food make it a popular resting place on a country ride. The interior includes real oak studded floorboards, oak beams and a blackboard menu offering a frequently changing selection of home-cooked food: perhaps cod in beer batter, freshly-made soup, curry or beef and ale pie.

OPEN: 12-3 6-11 (Sat open all day, Sun 12-10.30) Rest:Sun Closed eve **BAR MEALS:** L served all week 12-2.30 D served Mon-Sat 6.30-9 Av main course £10 **RESTAURANT:** L served all week D served Mon-Sat 6.30-9 Av 3 course à la carte £20 Av 3 course fixed price £17.25 **BREWERY/COMPANY:** Brakspear 🍺: Brakspear Bitter & Old Ale. **FACILITIES:** Children welcome Garden: Food served outside **NOTES:** Parking 20

The Shoulder of Mutton
Play Hatch RG4 9QU ☎ 0118 947 3908
e-mail: gmwillows@hotmail.com
Dir: Situated just off the Henley / Reading Rd. At the Sonning / Binfield Heath Rdbt towards Binfield. We are approx 5 miles from Henley & Reading (A4155)

Renowned locally for good food and a beautiful Victorian walled garden, this renovated pub remains full of authentic character with its low beamed ceilings and large open fireplace. There's plenty to choose from the menus, with a typical meal being button and oyster mushrooms in a garlic cream sauce with Stilton, and chicken breast filled with cream cheese, pinenut and coriander, wrapped in bacon and served with chilli jam. Handy for avoiding the Henley Regatta queues.

OPEN: 12-3 6-11 Closed: 26-27 Dec, 1-2 Jan **BAR MEALS:** L served all week 12-2 D served all week 6.30-9 Av 3 course à la carte £19.50 **BREWERY/COMPANY:** Greene King 🍺: Greene King IPA & Ruddles County. **FACILITIES:** Garden: Victorian walled garden, conservatory **NOTES:** Parking 40

Sweeney & Todd
10 Castle St RG1 7RD ☎ 0118 9586466

Town centre pie shop with well-stocked bar. The selection of pies is excellent, as are the pies themselves. A great stop after a hard day's shopping.

OPEN: 11-11 **BAR MEALS:** L served all week 12-10.30 D served all week Av main course £8 🍺: Wadworth 6X, Adnams Best, Badger Tanglefoot, plus guest ales. **FACILITIES:** Children welcome **NOTES:** No credit cards

SONNING

Map 05 SU77

Bull Inn
High St RG4 6UP ☎ 01189 693901 📠 01189 691057
e-mail: dennis1925@aol.com
Dir: Telephone for directions

16th-century timbered inn in a splendid setting next to the village church and featuring old beams, tiled floors, winter log fires and a recommendation from Jerome K. Jerome, who mentions the pub in his novel 'Three Men in a Boat'. It also featured in the film 'Highlander', starring Sean Connery. An extensive menu offers vegetarian, vegan, gluten-free and dairy-free options. Popular dishes include lamb shank, Tennessee beef, steak and kidney pie, and goat's cheese and red pepper cannellini.

OPEN: 11-3 5.30-11 **BAR MEALS:** L served all week 12-2 D served all week 6.30-9 Av main course £9.95 **RESTAURANT:** L served all week 12-2 D served all week 6.30-9.30
BREWERY/COMPANY: Gales 🍺: Gale's HSB, Best, Butser Bitter. **FACILITIES:** Children welcome Children's licence Garden: Patio area Dogs allowed Dog Bowls **NOTES:** Parking 20

STANFORD DINGLEY

Map 05 SU57

The Bull Inn
RG7 6LS ☎ 0118 9744409 📠 0118 974 5249
e-mail: robert.archard@btinternet.com
Dir: A4/A340 to Pangbourne. 1st L to Bradfield.Thru Bradfield, 0.3m L into Back Lane. At end L, pub 0.25m on L

Traditional 15th-century inn featuring a wealth of timbers and even the remains of an original wattle and daub wall. Classic cars, and Jaguars in particular, are the landlord's lifetime hobby and passion, and one of the bars reflects this deep interest. Among the interesting food selections are fillet of venison on grain mustard mash, saddle of lamb filled with apricot and rosemary stuffing, and tasty hot and cold snacks.

OPEN: 12-3 6-11 (Sun 7-10.30) **BAR MEALS:** L served all week 12-2.30 D served all week 6.30-9.30 Av main course £8.50

continued

RESTAURANT: L served Sun 12.30-2.30 D served Wed-Sat 6.30-9.30 Av 3 course à la carte £20 **BREWERY/COMPANY:** Free House ◖: West Berkshire Brewery Ales, Brakspear Bitter, Interbrew Bass. ♀: 7 **FACILITIES:** Children welcome Garden: Lrg secure area, plenty of tables Dogs allowed Water **NOTES:** Parking 32

The Old Boot Inn ◔ ♀
RG7 6LT ☎ 01189 744292 🖷 01189 744292
Dir: *M4 J12, A4/A340 to Pangbourne. 1st L to Bradfield. Through Bradfield & follow signs for Stanford Dingley*
Set in the glorious Pang Valley, in a village of Outstanding Natural Beauty, the original 18th-century Old Boot has been extended to include a popular conservatory. Fresh fish is announced daily on the blackboard, while further dining options range through lamb sweetbreads and sautéed chicken livers for starters, duck breast, guinea fowl with Calvados and lime, and ostrich fillet, and bar snacks like pork stir-fry, cod in batter, and steak and kidney pudding.
OPEN: 11-3 6-11 (Sun 12-3, 7-10.30) **BAR MEALS:** L served all week 12-2.15 D served all week 7-9.30 Av main course £8 **RESTAURANT:** L served all week 12-2.15 D served all week 7-9.30 Av 3 course à la carte £20 **BREWERY/COMPANY:** Free House ◖: Brakspear Bitter, Interbrew Bass, West Berkshire Dr Hexters, Archers Best. ♀: 8 **FACILITIES:** Children welcome Garden: 1/2 acre over-looking farmland Dogs allowed **NOTES:** Parking 40

SWALLOWFIELD   Map 05 SU76

Pick of the Pubs

The George & Dragon ♀
Church Rd RG7 1TJ ☎ 0118 9884 432 🖷 0118 9886474
Behind the unassuming façade of this old inn, set close to the River Blackwater on the village edge, is a smart and cosy interior featuring stripped low beams, terracotta-painted walls, log fires and rug-strewn floors. Very much a dining pub - booking essential. Start with a skewer of garlic tiger prawns on a minted tabouleh with sweet and sour dipping sauce, Malaysian squid salad with chargrilled marinated halloumi, or grilled Portuguese sardines with crispy seaweed; and continue with pan-fried red snapper with wild mushroom and spring onion risotto, whole-baked seabass in Thai marinade, or beef fillet with penny onion, mushroom and smoked bacon ragôut. Keep an eye on the blackboard for daily specials, and seasonal fish and game.
OPEN: 12-11 (Sat 12-4, 6-11, Sun 12-4, 7-10.30)
BAR MEALS: 12-2.30 7-10 **RESTAURANT:** L served all week 12-2.30 D served all week 7-10 **BREWERY/COMPANY:** Free House ◖: Fullers London Pride, Wadworth 6X plus Guest ale.
FACILITIES: Garden Dogs allowed **NOTES:** Parking 50

THATCHAM   Map 05 SU56

Pick of the Pubs

The Bladebone Inn
Chapel Row, Bucklebury RG7 6PD
☎ 0118 9712326 🖷 0118 9712326
Dir: *5m from Newbury and the A4, 2m from the A4 at Thatcham*
Within earshot of the M4 at the southern edge of the North Wessex Downs, but more easily accessed from the A4 east of Thatcham, this historic inn stands at the end of a stately avenue of oak trees planted to

commemorate a visit by Elizabeth I. Over the entrance hangs a bladebone which, according to local legend, came from a mammoth that once stalked the Downs. It is more likely that it was used to indicate that whale oil was sold here for use in oil-burning lamps and probably of 17th-century origin. What once was a traditional village local has been transformed into a dining venue with emphasis on modern pub food, comfortable furnishings and a relaxed atmosphere. Starters typically consist of crispy tempura prawns and warm Roquefort cheesecake, followed by chicken fillet stuffed with Toulouse sausage, roast seabass with tomato and chorizo on Parmesan risotto, or Tallegio cheese and Mediterranean vegetables on ciabatta bread.
OPEN: 12-3 6.30-11 Closed: 1-30 Jan **BAR MEALS:** L served Tue-Sun 12-3 D served Tue-Sat 7-9 Av main course £12.50 **RESTAURANT:** L served Tue-Sun 12-3 7-9 **BREWERY/COMPANY:** Whitbread ◖: Fuller's London Pride, Interbrew Flowers IPA, West Berks Dr Hexters Healer, Brakspear Bitter. **FACILITIES:** Garden **NOTES:** Parking 20

THEALE   Map 05 SU67

Thatchers Arms ♀
North St RG7 5EX ☎ 0118 930 2070 🖷 0118 930 2070
Dir: *Telephone for directions*
You'll find a warm welcome and good, home-cooked food at this classic country pub. Despite its location in a small village surrounded by open countryside, the Thatchers Arms is just five minutes drive from the centre of Theale and junction 12 of the M4. The menu changes regularly, but steak and kidney pie, wild boar sausages, and seafood kebabs are typical precursors to bread and butter pudding, apple crumble, or caramelised plums.

OPEN: 12-2.30 (Sat 12-3, 6-11) 5.30-11 (Sun 12-3, 7-10.30)
BAR MEALS: L served all week 12-2 D served all week 7-9.30 Av main course £7.95 **RESTAURANT:** L served all week 12-2 D served all week 7-9.30 **BREWERY/COMPANY:** ◖: Fuller's London Pride, Brakspear Bitter, Stella Artois, Dry Blackthorn. ♀: 8 **FACILITIES:** Children welcome Garden: Dogs allowed Water **NOTES:** Parking 15

WALTHAM ST LAWRENCE   Map 05 SU87

The Bell
The Street RG10 0JJ ☎ 0118 9341788
Dir: *on B3024 E of Twyford (from A4 turn at Hare Hatch)*
Since 1608, when it was left to the village in trust, the rent from this 14th-century inn has been donated to local charities. The same menu operates throughout, offering a variety of

continued   *continued*

WALTHAM ST LAWRENCE continued

meat pies and puddings, chilli, enchiladas, lamb and pork shanks, chicken tikka, and fresh fish on Fridays.
OPEN: 11.30-3 (Sun 12-7) 5-11 **BAR MEALS:** L served all week 12-2 D served Mon-Sat 7-9.30 Av main course £7.50 **RESTAURANT:** L served all week 12-2 D served Mon-Sat 7-9.30 **BREWERY/COMPANY:** Free House ◧: Waltham St Lawrence No.1 Ale, Hook Norton, plus 3 Guests. **FACILITIES:** Children welcome Garden: Food served outside Dogs allowed Water bowls provided **NOTES:** Parking 5

WEST ILSLEY — Map 05 SU48

Pick of the Pubs

Harrow Inn ⏣
RG20 7AR ☎ 01635 281260 ▤ 01635 281260
e-mail: theharrowilsley@aol.com

Historic inn where Morlands Brewery was founded in 1711, the Harrow lies in a peaceful settlement on the edge of the Berkshire Downs, close to the Ridgeway Path and surrounded by horseracing country. Thoroughbred English food is served in the open-plan bar, with wraps, filled French rolls, and beef burgers at lunchtime, in addition to more substantial dishes, such as classic French cassoulet with Toulouse sausage and green salad, or half shoulder of lamb with haggis, dauphinoise potatoes, braised green cabbage and port sauce, which might appear at either lunch or dinner. Lemon and sun-dried tomato risotto with Parmesan shavings serves as a starter or main course, and you could round off with tarte Tatin, or chocolate brownie with caramel sauce and vanilla ice cream. The inn has recently been repainted with a green and terracotta scheme, enhancing the warm and inviting atmosphere.
OPEN: 11-3 (open Sun eve, Mon in summer) 6-11 Rest:Sun (Winter) Closed eve **BAR MEALS:** L served Mon-Sun 12-2 D served Tue-Sun 7-9 **BREWERY/COMPANY:** Greene King ◧: Morland Original, Greene King & Abbot Ale. ⏣: 6 **FACILITIES:** Children welcome Garden Dogs allowed **NOTES:** Parking 10

WINKFIELD — Map 06 SU97

Pick of the Pubs

Rose & Crown ⌕
Woodside, Windsor Forest SL4 2DP
☎ 01344 882051 ▤ 01344 885346
Dir: M3 J3 from Ascot racecourse on A332 take 2nd exit from Heatherwood Hosp r'about, then 2nd L
A 200-year-old traditional pub complete with old beams and low ceilings. Hidden down a country lane, it has a

peaceful garden overlooking open fields where you can see horses and llamas at pasture. The tastefully-refurbished bar and restaurant provide comfortable seating in which to enjoy real ales, good wines and home-cooked food prepared with care and cooked in a confident and robust style. Starters like warm Portabella mushroom salad, and New Zealand mussel tempura with a herbed risotto are followed by pan-fried calves' liver on a bubble and squeak croquet, or corn-fed chicken filled with chorizo sausage and chargrilled peppers. Fish might be represented by pan-fried skate wing, or marinated salmon fillet with wok-fried vegetables. Greene King ales take pride of place at the bar.

OPEN: 11-11 (Sun 12-7) **BAR MEALS:** L served all week 12-2.30 D served Tue-Sat 7-9.30 Av main course £6.50 **RESTAURANT:** L served all week 12-2.30 D served Tue-Sat 7-9.30 Av 3 course à la carte £25 **BREWERY/COMPANY:** Greene King ◧: Greene King Abbot Ale, Morland Original-IPA. **FACILITIES:** Children welcome Garden: Next to large field **NOTES:** Parking 24

WINTERBOURNE — Map 05 SU47

Pick of the Pubs

The Winterbourne Arms ⏣
RG20 8BB ☎ 01635 248200 ▤ 01635 248824
Dir: From M4 S on A34, 1st slip road

This large black and white timber-framed freehouse must look very different from the bakery it was 300 years ago. You can still see where the old bread oven was before the building became the village local. A wide cross-section of society now finds sanctuary here - regulars, veteran drinkers (often one and the same), couples, families, and walkers are all welcomed. A cosy, relaxed feel is created inside by wall lighting, a large inglenook fireplace,

continued

continued

traditional pub furniture, exposed stone walls, beams and tasteful trinkets. In the words of the new owners, the 'spacious, well-decorated restaurant is ideal for informal country dining' - we'd welcome visitors' views of their uncomplicated, but catholic seasonal menus. Lunch is in the fresh fillet of cod, home-made burger with bacon and Mozzarella, and leek and ricotta cannelloni mould. A change of gear in the evenings produces fragrant green Thai curry, pan-fried sea bass, and seared duck breast. Daily specials are in similar vein. Beautifully kept gardens look across rolling countryside.

OPEN: 12-3 6-11 Rest:26 Dec 1 Jan Closed eve
BAR MEALS: L served Tue-Sun 12-2.30 D served Tue-Sat 7-9.30 Av main course £6.95 **RESTAURANT:** L served Tue-Sun 12-2.30 D served Tue-Sat 7-9.30 Av 3 course à la carte £18
BREWERY/COMPANY: Free House : Fuller's London Pride, West Berkshire Good Old Boy, Interbrew Bass. : 10
FACILITIES: Garden: Garden in front of pub with tables Dogs allowed **NOTES:** Parking 40

OPEN: 12-3 6-11 **BAR MEALS:** L served Mon-Sat 12-2.30 D served Mon-Sat 6-9.30 Av main course £10 **RESTAURANT:** L served all week 12-2.30 D served all week 6-10 Av 3 course à la carte £30
BREWERY/COMPANY: Free House : Interbrew Flowers Original & Boddingtons. : 20 **FACILITIES:** Garden: Japanese water garden
NOTES: Parking 40

WOKINGHAM
Map 05 SU86

The Crooked Billet
Honey Hill ☎ 0118 978 0438 ▤ 0118 9789256

An old white weather-boarded pub, reputed to have been moved piece by piece from the other side of the road! Inside there is an open fireplace, traditional decorations and a friendly atmosphere that draws in a strong local following. Most of the food is home made, including specials like calves' liver and bacon, honey-glazed duck, bangers and mash, and from the menu, chilli con carni, and mushroom and Stilton tagliatelle.
OPEN: 11-11.40 Closed: Dec 26 **BAR MEALS:** L served all week 12-2.30 D served Mon-Sat 7-9.30 Av main course £7.95 **RESTAURANT:** L served all week 12-2.30 D served all week 7-9.30 : Breakspear Special, Original. **FACILITIES:** Children welcome Garden: Food served outside Dogs allowed Water **NOTES:** Parking 300

WOOLHAMPTON
Map 05 SU56

The Angel
Bath Rd RG7 5RT ☎ 0118 9713307
e-mail: mail@a4angel.com

An impressive Virginia creeper-covered building, dating from around 1752,with a large front terrace. Many original features remain, like the splendid Regency board room with chandeliers. In an atmosphere that is both informal and relaxing, a wine list of more than 20 selections by the glass augments such fairly serious food as cream of home-smoked haddock with poached oysters, supreme of corn-fed chicken with rosti, roast parsnip dumpling and mushroom sauce, and steamed timbale of lemon sole and lobster with caviar.

YATTENDON
Map 05 SU57

Pick of the Pubs

The Royal Oak Hotel ★★
The Square RG18 0UG ☎ 01635 201325 ▤ 01635 201926
e-mail: theroyaloak@hotmail.com
Dir: From M4 J12, A4 to Newbury, R at 2nd rdbt to Pangbourne then 1st L. From J13, A34 N 1st L, R at T-junct. L then 2nd R to Yattendon

A 16th-century timber-framed coaching inn on the village square, later re-faced in the red brick that you will encounter today, The Oak - as it was then known - played host to such luminaries as King Charles I and Oliver Cromwell. It's a quintessentially English country inn, rarely interrupted by more than the footfall of passing horse-riders. While the popular village bar remains, emphasis is based on a brasserie-style menu rooted in local ingredients and sound cooking. Confit of duck leg with pineapple, and Thai fishcakes with sweet-and-sour pickle satisfy as a snack or a precursor to roast monkfish tails in goats' cheese and Parma ham, or classic-style steak béarnaise. Cap it off with rich chocolate bread and butter pudding or a selection of French and English cheeses.
OPEN: 11-3 6-11 **BAR MEALS:** L served all week 12-2.30 D served all week 7-10 **RESTAURANT:** L served Mon-sat 12-2.30 D served Mon-Sat 7-9.30 Av 3 course à la carte £26
BREWERY/COMPANY: : 6X, Boddingtons, Stella.
FACILITIES: Garden: Traditional Garden **NOTES:** Parking 15
ROOMS: 5 bedrooms 5 en suite no children overnight

continued

England

BRISTOL

BRISTOL Map 04 ST57

Brewery Tap ♀
Upper Maudlin St BS1 5BD ☎ 0117 921 3668 📄 0117 925 8235
e-mail: brewerytap@smiles.co.uk
Dir: *Telephone for directions*

Pub adjacent to Smiles Brewery so all the ales are freshly brewed next door. It's a traditional English pub with an emphasis on real beer, though lagers, Guinness, cider, wines and spirits are also served. A menu of pub favourites is offered - fish and chips, chilli, curry and burgers - all home made. New management, but same brewery ownership.
OPEN: 11-11 (Sun 11-4, 7-11) Closed: 25-26 Dec, 1 Jan
BAR MEALS: L served Mon-Sun 12-8 D served Mon-Fri 12-8 Av main course £4.50 **BREWERY/COMPANY:** Smiles 🍺: Smiles, Best, Original, Heritage. ♀: 7 **FACILITIES:** Children welcome Dogs allowed

Highbury Vaults
164 St Michaels Hill, Cotham BS2 8DE
☎ 0117 9733203 📄 0117 9744828
Dir: *Take main road to Cotham from inner ring dual carriageway*
Once a turnpike station, this 1840s pub retains a Victorian atmosphere and seating in its many nooks and crannies. In days when hangings took place on nearby St Michael's Hill, many victims partook of their last meal in the vaults. Today, its a business crowd by day and students at night feasting on chilli, meat and vegetable curries, casseroles and jacket potatoes. Young's beers, no music or fruit machines and a heated garden terrace in which to chill out.
OPEN: 12-11 (Sun 12-10.30) **BAR MEALS:** L served all week 12-3 D served Mon-Fri 5.30-8.30 Av main course £3.40
BREWERY/COMPANY: Young & Co 🍺: Smiles Best & Heritage, Brains SA, Young's Special & Bitter. **FACILITIES:** Children welcome Garden: Heated patio, seating for 100 people **NOTES:** No credit cards

> **Room prices show the minimum double and single rates charged.**
> **Room rates in hotels and B&Bs often vary depending on the facilities, so be sure to check prices with the establishment before booking.**

BUCKINGHAMSHIRE

AMERSHAM Map 06 SU99

The Hit or Miss ♀
Penn St Village HP7 0PX ☎ 01494 713109 📄 01494 718010
e-mail: enquiries@hitormiss.fsnet
Old deeds show that this 18th-century cottage was converted to a pub as long ago as 1798. Its name is a cricketing reference - after all, it is opposite the village cricket pitch. The menu serves both the bar and cricket-themed no-smoking dining area. Typical would be duck egg Benedict as a starter, followed by individual fillet of beef Wellington, and strawberry and rhubarb amaretti crumble. Sadly, no-one has recently seen Molly, the resident ghost.
OPEN: 11-3 5.30-11 (All day Sat-Sun, Summer) **BAR MEALS:** L served all week 12-2.30 D served all week 6.45-9.30 Av main course £9.50 **RESTAURANT:** L served all week 12-2.30 D served Mon-Sat 6.45-9.30 Av 3 course à la carte £17 **BREWERY/COMPANY:** Hall & Woodhouse 🍺: Badger Tanglefoot, Best, Sussex, Pilsner. ♀: 8 **FACILITIES:** Garden: Lawn and patio area with picnic tables Dogs allowed **NOTES:** Parking 40

The Kings Arms ♀
30 The High St, Old Amersham HP7 0DJ
☎ 01494 726333 📄 01494 433480
e-mail: info@kingsarmsamersham.co.uk

Historic atmosphere fills the bars of this 15th-century, black and white timbered inn. There are always four real ales on offer, two drawn directly from the cask behind the counter. The bar snack menu lists sandwiches, pies, pasta and chicken tikka, while the restaurant offers a three-month carte and four to five-week fixed-price menu. A sample from a restaurant menu offers mousseline of salmon with a crab sauce, duck breast with honey and peppercorns, sea bass with saffron and orange, and braised lamb with flageolet beans. The façade of the pub was used in the film 'Four Weddings and A Funeral'.
OPEN: 11-11 (Sun 12-10.30) **BAR MEALS:** L served all week 12-2.30 Av main course £7 **RESTAURANT:** L served Tue-Sun 12-2 D served Tue-Sat 7-9.30 Av 3 course à la carte £27 Av 3 course fixed price £15.50 **BREWERY/COMPANY:** Free House 🍺: Rebellion IPA, Burton Ale, Guest Beers. ♀: 9 **FACILITIES:** Children welcome Children's licence Garden **NOTES:** Parking 25

The Stag and Huntsman

Explore the countryside around picturesque Hambleden, a popular film and TV location.

From the pub turn left towards the church and then swing right. Pass pairs of cottages and then turn right at the footpath sign. Follow the track up the hill through the trees and keep ahead between fields. Pass a stile on the left and continue towards farm outbuildings. Turn sharp left just before them and cross a stile. Follow the track into woodland, keep left at the fork and cross a track with a 'no public right of way' sign seen on the left. Continue ahead on a grassy path.

Cross a stile and keep right at the road. Walk along to Rockwell End, swing left here and eventually pass a turning on the right for Marlow. Turn left just beyond St Katherine's, a retreat house, following the tarmac lane to a house with a balcony. The lane dwindles to a path here, descending gradually between trees and bushes.

Pass a path running off sharp right and on reaching the road, keep left. Walk down towards the junction at the southern end of the village of Skirmett, look for a stile on the left and join the Chiltern Way, heading south across fields. Cross six stiles to reach a house, keep to the left of it and follow the path through the trees.

Keep alongside a hedge, heading towards several houses set against trees. Cross the field and continue on a wide track. Go straight on at the road, passing Colstrope Farm on the left. Look for a kissing gate on the right bend. Continue ahead on the Chiltern Way, make for a gate and keep the field boundary on your right.

Head for a kissing gate and keep ahead with the field perimeter now on your left. Make for Pheasant's Hill, following the way through several gates. Cross a drive to a kissing gate and continue beside a paddock. Ahead lie a stile and kissing gate. Cross the next field, go through a gate and veer left to a kissing gate. Swing right, following the road back to Hambleden.

THE STAG AND HUNTSMAN INN,
HAMBLEDEN, RG9 6RP
☎ 01491 571227
Directions: 5m from Henley-on-Thames on A4155 towards Marlow, L at Mill End towards Hambleden. Welcoming old building made of brick and flint, attracting walkers and cyclists along with other passing and local customers. Looks familiar from being the set for many films and TV programmes. Choose between a cosy snug, public bar, lounge bar and dining room.
Open: 11-2.30 6-11 (Sat 11-3 6-11, Sun 12-3 7-10.30)
Bar Meals: 12-2 7-9.30
Notes: Children & dogs welcome. Garden. Parking.
(See page 49 for full entry)

DISTANCE: 6 miles/9.7km
MAP: OS Explorer 171
TERRAIN: Undulating Chilterns north of Hambleden
PATHS: Country roads, tracks and paths
GRADIENT: One moderate climb near the start

Walk submitted and checked by Nick Channer

ASTON CLINTON Map 05 SP81

The Oak ♀
119 Green End St HP22 5EU ☎ 01296 630466 📠 01296 631796
e-mail: jan.andrews2@BTOPENWORLD.com
Dir: *entry via Brook St, off the A41*

Thatched, 500-year-old coaching inn with flagstone floors, inglenook fireplace and bags of old-world charm. Set in the old part of the village, it offers a good family garden and a wide-ranging menu. Summer events include a beer festival and a charity fete. Expect traditional pub favourites, alongside beef Stroganoff, pan-fried salmon, and sweet and sour chicken with sweet peppers.
OPEN: 11.30-2.30 6-11 (Sun 12-3 6-11) (open all day Sat-Sun in summer) **BAR MEALS:** L 12-2 (later on Sun) D served all week 6-9.30 Av main course £5.25 **RESTAURANT:** L served all week 12-2 D Mon-Sat 6-9.30 Av 3 course à la carte £14.75
BREWERY/COMPANY: Fullers 🍺: Fullers London Pride, Fullers ESB + 1 Guest. **FACILITIES:** Garden: Food served outside Dogs allowed Water **NOTES:** Parking 30

AYLESBURY Map 11 SP81

Pick of the Pubs

Bottle & Glass 🐷 ♀
Gibraltar, Nr Dinton HP17 8TY
☎ 01296 748488 📠 01296 747673
Dir: *On A418 between Thame & Aylesbury*

In a peaceful rural setting close to the Chiltern Hills, this 17th-century thatched inn with low ceilings, flagstone floors, intimate alcoves, open fires and an appealing decor has an immediately warm and welcoming ambience. Fresh fish and seafood, delivered daily, is a real strength: simply cooked to enhance their best flavours may be tuna on garlic mash with thyme cream and vinaigrette, chargrilled cod with sweet pepper coulis and balsamic reduction, and salmon on Asian noodles with

orange dressing, basil oil and mango salsa. Meat dishes cover duck breast with wild mushroom sauce, beef fillet on rösti with Dijon mustard and tarragon sauce, and steak and kidney pie; excellent Sunday roasts with all the trimmings. With lunch in mind are open ciabatta sandwiches or a bowl of mussels served with fresh bread; follow with a home-made pudding, perhaps a tangy citron tart. Superb front terrace seating festooned with flowering hanging baskets and tubs.
OPEN: 11-3 6-11 (closed Sun eve) **BAR MEALS:** L served all week 12-2.30 D served Mon-Sat 7-9.30 Av main course £6
RESTAURANT: L served all week 12-2 D served Mon-Sat 7-9.30 Av 3 course à la carte £25 Av 3 course fixed price £15
BREWERY/COMPANY: Morrells 🍺: IPA, Ruddles County.
FACILITIES: Children welcome Garden: Plants and flower beds, heating lamps **NOTES:** Parking 50

BEACONSFIELD Map 06 SU99

The Greyhound 🐷 ♀
33 Windsor End HP9 2JN ☎ 01494 673823 📠 01494 673379
e-mail: greyhound.windsorend@eldridge-pope.co.uk
Dir: *Follow signs to Beaconsfield Old Town, left at central roundabout*
Comfortable 16th-century drovers' tavern enjoying a secluded location opposite the parish church. Traditional, home-cooked pub food is served, including garlic chicken breast, poached salmon with a dill sauce, tuna à la Maltese, vegetable Wellington, whole seabass with red pepper sauce, or quarter of lamb shoulder with red wine and mint sauce. Choice of sandwiches, baked potatoes and salads also available.
OPEN: 11-3 5-11 Closed: May 10 **BAR MEALS:** L served all week 12-2 D served Tue-Sat 6-9.30 Av main course £8 **RESTAURANT:** L served all week 12-2 D served Tue-Sat 7-9.45 Av 3 course à la carte £15 **BREWERY/COMPANY:** Eldridge Pope 🍺: Ansells, Fullers London Pride, Rebellion Beers, Guest Ales. ♀: 8
FACILITIES: Children welcome Garden: Food served outside. Dogs allowed **NOTES:** Parking 100

Pick of the Pubs

The Royal Standard of England 🐷
Brindle Ln, Forty Green HP9 1XT
☎ 01494 673382 📠 01494 523332
Dir: *A40 to Beaconsfield. R at Church rndbt onto B474 towards Penn. L onto Forty Green Rd, then 1m*
Country inn dating from the 12th century with striking stained glass windows, beams, flagstone floors, and a large inglenook fireplace. Situated in a part of the world renowned for Civil War battles and skirmishes, the inn became a Royalist headquarters, and it was this that led to its splendid and impressive name. The inn is a perfect base for walking and here you can rest after a long hike, licking your wounds and stoking up with beef and Owd Rodger ale pie, local speciality sausages, marinated paprika pork, traditional beer and herb-battered haddock or fillet of chicken, or spring vegetable pilaf timbale. Mediterranean fresh tuna stir-fry with buttered noodles, shank of lamb slow cooked with cider and Guinness, and baked goats' cheese with toasted walnut salad are typical examples of the specials board. A range of real ales including Marston's powerful Owd Roger - not suitable for drivers!

continued

continued

OPEN: 11-3 5.30-11 (Sun 12-3, 7-10.30) Rest:25 Dec closed eve **BAR MEALS:** L served all week 12-2.15 D served all week 6.30-9.15 Av main course £10 **BREWERY/COMPANY:** Free House 🍺: Marston's Pedigree, Brakspear Bitter, Fuller's London Pride & two Guest ales. **FACILITIES:** Children welcome Children's licence Garden: Paved seating area with floral borders Dogs allowed Water **NOTES:** Parking 90

BLEDLOW   Map 05 SP70

The Lions of Bledlow 🐾 ♀
Church End HP27 9PE ☎ 01844 343345 ▤ 01844 343345
Dir: M40 J6 take B4009 to Princes Risborough, through Chinnor into Bledlow

Unchanged since the early 20th century, this Grade II listed building nestles beneath the Chiltern escarpment and still retains the atmosphere of an old style country pub. The rambling low-beamed bar has a wealth of character, and the patio and large garden, overspilling onto the village green, are popular for summer drinking. Halibut fillet with cider sauce, fresh mussels in white wine, pork fillet in mushroom sauce, duck in hoi-sin sauce are supplemented by a list of ten or so daily specials.
OPEN: 11.30-3 6-11 (Sun 12-3, 7-10.30) Rest:25 Dec Closed eve **BAR MEALS:** L served all week 12-2.30 D served all week 7-9.30 Av main course £6.75 **RESTAURANT:** L served all week 12-2.30 D served all week 7-9.30 **BREWERY/COMPANY:** Free House 🍺: Wadworth 6X, Scottish Courage Courage Best, Marston's Pedigree, Brakspear Bitter. ♀: 8 **FACILITIES:** Garden: Lawns, patio, village green at front Dogs allowed Water, Biscuits, Toys **NOTES:** Parking 60

The Rosette is the AA award for food. Look out for it next to a pub's name.

BLETCHLEY   Map 11 SP83

Pick of the Pubs

Crooked Billet ◉◉ 🐾 ♀
2 Westbrook End, Newton Longville MK17 0DF
☎ 01908 373936 ▤ 01908 631979
e-mail: john@thebillet.co.uk
Dir: From M1 junct 13 take A421 towards Buckingham to Bottleaimp rdbt turn L into the village of Newton Longville. Pub on R

All you could dream of in a village local is offered at this 200-year-old former coaching inn - a thatched roof, original oak beams, open log fires and a quiet location in a country lane. It also offers a wine-themed restaurant serving innovative modern British food in informal pub surroundings, and a sublime wine list with an astonishing 300 wines available by the glass. Lunchtime options range from toasted ciabatta snacks to an interesting choice of hot dishes like smoked haddock and bubble and squeak fishcake with poached egg, and crispy maple-cured bacon and hollandaise. From the dinner menu come roasted turbot with lobster mash, wilted spinach and Pinot reduction, and duck three ways: roasted breast on fondant, confit leg and duck sausage on mash with duck jus. For dessert try plum and ginger bread and butter pudding with vanilla fudge and vanilla pod ice cream, or whole roasted figs with oatmeal tuilles, LBV port sorbet and spicy fig sauce. Cheeses from Neal's Yard and Longman Dairies are served with quince paste and prune and walnut cake. Booking is essential.
OPEN: 12-2.30 5.30-11 (Sun 12-4, 7-10.30) Closed: 1st 2 weeks Jan, 25-26 Dec **BAR MEALS:** L served Tue-Sun 12-2 D served Tue-Sat Av main course £12 **RESTAURANT:** L served Sun 12-3 D served Tues-Sat 7-10 Av 3 course à la carte £22 **BREWERY/COMPANY:** Greene King 🍺: Abbot Ale, Triumph, Old Speckled Hen, Badger Tanglefoot. ♀: 300 **FACILITIES:** Garden: Large open garden, 13 tables **NOTES:** Parking 25

BOLTER END   Map 05 SU79

The Peacock ♀
HP14 3LU ☎ 01494 881417
Dir: A40 through Stokenchurch, then B482
The oldest part of this pub dates from 1620, featuring original beams and a fireplace dating from the early 1800s. It is situated on top of the Chiltern Hills overlooking the common. A typical menu features Lincolnshire pork sausages, Aberdeen Angus steaks, cheesy mushroom pancakes, and spicy beef and bean chilli. Don't forget the daily specials.
OPEN: 12-2.30 6-11 (Sun 12-4 only) **BAR MEALS:** L served all week 12-2 D served Mon-Sat 6-9.30 Av main course £8 **BREWERY/COMPANY:** Punch Taverns 🍺: Brakspear Bitter, Fullers London Pride. **FACILITIES:** Children welcome Garden: Food served outside **NOTES:** Parking 30

England

BOVINGDON GREEN

Map 05 SU88

The Royal Oak ♀
Frieth Rd SL7 2JF ☎ 01628 488611 📷 01628 478680

In the three years since it opened, The Oak has become popular not only with the locals but also with Londoners seeking a taste of the country. It's a pretty, traditional-looking inn with a sun trap terrace and pétanque court, and prides itself on the quality and variety of its food. Choose from 'small plates' (perhaps home-made soup or crisped pork belly with lemon chutney) or main meals such as braised lamb shank with rowanberry jus or venison and roast apple stew.
OPEN: 11 -11 (Sun 12-10.30) **BAR MEALS:** L served all week 12-2.30 D served all week 7-10 Av main course £11.50 **RESTAURANT:** L served all week 12-2.30 D served all week 7-10 Av 3 course à la carte £21.25 🍺: London Pride, Brakspears, Rebellion, Stella Artois. ♀: 13 **FACILITIES:** Garden: Terrace with large tables and canopies Dogs allowed **NOTES:** Parking 42

BRILL

Map 11 SP61

The Pheasant Inn 🐾 ♀
Windmill St HP18 9TG ☎ 01844 237104
e-mail: mrcarr@btinternet.com
Set on the edge of Brill Common, the large garden and veranda at this 17th-century beamed inn make the most of its fine hilltop position, with impressive views over seven counties. The pub used to be a village shop, no doubt supplied with flour from Brill windmill, which is right next door! There are winter fires, and the popular blackboard menu offers fresh salmon, plus local steaks and pheasant in season. Roald Dahl and JRR Tolkien were both frequent visitors to the pub.
OPEN: 11-3 5.30-11 (Sun 12-10.30) Closed: Dec 25-26
BAR MEALS: L served all week 12-2 D served all week 7-9 Av main course £9.95 **RESTAURANT:** L served all week 12-2 D served all week 7-9 Av 3 course à la carte £18.50 **BREWERY/COMPANY:** Free House 🍺: Young's Special, Brakspear Bitter. ♀: 7 **FACILITIES:** Children welcome Garden: Beautiful views, seats 80 **NOTES:** Parking 25

BUCKINGHAM

Map 11 SP63

The Old Thatched Inn 🐾 ♀
Adstock MK18 2JN ☎ 01296 712584 📷 01296 715375
Thatched and beamed 17th-century inn which has come through a refurbishment with the traditional beams and inglenook fireplace intact. A modern conservatory and the timbered lounge provide a choice of eating place where the menu plus specials and light bites is offered. Oven-roasted fillet of cod, lamb kofta on lemongrass skewer, slow-braised lamb shank, salmon and prawn fishcakes, and grilled pork steaks with Hook Norton mustard gravy are all part of an interesting choice.
OPEN: 12-3 Open all day bank holidays & weekends 6-11 Rest:Closed

Eve **BAR MEALS:** L served all week 12-2.30 D served all week 6-9.30 Av main course £10.95 **RESTAURANT:** L served all week 12-2.30 D served all week 6-9.30 Av 3 course à la carte £25 🍺: Hook Norton Best, Bass, Hook Norton Seasonals, Staropomen. ♀: 8 **FACILITIES:** Children welcome Children's licence Garden: Floral terrace with tables, lawned area Dogs allowed Water provided **NOTES:** Parking 20

The Wheatsheaf 🐾 ♀
Main St, Maids Moreton MK18 1QR
☎ 01280 815433 📷 01280 814631
Dir: From M1 junc 15A, take A43 towards Oxford, take A413 towards Buckingham, follow signs for Maids Moreton
Old world village pub serving real ales, quality bar snacks and an à la carte menu in the spacious conservatory overlooking the secluded beer garden. Options include chicken breast in a cream and Stilton sauce, mushroom and brandy strudel, duck breast with Madeira sauce, or Stilton and broccoli pasta. Fish specialities include breaded Whitby fish and chips, smoked haddock topped with prawns and cheese, and salmon steak in a lemon and lime sauce.
OPEN: 12-3 6-11 (Sun 7-10.30) **BAR MEALS:** L served Mon-Sat 12-2.15 D served Tue-Sat 7-9.30 Av main course £6 **RESTAURANT:** L served Mon-Sat 12-2.15 D served Mon-Sat 7-9.30 Av 3 course à la carte £20 **BREWERY/COMPANY:** Free House 🍺: Hook Norton, Black Sheep, John Smiths, Side Pocket For A Toad. ♀: 30 **FACILITIES:** Children welcome Garden: Large secluded garden, chairs on lawn/patio Dogs allowed Water **NOTES:** Parking 15

CHALFONT ST GILES

Map 06 SU99

Pick of the Pubs

Ivy House ♀
London Rd HP8 4RS ☎ 01494 872184 📷 01494 872840
Dir: On A413 2m S of Amersham & 1.5m N of Chalfont St Giles

Within the sturdy flint and brick walls of this 200-year-old free house in the Chilterns, you enter the warm atmosphere that beams, open fires, books, brass and armchairs always seem to create. It's here that chef and co-owner Jane Mears (with husband Anthony) presides over gastro-style menus that are, they say, 'Not Just Food for Thought'. Indeed they are not, as a giant seafood-combo-with-dips starter for two might single-handedly prove. Other starters include potato skins with spicy salsa and melting Cheddar, and cheese-topped Feta and spinach crêpes. Next could be pan-fried ostrich with mango sauce, chicken enchiladas, chargrilled swordfish, or creamy paprika vegetable and bean casserole. For dessert, there's good old bread and butter pudding, and rich rum and raisin chocolate truffle torte. Fuller's London Pride and Hook Norton Old Hooky are among the real ales. Also available are children's and slimline menus, and traditional afternoon teas at weekends.

continued

continued

OPEN: 12-3.30 6-11 (Sat 12-11, Sun 12-10.30) Closed: 25 Dec
BAR MEALS: L served all week 12-2.30 D served all week 6.30-9.30 Av main course £10.95 **RESTAURANT:** L served all week 12-2.30 D served all week 6.30-9.30 Av 3 course à la carte £20
BREWERY/COMPANY: Free House ◀: Fuller's London Pride, Brakspear Bitter, Wadworth 6X, Hook Norton Old Hooky. ♀: 20
FACILITIES: Children welcome Garden: Courtyard & garden with good views Dogs allowed, but not in restaurant **NOTES:** Parking 45

The White Hart 🍸
Three Households HP8 4LP ☎ 01494 872441 📠 01494 876375
e-mail: thewhitehartinn@supanet.com
Dir: Off A413 (Denham/Amersham)
High standards and attention to detail are the hallmarks of this prettily located 100 year-old pub. Open fireplaces, comfy sofas and fresh flowers characterise the quiet, relaxed atmosphere in the bar, with its wide choice of cask ales. Book ahead for the popular lodge-style bedrooms and non-smoking restaurant, where four dedicated chefs deliver a varied menu that ranges from a simple sandwich to loin of pork with griddled aubergines, or linguine with salmon, cod and prawns.
OPEN: 11.30-2.30 6-11 (Sun 12-3, 7-10.30) Closed: 26-27 Dec
BAR MEALS: L served all week 12-2 D served all week 6.30-9.30 Av main course £12 **RESTAURANT:** L served all week 12-2 D served all week 6.30-9.30 **BREWERY/COMPANY:** Greene King ◀: Greene King Morland Original, IPA & Old Speckled Hen, Wadworth 6X. **FACILITIES:** Children welcome Garden: **NOTES:** Parking 40 **ROOMS:** 11 bedrooms 11 en suite 1 family rooms s£67.50 d£87.50 (♦♦♦♦)

CHENIES
Map 06 TQ09

Pick of the Pubs

The Red Lion ♀
WD3 6ED ☎ 01923 282722 📠 01923 283797
Dir: Between Rickmansworth & Amersham on A404, follow signs for Chenies & Latimer

Country free house located near to Chenies Manor and the River Chess. The menu is renowned for its freshly prepared, home-made dishes, particularly the range of popular pies which include Thai fish curry, lamb, and bison in red wine. Other dishes run along the lines of red mullet fillets on green pea guacamole, medallions of pork in a mild mustard sauce, fresh salmon supreme marinated in teriyaki and apricots, and the intriguing bangers and mash suprise. Jacket potatoes, French bread sticks and pasta dishes fill out the food choices.
OPEN: 11-2.30 5.30-11 Closed: 25 Dec **BAR MEALS:** L served all week 12-2 D served all week 7-10 Av main course £8.50
BREWERY/COMPANY: Free House ◀: Wadworth 6X, Rebellion, Maypole Lion's Pride, Vale Best. ♀: 10 **FACILITIES:** Garden: Benches beside main bar Dogs allowed Water **NOTES:** Parking 14

CHESHAM
Map 06 SP90

The Black Horse Inn 🍸
Chesham Vale HP5 3NS ☎ 01494 784656
Dir: A41 from Berkhamstead, A416 through Ashley Green, 0.75m before Chesham R to Vale Rd, btm of Mashleigh Hill follow rd for 1m, inn on L
Set in some beautiful valley countryside, this 500-year old pub is ideal for enjoying a cosy, traditional environment without electronic games or music. During the winter there are roaring log fires to take the chill off those who may spot one of the resident ghosts. An ever-changing menu includes an extensive range of snacks, while the main menu may feature steak and Stallion Ale pie, various home-made pies, steaks and gammons, stuffed plaice, salmon supreme.
OPEN: 11-3 5.30-11 (Sun 12-3, 7-10.30) **BAR MEALS:** L served all week 12-2.30 D served all week 6.30-9.30 Av main course £8.50
RESTAURANT: L served all week 12-2.30 D served all week 6-9.30 Av 3 course à la carte £15 ◀: Adnams Bitter + Guest ale. ♀: 12
FACILITIES: Garden: Food served outdoors, patio, pond Dogs allowed **NOTES:** Parking 80

The Swan 🍸 ♀
Ley Hill HP5 1UT ☎ 01494 783075
e-mail: swan@putland.com
Dir: E of Chesham by golf course
Well-known locally for real ales, good food and conversation, this 500-year-old pub boasts a large inglenook fireplace, leaded lights and original ship's timbers. The pub overlooks Ley Hill Common, and is handy for walks on the nearby Chiltern Hills. Freshly-cooked local ingredients feature on the menu, which includes pot-roasted pheasant in white wine, tarragon and mushroom sauce, Aberdeen Angus sirloin steak, bacon and mushroom pasta, grilled Barnsley lamb chops, and poached fresh salmon.
OPEN: 12-3 5.30-11 (Sun 12-3, 7-10.30) **BAR MEALS:** L served all week 12-2.15 D served all week Av main course £9.50
RESTAURANT: L served all week 12-2 D served all week 7-9 Av 3 course à la carte £18.50 **BREWERY/COMPANY:** ◀: Adnams Bitter, Fuller's London Pride, Timothy Taylor Landlord, Marston's Pedigree. ♀: 11 **FACILITIES:** Garden: Lrg garden, patio, benches Dogs allowed Water

---

CHICHELEY
Map 11 SP94

The Chester Arms 🍸 ♀
MK16 9JE ☎ 01234 391214 📠 01234 391214
Dir: On A422, 2m NE of Newport Pagnell. 4m from M1 J14

A philosophy of buying well and keeping it simple pays dividends at this comfortable roadside pub near Chicheley Hall (NT). From a shopping list of Angus beef, spring lamb, poultry and fresh fish, chalkboards are written up daily and presented at your table. On a typical day, choices might include avocado with lightly curried prawn starter, grilled cod

continued

England

CHICHELEY continued

fillet with garlic butter, English duck breast with orange sauce, and steak and kidney pie 'like Mum makes'.
OPEN: 11-3 6-11 **BAR MEALS:** L served Tues-Sun 12-2 D served Tues-Sat 6.30-9.30 **RESTAURANT:** L served Tues-Sun 12-2 D served Tues-Sat 6.30-9.30 Av 3 course à la carte £20
BREWERY/COMPANY: Greene King 🍺 Greene King IPA & Ruddles County. **FACILITIES:** Garden **NOTES:** Parking 25

CHOLESBURY   Map 06 SP90

The Full Moon 🐾 ♀
Hawridge Common HP5 2UH ☎ 01494 758959 📠 01494 758797
Dir: At Tring on A41 take turn for Wiggington & Cholesbury

A windmill behind the pub sets the scene for this 16th-century coaching inn, beautifully situated on the borders of Cholesbury Common and Hawridge Common. Inside, you'll find beamed ceilings, flagstone floors and winter fires. Six cask ales and an international wine list support the extensive menu, with organic meat and poultry supplied by Eastwoods of Berkhamstead. A range of fish dishes might include plaice, salmon supreme, or sea bass stuffed with crabmeat, spring onion and ginger, and there are daily chef's specials, too. Look out for beef braised in Guinness, or pheasant casserole.
OPEN: 12-3 5.30-11 (Sat open all day, Sun 12-10.30) Rest:Closed 25 Dec **BAR MEALS:** L served all week 12-2 D served Mon-Sat 6.15-9
RESTAURANT: L served all week 12-2 D served Mon-Sat 6.15-9
BREWERY/COMPANY: Enterprise Inns 🍺 Interbrew Bass & Boddingtons Bitter, Fuller's London Pride, Brakspear Special, Guest Ales. ♀: 7 **FACILITIES:** Children welcome Garden: Country pub garden, canopy, heat lamps Dogs allowed Water **NOTES:** Parking 28

CUDDINGTON   Map 05 SP71

Pick of the Pubs

The Crown 🐾 ♀
Spurt St HP18 0BB ☎ 01844 292222
e-mail: david@thecrowncuddington.co.uk
Dir: Telephone for directions
Having successfully run Annie Bailey's bar-cum-brasserie in Cuddington for a number of years, the Berrys turned their attention to improving the Crown, a delightful Grade II listed pub nearby. Customers will find plenty of character inside, with a popular locals' bar and several low-beamed dining areas filled with charming prints and the glow of evening candlelight. A choice of beers on tap, an extensive wine list and an eclectic menu add to the enjoyment of a visit here. A short menu may list various snacks, salads and sandwiches with starters including winter broth with leeks and pearl

barley, and white crab meat with prawns on mixed leaf with Marie Rose dressing. Main dishes may feature beef and mushroom casserole, breast of chicken with almonds, wild rice and Amaretto glaze, rib-eye steak, smoked haddock on a Cheddar and smoked bacon rösti, and chargrilled Mediterranean vegetables with grilled goats' cheese. Don't forget the treacle sponge pudding, if you can find space!

OPEN: 12-3 6-11 **BAR MEALS:** L served all week 12-2.30 D served all week 6.30-10 Av main course £10.50 **RESTAURANT:** L served all week 12-2.30 D served all week 6.30-10 Av 3 course à la carte £18 Av 3 course fixed price £20 **BREWERY/COMPANY:** Fullers 🍺: Fullers London Pride, Adnams, Stella Artois. **FACILITIES:** Children welcome Garden: Small patio area **NOTES:** Parking 12

DINTON   Map 05 SP71

Seven Stars 🐾 ♀
Stars Ln HP17 8UL ☎ 01296 748241 📠 01296 748241
e-mail: secretpub.company@virgin.net
Dir: Telephone for directions

A picturesque country pub in the charming village of Dinton close to Aylesbury Ring. Dating from around 1640, with inglenook fireplaces, wooden settles and a cosy old snug to prove it. Sandwiches, light bites, grills, burgers, and specials are served in the bar, while the restaurant menu runs to favourites like liver and bacon, and steak and kidney pudding, with tuna Mexicana among several fish options.
OPEN: 12-3 (Sun 12-3) 6-11 (Sun 7-10.30) **BAR MEALS:** L served all week 12-2.30 D served all week 6.30-8.45 Av main course £7.50
RESTAURANT: L served all week 12-2.30 D served all week 6.30-8.45 Av 3 course fixed price £12.50 **BREWERY/COMPANY:** 🍺: London Pride, Worthington 1774, Stella Artois, Carlsberg Export. ♀: 6
FACILITIES: Children welcome Garden: Lawn with small patio Dogs allowed in the garden only. Water provided **NOTES:** Parking 20

continued

FARNHAM COMMON
Map 06 SU98

The Foresters 🍽 ♀
The Broadway SL2 3QQ ☎ 01753 643340 🗎 01753 647524
e-mail: barforesters@aol.com

There's a real buzz at the Foresters - formerly the Foresters Arms, which was built in the 1930s to replace a Victorian building. Located close to Burnham Beeches, a large woodland area famous for its coppiced trees, it offers a combination of good drinking and a busy restaurant renowned for the quality of its food. The daily menu might include marlin steak on polenta, braised venison, and linguini with smoked salmon and dill.
OPEN: 11-11 Mon-Sat 12-10.30 Sun **BAR MEALS:** L served all week 12-3 D served all week 6.30-10 Av main course £10
RESTAURANT: L served all week 12-2.30 D served all week 6.30-10 Av 3 course à la carte £20 **BREWERY/COMPANY:** Simply Pubs Ltd
🍺: Fullers London Pride, Draught Bass, Youngs Special Bitter, Carling.
♀: 9 **FACILITIES:** Children welcome Dogs allowed Water provided

FAWLEY
Map 05 SU78

Pick of the Pubs

The Walnut Tree ♀
RG9 6JE ☎ 01491 638360 🗎 01491 639508
Dir: From Henley on A4155 towards Marlow, L at 2nd sign for Fawley. R at village green

Set in the Chiltern Hills with wonderful views some 400ft above Henley-on-Thames, the pub retains two gnarled walnut trees in a fine garden that boasts a barbecue, rustic swings and an original hitching-post: there is also walnut furniture in the restaurant reputedly made from a tree felled on the site. An up-to-date feel on the latest menus produces lunchtime fare such as seared sea bass fillets on smoked bacon mash, turkey escalope in a brioche crumb with red onion and celery sauce, Tuscan chicken wrapped in charred leeks with Parma ham, and grilled king scallops in cucumber and lemon butter. Also watch the blackboard menus for daily specials.
OPEN: 12-3 6-11 (Sat-Sun & Bhs 11-11) **BAR MEALS:** L served all week 12-3 D served all week 7-9.30 Av main course £7
RESTAURANT: L served all week 12-3 D served all week 7-9.30 Av 3 course à la carte £25 **BREWERY/COMPANY:** Brakspear
🍺: Brakspear. **FACILITIES:** Children welcome Garden: beer garden, patio, outdoor eating, BBQ Dogs allowed **NOTES:** Parking 50

FINGEST
Map 05 SU79

The Chequers Inn ♀
RG9 6QD ☎ 01491 638335
Dir: From M40 L towards Ibstone, L at T junc at end of rd, stay L, pub on R

Set deep in the Chiltern Hills, opposite a splendid Norman church, the Chequers is a 15th-century redbrick pub with log

continued

fires in the winter, and a delightful sun-trap garden with rural views for summer imbibing.
OPEN: 12-3 (open all day wknds) 6-11 **BAR MEALS:** L served all week 12-2.30 D served all week 6-10 Av main course £8.95
RESTAURANT: L served all week 12-2.30 D served all week 6-10 Av 3 course à la carte £17.50 Av 3 course fixed price £15
BREWERY/COMPANY: Brakspear 🍺: Brakspear Bitter, Ordinary Old Mild & Special. **FACILITIES:** Children welcome Garden: beer garden, food served outdoors Dogs allowed garden only
NOTES: Parking 60

FORD
Map 05 SP70

Pick of the Pubs

The Dinton Hermit ♀
Water Ln HP17 8XH ☎ 01296 747473 🗎 01296 748316
Dir: Off A418 between Aylesbury & Thame

Set back from the lane in an isolated hamlet, this 15th-century stone-built pub is named after John Biggs, clerk to one of the judges who condemned Charles I to death. So ashamed was he of his part in the execution that he became a hermit, and subsequently a local legend. Another John - John Bingham Chick - runs the pub these days, and offers a good range of beers - Hook Norton, Adnams, Morrells and Marstons - along with hearty, freshly-prepared food in both of the beamed and warmly decorated bars. Half a crisp roast Barbary duck (boneless except for the leg bone), served with ginger, chilli and papaya salsa, is a signature dish, and another favourite is seared fillet of Angus beef with pak choy, fresh lime and ginger. The pub has an acre of garden looking out over the countryside, and children are made welcome.
OPEN: 11-2.30 6-11 **BAR MEALS:** L served all week 12-2 D served all week 7-9.30 Av main course £10 **RESTAURANT:** L served all week 12-2 D served all week 7-9.30 Av 3 course à la carte £22 **BREWERY/COMPANY:** Free House 🍺: Hook Norton Best, Adnams Bitter, Marston's Bitter, Morrells.
FACILITIES: Garden: Food served outside **NOTES:** Parking 30

FRIETH
Map 05 SU79

The Prince Albert
RG9 6PY ☎ 01494 881683
Dir: From Marlow take Oxford Road

An old-fashioned country local, very much a community pub but also ideal for a stop-off when walking in the Chilterns. The customers are a mixed bunch, with vehicles in the car park ranging from four-wheel drives to Porsches and Rolls Royces, but they all mix well and there are no airs and graces. Brakspear beers are served alongside pub food ranging from sandwiches and jacket potatoes to salmon and rib of beef.
OPEN: 12-3 5.30-11 **BAR MEALS:** L served Tues-Sun 12-2.30 D served all week 6-9 Av main course £6.50
BREWERY/COMPANY: Brakspear 🍺: Barkspear Bitter, Special.
FACILITIES: Children welcome Garden: Food served outside Dogs allowed **NOTES:** Parking 20 No credit cards

---

Do you have a favourite pub that we have overlooked? Please use the Reader's Report form at the back of this guide to tell us all about it.

FRIETH continued

The Yew Tree
RG9 6PJ ☎ 01494 882330 📠 01494 882927
Dir: from M40 towards Stokenchurch, thru Cadmore End, Lane End R to Frieth

A huge yew tree spirals majestically outside this 16th-century red-brick pub in a truly rural Chilterns village. Sit in the pretty flower garden, or in the original beamed bar with its inglenook and tip-top ales, and enjoy a hot chicken sandwich, traditional fish and chips, smoked salmon tagliatelle, or grilled plaice.
OPEN: 11-3 (Sun 12-5) 6-11 (Sun 7-10.30) **BAR MEALS:** L served all week 11-2.30 D served all week 6.30-10 Av main course £9.95
RESTAURANT: L served all week 11-2.30 D served all week 6-10 Av 3 course à la carte £15 **BREWERY/COMPANY:** Free House
🍺: Brakspear Bitter, Fullers London Pride, Caledonian Deuchars.
FACILITIES: Children welcome Garden Dogs allowed
NOTES: Parking 60

GREAT BRICKHILL   Map 11 SP93

The Old Red Lion ♀
Ivy Ln MK17 9AH ☎ 01525 261715 📠 01525 261716
Dir: Signposted off A5, 10m S of Milton Keynes

This friendly local was first established as a pub in 1771. The garden overlooks the Aylesbury Vale, and is reckoned to have the best view in Buckinghamshire. Here you'll find fine ales and varied menus, freshly prepared with local ingredients where possible. Lunchtime dishes include warm baguettes, beef or vegetable lasagne, and a daily curry. In the evening, choose from sausage and mushroom casserole, Jamaican jerk chicken, or oven-baked salmon.
OPEN: 12-3 (Sun 12-10.30) 5-11 **BAR MEALS:** L served all week 12-2.30 D served all week 6-9 Av main course £8.50
RESTAURANT: L served all week 12-2 D served Tue-Sat 7-9 Av 3 course à la carte £20 **BREWERY/COMPANY:** Whitbread
🍺: Greene King IPA, Bass & Guest beer. **FACILITIES:** Garden: Food served outdoors Dogs allowed **NOTES:** Parking 6

GREAT HAMPDEN   Map 05 SP80

The Hampden Arms 🍴
HP16 9RQ ☎ 01494 488255 📠 01494 488255
e-mail: tezy@pubham.fsnet.co.uk
Dir: From M40 take A4010, R before Princes Risborough, Great Hampden signposted

Whether you're celebrating a special occasion or just want a quiet pint of real ale, you'll find a warm and friendly welcome at this mock Tudor pub restaurant in the heart of the beautifully wooded Hampden Estate. The menu features light lunches and a range of traditional home-cooked meals, with dishes like chicken Maryland, rib-eye steak, steak

Yucatan, Merry Berry Duck, and seafood lasagne. There's a selection of low fat dishes and a nice choice of hot puddings to finish off.
OPEN: 12-3 6.30-11 (Sun 6.30-10.30) **BAR MEALS:** L served Wed-Sun 12-2 D served Wed-Sat 6.30-9.30 Av main course £6.95
RESTAURANT: L served all week 12-2 D served all week 6.30-9.30
BREWERY/COMPANY: Free House 🍺: Adnams Bitter, Brakspear Bitter, Interbrew Boddingtons Bitter. **FACILITIES:** Children welcome Garden: Lrg wooden area **NOTES:** Parking 30

GREAT MISSENDEN   Map 06 SP80

The George Inn ♀
94 High St HP16 0BG ☎ 01494 862084 📠 01494 865622
Dir: off A413 between Aylesbury & Amersham

Established as a coaching inn in 1483, the George has always had strong ties with nearby Missenden Abbey. The small, cosy bars boast a wealth of old beams and fireplaces, whilst a tithe barn in the grounds houses the original stables. The restaurant offers a relaxed, non-smoking environment for lunchtime snacks, plus hot dishes like ham, egg and chips, salmon fishcakes, and spicy tomato pasta. Evenings bring a range of authentic Thai seafood and specials.
OPEN: 11-11 (Sun 12-3, 7-10.30) **BAR MEALS:** L served all week 12-2.30 D served Mon-Sat 6.30-9.30 Av main course £7
RESTAURANT: L served all week 12-2.30 D served Mon-Sat 6.30-9.30 Av 3 course à la carte £16 **BREWERY/COMPANY:** Inn Partnership 🍺: Adnams Bitter, Adnams Broadside, Interbrew Flowers Original. ♀: 6 **FACILITIES:** Children welcome Garden: Beer garden with tables and benches Dogs allowed Water
NOTES: Parking 25

Pick of the Pubs

The Polecat Inn 🍴 ♀
170 Wycombe Rd, Prestwood HP16 0HJ
☎ 01494 862253 📠 01494 868393
e-mail: polecatinn@btinternet.com
Dir: On the A4128 between Great Missenden and High Wycombe
Small, low-beamed rooms with rug-strewn floors radiate from the central bar of this charming 17th-century inn in the Chiltern Hills. The mix of furnishings includes cabinets full of stuffed birds, and there are open fires in the winter months. The inn has a three-acre garden, with tables for alfresco summer eating. Local ingredients and herbs from the garden are the foundation of the wide-ranging menu and interesting specials boards, with food freshly prepared on the premises. There are snack meals at lunchtime as well as a full menu both midday and in the evening. Expect starters like baked field mushrooms with melting cheese and a garlic and herb crust, and filo tartlet of smoked chicken with roast vegetables and Mozzarella.

continued

continued

Mains could include braised beef olives with crumbled Roquefort, or gratinated loin of pork layered with orchard fruits. To follow, what about chilled hazelnut soufflé with fudge sauce, or traditional syrup sponge and custard? **OPEN:** 11.30-2.30 6-11 (Sun 12-3) Closed: Dec 25-26, Jan 1 Rest:Dec 24, Dec 31, Sun closed pm **BAR MEALS:** L served all week 12-2 D served Mon-Sat 6.30-9 Av main course £8.50 **BREWERY/COMPANY:** Free House ◀: Marston's Pedigree, Wadworth 6X, Greene King Old Speckled Hen, Interbrew Flowers IPA. ♀: 16 **FACILITIES:** Children welcome Garden Dogs allowed **NOTES:** Parking 40 No credit cards

Pick of the Pubs

The Rising Sun 🐾 ♀
Little Hampden HP16 9PS
☎ 01494 488393 & 488360 🖻 01494 488788
e-mail: sunrise@rising-sun.demon.co.uk
Dir: From A413 N of Gt Missenden take Rignall Rd on L (signed Princes Risborough) 2.5m turn R signed 'Little Hampden only'
You'll find this 250-year-old country inn tucked away in the Chiltern Hills surrounded by beech woods and glorious scenery. A network of footpaths begins just outside the front door, so it's a perfect base for country walks. Reached down a single track no-through-road, the pub is seemingly miles from anywhere, yet London is only 40 minutes away by train from nearby Great Missenden. The proprietor prides himself on a well-run, clean and welcoming establishment, which offers an interesting snack menu, a popular Sunday lunch and a carte for lunch and dinner. A good choice of seafood includes poached halibut steak with mushrooms and prawns in a white wine sauce, while other regulars include roast home-smoked pork joint with a red wine and plum sauce and pan-fried slices of calves' liver served in a red wine and blackcurrant sauce.
OPEN: 11.30-2.30 6.30-11 **BAR MEALS:** L served Tue-Sun 12-2 D served Tue-Sat 7-9 Av main course £9.50 **RESTAURANT:** L served Tue-Sun 12-2 D served Tue-Sat 7-9 Av 3 course à la carte £19 **BREWERY/COMPANY:** Free House ◀: Adnams, Brakspear Bitter, Marstons Pedigree, Old Speckled Hen. ♀: 12 **FACILITIES:** Children welcome Garden: Fence enclosed garden with seating area Dogs allowed Water **NOTES:** Parking 20

HADDENHAM   Map 05 SP70

Pick of the Pubs

The Green Dragon ◉◉ 🐾 ♀
8 Churchway HP17 8AA ☎ 01844 291403
e-mail: paul@eatatthedragon.co.uk
See Pick of the Pubs on page 50

Pick of the Pubs have that extra special quality that makes them stand out from the crowd. Their entries are highlighted, and may be a full page.

Pick of the Pubs

The Stag & Huntsman Inn
RG9 6RP ☎ 01491 571227 🖻 01491 413810
Dir: 5m from Henley-on-Thames on A4155 toward Marlow, L at Mill End towards Hambleden
This warm and welcoming 400 year-old brick and flint inn lies close to the glorious beech-clad Chilterns. In addition to its local trade, customers range from walkers and cyclists to business people and tourists. The charming building and village have featured in many films and TV productions, including '101 Dalmatians', 'Midsomer Murders', 'As Time Goes By', 'Poirot', 'My Uncle Silas', 'Daniel Deronda', and 'A Band of Brothers'. After an exhilarating ramble in the hills, relax in the cosy snug, or choose the public bar for a traditional game of darts or dominoes. Alternatively, savour the bustling atmosphere of the L-shaped, half-panelled lounge, with its low ceilings, open fire, and upholstered seating. There's also a dining room, where you can sample marinated lamb gigot steak, pan-fried breast of Hambleden pheasant or fillet steak topped with Stilton cheese.
OPEN: 11-2.30 6-11 (Sun 12-3, 7-10.30, Sat 11-3, 6-11) Closed: Dec 25 **BAR MEALS:** L served all week 12-2 D served Mon-Sat 7-9.30 Av main course £8 **BREWERY/COMPANY:** Free House ◀: Brakspear Bitter, Wadworth 6X, guest ales.
FACILITIES: Children welcome Garden: Dogs allowed Water **NOTES:** Parking 60
See Pub Walk on page 41

KINGSWOOD   Map 11 SP61

Crooked Billet
Ham Green HP18 0QJ ☎ 01296 770239 🖻 01296 770094
e-mail: info@crookedbillet.com
Dir: On A41 between Aylesbury & Bicester

Located in peaceful Buckinghamshire countryside, The Crooked Billet has been a pub for about 200 years and is believed to be haunted by Fair Rosamund, a girlfriend of Charles I. A typical menu includes wild mushroom-crusted chicken breast with wilted spinach, crispy bacon and white wine cream, roast sirloin of beef with Yorkshire pudding, wild mushroom compote and roast Shiraz jus, and winter lamb braised in Beaujolais.
OPEN: 11-11 **BAR MEALS:** L served all week 12-6 D served all week 6-9 Av main course £7 **RESTAURANT:** D served all week 6.30-9 Av 3 course à la carte £20 ◀: Hook Norton, Wadworh 6X, Courage Directors. **FACILITIES:** Children welcome **NOTES:** Parking 50

Open: 11.30-2, 6.30-11
Closed: 1 Jan
Bar Meals: L served all week 12-2,
D served all week 7-9.30.
RESTAURANT: L served all week 12-2,
D served all week 7-9.30.
Av cost 3 courses £24
BREWERY/COMPANY:
ENTERPRISE INNS
☎: Vale Notley Ale, Fullers London
Pride, Timothy Taylor Landlord.
FACILITIES: Garden
NOTES: Parking 18

The Green Dragon

The Green Dragon is attractively located in the old part of
Haddenham, close to the village green and 12th-century church.

8 Churchway, Haddenham, HP17 8AA
☎ 01844 291403
✉ paul@eatatthedragon.co.uk
Dir: From M40 A329 to Thame,
then A418, 1st R after entering
Haddenham.

For some of its time, this 300-year-old building was a manorial courthouse, as the last man to be executed in Buckinghamshire discovered to his cost. Nearby is St Tiggywinkle's animal hospital, where Channel 4 records some episodes of Pet Rescue. In the four years he has been here, pub co-owner and chef Paul Berry has built up a formidable reputation for his food. He offers ten starters, any of which can double as a light lunch.

Among them are tian of smoked salmon and avocado salad with mango and vanilla dressing, crisp goats' cheese parcel on sun-dried tomato and red pepper risotto, and local pigeon on teisen datws (a potato cake once popular in North Wales) with black pudding and mustard and tarragon dressing. Next, go for rump of English lamb on confit garlic croquette with wild mushroom and sage jus, or perhaps sautéed calves' liver and bacon on leek mash with caramelised baby onion sauce. If you'd prefer fish, then how about fillet of monkfish on lightly-spiced butternut squash soup with coriander dressing, or

escalope of salmon on linguine and vegetable spaghetti with warm potted shrimp butter? On top of these and at least another half dozen possible main courses are usually several specials - toad in the hole with leek and onion gravy, or grilled chicken with avocado in batter salad with Caesar dressing, for instance. Finally, will it be home-made lemon and lime tart and raspberry sorbet, Bailey's cheesecake, or meringue with home-made lime and mascarpone ice cream and mixed fruits? Haddenham's own Vale Brewery supplies Notley and Wychert real ales. Outside are two grassed areas with tables and chairs.

England

LACEY GREEN
Map 05 SP80

Pink & Lily ♀
Pink Rd HP27 0RJ ☎ 01494 488308 🖷 01494 488013
Dir: Off A4010 S of Princes Risborough
The pub is named after a local butler (Mr Lily), who had a liaison with a chambermaid (Miss Pink). On being dismissed from service they set themselves up as innkeepers. The inn has several refurbished eating and drinking areas serving the likes of home-made pies, fresh cod in beer batter, and favourite sweets such as apple pie and sticky toffee pudding.
OPEN: 11.30-11 **BAR MEALS:** L served all week 12-2 D served Mon-Sat 7-9.30 Av main course £8.95 **BREWERY/COMPANY:** Free House 🍺: Brakspear Bitter & Special, Fullers London Pride, Courage Best, 12 Guest beers from local breweries. **FACILITIES:** Children welcome Garden: large sunny garden with tubs and flower beds Dogs allowed garden only (water) **NOTES:** Parking 40

LONG CRENDON
Map 05 SP60

Pick of the Pubs

The Angel Inn ✿ ♀
47 Bicester Rd HP18 9EE ☎ 01844 208268 🖷 01844 202497
Dir: A418 to Thame, B4011 to L Crendon, Inn on B4011

Attractive period features, like the wattle and daub walls and inglenook fireplace, testify to the age of this upgraded 16th-century coaching inn. There's plenty of character, too, in the assorted scrubbed pine and sturdy oak tables set on light wooden floors, and the comfy Chesterfields fronting the bar. Real ales are served, along with cocktails, champagne, and wine by the glass, but the commitment is to first-class pub dining, in the air-conditioned conservatory, or out on the patio or sun terrace. There's a daily blackboard of imaginative fish dishes - lightly-curried codling on wild mushroom risotto with coriander sabayon perhaps, and for lunch it's a choice of light bites - Oriental salad of deep-fried smoked turkey in plum vinaigrette, or speciality crostini breads. More substantially, at lunch or dinner, there might be roast fillet of Highland beef with caramelised red onion tart Tatin, confit of wild mushrooms and sweet garlic jus.
OPEN: 12-3 7-10 Rest:Sun Closed eve **BAR MEALS:** L served all week 12-2.30 D served Mon-Sat 7-9.30 Av main course £12.50 **RESTAURANT:** L served all week 12-2.30 D served Mon-Sat 7-9.30 Av 3 course à la carte £30 Av 2 course fixed price £13.95 **BREWERY/COMPANY:** Free House 🍺: Hook Norton Best, Adnams Broadside, Ridleys Rumpus. ♀: 11 **FACILITIES:** Children welcome Garden: Patio, terrace at rear of pub **NOTES:** Parking 25

Pick of the Pubs

Mole & Chicken 🐾 ♀
Easington Ter HP18 9EY ☎ 01844 208387 🖷 01844 208250
e-mail: shanepellis@hotmail.com
Dir: Off B4011 N of Thame

Legend has it that this fashionable dining pub was re-named after two latter day proprietors, Mr Mole and Mr Chicken. Once known as the Rising Sun, it was built in 1831 in a fold of the Chiltern Hills as a beer and cider house. A tastefully-decorated interior features cosy fireplaces, rag-washed walls and flagstone floors in the oak-beamed bar, while the tiered and terraced garden enjoys outstanding views across three counties. Menu specialities are posted on boards over the fireplace's oak lintel to support the carte: sautéed king prawns in garlic and chilli, bowl of creamed chilli mussels, and chicken Satay might appear as starters, while the main list runs to slow-roasted shoulder of lamb, deep-fried tomato and goats' cheese risotto, and beef 'welly' stuffed with chicken liver pâté.
OPEN: 12-3.30 6-12 Closed: 25 Dec **BAR MEALS:** L served all week 12-2 D served all week 6-10 Av main course £10.95 **RESTAURANT:** L served all week 12-2 D served all week 6-10 Av 3 course à la carte £22 **BREWERY/COMPANY:** Free House 🍺: Ruddles Best, Greene King IPA, London Pride & Old Speckled Hen. **FACILITIES:** Children welcome Garden: Good view of rural landscape **NOTES:** Parking 40

MARLOW
Map 05 SU88

The Kings Head 🐾 ♀
Church Rd, Little Marlow SL7 3RZ
☎ 01628 484407 🖷 01628 484407
Dir: M40 J4 take A4040 S 1st A4155
This flower-adorned pub, only 10 minutes from the Thames Footpath, dates back to 1654. It has a cosy, open-plan interior with original beams and open fires. From sandwiches and jacket potatoes, the menu extends to the likes of sea bass with ginger, sherry and spring onions, lamb shank with rich minty gravy, mash and fresh vegetables, and stir-fry duck with plum sauce.
OPEN: 11-3 5-11 (Sat-Sun 11-11) **BAR MEALS:** L served all week 12-2.15 D served all week 6.30-9.30 Av main course £8.50 **RESTAURANT:** L served all week 12-2.15 D served all week 6.30-9.30 Av 3 course à la carte £14 **BREWERY/COMPANY:** Enterprise Inns 🍺: Brakspear Bitter, Fuller's London Pride, Rebellion IPA, Timothy Taylor Landlord. **FACILITIES:** Children welcome Garden: Safely behind pub, lots of tables & chairs **NOTES:** Parking 50

England

MOULSOE

Map 11 SP94

The Carrington Arms 🕸 ♀
Cranfield Rd MK16 0HB ☎ 01908 218050 ▤ 01908 217850
e-mail: thecarringtonarms@4cinns.co.uk
Dir: *M1 J14 take rd signed 'Cranfield & Moulsoe'. Pub 1m on R*
For those who prefer to enjoy cooking as a spectator sport, this
should fit the bill. Orders are taken directly by the chef who
then cooks on a range in full view of his expectant customers.
Food includes excellent Aberdeenshire beef, monkfish, tiger
prawns and oysters. You can even decide exactly which
Canadian lobster you want the chef to pluck from its tank.
OPEN: 11-3 (Sun 12-3, 7-10.30) 5.30-11 **BAR MEALS:** L served all
week 12-2.30 D served all week 6.30-10 **RESTAURANT:** L served all
week 12-2 D served all week 6.30-10 Av 3 course à la carte £30
BREWERY/COMPANY: Free House 🍺: Abbot Ale, Green King IPA
& Guest Ales. ♀: 48 **FACILITIES:** Garden: Patio & lawned area
Dogs allowed in the garden only **NOTES:** Parking 100

PRINCES RISBOROUGH

Map 05 SP80

Red Lion 🕸
Upper Icknield Way, Whiteleaf HP27 0LL
☎ 01844 344476 ▤ 01844 273124
Dir: *A4010 thru Princes Risbro', then R into 'Holloway', go to end of road,
R, pub on L*

Family-owned 17th-century inn in the heart of the Chilterns,
surrounded by National Trust land and situated close to the
Ridgeway national trail. Plenty of good local walks with
wonderful views. A cosy fire in winter and a secluded summer
beer garden add to the appeal. Hearty pub fare includes
steaks, stirfries and home-made curries, as well as haddock
and chips, smoked haddock gratin, garlic and herb chicken,
and various pies.
OPEN: 12-3 (Sun 12-3, 7-10.30) 5-11 (All day Wkds May- Sept)
BAR MEALS: L served all week 12-2 D served Mon-Sat 7-9 Av main
course £7.50 **RESTAURANT:** L served all week 12-2 D served Mon-
Sat 7-9 Av 0 course fixed price £9.95 **BREWERY/COMPANY:** Free
House 🍺: Brakspear Bitter, Hook Norton Best, Carlsberg-Tetley
Tetley's. **FACILITIES:** Garden: Grass area, benches, tables, beautiful
views Dogs allowed Water provided **NOTES:** Parking 10

SKIRMETT

Map 05 SU79

Pick of the Pubs

The Frog ♀
RG9 6TG ☎ 01491 638996 ▤ 01491 638045
Dir: *Turn off A4155 at Mill End, pub 3 m on.*

From its pretty, clay-tiled dormer windows to its
overflowing flower tubs, this eye-catching whitewashed
free house exudes warmth and tranquillity. Set deep in
one of the loveliest valleys in the Chiltern Hills, The Frog
lies close to the heart of 'Vicar of Dibley' country. There
are attractive rural views from the delightful, tree-shaded
garden, and you may be tempted to enjoy one of the
recommended local walks. Once inside, this family-run pub
does not disappoint though in wintertime you may have to
queue for a place on the unusual wooden bench that
encircles the fireplace. In the reassuringly civilised non-
smoking restaurant, the wide ranging international menu is
changed monthly, and daily specials are featured on the
blackboard. Fresh ingredients and confident cooking
produce home-made soups, Irish fry-up, and braised lamb
shank. There's always a good selection of fish, too; expect
haddock in beer batter, red mullet, sea bass, or bream.
OPEN: 11-3 6.30-11 Closed Sun night Oct-May
BAR MEALS: L served all week 12-2.30 D served all week 6.30-
9.30 Av main course £8.50 **RESTAURANT:** L served all week
12-2.30 D served all week 6.30-9.30 Av 3 course à la carte £17.95
BREWERY/COMPANY: Free House 🍺: Adnams Best, Hook
Norton, Fullers London Pride. **FACILITIES:** Children welcome
Garden: beer garden, patio, outdoor eating Dogs allowed
NOTES: Parking 15

SPEEN

Map 05 SU89

King William IV
Hampden Rd HP27 0RU ☎ 01494 488329 ▤ 01494 488301
Dir: *Through Hughenden Valley, off A4128 N of High Wycombe*
Nestling in the Chiltern Hills, this 17th-century, family-run pub and
restaurant boasts log fires in winter and a popular terrace and
garden ideal for summer drinking. Choose from an interesting
range of blackboard specials that might include Thai green
chicken curry, grilled red snapper and trio of Welsh lamb cutlets.
OPEN: 12-3 (Sun 12-4) 6-11 Rest:Sun closed evenings
BAR MEALS: L served Tues-Sun 12-2.30 D served Tues -Sat 7-10 Av
main course £8 **RESTAURANT:** L served Tue-Sun 12-2 D served Tue-
Sat 7-10 Av 3 course à la carte £20 **BREWERY/COMPANY:** Free
House 🍺: Batemans, Hook Norton, Fullers London Pride Tetley.
FACILITIES: Children welcome Garden: lawned area with cast iron
feature, patio Dogs allowed **NOTES:** Parking 50

TURVILLE — Map 05 SU79

Pick of the Pubs

The Bull & Butcher ♀
RG9 6QU ☎ 01491 638283 📠 01491 638283
e-mail: nick@bullandbutcher.com
Dir: M40 J5 follow signs for Ibstone. Turn R T-junct. Pub 0.25m on L
Lovely, black and white timbered 16th-century pub tucked away in a secluded valley in a classic Chiltern village that is regularly used as a film set, including The Vicar of Dibley. Two unspoilt low-ceilinged bars with open fires provide a welcoming atmosphere, and good restaurant-style food in a traditional pub setting. Daily menus, served throughout, show imagination and flair and make good use of fresh local produce, including local estate game and fish bought direct from Billingsgate. Don't expect traditional pub food: light meals include salads - grilled goats' cheese salad with tapenade, warm salad of king scallops and wild mushrooms - or starters like hot home-smoked beef pastrami on rye, and smoked haddock, spinach and potato terrine. Hearty, rustic main dishes may feature Toulouse sausages with mash, roast shallots and gravy, and calves' liver with peccorino mash and smoked bacon. Tip-top Brakspear ales on tap, plenty of wines by the glass and excellent local walks; delightful summer garden.
OPEN: 11-3 (Sun 12-5, 7-10.30) 6-11 (Sat 11-3, 6.30-11)
BAR MEALS: L served Mon-Sun 12-2 D served Mon-Sat 6-11 Av main course £10.95 **RESTAURANT:** L served Mon-Sun 12-2 D served Mon-Sat 6-11 Av 3 course à la carte £17
BREWERY/COMPANY: Brakspear 🍺: Brakspear Mild, Bitter, Special, Old & Choice. ♀: 36 **FACILITIES:** Garden: BBQ, outdoor eating, beer garden Dogs allowed **NOTES:** Parking 20

WENDOVER — Map 05 SP80

Red Lion Hotel ♀
High St HP22 6DU ☎ 01296 622266 📠 01296 625077
e-mail: redlionhotel@wizardinns.co.uk
A 17th-century coaching inn located in the heart of the Chilterns, popular with regulars and providing a welcome break for cyclists and walkers. One menu is served throughout offering the likes of grilled fillet of sea bass with lime, ginger and coriander marinade on linguine pasta, seared barracuda supreme, or slow-cooked shoulder of lamb with cheddar mash and redcurrant, rosemary and red wine gravy. Dolly the waitress has worked here for over sixty years.
OPEN: 10-11 (Sun 10-10.30) **BAR MEALS:** L served all week 12-9.30 D served all week Av main course £7.50 **RESTAURANT:** L served all week 12-2 D served all week 5-9.30 Av 3 course à la carte £19 **BREWERY/COMPANY:** 🍺: Courage Spitfire, Red Lion, plus Guest ales. **FACILITIES:** Children welcome Garden: Food served outside **NOTES:** Parking 60

WEST WYCOMBE — Map 05 SU89

Pick of the Pubs

The George and Dragon Hotel ♀
High St HP14 3AB ☎ 01494 464414 📠 01494 462432
e-mail: enq@george-and-dragon.co.uk
Dir: On A40, close to M40

Built on the site of a 14th-century hostelry, this 18th-century former coaching inn has welcomed many generations of visitors. Indeed, some from a bygone era are rumoured still to haunt its corridors - notably the White Lady. The hotel is reached through a cobbled archway and comprises a delightful jumble of whitewashed, timber-framed buildings. The varied menu offers something for everybody, beginning with a choice of starters or snacks. Freshly-cooked main course specialities encompass venison casserole with juniper dumplings, lamb and spinach curry, spicy Creole jambalaya, and a Mediterranean vegetable pudding. As well as a good choice of well-kept real ales there are 12 wines served by the glass. Outside you'll find a large garden complete with children's play area.
OPEN: 11-2.30 5.30-11 (Sun 12-3, 7-10.30, Sat 12-3, 5.30-11)
BAR MEALS: L served all week 12-2 D served all week 6-9.30 Av main course £9 **BREWERY/COMPANY:** Unique Pub Co 🍺: Scottish Courage Courage Best, Wells Bombardier Premium, Greene King Abbot Ale, Adnams Broadside. ♀: 12 **FACILITIES:** Children welcome Garden: Large garden adjacent to car park Dogs allowed Water **NOTES:** Parking 35

WHEELEREND COMMON — Map 05 SU89

The Chequers 🏨
Bullocks Farm Ln HP14 3NH ☎ 01494 883070
e-mail: thechequers.inn@virgin.net
Dir: Between Marlow & High Wycombe
The Chequer dates back 300 years and retains many original features including low beams and open fires. It is known locally for its real ale and freshly-produced food. The menu changes regularly and features local game and seasonal fish and meat dishes, such as venison, pheasant in game sauce, wild duck breast in black cherry and brandy, and roast rack of English lamb.
OPEN: 12-3 5.30-11 (Sat-Sun all day) Rest:25 Dec, 31 Dec Closed eve
BAR MEALS: L served all week 12-2.30 D served Mon-Sat 7-10 Av main course £6 **RESTAURANT:** L served all week 12-2.30 D served all week 7-10 Av 3 course à la carte £20 Av 3 course fixed price £17
BREWERY/COMPANY: Fullers 🍺: Fuller's ESB, London Pride, Jack Frost & Summer Ale, Guest ale. **FACILITIES:** Children welcome Garden: Beer garden, benches Dogs allowed Water & biscuits
NOTES: Parking 18

WHITCHURCH
Map 11 SP82

The White Horse Inn
60 High St HP22 4JS ☎ 01296 641377 📠 01296 640454
e-mail: whitchurchhorse@aol.com
Dir: A413 4 M N of Aylesbury
In a picturesque village setting, this 16th-century inn boasts an open fire and a resident ghost. The kitchen uses best local produce and has a good neighbourhood reputation. Choose from more than twenty steak dishes (all Aberdeen Angus), or maybe sea bass or grilled mackerel.
OPEN: 12-3 6-11 (Sun 12-4.30) Rest:Mon Closed lunch
BAR MEALS: L served Tues-Sun 12-2 D served Mon-Sat 7-9 Av main course £7.50 **RESTAURANT:** L served Tues-Sun 12-2 D served Mon-Sat 7-9 Av 3 course à la carte £15
BREWERY/COMPANY: Punch Taverns 🍺: Brakspear Bitter, Young's Bitter, Batemans Bitter, Adnams Bitter. **FACILITIES:** Children welcome Garden: Patio, food served outside Dogs allowed Water
NOTES: Parking 20

WOOBURN COMMON
Map 06 SU98

Pick of the Pubs

Chequers Inn ★★ 🏵 ♀
Kiln Ln HP10 0JQ ☎ 01628 529575 📠 01628 850124
e-mail: info@chequers-inn.com
Dir: M40 J2 through Beaconsfield towards H Wycombe.1m turn L into Broad Lane. Inn 2.5m
Just two miles from the M40 at Junction 2, it's hard to believe that this deeply rural inn is only 24 miles by road from central London. Built in the 17th century, with a massive oak post-and-beam bar, it's a splendidly snug spot on a cold winter's night and delightful when sitting out with a drink on balmy summer evenings. Bedroom accommodation is convenient, up-to-date and thoroughly comfortable. Choose the brasserie or bar for relaxed, well-priced meals along the lines of chicken curry or a home-made beefburger with bacon, cheese, chips and salad. If you're after something more formal, try the atmospheric dining room, which is prettily decorated with palms and greenery. Here, the award-winning French and English cuisine might include seared salmon with Puy lentil salad and mustard dressing or pot-roast Barbary duck with braised baby beets and deep-fried foie gras.
OPEN: 10-11 **BAR MEALS:** L served all week 12-2.30 D served all week 6.30-9.30 Av main course £9.95
RESTAURANT: L served all week 12-2.30 D served all week 7-9.30 Av 3 course à la carte £30 Av 3 course fixed price £17.95
BREWERY/COMPANY: Free House 🍺: Ruddles, IPA, Abbot, Morland. **FACILITIES:** Children welcome Garden: Dogs allowed In the garden only **NOTES:** Parking 60 **ROOMS:** 17 bedrooms 17 en suite 1 family rooms s£72.50 d£77.50

CAMBRIDGESHIRE

BARRINGTON
Map 12 TL34

The Royal Oak
West Green CB2 5RZ ☎ 01223 870791 📠 01223 871845
Dir: From Barton off A14 S of Cambridge 1 mile.
Rambling timbered and thatched 14th-century pub. Overlooks village green and provides a wide range of fish and Italian dishes.

OPEN: 12-11 (Sun 12-10.30) **BAR MEALS:** L served all week 12-2.30 D served Mon- Sat 6.30-11 **RESTAURANT:** L served all week 12-2.30 D served Mon- Sat 6.30-11 Av 3 course à la carte £23
BREWERY/COMPANY: Old English Inns 🍺: IPA Potton Brewery, Adnams. **FACILITIES:** Children welcome **NOTES:** No credit cards

BYTHORN
Map 12 TL07

Pick of the Pubs

The White Hart
PE28 0QN ☎ 01832 710226 📠 01832 710226
Dir: 0.5m off A14 (Kettering/Huntingdon rd)
In a peaceful by-passed village just off the A1/M1 link, the White Hart plays host to the chef/patron's eponymous bistro and restaurant, Bennett's. Though the local pub trade is not ignored, it is in a succession of dining areas that one can expect to find the crowds, drawn by bar meals that encompass steak and mushroom pie, game and Guinness casserole, crispy loin of pork and grilled haddock in cheese sauce, with side orders that include proper chips. Restaurant menus include Thai fish soup, Gressingham duck with apple and herb stuffing, and burnt Cambridgeshire cream with toffee bananas. Three-course, fixed-price Sunday lunches.
OPEN: 11-11 (Sun 12-2.30) Closed: 26 Dec, 1 Jan
BAR MEALS: L served Tue-Sat 11-2 D served Tue-Fri 6-10 Av main course £8.50 **RESTAURANT:** L served Tue-Sun 12-2 D served Tue-Sat 7-10 Av 3 course à la carte £25
BREWERY/COMPANY: Free House 🍺: Greene King IPA & Abbott Ale. **FACILITIES:** Children welcome Garden Dogs allowed garden only **NOTES:** Parking 50

CAMBRIDGE
Map 12 TL45

The Anchor
Silver St CB3 9EL ☎ 01223 353554 📠 01223 327275
Waterside pub frequented by students from Queen's College opposite. There's a good selection of real ale, and the opportunity to hire a punt to go on the River Cam. Lots of bric-a-brac and a good atmosphere.
OPEN: 11-11 **BAR MEALS:** L served all week 12-3 D served all week Av main course £5.75 **BREWERY/COMPANY:** Whitbread 🍺: Flowers Original, Bass, Wadworth 6X, Pedigree. **FACILITIES:** Children welcome Dogs allowed **NOTES:** No credit cards

The Cambridge Blue
85 Gwydir St CB1 2LG ☎ 01223 361382 📠 01223 505110
e-mail: cambridgeblue@fsbdial.co.uk
Dir: Town centre
University Boat Race memorabilia features strongly in this Victorian non-smoking pub, including the bow of the 1984 boat that hit a barge and sank. The garden has a rabbit warren enclosure appealing to younger customers. The menu offers filled and toasted ciabatta rolls, burritos with a choice of chilli fillings, and a trio of meat or vegetarian sausages. Daily specials might include game casserole, aubergine and Mozzarella bake, or seafood pie. On Sunday lunchtimes traditional roasts are available.
OPEN: 12-2.30 5.30-11 (Sun 6-10.30) Rest:Dec 25-26 Half day
BAR MEALS: L served all week 12-2.30 D served all week 6-9.30 Av main course £5 **BREWERY/COMPANY:** Free House
🍺: Woodforde's Wherry, Nethergate IPA, Milton Pegasus.
FACILITIES: Children welcome Garden: Grass, wooden paving slabs, rabbit warren Dogs allowed Water (dogs on leads)

continued

The Eagle ♀
Benet St CB2 3QN ☎ 01223 505020
e-mail: 3004@greenking.co.uk
Dir: On foot, 5 mins from the Lion Yard Car Park
Splendidly atmospheric city-centre pub with a fascinating history, first recorded in 1667, and retaining many original features - mullioned windows, fireplaces, wall paintings and pine panelling. Good Greene King ales and a wide-ranging pub menu.
OPEN: 11-11 (Sun 12-10.30) **BAR MEALS:** L served all week 12-2.30 D served Mon-Thurs 5-9 Av main course £6
BREWERY/COMPANY: Greene King ◀: Greene King Martha Greene IPA & Abbot Ale, Old Speckled Hen. ♀: 16
FACILITIES: Children welcome Dogs allowed

Free Press ♀
Prospect Row CB1 1DU ☎ 01223 368337
e-mail: freepresspub@hotmail.com
Students, academics, locals and visitors rub shoulders - quite literally - in an atmospheric and picturesque back-street pub near the city centre: normally half a dozen customers can sit comfortably in the Snug, said on one occasion to have accommodated over 60! Non smoking for a decade and without music or gaming machines, punters are attracted by first-rate real ales and nourishing home-made soups, salads, chilli, filled toasted ciabattas, sausages, and pasta.
OPEN: 12-2.30 6-11 Closed: 25-26 Dec, 1 Jan **BAR MEALS:** L served all week 12-2 D served Mon-Sat 6-9 Av main course £6.50
BREWERY/COMPANY: Greene King ◀: Greene King IPA, Abbot Ale, Dark Mild plus Guest ales. ♀: 10 **FACILITIES:** Children welcome Garden: Small walled courtyard garden

Live & Let Live
40 Mawson Rd CB1 2EA ☎ 01223 460261 ▤ 01223 460261
e-mail: liveandletliveph@aol.com
A backstreet traditional pub with no electronic entertainment, only a few minutes from the bus and train stations. Theme nights are a regular event, as are performances by Dave, a local solo singer-guitarist. A hearty menu includes giant Yorkshire pudding with a variety of fillings, bangers and mash, suet puddings and casseroles.
OPEN: 11.30-2.30 5.30-11 Closed: 1 Jan **BAR MEALS:** L served all week 12-2 D served Mon-Sat 6-9 **BREWERY/COMPANY:** ◀: Everards Tiger Best, Adnams Bitter, Nethergates Umbel, Oakham JHB.
FACILITIES: Children welcome Dogs allowed

DRY DRAYTON   Map 12 TL36

The Black Horse ♀
Park St CB3 8DA ☎ 01954 781055 ▤ 01954 782628
e-mail: blackhorsedry@aol.com
Dir: Just outside Cambridge between A14 & A428
Exposed wooden beams and open fires characterise this welcoming 350-year-old village inn, where an extensive menu of traditional pub dishes is served. Expect lasagne, Chinese chicken curry, steak and kidney pie, seafood platter, liver and bacon casserole, battered cod, or gammon steak, along with baguettes, sandwiches, baked potatoes, and a selection of steaks. A courtesy bus is available. Contact the Black Horse for more details.
OPEN: 11.00-3 6.30-11 (Sun 12-3, 7-10.30) Closed: Dec 25/26
BAR MEALS: L served all week 12-2 D served Mon-Sat 6.30-9 Av main course £6.75 **RESTAURANT:** L served all week 12-2 D served Mon-Sat 6.30-9 **BREWERY/COMPANY:** Free House ◀: Greene King IPA, Adnams, Interbrew Bass & Guests. ♀: 8
FACILITIES: Children welcome Garden: Colourful lawned garden Dogs allowed **NOTES:** Parking 40

DUXFORD   Map 12 TL44

The John Barleycorn 🛏
3 Moorfield Rd CB2 4PP ☎ 01223 832699 ▤ 01223 832699
Dir: Turn off A505 into Duxford
Traditional thatched and beamed English country pub situated close to Cambridge. Originally built as a coaching house in 1660, it was renamed once or twice, until 1858 when the current name was attached. The same menu is served throughout and ranges from a cheese sandwich to tournedos Rossini. Typical dishes are large leg of lamb in mint gravy, and chicken breast with garlic and herbs.
OPEN: 11-11 (Sun 12-10.30) **BAR MEALS:** L served all week 12-11 D served all week 12-11 Av main course £7.50 **RESTAURANT:** L served all week D served all week à la carte £15
BREWERY/COMPANY: Greene King ◀: Greene King IPA, Abbot Ale, Old Speckled Hen, Ruddles Best & County. **FACILITIES:** Children welcome Garden: Lrg patio area **NOTES:** Parking 40

ELSWORTH   Map 12 TL36

The George & Dragon 🛏
41 Boxworth Rd CB3 8JQ ☎ 01954 267236 ▤ 01954 267080
Dir: SE of A14 between Cambridge & Huntingdon
Set in a pretty village just outside Cambridge, this pub, originally a row of shops, has recently undergone a change of hands. There's plenty of fish on the menu, and a patio garden to enjoy it in. Reader's reports welcome.
OPEN: 11-3 6-11 (Sun 12-3, 6.30-10.30) **BAR MEALS:** L served all week 12-2 D served Mon-Sat 6.30-9 Av main course £9.50 **RESTAURANT:** L served all week 12-2 D served Mon-Sat 6.30-9 Av 3 course à la carte £18 **BREWERY/COMPANY:** Free House ◀: Greene King IPA, Ruddles County, Greene King Old Speckled Hen. **FACILITIES:** Children welcome Garden: Patio area Guide dogs only **NOTES:** Parking 50

ELTISLEY   Map 12 TL25

The Leeds Arms 🛏
The Green PE19 6TG ☎ 01480 880283 ▤ 01480 880379
Dir: On A428 between Cambridge & St Neots
Village free house and motel, built towards the end of the 18th century and named after the local landowners, the Leeds Arms has been under the same management for a quarter of a century. It is situated opposite the village green where the cricket team plays in season. Sample from a typical menu that may feature grilled swordfish steak, steak Rossini, mushroom Stroganoff, spinach and Ricotta cannelloni, sizzling tiger prawns and fillet steak kebab, or chicken and beef combo.
OPEN: 11.30-2.30 6.30-11 (Sun 12-2.30, 7-10.30) Closed: Xmas/New Year week **BAR MEALS:** L served all week 12-2 D served all week 7-9.45 Av main course £8.50 **RESTAURANT:** L served all week 12-2 D served all week 7-9.45 **BREWERY/COMPANY:** Free House ◀: Greene King IPA, Adnams Broadside, Scottish Courage John Smith's Smooth. **FACILITIES:** Garden: Patio, tables, grass area **NOTES:** Parking 30

> **Restaurant and Bar Meal times indicate the times when food is available. Last orders may be approximately 30 minutes before the times stated.**

England

ELTON   Map 12 TL09

Pick of the Pubs

The Black Horse 🐾 ♀
14 Overend PE8 6RU ☎ 01832 280240 📠 01832 280875
Dir: Off A605 (Peterborough to Northampton rd)

Harry Kirk, the landlord here in the 1950s, was an assistant to Tom and Albert Pierrepoint, Britain's most famous hangmen. Harry's son is now said to haunt the bar. Once the village jail, the building later became a morgue, but today's rustic interior is a lot more agreeable. Pop in for a pint of Deuchars IPA, or a seasonal Nethergate brew, and a decent bar snack (lunchtime only), and perhaps a rare roast beef and horseradish sandwich, or home-baked gammon, egg and chips. Full meals include medallions of fillet steak in a crème fraîche, with prosciutto and Roquefort sauce, on a spinach tagliatelle, and daily fish specials such as fresh wild sea bass with a trio of king prawns in garlic, finished with a hollandaise sauce. Traditional set Sunday lunch menu. Good puddings. Delightful rear garden overlooking Elton's famous church and rolling open countryside.
OPEN: 12-3 6-11 **BAR MEALS:** L served all week 12-2 D served Mon-Sat 6-9 Av main course £10 **RESTAURANT:** L served all week 12-2 D served Mon-Sat 6-9 Av 3 course à la carte £25 **BREWERY/COMPANY:** Free House 🍺: Bass, Deuchars IPA, Nethergate, Archers. **FACILITIES:** Children welcome Garden: Food served outside. Patio area Dogs allowed in the garden only. Water provided **NOTES:** Parking 30

ELY   Map 12 TL58

Pick of the Pubs

The Anchor Inn ♦♦♦♦ ◎ 🐾 ♀
Sutton Gault CB6 2BD ☎ 01353 778537 📠 01353 776180
e-mail: anchorinnsg@aol.com
Dir: From A14, B1050 to Earith, take B1381 to Sutton. Sutton Gault on L
Situated on the banks of the New Bedford River, the Anchor was built in 1650 to house men conscripted to clear the diseased and crime-ridden fens - now a fine agricultural landscape rich in wildlife. The inn is fully modernised yet retains much of its original character, including scrubbed pine tables, gently undulating floors, gas lighting, welcoming log fires, and some first-class cooking. Daily deliveries of quality produce are reflected in the menu's seasonal delights of hand-dressed Cromer crab, spring lamb, samphire, Brancaster oysters and mussels, local game and wild duck from the marshes. Fish

dishes might include baked gilt head bream on niçoise salad or grilled fillet of smoked haddock with colcannon, spinach, poached egg and tartare sauce. A good selection of desserts and the excellent cheese board are also worthy of consideration. Spacious and charming accommodation is available.
OPEN: 12-3 (Sat 6.30-11) 7-11 Closed: Dec 25-26
BAR MEALS: L served all week 12-2 D served all week 7-9 Av main course £11 **RESTAURANT:** L served all week 12-2 D served all week 7-9 Av 3 course à la carte £22
BREWERY/COMPANY: Free House 🍺: Nethergate IPA, Wolf Bitter, Batemans XB, Adnams Bitter. ♀: 8 **FACILITIES:** Children welcome Garden: Terrace overlooking the river **NOTES:** Parking 16 **ROOMS:** 2 bedrooms 2 en suite 1 family rooms s£50 d£75

FEN DITTON   Map 12 TL46

Ancient Shepherds 🐾
High St CB5 8ST ☎ 01223 293280 📠 01223 293280
Dir: From A14 take B1047 signed Cambridge/Airport
Named after the ancient order of Shepherders who used to meet here, the pub was originally three cottages built in 1540. The building is heavily beamed, and has two bars, a lounge and a dining room. All rooms have inglenook fireplaces. A typical menu includes salmon fillet with lemon butter sauce, Barnsley lamb chops, half casseroled guinea fowl in Burgundy with roast vegetables, rainbow trout sautéed with mushrooms and bacon, and pork loin steaks in cream and mustard sauce.
OPEN: 12-3 6-11 (Fri-Sat 11-3, 6.30-11) Closed: 25-26 Dec Rest:Sun Closed eve **BAR MEALS:** L served all week 12-2 D served Mon-Sat Av main course £11.95 **RESTAURANT:** L served all week 12-2 D served Mon-Sat 6.30-9 **BREWERY/COMPANY:** Pubmaster 🍺: Adnams Bitter, Greene King IPA. **FACILITIES:** Garden: Lawned shady garden, garden furniture Dogs allowed Water, Fireplace **NOTES:** Parking 18

FEN DRAYTON   Map 12 TL36

The Three Tuns ♀
High St CB4 5SJ ☎ 01954 230242 📠 01954 230242
e-mail: mail@timspubs.com
Dir: Between Cambridge and Huntingdon
This thatched building dating back over 400 years was originally the Guildhall of Fen Drayton, and some wonderfully ornate details can still be seen on the original oak beams. Renovation work has recently restored the bar to its original layout, while outside there is a large enclosed garden with covered dining, children's play area and petanque pitch. Popular choices from the menu include tournedos Rossini, lamb noisettes, and layered medallions of fillet steak with bacon and Stilton cheese.
OPEN: 12-2.30 6-11 **BAR MEALS:** L served all week 12-2 D served all week 7-9 Av main course £8 **RESTAURANT:** L served all week 12-2 D served all week 7-9 Av 3 course à la carte £16 **BREWERY/COMPANY:** Greene King 🍺: Greene King IPA, Ruddles Best, Batemans XXXB. ♀: 6 **FACILITIES:** Children welcome Garden: Large enclosed, kids play area **NOTES:** Parking 20

FENSTANTON   Map 12 TL36

King William IV 🐾 ♀
High St PE28 9JF ☎ 01480 462467 📠 01480 466571
e-mail: jerry@kingbill.co.uk
Dir: Off A14 between Cambridge & Huntingdon (J27)
Originally three 17th-century cottages, this rambling, part cream-

continued

continued

painted, part red brick inn is in the centre of the village next to an old clock tower. Inside are low beams, a lively bar and the plant-festooned Garden Room. Tourists, business people and locals all stop by for a traditional bar meal or something more, shall we say, stylish from the carte menu, such as pan-seared venison, duck breast or medallions of pork tenderloin, French onion tart, penne pasta, and sausages and mash.
OPEN: 11-3.30 6-11 (Sun 12-10.30) **BAR MEALS:** L served all week 12-2.15 D served Mon-Sat 7-9.45 Av main course £12.60
RESTAURANT: L served all week 12-2.15 D served Mon-Sat 7-9.45 Av 3 course à la carte £25 **BREWERY/COMPANY:** Greene King
🍺: Greene King Abbot Ale & IPA, Guest Ales. **♀:** 10
FACILITIES: Children welcome Garden: Patio area Dogs allowed Water **NOTES:** Parking 14

FORDHAM
Map 12 TL67

White Pheasant 🐑 ♀
CB7 5LQ ☎ 01638 720414
Dir: From Newmarket. A142 to Ely, approx 5 miles to Fordham Village. On L as you enter Fordham
Rug-strewn wooden floors, tartan check fabrics, soft wall lighting and candle-topped scrubbed tables characterise this white-painted 17th-century free house. Set beside the A43 in a Fenland village between Newmarket and Ely, the inn is named after a protected white pheasant that was killed by a previous landlord. The menu includes roast duck breast with honey-roasted root vegetables, pan-fried sea bass, and vegetable Wellington with basil gnocchi and steamed wild mushrooms.
OPEN: 12-3 6-11 (Sun 7-10.30) Closed: 25-27Dec, 1Jan
BAR MEALS: L served all week 12-2.30 D served all week 6-10.30 Av main course £14.95 **RESTAURANT:** L served all week 12-2.30 D served all week 6-10.30 Av 3 course à la carte £25
BREWERY/COMPANY: Free House **🍺:** Woodforde's Nelson's Revenge, Norfolk Nog, Admirals Reserve. **♀:** 12
FACILITIES: Children welcome Garden: Pleasant area, child friendly **NOTES:** Parking 30

FOWLMERE
Map 12 TL44

Pick of the Pubs

The Chequers ♀
High St SG8 7SR ☎ 01763 208369 ▤ 01763 208944
Dir: From M11 A505, 2nd R to Fowlmere

There's a strong sense of history at this bustling inn, renovated by William Thrist in 1675 after much of the village was devastated by fire - you can still see his initials over the main door. Samuel Pepys stayed here in 1660, but the pub's sign reflects its more recent past with blue and red chequers honouring the British and American squadrons based at Fowlmere during World War II. Today

the Chequers is known for its imaginative cooking served formally in the smart galleried restaurant or the more relaxed surroundings of the bar or attractive garden. The extensive seasonal menu might include grilled escolar with shrimp and lobster bisque, or roast partridge with bread sauce, gravy, liver pâté croutons and game chips. The drinks range includes interesting guest ales, around 30 malt whiskies and 10 wines by the glass from a decent list.
OPEN: 12-2.30 6-11 Closed: 25 Dec **BAR MEALS:** L served all week 12-2 D served all week 7-10 Av main course £1080
RESTAURANT: L served all week 12-2 D served all week 7-10 Av 3 course à la carte £20.50 **BREWERY/COMPANY:** Free House
🍺: Adnams Bitter, Black Sheep Special, Fuller's ESB, Hook Norton Old Hooky. **♀:** 10 **FACILITIES:** Garden
NOTES: Parking 30

GODMANCHESTER
Map 12 TL27

The Black Bull Coaching Inn 🐑 ♀
32 Post St PE29 2AQ ☎ 01480 453310 ▤ 01480 435623
Dir: Off A1198 S of Huntington
Five minutes' walk from the Great Ouse River, this 17th-century inn sports beams and a large inglenook fireplace. Examples of fish main courses include sea bass, baked sardines, monkfish and poached salmon. Steak and ale pie and chips, braised knuckle of lamb, tournedos Rossini and baked leek and Stilton crêpes provide meat and vegetarian balance.
OPEN: 12-11 **BAR MEALS:** L served all week 12-2.30 D served all week 6-9 Av main course £10 **RESTAURANT:** L served all week 12-2.30 D served all week 6-9.30 **🍺:** Black Bull, Old Speckled Hen, Hobsons Choice, Bombadier. **FACILITIES:** Garden: Patio area Dogs allowed in the garden only **NOTES:** Parking 30

GOREFIELD
Map 12 TF41

Woodmans Cottage 🐑 ♀
90 High Rd PE13 4NB ☎ 01945 870669 ▤ 01945 870631
e-mail: magtuck@aol.com
Dir: A47 to Peterborough, ring road to A1M
Popular pub run by a hard-working brother and sister team. Their efforts have paid off, and Woodmans Cottage remains a successful local with live entertainment, well-kept beers and a good choice of bar food. Established favourites include lemon sole bonne femme, seafood mornay, filo prawns, minty lamb shank, and Chinese rack ribs.
OPEN: 11-2.30 7-11 Closed: 25 Dec **BAR MEALS:** L served all week 12-2.30 D served all week 7-10 Av main course £6.75
RESTAURANT: L served all week 12-2.30 D served all week 7-10 Av 3 course à la carte £20 **BREWERY/COMPANY:** Free House
🍺: Greene King IPA & Abbot Ale, Interbrew Worthington Bitter.
FACILITIES: Children welcome Garden **NOTES:** Parking 40

> **Restaurant and Bar Meal times indicate the times when food is available. Last orders may be approximately 30 minutes before the times stated.**

continued

GRANTCHESTER
Map 12 TL45

The Green Man 🛏️ ♀
High St, Grantchester CB3 9NF ☎ 01223 841178 📠 01223 847940
A delightful old pub retaining many original features, including low ceiling beams (beware!). In winter roaring log fires burn in the re-opened fireplaces, and in summer customers can sit out in the restored gardens. Real ales, lagers and fresh coffees are served, plus a list of wines available by the glass. The menu is augmented by frequently-changing blackboard specials. Bubble and squeak, home-made curry, Thai fishcakes, and lamb in Dijon mustard are typical of the range. The village cemetery contains a WWI memorial that includes poet Rupert Brooke.
OPEN: 11.30-3 (Summer all day) **BAR MEALS:** L served all week 12-2.30 D served all week 6-9 Av main course £7.50
BREWERY/COMPANY: Punch Taverns ⬤: Adnams Bitter, Broadside, Greene King IPA. **FACILITIES:** Children welcome Garden: Patio, food served outside **NOTES:** Parking 10

HEYDON
Map 12 TL43

The King William IV 🛏️ ♀
SG8 8PN ☎ 01763 838773 📠 01763 837179
Dir: A505
A 16th-century countryside inn with an old world interior. It has beams and an inglenook fireplace, and is full of antiques and farming implements, with unusual oak tables suspended from the ceiling by chains. A good range of freshly-prepared food is available with a particular emphasis on vegetarian dishes. On the menu there may be grilled swordfish steak with avocado and mango salad, confit leg of duck marinated in Rioja and oriental spices or spinach and spring onion cakes with Dijon mustard cream sauce.
OPEN: 12-2.30 6.30-11 Closed: 25-26 Dec Jan 1 **BAR MEALS:** L served all week 12-2 D served all week 6.30-10 Av main course £9.50
BREWERY/COMPANY: Free House ⬤: IPA Greene King, Adnams, Abbot Ale, Fullers London Pride. **FACILITIES:** Children welcome Garden: Food served outside Dogs allowed in the garden only **NOTES:** Parking 50

HILDERSHAM
Map 12 TL54

The Pear Tree
CB1 6BU ☎ 01223 891680 📠 01223 891970
e-mail: dgj-@lycos.com
Dir: Just off A1307
This small village pub, which stands facing the village green, retains its traditional atmosphere with bare beams and a stone floor. Popular with walkers and locals alike, it is particularly well known for its home-cooked food. Bar meals include grills, Lincolnshire sausages and jumbo battered cod, and daily specials like steak and kidney pudding. A choice of good old-fashioned puddings offers the likes of treacle tart, pecan pie and fruit crumbles.
OPEN: 11.45-2 (Sun 12-2, 7-10.30) 6.30-11 **BAR MEALS:** L served all week 12-2 D served all week 6.30-9.30 Av main course £6
BREWERY/COMPANY: Greene King ⬤: Greene King IPA & Abbot Ale. **FACILITIES:** Garden Dogs allowed **NOTES:** Parking 6

HILTON
Map 12 TL26

The Prince of Wales ◆◆◆◆
Potton Rd PE28 9NG ☎ 01480 830257 📠 01480 830257
e-mail: Princeofwales.hilton@talk21.com
Dir: on B1040 between A14 and A428 S of St Ives
Traditional two-bar village inn at the heart of rural Cambridgeshire, just a short drive from Cambridge, Peterborough and Huntingdon. Food options range from bar snacks to full meals, alongside a choice of grills, fish, curry and daily specials prepared from local produce. Home-made puddings include crème brûlée and sherry trifle. Four comfortable letting bedrooms. Recent change of hands.
OPEN: 11-2.30 (Sat 12-3, 7-11) (Sun 12-3, 7-10.30) 6-11 Winter Closed-Lunch Mon-Thurs Closed: 1 Jan Rest:Mon Closed lunch
BAR MEALS: L served Tue-Sun (Summer) 12-2 D served all week 7-9 Av main course £7 **BREWERY/COMPANY:** Free House ⬤: Adnams Southwold, Elgoods Black Dog Mild, Timothy Taylor Landlor, Greyhound. **FACILITIES:** Garden: Patio with tables and chairs **NOTES:** Parking 9 **ROOMS:** 4 bedrooms 4 en suite s£50 d£70 no children overnight

HINXTON
Map 12 TL44

The Red Lion
High St CB10 1QY ☎ 01799 530601 📠 01799 531201
e-mail: lynjim@lineone.net
Dir: 1m from M11 J9, 2m from M11 J10
Jim and Lynda Crawford have extended their 16th-century inn to create an excellent air-conditioned restaurant. Old clocks, horse brasses and stuffed animals pop up all over the place. Fresh local produce forms the basis of an extensive menu, including sandwiches, hot paninis and jacket potatoes (lunchtime only) and breast of Norfolk duck, fresh Scottish salmon, and chargrilled chicken fillet marinated in Marsala at both lunch and dinner.
OPEN: 11-2.30 6-11 (Sun 12-2.30, 7-10.30) Closed: Dec 25-26
BAR MEALS: L served all week 12-2 D served all week 7-9.30
RESTAURANT: L served all week 12-2 D served all week 7-9.30
BREWERY/COMPANY: Free House ⬤: Adnams, Greene King IPA, Woodforde's Wherry, plus Guest ales including Nethergates & Ridleys.
FACILITIES: Garden: Terrace with seating, Lawns with benches
NOTES: Parking 40

HOLYWELL
Map 12 TL37

The Old Ferryboat Inn 🛏️ ♀
PE27 4TG ☎ 01480 463227 📠 01480 463245
e-mail: theoldferryboatinn@hotmail.com
Dir: A14 then R onto A1096 then A1123 R to Holywell
Renowned as England's oldest inn, built some time in the 11th century, but with a hostelry history that goes back to the 6th, the Old Ferryboat has immaculately maintained thatch, white stone walls, and cosy interior. A pleasant atmosphere - despite resident ghost of a lovelorn teenager - in which to enjoy hot chicken curry, roast rack of lamb, steak and ale pie, fish and chips, and Greene King ales.
OPEN: 11.30-11 **BAR MEALS:** L served all week 12-2.30 D served all week 6-9.30 Av main course £7 **BREWERY/COMPANY:** Greene King ⬤: Greene King Abbot Ale/IPA, Old Speckled Hen.
FACILITIES: Children welcome Garden: Food served outside. River views Dogs allowed in the garden only. Water provided
NOTES: Parking 100

Pick of the Pubs

Crown & Punchbowl
CB5 9JG ☎ 01223 860643 ▤ 01223 441814
A 17th-century inn located in beautiful countryside in the
village of Horningsea, on the banks of the River Cam.
Enjoy bar food or candlelit dinners in the beamed dining
room, where classical music, rugs and antique pieces
enhance the atmosphere. Fresh local produce is used
extensively. The bar menu could include Newmarket
sausages with mash and onion gravy, honey-roast Suffolk
ham with honey and mustard glaze or Norfolk chicken
breast with a sherry and mushroom sauce. The à-la-carte
menu offers starters such as home-made paté, smoked
Arctic cod and crispy bacon bake or prawn spaghetti.
Follow with the likes of shank of lamb with boxty potato
and apricot sauce, or Gressingham duck breast with a
plum, spring onion and ginger sauce. The bar menu is
available in the conservatory and both bar areas, one of
which features a church pulpit and an original stained-
glass window.
OPEN: 12-2.30 6-10 Closed: 25 Dec Rest:26 Dec, 1 Jan Closed
eve **BAR MEALS:** L served all week 12-2.30 D served all week
6-10 **RESTAURANT:** L served all week 12-2.30 D served all
week 6-10 **BREWERY/COMPANY:** Free House ◀: Adnams
Broadside. **FACILITIES:** Children welcome Garden Dogs
allowed **NOTES:** Parking 50

Pick of the Pubs

The Old Bridge House ★★★ ◎◎ ♀
1 High St PE29 3TQ ☎ 01480 424300 ▤ 01480 411017
e-mail: oldbridge@huntsbridge.co.uk
Dir: Signposted from A1 & A14
One of a local partnership of chef-managed dining pubs,
this ivy-clad, 18th-century house overlooks the River Ouse
in Oliver Cromwell's birthplace. Once a private bank, the
much-extended building offers 24 stylish bedrooms with
air conditioning, satellite TV and CD players. Meals are
served in either the Restaurant or the more informal
Terrace. Starters might include seared scallops with
cauliflower and sultana-caper purée, or just a 'simple'
green salad of lettuce, avocado, olives and beans.
Caramelised endive with mushrooms, roast root
vegetables and celeriac sauce is a possible main dish, as
are shoulder of lamb with cumin potatoes and braised red
cabbage, and roast breast of Goosnargh duck with
sauerkraut, smoked bacon, rösti potato and quince
chutney. But there are lighter dishes as well: prosciutto
with marinated artichokes, and deep-fried cod with pease
pudding, for example. Among some imaginative sweets is
vanilla soufflé with a hot raspberry and grappa compote.
OPEN: 11-11 (Sun 12-10.30) **BAR MEALS:** L served all week
12-2.30 D served all week 6.30-10.30 Av main course £13
RESTAURANT: L served all week 12-2.30 D served all week
6.30-10.30 Av 3 course à la carte £25
BREWERY/COMPANY: ◀: Adnams Best, Hobsons Choice,
Bateman XXXB. **FACILITIES:** Children welcome Garden: Drinks
served only **NOTES:** Parking 60 **ROOMS:** 24 bedrooms 24 en
suite s£80 d£100

Pick of the Pubs

The Pheasant Inn ♀
Village Loop Rd PE28 0RE
☎ 01832 710241 ▤ 01832 710340
e-mail: pheasant.keyson@btopenworld.com
Dir: Signposted from A14, W of Huntingdon
Yet another of a small group of chef-managed dining pubs
in the area with an admirably egalitarian attitude to eating
out and continuing dedication to the provision of fine
wines and East Anglian ales. Housed in a fine 15th-century
thatched building of oak beams, open fires and simple
wooden furniture, The Pheasant offers a single menu
throughout in a modern eclectic style that recognises the
quality and value of freshly-available local produce.
Imaginative, unfussy snacks and simple dishes include
warm goats' cheese or classic Caesar salads, Gloucester
Old Spot sausages and mash in grain mustard sauce, and
tagliatelle with wild mushrooms, Jerusalem artichokes and
truffle oil. Main dishes are exemplified by rare chargrilled
tuna loin with Moroccan spiced quinoa, slow-braised
Aberdeenshire beef blade with foie gras sauce, and pan-
roast duck breast on spiced barley with braised pak choi.
Caramelised apple tart with Calvados ice cream, and
unpasteurised farmhouse cheeses; traditional roast beef
on Sunday and fixed-price mid-week lunches are models
of consistency.
OPEN: 12-2 6-11 (Sun eve, 7-8.45) Rest:25/26 Dec, 1 Jan closed
eve **BAR MEALS:** L served all week 12-2 D served all week
6.30-9.30 Av main course £12 **RESTAURANT:** L served all week
12-2 D served all week 6.30-9.30 Av 3 course à la carte £21.50
BREWERY/COMPANY: Huntsbridge ◀: Adnams, Village Bike
"Potton Brewery", Augustinian "Nethergate Brewery". ♀: 12
FACILITIES: Children welcome **NOTES:** Parking 40

The New Sun Inn 🍴 ♀
20-22 High St PE28 0HA ☎ 01480 860052 ▤ 01480 869353
Dir: From A1 N, B645 for 7m, From A1 S B661 for 7m, From A14 B660 for
5m

An impressive array of flowers greets visitors to this 16th-
century inn near Kimbolton Castle. As well as being a real ale
pub, it offers a good choice of wines by the glass. Dishes from
the restaurant menus include fresh grilled Dover sole, slow-
roast belly pork with wild mushrooms, roast rack of lamb with
dauphinoise potatoes, beef Stroganoff, roast loin of venison
on leek and bacon rösti, and three cheese and sun-dried

continued

England

tomato risotto. For a lighter meal, try a jacket potato or sandwich.
OPEN: 11-2.30 6-11 (All day Sun) **BAR MEALS:** L served all week 12-2.15 D served Tues - Sat 7-9.30 **RESTAURANT:** L served Tues-Sun 12-2 D served Tues-Sat 7-9.30 **BREWERY/COMPANY:** Charles Wells **:** Wells Bombardier & Eagle IPA, Greene King Old Speckled Hen. **:** 12 **FACILITIES:** Children welcome Garden: Patio Dogs allowed

---

MADINGLEY
Map 12 TL36

Pick of the Pubs

The Three Horseshoes
High St CB3 8AB **☎** 01954 210221 **▤** 01954 212043
Dir: M11 J13. 1.5m from A14
This picturesque old thatched inn is part of a group of chef-managed local dining pubs. Inside, the lively atmosphere is given a cosmopolitan edge by the guests drawn from the tourist and business centre of nearby Cambridge. Beside the small bustling bar, the pretty conservatory-restaurant overlooks the large garden and neighbouring cricket pitch. Chef Patron Richard Stokes, says the inn's brochure, claims to hate Christmas, 'but otherwise he's charming'. He certainly puts on a good show, preparing food that is well flavoured yet uncomplicated. Starters range from tataki of salmon, Vietnamese cucumber and prawn salad, to sugar-cured venison saddle, fried new potatoes, dukkah (an Egyptian spice blend of toasted nuts and seeds) and celery leaf salsa. His imaginative style also shows in main courses such as pan-fried black bream with chilli, and roast pigeon with Mascarpone and Cottechino sausage with celeriac mash. Vegetarian dishes are available in both the restaurant and bar-grill area.
OPEN: 12-2 6-11 **BAR MEALS:** L served all week 12-2 D served Mon-Sat 6.30-9.30 Av main course £12 **RESTAURANT:** L served all week 12-2 D served Mon-Sat 6.30-9.30 Av 3 course à la carte £25 **BREWERY/COMPANY:** Huntsbridge Inns
: Adnams Bitter, Hook Norton Old Hooky, Smile's Best. **:** 18
FACILITIES: Garden: Large garden, seating for 50
NOTES: Parking 70

NEWTON
Map 12 TL44

Pick of the Pubs

The Queen's Head
CB2 5PG **☎** 01223 870436
Dir: 6m S of Cambridge on B1368, 1.5m off A10 at Harston, 4m from A505
This quintessentially English pub, dating back to 1680 (though the cellar is much older), stands in the heart of the village by the green. There are no fruit machines or piped music to interrupt the lively conversation in the two small bars; nor for 40 years has there been a menu - or specials 'whatever they might be'. The daily home-made soup is best described by its colour, while the cut-to-order sandwiches - roast beef, smoked ham, salmon, and cheese with pickle or salad - are made with the freshest brown bread and butter. You could also try a Humphry (banana sandwich with lemon and sugar). Hot alternatives are limited to Aga-baked potatoes and toast with beef

dripping. Adnams' ales are dispensed direct from the barrel in studious avoidance of modernisation.
OPEN: 11.30-2.30 6-11 (Sun 12-2.30, 7-10.30) Closed: 25 Dec
BAR MEALS: L served all week 11.30-2.15 D served all week 6-9.30 Av main course £3 **BREWERY/COMPANY:** Free House
: Adnams Southwold, Broadside, Fisherman, Bitter & Regatta.
FACILITIES: Children welcome Dogs allowed **NOTES:** Parking 15 **NOTES:** No credit cards

---

PETERBOROUGH
Map 12 TL19

The Brewery Tap
80 Westgate PE1 2AA **☎** 01733 358500 **▤** 01733 310022
e-mail: brewerytap@hotmail.com
Visitors to this unusual American-style pub can view the operations of the large Oakham micro-brewery through a glass wall. The vast space of the pub was once a labour exchange. There is always a minimum of ten real ales available at any time. The Tap has a capacity of over 500, specialises in real Thai food, and runs a night-club Friday and Saturday.
OPEN: 12-11 (Mon-Thur 12-11, Fri-Sat 12-1.30am) (Sun 12-10.30) Closed: Dec 25-26, Jan 1 **BAR MEALS:** L served all week 12-2.30 D served all week 6-9.30 Av main course £5 **RESTAURANT:** L served all week 12-2.30 D served all week 6-9.30 **BREWERY/COMPANY:** Free House **:** Oakham, Jeffery Hudson Bitter, Bishops Farewell & White Dwarf. **FACILITIES:** Dogs allowed Water

Charters Cafe Bar
Town Bridge PE1 1FP
☎ 01733 315700 315702 For Bookings **▤** 01733 315700
e-mail: manager@charters-bar.fsnet.co.uk
Dir: A1/A47 Wisbech, 2m for city centre & town bridge (River Nene). Barge is moored at Town Bridge
Charters is a 176ft long barge which proprietor Paul Robert sailed over from Holland in 1991 and moored right in the heart of the city, on the River Nene. The East part of the name applies to the upper deck, which is an oriental restaurant with dishes from Vietnam, Japan, Thailand, Malaysia and elsewhere. Twelve hand pumps dispense a continually-changing repertoire of real ales. Friday and Saturday nights are a treat for blues lovers, with a late night live blues club starting at 11pm.
OPEN: 12-11.30 Mon-Thu 12-late Fri-Sat Closed: 25-26 Dec, 1 Jan
BAR MEALS: L served all week 12-2.30 **RESTAURANT:** L served all week 12-2.30 D served all week 6-10.30
BREWERY/COMPANY: Free House **:** Oakham JHB, Oakham White Dwarf & Bishops Farewell, Hop Back Summer Lightning, Interbrew Draught Bass. **FACILITIES:** Garden: Lrg beer garden Dogs allowed **NOTES:** Parking 15

ST IVES
Map 12 TL37

Pike & Eel Hotel
Overcote Ln, Needingworth PE27 4TW
☎ 01480 463336 **▤** 01480 465467
e-mail: enquiries@pikeandeelhotel.co,uk
Dir: From A14 take A1096 to St Ives, A1123 to Earith, turn R into Overcote Lane
17th-century listed inn with marina moorings on the River Ouse where the ferry once crossed: formerly well known also for its fine pike fishing. Good fish includes crevettes flambees and seafood platter. In the bar enjoy Welsh rarebit and steak and kidney pudding. Restaurant carte and Sunday lunch.
OPEN: 11-11 (Sun 12-10.30) **BAR MEALS:** L served all week 12-2 D served all week 7-9.30 Av main course £10 **RESTAURANT:** L served all week 12-2.30 D served all week 7-10.30 Av 3 course à la carte £23

continued

continued

BREWERY/COMPANY: Free House **:** Greene King IPA, Ruddles, Greene King Old Speckled Hen. **FACILITIES:** Children welcome Garden: outdoor eating, BBQ, Marina adjacent Dogs allowed **NOTES:** Parking 75

STILTON   Map 12 TL18

Pick of the Pubs

The Bell Inn ★★★ ◉ 🐭
Great North Rd PE7 3RA ☎ 01733 241066 📠 01733 245173
e-mail: reception@thebellstilton.co.uk
Dir: from A1 follow signs for Stilton, hotel is situated on the main road in the centre of the village.

The Bell is known as the birthplace of Stilton, and stories of the famous cheese, first sold to travellers around 1720, abound. It is also associated with famous highwaymen (Dick Turpin hid here for nine weeks), and numerous other historic visitors from the Duke of Marlborough to Lord Byron. Restoration work in the late 1990s added high quality bedrooms and conference facilities that have been blended into the ageless inn's stonework around the central courtyard. Beamed ceilings, a stone floor and open fires imbue the Village Bar with great character, which is enhanced by fine real ales and an extensive monthly menu with daily specials. The ubiquitous cheese appears in dishes as diverse as Stilton and broccoli soup, sirloin steak with Stilton sauce, and grilled field mushrooms topped with Stilton and smoked bacon. Rest assured, there are plenty of cheese-free options: perhaps whole baked sea bass with pesto couscous, and braised beef and ale stew.
OPEN: 12-2.30 6-11 (Sun 12-3, 7-10.30) Closed: Dec 25
BAR MEALS: L served all week 12-2 D served all week 6.30-9.30 Av main course £9 **RESTAURANT:** L served Sun-Fri 12-2 D served all week 7-9.30 Av 3 course fixed price £23.95
BREWERY/COMPANY: Free House **:** Marston's Pedigree, Greene King Abbot Ale, Oakham JHB, Interbrew Boddingtons.
FACILITIES: Garden: Stone Courtyard, food served outside
NOTES: Parking 30 **ROOMS:** 19 bedrooms 19 en suite 1 family rooms s£72.50 d£96.50 no children overnight

---

STRETHAM   Map 12 TL57

The Lazy Otter 🐭 ♀
Cambridge Rd CB6 3LU ☎ 01353 649780 📠 01442 876893
e-mail: swilkinson110454@aol.com
Dir: Telephone for directions
With its large beer garden and riverside restaurant overlooking the marina, the 'Lazy Otter' lies just off the A10 between Ely and Cambridge. The pub's location beside the Great Ouse river makes it very popular in summer. Typical dishes include jumbo cod, lemon sole topped with crab meat,

continued

---

or fisherman's medley, as well as a selection of steaks and grills. The marina holds 30 permanent boats, as well as up to 10 day boats.
OPEN: 11-11 **BAR MEALS:** L served all week 12-2.30 D served all week 6-9.30 Av main course £6 **RESTAURANT:** L served all week 12-2.30 D served all week 6-9.30 **:** Marston's Pedigree, Wadsworth 6X, Interbrew Flowers IPA, Scottish Courage John Smith's & Courage Best. ♀: 8 **FACILITIES:** Children welcome Garden: Large Beer garden along river front **NOTES:** Parking 50

CHESHIRE

ALDFORD   Map 15 SJ45

Pick of the Pubs

The Grosvenor Arms ♀
Chester Rd CH3 6HJ ☎ 01244 620228 📠 01244 620247
e-mail: grosvenor.arms@brunningandprice.co.uk
Dir: on B5130 S of Chester
A relaxing Victorian inn with a bustling atmosphere in its comfortably-refurbished bars. The spacious, open-plan interior includes an airy conservatory decorated with hanging baskets, a panelled library filled with books, and a suntrap terrace for summer eating and drinking. Decent wines accompany the interesting bistro-style food, and there's a nice range of Cognacs, ports and real ales. Starters from the daily menu might include deep fried brie with cranberry compote or potted confit of duck with hoi sin dressing. The main courses range from good old fashioned steak and chips (albeit a posh version, using local meat and herb butter) to tandoori lamb chops with roasted peppers, salad and yogurt dressing. If you prefer a light bite, there's a good selection of sandwiches. Round off with appetising desserts such as chocolate brownie with chocolate sauce and ice cream or prune and Armagnac tart.
OPEN: 11-11 (Sun 12-10.30) **BAR MEALS:** L served all week 12-10 D served all week Av main course £7
BREWERY/COMPANY: Free House **:** Interbrew Flowers IPA, Beartown Bearskinful, Robinson's Best, Caledonian Deuchars IPA.
♀: 16 **FACILITIES:** Children welcome Garden: Lrg terrace, ample seating, walled garden Dogs allowed Water bowls
NOTES: Parking 150

continued

ASTON · Map 15 SJ57

Map 15 SJ57

Pick of the Pubs

The Bhurtpore Inn 🐾 ♀
Wrenbury Rd CW5 8DQ ☎ 01270 780917
e-mail: simonbhurtpore@yahoo.co.uk
Dir: between Nantwich & Whitchurch just off the A530
Lively and popular at weekends, this unpretentious village pub offers an unusual combination of Indian cuisine and a really exceptional range of real ales. Its name comes from a city in central northern India, where a local landowner, Lord Combermere, was involved in a fierce battle in 1825. The emphasis is very much on traditional ales, freshly-prepared home-made food and a comfortable village pub atmosphere. Ten real ales produced by small independent 'craft' brewers are served alongside many of Europe's finest, including pump-drawn German and Belgian beers as well as about 80 bottled beers from all over the world. Food ranges through venison casserole in a blueberry and sloe wine sauce, steak, kidney and real ale pie, and cheese and leek cakes on a creamy Dijon sauce, to a choice of about six curries and baltis. Toasties, hot baguettes and jacket potatoes also served.
OPEN: 12-2.30 6.30-11 (Sun 12noon-10.30pm) Closed: Dec 25, 1 Jan **BAR MEALS:** L served all week 12-2 D served all week 7-9.30 Av main course £8.50 **RESTAURANT:** L served all week 12-2 D served all week 7-9.30 Av 3 course à la carte £15 **BREWERY/COMPANY:** Free House 🍺: Hanbys Drawwell Bitter, Salopian Shropshire Golden Thread, Abbeydale Absolution, Weetwood Oasthouse Gold. ♀: 9 **FACILITIES:** Garden: Lrg area behind pub with countryside views Dogs allowed Water **NOTES:** Parking 40

AUDLEM · Map 15 SJ64

Map 15 SJ64

The Shroppie Fly

The Wharf CW3 0DX ☎ 01270 811772 📠 01270 811334
e-mail: grmagnum@aol.com
Dir: Jct 16 M6,A500, then A529
Originally built as a canal warehouse for the Shropshire Union Canal, this interesting building was converted to a pub in 1974. The name comes from the salvaged horse-drawn barge that now serves as the bar and is a major feature. The main menu includes broccoli and cream cheese bake, mixed grill, Goan chicken curry, spinach and ricotta cannelloni, and a selection of sandwiches and ploughman's. There is a separate specials board usually offering some 20 or 30 extra dishes.
OPEN: 11-11 **BAR MEALS:** L served all week 12-2.30 D served all week 6-9 Av main course £6 🍺: Interbrew Boddingtons Bitter, Flowers Original,Old Speckled Hen. **FACILITIES:** Children welcome Garden: Food served outdoors Dogs allowed **NOTES:** Parking 60

> **Restaurant and Bar Meal times indicate the times when food is available. Last orders may be approximately 30 minutes before the times stated.**

BARTHOMLEY · Map 15 SJ75

Map 15 SJ75

The White Lion Inn

CW2 5PG ☎ 01270 882242 📠 01270 873348
Historic half-timbered and thatched inn with character bars and a lovely rural setting. It offers bar food ranging from hot beef "banjo", tuna mayonnaise, and paté with toast, to more substantial dishes such as pie with peas, mash and gravy, and a daily roast with creamed potatoes and vegetables.
OPEN: 11.30-11 (Thurs 5-11, Sun 12-10.30) **BAR MEALS:** L served Fri-Wed 12-2 Av main course £4
BREWERY/COMPANY: Burtonwood 🍺: Burtonwood Bitter, Top Hat & Guest ale. **FACILITIES:** Children welcome Garden Dogs allowed **NOTES:** Parking 20

BOLLINGTON · Map 16 SJ97

Map 16 SJ97

The Church House Inn ♀

Church St SK10 5PY ☎ 01625 574014
Dir: Macclesfield turnoff on A34, thru Prestbury, follow Bollington signs.
Convenient for both the natural landscape of the Peak District National Park and the bright lights of Manchester, this village inn has a varied menu. Diners may enjoy lunchtime specials such as casseroles and home-made pies. Fresh fish dishes feature on the evening menu.
OPEN: 12-3 5.30-11 **BAR MEALS:** L served all week 12-2 D served all week 6.30-9.30 Av main course £6 **BREWERY/COMPANY:** Free House 🍺: Greene King IPA, Timothy Taylor Landlord. ♀: 12 **FACILITIES:** Children welcome **NOTES:** Parking 4

BROXTON · Map 15 SJ45

Map 15 SJ45

The Copper Mine 🐾

Nantwich Rd CH3 9JH ☎ 01829 782293 📠 01829 782183
Dir: A41 from Chester, L at rdbt onto A534, pub 0.5m on R

Convenient for Cheshire Ice Cream Farm, the 14th-century Beeston Castle, and the Candle Factory at Cheshire Workshops, this pub has a conservatory with fine views of the surrounding countryside. Favourite dishes include spare ribs, chicken pastorella, lamb feast, the 16oz T-bone steak, and various fish dishes including monkfish, sea bass and red snapper. Patio and lawn with mature trees.
OPEN: 12-3 6-11 Rest:25 Dec, 1 Jan closed eve **BAR MEALS:** L served all week 12-2.30 D served all week 6-9 Av main course £8 **RESTAURANT:** L served all week 12-2.30 D served all week 6-9 **BREWERY/COMPANY:** Free House 🍺: Interbrew Bass & Flowers IPA. **FACILITIES:** Children welcome Garden **NOTES:** Parking 80

The Ship Inn

Explore a picturesque corner of rural Cheshire on this delightful walk to Hangingstone, a striking outcrop of rocks. This local landmark boasts two plaques, one of which commemorates a man who served in both World Wars and was killed on active service in 1942.

Turn left on leaving the Ship, walk down the lane and cross the bridge spanning the River Dane. Keep ahead up the hill until you come to a post on the left pointing to Back Forest and Gradbach. Follow the right of way up some steps to reach a farm track.

Turn right, heading away from a stone cottage, and when you reach the next track, turn left and then immediately right in front of Ashmount Cottage. Climb four stone steps to a stile and then continue ahead up a grassy track until you reach a wooden gate.

Pass over the stile to the right of it and then turn immediately left to follow the tarmac drive. This stretch of the walk reveals good views across the Dane Valley. Hangingstone and Hangingstone Farm can also be seen. Cross a cattle-grid and pass Park House Cottage on your right. Follow the drive as it veers left.

When you reach the hill on which stands Hangingstone, turn left along the farm track, heading towards Hangingstone Farm. On reaching it, turn left at the signpost and follow the clear path, keeping the outbuildings on your left. Cross the stile set in the wall and make for the stone waymark in the middle of the field. Allegedly, this is the grave of Robin Hood or King Arthur - though both claims are without foundation.

THE SHIP, WINCLE
SK11 0QE
☎ 01260 227217
Directions: Leave A54 at Fourways Motel x-rds, towards Danebridge, inn 0.5m before bridge on L
16th-century pub, reputedly the oldest in Cheshire. Good choice of real ales, and blackboard menu to supplement the printed one. Sandwiches & snacks also available.
Open: 12-3 7-11 (Sun 12-3 7-10.30)
Bar Meals: 12-2 7-9
Notes: Children welcome (high chairs, food-warming facs) & dogs. Lawned terrace. Parking.
(See page 71 for full entry)

Descend towards a line of trees, keeping to the left of the hollow. On reaching the trees, cross the stile into the wood, descend some stone steps and continue following the path. Keep ahead at the waymark and eventually you reach a series of steps leading to a stile. Turn left and follow the track to a stone stile. Cross it to the road, turn right and return to the inn.

DISTANCE: 2 miles
MAP: OS Explorer 268
TERRAIN: Mixture of farmland and woodland on the edge of the Pennines
PATHS: Mainly paths and tracks
GRADIENT: Quite steep in places

Walk submitted and checked by the Ship Inn, Wincle

BUNBURY — Map 15 SJ55

The Dysart Arms 🐾 ♀
Bowes Gate Rd CW6 9PH ☎ 01829 260183 📠 01829 261286
e-mail: dysart.arms@brunningandprice.co.uk
See Pick of the Pubs on opposite page

BURWARDSLEY — Map 15 SJ55

The Pheasant Inn ★★ 😊😊 🐾 ♀
CH3 9PF ☎ 01829 770434 📠 01829 771097
e-mail: reception@thepheasant-burwardsley.com
*Dir: From Chester A41 to Whitchurch, after 4m L to Burwardsley.
Follow signs 'Cheshire Workshops'*

A delightful old sandstone inn tucked away in a beautiful
rural setting with lofty views of the Cheshire plain. This
traditional country inn is cosy indoors with reputedly the
largest log fire in the county, while outside a flower-filled
courtyard is ideal for summer evening drinks. The half-
timbered former farmhouse makes a great setting for a
bar that boasts sophisticated cooking and well-kept ales.
Home-cooked specialities like smoked haddock risotto or
grilled black pudding might kick off a meal in the stone-
flagged conservatory, followed by twice-baked soufflé,
poached halibut, or pork and apple sausage, with
irresistible toffee and date pudding, or chocolate torte to
finish. The old outbuildings have been tastefully converted
to provide a range of comfortable modern en suite
bedrooms, each one individually decorated and furnished
in contemporary styles.
OPEN: 11-11 **BAR MEALS:** L served all week 12-2.30 D
served all week 6.30-9.30 Av main course £12 **RESTAURANT:** L
served all week 12-2.30 D served all week 6.30-9.30 Av 3 course à
la carte £18 **BREWERY/COMPANY:** Free House
🍺: Weetwood Old Dog, Eastgate, Outhouse, Best. ♀: 7
FACILITIES: Children welcome Garden: Ten tables, views of the
Cheshire Plains **NOTES:** Parking 40 **ROOMS:** 10 bedrooms 10
en suite 2 family rooms s£55 d£70

CHESTER — Map 15 SJ46

Albion Inn
Park St CH1 1RN ☎ 01244 340345
e-mail: mike@albioninn.freeserve.co.uk
*Dir: In Chester City centre adjacent to Citywalls and Newgate overlooking
the River Dee*
The home fires still burn on winter nights at this living
memorial to the 1914-18 war. It is a traditional Victorian street
corner pub, with a splendid cast-iron fireplace, enamelled
advertisements and World War I memorabilia adding to the
period atmosphere. Trench rations range from the 'Great
British Buttie' to lamb's liver, smoked bacon and onions in
rich cider gravy, and Staffordshire oatcakes with a cheese and
broccoli filling. Home-made puddings are offered from the
specials board.
OPEN: 11.30-3 5-11 Closed: 26 Dec-2 Jan **BAR MEALS:** L served
all week 12-2 D served all week 5-8 Av main course £6.75
BREWERY/COMPANY: Inn Partnership 🍺: Timothy Taylor
Landlord, Jennine Cumberland, Banks Mild. **FACILITIES:** Dogs
allowed Water/cold sausage **NOTES:** No credit cards

Old Harkers Arms 🐾 ♀
1 Russell St CH1 5AL ☎ 01244 344525 📠 01244 344526
This canalside Victorian former warehouse is one of Chester's
more unusual pubs, with its high windows, lofty ceilings and a
bar created from salvaged doors. Six guest beers are offered
in addition to the regulars. There's a good selection of both
toasted and plain sandwiches, and an interesting range of
dishes that might include chickpea, chilli and coriander cakes
with red onion salad, grilled tuna on a warm potato and
onion salad, sausage and mash in Yorkshire pudding, and
crispy roast duck breast on parsnip puree with cranberry
gravy.
OPEN: 11.30-11 Closed: Dec 26 & Jan 1 **BAR MEALS:** L served all
week 11.30-2.30 D served Sat-Thur 5.30-9.30 Av main course £7
RESTAURANT: L served all week 11.30-2.30 D served Sat-Thur 5.30-
9.30 **BREWERY/COMPANY:** 🍺: Thwaites Bitter, Interbrew
Boddingtons, Exmoor Gold, Fuller's London Pride.

CHOLMONDELEY — Map 15 SJ55

The Cholmondeley Arms ♦♦♦ 🐾 ♀
SY14 8HN ☎ 01829 720300 📠 01829 720123
e-mail: guy@cholmondeleyarms.co.uk
See Pick of the Pubs on page 66

Open: 11.30-11 (Sun 12-10.30)
Bar Meals: L served all week 12-2.15,
D served all week 6-9.30.
Av cost main course £9.
BREWERY/COMPANY:
Free House.
🍺: Timothy Taylor Landlord,
Weetwood Eastgate, Thwaites Bitter,
Coach House Dick Turpin, Caledonian
Deuchars IPA.
FACILITIES: Dogs allowed, Children
welcome, Garden - Great views of
church and Peckforton Hills.
NOTES: Parking 30

The Dysart Arms

Built on the Dysart estate in the mid-18th century as a farm, by the
late 1800s this Grade II-listed building had became a pub - with an
abattoir attached, although that part has long since been demolished.

🐕 ♀

Bowes Gate Road,
Bunbury, CW6 9PH
☎ 01829 260183 📠 01829 261286
@ dysart.arms@brunningandprice.co.uk
Dir: Between A49 & A51, by
Shropshire Union Canal, opp church.

Antique furniture, old prints
and bookshelves decorate a
succession of airy rooms with
open fires, set around a central
bar. At the top end of a rural
Cheshire village, this listed
farmhouse was converted to a
pub in Victorian times, and was
extensively refurbished in the
1990s. Within can be found a
treasure trove of antiques and
old prints, with a superb
atmosphere to match. From the

terrace and attractive mature
garden, there are fine views of
Peckforton hills and Beeston
castles in one direction, and the
old church from the other.
Home-grown herbs are used in
an enticing menu served
throughout the pub - check the
website for an up-to-date
example. On a miserable
February day there can be
nothing more welcome than
home-made soup with crusty
bread, followed by fisherman's
hotpot, including mussels,
squid, tuna, trout and cod.
Other choices run to black
pudding and field mushroom
gateau with a mustard and
thyme sauce, and main dishes

like braised lamb shoulder with
roasted rosemary and garlic
potatoes, confit of duck on stir-
fried noodles, rich braised beef
with winter vegetables, mustard
mash and glazed shallots, and
Bunbury bangers with mash
and onion gravy. Puddings like
glazed lemon tart with
raspberry sauce, and cherry
crumble flan with sweet
whipped cream are offered
alongside a selection of guest
cheeses that offers a great
opportunity to sample some
lesser-known varieties.
Changing guest ales and a
dozen house wines. Parking
space is limited, so take the
horse - there are hitching posts.

Open: 11-3, 7-11
Bar Meals: L served all week 12-2.30, D served all week 7-10.
Av main course £9
RESTAURANT: L served all week 12-2.30, D served all week 7-10.
Av cost 3 courses £15
BREWERY/COMPANY:
Free House.
🍺: Marston's Pedigree, Adnams Bitter, Banks's, Everards Tiger Best.
FACILITIES: Garden - large lawns. Dogs allowed. Children welcome
NOTES: Parking 60.
ROOMS: 6 en suite from s£45 d£60

The Cholmondeley Arms

Formerly the village school, the Cholmondeley Arms is set in countryside close to the grounds of Cholmondeley Castle. The school closed in 1984, re-opening as a pub four years later, much to the relief of the locals as an accident of history had left the area dry for a century.

◆◆◆ 🐾 ♀

CHOLMONDELEY, Malpas, SY14 8HN
☎ 01829 720300 📠 01829 720123
📧 guy@cholmondeleyarms.co.uk
Dir: On A49, between Whitchurch & Tarporley

In the 1890s the Marquis of Cholmondeley, a passionate teetotaller, had closed all the licensed premises on his estate - in those days a considerable area of some 25,000 acres. So the Cholmondeley Arms was the first pub on the old estate lands for 100 years. Meanwhile it has gone from strength to strength gaining plaudits and awards along the way in recognition of its quality as a pub, with its hand-pumped beers and selection of wines, and also for its excellent home-made food. Dishes are freshly prepared using local produce wherever possible, and specialities of the house are Cholmondeley salmon fishcakes with hollandaise sauce, and Cholmondeley steak and kidney pie. (So popular are some of the dishes, that the pub now offers a mail order facility from their 'fishcake factory'.) Fresh fish is well represented with, perhaps, fillets of sea bass on buttered samphire with a light velouté sauce, while other options include pheasant with apple and Calvados sauce, or leek and Cheddar soufflé grilled with cheese and served with salad. Home-made puddings feature strongly - the likes of Pavlova, Bakewell tart and chocolate roulade - and there is also a menu of children's favourites. The old school house, across the original playground, provides accommodation for guests in fully equipped en suite bedrooms, each with its own individual character.

CHURCH MINSHULL Map 15 SJ66

The Badger Inn 🐾 ♀
Over Rd CW5 6DY ☎ 01270 522607 📠 01270 522607

Originally known as the Brookes Arms, this 15th-century inn later changed its name to the Badger Inn and became a coach stop on the route between Nantwich and Middlewich. The badger was part of the Brookes's family crest and has been used as the inn sign for many years. The menu here concentrates on steak dishes, as well as grills and curries. Baguettes, bar snacks, and burgers also available. Open for breakfast.
OPEN: 12-12 (Sun 12-11) **BAR MEALS:** Food served all week 12-9 **RESTAURANT:** Food served all week 12-9 Av 3 course à la carte £18 🍺: Mansfield Bitters. ♀: 8 **FACILITIES:** Children welcome Garden: Beer garden with benches, umbrellas Dogs allowed Water bowls provided **NOTES:** Parking 30

CONGLETON Map 16 SJ86

The Egerton Arms Hotel ♦♦♦ ♀
Astbury Village CW12 4RQ ☎ 01260 273946 📠 01260 277273
e-mail: egertonastbury@totalise.co.uk
Dir: *Telephone for directions*
Named after Lord Egerton of Tatton, the local lord of the manor, this 16th-century village inn is situated in the picturesque village of Astbury, adjacent to the 11th-century church. A typical menu includes pork Aphelia (traditional Greek casserole), beef and potato pie, chicken, broccoli and Stilton pie, Brie, courgette and almond crumble, and Madras chicken curry. Bedrooms are attractive and well equipped.
OPEN: 11.15-11 (Sun 11-3, 7-10.30) **BAR MEALS:** L served all week 11.30-2 D served all week 6.30-9 Av main course £6 **RESTAURANT:** L served all week 11.30-2 D served all week 7-9 **BREWERY/COMPANY:** Robinsons 🍺: Robinsons Old Stockport, Fredericks & Robinson Best Bitter. ♀: 8 **FACILITIES:** Children welcome Garden: Large grassed area with tables Dogs allowed Water **NOTES:** Parking 100 **ROOMS:** 6 bedrooms 2 en suite s£43 d£55

Plough Inn Hotel 🐾 ♀
Macclesfield Rd, Eaton CW12 2NH
☎ 01260 280207 📠 01260 280207
e-mail: theploughateaton@computerplus.net
Dir: *on A536 (Congleton to Macclesfield road)*
A combination of small alcoves, comfortable corners and blazing open hearth fires makes this nicely-restored 17th-century coaching inn an attractive place to meet. The menu changes regularly, and is served in the bar and the Old Barn restaurant with its high beamed roof, intimate gallery and wealth of gnarled old timbers. Tuna steak and bean salad, pasta with a selection of sauces, spare ribs, Feta cheese and herb salad, pork stincotta and apricot pork fillet are typical.

OPEN: 11-11 (Sun 12-10.30) Closed: 25-26 Dec, 1 Jan **BAR MEALS:** L served all week 12-2.30 D served all week 5.30-9.30 Av main course £7.95 **RESTAURANT:** L served all week 12-2.30 D served all week 6-9.30 Av 3 course à la carte £15 Av 3 course fixed price £9.95 **BREWERY/COMPANY:** Free House 🍺: Boddingtons, Macclesfield Hards Jacklethroat. **FACILITIES:** Children welcome Garden: Food served outside. Secret garden **NOTES:** Parking 50 **ROOMS:** 8 bedrooms 8 en suite s£50 d£60 (♦♦♦♦)

GREAT BARROW Map 15 SJ46

The Foxcote 🐾 ♀ NEW
Station Ln CH3 7JN ☎ 01244 301343 363287 📠 01244 303287
e-mail: thefoxcote@hotmail.com
Dir: *Telephone for directions*
Stunning views make this seafood restaurant and pub a delightful place to visit, especially in the summer. The small Cheshire village is a popular destination with TV stars and well-known footballers who delight in the menus: at least fifteen fishy starters and main dishes include sea bass with crab and banana, lobster with scampi and king prawn thermidor, and fresh turbot. Good beers always on tap.
OPEN: 12-3 6-11 Closed: First 2 Wks of Jan **BAR MEALS:** 12-2.15 6-9.30 Av main course £14 **RESTAURANT:** 12-2.15 6-9.30 Av 3 course à la carte £24 **BREWERY/COMPANY:** Scottish Courage 🍺: Carling, Boddingtons, Theakstones, Kronenbourg. ♀: 11 **FACILITIES:** Children welcome **NOTES:** Parking 30

HANDLEY Map 15 SJ45

The Calveley Arms 🐾 ♀
Whitchurch Rd CH3 9DT ☎ 01829 770619 📠 01829 770619
Dir: *5m S of Chester, signed from A41*
First licensed in 1636, this coaching inn has plenty of old world charm, with beamed ceilings, open fires, and a choice of classic pub games, including cribbage, dominoes and boules. A broad spectrum of food is offered, from sandwiches and a choice of pasta dishes to home-made steak and kidney pie. Fresh fish and game feature on the specials board, with options such as pan-fried monkfish with bacon, cream and garlic, or salmon teriyaki.
OPEN: 12-3 6-11 (Sun eve 7-10.30) Closed: 25 Dec (eve) **BAR MEALS:** L served all week 12-2.15 D served all week 6-9.30 Av main course £7.50 **RESTAURANT:** D served Same as bar **BREWERY/COMPANY:** Enterprise Inns 🍺: Interbrew Boddingtons Bitter & Bass, Castle Eden Ale, Wadworth 6X, Marston's Pedigree. **FACILITIES:** Garden: Seating and Tables, Boules court Dogs allowed Water **NOTES:** Parking 20

♦ **Diamond rating for inspected guest accommodation**

continued

KNUTSFORD   Map 15 SJ77

Pick of the Pubs

The Dog Inn
Well Bank Ln, Over Peover WA16 8UP
☎ 01625 861421 🖷 01625 864800
Dir: *From Knutsford take A50 S. Turn L at 'The Whipping Stocks'. Pub 2m*
Originally a row of cottages, built in 1804 in Over Peover (pronounced Peever), it later became an inn called The Hen, and was then renamed The Gay Dog until the word 'gay' was dropped 20 years ago. The traditional timbered building is located in the heart of the Cheshire countryside between Knutsford and Holmes Chapel, and in summer it is bedecked with dazzling flowerbeds, tubs and hanging baskets. A wide use of fresh local produce - and guest ales from local micro-breweries - attracts a faithful following for its interesting cooking. Rack of lamb with apricot and ginger, ham shank with parsley sauce, braised steak in red wine, and rabbit in herb and mustard sauce, along with fish dishes like halibut with spinach, haddock and prawn au gratin, and smoked salmon and prawn pancakes.
OPEN: 11.30-3 4.30-11 **BAR MEALS:** L served all week 12-2.30 D served all week 6-9 Av main course £10.95
RESTAURANT: L served all week 12-2.30 D served all week 7-9.30 Av 3 course à la carte £17.50 **BREWERY/COMPANY:** Free House 🍺: Hydes Traditional Bitter, Jackals Gold.
FACILITIES: Garden: Large patio, food served outside Dogs allowed **NOTES:** Parking 100 **ROOMS:** 6 bedrooms 6 en suite s£55 d£75 (♦♦♦) no children overnight

---

LANGLEY   Map 16 SJ97

Leathers Smithy
Clarke Ln SK11 0NE ☎ 01260 252313 🖷 01260 252313

Beautifully located pub, overlooking Macclesfield Forest and the Ridgegate Reservoir with a country park to the rear, offering what the landlord describes as 'the most beautiful views in Cheshire'. The name commemorates William Leather, a licensee in the early 1800s, and the building's one-time use as a forge. Food options range from sandwiches and snacks to speciality dishes like Smithy pork fillet topped with mushrooms, grain mustard, cream and brandy sauce.
OPEN: 12-3 7-11 **BAR MEALS:** L served all week 12-2 D served all week 7-10 **RESTAURANT:** L served all week 12-2 D served all week 7-10 🍺: Theakstons Best, Pedigree, Directors, Guest cask ale.
FACILITIES: Garden: Dogs allowed in the garden only
NOTES: Parking 25

LOWER WHITLEY   Map 15 SJ67

Chetwode Arms
St Ln WA4 4EN ☎ 01925 730203
e-mail: gfidler6@aol.co.uk
Dir: *Chetwode Arms is on the A49 2 m S from J 10 M56, 6m S of Warrington*
A country inn comprising a series of small and intimate rooms and believed to be over 300 years old. It has one of the best crown green bowling greens in the country, and is the focal point of the village - a best-kept village award winner. Freshly cooked food is prepared from produce supplied by small local businesses, and is offered alongside a comprehensive wine list and a selection of lagers and real ales. Typical menu includes medley of butcher's sausage, Chetwode chicken curry, fish casserole, or pork and sage burger.
OPEN: 12-11 **BAR MEALS:** L served all week 12-3 D served all week 6-9 **RESTAURANT:** L served all week 12-3 D served all week 6-9 Av 3 course à la carte £28 **BREWERY/COMPANY:** Inn Partnership 🍺: Greenalls Bitter, Cains Bitter, Marston's Pedigree.
♀: 12 **FACILITIES:** Garden: Patio overlooking bowling green Dogs allowed **NOTES:** Parking 60

MACCLESFIELD   Map 16 SJ97

The Windmill Inn ♀
Holehouse Ln, Whitely Green, Adlington SK10 5SJ
☎ 01625 574222
Dir: *A523 to Adlington turn off to Holehouse Lane*
On the fringe of the Peak District - just by the Macclesfield Canal - stands this heavily-beamed former farmhouse that dates back to 1684. Rustic specials boards promise pepper-pot mushrooms, monkfish in Pernod and duck breast in wild berry sauce. More traditional steak and ale pie, roast middle leg of lamb and fish in Speckled Hen batter happily co-exist.
OPEN: 12-11 **BAR MEALS:** L served all week 12-3 D served all week 6-9.30 **RESTAURANT:** L served all week 12-3 D served all week 6-9.30 **BREWERY/COMPANY:** 🍺: Bass, Old Speckled Hen, Stones. **FACILITIES:** Children welcome Garden: Dogs allowed Water **NOTES:** Parking 100

MARBURY   Map 15 SJ54

The Swan Inn ♀
SY13 4LS ☎ 01948 663715 🖷 01948 663715

A country inn with a friendly atmosphere and a reputation locally for good food. Sitting amidst Tudor houses overlooking a small mere, it boasts a large rural beer garden, and plenty of good walks, as well as cycle and bridle paths. Snacks or full meals are served, including giant hot dog and chips, roast rack of lamb, beer-battered salmon, prawns and cod with chips,

continued

monkfish with oriental stirfry, and sea bass with mushroom risotto.
OPEN: 11-2.30 7-11 (Open all day wknds) Closed: Dec 25
BAR MEALS: L served Tue-Sun 12-2.30 D served Tue-Sun 7-9.30 Av main course £7 **RESTAURANT:** L served Tue-Sun 12-2.30 D served Tue-Sun 7-9 Av 3 course à la carte £16.99 ◀: Tetley Smooth, Adnams, Bombadier. **FACILITIES:** Children welcome Garden: Food served outside. Beer garden Dogs allowed Water provided
NOTES: Parking 40

NANTWICH   Map 15 SJ65

The Thatch Inn 🕥 ♀
Wrexham Rd, Faddiley CW5 8JE
☎ 01270 524223 🗐 01270 524674
Dir: Follow signs for Wrexham from Nantwich, inn is 4m from Nantwich
Claiming to be the oldest, and one of the prettiest, pubs in south Cheshire, the black-and-white Thatch Inn has been photographed and painted countless times. There is a three quarter-acre garden, and inside you'll find oak beams, and open fires in winter. Favourite dishes include mixed grill, steak and stout pie, crispy belly pork and Thatcher's Pie (potato-topped mince and vegetables served with pickled beetroot). Fish, sometimes including barracuda, have their own board.
OPEN: 12-3.30 6-11 **BAR MEALS:** L served all week 12-2 D served all week 6-9 Av main course £9.50 **RESTAURANT:** L served all week 12-2 D served all week 6-9 Av 3 course à la carte £15 Av 2 course fixed price £7.95 **BREWERY/COMPANY:** Free House ◀: John Smiths, Weetwood Best, Kheans Steamer, Directors & Guest Beers. ♀: 24
FACILITIES: Children welcome Garden: Landscaped garden with seating Dogs allowed Water **NOTES:** Parking 60

OVER PEOVER   Map 15 SJ77

Ye Olde Parkgate Inn
Stocks Ln WA16 8TU ☎ 01625 861455
Dir: A50 from Knutsford. Inn 3m on L after Radbroke Hall
Ivy-covered village pub surrounded by fields and woodland. Attractively furnished beamed bars and comfortable lounge where meals are served. Recent change of hands. Menu specialises in roasts and pies.
OPEN: 11.30-11 **BAR MEALS:** L served all week 12-2 D served Tue-Sun 6.30-9 **BREWERY/COMPANY:** Samuel Smith ◀: Samuel Smith Old Brewery Bitter. **FACILITIES:** Dogs allowed Water Provided **NOTES:** Parking 45

PENKETH   Map 15 SJ58

The Ferry Tavern 🕥 ♀
Station Rd WA5 2UJ ☎ 01925 791117 🗐 01925 791116
e-mail: ferrytavern@aol.com
Dir: A57, A562, Fiddler's Ferry signed

Set on its own island, this 12th-century ale house welcomes walkers and cyclists from the trans-Pennine Way. Beneath the low beams in the stone-flagged bar you'll find a range of unusual guest beers and over 300 different whiskies, including 60 Irish. No food available.
OPEN: 12-3 5.30-11 (open all day wknd)
BREWERY/COMPANY: Free House ◀: Scottish Courage Courage Directors, Interbrew Boddingtons Bitter, Greene King Abbot Ale & Old Speckled Hen. ♀: 10 **FACILITIES:** Children welcome Garden: Dogs allowed Water, Toys **NOTES:** Parking 46

PLUMLEY   Map 15 SJ77

The Golden Pheasant Hotel 🕥 ♀
Plumley Moor Rd WA16 9RX ☎ 01565 722261 🗐 01565 722125
e-mail: helena.george@care4free.net
Dir: From M6 J19, take A556 signed Chester. 2m turn L at signs for Plumley/Peover. Through Plumley, after 1m pub opposite rail station.
Set in the heart of the north Cheshire countryside, this century-old pub stands opposite Plumley railway station, enabling customers to enjoy well-kept J W Lees cask ales without driving home! The building has been refurbished to make the most of its nooks and crannies, open fires and traditional hospitality. Extensive menus offer quality home-cooked food. Examples include brewers' pie, liver and onions, roast beef sirloin, broccoli and Stilton bake, chicken breast stuffed with soft cheese and Parma ham, and pan-fried halibut in a white wine and grape sauce.
OPEN: 11-11 (Sun 12-10.30) **BAR MEALS:** L served all week 12-2.30 D served all week 6-9.30 Av main course £8 **RESTAURANT:** L served all week 12-2.30 D served all week 6-9.30 Av 3 course à la carte £15 Av 2 course fixed price £10 **BREWERY/COMPANY:** J W Lees ◀: J W Lees Bitter, GB Mild & Moonraker. ♀: 15
FACILITIES: Children welcome Garden: Large garden, seating front and back of pub Dogs allowed Water **NOTES:** Parking 80

The Smoker 🕥 ♀
WA16 0TY ☎ 01565 722338 🗐 01565 722093
e-mail: smoker@plumley.fsword.co.uk
Dir: from M6 J19 take A556 W. Pub is 1.75m on L
A 400-year-old thatched coaching inn named after an 18th-century horse - Smoker the white charger, bred as a racehorse by the Prince Regent and owned by local landowner, Lord de Tabley. The wood-panelled interior with beams, log fires and horse brasses provides a traditional atmosphere, while the menu offers a good choice of fish and seafood, light bites, and house specialities such as fillet steak de Tabley (stuffed with Stilton and topped with port wine).
OPEN: 11-3 6-11 (all day Sun) **BAR MEALS:** L served all week 11.30-2.30 D served all week 6.30-9.30 Av main course £7.95
RESTAURANT: L served all week 11.30-2.30 D served all week 6.30-9.30 Av 3 course à la carte £14.50
BREWERY/COMPANY: ◀: Robinson's Best & Hatters Mild.
FACILITIES: Children welcome Garden: Large lawned area, 15 large dining benches **NOTES:** Parking 100

PRESTBURY   Map 16 SJ87

The Legh Arms & Black Boy Restaurant 🕥 ♀
SK10 4DG ☎ 01625 829130 🗐 01625 827833
Dir: From M6 through Knutsford to Macclesfield, turn to Prestbury at Broken Cross. Pub in village centre
15th-century pub, centrally located in historic Prestbury village. An imaginative and varied restaurant menu includes pan-seared calves' liver with a Roquefort, celery and spinach salad and raspberry balsamic dressing, and roast Norfolk

continued

continued

England

PRESTBURY continued

duckling with an orange, sage and onion gateau and brandy mango sauce. From the bar menu expect wild mushroom risotto, spicy Thai beef, and bangers and mash, plus tasty sandwiches.
OPEN: 11.30 -11 **BAR MEALS:** L served all week 12-10 D served all week Av main course £6 **RESTAURANT:** L served all week 12-3 D served all week 7-10 Av 3 course à la carte £25 Av 3 course fixed price £12.95 **BREWERY/COMPANY:** Frederic Robinson **🍺:** Robinsons. **🍷:** 8 **FACILITIES:** Garden: **NOTES:** Parking 40

SWETTENHAM
Map 15 SJ86

Pick of the Pubs

The Swettenham Arms 🍷
Swettenham Ln CW12 2LF ☎ 01477 571284 📠 01477 571284
Dir: M6 J18 to Holmes Chapel, then A535 towards Jodrell Bank. In 3m take rd on R (Forty Acre Lane) to Swettenham
This charming, white-painted village inn is tucked away behind a 13th-century church in the lovely Dane valley. Formerly a nunnery, the pub once boasted an underground passage where bodies were stored before burial. Ghost stories abound, but there's nothing chilling about the large open fireplaces that warm the pub's heavily-beamed interior. In summer, this tranquil spot is deservedly popular with walkers and country lovers. Owners Frances and Jim Cunningham have planted a two-acre wildflower meadow, and customers are welcome to walk in the adjoining Quinta Arboretum. A select wine list supplements the extensive range of unusual real ales and draught cider, and the imaginative menu features home-cooked food and fresh local produce. Expect sautéed pigeon breast on a bed of oyster mushrooms; pan-fried sirloin steak; game pie; hake fillet with dill and smoked salmon; or vegetable strudel with mixed cheeses and toasted pine kernels.
OPEN: 12-3 6.30-11 (Sun 12-4, 7-11) Rest closed: 25 Dec eve **BAR MEALS:** L served all week 12-2.30 D served all week 7-9.30 **RESTAURANT:** 12-2.30 7-9.30
BREWERY/COMPANY: Free House **🍺:** Jennings Bitter, Carlsberg-Tetley Tetley Bitter. **🍷:** 70 **FACILITIES:** Children welcome Garden: Peaceful garden **NOTES:** Parking 150

TARPORLEY
Map 15 SJ56

Alvanley Arms Hotel ♦♦♦♦ 🐑 🍷
Forest Rd, Cotebrook CW6 9DS
☎ 01829 760200 📠 01829 760696
Dir: On the A49, 10m from Chester, 18m from M6 J16

Friendly family-run former coaching inn dating back 400 years, believed to be haunted by Ruth Ellis, the last woman to be hanged in England, who once stayed here with her lover. Local produce is a feature of the menu, and fresh fish is delivered direct from the coast up to five times a week. Specialities include sea bass dusted with Cajun spices, beer-battered cod, a wide selection of steaks and home-reared Aberdeen Angus dishes.
OPEN: 11.30-3 5.30-11 **BAR MEALS:** L served all week 12-2 D served all week 6-9 Av main course £8.95 **RESTAURANT:** L served all week 12-2 D served all week 6-9 Av 3 course à la carte £18 **BREWERY/COMPANY:** **🍺:** Robinsons Best & Guest Beers. **🍷:** 8 **FACILITIES:** Garden: Large beer garden, overlooks lake **NOTES:** Parking 75 **ROOMS:** 7 bedrooms 7 en suite s£35 d£60 no children overnight

The Boot Inn 🐑
Boothsdale, Willington CW6 0NH ☎ 01829 751375
Dir: off the A54 Kelsall by-pass or off the A51 Chester-Nantwich, follow signs to Willington
Originally a small beer house, now expanded along a charming row of red brick and sandstone cottages, where quarry-tiled floors, old beams and open fires give the interior a character of its own. Local walks prepare you for well-kept ales and freshly-prepared food. Sandwiches and hot panninis, pepper satay, and classic steak and kidney, with specials of breast of duck in an orange and cranberry sauce, and medallions of beef cater for all tastes.
OPEN: 11-3 6-11 (All day Sat-Sun & BHs) Closed: Dec 25 **BAR MEALS:** L served all week 11-2.30 D served all week 6-9.30 Av main course £11.95 **RESTAURANT:** L served all week 11-2.30 D served all week 6-9.30 Av 3 course à la carte £21.85 **BREWERY/COMPANY:** Inn Partnership **🍺:** Weetwood Oasthouse Gold, Ambush, Old Dog & Eastgate, Cains. **FACILITIES:** Children welcome Garden Dogs allowed Water **NOTES:** Parking 60

The Fox & Barrel 🐑 🍷
Forest Rd, Cotebrook CW6 9DZ
☎ 01829 760529 📠 01829 760529
e-mail: info@thefoxandbarrel.com
Dir: On the A49 just outside Tarporey, very close to Oulton Park Race Circuit

Set in the heart of the Cheshire countryside is this award-winning pub with an open fire, wooden floors, old tables and odd chairs. A cosy bar serves cask ales and a good choice of wine by the glass, and there's a no-smoking restaurant extending on to an enclosed patio area. Seasonal home-made specials like sea bass fillets with a citrus and chive dressing, and from the menu, roast rack of lamb, plus good choice of snacks.
OPEN: 12-3 5.30-11 Closed: 25 Dec **BAR MEALS:** L served all week 12-2.30 D served all week 6.30-9.30 Av main course £12 **RESTAURANT:** L served all week 12-2.30 D served all week 6.30-9

continued

continued

Av 3 course à la carte £20 **BREWERY/COMPANY:** Pubmaster **◀:** Scottish Courage John Smith's, Marston's Pedigree, Guest Beers. **♀:** 10 **FACILITIES:** Garden: Patio, picnic tables **NOTES:** Parking 40

TUSHINGHAM CUM GRINDLEY   Map 15 SJ54

Blue Bell Inn ☜
SY13 4QS ☎ 01948 662172
e-mail: patgage@btinternet.com
Dir: On the A41 N of Whitchurch
In what must be a unique tale from the annals of pub-haunting, this 17th-century, black and white magpie building that oozes character with its abundance of beams, open fires and horse brasses was once haunted by the spirit of a duck. Believe that or not, the Blue Bell remains a charming characterful pub with well-kept ales. Bar meals include Georgian-style lamb, breaded plaice and scampi and large, locally farmed trout. While soup, sandwiches, home-baked pies and steaks of similar ilk balance out the variety of choices.
OPEN: 12-3 6-11 (Sun 12-3, 7-11) Rest: 25 Dec Closed eve
BAR MEALS: L served all week 12-3 D served all week 6-9 Av main course £4.95 **RESTAURANT:** L served all week 12-3 D served all week 6-9 **BREWERY/COMPANY:** Free House **◀:** Hanby Ales, Guest Beers. **FACILITIES:** Children welcome Garden: Picnic benches Dogs allowed water, buscuits **NOTES:** No credit cards

WARMINGHAM   Map 15 SJ76

The Bears Paw Hotel ☜
School Ln CW11 3QN ☎ 01270 526317 ▤ 01270 526465
e-mail: enquiries@thebearspaw.co.uk
Dir: From M6 J18 take A54 then A533 towards Sandbach. Follow signs for village
A country house hotel where truly comprehensive menus offer so much choice it's hard to know where to start. Apart from sandwiches, jackets and wraps, a random selection includes giant filled Yorkshire puddings - chilli con carne and lamb rogan josh among them - grills, chicken jambalaya, braised oxtail with dumplings, magret of duck with black olives, bouillabaisse, and vegetarian dishes, including Greek spanakopita and a lentil curry known as sambhar. At lunchtime on Sundays there's a carvery.
OPEN: 5-11 (Sun 12-10.30) **BAR MEALS:** L served all week 12-2 D served all week 6-9.30 Av main course £10 **RESTAURANT:** L served Weekends 12-6 D served all week 6-9.30 Av 3 course à la carte £23 Av 4 course fixed price £12.95 **BREWERY/COMPANY:** Free House **◀:** Interbrew Bass, Boddingtons Bitter & Flowers IPA, Marston's Pedigree. **FACILITIES:** Children welcome Garden: Beer garden at front and rear **NOTES:** Parking 100

WARRINGTON   Map 15 SJ68

Ring O Bells ☜ ♀
Old Chester Rd, Daresbury WA4 4AJ
☎ 01925 740256 ▤ 01925 740972
The village of Daresbury is where the author Lewis Carroll was born and lived as a child. The pub was formerly a large farmhouse plus an old courthouse. There is a good choice of hand-pulled ales and wines and freshly prepared food. The daily changing chalkboards display the dishes of the day. Fresh fish is always available such as red snapper, tuna steak, red mullet, and whole seabass. Other popular dishes are beef and Theakston ale pie, red Thai curry, and a variety of sandwiches, salads and "Hot Hobs".
OPEN: 11-11 (Sun 12-10.30) Rest closed 25 Dec eve
BAR MEALS: L served all week 12-10 D served all week 12-10 Av

main course £6.95 **RESTAURANT:** L served all week 12-10 D served all week 12-10 **BREWERY/COMPANY:** **◀:** Carlsberg-Tetley Greenalls, Scottish Courage Theakstons, Courage Directors & John Smiths, Guest Ales. **♀:** 24 **FACILITIES:** Children welcome Garden: Terraced garden, seating for 130 people **NOTES:** Parking 100

WINCLE   Map 16 SJ96

The Ship Inn ☜
SK11 0QE ☎ 01260 227217
Dir: Leave A54 at Fourways Motel x-rds, towards Danebridge, Inn 0.5m before bridge on L

Quaint, 16th-century red-sandstone pub with connections to the Shackleton expedition to the Antarctic. Reputedly the oldest inn in Cheshire, the Ship is in the lower Pennines, close to some of the finest walking country in the north-west of England. An interesting choice of real ales is complemented by a frequently changing blackboard menu. Typical examples from the printed menu include Danebridge trout with mussels, sausages and mash, steak and ale pie, braised lamb shank with apple mash, and 'Farmer's Lunch'. Sandwiches and lighter meals available.
OPEN: 12-3 7-11 (Sun 12-3, 7-10.30) **BAR MEALS:** L served Tue-Sun 12-2 D served Tue-Sun 7-9 Av main course £8.50
RESTAURANT: 12-2 7-9 **BREWERY/COMPANY:** Free House **◀:** Wye Valley, Timothy Taylor Landlord, York, Beartown. **FACILITIES:** Children welcome Garden: Lawned Terrace Dogs allowed **NOTES:** Parking 15

See Pub Walk on page 63

WRENBURY   Map 15 SJ54

The Dusty Miller ♀
CW5 8HG ☎ 01270 780537
e-mail: admin@dustymiller-wrenbury.com

A black and white lift bridge, designed by Thomas Telford completes the picture postcard setting for this beautifully converted 16th-century mill building beside the Shropshire

continued

continued

England

WRENBURY continued

Union canal. The current landlord is the great grandson of Arthur Summer, who ran the mill up until WWII. The menu features freshly cooked dishes like chargrilled chicken fillet with crispy smoked bacon, Staffordshire oatcakes filled with spinach and garlic mushrooms, spiced roast salmon, or slow-roast duck breast. Watch the blackboard for daily seasonal specials and fresh fish dishes.

OPEN: 11.30-3 6.30-11 **BAR MEALS:** L served Tues-Sun 12-2 D served all week 6.30-9.30 Av main course £10 **RESTAURANT:** L served all week 12-2 D served all week 6.30-9.30

BREWERY/COMPANY: 🍺: Robinsons Best Bitter, Frederics, Old Tom, Hatters Mild & Hartleys XB. 🍷: 12 **FACILITIES:** Children welcome Garden: Canalside garden accessed via footbridge Dogs allowed Water, Kennel **NOTES:** Parking 60

WYBUNBURY — Map 15 SJ64

The Swan 🍺

Main Rd CW5 7NA 🕿 01270 841280
e-mail: richard@theswan77.freeserve.co.uk
Dir: M6 J16 towards Chester & Nantwich. Turn L at traffic lights in Wybunbury
The Swan, registered as an alehouse in 1580, is situated next to the church in the village centre. All the food is freshly prepared on the premises and includes prime steaks, grilled lamb cutlets, Tuscan vegetable roulade, smoked haddock rarebit, tuna fish and spring onion fishcakes, and cod and chips with mushy peas. Hot sandwiches, ploughman's, sandwiches and salads are also available.

OPEN: 12-11 (Mon open from 5pm) **BAR MEALS:** L served Tue-Sun 12-2 D served all week 6.30-9.30 Av main course £7.50 **RESTAURANT:** L served Tue-Sat D served all week Av 3 course à la carte £16 **BREWERY/COMPANY:** Jennings 🍺: Jennings Bitter, Cumberland Ale, Guest beers. **FACILITIES:** Children welcome Garden **NOTES:** Parking 40

CORNWALL & ISLES OF SCILLY

BODINNICK — Map 02 SX15

Old Ferry Inn 🍺

PL23 1LX 🕿 01726 870237 📠 01726 870116
e-mail: ferryinn@bodinnick.fsnet.co.uk
Astonishingly, this 16th-century former merchant's house, just fifty yards from Bodinnick ferry, once stood on the main route from Plymouth to the West Country. Now a friendly family inn, the Old Ferry is perfectly situated for walking, sailing or touring - the Eden Project and Heligan Gardens are both nearby. The comprehensive menus feature daily specials and popular pub favourites like home-made fish pie, cod and chips, home-made steak and kidney pie, and home-cooked ham and chips.

OPEN: 11-11 (Sun 12-10.30) (Nov-Feb, 11.30-2.30, 6.30-10.30) Closed: 25 Dec **BAR MEALS:** L served all week 12-2.30 D served all week 6-9 Av main course £9 **RESTAURANT:** L served Sun 12-2.30 D served all week 7-9 Av 3 course à la carte £17.50 🍺: Sharp's Bitter, Stella Artois. **FACILITIES:** Garden: Patio overlooking River Fowey Dogs allowed **NOTES:** Parking 10 **ROOMS:** 12 bedrooms 8 en suite s£55.80 d£55.80 (♦♦♦♦) no children overnight

---

BOSCASTLE — Map 02 SX09

The Wellington Hotel ★★ 🍺

The Harbour PL35 0AQ 🕿 01840 250202 📠 01840 250621
e-mail: vtobutt@enterprise.net
Dir: A30 onto A395, then A39, R onto B3314, R onto B3266

Imposing 16th-century coaching inn with an interesting history and a reputation for being haunted. Located in glorious National Trust countryside within easy reach of the Elizabethan harbour and heritage coastal footpath, it offers a cosy retreat with its log fires and original beams. New owners have maintained the extensive choice of food, ranging from twice-baked Cornish yarg soufflé, to traditional Cornish pasties. Traditional folk music is a regular feature.

OPEN: 11-3 5.30-11 Easter-Oct 11-11 **BAR MEALS:** L served all week 12-2.30 D served all week 6-10 **RESTAURANT:** D served all week 7-9.30 Av 3 course à la carte £18 **BREWERY/COMPANY:** Free House 🍺: Interbrew Flowers IPA, St Austell HSD, Bass, Greene King & Abbot Ale. **FACILITIES:** Children welcome Garden: National Trust walks, natural spring Dogs allowed **NOTES:** Parking 20 **ROOMS:** 16 bedrooms 16 en suite s£29 d£58

Drays and Horses

A few breweries still engagingly use Shire horses and old-style drays to deliver their as in days of yore. The older 18th-century drays were two-wheeled wagons drawn by a pair of horses in tandem, with the driver sitting on one of the barrels. From this developed the more familiar four-wheeled dray, drawn by two horses abreast, with the driver perched up on a high seat. Some of them had open sides, other rails or low boards, while some had iron stanchions supporting chains. Strong, hardy and weighing in at about a ton, Shire horses trace their ancestry from the vast, tank-like warhorses of the Middle Ages, which rumbled into battle at a ground-shaking trot. Their descendants today rumble through the streets on more peaceful and merciful errands.

The Halzephron Inn

One of Cornwall's loveliest and most spectacular coastal walks offers stunning views of Mount's Bay with its stretches of beautiful sandy beaches.

From the pub car park, cross the road and go down the lane towards a cove. From here there are many glorious views, along the shingle beach to Mousehole and Land's End. Turn left along the track, then head up steeply towards Halzephron Herb Farm. Follow the path round to the right and along the impressive cliffs - scene of many famous shipwrecks over the centuries. Look out along here for kittiwakes, cormorants, gulls and lapwings.

Continue round to Gwinian Head and at this point you begin to drop down gently to Dollar Cove, named after a Spanish galleon wrecked on the cliffs below in 1785 with a cargo of 2 1/2 tons of gold coins. Gold doubloons and other coins have been found on the beach. While here, have a look at the beautiful 13th-century church of St Winwaloe. The decorated panels inside were originally part of a 16th-century rood screen made from a ship, the St Anthony, wrecked in 1526 en route to Portugal from Flanders. The golden sands of Church Cove with Mullion golf links behind them and Poldhu cliffs across the bay - setting for Marconi's wireless station - create a spectacular scene.

Take the road up the hill, following it between traditional Cornish hedges filled with wild flowers and birds, and make for a magnificent view across Mount's Bay at the top. If time permits, call in and sample the produce at the Herb Farm before heading down the hill and back to the inn.

THE HALZEPHRON INN, GUNWALLOE
TR12 7QB
☎ 01326 240406

Dir: 3m S of Helston on A3083, R to Gunwalloe, then through village. Inn on L overlooking Mount's Bay. Spectacularly-located freehouse dating back 500 years (though it was dry for 50 years until 1956), and with a smuggling history. Real ales, and a twice-daily menu based on local produce.
Open: 11-2.30 6.30-11 (summer 6-11)
Bar Meals: 12-2 7-9
Notes: Children welcome (toys & blackboard). Garden, terrace, courtyard, raised area.
(See full entry on page 76)

DISTANCE: 3 miles/4.8km
MAP: OS Explorer 103
TERRAIN: Paths, tracks and roads
PATHS: Coastal - cliff path and tarmac road
GRADIENT: Steep cliff path and stretch of moderately steep road

Walk submitted and checked by A.M.Q. Thomas, The Halzephron Inn, Gunwalloe

CADGWITH
Map 02 SW71

Cadgwith Cove Inn 🐶
TR12 7JX ☎ 01326 290513 📠 01326 291018
e-mail: enquiries@cadgwithcoveinn.com

Set right on the Lizard Coastal Path overlooking a lovely cove on the peninsula, this inn is the focal point of the fishing and farming community. As might be expected, seafood is a speciality, with popular choices like grilled red mullet with bacon and garlic, monkfish in a light curry cream sauce, and fish and chips, plus steak, kidney and stout pie, and aubergine Charlotte. It is an ideal meeting place for walkers.
OPEN: 12-3 7-11 (Sat-Sun all day) (Jul-Aug open all day)
BAR MEALS: L served all week 12-2.30 D served all week 6-9.30 Av main course £7.95 **RESTAURANT:** L served all week 12-2.30 D served all week 6-9.30 Av 3 course à la carte £14
BREWERY/COMPANY: Inn Partnership 🍺: Interbrew Flowers IPA, Wadworth 6X, Marston's Pedigree, Sharp's.
FACILITIES: Garden: Large patio with sea view Dogs allowed Biscuits **NOTES:** Parking 4

CALLINGTON
Map 03 SX36

The Coachmakers Arms 🐶♇
6 Newport Square PL17 7AS ☎ 01579 382567 📠 01579 384679
Dir: Telephone for directions
A traditional stone-built pub appealing to a wide range of customers who enjoy a drink or meal in comfortable surroundings. Antique furniture, clocks, horse brasses and displays of foreign currency all contribute to the atmosphere. Home-made fare, from open ploughman's through grills and burgers to vegetable pasta bake and a good choice of fresh fish. The Sunday roast is also popular. Convenient for the Cornish coast, the Eden Project, Dartmoor and the Tamar Valley.
OPEN: 11-3 6-11 (Sun 12-3, 7-10.30) **BAR MEALS:** L served all week 12-2 D served all week 7-9.30 Av main course £4.50
RESTAURANT: L served all week 12-2 D served all week 7-9.30 Av 3 course à la carte £14 **BREWERY/COMPANY:** Enterprise Inns 🍺: Doombar, Cornish Knocker, Worthing Best Bitter, Abbot Ale. ♇: 7 **FACILITIES:** Children welcome Dogs allowed Water **NOTES:** Parking 10

Manor House Inn
Rilla Mill PL17 7NT ☎ 01579 362354
Dir: leave A30 and join B3254, L onto B3257 for 3m. R signed Rilla Mill
At the heart of a designated Cornish conservation area, the pub stands in its own mature gardens and orchard on the banks of the River Lynher. An extensive menu of daily home-made dishes and grills operates throughout with the steak and kidney pie, meat curry and vegetable lasagnes all prepared to the landlady's own recipes.

continued

OPEN: 11-3 6-11 **BAR MEALS:** L served Tue-Sun 12-2 D served all week 7-9 Av main course £6 **RESTAURANT:** L served all week 12-2 D served all week 7-9.30 Av 3 course à la carte £17
BREWERY/COMPANY: Free House 🍺: Bass, Local Ale.
FACILITIES: Children welcome Garden: beer garden, patio, outdoor eating, BBQ **NOTES:** Parking 41

CONSTANTINE
Map 02 SW72

Pick of the Pubs

Trengilly Wartha Inn ★★ ◉ 🐶♇
Nancenoy TR11 5RP ☎ 01326 340332 📠 01326 340332
e-mail: reception@trengilly.co.uk
Dir: SW of Falmouth
A choice of unusual ales is offered at this popular, family-run free house, together with an eclectic selection of wines from the pub's own shippers. The Trengilly Wartha stands in a peaceful wooded valley close to the Helford River, and its name means 'the settlement above the trees'. On warmer days, guests can enjoy alfresco meals beside the wisteria-covered pergola, or stroll in the extensive lakeside garden. The bar menu includes both traditional and more unusual dishes, with the emphasis on fresh local produce. Ploughman's lunches feature home-made breads, pickles and chutneys, supported by popular bar dishes such as real Cornish pasties or smoked chicken strudel. In the restaurant, starters like scallops or baby leek tart herald a main course menu that includes sea bass, rack of lamb, and three-cheese ravioli. There are six bedrooms in the main house, as well as newer garden rooms suitable for families.
OPEN: 11-3 6.30-11 Rest:25 Dec Closed **BAR MEALS:** L served all week 12-2.15 D served all week 6.30-9.30 Av main course £8 **RESTAURANT:** D served all week 7.30-9.30 Av 3 course fixed price £27 **BREWERY/COMPANY:** Free House 🍺: Sharps Cornish Coaster, St Austell HSD, Skinners, Exmoor Gold. ♇: 15 **FACILITIES:** Children welcome Garden: Walled garden, benches, pergola, terrace Dogs allowed **NOTES:** Parking 50 **ROOMS:** 8 bedrooms 8 en suite s£49 d£78

CRACKINGTON HAVEN
Map 02 SX19

Coombe Barton Inn ♦♦♦ 🐶♇
EX23 0JG ☎ 01840 230345 📠 01840 230788
e-mail: info@coombebartoninn.com
Dir: S from Bude on A39, turn off at Wainhouse Corner, then down lane to beach

Originally built for the 'Captain' of the local slate quarry, the Coombe Barton (it means 'valley farm' in Cornish) is over 200 years old and sits in a small cove surrounded by spectacular rock formations. Local seafood is a feature of the menu and

continued

includes crab, lemon sole, steaks, turbot, shark and plaice. Curries, pies, carvery, casseroles, pasta and vegetarian dishes are all available. Bedrooms are comfortable and one suite is suitable for families.
OPEN: 11-11 (Winter weekdays closed 3-6) **BAR MEALS:** L served all week 11-2.30 D served all week 6.30-9.30 Av main course £10 **RESTAURANT:** L served all week 11-2.30 D served all week 6-10 Av 3 course à la carte £12 **BREWERY/COMPANY:** Free House ☎: St Austell Dartmoor Best & Hick's special Draught, Sharp's Doom Bar Bitter. **FACILITIES:** Garden: Patio, food served outdoors **NOTES:** Parking 40 **ROOMS:** 6 bedrooms 3 en suite s£35 d£50 no children overnight

CRIPPLESEASE   Map 02 SW53

The Engine Inn
TR20 8NF ☎ 01736 740204
Dir: Pub is on B3311 between St Ives and Penzance

Homely inn high on the moor offering spectacular views and a quirky, cosy interior furnished with mining memorabilia, books, games, and musical instruments frequently played by customers. (Tuesday is quiz night and Thursday folk jam night.) Outside, a paddock provides parking for customers on horseback. Food includes home-made soups, doorstep sandwiches, ploughman's lunches, good vegetarian options and plenty of meat and chips combinations, including steak, gammon and scampi.

OPEN: 11-2.30 5-11 (Open all day Jul-Aug) **BAR MEALS:** L served all week 12-2 D served all week 6-10 Av main course £5.50 ☎: Sharp's Doom Bar Bitter, Marston's Pedigree, Greene King Old Speckled Hen. **FACILITIES:** Children welcome Garden: Terrace, paved area, picnic tables Dogs allowed Water **NOTES:** Parking 30

CUBERT   Map 02 SW75

The Smuggler's Den Inn 🏠 ♀
Trebellan TR8 5PY ☎ 01637 830209 ⌨ 01637 830580
e-mail: hankers@aol.com

Dir: From Newquay take A3075 to Cubert crossroads, then R, then L signed Trebellan, 0.5m
Two miles from the coast in an attractive valley, this thatched 16th-century pub features a long bar, barrel seats and inglenook wood-burner. A family room, beer garden and well-kept real ales tapped from the cask are among other attractions. For lunch, a range of sandwiches, snacks, salads, grills and puddings is on offer with a wider selection in the evening, including pastas. Specialities are the fresh fish dishes, especially Newlyn cod in beer batter, and prime quality steaks.
OPEN: 11-3 6-11 (Winter 12-2) Rest:Mon-Wed Closed Lunch Winter **BAR MEALS:** L served all week 12-2 D served all week 6-9.30 Av main course £10 **RESTAURANT:** L served all week 12-2 D served all week 6-9.30 Av 3 course à la carte £17 **BREWERY/COMPANY:** Free House ☎: Skinner's Cornish Knocker & Betty Stogs Bitter, Sharp's Doom Bar, St Austell Tribute & HSD. **FACILITIES:** Children welcome Garden: Small fenced beer garden, tables & chairs Dogs allowed Water **NOTES:** Parking 50

DULOE   Map 02 SX25

Ye Olde Plough House Inn 🏠 ♀
PL14 4PN ☎ 01503 262050 ⌨ 01503 264089
Dir: A38 to Dobwalls, take turning signed Looe
A welcoming 18th-century inn, with slate floors, wood-burning stoves, settles and old pews, located in a lovely village, handy for the coast and Cornish countryside. A choice of freshly-prepared dishes includes steak on hot stones, and wild boar with damson and plum sauce. The daily specials board always offers a selection of fresh fish dishes, such as monkfish and prawn Thai green curry, or fillets of John Dory with bacon and green peppercorn sauce.
OPEN: 12-2.30 6.30-11 (Sun 7-10.30) Closed: Dec 25-26 **BAR MEALS:** L served all week 12-2 D served all week 6.30-9.30 **RESTAURANT:** L served all week 12-2 D served all week 6.30-9.30 **BREWERY/COMPANY:** Free House ☎: Sharp's Doom Bar, Interbrew Bass, Worthington. **FACILITIES:** Children welcome Garden: Fenced grassed area, four tables Dogs allowed Water if requested **NOTES:** Parking 20

DUNMERE   Map 02 SX06

The Borough Arms
PL31 2RD ☎ 01208 73118 ⌨ 01208 76788
e-mail: Boroughharms@aol.com
Dir: From A30 take A389 to Wadebridge, pub approx 1m from Bodmin

Situated in glorious Cornish countryside, this popular pub lies on the Camel Trail, a 19-mile traffic-free walking, horse-riding and cycling route following the Camel river between Padstow and Bodmin Moor. Traditional pub fare includes a light menu of sandwiches, ploughman's and jacket potatoes; typical pub dishes like grills, a daily curry, lasagne, and jumbo cod, plus daily specials and a fill-your-own-plate carvery.

continued

continued

DUNMERE continued

OPEN: 11-11 (Sun 12-10.30) **BAR MEALS:** L served all week 12-2.15 D served all week 6.30-9.15 Av main course £5.50
RESTAURANT: L served all week 12-2.15 D served all week 6.30-9.15
BREWERY/COMPANY: Scottish & Newcastle ◀: Sharp's Bitter, Skinner's, Scottish Courage John Smith's Smooth.
FACILITIES: Children welcome Garden: Lrg with kids play area Dogs allowed Water **NOTES:** Parking 150

EGLOSHAYLE   Map 02 SX07

The Earl of St Vincent 🏠
PL27 6HT ☎ 01208 814807 📠 01208 814445
Dir: Telephone for directions
Dating from the Middle Ages, this atmospheric pub was built to house the masons who constructed the nearby church. Hidden away in a pretty village, it has wonderful floral displays in summer, and a collection of old clocks in its restored bar. Food is taken seriously here, whether it be roast duckling with orange sauce, tournedos Rossini, fresh grilled Dover sole, or a good choice of grills and salads.

OPEN: 11-3 6.30-11 **BAR MEALS:** L served all week D served Mon-Sat **RESTAURANT:** L served all week D served Mon-Sat
BREWERY/COMPANY: St Austell Brewery ◀: St Austell Tinners Ale & HSD, Tributo, Speciality beer every 3 months. **FACILITIES:** Garden: Patio with shrubs and plants Dogs allowed Water **NOTES:** Parking 20

FEOCK   Map 02 SW83

The Punch Bowl & Ladle 🏠
Penelewey TR3 6QY ☎ 01872 862237
Dir: Off A38 Falmouth Road
Thatched roadside inn, handy for Trelissik Gardens. The pub may have been a customs house, and contraband was destroyed in the fireplace. Typical menu includes fish pie, wild sea bass, lamb shoulder, and smoked haddock.
OPEN: 11.30-3 (open all day summer) 5.30-11 (Sun 12-10.30)
BAR MEALS: L served all week 12-2 D served all week 6.30-9 Av main course £7.95 ◀: IPA Tribute, HSD. **FACILITIES:** Children welcome Dogs allowed

FOWEY   Map 02 SX15

The Ship Inn 🏠 🍷
Trafalgar Square PL23 1AZ ☎ 01726 834931 📠 01726 834931
Dir: From A30, take B3269 & A390.
Authentic St Austell ales and good food uphold a long tradition of genuine hospitality at this traditional old inn.

Dating back to 1570, the Ship is handy for the Eden Project and the Lost Gardens of Heligan. The menu features lunchtime snacks like home-baked ham platters or Cornish Brie and grape sandwiches, whilst hot dishes include Cornish rump steak, local pan-fried scallops, and roasted vegetable lasagne. Arrive early to avoid disappointment.
OPEN: 11-11 (Winter times vary please telephone) **BAR MEALS:** L served all week 12-2 D served all week 6-8.30 **RESTAURANT:** L served all week 12-2 D served all week 6-8.30 **BREWERY/COMPANY:** St Austell Brewery ◀: St Austell Tinners Ale, Tribute & HSD.
FACILITIES: Children welcome Dogs allowed Water, biscuits

GUNNISLAKE   Map 03 SX47

The Rising Sun Inn
Calstock Rd PL18 9BX ☎ 01822 832201 📠 01822 832201
Dir: From Tavistock take A390 to Gunnislake, pub is through village and 0.25m on L. Left at traffic lights and 0.25m on R.
Quaint 17th-century pub with glorious gardens and fine views over the Tamar Valley. Cottagey interior featuring a fascinating collection of china, a wide range of real ales, and home-cooked food.
OPEN: 12-2.30 5-11 (Sun 12-3, 7-10.30) **BAR MEALS:** L served Tue-Sun 12-2 D served Tue-Sat 7-9 **RESTAURANT:** L served Tue-Sun 12-2 D served Wed-Sat 7-9 **BREWERY/COMPANY:** Free House ◀: Interbrew Bass, Sharp's Cornish Coaster, Skinner's Betty Stogs Bitter. **FACILITIES:** Children welcome Garden: Dogs allowed **NOTES:** Parking 14

GUNWALLOE   Map 02 SW62

Pick of the Pubs

The Halzephron Inn 🏠
TR12 7QB ☎ 01326 240406 📠 01326 241442
e-mail: halzephroninn@bandbcornwall.net
Dir: 3m S of Helston on A3083, R to Gunwalloe. Then through village, inn is on L overlooking Mount's Bay.

Five hundred-year-old freehouse, spectacularly situated on the South Cornwall Coastal Footpath overlooking Mount's Bay. Its name comes from the old Cornish Als Yfferin, or 'Cliffs of Hell', a name borne out by the numerous wrecks along this rugged coast. A shaft still connects the pub to an underground tunnel once used by smugglers. Formerly known as The Ship, the pub was 'dry' for half a century until 1956, when its licence was restored. Modern visitors will find a warm welcome, a good choice of real ales and a twice-daily menu of freshly-prepared food based on local produce. Options range from sandwiches (at lunchtime) to evening specials such as crab bisque with crab and Welsh rarebit croutons, straw potato and candied lemon, and peppered venison

continued

continued

fillet on spinach with potato fondant, celeriac purée and bramble jus.
OPEN: 11-2.30 6.30-11 (Summer evening 6-11) Closed: 25 Dec
BAR MEALS: L served all week 12-2 D served all week 7-9
RESTAURANT: L served all week 12-2 D served all week 7-9
BREWERY/COMPANY: Free House ◖: Sharp's Own, Doom Bar & Coaster, St Austell Tribute, Halzephron Gold.
FACILITIES: Garden: Terrace, courtyard, raised garden
NOTES: Parking 14

See Pub Walk on page 73

GWEEK Map 02 SW72

The Gweek Inn 🛏
TR12 6TU ☎ 01326 221502 📠 01326 221502
e-mail: gweek.inn@tesco.net
Dir: 2m E of Helston near Seal Sanctuary
A traditional family-run village pub and restaurant at the mouth of the Helford River. Nearby tourist attractions include the Lizard Peninsula, Goonhilly Earth Station and the National Seal Sanctuary. An extensive menu offers starters and snacks, traditional roasts, seafood, grills, chalkboard specials, and vegetarian and children's meals. Those stalwarts - steak, kidney and ale pie, and scampi, chips and peas - are always available. The pub claims the largest selection of real ales in the Lizard.
OPEN: 12-3 6.30-11 Sun Eve (7-10.30) **BAR MEALS:** L served all week 12-2 D served all week 6.30-9 Av main course £6.50
RESTAURANT: L served Sun 12-2 D served all week 6.30-9 Av 3 course à la carte £15 **BREWERY/COMPANY:** Pubmaster ◖: Interbrew Flowers IPA, Old Speckled Hen, Youngs, Whitbread.
FACILITIES: Children welcome Garden: BBQ, food served outdoors Dogs allowed on a lead Water **NOTES:** Parking 70

HAYLE Map 02 SW53

The Watermill 🛏 ♀
Old Coach Rd, Lelant Downs TR27 6LQ ☎ 01736 757912
Dir: From the A30 take the A3074 towards St Ives take L turns at the next two mini Rdbts
The old water mill here was in constant use as late as the 1970s. Converted from a restaurant into a classic 'local' just a few years ago, recent extensions to bar and restaurant allow for paella, baked local cod, fillet of beef tail, jambalaya, and ham hock glazed in honey. Chef's specials include lamb chops in balsamic and mint sauce, seafood linguine, baked cod in tomato and basil sauce, and twice-baked cheese soufflé. Under new management. Readers' reports welcome.
OPEN: 11-3 6-11 (Jul-Aug 11-11) **BAR MEALS:** L served all week 12-2.30 D served all week 6.30-9.30 **RESTAURANT:** L served all week 12-2.15 D served all week 6.30-9.30
BREWERY/COMPANY: Free House ◖: Sharp's Doombar Bitter, Dreckley Ring 'o' Bells. **FACILITIES:** Children welcome Garden: stream, pergola, ample seating, lawn Dogs allowed Water
NOTES: Parking 35

HELFORD Map 02 SW72

Pick of the Pubs

Shipwright Arms
TR12 6JX ☎ 01326 231235
Dir: A390 through Truro, A394 to Helston, before Goonhilly Down L for Helford/Manaccan
Superbly situated on the banks of the Helford River in an idyllic village, this small thatched pub is especially popular

in summer when customers relax on the three delightful terraces, complete with palm trees and glorious flowers, which lead down to the water's edge. Heavy nautical theme inside. Summer buffet offers crab and lobster subject to availablity, alongside various ploughman's lunches, salads, home-made pies, steaks and a wide range of international dishes. Barbecues in summer on the terrace.
OPEN: 11-2.30 6-11 (Closed Sun & Mon nights in Winter)
BAR MEALS: L served all week 12-2 D served all week 7-9
RESTAURANT: L served Sun 12-2 D served Tue-Sat 7-9
BREWERY/COMPANY: Free House ◖: Castle Eden, Greene King IPA, Sharps Doombar. **FACILITIES:** Children welcome Garden: Terrace, seating Dogs allowed

---

HELFORD PASSAGE Map 02 SW72

Ferryboat Inn 🛏 ♀
TR11 5LB ☎ 01326 250625 📠 01326 250916
e-mail: gav13@tinyworld.co.uk
Dir: From A39 at Falmouth, towards River Helford

Beautifully positioned on the north bank of the Helford River, this 300-year-old pub overlooks a safe beach and stands bang on the Cornish coastal path. Enjoy the views from the nautical-themed main bar, whose French windows open onto a spacious terrace. Well-kept St Austell ales are backed by a good range of wines, available by the glass. Food includes grills, light bites, daily-changing fish specials and Ferryboat ocean pie.
OPEN: 11-2.30 6.30-11 (Summer 11-11) **BAR MEALS:** L served all week 12-2.30 D served all week 6.30-9 Av main course £5.95
RESTAURANT: L served all week 12-2.30 D served all week 6.30-9 Av 3 course à la carte £10.95 **BREWERY/COMPANY:** St Austell Brewery ◖: St Austell HSD, Tinners & IPA. **FACILITIES:** Children welcome Garden: Patio, food served outdoors Dogs allowed
NOTES: Parking 80

HELSTON Map 02 SW62

Blue Anchor Inn
50 Coinagehall St TR13 8EX ☎ 01326 562821 📠 01326 565765
Dir: A30 to Penzance, then Helston signposted
One of the oldest pubs in Britain to brew its own beer, this unpretentious thatched pub dates from the 15th century when it was a monks' rest home. The inn has also been the haunt of Victorian tin miners, who collected their wages here. Sample excellent 'Spingo' ales in the low-ceilinged bars, tour the brewery, and tuck into stew and dumplings, fish pie, beef in Spingo, lamb hotpot, or a crusty filled roll.
OPEN: 10.30-11 **BAR MEALS:** L served all week 12-4 Av main

continued *continued*

England

HELSTON continued

course £4.75 **BREWERY/COMPANY:** Free House 🍺: Blue Anchor Middle, Best, Special & Extra Special, Braggit. **FACILITIES:** Children welcome Garden: Food served outside. Secluded, sunny garden Dogs allowed Water provided **NOTES:** No credit cards

KINGSAND
Map 03 SX45

Pick of the Pubs

The Halfway House Inn 🍴 ♀
Fore St PL10 1NA ☎ 01752 822279 ▤ 01752 823146
e-mail: halfway@eggconnect.net
Dir: From either Torpoint Ferry or Tamar Bridge follow signs to Mount Edgcombe

Tucked among the narrow lanes and colour-washed houses of this quaint fishing village is the family-run Halfway House Inn, set right on the coastal path. Named because it used to represent the border between Devon and Cornwall, it now signifies the dividing line between the conservation villages of Kingsand and Cawsand. The inn has been licensed since 1850, and has a pleasant stone-walled bar with low-beamed ceilings and a large central fireplace. Locally caught seafood is a feature of the small restaurant, and daily blackboard menus might feature assorted smoked fish platter, roast garlic monkfish, and scallops and seafood paella. Alternatives may include sautéed pork tenderloin with apple, rosemary and cider cream sauce, and braised lamb shank. For the casual diner there's a good selection of baguettes, baked potatoes, and ploughman's. The modern en suite bedrooms are furnished in pine.
OPEN: 12-3 7-11 **BAR MEALS:** L served all week 12-2 D served all week 7-9 Av main course £5 **RESTAURANT:** L served all week 12-2 D served all week 7-9 Av 3 course à la carte £19 **BREWERY/COMPANY:** Free House 🍺: Sharp's Doom Bar Bitter, Timothy Taylor Landlord, Scottish Courage Courage Best, Interbrew Boddingtons Bitter. ♀: 6 **FACILITIES:** Children welcome Dogs allowed Water, Dog chews **NOTES:** Parking 120 **ROOMS:** 6 bedrooms 6 en suite 1 family rooms s£27.50 d£55 (♦♦♦)

LAMORNA
Map 02 SW42

Lamorna Wink
TR19 6XH ☎ 01736 731566
Dir: 4m along B3315 towards Lands End, then 0.5m to turning on L
This oddly-named pub was one of the original Kiddleywinks, a product of the 1830 Beer Act that enabled any householder to buy a liquor licence. Popular with walkers and not far from the Merry Maidens standing stones, the Wink provides a selection

of local beers and a simple menu that includes sandwiches, jacket potatoes and fresh local crab. The management have been at the Wink for over thirty years, and prides itself on providing diners with as much local produce as possible.
OPEN: 11-11 (Winter 11-4, 6-11) **BAR MEALS:** L served all week 11-3 D served all week 6-9 Av main course £5.50
BREWERY/COMPANY: Free House 🍺: Sharp's Doom Bar, Skinners, Cornish Knocker Ale. **FACILITIES:** Children welcome Garden: Dogs allowed in Garden only **NOTES:** Parking 40 **NOTES:** No credit cards

LANLIVERY
Map 02 SX05

The Crown Inn 🍴
PL30 5BT ☎ 01208 872707 ▤ 01208 871208
Dir: From A30 S, follow signs 'Lanhydrock', L at mini rdbt 0.3m take A390, Lanlivery 2nd R
Built to accommodate masons constructing the church opposite, this 12th-century longhouse has three-foot-thick exterior walls, a large inglenook fireplace and a priest hole. Fresh fish from the quay is a feature of the comprehensive menu, as is 'Cornish under roast', a local speciality comprising rolled strips of steak topped with golden brown potato and onion. The Crown is set in a pretty cottage garden within 10 minutes' of the Eden Project and Lanhydrock House.
OPEN: 11-3 6-11 **BAR MEALS:** L served all week 12-2.15 D served all week 7-9.15 Av main course £6 **RESTAURANT:** L served all week 12-2.15 D served all week 7-9.15 Av 3 course à la carte £12.50
BREWERY/COMPANY: Free House 🍺: Sharp's Doom Bar & Eden Ale, Interbrew Worthington Bitter, Crown Inn Glory.
FACILITIES: Children welcome Garden: Cottage style, wrought iron furniture Dogs allowed Water, treats **NOTES:** Parking 40

LELANT
Map 02 SW53

The Badger Inn ♦♦♦♦ 🍴
Fore St TR26 3JT ☎ 01736 752181 ▤ 01736 759398
e-mail: marybadgerinn@aol.com
Dir: from rdbt at end of Hayle Bypass take A3074 to St Ives & Carbis Bay

The author Virginia Woolf used to stay in Room 1 of this village inn, and today devotees come from all over the world to follow in her footsteps. Situated in landscaped gardens close to the Hayle Estuary and St Ives Bay, the building has recently been brought up to date without sacrificing its charm. Fresh Cornish produce features strongly on a menu that includes casseroles, steaks, fish and pasta dishes along with tempting home-made puddings.
OPEN: 11-2.30 6-11 (Jun-Sep, open all day) **BAR MEALS:** L served all week 12-2 D served all week 6.30-10 **RESTAURANT:** L served all week 12-2 D served all week 6.30-10 Av 3 course à la carte £14 **BREWERY/COMPANY:** St Austell Brewery 🍺: St Austell Hicks & Tribute. **FACILITIES:** Garden: Landscaped with patio, umbrellas and shrubs **NOTES:** Parking 30 **ROOMS:** 5 bedrooms 5 en suite s£30 d£50 no children overnight

continued

England

LOSTWITHIEL — Map 02 SX15

Pick of the Pubs

Royal Oak Inn ♀
Duke St PL22 0AQ ☎ 01208 872552 📠 01208 872552
Dir: From Exeter take A30 to Bodmin then onto Lostwithiel or from Plymouth take A38 towards Bodmin then L onto A390 to Lostwithiel

An underground tunnel is said to connect the cellars of this 13th-century free house to the dungeons in the courtyard of nearby Restormel Castle. The friendly saloon bar is the place to mix with the locals in front of the open log fire. Alternatively, the lounge bar serves as a venue for a quiet drink, as well as offering a full à la carte service with a wide selection of wines and real ales. Lunchtime snacks include a range of sandwiches, ploughman's, chicken and seafood, whilst the specials menu offers ham or turkey salad; chargrilled T-bone steak; sautéed chicken in red wine; fresh local trout; and stuffed vegetarian crêpes with spinach, carrots and almonds. Leave space for home-made treacle tart or cherry pie with clotted cream.
OPEN: 11-11 (Sun 12-10.30) **BAR MEALS:** L served all week 12-2 D served all week 6.30-9.15 **RESTAURANT:** L served all week 12-2 D served all week 6.30-9.15
BREWERY/COMPANY: Free House 🍺: Interbrew Bass, Fuller's London Pride, Marston's Pedigree, Sharp's Own.
FACILITIES: Children welcome Garden Dogs allowed
NOTES: Parking 15

Ship Inn ◆◆◆◆ ♀
Lerryn PL22 0PT ☎ 01208 872374 📠 01208 872614
e-mail: shiplerryn@aol.com
Dir: 3m S of A390 at Lostwithiel

Dating back to the early 17th century, the Ship occupies a delightful riverside setting in the centre of a charming village. Close by lies woodland ideal for walkers. Handy for golf at nearby Lostwithiel and Lanhydrock. A sample menu includes

a variety of fish dishes, ranging from steamed salmon with pink peppercorn sauce to Cornish baked mullet. Steak and Guinness pie and fresh local meat are an integral part of the daily fare. Rooms are tastefully furnished.
OPEN: 11.30-3 6-11 (Sun 12-3, 7-10.30) **BAR MEALS:** L served all week 12-2 D served all week 6.30-9 Av main course £8
RESTAURANT: L served all week 12-2 D served all week 6.30-9 Av 3 course à la carte £15 **BREWERY/COMPANY:** Free House
🍺: Interbrew Bass, Sharp's, Skinner's, Otter Ale.
FACILITIES: Children welcome Garden: Food served outside Dogs allowed **NOTES:** Parking 36 **ROOMS:** 4 bedrooms 4 en suite s£35 d£60

LUDGVAN — Map 02 SW53

White Hart

Churchtown TR20 8EY ☎ 01736 740574
Dir: From A30 take B3309 at Crowlas
An early 14th-century pub with splendid views across St Michael's Mount and Bay. An old-fashioned atmosphere means no fruit machines or jukeboxes to disturb the peace. Cornish pasties made in the village, toad-in-the-hole, and fresh fish on Thursday and Friday are features of the menu, along with omelettes, pasta dishes and steaks. Tempting home-made puddings include apple pie, spotted dick, treacle tart and crumble, all served with clotted cream.
OPEN: 11-2.30 6-11 **BAR MEALS:** L served all week 12-2 D served Tues-Sun(all summer) 7-9 Av main course £5.50 **RESTAURANT:** L served all week 12-2 D served Tues-Sun (all summer) 7-9 Av 3 course à la carte £11 **BREWERY/COMPANY:** Inn Partnership
🍺: Marston's Pedigree, Interbrew Flowers & Bass.
FACILITIES: Garden Dogs allowed **NOTES:** Parking 12
NOTES: No credit cards

MANACCAN — Map 02 SW72

The New Inn ♀
TR12 6HA ☎ 01326 231323

With a thatched roof and porch, this small village pub deep in Daphne du Maurier country dates back to Cromwellian times. Enjoy the peaceful village setting, the large, flower-filled garden, and the homely and traditional bars. Fresh fish in season could be monkfish in bacon with lemon butter sauce, crispy herby squid with tartare sauce, or moules marinière. Otherwise try spaghetti with creamy crab and chilli sauce, or a home-made Cornish pasty with salad or chips.
OPEN: 12-3 6-11 (Sat-Sun all day in summer) **BAR MEALS:** L served all week 12-2.30 D served all week 6-9.30
BREWERY/COMPANY: Pubmaster 🍺: Wadworth 6X, Flowers IPA.
FACILITIES: Children welcome Garden: Food served outside Dogs welcome, Water **NOTES:** Parking 14

continued

England

Pick of the Pubs

Godolphin Arms ★★ 🛏 ⅋
TR17 0EN ☎ 01736 710202 📠 01736 710171
e-mail: enquiries@godolphinarms.co.uk

Few pubs can boast views this good: the Godolphin Arms sits directly opposite St Michael's Mount - so close, in fact, that the sea splashes at the windows in the winter. From the traditional style bar and beer terrace to the more homely restaurant and most of the bedrooms, the Mount is visible. It's a family run affair, with an emphasis on a friendly welcome and good service. The restaurant offers plenty of seafood - perhaps seabass, monkfish, squid, sardines, crab, red snapper or John Dory - alongside other pub favourites such as chargrilled steaks, chicken curry or beef Wellington. Less familiar options might include half a roasted duck with a cranberry and orange sauce, or vegetarian dishes such as mango and Cornish cheese strudel. A pared down menu is available in the bar, along with some imaginative light snacks.
OPEN: 10.30am-11pm **BAR MEALS:** L served all week 12-2.30 D served all week 5.30-9.30 Av main course £6 **RESTAURANT:** L served all week 12-2.30 D served all week 5.30-9.30 Av 3 course à la carte £19 **BREWERY/COMPANY:** Free House 🍺: Sharp's Eden Ale, Skinner's Cornish Knocker Ale, Interbrew Worthington Bitter, Scottish Courage John Smith's. ⅋: 8 **FACILITIES:** Children welcome Garden: Terrace overlooks waters edge, seating Dogs allowed **NOTES:** Parking 48 **ROOMS:** 10 bedrooms 10 en suite 2 family rooms s£40 d£70

Carpenters Arms 🛏
PL17 8BJ ☎ 01579 350242
Dir: From Saltash take A338 to Callington, then A390 to Tavistock, follow signs to pub
Set in the beautiful Tamar valley, this 15th-century building was originally the carpenter's workshop for nearby Cotehele House, and retains many original features including slate floors, an internal well and bare beams. Expect traditional pub food such as steak and ale pie, fisherman's pie and Sunday roasts. A good selection of fish and seafood dishes might include calamari, scallops or a pint of prawns.
OPEN: 12-3 7-11 (Open July-Sept at 6pm) (No food Mon Oct-July) **BAR MEALS:** L served all week 12-2 D served all week 7-9 Av main course £6 **RESTAURANT:** L served all week 12-2 D served all week 7-9 Av 3 course à la carte £12 **BREWERY/COMPANY:** Enterprise Inns 🍺: Sharp's Doom Bar & Own. **FACILITIES:** Children welcome Garden: Patio area, benches, wishing well feature Dogs allowed Water **NOTES:** Parking 12

The Rising Sun Inn 🛏 ⅋
Portmellon Cove PL26 6PL ☎ 01726 843235 📠 01726 843235
e-mail: cliffnsheila@tiscali.co.uk

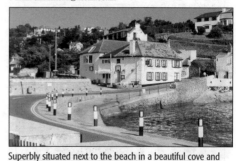

Superbly situated next to the beach in a beautiful cove and overlooking the sea, this 17th-century Grade II listed building is partly built of shipwreck timbers. Cosy beamed bar with snug for children and non-smokers and a cellar bar serving popular real ales and continental beers. Expect local seafood specialities in addition to Mediterranean chicken, gamekeepers pie, vegetable stirfry and black bean sauce, spicy pasta, and a variety of chargrilled steaks. (Please note that after 6pm only children over 13 are welcomed.)
OPEN: 11-3 6-11 (BHS, July-Aug 11-11) Closed: 1 Nov-28 Feb **BAR MEALS:** L served all week 12.30-3 D served all week 6-9.45 Av main course £8.95 **RESTAURANT:** L served all week 12.30-3 D served all week 6-9.45 Av 3 course à la carte £20 **BREWERY/COMPANY:** Free House 🍺: Adnams Bitter, St Austells HSD, Fuller's London Pride, Timothy Taylor Landlord. ⅋: 12 **FACILITIES:** Dogs allowed Water, beach **NOTES:** Parking 60 **ROOMS:** 7 bedrooms 7 en suite 3 family rooms s£43 d£66 (♦♦♦)

The Ship Inn ♦♦♦
Fore St PL26 6UQ ☎ 01726 843324 📠 01726 844368
Only one minute's walk from the harbour at Mevagissey, the Ship Inn offers plenty of fresh fish. Accomodation is en suite, and the area is convenient for attractions such as the Eden Project and the Gardens of Heligan.
OPEN: 11-11 Mon-Sat 12-10.30 Sun **BAR MEALS:** L served all week 12-3 D served all week 6-9 Av main course £8 **BREWERY/COMPANY:** St Austell Brewery 🍺: St Austell Ales. **FACILITIES:** Children welcome **ROOMS:** d£50

Miners Arms 🛏
TR5 0QF ☎ 01872 552375 📠 01872 552375
Dir: From A30 take B3277 to St Agnes. Take 1st R to Mithian

continued

Character pub with slate floors, wall paintings, a cobbled courtyard, exposed beams and ornate plasterwork ceilings that were made for a visit by Edward VII in 1896. Previously used as a courtroom and a pay house for local miners. Interesting bar food includes wild boar sausages, rosemary-roasted monkfish, ale and oyster pie, butternut squash and barley bake, as well as home-made favourites such as lamb pasanda and Sunday roasts.
OPEN: 12-3 6-11 **BAR MEALS:** L served all week 12-2.30 D served all week 7-9.30 Av main course £8
BREWERY/COMPANY: Pubmaster ■: Sharp's Doom Bar, Bass, Courage & Guest beers. **FACILITIES:** Children welcome Garden: Enclosed garden seats 40, courtyard seats 20 Dogs allowed Water provided **NOTES:** Parking 40

MORWENSTOW
Map 02 SS21

The Bush Inn
EX23 9SR ☎ 01288 331242
Dir: Telephone for directions
A historic country inn set in an isolated cliff-top hamlet close to bracing coastal path walks, the Bush is reputedly one of Britain's oldest pubs. It was originally built as a chapel in 950 for pilgrims from Wales en route to Spain, only becoming a pub some 700 years later. The unspoilt traditional interior, with stone-flagged floors and old stone fireplaces, has a Celtic piscina carved from serpentine and set into a wall behind the bar. Hearty lunchtime food includes generously-filled sandwiches, pasties and pasta dishes, and thick soup and home-made stews in winter.
OPEN: 12-3 7-11 (closed Mon) **BAR MEALS:** 12-2
BREWERY/COMPANY: Free House ■: St Austell HSD.
NOTES: Parking 30 **NOTES:** No credit cards

MOUSEHOLE
Map 02 SW42

Pick of the Pubs

The Old Coastguard Hotel ★★ ◎ 🍽 ♀
The Parade TR19 6PR ☎ 01736 731222 🖹 01736 731720
e-mail: bookings@oldcoastguardhotel.co.uk
Dir: A30 to Penzance, take coast road through Newlyn to Mousehole, pub is 1st building on L

Mousehole is a thriving and largely unspoilt village where the harbour was once the embarkation point for pilgrims to Rome. Situated above the village, the hotel is set in subtropical gardens leading down to the sea, and each of the en suite bedrooms enjoys spectacular views over Mounts Bay. With its stylish bar, brasserie and sun lounge, this is an excellent base to discover the landscape and legends of this delightful part of west Cornwall. Diners enjoy fresh regional produce, meats and cheeses

prepared and presented in a contemporary British style, with plenty of vegetarian and seafood options. Look out for Newlyn crab and mixed leaf salad with new potatoes; mussels and scallops on a spaghetti bed with herbs and salsa verde; fillet steak with smoked bacon and shallot rösti and garlic mushrooms; and chicken, crab and ginger in filo pastry with a rice noodle salad.
OPEN: 12-11 (closed 3-6 in winter) Closed: 25 Dec
BAR MEALS: L served all week 12-3 D served all week 6-9.30 Av main course £10 **RESTAURANT:** L served all week 12-3 D served all week 3-6 Av 3 course à la carte £19
BREWERY/COMPANY: Free House ■: Sharp's Doom Bar, Interbrew Bass. ♀: 8 **FACILITIES:** Garden: Large garden
NOTES: Parking 15 **ROOMS:** 21 bedrooms 21 en suite s£35 d£75 no children overnight

---

Ship Inn ♦♦♦
TR19 6QX ☎ 01736 731234 🖹 01736 732259
An old-world inn, with low beams and granite floors, overlooking the harbour. Seafood landed at nearby Newlyn figures prominently, with dishes such as crab bisque, seafood platter and fisherman's lunch (smoked mackerel with salad and brown bread). Other options might be monkfish, John Dory, or traditional meat specials.
OPEN: 11-11 (Sun 12-10.30) **BAR MEALS:** L served all week 12-2 D served all week 6-8.30 Av main course £6.50 **RESTAURANT:** L served Sun 12-2 D served all week 6-9 Av 3 course à la carte £16
BREWERY/COMPANY: St Austell Brewery ■: St Austell's HSD & Tinners Ale, Tribute, IPA. **FACILITIES:** Children welcome Dogs allowed **ROOMS:** 8 bedrooms 8 en suite s£32.50 d£55

MYLOR BRIDGE
Map 02 SW83

Pick of the Pubs

Pandora Inn 🍽 ♀
Restronguet Creek TR11 5ST
☎ 01326 372678 🖹 01326 372678
Dir: North of Falmouth off the A39
Medieval thatched pub on the shore of Restronguet Creek, especially popular with visiting yachtsmen who call here at high tide. The idyllic location is handy for Truro, Falmouth and the Lizard, and within easy reach of some of Britain's most beautiful coastal scenery. Low wooden ceilings and flagstone floors add to the charm of the pub's quaint old interconnecting rooms, and intimate alcoves are just the place for a quiet game of dominoes or crib. Solid fuel stoves and open log fires drive out the winter cold, and in summer you can sit out on the attractive riverside patio or floating pontoon. You'll find plenty of good home cooking: expect club sandwiches, as well as soups, pâté, and beef, pork or game pies. Other dishes include liver and onions, cottage pie, poached salmon, steak pie, lobster salad, grilled brill and fresh local crab. Finish off with Bakewell tart, apple and raspberry pie or bread-and-butter pudding.
OPEN: 11-11 (Sun 12-10.30) Winter 11.30-2.30, 7-11
BAR MEALS: L served all week 12-2 D served all week 7-9 Av main course £7 **RESTAURANT:** L served Sun only 12-2.30 D served all week 7-9 **BREWERY/COMPANY:** St Austell Brewery ■: St Austell Tinners Ale, HSD, Bass. **FACILITIES:** Children welcome Dogs allowed Water **NOTES:** Parking 30

continued

England

PELYNT
Map 02 SX25

Jubilee Inn ★★ 🛏
PL13 2JZ ☎ 01503 220312 🖷 01503 220920
e-mail: rickard@jubileeinn.freeserve.co.uk
Dir: take A390 signposted St Austell at village of East Taphouse, turn L onto B3359 signposted Looe & Polperro. Jubilee Inn on left on leaving Pelynt

The name commemorates Queen Victoria's Golden Jubilee in 1887, although the inn actually dates from the 16th century and was formerly known as The Axe. The interior has a homely, welcoming feel, with its oak-beamed ceilings, blazing winter fires, and Staffordshire figurines of the queen and her consort. Local seafood features, along with home-made ribs, curries and pies.
OPEN: 12-3 6-11 **BAR MEALS:** L served all week 12-2.30 D served all week 6-9.30 **RESTAURANT:** L served all week 12-2.30 D served all week 7-9.30 **BREWERY/COMPANY:** Free House **🍺:** Interbrew Bass, Sharp's Doom Bar, Skinner's Betty Stogs Bitter.
FACILITIES: Children welcome Garden Dogs allowed
NOTES: Parking 70 **ROOMS:** 11 bedrooms 11 en suite

PENDOGGETT
Map 02 SX07

The Cornish Arms 🛏 ♀
Port Isaac, Wadebridge PL30 3HH
☎ 01208 880263 🖷 01208 880335 e-mail: millstjanet@aol.com
Dir: From A30 Launceston, R onto A395, then L on to A39, then R onto B3314. Pub 7m along this road.
Atmospheric 16th-century coaching inn a mile or so from the beautiful and unspoiled Cornish coast. Hidden beaches and secret coves are just a short walk away and nearby is the fishing village of Port Isaac where you can watch the catch being landed. Solid beams and stone-flagged floors characterise the pub's interior, and bar food might include sirloin steak, prime beef-burger and butterfly chicken. Expect chargrilled monkfish, medallions of pork tenderloin, penne pasta with sausage, or mushroom Stroganoff on the daily-changing restaurant menu.
OPEN: 11-11 (Sun 12-10.30) **BAR MEALS:** L served all week 12-2 D served all week 6.30-9.00 Av main course £8 **RESTAURANT:** L served Sun 12-2 D served all week 6-9 Av 3 course à la carte £16 **BREWERY/COMPANY:** Free House **🍺:** Bass, Sharp's Doom Bar, Sharp's Eden, John Smiths & Guest Ales. **FACILITIES:** Children welcome Garden: Food served outside. Overlooking Port Isaac Dogs allowed Water provided **NOTES:** Parking 50

PENZANCE
Map 02 SW43

Dolphin Tavern 🛏 ♀
Quay St TR18 4BD ☎ 01736 364106 🖷 01736 364194
A 600-year-old harbourside pub overlooking St Michael's Mount across Mounts Bay. In this building, apparently, Sir Walter Raleigh first smoked tobacco on English soil and, the following century, Judge Jeffreys held court. Haunted by not one, but several ghosts. An old sea salt gazes out from menus offering local fish and seafood, steaks, mixed grills, lunchtime snacks, all-day bites and children's meals. Specials include grilled pilchards, mackerel and even shark, when available.
OPEN: 11-11 **BAR MEALS:** L served all week 11-2.30 D served all week 6.30-9.30 **BREWERY/COMPANY:** St Austell Brewery **🍺:** St Austell HSD, Tinners & Celtic Smooth. **FACILITIES:** Children welcome Garden: Pavement patio area Dogs allowed Water provided

The Turks Head Inn 🛏 ♀
Chapel St TR18 4AF ☎ 01736 363093 🖷 01736 360215
e-mail: veronica@turkspz.freeserve.co.uk
Dating from at least the 13th century and the oldest pub in Penzance although much of the original building was destroyed by a Spanish raiding party in the 16th century. Old flat irons, jugs and beams adorn the interior, and there is a sunny flower-filled garden at the rear. Typical dishes include Mexican hotpot, fish pie, spaghetti Bolognaise and moules marinière, along with steaks, salads, and daily puddings.
OPEN: 11-3 5.30-11 (Sun 12-3, 5.30-10.30) Closed: Dec 25
BAR MEALS: L served all week 11-2.30 D served all week 6-10 Av main course £7.98 **RESTAURANT:** L served all week 11-2.30 D served all week 6-10 **BREWERY/COMPANY:** Pubmaster
🍺: Marston's Pedigree, Young's Special, Greene King IPA, Sharp's Doom Bar Bitter. **♀:** 14 **FACILITIES:** Children welcome Garden: Walled garden

PERRANUTHNOE
Map 02 SW52

The Victoria Inn ♦♦♦ 🛏 ♀
TR20 9NP ☎ 01736 710309 🖷 01736 710309
Dir: Take the A394 Helston-Penzance road and turn down to the village following all the signs for Perranuthnoe

Mentioned in the Domesday Book and reputed to be the oldest hostelry in Cornwall, this 12th-century inn is idyllically close to a sandy beach and coastal footpath. With its en suite accommodation, pretty heated patio, and good food it makes a pleasant stopover for a pint of Abbot Ale, and dishes like mushroom and apple Stroganoff, breadcrumbed wholetail scampi, pan-fried breast of duck, 10oz rib-eye steak, mushroom and broccoli pasta, and spinach and ricotta cannelloni. Under new management.
OPEN: 11.30-2.30 6.30-11 (Aug open all day-12-11) **BAR MEALS:** L served all week 12-2 D served all week 6.30-9 Av main course £8 **RESTAURANT:** L served all week 12-2 D served all week 6.30-9 Av 3 course à la carte £16 **BREWERY/COMPANY:** **🍺:** Bass, Doom Bar, Abbot Ale. **♀:** 8 **FACILITIES:** Children welcome Garden: Paved Mediterranean style Dogs allowed Water provided **NOTES:** Parking 10 **ROOMS:** 3 bedrooms 2 en suite s£35 d£50

continued

PHILLEIGH   Map 02 SW83

Pick of the Pubs

The Roseland Inn
TR2 5NB ☎ 01872 580254 📠 01872 501528

A tiny village in rural surroundings provides the delightful setting for this 16th-century cob-built inn, on the old pilgrim route through Cornwall. The pub itself is worth paying homage to, peacefully positioned by the parish church just two miles from the King Harry Ferry that crosses the River Fal. In summer, the splendid front terrace, festooned with roses, is a perfect spot for outdoor eating, while inside the worn slate floors, old settles, low beams and log fire make for a cosy atmosphere. Children and dogs are welcome (especially springer spaniels), and cyclists drop in regularly as the inn is on the New Cycle Trail. A good range of food is served in two categories: large plates or small plates. Baked fillet of salmon, chicken breast stuffed with mango, and pan-fried Cornish scallops with orange, ginger and chilli sauce are typical of the dishes offered. Well worth the drive from St Mawes or Truro.

OPEN: 11-3 6-11 **BAR MEALS:** 12-2.15 6-9
RESTAURANT: 12-2.15 6-9 **BREWERY/COMPANY:** Greenalls
🍺: Sharp's Doom Bar, Ringwood Best, Interbrew Bass, Marston's Pedigree. **FACILITIES:** Children welcome Garden: Rose garden Dogs allowed Water **NOTES:** Parking 15

POLKERRIS   Map 02 SX05

The Rashleigh Inn
PL24 2TL ☎ 01726 813991
Dir: Off A3082 outside Fowey

Novelist Daphne du Maurier lived in the charming old pilchard fishing village of Polkerris, and knew the ancient 'Inn on the Beach' well. St Austell Bay provides some of the fresh

fish specials, while regular dishes include roast poussin with plum sauce, and pork noisettes in cider and cream sauce. Up to 300 guest ales a year in the main bar, which was once the coastguard station boathouse. Singalongs on Saturday nights after Easter.

OPEN: 11-11 **BAR MEALS:** L served all week 12-2 D served all week 6-9 Av main course £7 **RESTAURANT:** L served all week 12-2 D served all week 6-9 Av 3 course à la carte £20
BREWERY/COMPANY: Free House 🍺: Sharp's Doom Bar, St Austell HSD, Timothy Taylor Landlord, Rashleigh Bitter. 📖: 8
FACILITIES: Children welcome Garden: Multi-level terrace, overlooks Polkerris etc Dogs allowed Water bowls on terrace
NOTES: Parking 22

POLPERRO   Map 02 SX25

Old Mill House
Mill Hill PL13 2RP ☎ 01503 272362 📠 01503 272058
Dir: Telephone for directions
Stroll through the picturesque streets of Polperro and take a look at the colourful harbour before relaxing at this delightful old inn, where log fires and a riverside garden enhance the character of the place. Well-kept ales and good home-cooked food attract drinkers and diners alike. The menu offers a straightforward but winning selection of dishes: perhaps lamb tagine, home-made steak and ale pie, smoked haddock with poached egg, and West Country faggots in gravy.
OPEN: 11-11 (Winter open at 12) **BAR MEALS:** L served all week 12-2 D served all week 7-9 Av main course £6.20 🍺: Sharp's Eden Ale, Special, Shalds Old Mill Ale. **FACILITIES:** Children welcome Garden: By river, benched, grassed Dogs allowed Water & Bonio
NOTES: Parking 7

PORT GAVERNE   Map 02 SX08

Pick of the Pubs

Port Gaverne Hotel ★★
PL29 3SQ ☎ 01208 880244 📠 01208 880151
Dir: Signed from B3314, S of Delabole via B3267 on E of Port Isaac

With the sea and a beautiful little cove just down the road, this 17th-century inn is a magnet for holidaymakers as well as locals. The winding old building is a delight with its flagged floors, steep staircases and plenty of nooks and crannies that evoke its fishing origins. Smuggling might have been rife here once, but nowadays it is the day's fishing that forms part of the inn's raison d'être. Local produce is used wherever possible, and all bread is home made. Expect fruits de mer including grilled Dover sole with herb butter, monkfish goujons, or roast cod fillet on olive oil mash, and half pint of prawns with bread and butter. Pasta, salads and specials also on offer. Passing

continued

continued

PORT GAVERNE continued

walkers on the Heritage Coast Path can sit in the small beer garden, or at one of the tables in front of the hotel, to enjoy Greene King and Bass real ales.
OPEN: 11-2.30 6-11 (Summer 11-11) Closed: Early Jan - Mid Feb
BAR MEALS: L served all week 12-2.30 D served all week 6.30-9.30 **RESTAURANT:** D served all week 7-9.30 Av 3 course fixed price £25 **BREWERY/COMPANY:** Free House ◧: Sharp's Doom Bar, Bass, Greene King Abbot Ale. **FACILITIES:** Children welcome Garden Dogs allowed Water provided
NOTES: Parking 15 **ROOMS:** 15 bedrooms 15 en suite 2 family rooms s£35 d£70

PORTHLEVEN   Map 02 SW62

The Ship Inn 🍴
TR13 9JS ☎ 01326 564204
Built into steep cliffs and approached by a flight of stone steps, this 17th-century inn has wonderful views over the harbour, especially at night when it is floodlit. Inside is a knocked-through bar with log fires, and a family room converted from an old smithy. Real ales are properly served, and a good choice of food includes chicken tikka masala, pan-fried lamb fillet, seafood platter, Cornish fish pie, Mediterranean vegetable bake, nut and oatmeal roast, and a selection of toasties, crusties, sandwiches and jacket potatoes.
OPEN: 11.30-3 6.30-11 (all day mid Jul-mid Sept) **BAR MEALS:** L served all week 12-2 D served all week 7-9 Av main course £9.95
BREWERY/COMPANY: Free House ◧: Scottish Courage Courage Best, Greene King Abbot Ale, Sharp's Doom Bar.
FACILITIES: Children welcome Garden: Terraced. Overlooks the harbour Dogs allowed Water

PORTREATH   Map 02 SW64

Basset Arms
Tregea Ter TR16 4NG ☎ 01209 842077 ▤ 01209 843936
Dir: From Redruth take B3300 to Portreath
Typical Cornish stone cottage, built as a pub in the early 19th century to serve the harbour workers, with plenty of tin mining and shipwreck memorabilia adorning the low-beamed interior.
OPEN: 11.30-2 6-11 (all day in summer) **BAR MEALS:** L served all week 11-2 D served all week 6.30-9.30 Av main course £4.95
RESTAURANT: L served all week 12-2 D served all week 6.30-9.30 Av 3 course à la carte £15.95 Av 3 course fixed price £15.95
BREWERY/COMPANY: Free House ◧: St Austell Dartmoor Best, Bass, Sharps Courage. **FACILITIES:** Children welcome Garden: paved seating area, barbecue Dogs allowed on leads only
NOTES: Parking 25

RUAN LANIHORNE   Map 02 SW84

The Kings Head ⌾
TR2 5NX ☎ 01872 501263
Dir: 3m from Tregony Bridge on A3078
With its pretty sun-trap sunken garden overlooking the tidal River Fal, this popular Victorian summer pub enjoys a rural location in the heart of the Roseland Peninsula. Straightforward pub fare is supplemented by daily specials and more imaginative dishes such as chicken lemon couscous, Chinese pork hock and salmon and asparagus tart.
OPEN: 12-2.30 6.30-11 (closed Mon Sep-Etr) **BAR MEALS:** L served all 12-1.45 D served all 6.30-9 Av main course £6.50

continued

BREWERY/COMPANY: Free House ◧: Sharp's Best & Guest ale, Skinners Kings Ruan. **FACILITIES:** Children welcome Garden: Food served outside Dogs allowed **NOTES:** Parking 12

ST AGNES   Map 03 SW75

Driftwood Spars Hotel ◆◆◆ 🍴
Trevaunance Cove TR5 0RT ☎ 01872 552428 ▤ 01872 553701
e-mail: driftwoodsparshotel@hotmail.co.uk
Dir: A30 onto B3285, through St Agnes, down steep hill, L at Peterville Inn, onto road signed Trevaunance Cove

Situated just a few yards from the beach, this 300-year-old pub was originally a tin miner's store, a chandlery and a sail loft. Stunning sea views, massive oak beams, crackling log fires and a fascinating nautical theme make this one of the area's more distinctive watering holes. Smoked fish salad, sirloin steak, roast vegetable Stroganoff, barbecued ribs and chilli are typical examples of what to find on the bar menu.
OPEN: 11-11 (Fri-Sat 11-12, Sun 12-10.30) **BAR MEALS:** L served all week 12-2.30 D served all week 6.30-9.30 Av main course £9 **RESTAURANT:** L served all week 12-2.30 D served all week 6.30-9.30 **BREWERY/COMPANY:** Free House ◧: Carlsberg-Tetley Bitter, Interbrew Bass, Sharp's Own, St Austell HSD.
FACILITIES: Children welcome Garden Dogs allowed
NOTES: Parking 80 **ROOMS:** 15 bedrooms 15 en suite 5 family rooms s£40 d£80

ST AGNES (ISLES OF SCILLY)   Map 02 SV80

Turks Head
TR22 0PL ☎ 01720 422434 ▤ 01720 423331
Dir: By boat or helicopter to St Mary's and boat on to St Agnes

Former coastguard boathouse overlooking the cove and island quay, this gem of a pub, Britain's most southwesterly inn, is noted for its atmosphere and superb location. Inside are fascinating model ships and maritime photographs - among other features. The name comes from the Turkish pirates who came here from the Barbary Coast in the 16th century. Sample

continued

home-made quiche, mixed seafood, cold roast beef, vegetable pasta bake and breaded scampi from the straightforward but wholesome menu.
OPEN: 11-11 (Rest:Nov-Mar open Wed, Sat eve, Sun lunch only) **BAR MEALS:** L served all week 12-2.30 D served all week 6.30-9.30 Av main course £6.95 **BREWERY/COMPANY:** Free House **(:** St Austell Dartmoor Best &, Carlsberg-Tetley Ind Coope Burton Ale, Ales of Scilly Scuppered. **FACILITIES:** Children welcome Garden: Patio overlooking sea & enclosed garden Dogs allowed

---

ST BREWARD
Map 02 SX07

The Old Inn 🐾 ♀
Church Town, Bodmin Moor PL30 4PP
☎ 01208 850711 📠 01208 851671
e-mail: darren@theoldinn.fsnet.co.uk
Dir: 4 miles from A30 near Bodmin, or signed from B3266. Pub next to landmark St Breward church
Seven hundred feet up on Bodmin Moor, this is Cornwall's highest inn and, having been built by monks in the 11th century, among the oldest. A free house with slate floors, wooden beams, log fires and three bars, one family-friendly. Bar and restaurant menus, plus daily specials, among which are poached fillet of smoked salmon with Pernod and cream sauce, and lamb chops with minted mash and redcurrant and winterberry sauce. Pets' corner in the large beer garden.
OPEN: 11-3 6-11 (Summer open all day) (Fri-Sun) **BAR MEALS:** L served all week 11-1.50 D served all week 6-8.50 Av main course £5.95 **RESTAURANT:** L served all week 11-1.50 D served all week 6-8.50 Av 3 course à la carte £25 Av 3 course fixed price £10.95 **BREWERY/COMPANY:** Free House **(:** Bass, Sharp's Doom Bar Bitter, Sharps Special, Guest Ales. ♀: 24 **FACILITIES:** Children welcome Garden Dogs allowed Water **NOTES:** Parking 35

ST DOMINICK
Map 3 SX46

Who'd Have Thought It Inn ♀
St Dominic PL12 6TG ☎ 01579 350214
Village free house with beams, open fire, antique furnishings, and lovely views across the Tamar Valley to Plymouth. Handy for Cotehele House (NT). The village of St Dominic is well-known for its strawberries and daffodils. The "Silage bar" is the place to socialise with locals, while the lounge area is a touch more formal. Enjoy the likes of steak and kidney pie, smoked fish platter, and a variety of grills.
OPEN: 11.30-2.30 7-11 **BAR MEALS:** L served all week 12-2.30 D served all week 6.30-9.30 Av main course £8 **BREWERY/COMPANY:** Free House **(:** Bass, Betty Stoggs, Hicks, Stella CBL. ♀: 10 **FACILITIES:** Children welcome Garden: Small garden with spectacular views Dogs allowed Water provided **NOTES:** Parking 50

ST EWE
Map 02 SW94

The Crown Inn 🐾
PL26 6EY ☎ 01726 843322 📠 01726 844720
Dir: From St Austell take B3273. At Tregiskey x-rds turn R. St Ewe is signposted on R
Hanging baskets add plenty of brightness and colour to this delightful 16th-century inn, just a mile from the famous 'Lost gardens of Heligan.' The owner helped restore the gardens over a period of ten years. Well-kept St Austell ales complement an extensive menu and daily specials. Expect cod in beer batter, local steaks, rack of lamb, and liver and bacon among other favourites.

OPEN: 12-3 5-11 **BAR MEALS:** L served all week 12-2 D served all week 6-9 Av main course £6.50 **RESTAURANT:** L served all week 12-2 D served all week 6-9 **BREWERY/COMPANY:** St Austell Brewery **(:** Tribute, Hicks Special, Tinners, plus Guest ale. **FACILITIES:** Children welcome Garden: Two Marquees, heated, fenced, well lit Dogs allowed Water **NOTES:** Parking 60

ST IVES
Map 02 SW54

Pick of the Pubs

The Sloop Inn ♦♦♦♦ 🐾 ♀
The Wharf TR26 1LP ☎ 01736 796584 📠 01736 793322
e-mail: sloop@btinternet.com
Dir: On harbour front

Believed to date from around 1312AD, one of Cornwall's oldest and most famous inns is right on the harbour, separated from the sea only by a cobbled courtyard and The Wharf. A favourite haunt of local fishermen, artists and visitors alike, it offers a distinctly fishy slant to menus on display in the panelled Cellar Bar and low-beamed Lounge Bar, both adorned with colourful paintings by the St Ives School. Seafood chowder, home-made salmon and Cornish crab fishcakes, a trio of Cornish fish, and St Ives Bay mackerel fillets are perennial favourites. Alternative main meals include pasta dishes, sirloin steak, ham, egg and chips and chicken and bacon lasagne, while additional specials might be fish pie, chicken curry, and crab, prawn and mussel salad. Bedrooms differ in size but all exude an historic charm and contain modern facilities. Well placed for the Tate Gallery and the Barbara Hepworth Museum and Gallery.
OPEN: 10.30-11 (Sun 12-10.30) **BAR MEALS:** L served all week 12-3 D served all week 5-8.45 Av main course £6 **BREWERY/COMPANY:** Unique Pub Co **(:** Scottish Courage John Smiths, Sharp's Doom Bar, Greene King Old Speckled Hen & Morland, Interbrew Draught Bass. ♀: 12 **FACILITIES:** Children welcome **ROOMS:** 14 bedrooms 11 en suite 2 family rooms s£50 d£35

continued

England

Star Inn
TR19 7LL ☎ 01736 788767
Dir: Telephone for directions
Plenty of tin mining and fishing stories are told at this
traditional Cornish pub, reputedly built to house workmen
constructing the local church. Among those said to have
stayed here was John Wesley; today it is more recognisable
for having featured in several television and film productions.
Some good local beers are on offer, and to accompany them
there are homemade pies, soups, pasties and - in season -
crab dishes. Monday night entertainment features Irish and
folk music.
OPEN: 11-11 (Mon-Thu Oct-Etr 11-3, 6-11) (Sun 12-10.30)
BAR MEALS: L served all week 12-2 D served all week 6.30-8.30 Av
main course £5 **BREWERY/COMPANY:** St Austell Brewery 🍺: St
Austell HSD, Tinners Ale, Black Prince, Dartmoor & speciality beer
every 3 months. **FACILITIES:** Garden: Apple tree, roses, pine &
palm, patio Dogs allowed on a lead only **NOTES:** No credit cards

The Wellington Hotel ◆◆◆ 🐾
Market Square TR19 7HD ☎ 01736 787319 📠 01736 787906
e-mail: wellingtonhotel@msn.com
Named after the Iron Duke who stayed here, this family-run
hotel is an imposing granite-fronted building overlooking St
Just's market square. The town is on the scenic coastal road
between St Ives and Lands End, close to some of Cornwall's
finest cliffs, coves and beaches. Not surprising then that local
fish and crab are in great demand. Meat dishes are locally
sourced too. Large beer garden.
OPEN: 10.30-11 **BAR MEALS:** L served all week 12-2 D served all
week 6-9 **RESTAURANT:** L served all week 12-2 D served all week
6-9 **BREWERY/COMPANY:** St Austell Brewery 🍺: St Austell
Tinners, St Austell HSD, St Austell Cornish Cream Mild.
FACILITIES: Children welcome Garden: Enclosed by walls, filled with
flowers Dogs allowed Must provide own bedding £10 charge if dogs
staying **NOTES:** Parking 20 **ROOMS:** 11 bedrooms 11 en suite 4
family rooms s£27 d£45

The White Hart ◆◆◆ 🐾
The Square TR12 6ND ☎ 01326 280325 📠 01326 280325
e-mail: whitehart@easynet.co.uk
Opposite the 15th-century church, the White Hart is known for
the ghost of a former landlady, Lettie, who knocks things off
the shelves if customers get too rowdy! The lunchtime bar
menu offers ploughman's and huntsman's platters, various
sandwiches, baguettes and jacket potatoes. Also a good
choice of dishes for children. More extensive bistro menu -
also served in the evening - includes much locally-caught fish,
including whole hot baked crab, John Dory with herb crust on
Parmesan mash, and seared sea bass.
OPEN: 11-2.30 6-11 (July-Aug all day wkds) **BAR MEALS:** L served
all week 12-2 D served all week 6.30-9.30 Av main course £9
RESTAURANT: D served Wed-Sun 7-9.30
BREWERY/COMPANY: Pubmaster 🍺: Interbrew Flowers Original,
Greene King Old Speckled Hen, Sharp's Doom Bar.
FACILITIES: Children welcome Garden: Terrace & bench seating.
Herb Garden Dogs allowed Water, Bonios **NOTES:** Parking 15
ROOMS: 2 bedrooms 2 en suite s£35 d£50

St Kew Inn
PL30 3HB ☎ 01208 841259
e-mail: des@stkewinn.fsnet.co.uk
Dir: village signed 3m NE of Wadebridge on A39
Attractive stone-built 15th-century inn near the parish church
in a secluded valley. Retains much of its original character,
notably its large kitchen range and slate floors. One menu is
offered throughout, with dishes ranging from fish pie, and
beef in Guinness with herb dumplings, to specialities such as
steaks. Fresh fish comes straight from Padstow.
OPEN: 11-2.30 6-11(Sun 12-3, 7-10.30, all day Jun-Aug)
BAR MEALS: L served all week 12-2 D served all week 7-9.30 Av
main course £8.50 **RESTAURANT:** L served all week 12-2 D served
all week 7-9.30 Av 3 course à la carte £18 **BREWERY/COMPANY:** St
Austell Brewery 🍺: St Austell HSD, Tinners Ale & Tribute.
FACILITIES: Children welcome Garden **NOTES:** Parking 80

Pick of the Pubs

The Rising Sun ★★ 🏅 🐾 ♀
The Square TR2 5DJ ☎ 01326 270233 📠 01209 270198
e-mail: therisingsun@bt.click.com
St Mawes' central pub on the square is a deservedly
popular meeting-place for yachtsmen - who can moor by
the 19th-century harbour opposite - and locals for whom
it is the focus of village life. The decor is luxurious and
convivial, and the kitchen is overseen by the West
Country's only woman Masterchef. A typical menu
includes game and steak pudding, chicken breast filled
with duck and orange salad, grilled seabass with
blackcurrant dressing, and a simple, grilled sirloin steak.
OPEN: 11-11 (Sun 12-10.30) **BAR MEALS:** L served all week
12-2.30 D served all week 6.30-9.30 Av main course £8
RESTAURANT: L served Sun 12-2 D served all week 7-9.30 Av 3
course fixed price £29 **BREWERY/COMPANY:** St Austell
Brewery 🍺: Hicks Special Draught, St Austell Tinners Ale.
FACILITIES: Children welcome Garden: Paved terrace overlooking harbour Dogs allowed Water **NOTES:** Parking 6
ROOMS: 8 bedrooms 8 en suite s£40 d£80

Pick of the Pubs

The Victory Inn
Victory Hill TR2 5PQ ☎ 01326 270324 📠 01326 270238
Dir: In centre of village close to the harbour

A friendly fishermen's local that doubles as a modern
dining pub, just a stone's throw from the bustling harbour.

continued

Named after Nelson's flagship, it offers the freshest of local seafood in the bar. The blackboard specials change daily according to the catch, while the menu offers white crab and mushroom omelette, pesto pasta with roasted pine nuts and shaved Parmesan, beer-battered haddock and chips, and rib-eye steak with pepper sauce.
OPEN: 11-11 (Sun 12-10.30) **BAR MEALS:** L served all week 12-2 D served all week 6-9 Av main course £10
RESTAURANT: L served Mon-Sun 12-2 D served Mon-Sun 6-9 Av 3 course à la carte £17.50 🍺: Sharps, Bass, Ringwood, IPA.
FACILITIES: Children welcome Food served outside Dogs allowed Biscuits, water and toys

ST MAWGAN
Map 02 SW86

The Falcon Inn ♦♦♦♦ 🐑 ♀
TR8 4EP ☎ 01637 860225 🖷 01637 860884
e-mail: enquiries@falconinn.net
Dir: From A30 8m W of Bodmin, follow signs to Newquay/St Mawgan Airport. After 2m turn R into village, pub at bottom of hill

Taking its name from a falcon which, at the time of the Reformation, flew over the village to indicate a secret Catholic church service was being held, this 15th-century pub lies in the sheltered Vale of Lanherne. The dazzling gardens have won many awards and there are attractive terraces and wisteria-covered walls. Comprehensive menu and daily specials range from monkfish in coconut curry, or salmon en papillette, to hearty sirloin steaks, and steak and kidney pie. Well-equipped bedrooms are individual in style and size.
OPEN: 11-3 6-11 **BAR MEALS:** L served all week 12-2 D served all week 6.30-9.30 Av main course £7 **RESTAURANT:** L served all week 12-2 D served all week 6.30-9.30 Av 3 course à la carte £15
BREWERY/COMPANY: St Austell Brewery 🍺: St Austell HSD, Tinners Ale & Tribute. **FACILITIES:** Children welcome Garden: Large garden, sheltered, safe Dogs allowed Water **NOTES:** Parking 25 **ROOMS:** 3 bedrooms 2 en suite s£21 d£50

ST MERRYN
Map 02 SW87

The Farmers Arms ♦♦♦
PL28 8NP ☎ 01841 520303 🖷 01841 520643
Dir: B3275 Between Padstow and Newquay
A lively and vibrant community pub dating from the 17th century. Nearby is the fishing port of Padstow and the 'seven bays for seven days' and some of Britain's most beautiful beaches. Excellent golf courses and stunning coastal walks are also close by. One menu is available throughout, offering such dishes as beef in ale pie, lasagne, ham, egg and chips and rack of ribs in barbecue sauce. Accommodation is available in four en suite bedrooms.
OPEN: 11-11 (Apr-Oct 11-3, 5-11) **BAR MEALS:** L served all week

12-2 D served all week 6.30-9 Av main course £7 **RESTAURANT:** L served all week 12-2.30 D served all week 6-9.30 Av 3 course à la carte £9 **BREWERY/COMPANY:** St Austell Brewery 🍺: St Austell HSD, Tinners Ale, Tribute, plus Guest Ales. **FACILITIES:** Children welcome Dogs allowed Water **NOTES:** Parking 80 **ROOMS:** 4 bedrooms 4 en suite d£50

SALTASH
Map 03 SX45

The Crooked Inn ♦♦♦♦ 🐑 ♀
Stoketon Cottage, Trematon PL12 4RZ
☎ 01752 848177 🖷 01752 843203
e-mail: info@crooked-inn.co.uk

Originally two cottages, providing accommodation for the cooks and gardeners of Stoketon Manor (the remains of which are still evident across the courtyard), the building was converted into an inn some 15 years ago, now with adjacent bedroom blocks. It is set in 20 acres of grounds overlooking the Lynher Valley. The range of home-cooked meals includes locally-caught fish, traditional pies, vegetarian combo, steaks and curries.
OPEN: 11-11 (Sat 11-11, Sun 11-10.30) **BAR MEALS:** L served all week 12-2.30 D served all week 6-10 **RESTAURANT:** L served all week 12-2.30 D served all week 6-10 **BREWERY/COMPANY:** Free House 🍺: Hicks Special Draught, Sharp's Eden Ale, Skinner's Cornish Knocker Ale. **FACILITIES:** Children welcome Garden: 10 acres. Patio and decking with seating Dogs allowed **NOTES:** Parking 60 **ROOMS:** 15 bedrooms 15 en suite 15 family rooms s£45 d£75

The Weary Friar Inn ♦♦♦♦
Pillaton PL12 6QS ☎ 01579 350238 🖷 01579 350238
Dir: 2m W of A388 between Callington & Saltash

This whitewashed 12th-century inn with oak-beamed ceilings, an abundance of brass, and blazing fires lies next to the Church of St Adolphus, tucked away in a small Cornish village. A typical selection from the menu includes grilled haddock fillets, chicken Maryland, vegetarian nut roast, mushroom Stroganoff, Thai green chicken curry, and seafood platter.

continued

continued

SALTASH continued

Salads, sandwiches, afternoon cream teas and ploughman's are also available. Curry and other themed nights are popular. **OPEN:** 11.30-3 6.30-11 (Sun 12-3, 6-10.30) **BAR MEALS:** L served all week 12-2 D served all week 7-9.30 Av main course £8.50 **RESTAURANT:** L served all week 12-2 D served all week 7-9 **BREWERY/COMPANY:** Free House ◗: Wadworth 6X, Greene King Abbot Ale, Sharp's Doom Bar. **FACILITIES:** Garden **NOTES:** Parking 30 **ROOMS:** 12 bedrooms 12 en suite no children overnight

---

SEATON   Map 3 SX35

Smugglers Inn NEW
Tregunnick Ln PL11 3JD ☎ 01503 250646 🖹 01503 250646
Dating back to the 17th century, this is the oldest building in Seaton, idyllically located opposite the beach and on the edge of a country park. Inside the atmosphere is warm and friendly, and the décor in keeping with the pub's age. Pub food is served in the bar and restaurant, along with a choice of three or four local real ales. Several traditional pub games can be played, while outside there's a patio for summer drinking. **BAR MEALS:** L served all week 12pm D served all week 6pm Av main course £5.95 **RESTAURANT:** L served (Varies to season) 12-2.30 D served all week 7-9.30 Av 3 course à la carte £22.50 **BREWERY/COMPANY:** Free House ◗: Real ales from local brewery. **FACILITIES:** Children welcome Garden: Patio area Dogs allowed Water **NOTES:** Parking 10

SENNEN   Map 02 SW32

The Old Success Inn ★★ 🛏
Sennen Cove TR19 7DG ☎ 01736 871232 🖹 01736 871457
e-mail: oldsuccess@sennencove.fsbusiness.co.uk
A good catch of fish, especially mackerel, pilchards and grey mullet, explains the name of this late 17th-century inn. Once a rendezvous for smugglers and wreckers, Charlie's Bar is now a focal point for the local lifeboat crew, whose territory includes nearby Land's End. In a glorious location with expansive views to England's only cape - Cape Cornwall. Fresh local fish, including seafood paella and sea bass, as well as 'continental style' specials are popular. Live music every Saturday night all year round. **OPEN:** 11-11 **BAR MEALS:** L served all week 12-2.30 D served all week 6.15-9.30 Av main course £7 **RESTAURANT:** L served Sun 12-2.15 D served all week 7-9.30 Av 3 course à la carte £17 **BREWERY/COMPANY:** Free House ◗: Doom Bar, Sharps Special, Skinners. **FACILITIES:** Children welcome Garden: Food served outside. Beer terrace Dogs allowed **NOTES:** Parking 16 **ROOMS:** s£28 d£60

TINTAGEL   Map 02 SX08

Pick of the Pubs

The Port William ◆◆◆◆ 🛏
Trebarwith Strand PL34 0HB
☎ 01840 770230 🖹 01840 770936
e-mail: william@eurobell.co.uk
Dir: Off B3263 between Camelford & Tintagel
Occupying one of the best locations in Cornwall, this former harbourmaster's house lies directly on the coastal path. Overlooking the beach and cliffs, the inn is 50 yards from the sea and the building dates back about 300 years to a time when coal was brought ashore here and slate was shipped from Port William, an adjacent cove. Smuggling was also a regular activity in these parts. There

continued

is an entrance to a tunnel at the rear of the ladies' toilet! Focus on the daily-changing specials board for such dishes as seafood tagliatelle with crab, prawns, mussels and halibut, or local fresh cod in the Port William's own beer batter, shank of lamb with a honey balsamic sauce served with herb mashed potatoes and parsnips, smoked duck platter with cranberry sauce, and stuffed whole peppers served with wild rice. There is also an extensive selection of snacks and cold platters.

OPEN: 11-11 (Sun 12-10.30) 12 opening in winter **BAR MEALS:** L served all week 12-2.30 D served all week 6.30-9.30 Av main course £8 **RESTAURANT:** L served all week 12-2.30 D served all week 6-9.30 Av 3 course à la carte £15.20 **BREWERY/COMPANY:** Free House ◗: St Austell Tinners Ale & Hicks, Interbrew Bass. **FACILITIES:** Garden: Patio overlooking sea, food served outside Dogs allowed Water **NOTES:** Parking 75 **ROOMS:** 6 bedrooms 6 en suite d£75 no children overnight

---

Tintagel Arms Hotel 🛏
Fore St PL34 0DB ☎ 01840 770780
Dir: From M5 take A30 by pass Okehampton & Launceston, turn L onto dual rdbt B395 for North Cornwall, follow signs Camelford, hotel opposite Lloyds Bank
This 250-year-old stone-built inn, with its quaint beamed bedrooms and Cornish slate roof, is located in one of Britain's most famous villages, close to the remains of the legendary castle associated with King Arthur. The menu in Zorba's Taverna obviously has a Greek influence, with the expected moussaka, kebabs, stuffed vine leaves and Greek salad. Fresh fish dishes might include swordfish, tuna, cod, salmon and bass, and there is a choice for vegetarians. **OPEN:** 6-11 (Sun 7-10.30) Closed: Nov-Jan **BAR MEALS:** D served all week 6-9.30 Av main course £6 **RESTAURANT:** D served all week 6-9.30 Av 3 course à la carte £12.50 **BREWERY/COMPANY:** Free House ◗: Interbrew Bass, Sharp's Doom Bar. **FACILITIES:** Children welcome **NOTES:** Parking 7

TORPOINT   Map 03 SX45

The Edgcumbe Arms ◆◆◆ 🛏 ♀
Cremyll PL10 1HX ☎ 01752 822294 🖹 01752 822014
e-mail: edgcumbearms1@btopenworld.com
Dir: Please phone for directions
Right on the Tamar estuary and close to the foot ferry from Plymouth, the views from the bow window seats and waterside terrace are glorious. Real ales from St Austell and quality home-cooked food are added attractions for those staying in one of the Laura Ashley-style bedrooms. American oak-panelled bars and stone-flagged floors are the setting for fresh scallops, cod stuffed with crab, steak and ale pie and fresh Cornish beef steaks. Plenty of snacks on the bar menu.

continued

OPEN: 11-11 (Sun 12-10.30) (6 Jan-28 Feb, closed 3-6)
BAR MEALS: L served all week 12-2.30 D served all week 6-9 Av main course £5.95 **RESTAURANT:** L served all week 12-2.30 D served all week 7-9 Av 3 course à la carte £16
BREWERY/COMPANY: St Austell Brewery **◀:** St Austell HSD, Tinners Ale & Tribute HS, IPA, Cornish Cream. **FACILITIES:** Children welcome Garden: Large picnic area with tables Dogs allowed Water **NOTES:** Parking 12 **ROOMS:** 6 bedrooms 6 en suite 2 family rooms s£30 d£50

TREBURLEY
Map 03 SX37

Pick of the Pubs

The Springer Spaniel 🐾 ♀
PL15 9NS ☎ 01579 370424 🖂 01579 370113
Dir: On the A388 halfway between Launceston & Callington
This unassuming roadside hostelry, dating from the 18th century and formerly part of a farm, remains a warm, comfortable and friendly pub, but is these days particularly popular for its food. The neat parquet-floored main bar has a high-backed settle, farmhouse-style chairs set by the wood-burning stove, rustic tables and a relaxing atmosphere where conversation flows naturally. There is also a separate beamed dining room for a slightly more formal setting. Blackboards in the bar list the lighter snack options - freshly-filled sandwiches and rolls, decent soups and daily specials. Main menu options include imaginatively-conceived and attractively-presented dishes of pheasant breast on gingerbread sauce, West Country chicken with caramelised onions and balsamic vinegar, and cod fillet on provençale sauce. Children's meals are offered, a vegetarian selection (wild mushroom and cashew nut risotto), and tempting puddings like treacle and lemon tart with clotted cream or custard.
OPEN: 11-3 6-11 **BAR MEALS:** L served all week 12-2 D served all week 6.30-9 Av main course £8.95 **RESTAURANT:** L served all week 12-2 D served all week 6.30-9 Av 3 course à la carte £18 **BREWERY/COMPANY:** Free House **◀:** Sharp's Doom Bar, Eden & Cornish, Springer Ale. **FACILITIES:** Children welcome Garden: Landscaped with seating, food served outside Dogs allowed Water & Biscuits **NOTES:** Parking 30

TREEN
Map 02 SW32

The Logan Rock Inn 🐾
Treen, St Levan TR19 6LG ☎ 01736 810495 🖂 01736 810177
e-mail: anitageorge@loganrockinn.com
Logan Rock itself weighs some 60 tonnes and, so it's said, rocked at the slightest touch until being 'fixed' temporarily in 1824. The pub, thankfully, is solid enough with ancient beams, open fires and a host of memorabilia making it well worth a holiday visit. Home-made dishes include the Longship's bake – macaroni mixed with locally-caught fish, cheese and tomato in a celery sauce - or cheese, onion and potato pie. Other alternatives include a wide variety of steaks, various salads and basket meals.
OPEN: 10.30-2.30 5-11 (Sun 12-3, 7-10.30, Summer all day)
BAR MEALS: L served all week 12-2.30 D served all week 6.30-9 Av main course £5.75 **RESTAURANT:** L served all week 12-2.30 D served all week 6.30-9 **BREWERY/COMPANY:** St Austell Brewery **◀:** St Austell Hicks & Tinners. **FACILITIES:** Children welcome Garden: Patio area with seating, sun trap Dogs allowed Water, must be on lead **NOTES:** Parking 20

TREGADILLETT
Map 03 SX28

Eliot Arms (Square & Compass) 🐾 ♀
PL15 7EU ☎ 01566 772051
Dir: Turn off A30 for Tregadillett, (Bodmin side of Launceston)
Interesting old coaching inn built from Cornish stone, with a huge collection of clocks, Masonic regalia, horse brasses, pictures and documents, plus ghosts. Was believed to have been a Masonic lodge for Napoleonic prisoners, and boasts two real fires in winter and lovely hanging baskets in summer. Now known for its food, including steak and Stilton pie, lasagne, grilled tuna, doorstep sandwiches, plus a wide range of wines and champagnes by the glass.
OPEN: 11-3.00 6-11 (Sat-Sun all day) **BAR MEALS:** L served all week 12-2 D served all week 7-9 Av main course £6
RESTAURANT: L served all week 12-2 D served all week 7-9
BREWERY/COMPANY: Free House **◀:** Sharp's Eden Ale & Doom Bar, Scottish Courage Courage Best, Greene King Ruddles County.
FACILITIES: Children welcome Seating areas around pub Dogs allowed **NOTES:** Parking 20

TRESCO
Map 02 SV81

Pick of the Pubs

The New Inn ★★ ⊚ 🐾 ♀
New Grimsby TR24 0QQ ☎ 01720 422844 🖂 01720 423200
e-mail: newinn@tresco.co.uk
Dir: By New Grimsby Quay

This pub/hotel is in a sub-tropical island location, with beer gardens and a slate-roofed pavilion overlooking New Grimsby Harbour. Popular with islanders and visitors alike, the New Inn is the only pub on the island, drawing much of its character from Tresco's exposed location in the Western Approaches - indeed the main bar is fitted out with timber jettisoned from a passing cargo ship. Scillonian or Cornish ales are served across the bar counter, itself made from a 1960's shipwreck, and a choice of eight wines by the glass. Traditional bar food and local fish specials are offered in the bar, and light lunches in the Pavilion. For a more formal dinner there is a daily-changing menu in the restaurant, specialising in wonderfully fresh local seafood and Tresco-reared beef. Accommodation is provided in 15 double rooms, many with ocean views.
OPEN: 11-11 **BAR MEALS:** L served all week 12-2 D served all week 6-9 Av main course £8.95 **RESTAURANT:** D served all week 7-9 **BREWERY/COMPANY:** Free House **◀:** Skinner's Betty Stogs Bitter, Tresco Tipple, Ales of Scilly Maiden Voyage, St Austell IPA. ♀: 8 **FACILITIES:** Children welcome Garden: Patio area with sub-tropical plants Assistance dogs by arrangement **ROOMS:** 15 bedrooms 15 en suite d£138

England

TRURO
Map 02 SW84

Old Ale House ♀
7 Quay St TR1 2HD ☎ 01872 271122
Dir: A30, Truro City centre
Olde-worlde establishment with a large selection of real ales on display, as well as more than twenty flavours of fruit wine. Lots of attractions, including live music and various quiz and games nights. Food includes 'huge hands of hot bread', oven-baked jacket potatoes, ploughman's lunches and daily specials. Vegetable stirfry, five spice chicken and sizzling beef feature among the sizzling skillets.
OPEN: 11-11 (Sun 12-10.30) Closed: Dec 25 **BAR MEALS:** L served all week 12-3 D served Mon-Fri 7-9
BREWERY/COMPANY: Enterprise Inns ◗: Skinners Kiddlywink, Shepherd Neame Spitfire, Scottish Courage Bass, Greene King Abbot Ale. **FACILITIES:** Children welcome

The Wig & Pen Inn 🍲
Frances St TR1 3DP ☎ 01872 273028
Dir: City centre nr Law Courts, 10 mins from railway station
A listed city centre pub, originally known as the Star. It became the Wig & Pen when the county court moved to Truro. Good quality food is offered, with dishes ranging from cram o' mushroom and asparagus soup and pan-fried red mullet on a vegetable linguine to rack of English lamb on red onion confit with mint cream. Desserts may include bread and butter pudding on a butterscotch sauce or pear Condé with seasonal fruits
OPEN: 11-11 (Sun 12-10.30) **BAR MEALS:** L served all week 12-2.30 D served all week 6-9 **BREWERY/COMPANY:** St Austell Brewery ◗: St Austell Dartmoor & HSD plus guest ales.
FACILITIES: Children welcome Garden: Patio area Dogs allowed

VERYAN
Map 02 SW93

The New Inn ♦♦♦♦ 🍲 ♀
TR2 5QA ☎ 01872 501362 🖹 01872 501078
e-mail: jack@veryan44.freeserve.co.uk
Dir: Off A3078 towards Portloe

Based on a pair of 16th-century cottages, this unspoilt pub is set in the pretty Cornish village of Veryan, close to safe sandy beaches and interesting walks. It has a single bar, open fires and a beamed ceiling, and the emphasis is on good ales and home cooking. Favourite dishes are grilled whole bass, skate with caper sauce, duck braised in wine with forest mushrooms, and slow-roast lamb shank with oregano and olive oil.
OPEN: 12-3 6.30-11 (Winter 12-2.30) **BAR MEALS:** L served all week 12-2 D served Mon-Sat 7-9 Av main course £9
BREWERY/COMPANY: St Austell Brewery ◗: St Austell HSD, Tinners Ale & Tribute. ♀: 8 **FACILITIES:** Children's licence Garden: Secluded garden, Large tables **ROOMS:** 3 bedrooms 2 en suite s£26.50 d£53 no children overnight

WADEBRIDGE
Map 02 SW97

The Quarryman Inn
Edmonton PL27 7JA ☎ 01208 816444 🖹 01208 815674
Dir: off A39 opp Royal Cornwall Showground

Friendly 18th-century inn that evolved from a courtyard of quarrymen's cottages. Handy for the Royal Cornwall Showground and the Camel Trail. Among the many features at this unusual pub are a small health club and several bow windows, one of which includes a delightful stained-glass quarryman panel. Expect prime Aberdeen Angus steaks, fresh locally-caught fish, roasted duck breast, curries and pasta on the menu.
OPEN: 12-11 (Sun 12-10.30) **BAR MEALS:** L served all week 12-2.30 D served all week 6-9 Av main course £10 **RESTAURANT:** 12-2.30 6-9 **BREWERY/COMPANY:** Free House ◗: Sharps, Skinners, Timothy Taylor Landlord, Various Guest Ales.
FACILITIES: Garden: Dogs allowed Water provided
NOTES: Parking 100

Swan Hotel ♦♦♦♦ 🍲 ♀
9 Molesworth St PL27 7DD ☎ 01208 812526 🖹 01208 812526
A town centre hotel that is family friendly, and serves St Austell Hicks and Tinners as well as guest ales from the tap. Typical pub food includes scampi, cod, crab and prawns. There is outdoor seating on a patio area.
OPEN: 11-11 **BAR MEALS:** L served all week 12-9 D served all week 6.30-9 Av main course £5.75 **BREWERY/COMPANY:** St Austell Brewery ◗: St Austell Hicks, Tinners & Tribute, Guest Ale. ♀: 13 **FACILITIES:** Children welcome Garden: Patio area Dogs allowed In the garden only **ROOMS:** 5 bedrooms 5 en suite 2 family rooms s£35 d£60

ZENNOR
Map 02 SW43

Pick of the Pubs

The Gurnards Head Hotel 🍲 ♀
Treen, Zennor TR26 3DE ☎ 01736 796928 🖹 01736 795313
e-mail: enquiries@gurnardshead.free-online.co.uk
An imposing colour-washed building that dominates the coastal landscape above Gurnard's Head, this traditional Cornish pub (stone-flagged bar, open fires) is just the place to get stranded on a wind-swept winter's night. Here you can see Cornwall at its most brutal, but on warmer days there are some great walks along the coastal path or the rugged Penwith Moors, strewn with wild flowers and studded with ancient Celtic remains. The menu is based on wholesome local produce, so as you'd expect there's plenty of seafood - perhaps Cornish seafood broth, grilled gurnard with aubergine and pesto sauce, or sole with prawns and mushrooms. Other options could include

continued on page 92

The White Hart Inn

A spectacular walk in the southern Lake District with views of the Old Man of Coniston.

The Lake District covers a small and compact area of north-west England, yet within its 866-square mile (2,240 square-kilometre) National Park; there is more than enough to entertain the visitor. The southern part of Lakeland is the setting for this picturesque walk during which one of the region's most famous landmarks - the 2,633ft Old Man of Coniston - looms into view.

From the pub turn right, following the road for about 220yds/200m. Turn right at the bridleway sign and take the cart track up the hill, known locally as Dick Hill. Pass through a white gate and pause to enjoy the impressive view over the Rusland valley, Grizedale Forest and the Old Man of Coniston. In the other direction are the Leven estuary and the town of Ulverston.

Bear left to have a look at 19th-century Colton church, then retrace steps, follow track on the left to white gate. Look for a gate on the left, walk through the plantation to the road and turn right. Go down the hill and turn right at another white gate, following the path to the left and back to the bottom of Dick Hill. Retrace your steps back to the village and the White Hart Inn.

THE WHITE HART INN, BOUTH
LA12 8JB
☎ 01229 861229

Directions: Ring for details
Former coaching inn surrounded by fields, fells and woods. A good choice of ales, and fresh food made to order.
Open: 12-2 6-11
Bar Meals: 12-2 (Wed to Sun) 6-8.45
Notes: Children welcome (playground opposite). Garden, west-facing terrace.
(See full entry on page 97)

DISTANCE: 3 1/2 miles/5.7km
MAP: OS Explorer OL 7
TERRAIN: Undulating landscape at the southern end of the Lake District
PATHS: Roads, paths, tracks
GRADIENT: Some short, steep climbs

Walk submitted and checked by Nigel Barton of the White Hart Inn

England

ZENNOR continued

braised rabbit with its chargrilled tenderloin, home-cooked ham and chips with free-range eggs, and warming desserts like bread and butter pudding made with free-range eggs, double cream and sultanas soaked in brandy. Live music and storytelling evenings are regular events.

The Gurnards Head Hotel

OPEN: 12-3 6-11 (Sun eve 7-10.30) **BAR MEALS:** L served all week 12-2.15 D served all week 6.30-9.15 Av main course £12 **RESTAURANT:** L served all week 12-2.15 D served all week 6.30-9.15 Av 3 course à la carte £20 **BREWERY/COMPANY:** Free House ◀: Interbrew Flowers Original, Skinners Cornish Knocker Ale, Fuller's London Pride, Interbrew Boddingtons. ♀: 7 **FACILITIES:** Garden: Large patio & lawn area with sea views Dogs allowed Water **NOTES:** Parking 60

CUMBRIA

AMBLESIDE
Map 18 NY30

Pick of the Pubs

Drunken Duck Inn ◆◆◆◆ ◉ ⌂ ♀
Barngates LA22 0NG ☎ 015394 36347 📠 015394 36781
e-mail: info@drunkenduckinn.co.uk
See Pick of the Pubs on opposite page

White Lion Hotel ♀
Market Place LA22 9DB ☎ 015394 39901 📠 015394 39902
Dir: Jct 36 M6, follow A591 Kendal, from Windermere signposted to Keswick
Right in the heart of town, this Lakeland inn is superbly placed for both the tourist and business traveller. Varied bar menu.
OPEN: 11-11 **BAR MEALS:** L served all week 12-2.30 D served all week 6-9 Av main course £7 **BREWERY/COMPANY:** ◀: Bass, Worthington. **FACILITIES:** Children welcome Garden: beer garden, outdoor eating, BBQ Dogs allowed **NOTES:** Parking 9

APPLEBY-IN-WESTMORLAND
Map 18 NY62

The New Inn ⌂
Brampton Village CA16 6JS ☎ 017683 51231
At the heart of Brampton village with splendid Pennine views, a charming 18th-century inn with oak beams and an original range. One menu serves the bar and dining room with all home-cooked fare, from regulars like steak and ale pie and Cumberland sausage to specials of battered haddock, fisherman's platter and home-made mushroom balti.

OPEN: 12-3 7-11 **BAR MEALS:** L served all week 12-2 D served all week 7-9 Av main course £6.50 **RESTAURANT:** L served all week 12-2 D served all week 7-9 **BREWERY/COMPANY:** Free House ◀: Black Sheep, Charles Wells Bombardier, John Smiths. **FACILITIES:** Children welcome Garden: Food served outside Dogs allowed in the garden only **NOTES:** Parking 16 **NOTES:** No credit cards

Pick of the Pubs

The Royal Oak Inn ★★ ♀
Bongate CA16 6UN ☎ 017683 51463 📠 017683 52300
e-mail: royaloakinn@mortalmaninns.fsnet.co.uk
The Royal Oak has a long and venerable history with parts of the building dating back to 1100 and the rest to the 17th century, when it began life as a coaching inn. Today, sympathetically modernised and offering good food and ale, it proves popular with locals and tourists alike. The pub is especially popular as a touring base for both the Yorkshire Dales and the Lake District as it is situated conveniently between the two. Its well-maintained character interior comprises a classic tap-room with blackened beams, oak panelling and an open fire; a comfortable beamed lounge with a real fire and plenty of reading material; and two dining rooms. Ingredients for the wholesome food are sourced locally wherever possible, and the menus change on a daily or monthly basis. Dishes include home-made soups and desserts, Sunday lunches and vegetarian options, with specials served in the bar and dining rooms. Cumberland sausages, chicken carbonara, mussels, stuffed trout, pork medallions in Madeira and mushroom Stroganoff are typical choices, along with various steaks from Cumbrian fell-bred animals and home-smoked produce. A good choice of real ales includes a number from local brewers, augmented by some 50 malt whiskies. There are nine fully-modernised but traditionally-styled en suite bedrooms, so it's easy to make the most of the pub's excellent location.
OPEN: 11-11 (Sun 12-10.30) **BAR MEALS:** L served all week 12-2.30 D served all week 6-9 Av main course £8 **RESTAURANT:** L served Mon-Sun 12-2.30 D served Mon-Sun 6-9 Av 3 course à la carte £13 **BREWERY/COMPANY:** Free House ◀: Black Sheep, John Smiths & Guest Ales. ♀: 8 **FACILITIES:** Children welcome Dogs allowed Water **NOTES:** Parking 8 **ROOMS:** 9 bedrooms 7 en suite 1 family rooms s£35 d£60

continued

OPEN: 11.30-11.
BAR MEALS: L served all week 12-2.30,
D served all week 6-9.
Av main course £11
RESTAURANT: L served all week 12-2.30,
D served all week 6-9.
Av cost 3 courses £22
BREWERY/COMPANY:
Free House.
🍺: Guest Bitter, Barngates Cracker Ale,
Chesters Strong & Ugly, Tag Lag and
Cat Nap.
FACILITIES: Garden- Beer garden, patio,
food served outdoors. Dogs welcome.
NOTES: Parking 40.
ROOMS: 16 en suite from s£56 d£85

The Drunken Duck

Surrounded by 60 private acres of magnificent scenery, the 17th-century Drunken Duck, widely celebrated as a dining pub, stands high in the hills close to the beauty spot of Tarn Hows. Handy for Ambleside and Hawkshead, it enjoys some of the loveliest Lakeland views, with distant Lake Windermere and a backdrop of craggy fells.

◆◆◆◆ 🌐 🐏 🍸

Barngate, Ambleside LA22 0NG
☎ 015394 36347 📠 015394 36781
📧 info@drunkenduckinn.co.uk
Dir: A592 from Kendal, after reaching Ambleside, follow signs for Hawkshead, 2.5m sign for inn on R, 1m up the hill

The inn's name dates back to a Victorian landlady who, finding her ducks lifeless at the crossroads, proceeded to pluck them for the pot. Far from dead they were in fact dead drunk, from a barrel in the cellar that had slipped its hoops and seeped into their feeding ditch. The inn's own Barngates Brewery produces some fine beers, all named after the pub's pets, notably the refreshing Cracker Ale, the headier Chester's Strong and Ugly, the popular Tag Lag (a light golden bitter) and Cat Nap. At the heart of the inn is the timeless bar, unchanged for years, with its oak settles, log fires and large collection of pictures. The adjoining restaurant is candlelit at night for a relaxed and intimate atmosphere. Lunchtime options might include Cumbrian fell-bred steak, kidney and thyme pudding, or plaice grilled with Flookburgh shrimps. In the evening there are imaginative starters like smoked haddock with Roquefort rarebit, and pigeon breast marinated with liquorice on Agen prunes and Parmesan risotto. Equally creative mains encompass fillet of venison marinated in espresso, and plantain, chilli and polenta fritters with spinach, roast red peppers, ginger crème fraîche and mango vinaigrette. Stylish accommodation is provided in individually designed rooms, with the courtyard rooms affording splendid views of the Langdales.

APPLEBY-IN-WESTMORLAND continued

Pick of the Pubs

Tufton Arms Hotel ★★★ 🛏 ♀
Market Square CA16 6XA ☎ 017683 51593 📠 017683 52761
e-mail: info@tuftonarmshotel.co.uk
See Pick of the Pubs on opposite page

ARMATHWAITE
Map 18 NY54

The Dukes Head Hotel ♀
Front St CA4 9PB ☎ 016974 72226
e-mail: HH@hlynch.freeserve.co.uk
Dir: A6, turn at Armathwaite turning
A pub since the building of the Settle to Carlisle railway, and named after Queen Victoria's dissolute son, the Duke of Clarence. For nearly 15 years, the Lynch family have welcomed walkers, climbers, anglers, and all who appreciate comfort and courtesy. Meals could include Cumberland sausage with mash and local haggis, pan-fried tuna with spicy lime butter, or traditional roast duck. Other treats include home-made liqueurs and free cycle hire for residents.
OPEN: 12-3 5.30-11 Closed: 25 Dec **BAR MEALS:** L served all week 12-1.45 D served all week 6.15-9 Av main course £8.25
RESTAURANT: L served all week 12-1.45 D served all week 6.15-9 Av 3 course à la carte £15 **BREWERY/COMPANY:** Pubmaster
🍺: Jennings Cumberland Ale, Carlsberg-Tetley Tetley's Bitter. ♀: 6
FACILITIES: Children welcome Garden: Lawned area surrounded by trees Dogs allowed Back bar only Water **NOTES:** Parking 26

ASKHAM
Map 18 NY52

The Queen's Head 🛏
Lower Green CA10 2PF ☎ 01931 712225 📠 01931 712811
e-mail: d.nicholls@clara.net
Dir: From M6 N for 7 miles from motorway
Built in 1682, this welcoming village inn situated in the heart of the Lake District National Park has neat lounges, exposed beams, brass and copper memorabilia, and open fires. Facilities include a games room with pool and darts. Along with a range of curries, salads, cold and hot baguettes and burgers, the Queen's Head offers Cumberland sausage, steak and onion pie, chicken fajita, and three cheese broccoli bake.
OPEN: 12-11 **BAR MEALS:** L served all week 12-2 D served all week 6.30-9 Av main course £6.95 **RESTAURANT:** 12-2 6.30-9
BREWERY/COMPANY: Pubmaster 🍺: Black Sheep, Tetleys, Theakstons. **FACILITIES:** Children welcome Garden: Food served outdoors Dogs allowed Water, food, kennel **NOTES:** Parking 30

BARBON
Map 18 SD68

The Barbon Inn ♀
LA6 2LJ ☎ 015242 76233
Dir: 3.5m N of Kirkby Lonsdale on A683
A 17th-century coaching inn with oak beams and open fires, situated in a quiet village between the lakes and dales. Popular bar meals are smoked salmon baguette and Morecambe Bay shrimps; more substantial dishes include Lakeland lamb casserole, roast breast of duck, and halibut steak.
OPEN: 12-3 6.30-11 **BAR MEALS:** L served all week 12-2 D served all week 6.30-9 Av main course £6.25 **RESTAURANT:** L served Sun D served all week 7-9 Av 3 course à la carte £16.50
BREWERY/COMPANY: Free House 🍺: Theakston. ♀: 48

continued

FACILITIES: Children welcome Garden: beer garden, outdoor eating Dogs allowed **NOTES:** Parking 6

BASSENTHWAITE
Map 18 NY23

The Pheasant ★★★ 🏅 ♀
CA13 9YE ☎ 017687 76234 📠 017687 76002
e-mail: info@the-pheasant.co.uk
Dir: A66 to Cockermouth, 8m N of Keswick on L

Huntsman John Peel was a regular visitor to this former coaching inn, and the Cumbrian painter Edward Thompson bartered for beer in the pub - two of his originals hang in the bar. The inn dates back 500 years and is set in its own attractive gardens and woodland close to Bassenthwaite Lake. The interior is beautifully decorated, with period furnishings set against polished parquet flooring, fresh floral arrangements and blazing log fires. The mellow bar is richly inviting with its panelled walls and oak settles, and offers a selection of 50 malt whiskies and 12 wines by the glass. Light lunches are served in the lounge or bar, and there's a more formal lunch and dinner menu in the beamed dining room. Fish is a popular option, particularly the seafood platter, fillet of smoked haddock served with spinach, poached egg and new potatoes, and the pub's own potted Silloth shrimps.
OPEN: 11.30-2.30 5.30-10.30 Closed: Dec 25 **BAR MEALS:** L served all week 12-2 Av main course £8 **RESTAURANT:** L served all week 12.30-2 D served all week 7-9 Av 3 course à la carte £29.75 Av 3 course fixed price £17 **BREWERY/COMPANY:** Free House
🍺: Theakston Best, Interbrew Bass, Jennings Cumberland Ale. ♀: 12
FACILITIES: Garden: Garden seating 25 Dogs allowed Kennels
NOTES: Parking 50 **ROOMS:** 16 bedrooms 16 en suite s£70 d£120 no children overnight

---

BEETHAM
Map 18 SD47

Pick of the Pubs

The Wheatsheaf Hotel ◆◆◆◆ 🛏
LA7 7AL ☎ 015395 62123 📠 015395 64840
e-mail: wheatsheaf@beetham.plus.com
See Pick of the Pubs on page 96

Stars or Diamonds after the ROOMS information at the end of an entry denotes accommodation that has been inspected by an organisation other than the AA, eg the RAC, VisitBritain, VisitScotland or WTB.

Pick of the Pubs

OPEN: 11-11
CLOSED: 25-26 Dec
BAR MEALS: L served all week 12-2, D served all week 7-9. Av main course £6.50
RESTAURANT: L served all week 12-2, D served all week 7-9. Av cost 3 courses £23
BREWERY/COMPANY: Free House.
🍺: Tufton Arms Ale, Coors Worthington Bitter, Interbrew Flowers & Boddingtons.
FACILITIES: Dogs welcome. Children welcome.
NOTES: Parking 15.
ROOMS: 21 en suite from s£57 d£95

Tufton Arms Hotel

Located at the heart of the perfectly named and breathtakingly beautiful Eden Valley, this 16th-century coaching inn is renowned for its hospitality. Its sturdy presence is a landmark in the centre of the medieval town of Appleby-in-Westmorland, where it attracts visitors who come to enjoy the many countryside pursuits available locally, including angling and walking, as well as the charms of this former county town of Westmorland.

★★★ 🐾 ♇
Market Square,
Appleby-in-Westmorland, CA16 6XA
☎ 017683 51593   📠 017683 52761
📧 info@tuftonarmshotel.co.uk

On the doorstep lies an intricate network of paths and tracks running through idyllic countryside, and two of Britain's most popular National Parks, the Lake District and the Yorkshire Dales, are within easy reach. The Tufton Arms is elegantly furnished, with an inviting panelled bar, and a smart conservatory restaurant overlooking a cobbled mews courtyard. Light and airy in the daytime, this room takes on an attractive glow in the evening when the curtains are closed and the lighting is soft and romantic. The food is an appealing blend of the classical and the modern, with fresh local meat, game, fish and seafood appearing on the menu. Take your time to linger over mouth-watering starters like warm salad of wild sautéed mushrooms and chorizo sausage topped with melted Camembert, and tossed salad of smoked salmon and avocado pear. Imaginative dishes like lightly-grilled brill with buttered spinach and a red pepper sauce, and pan-fried venison steak in a whisky and green peppercorn sauce, might be followed by steamed chocolate pudding, or lemon cheesecake. Lighter fare including baguettes, sandwiches, omelettes and pasta dishes are served in the bar. Several smart, well-appointed en suite bedrooms make staying over a rare pleasure.

Open: 11-3, 6-11 (Sun 12-3, 7-10.30)
Bar Meals: L served all week 12-2,
D served all week 6-9.
Av cost main course £9.75.
RESTAURANT: L served all week 12-2,
D served all week 6-9.
Av cost 3 course £18.50
BREWERY/COMPANY:
Free House.
🍺: Jennings Cumberland Ale & Bitter,
Guest Ales.
FACILITIES: Children welcome, small
outside seating area.
NOTES: Parking 40

The Wheatsheaf at Beetham

Family owned and run, a 16th-century inn next to a 12th-century church, by a river in the attractive village of Beetham.

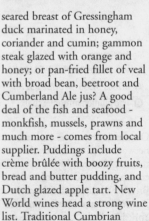

◆◆◆◆
Beetham, nr Milnthorpe, LA7 7AL
☎ 015395 62123 📠 015395 64840
📧 wheatsheaf@beetham.plus.com
Dir: On A6 5m N of J35, 5m S of J36.

The enthusiastic new owners have created smart, well-furnished dining rooms, where candlelight burns in the evenings, a welcoming beamed lounge, and a traditional, convivial bar. Despite its upmarket designation, this is still a place where you can just pop in for a pint or two of Jennings Cumberland ale. Throughout, you will find homely touches like fresh flowers and table decorations, as well as local and national newspapers and magazines. A commitment to purchasing fresh local produce underpins the home cooking. Lunch from Monday to Saturday could be a smoked salmon, melting Brie or honey-roast ham sandwich. Then again, it could be a prawn or poached salmon salad, ploughman's, or one of the many light or main meals, such as own-recipe bangers and mash, beef and ale pie or chickpea, spring onion and garlic bakes. For dinner, what about crab and salmon fish cakes; avocado, bacon and onion with Stilton sauce; pan-seared breast of Gressingham duck marinated in honey, coriander and cumin; gammon steak glazed with orange and honey; or pan-fried fillet of veal with broad bean, beetroot and Cumberland Ale jus? A good deal of the fish and seafood - monkfish, mussels, prawns and much more - comes from local supplier. Puddings include crème brûlée with boozy fruits, bread and butter pudding, and Dutch glazed apple tart. New World wines head a strong wine list. Traditional Cumbrian breakfasts get any day off to a good start.

BLENCOGO
Map 18 NY14

The New Inn 🛏 ♀
CA7 0BZ ☎ 016973 61091 ▤ 016973 61091
Dir: *From Carlisle, take A596 towards Wigton, then B5302 towards Silloth. After 4M Blencogo signed on L*
A late Victorian sandstone pub in a farming hamlet with superb views of the north Cumbrian fells and Solway Plain. Fish specialities include deep-fried large cod in beer batter, sea bass, plaice, halibut, and gambas. Selection of malt whiskies available.
OPEN: 7-11 (Sun 12-3, 6.30-10.30) **BAR MEALS:** L served Sun 12-2 D served Wed-Sun 7-9 Av main course £8 **RESTAURANT:** L served Sun D served Wed-Sun 7-9 **BREWERY/COMPANY:** Free House ◖: Yates, Carlisle State Bitter, Hesketh New Market. ♀: 10 **FACILITIES:** Children welcome Garden **NOTES:** Parking 50

BOOT
Map 18 NY10

The Burnmoor Inn ♀
CA19 1TG ☎ 019467 23224 ▤ 019467 23337
e-mail: stay@burnmoor.co.uk

Situated at the foot of Scafell Pike, this traditional 16th-century inn attracts many hill walkers. A fire burns in the beamed bar in cooler weather and there's a new conservatory and dining area affording spectacular views of the western fells in all seasons. Real ales and as many as 100 guest beers through the course of a year are available. Menu options include Cumberland sausage, chicken and ham pie, game stew and smoked haddock fishcake.
OPEN: 11-11 **BAR MEALS:** L served all week 11-5 D served all week 6-9 Av main course £7.50 **RESTAURANT:** L served all week 11-5 D served all week 6-9 Av 3 course à la carte £18.50
BREWERY/COMPANY: Free House ◖: Jennings Cumberland, Bitter, Black Sheep Best, Barngates Cracker Ale. ♀: 8
FACILITIES: Children welcome Garden: Part paved, part grassed, seating 40 people Dogs allowed Dog blankets, water **NOTES:** Parking 30 **ROOMS:** 9 bedrooms 9 en suite 2 family rooms s£29 d£58 (♦♦♦)

BOUTH
Map 18 SD38

The White Hart Inn
LA12 8JB ☎ 01229 861229 ▤ 01229 861229
e-mail: nigelwhitehart@aol.com
16th-century former coaching inn located in a quiet village in the Lake District National Park and surrounded by woods, fields and fells. Look out for plenty of bric-à-brac, including farm tools and long-stemmed clay pipes. A good choice of real ales are available and the menu offers fresh food made to order. A typical menu might include steak and stout pie,

papiette of sea bass, chicken balti, halibut steak, or five bean chilli.
OPEN: 12-2 6-11 **BAR MEALS:** L served Wed-Sun 12-2 D served Mon-Sun 6-8.45 Av main course £8.95 **RESTAURANT:** 12-2 D served Wed-Sun 6-8.45 Av 3 course à la carte £15.75
BREWERY/COMPANY: Free House ◖: Black Sheep Best, Jennings Cumberland Ale, Tetley, Yates Bitter. **FACILITIES:** Children welcome Children's licence Garden: West facing terrace **NOTES:** Parking 30

BRAITHWAITE
Map 18 NY22

Coledale Inn 🛏
CA12 5TN ☎ 017687 78272 ▤ 017687 78272
Dir: *From M6 J50 take A66 towards Cockermouth for 18 miles. Turn to Braithwaite then on towards Whinlatter Pass, follow sign on L, over bridge leading to hotel*
Built as a woollen mill in about 1824, this traditional pub was converted for pencil making before becoming an inn. Peacefully set above Braithwaite village, it is full of attractive Victorian prints, furnishings and antiques, with a fine cellar that includes cask-conditioned local ales. Its terrace and garden are very popular with walkers. Expect prawn salad, roast shoulder of lamb, beef in beer, and various fresh fish dishes.
OPEN: 11-11 **BAR MEALS:** L served all week 12-2 D served all week 6-9 Av main course £6.75 **RESTAURANT:** 12-2 6-9
BREWERY/COMPANY: Free House ◖: Yates, Theakstons Best, Jennings Best, Black Sheep. **FACILITIES:** Children welcome Garden: Lawn with benches Dogs allowed Water **NOTES:** Parking 20 **ROOMS:** 12 bedrooms 12 en suite s£21 d£52 (♦♦♦)

BRAMPTON
Map 21 NY56

Abbey Bridge Inn
Lanercost CA8 2HG ☎ 016977 2224 ▤ 016977 42184
e-mail: info@abbeybridge.co.uk
The pub is located by the bridge over the River Irthing, 400 metres from Lanercost Priory (1166), a mile from Hadrian's Wall and half a mile from Naworth Castle. In the 19th century the Naworth family were deeply involved in the Temperance Movement, so the Black Bull, as it was then, lost its licence until the 1960s. Now the pub has three bar areas, one specifically for walkers where dogs are welcome, a main bar area and a restaurant/lounge. The menu offers local and British favourites using locally-supplied produce. Look out for lasagne, chicken and apricot in orange sauce, battered cod and chips, and steak and kidney pie.
OPEN: 12-3 6-11 **BAR MEALS:** L served all week 12-2 D served Wed-Sun 6-9 Av main course £7.95 **RESTAURANT:** L served all week 12-2 D served Wed-Sun 6.30-9 Av 3 course à la carte £15 ◖: Black Sheep Special, Yates Bitter, Coniston Bluebird XB, Carlsberg-Tetley Tetley Smooth. **FACILITIES:** Children welcome Garden Dogs allowed **NOTES:** Parking 20 **ROOMS:** 5 bedrooms 3 en suite 1 family rooms s£26 d£52 (♦♦♦)

Blacksmiths Arms ♦♦♦ 🛏 ♀
Talkin Village CA8 1LE ☎ 016977 3452 ▤ 016977 3396
e-mail: blacksmithsarmstalkin@yahoo.co.uk
Dir: *from M6 take A69 E, after 7m straightover rdbt, follow signs to Talkin then Talkin Village*
Originally the local smithy, dating from around 1700, this attractive village inn is close to Talkin Tarn Country Park and handy for visiting Hadrian's Wall, the Borders and the Lake District. The well-balanced menu and blackboard specials offer a good variety of dishes, including lunchtime snacks and traditional Sunday roasts. Options include sweet and sour

continued

continued

BRAMPTON continued

chicken, local Cumberland sausage, beef lasagne, fresh haddock fillet, Blacksmiths vegetarian bake, tuna messicani, and beef Stroganoff. Specials board offers further choice.

Blacksmiths Arms

OPEN: 12-3 6-11 (Sun 12-3, 6-10.30) **BAR MEALS:** L served all week 12-2 D served all week 6.30-9 Av main course £7 **RESTAURANT:** L served all week 12-2 D served all week 6.30-9 Av 3 course à la carte £15 **BREWERY/COMPANY:** Free House ◗: Black Sheep Best, Jennings Cumberland Ale, Carlsberg-Tetley Bitter, Scottish Courage John Smith's. ♀: 12 **FACILITIES:** Children welcome Garden: Tables during summer months **NOTES:** Parking 20 **ROOMS:** 5 bedrooms 5 en suite 2 family rooms s£35 d£50

BROUGHTON-IN-FURNESS
Map 18 SD28

Blacksmiths Arms
Broughton Mills LA20 6AX ☎ 01229 716824 🖷 01229 716824 e-mail: blacksmithsarms@aol.com
Dir: A593 from Ambleside to Coniston then on to B-in-F, minor rd 2.5m from B-in-F

Originally a farmhouse, dating from before 1688, the inn is set in a secluded Lakeland valley. The interior is beautifully preserved, with the original farmhouse range, worn slate floors and low beams. Gaslights in the dining room and bar still work when the electricity fails. Traditional dishes such as lamb Henry, chicken casserole, and beef Wellington are offered alongside more exotic options such as Mexican crepes - all washed down with ales from nearby micro-breweries. **OPEN:** 12-11 (Sun 12-10.30)(Sat 12-11) (Winter Mon 5-11, Tue-Fri 12-2.30/5-11) Closed: Dec 25 **BAR MEALS:** L served Tue-Sun 12-2 D served Mon-Sun 6-9 Av main course £6 **RESTAURANT:** L served Tue-Sun 12-2 D served Mon-Sun 6-9 **BREWERY/COMPANY:** Free House ◗: Jennings Cumberland Ale, Dent Aviator, Barngates Tag Lag. **FACILITIES:** Children welcome Garden: Patio area tables and chairs, patio heater Dogs allowed **NOTES:** Parking 30

BUTTERMERE
Map 18 NY11

Bridge Hotel ★★
CA13 9UZ ☎ 017687 70252 🖷 017687 70215 e-mail: enquiries@bridge-hotel.com
Dir: Take B5289 from Keswick

Spend a weekend at this 18th-century former coaching inn and enjoy its stunning location in an area of outstanding natural beauty between Buttermere and Crummock Water. Guests can round off spectacular walks with afternoon tea, excellent ales in the beamed bar, or hearty food. Main courses include Cumberland hotpot, home-made steak and kidney pie, vegetable stirfry, and deep-fried haddock in crisp beer batter. For smaller appetites there's a good selection of salads, sandwiches and toasties. **OPEN:** 10.30-11 (open all day in summer) **BAR MEALS:** L served all week 12-2.30 D served all week 6-9.30 Av main course £6.50 **RESTAURANT:** D served all week 7-8.30 Av 5 course fixed price £21 **BREWERY/COMPANY:** Free House ◗: Theakston's Old Peculiar, Black Sheep Best, Interbrew Flowers IPA, Tirrell Old Faithfull. **FACILITIES:** Children welcome Garden Dogs allowed **NOTES:** Parking 60 **ROOMS:** 21 bedrooms 21 en suite s£60 d£90

CALDBECK
Map 18 NY34

Oddfellows Arms 🏠
CA7 8EA ☎ 016974 78227 🖷 016974 78134
Situated in a scenic conservation village in the northern fells, this 17th-century former coaching inn is in a stunning location and is popular with walkers on the Cumbrian Way and coast-to-coast cyclists. Lunchtime snacks and a specials board supplement the regular menu, and favourite fare includes roast duck, steak and ale pie, lamb Jennings, pork and cider casserole, poached salmon, double Barnsley chop, and Cumberland sausage. Sandwiches, jacket potatoes, and salads are also available. **OPEN:** 12-3 6-11 (Fri-Sun all day) (All day & all week in Summer) **BAR MEALS:** L served all week 12-2 D served all week 6-8.30 Av main course £7.95 **RESTAURANT:** L served all week 12-2 D served all week 6.30-8.30 Av 3 course à la carte £14.50 **BREWERY/COMPANY:** Jennings ◗: Jennings Bitter, Cumberland Ale. **FACILITIES:** Children welcome Garden: Beer garden Dogs allowed Water **NOTES:** Parking 10

★ **Star rating for inspected hotel accommodation**

CARTMEL
Map 18 SD37

Pick of the Pubs

The Cavendish
LA11 6QA ☎ 015395 36240 ▤ 015395 36243
e-mail: jmsmcwh@aol.com
Dir: M6 J36 take A590 follow signs for Barrow in Furness, Cartmel is signposted. In village take 1st R.
Cartmel's oldest hostelry, dating from the 15th century, with oak beams and log fires creating a cosy atmosphere. Bar food ranges from soup and sandwiches to lamb Henry or bangers and mash. Typical restaurant dishes might be stuffed fillet steak, sea bass and local ostrich. Top quality real ales and a good selection of wines by glass or bottle.
OPEN: 11.30-11 (Sun 12-10.30) **BAR MEALS:** L served all week 12-2 D served all week 6-9 Av main course £7
RESTAURANT: L served all week 12-2.15 D served all week 6-9.15 Av 3 course à la carte £20 **BREWERY/COMPANY:** Free House ☎: John Smiths, Cumberland, Bombadier, Cavendish.
NOTES: Parking 25

COCKERMOUTH
Map 18 NY13

The Trout Hotel ★★★ ◉ ⬡ ♀
Crown St CA13 0EJ ☎ 01900 823591 ▤ 01900 827514
e-mail: enquiries@trouthotel.co.uk
Dating from about 1670 and originally built as a private house, the Trout became a hotel in 1934. The hand-carved oak staircase and marble fireplace are among the many striking features, and the bedrooms are comfortable and well equipped. Choose between the bar menu - sandwiches, baked potatoes, steaks - the fixed price dinner menu or the carte. Options might include rosette of lamb on a rösti, steamed halibut with spinach and cheese velouté, and stuffed oven-baked butternut squash.
OPEN: 11-11 **BAR MEALS:** L served all week 11-9.30 D served Mon-Sat Av main course £5 **RESTAURANT:** L served all week 12-2 D served all week 7-9.30 Av 3 course à la carte £25.95
BREWERY/COMPANY: Free House ☎: Jennings Cumberland Ale, Theakston Bitter, John Smiths, Marston's Pedigree.
FACILITIES: Children welcome Garden: Riverside garden, food served outside Dogs allowed **NOTES:** Parking 70 **ROOMS:** 29 bedrooms 29 en suite s£89.95 d£109

CONISTON
Map 18 SD39

Black Bull Inn & Hotel ⬡ ♀
1 Yewdale Rd LA21 8DU ☎ 015394 41335 ▤ 015394 41168
e-mail: i.s.bradley@btinternet.com
The Romantic poets were familiar with this old coaching inn, built at the time of the Spanish Armada. The Black Bull has a lovely village setting, by the beck and in the shadow of the Old Man. Beers are brewed on the premises, and food is served in both the bar and restaurant. Snacks like toasted sandwiches and jacket potatoes, and local game dishes and fresh haddock fillet appear on the main menu.
OPEN: 11-11 (Sun 12-10.30) Closed: Dec 25 **BAR MEALS:** L served all week 12-9.30 D served all week **RESTAURANT:** L served by appointment D served all week 6-9 **BREWERY/COMPANY:** Free House ☎: Coniston Bluebird, Old Man Ale, Opium, Blacksmith & XB.
FACILITIES: Children welcome Children's licence Garden: Riverside patio outside Dogs allowed Walker, dog beds and meals
NOTES: Parking 12

Sun Hotel & 16th Century Inn ♀ NEW
LA21 8HQ ☎ 015394 41248 ▤ 015394 41219
e-mail: thesun@hotelconiston.com
Dir: From junction 36, take the A591, beyond Kendal and Windermere, then the A598 from Ambleside to Coniston. Sign posted from the bridge in the village.
A 16th-century inn with a 10-room hotel attached, located above the village on the road to Coniston Old Man. The bar has stone floors and walls, exposed beams and a lovely old range. A more recent addition is the conservatory, accessible from the bar and dining room, and a pleasant place to eat and enjoy the views. The English country menu offers broths, hot pot and game as available, supplemented by daily specials.
OPEN: 11-11 (Sun 12-10.30) **BAR MEALS:** L served all week 12-2.30 D served all week 6-9 Av main course £11 **RESTAURANT:** L served all week 12-2.30 D served all week 6-9 Av 3 course à la carte £20 ☎: Coniston Bluebird, Black Cat, Yates, Deuchards. ♀: 6
FACILITIES: Children's licence Garden: Large garden with benches, trees Dogs allowed Water in the bar **NOTES:** Parking 20 **ROOMS:** 10 bedrooms 9 en suite 3 family rooms s£35 d£40 (★★)

CROOK
Map 18 SD49

The Sun Inn ⬡ ♀
LA8 8LA ☎ 01539 821351 ▤ 01539 821351
Dir: off the B5284
A warmly welcoming inn dating from 1711, The Sun is steeped in tradition with winter fires and a summer terrace overlooking rolling countryside. The best local ingredients are used to create a variety of dishes, such as venison steak with wild mushroom sauce, game casserole, and fell-bred steaks. The bar snack and regular menus are supplemented by daily specials, and fresh fish is also featured.
OPEN: 12-2.30 (Sat 12-11, Sun 12-10.30) **BAR MEALS:** L served all week 12-2.30 D served all week 6-9 Av main course £6.50 **RESTAURANT:** L served all week 12-2.30 D served all week 6-9 Av 3 course à la carte £18 **BREWERY/COMPANY:** Free House ☎: Theakston, Scottish Courage John Smith's, Courage Directors, Wells Bombardier. **FACILITIES:** Children welcome Garden: Terrace Dogs allowed **NOTES:** Parking 40

CROSTHWAITE
Map 18 SD49

Pick of the Pubs

The Punch Bowl Inn ◉ ⬡ ♀
LA8 8HR ☎ 015395 68237 ▤ 015395 68875
e-mail: enquiries@punchbowl.fsnet.co.uk
Dir: From M6 J36 take A590 towards Barrow, then A5074 & follow signs for Crosthwaite. Pub next to church on L
Since ex-Gavroche chef Steven Doherty came to this 17th-century Lakeland pub it has been a serious and award-winning dining destination. With its warm and friendly atmosphere, the bar appeals to walkers and casual visitors who can relax amongst original beams, low ceilings and open fires. Theakston and Black Sheep ales are on tap, and imaginative sandwiches and light bites are served. Steven's exciting cooking skills are demonstrated on the carte and specials menu, which offer starters like oven-baked beetroot tart with crumbled goats' cheese, or home-made venison terrine, followed by boned and rolled saddle of rabbit with a grain mustard mash, and perhaps steamed white chocolate and vanilla sponge. In fine weather, food from the two lunch menus is also

continued

England

CROSTHWAITE continued

served on a terrace overlooking the Lyth Valley, featuring smoked haddock, duck leg confit, and perhaps pan-fried salmon fillet.
OPEN: 11-11 (Sun 12-10.30) Closed: 1wk Nov, 1wk Dec, 1wk Jan 1wk summer **BAR MEALS:** L served Mon-Sun 12-2 D served Mon-Sun 6-9 Av main course £13.50 **RESTAURANT:** L served Tues-Sun 12-2 D served Tues-Sat 6-9 Av 3 course à la carte £25 **BREWERY/COMPANY:** Free House ◖: Black Sheep Best, Barngates Cracker Ale, Greene King Old Speckled Hen. ♀: 21 **FACILITIES:** Children welcome Garden: Patio, terrace garden Dogs allowed Water Bowls **NOTES:** Parking 60

DALTON-IN-FURNESS   Map 18 SD27

Black Dog Inn 🐾 **NEW**
Holmes Green, Broughton Rd LA15 8JP
☎ 01229 462561 📖 01229 468036
e-mail: jack@blackdoginn.freeserve.co.uk
Dir: Telephone for directions
High above the Duddon Estuary stands this unassuming local at the junction of two turnpikes, one of them the main road to Scotland in the 18th century. Two fires warm the bar, which is divided into a quarry-tiled drinking area, and carpeted dining section. Tasty home-made food is an attractive aspect of this pub, and along with a standard menu and various snacks, a 'specials' list covers game casserole, black pudding platter, and salmon and asparagus pasta bake.
OPEN: 12-11 (Sun 12-10.30) (Winter 5-11) **BAR MEALS:** L served all week 12-2.30 D served all week 5.30-8.30 Av main course £5 ◖: Cambinus Deliverance, York Yorkshire Terrier, Barngates Cracker, Wye Valley Wholesome Stout. **FACILITIES:** Children welcome Children's licence Garden: Large patio area with tables and chairs Dogs allowed Water, charge for overnight staying **NOTES:** Parking 26

DENT   Map 18 SD78

Sun Inn
Main St LA10 5QL ☎ 015396 25208
e-mail: martin@dentbrewery.co.uk
Dir: From M6 through Sedburgh, Dent signed, 4.5m
Serving as a magnet for dale walkers and real ale buffs, the pub stands in picturesque Dentdale, surrounded by quaint whitewashed cottages and narrow cobbled streets. Its cosy bars, with original coin-studded beams, open coal fire and local photographs are entirely in keeping with the setting. Just up the road is the Dent Brewery, which owns the Sun Inn. Their award-winning real ales include T'owd Tup, Kamikaze and Aviator. No nonsense bar food is simple and filling, with local Cumberland sausages and home-made pies of the day dished up in trenchermen's portions.
OPEN: 11-2.30 6.30-11 Closed: Dec 25 **BAR MEALS:** L served all week 12-2 D served all week 6.30-8.30 Av main course £5.95 **BREWERY/COMPANY:** Dent Brewery ◖: Dent Bitter, T'Owd Tup, Aviator, Kamikaze. **FACILITIES:** Children welcome Garden Dogs allowed Water **NOTES:** Parking 15

DOCKRAY   Map 18 NY32

The Royal Hotel 🐾
CA11 0JY ☎ 017684 82356 📖 017684 82033
Dir: A66 towards Keswick for 8m, turn L onto A5091 signposted Dockray
Wordsworth and Mary Queen of Scots both visited this 16th-

century inn a mile from the shores of Ullswater. It's a family-run establishment, cosy with a flagstone floor and blazing log fire. A good selection of real ales, wines and malt whiskies is served in the bar, and the restaurant offers all home-made dishes. Whitby scampi and fresh haddock in batter are available every day, and other specialities are roast Herdwick mutton and royal game pie. Now under new management.
OPEN: 11-11 **BAR MEALS:** L served all week 12-2.30 D served all week 6-9 Av main course £7.50 **RESTAURANT:** L served all week 12-2.30 D served all week 6-9 **BREWERY/COMPANY:** Free House ◖: Castle Eden Ale, Black Sheep Best, Jennings Cumberland Ale, Greene King Old Speckled Hen. **FACILITIES:** Children welcome Children's licence Garden: Large grassed area, patio area and stream Dogs allowed by arrangement **NOTES:** Parking 30

ELTERWATER   Map 18 NY30

Pick of the Pubs

The Britannia Inn ★★
LA22 9HP ☎ 015394 37210 📖 015394 37311
e-mail: info@britinn.co.uk
Dir: A593 from Ambleside, then B5343 to Elterwater
Overlooking the village green in a famous scenic valley, the Britannia captures the essence of a traditional family-run Lakeland inn. Originally a farmhouse and the premises of a local cobbler, the Britannia really comes to life in summer when colourful hanging baskets dazzle the eye and the garden fills up with customers (and occasionally Morris dancers). In colder weather, real fires in the oak-beamed bar make it a good place to end a country walk. Lunches, afternoon snacks and dinner are served daily, with an extensive range of food and daily specials. Hearty home-made snacks include lamb rogan josh, Cumberland sausage and mash, quiche, and steak and kidney pie. The more ambitious evening menu might offer steak Diane, fresh bream with red and yellow pepper sauces, or Lakeland lamb Henry. Add to all this some attractively furnished bedrooms, and the Britannia is an ideal base for a holiday or weekend break.
OPEN: 11-11 (Sun 12-10.30) Closed: 25-26 Dec **BAR MEALS:** L served all week 12-2 D served all week 6.30-9.30 Av main course £8.95 **RESTAURANT:** L served all week 12-2 D served all week 6.30-9.30 **BREWERY/COMPANY:** Free House ◖: Jennings Bitter, Coniston Bluebird, Dent Aviator. **FACILITIES:** Children's licence Patio Dogs allowed Water **NOTES:** Parking 10 **ROOMS:** 9 bedrooms 8 en suite s£60 d£76 no children overnight

---

ESKDALE GREEN   Map 18 NY10

Pick of the Pubs

Bower House Inn ★★ 🐾
CA19 1TD ☎ 019467 23244 📖 019467 23308
e-mail: info@bowerhouseinn.co.uk
Dir: 4m off A595 0.5m W of Eskdale Green
Fine 17th-century stone-built former farmhouse with welcoming log fire and sheltered, well-established gardens overlooking Muncaster Fell. Oak-beamed bar and alcoves enhance the character of the place and a charming candlelit restaurant plays host to a varied selection of hearty, imaginative dishes. Cumberland wild duck, local pheasant in whisky, salmon with red pesto crust and

continued

continued

spinach and mushroom roulade may feature on the specials board, while the dinner menu may offer roast haunch of venison with red wine and juniper berry sauce, roast pheasant with whisky sauce, escalope of veal with ham and Gruyere, chicken breast with apple and tarragon sauce, grilled duck breast on roasted fruits with red wine and plum sauce, or poached salmon with white wine and cucumber sauce. Twenty five en suite rooms make the Bower House an ideal holiday retreat throughout the year.
OPEN: 11-11 **BAR MEALS:** L served all week 12-2 D served all week 6.30-9.30 Av main course £8.50 **RESTAURANT:** L served Sun D served all week 7-8.30 Av 3 course à la carte £22.50 **BREWERY/COMPANY:** Free House **◆:** Theakston Bitter, Jennings Bitter, Greene King Old Speckled Hen, Dent Ales.
FACILITIES: Children welcome Garden: Food served outside Dogs allowed In the garden only **NOTES:** Parking 50 **ROOMS:** 25 bedrooms 25 en suite s£35 d£60

King George IV Inn
CA19 1TS ☎ 019467 23262 ▤ 019467 23334
e-mail: kinggeorgeiv@eskdale83.fsnet.co.uk
Dir: A590 to Greenodd, A5092 to Broughton-in-Furness then over Ulpha Fell towards Eskdale
17th-century coaching inn located at the heart of one of Lakeland's finest hidden valleys close to picturesque Dalegarth Falls. Inside are open fires, oak beams, low ceilings and flagged floors with antiques to browse among before eating. Popular real ales and huge selection of almost 200 malt whiskies available. Home-cooked food includes dishes such as Cumberland sausage and egg, pan-fried liver and onions, steak and ale pie, seafood casserole and a range of steaks. Good vegetarian selection.
OPEN: 11-3 6-11 (Sun 12-3) (7 July-7 Sept 11-11, Open BHS) Closed: 25 Dec **BAR MEALS:** L served all week 12-2 D served all week 6-9 Av main course £7.50 **RESTAURANT:** L served all week 12-2 D served all week 6-9 **BREWERY/COMPANY:** Free House **◆:** Scottish Courage Theakston Best, Old Peculier & XB, Jennings Cumberland Ale. **FACILITIES:** Children welcome Garden: Beautiful views, ample tables Dogs allowed **NOTES:** Parking 12

GARRIGILL   Map 18 NY74

The George & Dragon Inn
CA9 3DS ☎ 01434 381293 ▤ 01434 382839
e-mail: thegeorgeanddragon@btopenworld.com
Once serving the local zinc and lead mining communities, this 17th-century coaching inn is popular with walkers, who enjoy log fires that stave off that brisk North Pennine weather. Recent change in ownership – reports please.
OPEN: 12-2 7-11 (Sat 12-11) (Sun 12-4.30, 7-10.30)
BAR MEALS: L served all week 12-2 D served all week 7-9 Av main course £6 **RESTAURANT:** L served all week 12-2 D served all week 7-9 Av 3 course à la carte £11 **BREWERY/COMPANY:** Free House **◆:** Lowenbrau, Guest Ales. **FACILITIES:** Children welcome Children's licence Dogs allowed Water, Biscuits, Toys, Leads

GRANGE-OVER-SANDS   Map 18 SD47

Hare & Hounds Country Inn ♀
Bowland Bridge LA11 6NN ☎ 015395 68333 ▤ 015395 68993
Dir: M6 onto A591, L after 3m onto A590, R after 3m onto A5074, after 4m sharp L & next L after 1m
Wonderfully located in Bowland Bridge in the beautiful Winster Valley, with stunning views over Cartmel Fell, this 17th-century coaching inn is 10 minutes from Lake

Windermere. Other Lake District attractions are easily reached. The new licensees are no strangers to the area, as they ran this self-same pub from 1979 to 1981. Current dishes on offer include Cumbrian fellbred meats, king scallops wrapped in bacon, and mussells cooked in a variety of guises.
OPEN: 11-11 (Sun 12-10.30) **BAR MEALS:** L served all week 12-2.30 D served all week 6-9 Av main course £7.50 **RESTAURANT:** L served all week 12-2.30 D served all week 6-9 Av 3 course à la carte £12.50 Av 3 course fixed price £6.50 **BREWERY/COMPANY:** Free House **◆:** Black Sheep, Jennings, Boddingtons. **♀:** 10 **FACILITIES:** Children welcome Garden: Orchard with tables and hard area with tables **NOTES:** Parking 80

GRASMERE   Map 18 NY30

The Travellers Rest Inn ◆◆◆
Keswick Rd LA22 9RR ☎ 015394 35604 ▤ 017687 72309
e-mail: stay@lakedistrictinns.co.uk
Dir: From M6 take A591 to Grasmere, pub 0.5m N of Grasmere

Some of the finest scenery in the country surrounds this 16th-century former coaching inn, which offers a good range of beers and an extensive menu of home-cooked traditional fare. Typical dishes from an interesting menu include Lakeland gammon and free range local eggs, chargrilled fillet steak bordelaise, bulgar wheat and walnut patties, or traditional Waberthwaite Cumberland sausage. Sandwiches and cold platters are also available, along with delicious home-made puddings.
OPEN: 12-11 (Sun 12-10.30) **BAR MEALS:** L served all week 12-3 D served all week 6-9.30 Av main course £7.95 **RESTAURANT:** L served all week 12-3 D served all week 6-9.30 Av 3 course à la carte £15 **BREWERY/COMPANY:** Free House **◆:** Jennings Bitter, Cumberland Ale, & Sneck Lifter, Jennings Cocker Hoop. **FACILITIES:** Children welcome Garden: beer garden, stunning views, picnic tables Dogs allowed Water bowls provided **NOTES:** Parking 60 **ROOMS:** 8 bedrooms 8 en suite s£25 d£50

GREAT LANGDALE   Map 18 NY20

The New Dungeon Ghyll Hotel
LA22 9JY ☎ 015394 37213 ▤ 015394 37666
e-mail: enquiries@dungeon-ghyll.com
Dir: From M6 into Kendal then A591 into Ambleside onto A593 to B5343, hotel 6m on R
Traditional Cumberland stone hotel dating back to medieval times, and full of character and charm. The hotel stands in its own lawned grounds in a spectacular position beneath the Langdale Pikes and Pavey Ark. Local specialities, expertly cooked, are served in the smart dining room. A sample dinner menu offers pan-fried venison steak on haggis mash, chargrilled salmon fillet on asparagus spears, roasted

continued   continued

England

GREAT LANGDALE continued

vegetable risotto, whole baked rainbow trout, and oven-roast chicken breast on stir-fried onion and spring cabbage.

The New Dungeon Ghyll Hotel

OPEN: 11-11 (Sun 11-10.30) **BAR MEALS:** L served all week D served all week **RESTAURANT:** D served all week 7-8.30 **BREWERY/COMPANY:** Free House ◑: Scottish Courage Courage Directors, Greene King Ruddles Best. **FACILITIES:** Children welcome Garden Dogs allowed **NOTES:** Parking 30

HAVERTHWAITE   Map 18 SD38

Rusland Pool Hotel Restaurant & Bar 🐾 ♀
LA12 8AA ☎ 01229 861384 ▤ 01229 861425
e-mail: enquires@ruslandpool.co.uk
Dir: M6 J36 take A590 towards Barrow-in-Furness for 17m, and the hotel is on the R hand side of the A590 Westbound
Licensed since 1841, a traditional coaching inn in open countryside in the South Lakes. The grounds include a paddock, patio and beer garden, while inside visitors can choose between the informal and spacious non-smoking restaurant, and the cosy Saddle Bar with real fire in winter. The comprehensive menu works its way from lunchtime specials such as Lancashire hotpot, chicken curry and burgers, to Oriental duck, lamb Henry, Cumberland sausage, breaded scampi and leek and mushroom crumble.
OPEN: 11-11 (food served all day, 12-9) **BAR MEALS:** L served all week 12-9 D served all week Av main course £7.50 **RESTAURANT:** L served all week 12-9 D served all week Av 3 course à la carte £15
BREWERY/COMPANY: Free House ◑: Tetleys, Boddingtons.
FACILITIES: Children welcome Children's licence Garden: Terraced area overlooking woodland Dogs allowed Water on request
NOTES: Parking 35

HAWKSHEAD   Map 18 SD39

Kings Arms Hotel ◆◆◆
The Square LA22 0NZ ☎ 015394 36372 ▤ 015394 36006

An impressive carved figure of a king now helps support the low beams in the bar of this charming 16th-century pub which overlooks the village square. Beatrix Potter and John Ruskin both lived nearby. Main course choices often include minted steaks of local lamb with sliced oven-baked potatoes and braised red cabbage; home-made steak and ale pie with a chunky mash of root vegetables; and roasted pheasant breast stuffed with apricot.
OPEN: 11-11 (Sun 12-10.30) 25 Dec Closed eve **BAR MEALS:** L served all week 12-2.30 D served all week 6-9.30 Av main course £7
RESTAURANT: L served all week 12-2.30 D served all week 6-9.30
BREWERY/COMPANY: Free House ◑: Carlsberg-Tetley Bitter, Black Sheep Best, Yates, Hawkshead Bitter. **FACILITIES:** Children welcome Children's licence Garden: Walled area, picnic tables Dogs allowed Water **ROOMS:** 9 bedrooms 8 en suite 3 family rooms s£36 d£62

Pick of the Pubs

Queens Head Hotel ★★ 🞉 🐾 ♀
Main St LA22 0NS ☎ 015394 36271 ▤ 015394 36722
e-mail: enquiries@queensheadhotel.co.uk
Dir: M6 J36 A590 to Newby Bridge. Take 1st R, 8m to Hawkshead

This hotel has been at the centre of picturesque Hawkshead since the 16th century. It was already very old when William Wordsworth attended the local grammar school, and Beatrix Potter, who adopted the Lake District in a big way, created Peter Rabbit. One of the curios on show in the bare-beamed interior is the 20-inch Girt Clog, worn in the 1820s by a mole catcher with elephantiasis. The surrounding lakes and fells provide many of the ingredients used in meals, including Esthwaite Water trout, Graythwaite estate pheasant, and Ms Potter's

continued

beloved Herdwick sheep. At lunch there are sandwiches, salads, light bites, grills and main meals, such as Westmoreland pie. From the equally extensive evening menu, many impressive dinner selections can be put together. How about pear, Roquefort and croûton salad, roast breast of guinea fowl with port and damson sauce, and mocha pannacotta with caramel and rum sauce, for instance?
OPEN: 11-11 (Sun 12-10.30) **BAR MEALS:** L served all week 12-2.30 D served all week 6.15-9.30 **RESTAURANT:** L served all week 12-2.30 D served all week 6.15-8.45 Av 3 course à la carte £20 Av 3 course fixed price £20
BREWERY/COMPANY: Frederick Robinson ▄: Robinsons Hartleys XB & Fredericks, Cumbrian Way. **FACILITIES:** Children welcome **NOTES:** Parking 13 **ROOMS:** 14 bedrooms 11 en suite 2 family rooms

The Sun Inn ◆◆◆◆
Main St LA22 0NT ☎ 015394 36236 🗎 015394 36155

Listed 17th-century coaching inn at the heart of the village where Wordsworth went to school. Bar dishes range from baguette with bacon and melted Brie to Cumbrian lamb cutlets seasoned with coriander and chilli and served with a mixed fruit couscous. The monthly-changing restaurant carte might have trio of local sausages on a creamed celeriac mash or fishcakes of Esthwaite Water trout served with sweet chilli and tomato crème fraîche.
OPEN: 11-11 **BAR MEALS:** L served all week 12-2.30 D served all week 6.15-9.30 Av main course £6 **RESTAURANT:** D served all week Av 3 course à la carte £15 **BREWERY/COMPANY:** Free House ▄: Black Sheep, Barn Gates Cracker, plus two Guest ales. **FACILITIES:** Children welcome Garden: beer garden, outdoor eating, patio Dogs allowed **NOTES:** Parking 8 **ROOMS:** 8 bedrooms 8 en suite s£45 d£60

HEVERSHAM
Map 18 SD48

Blue Bell Hotel 🗟
Princes Way LA7 7EE ☎ 015395 62018 🗎 015395 62455
e-mail: bluebellhotel@aol.com
Dir: On A6 between Kendal & Milnthorpe
Amazingly old - it dates from 1460 - the Blue Bell was once the local vicarage. Heversham is an ideal base for touring the scenic Lake District and Yorkshire Dales, but pleasant country scenery can also be viewed from the hotel's well-equipped bedrooms. On offer in the charming period lounge bar and separate restaurant are seared salmon fillet with a prawn nage, roast Barbary duckling with sweet black cherry sauce, and beef tenderloin with wild mushrooms and Dijonnaise sauce.
OPEN: 11-11 **BAR MEALS:** L served all week 11-9 D served all

week 6-9 Av main course £6.95 **RESTAURANT:** L served all week 11-9 D served all week 7-9 Av 3 course à la carte £21 Av 4 course fixed price £19.95 **BREWERY/COMPANY:** Samuel Smith ▄: Samuel Smith Old Brewery Bitter. **FACILITIES:** Children welcome Garden: Quiet garden, decoratively furnished Dogs allowed **NOTES:** Parking 100 **ROOMS:** 21 bedrooms 21 en suite s£49.50 d£72 (★★)

KENDAL
Map 18 SD59

Gateway Inn 🗟
Crook Rd LA8 8LX
☎ 01539 720605 & 724187 🗎 01539 720581
Dir: From M6 J36 take A590/A591, follow signs for Windermere, pub on L after 9m

Located within the Lake District National Park, this Victorian country inn offers delightful views, attractive gardens and welcoming log fires. A good range of appetising dishes includes chicken casserole with red wine and herb dumplings, grilled fillets of sea bass with ratatouille and mussels, and roasted butternut squash filled with leeks and Stilton. Traditional English favourites of liver and onions or rabbit pie are also a feature.
OPEN: 11-11 (all day wknds) **BAR MEALS:** L served all week 12-2 D served all week 6-9 Av main course £8.50 **RESTAURANT:** L served all week 12-2 D served all week 6-9 Av 3 course à la carte £15 **BREWERY/COMPANY:** Thwaites ▄: Thwaites Bitter, Thwaites Smooth. **FACILITIES:** Children welcome Garden: Terrace, food served outside Dogs allowed Water, dog food **NOTES:** Parking 50

The Gilpin Bridge Inn ◆◆◆ 🗟 NEW
Bridge End, Levens LA8 8EP
☎ 015395 52206 🗎 015395 52444
Dir: Telephone for directions
Good food is the chief attraction at this convivial pub where staff are unfailingly cheerful and service is efficient. Located just off the A590, it runs to the likes of mushroom Stroganoff, lasagne verde, 16oz T-bone steak, battered cod or haddock, and steak and mushroom pie, served in both the bar and restaurant at reasonable prices. A large selection of single malts boosts real ales like Old Stockport and Robinson's Best.
OPEN: 11.30-2.30 5.30-11 (Open all day Summer, BH's)
BAR MEALS: L served all week 11.30-2 D served all week 5.30-9 Av main course £9 **RESTAURANT:** 11.30-2 D served all week 6-9 Av 3 course à la carte £16.95 **BREWERY/COMPANY:** ▄: Robinsons Best Bitter, Old Stockport Hartleys XB. **FACILITIES:** Children welcome Children's licence **NOTES:** Parking 60 **ROOMS:** 10 bedrooms 10 en suite s£40 d£50

continued

KESWICK Map 18 NY22

Pick of the Pubs

The Horse & Farrier Inn 🐦 ♀
Threlkeld Village CA12 4SQ ☎ 017687 79688 📠 017687 79824
e-mail: enquiries@horseandferrier.com
Dir: Telephone for directions

For over 300 years this stone inn has stood in an idyllic position below Blencathra. Ever popular with hosts of fell walkers, it provides imaginative home cooking and real ales from the host brewer, Jennings's. New owners have maintained the warmly-welcoming atmosphere in the traditional-style bars and dining-room, with their hunting prints and cheerful log fire. The mouth-watering menu has plenty of choice including fresh fish and local produce. Starters like stir-fried king prawns and giant mussels with green chillies, and smoked haddock and sea trout terrine might come before fillets of red mullet with egg noodles and a Thai green curry sauce, pan-fried venison steak in a juniper marinade, and vegetarian choices such as warm leek, mushroom and sun-dried tomato tart. Additional lunchtime fare includes cold and hot open sandwiches, and seasonal salads.
OPEN: 11-11 (Sun 12-10.30) **BAR MEALS:** L served all week 12-2 D served all week 6.30-9 Av main course £12
RESTAURANT: L served all week 12-2 D served all week 6.30-9 Av 3 course à la carte £18 **BREWERY/COMPANY:** Jennings
🍺: Jennings Bitter, Cocker Hoop, Sneck Lifter, Cumberland Ale & Guest Ale. ♀: 13 **FACILITIES:** Children welcome Garden: Long garden with views of Blencathra Mountain **NOTES:** Parking 60

Pick of the Pubs

The Kings Head ★★★ ♀
Thirlspot CA12 4TN ☎ 017687 72393 📠 017687 72309
e-mail: stay@lakedistrictinns.co.uk
See Pick of the Pubs on opposite page

The Swinside Inn ♦♦♦
Newlands Valley CA12 5UE ☎ 017687 78253
e-mail: info@theswinsideinn.com
Situated in the quiet Newlands valley, the Swinside Inn is a listed building dating back to about 1642. From the pub there are superb views of Causey Pike and Cat Bells - among other landmarks. Nearby is the market town of Keswick, a good base for visiting the area's many attractions. Inside are two bars, traditional open fires and oak-beamed ceilings. Extensive bar menu may offer lamb Henry, Cumberland sausage, Swinside chicken, and fresh grilled Borrowdale trout.
OPEN: 11-11 (Sun 12-10.30) **BAR MEALS:** L served all week 12-2 D served all week 6-8.45 **RESTAURANT:** L served all week 12-2 D served all week 6-8.45 **BREWERY/COMPANY:** Scottish & Newcastle
🍺: Jennings Cumberland Ale, Scottish Courage John Smith's & Courage Directors, John Smiths Smooth & Theakstons Best Bitter,.
FACILITIES: Children welcome Garden Dogs allowed
NOTES: Parking 30 **ROOMS:** 7 bedrooms 4 en suite s£35 d£55

KIRKBY LONSDALE Map 18 SD67

Pick of the Pubs

Pheasant Inn 🐦 ♀
Casterton LA6 2RX ☎ 015242 71230 📠 015242 73877
e-mail: Pheasant.casterton@eggconnect.net
See Pick of the Pubs on page 106

Strange Games

Competition and ingenuity have thrown up a rich variety of pub games besides the best-known ones, from lawn billiards to maggot racing to clay pipe smoking contests, where the object is to keep a pipeful of tobacco alight longest. Cribbage and other once popular card games are not seen so often nowadays, but bagatelle is alive and well in Chester and Coventry. In Knur and Spell up North the players hit a small ball (the knur) as far as possible with a bat. Bat and Trap, an odd variety of cricket, has a long history going back at least to the 16th century in Kent. In Sussex the game of Toad in the Hole involves pitching flat discs into a hole in a table and in Lincolnshire they throw pennies into a hole and call it gnurdling. For all the video games and one-arm bandits, older and more convivial pastimes are still alive in British pubs.

Open: 12-11 (Sun 12-10.30)
Bar Meals: L served all week 12-3, D served all week 6-9.30. Av cost main course £7.95
RESTAURANT: L served all week 12-3, D served all week 7-9.
BREWERY/COMPANY: Free House.
: Scottish Courage Theakston Best Bitter & Old Peculier, Jennings Bitter, Bluebird Bitter, Greene King Abbot Ale.
FACILITIES: Dogs allowed, Children welcome, Garden - Spectacular views of fells.
NOTES: Parking 60
ROOMS: 17 en suite

The Kings Head

Stunning Lakeland scenery surrounds this 17th-century former coaching inn standing at the foot of Helvellyn. Real ales and fine wine are served with the excellent food, offering good value for money.

★★★ 🍷
Thirlspot, Keswick, CA12 4TN
☎ 017687 72393 📠 017687 72309
ⓔ stay@lakedistrictinns.co.uk
Dir: From M6 take A66 to Keswick then A591, pub 4m S of Keswick.

The King's Head is spectacularly located, with sweeping pasture and arable land all around, and lovely views of the Lakeland peaks of Blencathra and Skiddaw. On warm days and in the summer, the garden is the best place to enjoy a meal or a drink. Inside, old beams and inglenook fireplaces are traditional features of the bar, while a separate games room offers pool, snooker and darts. Popular real ales include beers from Theakstons and from Jennings' brewery in nearby Cockermouth, and there is a fine selection of wines and malt whiskies. An extensive menu of good value bar food including daily specials is served, with starters like black fin chilli crab cakes, or grilled polenta with wild mushroom, followed by steamed pork belly, braised minted joint of lamb, and grilled thyme, basil, and lemongrass salmon. Sandwiches and cold platters widen the choice, and puddings like banana and butterscotch crêpes round things off well. An elegant restaurant offers a fixed-price menu that changes daily with four excellent courses of high quality, freshly-made traditional English dishes and local specialities. Start with fettuccine carbonara, perhaps, or broccoli and almond soup, linger over a refreshing sorbet, then move on to baked fillet of Whitby cod wrapped in prosciutto, or roast loin of Cumbrian pork with spiced apple compote. Complete the meal with traditional apple and pear crumble with creamy vanilla custard sauce, or a choice of local cheeses. There are also facilities for banquets and wedding receptions of up to 100 guests, and seventeen comfortable bedrooms with a delightful residents' lounge.

Open: 11-3, 6-11 (Sun 11-3, 6-10.30)
Bar Meals: L served all week 12-2,
D served all week 6.30-9.
Av main course £8.50.
RESTAURANT: L Sun 12-2,
D Tue-Sun 6.30-9.
BREWERY/COMPANY:
Free House.
🍺: Scottish Courage Theakston Best &
Cool Cask, Black Sheep Best,
Marston's Pedigree, Dent Aviator.
FACILITIES: Garden - Lawn, tables,
beautiful views. Patio area. Dogs
welcome. Children welcome.

Pheasant Inn

Nestling beneath the Cumbrian fells in an idyllic location on the edge of the Lune valley, this traditional 18th-century free house makes an ideal touring base.

◆◆◆◆ 🏵 ♆

Casterton, Kirkby Lonsdale, LA6 2RX
☎ 015242 71230 📠 015242 73877
✉ Pheasant.casterton@eggconnect.net
Dir: From M6 J36 onto A65 for 7m,
L onto A683 at Devils Bridge, 1m to
Casterton. Village centre.

The inn offers eleven stylish and individually furnished en suite bedrooms, and there's a twin-bedded ground floor room that's ideal for disabled guests. The Lake District, the Forest of Bowland and the Yorkshire Dales are all within easy reach. Nearby Casterton School, which was attended by the Brontë sisters, was the model for Lowood School in Charlotte Brontë's *Jane Eyre*. From the lawn at the side of the inn,

guests can enjoy beautiful views of the fells and valley. The Pheasant is just ten minutes from the M6, and a mile away from the pretty market town of Kirkby Lonsdale, where there are excellent 18-hole and 9-hole golf courses. It has had its fair share of distinguished visitors, including Prince Michael of Yugoslavia. Traditional hand-pulled ales, a discerning selection of malt whiskies, and a small but well-chosen wine list complement a good choice of imaginative dishes. Relax over an informal bar meal, or enjoy the finest locally-sourced produce in the attractive oak-panelled dining room. A meal might start

with carrot and coriander soup; duck and tarragon paté; avocado with prawns and crabmeat; or perhaps a hot crêpe filled with shredded duck and asparagus with a port and honey sauce. Venison sausages or fillet of pork come straight from the chargrill, whilst more complex dishes include ratatouille and polenta casserole; braised pheasant with beer, potatoes, bacon, leeks and prunes; pan-fried duck stuffed with pork and sun-dried tomato sausage; or Loch Fyne mussels in white wine, garlic and parsley. A selection of home-made puddings, ices and cheese are available to round off your meal.

KIRKBY LONSDALE continued

Pick of the Pubs

Snooty Fox Tavern ♀
Main St LA6 2AH ☎ 015242 71308 ◨ 015242 72642
e-mail: info@snootyfox84.freeserve.co.uk
Dir: M6 J36 take A65, tavern 6m
One of a trio of privately-owned, well-run Cumbrian inns
(qv. Troutbeck's Mortal Man and the Royal Oak in
Appleby), the Snooty Fox is a listed Jacobean coaching inn
at the centre of town, the 'capital' of the scenic Lune
valley. Inside are roaring fires in rambling bars full of eye-
catching artefacts, while adjacent to a quaint cobbled
courtyard is the pub's own herb garden, which signals its
commitment to fresh food. A typical meal might start with
duck liver and pistachio parfait, followed by roasted rack
of lamb with spring onion mash and redcurrant jus. There
are some inspiring fish dishes (steamed cod with sautéed
potatoes, olives, crème fraîche and lumpfish caviar;
steamed huss wrapped in a banana leaf and served with a
creamy saffron sauce) and plenty of prime condition real
ales to wash it all down. The surroundings are
comfortably convivial and well-appointed bedrooms
promise a good night's sleep.
OPEN: 11-11 (Sun 12-10.30) **BAR MEALS:** L served all week
12-2.30 D served all week 6.30-9.30 Av main course £7.50
RESTAURANT: L served all week 12-2.30 D served all week
6.30-9.30 Av 3 course à la carte £25
BREWERY/COMPANY: Free House ◀: Timothy Taylor
Landlord, Theakstons, Black Sheep. ♀: 8 **FACILITIES:** Garden:
Beer Garden Dogs allowed Water **NOTES:** Parking 9
ROOMS: 9 bedrooms 9 en suite s£36 d£56 (♦♦♦) no
children overnight

The Sun Inn
Market St LA6 2AU ☎ 015242 71965 ◨ 015242 72489
Dir: From M6 J36 take A65
A popular 17th-century pub rumoured to have a resident
ghost, and with two open log fires to add to the atmosphere.
During excavations to the yard, a tunnel was found that
connects the pub with the church. Home-made food is
available in both the 30s-style restaurant (called Mad Carew's
after the poem by J Milton Hayes), and the bar. Try authentic
Cumberland sausage and mash, steak frites, lamb Devonshire
or the traditional Sunday lunch.
OPEN: 11-11 (Sun 12-10.30) **BAR MEALS:** L served all week
12.30-2.30 D served all week 6-9.30 Av main course £7.35
RESTAURANT: D served all week 6-9.30 Av 3 course à la carte £16
BREWERY/COMPANY: Free House ◀: Black Sheep Best, Timothy
Taylor Best, Moorhouse Pride of Kendal. **FACILITIES:** Children
welcome Dogs allowed Water, toys

Whoop Hall Inn ★★ 🐾 ♀
Skipton Rd LA6 2HP ☎ 015242 71284 ◨ 015242 72154
e-mail: info@whoophall.co.uk
Dir: From M6 take A65. Pub 1m SE of Kirkby Lonsdale
16th-century converted coaching inn, once the kennels for
local foxhounds. In an imaginatively-converted barn you can
relax and enjoy Yorkshire ales and a good range of dishes
based on local produce. Oven-baked fillet of sea bass with
tagliatelle verdi and tiger prawns, and stir-fried honey roast
duck with vegetables and water chestnuts are among the
popular favourites. The bar offers traditional hand-pulled ales

and roaring log fires, while outside is a terrace and children's
area.
OPEN: 7-11.30 **BAR MEALS:** L served all week 11.30-2.30 D
served all week 5-10 Av main course £5.95 **RESTAURANT:** L served
all week 12-2.30 D served all week 5-10 Av 3 course fixed price £17
BREWERY/COMPANY: Free House ◀: Black Sheep, Greene King
IPA, Tetley Smooth, Caffreys. ♀: 14 **FACILITIES:** Children welcome
Children's licence Garden: Terrace & lawn areas with good views
Dogs allowed Water provided **NOTES:** Parking 120 **ROOMS:** 23
bedrooms 23 en suite s£50 d£65

KIRKBY STEPHEN   Map 18 NY70

The Bay Horse
Winton CA17 4HS ☎ 017683 71451
e-mail: wintonpubks@whsmithnet.co.uk
Dir: Jct 38 M6, A685 To Brough via Kirkby Steven, 2m N

Standing in a moorland hamlet off the A685, the Bay Horse
offers home-cooked food.
OPEN: 12-2.30 6.30-11 **BAR MEALS:** L served Wed-Mon 12-2 D
served all week 6.30-9 Av main course £7 ◀: Black Sheep,
Theakstons plus Guest ales. **FACILITIES:** Children welcome Garden:
Food served outside. Views of North Pennines Dogs allowed

LITTLE LANGDALE   Map 18 NY30

Pick of the Pubs

Three Shires Inn ★★
LA22 9NZ ☎ 015394 37215 ◨ 015394 37127
e-mail: enquiries@threeshiresinn.co.uk
See Pick of the Pubs on page 108

continued

England

Open: 11-11 (Sun 12-10.30, Dec-Jan 12-3, 8-10.30)
Bar Meals: L served all week 12-2, D served all week 6-8.45.
Av cost main course £8
RESTAURANT:
D served all week 6.30-8.
BREWERY/COMPANY:
Free House.
🍺: Jennings Best & Cumberland, Ruddles County, Coniston Old Man, Hawkshead Bitter.
FACILITIES: Dogs allowed, Children welcome, Garden - Terrace and gardens next to stream.
NOTES: Parking 20
ROOMS: 10 en suite from d£64

Three Shires Inn

This 19th-century hotel stands in the beautiful valley of Little Langdale, close to the Three Shires Stone where Lancashire met the old counties of Cumberland and Westmoreland.

★★
Little Langdale, Ambleside, LA22 9NZ
☎ 015394 37215 📠 015394 37127
📧 enquiries@threeshiresinn.co.uk
Dir: Turn off A593, 2.3m from Ambleside at 2nd junct signposted for The Langdales. 1st L 0.5m, Hotel 1m up lane.

The traditional Cumbrian slate and stone building was erected in the 1880s, when it provided a much-needed resting place and watering hole for travellers on the journey over the high passes of Hardknott and Wrynose. The Three Shires still plays host to travellers, especially walkers, who are drawn to this majestic mountain country throughout the year. To make the most of the delightful views of the fells, relax in the landscaped garden, or on the terrace which overlooks a mountain stream. The interior has all the expected traditional charm: bare beams and slate walls in the bar and floral, country-house décor in other rooms. Guests always feel welcome - the inn has been run by the same family since 1983, so they know a thing or two about hospitality. Other comforts include wines, malt whiskies, and a good selection of real ales (Jennings' Best, Cumberland and Coniston Old Man from nearby breweries). Food is also a strength: dining options range from bar snacks to more elaborate evening menus. In the bar, expect steak and chips, Cumberland sausage and perhaps pan-fried cod with a crab cream sauce. The dinner menu shifts things up a gear with dishes such as oven-roasted pork loin marinated in fennel and garlic, with apple and wild herb potatoes and a Calvados and mustard cream, or lightly-grilled fillet of cod with wilted greens and a lightly-spiced tomato sauce.

LOWESWATER
Map 18 NY12

Kirkstile Inn ◆◆◆◆
CA13 0RU ☎ 01900 85219 ▤ 01900 85239
e-mail: info@kirkstile.com
Dir: Telephone for directions

This characterful inn has been providing food, drink and shelter for over 400 years. Beautifully situated, with superb views across Cumbria's fells, this is an ideal spot to enjoy a jar of local real ale. Bedrooms are comfortable and attractive, and there's a home-cooked bar menu with specialities including Cumberland sausage with black pudding and mustard mash; Kirkstile lamb cobble with a warm herb scone; and bacon chops on a bed of leaf spinach with cider and sage cream.
OPEN: 11-11 Closed: 25 Dec **BAR MEALS:** L served all week 12-2 D served all week 6-9 Av main course £7 **RESTAURANT:** L served Sun 12-2 D served Thur-Sat 7-8.30 **BREWERY/COMPANY:** Free House ◀: Jennings Bitter, Coniston Bluebird, Yates Bitter.
FACILITIES: Children welcome Children's licence Garden: Located away from road with river running by Dogs allowed Water
NOTES: Parking 40 **ROOMS:** 11 bedrooms 9 en suite s£37 d£64

MELMERBY
Map 18 NY63

The Shepherds Inn
CA10 1HF ☎ 01768 881217 ▤ 01768 881977
e-mail: theshepherdsinn@btopenworld.com
Dir: On A686 NE of Penrith

Well-known in the North Pennines, this unpretentious sandstone pub looks across the village green towards remote moorland country and close to miles of spectacular walks. Renowned for its extensive choice of country cheeses, including Lanark Blue, Westmorland Smoked and Allerdale Goat. Diners are drawn from far and wide to sample the lunchtime snack menu (baked potatoes, sandwiches and home-made scones) or specials such as rogan gosh,

Cumberland sausage hotpot or prime Cumberland grilled steaks. An interesting mix of well-kept real ales.
OPEN: 10.30-3 6-11 (Sun 12-3, 7-10.30) Closed: 25 Dec
BAR MEALS: L served all week 11.30-2.30 D served all week 6-9 Av main course £7.50 **RESTAURANT:** L served all week 11.30-2.30 D served all week 6-9 **BREWERY/COMPANY:** Enterprise Inns
◀: Jennings Cumberland Ale, Black Sheep Best, Boddingtons Cask, J S Magnet. **FACILITIES:** Children welcome Dogs allowed
NOTES: Parking 20

MUNGRISDALE
Map 18 NY33

The Mill Inn ◆◆◆ ♀
CA11 0XR ☎ 017687 79632 ▤ 017687 79981
e-mail: margaret@the-millinn.co.uk
Dir: From Penrith A66 to Keswick, after 10m R to Mungrisdale, 2m on L
Set in a peaceful village, this 16th-century coaching inn is handy for spectacular fell walks. Charles Dickens and John Peel once stayed here. The inn has a cask marque for its beer, and the food is also an attraction. All the hoped-for favourites are here (lunchtime sandwiches and ploughman's lunches, home-made pies, scampi and chips) whilst the specials menu offers more elaborate dishes such as grilled fresh salmon with a mushroom, white wine and cream sauce or pan-fried duck breast with honey, Port and coriander.
OPEN: 12-11 (Sun 12-10.30) **BAR MEALS:** L served all week 12-2.30 D served all week 6-8.30 Av main course £7 **RESTAURANT:** L served all week 12-2.30 D served all week 6-8.30 Av 3 course à la carte £15 **BREWERY/COMPANY:** Free House ◀: Jennings Bitter & Cumberland plus Guest ale. ♀: 6 **FACILITIES:** Children welcome Children's licence Garden: Landscaped, seats 30, overlooking river Dogs allowed, £5.00 to use bedrooms **NOTES:** Parking 40 **ROOMS:** 6 bedrooms 5 en suite 2 family rooms s£35 d£55

NEAR SAWREY
Map 18 SD39

Tower Banks Hotel ⌂ ♀
LA22 0LF ☎ 015394 36334 ▤ 015394 36334
e-mail: sales@towerbankarms.fsnet.co.uk
Dir: On B5285 SW of Windermere
This small 17th-century country inn featured in 'The Tales of Jemima Puddleduck', and stands next door to Hill Top, Beatrix Potter's former home. It makes an ideal base for exploring the Lake District, with its cosy bedrooms and good facilities. Inside it is quite unspoilt, and offers a good choice of beers. Interesting bar food like wild boar and pheasant pie, cheese flan, and locally-made sausages, with the evening choice expanding to include various tasty grills.
OPEN: 11-3 6-11 (Summer 6-10.30) Closed: 25 Dec
BAR MEALS: L served all week 12-2 D served all week 6.30-9 Av main course £6 **RESTAURANT:** L served all week 12-2 D served all week 6.30-9 **BREWERY/COMPANY:** Free House ◀: Theakston Best & Old Peculier, Wells Bombardier, Barngates Tag Lag. ♀: 7
FACILITIES: Children welcome Children's licence Garden: 5 tables, 30 seats Dogs allowed **NOTES:** Parking 8 **ROOMS:** 3 bedrooms 3 en suite (◆◆◆)

NETHER WASDALE
Map 18 NY10

The Screes Inn ⌂
CA20 1ET ☎ 019467 26262 ▤ 019467 26262
e-mail: info@thescreesinnwasdale.com
Dir: E of A595 between Whitehaven & Ravenglass
Nestling in the scenic Wasdale valley and only a short walk from Wastwater is this welcoming 300-year-old inn with its

continued

continued

NETHER WASDALE continued

cosy log fire and a large selection of malt whiskies. A good choice of dishes includes chicken satay, grilled halibut, and steak and kidney pie, with vegetarian specials like chick pea and sweet potato curry, and chilli with sour cream.

OPEN: 12-11 **BAR MEALS:** L served all week 12-2.30 D served all week 6-9.30 Av main course £6.50 **RESTAURANT:** L served all week 12-2.30 D served all week 6-9.30 **BREWERY/COMPANY:** Free House ◀: Black Sheep Best, Yates Bitter, Worthington's Bitter, Derwent. **FACILITIES:** Children welcome Children's licence Garden: Seating area to front & side of pub, BBQ area Dogs allowed Water **NOTES:** Parking 30

OUTGATE   Map 18 SD39

Outgate Inn
LA22 0NQ ☎ 015394 36413 ▤ 015394 36939
e-mail: info@theoutgateinn.co.uk
Dir: From M6, by-passing Kendal, A591 towards Ambleside. At Clappersgate take B5284 to Hawkshead then Outgate

In this literary part of the country it's no surprise to learn that Wordsworth went to school a mile down the road. No doubt he was inspired by the good walks and stunning scenery that surround this former tollhouse. Inside, many original features remain. Enjoy a pint or two of Robinsons' as a prelude to your meal, which can be enjoyed in the cosy dining room or the bar area. Among the popular dishes are lemon chicken, local Cumberland sausage, or the farmers' grill. **OPEN:** 11-3 6-11 **BAR MEALS:** L served all week 12-2 D served all week 6.30-9 Av main course £6.95 **RESTAURANT:** L served all week 12-2 D served all week 6.30-9 **BREWERY/COMPANY:** Hartleys ◀: Robinsons Best, Cumbria Way, Fredericks & Hartleys XB. **FACILITIES:** Children welcome Children's licence Garden: Beer garden at the rear Dogs allowed Water **NOTES:** Parking 30

RAVENSTONEDALE   Map 18 NY70

Black Swan Hotel ♀
CA17 4NG
☎ 015396 23204 & 0800 0741394 ▤ 015396 23604
e-mail: reservations@blackswanhotel.com
Dir: M6 J38 take A685 E towards Brough

In a peaceful village in the foothills of the Eden Valley, in the old county of Westmorland, this comfortable Lakeland stone hotel dates from 1899. The larger of two bars, with a bright air from its shiny copper-topped tables, is well placed for good value portions of steak pie in shortcrust pastry, Cumberland sausage with caramelised apples, and salmon marinated in lime and honey. The owners, who have been here for fifteen years, spend much of their day preparing dinner for their restaurant guests, with an emphasis on delights such as local beef, lamb and game and traditionally made cheeses. Flavours are a strong point in scallops with sweet potato purée and tartare of mussels, grilled sea bass with lobster tail and green pea mousse and chocolate torte with peppermint mousse. A perfect place to escape the pressures of the modern day world, there is tennis and fishing nearby, and a sheltered garden approached by way of a footbridge across the stream.
OPEN: 8.30-3 6-11 (wknds 8.30am-midnight) **BAR MEALS:** L served all week 12-2.15 D served all week 6-9 Av main course £6 **RESTAURANT:** L served all week 12-2.15 D served all week 7-9 Av 3 course à la carte £24 Av 5 course fixed price £20 **BREWERY/COMPANY:** Free House ◀: Black Sheep, Timothy Taylor Landlord, Scottish Courage John Smith's, Dent. ♀: 72 **FACILITIES:** Children welcome Children's licence Garden: River & garden Dogs allowed **NOTES:** Parking 40 **ROOMS:** 20 bedrooms 18 en suite 2 family rooms s£50 d£80 (★★)

The Fat Lamb Country Inn ★★ ⌂ ♀
Crossbank CA17 4LL ☎ 015396 23242 ▤ 015396 23285
e-mail: fatlamb@cumbria.com
Dir: On A683 between Sedbergh and Kirkby Stephen
Under the same ownership for 25 years, the Fat Lamb has seen some considerable development and these days boasts 12 guest bedrooms and a private nature reserve. Originally a 17th-century farmhouse, the inn is set in magnificent countryside above the old market town of Kirkby Stephen. The informal garden doubles as a pleasant eating area and wildlife haven, the grassed picnic area surrounded by shrubs and bushes specially chosen

continued

to attract birds and insects. Sheltered paths cut through the wooded areas lead to viewing points overlooking the seven-acre nature reserve to the rear. Chefs use local produce whenever possible, and the extensive bar snack menu ranges from soup and sandwiches to Whitby scampi and Yorkshire gammon. The carte, serving the bar and restaurant, includes grilled Bessy Beck trout with fennel and ginger butter sauce, and roast local leg of lamb with redcurrant jelly and mint gravy.

OPEN: 11-2 6-11 **BAR MEALS:** L served all week 12-2 D served all week 6-10 Av main course £7.50 **RESTAURANT:** L served all week 12-2 D served all week 6-9 Av 3 course à la carte £16 Av 4 course fixed price £20 **BREWERY/COMPANY:** Free House **:** Cask Condition Tetley's Bitter. **FACILITIES:** Children welcome Garden Dogs allowed **NOTES:** Parking 60 **ROOMS:** 12 bedrooms 12 en suite 4 family rooms s£48 d£76

Kings Head Hotel ♦♦♦ 🐑 NEW
CA17 4NH ☎ 015396 23284
e-mail: enquiries@kings-head.net
Dir: Ravenstonedale is less that 10 mins (7 miles) from J38 Tebay on A685 & 6 miles from Kirkby Stephen

With a history dating from the 16th century, this building has seen some changes, serving as an inn, a court and jail, cottages, a temperance hotel and latterly licensed premises again. Though recently refurbished, the Kings Head retains its old world charm and traditional values, with cask ales, 45 malt whiskies, home-cooked local produce and real log fires. Special dishes include 'cock and bull' with rice, smoked game platter, and grilled marlin fillet with stir-fried vegetables.
OPEN: 11-3 6-11 (Fri-Sat Open all day Spring & Summer) **BAR MEALS:** L served all week 12-2 D served all week 6-9 Av main course £7.50 **RESTAURANT:** L served all week 12-2 D served all week 6-9 Av 3 course à la carte £15.50 **:** Black Sheep, Dent, Scottish Courage John Smith's, Carlsberg-Tetley Tetley's Imperial. **FACILITIES:** Children welcome Children's licence Garden: By river,

offset from building, tree canopy Dogs allowed Water, food bowls **NOTES:** Parking 10 **ROOMS:** 3 bedrooms 2 en suite 1 family rooms s£35 d£50

SCALES
Map 18 NY32

White Horse Inn 🐑 ♀
CA12 4SY ☎ 017687 79241 📠 017687 79486
Dir: 4m E of Keswick of A66

Situated on the slopes of Blencathra, this traditional Lakeland inn overlooks outstanding mountain scenery and makes an ideal base for walkers. The building dates from 1610 and is full of character, with beamed ceilings, an open fire and antique furnishings. Favourite dishes include lamb Henry with minted gravy, venison haunch with port and wild mushroom sauce, and Barbary duck breast with cranberries and Stilton.
OPEN: 12-2.30 6.30-11 **BAR MEALS:** L served all week 12-2 D served all week 6.45-9 Av main course £8 **RESTAURANT:** L served all week 12-2 D served all week 6.45-9 Av 3 course à la carte £14 **BREWERY/COMPANY:** Free House **:** Jennings Bitter, Black Sheep Best & Guest beers. ♀: 9 **FACILITIES:** Children welcome **NOTES:** Parking 6

SEATHWAITE
Map 18 SD29

Newfield Inn ♀
LA20 6ED ☎ 01229 716208
e-mail: paul@seathwaite.freeserve.co.uk
Dir: A590 toward Barrow, then R onto A5092, becomes A595, follow for 1m, R at Duddon Bri, 6m to Seathwaite
Located in Wordsworth's favourite Duddon Valley, six miles from the market town of Broughton-in-Furness, this early 17th-century inn is understandably popular with walkers and climbers, with many good walks (long and short) starting close to its door. The bar has a rare slate floor, a real fire and a small collection of historic photographs. The menu encompasses steak pie, large gammon steaks, local beef, lasagne, spicy bean casserole, and an ever-changing specials board. The garden area offers some stunning views of the fells.
OPEN: 11-11 **BAR MEALS:** L served all week 12-9 D served all week 12-9 Av main course £6 **RESTAURANT:** L served all week 12-9 D served all week 12-9 Av 3 course à la carte £12 **BREWERY/COMPANY:** Free House **:** Scottish Courage Theakston Old Peculier, Jennings Cumberland Ale, Coniston Bluebird, Caledonian Deuchars IPA. ♀: 7 **FACILITIES:** Children welcome Garden: Sheltered, seating for 40, stunning views Dogs allowed Water **NOTES:** Parking 30

continued

SEDBERGH   Map 18 SD69

The Dalesman Country Inn ⌂ ♀
Main St LA10 5BN ☎ 015396 21183 ▤ 015396 21311
Dir: J37 on M6, follow signs to Sedbergh, 1st pub in town on L

A 16th-century coaching inn, renowned for its floral displays and handy for walks along the River Dee or up on Howgill Fells. The lunchtime menu concentrates on the likes of home-made pies, hot sandwiches, and fresh fish in crispy beer batter. The more ambitious evening choice extends to seared chicken fillet with caramelised shallots and spinach, seared lamb's liver with black pudding, grilled haddock with saffron potatoes, and game casserole with a puff pastry lid. There is a patio and garden, ideal for summer meals. Good wine selection.
OPEN: 11-11 **BAR MEALS:** L served all week 12-2.30 D served all week 6-9.30 Av main course £9 **RESTAURANT:** L served all week 12-2.30 D served all week 6-9.30 **BREWERY/COMPANY:** Free House ◖: Carlsberg-Tetley, Scottish Courage Theakston Best Bitter, Black Sheep. ♀: 9 **FACILITIES:** Children welcome Children's licence Garden: Wooden benches & tables at pubs front **NOTES:** Parking 8 **ROOMS:** 7 bedrooms 7 en suite 6 family rooms s£25 d£60 (♦♦♦♦)

SHAP   Map 18 NY51

Greyhound Hotel ♀
Main St CA10 3PW ☎ 01931 716474 ▤ 01931 716305
e-mail: postmaster@greyhoundshap.demon.co.uk
Dir: Telephone for directions

Built as a coaching inn in 1684, the Greyhound is recognised as the first inn travellers and tourists reach after crossing notorious Shap Fell. Bonnie Prince Charlie once stayed here overnight on the march south with his Highlanders in 1745. Appetising menu characterised by dishes such as steak and kidney pudding, haunch of venison, pot-roast brisket of beef, Dublin Bay prawns, grilled gammon with pineapple or egg, deep-fried fillet of fresh cod and Westmorland sirloin steak garni. Good choice of ales.

OPEN: 11-11 **BAR MEALS:** L served all week 12-2 D served all week 6-9 Av main course £7.50 **RESTAURANT:** L served all week 12-2 D served all week 6-9 Av 3 course à la carte £15 **BREWERY/COMPANY:** Free House ◖: Carlsberg-Tetley Bitter, Young's Bitter, Greene King Old Speckled Hen, Jennings Bitter plus Guest Ales. ♀: 7 **FACILITIES:** Children welcome Garden: Food served outside Dogs allowed **NOTES:** Parking 30

TEBAY   Map 18 NY60

Cross Keys Inn ♦♦♦ ⌂ NEW
CA10 3UY ☎ 015396 24240 ▤ 015396 24240
e-mail: www.stay@crosskeys-tebay.co.uk
Dir: Just off J38 M6. Along A685 to Kendal
A little gem of a free house, allegedly haunted by the ghost of Mary Baynes, the Tebay Witch, still looking for her black cat which was savagely disposed of by a former landlord. An extensive lunch and evening menu - available in both the restaurant and bar - offers steak and mushroom pie, Cumberland sausage, Catalan chicken, chicken and ham pudding, smoky bacon pasta, smoked haddock and spinach bake, and salmon and broccoli mornay. Black Sheep Best Bitter on tap.
OPEN: 12-3 6-11 (Open all day Fri-Sun) **BAR MEALS:** L served all week 12-2.30 D served all week 6-9 Av main course £6.25 **RESTAURANT:** L served all week 12-2.30 D served all week 6-9 **BREWERY/COMPANY:** Free House ◖: Black Sheep Cask, Carlsberg-Tetley Tetley's Cask, Smooth & Imperial. **FACILITIES:** Children welcome Children's licence Garden: Lrg patio area, lrg lawned area **NOTES:** Parking 50 **ROOMS:** 6 bedrooms 3 en suite s£25 d£35

TIRRIL   Map 18 NY52

Pick of the Pubs

Queens Head Inn ♦♦♦♦ ⌂ ♀
CA10 2JF ☎ 01768 863219 ▤ 01768 863243
e-mail: bookings@queensheadinn.co.uk
Dir: A66 towards Penrith then A6 S toward Shap. In Eamont Bridge take R just after Crown Hotel. Tirril 1m on B5320.
A Grade II listed property, this stone-built Cumbrian pub dates from about 1719 and has a long and colourful history. Formerly owned by the Wordsworth family in the early 1800s, there are signed deeds in the bar to establish the link with the great poet himself. The pub produced its own beers until 1899, and the current owners revived the Tirril brew exactly a century later. Award-winning Tirril ales are now on tap in the beamed and flagstoned front bar, which is also renowned for blazing log fires in a spectacular inglenook. Good-value accommodation and traditional English pub food are a bonus for appreciative locals, visiting tourists and walkers alike. Daily specials might include Thai fishcakes on dill hollandaise or Moroccan spiced lamb shank with apricot jus, while a favourite from the regular menu is brewer's pudding with a steak and Tirril's filling.
OPEN: 12-3 6-11 (Fri-Sun all day) Dec 25 closed evening **BAR MEALS:** L served all week 12-2 D served all week 6-9.30 **RESTAURANT:** L served all week 12-2 D served all week 6-9.30 Av 3 course à la carte £15 **BREWERY/COMPANY:** Free House ◖: Tirril Bewshers Best, Thomas Slee's Academy Ale, Charles Gough's Old Faithful, Brougham Ale. ♀: 10 **FACILITIES:** Children welcome Children's licence Dogs allowed Water **NOTES:** Parking 60 **ROOMS:** 7 bedrooms 7 en suite s£30 d£45

continued

TROUTBECK   Map 18 NY40

Pick of the Pubs

Queens Head Hotel ♦♦♦♦ ⊚ ♀
Townhead LA23 1PW ☎ 015394 32174 🖷 015394 31938
e-mail: enquiries@queensheadhotel.com
Dir: M6 J36, A590/591 westbound towards Windermere, R at mini-rdbt onto A592 signed Penrith/Ullswater, pub 2m on R

A classic Lakeland hostelry that is true to its roots as a thriving 17th-century coaching inn in the Troutbeck Valley. The Queens Head still offers accommodation in comfortable en suite bedrooms and even those just calling briefly will appreciate the stunning views across the Garburn Pass. Its rambling rooms are full of character, with solid beams, open fires, ancient carved settles and stone-flagged floors. Old prints adorn the walls of a bar servery created from an Elizabethan four-poster bed. Accomplished cooking ranges from simple braised dishes to imaginative seafood options served both in the bar and restaurant. Half-a-dozen good house wines and local Cumberland micro-brewed ales can accompany starters such as warm potted prawns cooked in cream and garlic or a salad of smoked pork and mixed berries, perhaps followed by peppered venison and redcurrant casserole; steak, ale and mushroom cobbler; or baked cod fillet on cumin-spiced butternut squash.
OPEN: 11-11 (Sun 12-10.30) Closed: 25 Dec **BAR MEALS:** L served all week 12-2 D served all week 6.30-9 Av main course £9.95 **RESTAURANT:** L served all week 12-2 D served all week 6.30-9 Av 3 course à la carte £20 Av 4 course fixed price £15.50 **BREWERY/COMPANY:** Free House 🍺: Interbrew Boddingtons Bitter, Coniston Bluebird, Old Man Bitter, Jennings Cumberland Ale. **FACILITIES:** Children welcome Children's licence Dogs allowed **NOTES:** Parking 100 **ROOMS:** 14 bedrooms 14 en suite s£55 d£75

ULVERSTON   Map 18 SD27

Pick of the Pubs

Farmers Arms 🍴 ♀
Market Place LA12 7BA ☎ 01229 584469
e-mail: roger@farmersrestaurant-thelakes.co.uk
A warm welcome is extended to locals and visitors alike at this lively 16th-century inn. Located at the centre of the market town overlooking the market cross, its cosy front bar is relaxed and comfortable with an open fire and traditional old beams. A patio area at the front of the inn provides a flower-filled spot to enjoy a drink or a summer meal, and watch the world, and the many local festivals,

go by. The beamed rear dining area is decorated with a collection of old and new mirrors, and landlord Roger Chattaway takes pride in the quality food. His famous Sunday lunch offers great value, while the specials list is imaginative and popular: fillets of charred swordfish with mussels, garlic and cream, baby lemon sole on courgette linguini, and stir-fried beef marinated in chilli and ginger. The lunchtime choice includes hot and cold sandwiches on baguette or ciabatta, and various salads.

OPEN: 10-11 **BAR MEALS:** L served all week 11.30-3 D served all week 5.30-8.30 Av main course £6.50 **RESTAURANT:** L served all week 11.30-3 D served all week 5.30-8.30 Av 3 course à la carte £12 **BREWERY/COMPANY:** Free House 🍺: Scottish Courage Directors & Theakston Best Bitter, Timothy Taylor Landlord, Hawkshead Best Bitter. **FACILITIES:** Children welcome Garden: Patio garden, outdoor heaters and canopy,

Royal Oak
Spark Bridge LA12 8BS ☎ 01229 861006
Dir: From Ulverston take A590 N. Village off A5092

Set in a small village, this large 18th-century pub offers a varied menu. Dishes include breaded sole filled with crab and prawn sauce, fillet steak stuffed with Stilton cheese and wrapped in bacon served on a port wine sauce, steak and mushroom pie, Cumberland sausage and chips, roasted sea bass served on creamy mashed potatoes, chicken and ham pie, or seared scallops on salad. Try the enormous Royal Grill (steak, sausage, porkloin, black pudding, gammon and eggs).
OPEN: 12-3 6-11 **BAR MEALS:** L served all week 12-2 D served all week 6-9 **BREWERY/COMPANY:** Enterprise Inns 🍺: Tetley, Jennings Cumberland. **FACILITIES:** Children welcome Garden: Food served outside Dogs allowed Water **NOTES:** Parking 30

continued

WASDALE HEAD
Map 18 NY10

Wasdale Head Inn 🐾 ⵏ
CA20 1EX ☎ 019467 26229 🖷 019467 26334
e-mail: wasdaleheadinn@msn.com
Dir: *Follow signs 'Wasdale' from A595, the inn is at the head of the valley*
Dramatically situated at the foot of England's highest
mountains and beside her deepest lake, this Lakeland inn is a
perfect base for walking and climbing. Slate floors and oak-
panelled walls are characteristic of its rustic interior, and the
walls are hung with photographs reflecting a passion for
climbing. Real ale is made exclusively for the inn, and local
Herdwick lamb is a speciality, along with traditional bangers -
Cumberland, pork and leek, and venison and herb.
OPEN: 11-11 (Sun 12-10.30) **BAR MEALS:** L served all week 11-9
D served all week 6.30-8.30 Av main course £6.50 **RESTAURANT:** D
served most 7-8 Av 3 course à la carte £22 Av 4 course fixed price £22
BREWERY/COMPANY: Free House ◖: Heskett Newmarket Kern
Knott's Cracking Stout, Great Gable Wasd Ale, Yates Bitter. ⵏ: 15
FACILITIES: Garden: View of mountains, food served outside Dogs
allowed Water **NOTES:** Parking 50 **ROOMS:** 15 bedrooms 15 en
suite s£49 d£98 (♦♦♦♦) no children overnight

WATERMILLOCK
Map 18 NY42

Pick of the Pubs

Brackenrigg Inn ♦♦♦ 🐾 ⵏ
CA11 0LP ☎ 017684 86206 🖷 017684 86945
e-mail: enquiries@brackenrigginn.co.uk
See Pick of the Pubs on opposite page

WINDERMERE
Map 18 SD49

Eagle & Child Inn ♦♦♦ ⵏ
Kendal Rd, Staveley LA8 9LP ☎ 01539 821320
e-mail: info@eaglechildinn.co.uk
Dir: *Follow M6 to Jct 36 then A590 towards Kendal join A591 towards
Windermere. Staveley approx 2m*

The name of this inn, in Staveley village at the foot of the
Kentmere valley, refers to the crest of arms of the Lonsdale
family who were local landowners. Excellent walking, cycling
and fishing country on the doorstep. Opposite the inn, the River
Kent rushes past the beer garden. Appetising range of dishes
might include whole Kentmere lamb shank on a minted mash,
pan-fried duck breast with plum sauce, local Cumberland
sausage and mash, and fresh grilled salmon supreme with herb
mustard and honey crust. Well-kept local beers also feature.
OPEN: 11-11 (Dec 25 Open 12-2) **BAR MEALS:** L served all week
12-3 D served all week 6-9 Av main course £7.50 **RESTAURANT:** L
served all week 12-3 D served all week 6-9 Av 3 course à la carte £15
◖: Black Sheep Best Bitter, Coniston Bluebird Bitter, Dent Ales,

continued

Jennings. ⵏ: 8 **FACILITIES:** Children welcome Garden: Riverside
location, secluded rear terrace **NOTES:** Parking 16 **ROOMS:** 5
bedrooms 5 en suite 1 family rooms s£35 d£50

New Hall Inn
Lowside, Bowness LA23 3DH ☎ 015394 43488
Dir: *Telephone for directions*
Complete with flagged-floors, exposed beams and open fires,
this historic pub was built in 1612, and was then used as a
blacksmiths. One of its best-known visitors was Charles Dickens.
Typical menu includes pheasant, fish pie, and crab claws.
OPEN: 11-11 Closed: 25 Dec **BAR MEALS:** L served all week 12-
2.30 D served all week 6-8.30 Av main course £6.50
BREWERY/COMPANY: ◖: Hartleys XB, Robinsons Best, Red
Robin. **FACILITIES:** Children welcome Garden: Patio Garden

The Watermill Inn ⵏ
Ings LA8 9PY ☎ 01539 821309 🖷 01539 822309
e-mail: all@watermillinn.co.uk
Once a timber mill crafting shuttles and bobbins for the
Lancashire cotton industry, this inn is very popular with
walkers, not least because of its impressive selection of real
ales - up to 16 on offer at any one time. To accompany them,
the menu has many daily specials, with popular choices being
venison sausage, beef and ale pie, Wrynose mixed grill,
Cumberland sausage, and Watermill chicken.
OPEN: 12-11 (Sun 12-10.30) Closed: 25 Dec **BAR MEALS:** L
served all week 12-4.30 D served all week 5-9 Av main course £8.25
BREWERY/COMPANY: Free House ◖: Coniston Blue Bird, Black
Sheep Special, Jennings Cumberland Ale, Hawkshead Bitter.
FACILITIES: Children's licence Garden: Paved area Dogs allowed
Biscuits/water provided

YANWATH
Map 18 NY52

Pick of the Pubs

The Yanwath Gate Inn 🐾
CA10 2LF ☎ 01768 862386 🖷 01768 864006
e-mail: ian.rhind@virgin.net
An unassuming 17th-century village pub popular with
walkers and visitors to the Lake District, not far from
scenic Ullswater but only a couple of miles from J40 of
the M6. A charming stone inglenook fireplace tends to
draw both regulars and newcomers. This is the place to
enjoy a pint of Black Sheep bitter while you choose
something from the appetising menu. If you prefer, relax
in the congenial surroundings of the inn's separate
restaurant with its pleasant views over the garden. Good
range of light bar meals, including sweet potato pie,
Gloucester pie (chicken, ham and eggs in a parsley sauce
with a crisp pastry topping), Cumberland sausage bake, or
salmon and haddock fish pie. Examples of blackboard
specials are fillet of beef Rutland, Derwentwater duck,
spinach, cherry tomato and pesto lasagne, and chargrilled
sirloin steak. Try mango and chocolate crème brûlée or
Eton mess from the dessert menu.
OPEN: 12-2.30 6.30-11 (Summer 12-3, 6-11) Closed: 2nd 2 weeks
of Jan **BAR MEALS:** L served all week 12-2 D served all week 6-9
Av main course £8 **RESTAURANT:** L served all week 12-2 D
served all week 6-9.15 Av 3 course à la carte £15
BREWERY/COMPANY: Free House ◖: Black Sheep Bitter,
Jennings Cumberland Bitter, Scottish Courage John Smith's Smooth.
FACILITIES: Children welcome Children's licence Garden:
Secluded terrace, lawns, landscaped garden **NOTES:** Parking 20

Open: 11-11 (Sun 12-10.30) (Nov-Mar closed between 3-5pm Mon-Fri)
Bar Meals: L served all week 12-2.30, D served all week 6.30-9.
Av cost main course £8.95
RESTAURANT: L served all week 12-2.30, D served all week 6.30-9.
Av cost 3 course £17.95
BREWERY/COMPANY:
Free House.
🍺: Theakstons Best, Jennings Cumberland, Black Sheep Special, Coniston Bluebird.
FACILITIES: Dogs allowed, Children welcome, Garden – Good views of Ullswater.
NOTES: Parking 40
ROOMS: 17 en suite from s£32 d£54

Brackenrigg Inn

This traditional 18th-century coaching inn boasts sweeping views across Lake Ullswater and the surrounding fells from its elevated terrace and fine gardens. Good quality food and comfortable modern accommodation are promised.

♦♦♦ 🐾 ⊈

Watermillock, Lake Ullswater, CA11 0LP
☎ 017684 86206 📠 017684 86945
📧 enquiries@brackenrigginn.co.uk
Dir: From M6 J40 take the A66 (signed Keswick), then A592 toward Ullswater. Pub is 6m from M6 and Penrith.

An unpretentious white-painted roadside hostelry that makes the most of its elevated position, the Brackenrigg Inn offers both casual visitors and overnight guests stunning views of Ullswater and distant peaks, including Helvellyn. Other attractions are the Black Sheep and Jennings ales served in the traditional bar lounge, and an imaginative choice of modern pub food offered in the no-smoking dining room and restaurant. Add to all of this a variety of accommodation to suit every taste, and you have the ideal base from which to explore the delights of the northern Lake District, whether it be walking, climbing, watersports, golfing, or just touring this area. You can enjoy a traditional bar snack in the homely bar or out on the terrace with its views over the lake, or sample modern British dishes in the restaurant. A weekly-changing menu may offer fresh mussels in various sauces, potato and smoked haddock dauphinoise, and king prawns with chermoula among some of the fish choices, while roast rump of lamb, honey-coated duck confit, and a variety of Cumbrian delicacies also make an appearance. For dessert there may be rum and raisin parfait or glazed lemon tart. Retire to one of the pleasantly-furnished en suite bedrooms, with their breathtaking lake and fell views, and spot the resident ghost if you're lucky. There are some rooms with ground floor access, one with full disabled facilities, and three rooms in which dogs are allowed. Some units can be combined to offer family/group rooms.

DERBYSHIRE

ALFRETON
Map 16 SK45

White Horse Inn 🐾 ♀
Badger Ln, Woolley Moor DE55 6FG ☎ 01246 590319
Dir: From A632 (Matlock/Chesterfield rd) take B6036. Pub 1m after Ashover. From A61 take B6036 to Woolley Moor
Situated on an old toll road, close to Ogston Reservoir, this 18th-century inn has outstanding views over the Amber Valley. Dishes from the bar menu or restaurant carte can be taken anywhere in the pub. Options range from sandwiches, paninis and traditional fish and chips to pan-seared salmon fillet on cherry tomato and asparagus confit; leek, chestnut and Stilton Wellington; pan-fried pork loin with black pudding, and slowly braised gigonette of lamb.
OPEN: 12-2 6-11 (Sun 12-10.30, all day summer wknds)
BAR MEALS: L served all week 12-2 D served all week 6-9 Av main course £8.95 **RESTAURANT:** L served all week 12-2 D served all week 6-9 Av 3 course à la carte £15.50 **BREWERY/COMPANY:** Free House 🍺: Jennings Cumberland, Adnams Broadside, Ruddles Best, Theakstons Old Peculiar. ♀: 8 **FACILITIES:** Children welcome Garden: Large patio with picnic benches Dogs allowed Water **NOTES:** Parking 50

ASHBOURNE
Map 10 SK14

Barley Mow Inn
Kirk Ireton DE6 3JP ☎ 01335 370306
On the edge of the Peak District National Park, this imposing inn at the head of the village street dates from 1683, and has remained largely unchanged over the years. Close to Carsington Water, ideal for sailing, fishing and bird watching. Ales from the cask and traditional cider; fresh granary rolls at lunchtime and evening meals for residents only.
OPEN: 12-2 7-11 (Sun, 7-10.30) Closed: Dec 25 & Dec 31
BAR MEALS: 12-2 **BREWERY/COMPANY:** Free House 🍺: Hook Norton, Burton Bridge, Whim Hartington, Archers. **FACILITIES:** Children welcome Garden Dogs allowed **NOTES:** No credit cards

Dog & Partridge Country Inn ★★ 🐾 ♀
Swinscoe DE6 2HS ☎ 01335 343183 📠 01335 342742
e-mail: dogpart@fsbdial.co.uk
Dir: Telephone for directions
Sporting and show business links distinguish this 17th-century coaching inn, where accommodation was expanded in 1966 for the Brazilian World Cup football team, who practised in a nearby field. Within easy reach of Alton Towers, the inn has a traditional bar and separate restaurant. Extensive menus feature fish, grills, curries, pasta and salads, and vegetarians are well catered for. Try a traditional Staffordshire oatcake with a choice of fillings accompanied by red cabbage, beetroot and salad.
OPEN: 11-11 **BAR MEALS:** L served all week 11-11 D served all week Av main course £7.50 **RESTAURANT:** L served all week 11-11 D served all week Av 3 course à la carte £20
BREWERY/COMPANY: Free House 🍺: Greene King Old Speckled Hen & Ruddles County, Hartington Best, Wells Bombardier, Scottish Courage Courage Directors. **FACILITIES:** Children welcome Garden: Good patio area with lovely views Dogs allowed **NOTES:** Parking 50 **ROOMS:** 29 bedrooms 29 en suite s£40 d£70

The Green Man ◆◆◆◆
St Johns St DE6 1GH ☎ 01335 345783 📠 01335 346613
Dir: In town centre off A52
Located in the heart of Ashbourne, this 17th-century coaching inn has two bars, the Johnson and the Boswell. On the specials board you'll find fresh fish and shellfish, local game, and

continued

traditional favourites like beef in Guinness and home-made pies. The comfortable en suite bedrooms are attractively decorated.
OPEN: 11-11 (Sun 12-10.30) Closed: Dec 25 **BAR MEALS:** L served all week 12-2.30 D served all week 6-8.30 Av main course £6
BREWERY/COMPANY: Free House 🍺: Marston's Pedigree, Bass, Worthingtons. **FACILITIES:** Children welcome Dogs not allowed during meal times **NOTES:** Parking 12 **ROOMS:** 18 bedrooms 18 en suite s£40 d£60

BAKEWELL
Map 16 SK26

George Hotel 🐾
Church St, Youlgreave DE45 1VW ☎ 01629 636292

Family-run pub close to many popular attractions, including Haddon Hall and Chatsworth House, and a handy base for walking and rock climbing in the Peak District and Derbyshire Dales. Try one of the game dishes - pheasant, rabbit or hare - or a good choice of vegetarian meals. Alternatively, go for salmon steak, home-made pies, or fresh trout.
OPEN: 11-11 open all day **BAR MEALS:** L served all week 11.30-9 D served all week Av main course £6.25
BREWERY/COMPANY: 🍺: Scottish Courage Courage Directors, Bateman XB, John Smiths, Theakston. **FACILITIES:** Children welcome Dogs allowed Water **NOTES:** Parking 20 **NOTES:** No credit cards

Pick of the Pubs

The Lathkil Hotel
Over Haddon DE45 1JE ☎ 01629 812501 📠 01629 812501
e-mail: info@lathkil.co.uk
Dir: 2m SW of Bakewell
Formerly 'The Miners Arms', named from the old lead mines that date back to Roman times, an overnight stay here remains in the memory for its panoramic views from the Victorian-style bar of the hills and dales of the Peak District. Home-cooked food has an enviable reputation locally, with a lunchtime hot and cold buffet in summer and more extensive evening choices supplemented by cooked-to-order pizzas. Following onion bhajis with cucumber raita, or tiger prawns in filo, indulge perhaps in a fruit sorbet before tackling sea bass with garlic and rosemary, Wootton Farm venison steak with Stilton sauce or Barbary duck breast with blackcurrant coulis. More conventional steaks with optional sauces, and steak, kidney and oyster pie, along with a daily vegetarian dish, are regular alternatives. To follow perhaps treacle tart or toffee and apple crumble from the home-made puddings list, or cheese and biscuits.
OPEN: 11.30-3 7-11 (all day Sat-Sun) Dec 25 no food
BAR MEALS: L served all week 12-2 Av main course £6.50
RESTAURANT: D served all week 7-9 Av 3 course à la carte £20
BREWERY/COMPANY: 🍺: Whim Hartington, Timothy Taylor Landlord, Wells Bombardier, Marston's Pedigree.
FACILITIES: Garden: beer garden, outdoor eating Dogs allowed Water **NOTES:** Parking 28

Yorkshire Bridge Inn

An exhilarating walk to the top of Win Hill, with its stunning Peak District views, and to Ladybower Reservoir and its magnificent dam.

On leaving the inn, turn right and follow the main road (A6013) for 110 yards (100m). Turn right, signed Thornhill, and follow the road downhill to cross the bridge (Yorkshire Bridge) over the River Derwent. Once over the bridge, bear left for 10metres then pass through the gate on your right and climb the track to a junction of paths. Proceed straight across and follow the track gently uphill for about 1/2m (0.8km) to the next footpath waymarker.

Take the track on the right and proceed along the side of the hill to a wooded area. Follow the waymarked path to the top of Win Hill. Pause to take in the magnificent view, then carry on down the opposite side and follow the track along the ridge for approximately a mile (1.6km) to where a stone wall crosses your path. Bear right and head for the gate giving access to woodland. Enter the woodland and follow the road downhill to Ladybower Reservoir.

Turn right and follow the access road to the dam. Cross the dam, enjoying the fine views up and down the valley, then turn right along the main road (A6013) back to the inn.

★★
YORKSHIRE BRIDGE INN, BAMFORD
Ashopton Road S33 0AZ.
☎ 01433 651361

Directions: A57 from M1, L onto A6013, pub 1m on R
Overlooking the Ladybower Reservoir and the Derwent Valley, this charming inn is located in the heart of Peak National Park - prime walking country. Generous bar food, good real ales and a warm welcome in the well-refurbished bars. Bedrooms
Open: 11-11. **Bar Meals:** 12-2, 6-9 (Sun 12-8.30).
Notes: Children welcome. Garden. Parking. No muddy boots. No dogs inside when food is being served.
(See page 119 for full entry)

DISTANCE: 6 miles (10km)
MAP: OS Landranger 110
TERRAIN: Woodland and heather covered moorland
PATHS: Moorland paths, field and woodland tracks
GRADIENT: Undulating; one fairly short steep climb

Walk submitted by: Nigel Palmer

England

BAKEWELL continued

Pick of the Pubs

The Monsal Head Hotel ★★ 🛏 ♀
Monsal Head DE45 1NL ☎ 01629 640250 ▤ 01629 640815
e-mail: Christine@monsalhead.com
Dir: A6 from Bakewell towards Buxton. 1.5m to Ashford. Follow Monsal Head signs, B6465 for 1m

Set against a spectacular backdrop of hills and dales, the disused viaduct at Monsal Head has long been a familiar landmark in the Peak District. It even crops up on television from time to time, most notably in the drama series 'Peak Practice', which is filmed locally. Long before the era of TV, horses pulled guests and their luggage from the railway station up the steep incline to the hotel. The old stable is now a cosy bar and part of the hotel. One menu operates throughout the restaurant, bar and eating area, with specials such as chargrilled wild boar, braised ham shank, and roast chump of lamb, as well as halibut, monkfish, salmon and scallops from a good fishy choice. Small plates, grills, salads, omelettes and jacket potatoes extend the range, and eight real ales are always available. **OPEN:** 11.30-11 (Sun 12-10.30) Closed: 25 Dec **BAR MEALS:** L served all week 12-9.30 D served all week Av main course £8 **RESTAURANT:** L served Sat-Sun 12-9.30 D served all week 7-9.30 Av 3 course à la carte £18 **BREWERY/COMPANY:** Free House 🍺: Scottish Courage Theakston Old Peculier, Timothy Taylor Landlord, Whim Hartington IPA, Abbeydale Moonshine. ♀: 15 **FACILITIES:** Children welcome Garden Dogs allowed **NOTES:** Parking 20 **ROOMS:** 7 bedrooms 7 en suite 1 family room s£40 d£45

BAMFORD
Map 16 SK28

Pick of the Pubs

Yorkshire Bridge Inn ★★ 🛏
Ashopton Rd S33 0AZ ☎ 01433 651361 ▤ 01433 651361
e-mail: mr@ybridge.force9.co.uk
See Pub Walk on page 117
See Pick of the Pubs on opposite page

BEELEY
Map 16 SK26

Pick of the Pubs

The Devonshire Arms 🛏 ♀
The Square DE4 2NR ☎ 01629 733259 ▤ 01629 733259
e-mail: jagrosvenor@devonshirearmsbeeley.co.uk
See Pick of the Pubs on page 120

BIRCHOVER
Map 16 SK26

Pick of the Pubs

The Druid Inn 🛏
Main St DE4 2BL ☎ 01629 650302 ▤ 01629 650559
e-mail: mail@druidinnbirchover.co.uk
Dir: From A6 between Matlock & Bakewell take B5056, signed Ashbourne.Take 2nd L to Birchover
This ivy-covered free house stands in a quiet village above Darley Dale, close to the edge of the Peak District National Park. The nearby caves, canopies and terracing at Row Tor Rocks were supposedly once inhabited by druids. In fact, most of these curious carvings were carried out in the 19th century by a delightfully eccentric local vicar, the Rev Thomas Eyres. A large two storey extension supplements the narrow bar with its open fire and blackboard menus, and there's a terrace garden for alfresco summer dining. The eclectic menu has long been popular with the pub's faithful clientele. You might start with spicy lamb meatballs, deep-fried Brie with redcurrant dip or salmon, cod and prawn fishcakes. Follow these with dishes such as roast Barbary duck breast with orange, honey and grape sauce, chicken tikka masala or Derbyshire beef and vegetable stew with herb dumplings. Puddings include warm Bakewell pudding and apple and marzipan torte. **OPEN:** 12-3 7-11 Closed: 25/26 Dec **BAR MEALS:** L served all week 12-2 D served all week 7-8.45 Av main course £8.90 **RESTAURANT:** L served all week 12-2 D served all week 7-8.45 **BREWERY/COMPANY:** Free House 🍺: Marstons Pedigree, Druid Bitter. **FACILITIES:** Children welcome Garden: Terraced Area **NOTES:** Parking 36

BIRCH VALE
Map 16 SK08

Pick of the Pubs

The Waltzing Weasel Inn
New Mills Rd SK22 1BT ☎ 01663 743402 ▤ 01663 743402
e-mail: w-weasel@zen.co.uk
Dir: W from M1 at Chesterfield
Set within the heart of the Peak District Hills, this traditional country inn is beloved of walkers and business people alike - no music or machines and no mobile phones permitted. Country antiques are a feature of the bar, while from the garden and mullion-windowed restaurant there are dramatic views of Kinder Scout. Solidly English bar menus are supplemented by dishes inspired by the owners' love of Italy. Regulars include fish of the day, game in season and Peak Pie (a bar menu speciality comprising meat, game, mushrooms and red wine topped with puff pastry), and there's always at least one hearty peasant stew or casserole. Fantasia Italiana is a selection of Italian delights which can be arranged as a vegetarian option, with others including torta peperonata or Moroccan vegetable casserole. On Sunday only, traditional roast beef with Yorkshire pudding is served.
OPEN: 12-3 6-11 (Sun 12-3, 6-10.30) **BAR MEALS:** L served Mon-Sun 12-2 D served Mon-Sun 7-9.30 Av main course £10 **RESTAURANT:** L served Mon-Sun 12-2 D served Mon-Sun 7-9 Av 3 course à la carte £25.50 **BREWERY/COMPANY:** Free House 🍺: Marston's Best & Pedigree, Timothy Taylor Landlord, Camerons Strongarm. **FACILITIES:** Garden: Large patio, lawn shrubbery Dogs allowed Water & Toys **NOTES:** Parking 42

Open: 11-11.
Bar Meals: L served all week 12-2,
D served all week 6-9.
Av cost main course £6.95
RESTAURANT: L served all week 12-2,
D served all week 6-9.30.
BREWERY/COMPANY:
Free House.
🍺: Black Sheep, Theakston Best & Old
Peculier, Stones, Worthington
Creamflow.
FACILITIES: Dogs allowed, Children
welcome, Garden - Walled courtyard.
NOTES: Parking 40
ROOMS: 14 en suite from s£45 d£60

Yorkshire Bridge Inn

A bagful of awards have been handed out to 'The Bridge' in recent years, not least the third place in Pub Garden of the Year. Still, you'd expect nothing less in this pristine part of the countryside, where the pub nestles in close to the famous Ladybower reservoir, scene of the Dambusters' rehearsals before their dramatic raid.

★★ 🐾
Ashopton Road, Bamford, Hope
Valley, S33 0AZ
☎ 01433 651361 📠 01433 651361
📧 mr@ybridge.force9.co.uk
Dir: A57 from M1, L onto A6013,
pub 1m on R.

Luckily, these dams are still in place, creating a majestic series of reservoirs that provide gorgeous views for motorist and rambler alike. In the summer, you'll want to make use of the courtyard and beer garden, while in more inclement weather the bars provide a cosy sanctuary. Whether inside or out, you'll appreciate the well stocked bar and the priority given to the real ales such as Black Sheep or Old Peculier. Food is available in the bar and dining room and starters can range from tandoori chicken strips to giant Yorkshire puddings. Main courses are equally varied with dishes such as chicken Italiano, giant prawn cocktail or, from the specials menu, rack of lamb on a caramelised onion, redcurrant and rosemary sauce or fresh dressed crab salad. An impressive selection of sandwiches, filled jacket potatoes and salad platters will more than satisfy those just popping in for a bite, while vegetarians are also catered for with dishes such as the Mediterranean vegetable tart with provençale sauce. If you decide to stay and savour this picturesque area of England for more than a few hours, you'll be pleased to know that the rooms here are of as high a standard as everything else.

Open: 11-11
Bar Meals: L & D served all week
12-9.30. Av cost main course £7
RESTAURANT: L & D served all week
12-9.30. Av cost 3 course £12.50
BREWERY/COMPANY:
Free House.
🍺: Black Sheep Best & Special,
Theakston Old Peculier & XB,
Interbrew Bass, Marstons Pedigree
and Guest ales.
FACILITIES: Children welcome, Garden.
NOTES: Parking 120.

The Devonshire Arms

Built as three honey-coloured stone cottages in 1726 and converted into a popular coaching inn in 1747, The Devonshire Arms has a long history. John Grosvenor, the present owner, keeps a list of all the innkeepers since that date.

🐾 ♀

The Square, Beeley, nr Matlock,
DE4 2NR
☎ 01629 733259 📠 01629 733259
📧 jagrosvenor@
   devonshirearmsbeeley.co.uk
Dir: From A6 onto B6012 at Rowsley.

In July 1872 a tremendous thunderstorm made the road here quite impassable. History was repeated in August 1997, and a marked beam in the bar records the water level of the second flood. King Edward VII is rumoured to have come here to meet his mistress, Alice Keppel, and Charles Dickens was another frequent visitor.

Today, you'll be greeted by the same oak beams, stone flagged floors and winter fires. This civilised dining pub can be found in a picturesque village at the gateway to Chatsworth House, one of Britain's most palatial stately homes. The twisting lanes leading to it lie within the Peak District National Park, and the village of Beeley is a designated conservation area. Families, walkers and cyclists are always welcome, and motorists will appreciate the large car park. Meals are freshly cooked to order, and the extensive menu is also served on the patio in warm weather. Home-made soup and a

baguette make ideal snacks, but there's a serious list beginning with roasted pepper and Mozzarella terrine, and smoked chicken and bacon salad. A fine selection of main courses offers steak and ale pie, beef and horseradish suet pudding, and braised knuckle of lamb. The weekend begins on Friday evenings with an extensive choice of fish - sole fillets hollandaise, tuna Niçoise, and seared fillet of salmon with avocado salsa are typical - and continues with a leisurely Victorian breakfast menu between 10.00 and 12.00 on Sundays.

BRADWELL
Map 16 SK18

The Bowling Green
Smalldale S33 9JQ ☎ 01433 620450 📠 01433 620280
e-mail: bowlinggreen@barbox.net
Dir: Telephone for directions
Complete with black oak beams, spectacular views of the valley, and a history stretching back to 1577, the Bowling Green Inn prides itself on providing a traditional setting for hearty meals. Look out for cod, haddock, homemade pies, and a carvery.
OPEN: 12 -11 **BAR MEALS:** L served all week 12-2 D served all week 7-9 Av main course £6.50 **RESTAURANT:** L served all week 12-2 D served all week 7-9 Av 3 course à la carte £14
BREWERY/COMPANY: Free House ◀: Stones, Timothy Taylor Landlord, 1774. **FACILITIES:** Children welcome Children's licence Garden: large patioed area, spectacular views **NOTES:** Parking 80

BRASSINGTON
Map 16 SK25

Ye Olde Gate Inne 🕮
Well St DE4 4HJ ☎ 01629 540448 📠 01629 540448
Dir: 3m NW of Carsington Water
The inn was built in 1616 of local stone and salvaged Armada timbers, and has one or two supernatural residents. There is a huge inglenook fireplace with a range, and a smaller one in the snug. Connections are claimed with Bonnie Prince Charlie's rebellion. Menu includes cod and prawn crumble, BBQ chicken with Parma ham and cheese, cod and mussels provençale, or monkfish kebabs.
OPEN: 12-2.30 6-11 (Sat 12-3, 6-11 Sun 12-3, 7-10.30)
BAR MEALS: L served Tue-Sun 12-1.45 D served Tue-Sat 7-8.45 Av main course £8.50 **BREWERY/COMPANY:** W'hampton & Dudley ◀: Marstons Pedigree, Hobgoblin. **FACILITIES:** Garden: Food served outside. Quaint garden Dogs allowed Water provided
NOTES: Parking 20

BUXTON
Map 16 SK07

Bull i' th' Horn 🕮
Flagg SK17 9QQ ☎ 01298 83348
Dir: Telephone for directions
Reputedly a watering hole of Dick Turpin, and frequented by several ghosts, this charming medieval hall dates back to 1472 and has oak-panelled walls setting off a display of armour, swords and pikes. The banquet room serves 'authentic medieval fare' (whole suckling pig, whole beef joints) whilst daily specials could include butterfish steak in lime and coriander sauce, or fillet steak filled with Brie, wrapped in bacon and served with red wine and mushroom sauce. Beautiful location in the heart of the Dales.
OPEN: 9.30 **BAR MEALS:** L served all week 12 D served all week 9 Av main course £8 **RESTAURANT:** L served all week D served all week ◀: Robinsons Best Bitter, Feiidnner. **FACILITIES:** Children welcome Garden: Large open plan walled garden Dogs allowed Water **NOTES:** Parking 70

The Sun Inn 🍺
33 High St SK17 6HA ☎ 01298 23452
Dir: Telephone for directions
Former coaching inn dating back some 400 years, full of beams, boards, open fires and a wealth of memorabilia. Low ceilings, small private areas and a no-smoking dining room allow for flexibility. Traditional cask ales and 14 wines by the glass are served along with a wide choice of main courses, specials and snacks. Food is cooked to order and served with

fresh vegetables - typically, liver and onions, lemon chicken and vegetable chilli.
OPEN: 11.30-11 **BAR MEALS:** L served Mon-Sun 12-2.30 D served Mon-Sun 5.30-9 Av main course £7.50 ◀: Marstons Bitter, Marston Pedigree, Banks Bitter, Camerons Strongarm. 🍺: 14
FACILITIES: Children welcome

CASTLETON
Map 16 SK18

The Castle NEW
Castle St S33 8WG ☎ 01433 620578
Dir: Exit the M1 for Chesterfield and follow signs for Chatsworth House. After reaching Chatsworth House follow signs for Castleton. The Castle is in the centre of the village
The Castle in the heart of the Peak District has been a coaching inn since Charles II's reign. The four resident ghosts may go back that far too. Open fires ensure that entering on a chilly day after some brisk fell-walking is a heart-warming experience. Food includes beef and ale pie, ribbon pasta with spinach, tomato and ricotta sauce, lemon chicken, and sirloin steak with peppercorn sauce.
OPEN: 12 -11 (Sun 12-10.30) **RESTAURANT:** L served all week D served all week **BREWERY/COMPANY:** Vintage Inns ◀: Tetley Bitter, Cask Bass. **FACILITIES:** Garden: Patio and outdoor furniture **NOTES:** Parking 18

The George
Castle St S33 8QG ☎ 01433 620238 📠 01433 620886
Dir: Telephone for directions
The earliest known reference to this pub comes from the Domesday Book, and the building has been used as an alehouse since at least 1557. This distinguished heritage is guarded and extended by the current team who serve an imaginative international menu. Typical menu includes pan-fried seared salmon fillet, beer-battered cod, steak and kidney pie, lamb curry, and chicken breast with a julienne of leeks.
OPEN: 12-3 6-11 **BAR MEALS:** L served all week 12-2 D served all week 12-2 **RESTAURANT:** L served all week 12-2 D served all week 7-9 **BREWERY/COMPANY:** ◀: Black Sheep, Pedigree, Boddingtons **FACILITIES:** Children welcome Garden Dogs allowed **NOTES:** Parking 20

The Olde Nag's Head
Cross St S33 8WH ☎ 01433 620248 📠 01433 621501
Dir: A57 from Sheffield to Bamford, through Hope Valley, turn R
Grey-stone 17th-century coaching inn situated in the heart of the Peak District National Park, close to Chatsworth House, Haddon Hall and miles of wonderful walks. Cosy lounge bar with open fire and antiques and a Victorian restaurant. Tea room, weekend lunchtime carvery.
OPEN: 9-11 **BAR MEALS:** L served all week 9-9 D served all week Av main course £6.50 ◀: Timothy Taylor Landlord, Black Sheep, Marstons Pedigree, plus Guest. **FACILITIES:** Children welcome Dogs allowed **NOTES:** No credit cards

DARLEY ABBEY
Map 11 SK33

The Abbey
Darley St DE22 1DX ☎ 01332 558297
Dir: A38 onto A6 to Duffield Rd
The Abbey was built in 1147 as part of an enormous monastery, most of which was destroyed in the Dissolution. What is now the pub was probably the bakehouse or brewery originally, and has served as cottages and shops in its time. It still has a spiral stone staircase, beehive bread oven and,

continued

continued

DARLEY ABBEY continued

apparently, some ghostly visitations. Church pews and tapestries retain the period feel, and pub food includes sandwiches, home-cooked ham, and chicken curry.
OPEN: 11.30-2.30 6-11 (all day Sat-Sun) Closed: Dec 25
BAR MEALS: L served all week 12-2 Av main course £5.50
BREWERY/COMPANY: Samuel Smith 🍺: Samuel Smith Old Brewery Bitter, Samuel Smith Stout. **FACILITIES:** Children welcome Dogs allowed Water **NOTES:** Parking 20 **NOTES:** No credit cards

DERBY   Map 11 SK33

The Alexandra Hotel
203 Siddals Rd DE1 2QE ☎ 01332 293993 📠 01332 293993
Two-roomed hotel filled with railway memorabilia. Noted for its real ale (450 different brews on tap each year), range of malt whiskies, and friendly atmosphere. Traditional pub food.
OPEN: 11-11 (Sun 12-3, 7-10.30) Closed: Dec 25 **BAR MEALS:** L served Sun 12-2.30 Av main course £3.25
BREWERY/COMPANY: Tynemill Ltd 🍺: Castle Rock, Nottingham Gold, Barnsley Bitter, York Yorkshire Terrier. **FACILITIES:** Dogs allowed **NOTES:** Parking 12 **NOTES:** No credit cards

DOE LEA   Map 16 SK46

Hardwick Inn 🐾 ♀
Hardwick Park S44 5QJ ☎ 01246 850245 📠 01246 856365
e-mail: Batty@hardwickinn.co.uk
Dir: M1 J29 take A6175. 0.5m L (signed Stainsby/Hardwick Hall). After Stainsby, 2m L at staggered junction. Follow brown Tourist Board signs.

Built in 1607 from locally-quarried sandstone by the south gate of Hardwick Hall, the pub has been in the same family since 1928. All meals are freshly prepared, with a menu offering a choice of steaks and roasts. There'll probably be trout, salmon, cod, haddock, home-made pies, lasagne and an extensive specials board featuring casseroles, and fish dishes based on that day's delivery. Mixed grills, ploughman's, various salads and sandwiches are also available.
OPEN: 11.30-11 **BAR MEALS:** L & D served all week 11.30-9.30 Av main course £6 **RESTAURANT:** L served Tues- Sun 12-2 D served Tues-Sat 7-9 Av 3 course à la carte £16 Av 3 course fixed price £12.75
BREWERY/COMPANY: Free House 🍺: Scottish Courage Theakston Old Peculier & XB, Greene King Old Speckled Hen & Ruddles County, Marston's Pedigree. **FACILITIES:** Children welcome Garden: Lrg garden with pond and picnic table

DRONFIELD   Map 16 SK37

The Old Sidings
91 Chesterfield Rd S18 2XE ☎ 01246 410023 📠 01246 292202
e-mail: theoldsidings@aol.com
Unpretentious, stone-built tavern, situated just 30 feet from

the main Sheffield railway line. A must for railway buffs, it's full of railway paraphernalia.
OPEN: 12-11 (Sun 12-10.30) **BAR MEALS:** L served all week D served all week Av main course £5 **RESTAURANT:** L served Sun 12-5 D served all week 5.30-11 Av 3 course à la carte £9 Av 3 course fixed price £12.95 **BREWERY/COMPANY:** Free House 🍺: Burton Ale, Stones, Bass. **FACILITIES:** Dogs allowed **NOTES:** Parking 24

The Trout Inn
33 Valley Rd, Barlow S18 7SL ☎ 0114 2890893 📠 0114 2891284
e-mail: troutinn@t.f.h.co.uk
A few miles outside Chesterfield this quaint country pub is located at the gateway to the superb Peak District, renowned for its walking and splendid scenery. There is a pleasant, cosy atmosphere inside where you can sample the inn's straightforward menu. Among the main courses are chicken and vegetable pie, steak and mushroom pie, sausage and mash, trout special, grilled gammon steak topped with pineapple, and pan-seared salmon steak. Under new management.
OPEN: 12-3 6-11 **BAR MEALS:** L served all week 12-2.30 D served all week 6.30-9 Av main course £5.95 **RESTAURANT:** L served all week 12-2.30 D served all week 6.30-9 **BREWERY/COMPANY:** Free House 🍺: Interbrew Flowers IPA, Scottish Courage John Smith's, Coors Worthington. **FACILITIES:** Children welcome Garden: Patio with bench style tables **NOTES:** Parking 20

EYAM   Map 16 SK27

Miners Arms ♦♦♦♦ 🐾 ♀
Water Ln S32 5RG ☎ 01433 630853 📠 01433 639050
e-mail: minersarmseyam@aol.com
Dir: Off B6521, 5m S of Bakewell
Expect a warm welcome at this 17th-century inn and restaurant in the famous plague village of Eyam. During Roman times the village was an important centre for lead mining - hence the pub name. Supposedly, the inn is haunted by the ghosts of two girls who died in a fire on this site before the inn was built. Food is freshly prepared with the use of local produce and the seasonally-changing dining room menu is traditionally English in style with some French influences. Good bar meals include beer-battered haddock, guinea fowl casserole, baby halibut, pork fillet in apple and cider sauce, and crayfish in garlic butter.
OPEN: 12-11 **BAR MEALS:** L served all week 12-3 D served Mon-Sat 5.30-9 Av main course £11.50 **RESTAURANT:** L served Sun 12-3 D served Tue-Sat 6-9 Av 3 course à la carte £20
BREWERY/COMPANY: Free House 🍺: Interbrew Bass, Stones Bitter, Coors Worthington's Creamflow. ♀: 7
FACILITIES: Garden: 12 outdoor benches front & back Dogs allowed Water, food for overnight dogs **NOTES:** Parking 50
ROOMS: 7 bedrooms 7 en suite 2 family rooms s£30 d£60 no children overnight

FENNY BENTLEY   Map 16 SK14

The Coach and Horses Inn 🐾 ♀
DE6 1LB ☎ 01335 350246 📠 01335 350178
e-mail: coachnhorses@aol.com
Beautifully located on the edge of the Peak District National Park, this family-run 17th-century coaching inn is handy for Dovedale and the Tissington Trail. The cosy interior features stripped wood furniture, low beams and memorabilia. The pub is locally renowned for its well-kept ales and good home

continued

continued

cooking: daily-changing menus could include rib-eye steak garni, rabbit pie or spicy crab cakes with chilli dips.

OPEN: 11-11 **BAR MEALS:** L served all week 12 D served all week 9 Av main course £6.95 **RESTAURANT:** L served all week 12 D served all week 9 Av 3 course à la carte £13
BREWERY/COMPANY: Free House ◑: Marston's Pedigree, Timothy Taylor Landlord, Black Sheep Best, Harrington Bitter. ♀: 6
FACILITIES: Children welcome Garden: Gravelled area seats 36, water feature **NOTES:** Parking 24

FOOLOW   Map 16 SK17

The Bulls Head Inn ◆◆◆◆ 🐑
S32 5QR ☎ 01433 630873 ▯ 01433 631738
Dir: Just off A623, N of Stoney Middleton

Typically English, family-owned inn with flagged floors, roaring fires and an inglenook fireplace in the oak-panelled dining room. Set in a tiny conservation village in the heart of the Peak National Park it's a welcoming venue for 'walkers and their boots and dogs'. Fresh fish such as sea bass and monkfish tails - perhaps with lime and ginger cream - are seasonally supplemented by the likes of rabbit and prune casserole and beef fillet in brandied gravy.
OPEN: 12-3 6.30-11 **BAR MEALS:** L served Tue-Sun 12-2 D served Tue-Sat 6.30-9 Av main course £9 **RESTAURANT:** L served Tue-Sun 12-2 D served Tue-Sat 6.30-9 Av 3 course à la carte £18
BREWERY/COMPANY: Free House ◑: Black Sheep Best, Marston's Pedigree, Carlsberg-Tetley Bitter, Fuller's London Pride.
FACILITIES: Children welcome Garden: Dogs allowed Water
NOTES: Parking 20 **ROOMS:** 3 bedrooms 3 en suite s£40 d£60

FROGGATT   Map 16 SK27

Pick of the Pubs

The Chequers Inn ◆◆◆◆ 🐑 ♀
Froggatt Edge S32 3ZJ ☎ 01433 630231 ▯ 01433 631072
e-mail: info@chequers-froggatt.com
A traditional country pub in the Hope Valley, in the heart of the Peak National Park. Sixteenth century in origin, its Grade II listing embraces a horse mounting block, and the old stables where logs for the crackling winter fires are kept. The smart interior has a bistro feel, with rag-washed yellow walls, bare board floors, prints and comfortable furnishings. One of the five cosy en suite bedrooms has a four-poster. The dinner menu is European and British in character, and may include whole John Dory with orange butter, roast pigeon with apricot and chestnut jus, beef bourguignon, or fusilli pasta. A daily-changing blackboard menu offers specials and puddings, and game in season. Hearty sandwiches include Mediterranean vegetable with melted feta cheese, and Cajun chicken. Behind the pub, a footpath from the landscaped beer garden leads directly up through steep, wild woodland to a wonderful panorama from Froggatt Edge.
OPEN: 12-3 6-11 (Open all day Sat & Sun) Closed: 25 Dec
BAR MEALS: L served all week 12-2 D served all week 6-9.30
BREWERY/COMPANY: Free House ◑: Charles Wells Bombardier Premium Bitter, Green King IPA, Scottish Courage Theakston. ♀: 8 **FACILITIES:** Garden: Private woodland garden seating **NOTES:** Parking 45 **ROOMS:** 5 bedrooms 5 en suite s£50 d£50 no children overnight

---

GREAT HUCKLOW   Map 16 SK17

The Queen Anne ◆◆◆ 🐑 ♀
Great Hucklow, nr Tideswell SK17 8RF ☎ 01298 871246
e-mail: malcom_hutton@bigfoot.com
Dir: A623 turn off at Anchor pub toward Bradwell, 2nd R to Great Hucklow A warm welcome awaits at this traditional country freehouse with its log fires, good food, and an ever-changing range of cask ales. The inn dates from 1621, and its comfortable en suite bedrooms make an ideal base for exploring the spectacular Peak District National Park. Bar food ranges from freshly-made sandwiches to grills, and includes favourites like steak and ale pie, beef stew and Yorkshire pudding, and Mediterranean vegetable lasagna.
OPEN: 12-3 (except Mon & Wed) 6-11 (Sat 11.30-11, Sun 7-10.30)
BAR MEALS: L served Mon-Sun 12-2 D served Mon-Sun 6.30-8.30 Av main course £5.50 **BREWERY/COMPANY:** Free House ◑: Mansfield Cask Ale, Barnsley Bitter, Storm Ale Force, Kelman Islands. ♀: 7 **FACILITIES:** Children welcome Garden: Lawn overlooking the hills Dogs allowed **NOTES:** Parking 30 **ROOMS:** 2 bedrooms 2 en suite s£35 d£55

> **Stars or Diamonds after the ROOMS information at the end of an entry denotes accommodation that has been inspected by an organisation other than the AA, eg the RAC, VisitBritain, VisitScotland or WTB.**

GRINDLEFORD   Map 16 SK27

Pick of the Pubs

The Maynard Arms ★★★ 🏨
Main Rd S32 2HE ☎ 01433 630321 🖹 01433 630445
e-mail: info@maynardarms.co.uk
Dir: *From M1 take A619 into Chesterfield, then onto Baslow. A623 to Calver, R into Grindleford*
Situated at the heart of the Peak District National Park, this fine 1898 coaching inn overlooks the village and the Derwent Valley beyond. During the 1950s and 60s it frequently accommodated touring Australian cricket teams. These days the pub has up-to-the minute interior design, and in both the Longshore Bar and Padley Restaurant, the menus show a confidently-contemporary approach. The former lists large, filled home-made Yorkshire puddings, all-day breakfast, and fish and chips, while dishes from the restaurant menu include braised oxtail or seared venison steak. Typical daily specials are local rabbit and leek pie or grilled sea bass with roasted Mediterranean vegetables. In addition to the original Bakewell pudding and custard, favourite desserts are orange-flavoured bread and butter pudding and fruit crumbles. The inn is set in immaculately-kept grounds, and offers accommodation and conference facilities.
OPEN: 11-3 5.30-11 (Sun 12-10.30) **BAR MEALS:** L served all week 12-2 D served all week 6-9.30 Av main course £5.95 **RESTAURANT:** L served Sun-Fri 12-2 D served all week 7-9.30 Av 3 course fixed price £22.40 **BREWERY/COMPANY:** Free House 🍺: Interbrew Boddingtons Bitter, Greene King Old Speckled Hen, Marston's Pedigree, Timothy Taylor Landlord. **FACILITIES:** Children welcome Children's licence Garden: Well kept gardens **NOTES:** Parking 60 **ROOMS:** 10 bedrooms 10 en suite 2 family rooms s£69 d£79

HASSOP   Map 16 SK27

Eyre Arms 🏨 ♀
DE45 1NS ☎ 01629 640390
Dir: *Take the A6 to Bakewell, then the A619 towards Sheffield, after 0.5m turn onto the B6001 to Hathersage & Hassop*
This 17th-century coaching inn, just a short drive north of Bakewell, is associated with the Civil War and has its own Cavalier ghost. Unaltered since the 1950s, it's a traditional pub with oak pews, beams, old photographs and maps creating a cosy atmosphere. The garden, with eight tables around the fountain, overlooks rolling Peak District countryside and there are some lovely local walks. Typical dishes are rabbit pie, minted lamb banquet, halibut steak with orange and basil sauce, braised pheasant in Madeira, and rainbow trout.
OPEN: 11.30-3 6.30-11 (Nov-March eve open from 7pm) Closed: 25 Dec **BAR MEALS:** L served all week 12-2 D served all week 6.30-9 Av main course £8 **BREWERY/COMPANY:** Free House 🍺: Marston's Pedigree, Scottish Courage John Smiths, Black Sheep Special. **FACILITIES:** Garden **NOTES:** Parking 20

HATHERSAGE   Map 16 SK28

Millstone Inn ♦♦♦♦ ♀
Sheffield Rd S32 1DA ☎ 01433 650258 🖹 01433 651664
e-mail: jerry@millstone.fsbusiness.co.uk
Tastefully-furnished former coaching inn with superb views over the unspoiled Hope Valley, that has been reinvented for the 21st century. There's an open fire in the bar, and the relaxed, civilised restaurant makes extensive use of fresh local

produce. Start with mussel and saffron risotto or chilled gazpacho soup, before moving on to lamb and asparagus with couscous, baked gnocchi with Wensleydale, or monkfish and Pernod. Comfortable well-equipped bedrooms are suitable for both the business and leisure guest.
OPEN: 11.30-3 6-11 (Sat 11-11, Sun 12-10.30) **BAR MEALS:** L served all week 12-2 D served all week 6-9 **RESTAURANT:** D served all week 6.30-9.30 **BREWERY/COMPANY:** Free House 🍺: Timothy Taylor Landlord, Black Sheep, Guest Beers. **FACILITIES:** Children welcome Garden **NOTES:** Parking 50 **ROOMS:** 7 bedrooms 7 en suite

The Plough Inn ♦♦♦♦ 🏨 ♀
Leadmill Bridge S32 1BA
☎ 01433 650319 & 650180 🖹 01433 651049
e-mail: theploughinn@leadmillbridgehathersage.co.uk

Situated in nine acres of its own grounds by the meandering River Derwent, this 17th-century stone-built inn was originally a farmstead. The public rooms are charming, with plenty of exposed beams and brickwork. Dishes range from pub favourites (home-made pies, scampi and chips) to imaginative creations such as Indian spiced monkfish with Bombay potatoes or honey-grilled chicken with sage and onion muffins, smoked bacon and green tomato chutney.
OPEN: 11-11 Closed: Dec 25 **BAR MEALS:** L served all week 11.30-2.30 D served all week 6.30-9.30 Av main course £12.95 **RESTAURANT:** L served all week 11.30-2.30 D served all week 6.30-9.30 **BREWERY/COMPANY:** Free House 🍺: Theakstons Old Peculier, Batemans, Adnams Bitter, Smiles Best. ♀: 8 **FACILITIES:** Children welcome Garden **NOTES:** Parking 50 **ROOMS:** 5 bedrooms 5 en suite no children overnight

---

HAYFIELD   Map 16 SK08

The Sportsman
Kinder Rd SK22 2LE ☎ 01663 741565
Dir: *Hayfield is 5m S of Glossop on A624*
Standing in the glorious Peak District, this comfortable, family-run inn is an obvious watering hole for those tackling the popular Kinder Scout Trail, which runs out of Hayfield village centre towards Kinder Scout. Wholesome home-cooked food and hand-pulled beers are available in the traditional bar, with its warming log fires and welcoming atmosphere. Expect Cumberland casserole, Thai style chicken, fresh plaice grilled in butter, Somerset pork chops with apples casseroled with herbs, and vegetable bourguignon among the range of blackboard dishes.
OPEN: 12-3 7-11 Closed: 1wk Mar/Oct **BAR MEALS:** L served Tue-Sun 12-2 D served Mon-Sat 7-9 Av main course £8 **RESTAURANT:** L served Tue-Sun 12-2 D served Mon-Sat 7-9 Av 3 course à la carte £12.50 **BREWERY/COMPANY:** Thwaites 🍺: Thwaites Bitter & Reward, Daniels Hammer. **FACILITIES:** Garden Dogs allowed Water bowl **NOTES:** Parking 3

continued

HOGNASTON
Map 16 SK25

Pick of the Pubs

The Red Lion Inn
Main St DE6 1PR ☎ 01335 370396 ▤ 01335 372145
e-mail: lionrouge@msn.com
Dir: M1 J25 take A52 towards Derby & Ashbourne. Hognaston on
B5035

A traditional pub atmosphere is retained at this 17th-century country inn, with its beamed ceilings and open fireplaces, yet it serves the kind of food you'd expect in a restaurant. The owners maintain a value for money philosophy, offering a good choice of dishes from an ever-changing blackboard menu. Typical of the range are home-made soup with warm bread, goats' cheese and herb bruschetta salad, flash-fried lamb's liver with crispy bacon and mashed potato, and cod kebabs coated in Thai ginger. The Red Lion is located in the main street of a small village, surrounded by attractive countryside, so it is popular with walkers who stop off for lunch or use the inn as a base for exploring the nearby Peak District National Park.
OPEN: 12-3 6-11 **BAR MEALS:** L served Tue-Sun 12-2 D
served Mon-Sat 6.30-9 Av main course £8.95 **RESTAURANT:** L
served Tue-Sun 12-2 D served Mon-Sat 6.30-9 Av 3 course à la
carte £17.85 **BREWERY/COMPANY:** Free House ●: Greene
King Old Speckled Hen, Interbrew Bass, Worthington's Creamflow,
Marston's Pedigree. **NOTES:** Parking 30

HOPE
Map 16 SK18

Cheshire Cheese Inn ♀
Edale Rd S33 6ZF ☎ 01433 620381 ▤ 01433 620411
e-mail: cheshire.cheese@barbox.net
Dir: On A6187 between Sheffield & Chapel-en-le-Frith
In the heart of the Peak District, close to the Pennine Way, this 16th-century inn offers a traditional pub experience in wonderful surroundings. It's on the old salt route, and payment for lodging in those days was made in cheese, hence the name. Expect real ales and home-cooked food such as lambs' liver and smoked bacon on a bed of mash, home-made steak pie, or grilled tuna steak in a garlic and tomato sauce. Bar snacks include giant filled Yorkshire puddings.
OPEN: 12-3 6.30-11 (all day Sat) **BAR MEALS:** L served all week
12-2 D served all week 6.30-9 **RESTAURANT:** L served all week 12-2
D served all week 6.30-9 Av 3 course à la carte £14
BREWERY/COMPANY: Free House ●: Barnsley Bitter,
Wentworthy Pale Ale, Black Sheep Best, Timothy Taylor Landlord.
♀: 13 **FACILITIES:** Garden Dogs allowed Water **NOTES:** Parking
8

LITTON
Map 16 SK17

Red Lion Inn
SK17 8QU ☎ 01298 871458 ▤ 01298 871458
e-mail: redlioninn@littonvillage.fsnet.co.uk
Dir: just off the A623 Chesterfield to Stockport rd 1m E of Tideswell
Overlooking the village green, a 17th-century pub where in summer visitors can enjoy a meal under the trees. Many local walks begin and end here, and it is therefore very popular with hikers. Indoors it's all beams and log fires in cosy rooms, where favourite dishes include garlic and rosemary lamb, rabbit stew, bobotie, steak and ale pie, and sausage and mash.
OPEN: 12-3 6-11 (Fri-Sun 11-11) **BAR MEALS:** L served all week
12-2 D served Sat 6-8.30 Av main course £6.25
BREWERY/COMPANY: Free House ●: Jennings Bitter, Barnsley
Bitter, Shepherd Neame Spitfire, Black Sheep Best.
FACILITIES: Garden: Four picnic tables on village green Dogs
allowed Water bowl, Dog chews

LONGSHAW
Map 16 SK27

Fox House ♀ NEW
S11 7TY
Dir: Leave M1 at J29 and follow signs for Chesterfield. Travel towards
Baslow & Bakefield. At Baslow roundabout turn right on to A621 towards
Sheffield, turn left after 5 miles on to B6054 and head towards Castleton.
The pub is at junction of B6954/A625
A delightfully original 17th-century coaching inn, and at 1,132 feet above sea level, one of the highest pubs in Britain. Assuming that at such a height they were safe from the law, wagon drivers used to drink here during the small hours, but local magistrates naturally took a dim view of such behaviour. A simple menu lists rib-eye steak béarnaise, hunter's chicken, ham hock with creamy wholegrain mustard sauce, Cajun chicken on bow-tie pasta, and sea bass.
OPEN: 12 -11 (Sun 12-10.30) **RESTAURANT:** L served all week D
served all week Av 3 course à la carte £16
BREWERY/COMPANY: Vintage Inns ●: Tetley Bitter, Cask Bass.
♀: 16 **FACILITIES:** Garden Patio area **NOTES:** Parking 80

MATLOCK
Map 16 SK35

The Red Lion ◆◆◆◆ NEW
65 Matlock Green DE4 3BT ☎ 01629 584888
Dir: From Chesterfield, A632 into Matlock, on R of road just before J of
A615
This friendly, family-run freehouse makes a good base for exploring local attractions like Chatsworth House, Carsington Water and Dovedale. Spectacular walks in the local countryside will help to work up an appetite for bar lunches, steaks and a wide selection of home-cooked meals. In the winter months, open fires burn in the lounge and games room, whilst there's a boules area in the garden for warmer days.
OPEN: 11-11 **BAR MEALS:** L served Tue-Fri, Sun 12-9 D served
Tue-Sun 12-9 Av main course £6 **RESTAURANT:** L served Tue-Fri,
Sun 12-2 D served Tue-Sat 7-9 Av 3 course à la carte £15 ●: Scottish
Courage Courage Directors, John Smiths & Theakstons Bitter, Maston's
Pedigree, Guest Ale. **FACILITIES:** Garden: Small, seating area
NOTES: Parking 20 **ROOMS:** 6 bedrooms 6 en suite 1 family
rooms s£25 d£50 no children overnight

The White Lion Inn
195 Starkholmes Rd DE4 5JA ☎ 01629 582511 ▦ 01629 582511
e-mail: info@whitelion-matlock.com
Dir: Telephone for directions

Right in the heart of the Peak District, with spectacular views over Matlock Bath, this 18th-century inn is the ideal venue for a relaxing break. Close to many beautiful dales and historic buildings, it makes a good starting point. Typical dishes are chargrilled fillet medallions of ostrich, wild mushroom risotto, venison fillet with fondant potatoe, marinated free-range Norfolk duck breast, and Aberdeen Angus steak. Ragout of mushrooms and baked goats' cheese feature among the appetising starters.
OPEN: 12-3 5-11 (All day Sat-Sun) **BAR MEALS:** L served all week 12-2 D served Mon-Sat 7-9.30 Av main course £7 **RESTAURANT:** L served all week 12-2 D served Mon-Sat 7-9.30 Av 3 course à la carte £25 **BREWERY/COMPANY:** Burtonwood ◀: Scottish Courage John Smiths, Marston's Pedigree plus Guest ales.
FACILITIES: Garden: Facing over Matlock bath, large boules pitch Dogs allowed Water **NOTES:** Parking 50

MELBOURNE   Map 11 SK32

Hardinge Arms 🐷 ♈
54-56 Main St, Kings Newton DE73 1BX ☎ 01332 865892
Handy for Donnington and Midlands Airports. Smart lounge area, children welcome, chalet-style bedrooms.
OPEN: 12-2.30 6-11 (Sun 12-9) **BAR MEALS:** L served Tues-Sun 12-2 D served Tues-Sun 6-9 Av main course £5.95 **RESTAURANT:** L served Tues-Sun 12-2 D served Tues-Sun 6-9 Av 3 course à la carte £11.95 ◀: Interbrew Bass. **FACILITIES:** Children welcome Garden: Patio, food served outside **NOTES:** Parking 80

RIPLEY   Map 16 SK35

The Moss Cottage 🐷
Nottingham Rd DE5 3JT ☎ 01773 742555 ▦ 01773 741063
This red-brick freehouse specialises in carvery dishes, with four roast joints each day. The Moss Cottage also offers regular 'two for the price of one' weekday meals, as well as blackboard specials and a selection of home-made puddings. Expect popular menu choices like prawn cocktail or mushroom dippers; ham, egg and chips; liver and onions; or battered haddock. Hot puddings include rhubarb crumble and chocolate fudge cake.
OPEN: 12-3 6-11 (All day wkds & BHS) **BAR MEALS:** L served all week 12-2.15 D served Mon-Sat 6-9 Av main course £5 **RESTAURANT:** L served all week 12-2.15 D served Mon-Sat 6-9 Av 3 course à la carte £10 **BREWERY/COMPANY:** Free House ◀: Interbrew Bass, Coors Worthington's 1744 & Worthington's, Shepherd Neame. **NOTES:** Parking 52

ROWSLEY   Map 16 SK26

The Grouse & Claret ♈
Station Rd DE4 2EB ☎ 01629 733233 ▦ 01629 733010
Dir: On A6 between Matlock & Bakewell
Situated in the heart of the Peak District, this refurbished pub is handy for touring the area. Several historic towns are close by, and Haddon Hall and Chatsworth House are only a few minutes' drive away. The name of the pub is taken from a kind of fishing fly, and the pub is very popular with local fly fishermen. Appetising menu features such perennial favourites as liver and sausage sizzler, Thai prawns, various pies and traditional Sunday roast.
OPEN: 11-11 (Sun 12-10.30) **BAR MEALS:** L served all week 12-9 D served all week **RESTAURANT:** L served all week 12-9 D served all week **BREWERY/COMPANY:** W'hampton & Dudley ◀: Marston's Pedigree, Mansfield Cask, Original, Bank's.
FACILITIES: Children welcome Garden: Food served outside, great views **NOTES:** Parking 60

SHARDLOW   Map 11 SK43

The Old Crown
Cavendish Bridge DE72 2HL ☎ 01332 792392
Dir: M1 J24 take A6 towards Derby turn L before river bridge into Shardlow
This bustling 17th-century pub stands by the old A6 next to the River Trent, over which the former toll bridge used to stand until washed away during the 1947 floods. Convicts en route to the Assizes were once held here. In addition to the comprehensive range of light meals, potato jackets, freshly-baked baguettes and sandwiches, customers can tuck into specials such as champagne salmon, lamb parcels, rabbit in red wine, game pie and Stilton chicken.
OPEN: 11.30-3 5-11 (Sun 12-5, 7-10.30) 25-26 & 31 Dec closed evenings **BAR MEALS:** L served all week 12-2 Av main course £6.95 **BREWERY/COMPANY:** Free House ◀: Marston's Pedigree, Interbrew Bass, Batemans XXXB, Fuller's London Pride.
FACILITIES: Children welcome Garden Dogs allowed Water **NOTES:** Parking 25

TIDESWELL   Map 16 SK17

Three Stags' Heads
Wardlow Mires SK17 8RW ☎ 01298 872268
Dir: Junct of the A623 & B6465 on the Chesterfield/Stockport road
Unspoilt 300-year-old Derbyshire longhouse located in the limestone uplands of the northern Peak District. Grade II listed and designated by English Heritage as one of over 200 heritage pubs throughout the UK, it was the site of the last public gibbeting in England, and is home to a petrified cat! Well-kept real ales and hearty home-cooked food for ramblers, cyclists and locals includes oxtail and chestnut stew, cottage pie, penne la sanchez, chicken chorizo, and game in season. No children under eight.
OPEN: Fri 7-11 Sat-Sun 12 noon-11pm Closed: Mon-Thur
BAR MEALS: L served Sat-Sun 12.30-3 D served Fri-Sun 7.30-9.30 Av main course £8.50 **BREWERY/COMPANY:** Free House ◀: Abbeydale Matins, Absolution, Black Lurcher. **FACILITIES:** Dogs allowed **NOTES:** Parking 14 No credit cards

England

WARDLOW
Map 16 SK17

The Bull's Head at Wardlow 🛏️ ♀
SK17 8RP ☎ 01298 871431

For over 300 years this pub has stood in the heart of the Peak National Park, adjacent to one of the country's oldest drovers' routes dating back to the Iron Age. Largely unaltered within, it is adorned with antique prints, clocks, coach lamps, brass and copperware. Locally famous for its chargrilled steaks which share a menu with steak and kidney and cottage pies, seafood mornay and large fillets of cod and halibut.
OPEN: 11.30-3 6.30-11 **BAR MEALS:** L served Sat-Sun 11.30-3 D served all week 6.30-9.30 **RESTAURANT:** L served Sat-Sun 11.30-3 D served all week 6.30-9.30 **BREWERY/COMPANY:** Free House 🍺: Scottish Courage John Smith's, Carlsberg-Tetley Tetley's Smooth. **FACILITIES:** Children welcome Garden: Grassed area, tables, seating Dogs allowed Water **NOTES:** Parking 50 No credit cards

DEVON

ASHBURTON
Map 03 SX77

Pick of the Pubs

The Rising Sun ♦♦♦♦ 🛏️ ♀
Woodland TQ13 7JT ☎ 01364 652544 📠 01364 653628
e-mail: mail@risingsunwoodland.co.uk
Dir: E of Ashburton from the A38 take lane signed to Woodland and Denbury, pub is on the L approx 1.5m

Standing in an isolated spot overlooking the beautiful Devon countryside, and originally a drovers' inn on the road from Dartmoor to Newton Abbot market. The name comes from the sun rising directly opposite the main building, and the sunny south-facing terrace is a delightful place for summer eating and drinking. Following a fire which gutted it, the inn was rebuilt in keeping with its past, including rough plaster walls and exposed beams, and two cosy en suite bedrooms. Providing good food from fresh market produce is the passion of dedicated landlady Heather Humphries, and her menus are updated on a daily basis. Her commitment to quality is evident from blackboard starters like smoked duck breast with griottine cherries, and shallot tart with mixed leaves, and such mains as blackened salmon with citrus yogurt, Brixham bass with roasted tomatoes, lamb and apricot pie, and bubble and squeak with black pudding. Don't miss the wonderful cheese list.
OPEN: 11.45-3 6-11 Closed Mon lunch in Summer except BHS (Sun 12-3, 7-10.30) Closed: Dec 25 Mon in winter
BAR MEALS: L served Tue-Sun 12-2.15 D served Tue-Sun 6-9.15 Av main course £7.95 **RESTAURANT:** L served Tue-

continued

Sun 12-2.15 D served Tue-Sun 6-9.15 Av 3 course à la carte £16
BREWERY/COMPANY: Free House 🍺: Princetown Jail Ale, IPA, Teignworthy Reel Ale & changing Guest ales. ♀: 10 **FACILITIES:** Children welcome Garden: Patio and lawn with seating Dogs allowed Water **NOTES:** Parking 30 **ROOMS:** 2 bedrooms 2 en suite 1 family rooms s£30 d£55

AVONWICK
Map 03 SX75

The Avon Inn
TQ10 9NB ☎ 01364 73475
Dir: From A38 take South Brent turning, Avonwick signed on B3210

Unassuming 18th-century pub beside the River Avon, where local real ales and cider are served and there's a large garden with children's play area. Mark and Natasha Benfield took over the free house in 2002 and offer a wide-ranging menu. Evening selections include wild boar pâté with apple and cider chutney; beef fillet served on a rösti topped with local Beenleigh cheese with wild mushroom and port jus; and chicken breast stuffed with Cornish Yarg cheese and spinach with a tarragon brandy cream.
OPEN: 11.30-2.30 6-11 (Sun 12-2.30, 7-10.30) **BAR MEALS:** L served all week 12-2 D served Mon-Sat 6.30-9.30 **RESTAURANT:** L served all week 12-2 D served Mon-Sat 6.45-9.30 Av 3 course à la carte £20 **BREWERY/COMPANY:** Free House 🍺: Interbrew Bass, Guest Ale. **FACILITIES:** Children welcome Garden: Lrg garden, play area Dogs allowed Water **NOTES:** Parking 30

AXMOUTH
Map 04 SY29

The Ship Inn 🛏️ ♀
EX12 4AF ☎ 01297 21838 📠 01297 22403
e-mail: theshipinn@axmouth.com
Dir: From Lyme Regis take A3052 W towards Seaton/Sidmouth, then L onto B3172 to Axmouth

Creeper-clad family-run inn built soon after the original Ship burnt down on Christmas Day 1879. There's a new beer garden, with long views over the Axe estuary. The pub traces its landlords back to 1769: the current licensee, Paul Chapman, is the grandson of TV's first celebrity cook Fanny Craddock. Well kept real ales complement an extensive menu, with specials like half a pheasant, sea bass and ginger fishcakes, or creamy vegetable Kiev.
OPEN: 11-2.30 6-11 (open all day Sunday) **BAR MEALS:** L served all week 12-2 D served all week 7-9 Av main course £7 **RESTAURANT:** L served all week 12-2 D served all week 7-9 **BREWERY/COMPANY:** Pubmaster 🍺: Interbrew Bass, Otter Bitter & Youngs Special. **FACILITIES:** Children welcome Garden: Lawn and patio area Dogs allowed on leads, water **NOTES:** Parking 20

England

BANTHAM Map 03 SX64

Sloop Inn ◆◆◆ 🐑 ⚍

TQ7 3AJ ☎ 01548 560489 & 560215 📠 01548 561940
Dir: *From Kingsbridge take A379. At rndbt after Churchstow follow signs for Bantham*

Just a short stroll from the beach, this 16th-century smugglers' inn features oak beams, a flagstone floor, and a bar made from half a rowing boat. Fresh local produce, especially seafood, is to the fore in a comprehensive choice of blackboard dishes, likes steamed fillet of bass on sea salad, and pan-fried halibut with saffron and chives. From the regular menu expect basket meals, salads, steaks and sandwiches.

OPEN: 11-2.30 6-11 (Sun 12-2.30, 7-10.30) **BAR MEALS:** L served all week 12-2 D served all week 7-10 Av main course £9.50 **RESTAURANT:** L served all week 12-2 D served all week 7-10 Av 3 course à la carte £16 **BREWERY/COMPANY:** Free House ⚍: Palmers IPA, Bass, Palmers Copper Ale. **FACILITIES:** Children welcome Garden: Patio area with six tables Dogs allowed **NOTES:** Parking 10 **ROOMS:** 5 bedrooms 5 en suite 2 family rooms s£34 d£68

BEER Map 04 SY28

The Anchor Inn

Fore St EX12 3ET ☎ 01297 20386 📠 01297 24474
Dir: *Turn off A3052 following signs for Beer, continue through the village to slip road for Beach Anchor Inn on the R.*

One of Britain's best sited inns, the Anchor overlooks the tiny working harbour and beach in this popular little resort. Good summer cliff-top garden and an open-plan bar where you can enjoy pub snacks and excellent fresh fish. From mussels and oysters, the choice extends to red mullet with crab and herb crust and white wine sauce, and sea bass with creamy tarragon and orange sauce.

OPEN: 12-11 **BAR MEALS:** L served all week 12-3 D served all week 7-9 Av main course £7 **RESTAURANT:** L served all week 12-2 D served all week 7-9.30 Av 3 course à la carte £20 **BREWERY/COMPANY:** Old English Inns ⚍: Otter Bitter, Greene King IPA, and Abbot.
FACILITIES: Children welcome Garden Dogs allowed

BERE FERRERS Map 03 SX46

Old Plough Inn 🐑

PL20 7JL ☎ 01822 840358
Dir: *A386 from Plymouth, A390 from Tavistock*

Originally three cottages, dating from the 16th century, this inn has bags of character, with its old timbers and flagstones, which on closer inspection are revealed to be headstones. To the rear is a fine patio overlooking the River Tavey, and there are lovely walks in the Bere Valley on the doorstep. Dishes on offer range through fresh fish, crab, local pies, curries and stirfries.

OPEN: 12-3 7-11.30 **BAR MEALS:** L served all week 12-2 D served all week 7-9 Av main course £6 **RESTAURANT:** L served all week

12-2 D served all week 7-9 **BREWERY/COMPANY:** Free House ⚍: Sharp's Doom Bar & Sharp's Own, Interbrew Flowers.
FACILITIES: Children welcome Garden: Safe beer garden with river views Dogs allowed Water

BICKLEIGH Map 03 SS90

Fisherman's Cot ⚍

EX16 8RW ☎ 01884 855237 📠 01884 855241
e-mail: fishermanscot.bickleigh@eldridge-pope.co.uk

Well-appointed inn by Bickleigh Bridge over the River Exe with food all day and large beer garden just a short drive from Tiverton and Exmoor. The Waterside Bar is the place for snacks and afternoon tea while the restaurant incorporates carvery and à la carte menus. Sunday lunch is served, and champagne and smoked salmon breakfast optional. The cosy bedrooms are comfortable and well equipped.

OPEN: 11-11 (Sun 12-10.30) **BAR MEALS:** L served all week 12-9.30 D served all week Av main course £7.55 **RESTAURANT:** L served all week 12-10 D served all week
BREWERY/COMPANY: Eldridge Pope ⚍: Courage Best, Tetley Cask, John Smiths. **FACILITIES:** Children welcome Garden: Food served outside. Dogs allowed **NOTES:** Parking 100 **ROOMS:** 21 bedrooms 21 en suite s£59 d£74 (◆◆◆◆)

BIGBURY-ON-SEA Map 03 SX64

Pilchard Inn 🐑 ⚍

Burgh Island TQ7 4BG ☎ 01548 810514 📠 01548 810514
e-mail: reception@burghisland.com
Dir: *From A38 turn off to Modbury then follow signs to Bigbury & Burgh Island*

Atmospheric 14th-century white-walled pub located on a tiny tidal island reached only by giant sea tractor when the tide is in. Once frequented by pirates and smugglers, the island was still said to be haunted by the notorious Tom Crocker. The main catch off the island was pilchard - hence the name. Unsurprisingly, seafood figures large on the menu, from fish soup and crab sandwiches to seafood risotto.

OPEN: 11.30-11 (Sun 12-10.30) **BAR MEALS:** L served all week 12-2.30 D served Thur-Sat 7-9 Av main course £6.50
BREWERY/COMPANY: Free House ⚍: Interbrew Bass, Greene King Abbot Ale, Black Sheep Best, Wells Bombardier. ⚍: 7
FACILITIES: Children welcome Children's licence Garden: Terrace overlooking sea, beach Dogs allowed **NOTES:** Parking 100

 Pubs offering a good choice of fish on their menu

continued

The Cleave

Some of Devon's loveliest countryside can be seen on this picturesque walk in the glorious Dartmoor foothills.

From the pub, walk through the village, keeping the church to your left. Head up the hill to the war memorial and turn left, with the Old Rectory on your right. Make for a gate at the end of the road and enter the field. Turn left to a kissing gate leading into a wood. Keep ahead, cross a stream and follow the track up to a lane. Turn right and ascend a steep hill, passing Ellimore Farm before turning right at the top. Continue for about 250yds (229m) to join a path signposted to Foxworthy. Further on are signs for Hunter's Tor.

The path cuts through attractive woodland and between rocky outcrops before reaching Sharpitor. From here there are impressive views over Lustleigh Cleave towards Manaton and Hound Tor. Keep ahead on the path, with stunning views over a glorious Devon landscape. Hunter's Tor reveals glimpses of North Bovey, Moretonhampstead and Dartmoor. On a good day you might even spot the sea!

Keep to the right of Hunter's Tor, go through the gate and down the hill to the farm. Pass through a gate signposted 'Foxworthy Bridge' and follow a high-hedged path to reach a thatched house and some cottages. Turn left at the waymarked path for Hammerslake and Horsham and follow the path signs through woodland adjoining the River Bovey. When the path forks go left towards Hammerslake. Climb gently up through the valley, keeping right at the fork for Manaton via Water, then left at the sign for Lustleigh via Pethybridge.

At the next junction follow the bridle path for Lustleigh, ascending the hill to reach a gate at the top. Keep ahead between hedges to join a farm track and follow it to a lane. Turn right, then left after about 75yds (69m) into Pethybridge. Follow the road down to a lane marked 'unsuitable for heavy vehicles'. At the bottom of the hill turn right and then left at the next T junction, returning to the church and Lustleigh village centre.

THE CLEAVE, LUSTLEIGH
TQ13 9TJ
☎ 01647 277223

Directions: Off A382 between Bovey Tracy and Moretonhampstead 15th-century former Devon longhouse on the edge of Dartmoor. A cosy lounge bar comes complete with an inglenook fireplace, and there's a larger Victorian bar. Interesting food served.
Open: 11-3 6.30-11 (summer 11-11)
Closed: Mon Nov-Feb
Bar Meals: 12-2.30 6.30-9
Notes: Children welcome (books, crayons, games). Cottage-style garden. Parking.
(See page 142 for full entry)

DISTANCE: 5 miles (8km)
MAP: OS Explorer 110
TERRAIN: Valley, farmland and rocky outcrops
PATHS: Lanes, footpaths and bridleways
GRADIENT: Undulating. Several steep and gentle climbs

Walk submitted and checked by A Perring

BLACKAWTON
Map 03 SX85

Normandy Arms
Chapel St TQ9 7BN ☎ 01803 712316 ◨ 01803 712619
Dir: A381 from Totnes, L onto A3122, 1st R to Blackawton after Kingsbridge turning

Venture off the beaten track to find this 15th-century inn, re-named in honour of the Normandy Landings, for which training exercises took place on nearby Slapton Beach. The pub has interesting memorabilia from that period. Mussels and Torbay sole feature along with grilled steaks and meat pies.
OPEN: 12-2.30 6-11 Sun eve no food in winter **BAR MEALS:** L served all week 12-2 D served all week 7-9 Av main course £3.95
RESTAURANT: L served all week 12-2 D served all week 7-9 Av 3 course à la carte £14 **BREWERY/COMPANY:** Free House
◨: Blackawton Bitter, Marstons. **FACILITIES:** Children welcome Garden: beer garden, outdoor eating Dogs allowed **NOTES:** Parking 10

BRANSCOMBE
Map 04 SY18

The Fountain Head
EX12 3BG ☎ 01297 680359
Approximately 500 years old, and set among some of the oldest dated houses in Branscombe. Its small interior has flagstone floors and wood-panelling; outside are stools made from tree trunks, and a stream. The dining area was once the village forge and retains its central chimney. Representative dishes include no-nonsense steak and kidney pie and fresh battered cod. Beer comes from the local Branscombe Vale micro-brewery. Popular with hikers and their dogs.
OPEN: 11.30-3 6.30-11 **BAR MEALS:** L served all week 12-2 D served all week 7-9 Av main course £6 **BREWERY/COMPANY:** Free House ◨: Guest ales. **FACILITIES:** Children welcome Food served outside. Dogs allowed Water & biscuits provided **NOTES:** Parking 12

Pick of the Pubs

The Masons Arms ★★ ◷ ♀
EX12 3DJ ☎ 01297 680300 ◨ 01297 680500
e-mail: reception@masonsarms.co.uk
Dir: Turn off A3052 towards Branscombe, down hill, hotel at bottom of hill

Delightful 14th-century creeper-clad inn, formerly a cider house and well-known smugglers' haunt. It stands in the centre of picturesque Branscombe, which lies in a steep valley, deep in National Trust land and only a ten-minute stroll from the sea. Beyond the pretty front terrace is the charming bar with stone walls, ancient ships' beams, slate floors and a splendid open fireplace, used for spit-roasts on a weekly basis and including Sunday lunch. Popular bar food ranges from specials like venison casserole, and oven-roasted sea bass with a black bean sauce, to a tried-and-tested selection of sandwiches, ploughman's lunches and hot filled baguettes. In the Waterfall Restaurant, a separate fixed-price menu might feature brochette of langoustines, pan-fried tenderloin of pork medallions flamed in Pernod, and an orange Pavlova with Chantilly cream. Several beautiful bedrooms are split between the main building and neighbouring terraces of cottages; all are attractive and tastefully decorated. Conference/function room.
OPEN: 11-11 (winter 11-3, 6-11) Times vary, please phone
BAR MEALS: L served all week 12-2 D served all week 7-9 Av main course £9.95 **RESTAURANT:** D served all week 7-8.45 Av 3 course à la carte £25 Av 3 course fixed price £25
BREWERY/COMPANY: Free House ◨: Otter Ale, Masons Ale, Interbrew Bass, Guest Ales. ♀: 12 **FACILITIES:** Children welcome Garden: Walled terrace with seating for around 100 Dogs allowed Water **NOTES:** Parking 30 **ROOMS:** 22 bedrooms 19 en suite s£28 d£48

BRENDON
Map 03 SS74

Rockford Inn ◷ ♀
EX35 6PT ☎ 01598 741214 ◨ 01598 741265
e-mail: enquiries@therockfordinn.com

Situated within the spectacular Exmoor National Park, on the banks of the East Lyn River at Brendon, this traditional West Country pub is ideally placed for touring Devon and Somerset on foot or by car. Nearby is the spectacular Doone Valley, made famous by R D Blackmore's classic 19th-century novel Lorna Doone. Sample battered cod, home-made cottage pie or Lancashire hotpot at lunchtime. Alternatively, choose local trout, 8oz rump steak or chicken tikka masala from the evening menu.
OPEN: 12-3 6-11 (Sun 6.30-10.30) Tues Nov-Mar Closed eve
BAR MEALS: L served all week 12-2.30 D served all week 7-9 Av main course £6 **BREWERY/COMPANY:** Free House ◨: Cotleigh Barn Owl, Tawny, Greene King, Golden Arrow. **FACILITIES:** Children welcome Garden: Food served outside Dogs allowed Water **NOTES:** Parking 12

BROADHEMBURY
Map 03 ST10

Pick of the Pubs

Drewe Arms
EX14 3NF ☎ 01404 841267
Dir: A373 halfway between Cullompton and Honiton

Set in an archetypal thatched Devon village in sprawling unspoiled countryside handy for Dartmoor and the spectacular Devon coast, its striking mullioned windows and quaint old furniture lend the Drewe Arms its particular tasteful character. The best available West Country produce forms the basis of the daily menus that major in fresh fish. Expect on any one day to feast on pollack baked with Cheddar and cream or sea bream with orange and chilli. Steamed mussels with garlic and herbs, griddled sardines and smoked haddock and Stilton rarebit are all offered in two portion sizes - large and very large. Alongside seared scallops with rouille and turbot fillet with hollandaise, on the fixed-price dining menu might be venison tenderloin with wild mushroom sauce, followed by chocolate St Emilion. For more dedicated meat-eaters are rare beef and hot chicken baguettes and a Bookmaker's fillet steak with anchovy butter. Good house wines from around the world are all offered by the glass.
OPEN: 11-3 6-11 (Sun 12-3 only) Closed: Dec 25 & Dec 31
BAR MEALS: L served all week 12-2 D served Mon-Sat 7-10 Av main course £10.50 **RESTAURANT:** L served all week 12-2 D served Mon-Sat 7-10 Av 3 course à la carte £27
BREWERY/COMPANY: Free House ◨: Otter Ale, Otter Bitter, Otter Head, Otter Bright. **FACILITIES:** Children welcome Garden: outdoor eating, patio Dogs allowed Water

BROADHEMPSTON
Map 03 SX86

The Monks Retreat Inn ♀ NEW
The Square TQ9 6BN
Dir: *From Newton Abbot to Totnes, take right turn through Ippleden and follow signs for Broadhempston.*
Apparently a friendly ghost inhabits this inn - certainly it's the sort of place you'd want to linger in: the building (listed as of outstanding architectural interest) is full of fascinating features, including a panelled oak screen typical of ancient Devon houses. Sit by one of the cosy log fires and enjoy good beer, wine, or food including home-made soup, jacket potatoes, home-made quiche, seafood platter or (in the evening) grilled steaks.
OPEN: 12-2.30 6-11 (Sun 12-3, 7-10.30) **BAR MEALS:** L served Tue-Sun 12-2 D served Tue-Sun 6.30-9.30 Av main course £9.60
RESTAURANT: L served Tue-Sun 12-2 D served Tue-Sun 6.30-9.30 Av 3 course à la carte £21 **◀:** Bass, Buttcombe, Fosters. ♀: 7
FACILITIES: Children welcome Children's licence Dogs allowed
NOTES: Parking 2

BUCKFASTLEIGH
Map 03 SX76

Dartbridge Inn 🍽 ♀
Totnes Rd TQ11 0JR ☎ 01364 642214 ▤ 01364 643839
e-mail: dartbridge.buckfastleigh@oldenglishinns.co.uk
Dir: *Turn off A38 onto A384. Dartbridge Inn 200yds on L*
Renowned for its colourful floral displays, this beamed inn lies on the banks of the River Dart and is handy for the Buckfastleigh to Totnes steam railway, as well as Buckfast Abbey. A good range of food is available, from jacket potatoes to whale of cod. Steak and kidney pie, wild mushroom risotto, Dartington chicken and game casserole are also available.
OPEN: Open all day **BAR MEALS:** L served all week 12-2 D served all week 6.30-9 Av main course £8.95 **RESTAURANT:** L served all week 12-2 D served all week 7-9.30 Av 3 course à la carte £20.50 **BREWERY/COMPANY:** Old English Inns **◀:** Scottish Courage Courage Best & Directors, Wadworth 6X. ♀: 12
FACILITIES: Children welcome **NOTES:** Parking 100

BUCKLAND BREWER
Map 03 SS42

The Coach & Horses 🍽
EX39 5LU ☎ 01237 451395
A popular, thatched free house dating from the 13th century, and once the village courthouse. Set in lovely countryside close to the Tarka Trail. Beneath its heavily-beamed ceilings, locals and tourists gather around the inglenook fireplaces, or spill out onto the terrace and garden. Fresh food cooked to order has a good local reputation, including pan-fried skate wing, beef fillets in port and mushroom sauce, spinach and stilton filo parcels, and lamb in red wine.
OPEN: 12-3 7-11 (Sun 7-10.30) **BAR MEALS:** L served all week 12-2 D served all week 7-9.30 Av main course £8 **RESTAURANT:** L served all week 12-2 D served all week 7-9.30 Av 3 course à la carte £18 **BREWERY/COMPANY:** Free House **◀:** Fuller's London Pride, Bass, Worthingtons. **FACILITIES:** Children welcome Garden Dogs allowed, but not overnight in bedrooms **NOTES:** Parking 12

BUCKLAND MONACHORUM
Map 03 SX46

Drake Manor Inn 🍽 ♀
The Village PL20 7NA ☎ 01822 853892 ▤ 01822 853892
Dir: *Off A386 near Yelverton*
Mainly 16th-century inn nestling between the church and the stream, named after local resident Sir Francis Drake. Heavy beams and fireplaces with wood-burning stoves are still in

continued

evidence, and the pub is renowned for its pretty gardens and award-winning floral displays. Meals take in bar snacks and daily specials, with a home-made pie of the day and dishes like monkfish with stir-fried vegetables and oyster sauce, or braised lamb shank with redcurrant and rosemary.

OPEN: 11.30-2.30 6.30-11 (Sun 12-3, 7-10.30) **BAR MEALS:** L served all week 12-2 D served all week 7-10 **RESTAURANT:** L served all week 12-2 D served all week 7-10 Av 3 course à la carte £15 **BREWERY/COMPANY:** **◀:** Scottish Courage John Smiths & Courage Best, Interbrew Bass, Wadworth 6X, Greene King Abbott Ale. ♀: 7 **FACILITIES:** Children welcome Garden: Pretty cottage garden Dogs allowed Water **NOTES:** Parking 4

BUTTERLEIGH
Map 03 SS90

The Butterleigh Inn
EX15 1PN ☎ 01884 855407 ▤ 01884 855600
Dir: *3m from J 28 on the M5 turn R by The Manor Hotel in Cullompton and follow Butterleigh signs*
Tucked away in a sleepy village amid glorious countryside south of Tiverton, this 400-year-old pub is worth seeking out for its traditional atmosphere and excellent Cotleigh Brewery ales. Here you can relax in the homely bars with their comfortable furniture, open fires and time-honoured pub games. Local beef is a feature of the freshly made steak and ale pie, lasagne, Butterleigh burgers, chilli skins and Sunday roast.
OPEN: 12-2.30 6-11 **BAR MEALS:** L served all week 12-2 D served all week 7-9.45 Av main course £7.50 **BREWERY/COMPANY:** Free House **◀:** Cotleigh Tawny Ale, Barn Owl Bitter, O'Hanlans "Yellow Hammer". **FACILITIES:** Children welcome Garden: Seating available for 30 plus Dogs allowed **NOTES:** Parking 30

CADELEIGH
Map 03 SS90

Cadeleigh Arms
Cadeleigh EX16 8HP ☎ 01884 855238 ▤ 01884 855385
Dir: *Telephone for directions*
Part of a small community in the hills above the Exe valley, and known as the New Inn until it burnt down in 1892. The skittle alley was once a stable for racehorses, and the place is reputedly haunted. The bar snack menu offers filled baguettes, ham, egg and chips, and the Cadeleigh burger, while the full menu runs to mushroom Stroganoff, sirloin steak with chasseur sauce, and chicken breast in a creamy grain mustard sauce.
OPEN: 12-2.30 6-11 (Sat 12-11, Sun 12-10.30) **BAR MEALS:** L served all week 12-2 D served Tues-Sat 6.30-9 Av main course £7.95 **RESTAURANT:** L served all week 12-2 D served Tues-Sat 6.30-9 **BREWERY/COMPANY:** Free House **◀:** Cotleigh Tawny Bitter, Scottish Courage John Smith's, Whitbread Best Bitter, Fullers London Pride. **FACILITIES:** Children welcome Garden: Large pretty garden with views Dogs allowed **NOTES:** Parking 30

CHAGFORD
Map 03 SX78

Ring O'Bells ♀
44 The Square TQ13 8AH ☎ 01647 432466 📠 01647 432466
Dir: From Exeter take A30 to Whiddon Down Rdbt, take 1st L onto A382 to Mortonhampstead. After 3.5m to Easton Cross turn R signed to Chagford
Twice burnt down during its 500-year history, this traditional West Country inn is nevertheless still thriving. The area is especially popular as a base for walking expeditions and tours of Dartmoor. Daily-changing menus use local produce as often as possible, with pork and apple griddlecakes, Italian pancakes filled with meat Bolognaise, and herb-roasted farmhouse chicken, perhaps followed by golden syrup sponge pudding. Traditional bar dishes like jacket potatoes, home-cooked ham, and butcher's sausages also feature.
OPEN: 9-3 5-11 (Sun 9-3, 6-10.30) Closed: 2 weeks Mid June
BAR MEALS: L served all week 12-2 D served all week 6-9 Av main course £7.95 **RESTAURANT:** L served all week 12-2 D served Wed-Mon 6-9 **BREWERY/COMPANY:** Free House ◖: Butcombe Bitter, Exmoor Ale, Devon Cream, Hicks HSD-Cornish Bitter. ♀: 8
FACILITIES: Children welcome Garden: Walled courtyard with lawn & covered area Dogs allowed Very dog friendly Water and biscuits provided

The Sandy Park Inn 🐾 ♀
Sandy Park TQ13 8JW ☎ 01647 432236 📠 01647 432236
Dir: on A382 between Moretonhampstead and Whiddon Down

A 16th-century thatched inn within Dartmoor National Park. Nearby are the National Trust's Castle Drogo and, no smirking please, Piddledown. Jukeboxes, loud music and gaming machines are banned, so the chatter of locals enjoying their pints of Otter, Porkers Pride and Reel Ale is the dominant sound. The pub specialises in fresh fish dishes, with six usually available, including lemon sole, sea trout, halibut and giant prawns. Alternatives include rack of lamb, Gressingham duck breast, and home-made beef and Murphy's pie.
OPEN: 12-2.30 6.00-11 **BAR MEALS:** L served Tue-Sun 12-2 D served Tue-Sun 6.30-9 Av main course £9 **RESTAURANT:** L served Tue-Sun 12-2 D served Tue-Sun 6.30-9 **BREWERY/COMPANY:** Free House ◖: Otter Bitter, Butcombe Bitter, Wadworth 6X, Porkers Pride. ♀: 12 **FACILITIES:** Garden: Patio area with benches seats 24 Dogs allowed Water **NOTES:** Parking 6

Three Crowns Hotel ★★
High St TQ13 8AJ ☎ 01647 433444 & 433441 📠 01647 433117
This 13th-century inn is a fine example of Chagford's striking architecture. A shooting in the nearby churchyard of the 15th-century church is said to have given R D Blackmore inspiration for part of his classic novel Lorna Doone. Sturdy oak beams and a wonderful open fireplace enhance the inn's delightful surroundings. Expect best end lamb, pork Dijonnaise, salmon

steak, red mullet and mushroom, and fresh Brixham fish and chips, among a wide-ranging choice of favourite dishes.
OPEN: all day **BAR MEALS:** L served all week 12-2.30 D served all week 6-9.30 Av main course £9 **RESTAURANT:** L served all week D served all week 6-9.30 Av 3 course à la carte £25 Av fixed price £17.50 **BREWERY/COMPANY:** Free House ◖: Interbrew Flowers Original, Boddingtons, Bass, Whitbread. **FACILITIES:** Children welcome Children's licence Dogs allowed **NOTES:** Parking 20 **ROOMS:** 20 bedrooms 17 en suite 20 family rooms s£55 d£50

CHARDSTOCK
Map 04 ST30

The George Inn 🐾 ♀
EX13 7BX ☎ 01460 220241 📠 01460 221037
e-mail: infogeorgeinn@aol.com
Dir: A358 to Chard, then A358 toward Axminster, R at Tytherleigh
The George is over 700 years old, has graffiti from 1648 and was once the church school. Underneath is a sealed-off crypt. Two resident ghosts, one a parson, haunt the main entrance and restaurant. On offer are likely to be 15 daily specials, including 'legendary' fillet steak gateau with Stilton, wrapped in smoked bacon, and served with red wine jus, Chinese stir fry, vegetable kebabs and moules marinière. Also pasta, fish, vegetarian and ploughman's.
OPEN: 12-2.30 6-11 **BAR MEALS:** L served all week 12-2 D served all week 6-9 Av main course £7.50 **RESTAURANT:** L served all week 12-2 D served all week 6-9 **BREWERY/COMPANY:** Free House ◖: Otter Ale, Otter Bitter. **FACILITIES:** Children welcome Garden: Food served outside. Garden & courtyard Dogs allowed Water provided
NOTES: Parking 50

CHERITON BISHOP
Map 03 SX79

The Old Thatch Inn
EX6 6HJ ☎ 01647 24204 📠 01647 24584
e-mail: theoldthatchinn@aol.com
Dir: Take A30 from M5, about 10m take turn on L signed Cheriton Bishop
Old world charm and modern comforts are effectively combined at this listed inn, originally built as a coaching house and licensed as a pub as recently as 1974. Close by is Fingle Bridge, described by R D Blackmore as 'the finest scene in all England'. Meals range from light snacks to a choice of chargrilled steaks and chops, and popular pub fare like fish and chips, bangers and mash, and steak and Otter Ale pie.
OPEN: 11.30-3 6-11 Closed: 25 Dec **BAR MEALS:** L served all week 12-2 D served all week 7-9.30 Av main course £7.95 **RESTAURANT:** L served all week 12-2 D served all week 7-9.30 Av 3 course à la carte £17 **BREWERY/COMPANY:** Free House ◖: Branscombe Vale Branoc, Sharp's Own, Otter Ale, Skinners Figgy's Brew plus Guest beers. **FACILITIES:** Children welcome Garden **NOTES:** Parking 30

CHUDLEIGH KNIGHTON
Map 03 SX87

The Claycutters Arms
TQ13 0EY ☎ 01626 853345
Dir: Turn off the Devon Expressway at Chudleigh Knighton
Thatched village pub, originally three Quaker cottages, on the flanks of Dartmoor, complete with beams, an open fire and an abundance of hanging baskets in summer. Dishes range from home-made pigeon pie, wild boar sausages and cider apple sauce, to duck with leeks and port, and venison with honey and juniper.
OPEN: 11.30-3 5-11 Dec 25 closed for food **BAR MEALS:** L served all week 12-2.30 D served all week 6-9.30 Av main course £6.95

continued

continued

England

RESTAURANT: L served all week 12-2.30 D served all week 6-9.30 Av 3 course à la carte £15 **BREWERY/COMPANY:** Heavitree **📥:** Bass, Otter, Fullers London Pride. **FACILITIES:** Children welcome Garden Dogs allowed **NOTES:** Parking 60

CLEARBROOK
Map 03 SX56

The Skylark Inn 🐑
PL20 6JD ☎ 01822 853258
e-mail: sueandroger@skylarkinn.fsnet.co.uk
Dir: 5m North of Plymouth, just off the A386 to Tavistock Road
Attractive village inn set in Dartmoor National Park, with a beamed bar and large fireplace with wood-burning stove. A good area for cyclists and walkers, yet only 10 minutes from Plymouth. Good wholesome food is served from an extensive menu, with courses like roast beef and Yorkshire pudding, meatballs in sweet and spicy sauce, moussaka, Skylark mixed grill, chicken Dijonnaise, smokey bacon and leek bake, Scottish salmon fillet, mushroom Stroganoff, or lamb pie. Good dessert choices.
OPEN: 11.30-2.30 6-11 (Summer 11.30-3) **BAR MEALS:** L served all week 11.30-2.30 D served all week 6.30-9.30 Av main course £7
BREWERY/COMPANY: 📥: Interbrew Bass, Greene King Old Speckled Hen & Moorland Original, Scottish Courage Courage Best.
FACILITIES: Garden: Lrg lawn, patio, tables, chairs, benches Dogs allowed Water Bowls **NOTES:** Parking 16

CLYST HYDON
Map 03 ST00

Pick of the Pubs

The Five Bells Inn 🐑 ♟
EX15 2NT ☎ 01884 277288 📠 01884 277693
Dir: B3181 3m out of Cullompton, L to Clyst Hydon then R to Clyst St Lawrence. Pub on R
So called because of its close proximity to the village church, this inn was moved lock, stock and literally barrel to its present position - in a 16th-century Devon longhouse - after the vicar objected to its presence a century ago. Many of the old outbuildings have been incorporated into the thatched inn, and its careful modernisation has left the old world atmosphere intact. Far-reaching country views can be enjoyed from the front terrace and raised side garden, and a warm welcome awaits inside. Main menu and specials board meals are available in the carpeted open-plan bar, where choices include cut-to-order sandwiches, some rather lovely ploughman's style platters, a good selection of children's food and plenty of comforting dishes such as steak and chips, home made soup or courgettes provençale. An à la carte menu served in the restaurant offers home-cooked choices like fresh mussels in cider and cream, steak and kidney suet pudding or lamb shank with honey and rosemary.
OPEN: 11.30-3 6.30-11 Closed: Dec 26 & Jan 1
BAR MEALS: L served all week 12-2 D served all week 7-10
RESTAURANT: L served all week 12-2 D served all week 7-10
BREWERY/COMPANY: Free House 📥: Cotleigh Tawny Ale, Otter Bitter, O'Hanlon's Blakeley's. **FACILITIES:** Children welcome Garden: Large well kept award winning floral display Dogs allowed Water **NOTES:** Parking 40

COCKWOOD
Map 03 SX98

The Anchor Inn 🐑 ♟
EX6 8RA ☎ 01626 890203 📠 01626 890355
Dir: Off A379 between Dawlish & Starcross
Historic smugglers' inn set on the broad estuary of the River Exe, overlooking a landlocked harbour. The interior is dark and cosy with snug areas and two real fires. Seemingly endless, the menu specialises in fish and shellfish from the Exe, including 30 mussel, eight oyster and 13 scallop dishes, and seasonal fish such as mackerel, bass, John Dory, skate, sand soles and megrim. There's also a good choice of bar snacks.
OPEN: 11-11 (Sun 12-10.30) **BAR MEALS:** L served all week 12-3 D served all week 6.30-10 Av main course £5.95 **RESTAURANT:** L served all week 12-3 D served all week 6.30-10 Av 3 course à la carte £25 **BREWERY/COMPANY:** Heavitree 📥: Interbrew Bass & Flowers Original, Wadworth 6X, Fuller's London Pride, Marston's Pedigree. ♟: 10 **FACILITIES:** Garden: Patio, verandah, overlooks harbour Dogs allowed Water **NOTES:** Parking 15

COLEFORD
Map 03 SS70

Pick of the Pubs

The New Inn ♦♦♦♦ 🐑 ♟
EX17 5BZ ☎ 01363 84242 📠 01363 85044
e-mail: new-inn@reallyreal-group.com
Dir: From Exeter take A377, 1.5m after Crediton turn L for Coleford. Pub in 1.5m

This 13th-century listed free house is beautifully situated in terraced gardens beside the Cole Brook, in the conservation village of Coleford. The building features whitewashed cob walls and original beams under an historic thatched roof, and the ancient bar blends successfully with extensions created from the old barns. The bars and restaurant are full of old-world charm, and the walls and ceilings are festooned with plates, tankards, copper and horse brasses. Guests are welcomed by crackling log fires - and by Captain, the pub's resident parrot! The inn has been tastefully converted over many generations, and now offers accommodation in six spacious, airy en suite bedrooms. But, to add a frisson of apprehension, the building is reputed to be haunted by Sebastian, a monk of ill repute, who sometimes appears in one of the bedrooms or along the adjacent corridors. The inn pursues a ruthless policy of using fresh local produce wherever possible, and you'll find the best choices on daily blackboards offering West Country dishes from local suppliers. Fish arrives fresh from Brixham; cheeses for ploughman's lunches are made in the West Country, whilst clotted cream and free-range eggs are

continued

COLEFORD continued

produced on a local farm. The restaurant menu offers an impressive choice: perhaps start with fish soup or duck and orange pâté, before moving on to pork tenderloin with bubble and squeak, navarin of lamb cobbler, seafood platter, or brocolli with walnuts and Stilton sauce. Otter ale and Badger bitter are always on tap, together with a variety of guest beers. There's an extensive list of malt whiskies and ports, and decent wines are offered by the glass.
OPEN: 12-3 6-11 (Sun 7-10.30) Closed: 25-26 Dec
BAR MEALS: L served all week 12-2 D served all week 7-10 Av main course £9.95 **RESTAURANT:** L served all week 12-2 D served all week 7-10 Av 3 course à la carte £18 Av 3 course fixed price £15.95 **BREWERY/COMPANY:** Free House
◀: Wadworth 6X, Otter Ale, Badger Bitter, Shepherd Neame Spitfire. **FACILITIES:** Children welcome Garden: Terraced, paved, decked area, stream **NOTES:** Parking 50 **ROOMS:** 6 bedrooms 6 en suite 1 family rooms s£55 d£65

CORNWORTHY   Map 03 SX85

Hunters Lodge Inn 🍽 ♀
TQ9 7ES ☎ 01803 732204
e-mail: rog.liz@hunterslodgeinn.com
Dir: Off A381 S of Totnes

Dating from the early 18th century, this country local is tucked away in a quiet village close to the River Dart. The interior is simply furnished and a real fire burns in the gorgeous fireplace. Fresh local produce is used in the cooking, and the water sold originates from a spring in the village. Smoked fish platter, roast rack of lamb, Angus sirloin steak, mushroom tortellini, and Moroccan lamb casserole are typical dishes.
OPEN: 11.30-2.30 6.30-11 **BAR MEALS:** L served all week 12-2 D served all week 7-9 Av main course £10 **RESTAURANT:** L served all week 12-2 D served all week 7-9 Av 3 course à la carte £17 **BREWERY/COMPANY:** Free House **◀:** Teignworthy Reel Ale & Springtide, Guest Ales. ♀: 13 **FACILITIES:** Children welcome Garden: Lrg paddock with shaded seating areas Dogs allowed Water, Dog chews **NOTES:** Parking 18

CULMSTOCK   Map 03 ST11

Culm Valley Inn 🍽 ♀
EX15 3JJ ☎ 01884 840354 🖷 01884 841659
A former station hotel in which the owners exposed a long-hidden bar during a renovation re-creating an 'inter-war years' look. The ever-changing blackboard menu displays a lengthy list of home-made dishes, mostly using locally-grown or raised ingredients, including braised belly pork with pak

choi, sweetbreads with red onion and fennel seeds, and rabbit with cider, mustard and cream. Fish and shellfish mostly come from South Devon, including hand-dived Ladram Bay scallops, served with pomegranate and molasses dressing.
OPEN: 12-3 6-11 (Open All Day Sun) Closed: 25 Dec
BAR MEALS: L served all week 12-2 D served Mon-Sat 7-9 Av main course £10 **RESTAURANT:** L served all week 12-2 D served Mon-Sat 7-9 Av 3 course à la carte £21.50 **BREWERY/COMPANY:** Free House **◀:** O'Hanlons-Blakelys & Wheat Beer, Otter Bright, Oakhill, Exmoor Ale. ♀: 50 **FACILITIES:** Garden: Old Railway embankment overlooking River Culm Dogs allowed Water **NOTES:** Parking 40 No credit cards

DALWOOD   Map 04 ST20

Pick of the Pubs

The Tuckers Arms 🍽 ♀
EX13 7EG ☎ 01404 881342 🖷 01404 881802
e-mail: tuckersarms@aol.com
See Pick of the Pubs on opposite page

DARTINGTON   Map 03 SX76

Cott Inn ♀
TQ9 6HE ☎ 01803 863777 🖷 01803 866629
Dir: On A384 between Totnes & Buckfastleigh
Picture-postcard pretty, 14th-century stone-and-cob-built inn, continuously licensed since 1320, with a wonderful 183ft thatched roof - one of the longest in England. Carpeted bar with open fires, a wealth of beams and a comfortable collection of antique and older-style furnishings. Popular buffet-style lunchtime menu; more elaborate evening dishes like wild sea bass dressed with dill and sweet pepper, and beef fillet stuffed with pâté with a rich game jus.
OPEN: 11-11 **BAR MEALS:** L served all week 12-2.30 D served all week 6-9.30 Av main course £9 **RESTAURANT:** L served all week 12-2.30 D served all week 6-9.30 Av 3 course à la carte £20 **BREWERY/COMPANY:** Old English Inns **◀:** Greene King IPA, Ruddles. **FACILITIES:** Children welcome Garden: Food served outside Dogs allowed **NOTES:** Parking 40

DARTMOUTH   Map 03 SX85

The Cherub Inn ♦♦♦♦ 🍽 ♀
13 Higher St TQ6 9RB ☎ 01803 832571
e-mail: enquiries@the-cherub.co.uk
The Cherub Inn is Dartmouth's oldest building. It dates from about 1380 and survived the threats of fire in 1864, World War II bombing and threatened demolition in 1958 to be finally restored and Grade II listed. Bar meals are available lunchtime and evenings, and the restaurant serves dinner every night, offering a selection of steak, poultry, game and fish dishes. Expect seafood salad, curry, and steak, mushroom and Guinness pie among many popular favourites.
OPEN: 11-11 (Sun 12-10.30) **BAR MEALS:** L served all week 12-2 D served all week 7-9.30 Av main course £7.50 **RESTAURANT:** L served all week D served all week 7-9.30 Av 3 course à la carte £18 **BREWERY/COMPANY:** Free House **◀:** Cherub Best Bitter, Brakspear Bitter, Shepherd Neame Best, Exmoor Ale. ♀: 10 **FACILITIES:** Children welcome Dogs allowed

continued

Open: 12-3, 6.30-11
Bar Meals: L served all week 12-2, D served all week.
Av cost main course £5.95
RESTAURANT: L served all week 12-2, D served all week 7-9.
Av cost 3 courses £17.50
BREWERY/COMPANY:
Free House.
🍺: Otter Bitter, Otter Ale, Scottish Courage Courage Directors, Courage Best, O'Hanlons Firefly.
FACILITIES: Garden - Old English country garden.
NOTES: Parking 6

The Tuckers Arms

The Tuckers Arms is a pretty thatched inn, decked with colourful hanging baskets in summer, set in a delightful Axe valley village in a quiet corner of East Devon.

Dalwood, Axminster, EX13 7EG
☎ 01404 881342   📠 01404 881802
📧 tuckersarms@aol.com
Dir: off A35 between Honiton & Axminster.

Although it has seen many changes through the centuries, for all its life the inn has been involved in the provision of hospitality, food and drink. The building is a typical Devon longhouse, and reputedly dates back to the 14th century, when it housed the artisans constructing the local church. The cosy interior features low beams, flagstone floors and inglenook fireplaces. The blackboard menus frequently list fresh fish, game and locally caught crab, and choices change daily according to market availability. Starters could include grilled goats' cheese, Dartmouth smoked salmon or seafood chowder with garlic cream. Expect at least three 'fish of the day' dishes - maybe lemon sole, paella or seafood roast. Other main courses could include local beef steak with traditional garnishes, veal cordon bleu or duck confit with shallots, red wine, redcurrant, Yorkshire pudding and creamy goats' cheese. Vegetarians are well catered for with dishes such as wild mushroom risotto or sweet potato and pine nut roulade with cherry tomatoes, yoghurt and chives. Finish with mouthwatering home-made desserts such as treacle tart, lemon meringue pie and chocolate soufflé - all served with Devonshire cream. Country pursuits, including walks, golfing and fishing, are all available nearby. Within easy striking distance are the city of Exeter, the antiques capital of Honiton and the coastal resorts of Sidmouth and Lyme Regis, where the cliff paths offer plenty of opportunities for fossil hunting.

DARTMOUTH continued

Pick of the Pubs

Royal Castle Hotel ★★★ 🐾 ♀
11 The Quay TQ6 9PS ☎ 01803 833033 📠 01803 835445
e-mail: enquiry@royalcastle.co.uk

The imposing quay front façade of the Royal Castle Hotel masks the considerable age of the building behind. With a commanding position overlooking the Dart estuary, the hotel offers lively bars and good food. The hotel was developed from two private residences dating from the 1630s. One became the New Inn a century later, frequented by thirsty seamen coming ashore. By 1782 the two houses were combined to become the Castle Inn, with the addition of a brew house and stables at the rear. In the 1800s, with the coming of the turnpike, the inn was extensively developed to provide a proper coaching house, with a third floor, the new façade topped by a castellated cornice, and two Doric columns at the entrance. Thus the Castle Hotel was established. The large oak beams in the Galleon Lounge are reputed to come from the wreckage of Spanish men o'war, and the Lydstone Range, opposite the bar, was forged in Dartmouth over 300 years ago (joints are still roasted on it during the winter months). Tudor fireplaces, spiral staircases, priest holes and period furniture contribute to the sense of history, as does the bell board in the courtyard, with each room's bell pitched to a different note. The lively Harbour Bar, with its nautical décor, retains a traditional pub atmosphere. Here you'll find local farm cider, cask ales, numerous malt whiskies and a good choice of wines by the glass. Morning coffee and decent pub food are also served in the Galleon Lounge, while imaginative food is available in the upstairs Adam Room Restaurant overlooking the river. Seafood specialities include lobster, crab, Dover sole, and oven-roasted sea bass with almond butter.
OPEN: 11-11 **BAR MEALS:** L served all week 11.30-6.30 D served all week 6.30-10 **RESTAURANT:** L served all week 12-2 D served all week 7-9.30 **BREWERY/COMPANY:** Free House 🍺: Exe Valley Dob's Bitter, Wadworth 6X, Scottish Courage Courage Directors, Interbrew Flowers IPA. **FACILITIES:** Children welcome Dogs allowed Water, Biscuits **NOTES:** Parking 14 **ROOMS:** 25 bedrooms 25 en suite

DENBURY   Map 03 SX86

The Union Inn 🐾 ♀
Denbury Green TQ12 6DQ ☎ 01803 812595 📠 01803 814206
Dir: Telephone for directions
A pretty country inn affectionately - and understandably -

continued

known as the Tardis. Inside are rustic stone walls, a log fire with adjacent settle, and an iron gantry used for the 'hanging' mixed grill - local meats are cooked on skewers, hung to let the hot juices drip on to chips, then flambéed at table and served with mushrooms, tomatoes and onions. A huge selection of other meat, local fish, seafood and vegetarian dishes, sweets and snacks.
OPEN: 11-3 6-11 (Sat 11-11, Sun 12-10.30) 25 Dec Closed eve
BAR MEALS: L served all week 12-2.30 D served all week 6.30-10 Av main course £5.95 **RESTAURANT:** L served all week 12-2.30 D served all week 6.30-10 Av 3 course à la carte £20
BREWERY/COMPANY: 🍺: Interbrew Bass, Flowers IPA, Black Sheep Special, Greene King Abbot Ale. ♀: 9 **FACILITIES:** Benches outside Dogs allowed Water **NOTES:** Parking 10

DITTISHAM   Map 03 SX85

The Ferry Boat ♀
Manor St TQ6 0EX ☎ 01803 722368
Now under new ownership, this traditional pub (the only riverside inn on the river Dart) continues to prove popular with walkers and boatmen. Its picture windows make the most of its enviable location, looking across the river to Greenway House, a National Trust property that was once Agatha Christie's home. The menu features simple pub food such as steaks, fish pies and baguettes.
OPEN: 11 -11 (Sun 12-10.30) **BAR MEALS:** L served all week 12-2.30 D served all week 7-9 Av main course £7.25
BREWERY/COMPANY: 🍺: Bass, Stella Artois, Ushers, Scrumpy. ♀: 8 **FACILITIES:** Children welcome Children's licence Dogs allowed Water, dog chews

DODDISCOMBSLEIGH   Map 03 SX88

Pick of the Pubs

The Nobody Inn 🐾 ♀
EX6 7PS ☎ 01647 252394 📠 01647 252978
e-mail: info@nobodyinn.co.uk
Dir: From A38 follow signs for Dunchideock and Doddiscombsleigh
This charming 16th-century inn, set amid lovely Devon countryside just off the old Plymouth to Exeter road, has a wealth of beams, ancient settles, antique tables and a huge inglenook fireplace. Its name reputedly comes from the days when travellers in need of refreshment were greeted from behind the door with calls of 'Nobody in'! These days visitors are assured of a warm welcome, a good choice of unusual ales, 260 whiskies, some 20 wines by the glass, and an imaginative range of food including around 40 local cheeses. Beef and oyster pie, lamb casserole and salmon and haddock fishcakes are typical bar dishes, while dinner in the restaurant might offer quail stuffed with rice and apricots with fig and apricot sauce, or pan-fried halibut with green peppercorn, tomato, bell pepper, coriander and white wine sauce.
OPEN: 12-2.30 6-11 (Sun 7-10.30) Closed: 25-26 & 31 Dec
BAR MEALS: L served all week 12-2 D served all week 7-10 Av main course £8 **RESTAURANT:** D served Tue-Sat 7.30-9 Av 3 course à la carte £22 **BREWERY/COMPANY:** Free House 🍺: Branscombe Nobody's Bitter, Teign Valley Tipple, Sharp's Doom Bar. ♀: 20 **FACILITIES:** Garden: Patio area Dogs allowed in the garden only **NOTES:** Parking 50

DOLTON   Map 03 SS51

Pick of the Pubs

The Union Inn ◆◆◆◆ 🍽
Fore St EX19 8QH ☎ 01805 804633 📠 01805 804633
e-mail: union.inn@eclipse.co.uk
Dir: From A361 take B3227 to S Moulton, then Atherington. L onto
B3217 then 6m to Dolton. Pub on R
This 17th century freehouse was originally built as a Devon
longhouse. Traditionally constructed of cob, the building was
converted to a hotel in the mid-19th century to serve the
local cattle markets. The inn now offers three en suite
bedrooms and, with its large Georgian rooms, sash windows
and traditional pub interior, visitors are guaranteed a warm
welcome. There's a homely beamed bar, oak settles and
sturdy wooden tables, plus good home cooking washed
down with West Country ales. The bar menu features freshly-
baked baguettes and Union toasties, as well as local ham and
sausages. In the restaurant, start with potato, artichoke and
bacon soup, or warm salad with pigeon breasts and bacon.
Main courses include marinated rib-eye steak, braised oxtail
with red wine and vegetables, char-roast chicken breast with
wild mushroom sauce and spinach and feta cheese pie.
OPEN: 12-2.30 6-11 Closed: 1st 2 wks Feb **BAR MEALS:** L
served Thur-Tue 12-2 D served Thur-Tue 7-9 Av main course £5.50
RESTAURANT: L served Sun 12-2 D served Thu-Tue 7-9 Av 3
course à la carte £17 **BREWERY/COMPANY:** Free House
🍺: Sharp's Doom Bar, St Austell HSD, Barum Original, Jollyboat
Freebooter. **FACILITIES:** Garden: Small area with three tables
Dogs allowed Dog bed and toys **NOTES:** Parking 15
ROOMS: 3 bedrooms 3 en suite d£60 no children overnight

DREWSTEIGNTON   Map 03 SX79

Pick of the Pubs

The Drewe Arms 🍷
The Square EX6 6QN ☎ 01647 281224
Dir: W of Exeter on A30 for 12m L at Woodleigh junction follow signs
for 3m to Drewsteignton
Picture-postcard, long and low-thatched inn tucked away
in a sleepy village square high above the wooded slopes of
the Teign Valley, close to Castle Drogo (NT), Dartmoor and
beautiful walks. A rural gem, once totally in a time warp
when Britain's longest-serving landlady Mabel Mudge (75
years) was at the helm until she officially retired in 1996
aged 99. Although sympathetically refurbished by
Whitbread, ales are still drawn from the cask and served
through two hatchways, one in a classic, unspoilt and
simply-adorned bar, and a pine-furnished room with
roaring log can also be found off the flagged passageway.
'Mabels Kitchen', now the dining-room, retains her old
black range and original dresser. Good food, listed on a
short blackboard menu, ranges from decent ploughman's
lunches, crispy belly pork with neeps and tatties, home-
made steak pudding, hock of ham with mash and cabbage
and Devonshire junket, to scallops with pesto, trio of
grilled fish and grilled bass on gratin leeks.
OPEN: 11-3 6-11 **BAR MEALS:** L served all week 12-2 D
served all week 6.30-9.30 Av main course £6.95
RESTAURANT: D served all week 6.30-9.30 Av 3 course à la
carte £20 **BREWERY/COMPANY:** Whitbread 🍺: Flowers IPA,
Bass ,Greene King, Greene King Old Speckled Hen.
FACILITIES: Children welcome beer garden, patio, outdoor
eating, Dogs allowed **NOTES:** Parking 12

EXETER   Map 03 SX99

Double Locks Hotel 🍷
Canal Bank EX2 6LT ☎ 01392 256947 📠 01392 250247
Dir: From M5 follow signs for Marsh Barton Trading Est, R at 2nd rdbt,
then onto slip rd to L of incinerator, R after bridge across canal
Enjoying a peaceful setting on the old Exeter ship canal within
sight of Exeter Cathedral, the Double Locks is cosy and
atmospheric in the winter, and a cheerful family day out in
the summer, with live music and a BBQ in the large canalside
garden. The real ale choice is good, as is a simple menu that
includes lasagne, turkey and mushroom pie, bangers and
mash, toasties, ratatouille, and Feta cheese and spinach pie.
OPEN: 11-11 (Sun 12-10.30) **BAR MEALS:** L served all week 11-
10.30 D served all week Av main course £6 **RESTAURANT:** L
served all week 11-10.30 D served all week
BREWERY/COMPANY: Young & Co 🍺: Adnams Broadside,
Everard's Original, Branscombe Vale Branoc, Young's PA. 🍷: 9
FACILITIES: Children welcome Garden: Approx 4 acres Dogs
allowed Water **NOTES:** Parking 100

Red Lion Inn 🍽 🍷
Broadclyst EX5 3EL ☎ 01392 461271
Dir: on the B3181 Exeter to Culompton.
At the centre of a National Trust village, close to Killerton
House and Gardens, this renowned 15th-century inn features
original beams and antique furniture inside and a cobbled
courtyard outside. Among the kitchen's dishes you may find
fisherman's pie, baked aubergine stuffed with Mozzarella,
tomatoes and pesto, wild mushroom nut roast, Mediterranean
vegetable roulade, Barbary duck breast with Savoy cabbage,
or whole baked seabass with capers and shallots.
OPEN: 11-2.30 5.30-11 (Sun 12-3, 7-10.30) **BAR MEALS:** L served
all week 12-2.30 D served all week 6-9.30 Av main course £6
RESTAURANT: L served all week 12-2 D served Mon-Sat 6-9.30 Av 3
course à la carte £17 **BREWERY/COMPANY:** Free House 🍺: Bass,
Fullers London Pride, Hardy Royal Oak, Worthington Best. 🍷: 7
FACILITIES: Children welcome Garden: Small garden with three
tables Dogs allowed in garden only. Water & biscuits provided
NOTES: Parking 70

EXMINSTER   Map 03 SX98

Swans Nest 🍽 🍷
Station Rd EX6 8DZ ☎ 01392 832371
Dir: From M5 follow A379 Dawlish Rd

A much-extended pub in a pleasant rural location whose
facilities, unusually, extend to a ballroom, dance floor and
stage. The carvery is a popular option for diners, with a choice
of meats served with freshly-prepared vegetables, though the
salad bar is a tempting alternative, with over 39 items,
including quiches, pies and home-smoked chicken. A carte of

continued

EXMINSTER continued

home-cooked fare includes grilled lamb steak, Devon pork chop, and five-bean vegetable curry. Interested diners might like to sample 'Plant Pot Pudding', as well as take a look at a jukebox that once belonged to Sir Elton John. **OPEN:** 10.30-2.30 6-11 Closed: Dec 26 **BAR MEALS:** L served all week 12-2 D served all week 6-9.45 **RESTAURANT:** L served all week 12-2 D served all week 6-9.30 Av 3 course à la carte £15 **BREWERY/COMPANY:** Free House ☎: Otter Bitter, Princetown Jail Ale. **FACILITIES:** Children welcome Garden **NOTES:** Parking 102

Turf Hotel ♀

Turf Lock EX6 8EE ☎ 01392 833128 ▤ 01392 832545
Dir: Off A379 turn L at end of Exminster by-pass/over rail bridge. Park by canal (pub is 0.75m on foot)
Built around 1830, and remotely situated on the Exeter Canal, this is one of only a few pubs in the country that cannot be reached by car. Follow the paths or travel there on the inn's own boat. The beautifully hand-drawn menu includes toasties, jacket potatoes, platters, sandwiches, snacks, and 'yummy specials'. Vegetarian dishes and daily specials are on the blackboard, and there is also a 'cook-your-own' BBQ menu. **OPEN:** 11-3 6-11 (Jul-Aug 11-11) Closed: Nov-Feb **BAR MEALS:** L served all week 12-2.30 D served Mon-Sat 6.30-9 Av main course £7.50 **BREWERY/COMPANY:** Free House ☎: Otter Bitter, Otter Ale, Otter Bright. **FACILITIES:** Children welcome Garden: Food served outside. Overlooks Estuary Dogs allowed Water & dog chews

---

EXTON   Map 03 SX98

The Puffing Billy 🐕 ♀ NEW

Station Rd EX3 0PR ☎ 01392 877888 ▤ 01392 876212
e-mail: billy@hotmail.com
Enjoy estuary views from this 16th-century village pub, popular for its live jazz, real ales and fine wines. Menus include a good range of seafood (cod, lobster, scallops, oysters) and imaginative dishes such as dried aged Aberdeen Angus beef fillet with shallots, red wine glaze, beetroot confit and leek and potato cake, or peppercorn and honey-glazed duck with rösti and Cassis reduction. **OPEN:** 11-3 5.30-11 Closed: 25 Dec, 1 Jan **BAR MEALS:** L served all week 12-3 D served all week 6-7 Av main course £12.95 **RESTAURANT:** L served all week 12-3 D served all week 6-10 Av 3 course à la carte £23.95 Av 3 course fixed price £13.75 ☎: Otter Ale, Pilsner, Cafferys, Dobs. ♀: 16 **FACILITIES:** Children welcome Children's licence Garden: Sun terrace, small garden **NOTES:** Parking 30

HARBERTON   Map 03 SX75

The Church House Inn 🐕 ♀

TQ9 7SF ☎ 01803 863707
e-mail: starkey@churchhouseinn.freeserve.co.uk
Dir: From Totnes take A381 S. Take turn for Harberton on R, adjacent to church in centre of village
Originally built to house the stonemasons working on the church next door around 1100, this charming inn has also been used as a chantry house for monks. Inside there is a medieval oak screen, original oak beams, and a latticed window containing 13th-century glass. The specials board changes regularly, but may include spinach and cream cheese pancake gateaux on white wine sauce, local venison steak with blackcurrant and thyme sauce, Devon chicken breast with

continued

Thai sauces, and Devon rabbit pie. Light bites are also available. **OPEN:** 12-3 6-11 (Sat 12-4, 6-11 Sun 12-3, 7-10.30) 25-26 Dec, 1 Jan closed evenings **BAR MEALS:** L served all week 12-2 D served all week 7-9.30 Av main course £7 **RESTAURANT:** L served all week 12-2 D served all week 7-9.30 Av 3 course à la carte £16 **BREWERY/COMPANY:** Free House ☎: Bass, Wells Bombardier, Palmers IPA, Marstons Pedigree. ♀: 7 **FACILITIES:** Children welcome Dogs allowed Water, dog biscuits, food **NOTES:** Parking 20

HATHERLEIGH   Map 03 SS50

Tally Ho Inn & Brewery ♀

14 Market St EX20 3JN ☎ 01837 810306
e-mail: adytaylor65@hotmail.com
Great food, good beer, and a welcoming atmosphere are promised at this 15th-century pub located in the heart of the historic town. With its beamed bar and open fires, own ales brewed on site, and prize-winning home-made dishes, it clearly succeeds in its philosophy. In the cosy dining room and beamed bar expect crispy duck breast served with a roasted pepper and red onion chutney, plus Tally Ho sausages made with the house beer. **OPEN:** 11-3 6-11.30 (Sun 11-10.30) **BAR MEALS:** L served all week 11-2.30 D served all week 6-9.30 Av main course £7.50 **RESTAURANT:** L served all week 11-2.30 D served all week 6-9.30 Av 3 course à la carte £20 **BREWERY/COMPANY:** Free House ☎: Cavalier, Courage Best, Oliver's Nectar & Guest ale. **FACILITIES:** Children welcome Garden: Food served outside Dogs allowed

---

HAYTOR VALE   Map 03 SX77

Pick of the Pubs

The Rock Inn ★★ ⊛ 🐕 ♀

TQ13 9XP ☎ 01364 661305 ▤ 01364 661242
e-mail: inn@rock-inn.co.uk
Dir: A38 from Exeter, at Drum Bridges rdbt take A382 for Bovey Tracey, 1st exit at 2nd rdbt (B3387), 3m L to Haytor Vale.
A coaching inn dating from around 1750, although in parts much older. The covered entrance and stone trough beside the old stables are reminders of its strategic position on the one-time coach road between Widecombe-in-the-Moor and Newton Abbot. The remains of the horse-drawn Haytor Granite Railway, opened in 1820, are nearby. Open fires, antique tables and sturdy furnishings lend a traditional feel to the rambling bars. Lunch choices include steak and kidney suet pudding, and fillet of salmon on spinach with sauce vierge. At dinner, start with River Teign mussels steamed in chilli, or warmed goat's cheese salad with bacon and walnut dressing, then perhaps duck breast with braised lentils and roasted shallots, chargrilled peppered steak, or pan-fried John Dory from Brixham. Round off with lemon syrup sponge pudding and custard, or biscuits and Hawkridge Farm cheese. Vegetarians have a four-way choice. Guests in the Four Poster Room are served champagne on arrival and at breakfast. **OPEN:** 11-11 Closed: Dec 25-26 **BAR MEALS:** L served all week 12-2.30 D served all week 6.30-9.30 **RESTAURANT:** L served all week 12-2.30 D served all week 7-9 **BREWERY/COMPANY:** Free House ☎: Hardy Royal Oak, St Austell Dartmoor Best, Interbrew Bass. **FACILITIES:** Children welcome Garden: Lrg well kept **NOTES:** Parking 35 **ROOMS:** 9 bedrooms 9 en suite

HOLBETON Map 03 SX65

Mildmay Colours Inn
PL8 1NA ☎ 01752 830248 ▤ 01752 830432
e-mail: louise@mildmaycolours.fsnet.co.uk
Dir: S from Exeter on A38, Yealmpton/Ermington, S past Ugborough & Ermington R onto A379. After 1.5m, turn L, signposted Mildmay Colours/Holbeton
A 17th-century pub which derives its unusual name from a famous jockey, Lord Anthony Mildmay, whose portrait and silks are hung in the pub. On the racing theme, the pub was used as a location for the film 'International Velvet' with Tatum O'Neil and Oliver Reed. Surrounded by thatched cottages and rolling hills, the inn also has a well-equipped family room. There are simple bar snacks and children's meals, along with daily specials such as cod in Mildmay beer batter, locally-caught mackerel, Modbury home-made Stilton sausages and organic local farm lamb racks.
OPEN: 11-3 6-11 (Sun 12-3, 7-10.30) **BAR MEALS:** L served all week 12-2 D served all week 6-9 Av main course £6.95
RESTAURANT: L served Sun 12-2 Av 3 course fixed price £11.95
BREWERY/COMPANY: Free House ◖: Mildmay Colours Bitter & Mildmay SP, Sharps Eden Ale, Bishops Ruin, Blackawton.
FACILITIES: Children welcome Garden: Nice flower arrangements, 10 picnic benches Dogs allowed Water **NOTES:** Parking 20

HOLNE Map 03 SX76

Church House Inn
TQ13 7SJ ☎ 01364 631208 ▤ 01364 631525
Dir: From A38 at Ashburton (Peartree Junction) take road to Dartmoor. Follow road over Holne bridge, up hill and take L turn, signed to Holne.

Tucked away in the tranquil south Devon countryside, this traditional 14th-century free house is on the southeast edge of Dartmoor and offers a warm welcome and old-fashioned service. This is a paradise for outdoor enthusiasts, and the owners are building a reputation for quality local fare. Examples from the blackboard include medallions of beef topped with cheese mousseline, skate wing on braised fennel, baby aubergines with curried vegetable couscous, and cod steak with cream cauliflower purée and pea and herb sauce.
OPEN: 12-2.30 7-11 **BAR MEALS:** L served all week 12-2.15 D served all week 7-9.15 Av main course £9 **RESTAURANT:** L served Sun 12-2.15 D served all week 7-9.15 Av 3 course à la carte £16
BREWERY/COMPANY: Free House ◖: Butcome, Palmer IPA, Ring Of Bells, Samerskills. ♀: 12 **FACILITIES:** Children welcome Garden: Small village green and patio Dogs allowed
NOTES: Parking 6

HONITON Map 04 ST10

Pick of the Pubs

The Otter Inn ♀
Weston EX14 3NZ ☎ 01404 42594
Dir: Just off A30 W of Honiton
On the banks of the idyllic River Otter, this ancient 14th-century inn is set in over two acres of grounds and was once a cider house. Enjoy one of the traditional real ales, try your hand at scrabble, dominoes or cards, or peruse the inn's extensive book collection. A wide-ranging menu caters for all tastes and includes fresh fish, game, steak, vegetarian dishes, bar meals and Sunday lunch.
OPEN: 12-11 (Fri-Sun 12-3) Dec 25-26 Closed eve
BAR MEALS: L served all week 12-2 D served all week 6-9 Av main course £5.95 **RESTAURANT:** L served all week 12-2 D served all week 6-9 Av 3 course à la carte £15.95
BREWERY/COMPANY: Free House ◖: Otter Ale, Flowers IPA.
♀: 15 **FACILITIES:** Children welcome Garden: Food served outside Dogs allowed Water **NOTES:** Parking 60

HORNDON Map 03 SX58

The Elephant's Nest Inn ♀
PL19 9NQ ☎ 01822 810273
Dir: Off A386 N of Tavistock

An isolated inn on the flanks of Dartmoor reached via narrow lanes from Mary Tavy. The 16th-century buildings retain their real fires, slate floors and low beamed ceilings, decorated with loads of elephant memorabilia, including 'Elephant's Nest' written on the beams in over 80 languages. The name comes from a humorous remark made by a regular about the then rather portly landlord. Traditional pub food is served from a daily-changing menu of fresh local produce. Range of bar snacks also available. Under new ownership.
OPEN: 12-3 6-11 (Sun 12-10.30) (May-Sept 12-11 wknd)
BAR MEALS: L served all week 12-2 D served all week 7-9 Av main course £8 **BREWERY/COMPANY:** Free House ◖: Palmers IPA, Copper, St Austell's HSB & changing guest ales.
FACILITIES: Children welcome Garden: Food served outside, views of Dartmoor Dogs allowed **NOTES:** Parking 30

> **Restaurant and Bar Meal times indicate the times when food is available. Last orders may be approximately 30 minutes before the times stated.**

England

Pick of the Pubs

Hoops Country Inn & Hotel ♀
'Hoops', nr Clovelly EX39 5DL
☎ 01237 451222 📠 01237 451247
e-mail: reservations@hoopsinn.co.uk
Dir: on the A39 between Bideford & Clovelly

Set in 16 acres of garden and meadow close to the
National Trust coastal path, the thatch-roofed, cob-walled
13th-century smugglers' inn combines olde worlde charm
with up-to-date fine cuisine. Throughout the bar and
dining-rooms, potted herring roes with cognac, and
chicken livers grilled in pancetta precede main dishes
such as Hoops crackly pork knuckle, seasonal game pie
and goose breast with apple tempura and onion mash.
Pride of place goes to the fish blackboards with daily-
changing offers of Clovelly mackerel with mustard mash
and monkfish collops with raspberry vinaigrette. Round
off with deep treacle tart or Chocolate Ectasy with
Cointreau cream.
OPEN: 8-11 (Sun 8.30-10.30) Closed: Dec 25 **BAR MEALS:** L
served all week 12-3 D served all week 6-9.30 Av main course £11
RESTAURANT: L served all week 12-3 D served all week 7-9.30
Av 3 course à la carte £23 **BREWERY/COMPANY:** Free House
🍺: Jollyboat Mainbrace, Cottage, Exe Valley, Cotleigh Barn Owl.
FACILITIES: Children welcome Garden: outdoor eating, BBQ
Dogs allowed **NOTES:** Parking 150

The Royal Inn
PL19 8PJ ☎ 01822 870214
e-mail: paul@royalinn.co.uk
Dir: South of B3362 Launceston/Tavistock road
The pub, with a façade enlivened by superb pointed arched
windows, was once a nunnery. Standing near a bridge built
over the Tamar in 1437 by Benedictine monks, it was the
Packhorse Inn until Charles I pitched up one day - his seal is
in the doorstep. Beef for the steaks, casseroles and stews, and
the pheasant and venison on the specials board are all locally
supplied. Chilli cheese tortillas are much appreciated. So is the
absence of noisy machines.
OPEN: 12-3 6.30-11 Dec 25 Closed eve **BAR MEALS:** L served all
week 12-2 D served all week 7-9 Av main course £6
RESTAURANT: L served all week 12-2 D served all week 7-9
BREWERY/COMPANY: Free House 🍺: Sharp's Doom Bar &
Special, Interbrew Bass, Ring O'Bells Tipsy Trotter.
FACILITIES: Garden: Three patio areas Dogs allowed
NOTES: Parking 30

Anchor Inn 🍴
Lutterburn St, Ugborough PL21 0NG ☎ 01752 892283
Although it has a nautical theme, this pub is nowhere near the
sea. It might be named after a local community of anchorite
monks from the 14th century. The menu has a definite
international feel, complete with flags and maps. Britain,
North America and various other countries are represented
with a variety of dishes. For example there is chicken
Maryland and carpet-bagger's steak from North America, veal
Romano from Italy and noisette of lamb from France.
OPEN: 11-11 **BAR MEALS:** L served all week 12-2.30 D served all
week 7-9 Av main course £7 **RESTAURANT:** L served all week 12-3
D served all week 7-10 **BREWERY/COMPANY:** Free House
🍺: TSB, Spitfire, Interbrew Bass. **FACILITIES:** Children welcome
Garden: Small walled area with two tables Dogs allowed Water &
biscuits provided **NOTES:** Parking 15

Devon Arms ◆◆◆
Fore St EX6 8LD ☎ 01626 890213 📠 01626 891678
e-mail: devon.arms@ukgateway.net
Dir: on A379 between Exeter & Dawlish 7m from Exeter, 5m from Dawlish,
adjacent to Powderham castle
This old coaching house dates back to 1592 and its 1846 lease
described an inn, posting house and brewery producing 'forty
hogsheads per week'. Today's modern comforts comprise a
garden with patio, barbecue, pets' corner and children's play
area, and comfortably furnished bedrooms. The menu
includes beer-battered cod fillet, vegetable tikka masala,
chicken in a creamy white wine and mushroom sauce, and
lasagne. Under new management.
OPEN: 11-2.30 6-11 (Sun 12-3, 7-10.30) **BAR MEALS:** L served all
week 12-2 D served all week 6.30-9 **RESTAURANT:** L served all
week 12-2 D served all week 6.30-9 **BREWERY/COMPANY:** Free
House 🍺: Teign Valley Tipple, Bass, Whitbread Best.
FACILITIES: Children welcome Garden **NOTES:** Parking 20
ROOMS: 6 bedrooms 6 en suite s£30 d£45

Church House Inn 🍴
Churchstow TQ7 3QW ☎ 01548 852237
Dir: On A379 0.5m W of Kingsbridge
Set in some lovely Devon countryside on the way to
Salcombe, this historic 15th-century inn was originally the site
of a rest house for Cistercian monks during the 13th century.
Look out for sea bass, steak and kidney pie, devilled chicken,
or smoked salmon. There is also a very popular hot carvery.
OPEN: 11-2.30 6-11 **BAR MEALS:** L served all week 12-2 D served
all week 6.30-9 Av main course £6.50 **RESTAURANT:** L served all
week 12-2 D served all week 7-9 Av 3 course à la carte £10.40
BREWERY/COMPANY: Free House 🍺: Interbrew Bass, Fuller's
London Pride, St Austell Dartmoor Best. **FACILITIES:** Children
welcome Garden: Patio with heaters, food served outside Dogs
allowed **NOTES:** Parking 26

The Crabshell Inn 🍴
Embankment Rd TQ7 1JZ ☎ 01548 852345 📠 01548 825262
You can fish for crab from the quay of this family-run
waterside inn that boasts 240 feet of free mooring for
customers. There are panoramic views of the Kingsbridge
estuary and occasionally seals playing right by the sea wall.
Fresh local fish is, of course, the highlight of the menu, with
pride of place going to the lobster and crab platters which

continued

sometimes need to be ordered a day ahead. Other dishes include traditional favourites (steak and kidney pie, steak and chips), curries, salads, pasta and plenty of children's meals.
OPEN: 11-11 (Sun 12-10.30) **BAR MEALS:** L served all week 12-2.30 D served all week 6-9.30 Av main course £5.50
RESTAURANT: L served all week 12-2.30 D served all week 6-9.30 Av 3 course à la carte £12 **BREWERY/COMPANY:** Free House
◀: Bass Bitter, Crabshell Bitter, Wadworth 6X. **FACILITIES:** Children welcome Garden: Patio area with tables & seats Dogs allowed Water **NOTES:** Parking 40

KINGSKERSWELL   Map 03 SX86

Barn Owl Inn ♀
Aller Mills TQ12 5AN ☎ 01803 872130 ▤ 01803 875279
This 16th-century former farmhouse at the heart of Devon boasts many charming features, including flagged floors, a black-leaded range and oak beams in a high-vaulted converted barn with a minstrel's gallery. Its location is handy for Dartmoor and the English Riviera towns, and there are six well-equipped and comfortable rooms for those wanting to stay over. The menu offers wholesome fare such as fisherman's crumble, minted half-shoulder of lamb, spatchcock chicken and tournedos Rossini.
OPEN: 11-11 (Sun 12-10.30) **BAR MEALS:** L served all week 12-3 D served all week 6-9.30 **RESTAURANT:** L served all week 6-9.30 **BREWERY/COMPANY:** Eldridge Pope **◀:** Bass, 6X, Tetley, Stella Artois. **FACILITIES:** Children welcome Garden: Large garden area Dogs allowed Water in garden **NOTES:** Parking 30

KINGSTEIGNTON   Map 03 SX87

Old Rydon Inn ♀
Rydon Rd TQ12 3QG ☎ 01626 354626 ▤ 01626 356980
Dir: From A380 take B3193 into Kingsteignton
A feature of this Grade II listed former farmhouse is its large family dining conservatory filled with flowering tropical plants and grape vines. Adjacent, the pub is housed in the old stables with a cider apple loft above it. A typical menu features Old Rydon seafood salad, grilled salmon on vegetable spaghetti, venison and wild boar steaks, and Nasi Goreng. Light bites include salads, jacket potatoes, toasted muffins, and ploughmans.
OPEN: 11-3 6-11 Closed: 25 Dec **BAR MEALS:** L served all week 12-2 D served all week 6.30-9.30 Av main course £7
RESTAURANT: D served Mon-Sat 7-9.30 Av 3 course à la carte £25
BREWERY/COMPANY: Heavitree **◀:** Bass, Fullers London Pride, plus Guest. **FACILITIES:** Children welcome Garden: beer garden, patio, outdoor eating Dogs allowed **NOTES:** Parking 40

KINGSTON   Map 03 SX64

The Dolphin Inn 🛏
TQ7 4QE ☎ 01548 810314 ▤ 01548 810314
Historic 16th-century beamed inn situated in a delightful South Hams village. Bigbury Bay and Burgh Island are nearby, and the pub is handy for rambling by the tranquil River Erme or strolling to the coast. Relax by the inglenook fireplace and enjoy a pint of real ale, or perhaps something from the appetising menu which uses locally-grown produce. Typical dishes include Stilton and vegetable crumble, gammon steak, pork medallions, chicken Maryland, and rainbow trout. Under new management.
OPEN: 11-3.00 6-11 (Sun 12-3, 7-10.30) **BAR MEALS:** L served all week 12-2 D served all week 6-9.30
BREWERY/COMPANY: **◀:** Thomas Hardy Founders & Four Seasons Ale, Scottish Courage Courage Best. **FACILITIES:** Children welcome Garden: Small patio area, lrg garden, seating Dogs allowed Water provided **NOTES:** Parking 40

KINGSWEAR   Map 03 SX8▫

The Ship 🛏
Higher St TQ6 0AG ☎ 01803 752348
Dir: Telephone for directions
Historic village pub overlooking the scenic River Dart towards Dartmouth and Dittisham. Located in one of South Devon's most picturesque corners, this tall, character inn is very much a village local with a friendly, welcoming atmosphere inside. Well-prepared fresh food is the hallmark of the menu. Sandwiches, baguettes and pies are available in the bar, while the restaurant menu offers crispy duck with stir-fried vegetables on egg noodles, or oven-baked cod with lemon and lime crust.
OPEN: 12-3 6-11 **BAR MEALS:** L served all week 12.30-2 D served all week 7-9.30 Av main course £9.95 **RESTAURANT:** D served all week 7-9.30 Av 3 course à la carte £16.50 **BREWERY/COMPANY:** Heavitree **◀:** Flowers IPA, Bass, Otter. **FACILITIES:** Children welcome Garden: Patio with several garden tables Dogs allowed Water

---

KNOWSTONE   Map 03 SS82

Pick of the Pubs

Masons Arms Inn ♀
EX36 4RY ☎ 01398 341231
e-mail: masonsarmsinn@aol.com
Dir: M5 J27 Off A361 between Tiverton & S Molton

Rolling farmland and steep forested valleys surround this 13th-century inn on the edge of Exmoor. Nestling in a sleepy thatched hamlet and untroubled by passing traffic, this is a classic medieval hostelry. Unspoilt and still complete with inglenook fireplaces, bread ovens, heavy black oak beams and beers from the cask, it is enthusiastically run by owners Jo and Paul Stretton-Downes. Home-cooked food may be enjoyed at lunchtime and in the evenings in the convivial bars, or the cosy atmospheric restaurant with its polished dark wood dining tables, tasteful prints and warming log fires, plus excellent views of Exmoor. For a light lunch try filled baguettes (bacon and Brie) or various ploughman's, while the carte offers chargrilled rib-eye steak, chicken breast in red wine, beer-battered cod, curried cauliflower and courgette crumble, and smoked haddock and prawn pie, with malted bread and butter pudding for an unusual dessert. Fabulous views of Exmoor from the garden.
OPEN: 12-3 6-11 (Sun 12-3, 7-10.30) Closed: Dec 25 Nov-Easter Closed Sun eve **BAR MEALS:** L served all week 12-2 D served all week 7-9 Av main course £9.50 **RESTAURANT:** L served all week 12-2 D served all week 7-9 Av 3 course à la carte £18
BREWERY/COMPANY: Free House **◀:** Cotleigh Tawny, Exmoor Ale, Badger. **FACILITIES:** Garden: Terrace & Lawn with views over valleys Dogs allowed on lead **NOTES:** Parking 10

Map 03 SX48

...... Arms 🍴 ♀
...0 4PZ ☎ 01566 783331
e-... grant@hotmail.com
Dir: From A30 take Lifton turning, halfway between Lifton and Lewdown
A former corn merchant's and church brewery, this 16th-century building stands on the former A30 as it runs through a particularly rural part of Devon. The family owners pride themselves on prompt service and good, unpretentious pub food, including fresh fish, steaks and grills, lasagne, curries and jacket potatoes. Specials are more sophisticated: typically marinated pork tenderloin with sherry and mustard sauce, and baked fillet of John Dory with tomatoes and olives.
OPEN: 11-3 5.30-11 (Sun 12-3, 7-10.30) (winter 12-3, 5.30-11)
BAR MEALS: L served all week 12-2.30 D served all week 6.30-9 Av main course £7.50 **RESTAURANT:** L served all week 12-2.30 D served all week 6.30-9 Av 3 course à la carte £16.95
BREWERY/COMPANY: Free House 🍺: Interbrew Bass, St Austell Tinners, Abbot Ale, Dartmoor. ♀: 7 **FACILITIES:** Garden: Lawned area with views towards Dartmoor **NOTES:** Parking 30

LIFTON   Map 03 SX38

Pick of the Pubs

The Arundell Arms ★★★ ⊛⊛⊛ ♀
PL16 0AA ☎ 01566 784666 📠 01566 784494
e-mail: reservations@arundellarms.com
Dir: 2/3m off the A30 dual carriageway, 3m E of Launceston
Under the same ownership for over 40 years, this creeper-clad 18th-century coaching inn lies at the heart of a delightful Devon village. It is a favourite with country sports enthusiasts, and the owner's passion for angling is shared by many guests who appreciate the 20 miles of private fishing, plus local shooting, riding and golf. The Courthouse Bar (originally the magistrates' court) has year-round appeal serving three local real ales, while the Arundell Bar is a focal point of the hotel proper. Bar food in the latter ranges from upmarket sandwiches (smoked salmon with cucumber and dill, fillet steak with Dijon mustard) to hot dishes such as smoked mackerel and horseradish fishcakes with lentils and leeks, and a choice of salads, including home-cured Gloucester Old Spot with Cumberland sauce, potato salad and tossed leaves. In the renowned restaurant à la carte dining of considerable class features top quality locally-sourced produce.
OPEN: 11.30-3 6-11 **BAR MEALS:** L served all week 12-2.30 D served all week 6-10 Av main course £12.50 **RESTAURANT:** L served all week 12.30-2 D served all week 7.30-9.30 Av 3 course à la carte £39.50 Av 5 course fixed price £33
BREWERY/COMPANY: Free House 🍺: Guest beers. ♀: 9
FACILITIES: Children welcome Garden: Terraced garden with fountain Dogs allowed **NOTES:** Parking 70 **ROOMS:** 27 bedrooms 27 en suite s£49.50 d£99

LITTLEHEMPSTON   Map 03 SX86

Tally Ho Inn 🍴
TQ9 6NF ☎ 01803 862316 📠 01803 862316
Dir: Off the A38 at Buckfastleigh
A traditional 14th-century inn very much at the centre of the community, and catering for visitors and locals alike. In summer the hanging baskets and flower-filled patios are a gardener's delight, while roaring log fires and cosy corners have their own charm in winter. An ever-changing specials board supplements

continued

---

dishes such as Yankee gammon steak, escalope of turkey, tournedos Rossini, grilled tuna steak, oven roasted chicken supreme, pork fillet medallions, or medley of grilled local fish.
OPEN: 12-3 6-11 Closed: Dec 25 **BAR MEALS:** L served all week 12-2 D served all week 7-9 **BREWERY/COMPANY:** Free House 🍺: Interbrew Bass, Carlsberg-Tetley Tetley's Smooth, Guest Ales. **FACILITIES:** Children welcome Garden: Patio area, picnic benches, grass area Dogs allowed **NOTES:** Parking 20

LOWER ASHTON   Map 03 SX88

Manor Inn 🍴 ♀
EX6 7QL ☎ 01647 252304
e-mail: cms.mann@virgin.net
Dir: A38, Teign Valley turning, follow signs for B3193, pub 5m on R, Just over the stone bridge
An authentic country pub in a small village way up the picturesque Teign Valley. Completely unspoilt inside, its traditional furnishings generate a cosy atmosphere all year round, so imagine the effect blazing log fires have in winter. In summer, the peaceful garden is a great attraction. Sandwiches, jacket potatoes, ploughman's, steaks, and chilli are always available. Specials boards are likely to list chicken cacciatore, lamb, leeks and mushroom in local cider, grilled trout, and macaroni cheese.
OPEN: 12-2 6.30-11 **BAR MEALS:** L served Tue-Sun 12-1.30 D served Tue-Sun 7-9.30 Av main course £6.95
BREWERY/COMPANY: Free House 🍺: Teignworthy Reel Ale, Wadworth 6X, Princetown Jail Ale, RCH Pitchfork. ♀: 8
FACILITIES: Garden: Sheltered overlooking fields and hills Dogs allowed Water **NOTES:** Parking 20

LUSTLEIGH   Map 03 SX78

The Cleave ♀
TQ13 9TJ ☎ 01647 277223 📠 01647 277223
e-mail: alisonperring@supanet.com
Dir: Off A382 between Bovey Tracy and Moretonhampstead
Originally a Devon longhouse, this 15th-century thatched inn, on Dartmoor's eastern flanks, is a perfect pit-stop for walkers. It appeared in the 1939 film 'Hound of the Baskervilles', and was the unofficial waiting-room for the now long-gone railway station. The cosy lounge bar has granite walls, and a vast inglenook fireplace; the bigger Victorian bar has an impressive collection of musical instruments. Menu includes baked local trout, pheasant braised with bacon, shallots, mushrooms and Madeira, and home-made chicken korma.
OPEN: 11-3 6.30-11 (summer 11-11) Closed: Mon Nov-Feb
BAR MEALS: L served all week 12-2.30 D served all week 6.30-9 Av main course £6.95 **RESTAURANT:** L served all week 12-2 D served all week 6.30 Av 3 course à la carte £16
BREWERY/COMPANY: Heavitree 🍺: Interbrew Flowers Original Bitter, Interbrew Bass, Wadworth 6X, Otter Ale. ♀: 12
FACILITIES: Children welcome Garden: Traditional cottage style garden Dogs allowed Water **NOTES:** Parking 10
See Pub Walk on page 129

LYDFORD   Map 03 SX58

Pick of the Pubs

Castle Inn & Hotel 🍴 ♀
EX20 4BH ☎ 01822 820242 & 820241 📠 01822 820454
Dir: Off A386 S of Okehampton
Located beside the medieval castle and within walking distance of Lydford Gorge (NT), this pretty, wisteria-clad inn dates from the 16th-century. The interior oozes atmosphere and period charm, with its slate floors, low,

continued

lamp-lit beams, decorative plates and huge Norman fireplace. A change of hands has inevitably resulted in some changes but there is plenty of enthusiasm for the task in hand. Freshly-prepared dishes are the mainstay of the short menu. Fresh fish appears daily such as fillet of salmon with coriander dressed noodles and lemon-butter sauce. Among starters, chicken liver and green peppercorn pâté and warm Stilton and plum tartlet with a redcurrant and port sauce are typical. Main courses may include several vegetarian dishes such as mixed bean curry with Canadian wild rice and long grain rice or wild mushroom and nut risotto with pimento sauce. Shrub-filled garden for summer alfresco eating. Close to Dartmoor and miles of beautiful walks.
OPEN: 11-11 **BAR MEALS:** L served all week 12-2.15 D served all week 7-9.15 Av main course £8 **RESTAURANT:** L served all week 12-2.15 D served all week 7-9.30 Av 3 course à la carte £17 Av 3 course fixed price £17 **BREWERY/COMPANY:** Heavitree
🍺: Fullers London Pride, Flowers IPA, Greene King Old Speckled Hen. **FACILITIES:** Children welcome Garden: Food served outside. Dogs allowed Allowed in bar & patio **NOTES:** Parking 10

Pick of the Pubs

Dartmoor Inn 🐑🐑🐑 🍺 ♀
EX20 4AY ☎ 01822 820221 📠 01822 820494
Dir: On A386 S of Okehampton

Set in the pretty village of Lydford on the western side of Dartmoor National Park is this 16th-century coaching house which is steeped in history. Charles Kingsley almost certainly used the inn in Westward Ho! as the place where Roger Rowe, King of Gubbinses, was slain. Nowadays the bar has a welcoming log fire, and fresh flowers brighten the intimate dining areas where light lunches and candlelit dinners are served. British classics form the basis of the menus, with devilled sprats, fish and chips, and casserole of seafood on the bar selection, along with various set lunches and light suppers. From the evening menu try lamb's kidneys with a wood mushroom and black pudding risotto to start, move on to slow-cooked daube of beef with croutons and bacon lardons, and finish with baked nectarines with Marsala and almonds.
OPEN: 11.30-3 6.30-11 (6-11 in Summer) Closed: BHs **BAR MEALS:** L served Tue-Sun 12-2.15 D served Tue-Sat 6.30-9.15 Av main course £13.75 **RESTAURANT:** L served Tue-Sun 12-2.15 D served Tue-Sat 6.30-10 Av 3 course à la carte £26 **BREWERY/COMPANY:** Free House 🍺: Interbrew Bass, Greene King Old Speckled Hen, St Austell Hicks Special & Dartmoor Best. ♀: 8 **FACILITIES:** Children welcome Garden: Paved area with umbrellas Dogs allowed Water & Food **NOTES:** Parking 35
See Pub Walk on page 144

LYMPSTONE   Map 03 SX98

The Globe Inn 🍺 ♀
The Strand EX8 5EY ☎ 01395 263166
Set in the estuary village of Lympstone, this traditional beamed inn has a good local reputation for seafood. The separate restaurant area serves as a coffee bar during the day. Look out for seafood platter, Thai-grilled haddock, bass with plum and ginger sauce, crab sandwiches, tapas, lasagne, and battered fish and chips on Thursdays. Weekend music nights. Quiz night weekly.
OPEN: 11-3 5.30-11 **BAR MEALS:** L served all week 12-2 D served Mon-Sat 6.30-9.30 Av main course £5 **RESTAURANT:** L served all week D served Mon-Sat 7-9.30 Av 3 course à la carte £16 **BREWERY/COMPANY:** Heavitree 🍺: Flowers IPA, Otter, Bass, Whitbread Best. ♀: 6 **FACILITIES:** Children welcome Dogs allowed Water & treats provided

LYNMOUTH   Map 03 SS74

Pick of the Pubs

Rising Sun Hotel ★★ 🏵 🍺 ♀
Harbourside EX35 6EG ☎ 01598 753223 📠 01598 753480
e-mail: risingsunlynmouth@easynet.co.uk
Dir: From M5 J25 to Minehead, A39 to Lynmouth

Overlooking Lynmouth's tiny harbour and bay is the Rising Sun, a 14th-century thatched smugglers' inn. In turn, overlooking them all, are Countisbury Cliffs, the highest in England. The building's long history is evident from the uneven oak floors, crooked ceilings and thick walls. Literary associations are plentiful: R D Blackmore wrote some of his wild Exmoor romance, 'Lorna Doone', here; the poet Shelley is believed to have honeymooned in the garden cottage; and Coleridge stayed too. Immediately behind rises Exmoor Forest and National Park, home to red deer, wild ponies and birds of prey. With sea and moor so close, game and seafood are in plentiful supply, and pheasant, venison, hare, wild boar, monkfish, crab or scallops, for example, will appear variously as starter or main course dishes. At night the oak-panelled, candlelit dining room is an example of romantic British inn-keeping at its best. Individually designed bedrooms offer harbour views.
OPEN: 11-11 (Open all day all year) **BAR MEALS:** L served all week 12-2 D served all week 7-9 Av main course £8 **RESTAURANT:** L served all week 12-2 D served all week 7-9 Av 3 course à la carte £29.50 Av 3 course fixed price £32.50 **BREWERY/COMPANY:** Free House 🍺: Exmoor Gold, Fox & Exmoor Ale, Cotleigh Tawny Ale. **FACILITIES:** Garden: Beautiful terraced garden, sea views **ROOMS:** 16 bedrooms 16 en suite 2 family rooms s£90 d£90 no children overnight
See Pub Walk on page 146

Dartmoor Inn

An enjoyable and beautiful walk on the western flanks of Dartmoor, following the course of a moorland river valley and returning via a high disused railway line, affording excellent moorland views.

Turn right out of the pub car park, then immediately right onto a track alongside the pub to reach a gate leading on to Dartmoor. Continue straight ahead, keeping the wall on your left, for 1/2m (0.8km) to the footbridge and stepping stones across the River Lyd. Cross the bridge, turn left and follow one of the numerous tracks parallel with the river. Continue past two fords within 1/2m (0.8km), and proceed beside the river, soon to follow an old dry leat close to the river. Head towards a large steep hill (Great Nodden) on the left side of the river, the valley sides gradually becoming much steeper. Walk round Great Nodden and pass a large old tree on the left bank of the river. Shortly, where the river bends sharp right, cross the river (now no more than a stream) and walk straight ahead.

Ascend to an old railway embankment with a small bridge. This is the old peat railway that connected with valley peat workings with Bridestowe station. Turn left along the railway and savour the superb views into Cornwall. Follow the track bed for 1 1/2 miles (2km) to Nodden Gate. Go through the gate, turn left and left again through a second gate and follow the footpath sign. At a junction of three paths, take the left-hand fork across the field, following the markers to a wall stile close to the footbridge and stepping stones negotiated earlier. Turn right along the track and retrace steps back to the inn.

DARTMOOR INN, LYDFORD
EX20 4AY.
☎ 01822 820221

Directions: on A386 south of Okehampton
Refurbished 16th-century roadside inn set on the edge of Dartmoor close to Lydford Gorge (NT). Fresh flowers adorn the well decorated bar and restaurant. Expect upmarket pub food, decent wines and a warm welcome; value for money set lunch, 2 courses £10.75 or 3 courses £13.50.
Open: 11.30-3 6.30-11 (from 6 in summer). Closed Mon.
Bar Meals: 12-2.15, 6.30-9.15.
Notes: Children and dogs welcome. Garden. Parking.
(See page 143 for full entry)

DISTANCE: 5 miles (8km)
MAP: OS Landranger 191
TERRAIN: Moorland; can be wet underfoot in places
PATHS: Bridleways, tracks and a disused railway line
GRADIENT: Fairly easy; one long gradual incline

Walk submitted by Ian Hardy

LYNTON
Map 03 SS74

The Bridge Inn ♦♦♦ 🐷 ⚲ NEW
Lynbridge Hill EX35 6NR ☎ 01589 753425 📠 01589 753225
e-mail: info@bridgeinnlynton.co.uk
Dir: *Turn off the A39 at Barbrook onto the B3234. Continue for 1 mile and pub located on the right just after the Sunny Lyn camp site.*
Attractive 17th-century riverside inn overlooked by National Trust woodlands. In the cellars the remains of 12th-century salmon fishermen's cottages are still visible, and the unusually shaped windows at the front originally belonged to Charles I's hunting lodge at Coombe House that were salvaged following flood damage in the 1680s. The 1952 Lynmouth Flood destroyed the Lyn Bridge and car park, but most of the pub survived intact. Typical bar food - steaks, chilli and pies - is served.
OPEN: 12-3 6-11 (Summer & X-mas open 12-11) (Sun 7-10.30)
BAR MEALS: L served all week 12-2.30 D served all week 6-9.30 Av main course £5.50 **RESTAURANT:** L served all week 12-2.30 D served all week 6-9.30 Av 3 course à la carte £16.50 Av 3 course fixed price £15 **BREWERY/COMPANY:** Free House ⚫: St. Austell Tribute, Clearwater Cavalier, Exmoor Fox. ⚲: 16
FACILITIES: Children welcome Children's licence Garden: Picnic tables, benches, patio Dogs allowed Water, toys **NOTES:** Parking 14
ROOMS: 8 bedrooms 8 en suite 1 family rooms s£25 d£50

MEAVY
Map 03 SX56

The Royal Oak Inn
PL20 6PJ ☎ 01822 852944
Dir: *Off A386 between Tavistock & Plymouth*
Standing on the edge of Dartmoor, between Tavistock and Plymouth, this 12th-century brew house is a popular watering hole for those touring and exploring the National Park. Good quality fare is prepared from produce bought locally and much of the meat is free range. A local fishmonger delivers fresh fish from Plymouth. Expect filled baguettes, local pasties and salads at lunchtime, while the evening menu consists of stuffed plaice, lemon butterfly chicken, gammon steak and salsa sardines.
OPEN: 11-3 6.30-11 (Sun 12-3, 6.30-10.30) **BAR MEALS:** L served all week 12-2.00 D served all week 6.30-9.00 Av main course £5 **BREWERY/COMPANY:** Free House ⚫: Bass, Princetown Jail Ale, IPA. **FACILITIES:** Dogs allowed

MOLLAND
Map 03 SS82

The London Inn NEW
EX36 3NG ☎ 01769 550269
Just below Exmoor lies peaceful Molland, and to find its church is to find this 15th-century inn. Historic features abound, but try and picture today's spacious dining room as the original inn, and the bar as the brewhouse. Every so often the frequently-changing menu will feature guinea fowl with red wine sauce and black cherries, grilled salmon with parsley butter, and tarragon chicken breast with wine sauce and grapes. Bar snacks lunchtime and evenings. No credit cards, though.
OPEN: 11.30-2.30 6-11 (Sun 12-3, 7-10.30) **BAR MEALS:** L served all week 12-2 D served all week 7-9 Av main course £6
RESTAURANT: L served all week D served all week Av 3 course à la carte £12 **BREWERY/COMPANY:** Free House ⚫: Exmoor Ale, Cotleigh Tawny Bitter. **FACILITIES:** Children welcome Garden: Dogs allowed Water **NOTES:** Parking 12 **NOTES:** No credit cards

NEWTON ABBOT
Map 03 SX87

The Linny Inn & Hayloft Dining Area ⚲
Coffinswell TQ12 4SR ☎ 01803 873192 📠 01803 873395
e-mail: markgilstone@aol.com
Dir: *follow signs from A380*
In a largely-thatched village near Torquay, the Linny dates from about 1368, but it's been a pub only since 1969 after 15 years as a country club. The name comes from linhay, an outbuilding, which the snugs originally were. The inn enjoys a high reputation with a range of tasty starters, pastas, salads, fresh Torbay fish and vegetarian dishes, as well as succulent steaks and mouth-watering roasts. A patio leads to the suntrap garden.
OPEN: 11.30-3 6.30-11 **BAR MEALS:** L served all week 12-2 D served all week 6.30-9.30 **RESTAURANT:** 12-2 6.30-9.30 **BREWERY/COMPANY:** Free House ⚫: Carlsberg-Tetley, Stella, Real Ales San Miguel. **FACILITIES:** Children welcome Garden **NOTES:** Parking 34

The Wild Goose Inn 🐷 ⚲
Combeinteignhead TQ12 4RA ☎ 01626 872241
Dir: *from A380 at the Newton Abbot rdbt, take the B3195 Shaldon rd, signed Milber, for 2.5m into village then R at signpost*
Virtually unchanged since it was first licensed in 1840, the name of this Devon longhouse immortalises a flock of geese that used to leap from a high field onto passers-by. Its peaceful beer garden overlooks a 14th-century church and a stream winding its way down to the River Teign. A good choice of traditional home-made food, including fresh local fish, pies, chilli, sausages or ham, egg and chips, and vegetarian meals. Real ales from West Country micro-breweries.
OPEN: 11.30-2.30 6.30-11 (Sun 12-2.30, 7-10.30) **BAR MEALS:** L served all week 12-2 D served all week 7-10 Av main course £7 **RESTAURANT:** L served all week 12-2 D served all week 7-10 Av 3 course à la carte £14 **BREWERY/COMPANY:** Free House ⚫: Otter Ale, Cotleigh, Sharps Bitter, Skinner's Bitter. **FACILITIES:** Garden: Overlooking farm yard, small stream Dogs allowed Water **NOTES:** Parking 40

NEWTON ST CYRES
Map 03 SX89

The Beer Engine 🐷
EX5 5AX ☎ 01392 851282 📠 01392 851876
e-mail: enquiries@thebeerengine.co.uk
Dir: *from Exeter take A377 towards Crediton, pub is opp train station in Newton St Cyres*

A pretty, whitewashed free house, formerly a railway hotel. The proprietors have been brewing their own beer for 20 years, making it the longest established Devon brewery, so your needs are well met in that respect. As for food, expect a

continued

Rising Sun Hotel

A classic coastal walk which begins by following the popular South West Coast Path and returns through a wooded valley by the East Lyn River.

Lynmouth, together with neighbouring Lynton above it, is typically West Country in the look of its picturesque whitewashed houses and cottages. The harbour, where the East and West Lyn rivers flow into Lynmouth Bay, is a delight.

In the summer of 1952, it was a very different picture when a sudden storm hit the area and the Lyn, already swollen from weeks of heavy rain, at last broke its banks and raged through Lynmouth. The village was devastated and 34 people died.

The charm of the place has inspired writers and poets over the years. Coleridge fell under its spell and in 1812 Shelley stayed here with his teenage bride, Mary Wollstonecraft,

using Lynmouth as a secret hideaway where for a while so they could escape the wrath of her parents.

One of the village's more popular attractions is the splendid Victorian cliff railway up to Lynton, operated by use of a water tank incorporated into each car and provided by Sir George Newnes, the publisher, who had a great affection for the place.

From the pub make for the South-West Coast Path, which celebrated its 25th anniversary in 2003, and climb up over Countisbury Hill towards Countisbury Common. Several paths lead out towards Foreland Point lighthouse and from this stretch of the walk

★★ ⓐ
RISING SUN HOTEL, LYNMOUTH
Harbourside EX35 6EG
☎ 01598 753223

Directions: From M5 junc 25 to Minehead, A39 to Lynmouth
Historic inn with literary associations (Shelley, Coleridge, R D Blackmore), and a plentiful supply of seafood and game.
Open: 11-11
Bar Meals: 12-2 7-9
Notes: Beautiful terraced garden.
(See page 143 for full entry)

there are magnificent views out over the Bristol Channel.

From Countisbury Hill join the inland path and follow it through ancient woodlands and down into the valley to reach the East Lyn River. Return to Lynmouth along the riverside path.

DISTANCE: 5 miles/8km
MAP: OS Explorer OL 9
TERRAIN: Magnificent coastline and picturesque valley
PATHS: Coastal, woodland and riverside paths
GRADIENT: Some steep climbing and a sometimes steep descent

Walk submitted and checked by the Rising Sun Hotel, Lynmouth

NEWTON ST CYRES
Map 03 SX89

home-cooked extravaganza: dishes range from haddock in the landlord's own Brewery Batter (made with wort) through to African spicy lamb, home-made steak pies and plenty of good vegetarian options. Sunday lunches draw people from far and wide.
OPEN: 11-11 (Sun 12-10.30) **BAR MEALS:** L served all week 12-2 D served all week 6.30-9.30 Av main course £5.50
BREWERY/COMPANY: Free House **:** Beer Engine Ales: Piston Bitter, Rail Ale, Sleeper Heavy. **FACILITIES:** Children welcome Garden: Terraced with paved area, flowers Dogs allowed
NOTES: Parking 30

Crown and Sceptre
EX5 5DA ☎ 01392 851278
Dir: 2m NW of Exeter on A377
Twice razed by fire (the last time in 1962), today's pub has still managed to keep original character with oak beams and open fires, while summer barbecues and children's play areas feature among its added attractions. From straightforward bar meals of pies of the day, curries and 'big plate specials' (such as the 24oz mixed grill), the dining menu extends to duck breast with plum sauce, Mexican chilli, and grilled steaks with saucy options such as chasseur and Diane.
OPEN: 11.30-11 (winter 11.30-3 6-11) **BAR MEALS:** L served all week 12-9 D served all week Av main course £5.25
RESTAURANT: L served all week 12-2 D served all week 6-9 Av 3 course à la carte £15 **BREWERY/COMPANY:** Heavitree **:** Otter Ale plus Guest beers. **FACILITIES:** Children welcome Garden: Patio area, food served outside **NOTES:** Parking 30

NOSS MAYO
Map 03 SX54

Pick of the Pubs

The Ship Inn 🐑 ♀
PL8 1EW ☎ 01752 872387 📠 01752 873294
e-mail: ship@nossmayo.com
Dir: 3m S of Yealmpton, on the S side of the Yealm estuary
The Ship is a traditional 16th-century waterside inn attracting walkers, tourists and yachtsmen alike (you can tie your boat up outside). It's fun to reach the pub at high tide and relax at one of the terrace tables overlooking the scenic estuary. A refit a few years ago returned the pub to its roots, with good local and regional beers, home-made food, and comfortable surroundings - wood floors, log fires, old furniture, papers and books. The daily menu is based on local produce, and there's a choice of granary bread sandwiches ranging from cheese and tomato to aromatic duck with spring onions. Favourite dishes earning a regular slot on the carte include classic prawn cocktail with Marie Rose dressing, braised shoulder of Devon lamb served with herb mash and mixed vegetables, and salmon fishcakes with chive mayonnaise and mixed salad.
OPEN: 11-11 **BAR MEALS:** L served all week 12-9.30 D served all week **BREWERY/COMPANY:** Free House **:** Tamar, Exmoor Gold, Shepherd Neame Spitfire Premium Ale, St Austell Dartmoor Best. **FACILITIES:** Garden: Waterside Dogs allowed downstairs only **NOTES:** Parking 100

OTTERY ST MARY
Map 03 SY19

The Talaton Inn 🐑
Talaton EX5 2RQ ☎ 01404 822214
Timber-framed, well-maintained 16th-century inn, recently taken over by a brother and sister partnership. A strong seafood emphasis means that the menu may feature poached salmon hollandaise, cod and chips, king prawns, or scampi. Blackboard specials change regularly, and there's a good selection of real ales and malts. Readers' reports welcome.
OPEN: 12-3 7-11 **BAR MEALS:** L served all week 12-2 D served Tue-Sat 7-9.15 Av main course £7.50 **RESTAURANT:** L served all week 12-2 D served Tue-Sat 7-9.15 Av 3 course à la carte £15
BREWERY/COMPANY: Free House **:** Otter, Fuller's London Pride, O'Hanlon's, Badger Tanglefoot. **FACILITIES:** Children welcome Dogs allowed **NOTES:** Parking 30

PARRACOMBE
Map 03 SS64

Pick of the Pubs

The Fox & Goose ♦♦♦ 🐑 ♀
EX31 4PE ☎ 01598 763239 📠 01598 763621
e-mail: foxandgoose@mrexcessive.net
Dir: The Fox is 1m from the A39 between Blackmoor Gate (2m) and Lynton (6m). Signposted to Parracombe (With a 'Fox & Goose' sign on approach)

Photographs in the bar show this pub to have been two farm cottages until around 1900 when the landlord decided to make it a bit grander. His extensions have not spoilt the atmosphere, and despite a sound reputation for good food this remains a relaxing place where drinkers are welcome. Benefitting from an early bypass (1925), the Fox is set in the heart of a pretty unspoilt village with a narrow street. It takes pride in offering a wide selection of dishes to suit all tastes, based on produce from the surrounding farms and the Devon coast. The blackboard menus keep up with the daily changes, which include the popular venison steak with cognac and redcurrant gravy, and a prize-winning steak and seaweed pie. Fish choices might be turbot fillet with saffron risotto, and red mullet in sambuca cream with pasta, with perhaps pina colada cheesecake with raspberry sauce to round things off.
OPEN: 12-3 6-11 **BAR MEALS:** L served all week 12-2 D served all week 6-9.30 Av main course £12.50
BREWERY/COMPANY: Free House **:** Cotleigh Barn Owl, Carlsberg, Dartmoor Best, Exmoor Gold. ♀: 10
FACILITIES: Garden: Paved courtyard overlooking river Dogs allowed in bar at lunch Water **NOTES:** Parking 30 **ROOMS:** 4 bedrooms 4 en suite s£45 d£45 no children overnight

England

PETER TAVY   Map 03 SX57

The Peter Tavy Inn ♀
PL19 9NN ☎ 01822 810348 ▤ 01822 810835
e-mail: Peter.tavy@virgin.net
See Pick of the Pubs on opposite page

PLYMOUTH   Map 03 SX45

The China House ♀
Marrowbone Slip, Sutton Harbour PL4 0DW
☎ 01752 661592 ▤ 01752 661593
Dir: *A38 to Plymouth centre, follow Exeter St to Sutton Rd, follow signs for Queen Anns Battery*
Built as a warehouse in the mid-17th century, this waterfront pub has also been used as a gun wharf, a bakehouse, a wool warehouse and even a prison. The current name comes from the short-lived local manufacture of porcelain by William Cookworthy in the 1770s. Expect dishes such as chargrilled tuna with warm potato salad, Cumberland sausage with cheese mash and onion gravy, or Bantry Bay mussels, on a typical menu. Fresh baguettes and doorstops served all day.
OPEN: 12-11 **BAR MEALS:** L served all week 12-10 D served all week Av main course £7 **RESTAURANT:** L served all week 12-10 D served all week 7-10.30 Av 3 course à la carte £17
BREWERY/COMPANY: Vintage Inns ◖: Bass, Tetley's.
FACILITIES: Children welcome Garden: Food served outside Dogs allowed **NOTES:** Parking 120

Langdon Court Hotel ★★ ⊛ 🐾 ♀
Down Thomas PL9 0DY ☎ 01752 862358 ▤ 01752 863428
e-mail: enquiries@langdoncourt.co.uk
Dir: *On A379 from Elburton follow brown tourist signs*
Once owned by Henry VIII, this historic, picturesque manor became the home of his last wife, Catherine Parr. The Elizabethan walled garden is Grade II listed. Close to outstanding coastal scenery. Primarily a hotel, Langdon Court offers a comfortable bar with freshly-cooked meals and real ale. Menu includes whole roasted John Dory with shellfish risotto, rack of Devon lamb, steak and kidney pudding, and baked cod with saffron mash and brown shrimp salsa.
OPEN: 12-3 6.30-11 Closed: 25-26 Dec **BAR MEALS:** L served all week 12-2 D served all week 6.30-9.30 Av main course £11 **RESTAURANT:** L served all week 12-2.30 D served all week 6.30-9.30 Av 3 course à la carte £25 **BREWERY/COMPANY:** Free House ◖: Dartmoor Best, Bass. **FACILITIES:** Children welcome Garden: Food served outside, Elizabethan gardens Dogs allowed
NOTES: Parking 50 **ROOMS:** 17 bedrooms 17 en suite s£45 d£75

POSTBRIDGE   Map 03 SX67

Warren House Inn
PL20 6TA ☎ 01822 880208
Dir: *Take B3212 through Moretonhampstead on for 5m*
High up on Dartmoor, this old tin miners' inn was cut off during the harsh winter of 1963 and supplies were delivered by helicopter. A peat fire has burned here continuously since 1845. Home-made cauliflower cheese, seafood platter, mushroom Stroganoff, rabbit pie and venison steak in a port and cranberry sauce feature among the popular dishes. Good choice of snacks and sandwiches.
OPEN: 11-2.30 6-11 (Sun til 10:30 May-Oct open all day)
BAR MEALS: L served all week 12-2 D served all week 6-9.30 Av main course £5 **BREWERY/COMPANY:** Free House ◖: Sharps

Doom Bar, Butcombe Bitter, Badger Tanglefoot, Old Freddy Walker.
FACILITIES: Children welcome Garden: Food served outside Dogs allowed Water **NOTES:** Parking 30

RACKENFORD   Map 03 SS81

The 12th Century Stag Inn ♀
EX16 8DT ☎ 01884 881369
It's hard to imagine a more traditional inn than the Stag, which as its name proclaims dates from the 12th century, and which has a thatched roof and all original features, including beams and open fireplace. There's even a ghost - Tom King, highwayman. The pub is located opposite a 12th-century church, and is ideal for families and dog lovers who enjoy walking. Dishes include home-made pasties, steaks, sticky ribs and freshly-made curries.
OPEN: 11-3.30 6-11 (Open all day in summer) **BAR MEALS:** L served all week 12-3 D served all week 7-10 Av main course £5.99
RESTAURANT: L served all week 12-3 D served all week 7-10
◖: Cotleigh Barn Owl & Tawny, Scottish Courage John Smith's Smooth. ♀: 10 **FACILITIES:** Children welcome Garden: 2 gardens, overlook open fields Dogs allowed Water & toys provided
NOTES: Parking 20

RATTERY   Map 03 SX76

Church House Inn 🐾 ♀
TQ10 9LD ☎ 01364 642220 ▤ 01364 642220
Dating from 1028, Devon's oldest inn is also one of the oldest in the UK. Large open fireplaces, sturdy oak beams and loads of nooks and crannies. Traditional English food includes snacks, light meals, sandwiches, lasagne, chicken and cranberry curry, and rump steak. Moussaka features as a special, as do duck, guinea fowl, venison and rabbit. Plaice, sea bass, brill, halibut, lemon and Dover sole are usually available. Always at least three real ales, including local St Austell Dartmoor Best.
OPEN: 11-3 6-11 (Winter 11-2.30, 6.30-10.30) **BAR MEALS:** L served all week 12-2 D served all week 7-9 **RESTAURANT:** L served all week 12-2 D served all week 7-9 **BREWERY/COMPANY:** Free House ◖: St Austell Dartmoor Best, Greene King Abbot Ale, Wells Bombardier, Adnams Broadside. ♀: 8 **FACILITIES:** Children welcome Children's licence Garden: Lrg lawn, seating, benches Dogs allowed Water **NOTES:** Parking 30

continued

Open: 12-2.30, 6.30-11 (Fri-Sat 6-11, Sun 6.30-10.30)
Bar Meals: L served all week 12-2, D served all week 7-9.
Av cost main course £10.95
RESTAURANT: L served all week 12-2, D served all week 7-9.
BREWERY/COMPANY:
Free House.
🍺: Princetown Jail Ale, Interbrew Bass, Summerskills Tamar, Badger Dorset Best.
FACILITIES: Dogs allowed, Children welcome, Garden - Small garden with views of Dartmoor.
NOTES: Parking 40

The Peter Tavy Inn

A true pub in the best English tradition, dating from the 15th century with blazing fires and a reputation for good food and well-kept real ales.

♀
Peter Tavy, Tavistock, PL19 9NN
☎ 01822 810348 📠 01822 810835
📧 peter.tavy@virgin.net
Dir: Off A386 NE of Tavistock.

The Peter Tavy was built as a tiny cottage to accommodate the masons working on the rebuilding of the village church. It later became a poorhouse, and by 1800 it had been granted a licence to sell alcohol, although it kept its original small dimensions for nearly 200 years until it was renovated and extended in 1988. Its character remains intact with slate floors, low beams and large fireplaces filled with blazing logs in cold weather. In summer the beautiful garden is popular, surrounded as it is by moorland on the edge of Dartmoor, and accessed down a long country lane. Food is at the centre of the operation nowadays, with a regularly-changing blackboard menu listing home-made dishes based on fresh local produce. At lunchtime the choice ranges around traditional bar meals like filled baguettes and ploughman's, and specials such as roast lamb shank, monkfish in creamy garlic sauce, and Devonshire lemon chicken. In the evening the tone is raised a few notches to include caramelised onion tart with Brie, and Stilton and pear paté starters, and main choices like medallions of beef fillet with a wild mushroom sauce, roast rack of lamb with minted gooseberry sauce, and mushroom, chestnut and leek pie. Home-made puddings are equally good at any time of the day: apple and apricot crumble, and chocolate truffle torte should please most palates. Known for its real ales, with at least eight wines by the glass among an extensive list of bottles.

ROCKBEARE   Map 03 SY09

Pick of the Pubs

Jack in the Green Inn ◉◉ 🍴 ♀
London Rd EX5 2EE ☎ 01404 822240 ▤ 01404 823445
e-mail: info@jackinthegreen.uk.com
Dir: *From M5 take old A30 towards Honiton, signed Rockbeare*

They take food very seriously here, designing it with 'those who live to eat' in mind. Whether you're stopping by for a bar snack, or a fuller meal in the restaurant, the quality is evident in everything produced, with consistency, attention to detail and use of fresh local produce central to the philosophy of the kitchen. Outside the kitchen, the young staff show confidence and a delightful willingness to please, going so far as to pass on tips from the chef on request! Seating extends outdoors in summer, with delightful views over the Devon countryside. Imaginative bar food might include sesame chicken with noodles and plum sauce or baked croissant with Brie, apple and celery. Restaurant meals range from classic (roast wood pigeon with wild mushrooms and winter vegetable purée) to modern creations such as grilled fillet of red mullet with ratatouille and tapenade sauce.
OPEN: 11-2.30 6-11 (Sun 12-10.30) Closed: Dec 25 - Jan 2 inclusive **BAR MEALS:** L served all week 11-2 D served all week 6-9.30 Av main course £10 **RESTAURANT:** L served all week 11-2 D served all week 6-9.30 Av 3 course fixed price £21.75
BREWERY/COMPANY: Free House 🍺: Cotleigh Tawny Ale, Thomas Hardy Hardy Country, Otter Ale, Royal Oak. ♀: 12
FACILITIES: Children welcome Garden **NOTES:** Parking 120

SHEEPWASH   Map 03 SS40

Half Moon Inn
EX21 5NE ☎ 01409 231376 ▤ 01409 231673
e-mail: lee@halfmoon.demon.co.uk
Dir: *from M5 take A30 to Okehampton then A386, at Hatheleigh, L onto A3072, after 4m R for Sheepwash*

This white-painted village inn overlooking the village square in a remote Devon village is a Grade II listed building with fishing rights for ten miles of the River Torridge (very popular with anglers). Inside you'll find slate floors and a huge inglenook fireplace where a log fire burns in cooler weather. Bar snacks are available at lunchtime and a set menu of traditional fare at dinner. Typical dishes are prawn cocktail and roast beef. Over sixty malts are available at the bar.
OPEN: 11-2.30 6-11 Closed: 20-27 Dec **BAR MEALS:** L served all week 12-1.45 **RESTAURANT:** D served all week at 8
BREWERY/COMPANY: Free House 🍺: Scottish Courage Courage Best, Sharpe's Own, Greene King Ruddles Best Bitter.
FACILITIES: Dogs allowed **NOTES:** Parking 30

SIDMOUTH   Map 03 SY18

The Blue Ball 🍴 ♀
Stevens Cross, Sidford EX10 9QL
☎ 01395 514062 ▤ 01395 514062
e-mail: rogernewton@blueballinn.net

Run by the same family for 90 years, this thatched-roofed pub dates back to the late 14th century and is built of cob and flint. Converted from its farmhouse origins, the bar occupies the old dairy, with beams and log fires inside and a garden with a terrace and playhouse outside. Food centres round fresh fish and other local produce, and options range from ploughman's and sandwiches to steak and kidney pudding and local sausages.
OPEN: 11-11 Closed: 25 Dec eve **BAR MEALS:** L served all week 12-2 D served all week 6-9.30 Av main course £6.50
BREWERY/COMPANY: Pubmaster 🍺: Interbrew Bass & Flowers IPA, Otter Bitter, Greene King Old Speckled Hen, Guest ale each week.
♀: 10 **FACILITIES:** Children welcome Garden: Lrg, colourful gardens, quiet areas Dogs allowed Water **NOTES:** Parking 100

SLAPTON   Map 03 SX84

Pick of the Pubs

The Tower Inn 🍴 ♀
Church Rd TQ7 2PN ☎ 01548 580216 ▤ 01548 580140
e-mail: towerinn@slapton.org
See Pick of the Pubs on opposite page

Darts

Although darts is now regarded as the archetypal pub game, its history is shrouded in almost total mystery and it may not have entered the pub scene until well into the 19th century. The original board may have been the end of a barrel, with the doubles ring as its outer ring. The accepted arrangement of numbers round the rim dates from the 1890s, but there are variant types of board in different areas of the country. The Yorkshire board, for instance, has no trebles ring. Nor does the Lancashire or Manchester board, which has a very narrow doubles ring and is customarily kept soaked in beer when not in use.

Open: 12-3, 6-11 (Sun 7-10.30)
Bar Meals: L served all week 12-2.30,
D served all week 6-9.30.
RESTAURANT: L served all week 12-2.30,
D served all week 7-9.30.
BREWERY/COMPANY:
Free House.
🍺: Adnams Southwold, Badger
Tanglefoot, St Austell Dartmoor Best,
Tower, & Guest.
FACILITIES: Dogs allowed, Children
welcome, Garden - Beautiful walled
garden.
NOTES: Parking 6

The Tower Inn

A charming 14th-century inn tucked away in a delightful historic village, approached down a narrow lane and through a rustic porch.

Church Road, Slapton,
Kingsbridge, TQ7 2PN
☎ 01548 580216 📠 01548 580140
📧 towerinn@slapton.org
Dir: Off A379 south of Dartmouth,
turn L at Slapton Sands.

The building originally housed workers constructing the Collegiate Chantry of St Mary, whose ruined tower still overlooks the pub's walled garden. Later it became the College's guesthouse, from where alms and hospitality were dispensed. Today's interior is a fascinating series of interconnecting rooms with stone walls, beams, pillars, pews and open fires. The low ceilings are bedecked with plants, herbs and a giant cart wheel, and interesting artefacts decorate the walls, including candelabra, tapestries, various brasses and pictures, and a pair of violins. Two large stone fireplaces provide comfort and warmth on cooler days, and the scrubbed oak tables and church pew seating look inviting against flagstone floors and bare boards. From both lunch and dinner menus you can try spinach and ricotta cannelloni in a four-cheese sauce, and seared salmon escalopes, with braised lentils, mushrooms, and thyme and rosemary sauce. Additional dishes at dinner might be beef fillet with chargrilled asparagus, maltaise sauce and smoked cherry tomato dressing. The daily-changing specials offer yet more choice, with pan-fried turbot on garlic-creamed spinach with red wine butter sauce, and roast wood pigeon with smoked bacon, lentils and cider and wholegrain sauce two of the options. Puddings include apple and cherry pie with Devon clotted cream, and sticky toffee pudding with toffee sauce. For those wanting a lighter meal at lunchtime, there are various sandwiches, and the likes of platter of locally-smoked fish with dill mustard sauce, and home-made fishcakes with a warm citrus and cream dressing. An excellent range of good beers includes Adnams Southwold, and there is local cider, and mulled wine in winter.

SOURTON

Map 03 SX59

The Highwayman Inn

EX20 4HN ☎ 01837 861243 ▯ 01837 861196
e-mail: info@thehighwaymaninn.net
*Dir: Situated on the A386 Okehampton to Tavistock Rd come off main A30
following directions for Tavistock. Pub is 4m from Okehampton and 12m
from Tavistock*

A fascinating old inn full of eccentric furniture, unusual
architectural designs, and strange bric-a-brac. Since 1959, the
vision of Welshman John 'Buster' Jones, and now run by his
daughter Sally, it is made from parts of sailing ships, wood
hauled from Dartmoor's bogs, and Gothic church arches.
Popular with holidaymakers and international tourists, the
menu consists of light snacks including pasties, platters and
organic nibbles.
OPEN: 11-2 6-10.30 (Sun 12-2, 7-10.30) **BAR MEALS:** L served all
week 11-2 D served all week Av main course £5
BREWERY/COMPANY: Free House ◖: St Anstell Duchy,
Teignworthy. **FACILITIES:** Garden Dogs allowed **NOTES:** Parking
150

SOUTH POOL

Map 03 SX74

Millbrook Inn ♀

TQ7 2RW ☎ 01548 531581 ▯ 01548 531868
Dir: Take A379 from Kingsbridge to Frogmore then E
Arrive by boat, if you like, at this quaint 16th-century village
pub close to Salcombe estuary when the tide is high. Inside, it
is small, cosy and unspoilt, with open fires, fresh flowers,
cushioned wheelback chairs, and original beams adorned with
old banknotes and clay pipes. Wholesome bar food includes
fresh crab dishes (heavenly crab sandwiches!), bouillabaisse,
kiln-roasted salmon, roasted cod, halibut au poivre, and prime
Scottish fillet steaks. Peaceful sunny rear terrace overlooking a
stream.
OPEN: 11.30-2.30 5.15-11 (Sun 12-3, 7-10.30) **BAR MEALS:** L
served all week 12-2 D served all week 7-9
BREWERY/COMPANY: Free House ◖: Interbrew Bass, Sutton
Brewery, Spitfire, Shepherd Neame. ♀: 9 **FACILITIES:** Children
welcome Garden **NOTES:** No credit cards

SOUTH ZEAL

Map 03 SX69

Oxenham Arms ★★ ▯

EX20 2JT ☎ 01837 840244 ▯ 01837 840791
e-mail: theoxenhamarms@aol.com
Dir: Just off A30 4m E of Okehampton in the centre of the village
First licensed in 1477, but probably built by monks in the 12th
century, the building is scheduled as an Ancient Monument. In
the small lounge behind the bar is a stone that was shaped by
prehistoric man, which archaeologists believe the monks built

around. Local produce figures in the choice of daily-changing
dishes. Curries and pork sausages on the bar menu; from the
dinner menu come seafood thermidor, and roast topside of
Devon beef chasseur.
OPEN: 11-2.30 5-11 **BAR MEALS:** L served all week 12-2 D served
all week 7-9.15 **RESTAURANT:** L served all week 12-2 D served all
week 7-9 Av 3 course fixed price £17.50
BREWERY/COMPANY: Free House ◖: Princetown Dartmoor IPA,
Sharp's Doom Bar Bitter. **FACILITIES:** Garden: Overlooking Cosdon
Beacon Dogs allowed Water **NOTES:** Parking 8 **ROOMS:** 8
bedrooms 7 en suite 3 family rooms s£45 d£70 no children overnight

SPREYTON

Map 03 SX69

The Tom Cobley Tavern

EX17 5AL ☎ 01647 231314
*Dir: From Merrymeet roundabout take A3124 N. Turn R off the Post Inn,
then 1st R again over bridge*

From this pub one day in 1802 a certain Thomas Cobley, his
hapless mare and a group of friends went on a lads' day out
to Widecombe Fair. Many years later someone recorded the
adventures of 'Uncle Tom Cobley and all' in the famous song.
Today, this traditional village local offers home made, locally
supplied main meals, with a good selection of bar snacks and
lighter fare. The garden is in a pretty setting.
OPEN: 12-2 6-11 (Mon open Summer, BHS) **BAR MEALS:** L
served Tue-Sun 12-2 D served Tue-Sun 7-9 Av main course £7.95
RESTAURANT: L served Sun 12-2 D served Wed-Sat 7-8.45 Av fixed
price £10.95 **BREWERY/COMPANY:** Free House ◖: Cotleigh
Tawny Ale, Interbrew Bass. **FACILITIES:** Children welcome Garden:
Wooden seated area, approx 8 benches **NOTES:** Parking 8
ROOMS: 4 bedrooms 1 family room s£22.50 d£22.50 (♦♦♦)
NOTES: No credit cards

STAVERTON

Map 03 SX76

Pick of the Pubs

The Sea Trout ★★ ⊚ ▯ ♀

TQ9 6PA ☎ 01803 762274 ▯ 01803 762506
e-mail: enquiries@seatroutinn.com
Dir: M5/A38
Set in the heart of a quiet Devon village, this attractive
15th-century inn is a firm favourite with both locals and
visitors. Inside the rambling, whitewashed building you'll
find an easy combination of relaxed hotel, elegant
restaurant and village pub. Comfortably furnished
en suite bedrooms make this an ideal base for touring
Dartmoor and the South Devon coast. Dartington Hall is
on the doorstep, and Dart Valley steam trains cover the
short journey to Buckfast Abbey. An interesting bar menu
features home-made soup and smoked mackerel terrine

continued

continued

among the starters, whilst main courses cover steaks, pies and other pub classics such as bangers and mash. The attractive conservatory style restaurant overlooks pretty gardens; starters here could include grilled fillet of red mullet, or chargrilled vegetable tian, with seared fillets of brill with crab risotto, or pan-fried rump of venison with rösti potato to follow. Round off with desserts such as steamed chocolate sponge, raspberry pannacotta or West country cheeses.

OPEN: 11-3 6-11 (Sun 12-3, 7-10.30) **BAR MEALS:** L served all week 12-2 D served all week 7-9 Av main course £7.50 **RESTAURANT:** L served Sun 12-2 D served all week 7-9 **BREWERY/COMPANY:** Palmers ◖: Palmers IPA, Dorset Gold, Palmers Bi-Centenary '200'. **FACILITIES:** Children welcome Garden: Large, walled patio garden with ponds Dogs allowed Water, dog walk map **NOTES:** Parking 80 **ROOMS:** 11 bedrooms 11 en suite 2 family rooms s£35 d£50

STOCKLAND   Map 04 ST20

Pick of the Pubs

Kings Arms ◆◆◆ 🐑 ♀
EX14 9BS ☎ 01404 881361 🖷 01404 881732
e-mail: info@kingsarms.net

By the Great West Way, at the heart of the Blackdown Hills, stands this long Grade II, thatched and whitewashed 16th-century inn. It boasts an impressive flag-stoned walkway entrance, a medieval oak screen and an original bread oven, as well as an old grey-painted phone box. The atmospheric Farmers bar is a lively and popular meeting place, while the Cotley restaurant bar offers a wide range of blackboard specials: fish choices like pasta marinara, king prawn Madras, and Cajun Scotch salmon fillet, and meaty pork tenderloin and wild mushroom risotto, calves' liver with bacon and onions, and Cotley rack of lamb. Mouthwatering desserts include lemon

continued

treacle sponge pudding, and blueberry and raspberry cheesecake. The British and classic cooking is complemented by well-kept real ales and an outstanding collection of cheeses.
OPEN: 12-3 6.30-11.30 Closed: Dec 25 **BAR MEALS:** L served Mon-Sat 12-2 **RESTAURANT:** L served all week 12-2 D served all week 6.30-9 Av 3 course à la carte £22.50
BREWERY/COMPANY: Free House ◖: Otter Ale, Exmoor Ale, Scottish Courage John Smiths, O'Hanlon's Yellowhammer. ♀: 21
FACILITIES: Children welcome Garden: Part lawn part patio, Seating for 30 Dogs allowed **NOTES:** Parking 45 **ROOMS:** 3 bedrooms 3 en suite 1 family rooms s£40 d£60

STOKE FLEMING   Map 03 SX84

The Green Dragon Inn 🐑 ♀
Church Rd TQ6 0PX ☎ 01803 770238 🖷 01803 770238
e-mail: pcrowther@btconnect.com
Dir: Telephone for directions
A smugglers, tunnel is said to connect this 12th-century pub to Blackpool Sands. Certainly the landlord is drawn to the sea: he's famous for his voyages across the Atlantic. Inside, you'll find a warm atmosphere and deceptively-simple cooking. Lunchtime snacks include fresh baguettes and locally-made beefburgers, whilst dinner menus allow you to order starters as light bites (perhaps prawn platter with aïoli and bread or Dartmouth smoked mackerel). Main courses include Italian meatloaf, venison pie and Glamorgan sausages.
OPEN: 11-3 7.30-11 **BAR MEALS:** L served Mon-Sun 12-2.30 D served Mon-Sun 6.30-9 Av main course £8 **RESTAURANT:** L served Mon-Sun 12-2.30 D served Mon-Sun Av 3 course à la carte £15
BREWERY/COMPANY: Heavitree ◖: Otter, Flowers IPA, Bass 6x.
♀: 9 **FACILITIES:** Children welcome Garden: Small, covered patio Dogs allowed **NOTES:** Parking 6 No credit cards

---

STOKENHAM   Map 03 SX84

Pick of the Pubs

Trademan's Arms 🐑
TQ7 2SZ ☎ 01548 580313 🖷 01548 580313
e-mail: elizabethsharman@hotmail.com
Dir: just off A379 between Kingsbridge & Dartmouth
This part-thatched free house dates from 1390 and forms the centrepiece of a picturesque old village that was given to Anne of Cleves by Henry VIII in 1539. Incorporating a former brewhouse and three cottages, the pub takes its name from the tradesmen who used to call at the brewhouse while working in the area. Unpretentious and simply furnished, the interior has a stone fireplace and enjoys fine views of the parish church. Chef/proprietor John Sharman is a keen angler and hunter, which gives the menu a strong emphasis on fish and game. This is shown in dishes such as seared tuna steak with piquant tomato sauce, rod-caught Start Bay baked sea bass, wild pigeon breast finished with cream and chorizo, local pheasant braised in white wine sauce, scallops flamed in brandy in onion sauce, and Trademan's home-made fish cakes. Interesting puddings, real ales, local cider and a fine range of malt whiskies round off the package.
OPEN: 6.30-11 (Tues-Sat 6.30-11, Sun lunch 12-2.30) Closed: 2wks Nov or Mar **BAR MEALS:** L served Sun 12-1.45 D served Tues-Sat 6.30-9 Av main course £11.50 **RESTAURANT:** L served Sun 12-1.45 D served Tues-Sat 6.30-9 Av 3 course à la carte £20
BREWERY/COMPANY: Free House ◖: Adnams Bitter, Otter Ale, Exmoor Gold, Princetown. **FACILITIES:** Garden: Raised garden overlooking the valley Dogs allowed Water **NOTES:** Parking 14

TEDBURN ST MARY Map 03 SX89

Kings Arms Inn ♀
EX6 6EG ☎ 01647 61224 🖹 01647 61324
e-mail: reception@kingsarmsinn.co.uk
Dir: A30 W to Okehampton, 1st exit R signed Tedburn St Mary

Log fires and exposed beams are features of this delightful
village centre inn which is a handy base for exploring
beautiful Dartmoor. Charles II may well have stayed here on
his journey through Cornwall - hence the pub's name. Expect
a good range of traditional bar meals and daily specials.
Typical favourites include scampi and chips, chicken Caesar
salad, oven-roast salmon and flamed steak.
OPEN: 11-3 6-11 **BAR MEALS:** L served all week 11-2.30 D served
all week 6-9.30 Av main course £6 **RESTAURANT:** L served all week
11-2.30 D served all week 6-9.30 Av 3 course à la carte £15
BREWERY/COMPANY: Free House 🍺: Interbrew Bass &
Worthington Best, Sharps Cornish Coaster, Whitbread Best,.
FACILITIES: Children welcome Garden: Large lawned gardens, large
covered courtyard **NOTES:** Parking 40

THURLESTONE Map 03 SX64

The Village Inn 🍺♀
TQ7 3NN ☎ 01548 563525 🖹 01548 561069
e-mail: mike@thurlestone.co.uk
Dir: Take A379 from Plymouth towards Kingsbridge at Bantham rdbt go
straight over on to the B3197, then right onto a lane signed Thurlestone
2.5m

In the same family ownership for over a century, a friendly
village local that draws seasonal trade from the nearby coastal
path to Bigbury Bay. Once a farmhouse B&B, the 16th-century
freehouse today prides itself on good service, well-kept ales
and decent food. Blackboards offer daily choices such as shell-
on prawns with garlic mayonnaise, seared scallops with
Parma ham, smoked chicken tagliatelle and ostrich medallions
with pink peppercorn sauce.
OPEN: 11.30-3 6-11 (July-Aug all day) (Sun 12-3, 7-10.30)

BAR MEALS: L served all week 12-2 D served all week 6.30-9.30 Av
main course £6.95 **BREWERY/COMPANY:** Free House
🍺: Palmers IPA, Interbrew Bass, Sharp's Doom Bar & Guest beer.
FACILITIES: Children welcome Garden: Patio, food served outside
Dogs allowed Water **NOTES:** Parking 50

TOPSHAM Map 03 SX98

Bridge Inn NEW
Bridge Hill EX3 0QQ ☎ 01392 873862 🖹 01392 877497
e-mail: bridge@cheffers.co.uk
Dir: 4 miles from Exeter city centre
Four generation of the same family have run this listed 16th-
century inn since 1897, and under their management it has
remained old-fashioned in the best sense of the word. It sits
peacefully beside the River Clyst, where benches are
strategically placed to watch the heron, egret and Canada
geese. Inside are quirky little rooms filled with atmosphere
and interesting local characters, and usually a minimum of
eight real ales on tap to help oil the conversation (Triple FFF's
I Can't Remember, O'Hanlon's Yellowhammer and
Blackawton's Dragonheart are just a few of these). Food is
limited to sandwiches (smoked chicken, Stilton cheese),
ploughmans, and hot meat and potato pasties, all made
freshly to order; but this is mainly a drinker's pub, and the
selection of beers changes daily. An 18th-century malthouse is
used for meetings and parties, and the Bridge Inn has the
distinction of being the first pub that the Queen has ever
officially visited.
OPEN: 12-2 6-10.30 (Sun 7-11.30 Sat 6-11) **BAR MEALS:** L served
all week 12-1.45 6-10 Av main course £4.95
BREWERY/COMPANY: Free House 🍺: Branscombe Vale-Branoc,
Adnams Broadside, Exe Valley O'Hanlons, Blackawton.
FACILITIES: Children welcome Garden: Benches overlooking River
Clyst Dogs allowed Water & Toys **NOTES:** Parking 20 No credit
cards

The Lighter Inn ♀
The Quay EX3 0HZ ☎ 01392 875439 🖹 01392 876013

The imposing 17th-century customs house on Topsham Quay
has been transformed into a popular waterside inn. A strong
nautical atmosphere is reinforced with pictures, ship's
instruments and oars beneath the pub's wooden ceilings, and
the attractive quayside sitting area is popular in summer.
Dishes may include whole sea bass or plaice, steaks, curries
and salads, or steak, ale and mushroom pie.
OPEN: 11-11 Closed: Dec 25 **BAR MEALS:** L served all week 12-
2.30 D served all week 6.30-9 Av main course £7.95
BREWERY/COMPANY: Woodhouse Inns 🍺: Badger Best, Badger
Tanglefoot, Sussex. **FACILITIES:** Children welcome Public quay
Dogs allowed Water provided **NOTES:** Parking 40

continued

England

TORCROSS　　　　　　　　　Map 03 SX84

Pick of the Pubs

Start Bay Inn 🐾 ♀
TQ7 2TQ ☎ 01548 580553 📠 01548 580941
e-mail: cstubbs@freeuk.com
Dir: between Dartmouth & Kingsbridge on the A379
For some great Devonshire fish served in glorious
surroundings, head to this 14th-century thatched pub
situated between Slapton Ley and the panoramic sweep of
Start Bay in the beautiful South Hams. The landlord dives
for plaice, scallops and skate, and hooks sea bass by rod
and line, while the rest of the catch is freshly delivered
from a local trawler. Arrive soon after opening, especially
in the summer, to sample cod, haddock and plaice deeply
fried in a light batter, lemon sole, giant prawns, and crab
and seafood platters, along with various steaks, freshly-
roasted chicken, spinach and mushroom lasagne, and
plenty of sandwiches, ploughman's lunches, and other
snacks. Treacle sponge pudding, spotted Dick, and locally-
made ice cream go down well whatever the season. The
bar and dining areas are simply furnished and decorated
with photographs of the storm-ravaged pub.
OPEN: 11.30-2.30 6-11.30 (Summer 11.30-11.30) **BAR MEALS:** L
served all week 11.30-2 D served all week 6-10 Av main course
£5.50 **BREWERY/COMPANY:** Heavitree 🍺: Interbrew Flowers
Original & Bass, Otter Ale. **FACILITIES:** Children welcome
Garden: Patio area overlooks Slapton Sands Dogs allowed on leads,
water **NOTES:** Parking 18

TOTNES　　　　　　　　　Map 03 SX86

Pick of the Pubs

Durant Arms ♦♦♦♦ 🐾
Ashprington TQ9 7UP ☎ 01803 732240
e-mail: info@thedurantarms.com
See Pick of the Pubs on page 156

The Steam Packet Inn ♦♦♦♦ 🐾 ♀
St Peter's Quay TQ9 5EW ☎ 01803 863880 📠 01803 862754
e-mail: esther@thesteampacketinn.co.uk
*Dir: Leave A38 at Totnes Junct, proceed to Dartington & Totnes. Straight
across lights & rdbt following signs for town centre with river on L, follow
The Plains in town centre for 100yds. Pub on river*
The inn's sign depicts the Amelia, a steam packet ship that
regularly called here, transporting passengers, parcels and
mail in times before roads and railways were developed. The
inn (and in particular its Riverside restaurant) still provides a
good vantage point for watching river traffic - these days
mostly wildlife - accompanied by meals such as smoked duck
salad, and grilled Dover sole with battered avocado and a
sharp tomato dressing. Bar snacks, pizzas and children's
meals are also available.
OPEN: 11 -11 (Sun 12-10.30) **BAR MEALS:** L served all week 12-
2.30 D served all week 6.30-9.30 Av main course £6.75
RESTAURANT: L served all week 12-2.30 D served all week 7-9.30
Av 3 course à la carte £22.50 **BREWERY/COMPANY:** Free House
🍺: Scottish Courage Directors, Courage Best, Interbrew Bass & Two
Real Ales. **FACILITIES:** Children welcome Garden: Riverside quay,
lights, raised terrace Dogs allowed Water, small dogs only in
bedrooms **NOTES:** Parking 16 **ROOMS:** 4 bedrooms 4 en suite 1
family rooms s£40 d£60

Pick of the Pubs

The Watermans Arms 🐾 ♀
Bow Bridge, Ashprington TQ9 7EG
☎ 01803 732214 📠 01803 732314
e-mail: watermansarms.ashprington@eldridge-pope.co.uk
*Dir: A38, A381, follow signs for Kingsbridge out of Totnes, at top of hill
turn L for Ashprington and Bow Bridge*
A charming old free house set in a wildlife paradise at the
head of Bow Creek, close to the ancient Bow Bridge. In
the 1850s the inn doubled as a brewery and a smithy, and
at one time it was a favourite haunt of the hated press-
gangs, who 'spirited away' their victims for military
service. Nothing could be further from the tranquil nature
of the pub today, with its delightful riverside garden and
15 beautifully furnished en suite bedrooms. New
managers and a new chef have revitalised the menus and
the restaurant, and there's plenty of choice. Haddock and
mushroom bake, and salmon and asparagus béarnaise
from the sea, and beef lasagne verdi, half shoulder of
lamb, and steak and ale pie, feature on the dinner menu.
At lunchtime expect liver and bacon, and crispy-battered
cod with chips, along with various jackets and baguettes.
OPEN: 11-11 (Sun 12-10.30) **BAR MEALS:** L served all week
12-2.30 D served all week 6.30-9.30 **RESTAURANT:** D served
Wed to Sun 6.30-9.30 **BREWERY/COMPANY:** Eldridge Pope
🍺: Interbrew Bass, Wadworth 6X, Carlsberg-Tetley Smooth.
♀: 8 **FACILITIES:** Children welcome Garden Dogs allowed
NOTES: Parking 60 **ROOMS:** 15 bedrooms 15 en suite 2 family
rooms s£54 d£69 (♦♦♦♦)

DOWN ON THE FARM

Cider has been drunk in Britain since
before Roman times and was originally made of
fermented crab apple juice. Farmers made their
own, especially in the West Country, and by the
17th century about 350 varieties of cider apple
tree were cultivated, with names like Redstreak
and Kingston Black, Sweet Coppin and
Handsome Maud.
The basic process of cider-making is to crush
apples in a press, run off the juice and leave it to
ferment narurally in casks for four months or so.
The Industrial Revolution, however, transferred
cider from the farm to the factory and by the
1960s the major producers were following the
same path as the brewers and efficiently turning
out a standardised product - weak, sweet and
fizzy - that had only a distant resemblance to the
powerful ' rough cider' or 'scrumpy' of earlier
days. Fortunately, a draught cider renaissance
has followed in the wake of the real ale revival,
and one of the Campaign for Real Ale's aim
is to prevent the disappearance of
rough cider and perry.

Open: 11.30-2.30, 6.30-11
(Sun 12-2.30, 7-10.30)
Bar Meals: L served all week 12-2.30, D served all week 7-9.15.
Av cost main course £6.95
RESTAURANT: L served all week 12-2.30, D served all week 7-9.15.
Av cost 3 courses £17.50
BREWERY/COMPANY:
Free House.
🍺: Dartmoor Bitter, Tetley, Bass Bitter.
FACILITIES: Children welcome, Garden terraced with rosewood furniture.
NOTES: Parking 8
ROOMS: 7 en suite from s£40 d£70

The Durant Arms

A beautiful South Hams village close to the River Dart and the Dart Valley is the location for the 18th-century Durant Arms, just a few miles from the Elizabethan town of Totnes.

◆◆◆◆

Ashprington, Totnes, TQ9 7UP
☎ 01803 732240
✉ info@thedurantarms.com
Dir: Leave A38 at Totnes Jct, proceed to Dartington & Totnes, at 1st set of traffic lights R for Knightsbridge on A381, after 1m L for Ashprington.

As such, it is ideally placed for touring this popular area. This award-winning inn takes its name from the owners of the original village estate, and is renowned for its cuisine: all food is freshly cooked to order and based on a wide variety of locally-sourced meat, fish and vegetables. The comfortable bar is fitted out in traditional style, and serves a good choice of real ales and bottled lagers. There are three separate dining rooms to choose from, all supervised by owners Eileen and Graham Ellis who pride themselves on the quality of service and hospitality. For lovers of meat and game there is steak and kidney pie, half an Aylesbury duckling, venison fillet with red wine and mushroom sauce, and roast pheasant among a host of both hearty and sophisticated offerings. Fish is also prominent on the blackboard menu, including plaice fillets filled with spinach and smoked salmon, grilled turbot garni, monkfish with tiger prawns in cream and garlic, poached salmon with dill and cucumber sauce, and halibut steak with a cheese and prawn sauce. The six tasteful en suite bedrooms offer visitors a chance to extend their stay. Each room is individually designed and furnished, with charming exposed beams a feature in some. A small terrace garden with a water feature makes a pleasant alternative to the bars in warm weather.

TOTNES continued

Pick of the Pubs

The White Hart Bar and Restaurant 🐾 ♀
Dartington Hall TQ9 6EL ☎ 01803 847111 📠 847107
e-mail: dhcc.reservations@btinternet.com
Dir: Totnes turning on A38 to Plymouth, approx 4m
The 1200 acres of lovely landscaped gardens, ancient deer parkland, woodland and farmland surrounding Dartington Hall make this a truly stunning location. Add to this heady pastoral cocktail a bar and restaurant sited beside a 14th-century Great Hall and medieval courtyard, and you have the recipe for unlimited hedonism. The White Hart began life as a private club in 1934 and is now a stylish dining venue. With its flagstoned floors, limed oak settles, roughcast walls and historic photographs, it exudes a warm and welcoming atmosphere that is hard to beat. West Country ales feature alongside organic produce at lunchtime and in the evenings on the interesting menus, and an accessible wine list classifies bottles by their flavours. For a light bar lunch you might try squid and chorizo noodles, smoked haddock on a bed of spinach with a cheese sauce, or cheese and ham croissants, while the main menu lists Thai fish curry set on soft noodles, confit of duck leg, and deep-fried wild mushroom risotto balls with chargrilled vegetables and a pesto dressing. In the evening, the restaurant menu might start with local scallops and oysters poached in fish consommé, or whole roasted baby quail with shallot purée, and black pudding. Move on to braised blade of beef with bubble and squeak and crispy oxtail, roast brill fillets with garlic mash and deep-fried oysters, or Gressingham duck breast with braised Puy lentils. The sublime desserts should not be ignored: glazed blood orange tartlet with its own sorbet, and confit of citrus fruits with orange and poppy seed tuiles might compete with steamed spotted Dick with soaked Medjool dates and vanilla sauce.
OPEN: 11-11 (Closed Mon, Sun nights Nov-Mar) Closed: 24 Dec-6 Jan **BAR MEALS:** L served all week 12-2.30 D served all week 6-9.30 Av main course £7.50 **RESTAURANT:** L served all week 12-2.30 D served all week 6-9.30 Av 3 course à la carte £22.50 **BREWERY/COMPANY:** Free House 🍺: Princetown Jail Ale, Butcombe Bitter, Blackawton Bitter, White Hart Ale.
FACILITIES: Garden: 29 acres, landscaped, river walks etc
NOTES: Parking 250

**Use the AA Hotel Booking Service on
0870 5050505
to book at AA recognised hotels and
B&B's in the UK and Ireland
or through our internet site at
www.theAA.com**

TRUSHAM   Map 03 SX88

Cridford Inn 🐾
TQ13 0NR ☎ 01626 853694 📠 01626 853694
e-mail: cridford@eclipse.co.uk
Dating from 825 AD but remodelled in 1081, this lovely thatched building spent many years as a nunnery and later a farm before finding its vocation as an archetypal country pub. Inside you'll find rough stone walls, slate floors and loads of atmosphere. The transept window in the bar is said to be the oldest domestic window in Britain. The present proprietor's wife is a Malaysian culinary expert from Kuala Lumpur, so Malaysian specialities are offered alongside traditional pub dishes like grilled salmon with tarragon sauce, and steak and chips.
OPEN: 12-3 7-11 Closed: 8 Jan- 31Mar **BAR MEALS:** L served all week 12-3 D served all week 7-10.30 Av main course £6.50
RESTAURANT: D served all week 7-9.30 Av 3 course à la carte £15
BREWERY/COMPANY: Free House 🍺: Teign Valley Tipple, Badger Best, Trusham Ale, Tinners. **FACILITIES:** Children welcome Garden Dogs allowed **NOTES:** Parking 35

TUCKENHAY   Map 03 SX85

Pick of the Pubs

The Maltsters Arms 🐾 ♀
TQ9 7EQ ☎ 01803 732350 📠 01803 732823
e-mail: pub@tuckenhay.demon.co.uk
In secluded, wooded Bow Creek off the River Dart, this splendid 18th-century pub is a classy place to eat and stay. Accessible only through high-banked Devon lanes, or by boat for about three hours either side of high tide. The daily changing menus are flexible - if you want roasted half guinea fowl, or pan-fried fillet of salmon with couscous for lunch, then you may. If you want a starter masquerading as a light bite, or a double decker sandwich, you only have to ask. At dinner, what about sweet and sour pork with brown rice, grilled fillets of gurnard with prawn sauce, or tortilla filled with creamy fennel, mushroom and melted Gruyère? Vegetarians have a good choice and children can choose from their own menu. Puddings range from crumbles to Salcombe ice cream, and on to West Country cheeses and biscuits. A good selection of Devonshire real ales.
OPEN: 11-11 (Sun 12-10.30) **BAR MEALS:** L served all week 12-2.30 D served all week 7-9.30 Av main course £10
RESTAURANT: L served all week 12-2.30 D served all week 7-9.30 Av 3 course à la carte £18 **BREWERY/COMPANY:** Free House 🍺: Princetown Dartmoor IPA, Young's Bitter, Otter Ale, Exe Valley Devon Glory. ♀: 20 **FACILITIES:** Children welcome Garden: Riverside paved quay with seating & tables Dogs allowed Dog Bowl, Biscuits, lots of pals **NOTES:** Parking 50

TYTHERLEIGH   Map 04 ST30

Tytherleigh Arms Hotel 🐾 ♀
EX13 7BE ☎ 01460 220400 & 220214 📠 01460 220406
e-mail: TytherleighArms@aol.com
Notable features of this 17th-century former coaching inn are the beamed ceilings, huge roaring fire and the lovely lady's loo. It is a family-run, food-led establishment, situated on the Devon, Somerset and Dorset borders, with accommodation also provided in the old stable block. Fresh home-cooked

continued

England

TYTHERLEIGH continued

dishes using local ingredients include local trout with bacon and mushroom, West Country cod in beer batter, Lyme Bay diver-caught scallops, pork tenderloin with black pudding, or a selection of pies. Comprehensive bar snack menu also available. **OPEN:** 11-2.30 6.30-11 **BAR MEALS:** L served all week 12-2.30 D served all week 6.30-9 Av main course £8.95 **RESTAURANT:** L served all week 12-2.30 D served all week 6.30-9 Av 3 course à la carte £16.95 **BREWERY/COMPANY:** Free House **◀:** Butcombe Bitter, Exmoor Fox. **FACILITIES:** Children welcome Children's licence Garden: Courtyard, very pretty Dogs allowed Water dishes **NOTES:** Parking 60

UMBERLEIGH   Map 03 SS62

Pick of the Pubs

The Rising Sun Inn ★★ ♀
EX37 9DU ☎ 01769 560447 ▤ 01769 564764
e-mail: risingsuninn@btinternet.com
Dir: Situated at Umberleigh Bridge on the A377, Exeter/Barnstaple road, at the junc of the B3227

Idyllically set beside the River Taw and with a very strong fly-fishing tradition, the Rising Sun dates back in part to the 13th century. The traditional flagstone bar is strewn with fishing memorabilia, comfortable chairs and daily papers and magazines for a very relaxing visit. Outside is a sunny raised terrace with beautiful rural views of the valley, and the riverside walk is equally enjoyable before or after a meal. The quality of food has put this friendly inn firmly on the map. As well as a familiar selection of bar snacks, the extensive carte tempts guests with quality local produce, including fish, game and steak dishes. You could start with seared fresh scallops with spicy chorizo sausage or moules marinère with crusty bread. Move on to main courses such as roasted lamb shank on crushed potato with vegetables and mint gravy, Cumberland sausages with mash and onion gravy, or hot chilli nachos with cheese, crème frâiche and salad. **OPEN:** 11-3 6-11 (open all day Sat-Sun) **BAR MEALS:** L served all week 12-2 D served all week 7-9 Av main course £6.50 **RESTAURANT:** L served all week 12-2 D served all week 7-9 Av 3 course à la carte £19 **BREWERY/COMPANY:** Free House **◀:** Exmoor, Cotleigh Tawny Bitter, Barn Owl, Heineken. **♀:** 10 **FACILITIES:** Children welcome Children's licence Garden: Patio garden overlooking the river Dogs allowed **NOTES:** Parking 30 **ROOMS:** 9 bedrooms 9 en suite s£46 d£80

WIDECOMBE IN THE MOOR   Map 03 SX77

The Old Inn ▧
TQ13 7TA ☎ 01364 621207 ▤ 01364 621407
e-mail: oldinn.wid@virgin.net
Dir: Telephone for directions
Dating from the 15th century, the Old Inn was partly ruined by fire but rebuilt around the original fireplaces. Two main bars and no fewer than five eating areas offer plenty of scope for visitors to enjoy the home-cooked food. From several menus plus blackboard specials, options range from filled Widecombe granary sticks through salads and steaks to lamb with gin sauce, an enormous fillet of cod in batter, or Butcher's Delight - a massive meat platter. **OPEN:** 11-3 7-11 (Summer 6.30-11) Closed: 25 Dec **BAR MEALS:** L served all week 11-2 D served all week 7-10 Av main course £6.60 **RESTAURANT:** L served all week 11-14 D served all week 7-10 Av 3 course à la carte £14.60 **BREWERY/COMPANY:** Free House **◀:** Interbrew Flowers IPA & Boddingtons. **FACILITIES:** Children welcome Garden: Streams, Ponds, Gazebos Dogs allowed Water **NOTES:** Parking 55

Rugglestone Inn
TQ13 7TF ☎ 01364 621327 ▤ 01364 621224
Dir: A38 Drumbridges exit towards Bovey Tracey, L at 2nd rdbt, L at sign Haytor & Widecombe, village is 5m
Converted from a farm cottage in 1832, this pretty Dartmoor inn has a large lawned garden with picnic tables and is surrounded by peaceful moorland. Open fires, beamed ceilings, real ales straight from the barrel and local farm cider help give the pub its special atmosphere. New owners Rod and Diane Williams plan to make the pub more child-friendly, and their new-look menu has home-cooked pies - using local produce wherever possible - at its heart. **OPEN:** 11-2.30 6-11 (Sat 11-3, Sun 12-3) (Winter 7-11, Sun 10.30) **BAR MEALS:** L served all week 12-2 D served all week 7-9 **BREWERY/COMPANY:** Free House **◀:** Butcombe Bitter, St Austells Dartmoor Best. **FACILITIES:** Children welcome Garden: Lrg lawn, picnic tables, cover if needed Dogs allowed Water and biscuits **NOTES:** Parking 40

WINKLEIGH   Map 03 SS60

Pick of the Pubs

The Duke of York ♀
Iddesleigh EX19 8BG ☎ 01837 810253 ▤ 01837 810253
Thatched 15th-century inn set in a sleepy village in the heart of rural mid-Devon, Originally three cottages, built to house workers restoring the parish church, it has all the timeless features of a classic country pub - heavy old beams, a huge inglenook fireplace with winter log fires, old scrubbed tables and farmhouse chairs, and an unspoilt atmosphere free from electronic games. Popular with local farmers, business people and visitors alike, it offers great real ale and hearty home cooking, with all dishes displayed on the large blackboard menu being freshly prepared in the pub kitchen using local produce, including meat reared on nearby farms. From starters or light meals like port and Stilton pâté, smoked trout fillet with dill, and home-made soups, the menu choice extends to freshly-battered cod and chips, beef and Guinness casserole, lamb and mint pie, Thai green chicken curry, and liver and bacon with mash and onion gravy. Delightful hosts. **OPEN:** 11-11 **BAR MEALS:** L served all week 12-10 D served all

continued

week Av main course £6.50 **RESTAURANT:** D served all week 7-10 Av 3 course à la carte £19 Av 3 course fixed price £19 **BREWERY/COMPANY:** Free House 🍺: Adnams Broadside, Cotleigh Tawny, Guest beers. **FACILITIES:** Children welcome Garden: patio/terrace, outdoor eating Dogs allowed water provided

The Kings Arms 🐾 ♀

Fore St EX19 8HQ ☎ 01837 83384
An ancient thatched country inn in this hilltop village set between the rivers Taw and Torridge. Three wood-burning stoves keep the beamed bar and dining room warm in chilly weather, and help to maintain a traditional atmosphere. Typical pub snacks like baked potato, baguettes and ploughman's are supported by a decent choice including lamb and mint pastry parcels, chicken breast wrapped in bacon, mixed grills, and all-day breakfast.
OPEN: 11-11 (Sun 12-10.30) **BAR MEALS:** L served all week 11-9.30 D served all week Av main course £6.50
BREWERY/COMPANY: Enterprise Inns 🍺: Wells Bombardier, Butcombe Bitter, plus guest. **FACILITIES:** Children welcome Garden: Small courtyard to side of property Dogs allowed

WONSON   Map 03 SX68

Northmore Arms NEW

EX20 2JA ☎ 01647 231428
Dir: *From M5 take A30 Towards Okehampton. At Merrymeet roundabout(Whiddon Down) take first left on to the old A30 through village then left, then right down lane, left at T Junction 0.75 to Wonson*
Located in a very rural corner of Dartmoor, this pub is an ideal destination for ramblers, cyclists and horse riders (own paddock). No juke boxes or one-armed bandits spoil the peace of the place, and visitors find it relaxing to chat to the friendly locals. Bar food is of the traditional variety, with the likes of ham, eggs and chips, and steak and kidney pudding with vegetables, chips and gravy.
OPEN: 11-11 (Sun 12-10.30) **BAR MEALS:** L served all week 12-2.30 D served all week 7-9.30 Av main course £6 🍺: Adnams, Broadside, Cotley, Tawney & Ex Valley Dob's. **FACILITIES:** Children welcome Garden: Park for horses, large playing area Dogs allowed Water **NOTES:** Parking 8

YARCOMBE   Map 04 ST20

The Yarcombe Angel

EX14 9BD ☎ 01404 861676
Dir: *On A30 between Chard and Honiton, 1m from A303*
With 9th century origins as a monastery, and later owned by Sir Francis Drake, this historic pub offers a range of imaginative chef's specials. Among them might be spiced lamb with apricots, local pork with cider and shallots, summer salads, and homemade pizzas (to eat in or take out). Specials include tuna and coriander with sun-dried tomatoes and penne, and various sausages. Ploughman's and open sandwiches are always available. Antiques and curios for sale are dotted around.
OPEN: 12-3 6-11 **BAR MEALS:** L served all week 12-2.30 D served Tues-Sun 7-9.30 Av main course £4.95 **BREWERY/COMPANY:** Free House 🍺: Interbrew Bass, Black Sheep Best, Timothy Taylor Landlord, Fuller's London Pride. **FACILITIES:** Children Children's licence Garden: Patio overlooking the Yarty valley Dogs allowed **NOTES:** Parking 20 **NOTES:** No credit cards

---

★ **Star rating for inspected hotel accommodation**

DORSET

ABBOTSBURY   Map 04 SY58

Ilchester Arms

9 Market St DT3 4JR ☎ 01305 871243 📠 01305 871225
Rambling 16th-century coaching inn set in the heart of one of Dorset's most picturesque villages. Abbotsbury is home to many crafts including woodwork and pottery. A good area for walkers, and handy for the Tropical Gardens and Swannery. Under new management as we went to press.
OPEN: 11-11 **BAR MEALS:** L served all week 12-2 D served all week 7-9 Av main course £7 🍺: Old Speckled Hen, Gales HSB, Badger Tanglefoot, Courage Best. **FACILITIES:** Children welcome Dogs allowed **NOTES:** No credit cards

BLANDFORD FORUM   Map 04 ST80

The Crown Hotel ★★★ ♀

West St DT11 7AJ ☎ 01258 456626 📠 01258 451084
e-mail: thecrownhotel@blandforddorset.freeserve.co.uk
Dir: *M27 W onto A31 to junction with A350 W to Blandford. 100mtrs from town bridge*
Classic Georgian coaching inn on the banks of the River Stour overlooking Blandford's handsome redbrick-and-stone town centre, with plenty of period atmosphere. Bar fare ranges from ploughman's and hot baguettes to spicy chorizo pasta, pan-fried lambs' liver, and baked gammon hock, while the restaurant menu may feature escalopes of pork loin, chargrilled lamb cutlets, and steak, kidney and mushroom pie. To finish, perhaps, try Dutch apple pie, bread and butter pudding, or chocolate caramel gateau.
OPEN: 10-2.30 6-11 Closed: 25-28 Dec **BAR MEALS:** L served all week 12-2 D served all week 7-9 Av main course £9
RESTAURANT: D served Mon-Sat 7.15-9.15 Av 3 course à la carte £17 Av 3 course fixed price £15 **BREWERY/COMPANY:** Hall & Woodhouse 🍺: Badger Tanglefoot & Best. ♀: 20 **FACILITIES:** Children welcome Garden: Food served outside Dogs allowed **NOTES:** Parking 70 **ROOMS:** 32 bedrooms 32 en suite s£75 d£96

BOURTON   Map 04 ST73

The White Lion Inn 🐾 ♀

High St SP8 5AT ☎ 01747 840866 📠 01747 841529
e-mail: whitelioninn@bourtondorset.fsnet.co.uk
Dir: *Off A303, opposite B3092 to Gillingham*
If, Hollywood-style, there were a Central Casting of English pubs, this stone-built village inn should certainly audition. Attributes include old beams, flagstones, log fires, real ales, and home-prepared English food. Hosts Mike and Scarlett Senior share decades of catering experience: Mike has clocked up more than 40 years in the business, while Scarlett's family have been innkeepers for some 100 years. One menu is used throughout, so you may choose to eat in one of the bars or in the non-smoking restaurant. Examples of what to expect are the intriguingly different starters of rustic bread and roasted garlic bulbs with extra-virgin olive oil, and zucchini fritters with yoghurt sauce. Main courses prove equally noteworthy - glazed ratatouille and spinach pancakes, for instance, and, from the specials board, jugged hare bourguignon, and Barbary duck in Pimm's and blackberry sauce. The addition of Mike's curry board, Sunday roast board, and lunchtime-only speciality sandwiches and wraps completes the picture.
OPEN: 12-3 6-11 (Sun 12-10.30) Closed: 26 Dec **BAR MEALS:** L served all week 12-2 D served all week 7-9 Av main course £9 **RESTAURANT:** L served all week 12-2 D served all week 7-9 Av 3 course à la carte £25
BREWERY/COMPANY: 🍺: Fullers London Pride, Youngs, Bitter & Guest Beer. ♀: 8 **FACILITIES:** Children welcome Garden: Grassed with trees, patio area Dogs allowed Water **NOTES:** Parking 30

See Pub Walk on page 160

The White Lion

See the stone that represents the meeting point of Dorset, Wiltshire and Somerset on this delightfully varied walk.

From the inn turn left and follow the lane to a kissing gate leading into the field on the left. Aiming slightly left, follow the well-used path across the pasture to the next gate. Go through it and join a wide grassy track running down to a small gate leading out to a lane. Cross it to several cottages and before reaching the entrance to Bullpits Golf Course, pass through a small gate on the right. Turn left and cross the fairways to a gate in the far corner. Exit to a lane and turn left, passing Ecgbertht's Stone.

Follow the road down into Pen Selwood, cross the bridge and just beyond a group of cottages take the waymarked path to Coombe Street and Pear Ash on the right. Follow the narrow path to a gate, cross the yard and go through a kissing gate into the field, keeping to the well-worn path as it climbs the hill towards a row of cottages. Aim to the right of them and cross a stile leading to a narrow path. Almost immediately cross the stile into the field on the right, walk down to the brook and cross over.

Walk up the bank to a stile and join an undulating path running through the wood and down to a bridge. Follow the fenced path and turn left on reaching the lane. As it bends right, turn left to join a grassy track. Avoid the stile on the right and go through the gate into the field. Keep ahead to a stile in the boundary, then follow a pretty path to the road. Turn left, pass some cottages, then fork left down the hill. Cross the bridge at the bottom and take the track on the right, just before the entrance to Swallowfield. Follow it through bluebell woods and at the top of the hill, turn left and follow the lane into Pear Ash.

Turn left in the village centre and when the road swings right, turn left towards a farm. Cross into the field on the

right, crossing several fields and gates before following a path to a cul-de-sac. Turn immediately left and join a tarmac path between houses. Turn left into Coombe Street and take the right-hand path signposted Bourton 3/4 mile (1.2km). Make for the kissing gate on the far side, then swing left across the field to a stile. Climb over to a drover's track and turn left. Turn right at the T junction, then left at the main road, returning to the pub.

THE WHITE LION, BOURTON
High Street SP8 5AT
☎ 01747 841529

Directions: Off A303, opposite B3092 to Gillingham
Quintessentially English country inn with old beams, flagstoned floors, log fires, real ales and home-made food. Same dishes served in the bars and restaurants, including curry board, Sunday roasts and speciality sandwiches and wraps.
Open: 12-3 6-11 (Sun 12-10.30)
Bar Meals: 12-2 7-9
Notes: Children & dogs welcome. Garden with grass, trees and patio. Parking.
(See page 159 for full entry)

DISTANCE: 4 1/2 miles (7.2km)
MAP: OS Explorer 142
TERRAIN: Rolling landscape of farmland, woodland and streams
PATHS: Country lanes, paths and tracks
GRADIENT: Undulating

Walk submitted and checked by The White Lion, Bourton

BRIDPORT
Map 04 SY49

The George Hotel ⚱
4 South St DT6 3NQ ☎ 01308 423187
Dir: *Town centre*
Handsome Georgian town house, with a Victorian-style bar and a mellow atmosphere. It bustles all day, offering a traditional English breakfast, decent morning coffee and a good menu featuring fish and crab from West Bay, home-made rabbit pie, Welsh rarebit, and lambs' kidneys in Madeira.
OPEN: 9.30-11.30 (Sun 9.30-10.30) Closed: Dec 25 **BAR MEALS:** L served all week 12-2.30 D served all week 6-9 Av main course £4.50 **BREWERY/COMPANY:** Palmers **◖:** Palmers - IPA, Copper & 200. **FACILITIES:** Children welcome Dogs allowed

Pick of the Pubs

Shave Cross Inn ⚱
Shave Cross, Marshwood Vale DT6 6HW ☎ 01308 868358
Dir: *From Bridport take B3162 2m turn L signed 'Broadoak/Shave Cross' then Marshwood*
Thatched, 13th-century cob and flint inn tucked away down narrow lanes in the heart of the beautiful Marshwood Vale. Once a resting place for pilgrims and travelling monks, and only a short drive from the coast, it has a delightful sun-trap garden. The classic flagstone-floored bar has a warming log fire in a huge inglenook. A typical menu offers monkfish with crayfish and light mustard sauce, duck breast with honey and orange glaze, and rack of lamb with redcurrant sauce, among others. Enjoy a pint of specially-brewed Branscombe Vale Shaver at the bar. Under new management, readers reports welcome.
OPEN: 11-3 7-10 (all day Sat-Sun in Summer, BHs) 25 Dec Closed eve **BAR MEALS:** L served Tue-Sun 12-2 D served Tue-Sun 7-9 **RESTAURANT:** L served Tue-Sun 12-2 D served Tue-Sat 7-9 **BREWERY/COMPANY:** Free House **◖:** Local guest beers, Branoc (Branscombe Valley). **FACILITIES:** Children welcome Children's licence Garden: Cottage garden Dogs allowed on leads only, water available **NOTES:** Parking 30

BROADWINDSOR
Map 04 ST40

The White Lion 🐾
The Square DT8 3QD ☎ 01308 867070 ▤ 01308 867740
e-mail: johnandsuebei@aol.com
Close to Marshwood Vale and the Dorset coast is this 17th-century village inn. The modernised interior has an open fire, and serves Palmer's ales on tap. A varied menu offers traditional home-made pub food with a specials board that changes daily. Look out for baked trout with prawns and mushrooms, tuna steaks in garlic butter, butterfish in parsley butter, and strips of fillet steak in horseradish and brandy cream.
OPEN: 12-2.30 6-11 (Sun 12-2.30, 7-10.30) **BAR MEALS:** L served Tue-Sun 12-2 D served all week 6.30-9 Av main course £7 **RESTAURANT:** L served Tue-Sun 12-2 D served all week 6.30-9 **BREWERY/COMPANY:** Palmers **◖:** Palmer IPA & 200, Bridport Bitter. **FACILITIES:** Children welcome Garden: Patio area Dogs allowed Water, Biscuits

---

⚱ 7   **Number of wines by the glass**

BUCKLAND NEWTON
Map 04 ST60

Gaggle of Geese ⚱
DT2 7BS ☎ 01300 345249
e-mail: gaggle@bucklandnewton.freeserve.co.uk
Dir: *On B3143 N of Dorchester*
When the former landlord started keeping geese 20 years ago, this pub changed its name from the Royal Oak. Built as a village shop in 1834, its menu includes plenty of traditional dishes. A random selection includes whole breaded plaice, lamb rogan josh, Scottish smoked salmon, cheesy pasta and broccoli, calamari, and pizza, as well as a selection of ploughman's, sandwiches, and salads.
OPEN: 12-2.30 6.30-11 **BAR MEALS:** L served all week 12-2 D served all week 7-10 Av main course £6 **RESTAURANT:** L served all week 12-2 D served all week 7-10 Av 3 course à la carte £12 **BREWERY/COMPANY:** Free House **◖:** Badger Dorset Best, Ringwood Best & Fourtyniner, Butcombe. **FACILITIES:** Children welcome Garden: Pub on 5 acres. Pond & stream Dogs allowed Water **NOTES:** Parking 30

BURTON BRADSTOCK
Map 04 SY48

Pick of the Pubs

The Anchor Inn 🐾 ⚱
High St DT6 4QF ☎ 01308 897228 ▤ 01308 897228
e-mail: sleepingsat@hotmail.com
Dir: *2m SE of Bridport on B3157 in the centre of the village of Burton Bradstock*
Just a few steps from the beach at the centre of the village you will find this cosy 300-year-old coaching inn. It lives up to its maritime name, with fishing nets draped across the ceilings, old fishing tools and shellfish art on the walls, created by the chef under cooking the contents. Seafood is the house speciality, as you might expect, with lobster brought in daily from Lyme Bay, and scallops hand picked by local divers. Villagers also bring in their own garden produce so that much of the menu is fresh and sourced nearby. Seafood choices include monkfish and Parma ham, cod and crab baked in the oven, steamed brill fillet stuffed with crab, and Cornish mackerel with a crab and cheese sauce. Those who preference is for meat can choose from lamb noisette, Barbary duck, chicken and Stilton mango, and stirfry pork. Several real ales are on sale, and over 50 different Scottish whiskies.
OPEN: 11-3 6-11.30 **BAR MEALS:** L served all week 12-2 D served all week 6.30-9 Av main course £16 **RESTAURANT:** L served all week 12-2 D served all week 6.30-9 **BREWERY/COMPANY:** **◖:** Ushers Best, Flowers IPA, Founders, Boddingtons. ⚱: 8 **FACILITIES:** Dogs allowed Water **NOTES:** Parking 24

CATTISTOCK
Map 04 SY59

Fox & Hounds Inn NEW
Duck St DT2 0JH ☎ 01300 320444 ▤ 01300 320444
e-mail: info@foxandhoundsinn.com
An attractive 16th century inn set in the beautiful village of Cattistock. Original features include bare beams, open fires and huge inglenooks, one with an original bread oven. It's a fascinating building, full of curiosities such as the 'hidden cupboard', reached by a staircase that winds around the chimney in one of the loft areas. Meals are traditional and

continued

CATTISTOCK continued

home made: typical examples include country lamb pie, beef Wellington and Dorset Blue Vinney chicken.
OPEN: 12-2.30 6.30-11 **BAR MEALS:** L served Tue-Sun 12-2 D served Tue-Sat 7-9 Av main course £8 **RESTAURANT:** L served Tue-Sun 12-2 D served Tue-Sat 7-9 Av 3 course à la carte £15
BREWERY/COMPANY: Palmers Brewery ◖: Palmers IPA, Copper Ale, Palmers 200, Tally Ho Ale. **FACILITIES:** Children welcome Children's licence Garden: Large and well maintained Dogs allowed Water and biscuits **NOTES:** Parking 12

CERNE ABBAS   Map 04 ST60

The Red Lion
24 Long St DT2 7JF ☎ 01300 341441
Dir: Halfway between Sherbourne and Dorchester on A35
Victorian pub built to replace the original inn which burnt down in the 1890s, and therefore far more modern than most of this picturesque village. The impressive fireplace was believed to have originated from the old abbey, and the Victorian windows are Grade II listed. Locals and tourists enjoy the food served in the separate eating area: lamb cutlets, three shire sausages and mash, or sandwiches and baked potatoes.
OPEN: 12-3 6-11 **BAR MEALS:** L served Wed-Sun 12-2 D served Wed-Sun 6-9 Av main course £7 **RESTAURANT:** L served Wed-Sun 12-2 D served Wed-Sun 6-9 **BREWERY/COMPANY:** Free House ◖: Palmer IPA. **FACILITIES:** Garden: Food served outdoors Dogs allowed Water, biscuits

The Royal Oak 🐾 ♀
23 Long St DT2 7JG ☎ 01300 341797 📠 01300 341797
Dir: On A352 N of Dorchester
Thatched, creeper-clad, 16th-century inn, formerly a coaching inn and blacksmiths, situated in a picturesque village below the Dorset Downs. A previous owner of the pub also owned land in America. In 1791 this land was given to the US government, and became the site of Capitol Hill. Home-cooked food is served in the cosy, traditional interior. An imaginative menu includes pan-fried black bream fillets, seafood chowder, poached salmon salad, venison sausages, and wild mushroom strüdel. Attractive courtyard garden.
OPEN: 11-3 6-11 Closed: Dec 25 **BAR MEALS:** L served all week 12-2 D served all week 7-9.30 Av main course £8
BREWERY/COMPANY: Free House ◖: St Austell Brewery.
FACILITIES: Children welcome Garden: Food served outside. Dogs allowed Water bowl in garden

---

CHIDEOCK   Map 04 SY49

Pick of the Pubs

The Anchor Inn
Seatown DT6 6JU ☎ 01297 489215
e-mail: david@theanchorinn.co.uk
Dir: On A35 turn S in Chideock opp church & follow single track rd for 0.75m to beach
The Anchor has a spectacular setting in a little cove surrounded by National Trust land, beneath Golden Cap, the highest point on the south coast. It is right on the Dorset coastal path (ideal for walkers) and to the west of the bustling market town of Bridport. The inn makes the most of its position with a large sun terrace and cliff-side beer garden overlooking the beach. On winter weekdays it is blissfully quiet, while the summer sees it thronging

continued

with holidaymakers. A wide-ranging menu offers something for everyone, from sandwiches, burgers and jacket potatoes to prime rump steak. There's plenty of freshly-caught seafood, including crab and lobster, and game in season. Typical dishes are monkfish in Thai sauce, game casserole, carbonade of beef, and vegetable and spinach pancakes.

OPEN: 11-2.30 6-11 (Summer 11-11) **BAR MEALS:** L served all week 12-2 D served all week 6.30-9.30
BREWERY/COMPANY: Palmers ◖: Palmers 200 Premium Ale, IPA, Copper Ale. **FACILITIES:** Children welcome Garden: Food served outside Dogs allowed Water, Dog treats
NOTES: Parking 20

The George Inn 🐾 ♀
Main St DT6 6JD ☎ 01297 489419 📠 01297 489411
e-mail: george.inn@virgin.net
Dir: On A35

Traditional Dorset thatched inn located close to the famous and spectacular sandstone-scarred cliff top known as Golden Cap, the highest cliff in southern England. Along with a patio garden and a popular choice of real ales, the George offers an impressive range of snacks, home-made pies and light lunches, plus more substantial dishes - fillet steak Rossini, steamed salmon supreme and moules marinière among them.
OPEN: 11-2.30 6-11 **BAR MEALS:** L served all week 12-2 D served all week 6-9 Av main course £6.95 **RESTAURANT:** L served all week 12-2 D served all week 6-9 Av 3 course à la carte £15.95 Av 3 course fixed price £12.95 **BREWERY/COMPANY:** Palmers ◖: Palmers IPA & 200, Dorset Gold. **FACILITIES:** Children welcome Garden: Patio, food served outside Dogs allowed **NOTES:** Parking 40

Pubs offering a good choice of fish on their menu

CHRISTCHURCH
Map 05 SZ19

Fishermans Haunt Hotel 🐾 ♀
Salisbury Rd, Winkton BH23 7AS
☎ 01202 477283 & 484071 📠 01202 478883
Dir: 2.5m north on B3347(Christchurch/Ringwood rd)
Dating from 1673, this inn overlooks the River Avon and is a popular place for walkers and anglers, for Winkton has its own fishery and there are many others locally. The area is also well endowed with golf courses. The menu offers a daily fish selection, usually including trout and whole plaice, and staples such as steak and kidney pie, battered cod, and mixed grill along with sandwiches and baked potatoes. There's a more extensive carte menu in the restaurant.
OPEN: 10.30-2.30 5-11 (Sat-Sun open all day) **BAR MEALS:** L served all week 12-2 D served all week 6-9 Av main course £6.50
RESTAURANT: L served Sat-Sun 12-2 D served Sat-Sun 6-9 Av 3 course à la carte £17 **BREWERY/COMPANY:** Gales 🍺: Gales GB & HSB, Ringwood Fortyniner, Interbrew Bass. ♀: 8
FACILITIES: Children welcome Garden: Food only Dogs allowed Water, two rooms available **NOTES:** Parking 80

The Ship In Distress
66 Stanpit BH23 3NA ☎ 01202 485123
e-mail: sally@shipindistress.com

A 200-year-old smugglers' pub close to Mudeford Quay, specialising in fish and seafood mainly caught by local fishermen. The name derives from a smuggling vessel rescued by regulars from a nearby creek where it had run aground. Legend says that the pub's owner, Mother Sellers, warned smugglers of the coastgards' presence by wearing a red dress. Nowadays the food provides the excitement: expect roasted monkfish tails, baked fillet of pollock, and stir-fried tiger prawns, plus braised duck breast.
OPEN: 10.30-11 **BAR MEALS:** L served all week 12-2 D served all week 7-9.30 Av main course £12 **RESTAURANT:** L served all week 12-2 D served all week 7-9 Av 3 course à la carte £23.50
BREWERY/COMPANY: Inn Partnership 🍺: Ringwood Best, Fourtyniner, Interbrew Bass, Courage Directors.
FACILITIES: Children welcome Garden: Patio, food served outside Dogs allowed Water **NOTES:** Parking 40

CHURCH KNOWLE
Map 04 SY98

The New Inn 🐾 ♀
BH20 5NQ ☎ 01929 480357 📠 01929 480357
Dir: Telephone for directions
In a charming village in the Purbeck hills, this partly thatched 16th-century inn has been run by the same family for 20 years and was originally part of a working farm. All dishes are freshly made and fresh fish is delivered daily, with at least 12 fish dishes always available. These may include grilled trout

continued

topped with roasted almonds, salmon steak in lobster cream and brandy sauce or large haddock in beer batter. English lamb is also a speciality, along with a selection of traditional dishes and specials.
OPEN: 11-3 6.30-11 **BAR MEALS:** L served all week 12-2.15 D served all week 6-9.15 Av main course £7 **RESTAURANT:** L served all week 12-2.15 D served all week 6-9.15
BREWERY/COMPANY: Inn Partnership 🍺: Wadworth 6X, Greene King Old Speckled Hen, Interbrew Flowers Original.
FACILITIES: Garden: Beer garden, food served outdoors Dogs allowed Only on lead, water available **NOTES:** Parking 100

CORFE CASTLE
Map 04 SY98

The Greyhound Inn 🐾 ♀
The Square BH20 5EZ ☎ 01929 480205 📠 01929 421696
e-mail: mjml@greyhound-inn.fsnet.co.uk
Dir: W from Bournemouth, take A35, after 5m L onto A351, 10m to Corfe Castle
Corfe Castle, once one of England's five royal castles, not only forms a dramatic backdrop, but probably furnished the stones to build the Greyhound in the 16th century. Traditional pub food includes filled panini rolls, jacket potatoes, seafood and meat baskets, and steak and Guinness pie. The charcoal grill offers Aberdeen sirloin and T-bone steaks, and flame-grilled chicken breast in bacon. Dorset lobster, crab and Scottish rope-grown mussels could well be on the fish board.
OPEN: 11-3 6-11.30 Summer open all day **BAR MEALS:** L served all week 12-2.30 D served all week 6-9 Av main course £8.95
RESTAURANT: L served all week 12-2.30 D served all week 6-9
BREWERY/COMPANY: Enterprise Inns 🍺: Fuller's London Pride, Adnams, Marston's Pedigree, Timothy Taylor Landlord. ♀: 10
FACILITIES: Children welcome Garden: 100 seats, BBQ & hog roast in summer Dogs allowed Water **NOTES:**

Scott Arms Hotel 🐾 ♀
West St, Kingston BH20 5LH ☎ 01929 480270 📠 01929 481570
The Scott Arms Hotel is a large creeper-clad stone-built inn with excellent views of the Purbeck Hills and Corfe Castle from its attractive garden. It's a family pub with excellent facilities. Staff are cheerful, and welcoming fires are lit in the winter months. Home-made pies, curries and fresh fish and seafood feature among the popular dishes.
OPEN: 11.30-3 6-11 (Summer open all day) **BAR MEALS:** L served all week 12-2.30 D served all week 6-9 **RESTAURANT:** L served all week 12-2.30 D served all week 6-9.30 🍺: Ringwood Best, Marston's Pedigree, Scottish Courage John Smith's. ♀: 14
FACILITIES: Children welcome Garden: Amazing views of Corfe Castle Dogs allowed **NOTES:** Parking 40

> **Room prices show the minimum double and single rates charged.**
> **Room rates in hotels and B&Bs often vary depending on the facilities, so be sure to check prices with the establishment before booking.**

England

EAST CHALDON   Map 04 SY78

The Sailors Return
DT2 8DN ☎ 01305 853847 ▤ 01305 851677
Dir: 1m S of A352 between Dorchester & Wool

Splendid 17th-century thatched country inn tucked away in rolling downland close to Lulworth Cove and miles of cliff walks. The comfortable beamed and flagstoned bar is where a blackboard lists available dishes, which may include half shoulder of lamb, gammon hock, whole plaice, and home-made steak and kidney pie. Meals can also be enjoyed in a grassy area outside.
OPEN: 11-3 6-11 (all day open from Easter-end Sept)
BAR MEALS: L served all week 12-2 D served all week 6.30-9.30
RESTAURANT: L served all week 12-2 D served all week 6.30-9.30
BREWERY/COMPANY: Free House ◖: Ringwood Best, Hampshire Strongs Best Bitter, Badger Tanglefoot.
FACILITIES: Children welcome Garden: Grassed area with wooden tables and benches Dogs allowed **NOTES:** Parking 100

EAST KNIGHTON   Map 04 SY88

The Countryman Inn ♀
Blacknoll Ln DT2 8LL ☎ 01305 852666 ▤ 01305 854125
Dir: On A352 between Warmwell Cross & Wool
There's a comfortable farmhouse atmosphere at this attractive whitewashed freehouse, tucked away just off the A352 in the heart of Hardy country. There are open fires in the bars, plus a family room, garden and play area. The menus cater for all tastes: everything from sandwiches, ploughman's and jacket potatoes to pan-fried chicken, lemon sole, or tomato and lentil lasagne. Daily carvery roasts and specials include old-fashioned, home-made puddings. Two guest beers changed weekly.
OPEN: 11-2.30 6-11 Closed: 25 Dec **BAR MEALS:** L served all week 12-2 D served all week 6.30-9.30 **RESTAURANT:** L served all week 12-2 D served all week 6.30-9.30 Av 2 course fixed price £12.75 **BREWERY/COMPANY:** Free House ◖: Greene King Old Speckled Hen, Scottish Courage Courage Directors & Best, Ringwood Best & Old Thumper. ♀: 6 **FACILITIES:** Children welcome Garden: Dogs allowed **NOTES:** Parking 200

EAST MORDEN   Map 04 SY99

Pick of the Pubs

The Cock & Bottle 🐑 ♀
BH20 7DL ☎ 01929 459238
Dir: From A35 W of Poole take B3075. Pub 2m on R

Originally a cob-walled Dorset longhouse, dating back some 400 years, this delightful pub was given a brick skin around 1800. From the modern rear extension there are lovely pastoral views and inside it is comfortably rustic with quaint low-beamed ceilings, attractive paintings and lots of nooks and crannies around its log fires. Outside, a large field occasionally hosts vintage car and motorcycle rallies during the summer. Alongside its popular locals' bar are a lounge bar and a restaurant with the accent on fresh produce, including fish and game. Typical starters might include wild mushroom tartlet with a seed mustard hollandaise sauce, grilled feta cheese or duck spring rolls served with a chilli jam. Main courses may feature fillet of Thai pork marinated in ginger sauce, pigeon pie, beef Wellington, braised lamb rump in rosemary and redcurrant sauce, or seabass fillets on stirfry vegetables.
OPEN: 11-3 6-11 (Sun 12-3, 7-10.30) **BAR MEALS:** L served all week 12-2 D served all week 6-9 Av main course £10
RESTAURANT: L served all week 12-2 D served all week 6-9 Av 3 course à la carte £20 **BREWERY/COMPANY:** Hall & Woodhouse ◖: Badger Dorset Best & Tanglefoot & Sussex.
FACILITIES: Children welcome Garden: Patio, grass area Dogs allowed Water **NOTES:** Parking 40

EVERSHOT   Map 04 ST50

Pick of the Pubs

The Acorn Inn ♦♦♦♦ 🏵 🐑 ♀
DT2 0JW ☎ 01935 83228 ▤ 01935 83707
e-mail: stay@acorn-inn.co.uk
See Pick of the Pubs on opposite page

Skittles
Skittles is a far older game than darts or dominoes, on record in London since the 15th century, when it was banned. Henry VIII enjoyed it and had his own skittle alley, but governments kept vainly trying to stop ordinary people playing, because they ought to have been practising their archery and because they gambled so heavily. Even so, the game became popular enough to make 'beer and skittles' proverbial. Basically, three wooden balls are propelled at nine pins to knock them down, but there are sharp variations in the rules between different areas and pubs. Varieties include London or Old English Skittles, West Country Skittles, Long Alley and Aunt Sally, as well as several types of table skittles.

Open: 11.30-3, 6-11
Closed: 1 Jan
Bar Meals: L served all week 12-2,
D served all week 6.30-9.30.
RESTAURANT: L served all week 12-2,
D served all week 6.30-9.30.
BREWERY/COMPANY:
Free House.
🍺: Fuller's London Pride, Butcombe,
Palmer.
FACILITIES: Children welcome, Dogs
allowed, Garden.
NOTES: Parking 30
ROOMS: 9 en suite rooms from
s£60 d£80

The Acorn Inn

A carefully-restored 16th-century inn that creates the perfect
rural base from which to explore Hardy Country and the beautiful
Dorset coastline.

Evershot, Dorchester, DT2 0JW
☎ 01935 83228 📠 01935 83707
✉ stay@acorn-inn.co.uk
Dir: A303 to Yeovil, Dorchester Rd,
on A37 R to Evershot.

This fine stone building
appeared as 'The Sow and
Acorn' in Thomas Hardy's Tess
of the D'Urbervilles, and he is
believed to have stayed here
when writing Jude the
Obscure. The pub still has a
sleepy village setting
surrounded by fabulous
countryside and some great
walks. The dining room used
to be a grand hall, thought to
have been used by Judge

Jeffreys as a court-house, and
the old stables have been
converted into a skittle alley.
There are two oak-panelled
bars with flagstone floors, and
log fires in caved Hamstone
fireplaces. The bars serve
traditional ales and a selection
of wines, and in addition to the
choice of bar food, such as
hearty soups and substantial
sandwiches, a full menu is
offered in the Harding Dining
Room or the no-smoking
restaurant. Fresh fish from
nearby Bridport and local game
are specialities frequently
featured on the short menu.
Fish options may range from

cod in beer batter with mushy
peas to grilled red snapper on
crushed potato with pesto.
Other options include local
estate game casserole with port
and juniper berries, or loin of
pork with wild mushroom
sauce. A tempting array of
puddings takes in a traditional
apple crumble and a white
chocolate parfait with dark
chocolate sauce.
Accommodation is provided in
individually-styled rooms, two
with four-poster beds, and
mid-week special breaks are
available all year. Now under
new ownership.

GILLINGHAM
Map 04 ST82

The Kings Arms Inn
East Stour Common SP8 5NB ☎ 01747 838325
e-mail: jenny@kings-arms.fsnet.co.uk
Dir: 4m W of Shaftesbury on A30
A 200-year-old country inn set in the beautiful Blackmore Vale,
where the visitor can spend days exploring the maze of small
roads, footpaths and bridleways in a lush pastoral landscape.
Alongside a warm welcome, the inn sports an extensive beer
garden and a selection of real ales. Traditional pub food
encompasses ploughman's lunches, tempting pizzas and house
specials such as orchard pork, home-made steak and kidney pie
and assorted grills.
OPEN: 12-2.30 5-11 Closed: 25 Dec **BAR MEALS:** L served all
week 12-2 D served all week 6-9 **RESTAURANT:** L served all week
12-2 D served all week 6-9 **BREWERY/COMPANY:** Free House
🍺: Cools Worthington's Bitter, Ringwood Best Bitter, Quay
Weymouth Best Bitter. **FACILITIES:** Children welcome Garden Dogs
allowed Water **NOTES:** Parking 40

GODMANSTONE
Map 04 SY69

Smiths Arms
DT2 7AQ ☎ 01300 341236
With only room for around six tables, the Smiths Arms is one
of the smallest pubs in Britain. Set in the Cerne Valley on the
riverside, this 15th-century thatched pub offers hearty meals
including home-cooked ham off the bone, chicken and leek
pie, tuna and spicy tomato lasagne, and delicious bread
pudding.
OPEN: 11-5.30 Closed: 1 week before Easter-Mid Oct
BAR MEALS: L served all week 12-3 Av main course £4.95
BREWERY/COMPANY: Free House 🍺 Wadworth 6X, Stowford
Press Cider. **FACILITIES:** Garden: Seating area by river
NOTES: Parking 15 **NOTES:** No credit cards

GUSSAGE ALL SAINTS
Map 04 SU01

The Drovers Inn
BH21 5ET ☎ 01258 840084
e-mail: info@thedroversinn.net
Dir: A31 Ashley Heath rdbt, R onto B3081

Rural 16th-century pub with a fine terrace and wonderful
views from the garden. Popular with walkers, its refurbished
interior retains plenty of traditional appeal with flagstone
floors and oak furniture. Ales include Ringwood's seasonal
ales and guest beers. The menu features home-cooked pub
favourites: fresh cod in home-made beer batter, curry, steak
and kidney pie, and steak and chips.
OPEN: 11.45-2.30 6-11 (Sat 11-3 6-11, Sun 12-3 6-11)
BAR MEALS: L served all week 12-2 D served all week 7-9 Av main

course £6.95 **RESTAURANT:** L served all week 12-2 D served all
week 6-9 **BREWERY/COMPANY:** 🍺: Ringwood Best, Old
Thumper, Ringwood Seasonal Ales, Fortyniner & Guest Beers.
FACILITIES: Garden: overlooking surrounding countryside Dogs
allowed Water **NOTES:** Parking 70

LODERS
Map 04 SY49

Loders Arms
DT6 3SA ☎ 01308 422431
Dir: off the A3066, 2m NE of Bridport
Unassuming stone-built local tucked away in a pretty thatched
village close to the Dorset coast. Arrive early to bag a seat in
the bar or in the homely (and tiny) dining room. Interesting
blackboard menus may list fish soup, smoked haddock
fishcakes and filled baguettes for bar diners, with the likes of
scallops in Pernod, steak and ale pie, rack of lamb, and sea
bass with salsa verde available throughout. Lovely summer
garden. New owners end of 2002.
OPEN: 11.30-3 6-11 (Sun 11.30-11) **BAR MEALS:** L served all week
12.30-2 D served all week 7.15-9 Av main course £7.25
RESTAURANT: L served all week 12.30-2 D served all week 7.15-9
BREWERY/COMPANY: Palmers Brewery 🍺: Palmers Bridport
Bitter, Palmers IPA, Palmers 200. **FACILITIES:** Children welcome
Garden Dogs allowed

LOWER ANSTY
Map 04 ST70

The Fox Inn ★★
DT2 7PN ☎ 01258 880328 📠 01258 881440
e-mail: foxinnansty@tiscali.co.uk
*Dir: A35 from Dorchester towards Poole, onto B3142, 1st R for
Cheselbourne, keep to road for 4 miles.*
This reassuringly-civilised brick and flint dining pub with its
delightful six en suite bedrooms makes a perfect base for touring
Hardy's Wessex. The Hall and Woodhouse brewing families
were both linked with The Fox, and old family photos
decorate the bar. Varied menus serve the bar and restaurants;
choices range from home-made pies and all the usual things
with chips, through to distinguished main courses such as
supreme of chicken with lobster or chateaubriand for two.
OPEN: 11-11 (Sun 12-10.30) **BAR MEALS:** L served all week 12-
2.30 D served all week 6.30-9 Av main course £5.50
RESTAURANT: L served all week 12-2.30 D served all week 6.30-9
Av 3 course à la carte £16 **BREWERY/COMPANY:** Hall &
Woodhouse 🍺: Badger Tanglefoot, Badger Best, Sussex, Dempseys.
FACILITIES: Garden: Grassed area at front, swimming pool at rear
Dogs allowed **NOTES:** Parking 40 **ROOMS:** 12 bedrooms 12 en
suite 4 family rooms s£35 d£50

LYME REGIS
Map 04 SY39

Pilot Boat Inn
Bridge St DT7 3QA ☎ 01297 443157
This busy town centre pub is close to the sea front and has a
number of old smuggling and sea rescue connections, but its
biggest claim to fame would seem to be as the possible
birthplace of the inspiration for Hollywood's favourite super-
collie, Lassie. Meals include a range of fish dishes, steaks and
grills, ploughman's, salads, sandwiches and a selection of
vegetarian options. Look to the blackboard for specials.
OPEN: 11-11 (Sun 12-10.30) Closed: Dec 25 **BAR MEALS:** L served
all week 12-10 D served all week Av main course £7
RESTAURANT: 12-10 **BREWERY/COMPANY:** Palmers 🍺: Palmers
Dorset Gold, IPA, 200, Bridport Bitter. ♀: 8 **FACILITIES:** Children
welcome Children's licence Garden: Patio Dogs allowed

continued

Victoria Hotel ♦♦♦ 🛏 ♀ NEW
Uplyme Rd DT7 3LP ☎ 01297 444801
e-mail: info@vichotel.co.uk
Dir: Telephone for directions
Built in 1906 as the railway hotel for the famous Bluebell line into Lyme Regis, the Victoria enjoys magnificent views of the countryside and the sea from its position high above the town. Fish and seafood from Lyme Bay features strongly on both the restaurant and bar menus in the form of fillet of hake on a warm rocket pesto, and pan-roasted fillet of brill. Other favourites include best end of lamb, and various snacks.
OPEN: 11-3 6-11 Closed: Last week in Jan **BAR MEALS:** L served Tue-Sun 12-2.30 D served Tue-Sun 6.30-9.30 Av main course £6.95 **RESTAURANT:** L served Tue-Sun 12-2.30 D served Tue-Sun 6.30-9.30 Av 3 course à la carte £21.50 🍺: Otter Bitter, Abbot Ale, Marston Pedigree, Bass. ♀: 8 **FACILITIES:** Children's licence Garden: Patio garden with nice views **NOTES:** Parking 18 **ROOMS:** 7 bedrooms 7 en suite 1 family rooms s£30 d£50 no children overnight

MARSHWOOD   Map 04 SY39

Pick of the Pubs

The Bottle Inn
DT6 5QJ ☎ 01297 678254 📠 01297 678739
e-mail: thebottleinn@msn.com
Dir: 4m inland from the A35 on the B3165
Standing beside the B3165 on the edge of the glorious Marshwood Vale, the thatched Bottle Inn was first mentioned as an ale house back in the 17th century. It was the first pub in the area during the 18th century to serve bottled beer rather than beer from the jug - hence the name. The rustic interior has simple wooden settles, scrubbed tables and a blazing fire. Diners will find pan-fried wild boar steak with honey, plums and balsamic vinegar, whole chicken breast wrapped in pancetta and served on a Caesar salad, kumara and lemongrass bake, and traditional beef and Guinness pie on the menu. Taking the organic food theme to its furthest reaches, the pub is home to the annual World Stinging-Nettle Eating Championships.
OPEN: 12-3 6.30-11 Closed: 31 Oct-Easter **BAR MEALS:** L served all week 12-2 D served all week 7.30-9 **RESTAURANT:** L served all week D served all week **BREWERY/COMPANY:** Free House 🍺: Otter Ale, Greene King Old Speckled Hen. **FACILITIES:** Children welcome Garden: **NOTES:** Parking 40

MILTON ABBAS   Map 04 ST80

The Hambro Arms 🛏 ♀
DT11 0BP ☎ 01258 880233
e-mail: info@hambroarms.co.uk
Traditional whitewashed 18th-century thatched pub located in a picturesque landscaped village. Enjoy an appetising bar snack or, perhaps, half shoulder of lamb with minted redcurrant sauce, liver and bacon, duck with orange sauce, venison sausages, or grilled sea bass, in the comfortable lounge bar or on the popular patio.
OPEN: 11-3 6.30-11 **BAR MEALS:** L served all week 12-2 D served all week 7-9 Av main course £10 **RESTAURANT:** L served all week 12-2 D served all week 7-9 **BREWERY/COMPANY:** Free House 🍺: Bass, Greene King Old Speckled Hen. **FACILITIES:** Dogs allowed In the garden only **NOTES:** Parking 20

MOTCOMBE   Map 04 ST82

The Coppleridge Inn 🛏 ♀
SP7 9HW ☎ 01747 851980 📠 01747 851858
e-mail: thecoppleridgeinn@btinternet.com
Family-run country inn set in 15 acres including a children's play area, tennis court, cricket pitch, wood, lawns and a pond. The former farmhouse is full of character, with flagstone floors, stripped pine and lovely views across the Blackmore Vale. Wide-ranging menus encompass children's dishes and daily specials such as chicken breast with creamy smoky bacon sauce, venison casserole, and grilled whole brill with tarragon butter.
OPEN: 11-3 5-11 All day Sat & Sun **BAR MEALS:** L served all week 12-2.30 D served all week 6-9.30 **RESTAURANT:** L served all week 12-2.30 D served all week 6-9.30
BREWERY/COMPANY: Free House 🍺: Butcombe Bitter, Adnams Southwold, Wadworth 6X, Fuller's London Pride.
FACILITIES: Children welcome Garden: 15 acres including lawns, wood, pond area Dogs allowed Garden only, water provided **NOTES:** Parking 60

NETTLECOMBE   Map 04 SY59

Marquis of Lorne ♦♦♦♦ 🛏 ♀
DT6 3SY ☎ 01308 485236 📠 01308 485666
e-mail: julie.woodroffe@btinternet.com
Dir: 3m E of A3066 Bridport-Beaminster rd, after Mangerton Mill & West Milton

A 16th-century farmhouse converted into a pub in 1871, when the Marquis himself named it to prove land ownership. Membership of the Campaign for Real Food means rattling the food chain on behalf of local growers and suppliers. Daily menus offer fillet steak, pork tenderloin, Barbary duck, pigeon breast, brill - all with delicious sauces - and a good vegetarian selection. Mangerton, the main dining room, and two cosy bars, Eggardon and Pitcher, are named after local hills. Superb gardens with beautiful views.
OPEN: 11.30-2.30 6.30-11 (Sun 12-3, 7-10.30) **BAR MEALS:** L served all week 12-2 D served all week 6.30-9 Av main course £9 **RESTAURANT:** L served all week 12-2 D served all week 6.30-9 Av 3 course à la carte £16.95 **BREWERY/COMPANY:** Palmers 🍺: Palmers Copper, IPA, 200 Premium Ale. ♀: 8 **FACILITIES:** Children welcome Garden: Well kept garden with good views & play area Dogs allowed Water **NOTES:** Parking 50 **ROOMS:** 7 bedrooms 7 en suite s£30 d£50

> ♦ **Diamond rating for inspected guest accommodation**

England

The Three Elms 🐑 ♀
DT9 5JW ☎ 01935 812881 🖹 01935 812881
Dir: From Sherborne take A352 towards Dorchester then A3030.
Pub 1m on R
Real ales and locally produced ciders await you at this family-run free house overlooking Blackmore Vale. There are stunning views from the pub's garden, and the landlord boasts a collection of around 1,300 model cars. The wide-ranging menu includes dishes like shark & bacon cassoulet, royal ocean platter (a mixture of hot and cold fish and seafood), lamb and mango casserole, and Thai-style salmon supreme with noodles and stir-fried vegetables.
OPEN: 11-2.30 6.30-11 (Sun 12-3, 7-10.30) Closed: 25-26 Dec
BAR MEALS: L served all week 12-2 D served all week 6.30-10 Av main course £7 **RESTAURANT:** L served all week 12-2 D served all week 6.30-10 **BREWERY/COMPANY:** Free House 🍺: Fuller's London Pride, Butcombe Bitter, Otter Ale. ♀: 10
FACILITIES: Children welcome Garden: Dogs allowed
NOTES: Parking 50

The Smugglers Inn 🐑
DT3 6HF ☎ 01305 833125 🖹 01305 832219
This 13th century inn was the headquarters of notorious French smuggler Pierre Latour, whose wife (the landlord's daughter) was mistakenly shot during a raid on the pub. Her husband was hiding up the chimney. More famously, John Constable painted the view of Weymouth Bay from the car park. Located bang on the coastal path, with a stream running through the garden and a play area for children, it's a good stop on a sunny day. The interior is cosy, with bare beams and flagstone floors. Food includes fresh fish (seafood sandwiches, fresh lobster), steaks, pies and popular Sunday dinners.
OPEN: 11 -11 (Sun 12-10.30) **BAR MEALS:** L served all week 12 D served all week 9.30 Av main course £7.50 **RESTAURANT:** L served all week 12 D served all week 9.30
BREWERY/COMPANY: Woodhouse Inns 🍺: Badger Best, Tanglefoot. **FACILITIES:** Children welcome Children's licence Garden: Large lawn with picnic benches & BBQ Dogs allowed Water & Treats **NOTES:** Parking 70

The Thimble Inn 🐑
DT2 7TD ☎ 01300 348270
Dir: A35 westbound, R onto B3143, Piddlehinton 4m
Good food, open fires and traditional pub games make this friendly village local a favourite spot with visitors. The pub stands in an unspoilt valley on the banks of the River Piddle, and the riverside patio is popular in summer. The extensive menu caters for all tastes, from sandwiches, jacket potatoes and children's meals, to grilled duck breast with pink grapefruit and ginger sauce, spaghetti Bolognaise, poached rolled sole filled with scallops and crab in a seafood sauce, or steak and oyster pudding. Warm sticky puddings, too, if you've room!
OPEN: 12-2.30 7-11 (Sun 12-2.30 7-10.30) Closed: 25 Dec
BAR MEALS: L served all week 12-2 D served all week 7-9 Av main course £6 **RESTAURANT:** L served all week 12-2 D served all week 7-9 **BREWERY/COMPANY:** Free House 🍺: Badger Best & Tanglefoot, Palmer Cooper Ale & Palmer IPA, Ringwood Old Thumper. **FACILITIES:** Children welcome Garden: Dogs allowed **NOTES:** Parking 50

Piddle Inn 🐑 ♀
DT2 7QF ☎ 01300 348468 🖹 01300 348102
e-mail: inn.piddle@btinternet.co.uk
Once a staging post for the exchange of prisoners from Sherborne and Dorchester, this friendly village local has been a pub since the 1760s, and has many a tale to tell of drunken prisoners and their escorts. Seafood is a speciality - duo of turbot and snapper, roast monkfish wrapped in bacon, and seared scallops thermidor are likely dishes, along with rack of lamb and magret of duck. The riverside patio is popular in summer.
OPEN: 11-3 6-11 (Closed Mon lunch) **BAR MEALS:** L served Tues-Sun 12-2 D served Tues-Sat 6.30-9.30 Av main course £12
RESTAURANT: L served Tues-Sun 12-2 D served Tues-Sat 6.30-9.30 Av 3 course à la carte £21 Av 3 course fixed price £10
BREWERY/COMPANY: Free House 🍺: Greene King Old Speckled Hen, IPA, Abbot Ale, Ruddle's County. ♀: 7 **FACILITIES:** Children welcome Garden: 36 seater patio area, riverside **NOTES:** Parking 20

The Poachers Inn ♦♦♦♦
DT2 7QX ☎ 01300 348358 🖹 01300 348153
e-mail: thepoachers@piddletrenthide.fsbusiness.co.uk
Dir: 8m from Dorchester on B3143

At the heart of Thomas Hardy country, this free house in a small village by the River Piddle has had the same management for nearly 20 years. Open fires and traditional pub games reflect its identity as a genuine English local, whose riverside patio is especially popular in summer. Home-made soups, steak and ale pie and vegetarian options such as mushroom Stroganoff and an impressive array of beef steaks and grills. Leave room for a treat to follow - hot home-made Dorset apple cake.
OPEN: 12-11 Closed: 24-26 Dec **BAR MEALS:** L served all week 12-6.30 D served all week 6.30-9 Av main course £6.50
RESTAURANT: L served all week 12-6.30 D served all week 6.30-9 Av 3 course à la carte £12.50 **BREWERY/COMPANY:** Free House 🍺: Interbrew Bass & Worthington Bitter, Carlsberg-Tetley Bitter, Poachers Ale, Badger Tanglefoot & IPA. **FACILITIES:** Children welcome Garden: Over-looks river, tables, seating Dogs allowed **NOTES:** Parking 40 **ROOMS:** 18 bedrooms 18 en suite 1 family rooms s£35 d£60

```
♀ 7    Number of wines by the glass
```

PLUSH Map 04 ST70

Pick of the Pubs

Brace of Pheasants 🛏 ⚲

DT2 7RQ ☎ 01300 348357

Dir: *A35 onto B3143, 5m to Piddletrenthide, then R to Mappowder & Plush*

Tucked away in a fold of the hills east of Cerne Abbas is one of Dorset's prettiest 16th-century thatched village inns, hidden at the heart of Hardy's beloved county. He is believed to have used Plush as the model for Flintcomb-Ash in Tess of the d'Urbervilles. Beginning life as two cottages, the Brace of Pheasants then became a village smithy. Over the years it has been transformed into one of the area's most popular pubs. Inside the ambience is warm and welcoming, with an open fire, oak beams and fresh flowers. Lunch, dinner and bar meals are available, and the choice of menu reflects the changing of the seasons. Game dishes include loin of venison with grain mustard and brandy, and roast partridge with Madeira and mushrooms. Crusty pies and warming soups also form part of the menu, together with roast monkfish, baked salmon herb crust, medallions of pork tenderloin and breast of chicken.

OPEN: 12-2.30 7-11 (Sun 12-3 7-10.30) Closed: Dec 25 and in winter **BAR MEALS:** L served all week 12.30-2 D served all week 7.30-9.30 Av main course £8.50 **RESTAURANT:** L served all week 12-1.30 D served all week 7-9.30 Av 3 course à la carte £20 **BREWERY/COMPANY:** Free House ◀: Fuller's London Pride, Butcombe Bitter, Ringwood Best, Adnams. ⚲: 9 **FACILITIES:** Children welcome Garden: Large, food served outside Dogs allowed Water **NOTES:** Parking 30

POOLE Map 04 SZ09

The Guildhall Tavern 🛏

15 Market St BH15 1NB ☎ 01202 671717 🗎 01202 242346

e-mail: sewerynsevfred@aol.com *Dir:* *2 minutes from Poole Quay*

Formerly a cider house, today's re-incarnation is decidedly French, from the staff to its food and smart nautical décor. Herring roes on toast, snails in garlic butter, and king-size scallops deep-fried in ale batter are typical starters, followed by pan-fried fresh duck breast with blackcurrant sauce, or grilled seabass with thyme and flambéed in Pernod.

OPEN: 11-3.30 6.30-11 Closed: 1st & 2nd week in Nov **BAR MEALS:** L served all week 11-2.30 D served all week 6.30-10 Av main course £12 **RESTAURANT:** L served all week 12-2.30 D served all week 6.30-10 Av 3 course à la carte £25 Av 3 course fixed price £16.95 **BREWERY/COMPANY:** Inn Partnership ◀: Ringwood Best, Interbrew Flowers IPA. **FACILITIES:** Children welcome **NOTES:** Parking 10

POWERSTOCK Map 04 SY59

Pick of the Pubs

Three Horseshoes Inn 🛏 ⚲

DT6 3TF ☎ 01308 485328 🗎 01308 485328

Dir: *E of A3066 (Bridport/Beaminster rd)*

The new hosts and head chef have brought a breath of fresh air to this picturesque stone-and-thatch pub, originally a blacksmith's forge. It blends seamlessly into the village of Powerstock, a popular destination for film crews seeking a quintessential English village. Plenty of walkers and cyclists find their way here too, and they can enjoy the garden with its glorious coastal views. Inside, you'll find a traditional bar area with an open fireplace and a cosy wood-panelled restaurant, also warmed by a real fire and decorated with paintings by a local artist (the landlord's father). There's a clear commitment to food, whether in the bar snacks (soups, baguettes, and salads) or the mouth-watering array of modern British dishes on the dinner menu: perhaps pan-fried fillet of lamb with Puy lentils, balsamic vinegar and crème frâiche or pan-fried fillet of venison on a bed of braised red cabbage with a griotte cherry jus. Another welcome addition is a 30-strong wine list.

OPEN: 12-3 6-11 **BAR MEALS:** L served all week 12-2 D served all week 7-9.30 Av main course £8 **RESTAURANT:** L served all week 12-2 D served all week 7-9.30 Av 3 course à la carte £17 **BREWERY/COMPANY:** Palmers ◀: Palmer Bridport Bitter & IPA. **FACILITIES:** Children welcome Garden: Patio leading to terraced garden Dogs allowed Water, food, toys, baskets **NOTES:** Parking 30

PUNCKNOWLE Map 04 SY58

The Crown Inn ⚲

Church St DT2 9BN ☎ 01308 897711 🗎 01308 898282

e-mail: thecrowninn@puncknowle48.fsnet.co.uk

Dir: *From A35, into Bridevalley, through Litton Cheney. From B3157, inland at Swyre.*

Picturesque 16th-century thatched inn retaining a traditional atmosphere within its rambling, low-beamed bars, which were once the haunt of smugglers from nearby Chesil Beach on their way to visit prosperous customers in Bath. Food ranges from light snacks to hearty home-made dishes like mild chicken curry, pork and apple casserole, and steak and kidney pie cooked in Guinness. A choice of children's and vegetarian dishes is also offered.

OPEN: 11-3 7-11 (Sun 12-3, 7-10.30) (Summer 6.30 opening) Closed: 25 Dec **BAR MEALS:** L served all week 12-2 D served all week 7-9 Av main course £7 **BREWERY/COMPANY:** Palmers ◀: Palmers IPA, 200 Premium Ale. ⚲: 10 **FACILITIES:** Children welcome Garden: Dogs allowed Water **NOTES:** Parking 12 No credit cards

---

SHERBORNE Map 04 ST61

The Digby Tap

Cooks Ln DT9 3NS ☎ 01935 813148

e-mail: peter@lefevre.fslife.co.uk

Old-fashioned town pub with stone-flagged floors, old beams and a wide-ranging choice of real ale. A hearty menu of pub grub includes lasagne, steak and kidney pie, rump steak, gammon steak, and plaice or cod. The pub was used as a location for the 1990 TV drama 'A Murder of Quality', that

continued

SHERBORNE continued

starred Denholm Elliot and Glenda Jackson. Scenes from the film can be seen on the pub walls.
OPEN: 11-2.30 5.30-11 (Sat 6-11, Sun 12-3, 7-10.30) Closed: 1 Jan
BAR MEALS: L served Mon-Sat 12-1.45 Av main course £3.95
BREWERY/COMPANY: Free House ◗: Ringwood Best, Otter Ale, Sharp's Cornish Coaster & Cornish Jack, St Austell Tinners.
FACILITIES: Dogs allowed **NOTES:** No credit cards

Half Moon 🐓 ♀
Half Moon St DT9 3LN ☎ 01935 812017 🖹 01935 815295
Standing close to Sherborne Abbey, this half-timbered Cotswold stone inn stands in the centre of town. Eat in the restaurant or the warm and inviting bar: daily specials might include chicken pomodoro, and Thai salmon supreme, while the main menu offers a choice of steaks, plus old favourites like steak and ale pie, lasagne, and chicken tikka masala.
OPEN: 11-11 (Sun 12-10.30) **BAR MEALS:** L served all week 12-2 D served all week 6-9 Av main course £5 **RESTAURANT:** L served all week 12-2 D served all week 6-9.30 Av 3 course à la carte £15
BREWERY/COMPANY: Eldridge Pope ◗: Bass, Ansell, Tetley.
FACILITIES: Children welcome Garden: **NOTES:** Parking 40

Queen's Head 🐓
High St, Milborne Port DT9 5DQ
☎ 01963 250314 🖹 01963 250339
Dir: On A30
A Grade II listed building, parts of it dating back to Elizabethan times, the pub has charm, character and a very friendly atmosphere in two comfortable bars and dining-room. Enthusiastic licensees oversee a wide-ranging menu in which they take great pride. The most accomplished dishes include beef Stroganoff, warm lemon chicken salad, swordfish steaks with lime and ginger sauce and vegetarian Mexican mixed-bean chilli. There are home-made beefburgers in adult and junior portions and an ice cream menu amongst the desserts.
OPEN: 12-2.30 5.30-11 (Sat 12-11, Sun 12-3.30, 6.30-10.30)
BAR MEALS: L served all week 12-2 D served all week 7-9.30 Av main course £9.50 **RESTAURANT:** L served all week 12-2 D served all week 7-9.30 **BREWERY/COMPANY:** Enterprise Inns
◗: Butcombe Bitters, Old Speckled Hen, Fullers London Pride.
FACILITIES: Children welcome Garden: patio/terrace, food served outside Dogs allowed Water **NOTES:** Parking 15

Skippers Inn 🐓 ♀
Horsecastles DT9 3HE ☎ 01935 812753
e-mail: chrisfrowde@lineone.net
Dir: From Yeovil A30 to Sherborne
End-of-terrace converted cider house, much larger inside than it looks from the outside. The extensive menu can change by the minute, but there is usually a choice of 12 fresh fish dishes - all seasonal from local coastal waters - and at least four vegetarian. Other options range from bar snacks (baguettes, ploughman's, soup and scampi) to local pork chops with sweet and sour sauce, venison sausages, or well-hung rump, sirloin or fillet steak.
OPEN: 11-2.30 6.00-11 **BAR MEALS:** L served all week 11.15-2 D served all week 6.30-9.30 Av main course £7.95 **RESTAURANT:** L served all week 11.15-2 D served all week 6.30-9.30
BREWERY/COMPANY: Wadworth ◗: Wadworth 6X & Henrys IPA, Butcombe Butter. **FACILITIES:** Garden: Small garden with shrubs
NOTES: Parking 30

White Hart 🐓
Bishops Caundle DT9 5ND
☎ 01963 23301 🖹 01963 23301 (by arrangement)
Dir: On A3030 between Sherborne & Sturminster Newton
Walkers who come to pretty Bishops Caundle owe a debt of thanks to whoever waymarked the route to start and end here. The 16th-century pub was once a monks' brewhouse, and later used by the notorious Judge Jeffreys. An extensive menu ranges through snacks, children's and vegetarian dishes, steaks and chef's specialities. Favourites include grilled duck with port and orange, and spicy sizzling pork. There's also a six-activity play trail and two sunken trampolines.
OPEN: 11.30-3 6.30-11 (Sun 12-3, 7-10.30) **BAR MEALS:** L served all week 12-2 D served all week 6.45-9.30 Av main course £8.50
RESTAURANT: L served all week 12-2 D served all week 6.30-9.30
BREWERY/COMPANY: Hall & Woodhouse ◗: Badger Best, Tanglefoot, Golden Champion, Sussex Golden Glory.
FACILITIES: Children welcome Garden: Patio area, 6 benches Dogs allowed Water provided **NOTES:** Parking 32

SHROTON OR IWERNE COURTNEY   Map 04 ST81

Pick of the Pubs

The Cricketers ◆◆◆◆◆ 🐓 ♀
DT11 8QD ☎ 01258 860421 🖹 01258 861800
Dir: Off the A350 Shaftesbury to Blandford

Nestling under Hambledon Hill, renowned for its Iron-Age hill-forts, this classically-English pub is a welcoming local, luring hikers from the Wessex Way which, conveniently, runs through the hostelry's garden. Members of the local cricket team also frequent the homely bar during the summer months. An extensive menu offers a good choice of starters, among them avocado, sun-dried tomato, mozzarella and couscous salad, and pan-fried lambs' kidneys served with a balsamic vinegar cream sauce topped with croutons. Main meals could include roasted duck breast with a mango and orange sauce, Thai-spiced fish cakes, spicy meat balls in a chilli sauce served with rice, and Cricketers' kedgeree with avocado, bacon, Stilton, cucumber, spring onion and egg.
OPEN: 11.30-2.30 7-11 **BAR MEALS:** L served all week 12-2 D served all week 6.30-9 Av main course £8 **RESTAURANT:** L served all week 12-2 D served all week 6.30-9 Av 3 course à la carte £15.50 **BREWERY/COMPANY:** Free House ◗: Ringwood 49er, Butcombe Bitter, Shepherds Neame Spitfire, Marstons Pedigree.
♀: 10 **FACILITIES:** Children welcome Garden: Bordered by trees and hedges, herb garden Dogs allowed Water in garden
NOTES: Parking 19 **ROOMS:** 1 bedrooms 1 en suite d£60

England

STOKE ABBOTT — Map 04 ST40

The New Inn
DT8 3JW ☎ 01308 868333
e-mail: webbs@newinnstokeabbott.fsnet.co.uk
Expect a traditional welcome at this 17th-century thatched village inn. An attractive large garden is among the features, and inside is a cosy beamed bar with a roaring log fire. The Sunday roast is particularly memorable. Specials may include fresh mussels in wine and garlic, pan-fried duck breast with gooseberry sauce, grilled salmon, and lamb noisettes. Wide range of vegetarian dishes.
OPEN: 11.30-3 7-11 (Winter Mon-Thur 7-10.30) (Sun 12-3, 7-10.30)
BAR MEALS: L served all week 12-2 D served all week 7-9.30 Av main course £7.25 **RESTAURANT:** L served all week 12-2 D served all week 7-9.30 Av 3 course à la carte £20
BREWERY/COMPANY: Palmers ■: Palmers IPA & 200 Premium Ale. **FACILITIES:** Children welcome Garden: Lrg, comfortable, beautiful views Dogs allowed **NOTES:** Parking 25

STRATTON — Map 04 SY69

Saxon Arms
DT2 9WG ☎ 01305 260020 ▤ 01305 264225
e-mail: saxonarms@btinternet.com
Dir: 3m NW of Dorchester on A37 Saxon arms is at the back of the village Green between the church and new village hall

A massive thatched roof, a patio overlooking the village green, solid oak beams, flagstone floors and a log-burning stove provide great atmosphere. Since opening a few years ago, experienced licensees, Ian and Anne Barrett, have aimed to provide a high quality village inn. Menus offer sirloin steaks, Dorset ham or chicken chasseur, while the specials boards may conjure up scallop & tiger prawn brochette, or beef in Guinness casserole. Either way, leave room for one of the many desserts.
OPEN: 11-2.30 5.30-11 **BAR MEALS:** L served all week 11.30-2 D served all week 6.30-9 Av main course £7.50
BREWERY/COMPANY: Free House ■: Fuller's London Pride, Palmers IPA, Saxon Ale. ♀: 8 **FACILITIES:** Garden: Portland stone patio area with table **NOTES:** Parking 35

STUDLAND — Map 05 SZ08

The Bankes Arms Hotel
Watery Ln BH19 3AU
☎ 01929 450225 & 450310 ▤ 01929 450307
Dir: B3369 from Poole, across on Sandbanks chain ferry, or A35 from Poole, A351 then B3351

Close to sweeping Studland Bay, across which can be seen the prime real estate enclave of Sandbanks, is this part 15th-century, creeper-clad inn, once a smugglers' dive. It specialises in fresh fish and seafood, including mussels, kebabs, crab gratin and lobster dishes. Others include game casserole, lamb noisettes in mint, honey and orange sauce, and spicy pork in chilli, coriander and caper sauce. The annual beer festival held in its large garden showcases 60 real ales, music, Morris dancing and stone carving.
OPEN: 11-11 Closed: Dec 25 **BAR MEALS:** L served all week 12-3.00 D served all week 6-9.30 Av main course £7.50
BREWERY/COMPANY: Free House ■: Badger Best, Hampshire King Alfred's. **FACILITIES:** Garden: Garden with views toward the Isle of Wight Dogs allowed **NOTES:** Parking 10 **ROOMS:** 8 bedrooms 7 en suite 1 family rooms s£28 d£58 (♦♦♦) no children overnight

SYDLING ST NICHOLAS — Map 04 SY69

The Greyhound Inn
DT2 9PD ☎ 01300 341303 ▤ 01300 341303
Dir: Off A37 Yeovil to Dorchester Road, turn off at Cerne Abbas/Sydling St Nicholas
Located in one of Dorset's loveliest villages and surrounded by picturesque countryside, this traditional inn is characterised by its relaxed, welcoming atmosphere and delightful walled garden. Fresh home-cooked food served daily includes rib-eye steak, rack of English lamb, pan-fried king scallops with a sweet chilli, roast duck breast with port and redcurrant jus, and goats' cheese topped with pesto and grilled on salad.
OPEN: 11-3.30 6-11 (Sun 12-3.30, 7-11) **BAR MEALS:** L served all week 12-2 D served all week 6-10 Av main course £10.95
RESTAURANT: L served all week 12-2 D served all week 6-10 Av 3 course à la carte £25 **BREWERY/COMPANY:** Free House ■: Fuller's London Pride, Palmer IPA, Butcombe. ♀: 12 **FACILITIES:** Garden: Dogs allowed **NOTES:** Parking 24

Top of the Tree

Pubs called the Royal Oak were originally named in loyal remembrance of the day in 1651 when the youthful King Charles II hid in an oak tree at Boscobel in Shropshire, while Roundhead soldiers unsuccessfully searched the woods for him. The Royal Oak sign often shows simply the oak tree, or the king is shown perched among the branches - in plain view from all directions, but conventionally accepted as invisible to the purblind Parliamentarian troops. Sometimes, more subtly, the tree has a large crown among the foliage. Rarer variants include the king holding an oak spray with acorns, or acorns below a crown.

England

TARRANT MONKTON — Map 04 ST90

Pick of the Pubs

The Langton Arms ◆◆◆◆ ♀

DT11 8RX ☎ 01258 830225 ▤ 01258 830053

e-mail: info@thelangtonarms.co.uk

Dir: A31 from Ringwood, or A357 from Shaftesbury, or A35 from Bournemouth

Deep in Thomas Hardy country, this 17th-century thatched free house offers guest accommodation in rustic brick outhouses around an attractive courtyard. Enjoy good real ales in the beamed bar where meals include smoked salmon salad and game pie. In The Stables an evening bistro menu could feature galantine of chicken followed by Wellington of smoked pheasant in redcurrant and apple jus. A children's adventure play area, function room and skittle alley complete the pub's universal appeal.

OPEN: 11.30-11 (Sun 12-10.30) **BAR MEALS:** L served all week 11.30-2.30 D served all week 6-9.30 Av main course £7.95 **RESTAURANT:** L served Sun 12-2 D served Wed-Sat 7-9 Av 3 course à la carte £28 Av 3 course fixed price £16.95 **BREWERY/COMPANY:** Free House ◖: Hop Back Best, Guest Beers. ♀: 6 **FACILITIES:** Children welcome Garden: Lrg beer garden **NOTES:** Parking 100 **ROOMS:** 6 bedrooms 6 en suite s£50 d£70

TOLPUDDLE — Map 04 SY79

The Martyrs Inn ▨ ♀

DT2 7ES ☎ 01305 848249 ▤ 01305 848977

e-mail: martyrs@scottz.co.uk

Dir: Off A35 between Bere Regis (A31/A35 Junction)

Tolpuddle is the somewhat unlikely birthplace of the Trades Union Congress. Its seeds were sown in 1834 by six impoverished farm labourers who tried to bargain with local landowners for better conditions. Their punishment was transportation to Australia. Martyrs' memorabilia abounds in the pub. Home-made starters include chicken liver and wild mushroom pâté, and garlic mushrooms en croûte; main courses include Tolpuddle sausages with mash and onion gravy, country vegetable pasta bake, and spicy chicken curry with rice and naan bread.

BAR MEALS: L served all week 12-3 D served all week 6.30-9 Av main course £6 **RESTAURANT:** L served all week D served all week **BREWERY/COMPANY:** Hall & Woodhouse ◖: Badger Dorset Best & Tanglefoot. **FACILITIES:** Children welcome Garden: Dogs allowed **NOTES:** Parking 25

TRENT — Map 04 ST51

Rose & Crown Inn ▨

DT9 4SL ☎ 01935 850776

Dir: W on A30 towards Yeovil. 3m from Sherborne R to Over Compton/Trent, 1.5m downhill, then R. Pub opp church

Workers building the 15th-century church constructed the oldest part of this thatched pub, which has been considerably added to over the centuries. The France-bound Charles II reputedly hid here, while in the mid 20th-century it was a favoured watering hole of Lord Fisher, the Archbishop of Canterbury who crowned Queen Elizabeth II. Today's visitors come for the bistro-style food, in particular fresh fish, local

continued

---

game, steaks, chicken and pastas. Bar meals, snacks and children's choices too.

OPEN: 12-2.30 7-11 (Sun 12-3 only) Closed: 1 Jan **BAR MEALS:** L served all week 12-2.15 D served all week 7-9.15 Av main course £8.50 **RESTAURANT:** L served all week 12-2.15 D served all week 7-9.15 **BREWERY/COMPANY:** Free House ◖: Doombar, Butcombe Bitter. **FACILITIES:** Children welcome Garden: table seating, fish pond Dogs allowed on lead only, water **NOTES:** Parking 30

WEST BEXINGTON — Map 04 SY58

The Manor Hotel ★★

DT2 9DF ☎ 01308 897616 ▤ 01308 897035

e-mail: themanorhotel@btconnect.com

Dir: on B3157, 5m E of Bridport

Just 500 yards from spectacular Chesil Beach and the clear waters of Lyme Bay lies this 16th-century manor house, featuring Jacobean oak panelling and flagstone floors. A handy base for exploring Dorset's numerous delights and enjoying stunning coastal walks. Imaginative cooking and freshly-prepared specialities, with dishes such as Murphy's steak and kidney pudding, game pie, lamb shank and chicken stirfry. Fish options include whole local plaice and sea bass with scallops and king prawns.

OPEN: 11-11 (Sun 12–10.30) **BAR MEALS:** L served all week 12-2 D served all week 6.30-9.30 **RESTAURANT:** L served all week 12-2 D served all week 7-9.30 **BREWERY/COMPANY:** Free House ◖: Butcombe Gold, Steam Beer. **FACILITIES:** Children welcome Garden: Food served outside **NOTES:** Parking 25 **ROOMS:** 13 bedrooms 13 en suite d£110 s£70

WEST KNIGHTON — Map 04 SY78

The New Inn

DT2 8PE ☎ 01305 852349

A 200-year-old pub with a listed archway, the New Inn was originally a row of farm cottages. Its rural location makes an ideal base for walks and exploring the surrounding countryside. The regular menu is supplemented by weekly specials, such as moules marinière, and braised beef in red wine and garlic sauce. Among the interesting puddings are kish-mish salad of dried fruit in brandy and rosewater, and squidgy chocolate roll.

OPEN: 11-3 7-11.30 (Winter 12-3, 7-11.30) **BAR MEALS:** L served all week 12-2 D served all week 7-9 Av main course £5 **RESTAURANT:** L served all week 11.30-2 D served all week 7-9 **BREWERY/COMPANY:** Pubmaster ◖: Ringwood Best, Old Speckled Hen, Directors. **FACILITIES:** Children welcome Garden: Fenced area safe for young children Dogs allowed Water **NOTES:** Parking 30

WEST LULWORTH — Map 04 SY88

The Castle Inn ▨ ♀

Main Rd BH20 5RN ☎ 01929 400311 ▤ 01929 400415

Dir: on the Wareham to Dorchester Rd, L approx 1m from Wareham

Picturesque thatched and beamed inn with a delightful setting near Lulworth Cove, close to plenty of good walks and popular attractions. Prize-winning gardens packed with plants, garden furniture and a water feature are an additional attraction. The wide-ranging menu offers a choice of some 50 dishes, from chicken and ham pie, sirloin steak, or liver and bacon, to exotic cuts like crocodile, ostrich or kangaroo, plus a variety of flambé dishes cooked at the table.

continued

England

OPEN: 11-2.30 6-11 (Winter 12-2.30, 7-11) Closed: 25 Dec
BAR MEALS: L served all week 11-2.30 D served all week 6-10.30
Av main course £9 **RESTAURANT:** L served all week D served Fri
& Sat 7-9.30 Av 3 course à la carte £15
BREWERY/COMPANY: Free House ◀: Ringwood Best, Gales,
Courage, John Smith. ♀: 8 **FACILITIES:** Children welcome
Garden: Large tiered garden lots of plants and flowers Dogs
allowed Water/Food **NOTES:** Parking 30

WEST STAFFORD Map 04 SY78

The Wise Man Inn 🦅 ♀
DT2 8AG ☎ 01305 263694 🖶 01305 751660
e-mail: ray3bears@supanet.com
Dir: 2m from A35

Set in the heart of Thomas Hardy country, this thatched 16th-
century pub is a regular stopping off point for those on the
Hardy trail, and is proud to use local produce on its menu.
Chargrilled steaks are a popular option alongside a good
range of seafood - monkfish in lemon and ginger, pan-fried
scallops wrapped in bacon, and skate in black butter. There's
also a large secluded garden with ample seating.
OPEN: 11-3 6.30-11 **BAR MEALS:** L served all week 12-2.30 D
served Mon-Sat 7-9.30 Av main course £6.95 **RESTAURANT:** L
served all week 12-2.30 D served Mon-Sat 7-9.30 Av 3 course à la carte
£18 **BREWERY/COMPANY:** Pubmaster ◀: 3 casked
ales each week. ♀: 6 **FACILITIES:** Children welcome Garden:
Large, plenty of seating, secluded Dogs allowed Water & biscuits
provided **NOTES:** Parking 25

WEYMOUTH Map 04 SY67

The Old Ship Inn 🦅 ♀
7 The Ridgeway DT3 5QQ ☎ 01305 812522
One of his regular watering holes, Thomas Hardy refers to this
historic pub in his novels 'Under the Greenwood Tree' and 'The
Trumpet Major'. The terrace offers views over Weymouth, while
inside there are copper pans, old clocks and a beamed open fire.
Wholesome menu ranges from home-made beef and ale pie,
chicken topped with goats' cheese and basil pesto, lamb's liver
and bacon, pan-fried crab cakes with a light chilli mayonnaise,
and supreme of guinea fowl with cider apples and shallots.
OPEN: 12-3 6-11 (Sun 12-3, 7-10.30) **BAR MEALS:** L served all
week 12-2 D served all week 6-9.30 Av main course £9.50
RESTAURANT: L served all week 12-2 D served all week 6-9.30 Av 3
course à la carte £18 Av 3 course fixed price £10.95
BREWERY/COMPANY: Inn Partnership ◀: Greene King Old
Speckled Hen, Ringwood Best, Scottish Courage. ♀: 7
FACILITIES: Children welcome Garden: Patio garden with enclosed
grass area Dogs allowed Water **NOTES:** Parking 12

CO DURHAM

AYCLIFFE Map 19 NZ22

The County 🦅 ♀
13 The Green, Aycliffe Village DL5 6LX ☎ 01325 312273
Dir: Off the A167 into Aycliffe Village
Historic pub overlooking a pretty village green within Tony
Blair's Sedgefield constituency, where the PM has entertained
France's President Jacques Chirac. The County offers a good
range of guest and local ales and an extensive wine list, but
the emphasis is on quality modern pub food with a daily-
changing specials board. Representative main courses are
slow-cooked confit of duck, pan-fried Deben duckling breast,
Harry Coats' prize-winning sausages, and chargrilled tuna
steak with fennel ragôut.
OPEN: 12-3 5.30-11 (Closed Sun nights) Closed: 25-26 Dec 1 Jan
BAR MEALS: L served all week 12-2 D served Mon-Sat 6-7
RESTAURANT: L served all week 12-2 D served Mon-Sat 6-9.30 Av 3
course à la carte £22 **BREWERY/COMPANY:** Free House
◀: Scottish Courage John Smith's Magnet, Wells Bombardier,
Jennings Cumberland Ale, Castle Eden & Camerons. ♀: 9
FACILITIES: Children welcome **NOTES:** Parking 30

BARNARD CASTLE Map 19 NZ01

Pick of the Pubs

The Morritt Arms Hotel ♀
Greta Bridge DL12 9SE ☎ 01833 627232 🖶 01833 627392
e-mail: relax@themorritt.co.uk
Dir: At Scotch Corner take A66 towards Penrith, after 9m turn at Greta
Bridge. Hotel over bridge on L
The present building began life as a 17th-century
farmhouse. Over the years the outbuildings have been
incorporated into the hotel to create a stylish inn, which
may be familiar to viewers of 'The Fast Show'. Log fires
warm the building in winter, and you can eat out in the
landscaped gardens on balmy summer days. During the
19th century, Greta Bridge became the second overnight
stop of the London-Carlisle coaches. The Dickens Bar,
decorated with murals by John Gilroy, commemorates the
most famous guest of that era (Dickens stayed here in 1839
when researching Nicholas Nicklelby). A variety of dining
options caters for every occasion: for relaxed, informal
meals choose the bar or Pallatt's bistro; for a more formal
affair, opt for the Copperfield restaurant. Food ranges from
bar snacks (sandwiches or hearty main courses like
sausages and mash or steak and chips) through to
restaurant specials such as pork fillet provençale with a rice
timbale or stir-fried duck in hoi sin sauce.
OPEN: 7-11 **BAR MEALS:** L served all week 12-3 D served all
week 6-9.30 Av main course £6 **RESTAURANT:** L served all
week 12-3 D served all week 7-9 Av 3 course à la carte £25 Av 4
course fixed price £18.95 **BREWERY/COMPANY:** Free House
◀: Scottish Courage John Smith's, Theakston Best Bitter, Timothy
Taylor Landlord, Black Sheep Best. ♀: 20 **FACILITIES:** Children
welcome Children's licence Garden: Terraced, traditional garden
with walk ways Dogs allowed Water **NOTES:** Parking 100

Rose & Crown

A delightful ramble that takes in great views of Teesdale and finishes with a majestic walk beside the River Tees.

Turn left on leaving the inn and walk down to the bottom of the village. Take the waymarked footpath left down a track (Primrose Lane), crossing a beck and then a wall stile. Head diagonally across the field to a stile on the brow, then follow the right-hand field edge to a further stile. Proceed beside the concrete wall, soon to bear left to a gate and road by a stone barn, opposite Eggleston House.

Turn right, cross Eggleston Bridge and turn immediately right along a lane. In 1/2 mile (0.8km), cross the ladder stile on your left and ascend steep steps through Great Wood to enter a field. Cross the wall stile ahead, then bear left across the field to a stile. Head to the left of East Barnley Farm, aiming for the telegraph pole and the gate beyond. Head for the stile and gate beyond the beck and proceed across marshy ground to

a stile in a wire fence. Bear left to a wall stile and join a track. Good views across Teesdale.

Walk along the track, passing through two field gates to enter a small wood. Continue past a waterfall and caravan site and head towards the River Tees, crossing the bridge ahead. Turn right and cross the stile at the top of the bank. Keep to the right-hand edge of the field to a stile, then head for stepping stones across a beck. Proceed to a gate in the top right-hand corner of the field and soon pass a large house (Woden Croft - one of the old Yorkshire schools which Charles Dickens researched for Nicholas Nickleby). Bear right past a farm cottage and barns to a gate, then follow the path immediately right down to the river.

At the river, bear left and follow it upstream through beautiful woodland to a wall

★★ ⊗⊛

ROSE & CROWN, ROMALDKIRK
Barnard Castle DL12 9EB.

☎ 01833 650213

Directions: 6m NW of Barnard Castle on B6277
Splendid, stone-built Jacobean coaching inn standing in the middle of three greens by the church in a pretty conservation village. Retains much of its original charm and offers tasteful accommodation. Innovative menus.
Open: 11.30-3 5.30-11 (Sun 12-3 7-10.30). Bar Meals: 12-1.30 6.30-9.30.
Notes: Children and dogs welcome, Parking.
(See page 176 for full entry)

stile. Climb towards abandoned farmhouse and pass through gate to its left. Follow drive through field, soon to bear off right to gate in hedge. Head for gate in top left-hand corner of field and follow footpath (Sennings Lane) back into Romaldkirk. Inn is across the green to your left.

DISTANCE: 6 miles (10km)
MAP: OS Landranger 92
TERRAIN: Farmland and woodland
PATHS: Field and woodland paths
GRADIENT: Gently undulating; one steep climb

Walk submitted by The Rose & Crown

COTHERSTONE
Map 19 NZ01

The Fox and Hounds 🏮♀
DL12 9PF ☎ 01833 650241 📠 01833 650518
Dir: 4m W of Barnard Castle, from A66 turn onto B6277, Cotherstone signposted

Traditional heavily-beamed coaching inn dating back to the 1700s standing close to the River Tees and overlooking the village green. Well placed for walks and touring. Bar food lunchtime and evening, with the dinner menu providing an imaginative selection. Vegetables usually sourced from local allotments. Expect shank of pork braised in sage, apple and cider; rack of Teesdale lamb; roast breast of duckling on parsnip and apple mash; and ratatouille-filled crêpe baked with Cotherstone cheese.

OPEN: 12-3 6.30-11 Closed: 25-26 Dec **BAR MEALS:** L served all week 12-2 D served all week 6-9.30 **RESTAURANT:** L served all week 12-2 D served all week 6-9.30 Av 3 course à la carte £17
BREWERY/COMPANY: Free House ▄: Black Sheep Best, Scottish Courage, John Smith's Smooth, Hambleton Best Bitter. ♀: 7
FACILITIES: Garden; Dogs allowed Kennel available
NOTES: Parking 20

DURHAM
Map 19 NZ24

Pick of the Pubs

Seven Stars Inn 🏮♀
High St North, Shincliffe Village DH1 2NU
☎ 0191 384 8454 📠 0191 386 0640
e-mail: enquiries@sevenstarsinn.co.uk

A little gem tucked away on the edge of picturesque Shincliffe, this quaint inn has remained virtually unaltered since 1724, although tasteful decoration and the addition of antique furnishings have improved levels of comfort for discerning local diners. Pretty in summer with its tubs and window boxes, and cosily lit during the winter, it offers a

fine setting for imaginative British cuisine with exotic influences. The bar/lounge menu offers sandwiches, soup, and steak and ale pie, while the restaurant menu (also available in the lounge and bar) has the likes of Thai crab cakes on tomato salad with coriander dressing, Cajun-spiced rump of lamb with tomato and olive ragôut, sautéed potatoes and red wine jus, and for pudding a white chocolate and blueberry brûlée. Accommodation is also available in individually-furnished bedrooms.
OPEN: 11.30-11 (Sun 12-10.30) **BAR MEALS:** L served all week 12-2.30 D served all week 6-9.30 Av main course £11
RESTAURANT: L served all week 12-2.30 D served all week 6-9.30 Av 3 course à la carte £23 **BREWERY/COMPANY:** Free House ▄: Theakstons Best Bitter, Castle Eden Ale, Blacksheep Bitter, Courage Directors. ♀: 8 **FACILITIES:** Children welcome Dogs allowed **ROOMS:** 8 bedrooms 8 en suite 1 family rooms s£40 d£55 (♦♦♦)

FIR TREE
Map 19 NZ13

Duke of York Residential Country Inn ♦♦♦♦
DL15 8DG ☎ 01388 762848 📠 01388 767055
e-mail: suggett@firtree-crook.fsnet.co.uk
Dir: on A68 trunk road to Scotland, 12m W of Durham City

A former drovers' and coaching inn on the old York to Edinburgh coach route, this 18th-century white-painted inn is noted for its furniture which contains the famous carved mouse trademark of Robert Thompson, a renowned Yorkshire woodcarver. There's also a collection of flint arrowheads, axes and Africana. Typical food includes home-made steak and kidney pie, pork Zaccharoff, and soups that are so popular, people often ask for the recipe. Large landscaped beer garden.
OPEN: 11-2.30 6.30-10.30 **BAR MEALS:** L served all week 12-2 D served all week 6.30-9 Av main course £7 **RESTAURANT:** L served all week 12-2 D served all week 6.30-9 Av 3 course à la carte £18
BREWERY/COMPANY: Free House ▄: Black Sheep, Worthington, Stones, Carling. **FACILITIES:** Children welcome Children's licence Garden: Garden at rear of pub , patio area Dogs allowed Water
NOTES: Parking 65 **ROOMS:** 5 bedrooms 5 en suite s£52 d£72

> **For a list of pubs with AA Inspected Accommodation Awards**
> ♦ **see pages 646-651** ★

continued

England

Open: 11.30-3, 5.30-11
Bar Meals: L served all week 12-1.30,
D served all week 6.30-9.30.
Av main course £9.50
RESTAURANT: L served all week
12-1.30,
D served all week 7.30-9.
BREWERY/COMPANY:
Free House.
🍺: Theakston Best, Black Sheep Best
FACILITIES: Dogs allowed (bedrooms
and garden only). Children welcome.
NOTES: Parking 24
ROOMS: 12 en suite from s£70 d£96

Rose and Crown

A classic old coaching inn that offers a civilised welcome in fine surroundings. Successfully embracing many roles, it manages to be a pub for locals, a hotel for residents, a restaurant for diners, but an inn above all else.

Romaldkirk, Barnard Castle,
DL12 9EB
☎ 01833 650213 📠 01833 650828
📧 hotel@rose-and-crown.co.uk
Dir: 6m NW from Barnard Castle
on B6277

The Rose & Crown was built in 1733 on the green of a typical English village, next to the church - the Cathedral of the Dale - and opposite the old stocks and water pump which still remain in place. Old oak beams, a large dog grate with a roaring fire in the stone fireplace, and lots of brass, copper and old sepia photographs complete the rustic charm of the wood-panelled bar. You can eat lunch here or in the Crown Room, where good quality bar meals are popular with all comers. These range from ploughman's and filled baps through roast confit of duck leg, and lamb's liver and bacon to broccoli and mushroom crêpe with herb crust and salad. Bar suppers are more elaborate, with Stroganoff of beef fillet, and trout wrapped around crabmeat with chive cream sauce. Desserts like chocolate torte, and hot walnut and syrup tart make it difficult to leave in a hurry. A set-price four-course dinner in the restaurant offers choices such as scallop and prawn tartlet, potato, leek and parsley soup, and chargrilled rump of venison with haggis mash and whisky cream sauce. The fourth option might involve some indecision between hot sticky toffee pudding and a plate of blue Wensleydale, smoked Cumberland and Mrs Kirkham's Lancashire. Overnighters or those enjoying a longer stay will appreciate the bedrooms, decorated in vibrant colours and rich fabrics, with luxurious modern bathrooms, and the use of the lounge, with its exposed stone walls and period furniture.

MIDDLESTONE
Map 19 NZ23

Ship Inn NEW
Low Rd DL14 8AB ☎ 01388 810904
e-mail: graham@snaithg.freeserve.co.uk
Dir: Telephone for directions
Beer drinkers will appreciate the string of CAMRA accolades received by this family-run pub on the village green. In the last two years regulars could have sampled well over 500 different beers. Ask about the pub's challenge for regulars to visit as many pubs as possible with 'ship' in their name. Home-cooked food in the bar and restaurant. The rooftop patio has spectacular views over the Tees Valley and Cleveland Hills.
BAR MEALS: L served Fri-Sun 12-2.30 D served Wed-Sat 5-9 Av main course £4.95 **RESTAURANT:** L served Fri-Sun D served Wed-Sat **FACILITIES:** Children welcome Village green Dogs allowed **NOTES:** Parking 6 No credit cards

MIDDLETON-IN-TEESDALE
Map 18 NY92

The Teesdale Hotel 🍴
Market Square DL12 0QG
☎ 01833 640264 & 640537 📠 01833 640651
Tastefully modernised, family-run coaching inn noted for its striking stone-built exterior and archway. Nearby lies some of the North of England's loveliest scenery. Inside, a friendly atmosphere and cosy log fires add to the charm. From the dinner menu you could try honeydew melon or mushrooms in garlic cream sauce, followed by fresh monk fish, diced veal or medallions of beef.
OPEN: 11-11 **BAR MEALS:** L served all week 12-2 D served all week 7-9 Av main course £7 **RESTAURANT:** L served Sun 12-1.30 D served all week 7.30-8.30 Av 3 course à la carte £19.95
BREWERY/COMPANY: Free House 🍺: Tetley, Smooth, Beerton.
FACILITIES: Children welcome Garden: Dogs allowed **ROOMS:** 12 bedrooms 10 en suite s£42.50 d£65.50 (★★)

NEWTON AYCLIFFE
Map 19 NZ22

Blacksmiths Arms 🍷
Preston le Skerne, (off Ricknall Lane) DL5 6JH
☎ 01325 314873 📠 01325 307417
e-mail: pub@blacksmithsarms.co.uk
Originally a blacksmith's shop dating from around 1800, the pub was built into a disused railway embankment. It is set in isolated farmland outside the new town of Newton Aycliffe. Now a family business, the emphasis is on good value home-cooked food (rib-eye steak with all the trimmings, perhaps). There's a weekly-changing range of real ales, as many as 150 each year, supporting micro-breweries wherever possible. The beer garden is a popular summer attraction.
OPEN: 12-3 6-11 Closed: 25 Dec 1 Jan **BAR MEALS:** L served Sun 12-2 D served Tue-Sat 5.30-9 Av main course £6.50
BREWERY/COMPANY: Free House 🍺: Everchanging selection of Real Ales. 🍷: 10 **FACILITIES:** Children welcome Garden: Fully enclosed rural setting, 0.75 acre Dogs allowed Water **NOTES:** Parking 25 No credit cards

ROMALDKIRK
Map 19 NY92

Pick of the Pubs

Rose and Crown ★★ 🏵️🏵️ 🍴 🍷
DL12 9EB ☎ 01833 650213 📠 01833 650828
e-mail: hotel@rose-and-crown.co.uk
See Pub Walk on page 174
See Pick of the Pubs on opposite page

SEDGEFIELD
Map 19 NZ32

Dun Cow Inn ♦♦♦ 🍴 🍷 **NEW**
43 Front St TS21 3AT ☎ 01740 620894 📠 01740 622163
e-mail: duncowinn@grayner.fsnet.co.uk
Dir: At junct of A177 & A689. Inn in centre of village
An interesting array of bric-a-brac can be viewed inside this splendid old village inn, which has many flower baskets bedecking its exterior in summer. It is also the pub that can claim to be Prime Minister Tony Blair's local, as he is the local MP. Typical offerings include Angus sirloin steaks, locally-made sausages, spring lamb cutlets, fresh Shetland mussels, and mushroom Stroganoff. Pudding choices often include gooseberry crumble and chocolate fudge cake with butterscotch sauce.
OPEN: 11-3 6.30-11 **BAR MEALS:** L served all week 12-2 D served all week 7-10 Av main course £8.95 **RESTAURANT:** L served all week 12-2 D served all week 7-10 Av 3 course à la carte £19
BREWERY/COMPANY: Free House 🍺: Theakston Best Bitter, John Smiths Smooth. 🍷: 8 **FACILITIES:** Children welcome **NOTES:** Parking 30 **ROOMS:** 6 bedrooms 6 en suite s£49.50 d£65

ESSEX

ARKESDEN
Map 12 TL43

Pick of the Pubs

Axe & Compasses 🍴 🍷
High St CB11 4EX ☎ 01799 550272 📠 01799 550906
See Pick of the Pubs on page 178

BLACKMORE END
Map 12 TL73

Pick of the Pubs

The Bull Inn 🍷
CM7 4DD ☎ 01371 851037 📠 01371 851037
Off-the-beaten-track at the heart of tranquil north Essex countryside, two 17th-century cottages and an adjoining barn form this traditional village pub, full of original beams and open hearths, that looks out over open farmland little changed over 300 years. An attractive garden also produces herbs for kitchen staff who are full of enthusiasm and up-to-date ideas. In the beginning are potted brown shrimps, chicken and sun-dried tomato terrine, and grilled goats' cheese with raspberry vinaigrette. In the middle come beef tournedos Rossini with Marsala jus, monkfish in bacon garnished with queen scallops and game and oyster suet pudding in rich gravy with creamed mash. Vegetarians at this point have their own menu - wild mushroom Stroganoff or aubergine and Stilton polenta gateau perhaps - before all join in at the end for apple and forest fruits crumble, chocolate and hazelnut roulade and ice cream sundae. Only on a Sunday is there a set-price lunch with similar starters, traditional roasts and nursery puddings.
OPEN: 12-3 6-11 (Summer open 12-3, 5-11) **BAR MEALS:** L served all week 12-3 D served all week 7-9.45 Av main course £10
BREWERY/COMPANY: Free House 🍺: Greene King IPA, Abbot Ale, Adnams Best. 🍷: 6 **FACILITIES:** Children welcome Garden: beer garden, outdoor eating, BBQ **NOTES:** Parking 36

Open: 11.30-2.30, 6-11
Bar Meals: L served all week 12-2,
D served all week 6.45-9.30.
Av cost main course £10.50
RESTAURANT: L served all week 12-2,
D served all week 6.45-9.30.
BREWERY/COMPANY: GREENE KING
🍺: Greene King IPA, Abbot Ale & Old
Speckled Hen.
FACILITIES: Garden - Patio, seats
around 30 people.
NOTES: Parking 12

Axe & Compasses

The narrow main street of this captivating village runs alongside Wicken Water - an occasional stream spanned by a succession of footbridges leading to white, cream and pink-washed thatched cottages.

High Street, Arkesden, CB11 4EX
☎ 01799 550272 📠 01799 550906
Dir: From Buntingford take
B1038 towards Newport. Then
L for Arkesden.

At the heart of the village is an inn of real character whose long-held motto is 'Relax at the Axe'. With good reason: the Axe's central thatched section, dating from around 1650, links the former stabling area with a 19th-century extension housing today's welcoming bar and a laid-back lounge with easy chairs, sofas, antique furniture and brass reflecting the glow of an open fire. Floral tubs and hanging baskets adorn the front of the inn and its side patio in summer, when customers are tempted by the sandwiches and home-produced bar meals selection, such as sausage and mash with onion gravy, that are its stock in trade. Greene King ales predominate alongside a fair wine selection, including up to 14 by the glass, and a collection of over 20 malt whiskies. In the separate restaurant area, which seats 50, customers can select from at least a dozen starters and an equal number of main course choices, including tasty fresh fish selections such as grilled sea bass fillets with leek and potato cake and nut brown butter; monkfish in roasted red pepper sauce; and halibut steak stacked with spinach, tomato and cheddar cheese, drizzled with white wine and cream. Meat choices are likely to include medallions of beef fillet with deep-fried quenelles of horseradish mash finished with Drambuie, mushrooms and cream; and pan-fried duck breast with Cointreau, orange and demi-glace, garnished with creamed parsnips. Round off with popular desserts from the trolley such raspberry and hazelnut Pavlova or tiramisù. Friendly service amid constant bustle adds to the Axe's charm.

BRAINTREE — Map 07 TL72

Pick of the Pubs

The Green Dragon at Young's End
Upper London Rd, Young's End CM77 8QN
☎ 01245 361030 🖷 01245 362575
e-mail: green.dragon@virgin.net
Dir: *M11 J8 take A120 towards Colchester. At Braintree Bypass take A131 S towards Chelmsford, exit at Youngs End on Great Leighs Bypass*
These days, this former private house and stables is a comfortable dining venue with a choice of dining options, a garden and a play area for children. Cosy bars lead through to the Barn, and the non-smoking, first-floor Hayloft, with their plain brick walls and old beams. Available throughout is a wide selection of starters, main courses and puddings, as well as a whole raft of seafood specials, such as spicy crab cakes, Loch Fyne rock oysters, seared tuna with salsa, fresh lobster salad, and seafood platter for two. Other mains include beef bourguignon, speciality sausages with mash and onion gravy, curry of the day, pastas and vegetarian dishes, which may be parsnip, chestnut and sweet potato bake. Sunday lunch goes beyond the traditional roasts to include beefsteak and Abbot ale pie, Scotch salmon supreme, and a pasta dish. Breaded chicken nuggets and other child-friendly options for the under-10s.
OPEN: 12-3 5.30-11 (Sat-Sun & BHs 12-11) **BAR MEALS:** L served all week 12-2.15 D served all week 6-9.30 Av main course £8 **RESTAURANT:** L served all week 12-2.15 D served all week 6-9.30 **BREWERY/COMPANY:** Greene King ◗: Greene King IPA , Abbot Ale, Ruddles County & Old Speckled Hen. ♀: 8
FACILITIES: Garden: **NOTES:** Parking 40

BURNHAM-ON-CROUCH — Map 07 TQ99

Ye Olde White Harte Hotel
The Quay CM0 8AS ☎ 01621 782106 🖷 01621 782106

Directly overlooking the River Crouch, the hotel dates from the 17th century and retains many original features, including exposed beams. The pub has its own private jetty. The food is mainly English-style with such dishes as roast leg of English lamb, local roast Dengie chicken and seasoning, and grilled fillet of plaice and lemon. There is also a range of bar snacks including toasted and plain sandwiches, jacket potatoes, and soup.
OPEN: 11-11 **BAR MEALS:** L served all week 12-2 D served all week 7-9 Av main course £6.70 **RESTAURANT:** L served all week 12-2 D served all week 7-9 Av 3 course à la carte £21 Av 3

continued

course fixed price £14.80 **BREWERY/COMPANY:** Free House ◗: Adnams Bitter, Crouch Vale Best. **FACILITIES:** Children welcome Jetty over river Dogs allowed **NOTES:** Parking 15

CASTLE HEDINGHAM — Map 13 TL73

The Bell Inn
St James St CO9 3EJ ☎ 01787 460350
e-mail: bell-inn@ic24.net
Dir: *On A1124(A604) N of Halstead, R to Castle Hedingham*
The 15th-century Bell, set in a charming medieval village, serves gravity-fed real ale straight from the barrel. Outside there's a fine walled garden and upstairs a splendid barrel-vaulted function room - a theatre, courthouse and assembly room in its time - and now the venue for live jazz the last Sunday lunchtime of the month. Monday is fish night, while other favourites include Thai chicken curry, liver and bacon casserole, and treacle tart.
OPEN: 11.30-3 6-11 Open all day Friday (Sun 12-3, 7-10.30) Closed: 25 Dec(eve) **BAR MEALS:** L served all week 12-2 D served all week 7-9.30 Av main course £7 **BREWERY/COMPANY:** Grays ◗: Old Speckled Hen, Greene King IPA , Adnams Bitter.
FACILITIES: Children welcome Garden: Large walled orchard garden Dogs allowed by arrangement only **NOTES:** Parking 15

CHAPPEL — Map 13 TL82

The Swan Inn
CO6 2DD ☎ 01787 222353 🖷 01787 220012
Dir: *Pub visible just off A1124 Colchester-Halstead road, from Colchester 1st L after viaduct*

Set in the shadow of a magnificent Victorian viaduct, this rambling, low-beamed old freehouse boasts a charming riverside garden, cobbled courtyard and overflowing flower tubs. Fresh market meat and fish arrives daily: expect scallops grilled with bacon, butterfish Florentine, Swan seafood special, plus calves' liver, chicken Kiev, gammon steak, and various lunchtime snacks such as filled rolls and sandwiches, and beef burgers with chips.
OPEN: 11-3 6-11 (Sat 11-11, Sun 12-10.30) **BAR MEALS:** L served all week 12-2.30 D served all week 7-10.30 **RESTAURANT:** L served all week 12-2.15 D served all week 7-10
BREWERY/COMPANY: Free House ◗: Greene King IPA, Abbot Ale. **FACILITIES:** Children welcome Garden: Food served outside Dogs allowed Water **NOTES:** Parking 55

> **Pick of the Pubs have that extra special quality that makes them stand out from the crowd. Their entries are highlighted, and may be a full page.**

Pick of the Pubs

The Cricketers 🐾 ♀
CB11 4QT ☎ 01799 550442 🖷 01799 550882
e-mail: info@thecricketers.co.uk
Dir: From M11 J10 take A505 E. Then A1301, B1383. At Newport take B1038

Owned and run by the parents of celebrity chef Jamie Oliver - who grew up and worked in the kitchen here - this popular 16th-century inn is at the heart of a beautiful and unspoilt Essex village. It stands opposite the local cricket pitch, and cricketing memorabilia dots the bars and restaurant with their beamed ceilings and log fires that serve to create a friendly atmosphere. Meal options may include light snacks like chargrilled crostini topped with roasted onions, sun-dried tomatoes and a soft blue cheese, or chicken satay with home-made peanut and coconut sauce, through to main dishes such as roasted crown of pheasant stuffed with lemon breadcrumbs, pine kernels and fresh sage; roasted cod fillet on a white bean and herb purée; and cutlets of lamb with a rosemary couscous and thick red onion and redcurrant sauce. Multi-choice dinner menus in the restaurant are available at a fixed price.
OPEN: 10.30-11 Closed: 25-26 Dec **BAR MEALS:** L served all week 12-2 D served all week 7-10 Av main course £10
RESTAURANT: L served all week 12-2 D served all week 7-10 Av 3 course à la carte £26 Av 3 course fixed price £26
BREWERY/COMPANY: Free House ◀: Adnams Bitter, Carlsberg-Tetley Tetley Bitter. ♀: 10 **FACILITIES:** Children welcome Garden: One patio and one courtyard
NOTES: Parking 100 **ROOMS:** 14 bedrooms 14 en suite s£70 d£100 (♦♦♦♦)

Rose & Crown Hotel ★★★
East St CO1 2TZ ☎ 01206 866677 🖷 01206 866616
e-mail: info@rose-and-crown.com
Dir: From M25 J28 take A12 N & follow signs for Colchester
Situated in the heart of Britain's oldest town, this splendid 14th-century posting house retains much of its Tudor character. With ancient timbers, smartly-decorated bedrooms, and wide-ranging menus, it is a popular destination. Part of the bar is made of cell doors from the old jail that was once on the site. The focus is on fresh seafood, with other options such as rack of lamb, calves' liver and bacon, breast of duck with orange sauce, or seared venison fillet.
OPEN: 12-2 7-11 **BAR MEALS:** L served all week 12-2 D served Mon-Sat 7-10 Av main course £10 **RESTAURANT:** L served all week 12-2 D served Mon-Sat 7-11 Av 3 course à la carte £22
BREWERY/COMPANY: Free House ◀: Carlsberg-Tetley Tetley's Bitter, Rose & Crown Bitter, Adnams Broadside.
FACILITIES: Children welcome **NOTES:** Parking 50 **ROOMS:** 29 bedrooms 29 en suite 2 family rooms

---

All AA rated accommodation can also be found on the AA's internet site
www.theAA.com

The Anchor 🐾 ♀
Runsell Green CM3 4QZ ☎ 01245 222457 🖷 01245 222457
e-mail: anchordanbury@ukonline.co.uk
Dir: From Chelmsford take the A414 towards Danbury, pub is 50yds from the main road behind Runsell Green village green.
A popular and attractive 16th-century timbered pub close to the River Chelmer, a number of nature reserves, and just a short drive from the Blackwater Estuary. The welcoming heavily-timbered interior has a wealth of stuffed fish and angling paraphernalia, and roaring log fires in winter. The pub is popular with walkers, and is determined to win more awards with the floral displays that decorate its garden. A sample from the evening menu includes butterfly Cajun chicken, The Anchor Mixed Grill (not for the faint-hearted), harvest vegetable crumble, seafood platter, chicken Americana, braised shank of lamb, chicken breast stuffed with Stilton and wrapped in bacon, and individual steak and kidney pudding.
OPEN: 12-3 6-11 (Fri-Sun 12-11) **BAR MEALS:** L served all week 12-2.30 D served all week 6-9.30 Av main course £8.95
RESTAURANT: L served all week 12-2.30 D served all week 6-9.30 Av 3 course à la carte £16.50 **BREWERY/COMPANY:** Ridley & Sons ◀: Ridleys IPA, Rumpus, Old Bob & Prospect. ♀: 6
FACILITIES: Children welcome Garden: Food served outside Dogs allowed Water **NOTES:** Parking 50

Marlborough Head Hotel ♀
Mill Ln CO7 6DH ☎ 01206 323250
Dir: E of A12, N of Colchester
Set in glorious Constable country, close to Flatford Mill and peaceful walks, this former wool merchant's house dates from 1455. It became an inn in 1704, the year of the Duke of Marlborough's famous victory over the French at the Battle of Blenheim. An extensive menu might feature fisherman's pie, king cod, hot cross bunny, or duck delight.
OPEN: 11-11 Dec 25-26 Closed eve **BAR MEALS:** L served all week 12-3 D served all week 6.30-9.30 Av main course £8.50
RESTAURANT: L served all week 12-2.30 D served all week 7-9.30 Av 3 course à la carte £16 **BREWERY/COMPANY:** ◀: Adnams Southwold, Greene King IPA, Adnams Broadside, plus guest.
FACILITIES: Children welcome Garden: beer garden outdoor eating Dogs allowed garden only **NOTES:** Parking 28

The Crown
The Cross, High St CM22 6DG ☎ 01279 812827
Dir: M11 J8 towards Takeley L at traffic lights
A pub for 300 years, with oak beams, open fireplaces and Essex pargetting at the front. The menu, which has a large selection of fresh fish, might offer cottage pie with cheese topping, gammon steak, three cheese pasta bake, lasagne, baked trout with almonds and honey, steak and mushroom pie, or steaks cooked to order. Recent change of hands.
OPEN: 11-3 6-11 (Sun 12-3, 7-10.30, Summer open all wkd)
BAR MEALS: L served all week 12-2 D served Tue-Sat 7-9 Av main course £6 **RESTAURANT:** L served all week 12-2 D served Tue-Sat 7-9 Av 3 course à la carte £18 **BREWERY/COMPANY:** ◀: Youngs PA, Adnams Broadside, Guest Beers. **FACILITIES:** Children welcome Garden: Grassed area, tables etc, Patio garden Dogs allowed Water
NOTES: Parking 28

FEERING

Map 07 TL82

The Sun Inn

Feering Hill CO5 9NH ☎ 01376 570442
Dir: On A12 between Colchester and Witham
Thought to date from 1525 and originally part of a gentleman's residence, this lively pub offers between 15 and 20 different beers a week and is home to the Feering Beer Festival. An ever-changing menu board of home-cooked dishes includes some Maltese specialities, courtesy of the landlord. Braised chicken liver and bacon cooked in Adnams Best Bitter, jugged hare, and sweet and sour pork casserole are fairly typical. Sandwiches, salads, ploughmans' and baked potatoes are available as a lighter option.
OPEN: 12-3 6-11 (Sun 12-3, 6-9.30) **BAR MEALS:** L served all week 12-3 D served all week 6-9.30 Av main course £7
BREWERY/COMPANY: Free House **FACILITIES:** Children welcome Garden: Enclosed, large lawn, hanging baskets Dogs allowed Water provided **NOTES:** Parking 19 **NOTES:** No credit cards

FINGRINGHOE

Map 07 TM02

The Whalebone 🍴

Chapel Rd CO5 7BG ☎ 01206 729307 📠 01206 729307
e-mail: whale.bone@virgin.net
Dir: Telephone for directions
The 250-year-old Whalebone sits beside the village green and pond, close to the Fingrinhoe Nature Reserve from which the foot ferry crosses the River Colne. Outside is believed to be the oldest oak tree in Essex. Interesting dishes might include sautéed chicken livers and walnuts, followed by pork and leek sausage toad in the hole, traditional steak and kidney pie, or baked monkfish on fried potato cake.
OPEN: 10-3 5.30-11 (all day Sat-Sun Summer) **BAR MEALS:** L served all week 12-2.30 D served all week 6.30-9.30 Av main course £8.50 **RESTAURANT:** L served all week 12-2.30 D served all week 6.30-9.30 **BREWERY/COMPANY:** Free House **🍺:** Greene King IPA, Old Speckled Hen & Abbot Ale, Mauldon Moletrap.
FACILITIES: Garden: Panoramic views across over Roman River Dogs allowed Water **NOTES:** Parking 25

GOSFIELD

Map 13 TL72

The Green Man 🍴 ♀

The Street CO9 1TP ☎ 01787 472746
Dir: Take A131 N from Braintree then A1017 to village
Smart yet traditional village dining pub with old beams, named after a pagan symbol of fertility. Popular for the relaxing atmosphere, Greene King ales and decent bar food. Blackboard menus may list lamb chops with a port and cranberry sauce, mixed grill, cod or haddock fillets, tuna steak with herby tomatoes, lasagne, steak and kidney pudding, or pork chops in a mustard sauce. Cold buffet table available at lunch time.
OPEN: 11-3 6.15-11 (Sun 12-3, 7-10.30) **BAR MEALS:** L served all week 12-2 D served Mon-Sat 6.45-9 Av main course £9
RESTAURANT: L served all week 12-2 D served Mon-Sat 6.45-9 Av 3 course à la carte £15 **BREWERY/COMPANY:** Greene King **🍺:** Greene King IPA & Abbot Ale. **♀:** 9 **FACILITIES:** Children welcome Garden: 10 Tables, paved patio area Dogs allowed Water **NOTES:** Parking 25

> 🌹 **The Rosette is the AA award for food. Look out for it next to a pub's name.**

GREAT BRAXTED

Map 07 TL81

Du Cane Arms 🍴 ♀

The Village CM8 3EJ ☎ 01621 891697 📠 01621 890009
Dir: Great Braxted signed between Witham and Kelvedon on A12

Walkers and cyclists mingle with the locals at this friendly pub, built in 1935 at the heart of a leafy village: handy for the A12 today, it is a popular spot and comes up with a variety of lively real ales and daily fresh fish. Adnams bitter boosts the beer batter for fresh cod or haddock, while the steak and kidney pie is livened up with a splash of Guinness. Seared tuna on a bed of crushed rosemary potatoes and linguine of salmon and prawns with tomato and cream sauce are among the other dishes.
OPEN: 11.30-3 6.30-11 **BAR MEALS:** L served all week 12-2 D served all week 7-9.30 Av main course £8.95 **RESTAURANT:** L served all week 12-2 D served all week 7-9.30 Av 3 course à la carte £17.50 Av 3 course fixed price £10.95 **BREWERY/COMPANY:** Free House **🍺:** Adnams Bitter, Greene King IPA. **♀:** 10
FACILITIES: Garden: Grassed area with table and umberellas **NOTES:** Parking 25

GREAT YELDHAM

Map 13 TL73

> ### Pick of the Pubs
>
> ### The White Hart 🌹 🍴 ♀
> Poole St CO9 4HJ ☎ 01787 237250 📠 01787 238044
> e-mail: reservations@whitehartyeldham.co.uk
> *See Pick of the Pubs on page 182*

HARLOW

Map 06 TL41

Rainbow & Dove

Hastingwood Rd CM17 9JX ☎ 01279 415419 📠 01279 415419
Dir: M11 J7 take A414 towards Chipping Ongar.
Then L into Hastingwood Rd
Quaint listed inn with many charming features, originally a farmhouse and staging post. It became a pub when Oliver Cromwell stationed his new model army on the common here in 1642. The Rainbow & Dove was also popular with RAF pilots stationed at North Weald Station during WWII. Relaxed atmosphere inside and good quality bar food.
OPEN: 11.30-3 6-11 **BAR MEALS:** L served all week 11.30-2.30 D served all week 7-9.30 Av main course £5.75
BREWERY/COMPANY: Inn Business **🍺:** Morland Old Speckled Hen, Courage Directors, Bass. **FACILITIES:** Children welcome Garden: beer garden, BBQ area Dogs allowed **NOTES:** Parking 50

Open: 11-11
Bar Meals: L & D served all week
12-9.30, Av cost main course £13
RESTAURANT: L served all week 12-2,
D served all week 6.30-9.30.
Av cost 3 courses £24
BREWERY/COMPANY:
Free House.
🍺: Guest ales (Local & Nationwide),
Bottled Belgian Ales.
FACILITIES: Children welcome,
Garden - Landscaped, with large patio
area and small river.
NOTES: Parking 40

The White Hart

Grade I star-listed inn dating from the 16th century, set in a huge
garden and offering excellent food and both real ales and an
interesting range of bottled beers.

 ♀

Poole Street, Great Yeldham,
Halstead, CO9 4HJ
☎ 01787 237250 📠 01787 238044
✉ reservations@whitehartyeldham.co.uk
Dir: On A1017 between Haverhill
& Halstead.

This stunning timber-framed
building dates back to 1505
and still has its own jail (a
legacy of the days of the
highwayman). It is timber
framed with oak beams and
magnificent chimney stacks
with gabled buttresses and
octagonal shafts, and
impressively set in four acres of
recently landscaped gardens
with a riverside walk. A roaring
log fire makes the bar
irresistible in the winter, while
the garden and patio are ideal
for lunch or evening drinks
when the weather is fine and
the spring apple blossom or
autumn leaves can be enjoyed.
Popular with drinkers,
especially beer enthusiasts as
real ales are a speciality, with an
ever-changing selection from
micro-breweries across the
country, plus a range of Belgian
and international bottled beers
served in 'proper' glasses. There
are a dozen wines by the glass,
organic fruit juices, natural
ginger beer and a superb choice
of malt whiskies and Cognacs.
The inn has long enjoyed a
good reputation for the
standard of its cooking. Food is
served in the main restaurant,
the Garden Room, or the bar
from a selection of menus. For
a light dish, there might be
turkey and leek pie, or fresh
pasta with creamy wild
mushrooms, spinach and
Parmesan cheese. For
something more elaborate the
menu offers local game terrine
with runner bean chutney, and
grilled goats' cheese with spiced
figs, red onions and walnuts,
followed by braised oxtail on a
cream leek mash, or grilled
calves' liver and bubble and
squeak cake. Tasty desserts
might include traditional sherry
trifle, and chocolate and pecan
tart with crème frâiche. Beer
cuisine evenings are highly
popular.

HORNDON ON THE HILL   Map 06 TQ68

Pick of the Pubs

Bell Inn & Hill House ♀
High Rd SS17 8LD ☎ 01375 642463 🖩 01375 361611
e-mail: info@bell-inn.co.uk
Dir: Off M25 J30/31 signed Thurrock. Lakeside A13 then B1007 to Horndon

Though it dates from the 15th century, this former coaching inn has retained many original features, including a courtyard balcony where luggage was lifted from coach roofs. However, since the present owner bought it in 1938 - with no running water or electricity - it has been transformed into a comfortable inn. The two bars and restaurant offer a good choice of real ales and guest beers, and 16 wines by the glass. Imaginative menus are available throughout, supplemented by daily specials. Options range from sandwiches, fishcakes and Caesar salad in the bar, to main menu dishes like roast rib-eye beef with pancetta, beef and chilli sausage with sweet potato purée, and roast maple garlic and lime halibut tranche with cauliflower and capers. Appearing among the interesting desserts are lime and mango tart with corn syrup, and hot dark chocolate with cinnamon brioche and pineapple.
OPEN: 11-2.30 5.30-11 (Wkds times vary) Closed: 25-26 Dec
BAR MEALS: L served all week 12-1.45 D served all week 6.45-9.45 Av main course £11.95 **RESTAURANT:** L served all week 12-1.45 D served all week 6.45-9.45 Av 3 course à la carte £23.95 Av 3 course fixed price £15.95 **BREWERY/COMPANY:** Free House 🍺: Greene King IPA, Interbrew Bass, Young's Special.
♀: 16 **FACILITIES:** Children welcome Garden: Paved courtyard Dogs allowed **NOTES:** Parking 50

LANGHAM   Map 13 TM03

The Shepherd and Dog ♀
Moor Rd CO4 5NR ☎ 01206 272711 🖩 01206 273136
Dir: A12 towards Ipswich, 1st turn on L out of Colchester, signed Langham
A much-loved local, deep in Dedham Vale, this friendly pub has an increasing range of regulars. Foodie theme evenings are a highlight - Indian night, Italian night and fish'n'chip night for example. Good wine and good beer accompany locally-sourced ingredients in dishes that encompass fresh market sardines, plaice and skate along with lasagne, various curries, grilled chump of lamb and Sunday lunch with up to four roasts to choose from.
OPEN: 11-3 5.30-11 **BAR MEALS:** L served all week 12-2.15 D served all week 6-10 **RESTAURANT:** L served all week 12-2.15 D served all week 6-10 **BREWERY/COMPANY:** Free House

---

🍺: Greene King IPA, Abbot Ale & Ruddles County.
FACILITIES: Children welcome Garden: Food served outside Dogs allowed **NOTES:** Parking 40

LEIGH-ON-SEA   Map 07 TQ88

Crooked Billet
51 High St, Old Town SS9 2EP ☎ 01702 480289
Dir: A13 towards Southend, follow signs for Old Leigh
The picturesque fishing village of Old Leigh is the setting for this fine 17th-century timbered alehouse. Once the home of Nelson's officer Sir Richard Haddock, its open fires, original beams, wattle and daub walls and local fishing pictures reinforce the impression that it has remained unchanged for years. Enjoy views of cockle boats and the estuary from the terrace, where Kent is also visible across the sea wall.
OPEN: 12-11 (Sun 12-10.30) **BAR MEALS:** L served Mon-Sat 12-2.30 Av main course £5.50 **BREWERY/COMPANY:** 🍺: Adnams, Interbrew Bass, Greene King IPA, Everards Tiger.
FACILITIES: Garden: Beer garden & pub front seating Dogs allowed

---

LITTLE CANFIELD   Map 06 TL52

The Lion & Lamb 🏨 ♀
CM6 1SR ☎ 01279 870257 🖩 01279 870423
e-mail: info@lionandlambtakeley.co.uk
Dir: M11 J8 A120 towards Braintree

There's a friendly welcome at this traditional country pub restaurant, with its soft red bricks, oak beams and winter log fires. Handy for Stansted airport and the M11, the pub's charm and individuality makes it a favourite for business or leisure. Jazz fans will enjoy the monthly live music. The full menu is served throughout: typical dishes include Dover sole, pan-fried calves' liver and bacon, and monkfish with scallops in saffron and champagne sauce.
OPEN: 11-11 (Sun 12-10.30) **BAR MEALS:** L served all week 11-10 D served all week 11-10 Av main course £8 **RESTAURANT:** L served all week 11-10 D served all week 11-10
BREWERY/COMPANY: Ridley & Sons 🍺: Ridleys IPA, Old Bob, Rumpus & Seasonal Beers. ♀: 7 **FACILITIES:** Children welcome Garden: Lrg enclosed garden over-looking farmland Dogs allowed Water **NOTES:** Parking 50

LITTLE DUNMOW   Map 06 TL62

Flitch of Bacon ♀
The Street CM6 3HT ☎ 01371 820323 🖩 01371 820338
Dir: A120 to Braintree for 10m, turn off at Little Dunmow, 0.5m pub on R
15th-century country inn whose name refers to the ancient award of half a salted pig, or 'flitch', to couples who have been married for a year and a day, and 'who have not had a

continued

continued

England

LITTLE DUNMOW continued

cross word'. Sit down to salmon and dill lasagne, steak and kidney pie, smoked haddock and spinach bake, lamb with redcurrant and rosemary, 8oz sirloin steak with trimmings, or scampi and chips. 15-mile Flitch Way nearby for walkers.
OPEN: 12-3 6-11 **BAR MEALS:** L served all week 12-2 D served Mon-Sat 7-9 **BREWERY/COMPANY:** Free House **🍺:** Greene King IPA & regular changing ales. **FACILITIES:** Children welcome Garden: Dogs allowed **NOTES:** Parking 6 **NOTES:** No credit cards

MANNINGTREE   Map 13 TM13

Thorn Hotel
High St, Mistley CO11 1HE **☎** 01206 392821 **▤** 01206 392133
Historic pub in the centre of Mistley, which stands on the estuary of the River Stour near Colchester and is the only surviving Georgian port in England today. Wide choice of freshly cooked food is available, with dishes such as chicken curry, home-made cottage pie, beef and ale pie, seafood platter and mixed grill.
OPEN: 12-11 **BAR MEALS:** L served all week 12-2 7-9 Av main course £4 **RESTAURANT:** L served all week 12-2.30 D served Mon-Sat 7-9 Av 3 course à la carte £10.50 **BREWERY/COMPANY:** Free House **🍺:** John Smiths, Greene King IPA, Adnams, Ridleys. **FACILITIES:** Children welcome **NOTES:** Parking 6

NORTH FAMBRIDGE   Map 07 TQ89

The Ferry Boat Inn
Ferry Ln CM3 6LR **☎** 01621 740208
e-mail: Sylviaferryboat@aol.com
Dir: From Chelmsford take A130 S then A132 to South Woodham Ferrers, then B1012. R to village
The 500-year-old Ferry Boat Inn is located on the River Crouch, close to the well-known yachting centre and the Essex Wildlife Trust's 600-acre sanctuary, with wonderful walks. Low beams and log fires characterise the interior, and there is reputed to be a poltergeist in residence. Typical pub fare includes dishes such as steak and kidney pie, smoked haddock, grilled salmon, and ham, egg and chips.
OPEN: 11.30-3 7-11 (Sun 12-4, 7-10.30) **BAR MEALS:** L served all week 12-2 D served all week 7-9.30 Av main course £7 **RESTAURANT:** L served all week 12-1.30 D served all week 7-9.30 Av 3 course à la carte £12.50 **BREWERY/COMPANY:** Free House **🍺:** Shepherd Neame Bishops Finger, Spitfire & Best Bitter. **FACILITIES:** Children welcome Garden: Acre, grassed, benches Dogs allowed **NOTES:** Parking 30 **ROOMS:** 6 bedrooms 6 en suite 3 family rooms s£30 d£40 (♦♦♦)

PAGLESHAM   Map 07 TQ99

Plough & Sail 🏠 ♀
East End SS4 2EQ **☎** 01702 258243 **▤** 01702 258242
Charming weather-boarded, 17th-century dining pub on the bracing Essex marshes, within easy reach of the rivers Crouch and Roach. Inside are pine tables, brasses and low beams, giving the place a quaint, traditional feel. The attractive, well-kept garden has an aviary and is a popular spot during the summer months. Renowned for its good quality food and fresh fish dishes, including fresh skate, tuna steaks, steak and Stilton pie, and Dover sole.
OPEN: 11.30-3 6.45-11 **BAR MEALS:** L served all week 12-2.15 D served all week 7-9.30 **RESTAURANT:** L served all week 12-2.15 D served all week 7-9.30 **BREWERY/COMPANY:** Free House **🍺:** Greene King IPA, Ridleys, Mighty Oak, Fuller's London Pride. **♀:** 10 **FACILITIES:** Children welcome Garden: Lrg garden with aviary **NOTES:** Parking 30

PATTISWICK   Map 13 TL82

The Compasses Inn ♀
CM77 8BG **☎** 01376 561322 **▤** 01376 561322
Dir: off A120 between Braintree & Coggeshall
Set in idyllic Essex countryside surrounded by woodland and rolling fields and much extended from the original, this inn dates back to the 13th century. Lighter bar bites are supplemented on the bistro menu by local favourites such as Trucker's Platter, liver and bacon, toad-in-the-hole, braised Scottish steak and kidney pie, and spinach and goats cheese cannelloni. Multi-choice Sunday lunch.
OPEN: 11-3 6-11 (open all day wknds and in summer) Dec 25-26 & Dec 31 Closed eve **BAR MEALS:** L served all week 12-2 D served all week 6-9 Av main course £8.95 **RESTAURANT:** L served all week 12-2 D served all week 6-9 Av 3 course à la carte £14.95 Av 4 course fixed price £12.95 **BREWERY/COMPANY:** Free House **🍺:** Greene King - IPA, Abbot Ale, Adnams. **FACILITIES:** Children welcome Garden: beer garden, patio, outdoor eating **NOTES:** Parking 40

RADWINTER   Map 12 TL63

The Plough Inn 🏠 ♀
CB10 2TL **☎** 01799 599222
Dir: 4m E of Saffron Walden, at Jct of B2153 & B2154
An Essex woodboard exterior, old beams and a thatched roof characterise this listed inn, once frequented by farm workers. The menu extends from lunchtime snacks to three course meals, with fresh fish from Lowestoft from Tuesday to Saturday - maybe cod or haddock fillet in beer batter or plaice fillet au gratin with prawns. Other favourites are 8oz fillet steak au poivre, Radwinter pie and veggie Wellington.
OPEN: 12-3 6-11 **BAR MEALS:** L served all week 12-2 D served all week 6.45-9.30 Av main course £6.50 **RESTAURANT:** L served all week 12-2.15 D served Mon-Sat 7-9 Av 3 course à la carte £15 **BREWERY/COMPANY:** Free House **🍺:** Adnams Best, IPA, Bass, Abbot Ale. **FACILITIES:** Children welcome Garden: Food served outside Dogs allowed Water **NOTES:** Parking 28

SAFFRON WALDEN   Map 12 TL53

The Cricketers' Arms 🏠 ♀
Rickling Green CB11 3YG **☎** 01799 543210 **▤** 01799 543512
e-mail: reservations@cricketers.demon.co.uk
Dir: exit B1383 at Quendon. Pub 300yds on L opp cricket ground

The cricketing connection began in the 1880's when Rickling Green became the venue for London society cricket matches; associations with the England team and the county game are still maintained. This historic inn was built as a terrace of timber-framed cottages, and one menu serves all three dining areas. Choices include seafood lasagne, sweet and sour king

continued

prawns, traditional rib-eye steak, and chicken chasseur, with plenty of light bites and snacks.
OPEN: 12-11 Sun 12-22.30 **BAR MEALS:** L served all week 12-2.30 D served all week 7-9.30 Av main course £10.50
RESTAURANT: L served all week 12-2.30 D served all week 7-9.30
BREWERY/COMPANY: Free House 🍺: Interbrew Flowers IPA, Wadworth 6X, Fuller's ESB. ♀: 12 **FACILITIES:** Children welcome Garden: two separated patios, one heated Dogs allowed On lead, water **NOTES:** Parking 40

STOCK
Map 06 TQ69

The Hoop
21 High St CM4 9BD ☎ 01277 841137
Dir: On B1007 between Chelmsford & Billericay
Built as weavers' cottages in the 15th-century, The Hoop became an alehouse in the 17th-century and has been serving good ale ever since. An annual beer festival is held at the end of May. The homely little bar offers a good selection of snacks and light meals. Expect sandwiches, steak and kidney pie, fish pie, and ploughmans', and don't forget to check the blackboards for today's specials.
OPEN: 11-11 (Sun 12-10.30) **BAR MEALS:** L served all week D served all week 5-9 **BREWERY/COMPANY:** Free House 🍺: Fuller's London Pride, Hop Back, Crouch Vale, Adnams Bitter. **FACILITIES:** Garden: Large garden, 30 tables, Gazebo

TILLINGHAM
Map 07 TL90

Cap & Feathers Inn 🏠 ♀
South St CM0 7TH ☎ 01621 779212 ▦ 01621 779212
Dir: From Chelmsford take A414, follow signs for Burnham-on-Crouch, then Tillingham
Originally built in 1500 by Dutch labourers working on land drainage, the classic white-painted, weather-boarded frontage is delightfully unspoiled, as is its timeless old-fashioned, quiet interior, traditional furnishings and unassuming pub food that attracts its fair share of hikers, cyclists, bird-watchers and fishermen. Fresh fish such as bream, skate, plaice, haddock and cod, and locally-smoked fish and meats are main-stays of the menu, supported by a host of meat pies, hand-made sausages and game in winter. Commendable real ales.
OPEN: 12-3 5.30-11 (Sat 12-11, Sun 12-10.30) 25 Dec closed evening **BAR MEALS:** L served all week 12-2.30 D served all week 7-9.30 Av main course £7.50 **RESTAURANT:** L served all week 12-2.30 D served all week 7-9.30 Av 3 course à la carte £15
BREWERY/COMPANY: Crouch Vale 🍺: Crouch Vale Best. **FACILITIES:** Children welcome Garden: Food served outside Dogs allowed **NOTES:** Parking 20

WENDENS AMBO
Map 12 TL53

The Bell 🏠
Royston Rd CB11 4JY ☎ 01799 540382
Dir: Near Audley End train station
Formerly a farmhouse and brewery, this 16th-century timber-framed building is set in a pretty Essex village close to Audley End House. The pub is surrounded by extensive gardens, and the cottage-style rooms have low ceilings and open fires in winter. An allegedly friendly ghost, Mrs Goddard, is also in residence. The kitchen offers fish pie, steak and kidney pie, sausage and garlic mash, and excellent steaks. Recent change of ownership.
OPEN: 11.30-2.30 6-11 (Sat-Sun all day) **BAR MEALS:** L served all week 12-2 D served Tue-Sun 7-9 Av main course £6

continued

RESTAURANT: L served all week 12-2 D served Tue-Sun 7-9 Av 3 course à la carte £12 **BREWERY/COMPANY:** Free House 🍺: Adnams Bitter, Carlsberg-Tetley Ansells Mild, Greene King Old Speckled Hen. **FACILITIES:** Garden Dogs allowed Water **NOTES:** Parking 40

WICKHAM BISHOPS
Map 07 TL81

The Mitre ♀
2 The Street CM8 3NN ☎ 01621 891378 ▦ 01621 894932
Dir: Off B1018 between Witham and Maldon
Noted for its friendly atmosphere and character, this 19th-century pub was often used for overnight stays by the Bishops of London - hence the name. Regular range of steak, chicken, and fish dishes, plus specials with an international flavour such as Caribbean chicken (chicken, bacon and pineapple in a creamy tomato sauce), lamb rogan josh, spaghetti Bolognese, and Hawaiian crumble (gammon and pineapple in a tomato salsa topped with savoury crumble).
OPEN: 11.30-11 (Winter 12-3, 6-11) **BAR MEALS:** L served all week 12-3 D served all week 7-9.30 **RESTAURANT:** L served all week 12-3 D served all week 7-9.30 **BREWERY/COMPANY:** Ridley & Sons 🍺: Ridleys Rumpus & IPA. **FACILITIES:** Garden: **NOTES:** Parking 20

WIVENHOE
Map 07 TM02

The Black Buoy Inn ♀
Black Buoy Hill CO7 9BS ☎ 01206 822425 ▦ 01206 827834
e-mail: enquiries@blackbuoy.com
Dir: From Colchester take A133 towards Clacton, then B1027, B1028. In Wivenhoe turn L after church into East St

Wivenhoe's oldest inn has a smugglers' tunnel running from the quay - though we are reliably informed that it is no longer in use. The landlord has a passion for food, particularly Far Eastern and Asian cooking, examples of which can be found on the extensive menu. Produce is locally sourced, and the daily blackboard menu depends on the day's catch and the chef's mood.
OPEN: 11.30-2.30 6.30-11 (Sun 12-3.30 7-10.30) **BAR MEALS:** L served all week 12-2 D served Mon-Sat 7-9 Av main course £7.95
RESTAURANT: L served all week 12-2 D served Mon-Sat 7-9.30 **BREWERY/COMPANY:** Pubmaster 🍺: Greene King IPA, Adnams Bitter, Broadside, Marston's Pedigree & Guest beer. ♀: 12 **FACILITIES:** Children welcome Garden: small patio area, food served outdoors Dogs allowed Water and biscuits available **NOTES:** Parking 12

Pubs offering a good choice of fish on their menu

England

GLOUCESTERSHIRE

ALMONDSBURY   Map 04 ST68

The Bowl ★★ 🏠 ♀
Church Rd BS32 4DT ☎ 01454 612757 📠 01454 619910
e-mail: reception@thebowlinn.co.uk

A picturesque whitewashed pub on the edge of the Severn Vale, originally home to monks building the adjoining church. The unusual name comes from the surrounding bowl-shaped countryside, and it's handy for Bristol and the M4 and M5 motorways. Bar menu with club sandwich, salads, pastas, pies and grills, and from the restaurant carte, chicken liver and bacon parfait, grilled pork chop with mustard seed sauce, and plum pudding with crème anglaise.
OPEN: 11-3 5-11 (Sun 12-10.30) 25 Dec Closed eve **BAR MEALS:** L served all week 12-2.30 D served all week 6-10 Av main course £8.85 **RESTAURANT:** L served all week 12-2.30 D served all week 7-10 Av 3 course à la carte £25.50 Av 3 course fixed price £19.95
BREWERY/COMPANY: Free House 🍺: Scottish Courage Courage Best, Smiles Best, Wickwar BOB, Moles Best. ♀: 9 **FACILITIES:** Children welcome Garden: Patio area at rear. Seating on frontage Dogs allowed **NOTES:** Parking 50 **ROOMS:** 13 bedrooms 13 en suite s£46.50 d£75

ANDOVERSFORD   Map 10 SP01

Pick of the Pubs

The Kilkeney Inn ♀
Kilkeney GL54 4LN ☎ 01242 820341 📠 01242 820133
Dir: On A436 1m W of Andoversford
Rolling Cotswold landscape stretches away from this charming country pub-restaurant. The views can be seen from both the conservatory dining area and the mature garden, originally individual plots belonging to six mid-19th-century terraced stone cottages. Inside, it is very much a dining venue serving real ales, including Hook Norton Best, in a cosy atmosphere created by log fires and exposed beams. The lunch menu ranges from filled ciabattas to home-made beef and onion pie, smoked haddock coated in pesto and served on black pudding mash with white wine sauce, and sirloin steak with grilled tomatoes, mushrooms and chips. At dinner, dishes include slow-roasted shoulder of lamb, fillet of Scotch salmon on steamed pak choi, and Barnsley chops with creamy mash and minted gravy. For pudding, chocolate and orange cheesecake with fruit sauce, and a basket of figs with cream and raspberry coulis. Best to book for traditional Sunday lunch.
OPEN: 11-3 5-11 **BAR MEALS:** L served all week 12-2 D served all week 7-9.30 Av main course £10.95 **RESTAURANT:** L served all week 12-2 D served all week 7-9.30 Av 3 course à la

continued

carte £18 **BREWERY/COMPANY:** Free House 🍺: Hook Norton Best, Interbrew Bass, Wadworth 6X, Guest Ales. ♀: 3 **FACILITIES:** Garden: Patio, small grassy area **NOTES:** Parking 50

The Royal Oak Inn 🏠 ♀
Old Gloucester Rd GL54 4HR ☎ 01242 820335
e-mail: bleninns@clara.net
Dir: 200metres from A40, 4m E of Cheltenham

The Royal Oak stands on the banks of the River Coln, one of a small chain of popular food-oriented pubs in the area. Originally a coaching inn, its main dining room, galleried on two levels, occupies the converted former stables. Lunchtime bar fare of filled ciabatta baguettes and home-made steak and kidney pie extends in the evening to stuffed baked local trout, medallions of beef fillet, liver and bacon casserole, and cheese and potato pie with salad.
OPEN: 11-2.30 5.30-11 **BAR MEALS:** L served all week 12-2.30 D served all week 7-9.30 Av main course £6.50 **RESTAURANT:** L served all week 12-2.30 D served all week 7-9.30 Av 3 course à la carte £16 **BREWERY/COMPANY:** Free House 🍺: Hook Norton Best, Tetleys Bitter, Draught Bass. ♀: 8 **FACILITIES:** Children welcome Garden: Patio area with tables on banks of the river Dogs allowed Water **NOTES:** Parking 44

ARLINGHAM   Map 04 SO71

The Old Passage Inn ♦♦♦♦ 🏵 🏠 ♀
Passage Rd GL2 7JR ☎ 01452 740547 📠 01452 741871
e-mail: oldpassage@ukonline.co.uk
Dir: Telephone for directions
When owner Somerset Moore came across this remote inn on the banks of the Severn, it was derelict, but in the four years since, it has been transformed into a renowned seafood restaurant. Painted deep green outside, the interior decorations and furnishings are similarly attention-grabbing - and that's a compliment. Fish and shellfish are sourced from all over the UK - the oysters alone, for example, come from three different counties. The menu lists so many delicious dishes that visitors will hardly know where to begin.
OPEN: 12-3 6.30-11.30 Closed: Dec 24-Dec 30 **BAR MEALS:** L served Tue-Sun 12-2.15 D served Tue-Sat 7-9.30 Av main course £13 **RESTAURANT:** L served Tue-Sun 12-2.15 D served Tue-Sat 7-9.30 Av 3 course à la carte £27 **BREWERY/COMPANY:** Free House 🍺: Bass, John Smiths. ♀: 14 **FACILITIES:** Children welcome Garden: Mostly grass, bordering river Dogs allowed **NOTES:** Parking 60 **ROOMS:** 3 bedrooms 3 en suite

The Rosette is the AA award for food. Look out for it next to a pub's name.

The Bell at Sapperton

A very pleasant walk in the Sapperton valley, exploring a quiet corner of the Cotswolds between Cirencester and Stroud.

From the pub descend the hill towards 14th-century St Kenhelm's Church, take the footpath to the left of it and go through the kissing gate into the meadow. Follow the unmarked path straight across the bank, keeping the garden of Upper Dorvel House to your right. The garden is extensive and includes some of the distinctive topiary for which Sapperton is noted.

The path runs down to a metal green gate that leads out to a no through road. Descend the steep hill to reach Lower Dorvel House. Turn left at the entrance, heading down a narrow track to pass over a small stream. This is the River Frome. The going can be very wet and muddy here - especially in winter. Follow the path uphill for about 200yds/183m, keeping left at the fork and climbing steeply to reach another track. Turn sharp left by a large beech tree and follow the track down a slight slope.

Continue through the woods for about 1/2 mile/800m and remain on the track as you emerge from the trees. Daneway House is seen on your left. Cross a lane to a stile and follow the path with fence to your left, soon reaching a gate. Once through it, turn left and follow the path across Daneway Banks, climbing very gradually to the next stile. Cross the lane into Sicarage Wood.

Follow the stony track through the wood for about 1/2 mile/800m to a junction of five paths. Take the path to the left, following it down a steep slope to a bridge over the old Thames & Severn Canal. Cross the bridge and turn sharp left at the end of the parapet to join the towpath. Follow this upstream to a narrow wooden footbridge, cross over and continue on the path to the next road. The Daneway pub is in front of you.

THE BELL AT SAPPERTON,
SAPPERTON, GL7 6LE
☎ 01285 760298
Directions: Halfway between Cirencester and Stroud on A419 take signs for Sapperton village. Near church in centre.
Local pub and fine dining venue, serving well-kept ales, rough old scrumpy and more refined versions, and adventurous dishes that appear on the menu alongside more traditional choices.
Open: 11-2.30 6.30-11 (Sun opening times vary)
Bar Meals: 12-2 7-9.30
Notes: No children under 10 after 6.30. Dogs welcome (water). Traditional pub garden & courtyard. Parking. (See page 210 for full entry)

Keep ahead on the towpath towards Sapperton, following the path to the tunnel entrance. Leave the canal at this point by crossing the stile into the adjacent meadow. Follow the steep, well-defined path towards a church steeple, rejoin the path encountered earlier in the walk and return to the Bell.

DISTANCE: 3 miles/4.8km
MAP: OS Explorer 165
TERRAIN: Valley and woodland
PATHS: Clear paths and tracks - one lengthy section which can be muddy
GRADIENT: Moderate climbing

Walk submitted and checked by the Bell, Sapperton

ASHLEWORTH
Map 10 SO82

Boat Inn
The Quay GL19 4HZ ☎ 01452 700272 📠 01452 700272

With historic connections to King Charles, the Boat stands beside Ashleworth quay and close by the medieval Tithe Barn and former Court House. In the same family for 400 years, it's a gem of a pub with its tiny front parlour, flagstone floors and ancient kitchen range; a magnet to the many walkers exploring the nearby Severn or the village itself (leaflets available from the bar). Interesting real ales from Wye Valley and Church End breweries, dispensed direct from the cask, are ideal to accompany perhaps a generously-filled roll or ploughman's lunch with pickle. There is plenty of seating outside to enjoy the location. Annual beer festival in late summer.

OPEN: 11-2.30 6-11 (Oct-Apr closed Mon & Wed lunch)
BREWERY/COMPANY: Free House 🍺: Wye Valley, Church End, Arkells, RCH Pitchfork. **FACILITIES:** Children welcome Garden:
NOTES: Parking 10 **NOTES:** No credit cards

Pick of the Pubs

The Queens Arms 🐾 ♀
The Village GL19 4HT ☎ 01452 700395

At the heart of this pretty village close to the banks of the Severn stands a brick-fronted 18th-century inn with Victorian additions. Original beams, lovely iron fireplaces and comfy chairs grace the immaculate but homely bar and dining room, along with an ever-growing collection of antiques. The restaurant has been divided into two intimate rooms while retaining its warm, pubby atmosphere. With an accent on the use of fresh local ingredients combined with the philosophy that consistency is the secret to good dining, results certainly live up to their promise. Prominently placed chalkboards list lunchtime baguettes, Greek salad and South African bobotie, a house favourite. Similarly-posted evening specials include fresh marlin loin on a bed of anchovy, pan-fried duck breast with a plum and port sauce, and fresh roast cod with roasted sweet potatoes, with home-made treats like Cape brandy pudding to follow.

OPEN: 12-2.30 7-11 Closed: Dec 25 **BAR MEALS:** L served all week 12-2 D served all week 7-9 Av main course £11.25
RESTAURANT: L served all week 12-2 D served all week 7-9 Av 3 course à la carte £18.95 **BREWERY/COMPANY:** Free House
🍺: Shepherd Neame Spitfire, Donnington BB, S A Brain & Company Rev James, Young's Special. ♀: 10
FACILITIES: Children welcome Garden: Courtyard, colourful surroundings **NOTES:** Parking 80

AUST
Map 04 ST58

The Boar's Head 🐾 ♀
Main Rd BS35 4AX ☎ 01454 632278
e-mail: boarshead.aust@eldridge-pope.co.uk
Dir: Off the M48 just before the first-built Seven Bridge, A403 to Avonmouth about 60 yds from rdbt L into Aust Village. 1/2 mile on L

For those in the know, this popular 16th-century pub close to the M48 Severn Road Bridge offers a fine alternative to the nearby motorway service area. Seasonal log fires and a large stone-walled garden still provide hospitality to travellers, as they did in the days of the old Aust ferry. Expect home-made Cumberland sausage and mustard mash, grilled tuna steak, Cajun chicken, vegetable nut roast, and steak and ale pie.
OPEN: 11.30-3 5.30-11.30 (Sun 12-3, 6-10.30) Closed: 25 Dec(eve)
BAR MEALS: L served all week 12-2.30 D served Tue-Sat 6-9.30 main course £8.50 **RESTAURANT:** L served all week 12-2.30 D served Tue-Sat 6.30-9.30 **BREWERY/COMPANY:** Eldridge Pope 🍺: Bass, Ansells, Wadworth 6X. ♀: 8 **FACILITIES:** Garden: lots of benches **NOTES:** Parking 30

AWRE
Map 04 SO70

The Red Hart Inn 🐾 ♀
GL14 1EW ☎ 01594 510220 📠 01594 517249
Dir: E of A48 between Gloucester & Chepstow, access is from Blakeney or Newnham villages

A cosy traditional pub with a history that goes back to 1483 when it was built to house workmen renovating the nearby 10th-century church. Close to the River Severn, the setting is ideal for hikers (check the map by the front door for inspiration). Plenty of charm inside, including a glass-covered, illuminated well. A meal could start with oak-smoked salmon with home-made blinis followed by fillet steak with bacon and Stilton. Imaginative vegetarian options.
OPEN: 12-3 6.30-11 Closed: Jan 1-2 **BAR MEALS:** L served Tue-Sun 12-2 D served all week 7-9 Av main course £8.50
RESTAURANT: L served Tue-Sun 12-2 D served all week 7-9 Av 3 course à la carte £22 **BREWERY/COMPANY:** Free House
🍺: Fuller's London Pride, Archers Special, Goff's Jouster, Wickwar BOB. ♀: 6 **FACILITIES:** Children welcome **NOTES:** Parking 30

> **Restaurant and Bar Meal times indicate the times when food is available. Last orders may be approximately 30 minutes before the times stated.**

Catherine Wheel

The Cotswolds capture the best of our green and pleasant land and the region's villages are equally lovely. Bibury, where the walk begins, was described by William Morris as 'the most beautiful village in England.' This very attractive ramble takes you across country to the delightful River Coln, then back to the pub via the National Trust cottages of Arlington Row.

From the inn turn left to join the footpath adjacent to the car park. Cross the stile and go forward across the field, passing through the gate towards a small wood. Continue ahead through two further gates and then keep alongside a long, low dry-stone wall. To the right lies open land.

Follow the wall for about 1/2 mile/800m, to the point where the path meets a waymarked bridle path. Turn left here and walk down to the River Coln, crossing over at Court Farm and Mill. On your left is Bibury Court, now a hotel.

Keep ahead up the slight incline and turn left at the road, heading back towards Bibury. On reaching the telephone kiosk, follow the path to the church and take a look inside. Return to the church gate and continue along the road. On reaching the river again, cross over at the first stone bridge to have a look at picturesque Arlington Row, one of Gloucestershire's most photographed landmarks.

Take the narrow path by the mill, following it around Rack Island Nature Reserve to emerge opposite Arlington Mill and Bibury Trout Farm. Turn left and return to the Catherine Wheel.

CATHERINE WHEEL, BIBURY
Arlington GL7 5ND
☎ 01285 740250
In an ideal walking area, a low-beamed 15th-century pub in a classic Cotswold village. Expect traditional pub food, all home made.
Open: 11-11 (Sun 12-10.30)
Bar Meals: 12-2 6-9
Notes: Children welcome (highchairs, baby changing) & dogs (water). Garden, food served, vintage orchard. Parking.
(See page 190 for full entry)

DISTANCE: 2 miles/3.2km
MAP: OS Explorer OL 45
TERRAIN: Valley of the River Cole and farmland
PATHS: Roads and footpaths
GRADIENT: No steep hills

Walk submitted and checked by the Catherine Wheel, Bibury

BARNSLEY
Map 05 SP00

Pick of the Pubs

The Village Pub ◎◎ ♀
GL7 5EF ☎ 01285 740421 ▤ 01285 740142
e-mail: reservations@thevillagepub.co.uk
Dir: *On B4425 4m NE of Cirencester*
There is plenty of atmosphere in the beautifully-restored dining rooms at the Village Pub, with their eclectic mix of furniture, flagstone floors, exposed beams and open fires. But despite the mellow-stoned country pub setting, this distinctive dining venue is light years away from the average local. This is an exemplary pub restaurant, with the emphasis firmly on the quality of the ingredients - locally-sourced produce, traceable or organic meats, and fresh seasonal fish from Cornwall - offered from a daily-changing menu. Ham hash with fried egg, tarragon and caper sauce, or fillet of cod with vegetable relish, artichokes and aïoli are typical lunchtime dishes, while the dinner menu might see suckling pig, local Shorthorn beef, or braised hare with cinnamon, orange and red cabbage. All main courses come with home-made bread, and appetising puddings include chocolate St Emilion and ginger cake with roasted banana.
OPEN: 11-3.30 6-11 **BAR MEALS:** L served all week 12-3 D served all week 7-10 Av main course £10 **RESTAURANT:** L served all week 12-3 D served all week 7-10
BREWERY/COMPANY: Free House ◖: Hook Norton Bitter, Wadworth 6X. ♀: 17 **FACILITIES:** Children welcome Children's licence Garden: Walled terrace Dogs allowed
NOTES: Parking 35

BERKELEY
Map 04 ST69

The Malthouse ◌
Marybrook St GL13 9BA ☎ 01453 511177 ▤ 01453 810257
e-mail: the-malthouse@btconnect.com
Dir: *From A38 towards Bristol from exit 13 or 14 of M5, after approx 8m Berkeley is signposted, the Malthouse is situated on the main road heading towards Sharpness*

Close by the Severn Way is this century-old former slaughterhouse. Over the years it has been turned into a comfortable inn with a range of menus to suit all tastes and pockets. A warm greeting is extended to all, be it for a refreshing pint, a snack or a full meal. Malthouse steak and ale pie and Cajun chicken in cream and pepper sauce are favourites. Home-made soup and liver and onions at a give-away price for Mature Students (60 years plus)!

OPEN: 11-11 (Sun 12-4, Mon 4-11) **BAR MEALS:** L served Tues-Sat 11-9.30 D served Mon-Sat 4-9.30 Av main course £8
RESTAURANT: L served Tues-Sat 12-2.30 D served Mon-Sat 7-9.30 Av 3 course à la carte £15 **BREWERY/COMPANY:** Free House
◖: Scottish Courage Courage Best, John Smiths, Pedigree, Theakstons. **FACILITIES:** Children welcome Garden: Small garden; Food served outside in summer **NOTES:** Parking 40

BIBURY
Map 05 SP10

Catherine Wheel ◌
Arlington GL7 5ND ☎ 01285 740250 ▤ 01285 740779
e-mail: Catherinewheel.bibury@eldridge-pope.co.uk
Low-beamed 15th-century pub situated in a classic Cotswold village, close to Arlington Row (NT) - a group of ancient cottages - and the River Coln. An ideal area for walking. Traditional home-made pub food includes grilled Bibury trout, medallions of pork with a blackberry and mint sauce, Jamaican chicken, leek and Gruyère crown, roast shoulder of lamb, and peppered beef casserole.
OPEN: 11-11 (Sun 12-10.30) **BAR MEALS:** L served all week 12-2 D served all week 6-9 Av main course £8.50 **RESTAURANT:** L served all week 12-2 D served all week 6-9
BREWERY/COMPANY: Eldridge Pope ◖: Adnams, Wadworth 6X.
FACILITIES: Garden: Food served outside. Vintage orchard Dogs allowed Water provided **NOTES:** Parking 20 **ROOMS:** 4 bedrooms 4 en suite s£39 d£49 (♦♦♦) no children overnight
See Pub Walk on page 189

BIRDLIP
Map 10 SO91

The Golden Heart ◌ ♀
Nettleton Bottom GL4 8LA ☎ 01242 870261 ▤ 01242 870599
Dir: *on the main road A417 Gloucester to Cirencester*
There are memorable views of the glorious Cotswold countryside from the terraced gardens of The Golden Heart, which offers equally memorable dishes featuring prize-winning meats and market-fresh vegetables. Menus change daily but always fuse traditional British tastes (lamb steaks, beef and ale pie) with more exotic meats, fish and game (ostrich fillet, crocodile) and there is always a good vegetarian and dessert selection. Popular twice-yearly beer festivals are hosted at the May and August Bank Holidays.
OPEN: 11-3 5.30-11 (Fri-Sat 11-11, Sun 12-10.30) **BAR MEALS:** L served all week 12-3 D served all week 6-10 Av main course £9
RESTAURANT: L served all week 12-3 D served all week 6-10 Av 3 course à la carte £18 **BREWERY/COMPANY:** Free House
◖: Interbrew Bass, Timothy Taylor Landlord & Golden Best, Archers Bitter, Young's Special. ♀: 10 **FACILITIES:** Children welcome Garden: Terrace, 3 levels, lrg patio area, seating Dogs allowed Kennel, water **NOTES:** Parking 60

BISLEY
Map 04 SO90

The Bear Inn
George St GL6 7BD ☎ 01452 770265
Dir: *E of Stroud off B4070*
A former courthouse, The Bear opened as a village inn around 1766, its outstanding features including a huge inglenook fireplace, a bread oven and an old priest hole, though the rock-hewn cellars (including a 60ft well) are more likely to be Tudor. Menu items include "bear burgers", "bear necessities" and "bear essentials" that include rabbit and vegetable pie, casserole of prawns and white fish in cider and vegetable pasty in white wine sauce.

continued   *continued*

England

OPEN: 11.30-3 6-11 Closed: 25-26 Dec **BAR MEALS:** L served all week 12-2 D served Mon-Sat 7-9 Av main course £8.50 **BREWERY/COMPANY:** Pubmaster 🍺: Tetley, Flowers IPA, Charles Wells Bombardier, Marstons. **FACILITIES:** Children welcome Garden: Food served outside Dogs allowed **NOTES:** Parking 20

BLEDINGTON
Map 10 SP22

Pick of the Pubs

Kings Head Inn & Restaurant ◆◆◆◆ ♀
The Green OX7 6XQ ☎ 01608 658365 🖥 01608 658902
e-mail: kingshead@orr-ewing.com
See Pick of the Pubs on page 192

BLOCKLEY
Map 10 SP13

The Crown Inn & Hotel
High St GL56 9EX ☎ 01386 700245 🖥 01386 700247
e-mail: info@crown-inn-blockley.co.uk
Often referred to as the 'hidden village of the Cotswolds', Blockley seems to muddle along at a pleasantly sedate pace. The large arch in the mellow stone frontage immediately declares the Crown's origin as a coaching inn, while the charming interior is filled with old beams, log fires and exposed stone walls, creating a warm and welcoming atmosphere. Fine home-made country dishes include seared tuna fillet, roast of the day, fillet of beef Rossini, grills and vegetarian dishes. **OPEN:** 12-11 **BAR MEALS:** L served all week 12-2.30 D served all week 6.30-9.30 Av main course £8 **RESTAURANT:** L served all week 12-2.30 D served all week 7-9.30 Av 3 course à la carte £25 **BREWERY/COMPANY:** Free House 🍺: Hook Norton Best, Scottish Courage John Smith's, Wadworth 6X. **FACILITIES:** Children welcome Garden: Dogs allowed Water **NOTES:** Parking 40 **ROOMS:** 24 bedrooms 24 en suite 4 family rooms (★★★)

BOURTON-ON-THE-WATER
Map 10 SP12

The Duke of Wellington 🍺
Sherborne St GL54 2BY ☎ 01451 820539 🖥 01451 810919
Standing right by the River Windrush, a pleasantly presented, 16th-century former coaching inn with large gardens that are a tourist trap in summer. The open-plan bar leads to a dining area where the pick of dishes is at dinner, with tempura chicken and Hoisin sauce, honey glazed ham and Cotswold sausages with mash and onion gravy. A bonus is the Early Bird menu until 7pm with faggots and mushy peas or beef stew and dumplings at a set price. Look out for the large 'Duke Pie'. Under new management.
OPEN: 12-3 6-11 (Summer all day) **BAR MEALS:** L served all week 12-2.30 D served all week 6-9.30 Av main course £7 **RESTAURANT:** L served all week 12-2.30 D served Mon-Sat 7-9 Av 3 course à la carte £20 **BREWERY/COMPANY:** Free House 🍺: Hook Norton Best, Abbot Ale, Wadworth 6X. **FACILITIES:** Children welcome Garden: Overlooking local river with seating **NOTES:** Parking 10

Kingsbridge Inn ♀
Riverside GL54 2BS ☎ 01451 820371 🖥 01451 810179
e-mail: kingsbridgeinn,bourtononthewater@eldridge-pope.co.uk
Village-centre inn with waterside bar, garden and patios by the Windrush, and a childrens' play area. Diverse menu choices include cod in home-made beer batter, guinea fowl with chicken and cranberry mousse, daily pies, curries and roast lunches; variously filled baguettes; childrens' menu and Sunday lunch.
OPEN: 11-11 (Sun 12-10.30) **BAR MEALS:** L served all week 11-3 D served all week 6-9 Av main course £5 **BREWERY/COMPANY:** Eldridge Pope 🍺: Deuchars IPA, Bass, Courage Best. **FACILITIES:** Children welcome Garden: outdoor eating, patio Dogs allowed **NOTES:** Parking 5

BROCKWEIR
Map 04 SO50

Brockweir Country Inn 🍺
NP16 7NG ☎ 01291 689548
Dir: From Chepstow A446 to Monmouth, 1 mile after Tintem Bridge on R
A 400-year-old inn, with a small garden and covered courtyard, close to the River Wye in the old village of Brockweir. It is popular with locals and retains many characteristics of a traditional alehouse. Ideal for walkers enjoying the unspoilt Wye Valley. Menu includes naturally-smoked haddock, home-cooked ham, Welsh steak, salmon in butter with chilli, lime and coriander, and Cajun chicken. **OPEN:** 12-3.30 6-11 (Sun 7-11.30) **BAR MEALS:** L served all week 12-2.30 D served all week 6-8.30 Av main course £5 **RESTAURANT:** 12-2.30 6-9 **BREWERY/COMPANY:** Free House 🍺: Butcombe Bitter, Wadworth 6X, Wye Valley Bitter, Bass. **FACILITIES:** Children welcome Garden: Food served outside Dogs allowed **NOTES:** No credit cards

---

CHEDWORTH
Map 05 SP01

Hare & Hounds 🍺 ♀
Foss Cross GL54 4NN ☎ 01285 720288 🖥 01285 720488
Dir: On A429(Fosse Way), 6m from Cirencester

Situated on a remote stretch of the ancient Fosse Way and surrounded by beautiful Cotswold countryside, this rustic stone pub features flagged floors, splendid open fires, spiral staircase and a working bread oven. Meals range from rustic rolls with bacon and Brie to pan-fried pheasant with blackberry red wine jus, and fillet of sea bass on a bed of curry, Puy lentils and white wine sauce.
OPEN: 11-3 6-11 **BAR MEALS:** L served all week 12-2.30 D served all week 7-9.45 Av main course £10.95 **RESTAURANT:** L served all week 11-2.30 D served all week 6.30-9.45 Av 3 course à la carte £18.95 **BREWERY/COMPANY:** 🍺: Arkells 3B JRA. ♀: 7 **FACILITIES:** Children welcome Garden: Large, colourful Dogs allowed Water **NOTES:** Parking 50

◆ **Pubs with Red Diamonds are the top places in the AA's three, four and five diamond ratings**

191

Open: 11-2.30, 6-11
Bar Meals: L served all week 12-2,
D served all week 7-9.30.
Av cost main course £7.50
RESTAURANT: L served all week 12-2,
D served all week 7-9.30.
BREWERY/COMPANY:
Free House.
🍺: Hook Norton Bitter, Wadworth 6X,
Shepherd Neame Spitfire, Timothy
Taylor Landlord, Brakspear Bitter.
FACILITIES: Garden - food served
outside in summer.
NOTES: Parking 45
ROOMS: 12 en suite from s£50 d£65

Kings Head Inn

Delightfully set between Gloucestershire and Oxfordshire, this 16th-century, honey-coloured stone building represents the best of Cotswold inns with its excellent food, wines and ales plus comfortable stylish accommodation.

◆◆◆◆ 🍷
The Green, Bledington, OX7 6XQ
☎ 01608 658365 📠 01608 658902
📧 kingshead@orr-ewing.com
Dir: On B4450 4m from
Stow-on-the-Wold.

In the 16th century it was used as a cider house, and parts of the original building have survived to add character to today's smart inn. Low ceilings, ancient beams, open fires, exposed stone walls and sturdy wooden furnishings have been carefully renovated, with high-backed wooden settles, gate-leg or pedestal tables and a large black kettle hanging in the stone inglenook enhancing the surroundings. The pub is located by the idyllic village green with its brook, stone bridge and patrolling ducks. Enthusiastic owners Archie and Nicola Orr-Ewing have established a fine reputation for good food and drink in the three years they have owned the King's Head, and they continue to make significant improvements. Real ales like Timothy Taylor or a guest from a local micro-brewery, and an extensive wine list complement a menu that utilises seasonal produce, notably local game and fresh fish, in an impressive choice of dishes. After a relaxing drink in the bar, a meal might begin with smooth duck liver pâté with red onion marmalade, or grilled scallops with sweet chilli sauce and crème frâiche, moving on to steak and Hook Norton stew with home-made mash and braised cabbage, or lamb shank with vegetable casserole. Desserts show that kitchen standards remain high throughout a meal: try apple and plum crumble with custard, or chocolate biscuit cake, unless the plate of cheeses like Daylesford Cheddar or Celtic Promise is more your cup of tea. Twelve lovely bedrooms offer en suite accommodation.

CHEDWORTH continued

Seven Tuns ♀
Queen St GL54 4AE ☎ 01285 720242 ▤ 01285 720242
Dir: *A40 then A429 towards Cirencester, after 5m R for Chedworth, 3m then 3rd turning on R*

Traditional village inn dating back to 1610, and the ideal place to relax in after an exhilarating walk in the Cotswolds. Handy also for visiting nearby Chedworth Roman villa which can be reached on foot. Directly opposite the inn, which takes its name from seven chimney pots, are a waterwheel, a spring and a raised terrace for summer drinking. The freshly prepared daily-changing menu might feature braised rabbit, cheese and walnuts with a Stilton sauce, steak and kidney pie and ravioli. Well-kept real ales.
OPEN: 11-11 (Sun 12-10.30) (Nov-Mar 11-3, 6-11) **BAR MEALS:** L served all week 12-3 D served Mon-Sat 6-10 Av main course £7 **RESTAURANT:** L served all week 12-3 D served all week 6-10 **BREWERY/COMPANY:** Free House ◀: Young's Bitter, Everards, Greene King Abbot Ale, Youngs Special. **FACILITIES:** Children welcome Garden: Dogs allowed Water, biscuits **NOTES:** Parking 30

CHELTENHAM   Map 10 SO92

The Little Owl ☜ ♀
Cirencester Rd, Charlton Kings GL53 8EB
☎ 01242 529404 ▤ 01242 252523
e-mail: littleowlpub@yahoo.com
Dir: *On A435 Cirencester road, 2.5m from Cheltenham Spa*
This substantial double-fronted pub is handy for the popular Cotswold Way and Cheltenham Racecourse, its unusual name commemorates the Gold Cup winner of 1981. Its latest addition is a luxurious function suite. Bar food includes many traditional favourites supplemented by more up-to-date renditions of green Thai chicken curry. Fresh fish delivered daily might include gilt head bream and whole sea bass.
OPEN: 12-11 (Sun 12-10.30) **BAR MEALS:** L served all week 12-9 D served all week Av main course £6 **RESTAURANT:** L served all week 12-9 D served all week Av 3 course à la carte £15
BREWERY/COMPANY: Whitbread ◀: Wadworth 6X, Goff's Jouster, guest ale. **FACILITIES:** Children welcome Garden: Food served outdoors, plum and apple trees Dogs allowed Water **NOTES:** Parking 40

CHIPPING CAMPDEN   Map 10 SP13

The Bakers Arms
Broad Campden GL55 6UR ☎ 01386 840515
Small Cotswold inn with a great atmosphere - visitors are welcomed and regulars are involved with the quiz, darts and crib teams. The traditional look of the place is reflected in its time-honoured values, with good meals at reasonable prices

continued

and a choice of four to five real ales. Typical main courses are chicken curry, pie of the day, tomato, broccoli and pasta bake, cottage pie, leek and mushroom crumble, and lasagne verdi. Specials also available.
OPEN: 11.30-2.30 6-11 (Sun 12-10.30 Summer open all day)
BAR MEALS: L served all week 12-2 D served all week 6-9
RESTAURANT: L served all week 12-2 D served all week 6-9
BREWERY/COMPANY: Free House ◀: Hook Norton, Donnington, Stanway Bitter, Bombardier. **FACILITIES:** Children welcome Garden: Large grassed area Dogs allowed Garden only. Water provided
NOTES: Parking 30 **NOTES:** No credit cards

Pick of the Pubs

Eight Bells Inn ☜ ♀
Church St GL55 6JG ☎ 01386 840371 ▤ 01386 841669
e-mail: neilhargreaves@bellinn.fsnet.co.uk
See Pick of the Pubs on page 194

The Noel Arms Hotel ★★★ ◉ ♀
High St GL55 6AT ☎ 01386 840317 ▤ 01386 841136
e-mail: bookings@cotswold-inns-hotels.co.uk
Dir: *Telephone for directions*
14th-century inn renowned for its hospitality to Charles II who rested here in 1651 after his defeat by Cromwell at Worcester. As a reminder, Civil War weaponry festoons the grand stone hall. Light meals are served in both the historic beamed bar and the modern conservatory: from the specials list expect game casserole, braised lamb shank, and whole baked plaice, with perhaps cappuccino mousse or pecan pie to finish. Interesting sandwiches also freshly made.
OPEN: 11-11 (Sun 12-10.30) **BAR MEALS:** L served all week 12-2 D served Sat 7-9 **RESTAURANT:** L served Sun 12-2 D served all week 7-9.30 **BREWERY/COMPANY:** Free House ◀: Hook Norton, Interbrew Bass, Scottish Courage John Smith's.
FACILITIES: Children welcome Dogs allowed **NOTES:** Parking 25
ROOMS: 26 bedrooms 26 en suite

The Volunteer
Lower High St GL55 6DY ☎ 01386 840688 ▤ 01386 840543
e-mail: saravol@aol.com
A 300-year-old inn where in the mid-19th century the able-bodied used to sign up for the militia - hence its name. In the same family hands for nearly twenty years, its unspoilt local charm attracts many visitors, particularly to the 'olde worlde' rear garden by the River Cam where Aunt Sally is played in summer. Ramblers set off from here to walk the Cotswold Way refreshed by a pint of one of the six real ales. The pub has also supported a local cheese festival, and the wonderful Great British Sprout Festival. Food choices include home-made pies and casseroles, honey-roast ham and sea bass flamed in Pernod.
OPEN: 11.30-3 5-11 (Sat 11.30-3, 6-11) (Sun 12-3, 7-10.30)
BAR MEALS: L served all week 12-2 D served all week 7-9 Av main course £6.95 **BREWERY/COMPANY:** Free House ◀: Hook Norton Best, North Cotswold Genesis, Stanway Bitter, Fuller's London Pride. **FACILITIES:** Garden: Large lawn, courtyard with tables and seating Dogs allowed Water

 The Rosette is the AA award for food. Look out for it next to a pub's name.

Open: 11.30-3, 5.30-11
(all day Jul-Aug)
Bar Meals: L served all week 12-2.30, D
served all week 6.30-9.30.
Av cost main course £10
RESTAURANT: L served all week 12-2.30,
D served all week 6.30-9.30.
BREWERY/COMPANY:
Free House.
☎: Hook Norton Best & Guest Beers,
Goff's Jouster.
FACILITIES: Dogs allowed, Children
welcome, Garden - Terrace, courtyard
with great views.

The Eight Bells Inn

Originally constructed in the 14th century to house the stonemasons
and store the bells during construction of the nearby church, this
tiny, low-built inn of Cotswold stone has two atmospheric bars
where the original oak beams, open fireplaces and even a priest's
hole still survive.

Church Street, Chipping Campden,
GL55 6JG
☎ 01386 840371 📠 01386 841669
✉ neilhargreaves@bellinn.fsnet.co.uk

For centuries the pub has
provided refreshment for the
good folk of this historic wool
and silversmith town. These
days many of the customers are
tourists, but traditions are
upheld with a range of good
local and guest ales and a
seasonal menu reflecting a
serious approach to food.
During the summer the pub is
hung with attractive flower
baskets, and can be entered
through a cobbled entranceway
where the bars lead on to the
more recently-built dining
room. There is also an enclosed
courtyard for drinking and
dining in fine weather, plus
terraced gardens overlooking
the almshouses and the church.
In these delightful
surroundings, freshly-prepared
local food is offered from a
daily-changing menu. Options
range from salads and light
dishes to full Sunday lunch.
You might start your meal with
a twice-baked cheese soufflé
served with salad, or a warm
salad of lambs' kidneys with
black pudding and toasted pine
kernels. Robust main courses
include Mr Lashford's pork,
leek and apple sausages with
creamed mash and onion gravy,
or slowly-braised lamb kleftico
set on a sweet potato purée. For
a fishy alternative try seared
fillets of brill on a tomato and
red onion compôte and drizzled
with crab bisque, or whole
lemon sole with a lemon, caper
and cherry tomato butter sauce.
Food theme nights are a
feature, with Indian, Thai, and
Mexican evenings, plus a good
old English celebration of pies
and sausages.

CIRENCESTER   Map 05 SP00

Bathurst Arms ♀
North Cerney GL7 7BZ ☎ 01285 831281 ▤ 01285 831155
Dir: The Bathurst Arms is setback from the Cheltenham Rd (A435)
Former coaching inn with bags of period charm - antique
settles on flagstone floors, stone fireplaces, beams and
panelled walls. The pretty garden stretches down to the River
Churn, and a large barbecue is in use most summer
weekends. Local delicacies include grilled Cerney goats'
cheese with mixed leaves and walnuts, and trio of organic
sausages with garlic mash and red onion gravy.
OPEN: 11-3 6-11 (Sun 12-2.30, 7-10.30) **BAR MEALS:** L served all
week 12-2 D served all week 7-9 Av main course £9.50
RESTAURANT: L served all week 12-2 D served all week 7-9
BREWERY/COMPANY: Free House ◖: Hook Norton, Wadworth
6X. **FACILITIES:** Children welcome Garden: Riverside with boules
pitch Dogs allowed **NOTES:** Parking 30

Pick of the Pubs

The Crown of Crucis ★★★ ◉ 🐾 ♀
Ampney Crucis GL7 5RS ☎ 01285 851806 ▤ 01285 851735
e-mail: info@thecrownofcrucis.co.uk
Dir: On A417 to Lechlade, 2m E of Cirencester
The unique name of this stylish 16th-century Cotswold
hotel comes from the old crucis, or cross, in the nearby
churchyard. Its tranquil setting is unmistakably English: a
picturesque Cotswold village, swans gliding along the
Ampney Brook, and the summer sound of leather on
willow from the cricket field. The bar and dining areas are
in the original building, while bedrooms are housed in a
modern block surrounding the courtyard. The relaxed
atmosphere appeals to a broad mix of people, attracted
by an equally broad choice of bar and restaurant food -
roast saddle of lamb with pine nuts, shark steak, and
smoked oyster, and mushroom and tomato risotto, for
instance. There are so many different dishes of the day
that, over a sample 28-day period, not one was repeated.
So, Monday: lamb hot pot; Tuesday: poached cod
mornay; Wednesday: lasagne; Thursday? Could be almost
anything. Desserts include warm apple and raspberry
crumble, ice creams and British cheeses.
OPEN: 10.30-11 (Sun 12-11) Closed: Dec 25 **BAR MEALS:** L
served all week 12-2.30 D served all week 6-10 Av main course £7
RESTAURANT: L served all week 12-2.30 D served all week 7-9.30
Av fixed price £25.50 **BREWERY/COMPANY:** Free House
◖: Wadworth 6X, Archers Village, Scottish Courage John Smith's.
♀: 10 **FACILITIES:** Children welcome Garden: Riverside Setting
Dogs allowed **NOTES:** Parking 70 **ROOMS:** 25 bedrooms 25 en
suite s£61 d£75

CLEARWELL   Map 04 SO50

Pick of the Pubs

Wyndham Arms ★★★ 🐾 ♀
GL16 8JT ☎ 01594 833666 ▤ 01594 836450
e-mail: nigel@thewyndhamhotel.co.uk
Dir: In village centre on B4231
Once a manor house, later a pub and now a highly
civilised small hotel at the heart of an enchanting village.
It has discernible origins back in the 14th century, with
additions in the 16th and a relatively new bedroom block
to meet guests' expectations of the 21st. Beautiful flower

displays are an attractive feature, and the hotel is run with
style and enthusiasm. A bustling bar offers hand-pulled real
ales, good wines and a notable malt whisky collection. In
here, a meal may start with lightly-spiced crab cake with a
basil butter sauce, and lead on to numerous grills, venison
and root vegetable casserole, and tempting desserts like
dark chocolate and almond terrine. In the restaurant, fixed-
price lunch and dinner are backed up by the interesting
carte: confit of duck terrine, paupiettes of lemon sole,
lemon tart with warm fruit compote are typical choices.

OPEN: 11-11 (Sun 12-10.30) **BAR MEALS:** L served all week
12-2 D served all week 6.45-9 Av main course £8.50
RESTAURANT: L served all week 12-2 D served all week 6.45-
9.30 Av 3 course à la carte £23 Av 3 course fixed price £14.95
BREWERY/COMPANY: Free House ◖: Interbrew Bass,
Freeminer Bitter. **FACILITIES:** Children welcome Garden: Dogs
allowed **NOTES:** Parking 50 **ROOMS:** 18 bedrooms 18 en
suite 2 family rooms s£45 d£65

COLD ASTON   Map 10 SP11

The Plough Inn
GL54 3BN ☎ 01451 821459
Dir: village signed from A436 & A429 SW of Stow-on-the-Wold

THE PLOUGH INN, COLD ASTON

A delightful 17th-century pub standing at the heart of this
lovely Cotswold village close to Stow-on-the-Wold, at a
convergence point of four major Cotswold walks. Full of old
beams, flagstone floors, cottagey windows and open log fires
in winter. Typical menu includes steak and kidney pie, chicken
and leek pie, shank of lamb, red Thai curry, and salmon
fishcakes. Patio and garden for summer alfresco drinking.
OPEN: 12-3 6.30-11 (Sun 12-3, 7-10.30) **BAR MEALS:** L served all
week 12-2.30 D served all week 6.30-9.30 Av main course £8.95
BREWERY/COMPANY: Free House ◖: Hook Norton,
Donningtons,Tetleys. **FACILITIES:** Children welcome Garden: Food
served outside Dogs allowed Garden only **NOTES:** Parking 30

continued

England

COLESBOURNE   Map 10 SP01

The Colesbourne Inn ♀
GL53 9NP ☎ 01242 870376 ▤ 01242 870397
e-mail: info@colesbourneinn.com
Dir: *On A435 (Cirencester to Cheltenham road)*

Large log fires, beams and a large garden overlooking wooded hills are all features of this 18th-century coaching inn. The interior is decorated with a wealth of bric-a-brac, and there are cask ales to sup and traditional food in both lounge bar and dining room. Lunch might offer boiled gammon and wild boar sausages with favourites at night that take in pan-fired king prawns and scallops and lamb or beef sizzlers.
OPEN: 11.30-3 6.30-11 **BAR MEALS:** L served all week 12-2 D served all week 7-9 Av main course £10.95 **RESTAURANT:** L served all week 12-2.30 D served all week 7-9.30 Av 3 course à la carte £25 **BREWERY/COMPANY:** Wadworth ◀: Wadworth 6X, Henrys IPA, Badger Tanglefoot. ♀: 6 **FACILITIES:** Children welcome Garden: Views overlooking Cotswold country side Dogs allowed Water, toys **NOTES:** Parking 40

COLN ST ALDWYNS   Map 05 SP10

Pick of the Pubs

The New Inn at Coln ★★ ◉◉ ☜♀
GL7 5AN ☎ 01285 750651 ▤ 01285 750657
e-mail: stay@new-inn.co.uk
See Pick of the Pubs on opposite page

COWLEY   Map 10 SO91

Pick of the Pubs

The Green Dragon Inn ☜
Cockleford GL53 9NW ☎ 01242 870271 ▤ 01242 870171
A handsome stone-built inn dating from the 17th century and located in the Cotswold hamlet of Cockleford. The fittings and furniture are the work of Richard Thompson, the 'Mouse Man of York' (so called for his trademark mouse) who lends his name to the popular Mouse Bar, with its stone-flagged floors, beamed ceilings and crackling log fires. The weekly menu includes sandwiches at lunchtime, children's favourites, and a choice of starters/light meals such as smoked haddock chowder or Caesar salad. Typical main courses are sea bass, red mullet and crayfish tails cooked en papillote with white wine, basil and baby vegetables, or tournedos of pork, garnished with sausage and set on a white bean purée. Other important features are the choice of real ales, and

the heated dining terrace and the comfortable courtyard bedrooms.
OPEN: 11-11 **BAR MEALS:** L served all week 12-2.30 D served all week 6.30-10.30 Av main course £9 **BREWERY/COMPANY:** Free House ◀: Hook Norton, Scottish Courage Courage Best, Directors & Theakston, Smiles Best Bitter. **FACILITIES:** Children welcome Garden: Dogs allowed Water **NOTES:** Parking 100

CRANHAM   Map 10 SO81

The Black Horse Inn ☜
GL4 8HP ☎ 01452 812217
Dir: *A46 towards Stroud, follow signs for Cranham*
Situated in a small village surrounded by woodland and commons, a mile from the Cotswold Way and Prinknash Abbey, this is a traditional inn with two open fires, a stone-tiled floor and two dining rooms upstairs. On the menu you may find kleftiko, chicken breast in Stilton sauce, homily pie, trout with garlic and herb butter, and haddock and prawn mornay. Any eggs used have probably come from the pub's own chickens. There's quite a bit of Morris dancing throughout the season, with the sloping garden offering lovely views across the valley.
OPEN: 11.30-2.30 6.30-11 (Sun 12-3, 7-10.30) Closed: 25 Dec **BAR MEALS:** L served all week 12-2 D served Mon-Sat 6.45-9.30 **RESTAURANT:** L served all week D served Mon-Sat **BREWERY/COMPANY:** Free House ◀: Wickwar Brand Oak, Hook Norton, Bass, Jennings Cumberland Ale. **FACILITIES:** Children welcome Garden: Sloping garden with good views, drinks served Dogs allowed Water, Dogs on leads **NOTES:** Parking 25

Inns, Taverns and Alehouses

As the middle ages wore on, a rough distinction grew up between three types of drinking-house: the inn, the tavern and the alehouse. At the top of the tree, the inn provided lodging, meals and drink for well-to-do travellers. The tavern was more like a wine bar, with no accommodation. Usually in a town, it dispensed wine and sometimes food to prosperous customers. A bunch of evergreen leaves above the door might identify it and it was associated, in puritanical minds at least, with gambling, loose women and disreputable songs.
At the bottom of the ladder and far more numerous, alehouses catered for ordinary people. As there name implies, they were simply dwelling houses where ale was brewed and sold. Often kept by women, they were generally one-room, wattle-and-daub hovels which supplied a take-out service for the neighbours. Inside there was no bar counter, customers and the alewife huddled close, pigs and chickens wandered in and out, and standards of hygiene would horrify patrons today. The quality of the ale was checked by a local official, the ale-conner, and the houses identified themselves with an alestake. This long pole with leaves at the end was the forerunner of today's pub sign.

continued

Open: 11-11 (Sun 12-10.30)
Bar Meals: L served all week 12-2,
D served all week 7-9.
Av cost main course £10.50
RESTAURANT: L served all week 12-2,
D served all week 7-9.
BREWERY/COMPANY:
Free House.
🍺: Hook Norton Best Bitter,
Wadworth 6X, Butcombe Bitter.
FACILITIES: Dogs allowed, Garden -
Terrace area, food served outside.
NOTES: Parking 24
ROOMS: 14 en suite from s£85 d£115

The New Inn at Coln

Nestling in the peaceful Coln valley, this remarkable inn was already old when Christopher Wren was building St Paul's.

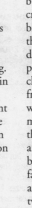

★★ ♀

Coln St-Aldwyns,
nr Cirencester, GL7 5AN
☎ 01285 750651 📠 01285 750657
✉ stay@new-inn.co.uk
Dir: Between Bibury (B4425) &
Fairford (A417), 8m E of Cirencester

The present owners rescued the building from near-dereliction over a decade ago, and although little of the inn's fabric has changed, the 16th century has ceded gracefully to the 21st. Queen Elizabeth I decreed that there should be a coaching inn within a day's travel of every major town, and twenty monarchs later, this place is still catering for the needs of visitors from near and afar. Its creeper-covered façade is a welcoming sight amongst the Cotswold stone buildings of this pretty village. Flagstone floors, exposed beams and open fires characterise the bars, where comfy mates chairs and bar stools offer a choice of seating. In summer, meals are served in the delightful flower-filled courtyard, while the restaurant is a stylish place to peruse the menus and savour the food in all seasons. The emphasis is on local produce and freshly-prepared ingredients, washed down with an abundance of real ales and quality wines. Delights like twice-baked goat's cheese soufflé, and local game pie feature on the bar menu, to be followed perhaps by pecan butter tart with fudge ice cream, or apple, cinnamon and blackberry crumble. At dinner, the imaginative restaurant dishes include roast local partridge, mixed fish grill with clams, mussels and crème fraîche, or roast pork fillet wrapped in Parma ham, and more delicious desserts. For those with time to linger, there are several very individual bedrooms offering en suite facilities along with half-testers and four-posters, or double and twin beds. Each room bears the name of a nearby village or estate, and is well equipped with plenty of home comforts.

England

DIDMARTON
Map 04 ST88

Pick of the Pubs

The Kings Arms ◆◆◆◆ 🛏 ♀
The Street GL9 1DT ☎ 01454 238245 🖨 01454 238249
e-mail: info@kadidmarton.com
Dir: *M4 Junct 18 take A46 N signed Stroud, after 8m take A433 signed Didmarton 2m*

An attractively-restored 17th-century former coaching inn on the edge of the Badminton Estate, home of the Duke of Beaufort and the world famous Badminton Horse Trials. Nearby are Westonbirt Arboretum, Highgrove and Gatcombe Park. The locally-renowned restaurant serves superb food using fresh, top quality ingredients. On offer in both bars and the restaurant, and depending on the monthly-changing menu, might be smoked duck and avocado salad, breast of chicken teriyaki, pork and hop sausages, and breast of pheasant with smoked bacon and rich orange and redcurrant sauce. Home-made puddings include brown sugar meringue with fresh fruit and cream, and banana and caramel cheesecake. Five Sunday menus rotate. Four real ales, including one named after Gloucestershire-born writer, Laurie Lee, are usually available. Accommodation includes four well-appointed, en suite bedrooms in the pub, and self-catering holiday cottages in the converted stable block and barn. There's a pétanque pitch in the beautiful garden.
OPEN: 12-3 6-11 (Sun 12-3, 7-10.30) **BAR MEALS:** L served all week 12-2 D served all week 7-9.30 Av main course £10.95 **RESTAURANT:** L served all week 12-2 D served all week 7-9.30 Av 3 course à la carte £22.50 **BREWERY/COMPANY:** Free House 🍺: Uley Bitter, Badger Best, Tanglefoot, Laurie Lee Bitter from Uley. **FACILITIES:** Garden: Enclosed garden, stone wall, benches Dogs allowed **NOTES:** Parking 28 **ROOMS:** 4 bedrooms 4 en suite s£45 d£70 no children overnight

DURSLEY
Map 04 ST79

Pickwick Inn 🛏
Lower Wick GL11 6DD ☎ 01453 810259 🖨 01453 810259
e-mail: gerry.richard@amserve.co.uk
Dir: *From Gloucester A38, turn L opposite Berkeley turnoff, pub on L*
Built in 1762, this has always been an inn, but has also doubled as a barber's and a slaughterhouse. The restaurant was built on in the mid-1980s, and the bar has an Old Codger Corner especially reserved for elderly regulars. Log burners warm the building in cooler months. Typical menu includes duck in black cherry sauce, Pickwick special mixed grill, steak and ale pie, and plenty of fish options.
OPEN: 11-3 6-11 (Sun 12-3,7-10.30) **BAR MEALS:** L served all

continued

week 12-2.30 D served all week 6.30-10 Av main course £7.95
RESTAURANT: L served all week 12-2.30 D served all week 6.30-10 Av 3 course à la carte £15 **BREWERY/COMPANY:** Youngs
🍺: Youngs Bitter, Youngs Special, Waggle Dance.
FACILITIES: Children welcome Garden: Food served outside. Lawn & flower beds Dogs allowed **NOTES:** Parking 80

EBRINGTON
Map 10 SP14

Ebrington Arms
Ebrington GL55 6NH ☎ 01386 593223 🖨 01386 593763
Dir: *Telephone for directions*
A charmingly down-to-earth village pub dating from the mid-18th century, with plenty of beams to go with traditional flagstone floors and large inglenook fireplaces. Walkers frequent the pub for its locally-brewed ales and good home-cooked food, including gammon with eggs or pineapple, steak and Guinness pie, and lasagne at lunchtime, and lamb shank in red wine, rosemary and redcurrant sauce or medallions of pork in cider in the evening.
OPEN: 11-2.30 6-11 **BAR MEALS:** L served Tues-Sun 12-2 D served Tues-Sat 6-9 Av main course £8 **RESTAURANT:** L served Tues-Sun 12-2 D served Tues-Sat 6-9 Av 3 course à la carte £18 **BREWERY/COMPANY:** Free House 🍺: Hook Norton Best, Donnington SBA, Carlsberg-Tetley, Tetley Smooth.
FACILITIES: Children welcome Children's licence Garden: Lawn and patio area Dogs allowed Water **NOTES:** Parking 12

EWEN
Map 04 SU09

Pick of the Pubs

The Wild Duck ★★ 🏵 🛏 ♀
Drakes Island GL7 6BY ☎ 01285 770310 🖨 01285 770924
e-mail: wduckinn@aol.com
See Pick of the Pubs on opposite page

FORD
Map 10 SP02

Plough Inn ♀
GL54 5RU ☎ 01386 584215 🖨 01386 584042
e-mail: craig.brown17@btopenworld.com
Dir: *4m from Stow-on-the-Wold on the Tewkesbury road*
Long a favourite of Cotswold ramblers, racing enthusiasts and lovers of the traditional English pub, the interior of the idyllic little 13th-century Plough Inn, with its flagstone floors, warming open fires, sturdy pine furnishings and lively conversation, has all the atmosphere you could wish for. Blackboards list the day's menu, where the interesting choice may include home-made soups and pâtés, steak and Guinness pie, home-baked gammon and eggs, beef and mushrooms in red wine, pork tenderloin in mustard sauce and fresh Donnington trout. Excellent Donnington ales.
OPEN: 11-11 (Sun 12-10.30) Closed: Dec 25 **BAR MEALS:** L served all week 12-2 D served Mon-Sun 6.30-9 Av main course £8.50 **RESTAURANT:** L served Everyday 11.30-2.00 D served all week 6.30-9.00 **BREWERY/COMPANY:** 🍺: Donnington BB & SBA, Bottled Double Donnington. **FACILITIES:** Children welcome Garden: Lrg court, beer garden with heat lamps Dogs allowed Water **NOTES:** Parking 50

> We endeavour to be as accurate as possible but changes to times and other information can occur after the guide has gone to press

Open: 8-11 (Sun 12-10.30)
Bar Meals: L served all week 12-2,
D served all week 7-10.
Av main course £9.95
RESTAURANT: L served all week 12-2,
D served all week 7-10.
Av cost 3 courses £25
BREWERY/COMPANY:
Free House.
🍺: Scottish Courage Theakston Old
Peculier, Wells Bombardier, Greene
King Old Speckled Hen, Smiles Best.
FACILITIES: Garden - Enclosed
courtyard, giant chess board. Dogs
welcome. Children welcome.
NOTES: Parking 50
ROOMS: 11 en suite from s£60 d£80

The Wild Duck

An Elizabethan inn of mellow Cotswold stone, the Wild Duck has
evolved over the years from a collection of barns, goat sheds and a
farm cottage, to exude all the character suggested by its provenance.

★★ ◎ 🐑 ♀

Drakes Island, Ewen,
Cirencester, GL7 6BY
☎ 01285 770310 📠 01285 770924
📧 wduckinn@aol.com
Dir: From Cirencester take A429, at
Kemble take L turn to Ewen, pub in
village centre.

In many ways it is a typical
local inn, with an abundance of
exposed beams, oak panelling,
open fires, and ancestral
English portraits adorning the
walls, but on an outside wall
there is an unusual clock
surrounded by a series of ducks
in flight, which light up in
sequence. The enclosed
courtyard, with its mature
trees, potted palms and giant
chessboard, is an ideal place for
summer eating. The country-
style dining room offers fresh
seasonal food, including game
in winter and fresh fish from
Brixham delivered overnight.
The food is traditionally British
with a hint of European and
Oriental influences, and
vegetarian choices are always
available. A daily board
highlights snacks served
throughout the day to
supplement such light lunches
as wok-fried tiger prawns with
coconut and chilli sauce on
penne pasta, and chargrilled
marinated lamb steak on
Moroccan couscous with roast
pepper dressing. From the
evening menu come roast duck
breast set on a goose liver
crôute, served with a rich red
wine sauce, or fillet of red
bream poached in a seafood
laska with prawns, mussels,
spring onion and lime. Real
ales are kept in tip-top
condition, and there's an
eclectic choice of wines from
an extensive list. A wide range
of cigars is also featured. Well-
equipped bedrooms offer an
inducement to stay; all are en
suite with fully up-to-date
facilities, and several with four-
poster beds.

England

FOSSEBRIDGE   Map 05 SP01

Pick of the Pubs

Fossebridge Inn 🐾 ♀
GL54 3JS ☎ 01285 720721 📠 01285 720793
e-mail: fossebridgeinn@aol.com
*Dir: From M4 J15, take A419 towards Cirencester, then take A429
towards Stow, pub approx 7m on L*
A long-standing favourite, the creeper-clad Fossebridge
makes an ideal base for touring the Cotswolds and for
visits to Bibury, Northleach and Chedworth whose Roman
villas date back to 180 AD. Today's family-run inn is
friendly and informal without ever overlooking standards
of service and comfort. The hotel is full of history, with
recent discoveries suggesting that a Roman settlement
stood here at the spot where the Fosse Way once crossed
the River Coln: the gardens that run alongside the river
are a picture in summer. Inside, the beamed Bridge Bar
with its flagstone floors and open fires is Tudor and the
main hotel building looking out on the gardens is certainly
Regency. The bar snack menu lives up to its promise to be
a little different in style and presentation of dishes that
use local supplies and are all prepared on the premises.
Typical of favourites are the smoked salmon with
scrambled eggs, home-made cheese and bacon
beefburgers with chunky chips and Mediterranean roast
vegetables on ciabatta topped with grilled goats' cheese.
The day's selection of baguettes, sandwiches and dishes
of the day are displayed on the blackboards and might
include salmon and halibut fishcakes, and home-
made fruit pie and chocolate fudge slice. Set-price and à
la carte menus change daily, offering a commendably
wide choice. From the former, select warm bacon and
cherry tomato salad, slow roast lamb shank with root
vegetables and tangy lemon tartlets. At the top of the
range, dinner runs to chilli tiger prawns on coriander
noodles, venison steak with sorrel cream sauce and
Parma ham potatoes and vanilla poached pear with
chocolate sauce.
OPEN: 11-3 6-11 **BAR MEALS:** L served all week 12-2.30 D
served all week 6.30-9.30 Av main course £8 **RESTAURANT:** L
served all week 12-2.30 D served all week 6.30-9.30 Av 3 course à
la carte £18 Av 3 course fixed price £11.95
BREWERY/COMPANY: Free House 🍺: Greene King Old
Speckled Hen, Worthington Bass. **FACILITIES:** Children
welcome Garden: 3.5 acres, food served outside Dogs allowed
NOTES: Parking 34

FRAMPTON MANSELL   Map 04 SO90

Pick of the Pubs

The Crown Inn 🐾 ♀
GL6 8JG ☎ 01285 760601 📠 01285 760681
e-mail: crowninn.framptonmansell@eldridge-pope.co.uk
Dir: A417 halfway between Cirencester and Stroud
A 17th-century coaching inn gloriously situated in the
heart of Stroud's Golden Valley. Nearby are the Royal
residences of Highgrove and Gatcombe Park. Honey-
coloured stone walls, old beams and an open fire from
September to May make for a warm atmosphere in the
bar, while the pub garden is a perfect summer spot, with
superb views of the surrounding countryside and, if

you're lucky, buzzards soaring overhead. Entirely home-
produced, seasonal menus featuring English lamb and
kiln-smoked salmon are supplemented by specials from
the chalkboard, such as hog roast with crispy crackling
and wild mushroom risotto with Parmesan shavings.
There is a selection of imaginative puds and a very decent
cheeseboard.
OPEN: 12-3 5-11 **BAR MEALS:** L served all week 12-2.30 D
served all week 6.30-9.30 Av main course £8.95
RESTAURANT: L served all week 12-2.30 D served all week
6.30-9.30 Av 3 course à la carte £25
BREWERY/COMPANY: Eldridge Pope 🍺: Tetley.
FACILITIES: Children welcome Garden: Patio, food served
outside Dogs allowed **NOTES:** Parking 100

The White Horse ♀ NEW
Cirencester Rd GL6 8HZ ☎ 01285 760960
Dir: 6 miles from Cirencester on the A419
A smart dining pub with a growing reputation for good food
but a warm welcome too for those who just want to enjoy a
quiet drink. A large sofa and comfy chairs encourage the
latter, whilst the daily-changing menu based on quality
ingredients will please the hungry. Pan-fried lambs' kidneys,
grilled black bream, and peach cheesecake are typical choices,
while traditional bar snacks should suit those looking for a
light bite.
OPEN: 11-3 6-11 Closed: 24-25 Dec **BAR MEALS:** L served
all week 12-2.30 D served Mon-Sat 7-9.45 Av main course £10.50
RESTAURANT: L served all week 12-2.30 D served Mon-Sat 7-
9.45 Av 3 course à la carte £21 🍺: Uley Bitter, Hook Norton
Best, Arkells Summer Ale. ♀: 7 **FACILITIES:** Children
welcome Garden: Lrg, attractive, tables Dogs allowed
NOTES: Parking 40

GLOUCESTER   Map 10 SO81

Queens Head 🐾 ♀
Tewkesbury Rd, Longford GL2 9EJ
☎ 01452 301882 📠 01452 524368
e-mail: finefoodpub@aol.com
Dir: On the A38 Tewkesbury to Gloucester road in the village of Longford

Festooned with hanging baskets in summer, this 250 year-
old pub/restaurant is just out of town looking back
towards the city. There's a lovely old locals' bar with
flagstoned floor and two dining areas. The signature dish
is Longford lamb - a two-and-a-half-pound joint, slow
cooked in mint gravy until it falls off the bone. Other
choices include chicken with Stilton and Dijon mustard
sauce and crispy leeks, and fillet of pork tenderloin with
plum and sage compote.

continued   *continued*

OPEN: 11-3 5.30-11 **BAR MEALS:** L served all week 12-2 D served all week 6.30-9.30 Av main course £4.95 **RESTAURANT:** L served all week 12-2 D served all week 6.30-9.30 Av 3 course à la carte £16 **BREWERY/COMPANY:** Free House 🍺: Interbrew Bass & Boddingtons, Greene King Old Speckled Hen, Ringwood, Goffs Jouster. ♀: 8 **NOTES:** Parking 40

GREAT BARRINGTON
Map 10 SP21

The Fox ♀
OX18 4TB ☎ 01451 844385
e-mail: info@foxinnbarrington.co.uk
Picturesquely set pub with a delightful patio and large beer garden overlooking the River Windrush - on warm days a perfect summer watering hole. Built of mellow Cotswold stone and characterised by low ceilings and log fires, the inn offers a range of well-kept Donnington beers and a choice of food which might include beef and ale pie, sea bass, Thai curry and various home-made chillies and casseroles.
OPEN: 11-11 **BAR MEALS:** L served all week 12-2.30 D served all week 6.30-9.30 Av main course £8 **RESTAURANT:** L served all week 12-2.30 D served all week 6.30-9.30
BREWERY/COMPANY: 🍺: Donnington BB, SBA. ♀: 7
FACILITIES: Children welcome Garden: Very large by river & lake, seats 100 people Dogs allowed **NOTES:** Parking 60

GREAT RISSINGTON
Map 10 SP11

The Lamb Inn 🛏 ♀
GL54 2LP ☎ 01451 820388 📠 01451 820724
e-mail: enquiries@thelamb-inn.com
Dir: Between Oxford & Cheltenham off A40

Make this delightful former farmhouse your base for exploring the picturesque Cotswold countryside on foot and touring the region's famous old towns by car. Many other popular attractions lie within easy reach of this busy inn, parts of which date back 300 years. Among the more unusual features here is part of a Wellington bomber which crashed in the garden in 1943. Home-cooked pub food might include shoulder of Cotswold lamb with redcurrant and red wine gravy, roast fillet of salmon, or a choice of casseroles.
OPEN: 11.30-2.30 6.30-11 **BAR MEALS:** L served all week 12-2 D served all week 7-9.30 Av main course £8.95 **RESTAURANT:** L served all week 12-2.30 D served all week 7-9.30 Av 3 course à la carte £16 **BREWERY/COMPANY:** Free House 🍺: Hook Norton, John Smiths, Wychwood. **FACILITIES:** Children welcome Garden: Food served outside. Overlooks Windrush Valley **NOTES:** Parking 15

GREET
Map 10 SP03

The Harvest Home 🛏 ♀
Evesham Rd GL54 5BH ☎ 01242 602430
e-mail: sworchardbarn@aol.com
Dir: M5 J9 take A435 towards Evesham, then B4077 & B4078 towards Winchcombe. 200yds from station.
Steam train enthusiasts are drawn to this traditional country inn, built in the early 1900s to serve the Great Western Railway, as a restored stretch of line runs past the end of the garden. Pretty Cotswold villages are all around, and the pub is handy for Cheltenham Racecourse and Sudeley Castle. Expect a good range of snacks and mains, including dishes featuring locally-reared beef and lamb such as fillet steak with brandy and tagine of lamb with apricots and almonds.
OPEN: 12-3 6-11 (Sun 6-10.30) 25 & 31 Dec closed eve
BAR MEALS: L served all week 12-2 D served all week 6-9.30 Av main course £9 **RESTAURANT:** L served all week 12-2 D served all week 6-9.30 Av 3 course à la carte £17
BREWERY/COMPANY: Enterprise Inns 🍺: Fuller's London Pride, Goffs Jouster. **FACILITIES:** Children welcome Children's licence Garden: Grass area, picnic tables, countryside views Dogs allowed Water **NOTES:** Parking 30

GUITING POWER
Map 10 SP02

The Hollow Bottom ♦♦♦ 🛏
GL54 5UX ☎ 01451 850392 📠 01451 850945
e-mail: hollow.bottom@virgin.net
Dir: Telephone for directions

An 18th-century Cotswold stone pub with a horse-racing theme, frequented by the racing fraternity associated with Cheltenham. Its nooks and crannies lend themselves to an intimate drink or meal, and there's a separate dining room plus tables outside for fine weather. Freshly-made dishes include grilled marlin, poached monkfish, bison steak in brandy sauce, and calves' liver with bacon and mash. Three smart bedrooms are available.
OPEN: 11-11 **BAR MEALS:** L served all week 12 D served all week 9.30 Av main course £10 **RESTAURANT:** L served all week 12 D served all week 9.30 Av 3 course à la carte £18.50
BREWERY/COMPANY: Free House 🍺: Hook Norton Bitter, Goff's Jouster, Timothy Taylor Landlord, Fullers London Pride.
FACILITIES: Children welcome Children's licence Garden: Bench, table, patio heaters Dogs allowed **NOTES:** Parking 15 **ROOMS:** 4 bedrooms 3 en suite s£35 d£60

♦ **Pubs with Red Diamonds are the top places in the AA's three, four and five diamond ratings**

HINTON

Map 04 ST77

The Bull Inn

SN14 8HG ☎ 0117 9372332 📠 0117 937 2332

Dir: *From M4 Junc 18, A46 to Bath for 1m then R, 1m down hill, Bull on R*

Converted to an inn about 100 years ago, a 15th-century farmhouse off the old London to Bath road with a traditional pub atmosphere. In the evening, the bars and a non-smoking area are candlelit. Food is freshly prepared on the premises, and the varied menu is offered throughout. Expect beef, ale and mushroom pie, shark and monkfish curry, and Moroccan spiced lamb with apricots, almonds and prunes. New owners summer 2002.

OPEN: 11.30-3 6-11 (Sun 6.30-10.30) **BAR MEALS:** L served all week 11.30-2 D served all week 6-9 Av main course £8.95 **RESTAURANT:** L served all week 11.30-2 D served all week 6-9 **BREWERY/COMPANY:** Wadworth 🍺: Wadworth 6X & Henrys IPA. **FACILITIES:** Children welcome Garden: Very large garden Dogs allowed **NOTES:** Parking 30

LECHLADE

Map 05 SU29

The Five Alls 🍴 ♀

Filkins GL7 3JQ ☎ 01367 860306 📠 01367 860776

Dir: *A40 exit Burford, Filkins 4m, A361 to Lechlade*

Set in a peaceful Cotswold village just outside Lechlade, this popular pub is offering home-made fare such as steak and kidney pudding, lamb's liver and bacon, chicken curry, salmon parcel, tuna fishcakes, salmon and spinach in watercress sauce, and trout in anise. The lawned garden has an over-sized chess set, quoits and a patio for a summer snack outdoors.

OPEN: 11-3 6-11 **BAR MEALS:** L served all week 11.30-2 D served all week 7-9.30 Av main course £10 **RESTAURANT:** L served all week 11.30-2 D served all week 7-9.30 Av 3 course à la carte £20 **BREWERY/COMPANY:** Free House 🍺: Hook Norton Best, Old Hooky. ♀: 8 **FACILITIES:** Children welcome Garden: Large lawn with patio **NOTES:** Parking 100

The Making of Beer

The traditional ingredients of beer are water, barley malt, hops, yeats and ripe judgement. One traditional brewery's products will taste different from another's because of variations in the blending of the ingredients and the timing of process. It all starts with barley, amlted in a kiln at the malting: the higher the temperature, the darker the beer. The powdered malt is mixed with hot water to make a mash. How the hot mash is and how long it is allowed to stand will affect the taste and in the old days local spring water gave beer a distinctive local flavour. Burton upon Trent's eminent reputation for bitter rested on the gypsum in the town's water.

The liquid from the mash is boiled up with hops - the more hops, the bitterer - and sugar is often added. Next the liquid is cooled and yeast is stirred in to make it ferment. The 'green beer' is eventually run into casks to mature. Keg beer is filtered, sterilised and carbonated, and then stored in sealed containers and taste more like bottled beers, which are put through the same process.

The Five Bells Broadwell ♦♦♦

Broadwell GL7 3QS ☎ 01367 860076

e-mail: trevorcooper@skynow.net

Dir: *A361 from Lechlade to Burford, after 2m R to Kencot Broadwell, then R after 200m, then R at crossrds*

Attractive 16th-century Cotswold stone inn overlooking the manor and parish church. The bars are full of character with beams and flagstones, and the conservatory leads to a pretty garden. An extensive choice of dishes includes salmon and prawn gratin, pheasant in red wine, and steak and kidney pie. Accommodation of five luxury chalets.

OPEN: 11.30-2.30 7-11 (Sun 12-3, 7-10.30) Closed: 25 & 26 Dec, closed Mon except BHs **BAR MEALS:** L served Tue-Sun 12-1.45 D served Tue-Sat 7-9 Av main course £6.50 **RESTAURANT:** L served Tue-Sun 12-1.45 D served Tue-Sat 7-9 **BREWERY/COMPANY:** Free House 🍺: Interbrew Bass Bitter, Archers Village. **FACILITIES:** Children welcome Garden: Beautifully kept, quiet, peaceful Dogs allowed **NOTES:** Parking 30 **ROOMS:** 5 bedrooms 5 en suite d£50

The Trout Inn 🍴 ♀

St Johns Bridge GL7 3HA ☎ 01367 252313

Dir: *From A40 take A361 then A417. From M4 to Lechlade then A417 to the Trout Inn*

Dating from around 1220, a former almshouse with a large garden on the banks of the Thames. Things are generally humming here, with tractor and steam events, jazz and folk festivals and sustenance for all, right down to baby food. The interior is all flagstone floors and beams in a bar that overflows into the old boat house. Soups, pizza and burgers graduate to grilled local trout, sausage and cider hotpot and mushrooms à la king in creamy pepper sauce.

OPEN: 10-3 6-11 Closed: Dec 25 **BAR MEALS:** L served all week 12-2 D served all week 7-10 Av main course £10 **BREWERY/COMPANY:** 🍺: Courage Best, John Smiths & Guest. ♀: 16 **FACILITIES:** Children welcome Garden: Food served outside, overlooking Weir Pool Dogs allowed Water **NOTES:** Parking 30

The Fox

Visit Chastleton House, a splendid Jacobean mansion, on this delightful walk to the village of Adlestrop, immortalised by the Edwardian poet Edward Thomas in his 1915 poem 'Yes, I Remember Adlestrop'.

From the pub turn right and walk through the village to a left turning opposite Forge House. Follow the lane to the church of St Nicholas. Keep it on your left, avoid a left-hand footpath and take the next left bridleway. Head down through fields, following waymarks, and turn right in the bottom corner to reach a footbridge.

Cross over to a gate and follow the track ahead over the railway line. Keep ahead alongside hedge and turn right at the road. Pass New Farm and turn left at the next bridleway sign. Head down towards Daylesford House, keep left at the fork and follow the drive between paddocks. Pass the estate office and turn left by Hill Farm Cottage. Pass between buildings, cross over at an intersection of tracks and break cover from the trees.

Swing right after several hundred yards and follow waymarks, cutting diagonally right across paddock to a gate in the corner. Continue ahead, through trees to the A436. Turn left, pass a turning to Adlestrop and turn right at the stile. Follow the woodland path to a track. Turn right to the road and cross over to Long Drive. Follow it to some gates and turn right. Skirt a field, keeping woodland on the right, and continue ahead between fields to reach the road on a bend.

Keep ahead to Chastleton House. Turn left beyond the bend and pass through an avenue of trees to join the Macmillan Way. Descend through fields and follow the path to a track. Keep ahead to the road and cross over to Adlestrop's preserved railway sign. Keep it on your left and

THE FOX, LOWER ODDINGTON
GL56 0UR
☎ 01451 870555

Directions: A436 from Stow-in-the-Wold then R to Lower Oddington 16th-century mellow-stone inn covered in dense Virginia creeper and located in an idyllic village. Noted for well-kept beers, good imaginative food and friendly service. The convivial interior has polished slate floors, fresh flowers and a blazing fire in winter.
Open: 12-3 6.30-11 (Sat-Sun 12-11)
Bar Meals: 12-2.30 6.30-10
Notes: Children welcome. Garden terrace with gas heating. Parking. (See page 205 for full entry)

walk through the village, veering right for the church. Join a track beyond it and make for a lake and kissing gate. Keep to the left of the cricket ground, pass between four trees and follow the sunken path to two stiles leading to the road. Turn left to the A436, turn right and then take the turning to Lower Oddington. Return to the pub.

DISTANCE: 7 miles/11.3km
MAP: OS Explorer OL 45
TERRAIN: Rolling Cotswold landscape
PATHS: Country roads, bridleways, field and woodland paths, drives and tracks
GRADIENT: Gentle climbing

Walk submitted and checked by Nick Channer

LITTLE WASHBOURNE

Map 10 SO93

Hobnail's Inn ♀

GL20 8NQ ☎ 01242 620237 📠 01242 620458
e-mail: finefoodpub@aol.com
Dir: From J9 of the M5 take A46 towards Evesham then B4077 to Stow on Wold. Hobnails is 1.5 m on the L

15th century exposed beams, a log fire and various other character features complement this charming old inn which, until recently, was owned by the same family for about 250 years. Well-known in the area, the pub is within easy reach of the region's many attractions, including the scenic Cotswolds, Beckford Silk Mill and Sudeley Castle. Food ranges from filled baps to marinated lamb, beef cooked in beer and herbs with creamed horseradish potato, and scampi.
OPEN: 11-3 6-11 (May-Sept 11-11) **BAR MEALS:** L served all week 11-2 D served all week 6.30-9.30 Av main course £6.25
RESTAURANT: D served all week 6.30-9.30 Av 3 course à la carte £15 **BREWERY/COMPANY:** Free House 🍺: Tetleys, Fullers London Pride. **FACILITIES:** Children welcome Garden: Food served outside Dogs allowed **NOTES:** Parking 80

LOWER APPERLEY

Map 10 SO82

The Farmers Arms 🍽 ♀

Ledbury Rd GL19 4DR ☎ 01452 780307 📠 01452 780307
Dir: On B4213 SE of Tewkesbury (off A38)

A traditional country pub delightfully set between the Cotswolds and the Malvern Hills, with extensive views towards Cheltenham. Low beams, open fire, and real ales ensure a warm setting to go with the extensive menu: anything from ploughman's lunches to braised lamb shanks, and lemon sponge with lemon sauce. Fresh fish is the house speciality, with the blackboard featuring grilled trout, fillet of cod mornay, and salmon supreme with a hollandaise and caviar sauce.
OPEN: 11-3 6-11 closed Mon (Nov-end Mar) **BAR MEALS:** L served all week 12-2.15 D served all week 6.30-9.30 Av main course £7
RESTAURANT: L served all week 12-2.15 D served all week 6.30-9.30
BREWERY/COMPANY: Wadworth 🍺: Wadworth 6X, Henry's Original IPA plus guest beers. ♀: 400 **FACILITIES:** Children welcome Garden: Patio enclosed garden Dogs allowed Water
NOTES: Parking 80

LOWER ODDINGTON

Map 10 SP22

Pick of the Pubs

The Fox ♀

GL56 0UR ☎ 01451 870555 📠 01451 870666
e-mail: info@foxinn.net

See Pub Walk on page 203
See Pick of the Pubs on page 205

LYDNEY

Map 04 SO60

The George Inn 🍽 ♀

St Briavels GL15 6TA ☎ 01594 530228 📠 01594 530260
e-mail: mail@ithegeorge.fsnet.co.uk
Dir: Telephone for directions

In a quiet village high above the Wye Valley and close to the Forest of Dean, the pub overlooks a moody 12th-century castle ruin. The pub possesses an interior of great character. Local produce features high on grills and specials menus. Ever popular are the traditional steak and kidney and beef and

Guinness pies, fresh fish such as prawns, plaice and sea bass alongside daily specials like assorted curries. Comfortable bedrooms and a flagstone terrace: walkers welcome - but no muddy boots please.

OPEN: 11-2.30 6.30-11 **BAR MEALS:** L served all week 11-2.30 D served all week 6.30-9.30 **RESTAURANT:** L served all week 11-2.30 D served all week 6.30-9.30 **BREWERY/COMPANY:** Free House 🍺: Marston's Pedigree, RCH Pitchfork, Greene King IPA, Freeminers. ♀: 10 **FACILITIES:** Children welcome Garden: Large courtyard with tables, benches Dogs allowed Water **NOTES:** Parking 20
ROOMS: 4 bedrooms 4 en suite 1 family rooms s£35 d£50 (♦♦♦)

MARSHFIELD

Map 04 ST77

The Catherine Wheel

39 High St ☎ 01225 892220
e-mail: info@thecatherinewheel.co.uk
Dir: Telephone for directions

A friendly country pub that appeals equally to locals and visitors from further afield. The old-style inn serves a good range of food such as fresh sea bass with salmon mousse, and luxury fish stew, as well as chicken stuffed with smoked cheese served with mango coulis, lamb shanks with mint and redcurrant gravy, and duck breast with plum sauce. Roasted Mediterranean tartlet in a smoked cheese sauce is one of several vegetarian choices.
OPEN: 11-3 6-11 **BAR MEALS:** L served Tue-Sun 12-2 D served Mon-Sat 7-10 Av main course £10 **RESTAURANT:** L served Tue-Sun 12-2 D served Mon-Sat 7-10 Av 3 course à la carte £17
BREWERY/COMPANY: Free House 🍺: Scottish Courage Courage Best, Abbey Ales Bellringer, Buckleys Best. **FACILITIES:** Children welcome Garden: Patio Area Dogs allowed **NOTES:** Parking 10

♀ 7   Number of wines by the glass

---

continued

OPEN: 12-11
BAR MEALS: L served all week 12-2.30
6.30-10, D served all week
Av main course £9
RESTAURANT: L served all week 12-2.30,
D served all week 6.30-10.00
BREWERY/COMPANY:
Free House.
🍺: Hook Norton Best,
BadgerTanglefoot, Abbot Ale, Tag
Ruddles County.
FACILITIES: Garden- Beer garden, patio,
food served outdoors. Children welcome
NOTES: Parking 14.
ROOMS: d£58.

The Fox

Under the still relatively new ownership of James Cathcart and Ian MacKenzie, the Fox benefits from one of the most idyllic and unspoilt village locations in the Cotswolds. Its 16th-century, mellow stone facade is largely hidden by dense Virginia creeper, while inside are polished slate floors, fresh flowers and candles on pine tables, tasteful prints on rag-washed walls, a blazing log fire in the convivial bar and daily papers.

🍷
GL56 0UR
☎ 01451 870555 📄 01451 870666
📧 info@foxinni.net
Dir: A436 from Stow-on-the-wold
then R to Lower Oddington

The Fox is very successful at enticing visitors away from the honeypots of Stow-on-the-Wold, Moreton-in-Marsh and Chipping Norton. And why shouldn't it be? It serves well-kept beers, fine wines, good, imaginative food, has three tasteful bedrooms, and offers warm, efficient and friendly service. The menu takes full advantage of the seasons and changes regularly.

Starters include rough and smooth patés with apple and fig chutney, and courgette and Stilton risotto. Coq au vin is always in demand, and fresh Scottish salmon baked in filo pastry with wild mushroom and chive sauce, and grilled organic sausages with celeriac and potato purée and Cumberland sauce, are also popular.

Other fresh fish comes up from Cornwall and features on both the regular menu - baked sea trout with creamed leeks and saffron, for example - and the daily specials board. For pudding try the delicious dark chocolate torte, or blueberry crème brûlée.

Booking is recommended for rare roast beef and Yorkshire pudding on Sundays. It has an awning-covered, heated terrace and a pretty, traditional cottage garden. We'd welcome your feedback, so please write or e-mail us.

MEYSEY HAMPTON
Map 05 SP10

The Masons Arms ◆◆◆ 🏠
28 High St GL7 5JT ☎ 01285 850164 📄 01285 850164
e-mail: jane@themasonsarms.freeserve.co.uk
Dir: A417 from Cirencester toward Fairford, after 6m R into village, pub on R by village green

This 17th-century stone-built inn is an ideal touring base for the southern Cotswolds, providing comfortable accommodation. Home-cooked food is served in both the bar and separate dining room. Salad bowls and hot filled baguettes are listed alongside braised lamb shank, Cotswold chicken and orchard pork, while the daily specials might include fresh sea bass with garlic prawns or trio of minted lamb chops with honey and redcurrant glaze.

OPEN: 11.30-2.45 6-11 **BAR MEALS:** L served all week 12-2 D served Mon-Sat 7-9.30 Av main course £6.95 **RESTAURANT:** L served all week 12-2 D served Mon-Sat 7-9.30 Av 3 course à la carte £12.50 **BREWERY/COMPANY:** Free House ◖: Interbrew Bass, Hook Norton Best, Guest Ales. **FACILITIES:** Garden: Village green beside the pub Dogs allowed Water (£5.00 charge to stay overnight) **NOTES:** Parking 5 **ROOMS:** 9 bedrooms 9 en suite s£45 d£65 no children overnight

---

MINCHINHAMPTON
Map 04 SO80

The Old Lodge Inn 🏠 ♀
Minchinhampton Common GL6 9AQ ☎ 01453 832047
Former 16th-century hunting lodge set in the middle of a 600-acre common. Pleasing rural outlook from pine-furnished rooms, good real ales and an imaginative choice of food. With sandwiches and jacket potatoes, the menu may also feature steak and ale pie, sausage and mash, halibut, and mixed grills. Watch out for cows and horses in the garden and car park!
OPEN: 12-3 6-11 **BAR MEALS:** L served all week 12-3 D served Mon-Sat 6.30-9 Av main course £7.50 **RESTAURANT:** L served all week 12-2 D served Mon-Sat 6-9.30
BREWERY/COMPANY: Youngs ◖: Smiles Bristol IPA, Young's Bitter, Special, Winter Warmer. **FACILITIES:** Children welcome Garden: Food served outside. Dogs allowed

---

Pick of the Pubs

The Weighbridge Inn ♀ NEW
GL6 9AL ☎ 01453 832520 📄 01453 835903
e-mail: enquiries@2in1pub.co.uk
Dir: Situated between Nailsworth and Avening on the B4014

Steeped in the local history of this lovely Cotswold area, the Weighbridge Inn has satisfied the appetites of walkers, passing motorists and locals for many years. Carefully renovated behind the scenes but with the original features of the bars and restaurant left unspoilt, this part-17th century inn is idyllically located. It stands literally on the

boundary of the Cotswolds, with a stream running past and a reputedly haunted bridge opposite. An old packhorse trail to Bristol, now a footpath and bridleway, is next to the old building. The original innkeeper also ran the nearby weighbridge, and much memorabilia from this and the nearby Longfords Mill - long disused - is displayed in the bar. The atmosphere inside is heavily reminiscent of its past, with massive roof beams reaching nearly to the floor in the upstairs restaurant, while the drinking areas are just as cosy. Popular with walkers, it claims to draw visitors from all over the world curious to try the famous '2 in 1' pie: a secret recipe served in a large bowl with one half given over to cauliflower cheese, and the other a filling of choice (steak and mushroom, salmon in creamy sauce, game in rich red wine with juniper berry sauce etc) topped with a pastry crust. Other dishes are equally gratifying, with salmon and seafood bake, moussaka, and steak bordelaise among the choices. Lighter bites and snacks run to filled baguettes, jacket potatoes and salads. Meringue surprise, and banana crumble are among the home-made desserts, and there are decent beers and wines to wash it all down. Outside, various patios and arbors make the most of the lovely scenery.
OPEN: 12-11 (Sun 12-10.30) **BAR MEALS:** L served all week 12-9.30 D served all week 12-9.30 Av main course £6.50 **RESTAURANT:** L served all week 12-9.30 D served all week 12-9.30 Av 3 course à la carte £15 ◖: Wadworth 6X, Old Spot, Laurie Lee. ♀: 16 **FACILITIES:** Children welcome Garden: Two large patio, heaters, awnings, abbors Dogs allowed Water **NOTES:** Parking 50

MISERDEN
Map 04 SO90

The Carpenters Arms 🏠 ♀
GL6 7JA ☎ 01285 821283
e-mail: Bleninns@clara.net
Dir: Leave A417 at Birdlip, take B4010 toward Stroud, after 3m Miserden signed

Named after the carpenter's workshop on the Miserden Park Estate, this old inn retains its inglenook fireplaces and original stone floors. Worn benches still carry the nameplates used by the locals a century ago to reserve their seats at the bar. Popular food in includes calves' liver and bacon, poached salmon in parsley sauce, and home-made beef curry. The unspoilt village is very popular with film crews.
OPEN: 11.30-2.30 6.30-11 (Sun 12-3, 7-10.30) **BAR MEALS:** L served all week 12-2.30 D served all week 7-9.30 Av main course £6.50 **RESTAURANT:** L served all week 12-2.30 D served all week 7-9.30 Av 3 course à la carte £14 **BREWERY/COMPANY:** Free House ◖: Greene King IPA, Wadworths, Guest beer. ♀: 8 **FACILITIES:** Children welcome Children's licence Garden: Patio area and gardens Dogs allowed Water **NOTES:** Parking 22

continued

NAILSWORTH · Map 04 ST89

The Britannia ♀
Cossack Square GL6 0DG ☎ 01453 832501 ▤ 01453 872228

Impressive 17th-century former manor house occupying a prominent position on the south side of Nailsworth's Cossack Square. The interior is bright and uncluttered with an open-plan design and a blue slate floor. Modern works of art separate the restaurant from the bar, which is heated by a large open fire. The Britannia's menu is a mix of modern British and continental food, like monkfish with oyster mushroom sauce, roast guinea fowl, peppered duck breast with plum and honey sauce, along with various light choices.
OPEN: 11-11 Closed: 25 Dec **BAR MEALS:** L served all week 11-2.45 D served all week 5.30-10 **RESTAURANT:** L served all week 11-2.45 D served all week 5.30-10 **BREWERY/COMPANY:** Free House
◀: Greene King Abbot Ale, Fuller's London pride.
FACILITIES: Garden: Dogs allowed Water **NOTES:** Parking 100

Pick of the Pubs

Egypt Mill ★★ ⊚ ☜ ♀
GL6 0AE ☎ 01453 833449 ▤ 01453 836098
e-mail: reception@egyptmill.co.uk
Situated in the charming Cotswold town of Nailsworth, this converted corn mill contains many features of great character, including the original millstones and lifting equipment. The recently-refurbished ground floor bar and bistro enjoy a picturesque setting and views over the pretty water gardens complete the scene. There is a choice of eating in the bistro or restaurant, and in both there is a good selection of wines by the glass. For those who like to savour an aperitif before dining, try the large Egypt Mill Lounge. Tempting starters might offer deep-fried spicy crab cakes, smoked salmon, or Portobello mushrooms. Main courses include the likes of grilled sirloin steak, confit of duck leg, roast tenderloin of pork, deep-fried haddock and Egypt Mill's popular steak and kidney suet pudding. Round off with butterscotch tart, dark chocolate and marshmallow cheesecake or a selection of well-chosen British cheeses.
OPEN: 10-3 6.30-11 **BAR MEALS:** L served all week 12-2 D served all week 7-10 **RESTAURANT:** L served all week 12-2 D served all week 7-10 Av 3 course à la carte £15
BREWERY/COMPANY: Free House ◀: Goffs Jouster, Adnams, Tetley Smoothflow. ♀: 10 **FACILITIES:** Children welcome Garden: Mill Garden, waterside **NOTES:** Parking 100
ROOMS: 17 bedrooms 17 en suite s£52.50 d£75

🐷 **Pubs offering a good choice of fish on their menu**

Tipputs Inn ☜ ♀ NEW
Bath Rd GL6 0QE ☎ 01453 832466 ▤ 01453 832010
Recent refurbishment has maintained and enhanced the charm of this 17th-century pub, which has a wide ranging clientele including shooting parties and special occasion diners, all of whom receive the same warm welcome. Light meals are available 11am-10pm, such as Caesar salad, steak sandwich, bouillabaisse or home-made nachos, while dishes from the main menu include ostrich fillet with roasted root vegetables and port wine jus, or pan-fried sea bass with creamed sorrel and spinach.
OPEN: 11-11 **BAR MEALS:** L served all week 11-10 D served all week Av main course £12 **RESTAURANT:** L served all week 11-10 D served all week Av 3 course à la carte £25
BREWERY/COMPANY: ◀: Greene King IPA, Ruddles County & Abbot Ale, Hook Norton. ♀: 12 **FACILITIES:** Garden: Terraced area, heaters, courtyard, grass area **NOTES:** Parking 75

NAUNTON · Map 10 SP12

The Black Horse
GL54 3AD ☎ 01454 850565

Renowned for its home-cooked food, Donnington real ales and utterly peaceful bed and breakfast, this friendly inn enjoys a typical Cotswold village setting beloved of ramblers and locals alike. Dishes range from ploughman's and jacket potatoes to some accomplished main dishes: steak and kidney pudding, grilled trout, chicken breasts with Stilton and bacon and salmon fillet in saffron sauce. Plus the day's selection of 'sinful sweets'!
OPEN: 11.30-3 6-11 **BAR MEALS:** L served all week 12-2 D served all week 6.30-9.30 Av main course £6.95 **RESTAURANT:** L served all week 12-2 D served all week 6.30-9.30 Av 3 course à la carte £14.95
BREWERY/COMPANY: ◀: Donnington BB, SBA.
FACILITIES: Children welcome Garden: Food served outside Dogs allowed **NOTES:** Parking 12

NEWENT · Map 10 SO72

Pick of the Pubs

The Yew Tree ☜ ♀
Clifford Mesne GL18 1JS ☎ 01531 820719
Dir: Follow A40 to Ross on Wye, 2m past Huntley turn R sign Mayhill/Cliffords Mesne, pass Glass House, turn L Yew Tree 50 Yds
Formerly an 18th-century cider press, The Yew Tree stands in glorious countryside overlooking the Malvern Hills. Its five acres of grounds include a patio (ablaze with floral colour in summer), garden seating and farmland where children can view sheep, chickens, ducks and geese. Both the open-plan bar and Hacketts restaurant are under the direction of chef/patron Paul Hackett, who shows a

continued

England

NEWENT continued

commitment to quality produce and local suppliers. The kitchen butchers and prepares all its own meats and fish; the pub's chickens, ducks and geese contribute their eggs; and herbs, salads and various fruits are all home grown. Straightforward bar and blackboard options are complemented by a more complex fixed-price dinner menu. Typical dishes include braised belly of Gloucester Old Spot slowly cooked with cider, onion and lentils; breast of Magret duck with orange and port sauce, and pan-fried beef fillet with dauphinoise potatoes and rich Teryaki sauce. Expect good wines and real such as Wye Valley and Shepherd's Neame on pump.
OPEN: 12-3 6.30-11 Closed: 1-14 Jan **BAR MEALS:** L served Tue-Sun 12-3 D served Tue-Sun 6.30-10.50 Av main course £13
RESTAURANT: L served Tue-Sun 12-3 D served Tue-Sun 6.30-10.30 Av 3 course à la carte £24.50 Av 3 course fixed price £24.50
BREWERY/COMPANY: Free House **:** Shepherds Neame Spitfire, Wye Valley Butty Bach, Fuller's London Pride. **:** 8
FACILITIES: Children welcome Garden: Spacious garden, furniture and parasoles Dogs allowed Toys, water
NOTES: Parking 30

NEWLAND   Map 04 SO50

The Ostrich Inn
GL16 8NP ☎ 01594 833260 ▤ 01594 833260
Dir: Follow Monmouth signs from Chepstow (A466), Newland is signed from Redbrook
A late 13th-century inn situated opposite the fine church known as the 'Cathedral of the Forest'. Huge open fireplace, old furniture, and friendly pub dog. A good choice of food is offered, from red brill with chilli and lime vinaigrette, or fishcakes with parsley sauce, to wild boar and apple sausages, ostrich fillet with plums and Marsala, or pork tenderloin with Calvados cream sauce. Specials board changes weekly. Eight constantly changing ales always available.
OPEN: 11-3 6-11 **BAR MEALS:** L served all week 12-2.30 D served all week 6.30-9.30 Av main course £8 **RESTAURANT:** L served all week 12-2.30 D served all week 6-9.30 Av 3 course à la carte £18 **BREWERY/COMPANY:** Free House **:** Timothy Taylor Landlord, Pitchfork, Butty Bach, Old Speckled Hen.
FACILITIES: Children welcome Garden: Food served outside. Lawn & patio areas Dogs allowed Water & companions to play with

---

NORTHLEACH   Map 10 SP11

The Puesdown Inn ◆◆◆ ♀ NEW
Compton Abdale GL54 4DN ☎ 01451 860262 ▤ 01451 861262
e-mail: inn4food@btopenworld.com
Dir: Located on A40 between Oxford and Cheltenham
High on a windy ridge overlooking the Cotswolds, this recently-refurbished inn provides a warm sanctuary for travellers on the Oxford-Cheltenham road, as it has done for over 200 years. Its imaginative dishes change with the availability of ingredients and you might find sea bass with peppers and pesto, ballotine of chicken filled with Cornish crab, or grilled calves' liver and bacon on the menu, as well as favourites like grilled T-bone steak.
OPEN: 11-3 6-11 (Fri-Sun 11-11) **BAR MEALS:** L served all week 12-3 D served Wed-Mon 7-10.30 Av main course £7
RESTAURANT: L served all week 12-3 D served Wed-Mon 7-10.30 Av 3 course à la carte £19.50 **:** Hook Norton, Guest Ales. **:** 7
FACILITIES: Garden: Large garden surrounded by dry stone walls

Dogs allowed Water Bowls **NOTES:** Parking 80 **ROOMS:** 3 bedrooms 3 en suite 1 family rooms s£40 d£50 no children overnight

Wheatsheaf Inn ◆◆◆ ◉ ♀
GL54 3EZ ☎ 01451 860244 ▤ 01451 861037

A 16th-century Cotswold stone coaching inn with simple, comfortable bedrooms, a civilised real ale bar, and dining areas with an adventurous new menu. There are plenty of choices from market fresh produce right down to marinated olives or garlic and Parmesan bread. Typically, enjoy roast pheasant, lamb shank with mash and onion gravy, and Bibury trout on Evesham asparagus.
OPEN: 12-11 all week **BAR MEALS:** L served all week 7-10 Av main course £9 **RESTAURANT:** L served all week 12-2.30 D served all week 7-10 Av 3 course à la carte £20
BREWERY/COMPANY: Free House **:** Wadsworth 6X, Hook Norton Best Bitter, Marstons Pedigree. **:** 6 **FACILITIES:** Children welcome Garden: Food served outside Dogs allowed except in restaurant
NOTES: Parking 20 **ROOMS:** 8 bedrooms 8 en suite s£55 d£55 no children overnight

---

OAKRIDGE   Map 04 SO90

The Butcher's Arms
GL6 7NZ ☎ 01285 760371 ▤ 01285 760602
Dir: From Stroud take A419 turn L for Eastcombe. Then follow signs for Bisley. Just before Bisley turn R to Oakridge. Look out for brown tourist sign
Traditional Cotswold country pub with stone walls, beams and log fires in the renowned Golden Valley. Once a slaughterhouse and butchers shop. A full and varied restaurant menu offers steak, fish and chicken dishes, while the bar menu ranges from ploughman's lunches to home-cooked daily specials.
OPEN: 11-3 6-11 Closed: 25-26 Dec, 1 Jan **BAR MEALS:** L served Tue-Sun 12-2 D served Tue-Sat 6.30-9 **RESTAURANT:** L served Tue-Sun 12-3 D served Tue-Sat 7.30-9 Av 3 course à la carte £20
BREWERY/COMPANY: Free House **:** Greene King Abbot Ale, Carlsberg-Tetley, Wickwar BOB, Archers Best. **FACILITIES:** Children welcome Garden: Food served outside. Overlooks Golden Valley Dogs allowed **NOTES:** Parking 50

OLDBURY-ON-SEVERN   Map 04 ST69

The Anchor Inn ♀
Church Rd BS35 1QA ☎ 01454 413331
Dir: From N A38 towards Bristol, 1.5m then R, village signed. From S A38 through Thornbury
A 17th-century pub built from Cotswold stone on the site of an old mill near the River Severn. There's a friendly atmosphere in the bar with its log fire and oak furniture, and summer dining in the garden overlooking a large boules area is increasingly popular. Real ales and 12 wines by the glass are

continued

continued

offered, and the same menu is served throughout, ranging from salads and baguettes to home-made faggots, Greek lamb, and seafood tagliatelle.
OPEN: 11.30-2.30 6.30-11 (Sat 11.30-11, Sun 12-10.30) Closed: Dec 25-26 evening **BAR MEALS:** L served all week 11.30-2.30 D served all week 6.30-9.30 Av main course £5.95 **RESTAURANT:** L served all week 11.30-2.30 D served all week 6.30-9.30 Av 3 course à la carte £13.50 Av 3 course fixed price £13.95 **BREWERY/COMPANY:** Free House 🍺: Interbrew Bass, Scottish Courage Theakston Old Peculier, Butcombe Best, Wickwar Bob Best. ⛄: 12 **FACILITIES:** Children welcome Garden: Lrg, by river, plenty of seats Dogs allowed **NOTES:** Parking 15

PAINSWICK
Map 04 SO80

The Falcon Inn 🏠 ⛄
New St GL6 6UN ☎ 01452 814222 📠 01452 813377
e-mail: bleninns@clara.net
Dir: On A46 in centre of Painswick

Boasting the world's oldest known bowling green in its grounds, the Falcon dates from 1554 and stands at the heart of a conservation village. For three centuries it was a courthouse, but today its comfy accommodation and friendly service extends to a drying room for walkers' gear. The seasonal menu might offer best end of lamb with herb crust and port and redcurrant sauce, and chargrilled pork, sage and apple kebabs with orange glaze and spicy couscous.
OPEN: 11-4 5.30-11 (Sun 12-4, 6-10.30) **BAR MEALS:** L served all week 12.00-2.30 D served all week 7-9.30 Av main course £6.50 **RESTAURANT:** L served all week 12-2.30 D served all week 7-9.30 Av 3 course à la carte £16 **BREWERY/COMPANY:** Free House 🍺: Hook Norton Best, Old Hooky, Wadworth 6X, Interbrew Boddingtons. ⛄: 10 **FACILITIES:** Children welcome Children's licence Garden: Courtyard and large bowling green to rear Dogs allowed Water **NOTES:** Parking 35 **ROOMS:** 12 bedrooms 12 en suite 4 family rooms s£45 d£65 (★★)

The Royal Oak Inn 🏠 ⛄
St Mary's St GL6 6QG ☎ 01452 813129
e-mail: bleninns@clara.net
Dir: In the centre of Painswick on the A46 between Stroud & Cheltenham
Tucked away behind the church of this conservation village, the Royal Oak features very low ceilings, old paintings and artefacts, and a huge, open fire. In summer, a sun-trap rear courtyard contribute to its atmosphere. A solidly old English approach to food includes pork, cider and leek casserole, chicken supreme stuffed with garlic mushrooms, and fish specials like halibut steak with lemon relish, and sea bass steak with balsamic dressing. Good snacks too.

OPEN: 11-2.30 5.30-11 **BAR MEALS:** L served all week 12-2.30 D served all week 7-9.30 Av main course £6 **RESTAURANT:** L served all week 12-2.30 D served all week 7-9.30 Av 3 course à la carte £13 **BREWERY/COMPANY:** Free House 🍺: Hook Norton Best, Wadworth 6X, Interbrew Flowers Original plus Guest Ales. ⛄: 8 **FACILITIES:** Children welcome Garden: Patio and courtyard Dogs allowed Water

PAXFORD
Map 10 SP13

Pick of the Pubs

The Churchill Arms ◉ ⛄
GL55 6XH ☎ 01386 594000 📠 01386 594005
e-mail: info@thechurchillarms.com
Dir: 2m E of Chipping Campden, 4m N of Moreton-in-Marsh
Part of the ever-growing Sonya Kidney stable of food-lovers' pubs and located in the heart of one of the most sought-after villages in the north Cotswolds, the pub enjoys magnificent views over the rolling countryside, popular with walkers and lovers of outdoor pursuits. Those lucky enough to visit can be confident of a warm welcome and cultured, modern-style pub food. Examples from menus that change daily are spiced tomato and herb soup, and duck salad with grapefruit and fennel, followed by slow-braised lamb shank with spring onion mash, rabbit loin with spiced aubergine lentils, and various vegetarian options compiled in a trice. To these, add saffron-marinated mackerel with cucumber sauce, pork fillet with prunes and ginger, and puddings like sticky toffee pudding, pistachio and orange parfait, and black coffee jelly to fully appreciate the range of treats on offer. The Churchill Arms deservedly continues to attract discerning custom.
OPEN: 11.30-3 6-11 **BAR MEALS:** L served all week 12-2 D served all week 7-9 Av main course £10.50 **RESTAURANT:** L served all week 12-2 D served all week 7-9 Av 3 course à la carte £20 **BREWERY/COMPANY:** Free House 🍺: Hook Norton Bitter, Arkells 3B. ⛄: 8 **FACILITIES:** Children welcome Garden: 25 Covers, parasoles Dogs allowed

REDMARLEY D'ABITOT
Map 10 SO73

Rose & Crown 🏠
Playley Green GL19 3NB ☎ 01531 650234
Dir: on the A417 Gloucester to Ledbury, 1m from exit 2 of the M50
This pretty old roadside building, dating from the 1720s with numerous later additions, is a blaze of summer colour from hanging baskets and flower troughs, and an array of daffodils in spring. The dishes on the main menu change very little, but the daily specials may offer fresh sea bream with lime butter, Moroccan spiced lamb with couscous, or beef and ale

continued

continued

England

REDMARLEY D'ABITOT continued

casserole. The prime Herefordshire beef steaks are a further plus, as are the Sunday roast lunches, that make booking advisable.
OPEN: 11-2.30 6-11 (Sun 12-3, 7-10.30) Closed: Dec 25
BAR MEALS: L served all week 12-2 D served Mon-Sat 6.30-9 Av main course £8 **RESTAURANT:** L served all week 12-2 D served Mon-Sat 6.30-9 Av 3 course à la carte £14.95
BREWERY/COMPANY: Pubmaster ◀: Interbrew Flowers Original IPA, Young's Special, Wadworth 6X, Greene King Old Speckled Hen & Ruddles County Ale. **FACILITIES:** Children welcome Garden: Food served outdoors, patio Dogs allowed Water **NOTES:** Parking 50

SAPPERTON

Map 04 SO90

The Bell at Sapperton ◔ ♀ NEW
GL7 6LE ☎ 01285 760298 ▤ 01285 760761
e-mail: thebell@sapperton66.freeserve.co.uk
Dir: Halfway between Cirencester & Stroud A419 take signs for Sapperton village. The Bell is in the centre near the Church.

Both a local pub and a fine dining venue, the Bell is elegant in an understated way and appeals to the business person and the hiker in equal measures. One of the attractions is the well-kept ales, all of them local and at any given time might include Uley's Hogshead, Old Spot and Hook's Norton. Cider lovers will be delighted to find rough old scrumpy along with more refined versions made in the area. For lovers of good food there is plenty of adventure on the menu along with the traditional: pan-fried breast of pigeon with black pudding and apples, or pan-fried herring roes with curry butter sauce, might be followed by hot goats' cheese baklava, or chargrilled spicy lamb burger with melted cheese and fries. Delicious chocolate and brandy mousse with Cointreau oranges makes a fitting ending.
OPEN: 11-2.30 6.30-11 (Sun times vary) Closed: 25 Dec, 31 Dec
BAR MEALS: L served all week 12-2 D served all week 7-9.30 Av main course £12 **RESTAURANT:** L served all week D served all week Av 3 course à la carte £22 **BREWERY/COMPANY:** Free House ◀: Uley Old Spot & Hogshead, Wickwar Cotswold Way, Hook Norton Best. ♀: 16 **FACILITIES:** Garden: Traditional pub garden at front, courtyard Dogs allowed Waterbowl **NOTES:** Parking 60

See Pub Walk on page 187

SHEEPSCOMBE

Map 04 SO81

The Butchers Arms ◔ ♀
GL6 7RH ☎ 01452 812113 ▤ 01452 814358
e-mail: bleninns@clara.net
Dir: 1.5m south of A46 (Cheltenham to Stroud road), N of Painswick
Once used to hang and butcher deer hunted by Henry VIII from his Royal deer park, this friendly hostelry boasts a sunny sheltered terrace and panoramic views. Laurie Lee, author of

'Cider with Rosie' was once a regular. A varied menu includes smoked duck and feta cheese with olives among the starters, and smoked haddock and prawn pancakes, trout fillets with a citrus crust, and various steaks.

OPEN: 11.30-2.30 6-11.30 (Sun 12-3, 7-10.30) **BAR MEALS:** L served all week 12-2.30 D served all week 7-9.30 Av main course £7.50 **RESTAURANT:** L served all week 12-2.30 D served all week 7-9.30 Av 3 course à la carte £15 **BREWERY/COMPANY:** Free House ◀: Hook Norton Best & Old Hooky, Uley old Spot, Wye Valley, Dorothy Goodbodys Summer Ale. ♀: 10 **FACILITIES:** Children welcome Garden: Beer garden, food served outdoors, patio Dogs allowed in garden and on terrace only **NOTES:** Parking 16

SHURDINGTON

Map 10 SO91

The Bell Inn ◔
Main Rd GL51 4XQ ☎ 01242 862245 ▤ 01242 862245
Late 18th-century pub - an alehouse and bakery until 1949 - set in a lovely spot overlooking the village green where cricket is played. It is also well placed for interesting walks on Cheltenham Ring and the Cotswold Way. Good food is served, including snacks, traditional pub favourites, vegetarian dishes such as parsnip, sweet potato and chestnut bake, and specials like Mediterranean chicken casserole, or pork en croûte with wild mushrooms and port sauce.
OPEN: 11-11 **BAR MEALS:** L served all week 12-2.15 D served all week 6-10 Av main course £7 **RESTAURANT:** L served all week 12-2.15 D served all week 6-10 ◀: Timothy Taylor Best, Greene King IPA & Old Speckled Hen, Uley Best. **FACILITIES:** Garden: Very large pebble & grass area Dogs allowed Water **NOTES:** Parking 25

SIDDINGTON

Map 05 SU09

The Greyhound ♀
Ashton Rd GL7 6HR ☎ 01285 653573 ▤ 01285 650054
Dir: A419 from Swindon, turn at sign for industrial estate, L at main rdbt, follow Siddington signs, pub at far end of village on R
Village pub, formally a coach house, built of Cotswold stone with flagstone floors inside. Friendly, relaxed atmosphere.
OPEN: 11.30-3 6.30-11 **BAR MEALS:** L served all week 12-2.30 D served all week 6-9 Av main course £7 **BREWERY/COMPANY:** Free House ◀: Wadworth 6X & Henry's IPA, Badger Tanglefoot. ♀: 9 **FACILITIES:** Garden: Dogs allowed **NOTES:** Parking 30

SOUTHROP

Map 05 SP10

The Swan
GL7 3NU ☎ 01367 850205 ▤ 01367 860331
Dir: Off A361 between Lechlade and Burford
Creeper-clad Cotswold pub, refurbished under new ownership. Emphasis on good quality pub food and classic country pub atmosphere. Expect crab risotto with spring

continued

continued

onions and chilli oil, and pan-fried calves' liver with mashed potato and red onion marmalade.

OPEN: 11.30-3 6.30-11 **BAR MEALS:** L served all week 12-2 D served all week 7-9 Av main course £7 **RESTAURANT:** L served all week 12-2 D served all week 7-9 Av 3 course à la carte £19 **BREWERY/COMPANY:** Free House 🍺: Hook Norton, Greene King IPA, Old Hooky and a guest ale. **FACILITIES:** Children welcome Dogs allowed

---

STONEHOUSE   Map 04 SO80

The George Inn ♦♦♦ 🐕

Bath Rd, Frocester GL10 3TQ ☎ 01453 822302 📠 01453 791612
e-mail: enquiries@georgeinn.fsnet.co.uk

A village pub in the traditional mould, undisturbed by music or games machines. This former coaching inn has huge inglenook fireplaces and the original stables surrounding the courtyard garden. The food is locally produced and cooked to order: look for British roast beef baguettes, chicken goujons with lemon mayonnaise, and Frocester Fayre faggots with creamy mash, followed by treacle pudding or Gaelic whiskey trifle. Sunday lunch carvery, occasional live music and a warm village welcome.
OPEN: 11.30-2.30 5-11 (Sat-Sun open all day) **BAR MEALS:** L served all week 12-2 D served all week 6.30-9.30 **RESTAURANT:** L served all week 12-2 D served all week 6.30-9.30
BREWERY/COMPANY: Enterprise Inns 🍺: Wadworth 6X, Ruddles County, Scottish Courage John Smith's. **FACILITIES:** Children welcome Garden: Courtyard, boules pitch **NOTES:** Parking 25
ROOMS: 8 bedrooms 4 en suite s£35 d£55

STOW-ON-THE-WOLD   Map 10 SP12

Pick of the Pubs

The Eagle and Child 🎍 ♀

C/o The Royalist Hotel, Digbeth St GL54 1BN
☎ 01451 830670 📠 01451 870048
e-mail: info@theroyalisthotel.co.uk
Dir: *From the A40 take the A429 towards Stow on the Wood, turn into town, and pub by the green on the L*

This cracking good pub is a popular watering hole for locals and visitors alike. Access is through the reception of the Royalist Hotel, dating from 947AD and certified as the oldest inn in England. Both hotel and pub have been totally refurbished by chef/owner Alan Thompson. The name Eagle & Child is said to come from the crest of the Earl of Derby dating back to the 16th century. With stone walls, polished flagstone floor, rustic wooden furnishings and airy rear conservatory, this is a relaxing venue in which to sample the excellent food that arrives from the hotel kitchen. Expect first-class steak and kidney pudding,

continued

local sausages with onion gravy and mash, clay-roast corn-fed chicken breast with olive and Feta spaghetti, local roast partridge, roast sea bass with aubergine caviar and mussel velouté, Cotswold lamb hotpot with champ mash and sautéed greens. Good puddings.

OPEN: 11-11 (Winter open at 12) **BAR MEALS:** L served all week 12-2.30 D served all week 6.30-10 Av main course £12 **RESTAURANT:** L served all week 12-2.30 D served all week 6.30-10 **BREWERY/COMPANY:** Free House 🍺: Hook Norton Best, Greene King Abbot Ale, Timothy Taylor Landlord. ♀: 8 **FACILITIES:** Children welcome Garden: Small paved terraced garden Dogs allowed **NOTES:** Parking 8

STROUD   Map 04 SO80

Pick of the Pubs

Bear of Rodborough Hotel ★★★ ♀

Rodborough Common GL5 5DE
☎ 01453 878522 📠 01453 872523
e-mail: bookings@cotswold-inns-hotels.co.uk
Dir: *From M5 J13 follow signs for Stonehouse then Rodborough*

300-year-old imposing former coaching inn situated high above Stroud in acres of National Trust parkland, with magnificent Cotswolds views. Minchinhampton and Rodborough Commons comprise open grassland and woodland which form a steep-sided plateau particularly important for wild flowers. The hotel is worth seeking out for the comfortable accommodation, open log fires, stone walls and solid wooden floors. There is certainly plenty of character here and the elegant Mulberry restaurant epitomises the inherent charm of the building. Appetising menu uses Cotswold produce where possible, including good local cheeses. Try the home-made chicken pie, Cotswold cheese platter, local hot buttered crumpets or the fish of the day.
OPEN: 10.30-11 **BAR MEALS:** L served all week 12.30-2.30 D served all week 6.30-9.30 Av main course £6.95
RESTAURANT: L served Sun 12.30-2.30 D served all week 7-9.30 Av cost 3 course £25.95 **BREWERY/COMPANY:** Free House 🍺: Bass, Uley Bitter, Laurie Lee. **FACILITIES:** Children welcome Garden: Food served outside. Patio area Dogs allowed Water provided **NOTES:** Parking 175 **ROOMS:** 46 bedrooms 46 en suite s£75 d£120

> **Pick of the Pubs have that extra special quality that makes them stand out from the crowd. Their entries are highlighted, and may be a full page.**

England

STROUD continued

Pick of the Pubs

Halfway Inn ◉ ♀
Box GL6 9AE ☎ 01453 832631 ▤ 01453 835275
e-mail: matt_halfwayinn@hotmail.com
Dir: From Cirencester A419

Once a wool store for the drovers of Michinhampton
common, this building has been stunningly converted to
create a pub that manages to feel fresh, modern and
rustic. There's plenty of bare wood, pine furniture and
brightly-painted walls, along with a rejuvenated garden for
summer drinks and dining. It's a popular destination after
a walk on the common, or perhaps a round of golf, and
despite a change of hands the reputation for good food
remains. The AA rosette-winning menu has a distinctly
modern feel. Dishes range from classic combinations such
as pan-fried steak with rösti potato, glazed baby
vegetables and port wine, through to creative or
internationally-inspired dishes - perhaps tuna spring roll
with a spiced avocado and aïoli salad or a trio of lobster
sausage, salmon fishcake and red mullet fillet with saffron.
OPEN: 12-3 5-11 (summer open all day) **BAR MEALS:** L
served all week 12-2 D served Mon-Sat 7-9.30 Av main course
£11 **RESTAURANT:** L served all week 12-2.30 D served Mon-
Sat 7-9.30 Av 3 course à la carte £20
BREWERY/COMPANY: Free House ◖▮: Wickwar Brand Oak
Bitter, Hook Norton, Smiles, plus guest ales.
FACILITIES: Children welcome Garden: Food served outside.
Landscape garden Dogs allowed **NOTES:** Parking 60

The Ram Inn 🐾
South Woodchester GL5 5EL ☎ 01453 873329 ▤ 01453 872880
e-mail: drink@raminn.com
Dir: A46 from Stroud to Nailsworth, R after 2m into S.Woodchester (brown
tourist signs)

Something for all seasons at the 400-year-old Ram, set in the
heart of the Cotswolds with lovely walks and a cycle track
nearby. In summer, the large patio provides splendid views of
the Stroud valley, but in winter months the huge fire is equally
appealing. Beef and Old Spot pie, venison sausages and giant
stuffed mushrooms can be washed down by regularly changing
real ales such as Old Peculier and Wychwood's Hobgoblin.
OPEN: 11-11 (Sun 12-10.30) **BAR MEALS:** L served all week 12-
2.30 D served all week 6.00-9.30 Av main course £6
RESTAURANT: L served all week 12-2.30 D served all week 6-9.30
Av 3 course à la carte £12.50 **BREWERY/COMPANY:** Free House
◖▮: Scottish Courage Theakston Old Peculier & John Smiths, Uley Old
Spot, Wickwar BOB, Wychwood Hobgoblin. **FACILITIES:** Children
welcome Garden: 2 Patio areas, seats approx 120 people Dogs
allowed **NOTES:** Parking 60

Pick of the Pubs

Rose & Crown Inn ♦♦♦ 🐾
The Cross, Nympsfield GL10 3TU
☎ 01453 860240 ▤ 01453 861564
e-mail: pubreliefcompany@tiscali.co.uk
Dir: M5 J13 off B4066 SW of Stroud

A 17th-century building of honey-coloured stone, the Rose
& Crown is located in the heart of the village close to the
Cotswold Way. It is a popular haunt for walkers and from
its lofty situation between Stroud and Dursley the
surrounding views of the Severn are breathtaking. The pub

has recently changed hands but maintains its traditional
appeal with log fire and cask ales in the bar, and an
intimate restaurant decorated in true Cotswold style with
balconies and exposed timbers. Sensibly-priced English
fare is served, favourite dishes including Gloucester Old
Spot sausage and mash, home-made faggots, and steamed
steak and kidney suet pudding. Fishy alternatives might be
grilled fillet of sea bass on straw potatoes with salsa verde,
or salmon with hollandaise sauce. The garden, overlooking
surrounding farmland, is large, shady and safe for
children. Accommodation is also available in spacious,
well-equipped bedrooms.

OPEN: 12-11 **BAR MEALS:** L served all week 12-9.30 D
served all week Av main course £8.95 **RESTAURANT:** L served
all week 12-9 D served all week Av 3 course à la carte £16.50
BREWERY/COMPANY: Free House ◖▮: Uley Best, Scottish
Courage Courage Directors & Best. **FACILITIES:** Children
welcome Garden: Large, shady, stunning views, safe Dogs
allowed Water provided **NOTES:** Parking 20 **ROOMS:** 3
bedrooms 3 en suite 2 family rooms s£42 d£55

The Woolpack Inn
Slad Rd, Slad GL6 7QA ☎ 01452 813429 ▤ 01452 813429
Dir: 2 miles from Stroud, 8 miles from Gloucester

Situated in the Slad valley close to the Cotswold Way, a friendly
local that offers good real ales, interesting wine selections and
middle-of-the-road food based largely on chargrills and popular
daily specials. Tempting starters include smoked mackerel and
country pâté, followed by butcher's faggots with mustard mash,
beef and ale stew and a mammoth mixed grill. Save room for
fruit crumble or treacle sponge. Booking advised for Richard's
good-value Sunday roast.
OPEN: 12-3 6-11 **BAR MEALS:** L served all week 12-2 D served
Tues-Sat 6-9 Av main course £7.95 **RESTAURANT:** L served all week
12-2 D served Tues-Sat 6.30-9 Av 3 course fixed price £18
BREWERY/COMPANY: Free House ◖▮: Uley Pig's Ear Strong Beer,
Flowers Original. **FACILITIES:** Children welcome Garden: Food
served outside Dogs allowed Water **NOTES:** Parking 8
NOTES: No credit cards

TETBURY   Map 04 ST89

Pick of the Pubs

Gumstool Inn 🐾 ♀
Calcot Manor GL8 8YJ ☎ 01666 890391 ▤ 01666 890394
e-mail: reception@calcotmanor.co.uk
Dir: In Calcot (on jct of A4135 & A46, 3m W of Tetbury)

The Gumstool is the pub at Calcot Manor Hotel, a lavishly-
converted farmhouse with a flower-filled central courtyard
and outbuildings dating back to the 13th century, when

continued

continued

the land was farmed by Cistercian monks. Here Cotswold produce is to the fore in a menu of modern English dishes served alongside cask ales and a selection of some 16 wines by the glass. Between the starters and main courses is a choice of dishes available in 'ample' or 'generous' portions - Caesar salad with Parmesan, smoked chicken and garlic croûtons, and Thai-spiced crab cakes with cucumber and crème fraîche, all served with the side dish of your choice (eg chips, veg, salad). For a more robust main course, try organic traditional Old Spot pork and leek sausages with sage mash, or crispy roast free-range pork confit with caramelised onions, bacon, mushrooms and red wine sauce.

OPEN: 11.30-2.30 6-11 (Sat 11.30-11, Sun 12-10.30)
BAR MEALS: L served all week 12-2 D served all week 7-9.30 Av main course £9.50 **RESTAURANT:** L served all week 12-2 D served all week 7-9.30 Av 3 course à la carte £20
BREWERY/COMPANY: Free House ◖: Scottish Courage Courage Directors, Best & Theakston XB, Greene King Spitfire, Wickwar BOB. ♀: 16 **FACILITIES:** Children welcome Garden **NOTES:** Parking 100

Pick of the Pubs

Trouble House Inn ⊛⊛ ♀
Cirencester Rd GL8 8SG ☎ 01666 502206 ▯ 01666 504508
e-mail: enquiries@troublehouse.co.uk
Dir: On A433 between Tetbury & Cirencester
The Trouble House has had a troubled past involving agricultural riots and suicidal landlords, but there's no looking back for chef/proprietor Michael Bedford, who has previously worked for Gary Rhodes and Raymond Blanc and is attracting many accolades for his cooking here. The historic Cotswold inn has been refurbished and now provides more seating, four open fires, low-beamed rooms, rustic wooden furnishings and a classic pub ambience. Used to heading up a brigade of 15, Michael runs the pub with his wife Sarah, and it's a very informal set up. Diners place their orders at the bar, choosing from options such as moules marinière or foie gras and apple terrine to start. From the main course range come calves' liver and bacon with onion gravy and mash, five-hour leg of lamb with white bean and tomato stew, or poached sea bass with creamed spinach, and you might finish with apple and blueberry frangipane or a selection of cheeses.
OPEN: 11-3 6.30-11 (Sun 12-3, 7-10.30) Closed: Dec 25, 2 weeks Jan, 1 week Autumn **BAR MEALS:** L served Tue-Sun 12-2 D served Tue-Sat 7-9.30 Av main course £12 **RESTAURANT:** L served Tue-Sun 12-2 D served Tue-Sat 7-9.30 Av 3 course à la carte £25 **BREWERY/COMPANY:** Wadworth ◖: Wadworth 6X & Henrys IPA. ♀: 8 **FACILITIES:** Garden: Benches Dogs allowed **NOTES:** Parking 30

TEWKESBURY   Map 10 SO83

The Fleet Inn
Twyning GL20 6DG ☎ 01684 274310 ▯ 01684 291612
e-mail: fleetinn@hotmail.com
Dir: 0.5m Junction 1 -M50
On the banks of the River Avon, this 15th-century pub with restaurant has lawns and patios that can seat up to 350. Fishing, boules, play area, pet's corner, bird garden, craft shop, tea room and a Japanese water garden are all to hand. The olde worlde bars and themed areas provide a wide range of dishes including jumbo cod fillet, Cajun chicken, Norwegian prawn salad, vegetarian cannelloni, traditional Sunday lunch and Atlantic tuna pasta bake.
OPEN: 11-11 **BAR MEALS:** L served all week 12-2.30 D served all week 6-9.30 **RESTAURANT:** 12-2.30 6.00-9.30
BREWERY/COMPANY: Whitbread ◖: Boddingtons, Greene King Abbot Ale, Bass, Fullers London Pride. **FACILITIES:** Children welcome Garden: Patios and water front garden **NOTES:** Parking 50

TORMARTON   Map 04 ST77

Compass Inn ★★ ⌂ ♀
GL9 1JB ☎ 01454 218242 ▯ 01454 218741
e-mail: info@compass-inn.co.uk
Dir: From M4 take A46 towards Stroud for 100yds then R
An extended former coaching inn, easily accessible from the M4 (J18), the Compass offers accommodation, conference facilities and a choice of bar and dining areas. It stands in four acres of grounds with terraces and a beer garden. Bar food includes a daily pie, grills and curry, while typical restaurant dishes are pan-fried breast of duck with stir-fried vegetables, and poached fillet of plaice with pomme dauphinoise. Horse riding, hot air ballooning and clay pigeon shooting can be arranged.
Closed: 25-26 Dec **BAR MEALS:** L served all week D served all week Av main course £6 **RESTAURANT:** L served all week D served all week 7-10 Av 3 course à la carte £20
BREWERY/COMPANY: Free House ◖: Interbrew Bass & Sussex, Badger. ♀: 7 **FACILITIES:** Children welcome Garden: Beer garden several terraces Dogs allowed Water **NOTES:** Parking 200
ROOMS: 26 bedrooms 26 en suite s£59.50 d£65

UPPER ODDINGTON   Map 10 SP22

Horse & Groom Inn
GL56 0XH ☎ 01451 830584 ▯ 01451 870494
Dir: Between A436 & B4450 E of Stow-on-the-Wold
Located just a mile from Stow-on-the-Wold in a pretty Cotswold village, this 16th-century inn is full of beamed ceilings and open log fires. Up-to-date bedrooms are popular with tourists, ramblers and lovers of horseracing, with Cheltenham just a short drive away. The menu includes lunchtime sandwiches, children's meals and dishes such as vegetarian sausages and mash, baked salmon with saffron potatoes, and noisettes of lamb with ratatouille and béarnaise sauce.
OPEN: 11 -11 (Sun 11-10.30) **BAR MEALS:** L served all week 12-2 D served all week 6.30-9.30 Av main course £8.50 **RESTAURANT:** L served all week 12-2 D served all week 6.30-9.30
BREWERY/COMPANY: Free House ◖: Hook Norton, Boddingtons, Old Speckled Hen, Wadworth 6X.
FACILITIES: Children welcome Garden: Beer garden Dogs allowed (not in restaurant) **NOTES:** Parking 40

England

WINCHCOMBE
Map 10 SP02

Royal Oak
Gretton GL54 5EP ☎ 01242 604999 ▤ 01242 602387
A local community syndicate recently bought this 18th-century Cotswold pub, and Goff's micro-brewery is responsible for the day-to-day running of it. Real ales are on tap, and there is also a huge selection of bottled beers. Lovely views across to the Malvern Hills can be enjoyed from the conservatory and gardens - at the bottom of which is a restored steam railway line. Food choices include smoked salmon and cucumber noodles, homemade fishcakes, wild mushroom tortellini, and game casserole.
OPEN: 12-3 6-11 Closed: Dec 25 **BAR MEALS:** L served all week 12-2.30 D served all week 6-7.30 Av main course £5.95
RESTAURANT: L served all week 12-2.30 D served all week 6-9.30 **BREWERY/COMPANY:** Free House 🍺: Goff's Jouster & White Knight, Scottish Courage John Smiths, Wickwar Brand Oak, Mighty Oak Burntwood. **FACILITIES:** Children welcome Garden Dogs allowed Water

WITHINGTON
Map 10 SP01

The Mill Inn
GL54 4BE ☎ 01242 890204 ▤ 01242 890195
Dir: 3m from the A40 between Cheltenham & Oxford
A 400-year-old former corn mill and local brewhouse set in a deep Cotswold valley. In summer you can snack at one of 40 tables on the banks of the River Coln, or choose to relax indoors where the stone-flagged floors, oak panelling and open log fires are features. Menu choices include minty lamb casserole, creamy pork and mushroom pepperpot, steak and ale pie, and a range of 'basket meals' - a food concept said to have originated here in the 1950s.
OPEN: 11.30-3 6.30-11 (Sun 12-3, 6.30-10.30) **BAR MEALS:** L served all week 12-2 D served all week 6.30-9 Av main course £6
BREWERY/COMPANY: Samuel Smith 🍺: Samuel Smith Old Brewery Bitter, Samuel Smith Sovereign. **FACILITIES:** Children welcome Garden: Lawned with 40 tables, Trees and river Dogs allowed Water, biscuits **NOTES:** Parking 80

WOODCHESTER
Map 04 SO80

The Old Fleece 🐾 ♀
Bath Rd, Rooksmoor GL5 5NB ☎ 01453 872582 ▤ 01453 872228
Dir: 2M S of Stroud on the A46

Popular 18th-century coaching inn built of Cotswold stone with a traditional stone roof. Cosy log fires bring a welcome glow to the inn's timeless, open-plan interior, characterised by wooden floors, wood panelling and exposed stone. Fine food cooked daily by the proprietor, with an extensive menu offering modern English and continental dishes. Sample

seared scallops wrapped in smoked bacon, tournedos Rossini or filo parcels with ricotta, basil and sun-dried tomatoes. Wide-ranging choice of starters and light meals, fish dishes and puddings.
OPEN: 11-11 Closed: 25 Dec **BAR MEALS:** L served all week 11-2.45 D served all week 5.30-10 Av main course £9.95
RESTAURANT: L served all week 11-2.45 D served all week 5.30-10 **BREWERY/COMPANY:** Pubmaster 🍺: Interbrew Boddington & Bass, Greene King Abbot Ale. ♀: 12 **FACILITIES:** Garden: Heated terrace Dogs allowed Water provided **NOTES:** Parking 40

The Royal Oak
Church Rd GL5 5PQ ☎ 01453 872735
Dir: Take A46 south from Stroud, R at N Woodchester sign onto Selsley Road. Church Rd on L
At the start of the popular Five Valleys Walk, in the heart of the glorious Cotswolds, it's not surprising that this welcoming 17th-century inn attracts many walkers and tourists. The rural views are stunning, and there's a popular beer garden. Expect a good range of local real ales, and traditional home cooking using fresh produce. Chicken pie, rib-eye steak, and venison casserole on the bar menu, with breast of duck with apple cider from the restaurant.
OPEN: 11-3 5.30-11 (Sun 12-4, 7-10.30) (all day Sat and in summer) Closed: 1 Jan **BAR MEALS:** L served Tues-Sun 12-2.30 D served Mon-Sat 6.30-9.30 Av main course £10 **RESTAURANT:** L served Tues-Sun 12-2.30 D served Mon-Sat 6.30-9.30 Av 3 course à la carte £15 **BREWERY/COMPANY:** Free House 🍺: Uley Old Spot, Archers Best, Bass plus guest. **FACILITIES:** Children welcome Garden: Patio, food served outside Dogs allowed Water **NOTES:** Parking 15

GREATER LONDON

CARSHALTON
Map 06 TQ26

Greyhound Hotel ★★★ ♀ NEW
2 High St SM5 3PE ☎ 020 8647 1511 ▤ 020 8647 4687
e-mail: greyhound@youngs.co.uk
Dir: Telephone for directions
Distinctive white-painted coaching inn directly opposite the ponds in Carshalton Park. Earliest records go back to 1706, but the building has been sympathetically refurbished, and the bar reflects both influences. A good choice of food with daily specials runs to seafood medley, grilled pork chops, pan-fried lamb's liver and tagliatelle verde, along with toasted sandwiches and ciabatta, and the likes of Cumberland sausages and mash.
OPEN: 11-11 Sun 12-10.30 **BAR MEALS:** L served all week 12-2.30 D served Mon-Sat 6.30-9.45 Av main course £8.25 **RESTAURANT:** L served all week D served Mon-Sat 6.30-9.45 Av 3 course à la carte £16.75 **BREWERY/COMPANY:** Young & Co 🍺: Youngs Special, Youngs Winter Warmer. ♀: 17 **FACILITIES:** Dogs allowed **NOTES:** Parking 46 **ROOMS:** 21 bedrooms 21 en suite 2 family rooms s£65 d£75 no children overnight

KESTON
Map 06 TQ46

The Crown 🐾 ♀
Leaves Green BR2 6DQ ☎ 01959 572920 ▤ 01959 572920
Dir: A21 onto A232, then L onto A233, pub 4m
Spitfire sausages and mash with onion gravy and parsnip crisps, Lancaster hotpot - braised lamb and vegetables with a potato topping - and Biggin Hill bomber burgers are appropriately-named selections on the menu at this old pub

continued

continued

not far from Biggin Hill airfield of Battle of Britain fame. There are good country walks from the pub, which was recently fully renovated and is now under new management. There is a large restaurant and extensive garden with play equipment for children.
OPEN: 11.30-11 (Sat-Sun, all week in summer 11-11)
BAR MEALS: L served all week 12 D served Mon-Sat 9.30 Av main course £7 **RESTAURANT:** L served all week 12 D served Mon-Sat 9.30 Av 3 course à la carte £15 **BREWERY/COMPANY:** Shepherd Neame ◀: Shepherd Neame Master Brew, Spitfire, Hurlimans. ♀: 8
FACILITIES: Garden: Very large Dogs allowed Water
NOTES: Parking 30

RICHMOND (UPON THAMES)　　　Map 06 TQ17

The White Cross ♀ NEW
Water Ln TW9 1TH ☎ 020 8940 6844
Dir: Telephone for directions
Set right beside the Thames, the view from this Grade II listed pub is much admired. An old fireplace uniquely fitted under a window is still lit on winter evenings, and the bar opens onto a patio in summer. All food is home cooked, including steak pie, roast pheasant with red wine sauce, lamb shanks, chilli con carne, and various pastas, sausages and fish dishes.
OPEN: 11-11 (Sun 12-10.30) **BAR MEALS:** L served all week 12-3.30 Av main course £6.75 **BREWERY/COMPANY:** Young & Co ◀: Youngs Bitter, Special, AAA. ♀: 13 **FACILITIES:** Garden: Large patio overlooking the Thames Dogs allowed Water

UXBRIDGE　　　Map 06 TQ08

The Turning Point ♀
Canal Cottages, Packet Boat Ln, Cowley Peachey UB8 2JS
☎ 01895 440550 📠 01895 422144
e-mail: bookings@turningpoint.co.uk
Dir: From M4 J4 2m N on A408

Housed in former workers' cottages on the Grand Union Canal, the last point where horse-drawn barges could be turned round. Explorers are rewarded with a waterside bar and restaurant whose daily output runs from sandwiches and salads to house favourites such as steak and vegetable pie and chicken curry. Saturday night menus for dinner and dancing offer liver pâté with red onion jam, calves' liver with mash and crispy bacon, and lobster thermidor (given 48 hours' notice and a good supplement).
OPEN: 12-11 Closed: 26 Dec, 1 Jan **BAR MEALS:** L served all week 12-9.30 D served Mon-Sat Av main course £10.95 **RESTAURANT:** L served all week 12-2.30 D served all week 6.30-9.30
BREWERY/COMPANY: Free House ◀: Fuller's London Pride, Interbrew Boddingtons Bitter. **FACILITIES:** Children welcome Garden: Patio, food served outside Dogs allowed **NOTES:** Parking 60

ALTRINCHAM　　　Map 15 SJ78

The Old Packet House ◆◆◆◆
Navigation Rd, Broadheath WA14 1LW
☎ 0161 929 1331 📠 0161 233 0048
Standing by the Bridgewater Canal, this charming black and white traditional inn takes its name from the horse-drawn post boat that once travelled the canal to Manchester. Colourful floral displays adorn the pub and garden in summer, and make outdoor dining a pleasure. Among the dishes on offer are haddock and prawn au gratin, braised steak casserole in red wine, roast Cheshire turkey, and chargrilled steak with plum tomatoes and mushrooms. Good wine list.
OPEN: 11-11 (Sun 12-10.30) **BAR MEALS:** L served all week 12-2.30 D served Tue-Sat 7-9.30 **BREWERY/COMPANY:** ◀: Hydes, Websters. **FACILITIES:** Children welcome Garden **NOTES:** Parking 10 **ROOMS:** 4 bedrooms 4 en suite

BAMFORD　　　Map 16 SD81

Egerton Arms ♀
Ashworth Rd, Ashworth Valley OL11 5UP
☎ 01706 646183 📠 01706 715343
e-mail: egertonarms@btconnect.com
Dir: Bamford on B6222
Old-world pub, next to the ancient chapel, haunted by the ghost of a tragic woman, killed with her lover while trying to defend him from crossbow attack. Bar favourites are the pies, daily roast and fish and chips, while the restaurant may offer Chateaubriand, and sole with asparagus mousse.
OPEN: 12.30-2.30 5.30-11 (Mon 5.30-11) **BAR MEALS:** L served Tue-Sun 12-2.30 D served all week 5.30-9.30 Av main course £6.50 **RESTAURANT:** L served Sun 12-2.30 D served all week 5.30-10.30 Av 3 course à la carte £18.50 **BREWERY/COMPANY:** Free House ◀: Theakston Old Peculier, John Smiths. **FACILITIES:** Children welcome Garden: BBQ, beer garden, patio, outdoor eating Dogs allowed garden only **NOTES:** Parking 100

DELPH　　　Map 16 SD90

Green Ash Hotel
New Tame, Denshaw Rd OL3 5TS
☎ 01457 871035 📠 01457 871414
Dir: Just off A670 NE of Oldham
Dating back to about 1800 and once a branch of the Co-op, this is a listed hotel with thoroughly modern bedrooms, and it stands in a half-acre garden surrounded by open countryside. An old-world-style dining room adjoining the bar and conservatory shares the fabulous views. In addition to a popular lunchtime carvery, specials might be king prawns with garlic and coriander, and lamb cutlets with minted gravy. Restaurant main courses at night take in lemon sole with warm green salsa, and fillet steak with Roquefort and bacon.
OPEN: 7am-midnight (Sun 8-11) **BAR MEALS:** L served Tue-Fri & Sun 12-2 D served all week 6-10 Av main course £11.50 **RESTAURANT:** L served Tue-Fri & Sun 12-2 D served all week 7-10 Av 3 course à la carte £19 **BREWERY/COMPANY:** Free House ◀: Black Sheep Best, Interbrew Boddington. **FACILITIES:** Garden: Food served outside, patio **NOTES:** Parking 37

England

England

DENSHAW — Map 16 SD91

The Rams Head Inn 🌳 ⚲ NEW
OL3 5UN ☎ 01457 874802 📠 01457 820978
Dir: From M62 towards Saddleworth, Denshaw 2m on R

A 400-year-old farmhouse-style pub with panoramic views of Saddleworth Moor, overlooking the former pack-horse route from Huddersfield to Rochdale. With its original beams and log fires in each room, the otherwise modest interior is a treasure trove of fascinating memorabilia. Menus offer specialities that include roast crispy suckling pig, grilled whole lemon sole, venison haunch steak on roast parsnips, seared king scallops, and grilled swordfish with mango and red pepper salsa.
OPEN: 12-2.30 6-11 (Sun, BHs 12-8.30 food, 12-10.30 drink) Closed: 25 Dec **BAR MEALS:** L served all week 12-2 D served all week 6-10 Av main course £10 **RESTAURANT:** L served all week 12-2 D served all week 6-10 **BREWERY/COMPANY:** Free House 🍺: Carlsberg-Tetley Bitter, Timothy Taylor Landlord, Golden Best & Best Bitter, Black Sheep Best. ⚲: 8 **FACILITIES:** Children welcome **NOTES:** Parking 30

DIDSBURY — Map 16 SJ89

The Royal Oak
729 Wilmslow Rd M20 6WF ☎ 0161 434 4788
Dir: Wilmslow Road Jct 6 M60

Character town pub gutted by fire in 1995 but now fully restored, and distinguished by Victorian fireplaces and old theatre memorabilia. Sources suggest the pub was once run by an ex-zookeeper who trained a monkey to clear glasses in the bar. Renowned for cheese and pâté lunches, with a daily choice of about 30 cheeses.
OPEN: 11-11 (Sun 12-10.30) **BAR MEALS:** L served Mon-Fri 12-2.15 Av main course £3.95 **BREWERY/COMPANY:** W'hampton & Dudley 🍺: Marstons Pedigree, Banks Bitter, plus Guest ales.

LITTLEBOROUGH — Map 16 SD91

The White House 🌳 ⚲
Blackstone Edge, Halifax Rd OL15 0LG ☎ 01706 378456
High on the Pennines, 1,300 feet above sea level, with panoramic views of the moors and Hollingworth Lake far below, this old coaching house dates from 1671. On the Pennine Way, which is popular with walkers and cyclists who sup on Theakston's and regular guest ales, and on Sundays can benefit from an all-day menu. Blackboard specials regularly include fresh fish: sea bass, marlin and grilled tuna, a seafood medley. Also various grilled steaks, 'lamb Henrietta' and steak and kidney pie. Children welcome until 9pm only.
OPEN: 12-3 6-11.30 Closed: 25 Dec **BAR MEALS:** L served all week 12-2 D served all week 6.30-9 **BREWERY/COMPANY:** Free House 🍺: Timothy Taylor Landlord, Theakstons Bitter, Exmoor Gold. **FACILITIES:** Children welcome **NOTES:** Parking 44

MANCHESTER — Map 16 SJ89

Dukes 92
14 Castle St, Castlefield M3 4LZ
☎ 0161 839 8646 📠 0161 832 3592
e-mail: dukes92@freenet.co.uk
Dir: Town centre
Beautifully-restored 19th-century stable building with a vast patio beside the 92nd lock of the Duke of Bridgewater canal. The interior is full of surprises, with minimalist décor downstairs and an upper gallery displaying local artistic talent.

The renowned cheese and pâté counter is a great draw, offering a huge range of British and continental cheeses, along with a salad selection, and a choice of platters for sharing.
OPEN: 11-11 (Fri-Sat 11-12, Sun 12-10.30) Closed: 25-26 Dec, 1 Jan **BAR MEALS:** L served all week 12-3 D served Sun-Thurs 5-8 Av main course £4.75 **RESTAURANT:** L served all week 12-3 D served Mon-Fri 5-8 **BREWERY/COMPANY:** Free House 🍺: Interbrew Boddingtons Bitter. **FACILITIES:** Children welcome Garden: Large front and back patio with seating **NOTES:** Parking 30

Lass O'Gowrie ⚲
36 Charles St, Chorlton-cum-Medlock M1 7DB ☎ 0161 273 6932
Not far from the BBC complex, this is a traditional pub with wooden floors, 20 constantly changing cask beers, and its own brewery. Very busy and popular with students, but has its quieter times. The real gas lamps add to the atmosphere. Straightforward bar menu includes lasagne, chicken tikka masala, steak and mushroom pudding, Glamorgan sausages, and chicken and bacon salad bowl.
OPEN: 11-11 **BAR MEALS:** L served all week 12-5 Av main course £3.50 **RESTAURANT:** L served all week 12-5
BREWERY/COMPANY: 🍺: Marstons Pedigree, Boddingtons, Old Speckled Hen.

MELLOR — Map 16 SJ98

The Oddfellows Arms 🌳 ⚲
73 Moor End Rd SK6 5PT ☎ 0161 449 7826
A friendly welcome can be expected in the stone-flagged bars and dining room of this old pub, which changed its name after extensions were carried out in 1860 to accommodate the Oddfellows Society, a forerunner of the trades unions. Pride of place goes to the selection of real ales and a choice of bar food including daily specials, many with an international flavour. Try Moroccan lamb casserole, Catalan pork tenderloin, Singapore-style chicken noodles, or mushroom and pepper goulash.
OPEN: 12-3 5.30-11 (Sun 12-3, 7-10.30) Closed: 25-26 Dec, 31 Dec-1 Jan **BAR MEALS:** L served Tues-Sun 12-2 D served Tues-Sat 6.30-9.30 Av main course £10 **RESTAURANT:** L served Sun 12-2 D served Tue-Sat 7-9.30 Av 3 course à la carte £17.50
BREWERY/COMPANY: Free House 🍺: Adnams Southwold, Marston's Pedigree & Bitter. ⚲: 8 **FACILITIES:** Garden: Small patio area Dogs allowed **NOTES:** Parking 21

OLDHAM — Map 16 SD90

The Roebuck Inn ⚲
Strinesdale OL4 3RB ☎ 0161 624 7819 📠 0161 624 7819
e-mail: smhowarth1@aol.com
Dir: From Oldham take A62 then A672 towards Ripponden. 1m turn R at Moorside PH into Turf Pit Lane. Pub 1m.
On the edge of Saddleworth Moor in the Pennines, this 18th-century inn has an upstairs room once used for the 'laying out' of bodies - often recovered from the reservoirs at Strinesdale! Fare includes rack of lamb coated in honey, garlic and mint sauce; steak, kidney and ale pudding; crispy roast duck with orange stuffing and Grand Marnier sauce; and chicken breast wrapped in bacon with mushroom sauce. Half portions of most dishes are available for children.
OPEN: 12-2.30 5-12 **BAR MEALS:** L served all week 12-2.15 D served all week 5-9.30 Av main course £9 **RESTAURANT:** L served all week 12-2.15 D served all week 5-9.30 Av 3 course fixed price £6.75 **BREWERY/COMPANY:** Free House 🍺: Boddingtons Smoothflow, Draft Bass. ⚲: 8 **FACILITIES:** Children welcome Garden: Dogs allowed **NOTES:** Parking 40

continued

Pick of the Pubs

The White Hart Inn ⓐⓐ 🛏 🍷
Stockport Rd, Lydgate OL4 4JJ
☎ 01457 872566 📠 01457 875190
e-mail: charles@thewhitehart.co.uk
Dir: From Manchester A62 to Oldham. R onto bypass, A669 through Lees. Inn 500yds past Grotton brow of hill turn R onto A6050
Dating from 1788, one part or other of this collection of buildings, high up on the moors, has been, in order, a tavern, brewery, doghouse, prison, school, weavers' cottages and Home Guard lookout post. Three regulars of this traditional inn were allegedly the inspiration for the old rascals in TV's 'Last of the Summer Wine'. Whichever dining option is chosen - bar, restaurant or brasserie - quality is stamped on every dish, with cooking based on the best available local produce. Starters on the combined brasserie/restaurant menu include braised shoulder of Welsh lamb with rocket mash and sun-dried tomato and basil pesto; pan-fried guinea fowl, with boulangère potatoes, sweet garlic, greens and artichokes; and grilled turbot fillet with tempura tiger prawns, citrus noodles and sauce Americaine. Saddleworth sausages come with mash and onion gravy. Super desserts and a selection of British and Irish cheeses.
OPEN: 12-11 (Sun 1-10.30) **BAR MEALS:** L served all week 12-2.30 D served all week 6-9.30 Av main course £14
RESTAURANT: L served all week 1-3.30 D served Tue-Sat 6.30-9.30 Av 3 course à la carte £25 Av fixed price £25.50
BREWERY/COMPANY: Free House 🍺: Timothy Taylor Landlord, J W Lees Bitter, Carlsberg-Tetley Bitter, Interbrew Bass Bitter. 🍷: 10 **FACILITIES:** Children welcome Garden: Lawned garden with view of Saddleworth Moor **NOTES:** Parking 70

SALFORD   Map 15 SJ89

Mark Addy
Stanley St M3 5EJ ☎ 0161 832 4080
On the banks of the River Irwell close to Salford Quays, a former river-ferry landing stage - where Mark Addy saved 50 passengers from drowning in Victorian times. Up to 50 cheeses from eight countries and eight Belgian pâtés are served with granary bread, and soup in winter. Wine tasting notes accompany: free doggy bags.
OPEN: 11.30-11 Closed: 25/26 Dec, Jan1 **BAR MEALS:** L served all week 11.30-9 D served all week Av main course £3.75
BREWERY/COMPANY: Free House 🍺: Guest Ales.
FACILITIES: Garden: Riverside patio

STALYBRIDGE   Map 16 SJ99

Stalybridge Station Buffet Bar 🍷
The Railway Station SK15 1RF ☎ 0161 303 0007
e-mail: esk@buffetbar.co.uk
Unique Victorian railway station refreshment rooms dating from 1885 and including original bar fittings, open fire and conservatory. The old living accommodation and first class ladies' waiting room are used to good effect. There have been over 4,300 real ales served here in the last six years, and the bar hosts regular beer festivals and folk nights. Expect pasta bake, pies and black peas, liver and onions, and sausage and mash on the bar menu.
OPEN: 11-11 Mon-Sat 12-10.30 Sun Closed: Dec 25
BAR MEALS: L served all week 11-8 Av main course £3
BREWERY/COMPANY: Free House 🍺: Interbrew Boddingtons,

continued

Bass & Flowers, Wadworth 6X, Guest Ales each week.
FACILITIES: Children welcome Garden: Platform Dogs allowed Water provided **NOTES:** Parking 60 No credit cards

STOCKPORT   Map 16 SJ89

The Nursery Inn NEW
Green Ln, Heaton Norris SK4 2NA
☎ 0161 432 2044 📠 0161 442 1857
The Nursery Inn has existed since 1869, though the present building was erected in 1939. Inside, original features such as 1930s wood panelling remain intact. Food is served at lunchtime - either sandwiches in the bar or home-cooked dishes in the restaurant, typically steak and kidney pie or fish with a choice of vegetables. Wash it down with excellent real ale from Hyde's of Manchester. In fine weather, the pub's patio and bowling green are good places to soak up the sun.
OPEN: 11.30 -11 **BAR MEALS:** L served all week 12-2 Av main course £4.95 **RESTAURANT:** L served all week 12-2 🍺: Hydes Bitter, Hydes Jekylls Gold, Hydes Seasonal Ales, Harp Irish.
FACILITIES: Garden: Bowling green with patio furniture
NOTES: Parking 20 **NOTES:** No credit cards

WIGAN   Map 15 SD50

Bird I'th Hand
Gathurst Rd, Orell WN5 0LH ☎ 01942 212006
Not far from Aintree racecourse, Orrell is noted for both its rugby club and this vibrant pub. Set in a large well-maintained garden, it possibly was the home of Dr Beecham of 'powders' fame. Home-made food, freshly prepared from market produce, typically offers plaice in brown butter, capers and prawns, chicken supreme in bacon with white wine sauce and rump steak with wild mushrooms and onions. Large garden and activity centre popular with families.
OPEN: 12-2 6-11 (Summer & Wknds open all day) **BAR MEALS:** L served all week 12-2 D served all week 6-9 Av main course £9
RESTAURANT: L served all week 12-2 D served all week 6-9 Av 3 course à la carte £19 Av 3 course fixed price £10 🍺: John Smiths, Theakstons Mild Cask. **FACILITIES:** Children welcome Garden: Large garden with BBQ and patio Dogs allowed Water
NOTES: Parking 35

HAMPSHIRE

ALRESFORD   Map 07 TM02

The Fox Inn 🍷
Bramdean SO24 0LP ☎ 01962 771363
e-mail: thefoxinn@callnet.com
400-year-old village pub situated in the beautiful Meon Valley surrounded by copper beech trees. Produce is locally sourced and a good choice of fresh fish is featured on blackboard menus written up twice a day. Options might include pan-fried wing of skate, whole sea bass with a chilli salsa, roast rack of lamb, and fillet steak in a mushroom cream sauce. No evening meals on Sundays or Mondays from Jan to Mar.
OPEN: 11-3 6-11 (Winter open at 6.30) Sun-Mon Closed eve in Jan-Feb **BAR MEALS:** L served all week 12-2 D served all week 7-9 Av main course £9.95 **BREWERY/COMPANY:** Greene King
🍺: Greene King Abbot Ale, Greene King IPA. **FACILITIES:** Garden: Food served outside **NOTES:** Parking 25

The Compasses Inn

A very pleasant walk in pretty countryside to the west of the New Forest.

From the pub car park turn left and follow the road for about 220yds/200m, crossing the Allen River where you might see signs of the local wildlife, including geese and ducks. Beyond Cross Ways Farm turn left to join a waymarked, paved footpath and pass alongside a smallholding. Make for a gate and turn left at the road. Pass a school on the right, keep along the road and cross a millstream to reach the Old Corn Mill.

Follow the road up an incline, pass a sign for Hill Farm and turn right at a barred gate before reaching the top. Join a waymarked footpath and cross three paddocks to reach a plank bridge spanning a deep ditch. Enter the field and follow the hedge round to the right.

In about 60yds/55m turn right, dropping down to a stile

and several sections of plank footway. Cross a footbridge over a stream and make for a paved road. Damerham Trout Lakes are on the left. Turn right and pass between houses. After about 440yds/400m turn right at a footpath sign and cross a stile.

Cut between tall hedges and fences, continue for over 100 yards/m and then keep to the right, following a narrow path between houses to reach the road. Turn right, re-cross the millstream and as you approach the 'Hill Farm- No Turning' sign turn left for Damerham's church of St George, which is usually locked.

Pass through a kissing gate at the top and enter the churchyard. Pass to the side of the church and note the attractive view of the valley.

♦♦♦
THE COMPASSES INN, DAMERHAM
SP6 3HQ
☎ 01725 518231

Directions: From Fordingbridge (A338) follow signs for Sandleheath/Damerham. Or signs from B3078.
Village centre pub close to the cricket pitch, 400 years old and full of character. Own-brewed and regular guest ales, and over 100 malt whiskies are served in the pine-furnished bars.
Open: 11-3 6-11
(Sat all day, Sun 12-4 7-10.30)
Bar Meals: 12-2.30 7-9.30
Notes: Children welcome (baby changing) & dogs. Large garden, water feature. Parking.
(See page 225 for full entry)

Make for the north end of the churchyard, go through gates and cross the road to another gate. The Compasses can be seen from here. Cross the village sports field to a stile in the left fence and enter the pub garden through the pergola arch.

DISTANCE: 2 1/2 miles/4km
MAP: OS Explorer OL 22
TERRAIN: Fields, valley and downland. Easy walking, muddy in places when wet
PATHS: Footpaths and roads
GRADIENT: Gentle climbing

Walk submitted and checked by the Compasses, Damerham

England

ALRESFORD continued

Pick of the Pubs

The Globe on the Lake
The Soke, Broad St SO24 9DB
☎ 01962 732294 ▤ 01962 736211
e-mail: duveen-conway@supanet.com
See Pick of the Pubs on page 220

BASINGSTOKE   Map 05 SU65

Hoddington Arms
Upton Grey RG25 2RL ☎ 01256 862371 ▤ 01256 862371
e-mail: monca777@aol.com
Dir: *Telephone for directions*
A traditional pub near the duck pond at Upton Grey,
Hampshire's best-kept village for several years. Cosy log fires
and 18th-century beams contribute to the relaxing atmosphere,
as does the lack of music and machines. A blackboard menu
broadcasts choices like breast of duck with apple and blackberry
sauce, and steak and Guinness pie, while lunchtime snacks
include hot foccacio sandwiches, and mushrooms and Stilton
cheese on toast. There's a peaceful rear terrace and garden.
OPEN: 12-3 6-11 **BAR MEALS:** L served Tue-Sun 12-2 D served
Tue-Sat 7-9.30 **RESTAURANT:** L served Tue-Sun 12-2 D served Tue-
Sat 7-9.30 **BREWERY/COMPANY:** Greene King ◖: Greene King
IPA, Old Speckled Hen, Ruddles Best, Fosters. ♀: 7
FACILITIES: Garden: Large patio with play area Dogs allowed Water
NOTES: Parking 30

BEAUWORTH   Map 05 SU52

The Milburys ♀
SO24 0PB ☎ 01962 771248 ▤ 01962 7771910
Dir: *A272 towards Petersfield, after 6m turn R for Beauworth*
Rustic hill-top pub dating from the 17th century and named
after the Bronze Age Mill-barrow nearby. Noted for its
massive, 250-year-old treadmill that used to draw water from
the 300ft well in the bar, and for the far-reaching views across
Hampshire that can be savoured from the lofty garden. Menu
includes chargrilled venison steak with woodland berry jus,
crispy aromatic duck, four cheese pasta, and pan-fried king
scallops on crispy bacon salad. Jacket potatoes, potato skins,
and sandwiches also available.
OPEN: 11-11 (Sun 12-10.30) **BAR MEALS:** L served all week 12-2 D
served all week 6.30-9.30 Av main course £8 **RESTAURANT:** L served all
week D served all week Av 3 course à la carte £20
BREWERY/COMPANY: Free House ◖: Cheriton Best Bitter & Diggers
Gold, Hop Back Best Bitter, Scottish Courage Theakstons Old Peculier,
Triple FFF Altons Pride. **FACILITIES:** Children welcome Garden: Beautiful
view of valley Dogs allowed Water provided **NOTES:** Parking 60

BENTLEY   Map 05 SU74

The Bull Inn
GU10 5JH ☎ 01420 22156 ▤ 01420 520772
Dir: *2m from Farnham on A31 towards Winchester*
A handy refuge from the A31 between Alton and Farnham, a
refurbished 16th-century road house that retains its old-
fashioned character with oak beams, inglenook and open fires.
Simple bar snacks stray little from the tried and tested baguettes,
jacket potatoes and ham, egg and chips. However, monthly-
changing dinner menus add pan-fried duck and Grand Marnier
parfait, roast chump of lamb and selections from the chargrill.

OPEN: 11-11 (Sun 12-10.30) **BAR MEALS:** L served all week 12-
2.30 D served all week 6.30-10 Av main course £25
RESTAURANT: L served all week 12-2.30 D served all week 6.30-10
Av 3 course à la carte £25 **BREWERY/COMPANY:** Free House
◖: Scottish Courage Courage Best, Hogs Back TEA, Young's Bitter,
Fullers London Pride. **FACILITIES:** Children welcome Garden: Dogs
allowed **NOTES:** Parking 40

BENTWORTH   Map 05 SU64

The Star Inn
GU34 5RB ☎ 01420 561224
e-mail: mk@star-inn.com
Dir: *N of Alton 3m off A339*
With its eye-catching floral displays in summer, The Star
occupies a charming spot opposite the village green. There's a
safe, secluded garden, and the pub is handy for the Woodland
Trust's property at Home Farm. Choose from ploughman's,
steak sandwiches and hot dishes in the bar, or move up to the
separate dining-room menu for monkfish with garlic and red
wine, lemon chicken, or spinach and mushroom pancakes.
OPEN: 12-3 5-11 **BAR MEALS:** L served all week 12-2 D served all
week 6.30-9 Av main course £8.45 **RESTAURANT:** L served all week
12-2 D served all week 6.30-9 Av 3 course à la carte £16
BREWERY/COMPANY: Free House ◖: Fullers London Pride,
Ringwood Best, Doombar, ESB. **FACILITIES:** Garden: Safe and
secluded **NOTES:** Parking 12

Smuggling and Skulduggery
All round Britain's coast an explosion of smuggling was the 18th-century response to high excise
duties on goods imported from abroad. There were villages in Kent where people were said to wash
their windows with smuggled gin, it was so cheap. Inns were often involved, because they had cellars where
casks and bales could conveniently be hidden and they could sell smuggled drink. Smugglers were nothing like
as romantic in real life as they are in fiction. Lawless and violent smuggling gangs could exercise a reign of terror.
Other criminal activities were often associated with some of the rougher pubs, where thieves planned
operations, the landlord fenced stolen goods and the 'gentlemen of the road' dropped in. Many
a pub on the Great North Road claims the famous highwayman Dick Turpin as a habitué.

Open: 11-3, 6-11 (Sun 12-7),
Summer open all day Sat & Sun
Bar Meals: L served Mon-Sat 12-2,
(Sun 12-5), all day during summer,
D served all week 6.30-9
Av cost main course £8
RESTAURANT: L served all week 12-2,
(Sun 12-5)
D served Mon-Sat 6.30-9
BREWERY/COMPANY:
UNIQUE PUB CO LTD
🍺: Wadworth 6X, Scottish Courage
Directors, Henley Brakspear Bitter,
Fullers London Pride.
FACILITIES: Children welcome for
lunch and early suppers. Non smoking
dining room. Baby changing facilities.
Garden - Large lakeside garden.

The Globe
on the Lake

In an outstanding setting on the banks of a reed-fringed lake and
wildfowl sanctuary, The Globe is a convivial hostelry serving good
food, good beer and good wine.

The Soke, Broad Street, Alresford,
SO24 9DB
☎ 01962 732294 📠 01962 736211
📧 duveen-conway@supanet.com
Dir: 7 miles from Winchester,
telephone for directions.

Located at the bottom of
Alresford's superb Georgian
main street is this popular
17th-century dining pub in an
enviable location beside
Alresford Pond. This huge
stretch of water is noted for its
waterfowl, which swim
amongst the reeds and sunbathe
between the picnic tables in the
lakeside gardens. Inside the bar,
a log fire blazes on cooler days,
while on the walls is a selection
of interesting artworks. A smart
dining room and unusual
garden room share the stunning
outlook over the water. Freshly-
prepared food is served
throughout the inn, and
summer meals can be enjoyed
in the garden and heated rear
terrace. The daily-changing
blackboard menus feature
several fresh fish dishes, like
pan-seared scallops in a rich
seafood velouté with leek and
tarragon mash, pan-roasted
salmon fillet with a spicy
oriental sauce, or fillet of hake
in beer batter. Other choices
might include fillet steak with a
red wine jus, chicken breast
with wild mushrooms, pancetta
and a creamy wine sauce, and
layered Mediterranean vegetable
bake. Popular desserts on a
separate blackboard might be
steamed toffee, banana and
pecan pudding, or cream-filled
profiteroles with hot chocolate
sauce. A fixed price menu is
served on Sunday with a choice
of four starters and four main
courses including a traditional
roast. Real ales and a good
selection of wines to
accompany the meal.

BENTWORTH continued

Pick of the Pubs

The Sun Inn ♀
Sun Hill GU34 5JT ☎ 01420 562338

First building in or last one out of the village, depending on your direction of travel. If you're leaving, it almost takes you by surprise, because it's not quite where you'd expect a pub to be. Inside the 17th-century building, however, it's everything you'd wish for - interconnecting rooms with open log fires, brick or boarded floors, low-beamed ceilings, and lots of old pews, settles and scrubbed pine tables. No wonder this pub makes such a strong impact on the senses when you enter, particularly in the evenings when the table candles are lit. Food conforms to pub traditional, including Cumberland sausage and mash, beef Stroganoff with rice, giant filled Yorkshire puddings, lamb casserole, cheesy haddock bake and chicken tikka. A thriving free house, it offers eight real ales, including Cheriton Pots and Ringwood's Old Thumper, both Hampshire breweries.
OPEN: 12-3 6-11 (Sun 12-10.30) **BAR MEALS:** L served all week 12-2 D served all week 7-9.30 Av main course £6.95 **BREWERY/COMPANY:** Free House ◗: Cheriton Pots Ale, Ringwood Best & Old Thumper, Brakspear Bitter, Fuller's London Pride. **FACILITIES:** Children welcome Garden: Dogs allowed Water

---

BOLDRE — Map 05 SZ39

The Red Lion Inn 🐾 ♀
Rope Hill SO41 8NE ☎ 01590 673177 📠 01590 676403
Dir: 0.25m E off A337, 1m N of Lymington
Though mentioned in the Domesday Book, today's inn harks back only to the 15th century when it was formed from two cottages and a stable. Inside you'll find a rambling series of beamed rooms full of interesting rural memorabilia. The lengthy menus range from light snacks (whitebait, home-made soup, sandwiches) through sausage, pies and scampi to extravagant specials such as wild boar steak with apple and cider sauce.
OPEN: 11-11 (Sun 12-10.30) **BAR MEALS:** L served all week 12-2.30 D served all week 6.30-9.30 Av main course £6 **RESTAURANT:** L served all week 12-2.30 D served all week 6.30-9.30 **BREWERY/COMPANY:** ELD ◗: Bass, Flowers IPA. ♀: 12 **FACILITIES:** Garden: Winner of the 2002 Best Floral Display Dogs allowed Water **NOTES:** Parking 50

BROCKENHURST — Map 05 SU30

The Filly Inn 🐾
Lymington Rd, Setley SO42 7UF
☎ 01590 623449 📠 01590 623449
e-mail: pub@fillyinn.co.uk
One of the most picturesque, cosy traditional pubs in the heart of the New Forest. Locals attest to frequent sightings of George, the resident ghost, thought to be a long-dead, repentant highwayman. The far from spooky menu offers standard pub snacks of baguettes and filled jacket potatoes, as well as home-cooked English ham with egg and chips, beef lasagne and home-baked pies of the day. Daily specials could include traditional battered cod, seafood platter and authentic curries. Cream teas in summer.
OPEN: 10-11 **BAR MEALS:** L served all week 10-2.15 D served all week 6.30-10 Av main course £5.50 **RESTAURANT:** L served all week 10-2.15 D served all week 6.30-10 **BREWERY/COMPANY:** Free House ◗: Ringwood Best, Old Thumper, Badger Tanglefoot. **FACILITIES:** Children welcome Garden: About 3/4 acres of lawn Dogs allowed Water **NOTES:** Parking 90

BROOK — Map 05 SU21

Pick of the Pubs

The Bell Inn ★★★ 🏵 🐾
SO43 7HE ☎ 023 80812214 📠 023 80813958
e-mail: bell@bramshaw.co.uk
Dir: From M27 J1 (Cadnam) take B3078 signed Brook, 0.5m on R

Dating from 1782, this handsome listed inn is part of Bramshaw Golf Club and includes facilities for conferences and golf societies. It also makes an ideal base for touring the New Forest and the nearby south coast. The inn retains many period features, particularly the imposing inglenook fireplace in the bar and the beamed bedrooms located in the oldest part of the building. Bar food stretches from hot and cold snacks (sandwiches, burgers, omelettes and so forth) to daily specials featuring fresh fish, local game in season and delightful home-made desserts. Comfortable country dishes like Test trout, chargrilled venison steak or roast Bramshaw estate pheasant are set beside more esoteric offerings, such as tempura haggis with gribiche sauce, or turkey bang bang with egg noodles. Among the favourite finishes are sticky toffee pudding, crème brûlée and pecan pie.
OPEN: 11-11 (Sun 12-10.30) **BAR MEALS:** L served all week 12-2.30 D served all week 6.30-9.30 Av main course £8.95 **RESTAURANT:** L served Sun 12-2 D served all week 6.30-9.30 Av 3 course fixed price £28.50 **BREWERY/COMPANY:** Free House ◗: Ringwood Best, Scottish Courage Courage Best, John Smith's. **FACILITIES:** Children welcome Garden **NOTES:** Parking 60 **ROOMS:** 25 bedrooms 25 en suite

England

BROUGHTON
Map 05 SU33

The Tally Ho!
High St SO20 8AA ☎ 01794 301280
Dir: *Winchester to Stockbridge rd then A30, 1st L to Broughton*
Traditional, well restored pub nestling in a pretty village close to the Test Valley and a popular refreshment stop for walkers undertaking the Clarendon Way.
OPEN: 12-3 6-11 (Sun 12-3 7-10.30) **BAR MEALS:** L served Wed-Mon 12-2 D served Wed-Mon 7-9 Av main course £5.95
BREWERY/COMPANY: Free House **◀:** Ringwood True Glory, Youngs and Bombadier. **FACILITIES:** Children welcome Garden: Patio, food served outdoors Dogs allowed On lead Water provided
NOTES: No credit cards

BUCKLERS HARD
Map 05 SU40

The Master Builders House Hotel ★★★ ◉◎ ♀
SO42 7XB ☎ 01590 616253 ▤ 01590 616297
e-mail: res@themasterbuilders.co.uk
On the banks of the Beaulieu River this former house of the master shipbuilder Henry Adams has been carefully refurbished. Grassy areas in front of this fine 18th-century building run right down to the river - a delightful spot. The beamed Yachtsman's Bar which is very popular in summer with tourists. Good light snacks and short evening menu offering the likes of fish pie and beef bourguignon. Imaginative restaurant menu, and stylish bedrooms in the upmarket hotel side of the operation.
OPEN: 11-11 (Sun 12-10.30) **BAR MEALS:** L served all week 12-2.30 D served all week 6-9 Av main course £9.50 **RESTAURANT:** L served all week 12-3 D served all week 7-10 Av 3 course à la carte £27.50
BREWERY/COMPANY: Free House **◀:** Greene King IPA, Youngs, Tetleys. **FACILITIES:** Children welcome Garden: Food served outdoors
NOTES: Parking 50 **ROOMS:** 25 bedrooms 25 en suite s£130 d£170

BURITON
Map 05 SU71

The Five Bells ◌ ♀
High St GU31 5RX ☎ 01730 263584 ▤ 01730 263584
Dir: *Village signposted off A3 S of Petersfield*
The South Downs Way runs through Buriton on its way to Winchester, and this characterful 17th-century village inn makes a welcome refreshment stop. In addition to its quaint beams, cosy fires and solid stone walls, the Five Bells has a fascinating history. The restaurant was formerly the farriers, then a clay pipe factory, and at one point even the village morgue! A typical menu may feature fresh red bream with onions and deep-fried prosciutto, steak and kidney pie, spinach and Brie filo parcels, and grilled whole plaice.
OPEN: 11-2.30 5.30-11 **BAR MEALS:** L served all week 12-2 D served all week 6-10 **RESTAURANT:** L served all week 12-2 D served all week 7-9.30 **BREWERY/COMPANY:** Hall & Woodhouse **◀:** Badger Best Bitter, Tanglefoot & Champion, King & Barnes Sussex, Gribble Fursty Ferret. **FACILITIES:** Children welcome Garden Dogs allowed Water & biscuits provided **NOTES:** Parking 12

BURLEY
Map 05 SU20

The Burley Inn ◌ ♀
BH24 4AB ☎ 01425 403448 ▤ 01425 402058
e-mail: info@theburleyinn.co.uk
Dir: *between the A31 & A35*
At the centre of a quiet New Forest village, this Edwardian doctor's house has been successfully converted into a

comfortable country inn, renowned for its tree house where the doctor himself once sold cream teas. The menu offers light bites, steaks, a good range of home-made pies, daily specials, sweet suet puddings and 15 wines by the glass. There are great country/forest walks, and cycle or horse rides right from the doorstep.

OPEN: 11-3 6-11 (Closed Sun pm, Summer open all day)
BAR MEALS: L served all week 12-2.15 D served Mon-Sat 6.30-9.00 Av main course £8 **RESTAURANT:** L served all week 12-2.15 D served Mon-Sat 6-9 Av 3 course à la carte £15
BREWERY/COMPANY: Wadworth **◀:** Wadworth 6X, Henry's IPA & JCB. **♀:** 15 **FACILITIES:** Garden: Outside terrace Dogs allowed Water **NOTES:** Parking 18

CADNAM
Map 05 SU31

The White Hart ♀
Old Romsey Rd SO40 2NP ☎ 023 80812277
Dir: *M27 J1. Just off rdbt to Lyndhurst*
Smartly refurbished old coaching inn located on the edge of the New Forest and a very convenient refreshment stopover for M27/A31 travellers. Rambling series of interconnecting rooms with open fires, a comfortable mix of old and new furniture, tiled floors and traditional decor. Food is the attraction here, the extensive blackboard menu listing home-cooked dishes prepared from fresh local produce, including fish and game. Typical dishes may include lamb noisettes on garlic mash with red wine sauce, pan-fried monkfish with Thai curry sauce, and game casserole; good snacks like open sandwiches and pasta dishes. Large rear garden.
OPEN: 11-11 (Sun 12-10.30) **BAR MEALS:** L served all week 12-9 D served all week Av main course £9.25
BREWERY/COMPANY: **◀:** Wadworth 6X, Ringwood Best, Boddingtons. **FACILITIES:** Children welcome Garden: Food served outside **NOTES:** Parking 60

CHALTON
Map 05 SU71

The Red Lion ♀
PO8 0BG ☎ 023 92592246 ▤ 023 92596915
e-mail: redlionchalton@aol.com
Dir: *Just off A3 between Horndean & Petersfield. Take exit near Queen Elizabeth Country Park*
Thatched and immaculately maintained, Hampshire's oldest pub dates back to 1147, and was originally a workshop for craftsmen building the Norman church opposite. Imaginative dishes from the daily menu include guinea fowl in Calvados, and fresh sea bass with roasted macadamia nuts and honey dressing, as well as the usual pub snacks. Large garden has spectacular views of the South Downs.

continued

continued

OPEN: 11-3 6-11 25-26 Dec closed evening **BAR MEALS:** L served all week 12-2 D served Mon-Sat 6.30-9.30 Av main course £8.50
RESTAURANT: L served all week 12-2 D served Mon-Sat 6.30-9.30
BREWERY/COMPANY: Gales ◖: Gales Butser, Winter Brew, GB & HSB. ♀: 20 **FACILITIES:** Children welcome Garden: Spectacular views over South Downs Dogs welcome in public bar
NOTES: Parking 80

CHARTER ALLEY   Map 05 SU55

The White Hart
White Hart Ln RG26 5QA ☎ 01256 850048 📠 01256 850524
e-mail: h4howard@aol.com
Dir: From M3 J6 take A339 towards Newbury. Take turning to Ramsdell. Turn R at church, then 1st L into White Hart Lane

Built in 1819, this village pub originally catered for local woodsmen and coaches visiting the farrier's next door. These days it's popular with cyclists and walkers from Basingstoke and Reading and real ale enthusiasts from all over, having sold more than 450 real ales from around the country in the last 10 years and won five CAMRA awards in recent times. Guest ales change weekly and home-made food is served in generous portions. Look out for steak and Stilton pie, White Hart smokie, venison and game pie, and Cajun tuna steak.
OPEN: 12-2.30 7-11 (Sun 12-3, 7-10.30) Closed: Dec 25-26
BAR MEALS: L served all week 12-2 D served Tue-Sun 7-9 Av main course £7.95 **RESTAURANT:** L served all week 12-2 D served Tue-Sun 7-9 Av 3 course à la carte £15 **BREWERY/COMPANY:** Free House ◖: Timothy Taylor Landlord, Otters Ale, West Berkshire Mild, Oakleaf. **FACILITIES:** Garden: Dogs allowed **NOTES:** Parking 30

CHAWTON   Map 05 SU73

The Greyfriar 🏠 ♀ NEW
Winchester Rd GU34 1SB ☎ 01420 83841
e-mail: info@thegreyfriar.co.uk
Dir: Chawton lies just off the A31 near Alton. Access to Chawton via the A31/A32 J. Sign posted Jane Austen's House
Built well over 400 years ago, the interior architecture clearly

continued

---

shows origins as a terrace of cottages. By 1847 the building was a 'beer shop', and by 1871 it had become a proper pub, the Chawton Arms. In 1894 a licence was granted in the name of the Greyfriar, but why the change isn't known. The Whitehead family's eminently laudable objective is to run it as a 'friendly place of refreshment and relaxation, where quality food from an imaginative and varied menu is available alongside excellent beers (from Fuller's), wines and spirits'. The simple lunch menu offers freshly-baked baguettes, ploughman's, Greyfriar burger and haddock and chips, for example, while on the daily main menu tuna, shark and mahi mahi may appear, alongside sirloin, fillet and rump steaks, sausage and mash and Thai curries - all fresh and home made. Opposite the pub is Jane Austen's house, a museum since 1949.
OPEN: 12-11 (Mon-Fri 12-11, Sun 12-10.30) **BAR MEALS:** L served all week 12-2.30 D served Mon-Sat 7-9.30 Av main course £8.95
RESTAURANT: L served all week 12-2.30 D served Mon-Sat 7-9.30 Av 3 course à la carte £16.95 ◖: Fuller's London Pride, Chiswick & ESB, Seasonal Ales. ♀: 7 **FACILITIES:** Children welcome Garden: Paved area, sun trap, picnic tables Dogs allowed Water
NOTES: Parking 16

CHERITON   Map 05 SU52

Pick of the Pubs

The Flower Pots Inn
SO24 0QQ ☎ 01962 771318 📠 01962 771318
Dir: A272 toward Petersfield, L onto B3046, pub 0.75m on R
Originally built as a farmhouse in the 1840s by the head gardener of nearby Avington House, this unassuming and homely brick village pub has become a popular place in which to sample award-winning ales, brewed in the micro-brewery across the car park, and simple, honest bar food. Two traditional bars are delightfully music- and electronic game-free, the rustic public bar being furnished with pine tables and benches and the cosy saloon having a relaxing sofa among other chairs; both have warming winter log fires. A short value-for-money menu offers home-cooked meals, including jacket potatoes with decent filling, giant baps (try the home-baked ham), hearty soups and casseroles and a bowl of delicious chilli served with garlic bread or rice. Come on a Wednesday night for an authentic Punjabi curry, and wash it down with a first-rate pint of Pots Ale or Diggers Gold. Beer Festival August Bank Holiday.
OPEN: 12-2.30 6-11 (Sun 12-3, 7-10.30) **BAR MEALS:** L served all week 12-2 D served Mon-Sat 7-9 Av main course £5.20
BREWERY/COMPANY: Free House ◖: Cheriton Pots Ale, Best Bitter, Diggers Gold (Brewed on premises).
FACILITIES: Garden: Lawns, flower beds with picnic benches Dogs allowed Dogs on leads **NOTES:** Parking 30 **NOTES:** No credit cards

---

CRAWLEY   Map 05 SU43

The Fox and Hounds ♀
SO21 2PR ☎ 01962 776006 📠 01962 776006
Dir: A34 onto A272 then 1st R into Crawley
A few miles north west of Winchester, at the heart of a peaceful Hampshire village, a mock Tudor inn that enjoys a burgeoning reputation for simple well-cooked food. Recently restored to former glories, it features beamed rooms warmed by log fires that create a welcoming, lived-in atmosphere.

continued

CRAWLEY continued

Blackboards display a wealth of options from chicken liver pâté and baked goats' cheese to Thai chicken curry, braised lamb shank and classic Sunday roasts.
OPEN: 12-3 6-11 **BAR MEALS:** L served all week 12-2 D served all week 6-9 Av main course £10 **RESTAURANT:** L served all week 12-2 D served all week 7-9 Av 3 course à la carte £21
BREWERY/COMPANY: Free House 🍺: Wadworth 6X, Ringwood Best, Gales HSB, Fullers London Pride. **FACILITIES:** Children welcome Garden: Food served outside, small terraced area
NOTES: Parking 13

CRONDALL
Map 05 SU74

Pick of the Pubs

The Hampshire Arms 🏠 🍷
Pankridge St GU10 5QU ☎ 01252 850418 🖷 01252 850418
e-mail: paulychef@hantsarms.freeserve.co.uk
See Pick of the Pubs on opposite page

DAMERHAM
Map 05 SU11

The Compasses Inn ♦♦♦ 🏠 🍷
SP6 3HQ ☎ 01725 518231 🖷 01725 518880
Dir: From Fordingbridge (A338) follow signs for Sandleheath/Damerham. Or signs from B3078

Located in the village centre next to the local cricket pitch, this 400-year-old coaching inn is full of character and atmosphere in both the cottagey bedrooms and pine-furnished bars. Real ales, including their own brew and regular guests, and a fine collection of over 100 malt whiskies. Locally-produced fresh food with offerings of smoked haddock with cream and cheese sauce, baked wolf-fish with ginger, soy and pak choi parcel, and spinach, red onion and Feta soufflé omelette. Notable for its cheeses, served with home-made pickles, and large garden with superb views. Take a look at the old brew tower.
OPEN: 11-3 6-11 (all day Sat, Sun 12-4, 7-10.30) **BAR MEALS:** L served all week 12-2.30 D served all week 7-9.30 Av main course £7.50 **RESTAURANT:** L served all week 12-2.30 D served all week 7-9.30 Av 3 course à la carte £17.50 **BREWERY/COMPANY:** Free House 🍺: Compasses Ale, Ringwood Best, Hop Back Summer Lightning, Interbrew Bass. 🍷: 8 **FACILITIES:** Children welcome Garden: water feature, play area Dogs allowed By arrangement
NOTES: Parking 30 **ROOMS:** 6 bedrooms 6 en suite 1 family room s£39.50 d£69

See Pub Walk on page 218

DOGMERSFIELD
Map 05 SU75

The Queens Head 🏠 🍷
Pilcot Ln RG27 8SY ☎ 01252 613531
A 17th-century coaching inn linked to Katherine of Aragon, set beside a stream and some pretty thatched cottages with Dogmersfield Park and lake nearby. An extensive international menu of over 120 dishes is served by friendly staff, including honey and ginger chicken, beef Stroganoff, Barnsley lamb chop, noisettes of lamb, and plenty of seafood such as halibut, turbot, whole seabass and king prawns.
OPEN: 11.30-3.30 5.30-11 **BAR MEALS:** L served Tue-Sun 12-2.15 D served Tue-Sun 6-9.15 Av main course £8.95 **RESTAURANT:** L served Tue-Sun 12-2.15 D served Tue-Sun 6-9.15 Av 3 course à la carte £20 **BREWERY/COMPANY:** Free House 🍺: Fuller's London Pride, Adnams Broadside, Scottish Courage Courage Best. 🍷: 10
FACILITIES: Children welcome Garden: Grass seated area, good views **NOTES:** Parking 20

DUMMER
Map 05 SU54

The Queen Inn
Down St RG25 2AD ☎ 01256 397367 🖷 01256 397601
Dir: from M3 J7, follow signs to Dummer

You can dine by candlelight at this 16th-century village pub, with its low beams and huge open log fire. Everything is home made, from the soup and light bites to the famous fish and chips with beer batter, fresh sea bass, and prime steaks. The steak and kidney pudding is only for the heartier appetite!
OPEN: 11.30-2.30 6-11 (Sun 12-3 7-10.30) **BAR MEALS:** L served all week 12-2.30 D served all week 6-9.30 Av main course £6.95 **RESTAURANT:** L served all week 12-2 D served all week 6-9.30 **BREWERY/COMPANY:** Unique Pub Co 🍺: Scottish Courage Courage Best & John Smiths, Greene King IPA, Fuller's London Pride, Adnams Broadside. **FACILITIES:** Children welcome Garden: Benches, tables, chairs **NOTES:** Parking 20

Open: 11-3.30, 5.30-11 (Sat all day, Sun 12-10.30)
Bar Meals: L served Tue-Sun 12-2.30, D served Mon-Sat 7-9.
Av cost main course £13.50
RESTAURANT: L served all week 12-2.30, D served Mon-Sat 7-9
BREWERY/COMPANY:
Greene King
🍺: Greene King IPA, Abbot Ale, Ruddles County.
FACILITIES: Dogs allowed, Children welcome, Garden - Large landscaped garden with river at the bottom.
NOTES: Parking 40

The Hampshire Arms

Originally two cottages, the Hampshire Arms dates back 250 years and has also been a courthouse, jail and baker's in its time.

Pankridge Street, Crondall, GU10 5QU
☎ 01252 850418 📠 01252 850418
📧 paulychef@hantsarms.freeserve.co.uk
Dir: From M3 junct 5 take A287 South towards Farnham. Follow signs to Crondall on R.

Since chef-proprietor Paul Morgan and his wife Gillian took over they have struck a balance between preserving the pub's traditional character and achieving an exceptional standard of food and service, attracting many awards and accolades in the process. The atmosphere is still delightfully pubby, with open fires, bare beams, hop bines and candlelight. There is also a large landscaped garden to be enjoyed with a pétanque pitch and a river running by at the bottom, complete with resident ducks. You can eat in the bar or the restaurant, where white linen and sparkling glassware provide the first clue that this won't be your average pub meal. To capture the flavour of the cooking you might try a trio of game birds, the dish comprising a pheasant set on boudin noir and served with apple, a pot-roasted quail and pigeon served with tatties-neeps, and a pan-fried poussin served with game chips on a purée of vegetables. For a fishy alternative, maybe cod and haddock wrapped in pancetta and served with haricot beans, hazelnut pesto and a rocket and Parmesan salad, or fillet of brill with green pea risotto, sautéed crayfish tails and clams in garlic. Special events at the pub include jazz nights, quiz nights, special menu gourmet evenings, gents' cooking evenings (prepare your own three-course gourmet meal supervised by Paul, then sit down and eat it!), and ladies' cooking evenings (the same as gents' evenings but strictly for the ladies).

England

Pick of the Pubs

The East End Arms 🦌

Main Rd SO41 5SY ☎ 01590 626223 🖹 01590 626223
e-mail: jennie@eastendarms.co.uk
Dir: From Lymington follow signs for Isle of Wight ferry. Pass ferry terminal on R & continue for 3m

Traditional New Forest pub tucked away down quiet lanes, close to Beaulieu and historic Buckler's Hard. Worth the short diversion off The Solent Way for the short, interesting range of modern, brasserie-style dishes served in the comfortably-refurbished lounge bar. Oven-baked ciabatta's, filled baguettes, rabbit casserole, and liver and bacon appear on the light snack menu, while the main fortnightly-changing menu could list duck and apple terrine, roast glazed duck with North African couscous, slow-roasted lamb shank with forest mushrooms, and pan-fried rib-eye steak with roast red pepper butter and freshly-cut chips. Fish specials may include fried Cornish sprats, grilled bream fillet, or fish pie. Rustic Foresters Bar with stone floor, open fires, Ringwood ales drawn straight from the wood, and gamekeepers with guns!
OPEN: 11.30-3 6-11 (Sun 12-9) Closed: 1 Jan **BAR MEALS:** L served Tue-Sun 12-2 Av main course £7 **RESTAURANT:** L served Tue-Sun 12-2 D served Tue-Sat 7-9 Av 3 course à la carte £20.50 **BREWERY/COMPANY:** Free House 🍺: Ringwood Best & Fortyniner. **FACILITIES:** Children welcome Garden: Fully enclosed lawn with bench style tables Dogs allowed Water provided **NOTES:** Parking 20

Ye Olde George Inn 🦌

Church St GU32 1NH ☎ 01730 823481 🖹 01730 823759
Dir: S of A272 (Winchester/Petersfield). 1.5m from Petersfield turn L opp church

In a lovely village on the River Meon, a charming 15th-century inn close to a magnificent Norman church, and near to Queen Elizabeth Country Park. Its open fires, heavy beams and rustic artefacts create an ideal setting for relaxing over a good choice of real ales or enjoying freshly-prepared bar food. Fish and seasonal game are the mainstays of the menu, with sea bass, monkfish and salmon regularly featured with steaks and racks of lamb for meat eaters. Cream teas in summer.
OPEN: 11-3 6-11 (Sun 12-3, 7-10.30) **BAR MEALS:** L served all week 12-2 D served all week 7-9 **RESTAURANT:** L served all week 12-2 D served all week 7-9 **BREWERY/COMPANY:** Hall & Woodhouse 🍺: Badger Best, Tanglefoot & King & Barnes Sussex,.
FACILITIES: Children welcome Garden: Patio Area Dogs allowed
NOTES: Parking 30

The Chestnut Horse 🦌 ♇

SO21 1EG ☎ 01962 779257 🖹 01962 779014
Dir: From M3 J9 take A33 towards Basingstoke, then B3047. Take 2nd R, then 1st L

A delightful dining pub at the heart of the Itchen Valley, the Chestnut Horse is great for walkers, with the Three Castles Path passing right by. The building dates from the 16th century, with low-beamed ceilings festooned with old beer mugs and chamber pots, and intimate dining areas divided by standing timbers. Log fires and candlelit tables play their part in the atmospheric interior, while outside there is a colourful decked patio with heating for cooler spells. A good selection of ales is kept, including Chestnut Horse Special, and a choice of 30 malt whiskies. The same menu is served throughout, with options ranging through fresh Dorset crab in a salad or cocktail, and freshly cooked fish and chips to confit of duck, comforting home-made steak and kidney pudding, or rack of English lamb with rosemary and thyme sauce.
OPEN: 11-3 5.30-11 (Sun eve Winter closes at 6pm)
BAR MEALS: L served all week 12-2.30 D served all week 6.30-9.30 Av main course £12 **RESTAURANT:** L served all week 12-2.30 D served all week 6.30-9.30 Av 3 course à la carte £22 Av 2 course fixed price £9.95 **BREWERY/COMPANY:** Free House 🍺: Interbrew Bass, Scottish Courage Courage Best, Chestnut Horse Special, Fuller's London Pride. ♇: 9 **FACILITIES:** Children welcome Garden: Decked patio, heaters Dogs allowed Water **NOTES:** Parking 40

Cricketers Inn 🦌

SO21 1EJ ☎ 01962 779353 🖹 01962 779010
e-mail: geoffgreen1382@aol.com
Dir: M3 J9, A33 towards Basingstoke. Turn R at Kingsworthy onto B3047. 0.75m turn R

A traditional free house in a pretty village close to the River Itchen. Regularly featuring well-kept real ales from independent brewers to complement extensive home-cooked menus, facilities include a non-smoking dining-room. Bar snacks include crusty doorstep sandwiches, hot baguettes and open toasties, while main dishes take in filled Yorkshire puddings, salmon fillet with tomato mascapone sauce, mint shoulder of lamb, Cumberland sausage and mash, steak and Ringwood ale pie, and gargantuan Cricketers' mixed grills. Vegetarian options also available.
OPEN: 12-3 6-11 (Sun 12-3 7-10.30) **BAR MEALS:** L served all week 12-2 D served Mon-Sat 7-9 Av main course £7.95 **RESTAURANT:** L served all week 12-2 D served Mon-Sat 7-9 **BREWERY/COMPANY:** Free House 🍺: Ringwood, Timothy Taylor Landlord, Fosters, Changing guest ales. **FACILITIES:** Children welcome Garden: Paved patio at front Dogs allowed **NOTES:** Parking 16

EAST STRATTON
Map 05 SU53

The Northbrook Arms 🏠
SO21 3DU ☎ 01962 774150
Dir: Just off A33, 9m S of Basingstoke, 7m N of Winchester, follow Kingsworthy signs from M3

In an idyllic setting adjoining the green and an assortment of thatched cottages, the pub was formerly known as the Plough. Built around 1847, it was once the village shop and bakery and has a skittle alley in converted stables. Home-produced fare includes steak and kidney pie, breast of Barbary duck, vegetable stirfry, cod and chips, and bangers and mash. Handy for Winchester and some of mid-Hampshire's loveliest walks.
OPEN: 12-3 6-11 (Sun 12-3, 7-10.30) Dec 25-26 Closed eve **BAR MEALS:** L served Tues-Sun 12-2 D served Tues-Sat 7-9 Av main course £8.95 **RESTAURANT:** L served Tues-Sun 12-2 D served Tues-Sat 7-9.30 **BREWERY/COMPANY:** Free House ◼: Gales HSB & GB, Otter Bitter, Ringwood Best, Scottish Courage John Smith's. **FACILITIES:** Garden: Very large, bench seating, volleyball pitch Dogs allowed Water **NOTES:** Parking 30

EAST TYTHERLEY
Map 05 SU22

Pick of the Pubs

Star Inn ♦♦♦♦ ◎◎ 🏠 ♀
SO51 0LW ☎ 01794 340225 📠 01794 340225
e-mail: info@starinn-uk.com
Dir: 5m N of Romsey off A3057. Take L turn Dunbridge B3084. Left for Awbridge & Lockerley. Through Lockerley then 1m

Brick-built 16th-century coaching inn overlooking the village cricket ground on a quiet back lane between Romsey and Salisbury, close to the attractions of the Test Valley. A blackboard menu hanging over the open fireplace in the modernised bar offers imaginative dishes with a contemporary slant. Dine where you like, in the bar or at dark-wood tables in the main dining room, and

continued

maybe stay over in one of the three bedrooms. In summer, drinks and meals can also be enjoyed outside in the patio loggia area. The menu offers a good selection of dishes using seasonally-available local produce. From the classical menu come cod and chips, and steak, kidney and Guinness pie, while from the à la carte menu you might choose seared scallops with roasted sweet potato, curried leeks and crispy Parma ham, or pan-fried fillet of beef with potato rösti, foie gras and Madeira jus.
OPEN: 11-2.30 6-11 Closed: 26 Dec **BAR MEALS:** L served Tues-Sun 12-2 D served Tues-Sun 7-9 Av main course £9.50 **RESTAURANT:** L served Tues-Sun 12-2 D served Tues-Sun 7-9 Av 3 course à la carte £20 **BREWERY/COMPANY:** Free House ◼: Ringwood Best plus guest beers. ♀: 10 **FACILITIES:** Children welcome Garden: Patio area Dogs allowed Water bowl **NOTES:** Parking 60 **ROOMS:** 3 bedrooms 3 en suite 2 family rooms s£50 d£70

EMSWORTH
Map 05 SU70

The Sussex Brewery 🏠 ♀
36 Main Rd PO10 8AU ☎ 01243 371533 📠 01243 379684
Dir: On A259 (coast road), between Havant & Chichester
A fresh 'carpet' of sawdust is laid daily in the bars of this traditional 17th-century pub that boasts wooden floors, large open fires and a typically warm welcome. Fully 50 sausage recipes are on offer, ranging from gluten-free Moroccan lamb and vegetarian varieties to the full-blown Feathered Platter, which includes spiced ostrich, chicken piri-piri, Sussex pigeon and pheasant. Non sausage-related daily specials might include fresh local fish, steaks, or rack of lamb.
OPEN: 11-11 **BAR MEALS:** L served all week 12-2.30 D served all week 7-10 Av main course £6.50 **RESTAURANT:** L served all week 12-2.30 D served all week 7-10 **BREWERY/COMPANY:** Young & Co ◼: Smiles Best Bitter, Young's PA, AAA & Special, Timothy Taylor Landlord. ♀: 8 **FACILITIES:** Children welcome Garden: Dogs allowed Water **NOTES:** Parking 30

EVERSLEY
Map 05 SU76

The Golden Pot ♀
Reading Rd RG27 0NB ☎ 0118 9732104
Dir: Between Reading and Camberley on the B3272 about 0.25m from the Eversley cricket ground

Dating back to the 1700s and located in a famous village where Charles Kingsley, author of 'The Water Babies', was once rector, this former standard local went more upmarket in the late 1990s when the pool bar was converted into a full à la carte restaurant. This operation has recently been taken over by Greene King, and is now run as a tied house. A sample menu includes pan-fried wild venison, brochette of

continued

England

EVERSLEY continued

salmon, king prawn and scallops, whole baked sea bass, and wild mushroom and rocket risotto. Readers reports welcome.
OPEN: 11-3 6-11 **BAR MEALS:** L served all week 12-2.15 D served all week 6.30-9.15 Av main course £14.50 **RESTAURANT:** L served Sun-Fri 12-2 D served Mon-Sat 7-9.15 Av 3 course à la carte £25 **BREWERY/COMPANY:** Greene King 🍺: Greene King Ruddles Best, Abbot Ale, Guest Ale. **FACILITIES:** Garden: Pergola, picnic tables **NOTES:** Parking 30

FACCOMBE
Map 05 SU35

The Jack Russell Inn
SP11 0DS ☎ 01264 737315
e-mail: simonandlizfroome@jackrussellinn.co.uk
Situated amongst some 4,500 acres of walking country just a step out of Newbury, an ivy-clad inn that overlooks the village pond and open farmland. Bar and conservatory menus feature ingredients such as fresh fish, game from the Faccombe estate and fresh meats delivered daily by the local butcher. Specials include home-made pies, seafood platter and Louisiana vegetable roast. At the weekends there are often popular theme nights.
OPEN: 12-3 7-11 Closed: Dec 25 eve **BAR MEALS:** L served all week 12-2 D served all week 7-9 Av main course £6.50 **RESTAURANT:** L served all week 12-2 D served all week 7-9.30 Av 3 course à la carte £11 **BREWERY/COMPANY:** Free House 🍺: Ruddles, IPA & Guest beer. **FACILITIES:** Children welcome Garden: Food served outside **NOTES:** Parking 30

FORDINGBRIDGE
Map 05 SU11

The Augustus John 🏠 ♀
116 Station Rd SP6 1DG ☎ 01425 652098
e-mail: peter@augustusjohn.com
Dir: Telephone for directions
Named after the renowned British painter who lived in the village (the pub was also his local), this unassuming brick buildings was transformed a few years ago into a smart dining pub. Of particular interest is the changing blackboard menu which may offer home-made soups, salmon and herb fishcakes, rack of lamb with redcurrant and mint, liver and bacon with mash and onion gravy and fresh Poole plaice. Good puddings and short list of good wines; 10 by the glass.
OPEN: 11.30-3.30 6-12 **BAR MEALS:** L served all week 11.30-2 D served all week 6.30-9 Av main course £10 **RESTAURANT:** L served all week 11.30-2 D served all week 6.30-9 **BREWERY/COMPANY:** Eldridge Pope 🍺: Bass, Tetley. **FACILITIES:** Children welcome Garden Dogs allowed **NOTES:** Parking 40

FRITHAM
Map 05 SU21

The Royal Oak
SO43 7HJ ☎ 02380 812606 ▤ 02380 814066
e-mail: royaloakfritham@btopenworld.com
Unaltered for some 100 years, this small thatched 17th-century country pub on a working farm deep in the New Forest maintains its long tradition of preferring conversation to the distractions of juke box and fruit machines. Ideally located for walkers and ramblers, warming open fires are maintained from October to March with ploughman's lunches and home-baked quiches to munch on, and home-made evening meals on two nights per week. The garden has lovely views of the valley, and a pétanque terrain.

continued

OPEN: 11-3 6-11 (Sat 11-11, Sun 12-11) **BAR MEALS:** L served all week 12-2.30 D served 2 days a wk winter only 7-9 Av main course £4.50 **BREWERY/COMPANY:** Free House 🍺: Ringwood Best & Fortyniner, Hop Back Summer Lightning, Palmers Dorset Gold, Cheriton Village Elder. **FACILITIES:** Children welcome Garden: Large, countryside views, ample benches Dogs allowed Water, biscuits **NOTES:** No credit cards

See Pub Walk on opposite page

HAVANT
Map 05 SU70

The Royal Oak 🏠 ♀
19 Langstone High St, Langstone PO9 1RY
☎ 023 92483125 ▤ 023 9247 6838

Occupying an outstanding position on Langstone Harbour, this historic 16th-century pub is noted for its rustic, unspoilt interior. Flagstone floors, exposed beams and winter fires contrast with the waterfront benches and secluded rear garden for alfresco summer drinking. Starters such as Feta cheese with sun-dried tomatoes, or battered squid and caper dip, precede minted loin of lamb, home-made fish pie, Cajun chicken sizzler or Brie and redcurrant tart.
OPEN: 11-11 (Sun 12-10.30) Closed: Dec 25 eve **BAR MEALS:** L served all week 12-9 D served all week Av main course £7.95 **RESTAURANT:** L served all week 12-2.30 D served all week 6-9 Av 3 course à la carte £15 **BREWERY/COMPANY:** Whitbread 🍺: Gales HSB, Interbrew Flowers. **FACILITIES:** Children welcome Garden: Patio, food served outside Dogs allowed Water

---

The Royal Oak

Discover the beauty of William the Conqueror's New Forest on this peaceful woodland walk.

With the pub garden behind you, set off along the narrow tarmac lane (a no through road) facing you. On the left are several houses and cottages and on the right is an open grassy expanse. Pass a chapel on your left and now the tarmac surface switches to gravel. Look for a gate on the right and enter woodland.

Soon the trees give way to open heath. Keep ahead on the obvious track, passing two wooden 'lids.' These conceal springs that feed drinking ponds. As you reach the second 'lid' the track forks. Take the right-hand path and soon Green Pond edges into view, visible against a semi-circle of trees and shrubs through which there are two openings.

With the pond on your left, take the left opening and follow a grassy track until you come to a junction with a gravel track. Turn right and almost immediately you reach a broad and very well defined gravel track. Turn left here and as the track approaches woodland and swings left, turn right and almost immediately pass through a gate on the left.

Follow the winding, well-used logging track through Sloden Inclosure for about 1 mile/1.6km, avoiding all tracks to the left and right, and pass several commemorative oak trees on the right. The track swings slightly right and then sharp right, with a less obvious track running almost straight ahead. Follow it over a slight incline to reach a gate.

Pass through the gate and turn right to join a pretty ride running between two Inclosures. Follow it for about 3/4 mile/1.2km, reaching a newly-

THE ROYAL OAK, FRITHAM
SO43 7HJ
☎ 02380 812606

Directions: Contact pub
Small, thatched 17th-century country pub deep in the New Forest. Ideal for walkers and ramblers, with hearty lunches served, and dinner available in the winter only, on two nights.
Open: 11-3 6-11 (Sat 11-11 Sun 12-11)
Bar Meals: 12-2.30 7-9 (dinner 2 days a week winter only)
Notes: Children & dogs welcome (water, biscuits). Large garden. (See full entry on opposite page)

established plantation surrounded by a high deer fence. Continue for a short distance to a gate. Here a narrow path forks left off the main track and winds through the trees and open ground to a junction of narrow stony paths. Keep ahead, passing through a holly wood to reach a track which soon rejoins the wide, well-defined track encountered earlier on the walk. Turn left and within about 1/2 mile/800m you reach the Royal Oak.

DISTANCE: 4 1/2 miles/7.2km
MAP: OS Explorer OL 22
TERRAIN: New Forest woodland and heath. Often very muddy in winter
PATHS: Forest paths and tracks. Quiet tarmac roads
GRADIENT: Gently undulating

Walk submitted and checked by Mr A Waldron of Romsey

HAWKLEY — Map 05 SU72

Hawkley Inn
Pococks Ln GU33 6NE ☎ 01730 827205
Dir: 2 mins W of A3 at Liss
Tucked away down narrow lanes on the Hangers Way Path, an unpretentious rural local with a fine reputation for quality ale from local micro-breweries and its own cider. Ambitious bar food offers Brie and bacon or spinach and Ricotta tart, duck breast in peppercorn sauce, Mediterranean chicken and green pesto spaghetti; for traditionalists, sausage and mash, and faggots with onion gravy. Frequent venue for live jazz and blues.
OPEN: 12-2.30 6-11 **BAR MEALS:** L served all week 12-2 D served Mon-Sat 7-9.30 Av main course £7.95 ◀: RCH East Street Cream, Itchen Valley Godfathers, Triple FFF Alton's Pride, Ballards Best Bitter.
FACILITIES: Garden: Food served outdoors Dogs allowed Water

HOLYBOURNE — Map 05 SU74

White Hart ♦♦♦ 🛏
GU34 4EY ☎ 01420 87654 🖥 01420 543982
Dir: off A31 between Farnham & Winchester
Traditional village inn popular with locals and business guests. Families are also welcome, and the children can play in the special play area which has swings and climbing frames. Comfortable bedrooms and a good selection of bar food, which may include fish dishes such as sea bass, grilled trout, or salmon.
OPEN: 11-3 5-11 **BAR MEALS:** L served all week 12-2.30 D served all week 7-10 Av main course £6 **RESTAURANT:** L served all week 12-2.30 D served all week 7-10 Av 3 course à la carte £12.50 **BREWERY/COMPANY:** Greene King ◀: Scottish Courage Courage Best, Greene King Abbot Ale & IPA.
FACILITIES: Children welcome Children's licence Garden: Large rear garden s£30 d£50 **NOTES:** Parking 40 **ROOMS:** 4 bedrooms s£30 d£50

HOOK — Map 05 SU75

Crooked Billet 🍷
London Rd RG27 9EH ☎ 01256 762118 🖥 01256 761011
e-mail: Richardbarwise@aol.com
Dir: From M3 take Hook Ring Road. At third Rdbt turn R on A30 towards London, pub on L 0.5m by river.

This traditional pub is exactly 100 years old; so too is the resident ghost. Barely had the cement set when a motorist - drunk, the coroner thought - on his way back from Cowes Week crashed into the building at 20mph, with fatal results. A large garden running down to the River Whitewater incorporates a play area and barbecue, and Morris Men meet here regularly. Food for all appetites includes meats, grills,

fish, vegetarian, salads, toasties and jackets. Surrey-brewed Hogs Back TEA from the pump.
OPEN: 11.30-3 6-11 **BAR MEALS:** L served all week 12-2.30 D served all week 7-9.30 **BREWERY/COMPANY:** Free House ◀: Scottish Courage Courage Best & Directors & John Smith's, Hogs Back TEA. **FACILITIES:** Children welcome Garden: Large garden next to Whitewater River Dogs allowed Water **NOTES:** Parking 60

HORSEBRIDGE — Map 05 SU33

John O'Gaunt Inn 🛏
SO20 6PU ☎ 01794 388394
Some five miles north of Romsey, a small country inn, popular with walkers from the nearby Test Way footpath, that scores highly for atmosphere, well-kept ales and generously-priced food. Frequented also by fishermen and the winter shooting fraternity, diners can expect trenchermen's portions of steak and kidney pudding, local pheasant in red wine and fresh local trout with almonds - 'a great meeting place for dogs, closely followed by their owners'.
OPEN: 11-2.30 6.30-11 (Fri- Sun 11-3) **BAR MEALS:** L served all week 12-2 D served all week 7-9.30 Av main course £7 **BREWERY/COMPANY:** Free House ◀: Ringwood Best Bitter, Ringwood Fortyniner, Palmers IPA. **FACILITIES:** Garden: Small area covered by attractive pergola Dogs allowed **NOTES:** Parking 12 **NOTES:** No credit cards

IBSLEY — Map 05 SU10

Olde Beams Inn 🍷
Salisbury Rd BH24 3PP ☎ 01425 473387
Dir: On A338 between Ringwood & Salisbury
The cruck beam is clearly visible from the outside of this thatched, 14th-century building. In addition to the restaurant there is also a popular buffet counter. Located in the Avon Valley and handy for the New Forest.
OPEN: 12-11 **BAR MEALS:** L served all week 12-9 D served all week Av main course £6.50 **BREWERY/COMPANY:** Old English Inns ◀: IPA, Abbotts Ale, Ringwood, Youngs. **FACILITIES:** Children welcome Garden: Outdoor eating **NOTES:** Parking 120

LONGPARISH — Map 05 SU44

The Plough Inn 🛏 🍷
SP11 6PB ☎ 01264 720358 🖥 01264 720377
Dir: Off A303 4m S of Andover

As it is only 100 yards away from the River Test, this 400-year old pub is regularly visited by the local duck population. It is also a popular meeting place for both family and business get-togethers. Typical menu includes a wide selection of fish, and game such as venison, partridge, wild boar, and ostrich.

continued

continued

England

OPEN: 11-3.30 6-11 (11-3, 6-11 in winter) Rest:Dec 25-26 closed evening **BAR MEALS:** L served all week 12-2.30 D served all week 6.30-9.30 Av main course £5.95 **RESTAURANT:** L served all week 12-2.30 D served all week 6.30-9.30 **BREWERY/COMPANY:** Enterprise Inns ◖: Hampshire Ironside, Greene King Old Speckled Hen, Ringwood, Warsteiner. **FACILITIES:** Children welcome Children's licence Garden: Garden with wooded/secluded area, wildlife Dogs allowed **NOTES:** Parking 60

LYMINGTON
Map 05 SZ39

The Kings Arms ◆◆◆ ♀
St Thomas St SO41 9NB ☎ 01590 672594
Dir: Approaching Lymington from N on A337, head L onto St Thomas St. Kings Arms 50yds on R
King Charles I is reputed to have patronised this historic coaching inn, which these days enjoys an enviable reputation for its cask ales, housed on 150-year-old stillages. Local Ringwood ales as well as national brews are served. It is a real community pub, with a dartboard and Sky TV, and the open brick fireplaces are used in winter. Good food includes home-cooked beefsteak and ale pie, jumbo cod, and sirloin steak.
OPEN: 11-1 (Sun 12-10.30) **BAR MEALS:** L served all week 12-2.30 D served all week 6.30-9 Av main course £5.95
RESTAURANT: L served all week 12-2 D served all week 6.30 Av 3 course à la carte £12 **BREWERY/COMPANY:** Whitbread
◖: Weekly rotating guest ales. **FACILITIES:** Garden: beer garden, outdoor eating Dogs allowed Water **NOTES:** Parking 8
ROOMS: 2 bedrooms 2 en suite s£48 d£48 no children overnight **NOTES:** No credit cards

Mayflower Inn ♀
Kings Saltern Rd SO41 3QD ☎ 01590 672160 ▯ 01590 679180
e-mail: info@themayflower.uk.com
Dir: A337 towards New Milton, L at rdbt by White Hart, L to Rookes Ln, R at mini-rdbt, pub 0.75m
Solidly built mock-Tudor inn located by the water's edge with views of the Solent and Lymington River. It has recently undergone extensive refurbishment in a contemporary style and has a brand new restaurant. There is a bar snack menu with paninis, salads and popular main meals, and a dinner menu in the restaurant offering chicken and prawn laska, Thai ribbons of beef or fillets of sole meunière, plus a good vegetarian selection.
OPEN: 11-11 (Sun 12-10.30) **BAR MEALS:** L served all week 12-9.30 D served all week 6.30-9.30 Av main course £8
RESTAURANT: L served all week 12-9.30 D served all week 6.30-9.30 Av 3 course à la carte £15 **BREWERY/COMPANY:** Enterprise Inns ◖: Ringwood Best, Fuller's London Pride, Greene King Abbot Ale & Old Speckled Hen. **FACILITIES:** Children welcome Garden: Lrg lawns, decking area Dogs allowed Water, baskets
NOTES: Parking 30

LYNDHURST
Map 05 SU30

New Forest Inn ⌂ ♀
Emery Down SO43 7DY ☎ 02380 282329 ▯ 02380 283216
Delightfully situated in the scenic New Forest, this rambling inn lies on land claimed from the crown by use of squatters' rights in the early 18th-century. Ale was once sold from a caravan which now forms the front lounge porchway. Lovely summer garden and welcoming bars with open fires, and an extensive menu listing local game in season and plenty of fresh fish - whole Dover sole, fresh tuna, monkfish thermidor - alongside traditional pub meals.
OPEN: 11-11 **BAR MEALS:** L served all week 12-3 D served all week 6-9.30 Av main course £6.50 **RESTAURANT:** L served all week 11-10 D served all week 6-10 **BREWERY/COMPANY:** Enterprise Inns ◖: Ringwood Best, Fullers London Pride, Abbot Ale, Old Hooky. **FACILITIES:** Children welcome Garden: Food served outside Dogs allowed Water **NOTES:** Parking 20

The Oak Inn ⌂
Pinkney Ln, Bank SO43 7FE ☎ 02380 282350
Ponies graze outside this 18th-century New Forest inn, which was once a cider house. Inside are bay windows, antique pine, and a traditional woodburner. There is also a large collection of antique bric-a-brac, and a distinct lack of modern electronic intrusions. Idyllically set in this Heritage Area, and with a beer garden for summer use, it specialises in freshly-prepared food including Mexican chilli, chicken Kiev, spicy Thai fish cakes, and vegetable Wellington. Expect also seafood chowder, cod and chips, and moules steamed in onion and garlic. There are plenty of real ales on offer.
OPEN: 11.30-3 6-11.30 (all day Sat-Sun) **BAR MEALS:** L served all week 12-3 D served all week 6-9.30 Av main course £7.50
BREWERY/COMPANY: Free House ◖: Ringwood Best, Holdens Black Country, Interbrew Bass, Hop Back Summer Lightning.
FACILITIES: Children welcome Garden: Dogs allowed Water
NOTES: Parking 40

The Trusty Servant ⌂
Minstead SO43 7FY ☎ 02380 812137

Popular Victorian pub in the picturesque New Forest. An ideal watering hole for visitors to the New Forest, just a stone's throw from Sir Arthur Conan Doyle's grave at Minstead Church. The famous pub sign depicts a strange mythical beast and is a copy of a picture belonging to Winchester College. Menu choices include medallions of beef, Thai-spiced crab cakes, mushroom, apple, leek and cherry tomato Stroganoff, and a variety of ploughman's,

continued

England

LYNDHURST continued

jacket potatoes, omelettes, giant Yorkshire puddings, and pies.
OPEN: 11-11 (Sun 12-10.30) **BAR MEALS:** L served all week 12-2.30 D served all week 7-10 Av main course £6.50
RESTAURANT: L served all week 12-2.30 D served all week 7-10 Av 3 course à la carte £17.95 **BREWERY/COMPANY:** Enterprise Inns ☜: Ringwood Best, Fuller's London Pride, Wadworth 6X, Gale's HSB. **FACILITIES:** Children welcome Garden: Heated barn area seats 30, picnic benches Dogs allowed Water
NOTES: Parking 16

MAPLEDURWELL   Map 05 SU65

The Gamekeepers 🐾
Tunworth Rd RG25 2LU ☎ 01256 322038 🖹 01256 357831
e-mail: shaunnother@ad.com
Dir: 3m from J6 M3. Turn R at the Hatch pub on A30 towards Hook. Gamekeepers is signposted
Welcoming 19th-century pub with a well in the centre, located in a very rural spot. All food is made on the premises from fresh produce, and the extensive menu includes plenty to tempt the palate. Fish choices include escalope of salmon laced with smoked halibut and Philadelphia, seabass fillets on roast fennel, chickpeas and herbs, and lemon sole fillets with prawns. An interesting choice for meat-eaters is the World Wide Mixed Grill, which features ostrich, wild boar, kudu (African antelope), crocodile and kangaroo.
OPEN: 12-3 6-11 **BAR MEALS:** L served all week 12-2.30 D served all week 6.30-9.30 Av main course £11 **RESTAURANT:** L served all week 12-2.30 D served all week 6.30-9.30
BREWERY/COMPANY: Hall & Woodhouse ☜: Badger Best, Tanglefoot. **FACILITIES:** Garden Dogs allowed Water
NOTES: Parking 50

MATTINGLEY   Map 05 SU75

The Leather Bottle ♀
Reading Rd RG27 8JU ☎ 01189 326371 🖹 01189 326547
e-mail: leatherbottle.mattingley@eldridge-pope.co.uk
Dir: From M3 J5 follow signs for Hook then B3349
Established in 1714, the Leather Bottle is a wisteria-clad pub with heavy beams, huge open winter fires and a dining extension leading to a summer terrace. Standard extensive menu.
OPEN: 11-11 (Sun 12-10.30) **BAR MEALS:** L served all week 12-2.30 D served all week 6-9.30 Av main course £8
RESTAURANT: L served all week 12-2 D served all week 6.30-10 Av 3 course à la carte £13 **BREWERY/COMPANY:** Eldridge Pope ☜: Courage Best, Abbott Ale, Bombadier. ♀: 8
FACILITIES: Children welcome Garden: beer garden, patio, food served outdoors Dogs allowed **NOTES:** Parking 60

MEONSTOKE   Map 05 SU61

The Bucks Head
Bucks Head Hill SO32 3NA ☎ 01489 877313
Dir: by the jct of A32 & B2150
A beautiful 16th-century inn on the banks of the River Meon, popular with locals as well as visitors. Surrounded by fields and woodland, it is ideal walking country with Winchester Hill and the old Watercress railway line nearby. Two character bars with open fires, and a range of home-cooked meals including sausages and mash, pork

steak in blue cheese sauce, liver and bacon, and home-made pies.
OPEN: 11-3 6-11 (Summer-open all day) **BAR MEALS:** L served all week 12-2.15 D served Mon-Sat 7-9.15 Av main course £6.95
RESTAURANT: L served all week 12-2.15 D served all week 7-9.15
BREWERY/COMPANY: Greene King ☜: Old Speckled Hen, Ruddles County, IPA, Guest Beer (changes regularly).
FACILITIES: Children welcome Garden: Riverside garden on village green Dogs allowed Water provided **NOTES:** Parking 40

MICHELDEVER   Map 05 SU53

Half Moon & Spread Eagle 🐾 ♀
Winchester Rd SO21 3DG ☎ 01962 774339 🖹 01962 774834
e-mail: rayhalfmoon@aol.com
Dir: Take A33 from Winchester towards Basingstoke. After 5m turn L after petrol station. Pub 0.5m on R
Old drovers' inn located in the heart of a pretty thatched and timbered Hampshire village, overlooking the cricket green. The pub, comprising three neatly-furnished interconnecting rooms, has a real local feel and has reverted to its old name having been the Dever Arms for eight years. An extensive menu ranges through Sunday roasts, Moon burgers, honeyed salmon supreme with lime courgettes, fresh battered cod, and half shoulder of minted lamb.
OPEN: 12-3 6-11 (Sun 7-10.30) **BAR MEALS:** L served all week 12-2 D served all week 6-9 Av main course £10
RESTAURANT: L served all week 12-2 D served all week 6-9 Av 3 course à la carte £19 **BREWERY/COMPANY:** Greene King ☜: Greene King IPA Abbot Ale, XX Mild and guest ales. ♀: 7
FACILITIES: Children welcome Garden: Patio area, tables, chairs, grass area Dogs allowed Water provided **NOTES:** Parking 20

NORTH WALTHAM   Map 05 SU54

The Fox
RG25 2BE ☎ 01256 397288 🖹 01256 397288
e-mail: info@thefoxinn.co.uk
Dir: From M3 J7 take A30 towards Winchester. Village signposted on R

Built as three farm cottages in 1624, this peacefully-situated village pub enjoys splendid views across fields and farmland and has its own award-winning garden. A varied bar menu features basket meals, baguettes and jacket potatoes. In the restaurant, look out for a variety of exotic meats - crocodile, kangaroo, wild boar - as well as plenty of game and fish choices.
OPEN: 11-3 5.30-12 (all day w/end) **BAR MEALS:** L served all week 12-2.30 D served all week 6.30-10 Av main course £6.50
RESTAURANT: L served all week 12-2.30 D served all week 6.30-10
BREWERY/COMPANY: ☜: Scottish Courage Courage Best, Jennings Cumberland Ale, Greene King Old Speckled Hen.

continued

continued

FACILITIES: Children welcome Garden: Dogs allowed Water
NOTES: Parking 40

OLD BASING
Map 05 SU65

The Millstone ♀
Bartons Mill Ln RG24 8AE ☎ 01256 331153
Dir: From M3 J6 follow brown signs to Basing House
Enjoying a rural location beside the River Loddon, close to a
country park and Old Basing House, one of Hampshire's Civil
War ruins, this attractive old building is a popular lunchtime
spot for summer alfresco imbibing.Typical dishes might
include chilli con carne, salmon goujons, Thai sweet and sour
pork, cod and chips, lamb balti and a traditional Sunday roast.
Basket meals, vegetarian options, jacket potatoes and
baguettes also feature.
OPEN: 11.30 -11 (Sun 12-10.30) **BAR MEALS:** L served all week
12-2 D served all week 6.30-9.30 Av main course £5.35
BREWERY/COMPANY: Wadworth ◖: Wadworth 6X, Wadworth
JCB, Adnams Broadside & Henrys IPA. ♀: 9 **FACILITIES:** Children
welcome Garden: Patio and lawn area Dogs allowed
NOTES: Parking 50

OVINGTON
Map 05 SU53

The Bush ♀
SO24 0RE ☎ 01962 732764 📠 01962 735130
e-mail: thebushinn@wadworth.co.uk
*Dir: A31 from Winchester, E to Alton & Farnham, approx 6m turn L off dual
carriageway to Ovington. 0.5m to pub*
Tucked away down a lane on the Pilgrim's Way, this delightful
rose-covered pub must have been a pleasant distraction from
spiritual matters. Take a riverside stroll before relaxing over a
meal in the characterful bars, furnished with pews and
warmed by roaring fires in winter. Fresh home-cooked meals
could include lasagne, local trout fillets with hazlenut butter,
pan-fried duck breast, or beef and ale pie. Heavenly desserts.
OPEN: 11-3 6-11 (Sun 12-2 7-10.30) Closed: Dec 25
BAR MEALS: L served all week 12-2 D served Mon-Sat 6.30-9.30 Av
main course £11.95 **BREWERY/COMPANY:** Wadworth
◖: Wadworth 6X, IPA & Farmers Glory, Badger Tanglefoot, Red Shoot
Tom's Tipple. ♀: 12 **FACILITIES:** Children welcome Garden: Pretty,
alongside river Dogs allowed Water **NOTES:** Parking 40

OWSLEBURY
Map 05 SU52

The Ship Inn 🐾 ♀
Whites Hill SO21 1LT ☎ 01962 777358 📠 01962 777458
e-mail: theshipinn@freeuk.com
Dir: M3 J11 take B3335 follow signs for Owslebury
Wonderful views of the South Downs to the Solent can be
relished from the huge garden, while indoors a host of
activities from crib and dominoes to winter quizzes and
musical entertainments keeps everyone happy. The Ship
stands high on a chalk ridge and is an ideal starting or
finishing point for country walking. The traditional trimmings
of a 300-year-old inn - old ship's timbers and a large fire -
lend this place a pleasing atmosphere, and it is often very
busy, particularly in summertime; families can relax in the
garden with its animal corner and bouncy castle. Sample a
snack like toasted ciabatta or steak and Guinness pie, or enjoy
a leisurely meal in the bistro-style restaurant, with braised
lamb shank in red wine gravy, venison steak with cranberry
sauce, and fillet steak and sweet potato mash leading the
choices.

OPEN: 11-3 6-11 (Sun 12-10.30, Sat Apr-Sep 11-11) (Jul-Aug 11-11 all
week) **BAR MEALS:** L served all week 12-2 D served all week 6.30-
9.30 Av main course £9 **RESTAURANT:** L served all week 12-2
D served all week 6.30-9.30 **BREWERY/COMPANY:** Greene King
◖: Greene King IPA, Moorland Original, & Greene King Ruddles
County, Cheriton Pots Ale. ♀: 12 **FACILITIES:** Children welcome
Garden: Garden with pond, horse park Dogs allowed Water
NOTES: Parking 50

PETERSFIELD
Map 05 SU72

The Good Intent ◆◆◆◆ 🐾 ♀
40-46 College St GU31 4AF ☎ 01730 263838 📠 01730 302239
e-mail: pstuart@goodintent.freeserve.co.uk
Candlelit tables, open fires and well-kept ales characterise this
16th-century pub, and in summer, flower tubs and hanging
baskets festoon the front patio. Regular gourmet evenings are
held and in summer, live music on Sunday evenings. Sausages are
a speciality (up to 12 varieties) alongside a daily pie and the
likes of seafood chowder and Thai fish curry. As members of
the Campaign For Real Food they have well-established links
with the local junior school.
OPEN: 11-3 5.30-11 **BAR MEALS:** L served all week 12-2.30 D
served all week 6-9.30 Av main course £7.95
RESTAURANT: L served all week 12-2 D served all week 6-9.30
BREWERY/COMPANY: Gales ◖: Gale's HSB, GB, Buster.
FACILITIES: Children welcome Garden: Small patio with lots of
flowers Dogs allowed Water **NOTES:** Parking 10 **ROOMS:** 3
bedrooms 2 en suite

The Trooper Inn ◆◆◆◆ ♀
Alton Rd, Froxfield GU32 1BD ☎ 01730 827293 📠 01730 827103
e-mail: info@trooperinn.com
*Dir: From A3/A272 Winchester exit, towards Petersfield then left at the 1st
rndt towards Steep. Stay on this road for 3m and pub is on right.*

An upgraded roadside inn enjoying an isolated downland
position west of Petersfield, the Trooper is also known as 'The
Pub at the Top of the Hill'. There is a relaxed atmosphere
throughout the spacious, rustic, pine-furnished interior;

continued

continued

PETERSFIELD continued

evening candlelight enhancing the overall ambience. In addition to changing guest ales and decent wines by the glass, expect interesting home-cooked food. A selection of main courses may include Aberdeen Angus fillet steak, salmon, ricotta, spinach and prawn en croûte, pork loin stuffed with a peach half and thyme butter, or free-range supreme of chicken. Attractively decorated bedrooms.
OPEN: 12-3 6-12 Closed: Dec 25-26, Jan 1 **BAR MEALS:** L served all week 12-2 D served all week 7-9.30 **RESTAURANT:** L served all week 12-2 D served all week 7-9.30 **BREWERY/COMPANY:** Free House ◀: Ringwood Best, Fortyniner, Interbrew Bass, guest ales. **FACILITIES:** Children welcome Garden: Attractive gardens **NOTES:** Parking 30 **ROOMS:** 8 bedrooms 8 en suite s£59 d£79

The White Horse Inn
Priors Dean GU32 1DA ☎ 01420 588387 ▤ 01420 588387
Dir: A3/A272 to Winchester/Petersfield. In Petersfield L to Steep, 5m then R at small X-rds to E Tisted, 2nd drive on R
Also known as the 'Pub With No Name' as it has no sign, this splendid 17th-century farmhouse was originally used as a forge for passing coaches. The blacksmith sold beer to the travellers while their horses were attended to. Hearty pub grub includes ciabattas, fillet steaks and beer-battered fish. Special fresh fish dishes are available on Fridays and Saturdays.
OPEN: 11-2.30 6-11 (Sun 12-4.30, 7-10.30) **BAR MEALS:** L served all week 12-2.30 D served Mon-Sat 7-9.30 Av main course £6.50 **RESTAURANT:** L served all week 12-2.30 D served Mon-Sat 7-9.30 Av 3 course à la carte £20 **BREWERY/COMPANY:** Gales ◀: No Name Best, No Name Strong, Fullers London Pride, Bass. **FACILITIES:** Children welcome Garden Dogs allowed Water, dog biscuits **NOTES:** Parking 60

PILLEY   Map 05 SZ39

The Fleur de Lys ♀
Pilley St SO41 5QG ☎ 01590 672158
Arguably the oldest pub in the New Forest, tracing its origins back to 1096, is this traditional thatched pub with stone-flagged hallway, low beamed ceilings and open log fires. Fresh food is prepared daily using local suppliers, and results include Lolly's fish or steak, kidney and Guinness pies, pork hocks and half shoulders of lamb. Fish from the specials board and a variety of inspired dishes with oriental influences keep customers - and the kitchen - on their toes.
OPEN: 11-2.30 6-11 (Sun 12-3, 7-10.30) 25 Dec Closed eve **BAR MEALS:** L served all week 12-2 D served all week 6.30-9.30 Av main course £6.50 **RESTAURANT:** 12-2 6.30-9.30 **BREWERY/COMPANY:** ◀: Ringwood Best, plus guest ales. **FACILITIES:** Children welcome Garden: Food served outside Dogs allowed Water **NOTES:** Parking 18

PORTSMOUTH & SOUTHSEA   Map 05 SZ69

The Still & West ☜ ♀
2 Bath Square, Old Portsmouth PO1 2JL ☎ 023 92821567
Dir: Bath Square, top of Broad Street
Nautically-themed pub close to HMS Victory and enjoying excellent views of Portsmouth Harbour and the Isle of Wight. Built in 1504, the main bar ceilings are hand painted with pictures relating to local shipping history. Plenty of fish on the menu including trout, black beam, seabass on red cabbage and risotto, and the famous Still & West fish grill of fresh fish and mussels.

OPEN: 12-11 **BAR MEALS:** L served all week 12-3 Av main course £7 **RESTAURANT:** L served all week 12-2.30 D served all week 6-9 Av 3 course à la carte £17 **BREWERY/COMPANY:** Gales ◀: HSB, GB, Butsers. **FACILITIES:** Children welcome Garden: Food served outside. Overlooks harbour Dogs allowed In the garden only

The Wine Vaults ♀
43-47 Albert Rd, Southsea PO5 2SF
☎ 023 92864712 ▤ 023 92865544
e-mail: winevaults@freeuk.com
Originally several Victorian shops, now converted into a Victorian-style alehouse with wooden floors, panelled walls, and seating from old churches and schools. Partly due to the absence of a jukebox or fruit machine, the atmosphere here is relaxed and there is a good range of real ales and good-value food. A typical menu includes beef Stroganoff, Tuscan vegetable bean stew, grilled gammon steak, salads, sandwiches, and Mexican specialities. Look out for celebs appearing at the local theatre.
OPEN: 12-11 (12-10.30 Sun) Closed: 1 Jan **BAR MEALS:** L served all week 12-9.30 D served all week Av main course £6.75 **RESTAURANT:** L served all week 12-9.30 D served all week Av 3 course à la carte £15 **BREWERY/COMPANY:** Free House ◀: Hop Back Gilbert's First Brew & Summer Lightning, Scottish Courage Best, Fuller's London Pride. ♀: 20 **FACILITIES:** Children welcome Children's licence Garden: Patio area Dogs allowed

---

PRESTON CANDOVER   Map 05 SU64

The Crown at Axford ♀
near Preston Candover RG25 2DZ
☎ 01256 389694 ▤ 01256 389149
Dir: Telephone for directions
Small country inn set at the northern edge of the pretty Candover Valley. Now under new management after a recent refurbishment. A selection of real ales is the ideal accompaniment to chicken, leek and bacon pie, Thai-style sea bass, braised lamb shank, and Hunters chicken, plus blackboard specials, all cooked to order and eaten in the two bars or in the dining area. A large garden for the summer.
OPEN: 12-3 6-11 Apr-Oct (Sat 11-1) (Sun12-10.30) **BAR MEALS:** L served Mon-Sun 12-2.30 D served Mon-Sun 6.30-9.30 Av main course £9 **RESTAURANT:** L served Mon-Sun 12-2.30 D served Mon-Sun 6.30-9.30 **BREWERY/COMPANY:** Free House ◀: Fuller's London Pride, Triple FFF Moondance, Becketts Whitewater, Triple FFF Alton Pride. ♀: 7 **FACILITIES:** Children welcome Garden: Large Patio, Garden Dogs allowed Water **NOTES:** Parking 30

ROCKBOURNE   Map 05 SU11

Pick of the Pubs

The Rose & Thistle ☜ ♀
SP6 3NL ☎ 01725 518236
e-mail: enquiries@roseandthistle.co.uk
See Pick of the Pubs on opposite page

All AA rated accommodation can also be found on the AA's internet site
www.theAA.com

continued

OPEN: 11-3, 6-11
CLOSED: Sun evenings in winter
BAR MEALS: L served all week 12-2.30,
D served all week 6.30-9.30.
Av main course £10
RESTAURANT: L served all week 12-2.30,
D served all week 6.30-9.30.
Av cost 3 courses £15
BREWERY/COMPANY:
Free House.
🍺: Fuller's London Pride, Marston's
Pedigree, Adnams Broadside, Wadworth
6X, Hop Back Summer Lightning.
FACILITIES: Children welcome,
Children's licence, Garden
NOTES: Parking 28.

The Rose & Thistle

An idyllic pub consisting of two long and low whitewashed 16th-century cottages, converted nearly 200 years ago and still full of charming original features. With its stunning rose arch, beautiful flowers all around the door, and pretty downland village setting, it is indeed picture postcard material. Located at the top of a delightful street filled with thatched cottages and period houses, it is handily placed for visiting the New Forest, Salisbury and Breamore House.

Rockbourne, Fordingbridge, SP6 3NL
☎ 01725 518236
✉ enquiries@roseandthistle.co.uk
Dir: Rockbourne is signposted from B3078 and from A354

Inside there are some tasteful features to add to the unspoilt low-beamed bar and dining area. Country-house fabrics, floral arrangements and magazines bring a civilised touch along with polished oak tables and chairs, cushioned settles and carved benches. Open fires make it a warm and relaxing haven in cool weather, while the summer sun brings visitors into the neat front garden where they can soak up the warmth under smart umbrellas, and watch the doves in the quaint dovecot. For ten years now, landlord Tim Norfolk has maintained a tradition of serving fine fresh food, cooked to order, along with good ales and decent wines. Lunchtime sees a choice of light favourites - bacon and mushrooms on toast, Welsh rarebit with bacon and tomato, and coarse wild boar terrine with red onion marmalade.

More robust dishes also feature, like pork and apple casserole with a sage scone. In the evening a meal might start with smoked salmon and prawn cornets, and move on to roast rack of lamb, or pork fillet stuffed with pistachios and apricots. Blackboard specials supplement the choice, such as pan-fried whole John Dory stuffed with lime and coriander butter, and medallions of beef fillet with a Stilton and port sauce. Puddings to match, like steamed syrup sponge, and lemon tart.

ROMSEY
Map 05 SU32

The Dukes Head ♀
Greatbridge Rd SO51 0HB ☎ 01794 514450 📠 01794 518102
This rambling 400-year-old pub has recently changed hands.
Covered in flowers during the summer, it nestles in the Test
Valley just a stone's throw from the famous trout river, fish
from which is delivered daily. Dishes are freshly cooked to
order, typically fillet of Test trout served on red cabbage with
lime butter, chicken breast stuffed with Stilton cheese, and
roast rack of lamb with a honey and rosemary crust.
OPEN: 11-11 **BAR MEALS:** L served all week 12-3 D served all week 6-
9.30 Av main course £8.95 **RESTAURANT:** L served all week 12-3
D served all week 6-9.30 Av 3 course à la carte £21.95
BREWERY/COMPANY: Free House 🍺: Fuller's London Pride, Greene
King IPA, Wychwood Hobgoblin. **FACILITIES:** Children welcome
Garden: Lrg garden near river, approx 60 seats Dogs allowed
NOTES: Parking 50

The Mill Arms ♦♦♦♦ 🐑
Barley Hill, Dunbridge SO51 0LF
☎ 01794 340401 📠 01794 340401
e-mail: info@themillarms.co.uk

Eighteenth-century coaching inn with large garden situated in
a picturesque Test Valley village. The real ales - including Test
Tickler, brewed specifically for the pub - enhance its
popularity, as does the private fishing on the River Itchen.
Indeed, catch-of-the-day might well be Test trout with
horseradish pâté. Tempting, too, is steak and ale pie or beer-
battered cod and chips. Tasty puddings may include
marmalade bread and butter pudding, and cinnamon
pannacotta with pear compote.
OPEN: 12-3 6-11 **BAR MEALS:** L served all week 12-2.30 D served
all week 7-9.30 **RESTAURANT:** L served all week 12-2.30 D served
all week 7-9.30 **BREWERY/COMPANY:** Free House
🍺: Dunbridge Test Tickler, Mottisfont Meddler.
FACILITIES: Children welcome Garden: Lrg garden, patio area,
Wendy House Dogs allowed Water **NOTES:** Parking 90
ROOMS: 6 bedrooms 6 en suite d£50

ROWLAND'S CASTLE
Map 05 SU71

Castle Inn
1 Finchdean Rd PO9 6DA ☎ 023 92412494 📠 023 92412494
*Dir: N of Havant take B2149 to Rowlands Castle. Pass green, under rail
bridge, pub 1st on L opp Stansted Park*
Victorian building directly opposite Stansted Park, part of the
Forest of Bere. Richard the Lionheart supposedly hunted here,
and the house and grounds are open to the public for part of
the year. Traditional atmosphere with wooden floors and
fires in both bars. The garden has a children's area with a
swing.

OPEN: 11.30-3 5-11.30 (Winter 12-3, 5-11.30)
BAR MEALS: L served all week 12-2 D served Tue-Sat Av main
course £6.50 **RESTAURANT:** L served all week 12-2 D served Tue-
Sat 7-9 Av 3 course à la carte £13 **BREWERY/COMPANY:** Gales
🍺: Gales Butser, HSB & GB. **FACILITIES:** Garden: Grassed area
with benches Dogs allowed Water, chews **NOTES:** Parking 30

The Fountain Inn ♦♦♦♦
34 The Green PO9 6AB ☎ 023 9241 2291 📠 023 9241 2291
e-mail: fountaininn@amserve.com
Music is of huge importance here - not surprising for an inn
owned by Irish musician and songwriter Herbie Armstrong
(former band member of Van Morrison, Yellow Dog, Fox and
others). Expect the walls of this lovingly-refurbished Georgian
building to resound with live music at least four days a week.
Also of note is the Thai restaurant, whose menu offers an
extensive range of dishes from the chef's homeland. Pretty
countryside location opposite village green.
OPEN: 12-2.30 5-11 (Fri-Sun 12-11) **BAR MEALS:** L served Tue-
Sun, Sat-Sun (Winter) 12-4 D served Tue-Sat 6-10.30 Av main course
£6.50 **RESTAURANT:** L served Tue-Sun 12-4 D served Tue-Sat 6-
10.30 Av 3 course à la carte £10 🍺: Ruddles IPA.
FACILITIES: Children welcome Garden: Enclosed back garden, four
tables Dogs allowed **NOTES:** Parking 20 **ROOMS:** 4 bedrooms 4
en suite 1 family rooms s£25 d£50

ST MARY BOURNE
Map 05 SU45

The Bourne Valley Inn 🐑
SP11 6BT ☎ 01264 738361 📠 01264 738126
e-mail: bournevalleyinn@wessexinns.fsnet.co.uk
Situated in the picturesque rural community of St Mary Bourne,
this charming traditional inn is the ideal location for
conferences, exhibitions, weddings or other celebrations. The
riverside garden abounds with wildlife, and the children can
play safely in the special play area. Typical menu includes lamb
shank with pot-roasted vegetables and red wine sauce, chicken
Stroganoff, cauliflower and broccoli bake, poached salmon, and
sausage and mash.
OPEN: 11-11 **BAR MEALS:** L served all week 12-2.30 D served all
week 6.30-9.30 Av main course £8 **RESTAURANT:** L served all week 12-
2 D served all week 7-9.30 Av 3 course fixed price £16
BREWERY/COMPANY: Free House 🍺: Draught Bass, Flowers,
Brakspeare. **FACILITIES:** Children welcome Garden: Riverside, secluded
garden Dogs allowed Water & biscuits provided **NOTES:** Parking 50

The George Inn
SP11 6BG ☎ 01264 738340 📠 01264 738877
*Dir: M3 J8/A303, then A34 towards Newbury. Turn at Whitchurch & follow
signs for St Mary Bourne*

Listed village inn in the picturesque Tarrant valley, with a bar
full of cricket memorabilia, one dining room decorated with

continued

continued

regimental battle scenes, and another one with a mural of the River Test. New owners offer steak and Tanglefoot pie, fajitas, and local sausage and mash, served indoors or in the courtyard patio.
OPEN: 11-3 5-11 (Open all day Sat-Sun in Summer)
BAR MEALS: L served all week 12-2 D served all week 7-9.30 Av main course £8 **RESTAURANT:** L served all week 12-3.30 D served all week 7-9.30 **BREWERY/COMPANY:** Hall & Woodhouse
🍺: Badger Best & Tanglefoot. **FACILITIES:** Children welcome Garden: Patio, courtyard Dogs allowed Water bowl, biscuits
NOTES: Parking 40

SOUTHAMPTON   Map 05 SU41

The Cowherds ♀ NEW
The Common SO15 7NN
Dir: *From J13 on M3, follow signs for Southampton onto the A33. The Cowherds is on the right hand side of the avenue (A33) after 1.5 miles*
Located at the heart of Southampton Common, the Cowherds offers easy access to both countryside and city. It was once a popular haunt of cattle drovers en route to London - hence the name. Inside is a variety of charming traditional features, including open fires, oak beams, flagstone floors and wood panelling, with hops hanging from the ceiling. Try the ham hock with a creamy wholegrain mustard sauce, 8oz sirloin grilled to individual preference, or the pork, apple and Somerset cider sausages with Cheddar mash.
OPEN: 12 -11 (Sun 12-10.30) **RESTAURANT:** L served all week D served all week Av 3 course à la carte £16.70
BREWERY/COMPANY: Vintage Inns 🍺: Tetley Bitter, Cask Bass.
♀: 16 **FACILITIES:** Garden: Patio with floral displays
NOTES: Parking 60

The Jolly Sailor 🏠 ♀
Lands End Rd, Bursledon SO31 8DN
☎ 023 8040 5557 📠 023 8040 2050
e-mail: jollysailor@freshnet.co.uk

In a hard-to-top location overlooking the River Hamble marina in Bursledon. The exterior of this famous waterside local will be familiar to anyone who recalls Howard's Way, BBC TV's salty soap of the late Eighties. As we write, however, owners Hall & Woodhouse have permission for interior remodelling that some feel will destroy the pub's character and traditional feel. Menus include moules marinière, bouillabaisse, ploughman's and chunky bloomer sandwiches.
OPEN: 11-11 (Sun 12-10.30) Closed: 25 Dec **BAR MEALS:** L served all week 12-9.30 D served all week Av main course £8.95
RESTAURANT: L served all week 12 D served all week 9.30
BREWERY/COMPANY: Woodhouse Inns 🍺: Badger Best, Tanglefoot, King & Barnes Sussex, Fursty Ferret. ♀: 7
FACILITIES: Children welcome Children's licence Garden: Terrace & Jetty alongside River Hamble Dogs allowed Water

St Jacques Bar & Restaurant 🏠 ♀
Romsey Rd, Copythorne SO40 2PE
☎ 023 8081 2321 & 8081 2800 📠 023 8081 2158
Dir: *On A31 between Cadnam & Ower, south of M27 between junctions 1 & 2*
Once called The Old Well, this large pub and restaurant caters for visitors to the New Forest. Set in attractive surroundings, it offers comfortable seating and a wide choice of well-cooked food. Light bites might include sausages and mash, cottage pie, and ham with eggs and chips, while the restaurant carte offers braised oxtail in a red wine sauce, breast of duckling with orange sauce, and seabass with king scallops. The Sunday lunch attracts diners from far and wide.
OPEN: 11-3 5.30-11 (Sun 12-10.30) **BAR MEALS:** L served all week 12-2.15 D served all week 6-9 Av main course £9
RESTAURANT: L served all week 1-2.15 D served all week 6-9.30 Av 3 course à la carte £20.50 Av 2 course fixed price £10
BREWERY/COMPANY: Free House 🍺: Ringwood Best.
FACILITIES: Children welcome Children's licence Garden
NOTES: Parking 100

SPARSHOLT   Map 05 SU43

Pick of the Pubs

The Plough Inn 🏠 ♀
Main Rd SO21 2NW ☎ 01962 776353 📠 01962 776400
See Pick of the Pubs on page 238

STEEP   Map 05 SU72

Pick of the Pubs

Harrow Inn ♀
GU32 2DA ☎ 01730 262685
Dir: *Off A3 to A272, L through Sheet, take road opp church (school lane) then over A3 by-pass bridge*
A gem of a rustic pub, run by the McCutchen family since 1929, that is totally unspoilt and tucked away down a sleepy lane that was once the drovers' route from Liss to Petersfield. Today the tile-hung 500-year-old building is a popular watering hole with hikers following the Hanger's Way, who stop to enjoy the delightful cottage garden. The two character bars, each with scrubbed wooden tables, boarded walls and seasonal flower arrangements, are the perfect environment to relax over a decent pint of local ale. This was an opportunity to contemplate choices of smoked salmon sandwiches, ploughman's lunches and maybe Stilton and broccoli quiche, followed by treacle tart or chocolate nut biscuits, all cooked in the long-serving Rayburn. Little has changed over the years - and why should it? A true survivor, the Harrow remains, as ever, resistant to change.
OPEN: 12-2.30 6-11 (Sat 11-3, 6-11, Sun 12-3, 7-10.30) Closed: Dec 25 evening **BAR MEALS:** L served all week 12-2 D served all week 7-9 Av main course £7 **BREWERY/COMPANY:** Free House 🍺: Ringwood Best, Cheriton Diggers Gold & Pots Ale, Ballards Best. **FACILITIES:** Garden: Wild cottage garden Dogs allowed Water **NOTES:** Parking 15

🐟 **Pubs offering a good choice of fish on their menu**

Open: 11-3, 6-11 (Sun 12-3, 6-10.30)
Bar Meals: L served all week 12-2,
D served all week 6-9.
RESTAURANT: L served all week 12-2,
D served all week 6-9.
BREWERY/COMPANY: WADWORTH
🍺: Wadworth Henry's IPA, 6X, Farmers
Glory & Old Timer.
FACILITIES: Dogs allowed,
Children welcome, Garden - Patio,
lawn, play area.
NOTES: Parking 90

The Plough Inn

Sparsholt, home of a well-known agricultural college, is just two
miles outside Winchester. The Plough is believed to have started life
about 200 years ago as a coach house for Sparsholt Manor on the
other side of the road, although only 50 years later it appears to
have become an alehouse.

🐑 ♀

Main Road, Sparsholt,
nr Winchester, SO21 2NW
☎ 01962 776353 🖹 01962 776400
Dir: From Winchester take
B3049(A272) W, take L turn to village
of Sparsholt. The Plough Inn is 1m
down the lane.

From the outside, it's easy to
tell that it has been greatly
extended but, once inside, the
main bar and dining areas - the
two in the original house are
cosily intimate - blend together
very well. Farmhouse-style pine
tables, a mix of wooden and
upholstered seats, clusters of
agricultural implements, stone
jars, wooden wine box end-
panels and garlands of dried
hops, all help to further
encourage this sense of
harmony. Real ales come from
Wadworth's and there's a decent
wine selection too. From the
dining tables to the left of the
entrance the views extend
across open fields to wooded
downland. It's at this end you'll
find a blackboard menu
offering lighter dishes, such as
peppered tomato and olive
pasta, tossed salad with strips of
beef fillet and oriental dressing,
salmon and smoked haddock
lasagne, and courgette, tomato
and chickpea pancake glazed
with cheese. The other board,
at the right-hand end of the
bar, offers meals that could be
regarded as a touch more
serious - maybe pan-fried
marlin with a gâteau of
vegetables and herb oil; sautéed
lamb's liver and bacon with
mash and onion gravy; or
teriyaki chicken breast with
mango on a sweet pepper stir
fry. Lunchtime regulars are
familiar with both the
'doorstep' sandwiches and the
locally made speciality sausages.
Puddings include fruit
crumbles, or British cheeses as a
popular alternative. Lunchtimes
can get very busy, and booking
is definitely advised for the
evenings. The car park is
generously proportioned, and
there's a delightful garden
overlooking fields.

STOCKBRIDGE

Map 05 SU33

Mayfly ♀
Testcombe SO20 6AZ ☎ 01264 860283
Dir: Between A303 & A30, on A3057

One of the county's most famous riverside pubs, this former farmhouse evolved into a watering hole in the early 1900s. It is a wonderful location for a summertime pint and lunch in the delightful garden beside the River Test. Winchester, Stockbridge and Romsey are within easy reach, and for walkers the long-distance Test Way runs close by. Up to 40 cheeses and a selection of hot and cold meats, quiches and pies are laid out buffet-style along with a few hot daily specials. Try the smoked River Test trout from a local smokery.
OPEN: 10-11 **BAR MEALS:** L served all week 11.30-9 D served all week Av main course £7.95
BREWERY/COMPANY: Enterprise Inns ◀: Wadworth 6X, Interbrew Flowers Original, Ringwood Best and Guest Beers.
♀: 20 **FACILITIES:** Children welcome Garden: Riverside Garden Dogs allowed **NOTES:** Parking 48

The Peat Spade ◎ ♀
Longstock SO20 6DR ☎ 01264 810612
e-mail: peat.spade@virgin.net
Dir: Telephone for directions
Tucked away in the Test Valley close to Hampshire's finest chalk stream is this red-brick and gabled Victorian pub with unusual paned windows. It offers an informal atmosphere in which to enjoy a decent pint of Hampshire ale and a satisfying meal chosen from the short, daily-changing blackboard menu. Orkney herring fillets in light mustard marinade may precede fish bourride of salmon, escalor and mussels, and rich chocolate roulade, with good use of local organic produce.
OPEN: 11.30-3 6.30-11 Closed: Dec 25-26 & 31Dec-1 Jan
BAR MEALS: L served Tue-Sun 12-2.30 D served Tue-Sun 7-9.30 Av main course £10.50 **RESTAURANT:** L served Tue-Sun 12-2 D served Tue-Sun 7-9.30 **BREWERY/COMPANY:** Free House ◀: Ringwood Best, Ringwood 49er & guest ales. **FACILITIES:** Children welcome Garden: Raised terrace, teak seating, lawn area Dogs allowed on a lead **NOTES:** Parking 22 No credit cards

STRATFIELD TURGIS

Map 05 SU65

The Wellington Arms ★★★ ♀
RG27 0AS ☎ 01256 882214 ▤ 01256 882934
e-mail: wellington.arms@virgin.net
Dir: On A33 between Basingstoke & Reading
Standing at an entrance to the ancestral home of the Duke of Wellington, this 17th-century former farmhouse is now an impressive hotel with some period bedrooms in the original building. A good range of snacks, sandwiches, omelettes, pastas, ploughman's and salads is available in the bar along

with main courses such as pan-fried cod fillet on aubergine mash, Chinese-style duck stir-fry, and blue cheese and leek tart with salad. A changing carte is offered in the restaurant.
OPEN: 11-11 (Sun 12-10.30) Restricted opening at Xmas
BAR MEALS: L served all week 12-2.30 D served all week 6-10 Av main course £15 **RESTAURANT:** L served Sun-Fri 12-2 D served Mon-Sat 6.30-9.30 Av 3 course à la carte £25
BREWERY/COMPANY: Woodhouse Inns ◀: Badger Best Bitter & Tanglefoot. **FACILITIES:** Children welcome Garden Dogs allowed **NOTES:** Parking 60 **ROOMS:** 30 bedrooms 30 en suite 2 family rooms s£65 d£75

TANGLEY

Map 05 SU35

The Fox Inn ♀
SP11 0RY ☎ 01264 730276 ▤ 01264 730478
e-mail: foxinn@wessexinns.fsworld.co.uk
Dir: 4m N of Andover
The 300-year-old brick and flint cottage that has been the Fox since 1830 stands on a small crossroads, miles, it seems, from anywhere. The blackboard menu offers reliably good lunchtime snacks and imaginative evening dishes. In the tiny, friendly bar, choose from steak and kidney pie, moussaka, or chicken tikka. In the unpretentious restaurant, look for fresh crab cakes, salmon en croûte, monkfish, or tenderloin of pork in Calvados.
OPEN: 12-3 6-11 **BAR MEALS:** L served all week 12-2 D served all week 6-9 Av main course £8.95 **RESTAURANT:** L served all week 12-2 D served all week 6-9
BREWERY/COMPANY: ◀: Flowers IPA, Fullers London Pride, Bass, Adnams. ♀: 12 **FACILITIES:** Children welcome Dogs allowed Water provided **NOTES:** Parking 50

TICHBORNE

Map 05 SU53

The Tichborne Arms ♀
SO24 0NA ☎ 01962 733760 ▤ 01962 733760
e-mail: kjjday@btinternet.com
Dir: off A31 towards Alresford, after 200yds R at sign for Tichborne

A heavily-thatched freehouse in the heart of the Itchen Valley, dating from 1423 but destroyed by fire and rebuilt three times; the present red-brick building was erected in 1939. An interesting history is attached to this idyllic rural hamlet, which was dramatised in the feature film The Tichborne Claimant. The pub displays much memorabilia connected with the film's subject, the impersonation and unsuccessful claim to the title and estates of Tichborne. Real ales straight from the cask are served in the comfortable atmospheric bars, and all food is home made. Traditional

continued

continued

TICHBORNE continued

choices range from steak, ale and Stilton pie, crab salad, mushroom crumble, chicken, tarragon and mushroom pie, and fish pie to toasted sandwiches and filled jacket potatoes. Expect hearty old-fashioned puddings. A large, well-stocked garden is ideal for summer eating and drinking.
OPEN: 11.30-2.30 6-11 25-26 Dec, 1 Jan Closed eve
BAR MEALS: L served all week 12-1.45 D served all week 6.30-9.45 Av main course £8 **BREWERY/COMPANY:** Free House **◖:** Ringwood Best, Wadworth 6X, Otter Ale, Several Guest Beers. **♀:** 12 **FACILITIES:** Garden: Large country garden seats around 70 Dogs allowed Water, biscuit **NOTES:** Parking 30

UPPER FROYLE   Map 05 SU74

The Hen & Chicken Inn ♀
GU34 4JH **☎** 01420 22115 **▤** 01420 23021
Dir: 6m from Farnham on A31 on R

Situated on the old Winchester to Canterbury road, this 16th-century inn was once the haunt of highwaymen. It retains its traditional atmosphere with large open fires, panelling and beams.
OPEN: 11-11 (Sun 12-10.30) **BAR MEALS:** L served all week 12 D served all week 9.30 Av main course £9 **RESTAURANT:** L served all week 12 D served all week 9 Av 3 course à la carte £25
BREWERY/COMPANY: Hall & Woodhouse **◖:** Badger Best, IPA, Tanglefoot, King & Barnes Sussex Ale. **♀:** 8 **FACILITIES:** Children welcome Garden: large, Food served outside Dogs allowed none **NOTES:** Parking 36

WARSASH   Map 05 SU40

The Jolly Farmer Country Inn 🐑 ♀
29 Fleet End Rd SO31 9JH **☎** 01489 572500 **▤** 01489 885847
Dir: Exit M27 Juct 9, head towards A27 Fareham, turn R onto Warsash Rd Follow for 2m then L onto Fleet End Rd
An abundance of hanging baskets decorate the outside of this white-painted pub, with its distinctive multi-coloured classic car parked on the forecourt. The bars are furnished in rustic style with farming equipment on walls and ceilings, and there's also a patio for al fresco eating. An interesting menu ranges through fresh salads and grills to specialities like chargrilled chicken breast; baked salmon fillet; or duck in port and red wine.
OPEN: 11-11 **BAR MEALS:** L served all week 12-2.30 D served all week 6-10 Av main course £9.95 **RESTAURANT:** L served all week 12-2.30 D served all week 6-10 **BREWERY/COMPANY:** Whitbread **◖:** Gale's HSB, Fuller's London Pride, Interbrew Flowers IPA. **FACILITIES:** Children welcome Garden: Lrg play area Dogs allowed Water **NOTES:** Parking 50

WELL   Map 05 SU74

The Chequers Inn
RG29 1TL **☎** 01256 862605 **▤** 01256 862133
e-mail: chequers.odiham.wi@freshnet.uk.com
Dir: from Odiham High St turn R into Long Lane, follow for 3m, L at T jct, pub 0.25m on top of hill

A charming, old-world 17th-century pub with a rustic, low-beamed bar, replete with log fire, scrubbed tables, and vine-covered front terrace, set deep in the heart of the Hampshire countryside. Choose from a menu including spinach and Feta cheese parcel, spicy Thai chicken, duck breast topped with red wine and plum sauce, Cumberland sausage wheel, grilled cod, or trout stuffed with Feta cheese and apricots.
OPEN: 11-3 6-11 (Sat 11-11, Sun 12-10.30) **BAR MEALS:** L served all week 12-2.30 D served all week 6-9.30 Av main course £9 **RESTAURANT:** L served all week 12-2.30 D served all week 6-10 Av 3 course à la carte £15 **BREWERY/COMPANY:** Hall & Woodhouse **◖:** Gribble Inn Fursty Ferret, Badger Tanglefoot & Best. **FACILITIES:** Children welcome Garden: Food served outside Dogs allowed **NOTES:** Parking 30

WHERWELL   Map 05 SU34

The White Lion 🐑 ♀
Fullerton Rd SP11 7JF **☎** 01264 860317 **▤** 01264 860317
Dir: Off A303 onto B3048, pub on B3420
Former coaching inn at the centre of one of Hampshire's most unspoilt villages, just a few minutes' walk from the River Test. The inn came under fire during the Civil War, when one of Oliver Cromwell's cannon balls reputedly dropped down the chimney. A lengthy daily specials menu lists the likes of smoked haddock and prawn bake, liver and bacon, roast duck with black cherry sauce, and minted lamb casserole; several light snacks.
OPEN: Times vary, phone for details. **BAR MEALS:** L served all week 12-2 D served all week 7-9.30 Av main course £7.50 **RESTAURANT:** L served all week 12-2 D served all week 7-9.30 **BREWERY/COMPANY:** Pubmaster **◖:** Interbrew Flowers Original, Adnams Bitter, Ringwood Best Bitter, Tetley Smooth Flow. **♀:** 7 **FACILITIES:** Garden: Enclosed courtyard seating for 50 Plus Dogs allowed **NOTES:** Parking 40

WHITCHURCH   Map 05 SU44

Pick of the Pubs

The Red House Inn ◎ 🐑 ♀
21 London St RG28 7LH **☎** 01256 895558
Dir: From M3 or M4 take A34 to Whitchurch
A busy 16th-century coaching inn with quaint flagstones and gnarled beams, set in the centre of a small

continued

Hampshire town, and only a short walk from southern England's only working silk mill. The Red House is counted among the fraternity of chef-owned free houses, where diners can expect to find first-rate, fresh local produce cooked in an imaginative modern guise. There are two bars, one very much a locals' bar and the other, with its stripped pine floor, large mirror and old fireplace is for eating. Specials on any one day might be fresh scallops with bacon and egg, or spinach salad, while the fixed-price menu might run to smoked salmon and goats' cheese rillettes on garlic croûton, teriyaki duck breast with tabouleh salad and special plum sauce, roast fillet of brill with Feta and artichoke ravioli and crab hollandaise, and double chocolate pie with butterscotch sauce and mint cream.
OPEN: 11.30-2.30 6-11 (Sun 12-3, 7-10.30) **BAR MEALS:** L served all week 12-2 D served all week 6.30-9.30 Av main course £10.95 **RESTAURANT:** L served all week 12-2 D served all week 6.30-9.30 Av 3 course à la carte £25
BREWERY/COMPANY: Free House ◖: Cheriton Diggers Gold & Pots Ale, Itchen Valley Fagins, Hop Back Summer Lightning.
FACILITIES: Children welcome Garden: Large, 25 seat patio Dogs allowed **NOTES:** Parking 25

Watership Down Inn
Freefolk Priors RG28 7NJ ☎ 01256 892254
Dir: On B3400 between Basingstoke & Andover
Enjoy an exhilarating walk on Watership Down itself before relaxing with a welcome pint at this homely 19th-century inn named after Richard Adams' classic tale of rabbit life. A popular beer garden, a conservatory and plenty of character are among the attractions, and the pub is renowned for its eclectic choice of beers. The same menu is offered throughout, including seafood platter, sausage and mash, ham, egg and chips and T-bone steak.
OPEN: 11.30-3.30 6-11 Closed: Dec 25-26 & 31 evening
BAR MEALS: L served all week 12-2.30 D served all week 6-9.30 Av main course £5.50 **BREWERY/COMPANY:** Free House
◖: Brakspear Bitter, Butts Barbus Barbus, Triple FFF Pressed Rat & Warthog, Hogs Back TEA. **FACILITIES:** Children welcome Garden: Beer garden, food served outdoors, patio **NOTES:** Parking 18

WHITSBURY
Map 05 SU11

The Cartwheel Inn ♀
Whitsbury Rd SP6 3PZ ☎ 01725 518362 ▤ 01725 518886
e-mail: thecartwheelinn@lineone.net
Dir: Off A338 between Salisbury & Fordingbridge
Handy for exploring the New Forest, visiting Breamore House and discovering the remote Mizmaze on the nearby downs, this extended, turn-of-the-century one-time wheelwright's and shop has been a pub since the 1920s. Venue for a beer festival held annually in August, with spit-roast pigs, barbecues, Morris dancing and a range of 30 real ales. Popular choice of well-kept beers in the bar too. Home-made food on daily specials boards - steak and kidney pudding, fisherman's pie and chicken curry. Like their postcard says: "Off the beaten track, but never in a rut!"
OPEN: 11-2.30 6-11 No food Mon pm (Oct-Apr)
BAR MEALS: L served all week 12-2 D served all week 7-9.30 Av main course £6.50 **RESTAURANT:** L served all week 12-2 D served all week 7-9.30 **BREWERY/COMPANY:** Free House ◖: Adnams Broadside, Ringwood Best, Smiles, Hop Back Summer Lightning.
♀: 12 **FACILITIES:** Children welcome Garden: Lawn, rockery borders Dogs allowed Water **NOTES:** Parking 25

WICKHAM
Map 05 SU51

Greens Restaurant & Pub NEW
The Square PO17 5JQ ☎ 01329 833197
e-mail: DuckworthGreens@aol.com
This mock-Tudor building - was it always a pub? - stands on a corner of Wickham's picturesque, though somewhat elongated square. It has been Greens since 1985, but following recent alterations the two-tier restaurant is now airier and more welcoming. Hands-on husband and wife team Frank and Carol Duckworth are sticklers for using the freshest ingredients for everything, including time-honoured pub favourites and specials, such as gammon steak and ale pie, and mussels. At lunchtime, try grilled goats' cheese and bacon salad.
OPEN: 11-3 6-11 (Summer Sun all day) Closed: Mon
BREWERY/COMPANY: Free House ◖: Fullers London Pride, Hop Back Summer Lighning, Bass **NOTES:** No credit cards

WINCHESTER
Map 05 SU42

The Westgate Hotel ♦♦♦♦ NEW
2 Romsey Rd SO23 8TP ☎ 01962 820222 ▤ 01962 820222

The hotel stands at the top end of Winchester's main shopping street, opposite the medieval West Gate and historic Great Hall. The popular bar serves home-cooked meals and snacks featuring fresh local ingredients, and there's live jazz on Monday evenings. Expect speciality sandwiches, jacket potatoes and salads at lunchtime. In the evening, typical dishes include Hampshire pork and pigeon terrine; salmon steak in lime and coriander; and wild mushroom and pine nut tortillas.
OPEN: 11-11 **BAR MEALS:** L served all week 12-2.30 D served Tue-Sun 6.30-9.30 Av main course £8.50 **RESTAURANT:** L served all week 12.00-2.30 D served Tue-Sun 6.30-9.30 Av 3 course à la carte £16 **BREWERY/COMPANY:** Eldridge Pope ◖: Interbrew Flowers & Bass, Ansells. **ROOMS:** 8 bedrooms 6 en suite d£65 no children overnight

Pick of the Pubs

Wykeham Arms ♦♦♦♦ ◉ ♀
75 Kingsgate St SO23 9PE ☎ 01962 853834 ▤ 01962 854411
Dir: Near Winchester College & Winchester Cathedral
Diligence pays off when seeking the 'Wyk' in Winchester's old back streets. When, at last, you open the curved, glazed doors into this historic pub's main bar you enter not just a local, but an institution. Its two bars are nearly always full of people talking, laughing and warming their behinds on the open fires. Photographs, paintings and ephemera fill most vertical surfaces, and a walking stick collection hangs from a ceiling. Recycled Winchester College desks, set inkwell to inkwell, allow lovers to gaze at one another. Willie Whitelaw carved 'Manners Makyth

continued

England

WINCHESTER continued

Man' on one. Both bars lead to small, intimate dining areas. The food is very good: exemplars from a daily menu are sautéed chicken breast on a chorizo, wild mushroom and mixed bean cassoulet with fresh asparagus, and grilled sea bass, new potatoes and baby corn on seafood chowder. Wyk cottage pie is a lunchtime favourite. Some 80 wines, with up to 20 by the glass. Spacious bedrooms upstairs and over the road.

OPEN: 11-11 (Sun 12-10.30) Closed: 25 Dec
BAR MEALS: L served Mon-Sat 12-2.30 D served Mon-Sat 6.30-8.45 **RESTAURANT:** L served all week 12-2.30 D served Mon-Sat 6.30-8.45 Av 3 course à la carte £22.50
BREWERY/COMPANY: Gales ◀: Interbrew Bass, Gales Butser Bitter, Special, HSB. ☷: 18 **FACILITIES:** Garden: Small walled garden 12 tables, seats 55 Dogs allowed
NOTES: Parking 12 **ROOMS:** 14 bedrooms 14 en suite s£50 d£90 no children overnight

---

WOODLANDS   Map 05 SU31

The Game Keeper
268 Woodlands Rd SO40 7GH ☎ 023 80293093
e-mail: mfa@thegamekeeper.fsworld.co.uk
Dir: *M27 J2 follow signs for Fawley(A326). At 1st rndbt after the Safeway rndbt turn R, then next L. 1m on L*
Backing onto open fields on the very edge of the New Forest, this 150-year-old extended cottage is the perfect resting place after a long forest walk. Comfortable modernised interior and traditional pub food.

OPEN: 11-11 **BAR MEALS:** L served all week 12-2.30 D served all week 6.30-9 Av main course £5.50 **RESTAURANT:** 12-2 D served all week 6.30-9.30 **BREWERY/COMPANY:** Wadworth ◀: Wadworth 6X, IPA, JCB & Guest. **FACILITIES:** Children welcome Garden: patio Dogs allowed **NOTES:** Parking 40

HEREFORDSHIRE

AYMESTREY   Map 09 SO46

Pick of the Pubs

Riverside Inn & Restaurant 🐾 ☷
HR6 9ST ☎ 01568 708440 📠 01568 709058
e-mail: richard.gresko@btinternet.com
Dir: *On A4110 between Hereford & Knighton*

An attractive black and white Welsh longhouse, dating from 1580, the inn is set on the banks of the River Lugg in the heart of the Welsh Marches. Its location halfway along

the Mortimer Way is great for walkers, while anglers will enjoy the mile of private trout and grayling fishing. The interior, with its low beams and log fires, provides a relaxing atmosphere reflecting 400 years of hospitality. The inn has a serious approach to food, and wherever possible locally-grown produce is used, including vegetables, salads and herbs from the garden. Specialities of the house include roast breast of duck with a sage and white wine sauce served on a bed of spiced pears, or roast saddle of rabbit with a sharp mustard and red wine jus on a bed of braised cabbage.

OPEN: 11-3 6-11 Open All day in summer Closed: Dec 25
BAR MEALS: L served all week 12-2 D served all week 7-9 Av main course £13.25 **RESTAURANT:** L served all week 12-2 D served all week 7-9 Av 3 course à la carte £23.50
BREWERY/COMPANY: Free House ◀: Wye Valley Seasonal, Black Sheep, Wood Seasonal. ☷: 7 **FACILITIES:** Children welcome Garden: Terraced. Overlooks river Dogs allowed Water, Food Bowls **NOTES:** Parking 40 **ROOMS:** 5 bedrooms 5 en suite 3 family rooms s£45 d£65 (♦♦♦♦)

BODENHAM   Map 10 SO55

England's Gate Inn
HR1 3HU ☎ 01568 797286 📠 01568 797768

A pretty black and white coaching inn dating from around 1540, with atmospheric beamed bars and blazing log fires in winter. A picturesque garden attracts a good summer following, and so does the food. Chef's specials like mixed grill, and pan-fried loin of pork steak glazed in red Leicester and herbs might be offered along with steak and ale pie, breast of duck in a port and redcurrant jus, and baked fillet of cod.

OPEN: 11-11 (Sunday 12-10.30) **BAR MEALS:** L served all week 12-2.30 D served Mon-Sat 6-9.30 Av main course £9
RESTAURANT: L served all week 12-2.30 D served Mon-Sat 6-9.30 Av 3 course à la carte £15 **BREWERY/COMPANY:** Free House ◀: Marston's Pedigree, Wye Valley Bitter & Butty Bach.
FACILITIES: Children welcome Garden: Large sunken garden with large patio area Dogs allowed Water **NOTES:** Parking 100

> Most of the pubs in this guide book pride themselves on the quality of their food. This may take a little time to prepare.

continued

Saracens Head Inn

The Forest of Dean and the glorious Wye Valley are renowned for their natural beauty, breathtaking views and miles of winding woodland trails just waiting to be discovered. Many writers and poets, including Wordsworth, have been inspired by the region's distinctive charm and magic and today it is a Mecca for outdoor enthusiasts.

★★
SARACENS HEAD INN,
SYMONDS YAT, HR9 6JL
☎ 01600 890435
On the banks of the River Wye beside an ancient ferry. Plenty of good home-baked food to choose from.
Open: 11-11 (Sun 12-10.30)
(Weekends only Dec-mid Feb)
Bar Meals: 12-2.30 7-9.15
Notes: Children & dogs welcome.
Garden - 2 riverside terraces.
(See page 251 for full entry)

Walking is one of the main pursuits here and this scenic linear route is one of the most popular in the area. When the walk is finished, return to the Saracens Head Inn via the local ferry service which operates on the Wye between mid February and the end of November. There is a small charge.

From the inn turn left and head south with the River Wye on your right. Keep on the lane and pass through the Royal Hotel car park - formerly the local railway station. Take the old railway track at the far end of the car park and soon you reach the Wye rapids on your right - a popular playground for canoeists and kayakers.

Take the lower track here and continue with the Forest of Dean on your left and the River Wye on your right. After about 1 1/2 miles/2.4km you come to Biblins Bridge, a wire suspension footbridge spanning the Wye. On your left here is the Lady Park Wood Nature Reserve. Cross the bridge and turn right, reaching Biblins Youth Campsite.

Continue north, passing a little waterfall on your left, as well as some toilets. Pass the canoe launch point at the edge of the campsite, with some small cliffs on your left and the river on your right. The track narrows here. With the roar of the rapids audible, take the lower track or remain on the same track. The former climbs some steps, the latter passes Woodlea Hotel before both reach a lane. Turn right here and the ferry across the Wye will be found on the right, a few yards/m down the lane. Use it to return to the inn.

DISTANCE: 3 miles/4.8km
MAP: Explorer OL 14
TERRAIN: Scenic Wye valley
PATHS: Riverside and disused railway tracks
GRADIENT: Level ground by the River Wye

Walk submitted and checked by the Saracens Head Inn

CANON PYON
Map 09 SO44

The Nags Head Inn
HR4 8NY ☎ 01432 830252
Dir: *Telephone for directions*

Flagstone floors, open fires and exposed beams feature in this 400-year-old pub, which is now a listed building. Six bedrooms are housed in an adjacent former brewery, while the large garden features a children's adventure playground. Food choices range from filled baguettes and baked potatoes to grilled steaks, fish dishes such as prawn-stuffed breaded plaice, and vegetarian options like wild mushroom parcel. Chicken breast with apricots, beef Stroganoff, and breast of Gressingham duck are also popular.

OPEN: 11-2.30 6-11 **BAR MEALS:** L served Tue-Sun 12-2.30 D served all week 6.30-9.30 Av main course £5.50 **RESTAURANT:** L served Tue-Sun 12-2.30 D served all week 6.30-9.30 Av 3 course à la carte £15 Av 2 course fixed price £4.95 **BREWERY/COMPANY:** Free House ◖: Wadworth 6X, Fuller's London Pride.
FACILITIES: Children welcome Garden: Beer garden, patio, table seating for 60 **NOTES:** Parking 50 **ROOMS:** 6 bedrooms 6 en suite 1 family rooms s£35 d£45 (◆◆◆)

CAREY
Map 10 SO53

Cottage of Content ♀
HR2 6NG ☎ 01432 840242
Dir: *From A40 W of Ross-on-Wye take A49 towards Hereford. Follow signs for Hoarwithy, then Carey*

Originally three cottages, the Cottage of Content is a charming Wye Valley inn, dating from 1485, in an attractive rural setting by a stream. Typical daily specials include tempura-battered hake with lettuce and sweet soy dressing, and chicken breast with a mango, coconut and chilli sauce. Vegetarian dishes are always available, such as Brie, potato, courgette and almond crumble.

OPEN: 12-2.30 7-11 Closed: 25 Dec **BAR MEALS:** L served all week 12-2 D served all week 7-9.30 Av main course £12 **RESTAURANT:** L served all week 12-2 D served all week 7-9.30 Av 3 course à la carte £17 **BREWERY/COMPANY:** Free House ◖: Hook Norton, Wye Valley. ♀: 10 **FACILITIES:** Children welcome Garden Dogs allowed **NOTES:** Parking 30

CRASWALL
Map 09 SO23

Bulls Head
HR2 0PN ☎ 01981 510616 ▤ 01981 510383
e-mail: bullshead@tesco.net

In the heart of some great walking country, this isolated 200 year-old drover's inn offers rough camping. The traditional atmosphere has been retained with flagstone floors, a farmhouse range and butler sink. Local ingredients drive the

menu: try the huge home-baked wholemeal sandwiches, Craswall pie, or Ledbury lamb chops. Lots of authentic curries, plus vegetarian options, and sticky puddings, too.

OPEN: 11-3 6-11 Closed: Sun eve **BAR MEALS:** L served all week 12-3 D served all week 6-9.30 Av main course £9 **RESTAURANT:** L served all week 11 D served all week 11
BREWERY/COMPANY: Free House ◖: Wye Valley Butty Bach.
FACILITIES: Garden: Large rustic with views to the Black Hill Dogs allowed **NOTES:** Parking 6

DORMINGTON
Map 10 SO54

Yew Tree Inn
Len Gee's Restaurant, Priors Frome HR1 4EH
☎ 01432 850467 ▤ 01432 850467
e-mail: len_gee@hotmail.com
Dir: *A438 Hereford to Ledbury, turn at Dormington towards Mordiford, 1/2 mile on L.*

Len Gee uses only the finest ingredients in his dining pub: local game and vegetables, butcher's meats plus an extensive selection of fresh fish. His weekend carvery is arguably the best for miles around. Imaginative bar snacks include smoked wild boar with raspberry vinaigrette, and main dishes such as seafood penne pasta, sirloin steak with Stilton sauce, and whole sole with caper butter. Leave room for the wild greengage ice cream. Panoramic views over the Lugg and Wye valleys toward Hereford and the Black Mountains from the terrace.

OPEN: 12-2 7-11 (Closed Tue Jan-Mar) **BAR MEALS:** L served all week 12-2 D served all week 7-9 Av main course £8.50 **RESTAURANT:** L served all week 12-2 D served all week 7-9 Av 3 course à la carte £18 Av 3 course fixed price £12.50
BREWERY/COMPANY: Free House ◖: Carlsberg-Tetley Tetley, Wye Valley, Greene King Old Speckled Hen. **FACILITIES:** Children welcome Garden: Terraced with views of Black Mountains Dogs allowed Waterbowls **NOTES:** Parking 40

DORSTONE
Map 09 SO34

The Pandy Inn ♀
HR3 6AN ☎ 01981 550273 ▤ 01981 550277
Dir: *Off B4348 W of Hereford*

Oliver Cromwell was a frequent visitor to the Pandy, the oldest inn in Herefordshire built in 1185 to house workers building Dorstone Church. Alongside the usual pub favourites, the South African owners offer traditional dishes from back home (bobotie and bredie) along with duck stirfry, courgette bake with goats' cheese, pork fillet with apricots, and steak and kidney pie, plus various hot and cold desserts.

OPEN: 12-3 6-11 (Mon 6-11 only) (Sat 12-11, Sun 12-10.30)
BAR MEALS: L served Tue-Sun 12-2.30 D served all week 7-9.30 Av main course £9 **RESTAURANT:** L served Tue-Sun 12-2.30 D served

continued

continued

all week 7-9.30 **BREWERY/COMPANY:** Free House ◀: Wye Valley Butty Bach & Dorothy Goodbody. ♀: 15 **FACILITIES:** Children welcome Garden: Large garden, lots of benches and tables Dogs allowed **NOTES:** Parking 50

FOWNHOPE
Map 10 SO53

The Green Man Inn ★★ 🛏
HR1 4PE ☎ 01432 860243 📠 01432 860207
e-mail: greenman.hereford@nhguk.com
Dir: From A449 then B4224 to Fownhope
Set in a charming garden close to the River Wye, this 15th-century country inn is white painted with a host of black beams inside and out. The former coaching inn is in picturesque countryside amidst wooded hills, an ideal base for walking, touring and local salmon fishing. The Petty Sessional Court was once held here, and Tom Spring, bare-fist fighter was a former owner. Under new management.
OPEN: 11-11 (Sun 12-10.30) **BAR MEALS:** L served all week 12-10 D served all week 12-10 Av main course £7.95 **RESTAURANT:** L served Sun 12-2 D served all week 7-9 Av 3 course à la carte £12.15 **BREWERY/COMPANY:** Free House ◀: Scottish Courage Courage Directors & John Smith's Smooth, Carlsberg-Tetley Tetley's Cask, Samuel Smith. **FACILITIES:** Children welcome Garden: Lawn area with seating overlooks countryside Dogs allowed **NOTES:** Parking 80 **ROOMS:** 22 bedrooms 22 en suite 4 family rooms s£39.50 d£67.50

HAMPTON BISHOP
Map 10 SO53

The Bunch of Carrots ♀
HR1 4JR ☎ 01432 870237 📠 01432 870237
Dir: From Hereford take A4103, A438, then B4224
Friendly pub with real fires, old beams and flagstones. Its name comes from a rock formation in the River Wye which runs alongside the pub. There is an extensive menu (steaks, salmon fillet and Cajun chicken) plus a daily specials board, a carvery, salad buffet and simple bar snacks.
OPEN: 11-3 6-11 **BAR MEALS:** L served all week 12-2 D served all week 6-10 **RESTAURANT:** L served all week 12-2 D served all week 6-10 **BREWERY/COMPANY:** Free House ◀: Bass, Hook Norton, Wye Valley. ♀: 11 **FACILITIES:** Children welcome Garden Dogs allowed **NOTES:** Parking 100

HEREFORD
Map 10 SO53

The Ancient Camp Inn ★★
Ruckhall HR2 9QX ☎ 01981 250449 📠 01981 251581
Dir: Take A465 from Hereford, then B4349. Follow signs 'Belmont Abbey/Ruckhall'
From its elevated position some 70 feet above the winding River Wye, the views across the river and Golden Valley from the terrace of the Ancient Camp Inn are stunning. The low-beamed interior with its stone-flagged floors and simple furnishings is typical of a country inn. Sample dishes include Shropshire hare casserole, Herefordshire cider brandy parfait, Frome Valley cider and onion soup, and local rabbit pie.
OPEN: 12-3 7-11 (Times vary, ring for details) Closed: 2 weeks Jan **BAR MEALS:** L served Sat-Sun 12-2.30 Av main course £6.95 **RESTAURANT:** L served Sat-Sun 12-2.30 D served All day to residents only Av 4 course fixed price £22.50 **BREWERY/COMPANY:** Free House ◀: Shepherd Neame Spitfire, Bishops Finger. **FACILITIES:** Garden: Terrace overlooking the River Wye, tables **NOTES:** Parking 30 **ROOMS:** 5 bedrooms 5 en suite s£50 d£60 no children overnight

The Crown & Anchor 🛏 ♀
Cotts Ln, Lugwardine HR1 4AB ☎ 01432 851303 📠 01432 851637
e-mail: jscrownandanchor@care4free.net
Dir: 2 miles from Hereford city centre on A438, turn left into Lugwardine down Cotts Lane
Old Herefordshire-style black-and-white pub with quarry tile floors and a large log fire, just up from the bridge over the River Lugg. Among the many interesting main courses are roast sea bass with fresh asparagus and fennel cream, supreme of escolar with ginger, coriander and lime, roast rack of lamb with blackberry and port wine sauce, pot-roast partridge with parsnip purée, and Brother Geoffrey's pork sausages with juniper and red wine sauce. A long lunchtime sandwich list.
OPEN: 12-11 Closed: 25 Dec **BAR MEALS:** L served all week 12-2 D served all week 7-10 Av main course £8 **BREWERY/COMPANY:** Free House ◀: Worthington Bitter, Theakstons XB, Timothy Taylors Landlord, Marstons Pedigree. ♀: 8 **FACILITIES:** Children welcome Garden: Patio area with tables and lots of plants **NOTES:** Parking 30

KIMBOLTON
Map 10 SO56

Stockton Cross Inn 🛏
HR6 0HD ☎ 01568 612509
Dir: On the A4112 off A49 between Leominster and Ludlow

A picturesque black and white building, regularly photographed by tourists and featured on calendars and chocolate boxes, Stockton Cross is a drovers' inn dating from the 17th century. It is set beside a crossroads where alleged witches, rounded up from the surrounding villages such as Ludlow, were hanged, a grisly historical aspect belied by the peace and beauty of the setting. Good home cooking using all local produce appears on a variety of menus, offering starters and light bites, main dishes and specials. Typical dishes are warm seafood salad, 'Old Percy's Rabbit', proper cod and chips, Cumberland venison sausage, various steaks and a good choice of fresh fish. Puddings have their own menu, with old favourites like treacle tart, fresh fruit Pavlova, and jam roly-poly. There is also a pretty country garden with umbrellas and two trees for shade.
OPEN: 12-3 7-11 (Mon 12-3 only) **BAR MEALS:** L served all week 12-2.15 D served Tues-Sun 7-9 **RESTAURANT:** L served all week 12-2.15 D served Tues-Sun 7-9 Av 3 course à la carte £22 **BREWERY/COMPANY:** Free House ◀: Castle Eden Ale, Wye Valley Butty Bach, Interbrew Bass, Black Sheep. **FACILITIES:** Garden: Pretty country garden with umbrellas Dogs allowed **NOTES:** Parking 30

KINGTON

Map 09 SO25

Pick of the Pubs

The Stagg Inn & Restaurant @@ ♀
Titley HR5 3RL ☎ 01544 230221
e-mail: reservations@thestagg.co.uk
Dir: Between Kington & Presteigne on the B4355

Situated at the meeting point of two drovers' roads, the Mortimer Trail and Offa's Dyke Path, the pub retains many original features from its often colourful past. Fireplaces with real fires, a bread oven, and antique furniture all add to the atmosphere, and make this a welcoming spot for a drink or a meal. The Stagg's chef/proprietor Steve Reynolds makes excellent use of the abundant quality produce for which the Marches area is renowned. Menus served throughout the homely bar with wood burner and large jug collection, and the separate informal dining room show the breadth of his imagination and skill. Seasonal cartes may start with pan-fried foie gras with Pembridge apple jelly, or mussel and saffron risotto, move on to saddle of venison with roast shallots, or fillet of Herefordshire beef with sautéed mushrooms, and finish with whole roasted baby pineapple with vanilla ice cream. Local Hobson Brewery ales, Dunkerton's organic cider, and a well-chosen wine list, with ten choices by the glass. Look out for the award-winning cheese trolley with more than twenty regional choices.
OPEN: 12-3 6.30-11 (Sun 12-3, 7-10.30) Closed: 1st 2wks Nov & 1wk Feb **BAR MEALS:** L served Tue-Sun 12-2 D served Tue-Sun 6.30-10 Av main course £7.50 **RESTAURANT:** L served Tue-Sun 12-2 D served Tue-Sun 6.30-10 Av 3 course à la carte £24
BREWERY/COMPANY: Free House ◀: Hobsons Town Crier, Hobsons Old Henry, Hobsons Best Bitter, Bass. ♀: 10
FACILITIES: Children welcome Garden: Food served outside Dogs allowed **NOTES:** Parking 20

LEDBURY

Map 10 SO73

The Farmers Arms ♀
Horse Rd, Wellington Heath HR8 1LS ☎ 01531 632010
Dir: Telephone for directions
Handy for the breathtaking high ground of the Malvern Hills and the seductive charms of Ross and the Wye Valley, this popular country inn offers a varied menu, with dishes cooked daily on the premises. The extensive menu and specials board feature perennial favourites such as fresh fish and game. Typical dishes include home-made steak and mushroom pie, slow-roasted half shoulder of lamb, and salsa chicken melt.
OPEN: 12-3 6-11 25-26 Dec, 1 Jan Closed evenings
BAR MEALS: L served all week 12-2 D served all week 7-10 Av main

course £8.95 **RESTAURANT:** L served all week 12-2 D served all week 7-10 Av 3 course à la carte £17.95
BREWERY/COMPANY: Free House ◀: Fuller's London Pride, Hancocks HB plus guest ales. ♀: 8 **FACILITIES:** Children welcome Children's licence Garden: Patio area small grassed area with rockery
NOTES: Parking 40

Pick of the Pubs

The Feathers Hotel ★★★ @ ♀
High St HR8 1DS ☎ 01531 635266 ◻ 01531 638955
e-mail: mary@feathers-ledbury.co.uk
Dir: S from Worcester A449, E from Hereford A438, N from Gloucester A417.

Long gone are the days when Royal Mail coaches carried the post through Ledbury to Aberystwyth, but any reincarnated coachman here today would still recognise the Feathers' striking black-and-white timbered frontage. In fact, travellers have been stopping at this fine old inn, full of oak beams, panelled walls and open log fires, since Elizabethan times. Eating takes place in Quills Restaurant, Fuggles Brasserie (named after a genus of hop) and the Top Bar, where lunchtime sandwiches and Herefordshire ciders are available. The daily 'Fish Box' usually offers four dishes, among them grilled Cornish hake fillet with garlic, lemon and chive butter, or lightly smoked salmon escalope with bean, garlic and potato salad. Meats tend to be prefixed by 'Herefordshire', whether tournedos with tarragon mustard and brandy sauce, pheasant breast with chestnuts, lardons and Madeira, or duck breast with plum, brandy and hoi sin sauce. Guests have included TV personalities, actors, and the current Poet Laureate.
OPEN: 11-11 (Sun 12-10.30) **BAR MEALS:** L served all week 12-2 D served all week 7-9.30 Av main course £13
RESTAURANT: L served all week 12-2 D served all week 7-9.30 Av 3 course à la carte £25 **BREWERY/COMPANY:** Free House ◀: Coors Worthington's Bitter, Interbrew Bass, Fuller's London Pride, Greene King Old Speckled Hen. ♀: 18
FACILITIES: Children welcome Garden: Courtyard garden, fountain, gazebo **NOTES:** Parking 30 **ROOMS:** 19 bedrooms 19 en suite 3 family rooms s£71.50 d£99.50

The Talbot ♀
14 New St HR8 2DX ☎ 01531 632963 ◻ 01531 633796
e-mail: talbot.ledbury@wadworth.co.uk
Dir: follow Ledbury signs, turn into Bye St, 2nd L into Woodley Rd, over bridge to jct, L into New St. Talbot on R
Take a step back in time at this historic black-and-white coaching inn dating from 1596. The oak-panelled dining room, with its fine carved overmantle, was once the scene of fighting between Roundheads and Cavaliers - the musket-holes are

continued

continued

still visible today. A good choice of local ales and wines by the glass accompanies deep-fried spicy chicken wings or moules marinières, followed by lamb cutlets chasseur, roast duck breast, and poached salmon steak.
OPEN: 11.30-3 5-11 **BAR MEALS:** L served all week 12-2.00 D served all week 6.30-9.00 Av main course £7.95 **RESTAURANT:** L served all week 12-2.00 D served all week 6.30-9.00 Av 3 course à la carte £17.22 **BREWERY/COMPANY:** Wadworth 🍺: Wadworth 6X & Henrys Original IPA, Wye Valley Butty Bach. **FACILITIES:** Children welcome **NOTES:** Parking 10 **ROOMS:** 7 bedrooms 6 en suite s£30 d£55 (★★)

The Trumpet Inn
Trumpet HR8 2RA ☎ 01531 670277 📠 01531 670277
e-mail: aa@trumpetinn.com
Dir: *4 miles from Ledbury on the Hereford Road, pub on the X-Roads of the A438 and A417*
This traditional black and white free house dates back to the late 1400s. Once a coaching inn and post house, it takes its name from the coachman's horn. The cosy bars feature a wealth of exposed beams, with open fireplaces and a separate dining area. Sandwiches, salads and baked potatoes are teamed with hot dishes like home-made steak and kidney pie; cod in batter; stifado; and cauliflower and leek bake.
OPEN: 11.30-2.30 6-11 **BAR MEALS:** L served all week 12-2 D served all week 6-9 Av main course £6.50 **RESTAURANT:** L served all week 12-2 D served all week 6-9 Av 3 course à la carte £10 **BREWERY/COMPANY:** Free House 🍺: Interbrew Flowers IPA, Scottish Courage John Smith's, Castle Eden Ale, Wye Valley HPA & Butty Bach. **FACILITIES:** Children welcome Garden: Small paddock adjacent to pub, sun trap Dogs allowed Water **NOTES:** Parking 60

Verzons Country Inn ★★ 🛏 🍷 NEW
Trumpet HR8 2PZ ☎ 01531 670381 📠 01531 670830
e-mail: info@theverzons.co.uk
Dir: *Situated 2.5 miles west of Ledbury on the A438 towards Hereford*
Once a Georgian farmhouse built on the Dutch-owned Verzons Estate, and converted to a hotel in the 1970s. Home to various vintage sports car clubs, and popular for its character bar and very smart restaurant. Bar snacks like filled potato skins, and stuffed tortilla wrap, are complemented by the likes of pan-roasted breast of Gressingham duck with spicy risotto, apricot and pear chutney and apricot jus, from the restaurant.
OPEN: 8 -11 Closed: 26 Dec **BAR MEALS:** L served all week 12-2 D served all week 7-9 Av main course £10.50 **RESTAURANT:** L served all week 12-2 D served all week 7-9 Av 3 course à la carte £27 🍺: Hook Norton Best Bitter, Tetley Best, Spitfire Kentish Ale. 🍷 7 **FACILITIES:** Children welcome Children's licence Garden: Large terrace and lawn, views of Malvern Hill **NOTES:** Parking 100 **ROOMS:** 8 bedrooms 8 en suite 1 family rooms s£45 d£88

LEOMINSTER   Map 10 SO45

The Grape Vaults 🛏 🍷 NEW
Broad St HR4 8BS
An unspoilt pub with a small, homely bar complete with real fire - in fact it's so authentic that it's Grade II- listed, even down to the fixed seating. Real ale is a popular feature (Banks Original & Bitter), and the good food includes fisherman's pie, bubble and squeak, steak and ale pie, and various fresh fish dishes using cod, plaice, salmon and whitebait.
OPEN: 11-11 **BAR MEALS:** L served all week 12-2 D served Mon-Sat 5.30-9 Av main course £5 **BREWERY/COMPANY:** 🍺: Banks Bitter, Pedigree, Banks Original & Guest Ales. 🍷 6 **FACILITIES:** Dogs allowed Water **NOTES:** No credit cards

The Royal Oak Hotel ★★ 🛏 🍷
South St HR6 8JA ☎ 01568 612610 📠 01568 612710
e-mail: reservations@theroyaloakhotel.net
Dir: *J A44/A49*

Coaching inn dating from around 1733, with log fires, antiques and a minstrels' gallery in the original ballroom. The pub was once part of a now blocked-off tunnel system that linked the Leominster Priory with other buildings in the town. Good choice of wines by the glass and major ales. Hearty menu includes Royal Oak double beef sandwiches, and fish dishes using cod, plaice, prawns or salmon.
OPEN: 10-2.30 6-11 (Sun 10.30-7, BHs 11-3, 7-10.30) **BAR MEALS:** L served all week 12-2 D served all week 6-9 Av main course £6 **RESTAURANT:** L served Sun 12-2 D served all week 7-9 Av 3 course à la carte £16 Av 3 course fixed price £15 **BREWERY/COMPANY:** Free House 🍺: Brains SA, Wood Special Bitter, Shepherd Neame Spitfire, Fuller's London Pride. 🍷: 10 **FACILITIES:** Children welcome Dogs allowed Water **NOTES:** Parking 30 **ROOMS:** 18 bedrooms 18 en suite s£45 d£59

LITTLE COWARNE   Map 10 SO65

The Three Horseshoes Inn 🛏 🍷
HR7 4RQ ☎ 01885 400276 📠 01885 400276
Dir: *Off A456 (Hereford/Bromyard). At Stokes Cross, take turning signed Little Cowarne/Pencombe*

Named after the horses brought for shoeing at the next-door blacksmiths', and an alehouse for nearly 200 years. This country inn offers home-made food using local produce, and served in the Garden Room conservatory at lunchtime. A selection of typical dishes includes prawn and haddock smokie, Steak and Wye Valley Ale pie, pork fillet in damson sauce, Cataplana (Portuguese fish stew) and pheasant in pear and perry sauce.
OPEN: 11-3 6.30-11 Closed: Dec 25 Sun eve in winter **BAR MEALS:** L served all week 12-2 D served all week 6.30-9.30 Av main course £5.50 **RESTAURANT:** L served all week 12-2 D served all week 6.30-9.30 Av 3 course à la carte £15

continued

LITTLE COWARNE continued

BREWERY/COMPANY: Free House **:** Marston's Pedigree, Greene King Old Speckled Hen, Websters Yorkshire Bitter, Wye Valley Bitter. **:** 6 **FACILITIES:** Garden: Patio/Lawn area with seating, flower beds Dogs allowed Water in the garden **NOTES:** Parking 50 **ROOMS:** 2 bedrooms 2 en suite s£28.50 d£48 (◆◆◆◆) no children overnight

MADLEY   Map 09 SO43

The Comet Inn
Stoney St HR2 9NJ ☎ 01981 250600 ◻ 01981 250643
Dir: approx 6m from Hereford on the B4352
Located on a prominent corner position and set in two and a half acres, this black and white 19th-century inn was originally three cottages, and retains many original features and a roaring open fire. A simple, hearty menu includes duck breast with port and cranberry sauce, chicken breast with wild mushroom sauce, lamb shank in port and mint gravy, and red mullet. Children's play area.
OPEN: 12-3 7-11 **BAR MEALS:** L served all week 12-2 D served Mon-Sun 7-9 Av main course £6.95 **RESTAURANT:** L served all week 12-2 D served Mon-Sat 7-9 Av 3 course à la carte £22
BREWERY/COMPANY: Free House **:** Hook Norton Best Bitter, Wye Valley Bitter, Tetley Smooth Flow. **FACILITIES:** Children welcome Garden: Large garden with shrubs **NOTES:** Parking 40

MICHAELCHURCH ESCLEY   Map 09 SO33

The Bridge Inn
HR2 0JW ☎ 01981 510646 ◻ 01981 510646
e-mail: embengiss@yahoo.co.uk
Dir: from Hereford take A465 towards Abergavenny, then B4348 towards Peterchurch. Turn L at Vowchurch for village
By Escley Brook, at the foot of the Black Mountains and close to Offa's Dyke, there are 14th-century parts to this oak-beamed family pub: where the dining room overlooks the river and garden, abundant in rose and begonias. An ideal area for walkers and nature lovers. Speciality dishes include steak and kidney with crispy dumplings.
OPEN: 12-2.30 6-11 (Sun 12-10.30) Closed: 25 Dec
BAR MEALS: L served Tue-Sun 12-2 D served all week 7-9.15 Av main course £7.50 **RESTAURANT:** L served Tue-Sun 12-2 D served all week 7-9.30 Av 3 course à la carte £15
BREWERY/COMPANY: Free House **:** Wye Valley Beers, Interbrew Flowers, Adnams. **:** 12 **FACILITIES:** Children welcome Garden: Lrg riverside patio, fenced garden, heaters Dogs allowed Water **NOTES:** Parking 25

MUCH COWARNE   Map 10 SO64

Fir Tree Inn
HR7 4JN ☎ 01531 640619 640725 ◻ 01531 640663
Dir: off the A4103 Hereford to Worcester
Set in three acres of grounds with fishing lake and small caravan site, this part 16th-century modernised inn is a versatile establishment situated in unspoilt countryside. Dishes may include home-made steak and ale pie, toad in the hole, lamb and apricot casserole, mixed grill, Dover sole, lasagne, and sirloin steak.
OPEN: 12-3 7-11 Closed: Dec 25 **BAR MEALS:** L served Tue-Sun 12-2 D served Tue-Sat 7-9 Av main course £7.25
RESTAURANT: L served Tue-Sun 12-2.30 D served all week 7-9.30 Av 3 course à la carte £11 Av 3 course fixed price £10
BREWERY/COMPANY: Free House **:** Carlsberg-Tetley

continued

Tetley Bitter, Ansells Best Bitter. **FACILITIES:** Children welcome Garden: Food served outdoors, orchard
NOTES: Parking 80

MUCH MARCLE   Map 10 SO63

The Scrumpy House Bar & Restaurant
The Bounds HR8 2NQ ☎ 01531 660626
e-mail: matt@scrumpyhouse.co.uk
Dir: approx 5 miles from Ledbury & Ross-on-Wye on A449, follow signs to Cidermill
A renovated hay barn on the site of a family-run cider mill with a bar and restaurant separated by a woodburner in the fireplace. Over 20 different ciders are offered alongside local bitters and a varied wine list. All food is prepared on the premises, including 16 kinds of ice cream, and fresh fish on Friday from Grimsby. Favourite dishes include award-winning local bangers and oven-baked sea bass stuffed with home-grown herbs.
OPEN: 11-3 7-12 (Fri-Sat 12-2.30, 6.30-12) Closed: 25-26 Dec
BAR MEALS: L served all week 12-2 D served Wed-Sat 7-9.30 Av main course £8 **RESTAURANT:** L served all week 12-2.30 D served Wed-Sat 7-11 Av 3 course à la carte £22
BREWERY/COMPANY: Free House **:** Hook Norton, Guest ales.
FACILITIES: Children welcome Garden: Patio, Food served outside
NOTES: Parking 30

The Slip Tavern
Watery Ln HR8 2NG ☎ 01531 660246
Dir: Follow signs off A449 at Much Marcle junction
Curiously named after a 1575 landslip which buried the local church, this country pub is delightfully surrounded by cider apple orchards. An attractive conservatory overlooking the award-winning garden, where summer dining is popular, and there's also a cosy bar. A comprehensive menu offers traditional pub food along with a wider choice of pasta dishes, curries, and steaks. From the evening carte expect liver Madeira, duck à l'orange, and leek and mushroom crumble.
OPEN: 11.30-2.30 Open all day wknds, BH's in the Summer 6.30-11 (Sun 12-2.30, 6.30-10.30) **BAR MEALS:** L served all week 11.30-2 D served all week 6.30-9.30 Av main course £8.50 **RESTAURANT:** L served all week 11.30-2 D served all week 6.30-9.30 Av 3 course à la carte £17.50 **BREWERY/COMPANY:** Free House **:** John Smiths, Hook Norton, Tetleys Smooth Flow, Ausells. **FACILITIES:** Children welcome Garden: Large terrace seating 50, lawns/flowerbeds
NOTES: Parking 45

ORLETON   Map 09 SO46

The Boot Inn NEW
SY8 4HD ☎ 01568 780228 ◻ 01568 780228
Dir: Follow the A49 S from London (approx 7 miles) to the B4362 (Woofferton), 1.5 miles off B4362 turn L. The Boot Inn is in the centre of the village
Relaxed and welcoming, this black and white timbered inn dates from the 16th century, and its peaceful atmosphere is undisturbed by music or games. In winter a blazing fire in the inglenook warms the bar, where an appetising selection of snacks and sandwiches extends the menu along with a list of specials: steak and kidney pie, Stilton chicken, and duck with plum and red wine sauce are options, with local real ales and cider on tap.

continued

Pubs offering a good choice of fish on their menu

OPEN: 12-3 6-11 (Sun 12-3, 6-10.30) **BAR MEALS:** L served Tue-Sun 12-2 D served all week 7-9 Av main course £4.50
RESTAURANT: D served all week 7-9 Av 3 course à la carte £12
BREWERY/COMPANY: Free House **◀:** Hobsons Best, Local Real Ales. **FACILITIES:** Children welcome Children's licence Garden: Lawn, BBQ area Dogs allowed Water **NOTES:** Parking 20

PEMBRIDGE
Map 09 SO35

The Cider House Restaurant
Dunkerton's Cider Mill, Luntley HR6 9ED
☎ 01544 388161 ▤ 01544 388654
Dir: W on A44 from Leominster, L in Pembridge centre by New Inn, 1m on L
A converted, half-timbered 16th-century barn with natural oak beams, and beautiful view over rolling countryside. Susie and Ivor Dunkerton started the restaurant after years of cidermaking on the farm, and are dedicated to fresh local produce and home cooking. Expect chicken, chive and pearl barley soup, and marinaded monkfish tails in basil, lemon and shallot sauce. Breads, cakes and desserts all made on the premises.
OPEN: 10-5 Closed: 1 Oct - Easter **BAR MEALS:** L served Mon-Sat 12-2.30 Av main course £10.20 **RESTAURANT:** L served Mon-Sat 12-2.30 Av 3 course à la carte £19.50 **BREWERY/COMPANY:** Free House **◀:** Caledonian Golden Promise. **FACILITIES:** Children welcome **NOTES:** Parking 30

New Inn 🍴
Market Square HR6 9DZ ☎ 01544 388427 ▤ 01544 388427
Dir: From M5 J7 take A44 W through Leominster towards Llandrindod Wells
A black and white timbered inn at the centre of a picture-postcard village full of quaint cottages. It dates from the early 14th century, and is one of the oldest pubs in England, once used as the local courthouse and reputedly haunted. Full of old beams, wonky walls and worn flagstones. The menu lists home-cooked dishes such as seafood stew, crab tart, lamb hotpot, lamb fillet in elderberry wine, pork steak in mustard and cream sauce, and beef casserole.
OPEN: 11-2.30 6-11 **BAR MEALS:** L served all week 12-2 D served all week 7-9.30 Av main course £7 **RESTAURANT:** 12-2 7-9.30
BREWERY/COMPANY: Free House **◀:** Fuller's London Pride, Kingdom Billes, Wood Shropshire Lad, Black Sheep Best.
FACILITIES: Children welcome Garden: Patio **NOTES:** Parking 25

> We endeavour to be as accurate as possible but changes to times and other information can occur after the guide has gone to press

---

Pick of the Pubs

The Moody Cow 🍴 ♀
Upton Bishop HR9 7TT ☎ 01989 780470
This old stone inn has found a winning formula that attracts people from a wide local area. The philosophy is simple: produce good home-baked food at sensible prices, present it attractively in pleasant, convivial surroundings, and enjoy the sight of satisfied customers. The buildings have been carefully and tastefully converted to create a choice of comfortable places to eat or drink. The restaurant used to be a barn, and is now a smart room on two levels with exposed beams, while the Fresco dining room has displays of crockery and plenty of cow-themed ornaments. The farmhouse-style bar is a friendly place in which to enjoy real ales or a meal under the exposed beams, and the Snug (wood-burning fire, cosy settees and armchairs) is for drinks only. The long menu of imaginative dishes shows why this has been a successful dining destination since the early 1990s. For a light snack or starter, you could choose deep-fried Brie, home-made fishcakes, or onion tartlet topped with melted goats' cheese. Main courses might include pork, apple and leek bangers, sautéed lamb's liver with bacon and mushrooms, tomato and chickpea curry, pan-fried duck breast with mixed berry compôte, or the irresistibly macho 'mad cow' pie - are you man (or woman) enough to order the large size? Kids' choices include perennial favourites, and there are desserts like raspberry crème brûlée, lemon and lime pannacotta, or home-made dime bar ice cream. A blackboard list of specials is changed daily.

OPEN: 12-2.30 6.30-11 (Sun 12-3, 7-10.30) **BAR MEALS:** L served all week 12-2 D served all week 6.30-9.30 Av main course £9.95 **RESTAURANT:** L served all week 12-2 D served all week 6.30-9.30 Av 3 course à la carte £19.95
BREWERY/COMPANY: Free House **◀:** Bass, Flowers IPA, Hook Norton Best. **FACILITIES:** Children welcome Garden: Patio area with iron table, chairs Dogs allowed Water provided
NOTES: Parking 40

Pick of the Pubs

The Lough Pool Inn 🍴🍴 ♀
HR9 6LX ☎ 01989 730236 ▤ 01989 730462
See Pick of the Pubs on page 250

England

Open: 11.30-2.30, 6.30-11
Bar Meals: L served 12-2,
D served 7-9.30.
RESTAURANT: L served 12-2, D served
7-9.30.
BREWERY/COMPANY:
Free House.
🍺: Wye Valley, Scottish Courage John
Smiths, Greene King Ruddles Country
& Old Speckled Hen.
FACILITIES: Children welcome,
Garden.
NOTES: Parking 40

The Lough Pool Inn

A typical Herefordshire black and white, half-timbered pub dating from the late 1500s, with flagstones, beams and open fires. Once a butchers' with a licence to sell beer brewed on the premises - a not uncommon practice in those days.

◎◎ ♟

Sellack, Ross-on-Wye, HR9 6LX
☎ 01989 730236 📠 01989 730462
Dir: A49 from Ross-on-Wye toward Hereford, side rd signed Sellack/ Hoarwithy, pub 2m from R-on-W.

In a fold of low hills and opposite a pond - that of the tautologous pub name - with waterfowl and weeping willows, and only a few strides away from the Wye Valley Walk. The remote location doesn't deter the die-hard followers of Stephen Bull. This renowned ex-London chef/restaurateur considers it very much a food pub, priding itself on its use of local produce. That said, he's equally happy to talk about the 'wet' side of the business, especially its ciders, perries, real ales and wines. The restaurant is at the rear of the pub, decorated in egg yellow. Wooden tables, smart place settings, a large fireplace and well-trained staff are just some of its joys. The daily carte is honest, rustic, and eminently satisfying. It features modern starters like broccoli and tarragon soup, and seared scallops with bacon and chorizo, and main courses of chargrilled Moroccan-spiced chicken, fillet of sea bass with clams and spiced garlic butter, and steak and kidney with Guinness and mash. The dessert menu not only has pear and frangipani tart and lime cheesecake, but home-made quince, damson, prune, Armagnac and liquorice ice creams. A lawned garden with pond and weeping willow is just across a quiet country lane, and ideal for summer relaxing.

SYMONDS YAT (EAST) — Map 10 SO51

The Saracens Head Inn ★★ 🛏 ♀

HR9 6JL ☎ 01600 890435 📠 01600 890034
e-mail: email@saracensheadinn.co.uk

Riverside inn on the east bank of the glorious Wye, situated by the ancient hand ferry which has been in use for 250 years. Handy for exploring the Wye Valley and Forest of Dean. Wide range of home-made bar food and restaurant dishes includes chargrilled chicken breast with port and Stilton sauce, grilled pink trout, Highland fillet filled with haggis, poached greenlip mussels, roasted quails, monkfish kebab, and prawn and black bean stirfry.
OPEN: 11-11 (Sun 12-10.30), (Wkds only in Dec-Jan) **BAR MEALS:** L served all week 12-2.30 D served all week 7-9.15 Av main course £7
RESTAURANT: D served all week 7-9.15
BREWERY/COMPANY: Free House 🍺: Scottish Courage Theakstons Best & Old Peculier, Greene King Old Speckled Hen, Wye Valley Hereford Pale Ale, Marston's Pedigree. ♀: 7 **FACILITIES:** Children welcome Garden: 2 riverside terraces Dogs allowed **NOTES:** Parking 38 **ROOMS:** 9 bedrooms 9 en suite 1 family rooms s£45 d£30
See Pub Walk on page 243

ULLINGSWICK — Map 10 SO54

Pick of the Pubs

Three Crowns Inn ⊚⊚ 🛏 ♀

HR1 3JQ ☎ 01432 820279 📠 01432 820279
e-mail: info@threecrownsinn.com
Dir: *From Burley Gate take A465 toward Bromyard, after 2m L to Ullingswick, L after 0.5m, pub 0.5m on R*
An unspoilt country pub in deepest rural Herefordshire, where food sources are so local their distance away is referred to in fields, rather than miles. A hand-written sign even offers to buy surplus garden fruit and veg from locals. New parterres in the garden give additional space for growing more varieties of herbs, fruit and vegetables that are not easy, or even possible, to buy commercially. There's even a pea whose provenance can be traced back to some Lord Carnarvon found in a phial in Tutankhamun's tomb. The menus change daily, but there is always fish, such as line-caught sea bass with green beans and champagne butter sauce. Soufflés often appear too. Meat dishes have included confit of belly and loin of pork with merguez sausage cassoulet, and glazed duck breast with prunes and red cabbage. Tuesday tasting evenings feature a set four-course dinner that changes week by week, with wines normally sold by the bottle, available by the glass.
OPEN: 12-2.30 7-11 (May-Aug 12-3, 6-11) Closed: 2wks from Dec 25 **BAR MEALS:** L served all week 12-3 D served all week 7-10.30 Av main course £13.75 **RESTAURANT:** L served all week 12-2 D served all week 7-9.30 Av 3 course à la carte £22.25

continued

BREWERY/COMPANY: Free House 🍺: Hobsons Best, Wye Valley Butty Bach & Dorothy Goodbody's. ♀: 9
FACILITIES: Children welcome Garden: Formal garden with patio, heaters Dogs allowed except when food is being served in bar **NOTES:** Parking 20

WALTERSTONE — Map 09 SO32

Carpenters Arms ♀

HR2 0DX ☎ 01873 890353
Dir: *Off the A465 between Hereford & Abergavenny at Pandy*
300-year-old country pub located on the edge of the Black Mountains where the owner, Mrs Watkins, was born. It has plenty of character, with beams, antique settles and a leaded range where open fires burn all winter. Popular options range from beef and Guinness pie, and thick lamb cutlets with a redcurrant and rosemary sauce, to home-made curries and lasagne.
OPEN: 12-3 7-11 **BAR MEALS:** L served all week 12-3 D served all week 7-9.30 **RESTAURANT:** 12-3 7-9.30
BREWERY/COMPANY: Free House 🍺: Wadworth 6X.
FACILITIES: Children welcome Garden Dogs allowed Only by arrangement **NOTES:** Parking 15 **NOTES:** No credit cards

WELLINGTON — Map 10 SO44

The Wellington 🛏 NEW

HR4 8AT ☎ 01432 830367
e-mail: thewellington@hotmail.com
Dir: *Turn for Wellington on A49 between Hereford & Leominster*
A Victorian country pub, with original open fireplaces, antique furniture, beers from Hobsons Brewery in Shropshire, guest ales, and locally made ciders. A sample meal might be glazed avocado with Stilton shavings and rocket salad, fillet of beef Wellington, with a red wine reduction, and sticky toffee pudding with clotted cream. Monday nights are given over to bangers and mash, and every first Thursday in the month is devoted to a Global Gourmet three-course dinner for £12.50.
OPEN: 12-3 6-11 (Sun 12-3, 7-10.30) **BAR MEALS:** L served Tue-Sun 12-2 D served Mon-Sat 6-9 Av main course £7.75
RESTAURANT: L served Tue-Sun 12-2 D served Mon-Sat 6-10 Av 3 course à la carte £22 Av 3 course fixed price £10 🍺: Hobsons, Wye Valley Butty Bach, Coors Hancocks HB, Guest Real Ales.
FACILITIES: Children welcome Garden: Beer garden, play area, ample seating Dogs allowed Water **NOTES:** Parking 20

WEOBLEY — Map 09 SO45

Pick of the Pubs

Ye Olde Salutation Inn ♦♦♦♦ ⊚ ♀

Market Pitch HR4 8SJ ☎ 01544 318443 📠 01544 318216
e-mail: info@salutationinn.co.uk
Dir: *In village centre opposite Broad Street*
A very popular pub, in a truly pretty mediaeval village in a county world famous for its cattle, apple orchards and hops. The 500-year-old black and white timber-framed building and adjoining cottage have been tastefully converted from an old ale and cider house into what you can see and enjoy today. Its good food has attracted more than the AA's attention, as national media reviews testify. With food at the forefront of the operation, it is perhaps not surprising that there are two separate areas for dining. Pitch up after a long walk or bike ride and have an informal meal in the traditional lounge bar, a pint of Wye

continued

England

WEOBLEY continued

Valley Butty Bach to hand, or maybe a glass of wine from the well stocked cellar. More formal dining in the stylish Oak Room restaurant, with its large open fireplace and partly exposed stone walls, is a comfortable experience. Modern English style dishes are prepared by talented young chefs using the best and freshest local ingredients to ensure that quality is never compromised. Depending on where you choose to eat, you should find old favourites like steak and ale pie, oak-smoked haddock, leg of Weobley lamb, and medallions of Herefordshire beef. The Salutation also offers delightful, non-smoking bedrooms, including one with a traditional brass bed and another with a four-poster.

OPEN: 11-11 (Sun 12-10.30) **BAR MEALS:** L served all week 12-2 D served all week 7-9.30 Av main course £8.95
RESTAURANT: L served all week 12-2 D served all week 7-9 Av 3 course à la carte £22 **BREWERY/COMPANY:** Free House
🍺: Hook Norton Best, Coors Worthington's 1744, Wye Valley Butty Bach, Shepherd Neame Bishops Finger. **FACILITIES:** Children welcome Children's licence Garden: Patio area with tables and umbrellas Dogs allowed Water **NOTES:** Parking 14 **ROOMS:** 4 bedrooms 4 en suite 1 family rooms s£47 d£75

WHITNEY-ON-WYE Map 09 SO24

Rhydspence Inn ★★ 🛏️
HR3 6EU ☎ 01497 831262 📠 01497 831751
e-mail: info@rhydspence-inn.co.uk
Dir: N side of A438 1m W of Whitney-on-Wye

Converted 14th-century manor house on the English side of the Welsh Borders with a spacious dining room overlooking the Wye Valley. For many years it was a meeting place for drovers on the Black Ox Trail, taking livestock as far as London. Imaginative menus range from bar bites, including house speciality pâté and Rhydspence salad, to rack of Welsh lamb with herb crust, and sea bas en papilotte.

continued

OPEN: 11-2.30 7-11 Closed: 2 wks in Jan **BAR MEALS:** L served all week 11-2 D served all week 7-9.30 Av main course £7
RESTAURANT: L served all week 11-2 D served all week 7-9.30 Av 3 course à la carte £23 **BREWERY/COMPANY:** Free House
🍺: Robinsons Best, Interbrew Bass. **FACILITIES:** Children welcome Garden: 2/3 acres, mostly lawn **NOTES:** Parking 30 **ROOMS:** 7 bedrooms 7 en suite s£32.50 d£65

WINFORTON Map 09 SO24

Pick of the Pubs

The Sun Inn
HR3 6EA ☎ 01544 327677 📠 01544 327677
e-mail: anne.bonney@btopenworld.com
Set in the heart of a typical black and white Herefordshire village, the Sun has recently come under new management. The kitchen now offers a range of curries, as well as traditional pub dishes such as pies, faggots and liver and bacon. In summer visitors can relax in the large garden which has a children's play area, crazy golf course and boules piste.
OPEN: 11.30-3 6.15-11 (closed Tue during winter)
BAR MEALS: L served Wed-Mon 12-2 D served Wed-Mon 6-9 Av main course £6.50 **BREWERY/COMPANY:** Free House
🍺: Timothy Taylor Landlord. **FACILITIES:** Children welcome Garden: Large garden with Boules Piste, crazy golf Guide dogs only **NOTES:** Parking 40

WOOLHOPE Map 10 SO63

The Butchers Arms 🛏️ 🍷
HR1 4RF ☎ 01432 860281
Dir: Off B4224 between Hereford & Ross-on-Wye
Set in glorious walking country close to the Marcle Ridge, this 14th-century pub welcomes you with low beams, comfortable old settles and roaring log fires. Well-kept ales complement substantial dishes like home-baked steak and ale pie, lamb and cranberry casserole or Woolhope pie (rabbit in local cider). The specials' board broadens the scope with dishes such as tuna steak with lime and coriander or guinea fowl in wild berry sauce. Extensive wine list.
OPEN: 12-2.30 6.30-11 **BAR MEALS:** L served all week 12-2 D served Mon-Sat 6.30-9 Av main course £7.50
RESTAURANT: L served Sat-Sun 12-2 D served Fri-Sat 6.30-9
BREWERY/COMPANY: Free House 🍺: Hook Norton Best & Old Hooky. Wye Valley Bitter, Shepherd Neame Spitfire. 🍷: 11
FACILITIES: Children welcome Garden: Small sheltered garden, rustic furniture Dogs allowed **NOTES:** Parking 50

The Crown Inn 🛏️
HR1 4QP ☎ 01432 860468 📠 01432 860770
e-mail: thecrowninn1382@aol.com
Dir: From Hereford take B4224 to Mordiford, L immediately after Moon Inn. Crown Inn in village centre
A mainly 18th-century rendered stone inn at the centre of a tiny village, which is part of a beautiful conservation area. A stone mounting block outside is dated 1520, and parts of the building go back 500 years. Now under new ownership, The Crown offers a comprehensive menu of home-made dishes ranging from ploughman's through grills, rabbit pie and fresh battered cod or haddock. There are also good vegetarian and children's choices.
OPEN: 12-3 6.30-11 **BAR MEALS:** L served all week 12-2 D served all week 6.30/7-9.30 Av main course £7.50 **RESTAURANT:** L served all week 12-2 D served all week 6.30/7-9.30 Av 3 course à la carte £15 **BREWERY/COMPANY:** Free House 🍺: Smiles Best, Wye Valley Best, Timothy Taylor Landlord, Carlsberg-Tetley Tetleys Cask.
FACILITIES: Children welcome Garden: Garden front and back with heaters **NOTES:** Parking 30

HERTFORDSHIRE

ALDBURY
Map 06 SP91

The Greyhound Inn
19 Stocks Rd HP23 5RT ☎ 01442 851228 ▤ 01442 851495
The Chiltern Hills begin at this peaceful village pub overlooking a duck pond and old stocks, making it popular with walkers. In winter visitors gravitate towards the blazing inglenook fireplace to enjoy a bar snack like steak and Tanglefoot pie or a filled baked potato, while in the evening the carte lists dishes such as halibut with prawns and cream sauce, rack of lamb, and duck breast.
OPEN: 11-11 Closed: 25 Dec **BAR MEALS:** L served all week 12-2.30 D served Mon-Sat 7-10 Av main course £10 **RESTAURANT:** L served all week 12-2.30 D served Mon-Sat 7-10 Av 3 course à la carte £18 **BREWERY/COMPANY:** Hall & Woodhouse ◖: Badger Best, Tanglefoot, Champion, IPA. **FACILITIES:** Children welcome Garden: Courtyard, Food served outside Dogs allowed Water
NOTES: Parking 9

The Valiant Trooper
Trooper Rd HP23 5RW ☎ 01442 851203 ▤ 01442 851071
Dir: A41 Tring jct, follow signs for railway station, go past for about 0.5m, once at village green turn R then 200yds on L
Family-run free house in a pretty village surrounded by the Chiltern Hills, where hikers, cyclists and dogs are all made welcome. Local and guest beers feature, and interesting daily specials from the blackboard are hot and spicy chicken stir fry, beef fillet Stroganoff, steak, kidney and ale pie, and shark and tuna Breton. The Duke of Wellington is rumoured to have held a tactical conference at the pub - hence the name.
OPEN: 11-11 (Sun 12-10.30) **BAR MEALS:** L served all week 12-2.30 D served Tue-Sat 6.30-9.15 **RESTAURANT:** L served Tue-Sun 12-2 D served Tue-Sun 6.30-9.15 **BREWERY/COMPANY:** Free House ◖: Fuller's London Pride, Scottish Courage John Smith's, Marston's Pedigree, Greene King Ruddles Best. **FACILITIES:** Children welcome Garden Dogs allowed **NOTES:** Parking 36

ARDELEY
Map 12 TL32

The Jolly Waggoner
SG2 7AH ☎ 01438 861350
A pink-washed, 500-year-old pub with open beams, real fires and antique furniture. It is set in a lovely village with a beautiful garden and great local walks. All the food is home made from fresh ingredients. The bar menu offers sandwiches, salads, steak and salmon, while dishes from the Rose Cottage restaurant menu include fillet of sea bass on creamed mash, or breast of chicken with blackberry sauce.
OPEN: 12-2.30 6.30-11 (Open BH Mon, closed Tue after BH)
BAR MEALS: L served Tue-Sun 12-2 D served Tue-Sat 6.30-9 Av main course £10 **RESTAURANT:** L served Sun 12.30-2 D served Tue-Sat 6.30-9 Av 3 course à la carte £30
BREWERY/COMPANY: Greene King ◖: Greene King IPA & Abbot Ale. **FACILITIES:** Children welcome Garden: Very well kept, large **NOTES:** Parking 15

ASHWELL
Map 12 TL23

Bushel & Strike
Mill St SG7 5LY ☎ 01462 742394 ▤ 01462 743768
Wooden floors, leather chesterfields and open fires in winter characterise the main bar of this popular inn - which stands in the shadow of Ashwell's Norman church tower - while the restaurant is a conversion of the old school hall with its

vaulted roof and oak floor. Try a traditional lamb and vegetable-filled Hertfordshire Pasty, braised lamb shank on ratatouille, or chicken breast with a wild mushroom and basil mousse. Spotted Dick and apple crumble are often among the sweet selections.
OPEN: 11.30-3 6-11 (all day Sun) **BAR MEALS:** L served all week 12-2.30 D served all week 7-9.30 Av main course £6.50
RESTAURANT: L served all week 12-2.30 D served all week 7-9.30 Av 3 course à la carte £22.50 **BREWERY/COMPANY:** Charles Wells ◖: Charles, Greene King Old Speckled Hen, Broadside. ♀: 7
FACILITIES: Children welcome Garden: Lrg garden, patio, tables, benches Dogs allowed Water **NOTES:** Parking 40

The Three Tuns
High St SG7 5NL ☎ 01462 742107 ▤ 01462 743662
e-mail: claire@tuns.co.uk
This 19th-century inn has a lot of original features, and is next to an ancient natural spring; parts of the building date back even further. The village itself has the Ashwell Springs, and its own museum. Old world atmosphere, and locally renowned home-made food. Typical menu includes pot-roast partridge with pork and leek stuffing, four grilled lamb chops in a mint sauce, vegetarian pasta bake, steak and kidney pie, and braised venison in a port and plum sauce.
OPEN: 11-11 (Sun 12-10.30) **BAR MEALS:** L served all week 12-2.30 D served all week 6.30-9.30 Av main course £9
RESTAURANT: L served all week 12-2.30 D served all week 6.30-9.30 Av 3 course à la carte £18 **BREWERY/COMPANY:** Greene King ◖: Greene King IPA, Ruddles, Abbot. **FACILITIES:** Children welcome Garden: Large, terrace at top, seats around 100 Dogs allowed **NOTES:** Parking 20

AYOT ST LAWRENCE
Map 06 TL11

Pick of the Pubs

The Brocket Arms ◆◆◆ ♀
AL6 9BT ☎ 01438 820250 ▤ 01438 820068

This delightful 14th-century inn stands in the village that was home to George Bernard Shaw for 40 years until his death in 1950. Before the Reformation, the building formed the monastic quarters for the Norman church. Henry VIII supposedly wooed his sixth wife, Catherine Parr, in the nearby manor house. There are many charming features inside the pub, including low oak beams, and the extensive walled garden is a glorious sun trap. The accommodation is in idiosyncratic bedrooms varying in shape and size. Some of the bedrooms are furnished with four-poster beds, which prove especially popular. Traditional English game and home-cooked dishes characterise the bar menu - among them perhaps game pie, sandwiches of fresh roast meats, and steak and

continued

continued

England

AYOT ST LAWRENCE continued

kidney pie. The dinner menu continues in the same vein, with starters such as smoked salmon, soup of the day or country-style Caesar salad followed by main courses like braised lamb with roast potatoes and spring vegetables, or seared salmon with sautéed spinach, potatoes and sweet onion and ginger glaze.
OPEN: 11-11 **BAR MEALS:** 12-2.30 7.30-10
RESTAURANT: 12-2.30 7.30-10 **BREWERY/COMPANY:** Free House **◀:** Greene King Abbot Ale & IPA, Adnams Broadside, Fullers London Pride, Youngs IPA. **FACILITIES:** Children welcome Garden: Large walled garden with tables Dogs must be supervised **NOTES:** Parking 6 **ROOMS:** 6 bedrooms 3 en suite s£70 d£80

BARLEY   Map 12 TL43

The Fox & Hounds
High St SG8 8HU ☎ 01763 848459 ⓘ 01763 849274
Dir: A505 onto B1368 at Flint Cross, pub 4m
Enjoying a pretty thatched village setting, this former 17th-century hunting lodge is notable for its pub sign which extends across the lane. Enjoy real fires and a warm welcome. The garden has a pétanque court, and boules are available for those interested in this fine Gallic pastime. The new owners have yet to finalise their menus at the time of going to press, but new children's' facilities are part of their plans.
OPEN: 12 -11 (Sun 12-10.30) **BAR MEALS:** L served all week 12-3 D served all week 6-8.30 **RESTAURANT:** 12-2 6-8.30
BREWERY/COMPANY: Punch Taverns **◀:** IPA.
FACILITIES: Children welcome Garden: "L" shaped garden with tables and chairs Dogs allowed **NOTES:** Parking 25 **NOTES:** No credit cards

BEDMOND   Map 06 TL00

The Swan 🐾 ♀ NEW
Bedmond Rd, Pimlico HP3 8SH
☎ 01923 263093 ⓘ 0118 375 1555
e-mail: johnvictorlucy@hotmail.com
Dir: Between Hemel Hempstead and Watford
An attractive, traditional pub, whose whitewashed front is adorned with colourful hanging baskets. Outside is a large lawn, play area and adults-only patio. Inside, you'll find a warm welcome and a wide selection of traditional pub food. Bar meals include burgers, jacket potatoes and sandwiches, whilst a meal from the main menu could include French fish soup followed by roast lamb, scampi and chips or perhaps pan-fried chicken and bacon.
OPEN: 11-11 (Sun 12-10.30) **BAR MEALS:** L served all week 12-3 D served all week 6.30-10 Av main course £9 **RESTAURANT:** L served all week 12-3 D served all week 6.30-10 Av 3 course à la carte £17 Av fixed price £9 **◀:** Mr Chubbs Lunchtime Bitter, Abbot Ale, Fullers London Pride. ♀: 8 **FACILITIES:** Children welcome Garden: Large lawn, adult only patio **NOTES:** Parking 70

BERKHAMSTED   Map 06 SP90

The Boat ♀
Gravel Path HP4 2EF ☎ 01442 877152
Very modern canalside pub that has a lot of character despite its relative youth. A summer terrace overlooks the canal.
OPEN: 11-11 **BAR MEALS:** L served all week 12-9 D served all week Av main course £6 **RESTAURANT:** L served all week 12-3 D served Mon-Thur 6-9 **BREWERY/COMPANY:** Fullers **◀:** Fuller's London Pride,

ESB, Chiswick,. **FACILITIES:** Children welcome Garden: Canal side garden, food served outside Dogs allowed Water **NOTES:** Parking 16

BUNTINGFORD   Map 12 TL32

The Sword in Hand 🐾 ♀
Westmill SG9 9LQ ☎ 01763 271356
e-mail: heather@swordinhand.ndo.co.uk
Dir: Off A10 1.5m S of Buntingford
Early 15th-century inn, once the home of the Scottish noble family, Gregs. The pub's name is taken from a motif within their family crest. The dining room looks out over open countryside, and offers a regularly changing menu. This may include swordfish steak with chilli and coriander couscous, chicken breast stuffed with Brie and wrapped in bacon, roasted skate wing with fresh mussels, and Barbary duck breast with honey and wholegrain mustard sauce.
OPEN: 12-3 5.30-11 **BAR MEALS:** L served Tues-Sun 12-2.30 D served Tues-Sun 6.30-9.30 Av main course £8 **RESTAURANT:** L served Tues-Sun 12-2.30 D served Tues-Sun 6.30-9.30 Av 3 course à la carte £18 **BREWERY/COMPANY:** Free House **◀:** Greene King IPA, Abbot Ale & Old Speckled Hen, Young's Bitter.
FACILITIES: Children welcome Garden: beautiful view, patio area, pergola Dogs allowed **NOTES:** Parking 25

COTTERED   Map 12 TL32

The Bull at Cottered 🐾
Cottered ☎ 01763 281243
Traditional local in an attractive village setting, with a good-sized garden outside and low-beamed ceilings, open log fires and pub games like cribbage and dominoes inside. Well-kept ales and a good choice of meals are served, ranging from ploughman's, home-made burgers and jacket potatoes to steak, Guinness and Stilton pie, or calves' liver with mustard mash and red wine and onion gravy.
OPEN: 12-2.30 6.30-11 **BAR MEALS:** L served all week 12-2 D served Wed-Mon 6.30-9 Av main course £8.50 **RESTAURANT:** L served all week 12-2 D served Wed-Mon 6.30-9 Av 3 course à la carte £21 Av 3 course fixed price £21.50 **BREWERY/COMPANY:** Greene King **◀:** Greene king IPA & Abbot Ale. **FACILITIES:** Children welcome Garden: Large well kept, rabbits **NOTES:** Parking 30

FLAUNDEN   Map 06 TL00

The Bricklayers Arms ♀
Hogpits Bottom HP3 0PH ☎ 01442 833322
Dir: M1 J8 through H Hempstead to Bovington then follow Flaunden sign. M25 J18 through Chorleywood to Chenies/Latimer then Flaunden

A traditional country pub clad with Virginia creeper, with a low-beamed bar and wooden wall seats within and dazzling floral baskets without. Popular with walkers and locals and

continued

continued

those who enjoy relaxing in the delightfully old-fashioned garden in the summer months. Once inside, the inn offers a friendly, informal ambience enhanced by good quality, freshly-prepared dishes such as grilled lamb cutlets, seared halibut, stuffed chicken and spinach and Ricotta roll.
OPEN: 11.30-3 6-11 **BAR MEALS:** L served all week 12-2 D served all week 7-9 **RESTAURANT:** L served all week 12-2 D served all week 7-9 **BREWERY/COMPANY:** Free House ◀: Fuller's London Pride, Brakspear Bitter, Ringwood Old Thumper, Marston's Pedigree.
FACILITIES: Children welcome Garden: Sunny & Secluded Dogs allowed Water **NOTES:** Parking 40

HARPENDEN
Map 06 TL11

Gibraltar Castle 🍴 ♀
70 Lower Luton Rd AL5 5AH ☎ 01582 460005
Bustling Fuller's pub located opposite a common in Batford. The pub may be up to 350 years old, and is believed to be the only pub with this name in the UK. In the past it was used as a magistrates court, and the remnants of an old cell are to be found in the beer cellar. Imaginative pub grub includes chicken wrapped in ham stuffed with Brie, and a variety of fresh fish. Now under new management.
OPEN: 11-3 5-11 (Sun 12-4, 6-10.30) **BAR MEALS:** L served all week 12-2.30 D served Mon-Sat 6-9 Av main course £10 **RESTAURANT:** L served all week D served Mon-Sat Av 3 course à la carte £17.50 **BREWERY/COMPANY:** Fullers ◀: Fuller's London Pride, ESB, Chiswick Bitter, Honey Dew & Red Fox. ♀: 7
FACILITIES: Children welcome Garden: Front garden lined with flower pots Dogs allowed Water **NOTES:** Parking 25

The Old Bell 🍴 ♀
177 Luton Rd AL5 3BN ☎ 01582 712484 🖷 01582 715015
Dir: Jct 10 M1, follow signs for Harpenden, 3 miles on R
A historic 18th-century pub which began selling beer to local straw-plaiters and farm workers, and later the railway navvies who built a branch line from Luton to Harpenden. It still serves full-bodied ales along with freshly-prepared food - fish is the house speciality. Expect Mediterranean swordfish, grilled plaice stuffed with prawn mousse, paella, and perhaps roast shoulder of lamb, beef and Theakston pie, and lemon-basted chicken.
OPEN: 11-11 (Sun 12-11) **BAR MEALS:** L served all week 11-10 D served all week Av main course £8 **RESTAURANT:** L served all week 11-10 D served all week **BREWERY/COMPANY:** Chef & Brewer ◀: Courage Best, guest ales. **FACILITIES:** Children welcome Garden: Food served outside **NOTES:** Parking 100

HEMEL HEMPSTEAD
Map 06 TL00

Pick of the Pubs

Alford Arms ♀
Frithsden HP1 3DD ☎ 01442 864480 🖷 01422 876893
A typically Victorian building surrounded by National Trust woodland. The Alford Arms is full of traditional finishes - log fires, old furniture and pictures, quarry tiles and reclaimed wooden floors - though the feel is still light and modern. The atmosphere is very relaxed - this is a pub that just happens to do great food. The same menu is served throughout, and whether you're after a pint and a sandwich or a slap-up feed, there is much to be recommended. Local, free-range and organic ingredients are used wherever possible, in 'small plates' like seared scallops with pea purée, and wild mushroom, thyme and Gruyère tart, and such main dishes as pan-fried pork tenderloin on creamy blue cheese, and braised lamb

continued

shank on spiced Puy lentils. A vegetarian option might be chargrilled Parmesan polenta with sautéed vegetables. On warm days the sunny terrace is always packed.
OPEN: 11-11 (Sun 12-10.30) Closed: 25 -26 Dec **BAR MEALS:** L served all week 12-2.30 D served all week 7-10 **RESTAURANT:** L served all week 12-2.30 D served all week 7-10 Av 3 course à la carte £21.50 **BREWERY/COMPANY:** Free House ◀: Marstons Pedigree, Brakspear, Interbrew Flowers, Carlsberg-Tetley Tetley. ♀: 13 **FACILITIES:** Children welcome Garden: Terrace with tables overlooking green Dogs allowed Water provided **NOTES:** Parking 25

HEXTON
Map 12 TL13

The Raven ♀
SG5 3JB ☎ 01582 881209 🖷 01582 881610
e-mail: jack@ravenathexton-f9.co.uk
Dir: Telephone for directions

Named after Ravensburgh Castle up in the neighbouring hills, this neat 1920s pub has comfortable bars and a large garden with terrace and play area. The traditional pub food menu is more comprehensive than many, with baguettes, filled jackets, pork ribs, steaks from the Duke of Buccleuch's Scottish estate, surf and turf, ribs, hot chicken and bacon salad, Mediterranean pasta bake and a whole lot more. Daily specials are on the blackboard.
OPEN: 11-3 6-11 (Sun 12-10.30) **BAR MEALS:** L served all week 12-2 D served all week 6-10 Av main course £7.95 **RESTAURANT:** L served all week 12-2 D served all week 6-10 **BREWERY/COMPANY:** Enterprise Inns ◀: Greene King Old Speckled Hen, Fullers London Pride. ♀: 16 **FACILITIES:** Children welcome Garden: Table and chair seating for 50 Dogs allowed garden only. Water provided **NOTES:** Parking 40

HINXWORTH
Map 12 TL24

Three Horseshoes 🍴
High St SG7 5HQ ☎ 01462 742280
Dir: E of A1 between Biggleswade and Baldock
Thatched 18th-century country pub with a dining extension into the garden. Parts of the building date back 500 years, and the walls are adorned with pictures and photos of the village's history. Samples from a typical menu include chicken of the wood, lamb cutlets with champ, rainbow trout with almonds, sea bass provençale, steak and Guinness pie, bacon and cheese pasta bake, and roasted Tuscan red peppers.
OPEN: 11.30-2.30 6-11 **BAR MEALS:** L served all week 12-2 D served Mon-Sat 7-9 Av main course £7.50 **RESTAURANT:** L served all week 12-2 D served Mon-Sat 7-9 Av 3 course à la carte £18 **BREWERY/COMPANY:** Greene King ◀: Greene King IPA, Abbot Ale. **FACILITIES:** Garden: Large, rustic, with trees and a petanque area Dogs allowed garden only **NOTES:** Parking 16

HITCHIN
Map 12 TL12

The Greyhound ◆◆◆ 🛏 ♀
London Rd, St Ippolyts SG4 7NL ☎ 01462 440989
e-mail: greyhound@freenet.co.uk

The Greyhound was rescued from dereliction by the present owners and is now a friendly, family-run inn surrounded by farmland yet conveniently located for the M1 and Luton Airport. The food is good, fresh and unpretentious, offering dishes such as fresh haddock fillet, duck breast, lamb kebabs, jugged hare, venison, steak and Adnams pie, and rabbit casserole. Due to popularity, the management suggest you book a table in advance.
OPEN: 11.30-2.30 5-11 Closed: Dec 25-26 **BAR MEALS:** L served all week 12-2 D served all week 7-10 Av main course £9 **RESTAURANT:** L served all week 12-2 D served all week 7-10 **BREWERY/COMPANY:** Free House 🍺: Adnams, Guest. **FACILITIES:** Garden: Patio area **NOTES:** Parking 25 **ROOMS:** 4 bedrooms 4 en suite s£50 d£60 no children overnight

KIMPTON
Map 06 TL11

The White Horse 🛏 ♀
22 High St SG4 8RJ ☎ 01438 832307 📠 01438 833842
e-mail: thewhitehorsepub@aol.com

Dating from the mid-1500s, this popular low-roofed pub features a priest hole behind the bar and, on winter evenings, welcomes customers with a roaring log fire. Located in a delightful country village, it also has a decked garden for dining outside. Varied menu with the likes of beef fillet steak filled with creamy horseradish on a rösti potato bed, and slow-roast lamb fillet topped with a mini rack of lamb all in a red wine jus.
OPEN: 12-2.30 6-11 (Sat 12-3, 6-11, Sun 12-4, 7-10.30)
BAR MEALS: L served Tues-Sun 12-2 D served Tues-Sat **RESTAURANT:** L served Tues-Sun 12-2 D served Tues-Sat 7-9 Av 3 course à la carte £16.50 🍺: Scottish Courage Courage Directors, Interbrew Bass, McMullen Original AK. ♀: 8 **FACILITIES:** Garden: Decked area, tables & chair **NOTES:** Parking 10

LITTLE HADHAM
Map 06 TL42

The Nags Head 🛏 ♀
The Ford SG11 2AX ☎ 01279 771555 📠 01279 771555
Dir: M11 J8 take A120 towards Puckeridge & A10. At lights in Little Hadnam turn L. Pub 0.75m on R
16th-century, former coaching inn that has doubled as a brewery, a bakery and an arsenal for the Home Guard during the War. It boasts an oak-beamed bar, and a restaurant area with open brickwork and an old bakery oven (now seating two people). Popular and wide-ranging menu includes Italian seafood salad, and grilled sardines followed by poached skate wing, Swiss lamb joint, and chicken chasseur.
OPEN: 11-2.30 6-11 (Sun 12-3.30 7-10.30) Dec 25-26 Closed eve **BAR MEALS:** L served all week 12-2 D served all week 6-9 Av main course £5.95 **RESTAURANT:** L served all week 12-2 D served all week 6-9 Av 3 course à la carte £15 **BREWERY/COMPANY:** Greene King 🍺: Greene King Abbot Ale, IPA, Old Speckled Hen & Ruddles County Ale, Marstons Pedigree. **FACILITIES:** Children welcome Garden: Patio area at the front of the pub Dogs allowed Water

MUCH HADHAM
Map 06 TL41

Jolly Waggoners 🛏 ♀
Widford Rd SG10 6EZ ☎ 01279 842102 📠 01279 842102
e-mail: Jollywaggoners@btinternet.com
Dir: On B1004 between Bishops Stortford & Ware
Daily fresh fish features on the evening menu at this Victorian pub built from two older cottages. A large open fire and beamed interior lend character to the non-smoking bar, and there are no noisy games machines to disturb the atmosphere. From the specials board expect several choices of fish, plus roast meats and grills, and the likes of omelettes, curries, pork Wellington and vegetarian dishes, all home made. Classic car meet held on the third Sunday of each month.
OPEN: 12-2.30 6.30-11 (Sun 12-3, 7-10.30) **BAR MEALS:** L served all week 12-2 D served all week 6.30-9 Av main course £6 **RESTAURANT:** L served all week 12-2.30 D served all week 6.30-9.00 Av 3 course à la carte £15 Av 2 course fixed price £5.95 **BREWERY/COMPANY:** McMullens 🍺: McMullen Original AK & Country Best Bitter, Scottish Courage Courage Directors. ♀: 8 **FACILITIES:** Children welcome Garden: picnic area with seating for over 40 people Dogs allowed Water **NOTES:** Parking 40

OLD KNEBWORTH
Map 06 TL22

The Lytton Arms ♀
Park Ln SG3 6QB ☎ 01438 812312 📠 01438 815289
e-mail: thelyttonarms@btinternet.com
Dir: From A1(M) take A602. At Knebworth turn R at rail station. Follow signs 'Codicote'. Pub 1.5m on R
Popular with ramblers, horse-riders and cyclists in picturesque north Hertfordshire countryside, this 1877 Lutyens-designed inn claims to have served over 4,000 real ales in 14 years. Without pool tables, video games or juke box, the pub offers a relaxing atmosphere in which to enjoy carefully-prepared pub food. Speciality sausages with English ale chutney, Thai chicken and banana curry, and treacle sponge with custard create a blend of traditional and exotic choices.
OPEN: 11-11 (Sun 12-10.30) **BAR MEALS:** L served Mon-Sun 12-2.30 D served Mon-Sat 7-9.30 Av main course £5.95 **RESTAURANT:** L served Mon-Sun 12-2 D served Mon-Sat 6.30-9.30 **BREWERY/COMPANY:** Free House 🍺: Fuller's London Pride, Adnams Best Bitter & Broadside. **FACILITIES:** Children welcome Garden: Food served outside Dogs allowed Water **NOTES:** Parking 40

POTTERS CROUCH
Map 06 TL10

The Hollybush ♀
AL2 3NN ☎ 01727 851792 ▯ 01727 851792
Dir: Ragged Ln off A405 or Bedmond Ln off A4147
Picturesque, attractively-furnished country pub with quaint, white-painted exterior and large, enclosed garden. Close to St Albans with its Roman ruins and good local walks. An antique dresser, a large fireplace and various prints and paintings help give the inn a delightfully welcoming atmosphere. Food is simple and unfussy, with a range of ploughman's, burgers, platters and toasted sandwiches. Smoked and peppered mackerel fillet, pasties and salads also feature.
OPEN: 11.30-2.30 6-11 (Sun 12-2.30, 7-10.30) **BAR MEALS:** L served Mon-Sat 12-2 **BREWERY/COMPANY:** Fullers ◄: Fuller's Chiswick Bitter, Fullers London Pride, ESB & Seasonal Ales. ♀: 7
FACILITIES: Garden: **NOTES:** Parking 50

PRESTON
Map 06 TL12

The Red Lion ▯
The Green SG4 7UD ☎ 01462 459585 ▯ 01462 442284
e-mail: janebaerlein@hotmail.com

Bought from Whitbread's in 1983, the Red Lion was the first community-owned pub in Britain. When the pub was threatened with closure, local people funded the purchase and renovation to ensure a continuing focal point for their village. Now, this award-winning free house offers a range of guest ales and a regularly-changing menu board that includes home-made pies, seasonal game, fresh fish and vegetarian options, as well as a selection of home-made puddings.
OPEN: 12-2.30 5.30-11 **BAR MEALS:** L served all week 12-2 D served Wed-Sat, Mon 7-9 Av main course £5.95
BREWERY/COMPANY: Free House ◄: Greene King IPA & Changing real ales. **FACILITIES:** Children welcome Garden Dogs allowed Water **NOTES:** Parking 60 No credit cards

ROYSTON
Map 12 TL34

The Green Man
Lower St, Thriplow SG8 7RJ ☎ 01763 208855 ▯ 01763 208431
e-mail: greenmanthriplow@ntlworld.com
Dir: 1m W of junction 10 on M11
A rejuvenated early 19th-century pub standing at the heart of a quaint rural village famous for its annual daffodil weekend and pig race. It offers fixed-price menus and guest ales that change regularly. Typical evening dishes include braised shoulder of lamb and foie gras, and roast duck breast, while the lunchtime selection might include goats' cheese and roast pepper cannelloni. Picnic tables in the large landscaped garden encourage al fresco meals.
OPEN: 12-2.30 6-11 **BAR MEALS:** L served Tue-Sun 12-2.30 D

continued

served Tue-Sat 7-9.30 Av main course £8 **RESTAURANT:** 12-2.30 D served Tue-Sat 7-9.30 **BREWERY/COMPANY:** Free House
◄: Eccleshall Slaters Original, Hop Back Summer Lightning, Batemans XXXB, Milton Klas Act. **FACILITIES:** Children welcome Garden Guide dogs only **NOTES:** Parking 12

ST ALBANS
Map 06 TL10

Rose & Crown ♀
10 St Michael St AL3 4SG ☎ 01727 851903 ▯ 01727 766450
e-mail: julia.dekker@ntlworld.com
Traditional 16th-century pub situated in a beautiful part of St Michael's 'village', opposite the entrance to Verulanium Park and the Roman Museum. It has a classic beamed bar with a huge inglenook, and a summer patio filled with flowers. Excellent American deli-style sandwiches are served with potato salad, kettle crisps and pickled cucumber. The 'Clark Gable', for example, has roast beef, American cheese, onions, cucumber, tomato, horseradish and mustard.
OPEN: 11.30-3 5.30-11 (Open all day Sun Open all day Sat Easter-Oct) **BAR MEALS:** L served Mon-Sat 12-2 Av main course £6
BREWERY/COMPANY: Pubmaster ◄: Adnams Bitter, Carlsberg-Tetley Tetley Bitter, Fuller's London Pride, Guest beers. ♀: 8
FACILITIES: Children welcome Children's licence Garden: Tables, hanging baskets etc Dogs allowed Water **NOTES:** Parking 6

SARRATT
Map 06 TQ09

The Cock Inn ♀
Church End, Church Ln WD3 6HH
☎ 01923 282908 ▯ 01923 286224
Dir: Between M25 J18 & A404 opposite St Clement Danes School
Cream-painted 17th-century pub opposite the 12th-century church and overlooking open countryside at the rear. The pub takes its name from the cock-horse that pulled carts up the hill from the nearby mill. Character interior includes a cosy snug with a vaulted ceiling and original bread oven. The restaurant is a converted barn with exposed beams and high-pitched roof. Good quality menu and daily specials feature the likes of bangers and mash, roast bell peppers stuffed with spicy couscous, seafood pasta, chicken and asparagus pie, and liver and bacon casserole. Under new management, reader's reports welcome.
OPEN: 11-3 5.30-11 (All day wknds) **BAR MEALS:** L served all week 12-2.30 D served all week 6-9.30 **RESTAURANT:** L served all week 12-2.30 D served all week 6-9.30 **BREWERY/COMPANY:** Hall & Woodhouse ◄: Badger Tanglefoot, Dorset Best & IPA, King and Barnes Sussex Bitter. ♀: 8 **FACILITIES:** Children welcome Garden: 30 benches Dogs allowed Water **NOTES:** Parking 40

STOTFOLD
Map 12 TL23

The Fox & Duck ♀
149 Arlesey Raod SG5 4HE ☎ 01462 732434 ▯ 01462 835962
e-mail: foxandduck@cragg-inns.co.uk
Set on a large site, this picturesque family pub has a big garden, a children's playground, a caravan site, weekly football matches, and regular barbecues. Children's birthday parties catered for. A sample menu selection includes 8oz fillet steak with Stilton and Madeira, sizzling black bean chicken, medallions of pork with honey and ginger, and a wide range of home-made soups and pâtés.
OPEN: 12-3 5-11 (Sat 12-11, Sun 12-10.30) **BAR MEALS:** L served all week 12-2 D served all week 5-8 Av main course £5.50
RESTAURANT: L served all week 12-2 D served all week 6-9 Av 3 course à la carte £21 **BREWERY/COMPANY:** Greene King ◄: Greene King Old Speckled Hen & IPA. **FACILITIES:** Children welcome Garden: Food served outdoors Dogs allowed **NOTES:** Parking 40

TEWIN   Map 06 TL21

The Plume of Feathers 🛏️ ♀
Upper Green Rd AL6 0LX ☎ 01438 717265 📠 01438 712596
Dir: *E from A1 J6 toward WGC, follow B1000 toward Hertford, Tewin signed on L*

Built in 1596, this historic inn, firstly an Elizabethan hunting lodge and later the haunt of highwaymen, boasts several ghosts including a 'lady in grey'. Interesting menus change daily, and now include a tapas bar from noon till close. Other options available are Moroccan spiced baby shark with king prawns and couscous, honey-roast duck with sweet potato wontons or slow-roasted belly pork with bacon and cabbage. Be sure to book in advance.
OPEN: 12-11 (Closed 3-6 Oct-Mar) **BAR MEALS:** L served all week 12-2 D served Mon-Sat 7-9 Av main course £10 **RESTAURANT:** L served all week 12-2 D served Mon-Sat 7-9 Av 3 course à la carte £20 **BREWERY/COMPANY:** Greene King ♀: 30 **FACILITIES:** Garden: Dogs allowed Garden only, water **NOTES:** Parking 40

WALKERN   Map 12 TL22

The White Lion
31 The High St SG2 7PA ☎ 01438 861251 📠 01438 861160
Dir: *B1037 from Stevenage*
Late 16th-century timber-framed building, originally a coaching inn on the Nottingham to London route, and ideal for walkers. The garden has a patio and a pétanque pitch. Very recent change of management.
OPEN: 12-3 5-11 (closed Sun eve & all Mon ex BHs)
BAR MEALS: L served Tues-Sun 12-3 D served Tues-Sat 5-11 Av main course £7 **RESTAURANT:** L served Tues-Sun 12-3 D served Tues-Sat 5-11 Av 3 course à la carte £16
BREWERY/COMPANY: Greene King 🍺: Greene King IPA & Abbot Ale. **FACILITIES:** Children welcome Garden **NOTES:** Parking 30

WELLPOND GREEN   Map 06 TL42

Nag's Head ♦♦♦♦ 🛏️
SG11 1NL ☎ 01920 821424
Dir: *Telephone for directions*
The Nag's Head is a family-run free house in a sleepy hamlet in pretty rolling countryside, half a mile off the A120. The menu offers four or more fish and seafood main courses, most likely including sea bass and lemon sole. Other popular dishes are beef Stilton, and grilled chicken with cheese and bacon. This is Greene King heartland, so IPA and Ruddles County will be on tap in the bar. Comfortable overnight accommodation in newly completed en suite bedrooms.
OPEN: 12-2.30 6-11 **BAR MEALS:** L served Tue-Sun 12-2 D served Tue-Sun 6.30-9.30 Av main course £6.95 **RESTAURANT:** L served Tue-Sun 12-2 D served Tue-Sat 6.30-9.30

BREWERY/COMPANY: Free House 🍺: Greene King IPA & Ruddles County. **FACILITIES:** Children welcome Garden: Lawn, full size boules pitch, Patio **NOTES:** Parking 28 **ROOMS:** 5 bedrooms 5 en suite 1 family rooms s£50 d£70

WESTON   Map 12 TL23

The Rising Sun 🛏️
21 Halls Green SG4 7DR ☎ 01462 790487 📠 01462 790846
e-mail: mike@therisingsun-hallsgreen.co.uk
Dir: *A1(M)J9 take A6141 towards Baldock & turn R towards Graveley. 100yds take 1st L*
Set in picturesque Hertfordshire countryside, the Rising Sun welcomes those with children in tow, providing an appropriate menu, play equipment, and tuck shop in summer. For adults, the regularly-changing menu offers starters such as Stilton mushrooms, and salmon fishcakes with dill sauce. Main courses include chargrilled steaks, salmon with dill and mustard sauce, or smoked fish crumble. There is a huge choice of sweets, and blackboards detailing specials are changed daily.
OPEN: 11-2.30 6-11 (open all day Sat Summer) **BAR MEALS:** L served all week 12-2 D served all week 6-9 Av main course £6.95 **RESTAURANT:** L served all week 12-2 D served all week 6-9 Av 3 course à la carte £15 **BREWERY/COMPANY:** McMullens 🍺: McMullen Original AK Ale, Fosters, Macs Country Best. **FACILITIES:** Garden: Well maintained with plenty of play equipment Dogs allowed **NOTES:** Parking 40

KENT

BENENDEN   Map 07 TQ83

The Bull at Benenden ♀
The Street TN17 4DE ☎ 01580 240054
e-mail: thebull@thebullatbenenden.co.uk
Dir: *Benenden is on the B2086 between Cranbrook and Tenterden*
Right on the village green, this listed family-run pub is thought to date back to 1608. It lies in the typically Kentish village where the Princess Royal went to school. Several of the bar snacks and Sunday main courses sensibly come in large or small portions, among them summer salads, grills, home-made lasagne, traditional roasts, battered cod and chips, and pasta Milano. Weekday main courses include vegetable curry, monkfish and Dijon pork. Harvey's and Shepherd Neame on tap.
OPEN: 11.30-3 6-11 (Sat 11-11.30) (Sun 12-10.30) **BAR MEALS:** L served all week 12-2.15 D served all week 7-9.15 Av main course £7.95 **RESTAURANT:** L served all week 12-2.15 D served all week 7-9.15 Av 3 course à la carte £17.50 **BREWERY/COMPANY:** Free House 🍺: Harveys, Spitfire. **FACILITIES:** Garden: Small sheltered garden **NOTES:** Parking 12 **ROOMS:** 3 bedrooms 3 en suite d£65 (♦♦♦♦) no children overnight

continued

Castle Inn

This delightful walk passes close to historic Hever Castle, in Tudor times the home of the Boleyn family and later the property of William Waldorf Astor, who spent a fortune on restoring it. He also built the village of Hever in Tudor style.

With the Castle Inn behind you and St Mary's Church on your right, take the road skirting the lake, keeping Chiddingstone Castle away to your left. Go over Gilwyns crossroads and straight ahead along the undulating road for about half a mile (800m).

When the road turns sharp left, go through an opening in the fence on your right to a path cutting through the grounds of Hever Castle. The path runs alongside a fence, next to a wood, with a private road to your left. Cross the road by a picturesque rustic bridge and continue between fences to a path crossing Hever churchyard to a lychgate. Noted for its slender spire, the church contains the tomb of Sir Thomas Bullen, father of Anne Boleyn, Henry VIII's mistress and then his tragic queen.

Make for the lychgate and turn left. When the road bends sharp right by the Henry VIII Inn, continue straight ahead via a path, passing the village school on your left. Follow the path to a quiet road and turn left. On reaching a junction, turn left over a stile and continue by a hedge. Turn right, skirt a wood and continue by hedging to a stile. Cross it, passing woodland on the right to reach the private road encountered early in the walk.

Don't join the road; instead turn right and follow a path alongside fencing. Cross the next road to a gate and go straight ahead between fences along the field edge. Turn right on reaching a wood, then sharp left, over a small footbridge and up a steep path. When the path reaches a track, turn left - if it

CASTLE INN, CHIDDINGSTONE
TN8 7AH
☎ 01892 870247

Directions: S of 2027 between Tonbridge & Edenbridge
Much used as a film set, dating back to 1420, and full of nooks and crannies. Beamed bar, vine-hung orchard and good ales are popular features. Good reputation for food, including typical bar meals and more sophisticated dishes.
Open: 11-11
Bar Meals: 12-2 7.30-9.30
Notes: Children welcome - highchairs, baby changing, bottle warmers. Water for dogs. Patio, lawn.
(See page 263 for full entry)

is muddy here then take the parallel track on the left. Pass alongside a half-timbered house called Withers and turn left down the road. Follow it for about 1/2 mile (800m) to reach Gilwyns crossroads again. Turn right and return to the inn.

DISTANCE: 4 1/2 miles (7.2km)
MAP: OS Explorer 147
TERRAIN: Woodland and farmland
PATHS: roads, sometimes muddy paths and tracks
GRADIENT: One steep climb

Walk submitted by the Castle Inn, Chiddingstone

England

BIDDENDEN — Map 07 TQ83

Pick of the Pubs

The Three Chimneys ♀
Biddenden Rd TN27 8LW ☎ 01580 291472
Dir: On A262 between Biddenden and Sissinghurst
During the Seven Years War (1756-1763) French prisoners were allowed to roam freely in the vicinity, as long as they went no farther than the signpost with the three ways on it. This became known as 'Les Trois Chemins' and was interpreted back into English as 'The Three Chimneys'. The interior of this 15th-century pub seems to have changed little since that time: the original small-room layout remains, as do old settles, low beams, wood-panelled walls, flagstone floors and warming fires. It is said that a friendly sentry used to light a candelabra in the sentry window by the front door to let soldiers know when there were no English officials inside. Food is cooked to order here, and the daily-changing menu features dishes such as sautéed lamb's liver and bacon in a Port and red onion gravy, seared tuna on avocado salsa with a sauce vierge, and grilled fillet of salmon in a brown butter with capers, lemon and Icelandic prawns. A classic, atmospheric country pub.
OPEN: 11.30-3 6-11 (Sun 12-3, 7-10.30) Closed: 25 Dec
BAR MEALS: L served all week 12-1.50 D served all week 6-9.45 Av main course £11.95 **RESTAURANT:** L served all week 12-2 D served all week 6-10 **BREWERY/COMPANY:** Free House ◀: Shepherd Neame, Adnams, Masterbrew, Spitfire.
♀: 10 **FACILITIES:** Garden: View of fields, nuttery at bottom of garden Dogs allowed **NOTES:** Parking 70

BOUGHTON ALUPH — Map 07 TR04

The Flying Horse Inn
TN25 4HH ☎ 01233 620914
15th-century inn with oak beams and open log fires. Comfortable minstrel bar with sunken wells. Regular cricket matches in summer on the spacious village green opposite. Good selection of real ales and a varied menu which might include roast rack of lamb, poached salmon, monkfish with mushroom, lemon and butter sauce, baked avocado with spinach, or braised lamb shank.
OPEN: 12-11 **BAR MEALS:** L served all week 12-2.30 D served all week 6-9 Av main course £5 **RESTAURANT:** L served all week 12-2 D served all week 7-9 Av 3 course à la carte £20
BREWERY/COMPANY: Unique Pub Co ◀: Fullers London Pride, Courage Best, Greene King IPA, Spitfire. **FACILITIES:** Garden: outdoor eating, patio/terrace, BBQ **NOTES:** Parking 40

BOYDEN GATE — Map 07 TR26

Pick of the Pubs

The Gate Inn ♀
Boyden Gate CT3 4EB ☎ 01227 860498
Dir: From Canterbury on A28 turn L at Upstreet
Surrounded by marshland and pasture, as rural a retreat as you'll find anywhere. On display is the Chislet Horse, which the locals will explain better than this guide. The garden is a picture, bounded by a stream and a pond with ducks and geese. Quarry-tiled floors and pine furniture feature in the family-friendly, interconnecting bars, while sustaining food includes jacket potatoes with 16 different fillings, Gateburgers (10 different), sandwiches (17) ploughman's, torpedoes and spicy home-made hotpots.
OPEN: 11-2.30 6-11 (Sun 12-4, 7-10.30) **BAR MEALS:** L served all week 12-2 D served all week 6-9
BREWERY/COMPANY: Shepherd Neame ◀: Shepherd Neame Master Brew, Spitfire & Bishops Finger, Seasonal Beers.
♀: 11 **FACILITIES:** Children welcome Garden: By the side of stream Dogs allowed Water & dog biscuits **NOTES:** Parking 14
NOTES: No credit cards

BRABOURNE — Map 07 TR14

The Five Bells ☜ ♀
The Street TN25 5LP ☎ 01303 813334 📠 01303 814667
e-mail: five.bells@lineone.net
Dir: 5m E of Ashford

Named after those rung out from the village church, this 16th-century inn lies below the scarp slope of the North Downs. Its old beams, inglenook fireplace and traditional upholstery help create a welcoming and hospitable atmosphere - and no piped music to spoil it. The garden is delightful. Extensive menus include fresh fish of the day, and home-made specialities such as steak and kidney pie, Wienerschnitzel, and chicken curry, plus snacks, salads and a children's menu.
OPEN: 11.30-3 6.30-11 **BAR MEALS:** L served all week 12-2 D served all week 7-10 Av main course £9 **RESTAURANT:** L served all week 12-2 D served all week 7-12 **BREWERY/COMPANY:** Free House ◀: Shepherd Neame Master Brew, Wells Bombardier, Interbrew Bass, Greene King IPA. **FACILITIES:** Children welcome Garden: Lawn, seating for 80 persons Dogs allowed Water
NOTES: Parking 65

BROOKLAND — Map 07 TQ92

Woolpack Inn ☜
TN29 9TJ ☎ 01797 344321
Partly built from old ship timbers and set in Kentish marshland, this 15th-century cottage inn was originally a beacon-keeper's house, and is particularly popular with birdwatchers. One of the long Victorian tables has penny games carved into the top. Homemade wholesome pub food includes steak pie, chicken Kiev, pork chops, lasagne, grilled trout, a variety of steaks, and the usual sandwiches, jackets and ploughmans. Chips with everything. See the blackboard for specials.
OPEN: 11-3 6-11 (Open all day Sat & Sun) **BAR MEALS:** L served all week 12-2 D served all week 6-9 Av main course £6
BREWERY/COMPANY: Shepherd Neame ◀: Shepherd Neame Spitfire Premium Ale, Master Brew Bitter. **FACILITIES:** Children welcome Garden: Large beer garden with 12 tables Dogs allowed Water **NOTES:** Parking 30

continued

England

BURHAM
Map 06 TQ76

The Golden Eagle
80 Church St ME1 3SD ☎ 01634 668975 🖺 01634 668975
Dir: South from M2 J3 or North M20 J6 on A229, signs to Burham

Set on the North Downs with fine views of the Medway Valley, this traditional free house has a friendly and informal atmosphere. The appearance of an old-fashioned English inn is belied by the fact that the kitchen specialises in oriental cooking, with an extensive menu that includes dishes from China, Malaysia, Thailand and Singapore. House specials include pork babibangang, king prawn sambal, wor-tip crispy chicken, vegetarian mee goreng, and chicken tom yam. As you would expect, vegetarians are well catered for.
OPEN: 11.30-2.30 6.15-11 Closed: Dec 25-26 **BAR MEALS:** L served all week 12-2 D served all week 7-10 **RESTAURANT:** L served all week 12-2 D served all week 7-10
BREWERY/COMPANY: Free House 🍺: Wadworth 6X, Marston's Pedigree. **NOTES:** Parking 45

CANTERBURY
Map 07 TR15

The Chapter Arms
New Town St, Chartham Hatch CT4 7LT
☎ 01227 738340 🖺 01227 732536
e-mail: chapterarms@clara.co.uk
Dir: 3 miles from Canterbury Off A28 in the village of Chartham Hatch

A flower-bedecked freehouse on the Pilgrims' Way with a garden featuring fish ponds and fruit trees. The property was once three cottages owned by nearby Canterbury Cathedral's Dean and Chapter - hence the name. Daily menus offer plenty of fresh fish, such as fillet of Sussex cod topped with cherry tomatoes, chives, Cheddar cheese and cream; or king prawns with fresh chillies and warm mixed breads. Or try beef suet pudding, home-made pie of the day, or a filled freshly-baked baguette.
OPEN: 11-3 6.30-11 Closed: 25 Dec (eve) **BAR MEALS:** L served all week 12-2 D served Mon-Sat 7-9 Av main course £8
RESTAURANT: L served all week 12-2 D served all week 7-9

BREWERY/COMPANY: Free House 🍺: Shepherd Neame Master Brew, Cambrinus Herald, Harveys Sussex Best, Adnams. 🍷: 8
FACILITIES: Children welcome Garden: 1 acre of fish ponds & Lawn Dogs allowed Water **NOTES:** Parking 40

Pick of the Pubs

The Dove Inn 🍷
Plum Pudding Ln, Dargate ME13 9HB ☎ 01227 751360
Tucked away in a sleepy hamlet on the delightfully named Plum Pudding Lane, the Dove is the sort of pub you dream of having as your local: roses round the door, a simple interior (stripped wooden floors and plain tables), tip-top Shepherd Neame ales, and a relaxed atmosphere. On top of all this, it has astonishingly good food. A series of blackboard menus feature fresh fish from Hythe and local game expertly prepared by talented chef/proprietor Nigel Morris. An inspiring selection of snacks might include caramelised pork with stir-fried vegetables, pan-fried crevettes with pickled ginger and garden herbs or avocado, bacon and rocket salad. Full meals could begin with crab and spring onion risotto or baked wild mushroom and Bayonne ham tart, followed by equally imaginative main courses: perhaps confit duck leg with braised red cabbage and roasted black pudding, or whole grilled sea bass with a confit of sweet pepper and fennel. Sunday lunch is impressive too, and there's a splendid sheltered garden for summer meals.
OPEN: 11-3 6-11 **BAR MEALS:** L served Tue-Sun 12-2 D served Wed-Sat 7-9 **RESTAURANT:** L served Tue-Sun 12-2 D served Wed-Sat 7-9 Av 3 course à la carte £25
BREWERY/COMPANY: Shepherd Neame 🍺: Shepherd Neame Master Brew. 🍷: 10 **FACILITIES:** Children welcome Garden **NOTES:** Parking 14

The Duke William 🍷
Ickham CT3 1QP ☎ 01227 721308 🖺 01227 722042
A family-run free house in a picturesque village between Canterbury and Sandwich, the Duke William dates from 1611. There's an open fire in the comfortable bar, with a summer garden and rural views. A good range of bar snacks is served, while the conservatory-style restaurant offers an extensive carte supplemented by a regularly-changing table d'hôte menu. Home-cooked dishes like 2lb half leg of lamb or boneless poussin stuffed with spinach are featured.
OPEN: 11-11 **BAR MEALS:** L served Tues-Sun 11-2 D served all week 6-10 **RESTAURANT:** L served Tues-Sun 11-2 D served all week 6-10 **BREWERY/COMPANY:** Free House 🍺: Shepherd Neame Master Brew, Young's Special, Adnams Bitter, Fuller's London Pride. **FACILITIES:** Children welcome Garden: Pretty pond, fountain, patio, conservatory Dogs allowed Water

The Old Coach House 🍷
A2 Barnham Downs CT4 6SA ☎ 01227 831218 🖺 01227 831932
Dir: 7M South bound of Canterbury on A2. Turn at Jet Petrol Station.
A former stop on the original London to Dover coaching route, and listed in the 1740 timetable, this inn stands some 300 metres from the Roman Way. Noteworthy gardens with home-grown herbs and vegetables, weekend spit-roasts, and unabashed continental cuisine mark it as an auberge in the finest Gallic tradition. Food options include seafood, venison and other game in season, plus perhaps rib of beef with rosemary, pot au feux, and grilled lobster with brandy sauce.
OPEN: 11-11 **BAR MEALS:** L served all week 12-2.30 D served all

continued

continued

CANTERBURY continued

week 6.30-9 Av main course £12 **RESTAURANT:** L served all week 12-2 D served all week 6.30-9 Av 3 course à la carte £20 **BREWERY/COMPANY:** Free House ◖: Interbrew Whitbread Best Bitter. **FACILITIES:** Children welcome Garden: Lrg sand pit, seating Dogs allowed **NOTES:** Parking 60 **ROOMS:** 10 bedrooms 10 en suite s£48 d£55 (★★)

CHIDDINGSTONE   Map 06 TQ54

Pick of the Pubs

Castle Inn 🏠
TN8 7AH ☎ 01892 870247 🗎 01892 870808
e-mail: info@castleinn.co.uk

See Pub Walk on page 259
See Pick of the Pubs on opposite page

CHILHAM   Map 07 TR05

The White Horse ♀
The Square CT4 8BY ☎ 01227 730355
Dir: Take A28 from Canterbury then A252, 1m turn L
One of the most photographed pubs in Britain, The White Horse stands next to St Mary's church facing onto the 15th-century village square, where the May Fair is an annual event. The pub offers a traditional atmosphere and modern cooking from a monthly-changing menu based on fresh local produce. Dishes include fillet steak poached in red wine, and cod and smoked haddock fishcakes served with a sweet chilli sauce.
OPEN: 11-11 (Sun 12-10.30, Jan-Feb 12-3, 7-11) **BAR MEALS:** L served all week 12-3 D served Mon-Sat 7-9
BREWERY/COMPANY: Free House ◖: Flowers Original Fullers London Pride, Greene King Abbot Ale Adnams Best.
FACILITIES: Garden Dogs allowed

CHILLENDEN   Map 07 TR25

Griffins Head 🏠
CT3 1PS ☎ 01304 840325 🗎 01304 841290
Dir: A2 from Canterbury towards Dover, then B2046. Village on R

A Kentish Wealden hall house, dating from 1286, with a lovely garden. Once occupied by monks who farmed the surrounding land, it features inglenook fireplaces, beamed bars, fine Kentish ales and home-made food. Typical dishes include game (in season), home-made pies, whole grilled seabass, roes on toast, fresh crab and Aberdeen Angus steaks. A vintage car club meets here on the first Sunday of every month.
OPEN: 10.30am-11pm **BAR MEALS:** L served all week 12-2 D

continued

served Mon-Sat 7-9.30 **RESTAURANT:** L served Sun-Fri 12-2 D served Mon-Sat 7-9.30 **BREWERY/COMPANY:** Shepherd Neame ◖: Shepherd Neame. **FACILITIES:** Garden: Large country garden, bat & trap pitch **NOTES:** Parking 25

DARTFORD   Map 06 TQ57

The Rising Sun Inn ♦♦♦ 🏠
Fawkham Green, Fawkham DA3 8NL
☎ 01474 872291 🗎 01474 872291

A pub since 1702, The Rising Sun is set in a peaceful, picturesque village not far from the Thames and Medway estuaries and convenient for the Brands Hatch racing circuit. Friendly atmosphere inside, with inglenook log fire and cosy restaurant. Traditional bacon, onion and thyme pudding, fish and chips, various steaks and chicken and mushroom pie are offered alongside crispy soy duck, chicken satay, pan-seared calves' liver, and Goosnargh duck breast served pink.
OPEN: 11.30-11 Sun 12-10.30 6-11 Closed: 1 Jan
BAR MEALS: L served all week 12-2.30 D served all week 6.30-9.30
RESTAURANT: L served all week 12-2.15 D served all week 6.30-9.30
Av 3 course à la carte £17 **BREWERY/COMPANY:** Free House
◖: Scottish Courage Courage Best, Courage Directors.
FACILITIES: Garden: Food served outside **NOTES:** Parking 30
ROOMS: 5 bedrooms 5 en suite 1 family rooms s£40 d£65 no children overnight

Shove Halfpenny

The game is still played with pre-decimal halfpennies, lovingly preserved, but is not as popular and widespread in pubs as it used to be. It is a scaled-down version of shuffleboard, which involved propelling flat metal discs along a smooth wooden table up to 30ft long. Down to the First World War a playing area was often drawn in chalk on the bar or a tabletop, but today a special wooden or slate board is used, 24 inches long by 15 inches wide. As usual, the house rules vary in detail from one pub to another.

Pick of the Pubs

CHIDDINGSTONE – KENT

Open: 11-11
Bar Meals: L served all week,
D served all week.
RESTAURANT: L served Wed-Mon 12-2,
D served Wed-Mon 7.30-9.30.
Av cost 3 course £20
BREWERY/COMPANY:
Free House.
🍺: Larkins Traditional, Harveys Sussex,
Young's Ordinary.
FACILITIES: Dogs allowed, Children
welcome, Garden - Patio, sheltered
lawn.

Castle Inn

Visitors arriving at the Castle Inn for the first time may sense they have seen it before, for the picturesque mellow tile-hung exterior is a much-used film set. 'Elizabeth R', 'Room with a View', 'The Life of Hogarth' and 'The Wicked Lady' are among films shot here.

Chiddingstone, TN8 7AH
☎ 01892 870247 📠 01892 870808
✉ info@castleinn.co.uk
Dir: S of B2027 between Tonbridge & Edenbridge.

The building dates back to 1420 when it was known as Waterslip House, but it was first licensed to sell ale in about 1730. Today it is full of nooks and crannies, period furniture and evocative curios, with the beamed bar having been remodelled carefully to preserve its unique character. Outside is the vine-hung courtyard with its own garden bar. The same family owners have dispensed good ales for 40 years, including Larkins Traditional, brewed nearby at Larkins Farm. The inn also has a strong reputation for its cooking. Typical pub food is available, including open sandwiches, salads, ploughman's and filled jacket potatoes, and more substantial dishes like chicken curry and chilli con carne. Chips are, however, definitely not on the menu in any form. Moving up a few notches is the Fireside Menu, offering the likes of terrine of ham hock and black pudding, or wild mushroom and Cashel Blue cheese tartlet, followed by chargrilled tuna on crushed lobster potatoes or roasted rump of lamb on a root vegetable purée. Typical sweets might include bitter chocolate tart with Amaretto ice cream, and pistachio and lemon grass crème brûlée. A selection of award-winning British cheeses is always on offer, perhaps tempting European visitors to sample them before paying in Euros, which is accepted currency here. In the small restaurant these dishes, and more, are on offer, with a serious selection of wines to match - including fine clarets - and an extensive choice of malt whiskies.

DEAL
Map 07 TR35

The King's Head
9 Beach St CT14 7AH ☎ 01304 368194 ▤ 01304 364182
e-mail: booking@kingsheaddeal.co.uk
Dir: A249 from Dover to Deal, on seafront

Traditional 18th-century seaside pub, overlooking the seafront and situated in one of the south-east's most picturesque coastal towns. Deal's famous Timeball Tower is a few yards away and the pub is within easy reach of Canterbury, Walmer Castle and the Channel Tunnel. Bar meals include steaks, sandwiches and seafood, and there is a daily-changing specials board.
OPEN: 10-11 (Sun 12-10.30) **BAR MEALS:** L served all week 11-2.30 D served all week 6-9 Av main course £5
BREWERY/COMPANY: Free House ◖: Shephard Neame Master Brew, Courage Best, Spitfire, Fullers London Pride.
FACILITIES: Children welcome Garden: Food served outside. Seafront terrace Dogs allowed **NOTES:** Parking 3

DOVER
Map 07 TR34

The Clyffe Hotel ♀
High St, St Margaret's at Cliffe CT15 6AT
☎ 01304 852400 ▤ 01304 851880
e-mail: info@theclyffeinn.com
Dir: 3m NE of Dover
Located opposite the parish church and just half a mile from the white cliffs north of Dover, this 16th-century Kentish clapboard building, formerly an 'academy for young gentlemen', has undergone major refurbishment since it was taken over a few years ago. Convivial main bar and neatly furnished lounge leading out to the delightful walled rose garden. Food now includes fresh local fish, traditional dishes like toad-in-the-hole, steak and ale pie, calves' liver and bacon, mushroom and herb tagliatelle, Thai curries, and home-made ice creams among the puddings.
OPEN: 11-3 (Sun 12-10.30) 5-11 **BAR MEALS:** L served all week 11.30-2.30 D served all week 7-9 Av main course £6
RESTAURANT: L served all week 12-2.30 D served Mon-Sat 6.30-9.30 Av 3 course à la carte £15 **BREWERY/COMPANY:** Free House ◖: Shepherd Neame Spitfire, Masterbrew, Fullers London Pride. **FACILITIES:** Children welcome Garden: Food served outside **NOTES:** Parking 35

The Swingate Inn & Hotel ♦♦♦ ⌂ NEW
Deal Rd CT15 5DP ☎ 01304 204043 ▤ 01304 204043
e-mail: terry@swingate.com
Dir: Telephone for directions
Just minutes from Dover's ferry port, this family-run free house makes an ideal touring base. There's a relaxed, friendly atmosphere, and the Thursday jazz evenings are particularly popular. Informal meals are served in the bar or garden, or

you can choose from the à la carte menu in the spacious restaurant. Expect mixed grill, rump of lamb with redcurrant jus, grilled red snapper with spinach, and vegetable Wellington with a sun-dried tomato sauce.
OPEN: 11-11 (Sun 12-10.30, Xmas 12-3) **BAR MEALS:** L served Mon-Sun 12-2.45 D served Mon-Sun 6-10 Av main course £6.25
RESTAURANT: L served Mon-Sun 12-2.45 D served Mon-Sun 6.30-10.00 Av 3 course à la carte £18 Av fixed price £10.95 ◖: Fullers London Pride, Abbot Ale. **FACILITIES:** Children welcome Garden: Large garden with gazebo, aviary **NOTES:** Parking 60 **ROOMS:** 14 bedrooms 14 en suite 2 family rooms s£42 d£50

EASTLING
Map 07 TQ95

Carpenters Arms ♦♦♦ ⌂
The Street ME13 0AZ ☎ 01795 890234 ▤ 01795 890654
e-mail: carpenters-arms@lineone.net
Dir: A251 towards Faversham, then A2, 1st L Brogdale Rd, 4m to Eastling
An early Kentish hall-house, built in 1380, this listed building soon became an ale house serving carpenters working in the nearby sawmill. It features oak beams, an inglenook fireplace, a brick-tiled floor, and a profusion of local bygones. The bar offers home-cooked pub fare, snacks and daily specials, while restaurant dishes include Tiger king prawns, shank of lamb, knuckle of pork, chicken fajita, and cod.
OPEN: 11-4 6-11 (Sun 12-6) **BAR MEALS:** L served all week 12-2.30 D served Mon-Sat 7-10 Av main course £6.50 **RESTAURANT:** L served all week 12-2.30 D served Mon-Sat 7-10 Av 3 course à la carte £20
BREWERY/COMPANY: Shepherd Neame ◖: Shepherd Neame Master Brew, Bishops Finger & Spitfire, Seasonal Beer.
FACILITIES: Children welcome Garden: Grassed area with garden furniture Dogs allowed on lead only, Water **NOTES:** Parking 20
ROOMS: 3 bedrooms 3 en suite s£41.50 d£49.50 no children overnight

EDENBRIDGE
Map 06 TQ44

The Kentish Horse ⌂
Cow Ln, Markbeech TN8 5NT ☎ 01342 850493
A recent extension at this white-painted inn has provided a new dining area, while the original part - dating from 1340 with a smuggling history - remains unchanged. The inn is popular in summer with families using the gardens, and all year round for food like traditional cod and chips, pies, puddings and casseroles, plus salads, ploughman's and sandwiches. Look out for the curious street-bridging Kentish sign.
OPEN: 12-11 (Sun 12-10.30) **BAR MEALS:** L served all week 12-2.30 D served Tues-Sat 7-9.30 Av main course £7.95
RESTAURANT: L served all week 12-2.30 D served all week 7-9.30 ◖: Harvey's Larking, plus guest ales. **FACILITIES:** Children welcome Garden: Food served outside Dogs allowed Water, biscuits **NOTES:** Parking 40

Ye Old Crown ♦♦♦♦
74-76 High St TN8 5AR ☎ 01732 867896 ▤ 01732 868316
An unmissable landmark on account of its unusual street-bridging Kentish inn sign, this has been an inn since the mid-14th century, and a concealed passage from the 1630s confirms its history as a smugglers' den. Today it dispenses local Larkins' ale, traditional English bar and restaurant food, and offers comfortable tourist accommodation. Simple menu includes baguettes, lasagne, jacket potatoes, sandwiches, and ploughman's.
OPEN: 11-11 (Sun 12-10.30) **BAR MEALS:** L served all week 12-2 D served all week 6-9 Av main course £7 **RESTAURANT:** L served all week 12-3 D served all week 6-10
BREWERY/COMPANY: ◖: Bombadier, Tetley, Bass.

continued

continued

FACILITIES: Children welcome Garden: Food served outside. Courtyard Dogs allowed **NOTES:** Parking 20 **ROOMS:** 6 bedrooms 6 en suite s£59 d£74

The Wheatsheaf

Hever Rd, Bough Beech TN8 7NU
☎ 01732 700254 📠 01732 700077
Dir: M25 & A21 take exit for Hever Castle & follow signs. 1 mile past Castle on R

Originally built as a hunting lodge for Henry V, this splendid medieval pub boasts lofty timbered ceilings and massive stone fireplaces. In the winter enjoy roast chestnuts and mulled wine, while the lovely gardens are at their best in summer. The Wheatsheaf has a well-deserved reputation for good food; expect beef goulash with dumplings, Thai green chicken curry, and poached smoked haddock, plus tasty snacks.
OPEN: 11-11 **BAR MEALS:** L served all week 12-10 D served all week 12-10 Av main course £8.95 **RESTAURANT:** L served all week 12-10 D served all week 12-10 Av 3 course à la carte £16
BREWERY/COMPANY: Free House 🍺: Harveys Sussex Bitter, Shepherds Neame, Fuller's London Pride, Greene King Old Speckled Hen. **FACILITIES:** Children welcome Garden: Sheltered, seats, benches Dogs allowed Water **NOTES:** Parking 30

EYNSFORD   Map 06 TQ56

Swallows' Malt Shovel Inn ♀

Station Rd DA4 0ER ☎ 01322 862164 📠 01322 864132
Dir: A20 to Brands Hatch, then A225, 1m to pub

Close to the River Darenth, this charming village pub is very popular with walkers and those visiting the Roman villa in Eynsford, or Lullingstone Castle. Fish is very well represented on the menu, and dishes may include grilled monkfish, best smoked Scotch salmon, whole lobster, sea bass, tiger prawns, tuna, plaice, trout, skate or dressed baby crab. Rack of ribs, venison pie, leek and lentil lasagne, and vegetable curry also turn up on a typical menu.

continued

OPEN: 11-3 7-11 Closed: 25-26 Dec **BAR MEALS:** L served all week 12-2.30 D served all week 7-10 **RESTAURANT:** L served all week 12-2.30 D served all week 7-10 **BREWERY/COMPANY:** Free House 🍺: Greene King Old Speckled Hen, Harvey's Armada, Fullers London Pride & ESB, Timothy Taylor Landlord. **FACILITIES:** Children welcome **NOTES:** Parking 26

FAVERSHAM   Map 07 TR06

The Albion Tavern

Front Brents, Faversham Creek ME13 7DH
☎ 01795 591411 📠 01795 591587
e-mail: jenniferkent@msn.com
Dir: From Faversham take A2 W. In Ospringe turn R just before Ship Inn, at Shepherd Neame Brewery 1m turn L over creek bridge

A quaint, white-weatherboarded gem built in 1748 overlooking historic Faversham Creek. On the opposite bank stands Shepherd Neame's brewery, Britain's oldest, and the Albion's owner. The small bar has a distinct nautical atmosphere with a hammock, old photographs of boats and other artefacts. A modern cooking style produces chicken, oyster, mushroom and tarragon crêpes, trio of salmon, sea bass and scallops, and daily specials. The small, vine-festooned rear conservatory leads out to a pretty garden with seating.
OPEN: 11.30-3 6.30-11 **BAR MEALS:** L served all week 12-2 D served all week 6.30-9.30 Av main course £10 **RESTAURANT:** L served all week 12-2 D served all week 7-9 Av 3 course à la carte £16
BREWERY/COMPANY: Shepherd Neame 🍺: Spitfire, Master Brew. **FACILITIES:** Children welcome Garden Dogs allowed Water **NOTES:** Parking 20

Shipwrights Arms

Hollowshore ME13 7TU ☎ 01795 590088
Dir: A2 through Osprince then R at rdbt. Turn R at T-junct then L opp Davington School & follow signs
Find this classic pub on the Kent marshes. First licensed in 1738, this was once a haunt of pirates and smugglers. There are numerous nooks and crannies inside and beer is served traditionally by gravity straight from the cask including a frequently changing range of Kent-brewed real ales. Self-sufficient landlord generates his own electricity and draws water from a well. Home-cooked food might include mushroom Stroganoff and sausage and mash, with an emphasis on English pies and puddings during the winter. Used as a location in the 1967 Oliver Reed movie 'The Shuttered Room'.
OPEN: 12-3 Summer Open all day 7-11 (Sun 12-3, 6-10.30)
BAR MEALS: L served Tue-Sun 12-2.30 D served Tue-Sat 7-9 Av main course £5.50 **BREWERY/COMPANY:** Free House 🍺: Local Beers. **FACILITIES:** Children welcome Garden: Large open area adjacent to Faversham Creek Dogs allowed **NOTES:** Parking 30
NOTES: No credit cards

England

FORDCOMBE   Map 06 TQ54

Chafford Arms 🐑 🍷
TN3 0SA ☎ 01892 740267 📠 01892 740703
Dir: On B2188 (off A264) between Tunbridge Wells & E Grinstead

Creeper-clad village pub with an award-winning garden, situated between Penshurst Place and Groombridge Place. Originally built in 1851 for the local paper works that made paper for the Royal Mint. The main emphasis is on fish, with perhaps skate wing, grilled trout and dressed crab, but there are meat choices like Dijon lamb chops and chicken Kiev, plus a good range of snacks, salads and vegetarian dishes. Ask about the skate-boarding dog.
OPEN: 11.45-3 6.30-11 **BAR MEALS:** L served all week 12.30-2 D served Tue-Sat 7.30-9 Av main course £7.45 **RESTAURANT:** L served all week 12.30-2 D served Tue-Sat 7.30-9 Av 3 course à la carte £15.45 **BREWERY/COMPANY:** 🍺 Larkins Bitter, Interbrew Bass. 🍷 9 **FACILITIES:** Children welcome Garden: Enclosed garden, patio for child safety Dogs allowed Water **NOTES:** Parking 16

FORDWICH   Map 07 TR15

Fordwich Arms 🍷
King St CT2 0DB ☎ 01227 710444 📠 01227 712811
Dir: From A2 take A28, on approaching Sturry turn R at 'Welsh Harp' pub into Fordwich Rd
Solid Tudor-style village pub situated opposite the tiny, half-timbered 16th-century town hall, a reminder of the days when Fordwich was a Borough. Large bar with log-burning fires, an oak-panelled dining room and delightful riverside patio and garden for summer sipping. Modern, daily-changing menus encompass Tuscan-style lamb with tomatoes in red wine, half-shoulder of herb-crusted lamb, pork fillet with Savoy cabbage and bacon, duck breast on noodles with plum and hoi sin sauce, garlic and herb ravioli, and rabbit in ale with dumplings. Good Sunday lunch menu.
OPEN: 11-11 (Sun 12-3, 7-10.30) **BAR MEALS:** L served all week 12-2.30 D served Mon-Sat 6.30-9.30 **RESTAURANT:** 12-2.30 6.30-9.30 **BREWERY/COMPANY:** Whitbread 🍺 Interbrew Flowers Original & Boddingtons Bitter, Shepherd Neame Masterbrew, Wadworth 6X. 🍷 10 **FACILITIES:** Garden: Terrace, River Stour runs along garden Dogs allowed **NOTES:** Parking 12

> **For a list of pubs with AA Inspected Accommodation Awards**
> ◆   see pages 646-651   ★

GOUDHURST   Map 06 TQ73

Pick of the Pubs

Green Cross Inn
TN17 1HA ☎ 01580 211200 📠 01580 212905
Dir: Tonbridge A21 toward Hastings turn L A262 leading to Ashford 2m from the turning on the A262 Station road, Goudhurst on the R
Food-orientated pub in a delightful unspoiled corner of Kent, ideally placed for visiting Tunbridge Wells, the Ashdown Forest and the remote fenland country of Pevensey Levels. The dining-room is prettily decorated with fresh flowers and white linen table cloths, and the whole pub is being upgraded by the chef/proprieter. Fresh seafood is the house speciality here, with all dishes cooked to order and incorporating the freshest ingredients. Main courses in the bar range from home-made steak, kidney and mushroom pie with shortcrust pastry, to calves' liver and bacon Lyonnaise. Restaurant fish dishes might include fillet of turbot with spinach and a creamy cheese sauce, grilled lemon sole with home-made tartare sauce, and Cornish cock crab with fresh dressed leaves.
OPEN: 11-3 6-11 Closed Sun eve in winter **BAR MEALS:** L served all week 12-2.30 D served Mon-Sat 7-9.45 Av main course £6.50 **RESTAURANT:** L served all week 12-2.30 D served Mon-Sat 7-9.45 Av 3 course à la carte £23 **BREWERY/COMPANY:** Free House 🍺 Harveys Best, Shepherd Neame Master Brew, Larkins. **FACILITIES:** Garden: Food served outside Dogs allowed **NOTES:** Parking 26

Pick of the Pubs

The Star & Eagle Hotel 🐑 🍷
High St TN17 1AL ☎ 01580 211512 📠 01580 212444
e-mail: StarandEagle@btconnect.com
Dir: On A262 E of Tunbridge Wells
A fine 14th-century timbered and gabled inn, reputed to have been an ancient monastery, with relics of vaulted stonework still visible in the building. A tunnel used to run from the cellars to a point underneath the parish church next door. Situated at the highest point of the village, 400ft above sea level, the inn commands outstanding views across the orchards and hop gardens of the Kentish Weald. In the split-level restaurant and atmospheric bar, a carte menu is supported by interesting daily specials, including Spanish-style hare in a rich chocolate sauce, fillet of pork in an apple and brandy cream sauce, and baked fillet of sea bass. For a lighter meal try mussels in white wine with chips, mushroom crêpes, or cannelloni pancakes filled with ricotta cheese and spinach. Tempting puddings might be Belgian chocolate torte, and treacle sponge with custard.
OPEN: 11-11 (Oct-May Sun 12-3 6-10.30) Dec 25 Closed eve **BAR MEALS:** L served all week 12-2.30 D served all week 7-9.30 Av main course £10 **RESTAURANT:** L served all week 12-2.30 D served all week 7-9.30 Av 3 course à la carte £23 **BREWERY/COMPANY:** Enterprise Inns 🍺 Interbrew Flowers Original & Bass Bitter, Adnams Bitter. **FACILITIES:** Garden: Patio overlooking Weald **NOTES:** Parking 25

GRAVESEND Map 06 TQ67

The Cock Inn
Henley St, Luddesdowne DA13 0XB
☎ 01474 814208 🗎 01474 812850
e-mail: andrew.r.turner@btinternet.com
No jukeboxes and no children permitted at this traditional
English alehouse. Set in the beautiful Luddesdowne Valley,
this is an ideal watering hole for walkers, who enjoy the
doorstep sandwiches served at lunchtimes only. Plenty of real
ale and a choice of ciders.
OPEN: 12-11 (Sun 12-10.30) **BAR MEALS:** L served Mon-Sat 12-
2.30 Av main course £6 **BREWERY/COMPANY:** Free House
🍺: Adnams Southwold, Adnams Broadside Shepherd Neame
Masterbrew, Goacher's Real Mild Ale, Draught Bass.
FACILITIES: Garden Dogs allowed Dog biscuits on sale
NOTES: Parking 60

HADLOW Map 06 TQ65

The Artichoke Inn 🍴
Park Rd, Hamptons TN11 9SR ☎ 01732 810763
Dir: From Tonbridge take A26. In Hadlow turn L into Carpenters Lane. L at
junction, 2nd on R
Built as a farmworker's cottage, and licensed in 1585 as a pub,
with large inglenook fireplace, and masses of brass and old
farm implements. A front terrace with awning is ideal for
summer dining, and it's handy for walking the Weald Way. Bar
food ranges through plaice stuffed with asparagus, salmon
and cream cheese, and steak and kidney pie.
OPEN: 12-3 7-11 Closed: 25/26 Dec & Sun evening
BAR MEALS: L served Tue-Sun 12-2 D served Tue-Sat 7-9 Av main
course £8.50 **BREWERY/COMPANY:** Free House 🍺: Young's PA,
Fuller's London Pride. **NOTES:** Parking 30

HARRIETSHAM Map 07 TQ85

The Pepper Box Inn 🍴
ME17 1LP ☎ 01622 842558 🗎 01622 844218
e-mail: pbox@nascr.net
Dir: Take the Fairbourne Heath turning from A20 in Harrietsham and
follow for 2m to crossroads, straight over, follow for 200 yds pub is on L

A delightful 15th-century country pub high up on the
Greensand Ridge, with far-reaching views over the Weald of
Kent from its terrace. The pub takes its name from an early
type of pistol, a replica of which hangs behind the bar. Typical
dishes might include sizzling Singapore beef with basmati rice,
home-made steak and kidney pudding, fillet of sea bass with
lobster bisque and stirfry vegetables in Thai spices.
OPEN: 11-3 6.30-11 **BAR MEALS:** L served all week 12-2.15 D
served Tue-Sat 7-9.45 Av main course £12 **RESTAURANT:** L served
Tue-Sat 12-2 D served Tue-Sat 7-9.45
BREWERY/COMPANY: Shepherd Neame 🍺: Shepherd Neame
Master Brew, Bishops Finger, Spitfire. **FACILITIES:** Garden: Country
cottage with terrace Dogs allowed **NOTES:** Parking 30

HERNHILL Map 07 TR06

Pick of the Pubs

Red Lion 🍴 ♟
The Green ME13 9JR ☎ 01227 751207 🗎 01227 752990
e-mail: theredlion@lineone.net
Dir: S of A299 between Faversham & Whitstable

Beams and flagstones, rustic pine tables and roaring
winter log fires are all part of the charm at this handsome
half-timbered, 14th-century hall house, which overlooks
the village green to the historic church. Visitors will find
local guest ales on tap, a monthly-changing carte and a
blackboard listing a good range of daily specials. Sample
from a menu that includes Thai chicken, liver and bacon,
fresh sea bass, seafood pancake, beef Wellington, or
braised beef in ale. Traditional puddings include chocolate
fudge cake, fruit crumble and apple pie.
OPEN: 11-3.30 6-11 (Sun 12-3.30, 7-10.30) Closed: 25 Dec
BAR MEALS: L served all week 12-2.30 D served all week 6-
9.30 Av main course £7.95 **RESTAURANT:** L served (Sun only)
D served all week 6-9.30 Av 3 course à la carte £15
BREWERY/COMPANY: Free House 🍺: Shepherd Neame
Master Brew & 2 Guest beers. ♟: 7 **FACILITIES:** Children
welcome Garden: Food served outside, attractive garden
NOTES: Parking 40

HOLLINGBOURNE Map 07 TQ85

The Dirty Habit 🍴
Upper St ME17 1UW ☎ 01622 880880 🗎 01622 880773
Historic pub on the old Pilgrim's Way to Canterbury, where
travellers could change their dusty clothes, and imbibe the
wine and ale introduced by monks as refreshments. The
tradition is upheld in a more sophisticated way today, where
visitors can dine on roast breast of duckling, poached salmon
fillets, and loin of beef along with various grilled dishes
including veal, spatchcock and swordfish, sizzling platters like
monkfish or chilli king prawns, and pasta choices.
OPEN: 11.30-3 6.30-11 (Sun 12-4, 7-10.30) Dec 25 closed evening
BAR MEALS: L served all week 12-2.45 D served all week 7-10
RESTAURANT: L served all week 12-2.45 D served all week 7-10.30
BREWERY/COMPANY: Enterprise Inns 🍺: Shepherd Neame
Spitfire, Interbrew Bass, Wadworth 6X, Harveys Sussex Best.
FACILITIES: Children welcome Garden: Patio garden
NOTES: Parking 30

**All AA rated accommodation can also be
found on the AA's internet site**

www.theAA.com

IDEN GREEN
Map 06 TQ73

The Peacock ♀
Goudhurst Rd TN17 2PB ☎ 01580 211233
e-mail: thepeacock@uk.online.co.uk
Dir: A21 from Tunbridge Wells to Hastings, onto A262, pub 1.5m past Goudhurst
Grade II listed building dating from the 12th century with low beams, an inglenook fireplace, old oak doors, real ales on tap, and a wide range of traditional pub food. A large enclosed garden with fruit trees and picnic tables on one side of the building is popular in summer, and there's also a patio and a permanent bouncy castle. Look out for grilled salmon with dill mayonnaise, omelettes, steak and ale pie, tagliatelle with salmon and prawns, and stuffed trout with almonds.
OPEN: 12-11 (Sun 12-10.30) **BAR MEALS:** L served all week 12-3 D served Mon-Sat 6-9 Av main course £6.95 **RESTAURANT:** L served all week 12-3 D served all week 6-9
BREWERY/COMPANY: Shepherd Neame ◀: Shepherd Neame Master Brew, Spitfire & Best and seasonal ales. ♀: 7
FACILITIES: Children welcome Garden: Patio seats 20, large garden with fruit trees Dogs allowed Water **NOTES:** Parking 50

IGHTHAM
Map 06 TQ55

Pick of the Pubs

George & Dragon 🐕 ♀
The Street TN15 9HH ☎ 01732 882440 ▤ 01732 883209
Dir: From M20, A20 then A227 towards Tonbridge
A beautiful Tudor country pub, dating from 1515, with beams and inglenook fireplaces. Among its many claims are: the Earl of Stafford lived here; the peripatetic Queen Elizabeth I visited it; Guy Fawkes hatched the Gunpowder Plot next door; and the Duke of Northumberland was imprisoned in the old restaurant for being a plot collaborator. There are several comfortable bars, a beer garden and an excellent restaurant offering a varied, season-following menu. Typical starters might be trio of smoked marlin, trout and salmon, chicken livers sautéed with apricots and peppers on polenta, or tomato and Mozzarella salad. Main courses have included carpaccio of Welsh beef with roasted aubergine, Bishops Finger (one of Shepherd Neame's fine beers) baked sausage with gammon, fennel, red onions and garlic, and tagliatelle with a wild mushroom, fresh herb, lemon grass and chilli ragoût. Close by is Ightham Mote, a 14th-century manor and one of England's oldest continuously-inhabited houses.
OPEN: 11-11 (Sun 12-10.30) Closed: 25-26 Dec eve, 1 Jan eve
BAR MEALS: L served all week 12-3 D served all week 6.30-9.30 **RESTAURANT:** L served all week 12-3 D served all week 6.30-9.30 **BREWERY/COMPANY:** Shepherd Neame
◀: Shepherd Neame Master Brew, Spitfire, Bishops Finger & Seasonal Ale. ♀: 20 **FACILITIES:** Children welcome Garden: Patio Dogs allowed **NOTES:** Parking 20

Pick of the Pubs

The Harrow Inn 🐕 ♀
Common Rd TN15 9EB ☎ 01732 885912
Dir: Off A25 between Sevenoaks & Borough Green. Signposted to Ightham common
Within easy reach of both M20 and M26 motorways, yet tucked away down country lanes close to the National Trust's Knole Park and Igtham Mote, this Virginia creeper-hung stone inn clearly dates back to the 17th century and beyond. The bar area comprises two rooms with a great brick fireplace, open to both sides and piled high with blazing logs; meanwhile the restaurant boasts a vine-clad conservatory that opens to a terrace that's ideal for summer dining. The menu displays good use of fresh produce, and even bar meals impress with dishes such as tureen of Tuscan bean soup, salmon and chive fishcakes or Suffolk sausages with mash and gravy. A meal from the main menu could begin with deep-fried Camembert or a plate of smoked salmon. Follow with imaginative main courses (perhaps smoked haddock with Welsh rarebit) or classically based dishes such as fillet of beef Rossini, or pan-fried calves' liver with bacon.
OPEN: 12-3 6-11 (Sun 12-3 only) Closed: Dec 26 Jan 1, BHs
BAR MEALS: 12-2.30 6-9.30 **RESTAURANT:** L served Tue-Sat 12-2 D served Tue-Sat 6-9 Av 3 course à la carte £22
BREWERY/COMPANY: Free House ◀: Greene King Abbot Ale, IPA. ♀: 10 **FACILITIES:** Garden: Terrace **NOTES:** Parking 20

IVY HATCH
Map 06 TQ55

Pick of the Pubs

The Plough ♀
High Cross Rd TN15 0NL ☎ 01732 810268 ▤ 01732 811287
e-mail: alisonhumbert@btconnect.com
Dir: M25 J5 take A25 towards Borough Green follow signs for Ivy Hatch

Long-established owners here have little to say except that they perennially produce more of the same - and if it ain't broke they don't fix it! Deep in Kent countryside and close to the National Trust's 14th-century Ightham Mote, this is a decidedly food-faceted dining pub whose special draw remains the variety of fish and sea-foods dished up according to market availability. Baked mushrooms filled with smoked salmon, chicken mousse wrapped in puff pastry, and gratin of fresh scallops Florentine with spinach and cheese sauce are precursors to fried fillets of Dover sole, steamed salmon fillet hollandaise, roast rack of English lamb, and braised game casserole as available. Vegetarian dishes might include ragôut of mushrooms, gratin of fresh vegetable cannelloni, and braised vegetable Stroganoff. More than a dozen wines by the glass and some perfectly acceptable Larkin's ales ensure none shall go thirsty!
OPEN: 12-3 6-11 Winter closed Sun pm **BAR MEALS:** L served all week 12-3 D served all week 7-11 **RESTAURANT:** L served all week 12-3 D served all week 7-11
BREWERY/COMPANY: Free House ◀: Larkins.
FACILITIES: Children welcome Garden: Large garden safe for children Dogs allowed In the garden only **NOTES:** Parking 30

continued

LINTON
Map 07 TQ75

The Bull Inn
Linton Hill ME17 4AW ☎ 01622 743612 📠 01622 749513
Dir: A229 through Maidstone to Linton

Traditional 17th-century coaching inn in the heart of the Weald with stunning views from the glorious garden. Popular with walkers and very handy for the Greensand Way. Large inglenook fireplace and a wealth of beams inside, as well as tunnels which once led to the nearby church. Bar snacks and freshly-prepared restaurant meals are available, ranging from Barnsley lamb chops with mint gravy and grilled salmon fillet to home-made lamb and apricot pie with Mediterranean vegetables and beef Wellington.

OPEN: 11-3 6-11 (Sun 12-10.30, Sat 11-11) **BAR MEALS:** L served all week 12-2.30 D served Mon-Sat 7-9.30 Av main course £6
RESTAURANT: L served Tue-Sun 12-2.30 D served Tue-Sat 7-9.30 Av 3 course à la carte £20 Av 2 course fixed price £10
BREWERY/COMPANY: Shepherd Neame 🍺: Shepherd Neame Master Brew & Spitfire, Seasonal Ale. **FACILITIES:** Children welcome Garden: Large garden, ample seating, stunning views Dogs allowed
NOTES: Parking 30

LITTLEBOURNE
Map 07 TR25

Pick of the Pubs

King William IV 🍃
4 High St CT3 1UN ☎ 01227 721244 📠 01227 721244
e-mail: paulharvey@kingwilliam04.fsbusiness.co.uk
Dir: From A2 follow signs to Howletts Zoo. After zoo & at end of road, pub is straight ahead

Located just outside the city of Canterbury, the King William IV overlooks the village green and is well placed for Sandwich and Herne Bay. With open log fires and exposed oak beams, this friendly inn is under new management. An ambitious sample menu offers sirloin of beef with Stilton and red wine jus, herb-crusted cod with caper butter sauce, breast of chicken on lightly spiced creamed leek, and supreme of duck on mustard mash with savoury cabbage and olive jus.

OPEN: 11-3 6-11 (Sat 11-11) **BAR MEALS:** L served all week 12-2.30 D served all week 7-9.30 Av main course £12
RESTAURANT: L served all week 12-2.30 D served all week 7-9.30 Av 3 course à la carte £20 Av 2 course fixed price £7.90
BREWERY/COMPANY: Free House 🍺: Shepherd Neame Master Brew Bitter, Scottish Courage John Smith's, Adnams Bitter. **FACILITIES:** Children welcome Garden: Patio to rear, External seating to front **NOTES:** Parking 15

MAIDSTONE
Map 07 TQ75

Pick of the Pubs

The Ringlestone Inn ◆◆◆◆◆ ♀
Ringlestone Hamlet, Nr Harrietsham ME17 1NX
☎ 01622 859900 📠 01622 859966
e-mail: bookings@ringlestone.com
Dir: Take A20 E from Maidstone/at rndbt opp Great Danes Hotel turn to Hollingbourne. Through village, R at crossroads at top of hill

It started out as a hospice for monks in 1533 on the ancient Pilgrim's Way, but less than a hundred years later Ringlestone found its present identity as an ale house. Very little has changed in the fabric of the building since those days, and the original brick and flint walls and floors, inglenooks and centuries-old furniture still fulfil their original functions. The Domesday Book mentions the 'ring stone' for tethering mounts, which can still be seen in the brickwork. The warm welcome awaiting visitors reflects the old promise of a 'ryghte joyeuse greetynge', and along with a mind-boggling selection of country fruit wines, ciders and real ales, the hearty home-cooked food should bring ample cheer. A hot and cold buffet is a popular lunchtime feature, with its seasonal choice of traditional country dishes. A traditional brunch menu is available from 11:30 until 3:00 and during the day there's also a good selection of sandwiches, paninis and snacks. Dinner is a more formal candle-lit affair, with starters like aubergine bruschetta, rustic patés, and mushroom and Stilton tartlets followed by pistachio stuffed duck, redcurrant lamb or pork and apple cutlets. A separate list of at least ten different home-made pies evokes a typically-English way of eating. Choices include chicken and asparagus in cowslip wine, beef in black beer and raisin, and vegetable and nut in birch wine sauce. Puddings continue in the same satisfying vein, though many look to Europe for inspiration: expect tarte Tatin, tiramisu and crème brûlée. Naturally, all are home made. A nearby converted farmhouse contains smart modern bedrooms, furnished with individual touches such as CD players and fresh milk in the fridge.

OPEN: 12-3 6-11 (Sat-Sun 12-11) Closed: 25 Dec
BAR MEALS: L served all week 12-2 D served all week 7-9.30 Av main course £13.20 **RESTAURANT:** L served all week 12-2 D served all week 7-9.30 Av 3 course à la carte £23 🍺: Shepherd Neame Bishops Finger & Spitfire, Greene King Abbot Ale, Theakston Old Peculiar. ♀: 40 **FACILITIES:** Children welcome Children's licence Garden: Five acres of landscaped gardens, seating Dogs allowed manager's discretion **NOTES:** Parking 50
ROOMS: 3 bedrooms 3 en suite s£89 d£99

NEWNHAM — Map 07 TQ95

Pick of the Pubs

The George Inn 🐕 ⏰
44 The Street ME9 0LL ☎ 01795 890237 🖨 01795 890726
Dir: 5m SW of Faversham

The George, in the ancient parish of Newnham, was built in the year 1540 and was used as a farm dwelling until it was licensed in 1718, during the reign of George I, and subsequently became a coaching inn. Despite the many changes it has seen, the inn retains much of its historic character, with beams festooned with hopbines, polished wooden floors, open fires and candlelit tables. It also has the advantage of a large garden. A good range of beer includes Shepherd Neame's Master Brew, Spitfire and Bishops Finger, plus a winter/summer ale. Bar snacks range from sandwiches to sausage and mash, while typical chef's specials are pan-fried fillet of sea bass with fresh asparagus and hollandaise sauce, or large half shoulder of lamb served with a thyme, redcurrant and port sauce.
OPEN: 11-3 6.30-11 **BAR MEALS:** L served all week 12-2 D served all week 7-9.30 Av main course £8 **RESTAURANT:** L served all week 12-2.30 D served all week 7-9.45 Av 3 course à la carte £19 **BREWERY/COMPANY:** Shepherd Neame 🍺: Shepherds Neame Master Brew, Spitfire, Bishops Finger, Porter Ale. **FACILITIES:** Children welcome Garden: Food served outside Dogs allowed **NOTES:** Parking 25

PENSHURST — Map 06 TQ54

The Leicester Arms 🐕 **NEW**
High St TN11 8BT ☎ 01892 870551 🖨 01892 870554
Dir: Take the second exit off A21 and follow signs to Penhurst Place

Once part of the Penshurst Place estate, the Leicester Arms was named after Viscount De L'isle, Earl of Leicester, who was

grandson of the former owner. Richard Burton and Elizabeth Taylor stayed here while filming 'Anne of a Thousand Days' at nearby Hever Castle. Ideally located for visiting a variety of well-established tourist attractions, this picturesque watering hole has a large secluded garden and fine views over pretty meadows. Expect a comprehensive menu which includes filled ciabattas, light lunch options, whole-roasted sea bass, lamb and spinach curry, roasted chump of lamb, steak and ale pie and pan-fried squid. Extensive popular wine list.
OPEN: 11 -11 **BAR MEALS:** L served all week 12-9.30 D served all week 12-9.30 Av main course £7.95 **RESTAURANT:** L served all week 12-9.30 D served all week 12-9.30 Av 3 course à la carte £14 **BREWERY/COMPANY:** Enterprise Inns 🍺: Old Speckled Hen, Shepherd Neame, Master Brew, Fullers London Pride.
FACILITIES: Garden: Lawns to the river, views over Medway Valley Dogs allowed Water & Biscuits **NOTES:** Parking 35

PLUCKLEY — Map 07 TQ94

Pick of the Pubs

The Dering Arms 🐕 ⏰
Station Rd TN27 0RR ☎ 01233 840371 🖨 01233 840498
e-mail: jim@deringarms.com
Dir: M20 J8 take A20 to Ashford.Then R onto B2077 at Charing to Pluckley

Located a mile from the village which featured in 'The Darling Buds of May', this impressive building with curved Dutch gables and uniquely arched windows was formerly a family hunting lodge for the Dering Estate. Splendid interior to match, with high ceilings, wood or stone floors, simple antique furniture and winter log fires. Expect a relaxing atmosphere, ale from Goacher's micro-brewery in Maidstone and good food using fresh vegetables from the family farm and herbs from the pub garden. Chef/patron James Buss' passion and enthusiasm for anything that swims is evident across the interesting menu, with starters like provençale fish soup, crab Newburg and Sussex smokies. Follow with monkfish with bacon, orange and cream sauce, fillet of halibut meunière, or - given twenty-four hour's notice - Jim's massive seafood special. Leg of lamb steak, guinea fowl in sherry and tarragon, and rib-eye steaks redress the balance. Impressive list of wines and regular gourmet evenings.
OPEN: 11-3 6-11 Closed: 26-29 Dec **BAR MEALS:** L served all week 12-2 D served all week 7-9.30 Av main course £11.95 **RESTAURANT:** L served all week 12-2 D served all week 7-9.30 Av 3 course à la carte £25 **BREWERY/COMPANY:** Free House 🍺: Goacher's Dering Ale, Maidstone Dark, Gold Star, Old Ale. ⏰: 7 **FACILITIES:** Children welcome Garden: Small grassed area with picnic tables Dogs allowed Water **NOTES:** Parking 20

continued

The Rose and Crown ♀

Munday Bois TN27 0ST ☎ 01233 840393 ▤ 01233 756530

An ale house since 1780, the Rose and Crown is set in a remote hamlet - allegedly part of England's most haunted parish. The bar menu offers local sausages, steak and kidney pie and hearty brunches. Specials might include chicken and Boursin en croûte, and lamb 'Shrewsbury'. Children's and Sunday lunch menus.

OPEN: 11.30-3 7-11 (Sun 12-4, 7-11) **BAR MEALS:** L served all week 12-2.30 D served all week 7-9.30 Av main course £7.95 **RESTAURANT:** L served all week 12-2.30 D served all week 7-9.30 Av 3 course à la carte £16 **BREWERY/COMPANY:** Free House **🍺:** Master Brew, IPA. **FACILITIES:** Children welcome Garden: Food served outside. Picnic tables Dogs allowed Garden only Water provided **NOTES:** Parking 30

SANDWICH
Map 07 TR35

St Crispin Inn 🐾 ♀

The Street, Worth CT14 0DF ☎ 01304 612081 ▤ 01304 614838
e-mail: job.tob@virgin.net

King William III was on the throne when the first licence was granted for the St Crispin Inn in 1604. It is a traditional country pub with exposed beams and open fires, set at the end of a dead-end country lane. Favourite dishes are pound pies (steak and ale, chicken and ham), venison stew and Oh My Cod! (enormous fish and chips). The game 'bat and trap' is played in the garden during the summer.

OPEN: 10.30-2.30 6-11 **BAR MEALS:** L served all week 12-2 D served all week 6-9.30 Av main course £6.50 **RESTAURANT:** L served all week 12-2 D served all week 6-9.30 Av 3 course à la carte £14.50 **🍺:** Shepherd Neame Master Brew, Wadworth 6X, Theakston Old Peculier. ♀: 7 **FACILITIES:** Children welcome Garden: Large with flower borders seats 100 **NOTES:** Parking 30

SELLING
Map 07 TR05

The Rose and Crown 🐾

Perry Wood ME13 9RY ☎ 01227 752214

Dir: A28 to Chilham R at Shottenden turning. R at Old Plough x roads, next R signed Perry Wood. Pub at top of hill

Set against 150 acres of natural woodland, this traditional 16th-century pub is decorated with local hop garlands and a unique corn dolly collection. Log fires in winter and a very attractive pub garden. Wide-ranging menu offers homemade steak and mushroom suet pudding, Moroccan lamb and couscous, goats' cheese with onion marmalade, or cod and smoked haddock mornay. In the garden, try your hand at Bat and Trap, the traditional pub game of Kent.

OPEN: 11-3 6.30-11 **BAR MEALS:** L served all week 12-2 D served Tue-Sat 7-9.30 Av main course £7 **RESTAURANT:** L served all week 12-2 D served Tue-Sat 7-9.30 **BREWERY/COMPANY:** Free House **🍺:** Adnams Southwold, Harveys Sussex Best Bitter, Goacher's Real Mild Ale. **FACILITIES:** Children welcome Garden: Dogs allowed Water, biscuit on welcome **NOTES:** Parking 25

SMARDEN
Map 07 TQ84

The Bell ♀

Bell Ln TN27 8PW ☎ 01233 770283 ▤ 01233 770726

Built in the year 1536, the Bell was originally a farm building on a large estate. It was used as a blacksmiths forge right up until 1907, but it had also been an alehouse since 1630. A typical menu includes seared king scallops with spinach and a crab sauce, chargrilled chicken breast with Mozzarella, basil

and wild mushroom sauce, gammon steak with beetroot mash and parsley sauce, and tournedos of monkfish Rossini.

OPEN: 11.30-3 5.30-11 (Sun all day) **BAR MEALS:** L served all week 12-2 D served all week 6.30-10 Av main course £11 **RESTAURANT:** L served all week 12-2 D served all week 6.30-10 **BREWERY/COMPANY:** Free House **🍺:** Shepherd Neame Master Brew, Spitfire, Interbrew Flowers IPA, Fuller's London Pride. **FACILITIES:** Garden: **NOTES:** Parking 20

Pick of the Pubs

The Chequers Inn ♦♦♦♦ 🐾 ♀

The Street TN27 8QA ☎ 01233 770217 ▤ 01233 770623
e-mail: charliebullock@lineone.net

Dir: Through Leeds village, L to Sutton Valence/Headcorn then L for Smarden. Pub in village centre

An atmospheric 14th-century inn in the centre of one of Kent's prettiest villages. A beautiful landscaped garden with a large pond makes a perfect setting for drinks or a meal. Two separate restaurants serve the same delicious food, with monkfish in a creamy wholegrain mustard sauce a typical fish dish. Otherwise expect lamb shank in red wine, hot prawn Thai curry, and roasted duck breast with a port and cranberry sauce.

OPEN: 11-11 (Sat all day Sun 12-10.30) **BAR MEALS:** L served all week 12-2.30 D served all week 6-9.30 Av main course £9 **RESTAURANT:** L served all week 12-2.30 D served all week 6-9.30 **BREWERY/COMPANY:** Free House **🍺:** Harveys, Interbrew Bass, Fuller's London Pride. ♀: 9 **FACILITIES:** Children welcome Garden: Landscaped garden with natural pond Dogs allowed **NOTES:** Parking 15 **ROOMS:** 4 bedrooms 4 en suite 1 family rooms s£40 d£70

♦ **Diamond rating for inspected guest accommodation**

continued

SMARTS HILL — Map 06 TQ54

Pick of the Pubs

The Bottle House Inn 🐾 ♀
Coldharbour Rd TN11 8ET ☎ 01892 870306 📠 01892 871094
e-mail: gordonmeer@aol.com
See Pick of the Pubs on page 273

Pick of the Pubs

The Spotted Dog ♀
TN11 8EP ☎ 01892 870253 📠 870107
Dir: Off B2188 between Penshurst & Fordcombe
Relax and enjoy far-reaching views over the Weald from the terraced gardens of this 15th-century weatherboarded pub, situated within easy reach of Penshurst Place and Hever Castle. The rambling interior with a wealth of beams, open log fires, tiled and oak floors and intimate nooks and crannies. Blackboards list the day's interesting choice of food - perhaps smoked cod and salmon fishcakes with white wine and parsley sauce, grilled swordfish with mango salsa, or rack of lamb with dauphinoise potatoes.
OPEN: 11-3 6-11 (Seasonal times vary, ring for details) Closed: 25 & 26 Dec **BAR MEALS:** L served all week 12-2.30 D served all week 6-9.30 **RESTAURANT:** L served all week 12-2.30 D served all week 6-9.30 Av 3 course à la carte £20
BREWERY/COMPANY: Free House 🍺: Harveys, Larkins.
FACILITIES: Garden: Terraced garden with views of Medway Valley Dogs allowed **NOTES:** Parking 60

SNARGATE — Map 07 TQ92

The Red Lion
TN29 9UQ ☎ 01797 344648
Few pubs invite you to picnic in their garden, but then they don't serve food at this one. Instead there's an emphasis on excellent ales, poured straight from the cask and served over the original marble-topped counter. Doris Jemison's family has run this free house since 1911, and little has changed here in fifty years. The result is delightfully nostalgic: expect bare floorboards, a real fire, wartime memorabilia and traditional games like shove ha'penny or toad-in-the-hole. Outside, chickens, guinea fowl and bantams roam in the pretty cottage garden.
OPEN: 12-3 7-11 (Sun 12-3, 7-10.30) **BREWERY/COMPANY:** Free House 🍺: Goachers Fine Light, Goachers Mild, Hop Daemon Golden Braid, Hop Daemon Skrimshander. **FACILITIES:** Children welcome Garden: Cottage garden with free range hens & bantams
NOTES: Parking 15 **NOTES:** No credit cards

STALISFIELD GREEN — Map 07 TQ95

The Plough 🐾 ♀
ME13 0HY ☎ 01795 890256
Dir: A20 to Charing, on dual carriageway turn L for Stalisfield
Originally a farmhouse, this 15th-century freehouse inn has been unspoilt by time, and boasts a lady ghost among its original beams and log fires. Set in a pretty village on top of the North Downs, it is run by Italian owners who hold regular theme evenings from their homeland. Interesting menus are supplemented by the specials, which might include salmon fillet with dill butter cream, pan-fried chicken supreme, duck brochettes with honey and orange sauce, and red mullet with

continued

mint new potatoes and herb jus. The Plough featured in an episode of the TV series, 'The Darling Buds of May'.

OPEN: 12-3 7-11 **BAR MEALS:** L served Tue-Sun 12-2.15 D served Tue-Sun 7-9.15 Av main course £5.95 **RESTAURANT:** L served Tue-Sun 12-3 D served Tue-Sun 7-11 Av 3 course à la carte £17.95 Av 2 course fixed price £18.95 **BREWERY/COMPANY:** Free House
🍺: Adnams Bitter, Wadworth 6X, Interbrew Flowers IPA.
FACILITIES: Children welcome Garden: Large beer garden, excellent view Dogs allowed **NOTES:** Parking 100

STOWTING — Map 07 TR14

The Tiger Inn ♀
TN25 6BA ☎ 01303 862130 📠 01303 862990
Dir: From M20 J11 take B2068 towards Canterbury. After 3m turn R to Stowting. Pub 2m on R
A lively pub with a good atmosphere, hosting regular jazz and Irish evenings and a popular annual beer festival. Renowned locally for good food, there is a separate restaurant (and in summer a large terrace) where dishes are listed on a daily-changing blackboard. Expect starters like tempura king prawns, and duck liver and Grand Marnier pâté, followed by Thai chicken stirfry, calves' liver with bacon, and poached salmon with fennel and lime hollandaise.
OPEN: 12-2.30 6.30-11 **BAR MEALS:** L served Tue-Sun 12-2 D served all week 6.30-9 Av main course £9.95 **RESTAURANT:** L served Tue-Sun 12-2 D served all week 6.30-9 Av 3 course à la carte £25 🍺: Fuller's London Pride, Shepherd Neame Master Brew Bitter, Spitfire, ESB. **FACILITIES:** Children welcome Garden: Food served outside Dogs allowed Water **NOTES:** Parking 50

TENTERDEN — Map 07 TQ83

White Lion Inn ♦♦♦♦ 🐾 ♀
57 High St TN30 6BD ☎ 01580 765077 📠 01580 764157
e-mail: whitelion@lionheartinns.co.uk
Dir: on the A28 Ashford/Hastings road
A 16th-century coaching inn on a tree-lined street of this old Cinque Port, with many original features retained. The area is known for its cricket connections, and the first recorded county match between Kent and London was played here in 1719. The menu offers plenty of choice, from calves' liver and bacon, shoulder of lamb, and Cumberland cottage pie to tuna pasta bake and various ploughman's.
OPEN: 11-11 (Sun 12-10.30) **BAR MEALS:** L served all week 12-2.30 D served all week 6-10 Av main course £5.50 **RESTAURANT:** L served all week 12-2.30 D served all week 6-10 Av 3 course à la carte £11.95 Av 2 course fixed price £7.75
BREWERY/COMPANY: Lionheart 🍺: Shepherd Neame, Interbrew Bass, Boddingtons Bitter, Wadworth 6X. **FACILITIES:** Children welcome Garden: Dogs allowed Water **NOTES:** Parking 30
ROOMS: 15 bedrooms 15 en suite 2 family rooms

Open: 11-11 (Sun 12-10.30pm).
Bar Meals: served all week 12-10.
Av main course £9.25
RESTAURANT: L served all week 12-10,
D served all week 6-10.
Av cost 3 courses £18
BREWERY/COMPANY:
Free House.
🍺: Larkins Ale, Harveys Sussex
Best Bitter.
FACILITIES: Garden - Front raised
terrace garden and side patio.
Children welcome.
NOTES: Parking 36

The Bottle House Inn

Built in 1492, and subsequently occupied by people with colourful
names like Grubbe, Qyll, Fagge, Stabbins, and Scraggy. Scraggy's
grandfather, a common beer seller from nearby Speldhurst, held a
licence to sell ales and ciders from the premises, although the first
full licence was not granted until 1938.

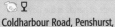

Coldharbour Road, Penshurst,
Tonbridge, TN11 8ET
☎ 01892 870306 📠 01892 871094
✉ gordonmeer@aol.com
Dir: From Tunbridge Wells take A264
W then B2188 N.

Today, this attractive and
characterful building is a dining
pub of some repute, with beams,
low ceilings, a copper-topped
bar and, in winter, open fires
that create a cosy atmosphere.
Run by the same friendly family
for eighteen years, it is well
positioned for refreshment
before or after visiting Penshurst
Place, Hever Castle and
Chartwell, Sir Winston

Churchill's former home. There
are also plenty of good walks
and striking views to be enjoyed
hereabouts. A considerable
range of dishes is offered on the
daily-changing menu, all made
from locally-supplied fresh
produce. A long list of starters
includes wild boar terrine with
redcurrants, English muffin with
Parma ham, poached eggs and
cheese sauce, crispy Peking duck
with pancakes, and whitebait
with garlic mayo, mixed leaves
and brown bread. Meat dishes
include pheasant breast with
venison and bacon stuffing en
croûte, shepherd's pie with fresh
vegetables, spicy chicken fajitas,
spaghetti with bacon,

mushrooms, roasted peppers and
olives, and the famous
Speldhurst sausages with garlic
mash and caramelised onion
gravy. For fish and seafood
lovers, mackerel fillets with
horseradish cream sauce, lemon
sole fillets stuffed with crab and
scallops, turbot with spring
onion and ginger sauce, and
skate wing with lemon butter
and caper sauce. All puddings
are home made too, including
pineapple cheesecake with fruit
coulis and Calvados crème
fraîche, and warm treacle and
pumpkin tart and custard. There
are separate vegetarian and
children's dishes. Harveys and
local Larkins bitters are on tap.

TUNBRIDGE WELLS (ROYAL)

Map 06 TQ53

The Beacon ☜ ☟

Tea Garden Ln, Rusthall TN3 9JH
☎ 01892 524252 ▤ 01892 534288
e-mail: beaconhotel@btopenworld.com
Dir: *From Tunbridge Wells take A264 towards East Grinstead. Pub 1m on L*

Built in 1895 as the home of one Sir Walter Harris, The Beacon's immaculate interior and oak-panelled bar retain plenty of country house charm (bookshelves, armchairs and stained glass windows). Outside is a dining terrace with lovely views across sixteen acres of grounds including lakes, woodland and a genuine chalybeate spring. Fresh local ingredients underpin dishes such as baked rack of lamb with a tomato, pancetta and brioche crust, roasted monkfish with crushed new potatoes, and apricot and leek potato cake with honey glazed vegetables and tarragon and Brie cream.
OPEN: 11-11 (Sun 12-10.30) **BAR MEALS:** L served all week 12-2.30 D served all week 6.30-9.30 Av main course £7.50
RESTAURANT: L served all week 12-2.30 D served all week 6-9.30 Av 3 course à la carte £23 **BREWERY/COMPANY:** Free House
◀: Harveys Best, Timothy Taylor Landlord, Breakspear Bitter. ☟: 10 **FACILITIES:** Children welcome Children's licence Garden: Decking area, 17 acres of garden Dogs allowed Water, Biscuits
NOTES: Parking 40

The Crown Inn ☟

The Green, Groombridge TN3 9QH ☎ 01892 864742
e-mail: crowngroombridge@aol.com
Dir: *Take A264 W of Tunbridge Wells, then B2110 S*

A cosy and inviting 16th-century inn situated by the village green and once frequented by the Groombridge smugglers, one of whom went on to become a cartographer and surveyor. Sir Arthur Conan Doyle wrote of seeing a ghost at the Crown. In winter there's a huge open fire in the beamed bar, and in summer a popular garden. Traditional bar food plus various salads with chips, filled bagels and steak and mushroom pie washed down with local real ales from Harveys or Larkins. Evening fare in the restaurant may offer diced curried lamb, seared salmon, or sirloin steak.
OPEN: 11-3 6-11 (Summer Fri-Sun open all day) **BAR MEALS:** L served all week 12-3 D served Mon-Sat 7-9.30 **RESTAURANT:** L served all week 12-3 D served Mon-Sat 7-9 Av 3 course à la carte £15
BREWERY/COMPANY: Free House ◀: Harveys IPA, Greene King IPA & Abbot Ale, Larkins. ☟: 8 **FACILITIES:** Children welcome Garden: Benches, over-looks village green Dogs allowed Water bowls
NOTES: Parking 35

★ Star rating for inspected hotel accommodation

The Hare on Langton Green ☟

Langton Rd, Langton Green TN3 0JA
☎ 01892 862419 ▤ 01892 861275
e-mail: hare@brunningandprice.co.uk
Dir: *On A264 W of Tunbridge Wells*

Rebuilt in 1901 following a fire, the pub has big windows, wooden floors and plenty of space for a collection of old books and bric-a-brac. In addition to real ales, there's an impressive range of malt whiskies and wines by the glass. Fish is well represented on the menu - fillet of salmon with prawn and crab crust, sea bass roasted with fennel and lemon served with champ - but there's plenty more to choose from, including Korkers sausages with mash and gravy, steakburger with onions, rabbit and smoked bacon casserole, and Stilton, celery and walnut tart.
OPEN: 12-11 (Sun 12-10.30) **BAR MEALS:** L served all week 12-9.30 D served all week 12-9 Av main course £10 **RESTAURANT:** served all week 12-9.30 D served all week Av 3 course à la carte £17.50
BREWERY/COMPANY: ◀: Greene King IPA & Abbot Ale. ☟: 16
FACILITIES: Garden: Long terrace over-looking Langton Green Dogs allowed **NOTES:** Parking 15

Pick of the Pubs

Royal Wells Inn ★★★ ◉ ☜ ☟

Mount Ephraim TN4 8BE ☎ 01892 511188 ▤ 01892 511908
e-mail: info@royalwells.co.uk
Dir: *75 yds from junction of A26 & A264*

There has been a recent change of hands at the Royal Wells Inn, a handsome white-painted hotel in a commanding position overlooking the common. The first-floor conservatory restaurant is something of a landmark, and food is also available in the informal brasserie and bar. Fine real ales are offered, and six wines by the glass. Classic car breaks are a special feature.
OPEN: 11-11 6.30-8.30 (Sun 12-10.30) **BAR MEALS:** L served all week 12.30-2.15 **RESTAURANT:** L served all week 12.15-9.30 D served all week 6.30-10.15 **BREWERY/COMPANY:** Free House ◀: Harveys Best, Shepherd Neame Master Brew, Bishop's Finger & Spitfire. **FACILITIES:** Children welcome Garden: Dogs allowed **NOTES:** Parking 28 **ROOMS:** 18 bedrooms 18 en suite

Pick of the Pubs

Sankey's Cellar Wine Bar ☜ ☟

39 Mount Ephraim TN4 8AA
☎ 01892 511422 ▤ 01892 511450
e-mail: seafood@sankeys.co.uk
Dir: *On A26*

Sankeys, a Tunbridge institution, is a wine bar specialising in seafood, and also a great supporter of small local and

continued

international brewers. The wine list offers quality wines at reasonable prices, including 10-12 by the glass, and most bottles are available to take home. Plus, there is an extensive choice of world classic bottled beers. The atmosphere is uniquely bustling and the place is cluttered with local memorabilia. Steps lead from the street down to the old cellars that open onto a sheltered garden protected from the weather by huge umbrellas and patio heaters. One sensibly-priced menu applies throughout, bringing diners the best of British seafood, with oysters from nearby Whitstable, Loch Fyne langoustines, and lobster and crab from Cornwall. House specialities are cock crabs with huge claws, hand dressed and served with salad and native British blue lobsters, claimed to be the best in the world.

OPEN: 11-3.30 6-12 (Open all day in summer) Closed: 25-26 Dec **BAR MEALS:** L served all week 12-2.30 D served all week 7-10 Av main course £8.50 **RESTAURANT:** L served all week 12-2.30 D served all week 7-10 Av 3 course à la carte £25 **BREWERY/COMPANY:** Free House ◖: Timothy Taylor Landlord, Larkins Traditional Bitter, Harveys Sussex Best. ♀: 11 **FACILITIES:** Garden: Patio, seats 50, heated

---

WARREN STREET
Map 07 TQ95

The Harrow Hill Hotel
Hubbards Hill ME.17 2ED ☎ 01622 858727 ▤ 01622 850026
e-mail: harrowhillhotel@hotmail.com
Dir: A20 to Lenham, follow sign for Warren St on L, pub on R
Situated high up on the North Downs, this country inn was once a forge and rest house for travellers heading for Canterbury on the Pilgrim's Way. Good food is served in the cosy bar, including sizzling platter, pasta silvana, lasagne, and vegetarian gateau. In the relaxed restaurant expect starters such as smoked duck and ginger salad or smoked seafood tower, followed by confit of guinea fowl, fan of lamb fillet, and chicken Hiawatha.
OPEN: 12-3 7-11 (Sun 7-10.30) Closed: 25-26 Dec **BAR MEALS:** L served all week 12-2.30 D served all week 7-9.15 Av main course £8.50 **RESTAURANT:** L served all week 12-1.30 D served all week 7-9.00 Av 3 course à la carte £25 **BREWERY/COMPANY:** Free House ◖: Greene King IPA, Adnams Bitter, Fuller's London Pride, Marston's Pedigree. **FACILITIES:** Garden: Courtyards with furniture and ponds Dogs allowed Water, dining area **NOTES:** Parking 80

WESTERHAM
Map 06 TQ45

The Fox & Hounds ♀
Toys Hill TN16 1QG ☎ 01732 750328
A traditional family-run country pub in the heart of National Trust land, with no music or gaming machines to disturb the convivial atmosphere. Beautiful gardens, open fires and comfortable old furniture inside. From the menu expect beef and Stilton pie, North African lamb stew, chicken Mozzarella, and Shirley's famous Sunday lunch. Plenty of good walks locally. Not far from Chartwell, home of Winston Churchill.
OPEN: 11.30-2.30 6-11 (Sun 12-4, 7-10.30) Closed: Dec 25 **BAR MEALS:** L served all week12-2 D served 6-9 all week Av main course £7 **RESTAURANT:** 12-2 6-9.30 **BREWERY/COMPANY:** Greene King ◖: Greene King IPA Abbot Ale. ♀: 9 **FACILITIES:** Children welcome Garden: Lrg garden with numerous tables with shade Dogs allowed at discretion of innkeeper **NOTES:** Parking 15 **NOTES:** No credit cards

---

WHITSTABLE
Map 07 TR16

Pick of the Pubs

The Sportsman 🐟
Faversham Rd CT5 4BP ☎ 01227 273370 ▤ 01227 262314
Reached via a winding lane across open marshland from Whitstable, and tucked beneath the sea wall, the Sportsman may seem an unlikely place to find such good food. The rustic yet comfortable interior is fuss free with wooden floors, sturdy tables and an interesting collection of prints. A first rate pint of Shepherd Neame Masterbrew is served and a decent glass of wine. Similar care is taken over the quality of the food, and the daily menu is based on local produce, mostly sourced from within a five-mile radius. There are usually three or four fresh fish dishes, depending on what's available - one day's offerings were Dover sole, brill, cod and smoked haddock. Speciality dishes are crispy duck with smoked chilli salsa, local brill fillet braised in vin jeune, and whole grilled Dover sole with a tartare of mussels. The pub is ideally positioned for walkers on the Saxon Shore Way.
OPEN: 12-3 6-11 (all day Sun) Closed: 25 Dec **BAR MEALS:** L served Tue-Sun 12-2 D served Tue-Sat Av main course £13.95 **RESTAURANT:** L served Tue-Sun 12-2 D served Tue-Sat 7-9 Av 3 course à la carte £22 **BREWERY/COMPANY:** Shepherd Neame ◖: Shepherd Neame Bishops Finger, Spitfire, Masterbrew. **FACILITIES:** Garden: Dogs allowed On leads **NOTES:** Parking 25

WROTHAM
Map 06 TQ65

The Green Man 🐟
Hodsoll St, Ash-cum-Ridley TN15 7LE ☎ 01732 823575
Dir: Off A227 between Wrotham & Meopham
Converted at some stage from three cottages, this village pub is at least 300 years old. A framed newspaper cutting recalls Hodsoll Street's brief fame as the 'forgotten village' because it was omitted from the 1931 census. Ladder-style blackboards show king scallops and bacon salad, skate wing with black butter and capers, lamb shank in red wine jus, roast duck with onion marmalade and plum sauce, and chicken stuffed with king prawns in filo pastry.
OPEN: 11-2.30 6.30-11 (Sat 11-3, 6.30-11/Sun 12-3, 7-10.30) **BAR MEALS:** L served all week 12-2 D served all week 6.30-9.30 Av main course £10 **RESTAURANT:** L served all week 12-2 D served all week 6.30-9.30 **BREWERY/COMPANY:** Enterprise Inns ◖: Youngs Bitter, Fuller's London Pride, Harveys, Flowers Original. **FACILITIES:** Children welcome Children's licence Garden: Large grassed area with many picnic benches Dogs allowed **NOTES:** Parking 35

WYE
Map 07 TR04

The New Flying Horse ♀
Upper Bridge St TN25 5AN ☎ 01233 812297 ▤ 01233 813487
e-mail: newflyhorse@shepherd-neame.co.uk
400-year-old Shepherd Neame inn, characterised by low ceilings, black beams and open fire. Tucked away in pretty village beneath the North Downs.
OPEN: 11-11 Closed 3-5.30 Winter **BAR MEALS:** L served all week 12-2 D served all week 6-9 Av main course £5 **RESTAURANT:** L served all week 12-2.30 D served all week 6-9 ◖: Masterbrew Spitfire, Plus guests. **FACILITIES:** Garden Dogs allowed in bar, garden

England

LANCASHIRE

BELMONT
Map 15 SD61

Black Dog
2/4 Church St BL7 8AB ☎ 01204 811218 ◻ 01204 811 694
Dir: M65 J3 onto A675

A traditional moorland pub, and a popular stopping point for walkers on the Witton Weavers Way, a 32-mile circuit around Blackburn and Darwen. Dating from the mid 19th-century, its new owners have pleased the locals by giving it a complete makeover. New customers welcome it too, clearly detecting what the proprietor calls its 'good feel factor'. Good value bar food includes toasted sandwiches, ploughman's, barm cakes, scampi or cod and chips, and Welsh dragon tart (cauliflower, leek and soft cheeses with a Caerphilly sauce). Specials include shoulder of lamb, peppered pork, liver and onions, steak and ale pie, chicken curry, chilli con carne and moussaka. Adorned with antiques and bric-a-brac, and noted for its New Year's Day classical music concert and occasional live jazz evenings. Real ale from the fiercely independent Holt family brewery in Manchester.

OPEN: 12-11 **BAR MEALS:** L served all week 12-3 D served Wed-Sun 7-9 Av main course £6.50 **BREWERY/COMPANY:** Holts
◖: Holt-Bitter, Diamond, Mild, Seasonal Guest Beer.
NOTES: Parking 28

BILSBORROW
Map 18 SD53

Owd Nell's Tavern 🏠 ♀
Guy's Thatched Hamlet, Canal Side PR3 0RS
☎ 01995 640010 ◻ 01995 640141
e-mail: info@guysthatchedhamlet.com
Dir: Telephone for directions

Great for families, Owd Nell's is situated by the Lancaster Canal in an all-thatched complex including bedroom lodges, a continental restaurant, cricket and crown green bowling. The tavern, a former farmhouse dating from the 16th century, offers a wide selection of guest ales, 50 malt whiskies and 40 wines available by the glass. Favourite dishes are home-made steak and kidney pie, huge battered cod and chips, mussel hot pot, and game in season.

OPEN: 11-11 Closed: 25 Dec **BAR MEALS:** L served all week 11-10.30 D served all week Av main course £5 **RESTAURANT:** L served all week 12-2.30 D served all week 5.30-10.30 Av 3 course à la carte £10.50 Av 2 course fixed price £7 **BREWERY/COMPANY:** Free House ◖: Interbrew Boddingtons Bitter & Flowers, Jennings Bitter, Castle Eden Ale, Owd Nells Bitter. ♀: 40 **FACILITIES:** Children welcome Garden: Patio areas by the Lancaster Canal Dogs allowed Water **NOTES:** Parking 300

BLACKBURN
Map 18 SD62

Pick of the Pubs

Millstone Hotel ★★ ◉ ♀
Church Ln, Mellor BB2 7JR
☎ 01254 813333 ◻ 01254 812628
e-mail: millstone.reception@shirehotels.co.uk
Dir: From M6 J31 take A59 towards Clitheroe, past British Aerospace. R at rdbt signed Blackburn/Mellor. Next rdbt 2nd L. Hotel top of hill on R

This fine inn, at the crossroads in a picturesque village, was the original flagship of Daniel Thwaites's Blackburn brewery. Developed from a 17th-century tithe barn, it retains original oak beams, linenfold panelling and the circular grinding-stone, incorporated in the façade, from which the hotel's name is derived. Equally well preserved is its traditional country inn ambience, characterised by good value bar and restaurant food. Likely starters include freshly-prepared soup, baked king prawns, or crispy duck pancakes with oriental salad and plum sauce. Lunch main courses include village-made sausages (lamb with apricot and mint), mash and onion gravy, and baked cèpe gnocchi, while at dinner try Pendle lamb rump, tournedos Rossini, grilled lemon sole, with ratatouille and red pepper syrup, and pan-fried chicken supreme, with wilted greens and white bean and grain mustard sauce. Daily specials appear on the blackboard. Real ales from, reasonably enough, Thwaites of Blackburn.

OPEN: 11-11 (Sun 12-10.30) **BAR MEALS:** L served all week 12-2.15 D served all week 6.30-9.15 Av main course £8.95 **RESTAURANT:** L served all week 12-2 D served all week 6.30-9.30 Av 3 course à la carte £23.50
BREWERY/COMPANY: Shire Hotels ◖: Thwaites, Warsteiner.
NOTES: Parking 45 **ROOMS:** 24 bedrooms 24 en suite 2 family rooms s£49 d£49 no children overnight

BLACKO
Map 18 SD84

Moorcock Inn 🏠
Gisburn Rd BB9 6NG ☎ 01282 614186 ◻ 01282 614186
e-mail: boo@patterson1047.freeserve.co.uk
Dir: M65 J13, A682 for Kendal

Family-run country inn with traditional log fires and good views towards the Pendle Way, ideally placed for non-motorway travel to the Lakes and the Yorkshire Dales. Home-cooked meals are a speciality, with a wide choice including salads and sandwiches, and vegetarian and children's meals. Tasty starters like cheesy mushrooms, and garlic prawns are followed by lasagne, various steak choices, pork in orange and cider, and trout grilled with lemon and herb butter.
OPEN: 12-2.30 6-9.30 **BAR MEALS:** L served all week 12-2 D served Tues-Sun 6-9.30 Av main course £6.25 **RESTAURANT:** L served all week 12-2.30 D served Tues-Sun 6-9.30
BREWERY/COMPANY: Thwaites ◖: Thwaites, Best Bitter, Smooth, Warfsteiner. **FACILITIES:** Children welcome Garden: Picnic benches, beautiful views Dogs allowed Water, food **NOTES:** Parking 80

The Rosette is the AA award for food. Look out for it next to a pub's name.

The Shireburn Arms

A very attractive and interesting walk in a part of Lancashire that may well have been the inspiration for Middle-earth in JRR Tolkien's epic 'Lord of the Rings.' Tolkien's son, a priest in training, was evacuated to a seminary next door to nearby Stonyhurst College, a Roman Catholic school and part of the route. Another of his son's was a teacher here and Tolkien was a regular visitor.

From the entrance to the Shireburn Arms Hotel, walk along the B6243 road, passing the war memorial, and turn into Avenue Road. Continue through the village, passing the Bayley Arms pub and some almshouses and then take the drive towards Stonyhurst College.

Turn sharp right at a statue and follow the drive to the bottom end of several lakes where it turns left. At the road junction turn right, then take the waymarked path on the right at a bend, following it to a driveway running between two large gate posts.

Keep ahead alongside the college and pass the church. Keep left, passing some observatories to reach a bend near some barns on the left. Leave the drive here and pass through a gate to join a track. Cut across farmland for about 1/2 mile (800m) to reach the B6243.

Turn right, then left into a field, passing through the right-hand gate. Follow an indistinct path to the right of a hedgerow, cross a stile and then descend to the left towards Fox Fields Farm. Pass through a gap in the hedge to the right of the farm and then through the farmyard. Follow the drive to the right, heading for the banks of the River Ribble.

Turn right, following the riverside Ribble Way and continue ahead beside the water for almost 1/2 mile (800m), eventually passing the aquaduct bridge. Follow the path over a footbridge beneath trees, then up a stepped hillside to reach a stile. Follow the waymarks, ascending through pasture, and make for the hotel, passing just to the right of it.

★★
THE SHIREBURN ARMS, CLITHEROE
Whalley Road, Hurst Green BB7 9QJ
☎ 01254 826518

Directions: Telephone for details Believed to have been the inspiration for Tolkien's Hobbiton, with blazing fires, low beams and real ales. Traditional food and snacks are served in the comfortable bar and smart restaurant. 18 individually-styled bedrooms.
Open: 11-11
Bar Meals: 12-2 5.30-9.30
Notes: Children welcome - small play area, toys - & dogs. Patio garden. Parking.
(See page 278 for full entry)

DISTANCE: 4 miles (6.4km)
MAP: OS Explorer OL 41
TERRAIN: Parkland, farmland a river valley
PATHS: Drives, tracks and field paths
GRADIENT: Undulating

Walk submitted by
The Shireburn Arms

England

BROOKHOUSE
Map 18 SD56

Black Bull Inn
LA2 9JP ☎ 01524 770329
Dir: Leave M6 at Jct 34, take A683 to Kirby Lonsdale for 2.5m, at mini rdbt turn R for 0.75m pub is located on R
16th-century coaching inn situated in a picture postcard village. Originally made up of three cottages, the inn was also used as a local courthouse in the 1820s. Lots of old beams and local atmosphere.
OPEN: 12-3 6-11 **BAR MEALS:** L served all week 12-2 D served all week 6-9 Av main course £5 **RESTAURANT:** L served all week 12-2 D served all week 6-9 Av 3 course à la carte £12.50 **◀:** Thwaites Lancaster Bomber. **FACILITIES:** Children welcome Dogs allowed **NOTES:** No credit cards

BURNLEY
Map 18 SD83

The Ram 🐾 ♀
399 Burnley Rd, Cliviger BB10 4SU ☎ 01282 418921
In the shadow of Thievely Peak, the pub dates back to 1630. The food is best described as leaning towards traditional home-style cooking with a contemporary twist. Best illustrated by its Vintage Collection platter of assorted salmon, cheese and salad tasters or baby leek and Caerphilly sausage plate with onion gravy and deep-fried parsnips. Also traditional Sunday roasts and lemon chicken with parsley butter from the main menu.
OPEN: 11-11 **BAR MEALS:** L served all week 12-10 D served all week Av main course £6.95 **BREWERY/COMPANY:** Vintage Inns **◀:** Tetleys, Bass. **FACILITIES:** Children welcome Garden: Large patio area with amazing views

CARNFORTH
Map 18 SD47

Dutton Arms 🐾 ♀
Station Ln, Burton LA6 1HR ☎ 01524 781225 ▤ 01524 782662
Dir: from M6 take A6 signed Milnthorpe (Kendal), 3m before Milnthorpe turn R signed Burton/Holme
Close to a host of tourist attractions, including Morecambe Bay, the Lancashire Canal and the Northern Yorkshire Dales. The Dutton Arms boasts a conservatory area that provides access to the pub's colourful gardens. Now under new management.
OPEN: 10-3.30 6-11 **BAR MEALS:** L served all week 11-2.30 D served all week 6-9.30 Av main course £10 **RESTAURANT:** L served all week 11-2.30 D served all week 6-9.30 **BREWERY/COMPANY:** Free House **◀:** Interbrew Boddingtons, Greene King Old Speckled Hen, Dent, Black Sheep Best. **FACILITIES:** Children welcome Garden: Lawned area with adventure playground Dogs allowed Water **NOTES:** Parking 30

CHIPPING
Map 18 SD64

Dog & Partridge
Hesketh Ln PR3 2TH ☎ 01995 61201 ▤ 01995 61446
Dating back to 1515, this comfortably modernised rural inn in the Ribble Valley enjoys wonderful views of the surrounding fells. The next door barn has been converted into an additional dining area, and the emphasis is on home-made food using local produce. Diners can choose from bar snacks, or à la carte in the restaurant. The latter includes poached salmon with prawn sauce, leek and mushroom crumble, roast Lancashire beef, or jumbo scampi in batter.
OPEN: 11.45-3 6.45-11 (Sun 11.45-10.30) **BAR MEALS:** L served all week 12-1.45 Av main course £9 **RESTAURANT:** L served all week 12-1.30 D served all week 7-9 Av 3 course à la carte £16 Av 4 course fixed price £13.50 **BREWERY/COMPANY:** Free House **◀:** Carlsberg-Tetley. **FACILITIES:** Children welcome **NOTES:** Parking 30

CLITHEROE
Map 18 SD74

Pick of the Pubs

Assheton Arms 🐾 ♀
Downham BB7 4BJ ☎ 01200 441227 ▤ 01200 440581
e-mail: asshetonarms@aol.com
Dir: From A59 take Chatburn turn. In Chatburn follow signs for Downham
The Assheton Arms (named after Lord Clitheroe's family who own the whole village) may be better known these days as the Signalman's Arms in the BBC drama series 'Born and Bred', and Downham itself features as Ormston, the picturesque village in the series. A single bar and sectioned rooms house an array of solid oak tables, wing back settees, window seats, an original stone fireplace, and a large blackboard listing the interesting range of daily dishes on offer. Typical choices begin with starters and snacks like home-made ham and vegetable broth, potted shrimps or a ploughman's. Seafood is well represented, including pan-fried monkfish with peppercorns in a cream and brandy sauce, and there are plenty of traditional pub favourites - grills, steak and kidney pie, and vegetarian chilli. The pub is well placed for a wild moorland walk up Pendle Hill, which looms high above the village.
OPEN: 12-3 7-11 (summer Sun open all day) Closed: 1st wk in Jan **BAR MEALS:** L served all week 12-2 D served all week 7-10 Av main course £9 **BREWERY/COMPANY:** Enterprise Inns **◀:** Marstons Pedigree, Interbrew Boddingtons Bitter. **♀:** 7 **FACILITIES:** Children welcome Dogs allowed **NOTES:** Parking 12

The Shireburn Arms ★★ 🐾 ♀
Whalley Rd, Hurst Green BB7 9QJ
☎ 01254 826518 ▤ 01254 826208
e-mail: steve@shireburnarmshotel.com
Dir: Telephone for directions

A favourite haunt of J R R Tolkien, the Shireburn stands in the heart of the village which some say was the inspiration for Tolkien's Hobbiton. Certainly the blazing fires, low beams and real ales of this 17th-century inn do little to dispel the rumour. The menu offers traditional snacks, plus Yorkshire pudding filled with chicken and mushrooms, leek and Gruyère parcel, liver and onions, and grilled halibut with lemon and dill butter.
OPEN: 11-11 **BAR MEALS:** L served all week 12-2 D served all week 5.30-9.30 Av main course £6.50 **RESTAURANT:** L served all week 12-2 D served all week 5.30-9.30 Av 3 course à la carte £15 **BREWERY/COMPANY:** Free House **◀:** Scottish Courage Theakstons Best Bitter, Mild & Guest Cask Ales. **♀:** 10 **FACILITIES:** Children welcome Garden: Patio garden, seating for 60 people Dogs allowed **NOTES:** Parking 100 **ROOMS:** 18 bedrooms 18 en suite 3 family rooms s£45 d£70

See Pub Walk on page 277

DARWEN
Map 15 SD62

Old Rosins Inn
Treacle Row, Pickup Bank, Hoddlesden BB3 3QD
☎ 01254 771264 ▤ 01254 873894
Dir: M65 J5, follow signs for Haslingdon then R after 2m signed Egworth. 0.5m R & continue for 0.5m

The original inn, set in the heart of the Lancashire Moors, has been extended to provide a variety of facilities. A typical menu includes halibut in lemon sauce, steak and ale pie, spinach tortellini, salmon with a herb crust, lasagne, lamb Jennings, cod in lemon and prawn butter, and mussels in cream and white wine.
OPEN: 11-11 (Sun 12-10.30) **BAR MEALS:** L served all week 12-2.30 D served all week 5.30-9 Av main course £5.95
RESTAURANT: L served all week 6.30-9 D served all week Av 3 course à la carte £12.95 Av 4 course fixed price £15
BREWERY/COMPANY: Jennings ▨: Directors, Worthington, 1744.
FACILITIES: Children welcome Garden: Lawns and shrubbery, food served outdoors Dogs allowed at manager's discretion only
NOTES: Parking 200 **ROOMS:** 15 bedrooms 15 en suite s£45 d£39.95 (♦♦♦)

EDGWORTH
Map 15 SD71

Strawberry Duck Hotel
Overshores Rd, Turton BL7 0LU ☎ 01204 852013
Surrounded by reservoirs and beautiful countryside, this cosy country pub is a favourite haunt of real ale lovers. The traditional bar also serves decent food, from platters of salad with choice of topping (beef, ham, cheese) to various grills and lamb Devonshire, chicken Stilton with asparagus, and Drunken Bullock (beef cooked slowly in Taylor's Landlord).
OPEN: 12-11 (Sun 12-10.30, 12pm bank holidays) **BAR MEALS:** L served all week 12-9.30 D served all week Av main course £7
RESTAURANT: L served all week 12-9.30 D served all week Av 3 course à la carte £15 **BREWERY/COMPANY:** Free House
▨: Timothy Taylors Landlord, Black Sheep, Boddingtons, plus Guest ales. **FACILITIES:** Children welcome Garden: Food served outside. Patio area Dogs allowed In the garden & overnight rooms
NOTES: Parking 30

FENCE
Map 18 SD83

Fence Gate Inn & Banqueting Centre
Wheatley Lane Rd BB12 9EE ☎ 01282 618101 ▤ 01282 615432
Dir: From M65 L 1.5m, set back on R opposite T-junction for Burnley

This substantial inn was originally a collection point for cotton delivered by barge and distributed to surrounding cottages to be spun into cloth. Wide-ranging menus are offered in the Topiary Brasserie.
OPEN: 12-11 **BAR MEALS:** L served all week 12.30-2.30 D served

all week 6.30-9.30 Av main course £6 **RESTAURANT:** L served all week 12-2.30 D served all week 6.30-9.30 Av 3 course à la carte £25 **BREWERY/COMPANY:** Free House ▨: Theakston, Directors.
FACILITIES: Children welcome Garden: patio, outdoor eating Dogs allowed at manager's discretion **NOTES:** Parking 100

FORTON
Map 18 SD45

Pick of the Pubs

The Bay Horse Inn ⛽ ♀
LA2 0HR ☎ 01524 791204 ▤ 01524 791204
e-mail: cwilki5769@aol.com
Dir: 1 M S off Junct 33 of M6

Bay Horse is the name given to the picturesque area to the south of Lancaster, stretching to Cockerham Sands and the Lune estuary. The inn dates from the early 17th century and was originally a farmhouse, and the function room is a conversion of a former barn. It is a traditional local with roughcast walls, bay windows and a small dining room, which these days serves food to the most discriminating of diners. The inn specialises in simple, fresh and imaginative food from a chef who is wholly self-taught (now a member of the Master Chefs of Great Britain), and whose shopping policy reveals his total commitment. The local speciality, potted Morecambe bay shrimps, is an obvious starter, and other representative dishes are roast halibut with rocket and potato purée, and pressing of foie gras and duck rillette with beer jelly.
OPEN: 12-3 6.30-11 (Sun 12-5, 8-10.30) **BAR MEALS:** L served Tue-Sun 12-1.45 D served Tue-Sat 7-9.15 Av main course £12.95 **RESTAURANT:** L served Tue-Sun 12-2 D served Tue-Sat 7-9.30 Av 3 course à la carte £30 Av 3 course fixed price £14.95
▨: Wadworth 6X, Everards Tiger. **FACILITIES:** Children welcome Garden: **NOTES:** Parking 30

GALGATE
Map 18 SD45

The Stork Hotel
Conder Green LA2 0AN ☎ 01524 751234 ▤ 01524 752660
e-mail: the.stork@virgin.net
Dir: M6 J33 take A6 north. At Galgate turn L & next L to Conder Green
White-painted coaching inn spread along the banks of the Conder Estuary, with a colourful 300-year-history that includes several name changes. The quaint sea port of Glasson Dock is a short walk along the Lancashire Coastal Way, and the Lake District is easily accessible. Seasonal specialities join home-cooked food like steak pie, locally-smoked haddock, salmon fillet with bonne femme sauce, and Cumberland sausage with onion gravy and mashed potatoes.
OPEN: 11-11 (Sun 12-10.30) **BAR MEALS:** L served all week 12-2.30 D served all week 6.30-9 Av main course £6.95
RESTAURANT: L served all week 12-2.30 D served all week 6-9
BREWERY/COMPANY: Free House ▨: Boddingtons, Pedigree.
FACILITIES: Children welcome Garden: Large seating area with wishing well Dogs allowed Water **NOTES:** Parking 35

> We endeavour to be as accurate as possible but changes to times and other information can occur after the guide has gone to press

continued

England

GOOSNARGH
Map 18 SD53

The Bushell's Arms 🏠 ♀
Church Ln PR3 2BH ☎ 01772 865235 📠 01772 865235
Dir: *Take A6 north to Garstang, turn right onto Whittingham Lane, drive for 3 miles, take left into Church Lane. The pub is situated to the right of the village green*

Dr Bushell was a philanthropic Georgian who built his villagers not just a hospital but this pub too. New owners arrived in 2002 and introduced a straightforward, modestly-priced menu comprising a fair selection of starters, and main courses: battered whole-tail scampi, traditional steak and ale pie, tagliatelle carbonara, chargrilled steaks, fish and seafood salads all feature, as well as snacks and children's favourites. A regular diner is the dad from a recent gravy commercial!
OPEN: 12-3 6-11 **BAR MEALS:** L served Tue-Sun 12-2 D served all week 6-9 Av main course £5.95 **RESTAURANT:** L served all week 12-2 D served all week 6-9 **BREWERY/COMPANY:** Enterprise Inns ⬤: Timothy Taylor Landlord, Interbrew Boddingtons Bitter. ♀: 8 **FACILITIES:** Children welcome Garden: Grassed area with several benches and trees Dogs allowed Water & Toys **NOTES:** Parking 10

Ye Horns Inn 🏠 ♀
Horns Ln PR3 2FJ ☎ 01772 865230 📠 01772 864299
e-mail: info@yehornsinn.co.uk
Dir: *From M6 J32 take A6 N towards Garstang. At traffic lights turn R onto B5269 towards Goosnargh. In Goosnargh follow Inn signs*

Elizabeth and Mark Woods have been welcoming guests to this 18th-century, black and white coaching inn for 20 years. Glorious open fires, original beams and luxurious furnishings await you indoors, whilst the patio and outdoor seating area is perfect for warmer days. Located in a peaceful country setting, the pub also provides a menu that includes roast pheasant in cranberry sauce, vegetarian stuffed peppers, and halibut with prawn sauce.
OPEN: 11.30-3 6-11 (Ex Mon) **BAR MEALS:** L served Tue-Sun 12-2 D served all week 7-9.15 Av main course £9 **RESTAURANT:** L served Tue-Sun 12-2 D served all week 7-9.15 Av 3 course à la carte £17 Av 5 course fixed price £18.95 **BREWERY/COMPANY:** Free House ⬤: No real ale. ♀: 8 **FACILITIES:** Children welcome Garden: Large patio area, tables, seating, pond, lawn **NOTES:** Parking 70

HASLINGDEN
Map 15 SD72

Farmers Glory 🏠
Roundhill Rd BB4 5TU ☎ 01706 215748 📠 01706 215748
Dir: *7 miles equidistant from Blackburn, Burnley and Bury, 1.5m from M66*

Stone-built 350-year-old pub situated high above Haslingden on the edge of the Pennines. Formerly a coaching inn on the ancient route to Whalley Abbey, it now offers locals and modern A667 travellers a wide-ranging traditional pub menu of steaks, roasts, seafood, pizzas, pasta, curries and sandwiches. Live folk music every Wednesday and a large beer garden with ornamental fishpond.
OPEN: 12-3 7-11.30 **BAR MEALS:** L served all week 12-2.30 D served all week 7-9.30 Av main course £6 **RESTAURANT:** L served all week 12-2.30 D served all week 7-9.30 Av 3 course à la carte £12 **BREWERY/COMPANY:** Pubmaster ⬤: Carlsberg-Tetley Tetley Bitter, Marston's Pedigree, Adnams, Jennings. **FACILITIES:** Children welcome Garden: 1/2 acre, fixed seating, fish pond **NOTES:** Parking 60

> ◆ Pubs with Red Diamonds are the top places in the AA's three, four and five diamond ratings

HESKIN GREEN
Map 15 SD51

Farmers Arms 🏠
85 Wood Ln PR7 5NP ☎ 01257 451276 📠 01257 453958
e-mail: andy@farmersarms.co.uk
Dir: *On B5250 between M6 & Eccleston*

Long, creeper-covered country inn with two cosy bars decorated in old pictures and farming memorabilia. Once known as the Pleasant Retreat, this is a family-run pub proud to offer a warm welcome. Typical dishes include steak pie, fresh salmon with prawns and mushroom, halibut, rack of lamb and chicken curry.
OPEN: 12-11 **BAR MEALS:** L served all week 12-9.30 D served all week **RESTAURANT:** L served all week 12-9.30 D served all week **BREWERY/COMPANY:** Enterprise Inns ⬤: Timothy Taylor Landlord, Castle Eden Ale, Interbrew Flowers IPA & Boddingtons, Carlsberg-Tetley Tetely Bitter. **FACILITIES:** Children welcome Garden: Dogs allowed **NOTES:** Parking 50 **ROOMS:** 5 bedrooms 5 en suite (♦♦♦)

HEST BANK
Map 18 SD46

Hest Bank Hotel 🏠
2 Hest Bank Ln LA2 6DN ☎ 01524 824339 📠 01524 824948
e-mail: hestbankhotel@hotmail.com
Dir: *From Lancaster take A6 N, after 2m L to Hest Bank*

First licensed in 1554 to brew mead, ale and sack, sell cooked game, and hold a weekly cock fight. Thankfully - at least in that last respect - times change and today this canalside, former staging post for coaches crossing Morecambe Bay concentrates on freshly-prepared food derived mostly from local suppliers. Cajun-dusted chicken breast with sweet chilli dip, Stilton-topped rump steak in red wine gravy, leek, Parmesan and parsnip bake, and fish dishes are typical.
OPEN: 11.30-11 (Sun 12-10.30) **BAR MEALS:** L served all week 12-9 D served all week Av main course £5.95 **BREWERY/COMPANY:** Pubmaster ⬤: Interbrew Boddingtons, Cains Bitter, Timothy Taylor Landlord. **FACILITIES:** Garden: Canalside, benches, lawn & patio area **NOTES:** Parking 20

MERECLOUGH
Map 18 SD83

Kettledrum Inn & Restaurant ♀
302 Red Lees Rd BB10 4RG ☎ 01282 424591 📠 01282 424591
Dir: *from Burnley town centre, past Burnley FC, 2.5m, 1st pub on L*

The Kettledrum is an inviting and well-kept country inn with superb views of the famous Pendle Hills. It offers real ales, malt whiskies, a choice of 12 wines by the glass and a good range of traditional pub food. Sandwiches, steaks and suet puddings are all part of the staple fare, along with creamy penne pasta, chicken curry, filled Yorkshire pudding and Barnsley lamb chops.
OPEN: 12-3 6-11 (Sun open all day) **BAR MEALS:** L served all week 12-2.30 D served all week 6-9 Av main course £6.50 **RESTAURANT:** L served all week 12-2.30 D served all week 6-9 Av 3 course à la carte £12 **BREWERY/COMPANY:** Pubmaster ⬤: Hancocks HSB, Tetley, Black Sheep. ♀: 12 **FACILITIES:** Children welcome **NOTES:** Parking 30

PARBOLD
Map 15 SD41

Pick of the Pubs

The Eagle & Child 🏠 ♀
Maltkiln Ln L40 3SG ☎ 01257 462297 📠 01257 464718
Dir: *From M6 J27 to Parbold. At bottom of Parbold Hill turn R on B5246 to Hilldale. Then 4th L to Bispham Green*

A dining-pub where the emphasis is firmly placed on good ales and cider, a daily-changing menu of freshly-

continued

cooked food, and a peaceful atmosphere conducive to conversation (no juke boxes or fruit machines). The interior is characterised by flagged floors, coir matting, oak settles, antique furniture and old prints, and includes a no-smoking room. Seven ever-changing real ales are served, and an interesting selection of wines. Options from the daily menu range from salads and snacks - BLT sandwich, club sandwich ciabatta - to full meals with dishes like roast rib-eye of beef with caramelised onion jus, grilled salmon with tomato couscous and lobster cream, and medallions of suckling pig, mustard mash and creamed Madeira. Perennially-popular special events include internationally-themed food nights and an annual beer festival in May. The pub also has its own bowling green.

OPEN: 12-3 5.30-11 (Sun 12-10.30) 25 Dec Closed eve **BAR MEALS:** L served all week 12-2 D served all week 6-8.30 Av main course £9 **RESTAURANT:** L served all week 12-2 D served all week 6-8.30 Av 3 course à la carte £16 **BREWERY/COMPANY:** Free House ◗: Moorhouses Black Cat, Thwaites Bitter, 5 changing guest beers. ♀: 6 **FACILITIES:** Children welcome Garden: Large patio, wooden benches, bowling green **NOTES:** Parking 50

PRESTON   Map 18 SD52

Pick of the Pubs

Cartford Country Inn & Hotel ⌂ ♀
Little Eccleston PR3 0YP ☎ 01995 670166 ▤ 01995 671785
This old, pleasantly rambling three-storey inn guards a historic toll bridge over the tidal River Wyre that enters the Irish Sea near Fleetwood. Inside, an open log fire may be blazing, and there's always pool, darts or dominoes to be played while enjoying a pint of Dishy Debbie, one of several real ales brewed behind the pub by the Hart brewery. A good range of food on the bar menu runs from sandwiches to pizzas, and from jacket potatoes to hot and cold platters with a choice of salads, Cumberland sausage with egg, chilli con carne, and lasagne. Various specials might include curries, and lemon sole with crabmeat. The choice for vegetarians has recently been extended. Meals can also be taken outside overlooking the river, along part of which runs a four-mile walk that conveniently starts and finishes at the pub.
OPEN: 12-3 7-11 (Sun 12-10.30) (Open 6.30 in summer) **BAR MEALS:** L served all week 12-2 D served all week 6.30-9.30 Av main course £5.50 **RESTAURANT:** L served all week D served all week **BREWERY/COMPANY:** Free House ◗: Hart Beers, Fullers London Pride, Moorhouse, Guest ales. **FACILITIES:** Children welcome Dogs allowed **NOTES:** Parking 60 **ROOMS:** 6 bedrooms 6 en suite s£36.95 d£48.95

RIBCHESTER   Map 18 SD63

The White Bull ⌂ ♀
Church St PR3 3XP ☎ 01254 878303
e-mail: whitebullrib@aol.com
Dir: Off A59 in village centre
Partly on the site of an old Roman town, a 17th-century, Grade II listed courthouse abounding in antiquity; the former Roman bathhouse can be seen from the beer garden. Cask beers in the lounge and bars accompany a comprehensive selection of traditional pub food and grills supplemented by regularly-changed specials. Look here for filo parcels of black pudding and onion, salmon supreme with black bream and sherry sauce, and home-made cheesecake.
OPEN: 11.30-3 6.30-11 (Sat in Summer all day, Sun 12-10.30) **BAR MEALS:** L served all week 12-2 D served Tue-Sun 6.30-9.30 Av main course £7 **RESTAURANT:** L served all week 11.30-2 D served Tue-Sun 6.30-9.30 Av 3 course à la carte £9.50 **BREWERY/COMPANY:** ◗: Interbrew Boddingtons Bitter, Black Sheep Best, Abbots Ale. ♀: 20 **FACILITIES:** Children welcome Garden: Food served outdoors **NOTES:** Parking 14

SLAIDBURN   Map 18 SD75

Hark to Bounty Inn
Townend BB7 3EP ☎ 01200 446246 ▤ 01200 446361
e-mail: manager@hark-to-bounty.co.uk
Dir: From M6 J31 take A59 to Clitheroe then B6478, through Waddington, Newton and onto Slaidburn
13th-century inn originally known as The Dog when the local squire, who was also the parson, had a pack of hounds. His favourite dog, known as Bounty, had a loud bark which could be heard above the rest of the pack. The inn also contains a remarkable courtroom which was still in use as a court as recently as 1937. Today's kitchen output remains largely traditional, with dishes such as home-made steak and kidney pie, slow-cooked lamb shank, fish pie and braised beef.
OPEN: 11-11 **BAR MEALS:** L served all week 12-2 D served all week 6-9 Av main course £8 **RESTAURANT:** L served Tue-Sun 12-2 D served Tue-Sat 6-9 Av 3 course fixed price £15.95 **BREWERY/COMPANY:** Scottish Courage ◗: Theakston Old Peculier, Scottish Courage Courage Directors. **FACILITIES:** Children welcome Children's licence Garden: Large enclosed area Dogs allowed **NOTES:** Parking 25

WHALLEY   Map 18 SD73

Freemasons Arms ♀
8 Vicarage Fold, Wiswell BB7 9DF ☎ 01254 822218
e-mail: freemasons@wiswell.co.uk
Dir: Telephone for directions
A traditional country dining pub in the quiet village of Wiswell. Numerous walks in the area take in some stunning views as the heart of the Ribble Valley. Formerly housing the monks from nearby Whalley Abbey, it was converted into a pub some four centuries ago and hosted secret freemasons' meetings - hence its 'new' name. The Livesey family have enhanced its fine reputation for good ales and food in the spacious bar area, the old tap room and in a more refined upstairs dining room.
OPEN: 12-2 6.30-12 (closed Mon-Tue) Closed: 25-26 Dec, 1-2 Jan **BAR MEALS:** L served Wed-Sun 12-2 D served Wed-Sun 6.30-9.30 **RESTAURANT:** L served Wed-Sun 12-2 D served Wed-Sun 6.30-9.30 **BREWERY/COMPANY:** Free House ◗: Jennings Bitter, John Smith Smooth, Black Sheep Best. ♀: 10

Pick of the Pubs

The Inn At Whitewell 🏨 ♀
Forest of Bowland BB7 3AT
☎ 01200 448222 📠 01200 448298
Dir: Take B6243 and follow signs for Whitewell

A slightly eccentric inn, packed with a haphazard arrangement of furnishings and bric-a-brac, that stands on the east bank of the River Hodder at the heart of the Forest of Bowland. Parts of the building date back to the 1300s, when it would have been the forest-keeper's house. The comprehensive bar lunch and supper menus are supplemented by daily specials that might include the ever-popular fisherman's pie, grilled black pudding with poached pear, and Cumberland sausages with champ. There are also substantial sandwiches at lunchtime, traditional home-made puddings and fine hand-made cheeses at any time. A la carte dining at night in a relaxing atmosphere where no-one stands on ceremony - a fine old inn.

OPEN: 11-3 6-11 **BAR MEALS:** L served all week 12-2 D served all week 7.30-9.30 **RESTAURANT:** D served all week 7.30-9.30 **BREWERY/COMPANY:** Free House 🍺: Marston's Pedigree, Interbrew Boddingtons Bitter. ♀: 12
FACILITIES: Children welcome Garden: Dogs allowed
NOTES: Parking 50 **ROOMS:** 17 bedrooms 17 en suite

The Grapes 🐾
Station Rd PR4 2PH ☎ 01772 682927 📠 01772 687304
Dir: From M55 J3 follow signs for Kirkham then Wrea Green

Once known as The Dumplings after a popular dish, this traditional pub is full of charm and character. It sits at the centre of the village opposite the duck pond and green where frequent entertainment is held. Chalkboards on the walls display the dishes - fresh fish is a speciality - and might include calves' liver pan-fried with black pudding and apple, and sirloin stirfry with black bean sauce and egg noodles. Extensive snacks and traditional pub food.

OPEN: 11-11 **BAR MEALS:** L served all week 12-10 D served all week 12-10 Av main course £8.50 **RESTAURANT:** L served all week 12-10 D served all week 12-10
BREWERY/COMPANY: Scottish & Newcastle 🍺: Scottish Courage Theakston & John Smith's, Interbrew Boddingtons, Marston's Pedigree. **NOTES:** Parking 30

Pick of the Pubs

The Mulberry Tree ⊗⊗ 🐾 ♀
WN6 9SE ☎ 01257 451400 📠 01257 451400
Dir: Jct 27 off M6 turn into Mossy Lea Road 2m on the right

With former Roux Brothers' head chef Mark Prescott running the show, the former Scarisbrick Arms continues to go from strength to strength. It remains popular with both locals and discerning diners who feel very much at home in its clean, airy ambience whilst choosing from a veritable feast of options. Bar menu starters might include Stilton and celery soup, and mussels with white wine, followed by traditional Irish stew with rösti dumplings, slow-roast belly pork with apple and sage, and chicken chasseur. More complex dishes feature on the specials list, such as pressed winter terrine with white truffle dressing, followed by breast of guinea fowl with wild mushrooms, honey and rosemary, or whole roast black bream with saffron and prawn risotto. In addition there are popular multi-choice Sunday lunches at fixed prices, and a good selection of house wines.

OPEN: 12-3 6-11 Closed: 26 Dec, 1 Jan **BAR MEALS:** L served Mon-Sun 12-2 D served Mon-Sun 6-9 Av main course £12.95 **RESTAURANT:** L served all week 12-2 D served all week 6-10 Av 3 course à la carte £26 Av 3 course fixed price £17.95
BREWERY/COMPANY: Free House 🍺: Interbrew Flowers IPA.
FACILITIES: Children welcome **NOTES:** Parking 100

The New Inn
40 Yealand Rd LA5 9SJ ☎ 01524 732938
e-mail: newinn.yealand@virgin.net
Dir: Join A6 between Carnforth & Milnthorpe, 3m then L after Yealand Conyers sign, .25m to pub

An ivy-clad building dating from the 1600s situated in an Area of Outstanding Natural Beauty close to Leighton Moss Nature Reserve. Good beers and home-cooked food are served in the oak-beamed bar, non-smoking dining room or out in the garden. Popular dishes include Cumberland sausage, beef in beer, and field mushrooms stuffed with peppers, shallots, goat's cheese and spinach. Local specialities often include roast Cumbrian duck, rack of Lakeland lamb and sticky toffee pudding with butterscotch sauce.

OPEN: 11.30-11 (Sun 12-10.30) **BAR MEALS:** L served all week 11.30-9.30 D served all week Av main course £8 **RESTAURANT:** L served all week 11.30-9.30 D served all week 11.30-9.30
BREWERY/COMPANY: Frederic Robinson 🍺: Hartleys XB, Robinson's Seasonal Bitter, Old Tom. **FACILITIES:** Children welcome Garden: Dogs allowed Water **NOTES:** Parking 50

LEICESTERSHIRE

CASTLE DONINGTON
Map 11 SK42

Pick of the Pubs

The Nag's Head
Hilltop DE74 2PR ☎ 01332 850652

The Nag's Head began life as four cottages, and spread out from the middle cottage until it had taken over all four after World War II. Low beamed ceilings, open coal fires and a friendly atmosphere can be found inside the plain, whitewashed building. There's a bistro feel to the large, well-decorated dining room, with its colour-washed walls and plain scrubbed tables. The extensive menu features an upmarket range of starters and snacks, including smoked salmon with cream cheese and chives, and garlic and cream mushrooms. Unusual and inventive dishes like pork fillet with pancetta risotto, braised oxtail with parsnip mash, and duck breast with stir-fried pak choi and curry oil lead on to an irresistible chocolate whisky trifle. The pub is ideal for those visiting the East Midlands airport or the nearby motor racing circuit.
OPEN: 11.30-2.30 5.30-11 (Sun 12-3, 7-10.30) Closed: 26 Dec-4 Jan **BAR MEALS:** L served Mon-Sat 12-2 D served Mon-Sat 5.30-7 Av main course £6 **RESTAURANT:** L served Mon-Sat 12-2 D served Mon-Sat 5.30-9.30 🍺: Bank's Bitter, Marston's Pedigree, Mansfield Cask Bitter. **FACILITIES:** Garden: Small enclosed area with boules pitch Dogs allowed **NOTES:** Parking 20

CROXTON KERRIAL
Map 11 SK82

Peacock Inn ⚲
1 School Ln NG32 1QR ☎ 01476 870324 🖹 01476 870171
e-mail: peacockcroxton@globalnet.co.uk
Dir: Situated on A607, 3m from junct with A1

A 300-year-old inn, set on the edge of the Vale of Belvoir with

continued

its famous castle just a mile away. Noted for its beautiful garden and views, the pub is popular with walkers, anglers and equestrians. Everything is prepared on the premises from fresh, local ingredients providing trendy bar food and specialities such as mushroom goulash, butter-glazed Dover sole and Scottish sirloin steak. Celebrated Sunday roasts.
OPEN: 12-3.30 6-11 **BAR MEALS:** L served all week 12-3.30 D served all week 6.30-10 Av main course £7.50 **RESTAURANT:** L served all week 12-3.30 D served all week 6.30-10
BREWERY/COMPANY: Free House 🍺: Scottish Courage John Smith's, Timothy Taylor Landlord and guest beers.
FACILITIES: Children welcome Garden: 1.5 acres of landscaped garden Dogs allowed Water **NOTES:** Parking 40

EAST LANGTON
Map 11 SP79

Pick of the Pubs

The Bell Inn
Main St LE16 7TW ☎ 01858 545278 🖹 01858 545748

A creeper-clad 16th-century listed building tucked away in a quiet village with good country walks around. The cosy inn is popular for its pretty walled garden, low beams and an open log fire. The Langton micro-brewery operates from outbuildings, and produces two regular brews as well as seasonal ales. There's a wide range of food on menus in both the Long Bar and non-smoking Green Room, from starters and light bites to more hearty fare such as pork stroganoff, minted lamb casserole, fish pie, chicken pancetta, stir-fried duck breast and a variety of steaks. Vegetarian choices may include wild mushroom pancake, roasted red pepper filled with brown rice, hazelnut and onion, and Stilton and celeriac savoury torte. There is a traditional Sunday roast carvery.
OPEN: 11.30-2.30 7-11 Closed: Dec 25 **BAR MEALS:** L served all week 12-2 D served all week 7-9.30 Av main course £10 **RESTAURANT:** L served all week D served all week Av 3 course à la carte £18 **BREWERY/COMPANY:** Free House 🍺: Greene King IPA & Abbot Ale, Langton Bowler Strong Ale & Caudle Bitter.
FACILITIES: Children welcome Garden: Dogs allowed **NOTES:** Parking 20

FLECKNEY   Map 11 SP69

The Old Crown ♀
High St LE8 8AJ ☎ 0116 2402223
e-mail: old-crown-inn@fleckney7.freeserve.co.uk

Close to the Grand Union Canal and Saddington Tunnel, a traditional village pub that is especially welcoming to hiking groups and families. Noted for good real ales and generous opening times (evening meals from 5pm) offering a wide choice of popular food and, as the landlady says, "Food your grandmother would cook". Curries of the day and boozy beef casserole with dumplings alongside baguettes, burgers, baked potatoes and children's options: home-made soup to start and 'Spotted Richard' to follow. Garden has lovely views of fields and the canal, as well as a pétanque court.
OPEN: 11-11 (Sun 12-10.30) **BAR MEALS:** L served all week 12-2 D served Tues-Sat 5-9 **RESTAURANT:** L served all week 12-2 D served Tues-Sat 5-9 Av 3 course à la carte £18 Av fixed price £3.45
BREWERY/COMPANY: Everards Brewery 🍺: Everards Tiger & Beacon, Scottish Courage Courage Directors, Adnams Bitter, Greene King Abbot Ale. **FACILITIES:** Children welcome Garden: Very lrg, wonderful views Dogs allowed Water **NOTES:** Parking 60 No credit cards

GLOOSTON   Map 11 SP79

Pick of the Pubs

The Old Barn Inn & Restaurant 🛏 ♀
Andrew's Ln LE16 7ST ☎ 01858 545215 📠 01858 545215
e-mail: theoldbarninn@yahoo.co.uk
Dir: *A6 from Market Harborough. At Kibworth follow signs to Langtons/Hallaton. Glooston signposted*

Well off the beaten track, yet within easy reach of Rutland Water and Rockingham Castle, the stylish old inn is opposite a row of charming stone cottages at a dead end of the original Roman road. Generally local produce produce is cooked by chef/patron John Buswell with enthusiasm and flair, the freshest fish showing the way in

continued

seafood crêpes, perhaps, and tuna fish Italienne with melted Mozzarella. Meanwhile from the bar menu are steak and kidney ale pie and fusilli carbonara with smoked ham and mushrooms. A la carte, expect to find whole grilled Dover sole, beef fillet with mushroom compote and home-made vegetable pie. Popular Gourmet Seafood Evenings are held every six weeks. Bar snacks include baguettes, ploughman's and soufflé omelettes and there will be four prime-condition real ales on offer on any one day.
OPEN: 12-3.00 6.30-11 **BAR MEALS:** L served all week 12-2 D served all week 7-9.30 Av main course £12
RESTAURANT: L served all week 12-2 D served all week 7-9.30 Av 3 course à la carte £22 **BREWERY/COMPANY:** Free House
🍺: Adnams Bitter, Fuller's London Pride, Shepherd Neame Spitfire.
FACILITIES: Garden: Small but attractive with seating
NOTES: Parking 8

GRIMSTON   Map 11 SK62

The Black Horse 🛏 ♀
3 Main St LE14 3BZ ☎ 01664 812358 📠 01664 813138
e-mail: joe.blackhorsepub@virgin.net
Dir: *Telephone for directions*
A traditional 16th-century coaching inn displaying much cricketing memorabilia in a quiet village with views over the Vale of Belvoir. Plenty of opportunities for country walks - or perhaps a game of pétanque on the pub's floodlit pitch? Dishes include sardines grilled in garlic and herbs; poached asparagus with orange hollandaise sauce; chicken fillet with Stilton and walnut sauce; and mint-glazed lamb shank. Extensive sweet menu changes weekly.
OPEN: 12-3 6-11 **BAR MEALS:** L served all week 12-2 D served Mon-Sat 6.30-9.30 Av main course £7.95 **RESTAURANT:** L served all week 12-2 D served Mon-Sat 6.30-9.30 Av 3 course à la carte £15.15
BREWERY/COMPANY: Free House 🍺: Belvoir, Interbrew Bass, Marstons Pedigree, Archers. ♀: 6 **FACILITIES:** Children welcome Children's licence Garden: Large beer garden, floodlights Dogs allowed Water **NOTES:** Parking 30

HALLATON   Map 11 SP79

Pick of the Pubs

The Bewicke Arms
1 Eastgate LE16 8UB ☎ 01858 555217 📠 01858 555598
Dir: *S of A47 between Leicester & junction of A47/A6003*

Film images of grown men being very silly here every Easter Monday have been seen all over the world. Hallaton is the home of the annual bottle-kicking and hare pie scramble, an ancient tradition in which the crowd jostles for pieces of pie (now containing beef) and teams

continued

of men from Hallaton and neighbouring Medbourne engage in a manic free-for-all as they try to capture three wooden casks (the bottles) for their respective villages. One contains ale, which they drink if they capture it. For the rest of the year, this 400-year-old thatched inn settles for quieter times, although healthy numbers of visitors still come for Langton's Caudle Bitter and other real ales, a good wine list, and a range of contemporary, home-made pub favourites. These include Mediterranean vegetable and potato bake, chicken with Boursin cream sauce, and salmon fillet with spring onion mash, asparagus and prawn sauce. Desserts are home made too. A play area has real animals.

OPEN: 12-3 6-11 (Open all day Sun, Winter months 7-11) **BAR MEALS:** L served all week 12-2 D served Mon-Sat 7-9.30 Av main course £8.95 **RESTAURANT:** L served all week 12-2 served Mon-Sat 7-9.30 Av 3 course à la carte £16.25 Av 2 course fixed price £5.95 **BREWERY/COMPANY:** Free House ☎: Caudle Bitter, IPA Flowers, Grainstore Triple B, Hook Norton. **FACILITIES:** Garden: Patio with picnic benches, enclosed with pond **NOTES:** Parking 20

HATHERN
Map 11 SK52

The Anchor Inn 🐾 ♀ NEW
Loughborough Rd LE12 5JB ☎ 01509 842309 🖷 01509 842312
Dir: 5 miles from motorway, 2 miles from railway station
Hathern's oldest pub, the Anchor was originally a coaching inn, with stables accessed through an archway off what is now the A6. It offers snacks galore, with vegetarian options, and a bar/restaurant menu presenting pasta, fish, and steaks, known here as Anchor Inn sizzlers. House specialities include supreme of chicken, and Barnsley lamb chop, pork chop and duck breast - all pan fried. Unquestionably family-friendly, with a fenced-off children's play area in the large garden.
OPEN: 11-11 **BAR MEALS:** L served all week 12-9.30 D served all week 12-9.30 Av main course £8.95 **RESTAURANT:** L served all week 12-9.30 D served all week 12-9.30 Av 3 course à la carte £16 **BREWERY/COMPANY:** Scottish & Newcastle ☎: John Smiths. ♀: 8 **FACILITIES:** Children welcome Children's licence Garden: Large garden, fenced area Dogs allowed **NOTES:** Parking 100

HOSE
Map 11 SK72

Rose & Crown
43 Bolton Ln LE14 4JE ☎ 01949 860424
e-mail: brian@rosehose.freeserve.co.uk
Dir: Off A606 N of Melton Mowbray
Renowned for its real ales and good food, a 200-year-old pub in the picturesque Vale of Belvoir. There is a large lounge bar with open fires, a heavily-beamed restaurant and, weather permitting, alfresco eating on the patio. Daily menus encompass sausages and fried egg, parsnip, sweet potato and chestnut bake, lamb rogan josh, gammon with pineapple and egg, chicken balti, or Mediterranean vegetable bake. For lighter appetites, filled jacket potatoes and hot baguettes.
OPEN: 12-2.30 7-11 (Sun 12-3, 7.30-10.30) **BAR MEALS:** L served Thur-Sun 12-2.30 D served Wed-Sat 7-9 Av main course £6 **RESTAURANT:** L served Thu-Sun 12-2.30 D served Thu-Sat 7-9.00 **BREWERY/COMPANY:** Free House ☎: Greene King IPA & Abbot Ale, Carlsberg-Tetley Ansells Mild, Guest. **FACILITIES:** Garden: Large grassy area, tables, sheltered patio **NOTES:** Parking 30

KEGWORTH
Map 11 SK42

Cap & Stocking
20 Borough St DE74 2FF ☎ 01509 674814
Dir: Village centre (chemist on L. Turn left and left again to Borough St)
A traditional, unspoilt country pub with comfortable, old-fashioned rooms and authentic features. Its award-winning garden has a barbecue area and pétanque piste. Appetising food includes soups, rolls (some hot) and burgers for the snack seeker; pizzas and ploughman's for those with a little more appetite; and, for the truly hungry, Hungarian goulash, chicken curry, beef Stroganoff, or vegetarian green lentil curry. Thai chicken, and minty lamb appear as specials. Bass is served from the jug.
OPEN: 11.30-2.30 6.30-11 (Sun 12-2.30,7-10.30) Rest:25 Dec Closed eve **BAR MEALS:** L served all week 11.30-2.15 D served all week 6.30-8.45 Av main course £6.25 **BREWERY/COMPANY:** Punch Taverns ☎: Bass & Greene King IPA. **FACILITIES:** Children welcome Garden: Enclosed walled garden, patio, conservatory Dogs allowed Water **NOTES:** Parking 4 **NOTES:** No credit cards

---

LOUGHBOROUGH
Map 11 SK51

The Swan in the Rushes ♀
21 The Rushes LE11 5BE ☎ 01509 217014 🖷 01509 217014
e-mail: tynemill@tynemill.co.uk
Dir: On A6 (Derby road)
A 1930s tile-fronted real ale pub with two drinking rooms, a cosmopolitan atmosphere and no frills. Ten ales always available, including six guests. Two annual beer festivals, acoustic open-mic nights (musical free-for-alls), folk club, and skittle alley. Simple menu lists dishes like Lincolnshire sausages, chilli, Kefalonian meat pie, or vegetables à la crème. Baguettes, jacket potatoes, and ploughman's also available.
OPEN: 11-11 (Sun 12-10.30) **BAR MEALS:** L served all week 12-2.30 D served Mon-Fri 6-8.30 Av main course £5.50 **BREWERY/COMPANY:** Tynemill Ltd ☎: Archers Golden, Carlsberg-Tetley Tetley Bitter, Guest Ales. ♀: 17 **FACILITIES:** Children welcome Dogs allowed Water if required **NOTES:** Parking 16

MARKET HARBOROUGH
Map 11 SP78

The Queens Head Inn ♀
Main St, Sutton Bassett LE16 8HP ☎ 01858 463530
Dir: *Heading towards Colby L into Uppingham Road*
Traditional English pub with real ale, bar meals and an upstairs restaurant specialising in regional Italian cuisine. Full range of pasta, pizza, fish, steak and chicken dishes, while the bar menu features chef's special grills, fresh Whitby scampi, beef Stroganoff, Harborough gammon and potato skins supreme. Well-kept real ales.
OPEN: 12-2.30 5-11 (Sat 12-11.30, Sun 12-10.30) **BAR MEALS:** L served all week 12-2.30 D served Mon-Sat 5-9.30 Av main course £7 **RESTAURANT:** D served Tue-Sat 7-11 Av 3 course à la carte £17 **BREWERY/COMPANY:** Free House ◖: Adnams, Timothy Taylor Landlord, Marstons Pedigree. **FACILITIES:** Children welcome Garden: patio, BBQ, food served outside Dogs allowed garden only **NOTES:** Parking 15

MEDBOURNE
Map 11 SP89

The Nevill Arms
12 Waterfall Way LE16 8EE ☎ 01858 565288 ▤ 01858 565509
e-mail: nevillarms@hotmail.com
Dir: *From Northampton take A508 to Market Harborough then B664 for 5m.L for Medbourne*
Warm golden stone and mullioned windows make this traditional old coaching inn, in its riverside setting by the village green, truly picturesque. Popular pub garden has its own dovecote and is a great attraction for children who like to feed the ducks. Handy for visiting Rutland Water, Burghley House, Bosworth Field and Stamford. A choice of appetising home-made soups, chicken in Stilton and leeks, lamb shank in redcurrant and mint, and smoked haddock bake are typical examples of the varied menu. Easter Monday is the right time to catch the spectacular bottle-kicking contest against nearby Hallaton.
OPEN: 12-2.30 6-11 (Sun 12-3, 7-10.30) 25 Dec, 31 Dec Closed eve **BAR MEALS:** L served all week 12-2 D served all week 7-9 Av main course £5.95 **BREWERY/COMPANY:** Free House ◖: Fuller's London Pride, Adnams Bitter, Greene King Abbot Ale, Guest Beers. **FACILITIES:** Children welcome Chairs and tables available **NOTES:** Parking 30

MELTON MOWBRAY
Map 11 SK71

Anne of Cleves House ♀
12 Burton St LE13 1AE ☎ 01664 481336
Fine old 14th-century building once used to house chantry priests. After Henry VIII dissolved the monasteries it was given to Anne of Cleves as part of her divorce settlement, and it is under a local heritage protection order. Log fires in winter and a picturesque garden for summer enjoyment. The menu includes home-made steak and kidney pie, traditional lasagne, and chicken breast on penne with roasted pepper, tomato and basil sauce.
OPEN: 11-11 (Sun 12-4, 7-10.30) **BAR MEALS:** L served all week 11.30-2.30 D served all week 6-9 **BREWERY/COMPANY:** Everards Brewery ◖: Everards Tiger Best, Everards Original, Guest ale. **FACILITIES:** Garden: Dogs allowed Water **NOTES:** Parking 20

MOUNTSORREL
Map 11 SK51

The Swan Inn
10 Loughborough Rd LE12 7AT
☎ 0116 2302340 ▤ 0116 2376115
e-mail: swan@jvf.co.uk
Dir: *On main road between Leicester & Loughborough*
Privately-owned former coaching inn between Loughborough and Leicester. Among the attractive interior features are various exposed beams, granite walls, flagstone floors and comfortable seating. Food is freshly cooked on the premises and the varied menu includes game and vegetarian dishes. Expect beef with onions casseroled in Old Peculier, Cajun-blackened chicken, salmon fillet poached in vermouth, pasta carbonara, prime Scottish fillet steak, or duck breast marinated in Eastern spices and pan fried with ginger. Good quality cask-conditioned ales and an extensive wine list.
OPEN: 12-2.30 5.30-11 (Sat all day & Sun 12-3, 7-10.30) **BAR MEALS:** L served all week 12-2 D served Mon-Sat 7-9.30 Av main course £7 **RESTAURANT:** L served all week 12-2 D served Mon-Sat 7-9.30 Av 3 course à la carte £13 **BREWERY/COMPANY:** Free House ◖: Theakston Best, XB, Old Peculier, Ruddles County. **FACILITIES:** Garden: Quiet, secluded riverside Dogs allowed manager's discretion **NOTES:** Parking 12

OLD DALBY
Map 11 SK62

Pick of the Pubs

The Crown Inn 🐟
Debdale Hill LE14 3LF ☎ 01664 823134 ▤ 01664 822638
e-mail: lynn@phoenixcons.demon.co.uk
Dir: *A46 turn R for Willougby / Broughton. Turn R into Nottingham Lane then L to Old Dalby*
Dating back to 1509, a classic old style pub set in extensive gardens and orchards, with small rooms, all with open fires. If playing solitaire or dominoes is what you like to do in a pub, then do so here undisturbed by background music, TV or gaming machines. Fish from Brixham is the only exception to a policy of supporting Lincolnshire suppliers, whose produce is the mainstay of bar meals like filled ciabattas and sandwiches and, in the restaurant, starters such as green-lipped mussels in cream, white wine and garlic sauce, and baby mushrooms marinated in a tomato jus, with chunky granary bread. Main courses include roast duck breast with plum sauce and honey-roasted parsnips, 'welfare friendly' veal saltimbocca, and a daily game dish. Real ales served straight from the cask include Hook Norton and Castle Rock Hemlock. In summer the gardens are full of flowers, shrubs, hanging baskets and pot plants.
OPEN: 12-3 6-11 (Winter 12-2.30, 6.30-11) 25-26 Dec, 1 Jan Closed in eve **BAR MEALS:** L served Tues-Sun 12-2.30 D served Mon-Sat 7-9.30 Av main course £13.50 **RESTAURANT:** L served Tues-Sun 12-2.30 D served Tue-Sat 7-9.30 Av 3 course à la carte £22.50 Av 3 course fixed price £12.95 **BREWERY/COMPANY:** Free House ◖: Wells Bombardier, Hook Norton, Scottish Courage Directors Castle Rock Hemlock. **FACILITIES:** Garden: 3/4 acre formal garden. Patio Dogs allowed Water **NOTES:** Parking 32

♀ 7   **Number of wines by the glass**

   Pubs offering a good choice of fish on their menu

REDMILE   Map 11 SK73

Pick of the Pubs

Peacock Inn 🍴
Church Corner NG13 0GB
☎ 01949 842554 ▤ 01949 843746
Dir: *From A1 take A52 towards Nottingham*

The Peacock is a 16th-century country inn set in the pretty village of Redmile, beside the Grantham Canal in the Vale of Belvoir, only two miles from the picturesque castle. It offers a relaxed and informal setting for wining, dining and socialising against a background of beamed ceilings and roaring log fires. The range of menus offer a good choice, from grilled goat's cheese on ciabatta to rondells of lamb on Bury mash, or pan-fried guinea fowl in redcurrant and tarragon jus. Vegetarians might consider the baked pineapple with vegetable jambalaya and salsa. A fine range of tempting desserts.
OPEN: 11-11 **BAR MEALS:** L served all week 12-2.30 D served all week 7-9.30 **RESTAURANT:** L served all week 12-2.30 D served all week 7-9.30 Av 3 course à la carte £21.50 **BREWERY/COMPANY:** 🍺: Marston's Pedigree, Timothy Taylor Landlord, Flowers IPA, Interbrew Bass. **FACILITIES:** Children welcome Garden: Dogs allowed **NOTES:** Parking 50

SADDINGTON   Map 11 SP69

The Queens Head 🍴
Main St LE8 0QH ☎ 0116 2402536
Dir: *Between A50 & A6 S of Leicester, NW of Market Harborough*
Traditional English pub with terrific views from the restaurant and garden over the Saddington Reservoir. Specialises in real ale and very good food, with four specials boards to supplement the evening menu. Foil-cooked cod fillet, roast Banbury duck, lamb shank with garlic mash, steak and ale pie, salmon in watercress sauce, and pan-fried tuna steak with sweet pepper and oyster sauce means something for everyone.
OPEN: 11-3 5.30-11 Dec 25-26 closed evenings **BAR MEALS:** L served all week 12-2 D served Mon-Sat 6.30-9.30 Av main course £6 **RESTAURANT:** L served all week 12-2 D served Mon-Sat 6.30-9.30 Av 3 course à la carte £19.50 Av 2 course fixed price £3.50 **BREWERY/COMPANY:** Everards Brewery 🍺: Everards Tiger Best & Beacon Bitter & Guest. **FACILITIES:** Children welcome Garden: Food served outdoors, over looking reservoir **NOTES:** Parking 50

SILEBY   Map 11 SK61

The White Swan 🍴
Swan St LE12 7NW ☎ 01509 814832 ▤ 01509 815995
A book-lined restaurant and homely bar with open fire lie beyond the unassuming exterior of this 1930s pub. There are always snack meals, hot baguettes and cold, filled rolls at lunchtimes alongside a more extensive menu that changes twice weekly for both lunchtime and evening dining. Popular choices include pan-fried sirloin steak with fried onions and a cheese soufflé topping; beef cobbler; salmon and prawn pasta; and mushroom and vegetable curry with rice.
OPEN: 11.45-3 7-11 (Closed Mon am, Sun pm) Closed: 1-7 Jan **BAR MEALS:** L served Tue-Sun 12-2 D served Tue-Sat 7-10 Av main course £7.95 **RESTAURANT:** L served Tue-Sun 12-2 D served Tue-Sat 7-10 Av 3 course à la carte £19.50 **BREWERY/COMPANY:** Free House 🍺: Marston's Pedigree, Carlsberg-Tetley Ansells, Banks, Fuller's London Pride. **FACILITIES:** Children welcome Garden: Small secluded courtyard **NOTES:** Parking 10

SOMERBY   Map 11 SK71

The Old Brewery 🍴
High St LE14 2PZ ☎ 01664 454777 ▤ 01664 454165
Dir: *Between Melton Mowbray & Oakham off the A606 at Leesthorpe*
Holder of the record for brewing the strongest beer in the world, (a mind pummelling 23% ABV!) this 15th-century coaching inn offers eight traditional cask ales. In addition to fine ale, the pub is also known for its food. Typical menu includes lemon sole, breaded haddock, and battered cod. Lots of good walking country around. Live music every Saturday night.
OPEN: 12-2.30 6.30-11 **BAR MEALS:** L served Tues-Sun 12-2 D served Tues-Sat 7-9 Av main course £5.95 **RESTAURANT:** L served all week D served all week Av 3 course à la carte £6 **BREWERY/COMPANY:** Free House 🍺: Parish, plus guest ales. **FACILITIES:** Children welcome Garden: Food served outside Dogs allowed On lead only **NOTES:** Parking 50

Stilton Cheese Inn 🍴
High St LE14 2QB ☎ 01664 454394

At the heart of a working village in beautiful countryside, this sandstone building dates from the 16th century. The same menus service both bar and restaurant areas, with good selections to be found on the Specials boards. Try monkfish on a rosemary skewer with butter sauce, Barnsley chops with mint and redcurrant glaze, salmon and prawns en croûte, braised steak and liver in ale and onion gravy, lambs' liver in chopped tomato sauce, or roulade of plaice and spinach coated in cheese sauce. Good selection of real ales.
OPEN: 12-3 6-11 **BAR MEALS:** L served all week 12-2 D served all week 6-9 Av main course £6.50 **RESTAURANT:** L served all week

continued

SOMERBY continued

12-2 D served all week 6-9 Av 3 course à la carte £12.50
BREWERY/COMPANY: Free House 🍺: Grainstore Ten Fifty,
Brewster's Hophead, Belvoir Star, Carlsberg-Tetley Tetley's Cask.
FACILITIES: Children welcome Garden: Small patio, seats around 20
NOTES: Parking 14

STATHERN   Map 11 SK73

Red Lion Inn 🛏 🍷 NEW
Red Lion St LE14 4HS ☎ 01949 860868 📠 01949 861579
e-mail: redlion@work.gb.com
Dir: *From A1 take sign for A52 Nottingham. Follow A52 towards
Nottingham, turn L off A52 signposted Belvoir Castle, Redmile. Follow road
for 2/3 miles. Stathern is turning on your L*
A large village pub, the Red Lion has recently been renovated,
rejuvenated and re-opened with the aim of serving good
quality traditional pub food, real ales, and interesting wines in
an informal and relaxed atmosphere. It is located in the heart
of the Vale of Belvoir, surrounded by open countryside, and is
understandably popular with walkers, shooting parties and
horse riders. Produce is drawn from the best local suppliers to
create the daily-changing menu, and seasonal highlights
include mulled wine and roast chestnuts by the open fire in
winter and home-made lemonade, Pimm's and barbecues in
the enclosed rear garden during the summer. Typical dishes
are Mrs King's Melton Mowbray pie with home-made piccalilli
and pickled shallots, pan-fried sea bream with tomato
couscous, spicy chicken kebab with Bombay potatoes and
lime salad, and warm rhubarb and ginger cream.
OPEN: 12-3 6-11 (Sat 12-11, Sun 12-5.30) Closed: 26 Dec, 1 Jan
BAR MEALS: L served all week 12-2 D served Mon-Sat 7-9.30 Av
main course £10 **RESTAURANT:** L served all week 12-2 D served
Mon-Sat 7-9.30 Av 3 course à la carte £21.50 Av 3 course fixed price
£10 **BREWERY/COMPANY:** 🍺: Grainstore Olive Oil, Brewster's
VPA. 🍷: 8 **FACILITIES:** Children welcome Garden: Enclosed,
decking area, tables, heaters Dogs allowed Water **NOTES:** Parking
25

THORPE LANGTON   Map 11 SP79

Pick of the Pubs

The Bakers Arms 🛏
Main St LE16 7TS ☎ 01858 545201
Dir: *Take A6 S from Leicester then L signed 'The Langtons'*
A charming thatched pub set in a pretty village, with
plenty of period charm and an enthusiastic following
locally and further afield. The first-class modern pub food
is one of the key attractions, though this remains an
informal pub rather than a serious dining pub or
restaurant. The Bakers Arms is located close to a popular
walk, the Leicestershire Round, which cuts across the
Candle Hills at the rear of the pub. The area is popular
with walkers, riders and mountain bikers. An intimate and
welcoming atmosphere is helped by low beams, rug-
strewn quarry-tiled floors and open fires. The inn is
furnished in character with large pine tables and antique
pews. In this relaxing and cosy setting, the food is well
worth sampling. There is a good choice of fish dishes
including whole baked sea bass with mussels and saffron
potatoes, cod fillet with Welsh rarebit crust and pesto
mash, supreme of salmon with creamed leeks and prawn
jus, and monkfish with Parma ham and tapenade. Meat
eaters are not ignored either, with a selection that might

include breast of chicken filled with salmon and Ricotta
cheese, or roast shank of lamb with shallots in a red wine
sauce. Vegetarians might try filo parcel filled with goats'
cheese and roasted vegetables.
OPEN: 12-3 6.30-11 (closed all Mon, Tue-Fri lunch, Sun eve)
BAR MEALS: D served Tue-Sat 6.30-9.30 Av main course £13
RESTAURANT: L served Sat-Sun 12-2.15 D served Tue-Sat 6.30-
9.30 Av 3 course à la carte £22 **BREWERY/COMPANY:** Free
House 🍺: Carlsberg-Tetley Bitter. **FACILITIES:** Garden: Cottage
style **NOTES:** Parking 12

WOODHOUSE EAVES   Map 11 SK51

The Pear Tree Inn
Church Hill LE12 8RT ☎ 01509 890243 📠 01509 890243
Dir: *Village centre*
Well-refurbished family-run inn at the centre of a lovely village
in the beauty spot known as Charnwood Forest. It is noted for
freshly-cooked starters like creamy Stilton and peppered
mushrooms, such main dishes as cobblestone lamb loin with
minted jus, or fishy choices like smoked mackerel and
mussels in cider sauce. Vegetarian dishes might be mushroom
Stroganoff or spicy provençale. There are excellent local
walks.
OPEN: 11-11 (Sun12-10.30) **BAR MEALS:** L served all week 12-10
D served Mon-Sat 6-10 Av main course £8 **RESTAURANT:** L served
all week 11-6 D served Mon-Sat 6-10 Av 3 course à la carte £15
BREWERY/COMPANY: Punch Taverns 🍺: Tetley, Marston's
Pedigree, Greene King Abbot Ale, Burton Ale. **FACILITIES:** Children
welcome Garden: **NOTES:** Parking 50

The Wheatsheaf Inn 🛏 🍷
Brand Hill LE12 8SS ☎ 01509 890320 📠 01509 890891
e-mail: wheatsheaf.woodhouse@virgin.net
Dir: *M1 Jct 22 follow directions for Quorn*

'The Wheatsheaf' Woodhouse Eaves, Leics. M. Frandt, 1989

A charming 18th-century pub accessed through an archway,
with a solid character imposed by the local slate quarrymen
who built it for their own use. Set in rural Charnwood Forest,
in a walker's paradise (ask for details of two local walks). The
appealing menu has something for everyone: chicken piri-piri,
Mexican burger, salmon and crab fishcakes, various salads
and vegetarian dishes, and tasty snacks like Woodhouse
smokies, and filled ciabatta.
OPEN: 12-2.30 6-11 **BAR MEALS:** L served all week 12-2 D served
Mon-Sat 7-9.30 Av main course £8.50 **RESTAURANT:** L served all
week 12-2 D served Mon-Sat 7-9.30 Av 3 course à la carte £16
BREWERY/COMPANY: Free House 🍺: Greene King Abbot Ale,
Interbrew Bass, Timothy Taylor Landlord, Marston's Pedigree. 🍷: 14
FACILITIES: Children welcome Garden: Enclosed patio with seating,
picnic tables Dogs allowed Water **NOTES:** Parking 70

continued

WYMONDHAM

Map 11 SK81

Pick of the Pubs

The Berkeley Arms
59 Main St LE14 2AG ☎ 01572 787587 🖷 01572 787587
e-mail: mikey-jones@msn.com

Equidistant from Oakham and Melton Mowbray in the heart of the county's largely unsung countryside, this chef-managed country inn has become a favoured dining destination since refurbishment several years ago. Its interior comprises a village bar of exposed stonework and original beams hung with dried hops, a carpeted, non-smoking dining-room with well-spaced pine tables and a garden that is popular with families and walkers in summer. The landlord prides himself on utilising the best available locally-produced meats, poultry and fresh herbs on monthly menus that are a modern mix of traditional and trendy. Typically, bar lunches might include garlic chicken and chorizo sausage with roast tomato and basil ciabatta and cornbeef hash with fried egg and herb butter sauce. At night, begin perhaps with pancetta with honey-glazed baby pears, herb and walnut dressing before seared calves' liver on a truffle spinach with horseradish mash and truffle oil. For dessert, chocolate cappuccino mousse or sticky toffee sponge.
OPEN: 12-3 6-11 **BAR MEALS:** L served Thu-Sun 12-2 D served Tue-Sat 6-9 Av main course £5.95 **RESTAURANT:** L served Thu-Sun 12-2 D served Tue-Sat 7-9 Av 3 course à la carte £21 **BREWERY/COMPANY:** Pubmaster ◖: Marstons Pedigree, Greene King Old Speckled Hen, Batemans XXXB.
FACILITIES: Children welcome Garden: Food served outside Dogs allowed Garden only **NOTES:** Parking 40

LINCOLNSHIRE

ALLINGTON

Map 11 SK84

Pick of the Pubs

The Welby Arms 🐾 ♀
The Green NG32 2EA ☎ 01400 281361 🖷 01400 281361
Dir: From Grantham take either A1 north, or A52 west. Allington is 1.5m

The new licensees used to work in the pub, and have successfully preserved and enhanced its character. With its views across the village green towards Allington Manor, this is quite an oasis - a village pub in the time-honoured style, with no loud music or pinball machines. Its warm lighting and pristine décor provide a welcome retreat for travellers on the A1. A fine selection of real ales and some good wines complement an ever-changing menu. The head chef has stayed, so existing customers can expect more of the fresh, seasonal produce they've come to expect. The style is predominantly British: starters could include deep-fried Brie, home-made soup or smoked mackerel with horseradish sauce. Follow these with main courses such as rack of lamb with a redcurrant and mint sauce, or fresh halibut with a pesto and cheese crumb crust.
OPEN: 12-2.30 6-11 (Sun 12-2.30 6-10.30) **BAR MEALS:** L served all week 12-2 D served all week 6.30-9.30 Av main course £8.50 **RESTAURANT:** L served all week 12-2 D served all week 6.30-9.30 **BREWERY/COMPANY:** Free House ◖: Scottish Courage John Smith's, Interbrew Bass, Timothy Taylor Landlord, Greene King Abbot. ♀: 8 **FACILITIES:** Children welcome Garden: Terrace with tables and chairs Dogs allowed garden only **NOTES:** Parking 35

ASWARBY

Map 12 TF03

The Tally Ho Inn ♦♦♦
NG34 8SA ☎ 01529 455205 🖷 01529 309024
Dir: From A1 take Grantham exit onto A52 towards Boston. Take A15 towards Sleaford. 5 miles S of Sleaford on A15

Part of the Aswarby Estate in deepest rural Lincolnshire, this 17th-century coaching inn has exposed stone walls, oak beams and open log fires; tables outside, under the fruit trees, overlook sheep-grazing meadows. A selection of representative dishes includes salmon and spinach fishcakes, beef and ale pie, sausage with cheese and onion mash, and halibut with spicy salsa.
OPEN: 12-3 6-11 (Sun 12-3, 7-10.30) Closed: Dec 26 **BAR MEALS:** L served all week 12-2.30 D served all week 6.30-10 Av main course £7.50 **RESTAURANT:** L served Sun 12-2.30 D served Mon-Sat 7-10 **BREWERY/COMPANY:** Free House ◖: Batemans, Interbrew Bass, Greene King Old Speckled Hen, Timothy Taylor Landlord. **FACILITIES:** Children welcome Garden: Old English garden, overlooks parkland etc Dogs allowed **NOTES:** Parking 40 **ROOMS:** 6 bedrooms 6 en suite s£35 d£50

BARNOLDBY LE BECK

Map 17 TA20

The Ship Inn 🐾 ♀
Main Rd DN37 0BG ☎ 01472 822308 🖷 01472 811148
Dir: Off A46/A18 SW of Grimsby

Situated on the edge of the Lincolnshire Wolds and the outskirts of Grimsby, this 200-year-old inn is filled with interesting bric-a-brac, and has a beautiful garden. Understandably it has a strong reputation for seafood. Award-winning cooking includes specials such as lobster thermidor, crab and prawn cakes, monkfish, fish pie, pan-fried breast of duck with fig and brandy sauce, and Mediterranean Wellington - seasonal vegetables with tomato, garlic and Mozzarella in puff pastry with saffron sauce.
OPEN: 12-3 6-11 **BAR MEALS:** L served all week 12-2 D served all week 7-9.30 Av main course £9 **RESTAURANT:** L served all week 12-2 D served all week 7-9.30 Av 3 course à la carte £16 **BREWERY/COMPANY:** Punch Taverns ◖: Black Sheep Best, Timothy Taylor Landlord, Carlsberg-Tetley Tetley's Smooth, Guest Beers. ♀: 8 **FACILITIES:** Garden: Dogs allowed Water **NOTES:** Parking 30

♦ **Diamond rating for inspected guest accommodation**

The Hare and Hounds

Beginning in Fulbeck, one of Lincolnshire's prettiest villages, located on a limestone ridge, this rural ramble enables you to discover the surrounding countryside and gain a flavour of the area's history.

From the pub car park turn left and follow the road towards the churchyard. On reaching the new village sign, just beyond the lychgate, cross the A607 to the waymarked footpath. Keep to the left edge of the sports field and continue to the left-hand corner where you will find a steep stile. Cross it and head uphill with the hedge now on your right.

Cross the abandoned railway line and continue straight ahead, with a small reservoir on your left. Continue uphill with the wood on your left and through the kissing gate to follow a pleasant lane enclosed by hedges, to an ancient road known as Pottergate. Turn right by Pottergate Farm, go straight over the crossroads and keep Gallipot Hall on your left and the site of the Holy Well on your right. Turn right a little over 350yds/320m beyond the crossroads and follow the waymarked path, cutting through the grounds of a nursery. Make sure you avoid the parallel path leading to Holywell Farm.

Turn right at the end of the nursery path to pass the farmhouse on your immediate left. Walk down the short bank and follow the hedge to an iron gate in the left-hand corner of the pasture. Keep ahead downhill through a gate and keep a hedge and stream on your right. In the next field make for the right-hand end of the nursery buildings and then follow the broad track to South Heath Lane.

♦♦♦

HARE AND HOUNDS, FULBECK

The Green NG32 3JJ
☎ 01400 272090

Directions: Contact pub directly
In one of Lincolnshire's prettiest villages, a family-owned inn dating from 1648. Top quality hand-prepared food is served in the bar and restaurant.
Open: 12-2 (All day Easter-Oct) 6-11 (Sun 7-10.30)
Bar Meals: 12-2 6.30-9.30
Notes: Children & dogs welcome. Garden, large patio-style courtyard. Parking.
(See page 293 for full entry)

Turn left, re-crossing the line of the disused railway, and just before you reach the main road, take the hard track on the right. Cross the road and return to the pub, which is on the right.

DISTANCE: 3 miles/4.8km
MAP: OS Explorer 272
TERRAIN: Mainly open farmland
PATHS: Mostly paths and tracks
GRADIENT: Undulating with one moderate climb

Walk submitted by Mrs Alison Nicholas of the Hare and Hounds, Fulbeck

BARNOLDBY LE BECK continued

The Wishing Well Inn 🛏 ♀

Main St, Dyke PE10 0AF ☎ 01778 422970 🖷 01778 394508
Dir: *Inn 1.5m from A15, 12m from A1, Colsterworth rdbt*
Modernised 300-year old country inn retaining old oak beams
and an inglenook fireplace with roaring open fires in winter;
named after the wishing well in the smaller of the two
restaurants. An annual family fun day is held in the nearby
paddock every August, but families are welcome all year.
Typical menu features Village grill, home-made pies, battered
jumbo cod, lasagne, and seafood platter.
OPEN: 11-3 6-11 **BAR MEALS:** L served all week 12-2 D served all
week 6.30-9 Av main course £7 **BREWERY/COMPANY:** Free House
🍺: Greene King Abbot Ale, Everards Tiger Bitter, 3 Guest's. ♀: 15
FACILITIES: Children welcome Garden: **NOTES:** Parking 100

BRIGG
Map 17 TA00

The Jolly Miller

Brigg Rd, Wrawby DN20 8RH ☎ 01652 655658 🖷 01652 657506
Dir: *1.5m E of Brigg on the A18, on L*
Popular country inn situated a few miles south of the Humber
estuary. Pleasant bar and dining area fitted out in traditional
pub style. Saturday night entertainment and facilities for
christenings, weddings and other functions. Straightforward
menu offers the likes of haddock, gammon, shepherd's pie
and curry.
OPEN: 11-3 5-11 (Sun 12-11) **BAR MEALS:** L served Thurs-Sun 12-2 D
served all week 6.30-9 Av main course £6 **BREWERY/COMPANY:** Free
House 🍺: Two changing guest ales. **FACILITIES:** Children welcome
Garden: outdoor eating, patio **NOTES:** Parking 40

COLEBY
Map 17 SK96

The Bell Inn 🛏

3 Far Ln LN5 0AH ☎ 01522 810240 🖷 01522 811800
Dir: *8m S of Lincoln on A607. In Coleby village turn right at church.*
The pub dates from 1759 and was originally three buildings - a
butcher's shop, house and pub. The location is rural with a log
fire and a barrel-shaped bar creating a cosy atmosphere. The
dining area comprises three parts - a brasserie, restaurant and
terrace room with a decking area outside. Speciality dishes
include fillet of John Dory on tomato tart with marinated

continued

artichokes and balsamic and pesto dressing, and crispy duck
breast on oriental vegetables and noodles.
OPEN: 11.30-3 5.30-11 (Sun 12-10.30) Closed: 2-4 Jan
BAR MEALS: L served all week 12-2.30 D served all week 5.30-9 Av
main course £8.95 **RESTAURANT:** L served all week 12-2.30 D
served all week 5.30-9.30 Av 3 course à la carte £17
BREWERY/COMPANY: Pubmaster 🍺: Interbrew Bass, Carlsberg-
Tetley Bitter, Batemans XB. **FACILITIES:** Children welcome Garden:
Enclosed by fence, decking area Dogs allowed **NOTES:** Parking 40

CONINGSBY
Map 17 TF25

The Old Lea Gate Inn 🛏 ♀

Leagate Rd LN4 4RS ☎ 01526 342370
e-mail: enquiries@theleagateinn.co.uk
Dir: *Off B1192 just outside Coningsby*

The Inn at Lea Gate

The oldest licensed premises in the county, dating from 1542, this
was the last of the Fen Guide Houses that provided shelter before
the treacherous marshes were drained. The oak-beamed pub has
a priest's hole and a very old inglenook fireplace among its
features. The gardens have a koi carp pond and play area.
Typical bar menus list pork cooked with Stilton, and confit of
duck.
OPEN: 11.30-2.30 6.30-11 (Sun 12-2.30, 6.30-10.30) Closed: Oct 19-
Oct 26 **BAR MEALS:** L served all week D served all
week 6.30-9.15 **BREWERY/COMPANY:** Free
House 🍺: Scottish Courage Theakstons XB, Marston's Pedigree.
♀: 7 **FACILITIES:** Children welcome Garden: Large with Koi carp
pond **NOTES:** Parking 60 **ROOMS:** 8 bedrooms 8 en suite 1 family
rooms s£49.50 d£65 (♦♦♦♦)

Curiouser and Curiouser

Some pub names are exceedingly old, and the suggested explanations often older still.
The Goat and Compasses is most unlikely to be a corruption of a supposed Puritan slogan 'God
encompasses us', the Bag o' Nails to come from Bacchanals of the Roman wine god or the Pig and
Whistle from Old English words for 'pail' and 'health'. The Cat and Fiddle may come from the
nursery rhyme, but then where did the nursery rhyme image itself come from? The device of the
Elephant and Castle is known in heraldry and was the badge of the Cutlers Company, so there is no
need to find an Infanta of Castile to derive it from.

Many strange names are the product of humour and sarcasm, such as the Quiet Woman (she
has no head), the Honest Lawyer (also beheaded), the Drop Inn, Nog Inn and Never Inn. Others,
like the Case is Altered, the Who'd Have Thought It, the Live and Let Live, the Labour in Vain
and the World Turned Upside Down are creations of rich and philosophical whimsy.

CORBY GLEN
Map 11 TF02

The Coachman Inn
NG33 4NS ☎ 01476 550316 ▤ 01476 550184
Dir: *4m E of A1 Colsterworth roundabout on the A151*

Old coaching inn complete with beams, woodburners and open fires, plus a newly-landscaped garden. An imaginative range of freshly-prepared dishes and a daily-changing menu includes baked seabass with lime butter, rack of lamb with herb crust, grilled rib-eye steak with pink peppercorn sauce, fillet of salmon with Punjabi spices, and wild mushroom risotto with balsamic dressing. Cabaret nights and a more spacious dining room have proved popular.
OPEN: 12-2.30 6.30-11 (All day bank holidays) **BAR MEALS:** L served all week 11.30-2.30 D served all week 6.30-9.30 Av main course £6.50 **RESTAURANT:** L served all week 11.30-2.30 D served all week 6.30-9.30 Av 3 course à la carte £16 Av 3 course fixed price £11.95 **BREWERY/COMPANY:** Free House **◀:** Timothy Taylor Landlord, Worthington, Adnams. **FACILITIES:** Children welcome Garden: Large, new patio and new landscaped garden Dogs allowed Water, Dog Biscuits **NOTES:** Parking 30

DONINGTON ON BAIN
Map 17 TF28

The Black Horse
Main Rd LN11 9TJ ☎ 01507 343640 ▤ 01507 343640
Ideal for walkers, this old-fashioned country pub is set in the heart of the Lincolnshire Wolds on the Viking Way. A large grassed area surrounded by trees is ideal for outdoor eating and drinking on sunny days. The specials are chalked up on a blackboard and include the likes of Black Horse pasta, fresh Grimsby haddock, Viking grill, many varieties of sausage and mash, seafood platter, and steaks.
OPEN: 11.30-3 6.30-11 Closed: 25 Dec **BAR MEALS:** L served all week 12-2 D served all week 7-9.30 Av main course £5.95 **RESTAURANT:** L served all week 12-2 D served all week 7-9.30 Av 3 course à la carte £13 **BREWERY/COMPANY:** Free House **◀:** John Smiths, Greene King, Tom Woods, Boddingtons.
FACILITIES: Children welcome Garden: Large grassed area surrounded by trees Dogs allowed Water provided, pre book for bedrooms **NOTES:** Parking 80

Use the AA Hotel Booking Service on
0870 5050505
to book at AA recognised hotels and
B&B's in the UK and Ireland
or through our internet site at
www.theAA.com

EWERBY
Map 12 TF14

Finch Hatton Arms
43 Main St NG34 9PH ☎ 01529 460363 ▤ 01529 461703
e-mail: bookings@finchhatton.fsnet.co.uk
Dir: *from A17 to Kirkby-la-Thorne, then 2m NE. Also 2m E of A153 between Sleaford & Anwick*
Originally known as the Angel Inn, this 19th-century pub was given the family name of Lord Winchelsea who bought it in 1875. After a short period of closure, it reopened as a new-style pub/restaurant in the 1980s. Extensive, varied menu includes salmon, sweet and sour chicken, steak and kidney pie, and seabass.
OPEN: 11.30-2.30 6.30-11 Closed: 25-26 Dec 1 Jan closed evening **BAR MEALS:** L served all week 11.30-2.30 D served all week 6.30-11 **RESTAURANT:** L served all week 11.30-2.30 D served all week 6.30-11 Av 3 course à la carte £15 **BREWERY/COMPANY:** Free House **◀:** Everards Tiger Best, Greene King Abbot Ale, Scottish Courage Courage Directors. **FACILITIES:** Children welcome Garden: **NOTES:** Parking 60

FREISTON
Map 12 TF34

Kings Head
Church Rd PE22 0NT ☎ 01205 760368
Dir: *from Boston take A52 towards Skegness. 3m turn R at Haltoft End to Freiston*
Originally two cottages, this village pub is renowned for its prize-winning hanging baskets and colourful window boxes. Inside, you can relax by an open fire and enjoy straightforward wholesome bar food. Home-made pies are a speciality and include steak and kidney, chicken and mushroom, and sausage. Also look out for Grimsby cod or haddock. The blackboard specials change on a weekly basis. Birdwatchers come from far and near to visit the newly opened RSPB reserve at Freiston Shore.
OPEN: 11-2.30 7-11 (Sun 12-3, 7.30-10.30) **BAR MEALS:** L served Tues-Sun 12-2 D served Wed-Sat 7-9 Av main course £7 **RESTAURANT:** L served Tue-Sun 12-2 7-9 Av 3 course à la carte £13.50 **BREWERY/COMPANY:** Batemans **◀:** Batemans XB & Dark Mild, Worthington Cream Flow, Stella. **FACILITIES:** Children welcome **NOTES:** Parking 30 **NOTES:** No credit cards

FROGNALL
Map 12 TF11

The Goat
155 Spalding Rd PE6 8SA ☎ 01778 347629
e-mail: goat.frognall@virgin.net
Dir: *A1 to Peterborough, A15 to Market Deeping, old A16 to Spalding, pub about 1.5m from jct of A15 & A16*

Welcoming country pub dating back to the 17th century, with a large beer garden and plenty to amuse the kids. This is a

continued

proud real ale pub, with four different guest ales every week, and a definite bias toward micro-breweries. A straightforward but comprehensive menu ranges through fish, grills and chicken dishes, while the chef's home-made selection includes sweet and sour pork, steak and kidney pie, spaghetti Bolognaise, and ham and mushroom tagliatelle. Regularly-changing specials are also available.

OPEN: 11-2.30 6-11 (Sun 12-3, 7-10.30) Closed: 25 Dec
BAR MEALS: L served all week 12-2 D served all week 6.30-9.30
RESTAURANT: L served all week 12-2 D served all week 6.30-9.30
BREWERY/COMPANY: Free House 🍺: Elgood's Cambridge, 4 Guest Cask Ales change each week, 3 German beers.
FACILITIES: Children welcome Garden: Covered patio, beer garden, seats approx 90 **NOTES:** Parking 50

FULBECK
Map 17 SK95

Hare & Hounds Country Inn ♦♦♦ ♀
The Green NG32 3JJ ☎ 01400 272090 ▤ 01400 273663
Family-owned inn dating from 1648, facing the church, vicarage and green of one of Lincolnshire's prettiest villages. The emphasis is on top quality, hand-prepared food in both the bar and restaurant. Steak and Stilton pie is a speciality in the bar, alongside filled baguettes, steaks, and fresh haddock in beer batter with mushy peas and home-made chips. A typical restaurant dish is stuffed chicken with cream cheese, garlic, sun-dried tomato and fresh basil.
OPEN: 12-2 6-11 (Open all day Easter-Oct) (Sun 7-10.30)
BAR MEALS: L served all week 12-2 D served all week 6.30-9.30 Av main course £8 **RESTAURANT:** L served all week 12-2 D served all week 7-9.30 Av 3 course à la carte £20 **BREWERY/COMPANY:** Free House 🍺: Fuller's London Pride, Hook Norton, Bateman, Scottish Courage John Smith's Smooth. ♀: 7 **FACILITIES:** Children welcome Garden: Lrg patio style courtyard Dogs allowed **NOTES:** Parking 32 **ROOMS:** 8 bedrooms 8 en suite 3 family rooms s£30 d£45

See Pub Walk on page 290

GEDNEY DYKE
Map 12 TF42

The Chequers 🍴 ♀
PE12 0AJ ☎ 01406 362666 ▤ 01406 362666
e-mail: enquiries@chequerspub.co.uk
Dir: From King's Lynn take A17, 1st roundabout after Long Sutton take B1359
Located in a remote fen-land village close to The Wash wildlife sanctuaries, an 18th-century country inn with an undimmed reputation for its food. Pan-fried red mullet on artichoke purée with a sundried tomato and red pepper coulis, loin of tuna marinated in five spices on a potato and fresh coriander salad, and seared halibut warm salad and a pink peppercorn butter feature on a heady fish list. Barnsley lamb chop with wild mushroom risotto and mint pesto, and confit of duck leg on herb and potato rosti with spring onions and orange & ginger jus are carefully sourced and imaginatively cooked for both bar and dining-room clientele. Well-chosen ales, patio garden and outdoor eating in summer.
OPEN: 12-2 7-11 (Sun 12-2 7-10.30) Closed: 26 Dec
BAR MEALS: L served all week 12-2 D served all week 7-9 Av main course £12 **RESTAURANT:** L served all week 12-2 D served all week 7-9 Av 3 course fixed price £19.95 **BREWERY/COMPANY:** Free House 🍺: Adnams Best, Greene King Abbot Ale.
FACILITIES: Children welcome Garden: Beer garden, patio, food served outside Dogs allowed **NOTES:** Parking 20

GRANTHAM
Map 11 SK93

The Beehive Inn
10/11 Castlegate NG31 6SE ☎ 01476 404554
Dir: A52 to town centre, L at Finkin St, pub at end
Grantham's oldest inn (1550) is notable for having England's only living pub sign - a working beehive high up in a lime tree. Otherwise, this simple town hostelry offers a good pint of Newby Wyke and good-value, yet basic bar food. Kids will enjoy the bouncy castle that appears during the summer.
OPEN: 11-11 **BAR MEALS:** L served all week 12-1.50 D served Tue-Thurs Av main course £4 **BREWERY/COMPANY:** Free House 🍺: Newby Wyke Real Ales, Worthingtons. **FACILITIES:** Children welcome Garden: Enclosed, block paved patio Dogs allowed Water

---

HECKINGTON
Map 12 TF14

The Nags Head
34 High St NG34 9QZ ☎ 01529 460218
Dir: 5m E of Sleaford on A17
Overlooking the green of a village boasting the only eight-sailed windmill in the country, this white-painted 17th-century coaching inn reputedly once played host to Dick Turpin. Garden and play area.
OPEN: 11-3 5-11 **BAR MEALS:** L served all week 12-2 D served all week 7-9 Av main course £6 **BREWERY/COMPANY:** Wards 🍺: Wards Best, Vaux Double Maxim. **FACILITIES:** Children welcome Garden: **NOTES:** Parking 50

LINCOLN
Map 17 SK97

Pyewipe Inn 🍴
Fossebank, Saxilby Rd LN1 2BG
☎ 01522 528708 ▤ 01522 525009
e-mail: robert@pyewipeinn.co.uk
Dir: Out of Lincoln on A57 past Lincoln A46 Bypass, pub signed after 0.5m

The Pyewipe is an 18th-century alehouse on the Roman Fossedyke Canal, set in four acres with great views of the city and the cathedral - a 20-minute walk away along the Fossedyke. All food from pâté to ice cream is freshly prepared from local sources and is offered from a daily board in the bar or seasonal carte in the restaurant. Look out for lamb fillet with rosemary on onion mash, pork and cheddar Wellington with port sauce, cod fillet topped with garlic cheese and wrapped in filo pastry, or sea bream fillet with bacon and basil sauce. The outdoor area seats up to 200.
OPEN: 11-11 (Mon-Sat 11-11, Sun 12-10.30) **BAR MEALS:** L served all week 12-9.30 D served all week **RESTAURANT:** L served all week 12-3 D served all week 7-9.30 **BREWERY/COMPANY:** Free House 🍺: Timothy Taylor Landlord, Greene King Abbot Ale, Interbrew Bass & Flowers Original, Wadworth 6X. **FACILITIES:** Garden: 200 seats along river. Patio, grassy areas **NOTES:** Parking 100

England

LINCOLN continued

The Victoria
6 Union Rd LN1 3BJ ☎ 01522 536048 📠 01522 536048
Situated right next to the Westgate entrance of the Castle and within a stone's throw of Lincoln Cathedral, a long-standing drinkers' pub with a range of real ales, including six changing guest beers, as well as two beer festivals a year. Nonetheless it also offers splendid meals with exclusively home-prepared food including hot baguettes and filled bacon rolls, Saturday breakfast and Sunday lunches. House specials include sausage and mash, various pies, chilli con carne and home-made lasagne.
OPEN: 11-11 (Sun 12-10.30) **BAR MEALS:** L served all week 12-2.30 D served None Av main course £4 **RESTAURANT:** L served Sun 12-2 **BREWERY/COMPANY:** Tynemill Ltd ◀: Timothy Taylor Landlord, Batemans XB, Castle Rock Hemlock, Guest Beers. **FACILITIES:** Garden: Patio area Dogs allowed

Pick of the Pubs

Wig & Mitre ◉ 🐾 ♀
30/32 Steep Hill LN2 1TL ☎ 01522 535190 📠 01522 532402
e-mail: email@wigandmitre.com
Dir: Town centre adjacent to cathedral & Lincoln Castle car park, at the top of Steep Hill
Situated in the heart of historic Lincoln, between the castle and magnificent cathedral, this is a reassuringly civilised pub-restaurant. In an ambience free of music and amusement machines, it offers continuous service from 8am to around midnight every day, all year round. Many 14th-century timbers have survived its numerous re-incarnations to provide an evocative interior. It is justifiably popular for its food and extensive wine selection, many available by the glass. Food choices range from sandwiches to set three course meals, with a wide variety of individual dishes in between. Specialities include baked cheese soufflé with roasted red onions and spinach; maple-glazed gammon with mustard mash, baby leeks and parsley velouté; and salmon escalope with tiger prawns on a herb couscous with sweet chilli dressing. Go out on a high with the house special bread and butter pudding, or perhaps raspberry and Marscapone crème brûlée - maybe accompanied by a glass of one of half-a-dozen dessert wines.
OPEN: 8-12 **BAR MEALS:** L served all week 8am-11pm D served all week 8am-11pm Av main course £8.45 **RESTAURANT:** L served all week 8-11 D served all week 8am-11pm Av 3 course à la carte £25 Av 3 course fixed price £12.95 **BREWERY/COMPANY:** Free House ◀: Greene King Ruddles County & Ruddles Best. ♀: 34 **FACILITIES:** Children welcome Dogs allowed

LONG BENNINGTON
Map 11 SK84

The Reindeer
Main Rd NG23 5EH ☎ 01400 281382
e-mail: terry@reindeerinn.co.uk
Dir: 7m North of Grantham on the A1
Welcoming pub, with exposed beams and open fireplaces, in a pretty village setting. A varied menu may include pork and leek sausages served with mustard creamed potatoes and onion gravy, Big John casserole with mushrooms, onions and carrots, Lasagne el Tel, "chuffing hot chilli", deep-fried breaded wholetails of scampi, or Dixie bird (chicken breast marinated in Cajun spices accompanied by Cumberland sauce).
OPEN: 12-3 7-11 (Sat/Sun 12-4, Sun 7-10.30) Dec 25-26, 31 closed evening **BAR MEALS:** L served Mon-Sat 12-2 D served Mon-Sat 7-9.30 Av main course £8 **RESTAURANT:** L served Mon-Sat 12-2 D served Mon-Sat 7-10 **BREWERY/COMPANY:** Free House ◀: John Smiths & Guest Ale. **FACILITIES:** Children welcome Garden

LOUTH
Map 17 TF38

Masons Arms ♦♦♦ 🐾 ♀
Cornmarket LN11 9PY ☎ 01507 609525 📠 0870 7066450
e-mail: justin@themasons.co.uk

A former coaching inn dating from 1725, known as the Bricklayers Arms until 1880, and located in the busy Cornmarket in the centre of town. Renowned locally for its quality food and the well-kept real ales on tap, the comfortable bars are open throughout the day for tea and coffee, as well as lunch. The lofty restaurant - Upstairs at the Masons - offers an award-winning menu of interesting dishes made from fresh local produce. The choice varies from week to week, with plenty of daily specials and extras on the blackboard. Expect fish dishes like moules marinière, monkfish, and lemon and thyme halibut, along with perhaps loin of local pork, chargrilled chicken breast, and pan-fried pigeon. Comfortable, well-equipped bedrooms make this an ideal base for touring the Lincolnshire Wolds and their capital Louth.
OPEN: 10-11 (Sun 12-10.30) **BAR MEALS:** L served all week 12-2 D served Mon-Sat 6-9 Av main course £6.95 **RESTAURANT:** L served Sun 12-2 D served Fri-Sat 7-9.30 Av 3 course à la carte £10 **BREWERY/COMPANY:** Free House ◀: Timothy Taylor Landlord, Marston's Pedigree, Samuel Smiths, Batemans XB Bitter. **FACILITIES:** Children welcome Children's licence **NOTES:** Parking 20 **ROOMS:** 10 bedrooms 5 en suite s£25 d£38
See Pub Walk on opposite page

NEWTON
Map 12 TF03

The Red Lion 🐾
NG34 0EE ☎ 01529 497256
e-mail: redlionnewton@aol.com
Dir: 10m E of Grantham on A52
The only pub in a tiny hamlet of around 20 houses, and a haven for walkers and cyclists. It dates from the 17th century and, with its low beams, exposed stone walls and an open fire in the bar, is very atmospheric. Popular dishes include haddock in beer batter, trout with lemon butter sauce, and home-made steak and ale pie, while the carvery dispenses cold meats and salads with a hot buffet on weekend evenings and Sunday lunch.
OPEN: 12-3 6-11 (Sun 12-4, 7-10.30) Closed: 26 Dec, 1 Jan **BAR MEALS:** L served all week 12-2 D served Mon-Sun 7-9 Av main course £7.95 **RESTAURANT:** L served Sun 12-2 D served Mon-Sat 7-9 Av 3 course à la carte £15.45 **BREWERY/COMPANY:** Free House ◀: Batemans XB, Guest Ale, Tetleys. **FACILITIES:** Garden: Patio area with lawn, shrubs Dogs allowed Water **NOTES:** Parking 40

> Most of the pubs in this guide book pride themselves on the quality of their food. This may take a little time to prepare.

Masons Arms

A pleasant rural walk from an historic market town. Some determined hill climbing is rewarded by excellent views east to the sea and west across the gently rolling Wolds.

From the inn, turn right along Rosemary Lane, then turn left to the church and head north along Bridge Street, crossing the River Lud. Turn left into Fanthorpe Lane, cross the A16 (great care) and continue along the lane to Northfield Farm, where it becomes a green lane, then a footpath. Pass through the edge of a clump of trees, cross a footbridge in the field corner and proceed along the hedge to a lane.

Turn left and walk uphill, passing through Acthorpe Farm, to reach 104m (343ft), and enjoy good views before descending to South Elkington. Cross the A631 and walk along Church Lane. Pass the church and footpaths left, go round the right-hand bend and take the signed bridleway left through a gate. The track becomes a path after exiting trees at Kirk Vale and continues along the left-hand hedge to a gate. Descend to a gate and turn left downhill along a track.

Where it veers sharp left, keep ahead into the wood and turn left along the bridleway through Sand Pit Plantation. Ignore paths left and right, go through a gate and continue alongside woodland. Eventually go through a gate to join a track, following it left around the end of a lake. Follow the waymarked footpath across a track, then over a stile and along the left-hand edge of fields to a footbridge on the left. Ascend the field towards a hedge gap and cross a stile and the A631. Continue uphill to a gate into woodland and follow the main track, which soon swings right to a stile and field. Continue with the trees to your left, downhill past Pasture Farm and uphill along the field edge to cross the Louth by-pass.

Follow arrows past houses and along the lane to cross the A157. Turn left, head downhill and cross the river. Continue into Louth, bearing left at the junction to St James' Church, then follow Rosemary Lane back to the pub.

♦♦♦
MASONS ARMS, LOUTH
Cornmarket LN11 9PY.
☎ 01507 609525

Directions: centre of town, off A16 between Skegness and Grimsby 18th-century former posting inn located right in the centre of the Cornmarket in this historic market town. Friendly welcome, imaginative menu, good range of ales and bedrooms - ideal base for exploring the Lincolnshire Wolds.
Open: 10am-11pm (Sun 12-10.30).
Bar Meals: 12-2 6-9.
Notes: Children welcome. Parking.
(See opposite page for full entry)

DISTANCE: 6 miles (10km)
MAP: OS Landranger 122
TERRAIN: Town streets, farmland and woodland
PATHS: Field and woodland path and track; metalled lanes
GRADIENT: Undulating; some steady climbs.

Walk submitted by: The Masons Arms

England

PARTNEY
Map 17 TF46

Red Lion Inn 🍴
PE23 4PG ☎ 01790 752271 📠 01790 753360
Dir: On A16 from Boston, or A158 from Horncastle
Parts of this Lincolnshire inn may date back 400 years, but reports of a ghost seem to be unsubstantiated, although you may be lucky enough to see something! The large menu lists some fifty home-made dishes, including steaks and grills, and a special Sunday roast.
OPEN: 11-3 7-11 (Sun 12-2.30, 7-10.30, closed Mon-Tue) Closed: 25 Dec **BAR MEALS:** L served Wed-Sun 12-2 D served all week 7-9.30 Av main course £7 **RESTAURANT:** L served Wed-Sun 12-2 D served Mon-Sun 7-9.30 **BREWERY/COMPANY:** Free House 🍺: Bateman, Tomwoods, XXXB, Tetleys. **FACILITIES:** Children welcome Garden **NOTES:** Parking 40

RAITHBY
Map 17 TF36

Red Lion Inn 🍴
PE23 4DS ☎ 01790 753727
Dir: Take A158 from Horncastle, R at Sausthorpe, keep L into Raithby

Traditional beamed black-and-white village pub, parts of which date back 300 years. Log fires provide a warm welcome in winter. A varied menu of home-made dishes includes seabass with lime stirfry vegetables, roast guinea fowl with tomato, garlic and bacon, and medallions of beef with peppercorn sauce.
OPEN: 12-3 7-11 **BAR MEALS:** L served Thu-Sun 12-2.30 D served Wed-Mon 7-9.30 Av main course £8 **RESTAURANT:** L served Sat-Sun 12-2.30 D served Wed-Mon 7-10 **BREWERY/COMPANY:** Free House 🍺: Raithby, Thwaites, Tetley, Batemans XB. **FACILITIES:** Children welcome Food served outside. Terrace patio Dogs allowed **NOTES:** Parking 20 **NOTES:** No credit cards

SAXILBY
Map 17 SK87

The Bridge Inn 🍴
Gainsborough Rd LN1 2LX ☎ 01522 702266
Dir: On A57 W of Lincoln
For some 14 years the landlady of the Bridge Inn has kept a tidy pub with traditional furnishings. Perching on the canal-side with its own moorings, it has safe areas for children and plenty of dining space. Two guest ales on offer to accompany bar snacks and more extensive menus taking in Grimsby fish, poached or pan-fried halibut and home-made fishcakes. Specials include white Stilton and vegetable crumble, broccoli and three cheese pasta bake, and chicken jalfrezi.
OPEN: 11.30-2.30 5.30-11 (open all day Sun, closed Mon) Closed: 25 Dec, 1 Jan **BAR MEALS:** L served Tue-Sun 11.30-1.30 D served Tue-Sat **RESTAURANT:** L served Tue-Sun 11.30-1.30 D served Tue-Sat **BREWERY/COMPANY:** 🍺: Tetley. **FACILITIES:** Children welcome Garden: Large enclosed, canalside with patio **NOTES:** Parking 60

SKEGNESS
Map 17 TF56

The Vine Hotel ★★★
Vine Rd, Seacroft PE25 3DB
☎ 01754 763018 & 610611 📠 01754 769845
e-mail: info@thevinehotel.com

Ivy-covered Victorian hotel, converted from a farmhouse and bought by Harry Bateman in 1928. Now this charming hostelry offers a fine selection of ales, silver service in the restaurant and comfortable accommodation, with weddings a speciality. Once a haunt of poet Alfred Lord Tennyson, who has given his name to The Tennyson Lounge.
OPEN: 11-11 (Sun 12-10.30) **BAR MEALS:** L served all week 12.15-2.15 D served all week 7-9.15 Av main course £5.95 **RESTAURANT:** L served all week 12.30 D served all week 7-9.30 Av 3 course à la carte £25 Av 3 course fixed price £18.50 **BREWERY/COMPANY:** Batemans 🍺: Batemans XB & XXXB. **FACILITIES:** Children welcome Garden: Secluded with pretty gardens Dogs allowed **NOTES:** Parking 50 **ROOMS:** 24 bedrooms 24 en suite 3 family rooms s£55 d£75

SOUTH WITHAM
Map 11 SK91

Blue Cow Inn & Brewery 🍴
High St NG33 5QB ☎ 01572 768432 📠 01572 768432
e-mail: richard@thirlwell.fslife.co.uk
Dir: Between Stamford & Grantham on the A1
Situated on the borders of Lincolnshire and Rutland, a once derelict and ruined local inn standing close to the source of the River Witham, which flows down to Lincoln. Named after the landlord, Thirwell's real ales are brewed on the premises - with guided tours of the micro-brewery an added attraction. Eclectic menus embrace Thai seafood curry and Malaysian chicken satay along with home-made pub pie, fresh Grimsby fish, and British steak grills that culminate in a king-size mixed grill. The Blue Cow provides a free minibus service to local diners; contact them for details.
OPEN: 12-11 **BAR MEALS:** L served all week 12-2.30 D served all week 6-9.30 **RESTAURANT:** L served all week 12-2.30 D served all week 6-9.30 **BREWERY/COMPANY:** Free House 🍺: Own beers. **FACILITIES:** Children welcome Garden: Seating for 32 Dogs allowed Water **NOTES:** Parking 45 **ROOMS:** 6 bedrooms 6 en suite 2 family rooms s£40 d£45 (♦♦♦)

STAMFORD
Map 11 TF00

The Blue Bell Inn 🍷
Shepherds Walk Belmesthorpe PE9 4JG ☎ 01780 763859
Dir: 2 m N of Stamford on the A6121 Bourn Road, turn R for Belmesthorpe and pub is on the L
At the time of going to press, this charming 500-year old stone building had just been taken over by new management. The

continued

menu still maintains a firm emphasis on good food and includes dishes such as supreme of chicken served on leaves of spinach with a white wine and tarragon sauce, honey and pepper roast duckling accompanied by an orange sauce, roast avocado served with vegetable ratatouille, and grilled sirloin steaks.
OPEN: 12-2.30 6-11 **BAR MEALS:** L served all week 12-2 D served Mon-Sat 7-9.00 Av main course £10 **RESTAURANT:** L served all week 12-2 D served Mon-Sat 7-9.30 **BREWERY/COMPANY:** Free House 🍺: Interbrew Bass, Greene King Old Speckled Hen & Ruddles County, Badger Best. ♀: 20 **FACILITIES:** Children welcome Children's licence Garden **NOTES:** Parking 30

Pick of the Pubs

The George of Stamford ★★★ ◉ 🛏 ♀
71 St Martins PE9 2LB ☎ 01780 750750 🖥 01780 750701
e-mail: reservations@georgehotelofstamford.com
Dir: take A1 N from Peterborough. From A1 roundabout signposted B1081 Stamford, down hill to lights. Hotel on L
The famous inn sign that straddles the road outside this 16th-century coaching inn said 'Welcome' to the honest traveller, but to the highwayman, it warned 'Do not mess with our clientele'. Just inside, doors marked London and York lead to panelled rooms in which passengers waited, depending on their route, while their horses were changed. But its coaching days are recent history compared with origins five hundred years earlier, and a medieval crypt still lurks underneath the cocktail bar. The restaurant's traditional approach to food is influenced by modern and international ideas, although you can't get much more traditional than sirloin of beef carved at table, or half a Woodbridge duck with sage and onion stuffing and apple sauce. But the other influences show through with grand Brittany seafood platter, and medallions of beef fillet on potato rösti with glazed shallots and a Burgundy jus. Dishes are simpler, but decision-making just as hard, in the plant-filled Garden Lounge and in the York Bar.
OPEN: 11-2.30 6-11 (Sat-Sun open all day from 11)
BAR MEALS: L served all week 7-11 Av main course £8.95
RESTAURANT: L served all week 12-2.30 D served all week 7-10 Av 3 course à la carte £33 Av 2 course fixed price £17.50
BREWERY/COMPANY: Free House 🍺: Adnams Broadside, Fuller's London Pride, Greene King Ruddles Bitter. ♀: 12
FACILITIES: Children welcome Garden: Sunken lawn, picturesque, well maintained Dogs allowed Dog Pack, Towel, Blanket, feeding mat **NOTES:** Parking 120 **ROOMS:** 47 bedrooms 47 en suite 20 family rooms s£78 d£115

WOODHALL SPA — Map 17 TF16

Village Limits Motel ◆◆◆◆ 🛏 NEW
Stixwould Rd LN10 6UJ ☎ 01526 353312 🖥 01526 353312
Dir: On reaching roundabout on main street of Woodhall Spa follow directions for Petwood Hotel. 500 yrds further on same road
Woodhall's spa waters were discovered by accident after analysis of water overflowing from an abandoned coalmine was found to contain iodine and bromide. In World War II, nearby Petwood House was the Officers' Mess for 617 Squadron, the famous Dambusters. Traditional pub food in the restaurant and bar includes steaks, chicken (perhaps char-grilled with rich pepper sauce), trout, battered and smoked haddock, and seafood omelette. Real ales include Tom Wood's Best Bitter from Lincolnshire brewery, Highwood.
OPEN: 12-2.30 6-11 **BAR MEALS:** L served all week 12-2 D served all week 6-9 Av main course £6.95 **RESTAURANT:** L served all week

continued

12-2 D served all week 6.30-9 Av 3 course à la carte £12.95
BREWERY/COMPANY: Free House 🍺: Bateman XB, Black Sheep Best, Barnsley Bitter, Carlsberg-Tetley Tetley's Smooth Flow.
FACILITIES: Children welcome Garden: Enclosed garden with superb views **NOTES:** Parking 30 **ROOMS:** 8 bedrooms 8 en suite 1 family rooms s£30 d£50

WOOLSTHORPE — Map 11 SK83

Rutland Arms
NG32 1NY ☎ 01476 870111
Better known to locals as the 'Dirty Duck' (or the 'Mucky Duck', or the 'Muddy Duck'!), this mid-18th-century family pub sits at the side of the Grantham canal, in the shadow of Belvoir Castle.
OPEN: 11-3 6-11 (Sun 12-10.30, Sat 11-11) **BAR MEALS:** L served all week 12-3 D served all week 6-9 Av main course £5.50
RESTAURANT: L served all week 11-3 D served all week 6-9.30 Av 3 course à la carte £12 **BREWERY/COMPANY:** Free House 🍺: Interbrew Bass, Robinsons. **FACILITIES:** Children welcome Garden **NOTES:** Parking 100

LONDON

E1

Prospect of Whitby 🛏 ♀ — Map GtL F4
57 Wapping Wall E1W 3SH ☎ 020 7481 1095 🖥 020 7481 9537
Originally known as The Devil's Tavern, this famous 16th century inn has been a meeting place for sailors and was also a gruesome setting for public executions. Samuel Pepys was a regular here before the tavern was renamed in 1777. Today, old ships timbers retain the seafaring traditions of this venerable riverside inn, which also boasts a rare pewter bar counter. Expect beef Wellington, minted lamb loins, and a good selection of fish dishes.
OPEN: 11.30-11 **BAR MEALS:** L served all week 11.30-9 D served all week **RESTAURANT:** L served Sun-Fri D served Mon-Sat **BREWERY/COMPANY:** Scottish & Newcastle
FACILITIES: Children welcome Garden Dogs allowed

Town of Ramsgate — Map GtL F4
62 Wapping High St E1W 2NP ☎ 020 7481 8000
Old pub close to The City. Plenty of bric-a-brac and old prints. Judge Jeffreys was caught here while trying to flee the country to escape the kind of justice he dealt out. Captain Kidd also met his end here in 1701. Value for money bar food.
OPEN: 12-11 (Sun 12-10.30) **BAR MEALS:** L served Tue-Sun 12-3 Av main course £6.95 🍺: Adnams, Youngs, Fullers London Pride.
FACILITIES: Children welcome **NOTES:** No credit cards

The Seven Stars

A fascinating walk through the streets of the capital, taking in Lincoln's Inn Fields and the Royal Courts of Justice.

From The Seven Stars turn right and walk along to the junction with Portugal Street. Turn left, passing the London School of Economics, then swing right into Sheffield Street leading to Portsmouth Street, passing the Old Curiosity Shop, immortalised by Charles Dickens in his novel of the same name.

Ahead now is Lincoln's Inns Fields, created by Inigo Jones. Cross it to the fascinating Sir John Soane's Museum. With the museum on your left, continue along Lincoln's Inn Fields and then swing right. On the left now is Lincoln's Inn, established in 1422. This is the oldest of the four Inns of Court - the centre of all things legal. It is where young barristers study before embarking on a career in law. If time allows and opening hours permitting, visit the Old Hall where Shakespeare's 'A Midsummer Night's Dream' was first performed, as well as Lincoln's Inn Chapel.

Just south of Lincoln's Inn is the delightful 17th-century New Square. Look for More's Passage or the more easterly gate by the porter's lodge and return to Carey Street. Turn left, head south along Bell Yard, then west along Fleet Street to reach the Royal Courts of Justice. Designed in the late 19th century by the architect George Edmund Street, this huge building is one of the best examples of High Victorian Gothic. Such was the scale of the building that the construction of it virtually

THE SEVEN STARS, LONDON WC2
53 Carey Street WC2A 2JB
☎ 0207 242 8521

Early 17th-century hostelry with two narrow rooms, a tiny Tudor staircase leading to the loos, and well-kept Adnams ales. Freshly-made food from the cookery-writer landlady is well worth trying.
Open: 11-11
Bar Meals: 12-4 5-9
Notes: Closed Sun. Dogs welcome, water provided.
(See page 318 for full entry)

drained Parliament's budget. However, work was eventually completed and today it serves as a monument to Street's skill and ingenuity. Inside is a lofty concourse leading to ornately finished courts, high vaulted ceilings and dark corridors.

Walk through the concourse, up a flight of steps and out through the north door into Carey Street. Almost directly opposite this exit is The Seven Stars where the walk started.

DISTANCE: 1 mile/1.6km
TERRAIN: Level surfaces and pavements
GRADIENT: No hills

Walk submitted and checked by the Seven Stars

E3

Pick of the Pubs

The Crown ♀   Map GtL F4
223 Grove Rd E3 5SN ☎ 020 8981 9998 📠 020 8980 2336
e-mail: crown@singhboulton.co.uk
Dir: Nearest tube: Mile End Central Line & District line. Buses 277 to Victoria Park
A beautifully-restored, listed building spread over two floors, with pleasant views across South Hackney's Victoria Park. The open-plan bar is equally suited to lively conversation or some peaceful newspaper reading on quiet afternoons (no juke boxes, pin ball machines, or TV). Upstairs, in a series of dining rooms with balconies, the European cuisine is presented on seasonal, twice-daily changing menus. Good value weekend breakfasts and brunch, a bargain weekday lunch, and a two-course dinner menu supplement the short carte, and all ingredients are strictly organic. Starters might run to tagliatelle with lemon cream, parsley and Parmesan, and asparagus and white bean minestrone, followed by the likes of polenta and Gorgonzola fritters with cauliflower, pine nut and raisin salad, or roast venison fillet with beetroot bubble and squeak and red wine sauce. Still pursuing the 'green' philosophy, pudding might be an irresistible apple compote with cinnamon custard.
OPEN: 12-11 (Mon 5-11, Wknd phone for details) Closed: 25Dec
BAR MEALS: L served Tue-Sun 12.30-3.30 D served Mon-Sun 6.30-10.30 Av main course £11 **RESTAURANT:** L served Tue-Sun 12.30-3.30 D served Mon-Sun 6.30-10.30 **BREWERY/COMPANY:** Free House 🍺: St Peter's Organic Ale & Best Bitter, Pitfield Eco Warrior & East Kent Goldings. ♀: 12 **FACILITIES:** Children welcome Children's licence Garden: Paved area at front of pub Dogs allowed

E10

King William IV ♀ NEW   Map GtL G5
816 High Rd, Leyton E10 6AE ☎ 020 8556 2460
e-mail: sweetwilliamiv@aol.com
An eye-catching street corner pub, adorned with colourful hanging baskets. The characterful interior is decorated with bric-a-brac and paintings, and behind it you'll find not only an attractive beer garden, but also a brewery, housed in a converted stable block. Sample its products in the bar, accompanied by another of the pub's unique features - genuine Thai cuisine. If, however, the traditional setting makes you long for something more homely, a full range of British bar snacks is available, including roasts on Sundays.
OPEN: 11 -11 (Sun 12-10.30) **BAR MEALS:** L served all week 12-10 D served all week 5-10 Av main course £7 🍺: Fullers ESB, Fullers London Pride. ♀: 13 **FACILITIES:** Garden: Terraced patio area

E14

Pick of the Pubs

The Grapes 🍴♀   Map GtL G4
76 Narrow St, Limehouse E14 8BP
☎ 020 7987 4396 📠 020 7987 3137
Dir: Docklands Light Railway stations: Limehouse or West Ferry
Dickens was a frequent visitor to The Grapes, which has been standing on its narrow riverside site since 1720. He based The Six Jolly Fellowship Porters on it in his novel 'Our Mutual Friend'. While the novelist might still

recognise the pub, the surroundings have changed dramatically with the development of Canary Wharf and the Docklands Light Railway. However, the traditional image is proudly maintained and appeals to a discerning clientele who appreciate good food, wine and cask-conditioned ales. Seafood is the speciality of the house and has attracted several awards in recent times. In the bar you can eat a pint of shell-on prawns, dressed crab, home-made fishcakes or pickled herring salad, while in the tiny upstairs restaurant you might sample whole baked sea bass with oriental sauce, king scallops wrapped in smoked back bacon, marinated chargrilled tuna, or sole meunière.
OPEN: 12-3 5.30-11 (Sat 12-11, Sun 12-10.30) Closed: BHs
BAR MEALS: L served all week 12-2 D served Mon-Sat 7-9 Av main course £6.50 **RESTAURANT:** L served Mon-Fri 12-2.15 D served Mon-Sat 7.30-9.15 Av 3 course à la carte £30
BREWERY/COMPANY: 🍺: Adnams, Burton Ale, Carlsberg-Tetley Tetley's Bitter, Interbrew Bass. **FACILITIES:** Dogs allowed Water

EC1

Pick of the Pubs

The Bleeding Heart Tavern ◉ ♀   Map E4
19 Greville St EC1N 8SQ ☎ 0207 4040333
e-mail: enquiries@bleedingheart.co.uk
The original tavern opened in 1746, its unusual name commemorating the brutal murder of Elizabeth Hatton in nearby Hatton Garden a century earlier. It ceased trading in 1946 but was restored to a contemporary version of its original glory in 1998, with plenty of glass, original stone and rustic scrubbed tables on wooden floors.
Supplementing the range of well-kept Adnam's ales and an impressive list of wines is a menu of traditional pub food with a modern twist. Spit-roast free range chicken, whole suckling pig and shoulder of lamb from the unusual French rotisserie are of particular note, as are the steak and oyster pudding, or braised duck and black pudding hot pot. The desserts are worth a mention too, from vanilla crème brûlée to steamed lemon and ginger pudding.
OPEN: 11-11 Closed: Sat/Sun BHs, 10 days at Christmas
BAR MEALS: L served Mon-Fri 11-10.30 D served Mon-Fri 6-10.30 **RESTAURANT:** L served Mon-Fri 12-3 D served Mon-Fri 6-10.30 **BREWERY/COMPANY:** Free House 🍺: Adnams Southwold Bitter, Broadside & Fisherman. **NOTES:** Parking 20

Pick of the Pubs

The Eagle ◉ ♀   Map E4
159 Farringdon Rd EC1R 3AL ☎ 020 7837 1353
Dir: Angel/Farringdon Stn. North end Farringdon Road
As a description, the term gastro-pub might fall short of universal acceptance, but the Eagle would probably happily acknowledge its part in pioneering the genre. In truth, it is probably more gastro than pub these days, but consider - if traditionally cynical journos from the Guardian and The Face nearby continue to turn up, then it can rest its case. Apart from media types (and, of course, others), the wooden-floored bar and dining area is filled with school chairs, bare tables and other randomly-sourced furniture. Aromas from the open kitchen waft enticingly around, encouraging visitors to eat as well as having 'just the one'. Dishes that recall Mediterranean

continued

continued

EC1 continued

holidays might include ribollita (Tuscan bean and bread stew), marinated rump steak sandwich - a house speciality, cuttlefish braised with peas, wine and garlic on bruschetta, and, for dessert, pecorino (ewe's milk cheese) with crispy flatbread and a pear or a Portuguese custard tart.
OPEN: 12-11 Closed: 1Wk Xmas, BHs **BAR MEALS:** L served all week 12.30-3.30 D served Mon-Sat 6.30-10.30 Av main course £10 **RESTAURANT:** L served all week D served Mon-Sat
BREWERY/COMPANY: Free House ■: Wells Eagle IPA & Bombardier. **FACILITIES:** Children welcome Dogs allowed

Pick of the Pubs

The Jerusalem Tavern ♀   Map F4
55 Britton St, Clerkenwell EC1M 5NA
☎ 020 7490 4281 ▤ 020 7490 4281
e-mail: beers@stpetersbrewery.co.uk
Dir: 100metres NE of Farringdon tube, 300metres N of Smithfield

Named after the Priory of St John of Jerusalem, this historic tavern can trace its history as an institution back to the 14th century. The current building dates from 1720, when a merchant lived here, although the frontage dates from around 1810, by when it had become one of Clerkenwell's many watch and clockmaker's workshops. This fascinating and atmospheric corner of London has only relatively recently been 'rediscovered', long, long after Samuel Johnson, David Garrick and the young Handel used to drink in this tavern. Its dimly-lit bar, with bare boards, rustic wooden tables, old tiles, candles, open fires and cosy corners, is the perfect film set - and that's what it has often been. Definitely one of the capital's finest pubs, it is open every weekday and offers the full range of bottled beers from St Peter's Brewery (which owns it), as well as simple bar food, including speciality sandwiches, sausage baguettes, steak and ale pie, and roast beef and Yorkshire pud.
OPEN: 10-11 (Mon-Fri only) Closed: Sat/Sun, 25 Dec, Etr, BH
BAR MEALS: L served Mon-Fri 12-3 Av main course £6
BREWERY/COMPANY: St Peters Brewery ■: St Peters (complete range). ♀: 8

> We endeavour to be as accurate as possible but changes to times and other information can occur after the guide has gone to press

Pick of the Pubs

The Peasant 🐽 ♀   Map D3
240 St John St EC1V 4PH
☎ 020 7336 7726 ▤ 020 7490 1089
e-mail: qapstairs@aol.com
Dir: Nearest tube: Angel & Faringdon Rd. On corner of St John Street & Percival Street.
Founded in 1993 as one of London's original gastro pubs, with a reputation based as much on consistently good bar mezze food as the restaurant carte. Once a Victorian pub, its original features have been restored to their former glory, including an inlaid mosaic floor, horseshoe bar and lovely conservatory. The upstairs restaurant has also been transformed, and beneath period chandeliers the inventive modern menu makes good reading. Peasant-style food with a Mediterranean leaning is the main thrust: pan-fried chorizo with sherry, pears and walnuts, fried calamari with sweet chilli sauce, seared sardines, and to follow perhaps, roast monkfish with spring greens and mussels, or marinated beef fillet with potato gratin and rosemary jus. White chocolate tiramisù, and passion fruit crème brûlée bring up the rear, while the acclaimed wine list is joined by real ales and cocktails.
CLOSED: Sun **BAR MEALS:** L served Mon-Fri 12.30-3 D served Mon-Sat 6.30-11 Av main course £10 **RESTAURANT:** L served Mon-Fri 12.30-3.30 D served Mon-Sat 6.30-11 Av 3 course à la carte £25 **BREWERY/COMPANY:** Free House ■: Bombadier, Watt Tyler. ♀: 40 **FACILITIES:** Garden terrace Dogs allowed

The Well ♀ **NEW**   Map F5
180 Saint John St, Clerkenwell EC1V 4JY
☎ 020 7251 9363 ▤ 020 7251 6611
e-mail: drink@downthewell.co.uk
Dir: Telephone for directions
Very much a gastro-pub where the emphasis is on modern European and Mediterranean-style food served on two floors. The lower ground features the leather-panelled aquarium bar with exotic tropical fish occupying huge tanks set into the walls. Try the crispy pork belly with roasted leeks, Jerusalem artichokes and pied bleu mushrooms with a mustard and brandy cream sauce; or slow-roasted rib-eye steak with dauphinoise potatoes, roasted garlic and crispy bacon.
OPEN: 11 -12 (Sun 11-10.30) **BAR MEALS:** L served Mon-Sun 12-3 D served Mon-Sun 6-10.30 Av main course £10 **RESTAURANT:** L served Mon-Sun 12-3 D served Mon-Sun 6-10.30 Av 3 course à la carte £20 ■: San Miguel, Budvar, Hoegadden, Leffe. ♀: 15 **FACILITIES:** Children welcome

Ye Olde Mitre   Map E4
1 Ely Court, Ely Place EC1N 6SJ ☎ 020 7405 4751
Located just off Holborn Circus at the edge of The City, this pub has been here since 1546, and retains its historic atmosphere with no music and no gaming machines. It is also a Heritage Inn, which means its preservation is bound to continue. In the bar is part of a cherry tree that Elizabeth I is thought to have danced around. Very busy at lunchtimes. Real ales from hand-pumps. Bar snacks include toasted sandwiches.
OPEN: 11-11 Closed: BHs **BAR MEALS:** L served Mon-Fri (Snack menu) 11-9.30 Av main course £1.75
BREWERY/COMPANY: ■: Adnams Bitter, Carlsberg-Tetley, Burton.

EC2

Old Dr Butler's Head
Map F4

Mason's Av, Coleman St, Moorgate EC2V 5BY
☎ 020 7606 3504 ▤ 020 7600 0417
Dir: *Telephone for directions*

Dr Butler was a quack selling 'medicinal ale' from taverns displaying his sign. This, the only survivor, was rebuilt after the Great Fire of London, while the frontage is probably Victorian. Pub lunches are served in the pleasantly Dickensian gas-lit bar, where Shepherd Neame real ales are on tap, and steak and suet pudding is a speciality. More intimate dining areas, including a carvery, are upstairs, where dinner is by arrangement. The City empties at weekends, so the pub closes.
OPEN: 11-11 **BAR MEALS:** L served Mon-Fri 12-3 D served Arrangement only Av main course £6.45
BREWERY/COMPANY: Shepherd Neame ◖: Spitfire, Shepherd Neame.

EC4

The Black Friar
Map F3

174 Queen Victoria St EC4V 4EG ☎ 020 7236 5474
Located on the site of Blackfriar's monastery, where Henry VIII dissolved his marriage to Catherine of Aragon and separated from the Catholic church. The pub has made several TV appearances because of its wonderful Art Noveau interior. The pub is close to Blackfriars Bridge and gets very busy with after-work drinkers. The traditional-style menu includes steak and ale pie, sausage and mash and sandwiches.
OPEN: 11.30-11 (Sat 12-4) **BAR MEALS:** L served Mon-Fri 12-2.30 Av main course £5.50 **BREWERY/COMPANY:** ◖: Fullers London Pride, Adnams. **FACILITIES:** Garden: Patio with plantation in the centre

The Centre Page
Map F3

29 Knightrider St EC4V 5BH ☎ 020 7236 3614 ▤ 020 7236 3614
e-mail: centrepage@frontpagepubs.com
Dir: *Telephone for directions*
Situated in the shadow of St Paul's Cathedral, this historic pub used to be known as the Horn Tavern and was mentioned by Charles Dickens in The Pickwick Papers, and in Samuel Pepys' diary. Varied menu could include provençale fish soup, beef and Guinness pie, fresh fish in beer batter, Thai fish cakes or veal escalope with a sage and Parmesan crust.
OPEN: 11-11 Closes 8pm Wkends (for hire at weekends) Closed: 25-26 Dec **BAR MEALS:** L served all week 12-3 3 Av main course £7.50
RESTAURANT: L served all week Av 3 course à la carte £16.50
BREWERY/COMPANY: Front Page Pubs Ltd ◖: Fullers London Pride, Pedigree. ♀: 11 **FACILITIES:** Children welcome Dogs allowed

The Old Bank of England ♀
Map E4

194 Fleet St EC4A 2LT ☎ 020 7430 2255 ▤ 020 7242 3092
e-mail: oldbankofengland@fullers.co.uk
This magnificent building was formerly the Law Courts branch of the Bank of England, and it lies between the site of Sweeney Todd's barbershop and his mistress' pie shop. It was in the tunnels and vaults below the present building that their unfortunate victims were butchered before being cooked and sold in Mrs Lovett's pies. The bar menu ranges from light snacks to the likes of lamb casserole with dumplings and jam sponge pudding with custard.
OPEN: 11-11 (closed wknds, BHs) **BAR MEALS:** L served Mon-Fri 12-8 D served Mon-Thurs Av main course £6.50
BREWERY/COMPANY: Fullers ◖: Fuller's London Pride, ESB, Chiswick Bitter.

Ye Olde Cheshire Cheese

Wine Office Court, 145 Fleet St EC4A 2BU
☎ 020 7353 6170 ▤ 020 7353 0845
A pub has stood on this site since 1538 and the present building, one of London's few remaining chop houses, was rebuilt after the Great Fire of 1666. It's a character setting, full of nooks and crannies, and has a long history of entertaining literary greats - Arthur Conan Doyle, Yeats and Dickens to name but a few. Food includes traditional steak and kidney pudding, roast beef and fish and chips.
OPEN: 11-11 Closed: Christmas & BH's **BAR MEALS:** L served all week 12-2.30 D served Mon-Sat 12-9.30 Av main course £5
RESTAURANT: L served all week 12-9 D served Mon-Sat Av 3 course à la carte £18 **BREWERY/COMPANY:** Samuel Smith ◖: Samuel Smith Old Brewery Bitter.

N1

The Albion ♀
Map GtL F4

10 Thornhill Rd, Barnsbury N1 1HW
☎ 020 7607 7450 ▤ 020 7607 8969
e-mail: keithinwood@aol.com
Dir: *Telephone for directions*

An ivy-clad pub of uncertain antiquity with a warren of homely rooms. The pub often plays host to local TV celebrities. Baguettes, burgers and jacket potatoes of choice clutter the chalkboards. Starters and 'lite bites' include spinach and Roquefort tart, and Thai fishcakes, with main dishes represented by beef and Theakston pie, minted lamb shoulder, and Louisiana meatballs, with vegetarian Cajun cream linguini, or rarebit strudel. Grilled steaks with multifarious side orders: outdoor eating in fine weather.
OPEN: 12-10 (Sun 12-10.30) **BAR MEALS:** L served all week 12-3 D served all week 6-9.30 Av main course £7.95 **RESTAURANT:** L served all week 12-3 D served all week 6-9.30
BREWERY/COMPANY: Scottish & Newcastle ◖: Fuller's London Pride, JSXS. **FACILITIES:** Garden

The Compton Arms ♀
Map GtL F4

4 Compton Av, Off Canonbury Rd N1 2XD ☎ 0207 3596883
e-mail: 4334@greeneking.co.uk
A country pub in the middle of town with a peaceful, rural feel. Real ales from the hand pump, and good value steaks, mixed grill, big breakfast and Sunday roast.
OPEN: 12-6 6-11 **BAR MEALS:** L served all week 12-2.30 D served all week 6-9 Av main course £3.50
BREWERY/COMPANY: Greene King ◖: Greene King IPA, Abbot Ale, Ruddles County, plus guest ale. **FACILITIES:** Children welcome Garden: Food served outside

N1 continued

The Crown ♀   Map GtL F4
116 Cloudsley Rd, Islington N1 0EB
☎ 020 7837 7107 📠 020 7833 1084
e-mail: crown.islington@fullers.co.uk

London's beer drinkers are usually happy to head for a Fuller's pub like the Grade II-listed Crown. To add to the appeal, it has a wealth of period features, and a modern menu designed for the diversity of tastes in this upmarket residential district. Alongside traditional chargrilled regular and veggie sausages and mash, there's open scallop and asparagus ravioli with chive cream sauce, pan-fried fillet of pork with Savoy cabbage, bacon and fondant potato, various casseroles, and the Crown's own burger.

OPEN: 12 -11 (Sun 12-11.30) **BAR MEALS:** L served all week 12-3 D served all week 6-10 Av main course £8
BREWERY/COMPANY: Fullers 🍺: Fullers London Pride, Honey Dew, Kirin, Staropramen & Guest ale. ♀: 8 **FACILITIES:** Children welcome Garden: Patio with six tables Dogs allowed

The Drapers Arms ♀ NEW   Map GtL F4
44 Barnsbury St N1 1ER ☎ 020 7619 0348 📠 020 7619 0413
Dir: Turn right outside tube station, walk along Upper street to Barnsbury Street opposite Town Hall

Located in the heart of Islington, where the Labour Party was founded. Many celebrities are drawn to the pub for its convivial atmosphere, good food and interesting wine list, along with decent ales (Old Speckled Hen & Courage). The menu offers an eclectic choice of dishes from gnocchi with roast tomatoes, tiger prawns and feta, to saltimbocca of veal with silver skin onions, spinach and gorgonzola, and grilled polenta. Delicious puddings deserve sampling.

OPEN: 11-11 (Sun 12-10.30) Closed: 25-28 Dec, 1 Jan
BAR MEALS: L served all week 12-3 D served Mon-Sat 7-10 Av main course £10.50 **RESTAURANT:** L served Sun 12-4 D served Mon-Sat 7-10.30 🍺: Old Speckled Hen, Courage, Budvar & Corona. ♀: 20 **FACILITIES:** Garden Dogs allowed

Pick of the Pubs

The Duke of Cambridge 🍴 ♀   Map GtL F4
30 St Peter's St N1 8JT ☎ 020 7359 3066 📠 020 7359 1877
e-mail: duke@singhboulton.co.uk

Running an organic gastro-pub in celeb-laden Islington imposes on owners and childhood friends Geetie Singh and Esther Boulton a stretching objective: to provide the highest quality organic food, wines and beers. Being one of only two Soil Association-certified pubs in the UK proves that they achieve it. Their careful restoration of this 1851 building in 'junkshop minimalist' style involved retaining many original features, and using reclaimed materials and second-hand furniture. Look in vain for juke box, TV and pin-ball machine - there's nothing so intrusive here. The twice-daily-changing blackboard menu is regional European in style, the cooking seasonal and uncomplicated. Examples from a summer menu include bacon-wrapped scallops with tartare potato cake and basil crème, home-smoked lamb fillet with potato aubergine and Feta gratin, and roast vegetable parmigiana with a hazelnut crust. Smaller meals for children, and organic baby food. Organic draught beers include the eponymous Singhboulton, Eco Warrior from Shoreditch, and a lager called Freedom.

OPEN: 12-11 12-10.30 (Mon 5-11) Closed: Dec 25-26, Jan 1
BAR MEALS: L served all week 12.30-3 D served all week 6.30-

10.30 Av main course £10 **RESTAURANT:** L served all week 12.30-3 D served all week 6.30-10.30 Av 3 course à la carte £15
BREWERY/COMPANY: Free House 🍺: Pitfield Singhboulton, Eco Warrior, St Peter's Best Bitter, East Kent Golding. ♀: 12
FACILITIES: Children welcome Children's licence Garden: Small courtyard Dogs allowed

The Northgate 🍴 ♀   Map GtL F4
113 Southgate Rd, Islington N1 3JS
☎ 020 7359 7392 📠 020 7359 7393
Dir: Telephone for directions

A popular gastropub that was transformed from a run-down community local into a friendly modern establishment serving excellent food. A regular guest beer supplements the two resident real ales, and there's also a good mix of draught lagers and imported bottled beers. An appealing list of fresh, seasonal dishes appears on the menu, including sweet potato and lemongrass soup, saffron risotto cakes with plum tomato sauce, and chocolate cake with blueberry cream.

OPEN: 5-11 (Sat 12-11, Sun 12-10.30) Closed: 24-26 Dec, 1 Jan
BAR MEALS: L served Sun 12-4 D served all week 6.30-10.30 Av main course £10.50 **RESTAURANT:** L served Sun 12-4 D served all week 6.30-10.30 Av 3 course à la carte £20
BREWERY/COMPANY: Punch Taverns 🍺: Adnams Bitter, Fuller's London Pride & Guest ales. ♀: 9 **FACILITIES:** Garden: Patio with seating Dogs allowed Water, Biscuits

N6

The Flask 🍴 ♀   Map GtL E5
Highgate West Hill N6 6BU ☎ 020 8348 7346
e-mail: info@theflaskhighgate.co.uk

17th-century former school in one of London's loveliest villages. Dick Turpin hid from his pursuers in the cellars, and TS Elliot and Sir John Betjeman enjoyed a glass or two of ale here. The interior is listed and includes the original bar with sash windows which lift up at opening time. Enjoy a glass of good real ale, mulled wine or a malt whisky while you peruse the menu. Choices range from sandwiches and platters to main courses such as hand-made sausages and mash or seared ginger duck with sweet potato and wilted baby spinach.

OPEN: 11-11 Closed: Dec 25
BAR MEALS: L served all week 12-3 D served all week 6-10 Av main course £8 **BREWERY/COMPANY:** 🍺: Rooster's Rooster, Adnams, Tim Taylor Landlord, Fullers Chiswick. ♀: 11 **FACILITIES:** Children welcome Garden: A large terrace at the front of the pub Dogs allowed Water, Doggie Snacks

N16

The Fox Reformed ♀   Map GtL F5
176 Stoke Newington Church St N16 0JL
☎ 020 7254 5975 📠 020 7254 5975

Wine bar at the heart of community life, with its own reading circle, backgammon club and wine tastings. Good food comes from regular and specials menus. Famed mystery writer Edgar Allen Poe attended school on this site in the 19th century.

OPEN: 5.30-12.00 (Mon-Fri) 12.00-12.00 (Sat-Sun) Closed: Dec 25-26, Jan 1 **BAR MEALS:** L served Weekends D served Everyday Av main course £10.75 ♀: 8 **FACILITIES:** Garden: 20 seater, heated, peaceful **NOTES:** No credit cards

---

> ♀ 7   **Number of wines by the glass**

continued

England

Pick of the Pubs

St Johns ♀   Map GtL E5
91 Junction Rd, Archway N19 5QU
☎ 020 7272 1587 ▤ 020 76872247
The exterior of this Victorian street corner pub is pure
Albert Square, yet, the airy bar and spectacular dining
room attract trendy North London thirty-somethings.
Beyond the long, attractively-converted bar, owner Nic
Sharp has transformed the adjoining snooker hall into a
vast, comfortable restaurant - idiosyncratic decor, solid
oak and pine tables, deep red walls hung with modern
works of art and comfy settees around the fire. You'll
need to book - and be sure to come hungry: St John's
portions are lavish, the food's very good, and the happy
staff generate a relaxed atmosphere. Starters like terrine
of Serrano ham, chorizo, chicken and rabbit or chargrilled
mackerel fillets are chalked up on huge daily-changing
blackboards. Main courses might be chargrilled sea bass
with red onion potato cake, or chicken with mussels and
tarragon. If you've space, dark chocolate and Amaretto
tart will round things off nicely.
OPEN: 11-11 Closed: Dec 25-26, Jan 1 **BAR MEALS:** L served
Tue-Sun 12-3 D served Mon-Sun 6.30-11 Av main course £11
RESTAURANT: L served Tue-Sun 12-3 D served Mon-Sun 6.30-
11 Av 3 course à la carte £20
BREWERY/COMPANY: 🍺: Marston's Pedigree, Fuller's
London Pride, Adnam's Broadside. ♀: 10 **FACILITIES:** Children
welcome Dogs allowed

Pick of the Pubs

The Chapel ♀   Map B4
48 Chapel St NW1 5DP ☎ 020 7402 9220 ▤ 020 7723 2337
e-mail: thechapel@btconnect.com
Dir: By A40 Marylebone Rd & Old Marylebone Rd junction. Off
Edgware Road by tube station
A modern, open-plan gastro-pub, the Chapel derives its
name from nothing more than its location: bright and airy
within, its stripped floors and pine furniture create a
relaxed, informal atmosphere. Menus posted daily on the
chalk-boards have a trendy Anglo-Mediterranean feel. On
any given day expect starters such as lamb, cumin and
chickpea soup, fish croquette salad with roast vegetables,
and turkey, sweet potato and chestnut tortilla. Follow with
ballottine of roasted Mediterranean vegetables and goats'
cheese en croûte, seared tuna steak with asparagus,
mash, saffron and anis, or tempura calamaris stuffed with
scallops, shrimps, Chinese leaf and noodle salad,
rounding off with pot au chocolate or banoffee pie.
OPEN: 12-11 (Sun 12-10.30) Closed: Dec 24-Jan 2
BAR MEALS: L served all week 12-2.30 D served all week 7-10
Av main course £10.75 **RESTAURANT:** L served all week 12-
2.30 D served all week 7-10 Av 3 course à la carte £19
BREWERY/COMPANY: Punch Taverns 🍺: Greene King IPA,
Adnams. ♀: 8 **FACILITIES:** Children welcome Garden Dogs
allowed

Pubs offering a good choice of
fish on their menu

Crown & Goose 🍺   Map GtL E4
100 Arlington Rd NW1 7HP ☎ 020 7485 2342 ▤ 020 7485 2342
Dir: Nearest tube: Camden Town
One of the original gastro-pubs with a relaxed atmosphere
attracting a fashionable media crowd. The food has an Anglo-
Mediterranean flavour with bar snacks like potato skins and
ciabatta rolls, and daily specials often feature fish. A typical
menu includes chargrilled tuna with mixed pepper salsa, pork
chop with apple sauce, red cabbage and mash, gigot lamb
with Greek salad and new potatoes, beer-battered cod and
chips, and fragrant Thai fish or chicken stew with coconut and
rice.
OPEN: 11-11 (Sun 12-10.30) Closed: 25 Dec **BAR MEALS:** L
served all week 12-3 D served all week 6-10 Av main course £7
RESTAURANT: L served all week 12-3 D served all week 6-10 Av 3
course à la carte £15 **BREWERY/COMPANY:** Scottish Courage
🍺: Fuller's London Pride. **FACILITIES:** Children welcome

Pick of the Pubs

The Engineer 🍺 ♀   Map GtL E4
65 Gloucester Av, Primrose Hill NW1 8JH
☎ 020 7722 0950 ▤ 020 7483 0592
e-mail: info@the-engineer.com
Dir: Nearest tube: Camden Town/Chalk Farm, on the corner of
Princess Rd and Gloucester Ave
Situated in a very residential part of Primrose Hill close to
Camden Market, this unassuming corner street pub, built
by Isambard Kingdom Brunel in 1841, attracts a discerning
dining crowd for imaginative and well-prepared food and
its friendly, laid-back atmosphere. Fashionably rustic
interior with a spacious bar area, sturdy wooden tables
with candles, simple decor and changing art exhibitions in
the restaurant area. A walled, paved and heated garden to
the rear is extremely popular in fine weather. A first-class,
fortnightly-changing menu features an eclectic mix of
home-made, Mediterranean inspired dishes and uses
organic or free-range meats. Start, perhaps, with split pea
and ham soup with truffle oil and home-made bread or
Mozzarella with figs and Parma ham with honey and grain
mustard dressing, following on with salmon fishcakes with
coriander, chilli and ginger served with roast garlic aïoli,
whole-roasted sea bass with coarse chopped tapenade, or
chargrilled organic sirloin steak with herb butter. Excellent
Sunday brunch.
OPEN: 11-11 Closed: 25-26 Dec, 1 Jan **BAR MEALS:** L served
all week 12.30-3 D served all week 7-10.30 Av main course £13
RESTAURANT: L served all week 12-3 D served all week 7-11
BREWERY/COMPANY: 🍺: Fullers London Pride, Youngs
Special. **FACILITIES:** Children welcome Garden: Food served
outside, paved garden Dogs allowed In the garden only

The Globe 🍺 ♀   Map B4
43-47 Marylebone Rd NW1 5JY
☎ 020 7935 6368 ▤ 020 7224 0154
Dir: Nr Baker St tube
Consisting of wine bar, main bar and restaurant, this 18th-
century, three-storey pub, opposite Baker Street tube station,
was once frequented by such luminaries as Charles Dickens,
Sir Arthur Conan Doyle, and Alfred Lord Tennyson. Typical
menu includes steak and Stilton pie, pork escalope with wild
mushroom sauce, light snacks, and the Globe's speciality: fish
and chips. Convenient for the Planetarium and Madame
Tussaud's.

continued

NW1 continued

OPEN: 11-11 (Sun 12-10.30) Closed: 25 Dec **BAR MEALS:** L served all week 11-11 D served all week Av main course £5 **RESTAURANT:** L served all week 11-10 D served all week Av 3 course à la carte £9 **BREWERY/COMPANY:** 🍺: Scottish Courage Courage Best & Directors, plus Guest ales. **FACILITIES:** Children welcome

Pick of the Pubs

The Lansdowne 🏠 ♀ Map GtL E4
90 Gloucester Av, Primrose Hill NW1 8HX
☎ 020 7483 0409 📠 0207 5861723
Dir: Nearest tube: Chalk Farm. Cross road turn R, 1st L over bridge, L again along Gloucester Ave, pub on L
One of the earlier dining pubs in Primrose Hill, The Lansdowne blends a light, spacious bar and outdoor seating area with a slightly more formal upper dining room. Here you'll find waiter service, and it's worth reserving your table. There's no music or other distractions, so this is an ideal venue for simply eating, drinking and talking with friends. All food is freshly prepared on the premises, using organic or free-range ingredients wherever possible. The seasonal menu offers such dishes as grilled Black Mountain rib-eye steak, chicken and chorizo stew, roast cod with Seville orange sauce, grilled sea bass with purple-sprouting broccoli, and pan-fried scallops.
OPEN: 12-11 (Sun 12-4, 7-10.30) **BAR MEALS:** L served Tue-Sun 12.30-2.30 D served Mon-Sun 7-10 Av main course £11 **RESTAURANT:** L served Sun 1-3 D served Tue-Sat 7-10 Av 3 course à la carte £23 Av 3 course fixed price £19.50 **BREWERY/COMPANY:** Bass 🍺: Fuller's London Pride, Woodforde's Wherry Best Bitter. ♀: 8

The Lord Stanley ♀ Map GtL E4
51 Camden Park Rd NW1 9BH
☎ 0207 428 9488 📠 020 7209 1347
In the mid-1990s, the Lord Stanley was stripped and re-kitted in a gastro-pub garb that has served the pub well. At an open grill, food is produced in full view - a typically-modern idiom producing, perhaps, chicken with mango salsa. Other dishes include seasonal soups, steaks, pasta or sausages with various accompaniments. Monday night jazz.
OPEN: 12-11 Closed: 26 Dec & 1 Jan **BAR MEALS:** L served Tue-Sun 12.30-3 D served all week 7-10 Av main course £11 **RESTAURANT:** L served Tue-Sun 12.30-3 D served all week 7-10 **BREWERY/COMPANY:** Free House 🍺: Young's Special, Adnams Broadside, Abbot Ale. **FACILITIES:** Children welcome Garden: Food served outside Dogs allowed

The Queens ♀ Map GtL E4
49 Regents Park Rd, Primrose Hill NW1 8XD
☎ 020 7586 0408 📠 020 7586 5677
Dir: Nearest tube station - Chalk Farm
In one of London's most affluent and personality-studded areas, this Victorian pub looks up at 206ft-high Primrose Hill. Main courses may include seared calves' liver with bacon and sage mash, roast vegetable Yorkshire pudding, smoked chicken with mango and mange-tout peas, and whole roasted plaice with prawns and pancetta. On Sundays there's a selection of roasts, as well as fish, pasta and salad. Beers include Youngs and guests.
OPEN: 11-11 (Sun 12-10.30) **BAR MEALS:** L served all week 12-

2.30 D served all week 7-9.45 Av main course £10 **RESTAURANT:** L served all week 12-2.30 D served all week 7-9.45 Av 3 course à la carte £20 **BREWERY/COMPANY:** Youngs 🍺: Youngs, guest ales. ♀: 12 **FACILITIES:** Children welcome Dogs allowed Water provided

NW3

The Flask ♀ Map GtL E5
14 Flask Walk, Hampstead NW3 1HE ☎ 020 7435 4580
Dir: Nearest tube: Hampstead. Turn L, then L again for Flask Walk
Friendly local with a fascinating clientele - writers, poets, actors, tourists, locals, workmen, shopkeepers, office-workers, professors and medics. The name reflects the time when flasks were made on site for the healing waters of the Hampstead spa. Dishes range through home-made soup, pies and burgers, fish and chips, chicken and leek pie, sausage and mash and various pastas.
OPEN: 11-11 (Sun 12-11) **BAR MEALS:** L served all week 12-3 served Tue-Sat 6-8.30 Av main course £6 **RESTAURANT:** 12-3 D served Tue-Sat 6-8.30 Av 3 course à la carte £11 **BREWERY/COMPANY:** Young & Co 🍺: Young's Special, Winter Warmer & WaggleDance. ♀: 17 **FACILITIES:** Children welcome Dogs allowed on lead

The Holly Bush Map GtL E5
Holly Mount, Hampstead NW3 6SG ☎ 020 7435 2892
Bought by English portraitist George Romney in 1796 and turned into a pub when he died in 1802, the Holly Bush is at the heart of Hampstead village. It retains a period atmosphere with lots of Edwardian fittings, though it is frequented by 21st-century pop/TV celebrities. Sausages, pies and puddings are the staple fare (with vegetarian and organic varieties), supplemented by daily specials. Real ales and a selection of malts and bourbons are served.
OPEN: 12-11.00 **BAR MEALS:** L served Tue-Sun 12.30-4.00 D served all week 6.30-10.00 Av main course £8.50 **BREWERY/COMPANY:** 🍺: Harveys Sussex Best, Adnams Bitter & Broadside. **FACILITIES:** Children welcome Garden: Small area outside pub with seating & tables Dogs allowed

Spaniards Inn 🏠 ♀ Map GtL E5
Spaniards Rd, Hampstead NW3 7JJ
☎ 020 8731 6571 📠 020 8731 6572
A famous landmark beside Hampstead Heath much frequented by celebrities, and birthplace of notorious highwayman Dick Turpin. This former tollhouse was mentioned in Bram Stoker's 'Dracula', and the poet Keats frequented the Spaniards Inn when he lived in Hampstead. The shaded and flagstoned courtyard is a delightful spot in the summer. Typical meals are steak and kidney pudding, roast beef, fish and chips, and open ciabatta sandwiches with various fillings.
OPEN: 11-11 (Sun 12-10.30) **BAR MEALS:** L served all week 12-10 D served all week 12-10 Av main course £7 **RESTAURANT:** L served all week D served all week 5-9 **BREWERY/COMPANY:** 🍺: Fullers London Pride, Adnams Best. **FACILITIES:** Children welcome Garden: Flagstone shaded courtyard Dogs allowed **NOTES:** Parking 50

Ye Olde White Bear ♀ Map GtL E5
Well Rd, Hampstead NW3 1LJ ☎ 0207 4353758
Victorian pub with a Hampstead village feel and varied clientele from dustmen to Hollywood stars, plus lots of theatrical memorabilia. Friendly and traditional, there has been a pub on this site since 1704. "A country pub in the heart of London." Patio at rear. All day bar food includes steak and Guinness pie, home-made cheeseburger, vegetarian lasagne, and tuna steak.

continued

continued

England

OPEN: 11-11 **BAR MEALS:** L served all week D served all week Av main course £6.50 **RESTAURANT:** L served all week D served all week **BREWERY/COMPANY:** Fuller's London Pride, Youngs. ♀: 12 **FACILITIES:** Children welcome Garden: Courtyard with seating Dogs allowed Water provided

NW5

Pick of the Pubs

The Vine — Map GtL E5
86 Highgate Rd NW5 1PB
☎ 020 7209 0038 ▤ 020 7209 3161
Dir: Telephone for directions
What looks like a Victorian pub on the outside has a very contemporary feel on the inside, with its copper bar, wooden floors, huge mirrors and funky art. The Vine is billed as a bar, restaurant and garden, and the latter is a great asset - fully covered in winter. Rooms are also available upstairs for private meetings or dinner parties. The pub is run by James and Paula Myers, and the head chef is Joel Gottlieb who has recently spent four years in Australia. Lunch, dinner and weekend brunch menus are offered, the latter including eggs Benedict, burgers and roast cod. Bar snack favourites include fish cakes, chicken satay and tempura sweetcorn, while restaurant fare features crispy duck pancakes with watercress, ginger and mango salsa, cassoulet, risottos and classic dishes like calves' liver with dried prosciutto, potato rösti and Madeira jus.
OPEN: 12.30-3.30 6.30-10.30 Closed: 25/26 Dec
BAR MEALS: L served all week 12.30-3.30 D served all week 6.30-10.30 Av main course £10.50 **RESTAURANT:** L served all week 12.30-3.30 D served all week 6.30-10.30 Av 3 course à la carte £25 Av 3 course fixed price £19.50
BREWERY/COMPANY: Punch Taverns Stella Artois, San Miguel, Fullers London Pride. **FACILITIES:** Children welcome Garden: pretty, brilliant for weddings **NOTES:** Parking 4

NW8

Pick of the Pubs

The Salt House ☺ ♀ — Map GtL E4
63 Abbey Rd NW8 0AE ☎ 020 7328 6626 ▤ 020 7625 9168
Situated in a leafy area of St Johns Wood, a compact and informal dining pub with a tiny open-plan kitchen that takes its food, though not itself, seriously. Expect nothing short of well-prepared fresh ingredients along with decent pints of real ale and numerous house wines served by the glass. A sample menu features Thai fishcakes with sweet chilli dressing, spiny artichoke, rocket and lentil salad with olive dressing or potato gnocchi with butternut squash, sage and Parmesan. For more substantial dishes try roast free range chicken with flageolet beans and roast garlic, duck breast with smashed celeriac, or fillet of sea bass with beetroot, mizuna and horseradish. For pudding try the wonderfully-named Rhubarb Eton mess from a tempting selection.
OPEN: 12-11 Closed: Dec 25 **BAR MEALS:** L served all week 12.30-3.30 D served all week 7-10.30 Av main course £13
RESTAURANT: L served all week 12-3 D served all week 6.30-10.30 Av 3 course à la carte £30 Av 3 course fixed price £11.75
BREWERY/COMPANY: Greene King Greene King IPA.
FACILITIES: Children welcome Garden: Food served outside

NW10

William IV Bar & Restaurant ♀ — Map GtL D4
786 Harrow Rd NW10 5JX ☎ 020 8969 5944 ▤ 020 8964 9218
Dir: Telephone for directions

A solid favourite with locals, and often used by pop bands and TV stars filming at nearby BBC studios. A new kitchen team was recruited in 2003 to take dining standards to new heights. One of the daily-changing menus offers deep-fried skate cheeks with aioli as a starter, and main courses of poached salt beef with lentils and mustard fruits, and rabbit, snail and cep stew with sage polenta.
OPEN: 12-11 (Thu-Sat 12-12, Sun 12-10.30) Closed: Dec 25 & Jan 01
BAR MEALS: L served all week 12-3 D served all week 6-10.30 Av main course £10 **RESTAURANT:** L served all week 12-3 D served all week 6-10.30 Av 3 course à la carte £20
BREWERY/COMPANY: Free House Fuller's London Pride, Greene King IPA, Interbrew Bass, Brakspear. **FACILITIES:** Children welcome Garden: Food served outside

SE1

The Anchor ☺ ♀ — Map F3
Bankside, 34 Park St SE1 9EF
☎ 020 7407 1577 & 7407 3003 ▤ 020 7407 0741
e-mail: southwick@premierlodge.co.uk
In the shadow of the Globe Theatre, this historic pub lies on one of London's most famous tourist trails. Samuel Pepys supposedly watched the Great Fire of London from here in 1666, and Dr Johnson was a regular, with Oliver Goldsmith, David Garrick and Sir Joshua Reynolds. The river views are excellent, and inside are black beams, old faded plasterwork, and a maze of tiny rooms. A varied menu includes fish and chips, pan-fried halibut with olives, and cod in crispy bacon served on wilted spinach.
OPEN: 11-11 (Sun 12-10.30) **BAR MEALS:** L served all week 11.30-8.30 D served all week Av main course £5.50 **RESTAURANT:** L served all week 12-2.30 D served all week 6-10 Av 3 course à la carte £22.50 **BREWERY/COMPANY:** Wadworth 6X, Scottish Courage Courage Directors, Greene King IPA. **FACILITIES:** Garden: Patio overlooking the River Thames

Pick of the Pubs

The Fire Station Restaurant & Bar ☺ ☺ ♀ Map D2
150 Waterloo Rd SE1 8SB
☎ 020 7620 2226 ▤ 020 7633 9161
e-mail: firestation@wizardinns.co.uk
Close to Waterloo Station, and handy for the Old Vic Theatre and the Imperial War Museum, this remarkable conversion of a genuine early-Edwardian fire station has kept many of its former trappings intact. Possibly the high

continued

England

SE1

point being a rear dining room facing the open kitchen. An interesting menu includes dishes such as Fire Station avocado Caesar salad, baked cod with cheese polenta and pimento and pesto dressing, roast spiced pork belly with sticky rice and pak choi. Alternatively try Tandoori seared yellowfin tuna loin, calves' liver with bacon or mustard mash or lemon sole with Jerusalem artichokes. There are also imaginative midweek and Sunday set-price lunches.
OPEN: 11-11 (Sun 12-10.30) Closed: 25/26 Dec
BAR MEALS: L served all week 12-5.30 D served all week 5.30-10.30 Av main course £11 **RESTAURANT:** L served all week 12-2.45 D served all week 5-11 Av 3 course à la carte £20 Av 2 course fixed price £10.95 **BREWERY/COMPANY:** ◖: Adnams Best Bitter & Broadside, Fuller's London Pride, Young's Bitters, Shepherd Neame Spitfire. ♀: 8 **FACILITIES:** Children welcome

Pick of the Pubs

The George Inn
Map G3
77 Borough High St SE1 1NH
☎ 020 7407 2056 ▯ 020 74036956
e-mail: info@georgeinn-southwark.co.uk
Dir: *London Bridge tube station, take Borough High Street exit, turn L, 200 yrds on left hand side.*
The only remaining galleried inn in London, this striking black and white building dates back at least to 1542 when it numbered one William Shakespeare among its clientele. Dickens mentioned it in 'Little Dorrit', and his original life assurance policy is displayed along with 18th-century rat traps. In the 18th and 19th centuries the George was a famous coaching terminus. Now owned by the National Trust, its river views are breathtaking, while inside there is fading plasterwork, black beams and a warren of tiny rooms. Food can be enjoyed here or in the large cobbled courtyard, with a straightforward choice including steak and ale pie, traditional fish and chips, and sausage and mash, along with some decent real ales. This is a 'real' olde English pub with plenty of buzz.
OPEN: 11-11 (Sunday 12-10.30) Closed: 25 Dec
BAR MEALS: L served all week 12-4 D served Mon-Sat Av fixed price £8.45 **BREWERY/COMPANY:** ◖: Fuller's London Pride, Greene King Abbot Ale, Adnams, George Inn Ale.
FACILITIES: Garden: Large courtyard, picnic tables, enclosed

The Market Porter ♀
Map F3
9 Stoney St, Borough Market, London Bridge SE1 9AA
☎ 020 7407 2495 403 7097 ▯ 020 7403 7697
Dir: *Close to London Bridge Station*
Traditional tavern serving a market community that has been flourishing for about 1,000 years. Excellent choice of real ales. Worth noting is an internal leaded bay window unique in London. The atmosphere is friendly, if rather rough and ready, and the pub has been used as a location in 'Lock, Stock and Two Smoking Barrels', 'Only Fools and Horses', and 'Entrapment'. Menu includes bangers and mash, roasted lamb shank, beetroot and lemon marinated salmon, and a hearty plate of fish and chips.
OPEN: 6.30-8.30am 11-11 (Sun 12-10.30) **BAR MEALS:** L served Mon-Sun 12-2.30 5-8.30 Av main course £5.50 **RESTAURANT:** L served Mon-Fri 12-2.30 5.30-8.30 Av 3 course à la carte £20 Av 3 course fixed price £20 **BREWERY/COMPANY:** Free House
◖: Harveys Best, Scottish Courage Courage Best, Lands End To John O'Groats. ♀: 6

The Old Thameside
Map F3
Pickford's Wharf, Clink St SE1 9DG
☎ 020 7403 4243 ▯ 020 7407 2063
Just two minutes' walk from Tate Modern, the Millennium Bridge and Shakespeare's Globe, this former spice warehouse is also close to the site of England's first prison, the Clink. The pub features a large outdoor seating area that overhangs the River Thames, and the friendly staff are always happy to point bewildered tourists in the right direction! Traditional pub fare includes fish and chips, sausage and mash, curries and vegetarian pies.
OPEN: 12-11 Closed: 25 Dec **BAR MEALS:** L served all week 12-5 Av main course £6.95 ◖: Fuller's London Pride, Adnams Bitter.
FACILITIES: Children welcome

SE5

The Sun and Doves ♀
Map GtL F3
61-63 Coldharbour Ln, Camberwell SE5 9NS
☎ 020 7924 9950 ▯ 020 7924 9330
A gastropub in recently-gentrified Camberwell, known for its food, drink and art. Much produce is free-range and specialities are skewers - haloumi and roast vegetables, swordfish tikka - prepared on beech skewers, marinated and grilled to order - and dishes such as moules marinière, bean and pepper lasagne, and pork and leek bangers. The drinks range extends to a good wine list and selection of cocktails. Bi-monthly art exhibitions include work by Anthony Gormley, Anish Kapoor, Chris Ofili and Sarah Raphael.
OPEN: 11-11 Closed: 25/26 Dec **BAR MEALS:** L served all week 12-10 D served all week 12-10 Av main course £8 **RESTAURANT:** L served all week 11-11 D served all week Av 3 course à la carte £16 **BREWERY/COMPANY:** Scottish & Newcastle ◖: Greene King Old Speckled Hen, Scottish Courage John Smith's Smooth. ♀: 8
FACILITIES: Children welcome Garden: Secluded, warm, spacious Dogs allowed

SE10

The Cutty Sark Tavern
Map GtL G3
4-7 Ballast Quay, Lassell St SE10 9PD ☎ 0208 858 3146
Originally the Union Tavern, this 1695 waterside pub was renamed when the world famous tea-clipper was dry-docked upriver in 1954. Inside, low beams, creaking floorboards, dark panelling and from the large bow window in the upstairs bar, commanding views of the Thames, Canary Wharf and the Millennium Dome. Well-kept beers, wines by the glass and a wide selection of malts. Bangers and mash, seafood and vegetarian specials and Sunday roasts. Busy at weekends, especially on fine days.
OPEN: 11-11 **BAR MEALS:** L served all week 12 D served all week 9 Av main course £7 ◖: Fullers London Pride.
FACILITIES: Children welcome Children's licence

Greenwich Union Pub NEW
Map GtL G3
56 Royal Hill SE10 8RT ☎ 020 8692 6258
A newly-refurbished pub (previously known as the Fox & Hounds) with an attractive bright colour scheme, several comfortable leather chairs and sofas, and flagstoned floors which help to keep the original character intact. Interesting beers and enjoyable food (Union club sandwich and Caesar salad among favourites), and a beer garden for summer eating and drinking make this a popular spot.
OPEN: 11-11 (Sun 12-10.30) **BAR MEALS:** L served Mon-Sun 12.30-3 D served Mon-Sun 5-8 Av main course £6 ◖: White Beer, Golden Beer, Blonde Ale, Red Beer. **FACILITIES:** Garden: Beer garden, tables and chairs, wooden fence Dogs allowed Water

Pick of the Pubs

North Pole Bar & Restaurant 🐾 ♀   Map GtL G3

131 Greenwich High Rd, Greenwich SE10 8JA
☎ 020 8853 3020 📠 020 8853 3501
e-mail: northpoleozzy@hotmail.com

This clubby, style-conscious establishment enjoys a prime Greenwich location. The ground floor bar features a cosmopolitan mix of cocktails and designer leather sofas, whilst the curving wooden staircase leads up to the comfortable restaurant. Here you'll find two calm, dignified rooms, decorated in red and green, with live goldfish swimming in the chandeliers. By contrast, the South Pole champagne and cocktail bar in the basement is themed on an aeroplane cabin, with cool blue and white décor, disco music and air conditioning to maintain the chilled atmosphere. The kitchen exhibits plenty of style, and the menu transcends the overworked gastro-pub image. Menus could include starters of warm crab cakes or confit of duck terrine, with main courses ranging from lamb chump with provençale vegetables to a trio of fish with crab sauce and fresh pasta.

OPEN: 12-12 **BAR MEALS:** L served all week 12-3 D served all week Av main course £5 **RESTAURANT:** L served Sun 12-4 D served all week 6-11 Av 3 course à la carte £25 Av 3 course fixed price £17.50 **BREWERY/COMPANY:** Free House
🍺: Stella Artois, Staropramen, Budvar, Hoegarden. ♀: 20

SE16

Mayflower Inn ♀   Map GtL F3

117 Rotherhithe St, Rotherhithe SE16 4NF
☎ 020 7237 4088 📠 020 7237 0548
Dir: Exit A2 at Surrey Keys roundabout onto Brunel Rd, 3rd L onto Swan Rd, at T jct L, 200m to pub on R

Before embarking on her historic voyage to the New World, The Mayflower was moored at the jetty you can still see today from the patio of the Mayflower Inn - then known as The Spread Eagle. Links with the voyage have been maintained through the memorabilia now on display. The pub has an unusual license to sell UK and US postage stamps. Pub fare includes sausage and mash, liver and bacon, and steak and Abbot Ale pie.

OPEN: 12-11.30 (Sun 12-10.30) **BAR MEALS:** L served all week 12-3 D served all week 7-10 Av main course £6 **RESTAURANT:** 12-4 6.30-9 **BREWERY/COMPANY:** Greene King 🍺: Greene King Abbot Ale, IPA, Old Speckled Hen. **FACILITIES:** Children welcome Jetty over river, food served outside Dogs allowed

SE21

The Crown & Greyhound ♀   Map GtL F2

73 Dulwich Village SE21 7BJ ☎ 020 8299 4976 📠 020 8693 8959
Large turn of the century pub which can easily absorb plenty of people, and is very welcoming towards families. The unusual name came from two inns which used to stand here, but it's known locally as The Dog. Meals can be eaten in the conservatory and adjoining restaurant, from daily-changing menus: chicken shitake, lamb shank, speciality sausage and mash, and specials like herb fishcakes, vegetable moussaka, plus a popular Sunday carvery.

OPEN: 11-11 (Sun 12-10.30) **BAR MEALS:** L served all week 12 D served all week 10 Av main course £8 **RESTAURANT:** L served all week 12 D served all week 10 🍺: Adnams Bitter, Fuller's London Pride, Bass Youngs Special. ♀: 10 **FACILITIES:** Children welcome Garden Dogs allowed

---

SW1

The Albert   Map D2

52 Victoria St SW1H 0NP
☎ 020 7222 5577 & 7222 7606 📠 020 7222 1044
e-mail: thealbert.westminster@snr.co.uk
Dir: Nearest tube - St James Park

Built in 1864, this Grade II Victorian pub is named after Queen Victoria's husband, Prince Albert. The main staircase is decorated with portraits of British Prime Ministers, from Salisbury to Blair, and the pub is often frequented by MPs. The pub was the only building in the area to survive the Blitz of WWII, with even its old cut-glass windows remaining intact. The traditional menu includes a carvery, buffet, a selection of light dishes and other classic fare.

OPEN: 11-11 (Sun 12-10.30) Closed: 25 Dec **BAR MEALS:** L served all week 11-10.30 D served all week Av main course £5.50 **RESTAURANT:** L served all week 12-9.30 D served all week 5-9.30 Av 3 course à la carte £16.50 Av 3 course fixed price £14.95
BREWERY/COMPANY: 🍺: Scottish Courage Courage Directors & Best, Greene King Abbott Ale, John Smiths, plus 2 Guest ales.
FACILITIES: Children welcome

The Buckingham Arms ♀   Map D2

62 Petty France SW1H 9EU ☎ 020 7222 3386
e-mail: buckinghamarms@youngs.co.uk
Dir: St James's Park tube

Known as the Black Horse until 1903, this elegant, busy Young's pub is situated close to Buckingham Palace. Popular with tourists, business people and real ale fans alike, it offers a good range of simple pub food, including the 'mighty' Buckingham burger, nachos with chilli, chicken ciabatta and old favourites like ham, egg and chips in its long bar with etched mirrors.

OPEN: 11-11 (Sat 12-5.30, Sun 12-5.30) **BAR MEALS:** L served all week 12-2.30 D served Mon-Fri 6-9 Av main course £4.80
BREWERY/COMPANY: Young & Co 🍺: Youngs Bitter, Special & Winter Warmer. ♀: 11

The Clarence   Map D3

55 Whitehall SW1A 2HP ☎ 020 7930 4808 📠 020 7321 0859
Dir: Between Big Ben & Trafalgar Sq

Haunted pub, situated five minutes' walk from Big Ben, the Houses of Parliament, Trafalgar Square and Buckingham Palace, with leaded windows and ancient ceiling beams from a Thames pier.
OPEN: 11-11 **BAR MEALS:** L served all week D served all week Av main course £6.95 **RESTAURANT:** L served all week D served all week **BREWERY/COMPANY:** 🍺: Bombardier, Fullers London Pride & Guest ale. **FACILITIES:** Children welcome

SW1 continued

The Grenadier 🏠 ♀ — Map B2
18 Wilton Row, Belgravia SW1X 7NR
☎ 020 7235 3074 ▤ 020 7235 3400
Regularly used for films and television series, once the Duke of Wellington's officers' mess and much frequented by King George IV, the ivy-clad Grenadier stands in a cobbled mews behind Hyde Park Corner, largely undiscovered by tourists. Outside is the remaining stone of the Duke's mounting block. Food ranges from black pudding stack, and spinach and Roquefort tart starters, to minted lamb shoulder, duck in red wine, and chicken breast with thyme dumplings.
OPEN: 12-11 (Sun 12-10.30 and BHs) **BAR MEALS:** L served all week 12-2.30 D served all week 6-9.30 Av main course £6.95
RESTAURANT: L served all week 12-2 D served all week 6-9.30 Av 3 course à la carte £25 **BREWERY/COMPANY:** ◖: Scottish Courage Best, Greene King Old Speckled Hen, Fuller's London Pride, Charles Wells Bombardier Premium Bitter. ♀: 8 **FACILITIES:** Children welcome

Nags Head — Map B2
53 Kinnerton St SW1X 8ED ☎ 020 7235 1135
In a quiet mews near Harrods, this old pub has the feel of a homely local. Once described as the smallest pub in London, it changed hands in 1921 for £11 7s and 6d - the price of a few drinks today! The pub boasts a 'What the Butler Saw' kinescope, used for donations to Queen Charlotte's Hospital. A good choice of decent, home-cooked food and kitchen favourites might include steak and mushroom pie, Mediterranean quiche, pork pies, roast chicken, and shepherd's pie.
OPEN: 11-11 (Sun 12-11) **BAR MEALS:** L served all week 11-9.30 D served all week Av main course £6 **BREWERY/COMPANY:** Free House ◖: Adnams Best, Broadside, Fisherman & Regatta.
FACILITIES: Children welcome **NOTES:** No credit cards

The Orange Brewery ♀ — Map C1
37-39 Pimlico Rd SW1 W8NE ☎ 020 7730 5984
Dir: Nearest tube: Sloane Square or Victoria
The name comes from local associations with Nell Gwynne, a 17th-century purveyor of oranges and a favourite of Charles II. The building dates from 1790, and fronts onto an appealing square. Beers are brewed in the cellar, including SW1, SW2 and Pimlico Porter, and regulars will find a different guest beer every month. Expect traditional pub food; steak, Guinness and suet pudding, chicken curry, or scampi and chips are favourites.
OPEN: 11-11 (Sun 12-10.30, bar food all day) 24 Dec Close at 6 **BAR MEALS:** L served all week 11-9 D served all week Av main course £5.45 **BREWERY/COMPANY:** ◖: Scottish Courage Courage Directors & Courage Best, Theakston Best, Greene King, Ruddles County & Old Speckled Hen. **FACILITIES:** Children welcome Dogs allowed

The Wilton Arms NEW — Map B2
71 Kinnerton St SW1X 8ED ☎ 020 7235 4854
Named after the 1st Earl of Wilton but known locally as the Village Pub, with exuberant hanging baskets and window boxes. The early 19th-century inn boasts high settles and bookcases which create individual seating areas, and a tasteful conservatory covers the garden. Fine ales and good homecooking are served, including beef and Guinness pie, fish and chips, various curries, and traditional pub snacks.
OPEN: 11-11 Sun (12-10.30) **BAR MEALS:** L served Mon-Sat 12-3.45 D served Mon-Fri 5.30-10 ◖: Spitfire, Bishops Finger.
FACILITIES: Children welcome

SW3

Pick of the Pubs

The Admiral Codrington ♀ — Map B2
17 Mossop St SW3 2LY ☎ 020 7581 0005 ▤ 020 7589 2452
e-mail: admiralcodrington@longshotplc.com
Dir: Telephone for directions
Affectionately known as The Cod, this old Chelsea pub has been given a make-over to create a smart but homely neighbourhood restaurant. The emphasis is on serving quality food in comfortable surroundings, and the restaurant is bright and warm, with a large skylight to let the sun in on the bare wooden floor. There's a separate bar with its own distinct identity, where you can have a drink or a bar meal: expect home-made linguini with fresh salmon and dill, a grilled chicken, avocado and tomato sandwich, and goats' cheese and roast peppers on ciabatta. In the restaurant the carte might offer starters like wild mushroom tartlet, foie gras and chicken liver parfait, and steamed moules, with such main choices as crispy salmon fishcake, caramelised breast of duck, roast lamb chops, grilled Scotch sirloin steak, and pan-fried seabass fillet. Virtually all the well-chosen wines are available by the glass.
OPEN: 11.30-11 (Sun 12-10.30) **BAR MEALS:** L served all week 12-2.30 D served all week Av main course £12.75
RESTAURANT: L served all week 12-2.30 D served all week 7-10.30 Av 3 course à la carte £33 Av 3 course fixed price £30
BREWERY/COMPANY: Free House ◖: Stella, Heineken, Becks, Cobra. ♀: 30 **FACILITIES:** Children welcome Garden: Beer garden/patio

Pick of the Pubs

The Coopers of Flood Street ♀ — Map B1
87 Flood St, Chelsea SW3 5TB
☎ 020 7376 3120 ▤ 020 7352 9187
e-mail: drinks@thecoopers.co.uk
A quiet backstreet Chelsea pub close to the Kings Road and the river. Celebrities and the notorious rub shoulders with the aristocracy and the local road sweeper in the bright, vibrant atmosphere, while the stuffed brown bear, Canadian moose and boar bring a character of their own to the bar. Food is served here and in the quiet upstairs dining room, with a focus on meat from the pub's own organic farm. The fresh, adventurous menu also offers traditional favourites: from a secret recipe there's Aberdeen Angus 'steak les Hooches', along with the likes of seared king scallops with rocket, crème frâiche and sweet chilli sauce, Cooper's Welsh rarebit with crisp prosciutto and Worcestershire sauce, and garlic and chilli prawn linguine in a white wine and cream sauce. Good staff-customer repartee makes for an entertaining atmosphere.
OPEN: 11-11 Closed: 25 Dec & Good Friday **BAR MEALS:** L served all week 12.30-3 D served Mon-Sat 6.30-9.30 Av main course £8 **BREWERY/COMPANY:** Young & Co ◖: Youngs Special, Smiles Bitter, Youngs Bitter.

England

Pick of the Pubs

The Cross Keys ♀ — Map GtL E3
1 Lawrence St, Chelsea SW3 5NB
☎ 020 7349 9111 ▤ 020 7349 9333
A fine Chelsea pub dating from 1765 which has been a famous bolthole for the rich and famous since the 1960s. The stylish interior includes a Bohemian-style banqueting room and open-plan conservatory, plus a restaurant and a first-floor gallery that is adorned with works of modern art. A modern European flavour adds to the menu, although Sunday is mainly traditional with some adventurous forays. The set meals offer good value around dishes likes smoked duck terrine, Toulouse sausages with mash, and date and pecan sponge pudding for lunch. Evening fare differs only in the extra choice on the carte: asparagus and broad bean risotto, or deep-fried Oriental samosas, followed by grilled marinated lamb steak, or baked tranche of cod with seafood linguine.
OPEN: 12-11 (Sun 12-10) Closed: Dec 25-26 Jan1, Easter Mon **BAR MEALS:** L served all week 12-3 D served all week 6-7 Av main course £10 **RESTAURANT:** L served Mon-Sat 12-3 D served Mon-Sat 7-11 Av 3 course à la carte £28.50
BREWERY/COMPANY: ◖: Courage Directors, John Smiths.
FACILITIES: Children welcome

The Crown at Chelsea ♀ NEW — Map A1
153 Dovehouse St, Chelsea SW3 6LB
☎ 020 7352 9505 ▤ 020 7352 9535
Dir: Just off Fulham Road, beside Royal Marsden Hospital
Traditional London pub which has been recently refurbished, located between the Royal Marsden and Brompton Hospitals. Popular with locals including celebrities and musicians who live in the area, it is known for its quality food and real ales. Big bites include lemon chicken supreme, and Hawaiian gammon, while lighter snacks come in the guise of filled potato skins, and baked potatoes. Daily specials also served.
OPEN: 11-11 (Sun 12-10.30) **BAR MEALS:** L served Mon-Fri 12-3 D served Mon-Fri 6-9 Av main course £6.95 **RESTAURANT:** 12-2.30
BREWERY/COMPANY: Whitbread ◖: Adnams Best, Fullers London Pride. ♀: 8

The Phene Arms — Map B1
Phene St, Chelsea SW3 5NY ☎ 020 7352 3294 ▤ 020 7352 7026
Dir: Nearest tubes: Sloane Square & South Kensington
Hidden away down a quiet Chelsea cul-de-sac, a short stroll from The Embankment, this welcoming neighbourhood pub has a charming roof terrace and large garden for summer alfresco eating. Food options range from Jerusalem salad, burgers and Cumberland sausage through to oven-baked cod and fillet steak.
OPEN: 11-11 (Sun 12-10.30) **BAR MEALS:** L served all week 12-3 D served all week 6-10 Av main course £6.95 **RESTAURANT:** L served all week 12-3 D served all week 6-10 Av 3 course à la carte £15
BREWERY/COMPANY: Free House ◖: Adnams Bitter Broadside, Courage Best & Directors, Greene King Old Speckled Hen, Fullers London Pride. **FACILITIES:** Children welcome Garden Dogs allowed

SW4

The Belle Vue — Map GtL E3
1 Clapham Common Southside SW4 7AA
☎ 0207 498 9473 ▤ 0207 627 0716
Overlooking Clapham Common, the Belle Vue is a popular dining-pub that provides a relaxing atmosphere for enjoyment

continued

of its bistro-style food. Comfortable sofas, scrubbed wood panelling and modern art around the walls are the setting for daily dishes posted on chalkboards: lamb shank with winter vegetables, perhaps, or roast cod with scallop gratin.
OPEN: 11-11 (Sun 12-10.30) Closed: 4-5 days at Xmas
BAR MEALS: L served all week 12.30-4 D served all week 6.30-10.30 Av main course £8 **BREWERY/COMPANY:** Free House
◖: Harveys Sussex Ale, Boddingtons.

The Coach & Horses NEW — Map GtL E3
173 Clapham Park Rd SW4 7EX
☎ 020 7622 3815 ▤ 020 7622 3832
e-mail: info@barbeerian-inns.com
Despite its city location, this attractive coaching inn feels like a country pub. It draws a wide clientele, from the old man in the corner to trendy young professionals. Good roast dinners make it particularly busy on Sundays, whilst Saturday is barbeque day. Wholesome home-cooked pub grub includes steak and ale pie, salmon with herb mash, wilted spinach and dill sauce, and sticky toffee pudding.
OPEN: 11-11 (Sun 12-10.30) Closed: 25-26 Dec **BAR MEALS:** L served all week 12.30-2.30 D served all week 6-9.30 Av main course £7.50 ◖: Fullers London Pride, Tetleys, Adnams.
FACILITIES: Garden: Large patio in front of pub seats 64 Dogs allowed Water bowls

The Royal Oak ◌ ♀ NEW — Map GtL E3
8-10 Clapham High St SW4 7UT
Dir: Telephone for directions
Set in the heart of Clapham, the Royal Oak is a traditional London pub that includes the modern tradition of a large screen TV for sporting events, and a funky gastro-pub interior that belies its rather drab exterior. A typical menu includes rib of English beef and horseradish, mushroom and tarragon sausage, toad-in-the-hole, and chicken and leek pie.
OPEN: 12 -11 (Sun 12-10.30) **BAR MEALS:** L served all week 12-6 D served all week 6-10.30 Av main course £6.50
BREWERY/COMPANY: ◖: Adnams Broadside, Adnams Bitter.
♀: 8 **FACILITIES:** Children welcome Children's licence Dogs allowed

The Windmill on the Common ★★★ ◌ ♀ Map GtL E2
Clapham Common South Side SW4 9DE
☎ 020 8673 4578 ▤ 020 8675 1486
Dir: Nearest tube: Clapham Common or Clapham South
The windmill on this site in 1655 is long gone, but in more recent times the building has been a popular watering hole for crowds returning from the Epsom Derby. There are two spacious bars, a conservatory and a back room with a roof shaped like a flattened Byzantine dome. Food ranges from filled baguettes and burgers to crab fishcakes, curries and steak and ale pie. There is separate oak-panelled restaurant and hotel accommodation.
OPEN: 11-11 (Sun 12-10.30) **BAR MEALS:** L served all week 12-2.30 D served all week 7-10 Av main course £6 **RESTAURANT:** L served all week 12-2.30 D served all week 7-10
BREWERY/COMPANY: Young & Co ◖: Youngs Bitter, Special, Winter Warmer. ♀: 20 **FACILITIES:** Children welcome Children's licence Garden: Benches, seats approx 50, garden bar Dogs allowed Water bowl **NOTES:** Parking 16 **ROOMS:** 29 bedrooms 29 en suite s£99 d£115

SW6

Pick of the Pubs

The Atlas ♀ — Map GtL D3
16 Seagrave Rd, Fulham SW6 1RX
☎ 020 7385 9129 📠 020 7386 9113
e-mail: atlas@ogh.demon.co.uk
Dir: 2mins walk from West Brompton underground
In an area where so many former pubs have become
diners or restaurants, here is an establishment that remains
true to its cause. The large bar area - divided into drinking
and eating parts - attracts what in a rural village would be
called outsiders, but to be a local round here you can even
come from Chelsea, Hammersmith or Earl's Court. Mostly
Mediterranean dishes - particularly from Italy, Spain,
France and North Africa - on a twice-daily changing menu.
Lunch is always soup, pasta, risotto, sandwiches and some
main meals. Dinner menus feature risotto or pasta, tapas
or antipasti, and usually two fish, a chicken or game, and
two other meat main dishes. Sicilian beef casserole, and
pan-roast lamb chop with chickpea tagine are typical. Fresh
produce comes daily from the markets and the global wine
list is updated regularly. Relatively few inner city pubs have
a walled beer garden, but there's one here.
OPEN: 12-11 (Sun 12-10) Closed: Dec 24-Jan 1, Easter
BAR MEALS: L served all week 12.30-3 D served all week 7-10.30
Av main course £9.50 **BREWERY/COMPANY:** Free House
🍺: Wells Bombardier, Fuller's London Pride, Brakspear. ♀: 12
FACILITIES: Children welcome Garden: Lrg suntrap, heaters, awning

The Imperial Arms ♀ — Map B1
577 Kings Rd SW6 2EH ☎ 020 7736 8549 📠 020 7731 3780
e-mail: imperial@fulham.co.uk
Dir: Telephone for directions
Mid 19th-century food pub in one of London's most famous
and fashionable streets, with a paved terrace at the back.
Vibrant and spacious inside, with wooden floors, striking
features, and a lively and varied clientele. A selection of
pizzas, sandwiches, salads, and burgers feature on the
popular menu. Look out for the wild boar sausage with
bubble and squeak.
OPEN: 11-11 Closed: BHs **BAR MEALS:** L served all week 12-2.30
D served Mon-Fri 7-9.30 Av main course £6
BREWERY/COMPANY: Free House 🍺: Wells Bombardier,
Haggard's Imperial Best Bitter. ♀: 8 **FACILITIES:** Garden: Paving,
seven benches, plants, lights Dogs allowed

Pick of the Pubs

The White Horse ♀ — Map A1
1-3 Parson's Green, Fulham SW6 4UL
☎ 020 7736 2115 📠 020 7610 6091
e-mail: inn@whitehorsesw6.com
Dir: 140 mtrs from Parson's Green tube
The rich history of the coaching inn that has stood on this
site since at least 1688 has been well documented. The
inn has advanced impressively since then, with its
polished mahogany bar and wall panels, open fires and
contemporary art on the walls. A large modern kitchen is
behind the imaginative, good value meals served in the
bar and Coach House restaurant. For lunch, you might try
basil-infused seared tuna with Greek salad, or pork
sausages with mash, summer cabbage and beer onion

gravy. In the evening starters like chilli-salt squid with a
red pepper and tomato salsa, might precede duck confit
with truffled mushroom and herb risotto, or braised lamb
shank with preserved lemon couscous. Every dish from
the starters through to the desserts comes with a
recommended beer or wine, and the choice of both is
considerable.
OPEN: 11-11 (Sun 12-10.30) **BAR MEALS:** L served all week
12-3.30 D served all week 6-10.30 Av main course £10.25
RESTAURANT: L served all week 12-3.30 D served all week 6-11
Av 3 course à la carte £22.50 🍺: Adnams Broadside, Interbrew
Bass, Harveys Sussex Best Bitter, Oakam JHB. ♀: 20
FACILITIES: Children welcome Garden: 80 seats in front of pub
overlooking Green

SW7

The Anglesea Arms ♀ — Map A1
15 Selwood Ter, South Kensington SW7 3QG
☎ 020 7373 7960 📠 020 73705611
Dir: Telephone for directions
This South Kensington pub is one of very few privately-owned
free houses in West London. Its interior is little changed since
1827, though the added-on dining area has proved a popular
addition. The style is clubby with panelled walls and leather-
clad chairs. Recent change of hands.
OPEN: 11-11 (Sun 12-10.30) Closed: Xmas pm only
BAR MEALS: L served all week 12-3 D served all week 6.30-10 Av
main course £9 **RESTAURANT:** L served all week 12-3 D served all
week 6.30-10 Av 3 course à la carte £17
BREWERY/COMPANY: Free House 🍺: Fuller's London Pride,
Brakspear Bitter, Youngs Special, Adnams Bitter. ♀: 10
FACILITIES: Children welcome Garden: Terrace at front and side of
the pub Dogs allowed Water

Pick of the Pubs

Swag and Tails 🏵 🐾 ♀ — Map B2
10/11 Fairholt St SW7 1EG
☎ 020 7584 6926 📠 020 7581 9935
e-mail: swag&tails@mway.com
See Pick of the Pubs on opposite page

SW8

The Artesian Well 🐾 ♀ — Map GtL E3
SW8 3JF ☎ 020 7627 3353 📠 020 7627 2850
e-mail: max@artesianwell.co.uk
Near Clapham Common, this Italian bar and eatery has a very
eccentric interior, with a fireplace as the open mouth of a
huge bearded face, and a glass skylight forming part of the
floor of the Moody Room and also the ceiling of the bar. Live
music is a weekly feature, with open mics on Mondays
(acoustic) and Wednesdays (electrified) and a DJ every Friday
and Saturday. The menu is wholly Italian, with dishes such as
bistecca artesiana, timballo vegetariano, and scaloppine alla
principessa.
OPEN: 12-3 6-11 **BAR MEALS:** L served all week 12-3 D served
Tues-Sat 6-8 Av main course £10.95 **RESTAURANT:** L served all
week 12-4 D served Tues-Sat 6-11 Av 3 course à la carte £19.90 Av 2
course fixed price £15.90 🍺: Scottish Courage John Smith's.
FACILITIES: Children welcome

continued

OPEN: Mon-Fri 11-11 (closed wknds)
CLOSED: All Bank Holidays
BAR MEALS: L served Mon-Fri 12-3,
D served Mon-Fri 6-10.
Av main course £10.50
RESTAURANT: L served Mon-Fri 12-3,
D served Mon-Fri 6-10.
Av cost 3 courses £25
BREWERY/COMPANY:
Free House.
🍺: Marston's Pedigree, Charles Wells
Bombardier Premium Bitter, Scottish
Courage John Smiths Smooth
FACILITIES: Dogs allowed (evenings
only), Children welcome

Swag and Tails

Tucked well away from the hustle and bustle of Knightsbridge, the Swag and Tails is a civilised retreat with warm, friendly service and modern pub food cooked to restaurant standards. The pretty, flower-decked Victorian pub sits in a tiny back street just a two-minute stroll from Harrods.

10/11 Fairholt Street, London,
SW7 1EG
☎ 020 7584 6926 📠 020 7581 9935
✉ swag&tails@mway.com
Dir: Nearest tube: Knightsbridge

Over the last fourteen years, owners Annemaria and Stuart Boomer-Davies have created a successful and welcoming neighbourhood pub-restaurant with a discerning local trade. Good quality food is served in a warm, relaxing and civilised environment, with high standards of cleanliness and presentation. Open fires, original panelling and pine tables complement the stripped wooden floors, whilst the windows with their attractive 'swag and tailed' curtains set the scene in which to savour freshly-prepared seasonal dishes, inspired by Mediterranean cuisine. You can just pop in for a pint of Wells Bombardier and peruse the daily papers over a decent steak sandwich at the bar, or look to the interesting and constantly-changing blackboard menu for something more substantial. Adventurous starters like pan-seared foie gras with rhubarb jam, and monkfish brandade sit alongside the more simple rocket salad with chargrilled red onions, Caesar salad, and sweetcorn and spring onion broth. There are main courses for every taste, from a classic burger in a sesame bap with shoestring fries, through roast fillet of sea bass with tartar crushed potatoes, lobster bisque and rocket, to roast breast of duck with chilli noodles, choi sum, sesame roast cucumber, and a shitake mushroom broth. Round off the meal with Morello cherry sorbet, steamed chocolate and pecan sponge or a selection of English cheeses with pear and date chutney. A decent wine list with tasting notes features a dozen wines by the glass - including champagne.

England

SW8 continued

The Masons Arms 🐖 🍷 Map GtL E3
169 Battersea Park Rd SW8 4BT
☎ 020 7622 2007 📠 020 7622 4662
e-mail: themasonsarms@ukonline.co.uk
Dir: Opposite Battersea Park BR Station
More a neighbourhood local with tempting food than a
gastro-pub, the worn wooden floors and tables support
refreshingly delightful staff and honest, modern cuisine. Here
you'll find a warm and welcoming atmosphere, equally suited
for a quiet romantic dinner or partying with friends. Open
fires in winter and a summer dining terrace. Daily-changing
menus feature wasabi salmon cake, pan-fried blackened tuna,
or spinach and duck spring roll.
OPEN: 12-11 BAR MEALS: L served all week 12-3.30 D served all
week 6-10 Av main course £8.50 RESTAURANT: 12-4 6-10 Av 3
course à la carte £15 BREWERY/COMPANY: Free House
🍺: Adnams, Flowers Original, IPA, Boddingtons.
FACILITIES: Children welcome Garden: Food served outdoors,
patio/terrace Dogs allowed

SW10

Pick of the Pubs

The Chelsea Ram 🍷 Map GtL E3
32 Burnaby St SW10 0PL ☎ 020 7351 4008 📠 020 73490885
e-mail: chelsearam@establishment.ltd.uk
Dir: Nearest tube - Earls Court
A busy neighbourhood gastro-pub located just off the
beaten track close to Chelsea Harbour and Lots Road. It
offers a distinct emphasis on fresh produce, including
market fish and meat from Smithfield. The set monthly
menu has a manifestly modern flavour, exemplified by
interesting and eclectic starters like crispy Thai duck salad,
and ballotine of chicken with pancetta and artichokes.
Main dishes, which include special market selections from
the blackboard, range from braised lamb shanks with
olive oil mash, Chelsea Ram salad with grilled chicken,
bacon avocado and sour cream dressing, and bangers
and mash with roast field mushrooms and spinach. Wild
mushroom risotto is suitable for vegetarians, while
Sunday roasts might finish with puddings like glazed
lemon tart with lemon sorbet, and caramelised pineapple
with raspberry and mint sorbet. Other pubs in the same
ownership are the Thatched House at Hammersmith, and
the Fox and Hounds off Sloane Square.
OPEN: 11-11 (Sun 12-10.30) BAR MEALS: L served all week
12-3 D served all week 7-10 Av main course £9
RESTAURANT: L served all week 12-3 D served all week 7-10
BREWERY/COMPANY: Young & Co 🍺: Youngs Bitter, Special
& Winter Warmer. 🍷: 16

The Sporting Page 🍷 Map A1
6 Camera Place SW10 0BH ☎ 020 7349 0455 📠 020 7352 8162
e-mail: sportingpage@frontpagepubs.com
Dir: Telephone for directions
Smart Chelsea pub offering good quality food - modern
British and European - with friendly service. Popular with
Chelsea fans meeting up before heading off to Stamford
Bridge. If you don't have a ticket, you can still watch the
action on the large screen TV. Menu includes Cumberland
sausages, pie of the day, lamb shank with new potatoes, and
The Sporting Page Burger. Reasonable wine list.

OPEN: 11-11 (Sun 12-10.30) Closed: 25-26 Dec BAR MEALS: L
served all week 12-2.30 D served Mon-Fri 7-10
BREWERY/COMPANY: Front Page Pubs Ltd 🍺: Shepherd Neame
Spitfire Premium Ale, Charles wells Bombardier, Fuller London Pride.
FACILITIES: Children welcome Garden: terrace Dogs allowed

SW11

The Castle 🍷 Map GtL E3
115 Battersea High St SW11 3HS
☎ 020 7228 8181 📠 020 7924 5887
Dir: Nearest tube - Clapham Junction
Built in the mid-1960s to replace an older coaching inn, this
ivy-covered pub tucked away in 'Battersea Village', has rugs
and rustic furnishings on bare boards inside, and an outside
enclosed patio garden. A typical menu offers fresh salmon
and dill fishcakes, Parma ham-wrapped chicken breast stuffed
with Brie, avocado and spring onion, Cajun chicken sandwich,
organic lamb steak, herb pancakes with leek, Gorgonzola and
mushroom, and fresh swordfish steak with avocado salsa.
OPEN: 12-11 (Sun 12-10.30) Closed: 25-26 Dec BAR MEALS: L
served all week 12-3 D served all week 7-9.45 Av main course £8
BREWERY/COMPANY: Young & Co 🍺: Youngs Bitter & Special,
Goddard's Winter Warmer. 🍷: 13 FACILITIES: Children welcome
Dogs allowed NOTES: Parking 6

Duke of Cambridge 🍷 Map GtL E3
228 Battersea Bridge Rd SW11 3AA
☎ 020 7223 5662 📠 020 7801 9684
e-mail: info@geronimo-inns.co.uk
An award-winning community pub with an eclectic mix of
locals and just a stone's throw from Battersea Park and two of
London's most famous Thames crossings - Battersea Bridge
and Albert Bridge. Popular Saturday brunch menu and
traditional Sunday roasts. The interesting range of dishes
includes chicken and leek pie with Irish champ, confit of duck
on fondant potato jus, asparagus and wild mushroom risotto
and saffron-infused fillet of red mullet with marinated roast
pepper couscous.
OPEN: 11-11 (Sun 12-10.30) BAR MEALS: L served all week 12-
2.30 D served all week 7-9.45 Av main course £9 RESTAURANT: L
served all week 12-2.30 D served all week 7-9.45 Av 3 course à la
carte £16 BREWERY/COMPANY: Young & Co 🍺: Youngs Bitter &
Special. FACILITIES: Children welcome Dogs allowed Garden: Beer
garden, patio, food served outdoors, BBQ

The Fox & Hounds 🍷 Map GtL E3
66 Latchmere Rd, Battersea SW11 2JU
☎ 020 7924 5483 📠 020 7738 2678
e-mail: richardmanners@ogh.demon.co.uk
Dir: Nearest startion is Clapham Junction. From the station turn left to go
down St John's Hill then up Lavender Hill. Turn left at the first set of traffic
lights down Latchmere Road. Pub is 200 yards on the left
A late 19th-century pub, restored rather than refurbished,
with a walled garden, extensive patio planting and a new
covered and heated seating area. Fresh, best quality
ingredients are delivered daily from London's markets, and
the Mediterranean-style menu changes accordingly. There are
a few starters/snacks, half a dozen main dishes, one cheese
and one pudding. Typical offerings: smoked salmon
bruschetta, Catalan beef casserole with parsley-mashed
potatoes, and a chocolate, hazelnut and sherry cake with
raisin cream.
OPEN: 12-3 5-11 (Sat 12-11, Sun 12-10.30, Mon 5-11) Closed: Easter
Day, 24 Dec- 01 Jan BAR MEALS: L served Tue-Sun 12.30-3 D
served all week 7-10.30 Av main course £10

continued

continued

BREWERY/COMPANY: Free House 🍺: Interbrew Bass, Greene King IPA, Fullers London Pride. ♀: 12 **FACILITIES:** Children welcome Garden: Walled garden, covered area with heaters Dogs allowed

SW13

The Bull's Head 🛏️ ♀   Map GtL D3
373 Lonsdale Rd, Barnes SW13 9PY
☎ 020 8876 5241 🖥 020 8876 1546
e-mail: jazz@thebullshead.com
Established in 1684, overlooking the Thames, the Bull has made its reputation over the last 40 years as a top venue for mainstream, modern jazz and blues. Nightly concerts draw music lovers from miles around encouraged by some fine cask-conditioned ales, more than 200 wines, and over 80 malt whiskies. Traditional, home-cooked meals are on offer in the bar, and from the Nuay Thai Bistro in the converted stable, fine Thai cooking is available throughout the pub in the evening.
OPEN: 11-11 (Sun 12-10.30) **BAR MEALS:** L served all week 12-3 D served all week 6-11 Av main course £5 **RESTAURANT:** D served all week 6-11 Av 3 course à la carte £14
BREWERY/COMPANY: Young & Co 🍺: Young's Special, Winter Warmer. **FACILITIES:** Children welcome Garden: Patio, food served outside Dogs allowed

The Old Sergeant 🛏️ ♀ NEW   Map GtL D2
104 Garrett Ln, Wandsworth SW18 4DJ
☎ 020 8874 4099 🖥 020 8874 4099
Traditional, friendly and oozing with character, The Old Sergeant enjoys a good reputation for its beers, but also offers some good malt whiskies and up to 15 different wines. It a good place to enjoy home-cooked food too: the menu could include soup, home-made burgers, steaks and light bites including sandwiches and rolls.
OPEN: 11-11 (12-10.30 Sun) **BAR MEALS:** L served Mon-Fri 12-3 D served Mon-Fri 5-9 Av main course £5 **RESTAURANT:** L served Mon-Fri D served Mon-Fr **BREWERY/COMPANY:** Youngs 🍺: Youngs Ordinary, Youngs Special, Winter Warmer, Light Ales. ♀: 15 **FACILITIES:** Children welcome Children's licence Dogs allowed Guide dogs only **NOTES:** Parking 20

The Ship Inn ♀   Map GtL E3
Jew's Row SW18 1TB ☎ 020 8870 9667 🖥 020 8874 9055
e-mail: drinks@theship.co.uk
Dir: *Wandsworth Town BR station nearby*
Situated next to Wandsworth Bridge on the Thames, the Ship exudes a lively, bustling atmosphere. Saloon bar and

continued

extended conservatory area lead out to a large beer garden and in the summer months an outside bar is open for business. There is a popular restaurant, and all-day food is chosen from a single menu, with the emphasis on free-range produce from the landlord's organic farm. Expect the likes of lamb cutlets, chargrilled marlin fillet, shepherds pie, and peppers stuffed with hazelnuts and goats cheese.
OPEN: 11-11 (Sun 12-10.30) **BAR MEALS:** L served all week 12-10 D served all week 7-10.30 Av main course £11.50 **RESTAURANT:** L served all week 12-10.30 D served all week Av 3 course à la carte £17
BREWERY/COMPANY: Young & Co 🍺: Youngs:PA, SPA, Triple A, Waggle Dance. **FACILITIES:** Garden: Food served outside Dogs allowed Water provided

SW19

The Brewery Tap NEW   Map GtL D2
68-69 High St, Wimbledon SW19 5EE ☎ 020 8947 9331
e-mail: thebrewerytap@hotmail.com
The closest pub to the Wimbledon tennis championships, and popular with players as well as fans. This welcoming open-plan pub is also often used as a backdrop for episodes of The Bill. Various guest beers from micro-breweries are served along with a choice of 'doorstep sarnies' and award-winning sausages at lunchtime, and fish and chips on Monday evenings. The only other evening food is the tapas bar on Wednesdays.
OPEN: 11-11 (Sun 11-10.30, 25 Dec 12-2) **BAR MEALS:** L served all week 11-2.30 D served Mon, Wed 6-10 Av main course £6
BREWERY/COMPANY: Enterprise Inns 🍺: Fuller's London Pride, Adnams, Guest Beers. **FACILITIES:** Dogs allowed Water

W1

The Argyll Arms   Map C4
18 Argyll St, Oxford Circus W1F 7TP ☎ 020 7734 6117
Dir: *Nearest tube - Oxford Circus*
A tavern has stood on this site since 1740, but the present building is mid-Victorian and is notable for its stunning floral displays. There's a popular range of sandwiches and the hot food menu might offer vegetarian moussaka, beef and Guinness pie, chicken and leek pie, haddock and lasagne.
OPEN: 11-11 (Sun 12-9) Closed: 25 Dec **BAR MEALS:** L served all week 11-3 D served Mon-Sat Av main course £5.95
BREWERY/COMPANY: 🍺: Tetley, Bass, Fullers London Pride, Greene King IPA.

BAR BILLIARDS

The ingenious blend of billiards and skittles is a relative newcomer to the pub scene. It was introduced here from Belgium in the 1930s, with support from billiard table manufacturers. The game caught on rapidly, especially in the South and Midlands, and leagues had been organised by the time the Second World War began. Its much more recent rival is pool, which came here from America in the 1960s in the wake of the Paul Newman film The Hustler.

England

W1 continued

French House 𝒴   Map D4
49 Dean St, Soho W1D 5BG ☎ 020 7437 2799 ▤ 020 7287 9109
Notable for its custom of only serving half pints of beer, this
small Bohemian bar holds an annual 'Pint Day' in aid of the
NSPCC. The bar remains much as it was in the 1950s, when it
was popular with writers, artists and actors - Brendan Behan,
Dylan Thomas and Francis Bacon to name but a few. Weekly-
changing menus might feature navarin of lamb, roast
monkfish with Parma ham, confit of duck with braised lentils
and red cabbage, or risotto of roast pumpkin.
OPEN: 11-11 (Sun 12-9) Closed: 25 Dec **BAR MEALS:** L served all
week 11-3 D served Mon-Sat **RESTAURANT:** L served all week 12-3
D served Mon-Sat 5.30-11.30 **BREWERY/COMPANY:** ◖: Tetley,
Bass, Fullers London Pride, Greene King IPA.

The Glassblower   Map D3
42 Glasshouse St W1V 5JY ☎ 020 7734 8547 ▤ 020 7494 1049
Ideally placed for visiting the shops and theatres, this wine bar
is in the heart of the West End.
OPEN: 11-11 (Sun 12-10.30) Closed: 25 Dec **BAR MEALS:** L
served all week 12 D served all week 8 Av main course £5.45
BREWERY/COMPANY: Scottish Courage ◖: Theakston Best,
Pedigree. **FACILITIES:** Children welcome

Red Lion 🐾   Map C3
No 1 Waverton St, Mayfair W1X 5QN
☎ 020 7499 1307 ▤ 020 7409 7752
e-mail: gregpeck@redlionmayfair.co.uk
Dir: Nearest tube - Green Park
Built in 1752, The Red Lion is one of Mayfair's most historic
pubs. Originally used mainly by 18th-century builders, the
clientele is now more likely to be the rich and famous of
Mayfair, yet the friendly welcome remains. The pub was used
as a location in the recent Brad Pitt and Robert Redford
movie, 'Spy Game'. The bar menu has a traditional pub feel,
offering the likes of steak and Stilton pie, Cumberland
sausage, chicken masala, rack of pork ribs, and steak
sandwich.
OPEN: 11.30-11.20 Closed: 25-26 Dec, 1 Jan **BAR MEALS:** L
served all week 12-2.30 D served all week 6-9.45 Av main course £7
RESTAURANT: L served all week 12-2.30 D served all week 6-9.45
BREWERY/COMPANY: ◖: Greene King IPA, Scottish Courage Best
& Directors. **FACILITIES:** Children welcome

Zebrano   Map C3
14-16 Gantan St W1V 1LB ☎ 020 7287 5267 ▤ 020 7287 2729
e-mail: info@freedombrew.com
Dir: 5 min walk from Oxford Circus Tube, the micro brew bar is half way
down Carnaby Street
The second of the Fulham-based Freedom Brewing
Company's new micro-brew bars, this popular watering hole
opened in 1999, taking advantage of the growing demand for
fresh, hand-crafted beer. The bar sells a range of six ales
made on the premises, as well as offering a varied choice of
freshly-prepared salads, sandwiches, tortilla wraps and main
dishes. Expect fish and chips, baked chicken with steamed
greens, Thai spiced mussels, and lamb steak with grilled
vegetables.
OPEN: 11-11 (Thu-Sat 11-12) Closed: 25-26 Dec, 1 Jan
BAR MEALS: L served Mon-Sat 12-5 D served Mon-Sat 6-10 Av
main course £6.50 **BREWERY/COMPANY:** ◖: Freedom Beers.

W2

Pick of the Pubs

The Cow Saloon Bar & Dining Rooms 🐾 𝒴
     Map GtL D4
89 Westbourne Park Rd W2 5QH
☎ 020 7221 5400 ▤ 020 7727 8687
e-mail: thecow@thecow.freeserve.co.uk
Dir: Nearest tubes - Royal Oak & Westbourne Park
Once known as the Railway Tavern, but reputedly renamed
after a former landlady with an attitude problem. Maybe a
more plausible reason is that drovers and their livestock
once trudged by near here as they headed east to London's
Smithfield Market. Whatever the true derivation, the Cow's
reputation for an enterprising approach to food stands firm,
its slogan being 'Eat heartily, and give the house a good
name'. The menu is strong on fish and seafood, with rock
and native oysters, crab chowder, Catalan fish stew and
kedgeree. Meat lovers can go for braised oxtails with mash,
cassoulet with confit of duck, and fillet of Angus beef with
cep mushrooms and rösti potato. Try to arrive early to get
the table of your choice - ideally in the upper dining room -
as the place can get very busy. It serves Fuller's beers on
tap and some fairly-priced wines.
OPEN: 12-11 Closed: 25 Dec **BAR MEALS:** L served all week
12.00-3.30 D served all week 6.00-10.30 Av main course £8
RESTAURANT: L served Sat-Sun 12.30-3.30 D served all week 6.30-
10.30 Av 3 course à la carte £35 **BREWERY/COMPANY:** Free
House ◖: Fuller's ESB & London Pride. 𝒴: 10

The Prince Bonaparte 𝒴   Map GtL D4
80 Chepstow Rd W2 5BE ☎ 020 7313 9491 ▤ 020 7792 0911
A first-generation gastro pub where Johnny Vaughan filmed the
Strongbow ads. Renowned for its bloody Marys, good music
and quick, friendly service, the pub proves popular with young
professionals and has DJ nights on Fridays and Saturdays. The
building is Victorian, with an airy and open plan interior. Typical
meals include sausages and mash, tomato and Mozzarella
bruschetta, sea bass with spinach, and spicy chicken gnocchi.
OPEN: 12-11 12-10.30 Closed: 25-26 Dec, 1 Jan **BAR MEALS:**
L served all week 12.30-3 D served all week 6.30-10 Av main course
£8.50 **RESTAURANT:** L served all week 12.30-3 D served all week
6.30-10 Av 3 course à la carte £15 **BREWERY/COMPANY:** Bass
◖: Fullers London Pride, Cafferys. 𝒴: 13 **FACILITIES:** Children
welcome Dogs allowed On a leash only

The Westbourne 𝒴   Map GtL D4
101 Westbourne Park Villas W2 5ED
☎ 020 7221 1332 ▤ 020 7243 8081
Classic Notting Hill pub/restaurant favoured by a Bohemian
clientele, including a sprinkling of celebrities. Sunny terrace is
very popular in summer. Tempting, twice-daily-changing menu
is listed on a board behind the bar and might include pot
roasted pheasant with bacon, shallots, oyster mushrooms,
garlic mash and winter greens; chargrilled red mullet, rocket,
olives, roasted fennel, charlotte potatoes and olive oil; or
baked filo roll with butternut squash.
OPEN: 11-11 (Mon 5.30-1 only, Sun 12-10.30) Closed: 24 Dec-5 Jan
BAR MEALS: L served Tue-Sun 12.30-3.30 D served all week 7-9.30
Av main course £11 **RESTAURANT:** L served all week 12.30-3.30 D
served all week 7-9.30 Av 3 course à la carte £20
BREWERY/COMPANY: Free House ◖: Interbrew Boddingtons,
Greene King Old Speckled Hen. **FACILITIES:** Garden: Large
forecourt with tables & chairs Dogs allowed Water

W4

The Pilot NEW
Map GtL C3
56 Wellesley Rd W4 4BZ ☎ 020 8994 0828 🖷 020 8994 2785
e-mail: the.pilotpub@ukonline.co.uk
Dir: Telephone for directions
A large garden makes this Chiswick pub a real winner,
especially in summer, while indoors the atmosphere is always
friendly and welcoming. Food is taken seriously here, and the
menu runs along the lines of starters like terrine of foie gras,
chestnut mushrooms, pork, sage and apple with gooseberry
chutney and toast, followed by rare grilled steak with parsley
mash, wild mushrooms, salsify and horseradish cream.
OPEN: 12-11 (Sun 12.00-10.30) Closed: 25-26 Dec **BAR MEALS:** L
served Mon-Sun 12-3.30 D served Mon-Sun 6.30-10 Av main course
£8.50 **RESTAURANT:** L served all week 12-3.30 D served all week
6.30-22 Av 3 course à la carte £18 🍺: Stella Artois, Heineken,
Adnams, Staropramen. **FACILITIES:** Garden: Large garden, capacity
for 60 seated

W5

The Red Lion 🍷 NEW
Map GtL C3
13 St Mary's Rd, Ealing W5 5RA
Dir: Telephone for directions
The pub opposite the old Ealing Studios, the Red Lion is
affectionately known as the 'Stage Six' (the studios have five),
and has a unique collection of film stills celebrating the Ealing
comedies of the 50s. Recent sympathetic refurbishment has
broadened the pub's appeal and the location by Ealing Green
has a leafy, almost rural feel, plus there's an award-winning
walled garden. Pub food ranges through oysters, burgers,
bangers and mash, and fillet steak.
OPEN: 11-11 Sun (12-10.30) **BAR MEALS:** L served all week 12-
2.30 D served Mon-Sat 7-9.30 Av main course £8.50
BREWERY/COMPANY: Fullers 🍺: Fullers London Pride, Chiswick,
ESB. 🍷: 50 **FACILITIES:** Garden: Walled Garden, can seat 60 Dogs
allowed Water

The Wheatsheaf 🍷
Map GtL C4
41 Haven Ln, Ealing W5 2HZ ☎ 020 8997 5240
Dir: 1m from A40 junction with North Circular
Just a few minutes from Ealing Broadway, this large Victorian
pub has a rustic appearance inside. Ideal place to enjoy a big
screen sporting event or a warm drink among wooden floors,
panelled walls, beams from an old barn, and real fires in
winter. Trad pub grub includes cottage pie, beer-battered cod
and chips, steak, ale and mushroom pie, pork and leek
sausage and mash, and vegetable lasagne.
OPEN: 11-11 (Sun 12-10.30) **BAR MEALS:** L served all week 12-9
D served Mon-Sat Av main course £5.25
BREWERY/COMPANY: Fullers 🍺: Fullers London Pride, ESB &
Chiswick, Seasonal ales. 🍷: 10 **FACILITIES:** Children welcome
Garden: Side alleyway Dogs allowed

W6

Pick of the Pubs

Anglesea Arms ⌾ 🍷
Map GtL D3
35 Wingate Rd W6 0UR ☎ 020 8749 1291 🖷 020 8749 1254
e-mail: Fievans@aol.com
Real fires and a relaxed, smokey atmosphere are all part
of the attraction at this traditional corner pub. Behind the
Georgian façade the decor is basic but welcoming, and
the place positively hums with people eagerly seeking out
the highly reputable food. A range of simple, robust
dishes might include starters like pigeon, duck and foie
gras terrine, Anglesea charcuterie platter, or butternut
squash and goats' curd risotto. Among main courses
could be slow-cooked belly of pork, Brittany 'Cotriade' fish
stew, pot-roast stuffed saddle of lamb, and toasted sea
bass with saffron potatoes. Puddings are also exemplary:
expect poached pear, brandy snap and pear sorbet,
chocolate, pecan and hazelnut 'brownie' cake with vanilla
ice cream, or perhaps buttermilk pudding with pineapple
and almond biscotti. A savoury alternative might be
Cornish yarm with chutney and water biscuits.
OPEN: 11-11 (Sun 12-10.30) Closed: 24-31 Dec
BAR MEALS: L served all week 12.30-2.45 D served all week
7.30-10.45 Av main course £8.95 **RESTAURANT:** L served all
week 12.30-2.45 D served all week 7.30-10.45 Av 3 course à la
carte £18 Av 3 course fixed price £12.95
BREWERY/COMPANY: Free House 🍺: Scottish Courage
Courage Best, Greene King Old Speckled Hen, Fuller's London
Pride. 🍷: 15 **FACILITIES:** Children welcome

The Stonemasons Arms 🍷
Map GtL D3
54 Cambridge Grove W6 0LA ☎ 020 8748 1397 🖷 020 8748 6086
A trendy yet welcoming London gastro-pub with warm
wooden floors and trestle tables, serving "modern, but honest
British cuisine." Sample such delights as coriander and corn
pancakes, Cumberland sausages with mash and onion gravy,
grilled blackened tuna on sweet potato and roast garlic
ragout, spinach and duck spring roll on pak choi, and stuffed
chicken breast with goats cheese and beetroot on parsnip
mash.
OPEN: 12-11 (Sun 12-10.30) Closed: Dec 25, Jan 1 **BAR MEALS:** L
served all week 12-3 D served all week 6.30-10 Av main course £9
RESTAURANT: L served all week 12-4 D served all week 6-10 Av 3
course à la carte £15 **BREWERY/COMPANY:** Free House
🍺: Adnams, Flowers Original. **FACILITIES:** Children welcome
Garden: Food served outdoors

Pick of the Pubs

The Thatched House 🍷
Map GtL D3
115 Dalling Rd W6 0ET ☎ 020 87486174 🖷 020 8563 2735
e-mail: thatchedhouse@establishment.ltd.uk
This newly sister pub to the Chelsea Ram (qv), the
Thatched House, in a leafy Hammersmith backwater, is
not thatched at all - nor do the Mediterranean-style
features of a 'modern British' menu evoke the English
countryside. Cosmopolitan gastro-pub fare delivers
monthly-changing menus of freshly-prepared modern
dishes. Expect the likes of roasted red pepper soup,
seared scallops with ginger and stir-fried vegetables and
American-style doughnuts with coffee cream and
chocolate sauce. The popular English breakfast salad is
borrowed from Gary Rhodes: grilled black pudding and
sausage with bacon and poached egg on crisp salad
leaves. There is a full range of Youngs' beers on tap plus
some 20 wines-by-glass on the list. The pub also acts as a
gallery for artists as the walls are decorated with paintings
that are for sale.
OPEN: 11-11 (Sun 12-10.30) **BAR MEALS:** L served all week
12-3 D served all week 6-10 Av main course £9
RESTAURANT: L served all week 12-2.30 D served all week 7-10
Av 3 course à la carte £22 **BREWERY/COMPANY:** Young & Co
🍺: Youngs Bitter, Special & Guest beer. **FACILITIES:** Children
welcome Garden: Food served outside Dogs allowed

continued

W8

The Churchill Arms ♀   Map GtL D3
119 Kensington Church St W8 7LN ☎ 020 7727 4242
Dir: Off A40 (Westway). Nearest tube-Notting Hill Gate
Thai food is the speciality at this traditional 200-year-old pub
with strong emphasis on exotic chicken, beef and pork dishes.
Try Thai rice noodles with ground peanuts, spicy sauce and a
choice of pork, chicken or prawns (Kwaitiew Pad Thai), or
special Thai roast duck curry served with rice (Kaeng Ped Phed
Yang). This Oriental feast notwithstanding, the Churchill Arms
has many traditional British aspects including oak beams, log
fires and an annual celebration of Winston Churchill's birthday.
OPEN: 11-11 (Sun 12-10.30) **BAR MEALS:** L served all week 12-
9.30 D served Mon-Sat Av main course £5.85 **RESTAURANT:** L
served all week 12-9.30 D served Mon-Sat Av 1 course fixed price
£5.50 **BREWERY/COMPANY:** Fullers 🍺: Fullers London Pride,
ESB & Chiswick Bitter & seasonal ales. **FACILITIES:** Children
welcome Garden: converted to Conservatory, food served Dogs
allowed (water)

The Windsor Castle ♀ NEW   Map GtL D4
114 Campden Hill Rd W8 7AR ☎ 0207 243 9551
*Dir: From Notting Hill Gate, take south exit towards Holland Park, left
opposite Pharmacy*
Built around 1830, this pub takes its name from the royal castle
which could once be seen from the upper-floor windows.
Unchanged for years, it boasts oak panelling and open fires
and, reputedly, the ghost of Thomas Paine (Rights of Man
author). A good variety of food is served in the bar, from
speciality sausages and mash, to salads, sandwiches, snacks
like half-a-dozen oysters, and lamb with roasted vegetables.
OPEN: 12-11 (Sun 12-10.30) Closed: 25-26 Dec **BAR MEALS:** L
served all week 12-10 D served all week Av main course £8.50
BREWERY/COMPANY: 🍺: Grolsch, Staropramen, Fullers London
Pride, Adnams. ♀: 7 **FACILITIES:** Garden: Walled garden, Ivy
Covered, tables and chairs Dogs allowed Dog Bowl

W10

Golborne House 🐾 ♀   Map GtL D4
36 Golborne Rd W10 5PR ☎ 020 8960 6260 ▤ 020 8960 6961
*Dir: Turn R out of the station onto Ladbroke Grove. Take 1st L and follow
road up to Portobello Rd. Turn L at Portobello Rd and follow road until
Golborne Res. Turn R*
Thriving gastro-pub in a fashionable West London location,
boasting many local celebrity regulars. In addition to the
choice of beers, the pub offers a cocktail menu and a
reasonable wine list, including 10 wines by the glass. Typical
dishes are red mullet and sea bass with bouillabaisse fennel
soup, rouille and croutons, and Buccleuch Estate sirloin steak
with paysanne potatoes, bacon, garlic butter and broccoli.
OPEN: 12-11 (Sat 12-12, Sun 12-10.30) Closed: 25-26 Dec, 1 Jan
BAR MEALS: L served all week 12.30-3.45 D served all week 6.30-
10.15 Av main course £9.95 **RESTAURANT:** L served all week 12.30-
3.45 D served all week 6.30-10.15 Av 3 course à la carte £25
BREWERY/COMPANY: Free House 🍺: Fuller's London Pride.
♀: 10 **FACILITIES:** Children welcome Dogs allowed

The North Pole   Map GtL D4
13-15 North Pole Rd W10 6QH
☎ 020 8964 9384 ▤ 020 8960 3774
e-mail: northpole@massivepub.com
A modern gastro-pub with large windows and a bright decor.
Expect leather sofas, armchairs, daily papers, a good range of
wines by the glass and a lively atmosphere in the bar.
Separate bar and restaurant menus continue to show real
interest, dishes are modern in style and simply described.

'Small Plates' may include seared scallops with pineapple
salsa, chicken Caesar salad and rocket and Parmesan salad.
'Main Flavours' include rib-eye steak with roasted potatoes
and asparagus risotto.
OPEN: 12-11 (Sun 12-10.30) **BAR MEALS:** L served all week 12-4 D
served all week 6-10 Av main course £8.95 **RESTAURANT:** L served
all week 12-10 D served all week **BREWERY/COMPANY:** Free House
🍺: Fullers London Pride, Fosters, Stella Artois, Kronenburg.
FACILITIES: Children welcome Dogs allowed

Pick of the Pubs

Paradise by Way of Kensal Green ♀   Map GtL D4
19 Kilburn Ln, Kensal Rise W10 4AE
☎ 020 8969 0098 ▤ 020 8960 9968
A truly eclectic pub atmosphere with bare boards, bric-à-brac,
oriental tapestries and wrought iron chandeliers creating a
Bohemian setting for working artists, musicians and actors.
The unusual name derives from the last line of G K
Chesterton's poem 'The Rolling English Road', and there are
plenty of original Victorian features in keeping with its late
19th-century origins. The food at this lively venue stands up
well to the demands placed on it by weekly live jazz and
special events like weddings, but don't expect bar snacks or
too much flexibility. The self-styled gastro-pub serves classy
food from the carte, such as Parma ham with rocket and
roasted figs, or crispy-fried squid salsa to start, followed by
monkfish and mussels in a creamy garlic sauce with linguine,
and Moroccan spiced haddock with roast vegetable couscous.
OPEN: 12-11 (Sun 12-10.30) Closed: 25 Dec & Jan 1
BAR MEALS: L served all week 12-4 D served all week 7.30-11 Av
main course £11 **RESTAURANT:** L served all week 12.30-4 D served
all week 7.30-11 Av 3 course à la carte £21 Av 2 course fixed price £18
BREWERY/COMPANY: Free House 🍺: Shepherds Neame
Spitfire. ♀: 8 **FACILITIES:** Children welcome Garden: Courtyard
Dogs allowed Water provided

W11

Pick of the Pubs

The Ladbroke Arms ♀   Map GtL D4
54 Ladbroke Rd W11 3NW
☎ 020 7727 6648 ▤ 020 7727 2127
e-mail: enquiries@ladbrokearms.com
One of London's trendier districts is the location of this
pub, close to Holland Park and fashionable Notting Hill,
renowned for its street market, chic restaurants and film
location image. A broad spectrum of regulars, including the
young well-heeled, is drawn to the chatty atmosphere, and
seating areas which encompassthe popular front courtyard
and a split-level dining area to the rear. The menu changes
daily, and offers imaginative but not outlandish choices:
confit tuna with garlic lentils, soft boiled egg and bottarga,
or prawns wrapped in betel leaves (Miang Gung) to start
perhaps, then linguini with sweet tomato and basil, or pan-
fried salmon with proscuitto, pea and mint risotto. Don't
leave without trying banana cake with mascarpone sorbet
and custard, or blood orange and chocolate parfait.
OPEN: 11-11 Closed: Dec 25 **BAR MEALS:** L served all week
12-2.30 D served all week 7-9.45 Av main course £12.50
RESTAURANT: D served Same as bar
BREWERY/COMPANY: Free House 🍺: Greene King Old
Speckled Hen & Abbot Ale, Fuller's London Pride, Adnams.
FACILITIES: Children welcome Dogs allowed

continued

The Pelican ♀
Map GtL D4

45 All Saints Rd W11 1HE ☎ 020 7792 3073 📠 020 7792 1134
e-mail: thepelican@btconnect.com

Built as a pub in 1869, The Pelican organic pub is spread over two floors and has a ground floor bar with outside seating on All Saints Road. There's a wide choice of real ales and over 50 organic wines; upstairs, the dining room is bright, with a view of the working kitchens. The menu changes twice daily. Typical choices include crab and parsley risotto, grilled swordfish, and roast lamb chump.
OPEN: 12-11 Closed: Dec 25&26 Closed: Mon morning
BAR MEALS: L served all week 12-4 D served all week 6-10 Av main course £7 **RESTAURANT:** L served Tues-Sun 12.30-3 D served all week 6.30-10.30 **BREWERY/COMPANY:** Free House 🍺: Bombardier, plus Guests. **FACILITIES:** Children welcome Dogs allowed

W14

The Cumberland Arms ♀ NEW
Map GtL D3

29 North End Rd, Hammersmith W14 8SZ
☎ 020 7371 6806 📠 020 7371 6848
e-mail: cumberlandarms@ogh.co.uk

Situated close to the Olympia exhibition halls, the blue-painted Cumberland Arms is one of four 'gastro pubs' owned by Richard & George Manners. Old couches, comfy chairs and a piano all add to the relaxed ambience. The menu is changed daily, but reflects a strong Mediterranean influence. Try the bream with couscous salad, or the Portuguese seafood stew as a main dish, with star anise and chocolate cake mousse to finish.
OPEN: Closed: 23 Dec-2 Jan **BAR MEALS:** L served all week 12.30-3 D served all week 7-10.30 Av main course £6.50
RESTAURANT: L served all week 12.30-3 D served all week 7-10.30 Av 3 course à la carte £18 🍺: Hoegaarden, Stella Artois, London Pride. ♀: 12 **FACILITIES:** Garden: Eight wooden tables, tiled courtyard Dogs allowed Water

Pick of the Pubs

The Havelock Tavern ♀
Map GtL D4

57 Masbro Rd, Brook Green W14 0LS
☎ 020 7603 5374 📠 020 7602 1163
Dir: Nearest tubes: Shepherd's Bush & Olympia

Renowned as one of the first gastro-pubs, the popular Havelock Tavern occupies a spacious, sunny corner site between Shepherd's Bush and Olympia. The emphasis is very much on an eclectic, ever-changing menu, presented in comfortable informal surroundings with large wooden tables and dark floorboards. A broadly-based clientele helps to give the place its distinctive character and atmosphere. The food is reasonably priced and the menu changes twice daily. The pub is often busy at lunchtime, with working diners who have little time to unwind and savour their meal; but, while it's just as crowded in the evening, most of the regulars are much more relaxed and stress-free. Typical dishes might include home-made grilled hamburger, chargrilled mackerel fillets with salad, penne with wild and field mushrooms, roast chicken breast with chips, rocket and aïoli, or pan-fried monkfish fillet.
OPEN: 11-11 (Sun 12-10.30) Closed: Xmas 5 days
BAR MEALS: L served all week 12.30-2.30 D served all week 7-10 Av main course £10 **BREWERY/COMPANY:** Free House 🍺: Brakspear, Marston's Pedigree, Fuller's London Pride. ♀: 9 **FACILITIES:** Garden: Small walled garden, pergola **NOTES:** No credit cards

WC1

Pick of the Pubs

Cittie of Yorke ♀
Map E4

22 High Holborn WC1V 6BN
☎ 020 7242 7670 📠 020 7405 6371

A pub has stood on this site since 1430. In 1695, it was rebuilt as the Gray's Inn Coffee House and the large cellar bar dates from this period. The panelled front bar features an original chandelier and portraits of illustrious locals, including Dickens and Sir Thomas More. In addition to a variety of sandwiches, salads and soups, six hot dishes are freshly prepared each day.
OPEN: 11.30-11 (closed Sun) Closed: Dec 25-26
BAR MEALS: L served all week D served all week 12-9 Av main course £5 **BREWERY/COMPANY:** Samuel Smith 🍺: Samuel Smith Old Brewery Bitter. **FACILITIES:** Children welcome

Pick of the Pubs

The Lamb ♀
Map E4

94 Lamb's Conduit St WC1N 3LZ ☎ 020 7405 0713
Dir: Nearest tube: Holborn or Russell Square

Dickens, and later the Bloomsbury Group, reputedly enjoyed a drink at this traditional watering hole, dating from around 1729. It really is a gem of a place, with its distinctive green-tiled façade, very rare glass snob screens, dark polished wood, and original sepia photographs of music hall stars who performed at the nearby Holborn Empire. The absence of television, piped music and fruit machines allows the art of conversation to thrive, although a polyphon in the bar can be wound up to play a selection of discs by customer request. Home-cooked bar food includes a vegetarian corner (veg curry, burger), a fish choice including traditional fish and chips, steaks from the griddle, and pies and baked dishes from the stove. Favourites are home-baked ham, egg and chips, lamb's liver and bacon, and sausage and mash. For something lighter, try a ploughman's or a samosa with mango chutney.
OPEN: 11-11 (Sun 12-4, 7-10.30) **BAR MEALS:** L served all week 12-2.30 D served Mon-Sat 6-9
BREWERY/COMPANY: Young & Co 🍺: Youngs (full range). ♀: 13 **FACILITIES:** Garden: Patio with benches and out-door heaters

The Museum Tavern
Map D4

49 Great Russell St WC1B 3BA ☎ 020 7242 8987

Built long before the British Museum, which is just across the road, this historic inn first opened its doors in 1723. Real ales from the pump and wines by the glass. Food available all day.
OPEN: 11-11 (Sun 12-10.30) **BAR MEALS:** L served all week 11-4 D served all week 5-10 Av main course £6.50 🍺: Fullers London Pride, Theakstons, Courage Directors, Bombardier. **NOTES:** No credit cards

⭐ **Pubs with Red Stars are part of the AA's Top 200 Hotels in Britain & Ireland**

England

WC1 continued

The Perseverance ♀   Map E4
63 Lambs Conduit St WC1N 3NB
☎ 020 7405 8278 📠 020 7831 0031
A Central London haven of good food, fine wine and abundant
conviviality. The elegant candlelit dining room upstairs offers
six starters: home-made gnocchi, courgettes and mussels,
maybe, while mains might include gilt-head sea bream with
globe artichokes, confit potatoes and red wine sauce, or daube
of pork with cep casserole. Sunday lunch requires booking.
OPEN: 12-11 Closed: Xmas **BAR MEALS:** L served Sun-Fri 12.30-3
D served Mon-Sat 7-10 **RESTAURANT:** L served Sun-Fri 12.30-3 D
served Mon-Sat 7-10 Av 3 course à la carte £25 Av 3 course fixed price
£22 **BREWERY/COMPANY:** 🍺 Scottish Courage, Courage
Directors. **FACILITIES:** Children welcome

WC2

Freedom Brewing Company ♀   Map D4
41 Earlham St WC2H 9LD ☎ 020 7240 0606 📠 020 7240 4422
e-mail: info@freedombrewery.com
Dir: 5 min walk from Leicester Square or Covent Garden tube station
Launched in 1995, the Freedom Brewing Company is Britain's
first dedicated lager micro-brewery, establishing a reputation
for quality beer and lager among London's more discerning
drinkers. The Earlham Street bar in Covent Garden was
originally part of the Soho Brewing Company, and when it
opened it was the new company's first branded micro-brew
bar. Interesting restaurant and bar menus offering grilled
chicken, rocket salad and bacon, seafood hotpot, calves' liver
with bacon and mash, steak sandwich, fish and chips, and a
daily-changing risotto.
OPEN: 12-11 Closed: 25-26 Dec, 1 Jan **BAR MEALS:** L served all week
12-10 D served all week 12-10 Av main course £7 **RESTAURANT:** L
served all week 12-5 D served all week 5-10 Av 3 course à la carte £12
BREWERY/COMPANY: 🍺 Freedom Beers: Pilsner, Soho Red, Pale
Ale, Organic Pilsner. **FACILITIES:** Children welcome

The Lamb and Flag ♀   Map D3
33 Rose St, Covent Garden WC2E 9EB
☎ 020 7497 9504 📠 0207 379 7655
Dir: Telephone for directions
Licensed in the reign of Elizabeth I, the Lamb and Flag is filled
with atmosphere, especially in the low-ceilinged bar with high-
backed settles. In 1679 the poet Dryden was almost killed in
an alley nearby, where nowadays Londoners spill out onto the
streets with a drink after work. Typical food includes lamb
hotpot, Cornish pastie, macaroni cheese and chips, and spicy
Cumberland sausage. No electronic games or music except
jazz on Sunday nights.
OPEN: Mon-Thur 11-11 Fri-Sat 11-10.45, Sun 12-10.30 Closed: 25-26
Dec, Jan 1 **BAR MEALS:** L served all week 12-3 Av main course
£4.50 🍺 Scottish Courage Courage Best & Directors, Young's IPA &
Special, Charles Wells Bombardier. ♀: 10 **NOTES:** No credit cards

Pick of the Pubs

The Seven Stars   Map E4
53 Carey St WC2A 2JB ☎ 020 7242 8521
e-mail: nathan.silver@ntlworld.com
Shakespeare was living in the locality when the Seven
Stars was constructed in 1602, and somehow the pub
survived the Great Fire of London in 1666, which
destroyed most of the nearby buildings. It was originally
called The League of Seven Stars, after the seven

provinces of the Netherlands, and its first customers were
Dutch sailors who had settled in the area. Nowadays, the
pub's clientele is drawn from the nearby Law Courts, and
'Spy' cartoons of eminent lawyers decorate the walls. The
Grade II listed establishment comprises two narrow
rooms, with a tiny Elizabethan staircase leading up to the
lavatories. This highly individual free house serves
Adnams ales, and freshly cooked home-made dishes
arrive from the kitchen in a glass-panelled hoist redolent
of an old British telephone booth. Landlady Roxy
Beaujolais, author of 'Home From the Inn Contented', a
cookbook of popular pub food, offers the likes of braised
lamb shanks with barley, dill cured herring with potato
salad, and duck breast with black pudding and polenta.
OPEN: 11-11 Closed: 25-26 Dec, 1 Jan, Easter Mon
BAR MEALS: L served all week 12-4 D served all week 5-9 Av
main course £8 **BREWERY/COMPANY:** Free House
🍺 Adnams Best, Broadside, Fuller's London Pride, Harveys.
FACILITIES: Dogs allowed Water
See Pub Walk on page 298

MERSEYSIDE

BARNSTON   Map 15 SJ28

Fox and Hounds 🛏 ♀
Barnston Rd CH61 1BW ☎ 0151 6487685
Dir: From M53 J4 take A5137 to Heswell. R to Barnston on B5138

Situated in the conservation area of Barnston, the décor of this
pub is true to its origins, featuring an assortment of 1920s/1930s
memorabilia. Much of the Edwardian building's character has
been preserved, including pitch pine woodwork and leaded
windows. Alongside a superb range of bar snacks (platters, open
sandwiches, baked potatoes, home-made soup) expect daily-
changing home-cooked specials including meat pies, curries, hot
pots, bangers and mash, fish and chips and lamb shank.
OPEN: 11-11 (Sun 12-10.30) **BAR MEALS:** L served all week 12-2
Av main course £5.45 **BREWERY/COMPANY:** Free House
🍺 Websters Yorkshire Bitter, Theakston, Best & Old Peculier, Bass two
Guest beers. **FACILITIES:** Children welcome Garden: lots of flowers
& baskets Dogs allowed No dogs at lunchtime **NOTES:** Parking 60

LIVERPOOL   Map 15 SJ39

Everyman Bistro ♀
9-11 Hope St L1 9BH ☎ 0151 708 9545 📠 0151 708 9545
e-mail: info@everyman.co.uk
Dir: Town centre. Bistro in basement of Everyman Theatre, between the
two cathedrals
This is the bistro under the Everyman Theatre, which is
popular with the theatrical and artist communities. The menu

continued

continued

changes twice a day and offers international casserole-type dishes, such as Thai pork, lamb goulash, and pesto pasta with artichokes, and is particularly renowned for its home-made puddings. After 8pm the atmosphere is more that of a candlelit pub, with cask beers and wines by the bottle or glass. Live music is also a feature.

OPEN: 12-12 (Thur 12-1, Fri 12-2, Sat 11-2) Closed: BHs
BAR MEALS: L served Mon-Sat 10-4 D served Mon-Sat 5-11.30 Av main course £6.50 **RESTAURANT:** L served Mon-Sat 12-4 D served Mon-Sat 4-11.30 Av 3 course à la carte £12.50
BREWERY/COMPANY: Free House 🍺: Cains, Black Sheep, Archers Village Bitter, Pedigree. 🍷: 11

Ship & Mitre
133 Dale St L2 2JH ☎ 0151 236 0859 📠 0151 236 0855
e-mail: dave@shipandmitre.co.uk
Dir: 5mins from Moorfields underground, 5mins from Lime St Station
Award-winning pub in the heart of bustling Liverpool. Built in the art deco style of the 1930s and boasting the city's largest and most varied range of independent or micro-brewery ales; regular beer festivals. Choose something from the frequently-changing menu, perhaps chicken and mushroom pie or cassoulet. There is always a selection of sausages, provided by a local butcher, as well as at least three vegetarian options.
OPEN: 11.30-11 (Sat 12.30-11, Sun 12.30-10.30) Closed: Dec 25-26, Jan 1 **BAR MEALS:** L served Mon-Fri 11.30-2.30
BREWERY/COMPANY: Free House 🍺: Roosters, Salopian, Hyde's Mild, Hydes Miller. **FACILITIES:** Dogs allowed **NOTES:** No credit cards

ST HELENS   Map 15 SJ59

Pick of the Pubs

The Red Cat 🐱
8 Red Cat Ln WA11 8RU ☎ 01744 882422 📠 01744 886693
e-mail: redcat@amserve.net
Dir: From A580/A570 Junct follow signs for Crank
Reputedly named after a local witch, executed in 1612, the Red Cat dates back at least 700 years. Whatever changes it may have seen in all that time, the most recent is the transformation of the pub restaurant by chef/proprietor Ian Martin, who offers well-sourced, home-cooked food. His own versions of classics like ploughman's, beef steak and mushroom pie, and deep-fried fillet of fresh cod are served in the bar, while the restaurant menu has a good choice of fish: maybe deep-fried monkfish with roast vegetables and garlic butter, or sea bass with oyster fritter and tomato and coriander sauce. Alternatives are corn-fed Goosenargh chicken with Burgos black pudding and girolle mushroom and cream sauce, or grilled fillet steak with fresh foie gras and wild mushrooms. There is also an excellent wine list, plus a large selection of malt whiskies and brandies.
OPEN: 12-11 (Sun 12-10.30) **BAR MEALS:** L served Wed-Sun 12-2 D served Wed-Sun 6-9.30 Av main course £6.95
RESTAURANT: L served Wed-Sun 12-2 D served Wed-Sun 6-9.30 Av 3 course à la carte £20 Av 2 course fixed price £8.95
BREWERY/COMPANY: Inn Partnership 🍺: Carlsberg-Tetley Greenalls Bitter, Scottish Courage Theakston Best Bitter, Timothy Taylor Landlord, Greene King Old Speckled Hen.
FACILITIES: Children welcome Dogs allowed Water
NOTES: Parking 60

NORFOLK

ATTLEBOROUGH   Map 13 TM09

Griffin Hotel
Church St NR17 2AH ☎ 01953 452149
e-mail: griffinattleboro@aol.co.uk
Dir: Telephone for directions
Charming 16th-century free house featuring original beams and mellow brick walls, and with local links with Abraham Lincoln. Outside, you'll find a secluded shingled suntrap, sheltered by a high flint wall with overhanging dog roses. Home-made soups and local steaks are supplemented by specialities such as breast of chicken with leeks and Stilton, pork with honey and ginger, or salmon in a prawn and dill sauce.
OPEN: 10.30-3 5.30-11 (Fri-Sat 10.30-11, Sun 12-4, 7-10.30)
BAR MEALS: L served Mon-Sun 12-2 D served Mon-Sat 6.30-9 Av main course £7 **RESTAURANT:** L served Mon-Sun 12-2 D served Mon-Sat 6.30-9 Av 3 course à la carte £13.50 🍺: Wolf Ale, Abbot Ale.
FACILITIES: Children welcome Garden: Secluded sun trap Dogs allowed Water/Biscuits. **NOTES:** Parking 12

BAWBURGH   Map 13 TG10

Kings Head 🛏 🍷
Harts Ln NR9 3LS ☎ 01603 744977 📠 01603 744990
e-mail: anton@kingshead-bawburgh.co.uk
Dir: From A47 W of Norwich take B1108 W
Beautiful views of the River Yare and the old mill can be enjoyed from this village pub, which dates from 1602 but which is now named after the 20th-century monarch Edward VII. Enjoy log fires in the winter and the pretty garden in summer. A good range of real beer is offered alongside a varied menu including gratin of smoked haddock; bass, scallop, tiger prawn and bream in a saffron vegetable nage; and the house special - steak and kidney pudding.
OPEN: 11.30-11 (Sun 12-10.30) Closed: 25-27 Dec(eve) 1 Jan(eve)
BAR MEALS: L served all week 12-2 D served all week 6.30-9.30 Av main course £11.95 **RESTAURANT:** L served all week 12-2 D served all week 6.30-9.30 **BREWERY/COMPANY:** Free House
🍺: Adnams, Woodforde's Wherry, Green King IPA, Courage Directors.
🍷: 15 **FACILITIES:** Children's licence Garden: Secluded garden with flower beds **NOTES:** Parking 100

BINHAM   Map 13 TF93

Chequers Inn ♦♦♦ 🛏
Front St NR21 0AL ☎ 01328 830297
Dir: On B1388 between Wells-next-the-Sea & Walsingham
Located between the picturesque yachting harbour at Blakeney and the village of Walsingham, famous for its shrine, the 17th-century Chequers is ideally placed for exploring North Norfolk's scenic coastline and the famous Stiffkey salt marshes. Popular for good food and real ales, served throughout the beamed bars with open fires. Extensive menu featuring grilled Dover sole, sweet and sour king prawns, and salmon Creole, plus fish and vegetarian options and snacks.
OPEN: 11.30-3 5.30-11 (Sun 11.30-2.30, 7-10.30) Closed: 25 Dec Dec 26 Closed eve **BAR MEALS:** L served all week 12-2 D served all week 6-9 Av main course £6.50 **RESTAURANT:** L served all week 12-2 D served all week 6-9 Av 3 course à la carte £15
BREWERY/COMPANY: Free House 🍺: Greene King Abbot Ale & IPA, Woodforde's Wherry, Adnams Bitter. **FACILITIES:** Garden: Beer garden, food served outdoors **NOTES:** Parking 20 **ROOMS:** 2 bedrooms 2 en suite s£30 d£50 no children overnight

Titchwell Manor

Magnificent coastal views, abundant bird-life and Roman remains all add to the pleasure of this coastal walk.

From the hotel turn right along the A149 to a bridle path (Gipsy Lane) at the end of the village. The bank here is part of the local sea defences. Follow the right of way for about 3/4 mile/1.2km to reach the beach by the Royal West Norfolk Golf Club. On the shore are the remains of trees that grew here some 6,000 years ago. Keep ahead along the beach, looking out for sandpipers, plovers and dunlin searching for food on the shoreline.

Turn right to join a road heading towards Brancaster and when you see the church and village buildings, turn left along the edge of reed beds, following the board walk to the National Trust harbour at Brancaster Staithe. Soon you reach redundant whelk sheds looking across to the nature reserve on Scolt Head Island, an important breeding ground. Fishermen supply Titchwell Manor with fresh crab, lobster, mussels and oysters from this stretch of coast.

From the harbour walk inland to the A149 and turn right towards Brancaster village. There is a pavement here. The fields beside the road represent the site of an old Roman fort known as Branodunum from which Brancaster takes its name. The fort's walls were 11ft thick and backed by ramparts with a wide ditch. Branodunum was built to guard the approaches of The Wash and during the Roman Occupation it became a well-fortified base with naval patrols and a garrison for a cavalry regiment.

As well as offering stunning views of the sea, this final stretch of the walk reveals rows of picturesque cottages lining the road. Walk back to the hotel at Titchwell and you may be lucky enough to witness thousands of geese flying low overhead as they return from their feeding grounds to roost on the mud flats.

★★
TITCHWELL MANOR HOTEL,
TITCHWELL, PE31 8BB
☎ 01485 210221

Directions: A149 (coast rd) between Brancaster & Thornham
Attractive Victorian manor house particularly popular with families. Wonderful views of the beach, and next door to a famous RSPB reserve. Well known for seafood among other well-cooked meals.
Open: 11-11
Bar Meals: 12-2 6.30-9.30
Notes: Children welcome (books, games, TV, VCR) & dogs (water, kennel). Large walled garden & summerhouse. Parking.
(See page 334 for full entry)

DISTANCE: 5 miles/8km
MAP: OS Explorer 250
TERRAIN: Coastal - marshes and reedbeds
PATHS: Pavements, boardwalk (can be slippery after rain) and quiet coastal roadway
GRADIENT: Flat, no hills

Walk submitted and checked by Margaret Snaith of Titchwell Manor

BLAKENEY
Map 13 TG04

The Kings Arms 🐑 ♀
Westgate St NR25 7NQ ☎ 01263 740341 📠 01263 740391
e-mail: kingsarms.blakeney@btopenworld.com
Grade II listed building on the North Norfolk coast - an ideal
spot for walking and birdwatching. Regular ferry trips to seal
colony and world-famous bird sanctuaries. Large beer garden
with swings for children. Many photographs of the theatrical
career of hosts Howard and Marjorie Davies are displayed
inside. Menu offers locally-caught fish, local game and a range
of homemade pies and pastas. Other food choices include
steaks, sandwiches, jacket potatoes and vegetarian dishes.
OPEN: 11-11 **BAR MEALS:** L served all week 12-9.30 D served all
week Av main course £5.95 **BREWERY/COMPANY:** Free House
🍺: Greene King Old Speckled Hen, Woodfordes Wherry Best Bitter,
Marston's Pedigree, Adnams Best Bitter. ♀: 12
FACILITIES: Children welcome Garden: Very safe large patio and
grass area Dogs allowed Water **NOTES:** Parking 10

Pick of the Pubs

White Horse Hotel 🐑 ♀
4 High St NR25 7AL ☎ 01263 740574 📠 01263 741303
e-mail: whitehorse4@lineone.net
Dir: *From A148 (Cromer to King's Lynn rd) turn onto A149 signed to
Blakeney.*

A short, steep stroll from the quayside, with fine views
across the harbour, lies Blakeney's earliest hotel, built in the
17th century. Run by the same team for thirteen years, it has
a deserved reputation for its accommodation and food. With
the sea so close, lovers of seafood and fish won't be
disappointed, with mussels and crabs in season, cockle
chowder, and Thai fish cakes as both starter and main course
on offer. By no means, though, does the North Sea provide
everything: daily blackboard specials include Glamorgan
sausages with tomato and basil sauce, lamb tagine and
couscous, and roasted celeriac, and mushroom and
Parmesan tartlet, while salads, sandwiches and children's
items are available too. The restaurant, overlooking a
courtyard where the stagecoaches once arrived and
departed, offers grilled breast of corn-fed chicken, and deep-
fried spicy chickpea cakes on cucumber and passion fruit
raita. Homemade desserts include treacle tart and apple pie.
OPEN: 11-3 6-11 (Sun 12-3, 7-10.30) Closed: 7-21 Jan
BAR MEALS: L served all week 12-2 D served all week 6-9 Av
main course £7.50 **RESTAURANT:** D served Tue-Sun 7-9 Av 3
course à la carte £23.50 **BREWERY/COMPANY:** Free House
🍺: Adnams Bitter, Adnams Broadside, Woodfordes Wherry,
Woodfordes Nelson. ♀: 8 **FACILITIES:** Children welcome
Garden: Courtyard, picnic tables and umbrellas **NOTES:** Parking 14

BLICKLING
Map 13 TG12

Pick of the Pubs

The Buckinghamshire Arms 🐑
Blickling Rd NR11 6NF ☎ 01263 732133 📠 01263 734541
Dir: *From Cromer (A140) take exit at Aylsham onto B1354*
A handsome late 17th-century coaching inn located right
by the gates of the National Trust's Blickling Hall in a
lovely Norfolk village. The inn was originally built for
houseguests and their servants, and the ghost of Anne
Boleyn is said to wander in the adjacent courtyard and
charming garden. There is nothing ethereal, however,
about the pub's strong local following, or the solid
furniture and wood-burning stoves in the lounge bar and
restaurant. A carte menu is offered in the restaurant for
lunch and dinner, and a bar snack selection at lunch and
supper, supplemented by daily specials. There's a good
choice of real ales and favourite dishes are Betty's steak
and kidney pie, Morston mussels and local game in
season. Houseguests are still welcome in the three
recently renovated four-poster bedrooms, two of which
have majestic views of Blickling Hall.
OPEN: 11-3.30 6.15-11 Closed: 25 Dec **BAR MEALS:** L served
all week 12-2 D served all week 7-9 Av main course £7.95
RESTAURANT: L served all week 12-2 D served all week 7-9 Av
3 course à la carte £15.90 **BREWERY/COMPANY:** Free House
🍺: Adnams, Woodforde's Wherry, Nelson's Revenge & Admirals
Reserve, Shepherd Neame Spitfire. **FACILITIES:** Garden:
Sheltered garden & lawn, picnic tables Dogs allowed Water
NOTES: Parking 60 **ROOMS:** 3 bedrooms 1 en suite s£40
d£70 (♦♦♦) no children overnight

BRANCASTER STAITHE
Map 13 TF74

Pick of the Pubs

The White Horse ★★ ◉ 🐑 ♀
Main Rd PE31 8BY ☎ 01485 210262 📠 01485 210930
e-mail: reception@whitehorsebrancaster.co.uk
See Pick of the Pubs on page 322

The Green Man
The most uncanny and enigmatic
of inn signs represents a figure of folk
custom from the distant past, the Jack in the
Green who appeared at May Day revels. He
was a man covered with green leaves and
branches, who probably stood for the rebirth
of plants, trees and greenery in the spring.
Virile and wild, part human and part tree, he is
often found carved eerily in churches. A
connection grew up between him and Robin
Hood, the forest outlaw, and this is
perpetuated in some Green Man pub
signs, which show an archer or a
forester in Lincoln green.

Pick of the Pubs

BRANCASTER STAITHE – NORFOLK

Open: 11.30-11 (Sun 12-10.30)
Bar Meals: L served all week 12-2.
Av cost main course £12.50
RESTAURANT: L served all week 12-2,
D served all week 7-9.
Av cost 3 course £22
BREWERY/COMPANY:
Free House.
🍺: Adnams Bitter, Regatta, Southwold
& Fisherman, Fullers E.S.B, Greene
King IPA plus guest beers.
FACILITIES: Dogs allowed, Children
welcome, Garden - Sun deck
overlooking tidal marshes.
NOTES: Parking 80.
ROOMS: 15 en suite from s£38 d£76

The White Horse

Stunning views across the tidal marshes can be enjoyed from this elevated dining pub at Brancaster Staithe, a paradise for birdwatchers and walkers who are drawn to the wildlife-rich coastline.

★★ 🏵 🐑 ♟

Main Road, Brancaster Staithe,
King's Lynn, PE31 8BY
☎ 01485 210262 📄 01485 210930
📧 reception@whitehorsebrancaster.co.uk
Dir: Mid-way between King's Lynn
and Wells-next-the-Sea on the A149
coastal road.

It is renowned for its seafood which can be enjoyed in the airy conservatory restaurant, the traditional bar, or the summer sun deck. Expect a friendly welcome at this stylish pub, which can be found in an unspoilt part of North Norfolk near the coastal path and Scolt Head Island. Scrubbed pine tables, high-backed settles, an open log fire in winter and cream-painted walls adorned with local sepia photographs of days gone by, contribute to the bright, welcoming atmosphere. In summer the sun deck is a popular spot for diners to watch the small sailing boats heading for the harbour entrance, and the sea retreating from the salt marsh. Local seafood is the reason for the pub's enviable reputation, with freshly-harvested local mussels, oysters and samphire often appearing on the menu. The daily-changing choice is inspirational: at lunchtime, seafood chowder with saffron oil starter, or perhaps warm salad of red mullet, chorizo sausage, rocket and sun-blanched tomatoes. Move on to pan-fried lemon sole, baked fillet of brill, or grilled fillet of plaice with Catalan bean stew. There are meat dishes too, like roast breast of chicken with coriander chilli pesto and tom yam vegetable noodle broth. The evening dishes are similarly outstanding, with seared peppered tuna and caviar, or chargrilled sardines with aubergine caviar, and to follow, confit of sea bass and chorizo risotto, or duck breast with garlic-roasted baby potatoes. There is no need to rush off after a meal: fifteen tasteful bedrooms, some with terrace and one on a split level with internal balcony, enjoy the same fantastic views.

BRISTON

Map 13 TG03

The John H Stracey ◆◆◆ 🛏 🍷
West End NR24 2JA ☎ 01263 860891 📠 01263 862984
e-mail: thejohnhstracey@btinternet.com

A 16th-century inn, renamed in the mid-1970s after the famous British welterweight champion, who used to spar with the then owner's son. Characterful interior, with log fire and knick-knacks. The wide choice of straightforward pub food includes ploughman's, sandwiches, 'lite bites', steaks cooked in various styles, home-made steak and ale pie, duck à l'orange, curries, pastas, scampi, lobster, Dover sole and salads. Vegetarian and children's selections too. Old Speckled Hen and Ruddles County in the bar.
OPEN: 11-2.30 6.30-11 **BAR MEALS:** L served all week 12-2 D served all week 6.30-9.30 Av main course £8 **RESTAURANT:** L served all week 12-2 D served all week 6.30-9.30
BREWERY/COMPANY: Free House 🍺 Greene King Old Speckled Hen & IPA, Greene King Ruddles County. **FACILITIES:** Children welcome Garden: Bench tables on grass Dogs allowed
NOTES: Parking 30 **ROOMS:** 3 bedrooms 1 en suite d£53

BURNHAM MARKET

Map 13 TF84

Pick of the Pubs

The Hoste Arms ★★ 🍴🍴 🛏 🍷
The Green PE31 8HD ☎ 01328 738777 📠 01328 730103
e-mail: reception@hostearms.co.uk
AA Seafood Pub of the Year for England 2004
See Pick of the Pubs on page 324

BURNHAM THORPE

Map 13 TF84

Pick of the Pubs

The Lord Nelson 🌐 🛏 🍷
Walsingham Rd PE31 8HL ☎ 01328 738241
e-mail: lucy@nelsonslocal.co.uk
Step inside this 350-year-old cottage, with its huge high-backed settles, old brick floors, open fires and traditional atmosphere. This unspoilt gem was named after England's most famous seafarer who was born in the rectory of this sleepy village in 1758. Nelson memorabilia can also be seen in the pub. Greene King and Woodforde ales are tapped from the cask in the cellar room, or a dram of the popular rum concoction called 'Nelson's Blood', made to a secret recipe, can be sampled here. The food also makes a visit worthwhile, with its seafood, vegetarian choices, grills and baguettes: starters like chicken leg terrine with red onion marmalade, and star anise confit, might be followed by chicken and wild mushroom pasta bake, and braised lamb shank with tomato cassoulet. Families are warmly welcomed, and children will enjoy the garden with its climbing frame, wooden play area and basketball net.
OPEN: 11-3 6-11 (Sun 12-3, 7-10.30, Sun Winter 11-2.30) Mon Closed in Winter **BAR MEALS:** 12-2 7-9 Av main course £9.95
BREWERY/COMPANY: Greene King 🍺 Greene King Abbot Ale & IPA, Woodforde's Wherry Best. 🍷 7
FACILITIES: Children welcome Garden: Very large Dogs allowed Water **NOTES:** Parking 30

CLEY NEXT THE SEA

Map 13 TG04

George & Dragon Hotel 🛏 🍷
High St NR25 7RN ☎ 01263 740652 📠 01263 741275
e-mail: thegeorge@cleynextthesea.com
Dir: On coast road (A149). Centre of village

The George and Dragon is a classic Edwardian Inn near the sea and marshes, where the first naturalist trust was formed in 1926. Sandwiches, ploughman's and jacket potatoes are available until 6pm, in addition to the main menu. Typical dishes from the latter are mixed seafood salad, Norfolk chicken breast stuffed with Brie and bacon and served with rosemary risotto, and smoked Norfolk ham with egg and chips.
OPEN: 11-3 6-11 (Winter 11.30-2.30, 6.30-11) (Open all day Apr-Oct)
BAR MEALS: L served all week 12-2.30 D served all week 6.30-9
RESTAURANT: L served all week 12-2.30 D served all week 6.30-9
Av 3 course à la carte £13 **BREWERY/COMPANY:** Free House
🍺 Greene King IPA, Abbot Ale & Old Speckled Hen, Adnams Bitter, Woodforde's Wherry. **FACILITIES:** Children welcome Garden: Mature garden Dogs allowed **NOTES:** Parking 15

Open: 11-11.
Bar Meals: No food in bar
RESTAURANT: L served all week 12-2, D served all week 7-9.
BREWERY/COMPANY: Free House.
🍺: Woodforde's Wherry Best, Greene King Abbot Ale & IPA.
FACILITIES: Garden - Grassy area, seating for 100, outside heaters.
NOTES: Parking 45
ROOMS: 36 en suite from s£71 d£100

The Hoste Arms

With huge support from the village, dedicated owners Paul and Jeanne Whittome have transformed a lacklustre village pub into a great dining pub and hotel.

AA Seafood Pub of the Year for England 2004

★★ ⬡⬡ 🐇 🍷

The Green, Burnham Market,
PE31 8HD
☎ 01328 738777 📠 01328 730103
📧 reception@hostearms.co.uk
Dir: Signposted off B1155, 5m w of Wells-next-the-Sea.

Built as a manor house in 1550, it became an inn a century later, subsequently to be owned by, and indeed named after, the Pitt family of parliamentary fame. While unemployed between 1788 and 1793, Lord Nelson visited weekly to receive his despatches. In 1811 it was renamed the Hoste Arms, and by late Victorian times was even doing brisk trade as a brothel. When former potato merchant Paul bought it in 1989, he ended virtually overnight a 130-year

process of decline under the ownership of successive, uncaring breweries. Probably its nadir was when, doubtless trying to exploit the Nelson connection, one of them attempted to turn it into a seafaring theme pub - with dire results. Since its rescue, the whole place has been transformed: Jeanne has designed the 36 comfortable bedrooms, the non-dining village bar has been restored, and several interlinked and air-conditioned dining areas have been added. The well-run kitchen copes well with popular demand. Starters and light meals might include stir-fry chilli beef with pak choi and noodles, Burnham Creek oysters, or pan-fried foie gras

with black pudding risotto. For a main course, consider baked sea trout, tabbouleh and asparagus; roasted corn-fed chicken, curried houmus and celeriac chips; or hoi sin-marinated pork belly with Thai-style rice noodles. Pasta dishes appear separately. There are irresistible puddings like apple and cider crumble, mango and nougat parfait, and Welsh rarebit with Parma ham and poached egg. A list of over 180 wines features some of the world's finest, and Woodforde's Wherry Best Bitter from Norwich is on tap. Paul's 'semi-educated ramblings' about world hotels and restaurants can be read in a book on sale in reception.

England

COLKIRK
Map 13 TF92

The Crown ♀
Crown Rd NR21 7AA ☎ 01328 862172 🖹 01328 863916
e-mail: thecrown@paston.co.uk
Dir: *2m from B1146 Fakenham-Dereham rd*

A quietly-located inn in a country village with plenty of enjoyable walks nearby. Open fires in winter, and a sunny terrace on warmer days make this a popular haunt with a lively atmosphere. The menu offers oriental tiger prawns and mushrooms, pan-fried chicken fillet, and various steaks, plus blackboard specials like fruity pork curry, chicken with Stilton sauce, and fillet of salmon with lemon sauce.
OPEN: 11-2.30 6-11 **BAR MEALS:** L served all week 12-1.45 D served all week 7-9.30 Av main course £7.95 **RESTAURANT:** L served all week 12-1.45 D served all week 7-9.30
BREWERY/COMPANY: Greene King 🍺: Greene King - IPA, Abbot Ale, Mild, Ruddles County. ♀: 25 **FACILITIES:** Children welcome Garden Dogs allowed **NOTES:** Parking 30

COLTISHALL
Map 13 TG21

Pick of the Pubs

Kings Head ♦♦♦ ⊛⊛ 🐄 ♀
26 Wroxham Rd NR12 7EA ☎ 01603 737426 🖹 01603 736542
Dir: *A47 Norwich ring road onto B1150 to North Walsham at Coltishall. R at petrol station, follow rd to R past church, on R next to car park*

Right in the heart of the Norfolk Broads, this 17th-century free house stands on the banks of the River Bure. Cruisers can be hired at nearby Wroxham, and fishing boats are available at the pub - but, if you prefer to stay on dry land, you'll find comfortable bedrooms with en suite or private facilities at the pub. Bar meals are available at lunchtime, and the evening à la carte menu can be served in the bar or no-smoking restaurant. Popular starters include Scottish smoked salmon, avocado and prawns

continued

---

with a Cognac Marie Rose sauce, and ravioli of rabbit with wild mushrooms. Main course options take in grilled fillet of Scotch beef, chicken breast stuffed with spinach and wild mushrooms, fillet of wild sea bass, and wild mushroom risotto with fresh Parmesan. Round things off with a steamed orange and Cointreau sponge, or dark chocolate mousse with white chocolate and Malibu sauce.
OPEN: 11-3 6-11 (Sun all day) Closed: 25-26 Dec
BAR MEALS: L served all week 12-2 D served all week 7-9 Av main course £6.95 **RESTAURANT:** L served all week 12-2 D served all week 7-9 Av 3 course à la carte £22
BREWERY/COMPANY: Free House 🍺: Adnams Bitter, Directors, Marston's Pedigree. ♀: 8 **FACILITIES:** Children welcome **NOTES:** Parking 20 **ROOMS:** 4 bedrooms 2 en suite 1 family rooms s£25 d£50

DEREHAM
Map 13 TF91

Yaxham Mill ♦♦♦ NEW
Norwich Rd, Yaxham NR19 1RP ☎ 01362 851182
A converted windmill stands in the grounds of this peaceful country pub, situated in open countryside not far from East Dereham. A caravan club campsite, well-kept lawns and childrens' play fort make it a popular choice for families. Menus cater well for all tastes, with a good selection of vegetarian dishes, baguettes and traditional favourites including steak and chips, cod in beer batter and home cooked lamb casserole or shepherd's pie. A good selection of roasts on Sundays.
OPEN: 12-3 6-11.30 **BAR MEALS:** L served all week 12-2 D served all week 6.30-9 Av main course £5 **RESTAURANT:** L served all week 12-2 D served all week 6.30-9 Av 3 course à la carte £12
🍺: Interbrew Boddingtons, Woodforde's Wherry.
FACILITIES: Children welcome Garden: Lawn, picnic tables Dogs allowed Outside compund with kennel **NOTES:** Parking 40 **ROOMS:** 8 bedrooms 8 en suite 2 family rooms s£30 d£39.50

EASTGATE
Map 13 TG12

Pick of the Pubs

Ratcatchers Inn 🐄 ♀
Easton Way NR10 4HA ☎ 01603 871430 🖹 01603 873343
Dir: *Off A140, past Norwich Airport take B1149 to Holt, thru Horsford, 6m then pub signed*

A white pan-tiled Norfolk country inn that, 'tis said, derives its unusual name from the 'one-penny-per-tail' bounty paid to local rat catchers in the 19th. Today's home-made, home-cooked policy includes no such delicacy but promises their own bread baked on the premises, herb oils, chutneys, purées and stocks. All menu

continued

EASTGATE continued

items are cooked to order, so do not expect to cut and run. Enjoy instead a choice of real ales and a sensible selection of wines by glass or bottle whilst awaiting smoked salmon, local smoked sausage or deep-fried cheese fritters. Move on to poacher's game pie, Madras curry or one of many vegetarian dishes - perhaps vegetable Stroganoff or Indonesian stir fry. For massive appetites there are steaks with speciality sauces, whilst others might prefer salads, sandwiches or dishes from the light eaters menu. Don't miss the excellent fresh fish listed daily on blackboards. Youngsters are well catered for and any meal will be nicely rounded off with adventurous home-made desserts.
OPEN: 11.45-3 6-11 (Sat all day, Sun 12-9) Closed: 26 Dec **BAR MEALS:** L served all week 11.45-2 D served all week 6-10 Av main course £9.50 **RESTAURANT:** L served all week 11.45-2 D served all week 6-10 **BREWERY/COMPANY:** Free House **🍺:** Adnams, Hancocks, Greene King IPA. **♀:** 8 **FACILITIES:** Children welcome Garden: 7 lunch tables Dogs allowed In the garden only, water **NOTES:** Parking 30

EATON   Map 13 TG20

Red Lion 🍺 ♀
50 Eaton St NR4 7LD ☎ 01603 454787 📠 01603 456939
Dir: off the A11
17th-century coaching inn retaining original features such as Dutch gables, beams, panelled walls and inglenook fireplaces. Bar food includes home-made soups, freshly-cut sandwiches, and sausages and mash. The restaurant offers Norfolk duck, prime beef ribs and steaks, game in season, Scotch salmon, Dover sole, and Norfolk skate.
OPEN: 11-3 6-11 (Sun 12-3, 7-10.30) **BAR MEALS:** L served all week 12-2.15 D served all week 7-9 **RESTAURANT:** L served all week 12-2 D served all week 7-9 **BREWERY/COMPANY:** Free House **🍺:** Theakston Bitter, Scottish Courage Courage Best, Courage Directors, Greene King IPA. **FACILITIES:** Garden: Covered patio area **NOTES:** Parking 40

ERPINGHAM   Map 13 TG13

Pick of the Pubs

The Saracen's Head 🍺
NR11 7LZ ☎ 01263 768909 📠 01263 768993
e-mail: saracenshead@wolterton.freeserve.co.uk
See Pick of the Pubs on opposite page

FAKENHAM   Map 13 TF92

The Wensum Lodge Hotel 🍺
Bridge St NR21 9AY ☎ 01328 862100 📠 01328 863365
e-mail: enquiries@wensumlodge.fsnet.co.uk
Originally built around 1750 as the grain store to Fakenham Mill, this privately-owned family establishment opened as a restaurant in 1983. It later became the Wensum Lodge Hotel, taking its name from the river it overlooks. The emphasis is on friendly service and quality home-cooked food. Expect mixed seafood, steak, mushroom and Guinness pie, pan-fried peppered fillet of lamb, griddled salmon fillet, roast vegetable lasagne, and a variety of 'Sizzling Combos', savoury pancakes, salads, jacket potatoes, baguettes, and chargrills.
OPEN: 11-11 **BAR MEALS:** L served all week 11.30-3 D served all

week 6.30-10 **RESTAURANT:** L served all week 11.30-3 D served all week 6.30-10 **BREWERY/COMPANY:** Free House **🍺:** Greene King Abbot Ale & IPA, Scottish Courage John Smith's, Norfolk Wherry. **FACILITIES:** Children welcome Garden: Small garden with stream **NOTES:** Parking 20

The White Horse Inn ♦♦♦ 🍺
Fakenham Rd, East Barsham NR21 0LH
☎ 01328 820645 📠 01328 820645
e-mail: rsteele@btinternet.com

Near 10th-century East Barsham Manor, this refurbished 17th-century inn with its log-burning inglenook has lost none of its character. Freshest ingredients are assured in daily specials that may include seafood platter, grilled chicken spiced chicken breast, steak and kidney suet pudding, chargrilled leg of lamb steak, or green leaves with goats cheese and roasted peppers. **OPEN:** 11-3 6-11 **BAR MEALS:** L served all week 12-2 D served all week 7-9.30 **RESTAURANT:** L served all week 12-2 D served all week 7-9.30 **BREWERY/COMPANY:** **🍺:** Adnams Best, Greene King, Woodforde's, Wells Eagle IPA. **FACILITIES:** Children welcome Garden: Patio area **NOTES:** Parking 50 **ROOMS:** 3 bedrooms 3 en suite 2 family rooms s£35 d£58

GREAT BIRCHAM   Map 13 TF73

King's Head Hotel
PE31 6RJ ☎ 01485 578265
Dir: Telephone for directions

Attractive 17th-century inn with a beamed snug, comfortable lounge and a wood-burning stove in the inglenook fireplace. The village has an impressive restored windmill, and is close to Haughton Hall. Food and drink are served in the garden.
OPEN: 11-2.30 7-11 **BAR MEALS:** L served all week 12-2 D served all week 7-9.30 **RESTAURANT:** L served Sun-Mon, Wed-Sat 12-2.30 D served Mon, Wed-Sat 7-9.30 Av 3 course à la carte £18 **BREWERY/COMPANY:** Free House **🍺:** Interbrew Worthington Best & Bass, Adnams Bitter. **FACILITIES:** Children welcome Garden Dogs allowed **NOTES:** Parking 50

continued

Open: 12-3, 6-11.30 (Sun 12-3, 7-10.30)
Bar Meals: L served all week 12.30-2,
D served all week 7.30-9.
Av cost main course £9.95
RESTAURANT: L served all week
12.30-2
D served all week 7.30-9.
BREWERY/COMPANY:
Free House.
🍺: Adnams Bitter & Broadside or
Woodforde's Wherry Best.
FACILITIES: Garden - Courtyard
garden.
NOTES: Parking 50

The Saracen's Head

Modelled on a Tuscan farmhouse, and built in 1806 around a
beautiful courtyard, this was once the coach house for Wolferton
Hall, the home of Horace Walpole.

Wolterton, Norwich, NR11 7LZ
☎ 01263 768909 📄 01263 768993
📧 saracenshead@wolterton.freeserve.co.uk
Dir: A140 2.5m N of Aylsham, L
through Erpingham, pass Spread
Eagle on L and continue straight on,
signed 'Calthorpe'. Through
Calthorpe 1m on R (in field).

In the same hands for some 13
years, the Saracen's Head is
known as north Norfolk's 'Lost
Inn' and merits both the name
and the detour to find it. There
is a great sense of fun in its
mildly eccentric approach and
inventive menus that ignore the
ubiquitous presence elsewhere
of the chip and the pea.

Unexpected pleasures include
the possibility of dining alfresco
in the garden, and a lack of
piped music or amusement
machines to disturb the
delightful parlour-room
atmosphere of the interior,
warmed by welcoming open
fires on colder days. Seasonally
changing blackboard menus
reflect the enthusiasm,
undimmed over many years, of
chef/ proprietor Robert
Dawson-Smith. Pan-fried
monkfish with orange and
ginger, scallops with bacon and
white wine, and the delicious
Morston mussels cooked in
cider and cream remain the
stars of his fish list. On a par

for meat lovers are pot-roast leg
of lamb with red and white
beans, roast Norfolk pheasant
with Calvados and cream, and
pan-fried venison liver with
ham and mushrooms.
Vegetarians are amply catered
for too, with red onion and
goats' cheese tart, followed
perhaps by baked avocado and
sweet pear with Mozzarella.
Nursery puddings are a house
speciality, with old-fashioned
treacle tart, and brown bread
and butter pudding vying with
the more sophisticated mulled
wine and red fruit pudding,
and chocolate pot with orange
jus.

GREAT RYBURGH · Map 13 TF92

The Boar Inn
NR21 0DX ☎ 01328 829212 📠 01328 829421
Dir: Off A1067 4m S of Fakenham

Deep in rural Norfolk, this 300-year-old inn sits opposite the village's round-towered Saxon church. Its owners offer a good variety of food, including bar/alfresco snacks and children's meals. Try beef Madras served with rice 'and things', sweet and sour chicken with noodles, plaice fillet with prawns in Mornay sauce, or prime Norfolk steaks. Specials include skate wing with garlic and herb butter, and wild boar steak with cranberry and red wine jus.
OPEN: 11-2.30 6.30-11 **BAR MEALS:** L served all week 12-2 D served all week 7-9.30 Av main course £6.95 **RESTAURANT:** 12-2 7-9.30 **BREWERY/COMPANY:** Free House 🍺: Adnams & Guest ale. **FACILITIES:** Children welcome Garden: Food served outside.
NOTES: Parking 30

HAPPISBURGH · Map 13 TG33

The Hill House
NR12 0PW ☎ 01692 650004 📠 01692 650004
Dir: 5m from Stalham, 8m from North Walsham
16th-century coaching inn with original timbers situated in an attractive North Norfolk coastal village. Sir Arthur Conan Doyle stayed here and was inspired to write a Sherlock Holmes story called 'The Dancing Men'. Changing guest ales good value bar food, and large summer garden. Look out for the likes of steaks, chicken breast with leek and Stilton, or seafood platter, plus various Greek, Italian and French dishes. Beer festival each June, on the Summer Solstice.
OPEN: 12-3 7-11 (Thu-Sun all day) (Summer all day) 25 Dec Closed eve **BAR MEALS:** L served all week 12-2.30 D served all week 7-9.30 Av main course £6 **RESTAURANT:** L served all week 12-2.30 D served all week 7-9.30 Av 3 course à la carte £14
BREWERY/COMPANY: Free House 🍺: Shepherd Neame Spitfire, Buffy's, Woodforde's Wherry, Adnams Bitter. **FACILITIES:** Children welcome Garden: Large, by the sea Dogs allowed Water
NOTES: Parking 20

HETHERSETT · Map 13 TG10

Kings Head Public House
36 Norwich Rd NR9 3DD ☎ 01603 810206
Dir: Old Norwich Road just off B1172 Cringleford to Wymondham road. 5m SW of Norwich
Attractive 17th-century roadside inn with a wealth of original beams and a large inglenook fireplace. There is also a pleasant enclosed rear garden that was once a bowling green. In October 1818 following the murder of a local glove-maker Hethersett's police constables arrested one James Johnson at

the pub. A good range of food, with typical dishes on the menu including steak and kidney pie, Thai salmon, rack of lamb, and lasagne. Daily specials vary from Cajun chicken to fillet of beef.
OPEN: 11-2.30 5.30-11 (Sun 12-3, 7-10.30 all day wknd May 3-Sep 13) **BAR MEALS:** L served all week 12-2 D served Mon-Sat 6.30-9 Av main course £6.25 **RESTAURANT:** L served all week 12-2 D served Mon-Sat 6.30-9.30 **BREWERY/COMPANY:** Unique Pub Co 🍺: Adnams Best Bitter, Greene King Abbot Ale, IPA, Tetley Smoothflow. **FACILITIES:** Children welcome Garden: Seating surrounded by trees, benches & tables Dogs allowed Water only
NOTES: Parking 20

HEVINGHAM · Map 13 TG12

Marsham Arms Freehouse ♦♦♦♦
Holt Rd NR10 5NP ☎ 01603 754268 📠 01603 754839
e-mail: nigelbradley@marshamarms.co.uk
Dir: 4M N of Norwich Airport on B1149 through Horsford

Victorian philanthropist and landowner Robert Marsham built what is now the Marsham Arms as a hostel for poor farm labourers, and some original features remain - including the large open fireplace. Cabaret and live music often feature thanks to the recent addition of a function suite. A good range of traditional pub fare is offered, including baguettes, steaks, ploughman's and various fish, chicken and vegetarian dishes. Specialities include steak and kidney pie, beef and mushroom casserole, and homemade lasagne.
OPEN: 10-3 6-11 (open all day Summer) Closed: 25 Dec
BAR MEALS: L served all week 11-3 D served all week 6-9.30
RESTAURANT: L served all week 12-3 D served all week 6-9.30
BREWERY/COMPANY: Free House 🍺: Adnams Best, Woodforde's Wherry Best Bitter, Greene King IPA, Interbrew Bass.
FACILITIES: Children welcome Garden: Patio front, lawn area.
NOTES: Parking 100 **ROOMS:** 10 bedrooms 10 en suite

HEYDON · Map 13 TG12

Earle Arms
The Street NR11 6AD ☎ 01263 587376
e-mail: ahtaylor@freeuk.com
Dir: signed off the main Holt to Norwich rd, between Cawston & Corpusty
The Earle Arms is a 17th-century pub situated opposite the village green in a classic estate village - a great base for exploring the North Norfolk Coast. The interior retains much of this timeless quality, with log fires, attractive wallpapers, prints and a collection of china and other bric-a-brac. It comprises two rooms, one with service through a hatch, and there are more tables outside in the pretty back garden, a blaze of colour in the summer months. You can expect a good pint of Adnams bitter, Woodforde's Wherry or a third guest ale, and proper home-cooked food from the bar menu. Local

continued

continued

fish features, and popular dishes include baked crab, blackened salmon fillet with shallots and tomatoes, chicken and mushroom Stroganoff, and aubergine and pepper au gratin.
OPEN: 12-3 6-11 (Sun 12-3, 7-10.30) **BAR MEALS:** L served all week 12-2 D served all week 7-9 Av main course £7.50
RESTAURANT: L served all week **BREWERY/COMPANY:** Free House ◖: Adnams, Woodfordes Wherry, Adnams Broadside, Bass.
FACILITIES: Children welcome Garden: Marquee, lawn
NOTES: Parking 20 No credit cards

HORSEY
Map 13 TG42

Nelson Head 🐾
The Street NR29 4AD ☎ 01493 393378 & 01692 670383
Dir: On coast rd (B1159) between West Somerton & Sea Palling
Located on a National Trust estate, just a short walk from the beach and Horsey Mere, this 17th-century inn has a cosy country pub atmosphere with a log fire in the winter. Hearty menu includes plaice in lemon and dill butter, Nelson pie (fish and prawns), cod or haddock in beer batter, cauliflower cheese, cottage pie, and a variety of filled baguettes. Sheltered gardens look out towards the dunes and water meadows.
OPEN: 11-3 6-11 **BAR MEALS:** L served all week 12-2 D served all week 6-9 **RESTAURANT:** L served all week 12-2 D served all week 6-9 **BREWERY/COMPANY:** Free House ◖: Woodforde's Wherry & Nelson's Revenge, Greene King IPA. **FACILITIES:** Garden: Sheltered with amazing views **NOTES:** Parking 30 **NOTES:** No credit cards

HORSTEAD
Map 13 TG21

Recruiting Sergeant 🐾 ♀
Norwich Rd NR12 7EE ☎ 01603 737077 ▤ 01603 738827
Dir: on the B1150 between Norwich & North Walsham
The name of this inviting country pub comes from the tradition of recruiting servicemen by giving them the King or Queen's shilling in a pint of beer. It offers good food, ales and wines in homely surroundings with a patio and lawned garden for alfresco dining. The menu is ever changing, with inventive specials such as chicken breast stuffed with chorizo and foie gras, chargrilled swordfish with lime and mango pickle, and seared saddle of venison with rosemary and redcurrant jus.
OPEN: 11-11 **BAR MEALS:** L served all week 12-2 D served all week 6.30-9.30 Av main course £16.95 **RESTAURANT:** L served all week 12-2 D served all week 6.30-9.30 Av 3 course à la carte £15.50
BREWERY/COMPANY: Free House ◖: Elgoods, Adnams, Interbrew Boddington, Greene King Abbot Ale. ♀: 13
FACILITIES: Children welcome Garden: Large patio, seats approx 40, enclosed lawn Dogs allowed Water **NOTES:** Parking 50

ITTERINGHAM
Map 13 TG13

Pick of the Pubs

Walpole Arms ♀
NR11 7AR ☎ 01263 587258 ▤ 01263 587074
e-mail: goodfood@thewalpolearms.co.uk
Dir: Leave Aylsham in Blickling direction. After Blickling Hall take 1st R turn to Itteringham
A handsome country inn with a restaurant and garden, on the edge of the village. The 18th-century, oak-beamed inn is run by a formidable team that comprises the former producer/director of BBC's Masterchef, a highly respected

wine merchant, and a chef with stints at top London and Norwich restaurants on his cv. Adding their skills to that of local suppliers means that if it's on the menu, it'll be good. Such produce includes mussels from Morston, venison reared at nearby Gunton Hall, and organic meat from Fellbrigg (NT) Estate. Examples from the carte are escabeche and baked sardines on sourdough toast to start, tranche of calves' liver with butter beans, morcilla and leeks, and filo tart of Greek yoghurt, lemon curd, honey and toasted seeds. Imaginative bar meals might run to chunky shepherd's pie with green beans, lamb tagine with couscous and Feta salad, and steamed mussels with three-pepper salsa. Good local real ales, and some carefully-sourced wines, including weekly specials and house wines by the glass.

OPEN: 12-3 6-11 (Summer open all day Sat, Sun) (Winter Sun 7-10.30) **BAR MEALS:** L served all week 12-2.00 D served Mon-Sat 7-9.30 Av main course £10.50 **RESTAURANT:** L served Wkds 12-2.30 D served Mon-Sat 7-9.30 Av 3 course à la carte £20
BREWERY/COMPANY: ◖: Adnams Broadside & Bitter, Woodfordes Wherry Best Bitter & Walpole. ♀: 12
FACILITIES: Children welcome Garden: 2 Large grassy areas with tables, patio area Dogs allowed Water **NOTES:** Parking 100

KING'S LYNN
Map 12 TF62

The Tudor Rose Hotel ★★
St Nicholas St PE30 1LR ☎ 01553 762824 ▤ 01553 764894
e-mail: enquiries@tudorrose-hotel.co.uk
Dir: Hotel is off Tuesday Market Place in the centre of Kings Lynn
Built by a local wool merchant and situated in the heart of King's Lynn, the oldest part of this historic inn dates back to 1187 and was originally part of the winter palace of a Norfolk bishop. The Dutch gable extension of 1645 remains one of the best examples of its kind in the town. Cosy snug and medieval-style tapestries inside. Dishes range from steak and kidney pie and ham, egg and chips to Mexican chilli and prawn salad. Various light bites and starters and a good choice of well-kept beers, whiskies and popular wines.
OPEN: 11-11 (Sun 7-10.30) **BAR MEALS:** L served Mon-Sat 12-2 D served Mon-Sat 7-9 **RESTAURANT:** L served Sun 12-3 D served Mon-Sat 7-9 **BREWERY/COMPANY:** Free House ◖: Fullers London Pride & 3 Guest ales. **FACILITIES:** Children welcome Garden **ROOMS:** 13 bedrooms 11 en suite 1 family rooms s£45 d£60

★ **Star rating for inspected hotel accommodation**

continued

England

LARLING
Map 13 TL98

Angel Inn 🛏 ☕
NR16 2QU ☎ 01953 717963 ▤ 01953 718561
A list of proprietors since 1631, when the pub was built, records a certain Arthur Stammers from 1913 to 1949. In 1983 great-grandson Brian and his wife Geraldine took on the tenancy at this charming roadside pub. In 1994 Brian became its owner, with son Andrew. The menu includes light bites, steaks, with a variety of sauces, grills, seafood, including fisherman's crumble, Indian dishes, a vegetarian selection, burgers, salads and sandwiches. Rhythm and Booze Festival every August.
OPEN: 10-11 **BAR MEALS:** L served Sun-Sat 12-2 D served Sun-Sat 6.30-9.30 Av main course £7.25 **RESTAURANT:** L served all week 12-2 D served all week 6.30-9.30 Av 3 course à la carte £14
BREWERY/COMPANY: Free House **◀:** Adnams Bitter, Buffy's Bitter, Wolf Bitter, Caledonian Deuchars IPA. ☕: 7
FACILITIES: Children welcome Garden: Large, garden tables
NOTES: Parking 100

LITTLE FRANSHAM
Map 13 TF91

The Canary and Linnet 🛏
Main Rd NR19 2JW ☎ 01362 687027 ▤ 01362 687021
e-mail: ben@canaryandlinnet.co.uk
Dir: Situated on A47 between Dereham and Swaffham
Pretty former blacksmith's cottage with exposed beams, low ceilings, inglenook fireplace and a conservatory dining area overlooking the rear garden. Food is offered in the bar, restaurant or garden from daily specials, carte or bar menu. Typical dishes include cod in beer batter, steak and ale pie, salmon fillet with wholegrain mustard sauce, medallions of pork in a Stilton sauce, or smoked haddock with spinach and cheddar. A selection of malt whiskies.
OPEN: 12-3 6-11 (Sun 12-3 7-10) **BAR MEALS:** L served Mon-Sun 12-2 D served all week 6-9.30 **RESTAURANT:** L served all week 12-2 D served Mon-Sun 6-9.30 **BREWERY/COMPANY:** Free House
◀: Greene King IPA, Woodforde's Wherry, Adnams Bitter, Wolf.
FACILITIES: Children welcome Garden Dogs allowed
NOTES: Parking 70

LITTLE WALSINGHAM
Map 13 TF93

The Black Lion Hotel ♦♦♦♦ 🛏
Friday Market Place NR22 6DB
☎ 01328 820235 ▤ 01328 821406
e-mail: blacklionwalsingham@btinternet.com
Dir: From Kings Lynn take A148 and B1105 or from Norwich take A1067 and B1105.
Frequented by Edward III on his numerous pilgrimages to one of England's oldest shrines at Walsingham, it became a coaching inn in the 17th century, and later hosted the Petty Sessions. Nowadays catering for discerning diners and drinkers, it offers interesting bar snacks like hot smoked mackerel fillets, and classic Greek salad, alongside large filled baps and seafood salad. The à la carte choice includes venison sausages with herb mash, and shank of lamb.
OPEN: 12-3 6-11 (Easter-Oct 11.30-11) (Sat 11.30-11, Sun 12-10.30)
BAR MEALS: L served all week 12-2 D served all week 7-9.30 Av main course £7.50 **RESTAURANT:** L served all week D served all week 7-9.30 Av 3 course à la carte £14.50
BREWERY/COMPANY: Free House **◀:** Greene King IPA, Carlsberg-Tetley Tetley Bitter, Abbott Ale. **FACILITIES:** Children welcome Garden: Courtyard garden, Picnic tables, Well Dogs allowed Water, food **ROOMS:** 6 bedrooms 6 en suite 1 family rooms s£40 d£60

MARSHAM
Map 13 TG12

The Plough Inn 🛏
Old Norwich Rd NR10 5PS ☎ 01263 735000 ▤ 01263 735407
e-mail: enquiries@ploughinnmarsham.co.uk
Dir: Telephone for directions
Smart, traditional-style country pub and restaurant close to the historic town of Aylsham and ideally placed for the Norfolk Broads. Good base for fishing and walking; 10 en suite bedrooms. A typical menu includes dishes like home-made pies, vegetarian options, and fish choices such as plaice, cod and red snapper.
OPEN: 11-3 6-11 25/26 Dec Restaurant closed **BAR MEALS:** L served all week 12-2.30 D served all week 6.30-9 Av main course £9 **RESTAURANT:** L served Mon-Sat 12-2.30 D served all week 6.30-9.00 Av 3 course à la carte £19.50 Av 2 course fixed price £6.95
BREWERY/COMPANY: Free House **◀:** Adnams, Greene King IPA, Woodforde's. **FACILITIES:** Children welcome Garden: Large lawned garden, trees & shrubs **NOTES:** Parking 80 **ROOMS:** 2 family rooms s£43.50 d£60 (♦♦♦)

MUNDFORD
Map 13 TL89

Crown Hotel
Crown Rd IP26 5HQ ☎ 01842 878233 ▤ 01842 878982
Dir: Take A11 until Barton Mills interception, then A1065 to Brandon & thru to Mundford
Ideal for those who enjoy walking, the Crown is surrounded by the Thetford Forest and was once a hunting inn. Unusually for Norfolk, the property is built on a hill so the garden is on the first floor. The Court Restaurant was once used as a magistrate's court. Today's menu may offer monkfish and lobster tails with savoury citrus butter, or beef roulade with pork forcemeat.
OPEN: 11-11 **BAR MEALS:** L served all week 12-3 D served all week 7-10 Av main course £6 **RESTAURANT:** L served all week 12-3 D served all week 7-10 Av 3 course à la carte £20
BREWERY/COMPANY: Free House **◀:** Courage Directors, Courage Best & Guest ales. **FACILITIES:** Children welcome Garden: beer garden patio, food served outside Dogs allowed

NORWICH
Map 13 TG20

Adam & Eve ☕
Bishopsgate NR3 1RZ ☎ 01603 667423 ▤ 01603 667438
e-mail: theadamandeve@hotmail.com
Customers have been quenching their thirst at this historic, award-winning pub in the heart of Norwich for centuries. The Adam & Eve was first recorded as an alehouse in 1249 when it was used by workmen building the nearby cathedral. The building grew in the 14th and 15th centuries when living accommodation and the Flemish gables were added. A varied menu offers dishes like beef and ale pie with mushrooms, battered cod or plaice, Elizabethan pork and salmon goujons.
OPEN: 11-11 (Sun 12-10.30) Closed: 25-26 Dec, 1 Jan **BAR MEALS:** L served all week 12-7 Av main course £5
BREWERY/COMPANY: **◀:** Adnams Bitter, Scottish Courage Theakston Old Peculiar, Greene King IPA, Wells Bombardier. ☕: 10 **NOTES:** Parking 10

The Fat Cat ☕
49 West End St NR2 4NA ☎ 01603 624364
Back street pub with a wide choice of up to 26 real ales and four Belgian draught beers. Food is limited to filled rolls, and there are tables outside in summer.
OPEN: 12-11 (Sat 11-11, Sun 12-10.30) **◀:** Adnams Best Bitter, Timothy Taylors Landlord, Hop Back Summer Lightning, Greene King Abbot Ale. ☕: 16 **NOTES:** No credit cards

Ribs of Beef ♀

24 Wensum St NR3 1HY ☎ 01603 619517 ▤ 01603 625446
e-mail: gary@ribsofbeef.co.uk
Welcoming riverside pub incorporating remnants of the
original 14th-century building destroyed in the Great Fire in
1507. Once used by the Norfolk wherry skippers, it is still
popular among boat owners cruising the Broads. The pub is
named after one of Henry VIII's favourite dishes. Wide range
of real ales.
OPEN: 10.30-11 **BAR MEALS:** L served all week 12-2.30 D served
by arrangement **BREWERY/COMPANY:** Free House
◑: Woodforde's Wherry, Adnams Bitter, Interbrew Whitbread Bitter,
Marston's Pedigree. **FACILITIES:** Children welcome

REEDHAM   Map 13 TG40

Pick of the Pubs

Railway Tavern 🕭 ♀

17 The Havaker NR13 3HG ☎ 01493 700340
e-mail: railwaytavern@tiscali.co.uk
A quiet country pub in the middle of the Norfolk Broads,
where visitors are as likely to arrive by boat as by car. It
also makes an ideal meeting place for friends or
business colleagues but whatever the reason for calling
in here, you won't be disappointed. Truly a railway
tavern as it is next to Reedham Station where trains from
Norwich, Lowestoft and Great Yarmouth make frequent
stops. The classic Victorian pub serves its own Humpty
Dumpty beers brewed in the village, and organises tours
of the brewery with a buffet afterwards. The Tavern also
plays host to beer festivals twice a year when over 70
real ales from all around the county can be sampled,
and imbibers can take part in a traditional hog roast.
Good home-cooked meals are served at other times in
the restaurant, bar or beer garden from a varied and
innovative menu. Starters run along the lines of red Thai
salmon fishcakes with coriander and lemongrass
mayonnaise, baked Feta with olives and red peppers,
and orange and Cointreau pâté. These can be followed
by main courses like haloumi salad with chargrilled
vegetables, home-made fish pie, beer-battered cod with
chips and mushy peas, wild mushroom risotto with
rocket and shaved Parmesan, and fillet of beef
Wellington. Weekly fish specials might include mixed
seafood tagliatelle, skate wing, and salmon en croûte. No
meal would be complete without one of the tasty sweets,
notably poached pears with cinnamon cream, and apple
and blackberry crumble.
OPEN: 11-3 6-11 (Fri-Sun 11-11) **BAR MEALS:** L served all
week 11.30-3 D served all week 6-9 Av main course £7
RESTAURANT: L served all week 11.30-3 D served all week 6-
9.30 Av 3 course à la carte £12 **BREWERY/COMPANY:** Free
House ◑: Adnams, plus Guest ales. **FACILITIES:** Children
welcome Garden: Food served outside. Overlooking stables
Dogs allowed Water provided **NOTES:** Parking 20

The Reedham Ferry Inn 🕭

Ferry Rd NR13 3HA ☎ 01493 700429 ▤ 01493 700999
Dir: 6m S of Acle on follow signs from Acle or Loddon (Acle to Beccles rd)
Quaint 17th-century inn in lovely Norfolk Broads country and
associated with the last working chain ferry in East Anglia.
With the same name over the door for more than fifty years,
this is one of the longest running family inns in East Anglia.

Typical fare ranges from salads, baguettes, sausage and chips
or pizzas, to joint of the day with all the trimmings, scampi
and chips, or steak and ale pie. The specials boards are
always worth examining.
OPEN: 11-3 6.30-11 (Sun 12-10.30) **BAR MEALS:** L served Mon-
Sat 12-2 D served all week 7-9 Av main course £6.50
RESTAURANT: L served Mon-Sat 12-2 D served all week 7-9
BREWERY/COMPANY: Free House ◑: Woodforde's Wherry,
Adnams - Best & Broadside, Greene King Abbot Ale.
FACILITIES: Children welcome Garden: Beside the River Yare on
the Norfolk Broads Dogs allowed Water provided **NOTES:** Parking
50

REEPHAM   Map 13 TG12

The Old Brewery House Hotel ★★

Mallet Place NR10 4JJ ☎ 01603 870881 ▤ 01603 870969
e-mail: enquiries@oldbreweryhousehotel.co.uk
Dir: Off the A1067 Norwich to Fakenham rd, B1145 signed Aylsham
A grand staircase, highly-polished floors and wooden
panelling characterise this fine hotel, originally built as a
private residence in 1729. It became a hotel in the 1970s,
retaining many of its Georgian features. Alongside the real
ales and fine wines, there's a bar menu of freshly-produced
dishes. Full hotel facilities are also available, including 23
bedrooms, restaurants, conference rooms and a licence to
hold marriage ceremonies.
OPEN: 11-11 (Sun 12-10.30) **BAR MEALS:** L served all week 12-2
D served all week 6.30-9.30 Av main course £6.50 **RESTAURANT:** L
served all week 12-2 D served all week 6.30-9.30 Av 3 course à la
carte £17.95 **BREWERY/COMPANY:** Free House ◑: Adnams
Bitter, Greene King Abbot Ale, Reepham Brewery Ales & Old Speckled
Hen. **FACILITIES:** Children welcome Garden: pond & benches
Dogs allowed **NOTES:** Parking 80 **ROOMS:** 23 bedrooms 23 en
suite s£47.50 d£75

RINGSTEAD   Map 12 TF74

Gin Trap Inn

High St PE36 5JU ☎ 01485 525264
Dir: take A149 from Kings Lynn to Hunstanton, after 15m R at Heacham
Gin traps adorn the beamed interior of this 17th-century
former coaching inn set in a peaceful village on the Peddars
Way, a short drive from the North Norfolk coast. Good range
of traditional pub food on varied menus, including steak and
kidney pie, fresh local sausages, vegetable Kiev, lasagne and a
specials board listing fish and chicken options, all served in
the split-level bar.
OPEN: 11-3 6-11 (open all day summer) Closed: 25 Dec
BAR MEALS: L served all week 12-2 D served all week 7-9 Av main
course £7.50 **RESTAURANT:** L served all week 12-2 D served all
week 7-9 **BREWERY/COMPANY:** Free House ◑: Adnams Best,
Woodfordes Norfolk Nog, Plus guest ales. **FACILITIES:** Garden:
Patio, food served outside Dogs allowed **NOTES:** Parking 50
NOTES: No credit cards

SALTHOUSE   Map 13 TG04

The Dun Cow 🕭

Coast Rd NR25 7XG ☎ 01263 740467
*Dir: Situated on A149 main coast road, 3 miles E from Blakeney, 6 miles
West from Sheringham*
Overlooking some of the country's finest freshwater marshes,
the front garden of this attractive pub is inevitably popular
with birdwatchers and walkers. The bar area was formerly a
blacksmith's forge, and many original 17th-century beams

continued   *continued*

SALTHOUSE continued

have been retained. Children are welcome, but there's also a walled rear garden reserved for adults. The menu includes snacks, pub staples like burgers and baked potatoes, and specials like lamb hotpot, wild mushroom lasagne, chicken provençale or seasonal crab salad.

The Dun Cow

OPEN: 11-11 (Sun 12-10.30) Closed: 25 Dec **BAR MEALS:** L served all week 12-9 D served all week 12-9 Av main course £6.50 **BREWERY/COMPANY:** Pubmaster **◀:** Greene King IPA & Abbot Ale, Adnams Broadside. **FACILITIES:** Children welcome Garden: Front garden, secluded, tables, adults only Dogs allowed **NOTES:** Parking 12

SCOLE
Map 13 TM17

Scole Inn ♀
Ipswich Rd IP21 4DR ☎ 01379 740481 ▤ 01379 740762
Dir: *Telephone for directions*
Just off the Ipswich to Norfolk road, built in 1655, this fine old Grade I listed inn was once the area's prime coaching inn. It has a striking Dutch façade and a wealth of authentic features within its old-fashioned bars and intimate restaurant. Bar food includes lasagne, fresh Lowestoft plaice, steak and ale pie, liver and bacon, and a selection of sandwiches. Fixed-price restaurant dinners are rather more formal.
OPEN: 11-11 (Sun 12-10.30) **BAR MEALS:** L served all week 12-2.15 D served all week 7-9.30 Av main course £6
RESTAURANT: L served Sun-Fri 12-2 D served all week 7-9.30 **BREWERY/COMPANY:** Greene King **◀:** Greene King IPA, Abbot Ale, Speckled Hen. **FACILITIES:** Children welcome Garden: Basic with benches and tables Dogs allowed Water **NOTES:** Parking 48

SCULTHORPE
Map 13 TF83

Sculthorpe Mill
Lynn Rd NR21 9QG ☎ 01328 856161 ▤ 01328 856651
e-mail: sculthorpe@mill4228.fsnet.co.uk
Dir: *0.25m off A148, 2m from Fakenham*
Splendid 18th-century listed watermill straddling the River Wensum, with extensive riverside gardens for summer alfresco drinking. There's a cosy oak-beamed bar and upstairs non-smoking restaurant with river views. The pub menu includes steak and kidney pudding, fish and chips, vegetable stirfry, and paella; the restaurant offers dishes such as roasted loin of pork and Brie, strips of chicken with Cajun seasoning, and goat's cheese and aubergine gateau.
OPEN: 11-3 6-11 (Summer 11-11) **BAR MEALS:** L served all week 11.30-2.30 D served all week 6.30-9.30 Av main course £5.50

RESTAURANT: L served Sun-Sat 12-2.30 D served all week 7-9.30 Av 3 course à la carte £20 **BREWERY/COMPANY:** Free House **◀:** Fosters, Greene King Ipa, Old Speckled Hen. **FACILITIES:** Garden Dogs allowed **NOTES:** Parking 60

SNETTISHAM
Map 12 TF63

Pick of the Pubs

The Rose & Crown ★★ ◉ 🐾 ♀
Old Church Rd PE31 7LX ☎ 01485 541382 ▤ 01485 543172
e-mail: info@roseandcrownsnettisham.co.uk
Dir: *Head N from Kings Lynn on A149 signed to Hunstanton. Inn in centre of Snettisham between market square and the church*

Built in the 14th century to house the craftsmen building Snettisham's famous church, the Rose & Crown is a charming family-run inn. Situated opposite the village cricket pitch, it offers an ideal base from which to visit Sandringham, the nearby bird reserves, and the lovely North Norfolk beaches. With a growing reputation for exciting, good quality food and a regularly-changing menu encompassing both traditional pub favourites and more exotic dishes, it's hardly surprising that large numbers of drinkers and diners are drawn here. Expect crunchy Vietnamese duck salad, and pan-roasted hake with lime polenta fries from the specials list, with whole citrus-roasted sea bass with Mexican spiced potatoes, and fillet of cod with spinach and Gruyère croquettes from the menu. Starters and lighter meals might include toasted ciabatta with garlic prawns, and salt and pepper squid with chilli ginger. A wide range of real ales and wines by the glass.
OPEN: 11-11 (Sun 12-10.30) **BAR MEALS:** L served all week 12-2 D served all week 6.30-9 Av main course £10
RESTAURANT: L served all week 12-2 D served all week 6-9 Av 3 course à la carte £20 **BREWERY/COMPANY:** Free House **◀:** Adnams Bitter & Broadside, Interbrew Bass, Fuller's London Pride, Greene King IPA. **♀:** 20 **FACILITIES:** Children welcome Garden: Large walled garden, seating & shade, chipmunks Dogs allowed Water **NOTES:** Parking 70 **ROOMS:** 11 bedrooms 11 en suite 4 family rooms s£55 d£90

STIFFKEY
Map 13 TF94

Pick of the Pubs

Stiffkey Red Lion 🐾 ♀
44 Wells Rd NR23 1AJ ☎ 01328 830552 ▤ 01328 830882
e-mail: mail@redlion.freeserve.co.uk
Dir: *Take A149 from Wells toward Sheringham, 4m onL*
Rustic 16th-century brick-and-flint cottage standing amid rolling Norfolk countryside. Popular with walkers,

continued

continued

birdwatchers, holidaymakers and devoted fish fanciers, the many charms of this welcoming watering-hole include fresh fish from King's Lynn, crab from Cromer, mussels from local beds, and first-rate ales from East Anglian brewers like Woodfordes, Elgoods, Adnams and Greene King. The interior comprises three wooden-floored or quarry-tiled rooms with open fires and a simple mix of wooden settles, pews and scrubbed tables. Ever-changing blackboard menus may list deep-fried Blakeney whitebait, Stiffkey mussels, and grilled local fish, alongside hearty home-made steak and kidney pie, hand-made sausages with mash, and seared local venison with a port and plum compôte. Lighter bites include home-made soup and imaginative salads. After a day on the beach or strolling the Peddars Way, this is a good stop for families who have use of a large and airy rear conservatory with access to the terraced garden.
OPEN: 11-3 6-11 **BAR MEALS:** L served all week 12-2 D served all week 6-9 Av main course £7.95 **RESTAURANT:** L served all week D served all week **BREWERY/COMPANY:** Free House ◗: Woodforde's Wherry, Adnams Bitter, Greene King Abbot Ale. **FACILITIES:** Children welcome Garden: Terraced patio & garden overlooking valley Dogs allowed Water **NOTES:** Parking 40

STOKE HOLY CROSS   Map 13 TG20

Pick of the Pubs

The Wildebeest Arms ☺ ♀
82-86 Norwich Rd NR14 8QJ
☎ 01508 492497 ▤ 01508 494353
e-mail: wildebeest@animalinns.co.uk
A passion for fine food underpins the operation of this unusually named dining pub, situated just two miles south of Norwich. Formerly the Red Lion, about eight years ago the old pub was opened up to create a wonderful space with low ceilings and beams on one side, and higher ceilings on the other, working fireplaces at either end and a horseshoe bar in the middle. The interior is striking and sophisticated, but the atmosphere casual and relaxed, attracting a good range of clients from country and city. Good quality local produce forms the basis of dishes along the lines of confit guinea fowl leg with warm apple boudin, roast celeriac and mustard seed jus, and peppered monkfish with saffron risotto, etuvée leeks and courgette tagliatelle. There is an extensive wine list and a good monthly choice by the glass.
OPEN: 12-3 6-11 (Sun 12-3 7-10.30) Closed: Dec 25-26 **RESTAURANT:** L served all week 12-2 D served all week 7-10 Av 3 course à la carte £22.50 Av 3 course fixed price £18 **BREWERY/COMPANY:** Free House ◗: Adnams, Greene King Old Speckled Hen. **FACILITIES:** Children welcome Garden: Beer garden, food served outdoors **NOTES:** Parking 30

STOW BARDOLPH   Map 12 TF60

Pick of the Pubs

The Hare Arms ☺ ♀
PE34 3HT ☎ 01366 382229 ▤ 01366 385522
e-mail: info@harearms.freeserve.co.uk
Dir: From King's Lynn take A10 to Downham Market. After 9m village signed on L
At the heart of a Norfolk village, this attractive ivy-clad pub took its name from the surrounding Hare estate over

200 years ago. Today there's a conservatory and terrace overlooking the garden, where peacocks and chickens roam freely, and the old coach house and stables have been converted to a functions room. The welcoming atmosphere and excellent food - the pub won its brewer's national food pub of the year award in 2002 - justifiably has wide appeal. Fresh produce is used: seasonal game, fish and shellfish from the coast, and local lamb, beef and vegetables. Bar and restaurant menus are offered, plus many daily specials, including vegetarian options. Choices typically include Stilton and bacon soup; slow-braised lamb shank with garlic, rosemary and red wine; steak and peppercorn pie; chicken breast stuffed with goat's cheese in a red pepper sauce; and asparagus and pea risotto flavoured with Parmesan, lemon and mint.
OPEN: 11-2.30 6-11 Closed: 25-26 Dec **BAR MEALS:** L served all week 12-2 D served all week 7-10 Av main course £8 **RESTAURANT:** L served Sun 12-2 D served Mon-Sat 7-9.30 Av 3 course à la carte £25 Av 3 course fixed price £21 **BREWERY/COMPANY:** Greene King ◗: Greene King, Abbot Ale, IPA & Old Speckled Hen, Strong Suffolk. ♀: 7 **FACILITIES:** Garden: Picnic tables, spacious, chickens, peacocks **NOTES:** Parking 50

SWANTON MORLEY   Map 13 TG01

Darbys Freehouse
1&2 Elsing Rd NR20 4NY ☎ 01362 637647 ▤ 01362 637987
Dir: From A47 (Norwich to King's Lynn) take B1147 to Dereham
Converted from two cottages in 1988 and originally built as a large country house in the 1700s, this popular freehouse opened when the village's last traditional pub closed. Named after the woman who lived here in the 1890s and farmed the adjacent land. Stripped pine tables, exposed beams and inglenook fireplaces enhance the authentic country pub atmosphere. Up to eight real ales are available, and home-cooked food includes pigeon breast, steak and mushroom pudding, pesto pasta and salmon fillet.
OPEN: 11.30-3 6-11 (Sat 11.30-11, Sun 12-10.30) Dec 25 Closed Eve **BAR MEALS:** L served all week 12-2.15 D served all week 6.30-9.45 Av main course £6.95 **RESTAURANT:** L served all week 12-2.15 D served all week 6.30-9.45 Av 3 course à la carte £17.50 **BREWERY/COMPANY:** Free House ◗: Woodforde's Wherry, Badger Tanglefoot, Greene King IPA, Adnams Broadside. **FACILITIES:** Children welcome Garden: beer garden, outdoor eating, Dogs allowed **NOTES:** Parking 75

THOMPSON   Map 13 TL99

Pick of the Pubs

Chequers Inn ♦♦♦♦ ☺
Griston Rd IP24 1PX ☎ 01953 483360 ▤ 01953 488092
e-mail: themcdowalls@barbox.net
Dir: Telephone for directions
A long building with Norfolk reed thatch sweeping almost to the ground, this historic inn is set in a country garden surrounded by fields in a village close to Thompson Water. It was sold as a pub in the 16th century but is probably older, and in its time has served as manor court, doctor's surgery and meeting room. These days, as a popular pub and restaurant, visitors can expect good beers and freshly-cooked food amid the beams, gleaming horse brasses and bucolic bygones. The bar snack menu,

continued

continued

THOMPSON continued — Map 13 TL99

carte and daily specials board offer a varied choice, including fresh fish and local game. Popular specials include medallions of ostrich on a Madeira sauce, roast pheasant, deep-fried cod, and double lamb chops with cheese and mushrooms. Home-made puddings like Bakewell tart and apple and blackberry pie also go down well. Purpose-built accommodation is available next to the inn.

OPEN: 11.30-2.30 6.30-11 (Sun 12-3, 6.30-10.30)
BAR MEALS: L served all week 12-2 D served all week 6.30-9.30 Av main course £6.50 **RESTAURANT:** L served all week 12-2 D served all week 6.30-9.30 Av 3 course à la carte £19 **BREWERY/COMPANY:** Free House ◆: Fuller's London Pride, Adnams Best, Wolf Best, Greene King IPA. **FACILITIES:** Children welcome Garden: Childrens climbing frame lawned area Dogs allowed Water, Sweeties **NOTES:** Parking 35 **ROOMS:** 3 bedrooms 3 en suite 1 family rooms s£40 d£60

THORNHAM — Map 12 TF74

Pick of the Pubs

Lifeboat Inn ★★ ◎ 🍴
Ship Ln PE36 6LT ☎ 01485 512236 🖷 01485 512323
e-mail: reception@lifeboatinn.co.uk
Dir: A149 to Hunstanton, follow coast rd to Thornham, pub 1st L

A long and colourful history attaches to this 16th-century inn overlooking the salt marshes and Thornham Harbour, and despite being much extended, its original character has been retained. There are roaring log fires in winter and fine summer views across open meadows to a sandy beach. Beyond the centuries-old Smugglers' Bar, with its hanging paraffin lamps and creaking oak door, is the conservatory, renowned for its ancient vine and adjacent walled patio garden. The best available fish and game

feature on the menus in the form of traditional country fare. Mussels are a speciality, along with fish and chips - fillet of finest fresh cod in a crisp beer batter. Other specials include local game casseroled in cider, beef and five bean chilli, and pan-seared tuna loin with peppery noodles, joining a list of light snacks and vegetarian dishes. Most bedrooms have sea views, with children and well-behaved dogs welcome.
OPEN: 11-11 (Sun 11-10.30) **BAR MEALS:** L served all week 12-2.30 D served all week 6.30-9.30 Av main course £8.95
RESTAURANT: D served all week 7-9.30 Av 3 course fixed price £25 **BREWERY/COMPANY:** Free House ◆: Adnams, Woodforde's Wherry, Greene King Abbot Ale.
FACILITIES: Children welcome Garden: Enclosed wall patio garden Dogs allowed Water provided **NOTES:** Parking 100 **ROOMS:** 22 bedrooms 22 en suite

THORPE MARKET — Map 13 TG23

Green Farm Restaurant & Hotel ★★
North Walsham Rd NR11 8TH ☎ 01263 833602 🖷 01263 833163
e-mail: grfarmh@aol.com
Dir: Situated on A149
Conveniently situated for exploring the Norfolk Broads, or the historic houses at Blickling, Felbrigg and Sandringham, this 16th-century flint-faced former farmhouse features a pubby bar and an interesting menu. Typical dishes may include grilled marinated breast of duck served on a herbal ratatouille with a sage and balsamic jus, roasted pork cutlet with a sweet pepper crust and spicy garlic and okra sauce, baked fillet of turbot filled with spring onion and prawn mousseline wrapped in filo pastry, or baked cherry tomato and sweet onion tartlet topped with Brie and served with a tomato salsa.
OPEN: 11-11 **BAR MEALS:** L served Sun D served all week 7-9 Av main course £11.95 **RESTAURANT:** L served Sun D served all week 7-8.30 **BREWERY/COMPANY:** Free House ◆: Greene King IPA, Abbot, Morlands. **FACILITIES:** Children welcome Garden: Food served outside Dogs allowed at manager's discretion
NOTES: Parking 75 **ROOMS:** 14 bedrooms 14 en suite s£55 d£70

TITCHWELL — Map 13 TF74

Pick of the Pubs

Titchwell Manor Hotel ★★ 🍴
PE31 8BB ☎ 01485 210221 🖷 01485 210104
e-mail: margaret@titchwellmanor.co.uk
Dir: A149 (coast rd) between Brancaster & Thornham

A century-old manor house with many Victorian features tastefully retained within a light modern décor. It has an all-round appeal, and is particularly popular with family

continued

continued

parties. Outside, the walled garden is full of interesting specimen plants, with wonderful views to the sandy beaches. The hamlet of Titchwell grew around the manor farm and the charming round-towered church, but is best known these days for the important RSPB reserve here, which attracts visitors from all over the world. Two championship golf courses are just minutes away. The seafood bar menu makes no secret of the house speciality, with dishes ranging from dressed Brancaster crab, and Madeira-marinated herring fillet, to baked sea bass, and deep-fried cod with mushy peas and chips. It's not all fish: chargrilled loin of lamb with redcurrant and caper jus, and sautéed duckling breast with a port and black cherry sauce are delicious alternatives.
OPEN: 11-11 **BAR MEALS:** L served all week 12-2 D served all week 6.30-9.30 Av main course £10 **RESTAURANT:** L served all week 12-2 D served all week 6.30-9.30 Av 3 course à la carte £25 Av 3 course fixed price £25 **BREWERY/COMPANY:** Free House **:** Greene King IPA & Abbot Ale. **FACILITIES:** Children welcome Garden: Large walled garden, summerhouse Dogs allowed Water, kennel **NOTES:** Parking 50 **ROOMS:** 16 bedrooms 16 en suite 6 family rooms s£35 d£70

See Pub Walk on page 320

TIVETSHALL ST MARY   Map 13 TM18

The Old Ram Coaching Inn ★★
Ipswich Rd NR15 2DE ☎ 01379 676794 ▤ 01379 608399
e-mail: theoldram@btinternet.com
Dir: On A140 approx 15m S of Norwich
Sympathetically refurbished with exposed brickwork and original beams throughout, this 17th-century inn features a terraced garden and comfortably-furnished bedrooms. Standing menu with very wide selection of meats, fish, salads, pastas, snacks and vegetarian dishes, including dedicated selections for children and the over-60s. Service starts with breakfast from 7.30am. Daily specials might include salmon supreme on a parsnip and honey potato cake with leek and ginger sauce, and medallions of venison with celeriac mash and blackberry sauce.
OPEN: 7.30-11 Closed: Dec 25-26 **BAR MEALS:** L served all week 11.30-10 D served all week Av main course £12.50
BREWERY/COMPANY: Free House **:** Adnams Bitter, Woodforde's Wherry Best Bitter, Coors Bass. **:** 22
FACILITIES: Children welcome Garden: Terraced, herb garden, patio heaters Dogs allowed Water **NOTES:** Parking 150 **ROOMS:** 11 bedrooms 11 en suite 1 family room s£45 d£57

UPPER SHERINGHAM   Map 13 TG14

The Red Lion Inn
The Street NR26 8AD ☎ 01263 825408
Dir: A140(Norwich to Cromer) then A148 to Sheringham/Upper Sheringham
A small village setting for this 17th-century cottage inn, close to the steam railway and North Norfolk's splendidly isolated coast. It's a flint building, with original floors, natural pine furniture and a large wood-burning stove. All food is cooked on the premises, with local produce used whenever possible, including plenty of grilled fish with a variety of fresh sauces. Other options are steak and Norfolk Ale pie, cottage pie with leek, cheese and potato topping, and Thai style red chicken curry.
OPEN: 11.30-3 6.30-11 Summer Hols Open all day Sun
BAR MEALS: L served all week 12-2 D served all week 6.30-9 Av main course £7.50 **RESTAURANT:** L served all week 12-2 D served all week 6.30-9 Av 3 course à la carte £14 **BREWERY/COMPANY:** Free House

: Woodforde's Wherry, Greene King IPA. **FACILITIES:** Children welcome Garden: Large lawned area with fruit trees Dogs allowed Water **NOTES:** Parking 16 **NOTES:** No credit cards

WARHAM ALL SAINTS   Map 13 TF94

Pick of the Pubs

Three Horseshoes
NR23 1NL ☎ 01328 710547
Dir: From Wells A149 to Cromer, then R onto B1105 to Warham
This fascinating free house was an alehouse in 1725, and has remained one ever since. It has one of the best original interiors in the area, with gaslights in the main bar, scrubbed deal tables, and grandfather clock that was made in nearby Dereham in 1830. There's a rare example of a Norfolk 'twister' set into the ceiling - a curious red and green dial for playing village roulette. Memorabilia from all the original Norfolk breweries is displayed in the bar, another room has royal mementos and a third is full of old vacuum cleaners, cooking implements and local artefacts. Outside, there's a sheltered lawn with picnic tables, as well as a new courtyard garden featuring a well. Expect East Anglian ales from the cask and hearty Norfolk cooking using fresh local ingredients. Typical dishes include rabbit with spinach; garlic lamb pie; and grilled local trout.
OPEN: 11.30-2.30 6-11 (Sun 12-3 6-10.30) **BAR MEALS:** L served all week 12-1.45 D served all week 6.00-8.30 Av main course £7.50 **BREWERY/COMPANY:** Free House **:** Greene King IPA, Woodforde's Wherry. **FACILITIES:** Children welcome Garden: Grassed area with seating for around 40 Dogs allowed Water, Dog food and biscuits **NOTES:** No credit cards

WELLS-NEXT-THE-SEA   Map 13 TF94

Pick of the Pubs

The Crown Hotel
The Buttlands NR23 1EX ☎ 01328 710209 ▤ 01328 711432
e-mail: reception@thecrownhotelwells.com
Dir: 10m from Fakenham on B1105
With the only safe harbour for yachtsmen along the north Norfolk coast, the picturesque fishing port of Wells was where Horatio Nelson's wife Fanny rented a house while he was at sea. This 16th-century coaching inn underwent a wholesale makeover a little while ago, but although now bright and uncluttered, its old world charm is as apparent as ever. For proof, have a drink or a light meal in the Crown Bar, with its open fire and ancient beams. Try the sampler of European and Asian appetisers served on a black slate tile. In the more formal restaurant, the menu features traditional favourites such as roast rack of lamb, modern British cooking such as duck breast with seared scallop and crushed potato, or maybe tiger prawns flash fried in garlic butter with watermelon curry and fragrant rice, just one of the dishes influenced by Pacific Rim cuisine. A superb wine list complements the menus.
OPEN: 11 -11 **BAR MEALS:** L served all week 12-2 D served all week 6-9 Av main course £9 **RESTAURANT:** L served Sun D served all week 7-10 Av 3 course fixed price £29.95
BREWERY/COMPANY: Free House **:** Adnams Bitter, Fisherman, Adnams Guest Ale, Bitburger. **:** 12 **FACILITIES:** Children welcome Decking area Dogs allowed on leads

continued

Open: 11.30-3, 6-11
Bar Meals: L served all week 12-2,
D served all week 6-9.30.
Av cost main course £7.95
RESTAURANT: L served all week 12-2,
D served all week 6-9.30.
BREWERY/COMPANY:
Free House.
🍺: Adnams, Woodforde's Wherry,
Fullers London Pride, Marstons Pedigree
John Smiths Smooth.
FACILITIES: Children welcome,
Garden - Landscaped beer garden.
NOTES: Parking 55

Bird in Hand

An eclectic mixture of styles characterises this interesting pub-restaurant in the heart of the Norfolk countryside.

Church Road, Wreningham,
Norwich, NR16 1BH
☎ 01508 489438 📠 01508 488004
Dir: 6m S of Norwich on the B1113.

The quarry-tiled bar features an attractive open-beamed roof, whilst diners can choose between the elegant Victorian-style dining room and the more traditional farmhouse restaurant. The Bird in Hand uses only local suppliers who grow much of their own produce, while a wide variety of herbs are grown in the pub garden. Fresh fish is bought from an old-established Norwich fishmonger who specialises only in top quality fish from Lowestoft and delivers on a daily basis. Meat comes from a local butcher. The menus are written to include an assortment of traditional favourites combined with a choice of more adventurous dishes which have the chef's reputation for flair and innovation stamped on them. Diner profiling also helps the Bird in Hand to recognise its customer requirements. Traditional bar favourites might include seared breast of Gressingham duck on a pool of mixed peppercorn and orange sauce and flavoured with Cointreau, chargrilled thick-cut salmon steak with a white wine cream sauce, and oven-roasted bell peppers stuffed with couscous, spring onions, Mozzarella cheese and basil served with pesto. Alternatively, try slow-braised game casserole, baked herb pancakes, pan-fried veal escalope, flaked pieces of salmon, cod, haddock and peeled prawns, or braised lamb's liver and kidneys in sweet and sour sauce with strips of peppers and shallots served with wild rice. For something lighter, you might like to choose from an appetising selection of baguettes and filled jacket potatoes.

WEST BECKHAM
Map 13 TG13

The Wheatsheaf ☺ ♀
Manor Farm, Church Rd NR25 6NX ☎ 01263 822110
Dir: off the A148 (between Holt & Cromer) opp Sheringham Park, signed Baconsthorpe Castle, L at village triangle after 1m
Former manor house converted to a pub in 1984 and retaining many original features. Sample one of the real ales from Woodfordes Brewery and relax in the large garden where a fully-restored gypsy caravan is on display. On summer evenings you can even enjoy a game of floodlit pétanque. Great pub atmosphere inside and a mix of traditional pub food and more adventurous specials. Expect pan-fried lemon sole with hot tartare sauce, baked duck breast in puff pastry stuffed with mushroom and thyme pate, or Brie-stuffed chicken supreme on lavender risotto.
OPEN: 11.30-3 6.30-11 (Winter 12-3, 6.30-11) **BAR MEALS:** L served all week 12-2 D served Mon-Sat 7-9 Av main course £7.95 **RESTAURANT:** L served all week 12-2 D served Mon-Sat 7-9 **BREWERY/COMPANY:** Free House ◖: Woodforde's Wherry Best Bitter, Nelson's Revenge, Norfolk Nog, Admirals Reserve & Guest Ales. ♀: 7 **FACILITIES:** Children welcome Garden: Large garden with gazebo and covered patio Dogs allowed Water **NOTES:** Parking 50

WINTERTON-ON-SEA
Map 13 TG41

Fishermans Return ☺
The Lane NR29 4BN ☎ 01493 393305 ▤ 01493 393951
e-mail: fishermans_return@btopenworld.com
Dir: 8 miles N of Gt Yarmouth on B1159

Close to the beach (sensible shoes essential for clambering over dunes!), this 300-year-old brick and flint pub is popular with visiting walkers and birdwatchers as well as locals. Dogs, too, are welcome. In addition to the standard pub fare, there are daily specials - often drawing on local produce. They might include seafood lasagne, hot Winterton smoked salmon, and various chicken dishes (such as orange and tarragon or lime and coriander) served on wild and basmati rice.
OPEN: 11-2.30 6.30-11 (Sat 11-11, Sun 12-10.30) **BAR MEALS:** L served all week 11.30-2 D served all week 6.30-9 Av main course £7 **BREWERY/COMPANY:** Free House ◖: Woodforde's Wherry & Norfolk Nog, Adnams Best Bitter & Broadside and John Smiths Bitter. **FACILITIES:** Children welcome Garden: Large enclosed, with tables, play equipment Dogs allowed Water, chews **NOTES:** Parking 50

WIVETON
Map 13 TG04

Wiveton Bell ☺
Blakeney Rd NR25 7TL ☎ 01263 740101
e-mail: enquiries@wivetonbell.co.uk
Picturesque village inn close to the green and church, with cosy beamed bar and spacious non-smoking conservatory

continued

restaurant. The owner is Danish so expect some native influence here, though the ingredients are largely local. Dishes might include pork tenderloin, venison steak with a cranberry and ginger sauce, chicken stirfry in noodles, cod fillet in home-made batter, and mussels and crab in season.
OPEN: 12-2.30 6.30-11 (Closed Sun eve & Mon in winter) Closed: Closed 2 wks Jan/Feb **BAR MEALS:** L served all week 12-2 D served all week 7-9 Av main course £10 **RESTAURANT:** L served all week 12-2 D served all week 7-9 Av 3 course à la carte £17 **BREWERY/COMPANY:** Free House ◖: Woodeforde's Nelson's Revenge, Adnams Bitter. **FACILITIES:** Garden: Grass lawn and tables Dogs allowed Water **NOTES:** Parking 5

WOODBASTWICK
Map 13 TG31

The Fur & Feather ♀
Slad Ln NR13 6HQ ☎ 01603 720003 ▤ 01603 722266
Dir: 1.5m N of B1140, 8m NE of Norwich
An idyllic country pub in a peaceful location, it was originally two farm cottages and now boasts three cosy bar areas and a smart restaurant. Next door is Woodforde's Brewery, and all eight ales are offered here, served straight from the cask. Two of these ales feature in the inn's signature dishes of Nogin Yorky and bangers and mash with crispy onions. From an interesting menu expect gamekeepers sausage with onion marmalade to start, to pan-fried salmon with tempura vegetables, or cod in Great Eastern beer batter as a main course.
OPEN: 11.30-3 6-11 (Summer Mon-Sat 11.30-11, Sun 11.30-11) **BAR MEALS:** L served all week 12-2 D served all week 6-9 Av main course £8 **RESTAURANT:** L served all week 12-2 D served all week 6-9 **BREWERY/COMPANY:** Woodforde's ◖: Woodforde's Wherry, Great Eastern, Norfolk Nog, Nelsons Revenge. ♀: 8 **FACILITIES:** Garden: Large garden with fenced pond **NOTES:** Parking 100

WRENINGHAM
Map 13 TM19

Pick of the Pubs

Bird in Hand ☺ ♀
Church Rd NR16 1BH ☎ 01508 489438 ▤ 01508 488004
See Pick of the Pubs on opposite page

NORTHAMPTONSHIRE

ASHBY ST LEDGERS
Map 11 SP56

The Olde Coach House Inn ☺ ♀
CV23 8UN ☎ 01788 890349 ▤ 01788 891922
e-mail: oldcoachhouse@traditionalfreehouses.com
Dir: M1 J18 follow signs A361/Daventry.Village on L
A late 19th-century farmhouse and outbuildings, skilfully converted into a pub with dining areas, accommodation and meeting rooms, set in a village that dates way back to the Domesday Book of 1086. Beer is taken seriously here with up to eight regularly changing real ales and legendary beer festivals, the pub also serves fresh, high quality food in comfortable surroundings, featuring game casserole, seafood linguine, massive mixed grills and summer barbecues.
OPEN: 12-2.30 6-11 (Sat 12-11, Sun 12-10.30) **BAR MEALS:** L served all week 12-2 D served all week 6-9.30 Av main course £7 **RESTAURANT:** L served all week 12-2 D served all week 6-9.30 **BREWERY/COMPANY:** Free House ◖: Everards Original, Interbrew Flowers Original, Fuller's London Pride, Hook Norton Best. **FACILITIES:** Children welcome Garden: Landscaped garden Dogs allowed Water **NOTES:** Parking 50

The Falcon Inn

Cross picturesque water meadows and pasture on this gentle walk by the Nene.

From the pub turn right and take the turning opposite, signposted Nassington. Cross the Willow Brook and take a waymarked footpath on the right to the far boundary, crossing into the next field by an oak tree. Follow the clear path diagonally right towards farm outbuildings.

With the house facing you, veer right, then left alongside the buildings, keeping three trees over to the right in the field. Follow the clear path towards hedge and trees, making for the field's left-hand corner. Cross a wooden footbridge and aim diagonally across the field to a dismantled railway track. Cross over and follow a grassy track through the fields to a footbridge spanning the River Nene.

Walk along to the next bridge and cross the river by Elton Lock. Make for the village

green at Elton and turn right at the road. Turn right after a few paces into Chapel Lane and head out of the village, passing alongside Elton Park and some cottages and then continue on a bridleway. Cross a wooden footbridge and then ascend a slope towards trees. Make for a gate and join a track leading to a woodland path. Keep ahead.

Emerge from the trees, follow the field edge to a mast in the corner, drop down the bank to a gate and turn right. Make for two kissing gates, cross the A605 to two more gates and then turn right in the field. Look for a stile in the boundary, with two gates just beyond it. Turn right and follow the road round to the left. Turn right at the Nene Way sign, pass under the A605 and keep right in front of Eaglethorpe Mill.

THE FALCON INN, FOTHERINGHAY
PE8 5HZ
☎ 01832 226254
Directions: N of A605 between Peterborough & Oundle
Attractive 18th-century stone-built inn close to the site of Fotheringhay Castle. Sit in the local's tap room, the smart dining room or conservatory extension, and choose food from blackboard or seasonal carte.
Open: 11.30-3 6-11 (Sun 12-3 7-10.30)
Bar Meals: 12-2.15 7-9.30
Notes: Children welcome (toys, highchairs). Garden with views. Parking. (See page 340 for full entry)

Turn left immediately beyond it, cross a stile and veer away from the water to a stile and footbridge. Continue ahead to Warmington Lock. Veer slightly left towards Fotheringhay Church and join a track. When it bends right, go straight on along the field path to the next track. Turn left, pass sheep pens and head for the site of Fotheringhay Castle. Turn right here, follow the track and return to the pub.

DISTANCE: 6 miles/9.7km
MAP: OS Explorer 227
TERRAIN: Low-lying water meadows, pasture and parkland
PATHS: Field paths, tracks and bridleways. Some road walking
GRADIENT: Mainly level ground

Walk submitted and checked by Nick Channer

England

ASHTON
Map 12 TL08

The Old Crown 🛏 ♀ NEW
1 Stoke Rd NN7 2JN ☎ 01604 862268
Dir: 5 mins from J15 off the A1. 1 mile from A508 from Roade Village, 5 mins from National Waterways Museum at Stoke Bruerne

Attractive 17th-century inn with traditional beamed interior and walls decorated with many prints and mirrors. Outside there are two attractively-planted gardens for alfresco dining. Snacks such as soups, sandwiches and salads are available, along with main courses like seared fennel-crusted tuna on Mediterranean couscous; charred aubergine and coconut curry; five-herb roasted chicken breast with potato and celeriac mash; and steamed steak, mushroom, bacon, Stilton and herb suet pudding.
OPEN: 12-3 6-11 **BAR MEALS:** L served Mon-Sun 12-2.15 D served Mon-Sun 6.30-9.30 Av main course £8.50 **RESTAURANT:** L served Mon-Sun 12-2.15 D served Mon-Sun 6.30-9.15 Av 3 course à la carte £22.50 **◀:** Charles Wells, Bombardier. ♀: 7
FACILITIES: Garden: Two large gardens, seating **NOTES:** Parking 20

BADBY
Map 11 SP55

The Windmill Inn
Main St NN11 3AN ☎ 01327 702363 ▤ 01327 311521
e-mail: windmill_badby@fsmail.net
Dir: M1 J16 take A45 to Daventry then A361 S. Village 2m

A friendly and relaxed atmosphere prevails in the beamed and flag-stoned bars of this 17th-century thatched inn. It is set at the centre of the village, overlooking the green, close to Blenheim Palace, Stratford and Silverstone. A varied menu includes steamed sea bream fillets with lemon and thyme, linguine with wild mushrooms, and loin of lamb wrapped in bacon with orange, redcurrant and port sauce.
OPEN: 11.30-3.30 5.30-11 **BAR MEALS:** L served all week 12-2 D served all week 7-9.30 Av main course £9.25 **RESTAURANT:** L served all week 12-2 D served all week 7-9.30 Av 3 course à la carte £21.50 **BREWERY/COMPANY:** Free House **◀:** Bass, Flowers, Brains, Wadworth 6X. **FACILITIES:** Children welcome Garden: Front of pub, adjacent to village, 10 tables Dogs allowed **NOTES:** Parking 25

BULWICK
Map 11 SP99

Pick of the Pubs

The Queen's Head 🛏 ♀
High St NN17 3DY ☎ 01780 450272
Dir: Just off the A43 nr Corby, 12m from Peterborough, 2m from Dene Park

No changes to the charm of this 17th-century inn overlooking the village church and open countryside. Inside, it's a warren of small rooms with stone floors and log fires - perfect for enjoying a wide selection of ales, wines and modern pub food. Dishes could include roasted duck breast with Cassis sauce, chicken breast filled with wild mushroom and smoked bacon or whole steamed sea bass with herbs and a saffron butter sauce.
OPEN: 12-2 6-11 **BAR MEALS:** L served Tue-Sun 12-2 D served Tue-Sat 6-9 Av main course £9.95 **RESTAURANT:** L served Tue-Sun 12-2 D served Tue-Sat 6-10 Av 3 course fixed price £20 **BREWERY/COMPANY:** Free House **◀:** Timothy Taylor Landlord, Greene King Old Speckled Hen, Fullers London Pride, Jennings Sneck Lifter. **FACILITIES:** Garden: Food served outside. Patio area Dogs allowed Children welcome Water provided **NOTES:** Parking 40

CASTLE ASHBY
Map 11 SP85

Falcon Hotel ★★ ☺ 🛏 ♀
NN7 1LF ☎ 01604 696200 ▤ 01604 696673
e-mail: falcon@castleashby.co.uk
Dir: A428 between Bedford & Northampton. Opposite war memorial

In tranquil village surroundings, the Falcon is perhaps the archetypal Northamptonshire country-cottage hotel. In the 60-seat restaurant everything is prepared from fresh ingredients. The fixed-price lunch menu offers salad of home-cured gravadlax, with artichokes and olives, breast of guinea fowl, with tarragon mousse and Parma ham, and grilled pavé of salmon, topped with a mustard and herb crust. At dinner try spiced mussel broth, followed perhaps by pan-fried fillet of venison, or grilled sea bass.
OPEN: 12-3 6-11 **BAR MEALS:** L served all week 12-2 D served all week 7-9.30 Av main course £9 **RESTAURANT:** L served all week 12-2 D served all week 7-10 Av 3 course à la carte £28.50 Av 3 course fixed price £23.50 **BREWERY/COMPANY:** Old English Inns **◀:** Scottish Courage John Smith's, Greene King Ruddles County & IPA. **FACILITIES:** Children welcome Garden: Food served outdoors, herb garden Dogs allowed **NOTES:** Parking 60 **ROOMS:** 16 bedrooms 16 en suite s£69.50 d£85

CHACOMBE
Map 11 SP44

Pick of the Pubs

George and Dragon 🛏
Silver St OX17 2JR ☎ 01295 711500 ▤ 01295 758827
e-mail: chacombepub@aol.com
Dir: From M40 take A361 to Daventry, 1st R to Chacombe, 2nd L in village

Well placed for M40 travellers and popular with business folk from nearby Banbury, the George & Dragon is an attractive, honey-stoned, 16th-century pub tucked away by the church in a pretty conservation village. Expect a welcoming atmosphere within the three comfortable bars, with low beams, log fires, simple wooden chairs and settles, and a warm terracotta decor enhancing the overall charm of the inn. Blackboards list the interesting choice of food, from sandwiches, filled jacket potatoes and unusual pasta dishes to crispy duck breast with chilli and cranberry sauce, collops of pork with creamy leek and sage sauce, and decent fish specials - roasted monkfish with spring onion and mushroom sauce.
OPEN: 12-11 **BAR MEALS:** L served all week 12-2 D served Mon-Sat 7-9.30 Av main course £10 **RESTAURANT:** L served all week 12-2 D served all week 7-9.30 Av 3 course à la carte £17 **BREWERY/COMPANY:** Free House **◀:** Theakston Best, Scottish Courage Courage Directors. **FACILITIES:** Children welcome Dogs allowed **NOTES:** Parking 40

England

CLIPSTON
Map 11 SP78

The Bulls Head 🛏 ♀
Harborough Rd LE16 9RT ☎ 01858 525268 📠 01858 525266
e-mail: george@bullsheadclipston.co.uk .
Dir: *On B4036 S of Market Harborough*
American airmen once pushed coins between the beams as a good luck charm before bombing raids, and the trend continues with foreign paper money pinned all over the inn. In addition to its good choice of real ales, the pub has an amazing collection of over 600 whiskies. The menu offers a comprehensive choice including liver and onions, Barnsley lamb chop, and specials like noisettes of lamb with a honey and rosemary gravy.
OPEN: 11.30-3 5.30-11 **BAR MEALS:** L served Tue-Sun 11.30-2 D served all week 6.30-9.30 Av main course £9 **RESTAURANT:** L served Tue-Sun 11.30-2 D served all week 6.30-9.30 Av 3 course à la carte £17.50
BREWERY/COMPANY: Free House ◀: Bass, Marston's Pedigree, Greene King, Abbot Ale. **FACILITIES:** Children welcome Garden: Patio Dogs allowed **NOTES:** Parking 40

CRICK
Map 11 SP57

The Red Lion Inn 🛏
52 Main Rd NN6 7TX ☎ 01788 822342 📠 01788 822342
Dir: *From M1 J18, 0.75m E on A428*
A thatched, stone-built former coaching inn dating from the 1600s, with open fires, beams and horse brasses. Family run for nearly 25 years, continuity is the secret of the Red Lion Inn's success. People know just what to expect - a clean and tidy pub, a friendly atmosphere, real ales and traditional food. The daily home-made pie is a lunchtime favourite, and steaks are a speciality of the evening menu.
OPEN: 11-2.30 6.15-11 (Sun 12-3, 7-10.30) **BAR MEALS:** L served all week 12-2 D served Mon-Sat 7-9 **BREWERY/COMPANY:** Wellington Pub Co ◀: Websters, Marston's Pedigree, Scottish Courage Theakston Best, Greene King Old Speckled Hen. **FACILITIES:** Garden: Terrace, picnic tables, chairs etc Dogs allowed Water **NOTES:** Parking 40

EASTCOTE
Map 11 SP65

Eastcote Arms ♀
6 Gayton Rd NN12 8NG ☎ 01327 830731
Dir: *Telephone for directions*
Brick and stone village inn dating from 1670 with inglenook fireplaces, original beams, a welcoming atmosphere, and a splendid south-facing garden. Look out for the ghost of an old landlord, and racing drivers from the nearby Silverstone track. Good value lunchtime snacks include filled baguettes, old favourites like ham, egg and chips, and fish and chips, while evening fare features Cumberland sausage in onion gravy, steak and ale pie, and lobster pastry purse.
OPEN: 12-3 6-11 (Sun 12-10.30, Fri-Sat 12-11) **BAR MEALS:** L served Tue-Sat 12-2 D served Wed-Sun 7-9.30 Av course £8.50 **RESTAURANT:** L served Tue-Sun 12-2 D served Wed-Sun 7-9.30 Av 3 course à la carte £16 **BREWERY/COMPANY:** ◀: Adnams, Greene King IPA, Pedigree, Tim Taylor Landlord. ♀: 10 **FACILITIES:** Children welcome Garden: Walled beer garden Dogs allowed In the garden only. Water provided **NOTES:** Parking 20

EAST HADDON
Map 11 SP66

Red Lion Hotel 🛏 ♀
NN6 8BU ☎ 01604 770223 📠 01604 770767
Dir: *7m NW of Northampton on A428, 8m from J18 of M1. Midway between Northampton & Rugby.*
Handy for visiting nearby Althorp Park, this smart 17th-century inn is built of eye-catching golden stone and thatch, with a popular walled side garden filled with lilac, roses and fruit trees. Oak panelled settles, cast-iron framed tables and recessed china cabinets characterise the interior. A wide-ranging menu features the likes of pheasant casserole, and rabbit cobbler in the bar, and perhaps local game terrine, and roast crown of partridge and mulled wine pear from the restaurant menu.
OPEN: 11-2.30 6-11 Closed: Dec 25 **BAR MEALS:** L served all week 12.15-2 D served Mon-Sat 7-9.30 Av main course £10 **RESTAURANT:** L served all week 12.15-2 D served Mon-Sat 7-9.30 Av 3 course à la carte £25 Av 3 course fixed price £21 **BREWERY/COMPANY:** Charles Wells ◀: Wells Eagle IPA, & Bombardier, Adnams Broadside. ♀: 7 **FACILITIES:** Children welcome Garden: Large lawns, well maintained **NOTES:** Parking 40

FARTHINGSTONE
Map 11 SP65

The Kings Arms
Main St NN12 8EZ ☎ 01327 361604 📠 01327 361604
e-mail: paul@kingsarms.fsbusiness.co.uk
Dir: *from M1 take A45 W, at Weedon join A5 then R on road signed Farthingstone*
Tucked away in unspoilt countryside near Canons Ashby (NT), this cosy 18th-century Grade II listed inn is adorned with a collection of stone gargoyles. Excellent real ales are served here. The menu is short and consists of things like British cheese platters, mixed leaf salad with smoked salmon, or Yorkshire pudding filled with steak and kidney or beef in Guinness. The landlord also sells cheeses and a variety of speciality regional foods.
OPEN: 12-3 7-11 Mon-Fri open evenings only **BAR MEALS:** L served Sat-Sun 12-2 Av main course £6 **BREWERY/COMPANY:** Free House ◀: Hook Norton, Timothy Taylor Landlord, Shepherd Neame Spitfire Premium Ale, Jennings Bitter. **FACILITIES:** Children welcome Garden: Many plants, herb garden, innovative design Dogs allowed Water **NOTES:** Parking 20 No credit cards

FOTHERINGHAY
Map 12 TL09

Pick of the Pubs

The Falcon Inn ◉ ♀
PE8 5HZ ☎ 01832 226254 📠 01832 226046
Dir: *N of A605 between Peterborough & Oundle*

Overlooking Fotheringhay Church and close to the site of Fotheringhay Castle, where Mary Queen of Scots was beheaded and Richard III was born, this attractive 18th-century stone-built inn is set in a garden recently redesigned by landscape architect Bunny Guinness. The Falcon and chef/patron Ray Smikle are members of the

continued

continued

Huntsbridge Inns group, each member producing innovative food in a relaxing pub environment. Eat what you like where you like, and accompany your meal with excellent wines or a pint of good ale. Settle in the locals' tap bar, the smart rear dining room or the conservatory extension and choose from the blackboard snack selection or the seasonal carte. Typical dishes are crispy duck spring rolls with spiced Asian coleslaw, couscous with roast Mediterranean vegetables and Feta cheese, duck breast with bubble and squeak and chorizo sausage salad, and shank of lamb with colcannon, spinach and fried carrots.

OPEN: 11.30-3 6-11 (Sun 12-3,7-10.30) **BAR MEALS:** L served all week 12-2.15 D served all week 7-9.30 Av main course £9.50 **RESTAURANT:** L served all week 12-2.15 D served all week 7-9.30 **BREWERY/COMPANY:** Free House ◨: Adnams Bitter, Greene King IPA, Scottish Courage John Smith's, Nethergate. ♀: 15 **FACILITIES:** Children welcome Garden: Very nice views **NOTES:** Parking 30

See Pub Walk on page 338

GRAFTON REGIS   Map 11 SP74

The White Hart 🛏 ♀
Northampton Rd NN12 7SR ☎ 01908 542123
Dir: M1 J15 on A508 between Northampton & Milton Keynes

Set in the historic village of Grafton Regis, where Edward IV married Elizabeth Woodville in 1464, the White Hart is a stone-built thatched pub that has been licensed since 1750. Extensive blackboard and carte menus and a good choice of wines by the glass. Try the home-made soups and pies, quality steaks or fresh fish dishes, including battered cod and smoked haddock in a cream sauce topped with cheese. Round off with chocolate suet pudding with black cherry filling. Wicked!

OPEN: 12-2.30 6-11 (Sun 12-2.30, 7-10.30) **BAR MEALS:** L served Tue-Sun 12-2 D served Tue-Sat 6-9.30 Av main course £7.50 **RESTAURANT:** L served Tue-Sun 12-1.30 D served Tue-Sat 6.30-9 Av 3 course à la carte £17 **BREWERY/COMPANY:** Free House ◨: Greene King Abbot Ale & IPA. ♀: 14 **FACILITIES:** Garden: Large floral garden, food served at lunchtime Dogs allowed Toys, water **NOTES:** Parking 40

GREAT OXENDON   Map 11 SP78

The George Inn 🛏 ♀
LE16 8NA ☎ 01858 465205 📠 01858 465205
Dir: Telephone for directions

Dishes based on fresh local produce are cooked to order at this country inn where you can enjoy a pint, a snack or a full-scale meal, including a traditional Sunday lunch. Bar choices include beef and Guinness pie, honey roast shank of lamb, fillet of salmon and asparagus in filo with a light cheese sauce, chargrilled Mediterranean pasta with chilli tomato sauce, or roast cod and butterbean casserole. There's a further selection with full service in the restaurant.

OPEN: 11.30-3 6-11 **BAR MEALS:** L served all week 12-2.30 D served Mon-Sat 7-10 Av main course £8 **RESTAURANT:** L served Tues-Sun 12-2.30 D served Mon-Sat 7-10 Av 3 course à la carte £20 Av 3 course fixed price £14.25 **BREWERY/COMPANY:** Free House ◨: Interbrew Bass, Adnams Bitter. ♀: 9 **FACILITIES:** Children welcome Garden: Large formal, large patio for dining Dogs allowed Water **NOTES:** Parking 34

HARRINGTON   Map 11 SP78

The Tollemache Arms 🛏 ♀
High St NN6 9NU ☎ 01536 710469 📠 01536 713447
e-mail: enquires@tollemache-harrington.co.uk
Dir: 6m from Kettering, off A14. Follow signs for Harrington

Situated near to Harrington airfield and museums is this pretty, thatched 16th-century village inn, named in the 19th century, after a local vicar who was incumbent for 60 years. In addition to ales from Wells and Greene King, freshly-prepared food made from local produce is served throughout the character bars and restaurant. Typical dishes include sole Véronique, fresh lemon sole fillet with vermouth, and various creations involving locally-reared beef, duck, venison and pheasant. Popular Sunday lunch menu.

OPEN: 12-3 6-11 25 Dec Closed eve **BAR MEALS:** L served all week 12-2.30 D served all week 6.30-9 Av main course £12 **RESTAURANT:** L served all week 12-2.30 D served all week 6.30-9 Av 3 course à la carte £22 **BREWERY/COMPANY:** Charles Wells ◨: Wells Eagle IPA & Bombardier Premium Bitter, Adnams Broadside, Greene King Triumph & Old Speckled Hen. ♀: 8 **FACILITIES:** Garden: over-looking countryside **NOTES:** Parking 60

HARRINGWORTH

Map 11 SP99

The White Swan
Seaton Rd NN17 3AF ☎ 01572 747543 🖺 01572 747323
e-mail: thewhiteswan@fsmail.net
Dir: Off B672 NE of Corby

Photographs recalling the nearby World War II airbase decorate the bar of this stone-built 15th century coaching inn. The prettily-situated free house also displays an old collection of craftsman's tools and memorabilia. There's a nice selection of well-kept real ales, and the constantly-changing blackboard menu is complemented by a carte that offers pan-roast loin of lamb, roast hazelnut and dill risotto, chicken Harringworth supreme, and pan-fried saddle of venison. Under new management.
OPEN: 11.45-2.30 6.30-11 (Sun 12-3, 7-10.30) Closed: 25 Dec, 1 Jan **BAR MEALS:** L served all week 12-2 D served all week 7-9 Av main course £9 **RESTAURANT:** L served all week 12-2 D served all week 7-9 Av 3 course à la carte £18 **BREWERY/COMPANY:** Free House ◑: Timothy Taylor Landlord, Greene King Old Speckled Hen.
FACILITIES: Garden: Patio **NOTES:** Parking 10 **ROOMS:** 6 bedrooms 6 en suite s£45 d£65 (♦♦♦♦) no children overnight

KETTERING

Map 11 SP87

The Overstone Arms 🐾 ♀
Stringers Hill, Pytchley NN14 1EU
☎ 01536 790215 🖺 01536 791098
Dir: 1m from Kettering, 5m from Wellingborough
The 18th-century coaching inn is at the heart of the village and has been home to the Pytchley Hunt, which over the years has attracted many royal visitors. Years ago guests would travel up from London, staying here or at Althorp Hall, mainly for the hunting. Despite its rural location, the pub is just a mile from the busy A1-M1 link road (A14). Home-made pies, grilled trout, steaks, lasagne and curry are typical dishes.
OPEN: 12-2.30 7-11 Closed: 1 Jan **BAR MEALS:** L served all week 12-2 D served all week 7-10 **RESTAURANT:** L served all week 12-2 D served all week 7-10 **BREWERY/COMPANY:** ◑: Greene King, Marston's Pedigree, Interbrew Bass, Adnams Bitter.
FACILITIES: Garden: **NOTES:** Parking 50

LITTLE HARROWDEN

Map 11 SP87

The Lamb
Orlingbury Rd NN9 5BH ☎ 01933 673300 🖺 01933 403131
Tucked away in a delightful village, this neatly refurbished 17th-century pub offers a friendly welcome in its comfortable lounge bar and adjoining public bar with games area.
OPEN: 12-11 **BAR MEALS:** L served all week 12-2.30 D served Thur-Sat 7-9 **RESTAURANT:** L served all week 12-2.30 D served Thur-Sat 7-9 **BREWERY/COMPANY:** Charles Wells ◑: Wells Eagle IPA & Bombardier, Greene King Old Speckled Hen, Guest.
FACILITIES: Children welcome Garden: Dogs allowed
NOTES: Parking 14

LOWICK

Map 11 SP98

The Snooty Fox
NN14 3BS ☎ 01832 733434
Dir: off the A14 5m E of Kettering on A6116. Straight over at 1st roundabout and L into Lowick
Exquisite carved beams are among the more unusual features at this 16th-century pub. Originally the manor house, it is supposedly haunted by a horse and its rider killed at the Battle of Naseby. Varied bar food includes steaks, chicken and pork; a good vegetarian selection, and fresh fish delivered daily.
OPEN: 12-3 6.30-11 **BAR MEALS:** L served all week 12-2 D served all week 7-10 Av main course £6.95 **RESTAURANT:** L served all week 12-2 D served all week 7-10 ◑: Greene King, Hook Norton Best, Batemans XB. **FACILITIES:** Children welcome Garden: Dogs allowed **NOTES:** Parking 100

MARSTON TRUSSELL

Map 11 SP68

Pick of the Pubs

The Sun Inn ★★
Main St LE16 9TY ☎ 01858 465531 🖺 01858 433155
e-mail: manager@suninn.com
Dir: S of A4304 between Market Harborough & Lutterworth
Head for Marston Trussell, in the heart of the Leicestershire countryside some three miles southwest of Market Harborough, to find this late 17th-century coaching inn offering cosy, up-to-date accommodation and modern amenities subtly combined with historic charm. Three separate dining areas include a popular locals' bar and an informal restaurant. Expect roaring fires, a friendly welcome, well-kept ales and a fair selection of wines by the glass. Fresh local produce plays a major part in the regularly-updated menus. These offer a winning combination of traditional favourites such as roast rack of lamb or deep-fried monkfish with French fries, and dishes with a modern, international appeal - perhaps Indonesian chicken and prawn laksa or fillets of sea bass with a saffron risotto and fine ratatouille. Charming waitress service and equally good breakfasts create a feeling of all round quality.
OPEN: 12-2 6-11 Closed: Dec 25, Jan 1 **BAR MEALS:** L served Sat-Sun 12-2.30 D served all week 7-10 Av main course £10.95 **RESTAURANT:** L served Sat-Sun 12-2.30 D served all week 7-10 **BREWERY/COMPANY:** Free House ◑: Bass, Hook Norton Best, Marstons Pedigree, Charles wells Bombardier.
FACILITIES: Children welcome **NOTES:** Parking 60
ROOMS: 20 bedrooms 20 en suite s£69 d£69

The Red Lion

A very pleasant country walk on the
Leicestershire/Northamptonshire border.

This walk is in a rural district bounded by Market Harborough, Kettering, Rugby and Northampton. Along the way there are good views over a patchwork of fields and hedgerows and close by are the River Avon and the Grand Union Canal.

From the Red Lion turn left and walk along to the junction with Welland Rise and Welford Road. Turn right, passing Beeches Close to reach the next turning on the right - Westhorpe. Follow it to the top to join a footpath running out across a large flat field. Look for waymarks along here, following the right of way as it turns left and then right.

Make for a gate at the top of the hill. Keep dogs on a lead in the next field as there might be sheep here. Continue ahead down the hill, keeping a wood on the right, and head for the road. Turn right at the gate and follow the road as it undulates between fields, back to the Red Lion at Sibbertoft.

THE RED LION, SIBBERTOFT
43 Welland Rise LE16 9UD
☎ 01858 880011

Directions: From Market Harborough take A4304, then A50. After 1m turn L. Civilised and friendly village pub with beamed restaurant and comfortable bar, and the same menu served in both. Baguettes and sandwiches also available.
Open: 12-2 6.30-11
Bar Meals: 12-2 (Wed-Sun only) 7-9.45
Notes: Garden, patio. Parking. (See page 344 for full entry)

DISTANCE: 4 miles/6.4km
MAP: OS Explorer 223
TERRAIN: Farmland
PATHS: Roads, bridleways and footpaths. Muddy in winter
GRADIENT: One steep incline and descent

Walk submitted and checked by Karen and Anna Raven of the Red Lion, Sibbertoft

England

NORTHAMPTON   Map 11 SP76

The Fox & Hounds 🐑 ♀
Main St, Great Brington NN7 4JA
☎ 01604 770651 🖹 01604 770164
e-mail: althorpcoachinn@aol.com
Dir: Telephone for directions

Located just a mile from Althorp House, ancestral home of the Spencer family, the Fox and Hounds is a much-photographed stone and thatch coaching inn dating from the 16th century. Its many charms include a pretty courtyard and garden, real fires, numerous guest ales and a reputation for quality food. Expect plenty of game in season, Sunday roasts and main courses ranging from traditional (beef and Guinness casserole; sirloin steak) to international favourites such as Thai curry or tagine of lamb.

OPEN: 11-11 (Sun 12-10.30) **BAR MEALS:** L served all week 12-2.30 D served all week 6.30-9.30 Av main course £5.95 **RESTAURANT:** L served all week 12-2.30 D served all week 6.30-9.30 Av 3 course à la carte £18 🍺: Green King IPA, Speckled Hen, London Pride Abbot Ale, 6 Guest Ales. ♀: 8

FACILITIES: Children welcome Garden: Secluded wall area, lots of trees Dogs allowed Water bowls, toys, dog chews
NOTES: Parking 5

OUNDLE   Map 11 TL08

The Mill at Oundle 🐑 ♀
Barnwell Rd PE8 5PB ☎ 01832 272621 🖹 01832 272221
e-mail: reservations@millatoundle.com
Dir: A14 Thrapston exit, A605 toward Peterborough, 8m Oundle turning, 1m to pub

Set on the banks of the River Nene, this converted watermill dates back to the Domesday Book. These days it comprises a waterside bar and two restaurants. One of these, The Granary on the top floor, is ideal for wedding receptions and other private functions. The menu ranges through a choice of grills, Tex Mex dishes, fish and pasta to other popular options like Caribbean chicken, home-made lasagne, and the speciality sausage of the day.

OPEN: 11-3 6.30-11 (Summer all day Sat-Sun) Closed: Dec 26/27 **BAR MEALS:** L served all week 12-2 D served all week 6.30-9 Av main course £8.95 **RESTAURANT:** L served all week 12-2 D served all week 6.30-9 **BREWERY/COMPANY:** Free House 🍺: Scottish Courage Theakston Best & XB, Marston's Pedigree.
FACILITIES: Children welcome Garden: **NOTES:** Parking 80

The Montagu Arms 🐑
Barnwell PE8 5PH ☎ 01832 273726 🖹 01832 275555
e-mail: ianmsimmons@aol.com
Dir: off A605 opposite Oundle slip Rd, access to A605 via A14 or A1

Originally three cottages built in 1601 for workmen constructing the nearby manor house, The Montagu Arms is now one of Northamptonshire's oldest inns. Overlooking the brook and village green in the royal village of Barnwell, the inn has a large garden well equipped for children's play. The extensive menu offers fajitas, nachos and chimichangas as well as chargrilled steaks, glazed ham hock and chicken breast in puff pastry shell with Stilton sauce. Good fish dish selection Fridays and Saturdays.

OPEN: 12-3 6-11 (Sat-Sun all day) **BAR MEALS:** L served all week 12-2.30 D served all week 7-10 Av main course £6.25 **RESTAURANT:** L served all week 12-2.30 D served all week 7-10 Av 3 course à la carte £15 **BREWERY/COMPANY:** Free House 🍺: Adnams Broadside, Southwold Bitter, Interbrew Flowers IPA & Original, Hop Back Summer Lightning. **FACILITIES:** Children welcome Garden: Large lawn, ample benches **NOTES:** Parking 25

SIBBERTOFT   Map 11 SP68

The Red Lion 🐑 ♀
43 Welland Rise LE16 9UD ☎ 01858 880011 🖹 01858 880011
e-mail: redlion@sibbertoft.demon.co.uk
Dir: From Market Harborough take A4304, then A50. After 1m turn L

Friendly and civilised village pub, believed to be 300 years old, with a cottage-like frontage. The same menu is offered in both the beamed restaurant and the comfortably-furnished bar, and may feature Thai green curry, sweet cure ham with egg and chips, lamb's liver and onions, steak and Stilton pie, or chicken Mississippi. A sample specials board features roast beef with Yorkshire pudding, rack of lamb, and kleftiko. Baguettes and sandwiches also available.

OPEN: 12-2 6.30-11 **BAR MEALS:** L served Wed-Sun 12-2 D served all week 7-9.45 Av main course £9 **RESTAURANT:** L served Wed-Sun 12-2 D served all week 7-9.45 Av 3 course à la carte £16 **BREWERY/COMPANY:** Free House 🍺: Everards Tiger, Adnams Bitter, Interbrew Bass. ♀: 8 **FACILITIES:** Garden: Patio area **NOTES:** Parking 15

See Pub Walk on page 343

STOKE BRUERNE   Map 11 SP74

The Boat Inn 🐑
NN12 7SB ☎ 01604 862428 🖹 01604 864314
e-mail: info@boatinn.co.uk
Dir: Just off A508

Thatched canal-side inn, right by a working lock and opposite the canal museum, owned and run by the Woodward family since 1877. Narrowboat trips on the pub's own 40-seater 'Indian Chief 'are a feature. Pub favourites are available in the bar, and a full menu in the restaurant - an extension to the original inn overlooking the locks. Dishes include monkfish, cod and salmon provençale, spiced Gressingham duck breast and well-matured steaks.

OPEN: 9-11 (3-5 closed Mon-Thu in winter) **BAR MEALS:** L served all week 9.30-9 D served all week Av main course £6 **RESTAURANT:** L served Tue-Sun 12-2 D served all week 7-9 Av 3 course fixed price £16 **BREWERY/COMPANY:** Free House 🍺: Banks Bitter, Marstons Pedigree, Adnams Southwold, Thwaites. **FACILITIES:** Children welcome Children's licence Garden: Table and grass area by canal Dogs allowed Water **NOTES:** Parking 50

See Pub Walk on page 345

> **Most of the pubs in this guide book
> pride themselves on the quality of their food.
> This may take a little time to prepare.**

The Boat Inn

With its charming canalside cottages, working locks and 15th-century church, the Northamptonshire village of Stoke Bruerne is the perfect starting point for a varied country walk in the area.

From the pub make for the canal entrance and cross the footbridge. Turn left and note the 1835 hump-backed bridge, the picturesque waterside cottages and the adjoining museum. Follow the towpath until you reach the tunnel. Completed in 1805, it stretches for 1 3/4 miles and took five years to build. Leave the canal at this point, walk up the slope and along the boat road, used by the horses pulling the narrow boats.

At the end of the road turn right and follow a quiet country road for a few paces, turning left at the bridleway. Keep the hedge and Nunn Wood on the right and walk along to a gate by a barn. Turn left and follow the lane to the T-junction. Turn left and pass the Plough Inn on your left.

Take the first right (Water Lane) and on the corner you have a fine view of the Old Monastery. Built as a hall house in 1310, this fascinating old building includes a striking porch dating back to 1350.

With the Old Monastery to your left, continue down Water Lane to a bridle path, go through a gate and across a meadow to a small footbridge over a brook. Turn left and follow the bridleway with a hedge and the brook to your left. At the end of the hedge line turn left to cross a stile. Follow the footpath to a lane, cross over and look for a waymark. Follow the footpath through an avenue of poplars, go through a metal gate and walk along a farm track to find a white gate at the end. The Boat Inn is directly opposite.

THE BOAT INN, STOKE BRUERNE
NN12 7SB
☎ 01604 862428
Directions: Just off A508
Beside a working lock and opposite the canal museum, a thatched inn. Pub favourites are served in the bar, and a full menu in the restaurant, an extension overlooking the lock.
Open: 9-11
(closed 3-5 Mon-Thur in winter)
Bar Meals: 9.30-9
(no food 3-7 Mon-Fri in winter)
Notes: Children welcome, & dogs (water provided). Garden on grassy area by canal.
(See page 344 for full entry)

DISTANCE: 5 miles/7.8km
MAP: OS Explorer 207
TERRAIN: Canal bank, woodland, farmland and pasture
PATHS: Towpath, boat road, country lanes, footpaths and bridleways
GRADIENT: Gently undulating

Walk submitted and checked by Ellen Shawe and Julian Clarke-Lowes

SULGRAVE
Map 11 SP54

The Star Inn
Manor Rd OX17 2SA ☎ 01295 760389 🖷 01295 760991
Dir: M1 J15A follow signs for Silverstone race circuit or M40 J11 follow brown signs for golf course, then for Sulgrave Manor

300-year-old creeper-covered inn with a large inglenook fireplace, cosy bar area and polished flagstones. During the summer the vine-covered patio attracts drinkers and diners. Expect deep-fried scallops, parsley and garlic risotto, and chicken and duck liver terrine among the starters, while breast of Gressingham duck, roast monkfish, field mushroom and spinach lasagne, and roast organic salmon feature as main course options. Lighter fare includes sandwiches and burgers.
OPEN: 11-2.30 6-11 (Sun 12-5 only) Closed: 26 Dec
BAR MEALS: L served Tue-Sun 12-2 D served Tue-Sat 6.30-9 Av main course £11 **RESTAURANT:** L served Tue-Sun 12-2 D served Tue-Sat 6.30-9.30 Av 3 course à la carte £20
BREWERY/COMPANY: Hook Norton ◀: Hook Norton Best, Old Hooky, Generation, & Haymaker. **FACILITIES:** Garden: Vine covered patio with wooden benches Dogs allowed Water **NOTES:** Parking 20

WADENHOE
Map 11 TL08

Pick of the Pubs

The King's Head
Church St PE8 5ST ☎ 01832 720024
e-mail: lou@kingzed.co.uk
A genuine drinker's pub with a separate bar serving real ales, although food is also taken quite seriously. Part-thatched and dating from the 17th-century, this stone inn stands peacefully beside the River Nene. Oak beams, quarry-tiled floors and open fires characterise the welcoming and neatly-refurbished interior, while a ban on mobile phones is vigilantly enforced. Popular with local villagers, boating types, cyclists and walkers who drop by for a pint. Sandwiches, and snacks like paté, quiche and broth feature at lunchtime, while in the evening, the cooking shifts up a notch with the likes of grilled red snapper, sautéed king scallops, calves' liver with Cumberland sausage, and home-made puddings. In the summer it's possible to dine alfresco by the river, when folk music and fen dancing take place in the paddock.
OPEN: 12-3 7-11 (Wed-Sat 6.30-11 all day Sat-Sun in sum)
BAR MEALS: L served all week 12-2 D served Wed-Sat 7-9 Av main course £6.50 **RESTAURANT:** L served all week D served Wed-Sat 7-9 Av 3 course à la carte £13.50
BREWERY/COMPANY: Free House ◀: Adnams, Timothy Taylor Landlord, Oakham JHB, Marston's Pedigree.
FACILITIES: Children welcome Garden: Lrg paddock, courtyard, patio, seating Dogs allowed Water **NOTES:** Parking 20

WESTON
Map 11 SP54

The Crown ♀
Helmdon Rd NN12 8PX ☎ 01295 760310 🖷 01295 760310
e-mail: terry@thearty.freeserve.co.uk
This 16th-century listed building has exposed beams and an inglenook fireplace, and is very good for local walks. The beamed function room is also a live music venue. Reputedly this was the last place that Lord Lucan was seen before his mysterious disappearance. A typical menu includes steak and ale pie, marlin in tarragon and white wine sauce, lamb shank with garlic and rosemary, tuna steak with lime and chillies, and Barbary duck in plum and ginger sauce.
OPEN: 6-11 (sat 11-11) (Sun 12-10.30) Closed: 26 Dec & Easter Sunday **BAR MEALS:** L served Fri-Sun 12-2 D served Tue-Sun 6.30-9 Av main course £7 ◀: Greene King IPA & Abbot Ale, Timothy Tailor Landlord, Interbrew Flowers IPA. **FACILITIES:** Children welcome Garden: Food served outdoors Dogs allowed water **NOTES:** Parking 10

WOODNEWTON
Map 11 TL09

The White Swan
22 Main St PE8 5EB ☎ 01780 470381 🖷 01780 470422
e-mail: whiteswan.woodnewton@tesco.net
Welcoming village local comprising a simple, single oblong room, one end focusing on the bar and wood-burning stove, the other set up as a dining area. The regularly-changing blackboard menu may offer home-made soup, fresh cod fillet in beer batter, stuffed chicken, pies, curries and steaks. Finish with a traditional home-made sweet, like fruit crumble or sticky toffee pudding.
OPEN: 12-2.30 7-11 (Fri from 6, Sat from 6.30) Sun Closed eve
BAR MEALS: L served Tue-Sun 12-1.45 D served Tue-Sat 7-9 Av main course £6 **RESTAURANT:** L served Tue-Sun 12-1.45 D served Tue-Sat 7-9 Av 3 course à la carte £17 **BREWERY/COMPANY:** Free House ◀: Adnams Southwold, Marstons Pedigree, Otter Bright, Camerons Creamy. **FACILITIES:** Garden: **NOTES:** Parking 20

NORTHUMBERLAND

ALLENDALE
Map 18 NY85

Kings Head Hotel ♀
Market Place NE47 9BD ☎ 01434 683681
Dir: From Hexham take B6305, B6304, B6295
Dating from 1754, the Kings Head is the oldest inn in Allendale, situated in the centre of the North Dales village. It's cosy and welcoming inside with its spacious bar/lounge and warming log fire in winter. Expect traditional food and well-kept ales, plus around 60 malt whiskies.
OPEN: 11-11 (Sun 12-10.30) **BAR MEALS:** L served all week 12-2.30 D served all week 6.30-9 Av main course £5.95
BREWERY/COMPANY: Free House ◀: Jennings Cumberland, John Smiths, Abbotts Ale. ♀: 7 **FACILITIES:** Children welcome patio

> The Rosette is the AA award for food. Look out for it next to a pub's name.

England

ALLENHEADS
Map 18 NY84

The Allenheads Inn
NE47 9HJ ☎ 01434 685200 🖨 01434 685200
e-mail: theallenheadsinn@yahoo.co.uk
Dir: From Hexham take B6305, then B6295 to Allenheads
Situated in the remote high country of the North Pennines, perfect for walking and exploring, this 18th-century pub is full of charm and character. A useful watering hole for those using the coast-to-coast cycle route, the Allenheads has a friendly, welcoming atmosphere in the popular Antiques Bar, or the unusually-named Forces Room, and enjoy steak pie, lasagne, battered cod or one of the pub's seasonal specials.
OPEN: 12-4 7-11 (all day Fri-Sat) **BAR MEALS:** L served all week 12-2.30 D served all week 7-9 Av main course £5.50
RESTAURANT: L served Sun **BREWERY/COMPANY:** Free House ◀: Greene King Abbott Ale, Carlsberg-Tetley Tetley Bitter, Timothy Taylor Landlord, Black Sheep Bitter. **FACILITIES:** Garden
NOTES: Parking 10

ALNWICK
Map 21 NU11

Masons Arms 🐾 ♀
Stamford, Nr Rennington NE66 3RX
☎ 01665 577275 🖨 01665 577894
e-mail: bookings@masonsarms.net
Dir: 3.5m from A1 on B1340
Known locally by farmers as the Stamford Cott, and a useful staging post for visitors to Hadrian's Wall, Lindisfarne and the large number of nearby golf courses, this 300-year-old coaching inn has been tastefully modernised. The same substantial home-cooked food is available in the bar and restaurant: beef and wild venison casserole, local lamb cutlets, and cannelloni verdi, plus fresh fish (haddock, lemon sole, and scampi) and chef's specials like seafood gratin.
OPEN: 12-2 6.30-11 (Sun 12-2 7-10.30) **BAR MEALS:** L served all week 12-2 D served all week 6.30-9 Av main course £6.50
RESTAURANT: L served all week 12-2 D served all week 7-9
BREWERY/COMPANY: Free House ◀: Scottish Courage John Smith's, Theakston Best, Secret Kingdom, Gladiator.
FACILITIES: Children welcome Children's licence Garden: Dogs allowed Kennels, dogs welcome by arrangement **NOTES:** Parking 50
ROOMS: 12 bedrooms 12 en suite 3 family rooms s£35 d£29.50 (♦♦♦♦)

BAMBURGH
Map 21 NU13

Lord Crewe Arms Hotel ★★ 🐾
Front St NE69 7BL ☎ 01668 214243 🖨 01668 214273
e-mail: lca@tinyonline.co.uk
Historic coaching inn named after Lord Crewe, who was one of the Prince Bishops of Durham. Perfect base for touring Northumberland, exploring the Cheviot Hills and visiting nearby Holy Island. Good, wholesome pub food ranges from local kipper pâté, wild boar and apple sausages, and pan-fried supreme of chicken, to breast of guinea fowl with an apricot, apple and raisin stuffing.
OPEN: 12-3 6-11 Closed: Jan-Feb **BAR MEALS:** L served all week 12-2.30 D served all week 6.30-9 Av main course £7.25
RESTAURANT: L served all week 12-2.30 D served all week 6.30-9 Av 3 course à la carte £25 **BREWERY/COMPANY:** Free House
◀: Interbrew Bass, Black Sheep Best, Fullers London Pride.
FACILITIES: Children welcome Garden: Food served outside
NOTES: Parking 20 **ROOMS:** 18 bedrooms 17 en suite s£45 d£43

Victoria Hotel ★★ ◎ 🐾 ♀
Front St NE69 7BP ☎ 01668 214431 🖨 01668 214404
e-mail: enquiries@victoriahotel.net
Dir: In centre of Bamburgh village green
Friendly, attentive service is just one feature of this stylishly-refurbished hotel, overlooking Bamburgh's historic village green. The exuberant stone building is late 19th century but the welcome is uncompromisingly modern. There's an airy candlelit brasserie, a children's playden and 29 cheerful, well-equipped bedrooms. Two real ales are always available in the popular bar. The brasserie has a domed glass ceiling, a white tiled floor and well-spaced tables. Starters could include oak-smoked local salmon with a parsley and walnut pesto or black pudding and toasted muffin stack served on a grain mustard honey dressing. For main courses expect the likes of pan-fried Bamburgh sausages with aïoli mash and a carbonnade of onions, or fillet of beef with wild mushrooms and malt whiskey jus followed by appetising sweets or Northumbrian cheeses. Morning coffee and afternoon tea are also available.

OPEN: 11-11 (Fri-Sat 11-12) **BAR MEALS:** L served all week 12-9 D served all week Av main course £5.50 **RESTAURANT:** L served Sun 12-3 D served all week 7-9 Av 3 course à la carte £20
BREWERY/COMPANY: Free House ◀: John Smiths, Theakstons Cool Keg, plus guests. **FACILITIES:** Children welcome Dogs allowed Water provided **NOTES:** Parking 6
ROOMS: 29 bedrooms 29 en suite s£52.50 d£94

BELFORD
Map 21 NU13

Blue Bell Inn 🐾
Market Place NE70 7NE ☎ 01668 213543 🖨 01668 213787
e-mail: bluebell@globalnet.co.uk
A long-established and creeper-clad coaching inn located in the centre of Belford. The inn offers a friendly, relaxed atmosphere, and a good range of real ales. Choices from the menu in the elegant restaurant may include tournedos of Aberdeen Angus steak with wild mushroom sauce, and roasted monkfish in a light tomato concassé, while lamb balti, chicken fajitas, and steak and kidney pie with Newcastle brown are typical of the bar and buttery. Three acres of garden with an orchard and vegetable garden.
OPEN: 11-2.30 6.30-11 **BAR MEALS:** L served all week 11-2.30 D served all week 6.30-9 Av main course £7.25 **RESTAURANT:** L served Sun 12-2 D served all week 7-8.45 Av 3 course à la carte £24
BREWERY/COMPANY: Free House ◀: Interbrew Boddingtons Bitter, Northumbrian Smoothe, Calders 80/-. **FACILITIES:** Children welcome Garden: 3 acres **NOTES:** Parking 17

Dipton Mill Inn

A pleasant, undulating ramble that meanders through woodland beside Dipton Burn before climbing to Hexham Racecourse and fine views across rolling Northumberland countryside.

Turn left from the inn, cross the bridge over Dipton Burn and turn immediately left into woodland, waymarked West Dipton Wood. Cross a stile and proceed through the wood with stream on your left. Where the trees thin on your right, with meadow beyond, follow the path alongside the fence. In the corner, pass beneath beech trees and then follow rocky path beside the stream again.

Pass a footbridge, then soon veer half-right to follow a zig-zag path up the bank, then along a sunken path to a gate on the woodland fringe. Walk straight across the field, with Hexham Racecourse soon coming into view. Go through several gates, draw level with the grandstand and pass through a further gate, heading towards woodland.

Join a drive leading to a house called Black Hill and pass beneath trees to a junction. Turn right along the lane, pass racecourse entrance and footpath to Dipton Burn, then at main junction, cross over and follow road uphill. Take the path right, signed to Hole House, and cross stile in the field corner. Turn right, then immediately left by old building and follow left-hand field edge towards Hole House.

Cross several stiles towards woodland and cross a stile into the wood. Pass Hole House, climb a stile on the right and follow the grassy swathe beside paddocks to a stile. Go through the gate ahead and follow the track beside Dipton Burn to the road. Turn left for the pub.

DIPTON MILL INN, HEXHAM
Dipton Mill Road NE46 1YA.
☎ 01434 606577
Directions: 2m S of Hexham on B6306 to Blanchland
Former mill house with beamed and panelled bars, built around 1750 and tucked away in a quiet wooded valley south of Hexham. Offers excellent beers from the family-owned Hexhamshire Brewery and wholesome home-cooked food.
Open: 12-2.30 6-11
(Sun 12-4. 7-10.30).
Bar Meals: 12-2.30 6.30-8.30.
Notes: Children welcome. Small aviary. Streamside garden and patio.
(See page 352 for full entry)

DISTANCE: 4 miles (6.4km)
MAP: OS Landranger 87
TERRAIN: Woodland, farmland, country lanes
PATHS: Riverside, woodland and field paths; lanes
GRADIENT: Undulating; steady climb to racecourse

Walk submitted by Nick Channer

BELSAY
Map 21 NZ07

The Highlander ♀
NE20 0DN ☎ 01661 881220
Dir: (On A696, 2m S of Belsay & 4m N of Ponteland)

Traditional pub meals, interesting home-cooked specials and all-day food are available at this popular, flower-adorned roadside hostelry. Choose from salads, casseroles, pasta meals, and substantial dishes like rack of lamb with minted jus, and pork with apple and cider sauce.
OPEN: 11-11 (Sun 12-10.30) **BAR MEALS:** L served all week 12-6 D served all week 6-9.30 Av main course £6.50
BREWERY/COMPANY: Enterprise Inns ◖: John Smiths & Guest ale. **FACILITIES:** Children welcome Garden: Heated Dogs allowed
NOTES: Parking 60

BERWICK-UPON-TWEED
Map 21 NT95

The Rob Roy 🐾 ♀
Dock Rd, Tweedmouth TD15 2BE
☎ 01289 306428 🖷 01289 303629
e-mail: therobroy@btinternet.com
Dir: Exit A1 2m S of Berwick at A1167 signed Scremerston, to rdbt signed Spittal, then R. 1m to Albion PH, L, 1m to pub

A single-storey stone cottage until thirty years ago, the Rob Roy overlooks the point where the Tweed widens to its estuary. Both the river and the sea provide fresh produce for this blatantly seafood restaurant. Crab, salmon sea trout (in season), and various white fish are caught locally, while rod-caught sea bass comes from Dunbar, and the oysters from Lindisfarne, north and south respectively. Alternatives include duckling cassis, and steak and lamb chops.
OPEN: 12-2.30 7-11 Closed: 3wks Feb or Mar. Xmas & New Year Closed: Wed lunch Nov-Mar **BAR MEALS:** L served Mon, Wed-Sun 12-2 D served Mon, Wed-Sun 7-9 Av main course £7.80
RESTAURANT: L served Wed-Mon 12-1.45 D served Wed-Mon 7-9.30 Av 3 course à la carte £25 **BREWERY/COMPANY:** Free House ◖: Tennants 70/-. **ROOMS:** 2 bedrooms 2 en suite s£28 d£44 (♦♦♦♦) no children overnight

BLANCHLAND
Map 18 NY95

Lord Crewe Arms ★★
DH8 9SP ☎ 01434 675251 🖷 01434 675337
e-mail: info@lordcrewehotel.com
Dir: 10m S of Hexham via B6306
Once the abbot's house of Blanchland Abbey, this is one of England's oldest inns. Antique furniture, blazing log fires and flagstone floors make for an atmospheric setting. Wide-ranging bar and restaurant menus, and well equipped period bedrooms split between the main hotel and a former estate building.
OPEN: 11-11 **BAR MEALS:** L served Mon-Sat 12-2 D served all week 7-9 Av main course £6 **RESTAURANT:** L served Sun 12-2 D served all week 7-9.15 Av 4 course fixed price £28
BREWERY/COMPANY: Free House ◖: Castle Eden Ale.
FACILITIES: Children welcome Garden: Dogs allowed **ROOMS:** 19 bedrooms 19 en suite 2 family rooms s£80 d£110

CARTERWAY HEADS
Map 19 NZ05

Pick of the Pubs

The Manor House Inn 🐾 ♀
DH8 9LX ☎ 01207 255268

Dir: A69 W from Newcastle, L onto A68 then S for 8m. Inn on R
From its lonely position high on the A68, this small family-run free house enjoys spectacular views across open moorland and the Derwent Reservoir. The cosy stone-walled bar, with its log fires, low beamed ceiling and massive timber support, offers a good range of well-kept real ales and around 70 malt whiskies. Built circa 1760, the inn has a succession of dining areas, and a huge collection of mugs and jugs hangs from the beams in the candlelit restaurant. Dishes range through Cumberland sausage and mash, Cajun blackened salmon with roasted vegetables, roast boneless quail with black pudding and Savoy cabbage, and sweet cured herrings with crème fraîche. Home-made puddings are a feature, with the likes of ginger grundy, and fig and almond cake with Baileys and butterscotch sauce. There's also a selection of up to 16 local cheeses.
OPEN: 11-3 5.30-11 25 Dec closed evening **BAR MEALS:** L served all week 12-2.30 D served all week 5.30-9.30
RESTAURANT: L served all week 12-2.30 D served all week 7-9.30 Av 3 course à la carte £27.50 **BREWERY/COMPANY:** Free House ◖: Theakstons Best, Mordue Workie Ticket, Greene King Ruddles County, Scottish Courage Courage Directors. ♀: 12
FACILITIES: Children welcome Children's licence Garden: Small picnic area Dogs allowed Dogs in bedroom by arrangement **NOTES:** Parking 60

England

CHATTON

Map 21 NU02

The Percy Arms Hotel ♀
Main Rd NE66 5PS ☎ 01668 215244
Dir: From Alnwick take A1 N, then B6348 to Chatton
Built in the early 19th-century as a hunting lodge by the Duke of Northumberland, this ivy-covered pub enjoys a peaceful village setting in the unspoilt Till Valley. Bar food includes game and vegetable pie, grilled lamb chops with rosemary and garlic butter, Aberdeen Angus fillet and fresh Lindisfarne crab salad.
OPEN: 11-3 6-11 (Sun 12-3, 7-10.30) **BAR MEALS:** L served all week 12-2.30 D served all week 6.30-9.30 Av main course £6.95 **RESTAURANT:** L served all week 12-2.30 D served all week 6.30-9.30 Av 3 course à la carte £13.50 **BREWERY/COMPANY:** Free House ◑: Scottish & Newcastle Ales. ♀: 12 **FACILITIES:** Children welcome Garden: patio/terrace, outdoor eating **NOTES:** Parking 30

CORBRIDGE

Map 21 NY96

The Angel of Corbridge 🏚
Main St NE45 5LA ☎ 01434 632119 🖹 01434 633496
Dir: 0.5m off A69, signed Corbridge
Stylish 17th-century coaching inn overlooking the River Tyne. Relax with the daily papers in the wood-panelled lounge or attractive bars, or enjoy a home-made dish or two from the extensive menu choice. Options include tempura of sole, oven-baked salmon en croûte with buttered spinach, baked peppered goats' cheese with spicy turmeric tomatoes, and roasted duck breast with hotpot potatoes and sautéed Savoy cabbage.
OPEN: 11-11 (Sun 12-10.30) **BAR MEALS:** L served all week 12-2.30 D served Mon-Sat 6-9.30 Av main course £14 **RESTAURANT:** L served all week 12-2.30 D served Mon-Sat 6-9.30 Av 3 course à la carte £25 **BREWERY/COMPANY:** Free House ◑: Black Sheep Best, Mordue, Boddingtons. **FACILITIES:** Children's licence Garden: Walled garden with seats and grassed area Dogs allowed Water **NOTES:** Parking 25

CRASTER

Map 21 NU21

Cottage Inn ♦♦♦ 🏚 ♀
Dunstan Village NE66 3SZ ☎ 01665 576658 🖹 01665 576788
Dir: NW of Howick to Embleton road
In an area of outstanding natural beauty, easily accessible from the A1, this 18th-century inn is located in a hamlet close to the sea. There is a beamed bar, Harry Hotspur Restaurant, conservatory, loggia and patio. One menu serves all - a comprehensive choice of snacks, full meals, kids' and vegetarian options, supplemented by daily specials. Local ingredients are used wherever possible in dishes such as Craster fish stew and whole joint of lamb.
OPEN: 11-11 (Sun 12-3, 7-10.30) **BAR MEALS:** L served all week 12-2.30 D served all week 6-9.30 Av main course £7.50 **RESTAURANT:** L served all week 12-2.30 D served all week 6-9.30 **BREWERY/COMPANY:** Free House ◑: Belhaven 80/-, Wylam Bitter. **FACILITIES:** Children welcome Garden: **NOTES:** Parking 60 **ROOMS:** 10 bedrooms 10 en suite s£39 d£69

Jolly Fisherman Inn
Haven Hill NE66 3TR ☎ 01665 576461
e-mail: muriel@silk827.fsnet.co.uk
Authentic, unpretentious pub situated in a tiny fishing village famous for its kipper sheds. Handy for local walks, visiting Dunstanburgh Castle and exploring the scenic delights of Northumberland and the beautiful Scottish Borders. Delicious home-made crabmeat soup, kipper paté and crab sandwiches feature on the menu.
OPEN: 11-3 6.30-11 (all day Jun-Aug) **BAR MEALS:** L served all week 11-2.30 Av main course £2.80
BREWERY/COMPANY: Pubmaster ◑: Carlsberg-Tetley Tetley Bitter, John Smith's, Timothy Taylor Landlord. **FACILITIES:** Children welcome Garden: Dogs allowed **NOTES:** Parking 10 No credit cards

EGLINGHAM

Map 21 NU11

Tankerville Arms 🏚
NE66 2TX ☎ 01665 578444 🖹 01665 578444
Dir: B6346 from Alnwick

In the foothills of the Cheviots, this traditional stone-built pub has a good reputation for its real ales and food. The historic village, local castles (including Alnwick, featured in the Harry Potter movies) and nearby beaches, make the pub a favourite with walkers and cyclists alike. Snacks, salads and entrées are supplemented by specials like slivers of roasted goose set on a salad with crispy bacon and herbs, and supreme of halibut wrapped in Craster smoked salmon with watercress sauce.
OPEN: 12-2 7-11 (Times may vary, ring for details) Closed: 25 Dec **BAR MEALS:** L served all week 12-2 D served all week 6-9 Av main course £7.50 **RESTAURANT:** L served all week 12-2 D served all week 6-9 Av 3 course à la carte £20 **BREWERY/COMPANY:** Free House ◑: Greene King Ruddles Best, Scottish Courage Courage Directors, Black Sheep Best, Mordue Workie Ticket.
FACILITIES: Children welcome Garden: Country garden, seating for 25, good views **NOTES:** Parking 15

ETAL

Map 21 NT93

Black Bull
TD12 4TL ☎ 01890 820200 🖹 070923 67733
e-mail: blackbulletal@aol.com
Dir: 10m N of Wooler R off A697, L at Jct for 1m then L into Etal.
This 300-year-old hostelry is the only thatched pub in Northumberland, located by the ruins of Etal Castle. Close to the River Till and a short distance from the grand walking country of the Cheviots. An imaginative menu includes a wide selection of traditional British food, with a variety of vegetarian options. Typical dishes include pork in Dijon mustard, pan-fried whole seabass, mushroom Stroganoff, roast beef Yorkshire pudding, and pasta with tomato, black olive, mushroom and Mozzarella salad.
OPEN: 11-3.30 5.30-11 **BAR MEALS:** L served all week 12-2 D served all week 6-9 Av main course £8 **RESTAURANT:** L served all week 11.30-2.30 D served all week 6-9.30 **BREWERY/COMPANY:** Pubmaster ◑: Jennings, Deuchers, John Smith Smooth, Fosters. **FACILITIES:** Garden: Concrete/grass area **NOTES:** Parking 10

continued

FALSTONE

Map 21 NY78

The Blackcock Inn ♦♦♦ 🛏 ♀
NE48 1AA ☎ 01434 240200 📠 01434 240200
e-mail: blackcock@falstone.fsbusiness.co.uk
Dir: off unclassified rd from Bellingham (accessed from A68 or B6320)
A traditional 18th-century stone-built inn, close to Keilder
Reservoir and Forest, with some lovely walks accessible from the
village. The pub is also handy for the Rievers Cycle Route. Old
beams and open log fires make for a cosy atmosphere, and food
is served in the bar, lounge and dining area alongside a good
choice of beers. Dishes are based on the best local produce,
ranging from snacks to steaks, with fish and vegetarian options.
Try one of the Yorkshire puddings with a variety of fillings.
OPEN: 11-3 6-11 (Winter 7-11) **BAR MEALS:** L served all week 11-2 D
served all week 7-9 Av main course £6.95 **RESTAURANT:** L served all
week D served Fri-Sun 7-9 Av 3 course à la carte £15
BREWERY/COMPANY: Free House 🍺: Blackcock Ale, Scottish
Courage Theakston Cool Cask, Magnet Ale, Marston's Pedigree. ♀: 8
FACILITIES: Children welcome Garden: Dogs allowed **NOTES:** Parking
20 **ROOMS:** 5 bedrooms 5 en suite 1 family rooms s£32 d£55

Pick of the Pubs

The Pheasant ♦♦♦♦ 🛏
Stannersburn NE48 1DD ☎ 01434 240382 📠 01434 240382
e-mail: enquiries@thepheasantinn.com
Dir: From A68 onto B6320, or from A69, B6079, B6320, follow signs
'Kielder Water'

Situated close to Kielder Water, this 17th-century building
was originally a farmstead with some 250 acres, but even
then it included a bar. Its long farming history is evident in
the cosy interior, which includes farming memorabilia
among a wealth of beams, exposed stone walls and open
fires. Nowadays guests who wish to extend their stay can
book one of eight attractive en suite bedrooms, arranged
around a courtyard. The restaurant is furnished in mellow
pine and has warm terracotta walls. It's a relaxing
environment in which to enjoy a good selection of
traditional home cooked food. Dishes are carefully
prepared and make use of the very best local produce
wherever possible. Typical examples include cider-baked
gammon, slow roasted Northumbrian lamb, marinated
chicken with roast peppers, and grilled fresh salmon with
lemon and dill sauce. Finish with desserts such as home-
made sticky toffee pudding, crème brûlée or kiwi and
passion fruit Pavlova.
OPEN: 11-3 6-11 (opening times vary, ring for details) Closed:
Dec 25-26 (Mon-Tues closed in Jan and Feb) **BAR MEALS:** L
served all week 12-2.30 D served all week 7-9 Av main course
£6.50 **RESTAURANT:** L served all week 12-2.30 D served all
week 7-9 Av 3 course à la carte £16

BREWERY/COMPANY: Free House 🍺: Theakston Best,
Marstons Pedigree, Timothy Taylor Landlord, Greene King Old
Speckled Hen. **FACILITIES:** Children welcome Garden: Dogs
allowed By arrangement only **NOTES:** Parking 30 **ROOMS:** 8
bedrooms 8 en suite 1 family rooms s£40 d£65

GREAT WHITTINGTON

Map 21 NZ07

Pick of the Pubs

Queens Head Inn & Restaurant 🛏
NE19 2HP ☎ 01434 672267
Dir: Off A68 & B6318 W of Newcastle upon Tyne
At the heart of Hadrian's Wall country this old
pub/restaurant, once a coaching inn, radiates a
welcoming atmosphere in comfortable surroundings of
beamed rooms, oak settles and open fires. In addition to
Black Sheep beers there are some three dozen wines of
choice and nearly as many malt whiskies. Menus combine
the best of local and European ingredients, without losing
touch with the classics. Expect the likes of seared fillet of
salmon with ratatouille and a tomato and herb couscous
or herb-crusted rack of lamb with a basket of turned roast
vegetables with a rosemary and redcurrant jus. Speciality
dishes could include breast of wood pigeon on a black
pudding mash with a tomato salsa, roast garlic and
Burgundy, or prime fillet steak topped with a mushroom
and Stilton sabayon served on a Madeira sauce. A long
and beguiling Sunday lunch menu begins with something
like deep-fried black pudding with beetroot relish, or
warm ciabatta bread with smoked mackerel and a coarse
wholegrain mustard. Follow with anything from traditional
roast sirloin with Yorkshire pudding and gravy to roast
vegetable and nut gateau with roast garlic coulis, or
seared fillet of salmon on a tagliatelle of vegetables.
OPEN: 12-3 6-11 **BAR MEALS:** L served Tues-Sun 12-2 D
served Tues-Sun 6.30-9 Av main course £10 **RESTAURANT:** L
served Tues-Sun 12-2 D served Tues-Sun 6.30-9
BREWERY/COMPANY: Free House 🍺: Black Sheep, Queens
Head, Hambleton. **FACILITIES:** Children welcome Garden:
Drink served in the garden **NOTES:** Parking 20

Nine Men's Morris

A certain eeriness clings to one of
the world's oldest games, which was
played in Ancient Egypt 3,000 years ago
and in Ireland in prehistoric times. It
involves moving pegs or counters to form
rows of three on a board or playing
surface with 24 holes marked on
it in an intricate pattern.

continued

England

HALTWHISTLE

Map 21 NY76

Milecastle Inn
Military Rd, Cawfields NE49 9NN
☎ 01434 321372 & 320682 ▤ 01434 321671
Dir: Leave A69 at Haltwhistle, pub about 2 miles from Haltwhistle at junction with B6318

Overlooking Hadrian's Wall, this stone-built rural inn attracts loyal locals and tourists alike. The beamed bar has old horse brasses, open fires and even a resident ghost. The walled gardens enjoy spectacular views. There's a long-standing tradition of home-made pies and casseroles - wild boar and duckling pie or minted lamb casserole, for example. Other dishes could include bangers and mash with onion gravy, or chicken breast stuffed with Stilton and leeks.
OPEN: 12-2.30 6.30-11 **BAR MEALS:** L served all week 12-2 D served all week 6.30-9 Av main course £6.25 **RESTAURANT:** L served Sun 12-2 D served Tue-Sat 7-8.30 Av 3 course à la carte £17
BREWERY/COMPANY: Free House ◫: Northumberland Castle, Carlsberg-Tetley Tetley Bitter, Marsdens Pedigree, Old Speckled Hen.
FACILITIES: Garden: Walled with benches, seats 25 **NOTES:** Parking 30

HAYDON BRIDGE

Map 21 NY86

The General Havelock Inn
Ratcliffe Rd NE47 6ER ☎ 01434 684376 ▤ 01434 684283
e-mail: GeneralHavelock@aol.com
Dir: On A69, 7m west of Hexham

In a pleasant riverside setting not far from Hadrian's Wall, the General Havelock takes its name from a 19th-century British Army officer. The pub, which has links with several show business personalities, was built as a private house in 1840 but has been licensed since 1890. The restaurant at the back of the building is a converted barn that overlooks the River Tyne. Outside, the tranquil south-facing patio is framed by trees and potted plants, and a grassy path leads to a lovely riverside walk. Local ingredients are the foundation of an adventurous menu. Starters like parsnip soup or chargrilled peppered pineapple herald main

courses such as pan-fried pigeon breast on red cabbage, lamb shank and rosemary, or seafood filo pastry money-bag. Leave room for white chocolate and raspberry crème brûlée, or bread and butter pudding with apricot compôte.
OPEN: 12-2.30 7-11 **BAR MEALS:** L served Tue-Sun 12-2 D served Tue-Sat 7-9 Av main course £6.50 **RESTAURANT:** L served Tue-Sun 12-2 D served Tue-Sat 7-9 Av 3 course à la carte £19.25
BREWERY/COMPANY: Free House ◫: Turbina, Old Speckled Hen, Skiddaw, Jennings Cumberland Ale. **FACILITIES:** Children welcome Garden: Patio area on river bank, lots of plants Dogs allowed

HEDLEY ON THE HILL

Map 19 NZ05

Pick of the Pubs

The Feathers Inn
NE43 7SW ☎ 01661 843607 ▤ 01661 843607
From its hilltop position, this small stone-built free house overlooks the splendid country of the Cheviots. The three-roomed pub is well patronised by the local community, but strangers, too, are frequently charmed by its friendly and relaxed atmosphere. Families are welcome, and a small side room can be booked in advance if required. Old oak beams, coal fires and rustic settles set the scene and there's a good selection of traditional pub games like shove ha'penny and bar skittles. The stone walls are decorated with local photographs of rural life. Although the pub has no garden, food and drinks can be served at tables on the green in good weather. The menus change regularly, and the imaginative home cooking includes an extensive choice of vegetarian meals. Expect spiced lentil and vegetable hotpot with naan bread, gingered salmon cakes with coriander salsa, pork casseroled with tarragon and Dijon mustard, and seafood pancake. An appetising range of puddings.
OPEN: 12-3 6-11 (Sun 12-3, 7-10.30) Closed: Dec 25
BAR MEALS: L served Sat-Sun 12-2.30 D served Tue-Sun 7-9 Av main course £6.95 **BREWERY/COMPANY:** Free House ◫: Mordue Workie Ticket, Big Lamp Bitter, Fuller's London Pride, Yates Bitter. **FACILITIES:** Children welcome Children's licence Tables outside at the front Dogs allowed Water
NOTES: Parking 12

HEXHAM

Map 21 NY96

Pick of the Pubs

Dipton Mill Inn ♀
Dipton Mill Rd NE46 1YA ☎ 01434 606577
Dir: 2m S of Hexham on HGV route to Blanchland (B6306)
Everything you would expect a country inn to be, with a stream running through its garden, and real fires warming the bar in cold weather. Originally part of a farmhouse, the inn has occupied its wooded setting since the 1800s. Enjoy a delightful walk through the trees to Hexham racecourse and back before relaxing with a pint of home-brewed Hexhamshire ale in the low-ceilinged bar. Freshly-prepared meals and snacks utilise ingredients from local suppliers; rolls are made by a local baker and the inn offers an interesting selection of around a dozen local and other cheeses. A tasty bowl of home-made soup (leek and potato, or roasted red pepper, tomato and orange) might be followed by chicken breast in sherry sauce, or lamb steak in a wine and mushroom sauce. Ploughman's and salads are also available, and

continued

continued

good puds like syrup sponge with custard, or triple chocolate cheesecake.
OPEN: 12-2.30 6-11 (Sun 12-4, 7-10.30) Closed: 25 Dec
BAR MEALS: L served all week 12-2.30 D served all week 6.30-8.30 Av main course £5.40 **BREWERY/COMPANY:** Free House ◀: Hexhamshire Shire Bitter, Old Humbug, Devil's Water, Devil's Elbow & Whapweasel. ⅊: 11 **FACILITIES:** Children welcome Children's licence Garden: Grassed and terraced area, small aviary **NOTES:** No credit cards

See Pub Walk on page 348

Miners Arms Inn
Main St, Acomb NE46 4PW ☎ 01434 603909
Dir: 17 miles W of Newcastle on A69, 2 miles W of Hexham.
Close to Hadrian's Wall in a peaceful village, this charming 18th-century pub has stone walls, beamed ceilings and open fires. Real ales are a speciality, as is good home-cooked food. There is no jukebox or pool table, so visitors will have to entertain themselves with conversation, and some choices from a menu that includes lasagne, curry, Italian chicken, steak and kidney pie, chilli, and a special trifle. Good setting for cyclists and walkers, and the garden has a new aviary.
OPEN: 12-11 5-11 (Mon-Fri 5-11, Sat 12-11, Sun 12-10.30)
BAR MEALS: L served all week 12-2 D served all week 5-9 Av main course £4.95 **RESTAURANT:** L served all week 12-2 D served all week 5-9 **BREWERY/COMPANY:** Free House ◀: Jennings Best, Mordue, Yates, Black Sheep Best. **FACILITIES:** Children welcome Garden: Secluded sun trap beer garden, seating Dogs allowed Water **NOTES:** No credit cards

The Rose & Crown Inn ♦♦♦ 🛏 ⅊
Main St, Slaley NE47 0AA ☎ 01434 673263
A 200-year-old listed building combining the charm of a traditional country inn with modern service and comfort. Conveniently situated for exploring Keilder Forest and the delights of the Borders, as well as the Roman sites of Vindolanda and Howsteads. Handy, too, for fishing, horse-riding, hunting, sailing and shooting. Appetising food is on offer, and among the dishes on the menu you might find beef casserole, turkey and ham pie, poached chicken breast and salmon and mushroom tagliatelle.
OPEN: 12-3 6-11 **BAR MEALS:** L served all week 12-2 D served all week 7-9 Av main course £6.95 **RESTAURANT:** L served all week 12-2.15 D served all week 6.30-9.30 Av 3 course à la carte £16 **BREWERY/COMPANY:** Free House ◀: Woodpecker, Jennings, plus guest ales. **FACILITIES:** Children welcome Garden: Food served outside **NOTES:** Parking 36 **ROOMS:** 3 bedrooms 3 en suite s£32.50 d£45

LONGFRAMLINGTON   Map 21 NU10

The Anglers Arms 🛏 NEW
Weldon Bridge NE65 8AX
The appropriately-named Anglers Arms offers free fishing for residents on the inn's own one-mile stretch of river. The theme carries over into the pub as well, with the walls festooned with fishing memorabilia and bric-a-brac, including hand-painted wall tiles. Meals are available either at the bar or in the delightfully-sophisticated Pullman railway carriage restaurant. Typical dishes include steaks, mixed grills, cod or salmon.
OPEN: 11-3 6-11 **BAR MEALS:** L served all week 12-2 D served all week 6-9.30 Av main course £9 **RESTAURANT:** L served all week 12-2 D served all week 6-9.30 Av 3 course à la carte £26 Av fixed price £26 ◀: Worthington, Carling, Boddingtons & 3 Guest Ales.
FACILITIES: Children welcome Children's licence Garden: Well looked after 0.5 acre garden Dogs allowed **NOTES:** Parking 30

Granby Inn 🛏
Front St NE65 8DP ☎ 01665 570228 🖷 01665 570736
Dir: On A697, 11m N of Morpeth
A friendly 200-year-old coaching inn that retains much of its original character, including fine old oak beams. Set at the heart of Northumberland, between the Cheviots and the coast, the family-run business specialises in good home-cooked food: moules marinière, chicken chasseur, roast duckling, grilled trout, and entrecôte bordelaise. These might be followed by treacle sponge with custard, or toffee and pecan sponge pudding, all served in the convivial bar and restaurant.
OPEN: 11-3 6-11 Closed: 25-26 Dec **BAR MEALS:** L served all week 11.30-2 D served all week 6-9.30 Av main course £8.90 **RESTAURANT:** L served all week 11.30-2 D served all week 6-9.30 Av 3 course à la carte £12 Av 3 course fixed price £11.50 **BREWERY/COMPANY:** Free House ◀: Stones Best Bitter, Worthington E. **FACILITIES:** Children welcome **NOTES:** Parking 20

LONGHORSLEY   Map 21 NZ19

Linden Tree ⅊
Linden Hall NE65 8XF ☎ 01670 500033 🖷 01670 500001
e-mail: stay@lindenhall.co.uk
Dir: Off the A1 on the A697 1m N of Longhorsley

Originally two large cattle byres, this popular bar takes its name from the linden trees in the grounds of Linden Hall Hotel, an impressive Georgian mansion offering smartly-furnished bedrooms. Straightforward meals range from aubergine and broccoli bake, braised lamb shank, or medallions of pork, to grilled salmon, or poached smoked cod fillets.
OPEN: 11-11 (Sun 12-10.30) Closed: 1 Jan **BAR MEALS:** L served all week 12-2 D served all week 6-9.30 Av main course £6.95 **RESTAURANT:** L served all week 12.00-2.00 D served 7.00-9.30 **BREWERY/COMPANY:** Free House ◀: Black Bull, Greene King Ruddles Best, Scottish Courage John Smiths. ⅊: 7 **FACILITIES:** Children welcome Garden: Dogs allowed **NOTES:** Parking 200 **ROOMS:** 50 bedrooms 50 en suite s£79.50 d£115 (★★★)

LOW NEWTON BY THE SEA   Map 21 NU22

The Ship
The Square NE66 3EL ☎ 01665 576262
e-mail: forsythchristine@hotmail.com
Dir: NW from A1 at Alnwick
The village of Low Newton was purpose-built as a fishing village in the 18th century and is in the shape of an open-sided square. The unspoilt Ship overlooks the green and is just a stroll away from the beach. Bustling in summer and a

continued

LOW NEWTON BY THE SEA continued

peaceful retreat in winter, it offers a menu that includes plenty of fresh, locally-caught fish and shellfish, venison rump steaks, Greek salad with houmous, and maybe Ship Inn trifle with ratafia and Madeira to finish.

OPEN: 11-4 6.30-11 (During school holidays open all day)
BAR MEALS: L served all week 12-2.30 6.30-8 Av main course £10
BREWERY/COMPANY: Free House ◀: Original Northumberland, Black Sheep, Guest beers. **FACILITIES:** Children welcome Garden: Food served outside Dogs allowed Water provided **NOTES:** No credit cards

---

MATFEN
Map 21 NZ07

The Black Bull
NE20 0RP ☎ 01661 886330
Dir: Leave A69 at Corbridge, join B6318. 2m N sign to Matfen
A 200-year-old, creeper-covered inn fronting the village green, which has a river running through it. The comfortable restaurant and carpeted bar have low beams and open fires.

OPEN: 11-3 6-11 (June-Sept 11-11) **BAR MEALS:** L served all week 12-2 D served all week Av main course £5.95 **RESTAURANT:** L served all week 12-2.30 D served Mon-Sat 6.30-9.30
BREWERY/COMPANY: Free House ◀: Theakston Black Bull.
FACILITIES: Children welcome Garden: beer garden, outdoor eating Dogs allowed garden only **NOTES:** Parking 60

NEWTON ON THE MOOR
Map 21 NU10

Cook and Barker Inn ♀
NE65 9JY ☎ 01665 575234 ▤ 01665 575234
Dir: 0.5m from A1 S of Alnwick

Traditional Northumbrian inn located in a picturesque village with outstanding views over the coast. Good quality fare, including some exotic specialities produced by five chefs, a welcoming atmosphere and various character features make the Cook and Barker a popular watering hole in the area. There is a good selection of real ales and a long list of wines to accompany the extensive bar menus, which suit most tastes and pockets. On the specials menu you might find purée of carrot and coriander soup with Welsh rarebit among the starters, while braised lamb shank, confit of duck, and Spanish chicken casserole may feature as main dishes. Fish options include poached salmon fillet, west coast scallops and bread-crumbed scampi tails.

OPEN: 12-3 6-11 **BAR MEALS:** L served all week 12-2 D served all week 6-9 **RESTAURANT:** L served all week 12-2 D served all week 7-9 Av 3 course fixed price £18.50 **BREWERY/COMPANY:** Free House ◀: Timothy Taylor Landlord, Theakstons Best Bitter, Fuller's London Pride, Batemans XXXB. ♀: 12 **FACILITIES:** Children

continued

welcome Garden: Pretty area with lots of space for children
NOTES: Parking 60

ROWFOOT
Map 21 NY66

The Wallace Arms 🐾
NE49 0JF ☎ 01434 321872 ▤ 01434 321872
The pub was rebuilt in 1850 as the Railway Hotel at Featherstone Park station, when the now long-closed Haltwhistle-Alston line (today's South Tyne Trail) was engineered. All around is great walking country, and just half a mile away is Featherstone Castle in its beautiful parkland. Nothing pretentious on the menu, just good, modestly-priced battered cod, chicken Kiev, vegetable curry, grilled sirloin steak, and Cumberland sausage with egg. There are light snacks, burgers and sandwiches, if you prefer.

OPEN: 11-2.30 4-11 (opening times vary, ring for details)
BAR MEALS: L served all week 12-2 D served all week 7-9 Av main course £6.50 **RESTAURANT:** L served all week 12-2 D served all week 7-9 Av 3 course à la carte £15 **BREWERY/COMPANY:** Free House ◀: Hook Norton Old Hooky, Timothy Taylor Landlord, Young's Special, Batemans. **FACILITIES:** Children welcome Garden: Large lawn surrounded by stone wall **NOTES:** Parking 30 **NOTES:** No credit cards

---

SEAHOUSES
Map 21 NU23

The Olde Ship Hotel ★★ 🐾 ♀
9 Main St NE68 7RD ☎ 01665 720200 ▤ 01665 721383
e-mail: theoldeship@seahouses.co.uk
Dir: lower end of main street above harbour

Sitting above a tiny bustling harbour, this historic hotel has been managed by the same family for over 90 years. There is a strong nautical theme to the cosy, comfortable bars, with plenty of seafaring memorabilia. Ideal location for a weekend break, with bracing country walks. Many fish dishes are featured, including smoked fish chowder, Craster kippers and bosun's fish stew. Other choices include beef stovies, chicken and mushroom casserole and spicy lamb stew. Good range of traditional puddings.

OPEN: 11-11 (Sun 12-10.30, Xmas 12-2, 8-10.30) **BAR MEALS:** L served all week 12-2 D served all week 7-8.30 Av main course £5.75 **RESTAURANT:** L served all week 12-2 D served all week 7-8.30 **BREWERY/COMPANY:** Free House ◀: Scottish Courage John Smith's, Theakston Best, Interbrew Bass, McEwans. ♀: 10 **FACILITIES:** Children's licence Garden: Grassed area with summer house Dogs allowed Water **NOTES:** Parking 18 **ROOMS:** 18 bedrooms 18 en suite s£46 d£40 no children overnight

---

> ★ **Star rating for inspected hotel accommodation**

England

WARDEN
Map 21 NY96

The Boatside Inn
NE46 4SQ ☎ 01434 602233
Dir: *Just off A69 west of Hexham, follow signs to Warden Newborough & Fourstones*

The name comes from the rowing boat that ferried people across the River Tyne before the bridge was built. This attractive stone pub nestles beneath Warden Hill Iron Age fort, a popular destination for walkers, and promises real ale and good food cooked from local produce. Expect interesting sandwiches and snacks, plus seafood thermidor, halibut steaks, Indian and Thai curries, game in season, and Cumberland sausage. Plenty of art and antiques for sale.
OPEN: 11-3 6-11 **BAR MEALS:** L served all week 12-2 D served all week 6.30-9.30 Av main course £7.50 **RESTAURANT:** L served all week 12-2 D served all week 6.30-9.30 **BREWERY/COMPANY:** Free House ◗: Jennings, Cumberland, Cumberland Cream, Jennings Bitter. **FACILITIES:** Children welcome Garden: Paved patio with lawn area, hanging baskets Dogs allowed Water **NOTES:** Parking 70

WARENFORD
Map 21 NU12

Pick of the Pubs

Warenford Lodge
NE70 7HY ☎ 01668 213453 ▤ 01668 213453
e-mail: warenfordlodge@aol.com
Dir: *100yds E of A1, 10m N of Alnwick*
By the original toll bridge over the Waren Burn, this 200-year-old coaching inn was once on the Great North Road. The A1, as it later became, today by-passes the village, leaving the pub a welcome stone's throw away. Inside, one is struck by the thick stone walls and open fireplaces, merrily blazing away on colder days. Visitors and locals alike enjoy the country atmosphere and award-winning Northumbrian dishes. From the specials menu start with, say, artichoke and leek pancakes, and then choose one of either six fish or meat dishes. East Coast haddock comes with a garlic butter and vermouth crumb crust, and seaside fish platter with home-made sauce tartare. Otherwise, opt for lamb and vegetable moussaka, or wild duck with cider and quince. Regular mains include spinach and ricotta cannelloni, Seahouses chowder, and Bamburgh pork and chive sausages. Baked lemon pudding with thick cream is a house speciality.
OPEN: 12-2 7-11 Closed Sun Eve, Mon-Tue(Nov-Easter) Closed: 25/26 Dec, 1 Jan-31 Jan **BAR MEALS:** L served Sat-Sun 12-1.30 D served Tues-Sun 7-9.30 Av main course £8.10
RESTAURANT: L served Sat-Sun 12-1.30 D served Tues-Sun 7-9.30 Av 3 course à la carte £14.85

BREWERY/COMPANY: Free House ◗: Scottish Courage john Smith's. ℡: 8 **FACILITIES:** Children welcome Garden: More a field than a garden Dogs allowed Water in the car park **NOTES:** Parking 60

NOTTINGHAMSHIRE

BEESTON
Map 11 SK53

Pick of the Pubs

Victoria Hotel ℡
Dovecote Ln NG9 1JG ☎ 0115 925 4049 ▤ 0115 922 3537
e-mail: hopco.victoriabeeston@virgin.net
Dir: *M1 J25 take A52 E. R at Nurseryman PH & R opp Rockaway Hotel into Barton St 1st L*
The original hotel came to life in the hey-day of the railways, and the large patio garden is still handy for a touch of train-spotting. The pub was transformed less than a decade ago from a state of dilapidation into a characterful free house serving an excellent range of traditional ales, continental beers and lagers, farm ciders and 150 malt whiskies. Several awards have followed over the past few years in recognition not only of the beers but also the home-cooked food. Dishes on the daily-changing menu might include local sausages and mash, sautéed chicken fillet with honey, ginger and chilli, pork Portugese (loin steaks with chorizo sausage, pancetta, tomato, oregano and sherry) or, from the extensive vegetarian menu, shepherdess pie (braised vegetable and bean casserole topped with mash). Finish with equally inspiring desserts: perhaps 18th-century Irish trifle or warm pecan pie. The pub hosts an annual Festival of Ale, Food and Music, which gets bigger and better every year.
OPEN: 11-11 (Sun 12-10.30) 25 Dec Open 12-3
BAR MEALS: L served all week 12-8.45 D served all week Av main course £7.50 **RESTAURANT:** L served all week D served all week 12-8.45 **BREWERY/COMPANY:** Tynemill Ltd
◗: Batemans XB, Caledonian Deuchers IPA, Castle Rock Hemlock, Everards Tiger & 6 Guests. ℡: 30 **FACILITIES:** Garden: Patio area Dogs allowed **NOTES:** Parking 10

CAUNTON
Map 17 SK76

Caunton Beck ℡
NG23 6AB ☎ 01636 636793 ▤ 01636 636828
Dir: *5m NW of Newark on A616*

Civilised pub-restaurant constructed around a 16th-century cottage set amid herb gardens with a dazzling rose arbour.

continued

continued

England

CAUNTON continued

Food is available non-stop from 8am to around midnight every day, so you can pop in for breakfast, a sandwich or a full meal. Menu favourites include confit of duck with apple and cider compote, beef fillet medallions with béarnaise sauce, and classic Caesar salad. For dessert, be tempted by warm date and walnut pudding or orange and mint pannacotta.
OPEN: 8-12 **BAR MEALS:** L served all week 8-11 D served all week Av main course £8.20 **RESTAURANT:** L served all week 8-11 D served all week Av 3 course à la carte £22.50 Av 3 course fixed price £12 **BREWERY/COMPANY:** Free House **:** Greene King Ruddles Best & Ruddles County, Scottish Courage John Smith's. **:** 7
FACILITIES: Children welcome Children's licence Garden: Terrace & lawns Dogs allowed **NOTES:** Parking 40

CAYTHORPE   Map 11 SK64

Black Horse Inn
NG14 7ED ☎ 0115 966 3520
Three generations of the same family have run this small, beamed country pub where old-fashioned hospitality is guaranteed. In winter, coal fires burn, and if the toilets are outside (they are still trying to fix that!), at least there are no slot machines or music. The inn has its own small brewery, producing Dover Beck Bitter, and food ranges from crispy bacon sandwiches to fresh fish specials, mixed grill, and fresh game.
OPEN: 12-3 5.30-11 (Sat 6-11, Sun 7-10.30) **BAR MEALS:** L served Tue-Sat 12-1.45 D served Tue-Fri 7-8.30 **RESTAURANT:** L served Tue-Sat 12-1.45 D served Mon-Sat 7-8.30 Av 3 course à la carte £16 **BREWERY/COMPANY:** Free House **:** Interbrew Bass, Adnams Bitter, Greene King Abbot Ale, Black Sheep. **FACILITIES:** Garden: Dogs allowed Water **NOTES:** Parking 30 **NOTES:** No credit cards

COLSTON BASSETT   Map 11 SK73

Pick of the Pubs

The Martins Arms Inn
School Ln NG12 3FD ☎ 01949 81361 ✉ 01949 81039
Dir: *From M1 J22 take A50 then A46 N towards Newark. Colston Bassett is E of Cotgrave*
There may be an air of recognition about this picturesque inn, for it has been featured on television in both programmes and advertisements. It was converted from a 17th-century farmhouse to an inn during the middle years of the 19th century by local Squire Martin, hence the name. Today the listed building has a county house feel, with period furnishings, traditional hunting prints and seasonal fires in the Jacobean fireplace. The acre of landscaped grounds - backing on to National Trust land - includes a herb garden and well-established lawns. Regional ingredients are a feature of the menu, with an outstanding ploughman's lunch comprising Melton Mowbray pork pie, Colston Bassett Stilton, home-cured ham, house pickles, apple slices, salad garnish and a crusty bread roll. If you prefer, try the cumin-roasted loin of lamb; Martins Arms potato cake with local Stilton or mature cheddar; ham hock, pease pudding and new potatoes; or one of the speciality sandwiches like seared haloumi, fig and grape chutney bruschetta.
OPEN: 12-3 6-11 25 Dec Closed eve **BAR MEALS:** L served all week 12-2 D served all week 6-10 Av main course £14 **RESTAURANT:** L served all week 12-2 D served Mon-Sat 6-9.30 Av 3 course à la carte £25 **BREWERY/COMPANY:** Free House **:** Marston's Pedigree, Interbrew Bass, Greene King Abbot Ale,

continued

Timothy Taylor Landlord. **:** 7 **FACILITIES:** Children welcome Garden: Acre of landscaped garden with 80 covers
NOTES: Parking 35

ELKESLEY   Map 17 SK67

Pick of the Pubs

Robin Hood Inn
High St DN22 8AJ ☎ 01777 838259

An unassuming village local, but one worth a detour from the tedious A1. It may not look it from the outside, but in parts the building dates back to the 14th century. Its enthusiastic landlord/chef, Alan Draper, has run the pub for at least a decade, and his relatively-recent refurbishment has maintained its traditional, homely feel. Ceilings and floors are deep red, while the green walls are adorned with pictures of food. Bar meals range from sandwiches, filled baguettes and ploughman's, through to ham, egg and chips, battered fillet of haddock, chips and minted mushy peas, and 'open' seafood omelette, topped with a grill-glazed mornay sauce. For something more ambitious, the main menu, complemented by a daily-changing specials board is at hand, with starters including chargrilled bell peppers, capers and melted Brie, potted crab, and avocado salad with crispy pancetta and garlic croutons. Next might come slow-cooked confit shoulder of lamb, with garlic and rosemary sauce and mint pesto; grilled gammon steak, with vine tomato, fried egg, pineapple, chips and peas; or deep-fried wholetail scampi, pea purée, chips and tartare sauce. Follow with a platter of English regional cheeses, or one of Alan's many delicious puddings, such as syrup sponge and custard, apple tarte Tatin, or chocolate nemesis - 'the ultimate dessert'. An excellent value mid-week menu offers four courses for £12.50. A dozen wines from eight countries. While here, visit the adjacent 14th-century church, the village pottery, or the National Trust's Clumber Park nearby.
OPEN: 11.30-3 6.30-11 **BAR MEALS:** L served all week 12-2 D served Mon-Sat 7-9.30 Av main course £7.50 **RESTAURANT:** L served all week 12-2 D served Mon-Sat 7-9.30 Av 3 course à la carte £18 Av 3 course fixed price £11.50
BREWERY/COMPANY: Enterprise Inns **:** Interbrew Flowers IPA & Boddingtons Bitter, Marston's Pedigree, Carlsberg-Tetley Bitter. **:** 8 **NOTES:** Parking 40

♦ **Diamond rating for inspected guest accommodation**

KIMBERLEY
Map 11 SK44

The Nelson & Railway Inn
12 Station Rd NG16 2NR ☎ 0115 938 2177
Dir: 1m N of J26 M1
This unusual 17th-century village pub, with various Victorian and 20th-century additions, has an eccentric atmosphere, nurtured by the landlord who has been here for over thirty years. Nearby, the two competing railway stations that once gave the inn its major business are now derelict and next door is the Hardy & Hanson brewery that supplies the bar with many of its beers. A hearty menu includes steak and kidney pie, cod in batter, lasagne, monster mixed grill, stirfry egg noodles and seafood platter.
OPEN: 11-11 (Sun 12-10.30) **BAR MEALS:** L served all week 12-2.30 D served all week 5.30-9 Av main course £5 **RESTAURANT:** L served all week 12-2.30 D served all week 5.30-9 Av 3 course à la carte £10 **BREWERY/COMPANY:** Hardy & Hansons 🍺: Hardys, Hansons Best Bitter, Classic, Cool & Dark. **FACILITIES:** Children welcome Garden: Food served outdoors, patio/terrace Dogs allowed water provided **NOTES:** Parking 50

LAXTON
Map 17 SK76

The Dovecote Inn ♀
Moorhouse Rd NG22 0NU ☎ 01777 871586 📠 01777 871586
e-mail: dovecoteinn@yahoo.co.uk
Dir: Telephone for directions
Set in the only village that still uses the '3 field system', (pop into the local Visitor Centre to find out what that is), this 18th-century pub is an ideal stopping point for walkers, who can relax over a pint in the large front and rear gardens. A typical menu mixes grills, salads and light bites with other dishes such as mushroom Stroganoff, cottage pie, seafood platter, steak in Guinness pie, and lasagne.
OPEN: 11.30-3 6.30-11.30 **BAR MEALS:** L served all week 12-2 D served all week 6.30-9.30 **RESTAURANT:** 12-2 6.30-9.30
BREWERY/COMPANY: Free House 🍺: Mansfield Smooth, Banks Smooth, Marston's Pedigree. **FACILITIES:** Children welcome Garden: Dogs allowed **NOTES:** Parking 45

NORMANTON ON TRENT
Map 17 SK76

The Square & Compass 🍴 ♀
Eastgate NG23 6RN ☎ 01636 821439 📠 01636 822794
e-mail: info@squareandcompass.co.uk
Dir: Off A1 & B1164 N of Newark-on-Trent

Full of charm and character, this beamed pub is almost 500 years old, and is said to be haunted by the ghost of a traveller who was hung for stealing. A typical menu includes stuffed woodland mushrooms, seafood platter, game casserole, and roulade of chicken. The pub also owns the Maypole Brewery, which produces real ales for local hostelries. A new building nearby houses three bedrooms.

OPEN: 12-3 5-11 **BAR MEALS:** L served all week 12-3 D served all week 6-10 Av main course £6 **RESTAURANT:** L served all week 12-3 D served all week 6-11 **BREWERY/COMPANY:** Free House 🍺: Maypole Lion's Pride, Wells Bombadier Premium, Shepherd Neame Spitfire. **FACILITIES:** Children welcome Garden: Beer garden, ample seating, parasols **NOTES:** Parking 80 **ROOMS:** 3 bedrooms 3 en suite d£45 (♦♦♦♦)

NOTTINGHAM
Map 11 SK53

Fellows Morton & Clayton ♀
54 Canal St NG1 7EH ☎ 0115 950 6795 📠 0115 953 9838
e-mail: info@fellowsmortonandclayton.co.uk
Dir: Telephone for directions
Atmospheric city-centre pub, originally a warehouse belonging to the brewers Samuel Fellows and Matthew Clayton, with a cobbled courtyard overlooking the canal. It has been a pub and restaurant since 1981 and a regular Nottingham in Bloom award winner (flowers on display from the end of May to mid September). Favourite dishes are home-made steak and kidney pie, and Moby Dick haddock weighing approximately 16oz.
OPEN: 11-11 (Sun 12-10.30) Fri-Sat close at - 12 **BAR MEALS:** L served all week 11.30-10 D served Tue-Sat Av main course £6 **RESTAURANT:** L served all week 11.30-2.30 D served Tue-Sat 5.30-9.30 Av 2 course fixed price £4.99 **BREWERY/COMPANY:** Free House 🍺: Timothy Taylor Landlord, Fuller's London Pride, Castle Eden Ale, Mallard Bitter. **FACILITIES:** Garden: **NOTES:** Parking 4

Lincolnshire Poacher
161-163 Mansfield Rd NG1 3FR ☎ 0115 941 1584
Dir: M1 J26.Town centre
Traditional wooden-floored town pub with settles and sturdy wooden tables. Bustles with real ale fans in search of the 12 real ales on tap - regular brewery evenings and wine tastings. Also, good cider and 70 malt whiskies - a great drinkers pub. Large summer terrace.
OPEN: 11-11 (Sun 12-10.30, bar food 12-4) (bar food Mon 12-3, Fri-Sun 12-4) Closed: Jan 1 **BAR MEALS:** L served all week 12-8 D served Mon-Fri Av main course £4.95
BREWERY/COMPANY: Tynemill Ltd 🍺: Bateman XB, XXXB, Castle Rock, JHB. **FACILITIES:** Children welcome Garden: beer garden, food served in garden Dogs allowed

Ye Olde Trip to Jerusalem
1 Brewhouse Yard, Castle Rd NG1 6AD ☎ 0115 9473171
e-mail: yeoldtrip@hardysandhansons.plc.uk
Travellers, it is said, will always find their way to the quaint old inn below Castle Rock. With so many relics of bygone days, it feels like a museum too. In Middle English, a 'trip' was a resting place - hence it began as a refreshment stop for Richard the Lionheart's Holy Land-bound Crusaders in 1189. Before that, the inhabitants of William the Conqueror's castle used caves here for brewing, ale being considerably healthier than water. Indeed, the first bar is a cave, with sandstone walls. Giant meat-filled Yorkshire puddings, steak and kidney pudding, Cajun chicken, and cod, chips and mushy peas, and Kimberley pie are popular main courses. There's a good vegetarian selection, as well as salads, jacket potatoes, burgers, sandwiches and a Young Crusaders menu. In the Rock Lounge look for the 'cursed galleon'; the last three people to clean it all died mysteriously!
OPEN: 11-11 (Sun 12-10.30) **BAR MEALS:** L served all week 11-6 D served None Av main course £5.49
BREWERY/COMPANY: 🍺: Hardys & Hansons Kimberley Best Bitter, Best Mild, Classic, & Ye Olde Trip Ale. **FACILITIES:** Children welcome Children's licence Garden: Seating in front & rear courtyard

continued

England

SOUTHWELL

Map 17 SK65

French Horn ♀

Main St, Upton NG23 5ST ☎ 01636 812394 ▤ 01636 815497
e-mail: duckstock@hotmail.com

An 18th-century former farmhouse handy for visiting the racecourse and nearby Southwell Minster. It offers real ales, eight wines by the glass and good food. One menu is served throughout, and typical dishes are pan-roasted salmon with a warm salad of baby potatoes, green beans and lemon butter, or rack of lamb with Mediterranean vegetables and creamed spinach tartlet. Children are welcome and there is a large enclosed garden to the rear.

OPEN: 11.30-3 5.30-11 **BAR MEALS:** L served all week 12-2.30 D served all week 6-9.30 Av main course £8 **RESTAURANT:** L served Sun 12-2.30 D served Tue-Sat 7-9.30 Av 3 course à la carte £22.50 Av 4 course fixed price £22.50 ☎: Directors, Adnams. ♀: 8
FACILITIES: Children welcome Children's licence Garden: Large enclosed garden Dogs allowed Water **NOTES:** Parking 100

SUTTON BONINGTON

Map 11 SK52

Star Inn ♦♦♦ 🐄 ♀

Melton Ln LE12 5RQ ☎ 01509 852233
Dir: A6 toward Loughborough, 0.33m L to Kingston, over canal, R to Sutt Bonn, over crossroad, 1m Star on L

Whitewashed walls and flowering window boxes and tubs add a touch of colour to this picturesque inn, which was once used for housing cows and chickens. Look out for the cock-fighting prints and foxes' masks on the ochre-painted walls in the public bar. Straightforward yet appetising pub food includes casseroles, grills, pies, pasta bakes, and fresh fish and chips. Evening specials include Burgundy chicken breast, tuna provençale, and Dijon pork.
OPEN: 11-2.30 6-11 (Sun 12-4, 7-10.30) **BAR MEALS:** L served all week 12.15-2 D served Tue-Sat 6.30-8.30 Av main course £6
RESTAURANT: L served all week 12.15-2 D served Tue-Sat 6.30-8.30 Av 3 course à la carte £11.50 **BREWERY/COMPANY:** Enterprise Inns ☎: Interbrew Bass, Adnams Broadside & Best, Greene King IPA, Fuller's London Pride. ♀: 12 **FACILITIES:** Children welcome Garden: Terrace, benches, lrg lawn Dogs allowed **NOTES:** Parking 40 **ROOMS:** 2 bedrooms 2 en suite 2 family rooms s£45 d£45

THURGARTON

Map 17 SK64

The Red Lion

Southwell Rd NG14 7GP ☎ 01636 830351
Dir: On A612 between Nottingham & Southwell

The 16th-century inn that was once a monk's alehouse. Try not to be put off your meal by the 1936 Nottingham Guardian cutting on the wall that tells of the murder of a previous landlady, Sarah Ellen Clarke, by her niece! A parlour extension and smartly-refurbished interior make this a popular place, and the kitchen has a good local reputation. Not far from Thurgarton Priory.

OPEN: 11.30-2.30 6.30-11 **BAR MEALS:** L served all week 12-2 D served all week 7-10 **RESTAURANT:** L served all week 12-2 D served all week 7-10 **BREWERY/COMPANY:** Free House
☎: Interbrew Bass, Greene King Ruddles Best & Abbot Ale, Jenning Cumberland, Carlsberg-Tetley. **FACILITIES:** Children welcome Garden: Large spacious, well kept **NOTES:** Parking 40

TUXFORD

Map 17 SK77

The Mussel & Crab 🍴 ♀

NG22 0PJ ☎ 01777 870491 ▤ 01777 871096
e-mail: musselandcrab1@hotmail.com
Dir: From the Ollerton/Tuxford Junction of the A1 & the A57 go N on the B1164 to Sibthorpe Hill and the pub is 800 yds on the R

As its name suggests, fish and seafood dominate the menu at this quirky pub. You can play liar dice, watch the fish in the gents' toilets, and ponder over the large carved wooden hands in the bar area. The large selection of blackboard dishes (over 22!) is less idiosyncratic: smoked fish platter, salmon and pesto fishcakes, oven-baked swordfish, and grilled Torbay witch sole, plus pork Wellington, Gressingham duck, and a vegetarian combination of three curries. The management boast that there are never fewer than 30 seafood dishes on offer.
OPEN: 11.30-2.30 6-11 **BAR MEALS:** L served all week 11.30-2 D served all week 6.30-10 Av main course £11 **RESTAURANT:** L served all week 12-2 D served all week 6.30-9 Av 3 course à la carte £19 **BREWERY/COMPANY:** Free House ☎: Carlsberg-Tetley Tetley Smooth, Tetley Cask. ♀: 15 **FACILITIES:** Garden: Food served outside, patio area Dogs allowed **NOTES:** Parking 74

WALKERINGHAM

Map 17 SK79

The Three Horse Shoes

High St DN10 4HR ☎ 01427 890959
e-mail: johnturner@barbox.net

A quiet village pub festooned with hanging baskets and some 10,000 bedding plants, all grown and tended by the owner. There's also an aviary, and a Japanese water garden. Medallions

continued

continued

of pork in a white wine herb mustard and cream sauce, roast stuffed breast of lamb, spinach and courgette lasagne, or home-made steak and kidney pie may be on today's menu.
OPEN: 11.30-3 7-11 **BAR MEALS:** L served all week 12-2 D served Mon-Sat 7-9 Av main course £8 **RESTAURANT:** L served Sun 12-2 D served Mon-Sat 7-9 Av 3 course à la carte £13
BREWERY/COMPANY: Free House ◼: Stones, Bass, Worthington, plus guest ale. **FACILITIES:** Children welcome Garden: **NOTES:** Parking 40

WELLOW
Map 17 SK66

Olde Red Lion
Eakring Rd NG22 0EG ☎ 01623 861000
Dir: From Ollerton on the A616 to Newark after 2 miles, Wellow village turn R.
400-year-old pub opposite the maypole in a quiet Nottinghamshire village, and perennially popular with walkers. The unspoilt atmosphere is one of the attractions, and the traditional pub food is another.
OPEN: 11.30-3.15 6-11 (all day wknds) **BAR MEALS:** L served all week 11.30-2.30 D served all week 6-10 Av main course £4.50
RESTAURANT: L served all week 11.30-2.30 D served all week 6-10 Av 3 course à la carte £9 **BREWERY/COMPANY:** Free House
◼: Castle Eden, Bromsbrooke, plus guests. **FACILITIES:** Children welcome Garden: beer garden, patio, outdoor eating
NOTES: Parking 24

OXFORDSHIRE

ABINGDON
Map 05 SU49

The Merry Miller ♀
Cothill OX13 6JW ☎ 01865 390390 ▤ 01865 390040
e-mail: rob@merrymiller.fsbusiness.co.uk
Dir: 1m from the Marcham interchange on the A34
A 17th-century former granary situated in a quiet village close to Oxford. Beams, flagstones, log fires and pine furnishings characterise the tasteful bar and restaurant, where either snacks or main meals may be taken. As a starter try smoked salmon tagliatelle, or Thai-style mussels. Main courses include braised half shoulder of lamb, smoked haddock fishcakes, poacher's casserole, roasted breast of Gressingham duck, and curried leek tartlets.
OPEN: 12-11 (Sun 12-10.30) **BAR MEALS:** L served all week 12-2.45 D served all week 6.30-9.45 **RESTAURANT:** L served all week 12-2.45 D served all week 6.30-9.45 Av 3 course à la carte £20
BREWERY/COMPANY: Greene King ◼: Greene King IPA & Old Speckled Hen. ♀: 15 **FACILITIES:** Children welcome Dogs allowed
NOTES: Parking 60

ADDERBURY
Map 11 SP43

The Red Lion
The Green OX17 3LU ☎ 01295 810269 ▤ 01295 811906
Dir: Off M40 3 miles from Banbury
Civilised old stone coaching inn on the Banbury to Oxford road. Once known as the King's Arms, it had a tunnel in the cellar used by Royalists in hiding during the Civil War. Expect a rambling, beamed interior, daily papers, good wines and a varied menu.
OPEN: 11-11 **BAR MEALS:** L served all week 12-2.30 D served all week 7-9 ◼: Greene King IPA, Hook Norton, Abbot Ale.
FACILITIES: Children welcome **NOTES:** No credit cards

ARDINGTON
Map 05 SU48

Pick of the Pubs

The Boars Head ♀
Church St OX12 8QA ☎ 01235 833254 ▤ 01235 833254
e-mail: bruce-buchan@theboarshead.freeserve.co.uk
Dir: Off A417 W of Wantage

The Boars Head is an attractive 400-year-old timbered pub set beside the church in a timeless estate village. Chef/patron Bruce Buchan has been here for a few years now, having established a fine reputation at several Oxfordshire dining pubs. There's a series of rooms, easy on the eye, and mainly given over to eating, though there is still a locals' bar. Log fires, evening candlelight and fresh flowers set the stage for an innovative choice of pub food. A short menu lists simply-described dishes based on fresh local produce. Starters like assiette of oysters, langoustines and scallops, and stuffed breast of pigeon with haricot bean cassoulet, might be followed by roast suckling pig with sweet and sour beetroots and fondant potato, roast Cornish cod with rösti and hollandaise or poached fillet of roe deer, potato and apple galette, Port Lees sauce and glazed salsify. You can finish in some style with hot Grand Marnier soufflé with iced chocolate cream, perhaps followed by a dessert wine or Port.
OPEN: 12-3 6.30-11 **BAR MEALS:** L served all week 12-2.30 D served all week 7-10 Av main course £8.50 **RESTAURANT:** L served all week 12-2.30 D served all week 7-10 Av 3 course fixed price £16.95 **BREWERY/COMPANY:** Free House
◼: Brakspear Bitter, Hook Norton Old Hooky, West Berkshire Berwery Dr. Hexter's, Warsteiner. **FACILITIES:** Children welcome Garden: Patio area, three tables Dogs allowed
NOTES: Parking 10

See Pub Walk on page 360

Room prices show the minimum double and single rates charged. Room rates in hotels and B&Bs often vary depending on the facilities, so be sure to check prices with the establishment before booking.

The Boars Head

Crossing open countryside to the north of the Ridgeway, this delightful walk makes for a village closely associated with cloth-making.

From the pub turn right, pass the entrance to Ardington House and turn right to a brick arch. Go through it and follow the path to the road opposite a timber-framed cottage. Turn right, pass a turning on the left and keep left at the next intersection of tracks.

Pass the buildings of Red Barn and when the farm track bends right, go straight on along a grassy path between fields and through trees to reach a stile, crossing Ginge Brook. Pass West Hendred Church and cross the road to a stile and sign for East Hendred. Cross the field, keeping fence and trees on the right, to the next stile and cross a track, following the bridleway between fences towards East Hendred.

On reaching the outskirts of the village, pass between houses and bungalows and follow Horn Lane down to the junction. To visit East Hendred village centre turn left. In the 16th and 17th centuries the village was a centre for clothmaking, and many of the houses date from that period. To continue the walk turn right. Pass a turning to Hendred Farm on the left and then turn right immediately beyond a belt of trees. Follow the byway alongside woodland and between fields.

Cross a road and continue on the next section of byway, following the field edge down to Ginge Brook. Cross it to a track and keep ahead between fields. On reaching the road on

THE BOARS HEAD, ARDINGTON
Church Street OX12 8QA
☎ 01235 833254

Directions: Off A417 W of Wantage
Attractive 400-year-old timbered pub with a fine reputation for dining. Still a local's bar, but mainly given over to eating in a series of rooms with log fires, candlelight and fresh flowers. Simply-described dishes on a short menu.
Open: 12-3 6.30-11
Bar Meals: 12-2.30 7-10
Notes: Children & dogs welcome. Patio area. Parking.
(See page 359 for full entry)

a bend, go forward and round to the right towards Ardington House. Cross the Ardington Brook, turn right and pass the entrance to Holy Trinity Church on your right. Just beyond it is the Boars Head.

DISTANCE: 5 1/2 miles/8.8km
MAP: OS Explorer 170
TERRAIN: Open landscape at the foot of the Ridgeway
PATHS: Bridleways, field paths and roads
GRADIENT: Gentle climbing

Walk submitted and checked by Nick Channer

BAMPTON
Map 05 SP30

The Romany
Bridge St OX18 2HA ☎ 01993 850237 📠 01993 852133
e-mail: romany@barbox.net

A shop until 20 years ago, The Romany is housed in an 18th-century building of Cotswold stone with a beamed bar, log fires and intimate dining room. Food ranges from ploughman's to steaks, with home-made specials like hotpot or steak and ale pie. Regional singers provide live entertainment a couple of times a month.
OPEN: 11-11 **BAR MEALS:** L served all week 1-2 D served all week 6.30-9 Av main course £4 **RESTAURANT:** L served all week 12-2 D served all week 6.30-9 Av 3 course à la carte £12
BREWERY/COMPANY: Free House 🍺: Archers Village, plus guests. **FACILITIES:** Children welcome Garden: Food served outside Dogs allowed Water **NOTES:** Parking 8

BANBURY
Map 11 SP44

The George Inn 🐑
Lower St, Barford St Michael OX15 0RH
☎ 01869 338226 📠 01869 337804

Handy for both Banbury and Oxford, this 300-year-old thatched village pub features old beams, exposed stone walls and open fireplaces. It stands in a large garden, with a patio and orchard, overlooking open countryside. Live music is an established tradition, and the pub hosts a variety of rock, folk and solo artists. There's a good choice of real ales, and options from the single menu include baguettes, baked potatoes, pasta, pies, and fish and chips.
OPEN: 12-3 (Sun 12-4) 7-11 **BAR MEALS:** 7-9
BREWERY/COMPANY: Free House 🍺: Hook Norton Best, Timothy Taylor Landlord, IPA, Copper Ale. **FACILITIES:** Children welcome Garden: Patio, orchard, food served outside Dogs allowed **NOTES:** Parking 20 **NOTES:** No credit cards

Pick of the Pubs

The Wykham Arms 🐑 ♀
Sibford Gower OX15 5RX ☎ 01295 788808

Pretty 17th-century village pub, built of mellow Hornton stone with a thatched roof and a gorgeous setting overlooking rolling Oxfordshire countryside. A series of cosy bars and eating areas provide an inviting place for a drink and a meal from the extensive menu. Previously known as the Moody Cow, this pub was rescued from a dilapidated state some years ago, and transformed into a smart and stylish country pub and restaurant. Although there is an upmarket, modern feel throughout the rambling series of five rooms, you can still expect original features such as slate floors, exposed stone, sturdy pine furnishings, tasteful prints and inglenook fireplaces. A

choice of bars welcome locals and visitors who have just come for a pint, while the Parlour and Dairy are more geared to eating, although food can be enjoyed in any of the rooms. Interesting home-made food, freshly prepared from local produce, matches the style of the place. From starters like Thai fishcakes with chilli dipping sauce, deep-fried Brie with cranberry and red wine sauce, and asparagus and pea risotto with Parmesan shavings (also available as a main course), the choice extends to slow-braised shank of lamb with Madeira, half a crispy duck with orange and rosemary sauce, and avocado, spinach, couscous and Feta cheese spring rolls with tomato and fresh basil sauce. Puddings include sticky toffee pudding and raspberry crème brûlée, all of which can be enjoyed on the south-facing terrace. New owners in Spring 2003.
OPEN: 12-2.30 6.30-11 **BAR MEALS:** L served all week 12-2 D served all week 6.30-9.30 Av main course £10.95
RESTAURANT: L served all week 12-2 D served all week 6.30-9.30 Av 3 course à la carte £19.50 **BREWERY/COMPANY:** Free House 🍺: Hook Norton Best, Flowers IPA, Wadworth 6X. **FACILITIES:** Children welcome Garden: Patio and Lawn area with trees Dogs allowed Water provided **NOTES:** Parking 30

BARNARD GATE
Map 05 SP41

Pick of the Pubs

The Boot Inn ♀
OX29 6XE ☎ 01865 881231 📠 01865 882119
e-mail: boot@traditionalfreehouses.com
Dir: off the A40 between Witney & Eynsham

For reasons unexplained, the good-and-famous who have donated footwear to this extraordinary Cotswold stone pub include Ian Botham, George Best, Eddie Irvine, The Bee Gees and Sir Ranulph Fiennes: the licencees have pledged to continue the tradition, adding recently the coveted boots that once belonged to Sir Stanley Matthews. Set back from the hum-drum of the busy A40 and surrounded by open fields and hedgerows, the accent here is on brasserie-style pub food in a modern idiom. Smart and civilised interior with a spacious quarry-tiled bar and attractively-decorated dining areas either side. A typical meal may begin with classic Caesar salad, smoked mackerel and crab fishcakes, or tagliatelle, followed by seared tuna niçoise, calves' liver and back bacon, chargrilled breast of guinea fowl with a kumquat compot, or 'Lamboot' - slow-roasted lamb shank with mashed roots, with beetroot and mint jus. Interesting list of wines; 12 by the glass.
OPEN: 11-3 6-11 (open all day in summer) **BAR MEALS:** L served all week 12-2 D served all week 7-9 Av main course £13 **RESTAURANT:** L served all week 12-2.30 D served all week 7-9.30 **BREWERY/COMPANY:** Free House 🍺: Hook Norton Best Bitter, Greene King Old Speckled Hen. **FACILITIES:** Children welcome Courtyard, **NOTES:** Parking 30

continued

BLACK BOURTON
Map 05 SP20

The Vines ♀
Burford Rd OX18 2PF ☎ 01993 843559 📠 01993 840080
Dir: From A40 Witney, take A4095 to Faringdon, then 1st R after Bampton to Black Bourton

This traditional Cotswold stone building features a stylish contemporary bar with cosy leather sofas beside an open log fire. The bar and restaurant menu, which offers a choice of light bites, salads and pastas in addition to main meals, changes with the seasons. Favourites include Cajun-style salmon; duck breast marinated in Chinese five-spice and cherry brandy; and chicken breast stuffed with goats' cheese. New owners Andy and Karen Gerges also offer a selection of wines from the local vineyard.
OPEN: 11-2.30 6-11 (Sun 12-10.30) **BAR MEALS:** L served Tue-Sun 12-2 D served Tue-Sun 6.30-9.30 Av main course £10 **RESTAURANT:** L served Tue-Sun 12-2 D served Tue-Sun 6.30-9.30 Av 3 course à la carte £20 **BREWERY/COMPANY:** Free House 🍺: Greene King IPA, Marston's Pedigree, Carlsberg-Tetley Tetley's Smooth.
FACILITIES: Children welcome Children's licence Garden: Lrg lawn area, seating Dogs allowed In the garden only **NOTES:** Parking 70

BLEWBURY
Map 05 SU58

Pick of the Pubs

Blewbury Inn ⊛⊛
London Rd OX11 9PD ☎ 01235 850496 📠 01235 850496
See Pub Walk on page 364
See Pick of the Pubs on opposite page

BLOXHAM
Map 11 SP43

The Elephant & Castle
OX15 4LZ ☎ 01295 720383
e-mail: elephantandcastle@hooknorton.tablesir.com
Dir: Just off A361
The arch of this 15th-century, Cotswold-stone coaching inn still straddles the former Banbury to Chipping Norton turnpike. Locals play darts or shove-ha'penny in the big wood-floored bar, whilst the two-roomed lounge boasts a bar-billiards table and a large inglenook fireplace. The reasonably-priced menu starts with a range of sandwiches and crusty filled baguettes, whilst hot dishes include pub favourites like steak and kidney pie, lasagne, haddock, and rump steak.
OPEN: 10-3 5-11 (Sat, Sun-open all day) **BAR MEALS:** L served Mon-Sat 12-2 Av main course £11 **RESTAURANT:** L served Mon-Sat 12-2 Av 3 course à la carte £6.50 **BREWERY/COMPANY:** Hook Norton 🍺: Hook Norton Best Bitter. **FACILITIES:** Children welcome Garden: Raised lawn in flower filled garden, patio Dogs allowed Water **NOTES:** Parking 20

BRIGHTWELL BALDWIN
Map 05 SU69

Pick of the Pubs

The Lord Nelson Inn ♀
OX9 5NP ☎ 01491 612330 & 612497 📠 01491 612118
Dir: Off the B4009 between Watlington & Benson
A charming 18th-century inn whose exterior will be familiar to viewers of Midsomer Murders. Situated in an unspoilt rural hamlet, the 300-year-old building started life as a thatched cottage and is filled with beautiful antique furniture, not to mention sofas, open log fires and a splendid inglenook fireplace - perfect for recuperating after a country walk. During summer the pretty garden, with its weeping willow and rear terrace prove to be a popular attraction. Brakspears real ale is served in the attractive beamed bar, there is a comprehensive wine list and all food is freshly cooked to order by the inn's experienced chefs. Interesting, well-designed specials might include half a roast pheasant, braised with shallots and thyme, grilled lamb cutlets with Shrewsbury sauce or fillet of beef with a wild mushroom sauce. Some good hearty bar snacks and an imaginative Sunday lunch menu complete the picture.
OPEN: 11-3 6-11 **BAR MEALS:** L served all week 12-2.30 D served all week 6-10.30 Av main course £10.95
RESTAURANT: L served all week 12-3 D served all week 6-10.30 Av 3 course à la carte £21 **BREWERY/COMPANY:** Free House 🍺: Brakspears, Hook, Morton, Fullers London Pride. ♀: 10
FACILITIES: Garden: Lawn terrace and borders **NOTES:** Parking 20

BURCOT
Map 05 SU59

The Chequers
OX14 3DP ☎ 01865 407771
Dir: On A415 (Dorchester/Abingdon rd)
Partly dating back to the 16th century and originally a staging post for barges on the Thames. A varied menu might include bacon, mushroom and pine nut salad, seared salmon with charred potatoes, braised leek, orange and ginger, braised shank of lamb, pan-fried duck breast with red cabbage and garlic mash, and grilled cod with chive mash and mild curry cream. Good choice of real ales, and German draught lagers.
OPEN: 11.30-2.30 6-11 (Sun 7-10.30) **BAR MEALS:** L served all week 12-2 D served all week 6.30-9.30 **RESTAURANT:** L served all week 12-2 D served all week 6.30-9.30 **BREWERY/COMPANY:** Free House 🍺: Brakspear Bitter, West Berkshire Dr. Hexter's, Seasonal Ales. **FACILITIES:** Children welcome Garden: Dogs allowed **NOTES:** Parking 30

BURFORD
Map 05 SP21

Golden Pheasant ★★ ♀
91 High St OX18 4QA ☎ 01993 823223 📠 01993 822621
Dir: Leave M40 at junction 8 and follow signs A40 Cheltenham into Burford
Attractive honey-coloured, 17th-century stone inn in the centre of Burford, with cosy log fires bringing warmth in winter. Expect an informal atmosphere in the brasserie-style lounge bar and smart restaurant, where the food has an enthusiastic following. Warm mussels with chorizo and wild mushroom salad might be followed by beef bourguignon, or rack of lamb, with the likes of blackberry and port trifle, or apple and

continued on page 365

Open: 12-3, 6-11
Closed: Mon
Bar Meals: L served Tue-Sun 12-2,
D served Tue-Sun 7-9.
Av cost main course £13.50
RESTAURANT: L served Tue-Sun 12-2,
D served Tue-Sat 6-11.
BREWERY/COMPANY:
Free House.
🍺: Hook Norton Best, Old Hookey &
Generation, Wadworth 6X, Timothy
Taylor Landlord, Batemans.
FACILITIES: Dogs allowed, Garden.
NOTES: Parking 20

Blewbury Inn

Tucked beneath the Berkshire Downs, Blewbury is a small springline village with thatched walls and ducks on the millstream. Kenneth Grahame of 'Wind in the Willows' fame once lived here.

London Road, Blewbury, nr Didcot,
OX11 9PD
☎ 01235 850496 📠 01235 850496
Dir: At the junction of the A417 and
B4016 below Didcot.

Franck and Kalpana Péigne's homely, 200-year-old free house stands back from the A417 on the village edge. It has just two public rooms - a bar with beams and log fire, and an intimate restaurant. Franck's inventive Modern British and French cooking - the latter reflecting his Brittany origins - becomes more popular every year, partly because he keeps his seasonally-changing menus short, but truly inventive. At lunchtimes the atmosphere is relaxed, the light and simple menu perhaps offering Parma ham, or Cornish mussel soup with chervil and fennel. In the evening though, the serious dining takes over, with the bar staff serving pre-dinner drinks (although don't be deterred from popping in for a for a pint, or glass of wine. Booking is advisable for the fixed-price menu offering three choices at each course. Starters might include tartlette of Welsh goat's cheese and red onion marmalade, with apple and chorizo macédoine, or scallop terrine with mesclun (a sophisticated mixed salad) of green beans, smoked salmon strips and grilled peppers, with truffle oil and prawn sauce. Main courses could be medallions of beef fillet with horseradish and potato mash, shallots confit, cheddar crust, and a basil and red wine jus, or halibut steak with grilled provençale vegetables, lemon thyme beurre Nantais, and tempura king prawns. Finish with iced terrine parfait of Bailey's cream with dark chocolate brownie and anglaise sauce, or French regional cheeses and grapes. The real ale aficionado who is your reviewer can recommend the Hook Norton and Wadworth's beers too.

The Blewbury Inn

Savour the stillness and solitude of Oxfordshire's racing country on this spectacular downland walk.

From the pub turn left and walk along to the junction with Westbrook Street. Turn left here at the bridleway sign for the Ridgeway. Head south-west on the path, pass a seat and climb gently on to the downs. Cross a track and continue to Churn Farm. Turn right here, joining a concrete farm road running between houses and outbuildings.

Turn left at the next junction and soon you will see an old railway bridge in front of you. This is virtually all that remains of Churn Halt. Before the First World War soldiers came here by train to use the nearby rifle ranges, part of a tented army camp opened towards the end of the 19th century by Baron

Wantage, who was a keen shot and pioneer of the territorial volunteers. The halt was on the old Didcot, Newbury and Southampton line.

Turn left in front of the bridge by a single-storey dwelling, and follow the straight track. When it curves left, go straight on alongside a hedge. Follow a broad rutted track to the Ridgeway and continue ahead up a gentle slope. Keep left at the next fork, draw level with a copse on the right and turn left at a crossroads. Cut between racing gallops, pass the buildings of Woodway and now the track graduates to a metalled lane. Follow it down to the A417, turn left and return to the Blewbury Inn.

THE BLEWBURY INN, BLEWBURY
London Road OX11 9PD
☎ 01235 850496

Directions: At junc of A417 & B4016 below Didcot
Homely 200-year-old freehouse on the edge of a pretty village, with a beamed bar and intimate restaurant. Real ales are served, along with a light and simple menu at lunchtime and a fixed-price choice in the evening.
Open: 12-3 6-11
Bar Meals: 12-2 7-9
Notes: Children & dogs welcome. Food served in the garden. Parking. (See page 363 for full entry)

DISTANCE: 7 1/2 miles/12.1km
MAP: OS Explorer 170
TERRAIN: Open downland to the south of Blewbury
PATHS: Paths and tracks
GRADIENT: Gentle climbing

Walk submitted and checked by Nick Channer

BURFORD continued

Map 05 SP21

pear harvest crumble bringing up the rear. The comfortable bedrooms include several four-posters.
OPEN: 9-11 **BAR MEALS:** L served all week 12-2.30 Av main course £9.95 **RESTAURANT:** D served all week 6.30-9 Av 3 course à la carte £25 **BREWERY/COMPANY:** ◖: Abbot, IPA. ♀: 15 **FACILITIES:** Children welcome Garden: Patio Dogs allowed Manager's discretion **NOTES:** Parking 12 **ROOMS:** 12 bedrooms 12 en suite s£60 d£95

Pick of the Pubs

The Inn for All Seasons ★★★ ◉ 🐾 ♀
The Barringtons OX18 4TN ☎ 01451 844324 📠 01451 844375
e-mail: sharp@innforallseasons.com
See Pick of the Pubs on page 366

Pick of the Pubs

The Lamb Inn ★★★ ◉◉ 🐾 ♀
Sheep St OX18 4LR ☎ 01993 823155 📠 01993 822228
e-mail: info@lambinn-burford.co.uk
Dir: From M40 J8 follow signs for A40 & Burford. Off High Street

Honey-coloured stone-built coaching inn with 500 years of history in a stunning Cotwold location, away from the bustle of the centre of Burford but close enough to the shops. Inside you'll find log fires, gleaming brass and copper, and highly-polished antique furniture. In summer you can visit the walled cottage garden, admire the herbaceous borders and perhaps take lunch on the lawn. Lunchtime options include sandwiches and filled baguettes, crispy cod and chips with tartare sauce, or roast partridge with spicy butternut squash. Other typically interesting offerings are haggis fritters with beetroot relish, and goats' cheese soufflés with celery and hazelnut sauce.
OPEN: 11-2.30 6-11 (Sun 12-3, 7-10.30) **BAR MEALS:** L served Mon-Sat 12-2 Av main course £8 **RESTAURANT:** L served Mon-Sun 12.30-1.45 D served Mon-Sun 7-9 Av 3 course fixed price £32 **BREWERY/COMPANY:** Free House ◖: Wadworth 6X, Hook Norton Best, Badger Dorset Bitter. ♀: 14 **FACILITIES:** Garden: walled cottage garden Dogs allowed Water **ROOMS:** 15 bedrooms 15 en suite s£80 d£125 no children overnight

The Maytime Inn ◆◆◆ 🐾 ♀
OX18 4HW ☎ 01993 822068 📠 01993 822635
e-mail: timmorgan@themaytime.fsnet.co.uk
Dir: A361 from Swindon, R onto A40 then onto B4047 to Asthall

Traditional Cotswold pub in the Windrush valley, near the former home of the famous Mitford sisters (Nancy wrote 'Love in a Cold Climate'). The present owners acquired the then derelict local in 1975 and set about transforming it into a character inn. There's a daily fresh fish board, with dishes such as fillet of sole stuffed with salmon, in addition to steaks, or breast of chicken stuffed with spinach. Comfortable accommodation is also available.
OPEN: 11-3 6-11 **BAR MEALS:** L served all week 12.15-2.15 D served all week 7-9.15 Av main course £8.95 **RESTAURANT:** L served all week 12.15-2.15 D served all week 7-9.15 Av 3 course à la carte £18.50 **BREWERY/COMPANY:** Free House ◖: Timothy Taylor. ♀: 8 **FACILITIES:** Children welcome Garden: Patio Dogs allowed Water **NOTES:** Parking 100 **ROOMS:** 6 bedrooms 6 en suite 1 family rooms s£52.50 d£69.50

★ **Pubs with Red Stars are part of the AA's Top 200 Hotels in Britain & Ireland**

Open: 11.30-2.30, 6-11
(Sun 12-3, 7-10.30)
Bar Meals: L served all week 11.30-2.20,
D served all week 6.30-9.30.
Av cost main course £9.50
RESTAURANT: L served all week 12-2.30,
D served all week 6.30-9.30.
Av cost 3 courses £21
BREWERY/COMPANY:
Free House.
🍺: Wadworth 6X, Interbrew Bass,
Wychwood, Badger.
FACILITIES: Dogs allowed, Children
welcome. Garden - Small grassy area
with tables and good views.
NOTES: Parking 80
ROOMS: 10 en suite from s£51 d£85

The Inn for All Seasons

Some three miles west of Burford on the A40, this engaging 16th-century Grade II listed coaching inn has lost nothing of its charm following conversion into a 10-bedroom country inn.

★★★ ◉ ⬡ ♟
The Barringtons, Burford, OX18 4TN
☎ 01451 844324 📠 01451 844375
✉ sharp@innforallseasons.com
Dir: 3m W of Burford on A40.

It reveals a treasure-trove of ancient oak beams, original fireplaces and complementary period furniture. Residents are assured of a warm and friendly welcome and the en suite bedrooms are both spacious and comfortably furnished, with a hint of romance thrown in for good measure. Close by is the National Trust's Sherborne Estate with its remarkable collection of early spring flowers - snowdrops, winter aconites and wild daffodils - a joy to behold in the course of a bracing walk. There are a number of guest ales and always a Wadworth from Devizes or Wiltshire to accompany a simple bar snack or a more formal restaurant meal. Menus plough an 'all-seasons' furrow, taking in everything from red Thai fish curry with Basmati rice and chunky crisp vegetables to fillet of Hereford beef served on a smoked bacon rösti cake with a horseradish and port sauce. Vegetarians are imaginatively catered for (how about baked butternut squash with goats' cheese and a sauté of button mushrooms and spinach?) but pride of place undoubtedly goes to the selection of fish, fresh from Brixham. Samples from the fish board include grilled tronçon of turbot with tarragon potatoes and Béarnaise sauce, whole roast John Dory on a bed of egg noodle with a red wine and shallot sauce and, of course, classic battered cod and chips. For dessert try iced banana and rum parfait with a mocha and vanilla sauce, chocolate roasted hazelnut tart with a caramel butter sauce or fresh berries in Pernod jelly with a citrus crème fraîche.

CHADLINGTON
Map 10 SP32

The Tite Inn ♀
Mill End OX7 3NY ☎ 01608 676475 🖷 0870 7059308
e-mail: willis@titeinn.com
Dir: 3m S of Chipping Norton

Cotswold stone inn where troops stopped en route to the
Battle of Edge Hill, and which takes its name from the stream,
or tite, running underneath. Roses climbing the walls are a
delight in summer, as are log fires and mulled wine in winter.
A variety of draught beers and eight wines by the glass are
served, alongside sandwiches, salads and meatloaf at lunch,
and in the evening perhaps beef bourguignon, local sausages
or chicken jalfrezi. Home-made puddings too.
OPEN: 12-2.30 6.30-11 (Sun 12-3, 7-10.30) Closed: Dec 25-26
BAR MEALS: L served Tue-Sun 12-2 D served Tue-Sun 7-9
RESTAURANT: L served Sun 12-2 D served Tue-Sat 6.30-11 Av 3
course à la carte £15 **BREWERY/COMPANY:** Free House
🍺: Fullers, Youngs, Guest Beers, Brakspears. ♀: 8
FACILITIES: Children welcome Garden: Lrg beer garden, outstanding
views Dogs allowed Water provided **NOTES:** Parking 30

CHALGROVE
Map 05 SU69

Pick of the Pubs

The Red Lion Inn 🐾 ♀
The High St OX44 7SS ☎ 01865 890625 🖷 01865 890795
Dir: B480 from Oxford Ring rd, thru Stadhampton, L then R at mini-rdbt, at Chalgrove Airfield R fork into village

A lovely cream-painted pub dating from the 11th century,
owned by the parish church since 1637. This traditional inn is
set back from the road beside a running brook in the
delightful village of Chalgrove, with a lovely rear garden for
summer visitors. It enjoys a good following from the village
teams it supports, and an upmarket clientele drawn to the
imaginative food. Expect a civilised atmosphere in the
beamed and tastefully-refurbished bar and dining area,
where perennial pub favourites are given a welcome
modern twist alongside more serious dishes. Lunchtime fare
ranges from chargrilled haggis with whisky, and beef
dumplings with mash, to filled ciabatta rolls and baguettes,
while evening specials might include roast figs with fresh
basil and Brie, and steamed lamb and leek suet pudding.
The menu offers crab cakes with red onion tartar sauce,
chicken cassoulet, and steamed treacle pudding and custard.
OPEN: 12-3 6-11 (Sun 7-10.30) Limited opening 26Dec-2Jan
BAR MEALS: L served all week 12-2 D served Mon-Sat 7-9 Av
main course £7.50 **RESTAURANT:** L served all week 12-2 D
served Mon-Sat 7-9 Av 3 course à la carte £16
BREWERY/COMPANY: Free House 🍺: Fuller's London Pride,
Adnams Best, Guest beers. ♀: 8 **FACILITIES:** Garden: Large,
with seating Dogs allowed Water **NOTES:** Parking 20

CHARLBURY
Map 11 SP31

Pick of the Pubs

The Bull Inn 🐾
Sheep St OX7 3RR ☎ 01608 810689
See Pick of the Pubs on page 368

CHECKENDON
Map 05 SU68

Pick of the Pubs

The Highwayman 🐾 ♀
Exlade St RG8 0UA ☎ 01491 682020 🖷 01491 682229
e-mail: thehighwayman@skyeinns670.fsnet.co.uk
See Pick of the Pubs on page 370

CHINNOR
Map 05 SP70

Pick of the Pubs

Sir Charles Napier ◎◎◎ 🐾 ♀
Spriggs Alley OX39 4BX ☎ 01494 483011 🖷 01494 485311
Dir: M40 J6 to Chinnor. Turn R at rdbt carry on straight up hill to Spriggs Alley

Situated amongst beechwoods and fields in the Chiltern
Hills, this is a genuine people's pub. Here you'll find a
welcoming atmosphere, excellent real ales, and a serious
approach to cooking. Huge log fires and an eclectic mix of
furniture and exhibition sculptures will encourage you to
linger, and Sunday lunch can go on all day! In summer,
lunch is served on the terrace beneath vines and wisteria,
looking out over the pub's extensive herb gardens and
lawns. An exhaustive wine list complements the
blackboard dishes and imaginative seasonal menus.
Parsnip and chestnut soup, cappuchino of asparagus and
tarragon, or pigeon breast with quince and apple might
precede baked salmon with Jerusalem artichoke purée,
roast guinea fowl with shallots and Madeira jus, and
butternut squash risotto. A selection of puddings and
English cheeses offer a rounded finale.
OPEN: 12-3.30 6.30-12 (closed Mon, Sun Night) Closed: 25/26
Dec **BAR MEALS:** L served Tue-Sat 12-2.30 D served Tues-
Thurs 7-9 Av main course £10.50 **RESTAURANT:** L served Tue-
Sun 12-2.30 D served Tue-Sat 7-10 Av 3 course à la carte £30 Av 2
course fixed price £16.50 **BREWERY/COMPANY:** Free House
🍺: Wadworth 6X. ♀: 10 **FACILITIES:** Children welcome
Garden: Large garden and terrace **NOTES:** Parking 50

Open: 12-2.30, 7-11
Closed: Sun evening & Mon all day
Bar Meals: L served Tue-Sun 12-2,
D served Tue-Sat 7-9.
RESTAURANT: L served Tue-Sun
(booking only) 12-1.30,
D served Tue-Sat 7-9.
BREWERY/COMPANY:
Free House.
🍺: Greene King IPA, Abbot Ale &
Ruddles County, Hooky.
FACILITIES: Garden - Terrace.
NOTES: Parking 14

The Bull Inn

You can expect good old-fashioned hospitality at this friendly pub in Charlbury's main street.

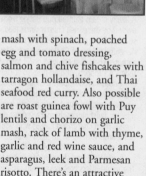

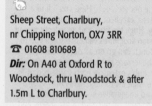

Sheep Street, Charlbury,
nr Chipping Norton, OX7 3RR
☎ 01608 810689
Dir: On A40 at Oxford R to
Woodstock, thru Woodstock & after
1.5m L to Charlbury.

A handsome, unspoilt Cotswold town, Charlbury is surrounded by excellent walking country, including the Blenheim and Cornbury estates, and a multitude of picturesque villages. The Bull, which dates from the 16th century, has a smart Cotswold stone exterior, while inside there are inglenook fireplaces, a tastefully-furnished lounge and dining room, and a traditional bar with wooden floors. Music and fruit machines are banned. Roy and Suzanne Flynn, helped by their son and daughter, have put a great deal of effort into creating an appealing inn that attracts people from far and wide seeking a simple drink or two, or a high quality meal. As you might expect, the restaurant offers a more adventurous menu than the bar, but whichever you choose, the food is home made. There's a good choice of fish and seafood, including undyed smoked haddock on cheese mash with spinach, poached egg and tomato dressing, salmon and chive fishcakes with tarragon hollandaise, and Thai seafood red curry. Also possible are roast guinea fowl with Puy lentils and chorizo on garlic mash, rack of lamb with thyme, garlic and red wine sauce, and asparagus, leek and Parmesan risotto. There's an attractive vine-covered terrace for summer days and evenings.

CHIPPING NORTON Map 10 SP32

Chequers 🍴 ⚲
Goddards Ln OX7 5NP ☎ 01608 644717 📠 01608 646237
e-mail: enquiries@chequers-pub.co.uk
Dir: Town centre, next to theatre

This old coaching inn is next door to the renowned theatre. An alehouse in the 16th century, it also provided lodgings for stonemasons working on the local church. The cosy bar has log fires, low ceilings and soft lighting, while the restaurant is a bright and airy. Well-kept real ale, good wines and decent coffee are served along with freshly-prepared dishes. These include roasted half shoulder of lamb, sea bass on roasted Mediterranean vegetables, salmon fillet on chive mash, pork and leek sausages, or Thai curry. Sandwiches and ploughman's also available.
OPEN: 11-11 (Sun 11-10.30) Closed: 25 Dec **BAR MEALS:** L served all week 12-2.30 D served Mon-Sat 6-9 Av main course £6.50 **RESTAURANT:** L served all week 12-2.30 D served Mon-Sat 6-9 Av 3 course à la carte £16 **BREWERY/COMPANY:** Fullers 🍺 Fuller's Chiswick Bitter, London Pride & ESB, Organic Honeydew. ⚲ 10

CHISLEHAMPTON Map 05 SU59

Coach And Horses Inn ♦♦♦ 🍴 ⚲
Watlington Rd OX44 7UX ☎ 01865 890255 📠 01865 891995
e-mail: enquires@coachhorsesinn.co.uk

A 16th-century former coaching inn situated in quiet countryside within a short distance of Oxford city centre. It retains plenty of character, with its beams, large fireplaces, old bread oven and well, and is believed to be haunted by Alice, a young girl killed during the Civil War. Set price and carte menus are available, and speciality dishes include medallions of pork Elizabeth, sirloin steak Diane, half a roast Devon duckling, guinea fowl forestière, and breast of chicken Chislehampton. Vegetarian selection also available.
OPEN: 11.30-3 6-11 **BAR MEALS:** L served all week 12-2 D served Mon-Sat 7-10 Av main course £8 **RESTAURANT:** L served all week

continued

12-2 D served Mon-Sat 7-10 Av 3 course à la carte £20 Av 2 course fixed price £13.95 **BREWERY/COMPANY:** Free House 🍺 Hook Norton Best, Interbrew Flowers Original. **FACILITIES:** Garden: Landscape courtyard, large lawn area Dogs allowed Water **NOTES:** Parking 40 **ROOMS:** 9 bedrooms 9 en suite 1 family rooms s£53.50 d£60 no children overnight

CHRISTMAS COMMON Map 05 SU79

The Fox and Hounds
OX49 5HL ☎ 01491 612599
Dir: Junct 5 off M40 2.5 miles to Christmas Common (On road to Henley)

A charming flint-built inn whose immaculate interior includes a large restaurant with open plan kitchen, four cosy bar areas and an eye-catching fireplace where logs are burned upright (in the manner of the rich, apparently). Typical dishes include pork loin with black pudding and mustard mash, and pan-fried tuna with Asian coleslaw. Snacks include kippers, soup and sandwiches. Wash it down with well-kept real ale.
OPEN: 11.30-3 6-11 (open all day Fri-Sun) 25 Dec 2pm closure **BAR MEALS:** L served all week 12-2.30 D served Mon-Sat 6-9.30 Av main course £12 **RESTAURANT:** L served all week 12-2.30 D served Mon-Sat 7-9.30 Av 3 course à la carte £24
BREWERY/COMPANY: Brakspear 🍺 Brakspear Bitter, Special & seasonal beers. **FACILITIES:** Garden: Small herb garden Dogs allowed Water **NOTES:** Parking 30

CHURCH ENSTONE Map 11 SP32

Crown Inn 🌀
Mill Ln OX7 4NN ☎ 01608 677262 📠 01608 677394
Dir: Telephone for directions
A 17th-century free house in a village setting on the edge of the Cotswolds, with a small cottage garden adding to the atmospheric facilities in the bar and restaurant. All of the food served here is home cooked, and may include scallops with watercress and bacon salad, rib-eye of beef with bearnaise sauce, and black bream with aioli. New owners in early 2003.
OPEN: 12-3 6-11 (Sun 7-10.30) **BAR MEALS:** L served Tue-Sun 12-2 D served Tue-Sat 7-9 Av main course £7 **RESTAURANT:** L served Tue-Sun 12-2 D served Tue-Sat 7-9 Av 3 course à la carte £18.50 **BREWERY/COMPANY:** Free House 🍺 Everards, Hook Norton. **FACILITIES:** Children welcome Garden: Small cottage garden Dogs allowed Water **NOTES:** Parking 8

♦ **Diamond rating for inspected guest accommodation**

Open: 12-3, 6-11.
Bar Meals: L served all week 12-2.30, D served all week 7-9.30.
Av cost main course £10.95
RESTAURANT: L served all week 12-2.30, D served all week 7-9.30.
Av cost 3 course £25
BREWERY/COMPANY:
Free House.
🍺: Gales HSB, Fullers London Pride, Black Sheep Best, Young's Special, Shepherd Neame Spitfire.
FACILITIES: Dogs allowed, Children welcome, Garden.
NOTES: Parking 30.
ROOMS: 4 en suite from s£49.50 d£49.50 (♦♦♦)

The Highwayman

The date 1625 painted on the wall of this country inn prompts speculation as to what it might have been like here nearly 380 years ago. Fields probably not so open, and the surrounding Chiltern Hills even more wooded, providing ample cover and escape routes for highwaymen.

🐷 🍷

Exlade Street, Checkendon, RG8 0UA
☎ 01491 682020 📄 01491 682229
📧 thehighwayman@skyeinns670.fsnet.co.uk
Dir: On A4074 Reading to Wallingford Rd

Armed robbery involving a blunderbuss is pretty unlikely today, despite the pub's slogan 'No finer place to be waylaid'. Its rambling interior is packed with curios and old artefacts, and at night you can dine at sunken tables by glimmering candlelight. The character bar, with its warm atmosphere, is just the place to relax with a pint of Gales HSB, Fuller's London Pride, or any of the other real ales on offer. The inter-connecting dining rooms and adjoining conservatory, with cane chairs and tiled floor, create a comfortable atmosphere in which to enjoy imaginative pub food. The kitchen uses the best and freshest ingredients, even for the simplest sandwich or home-made soup. Lunch could begin with terrine of pressed duck, foie gras and prune compôte, or baked Arbroath smokies with mushrooms, cheese and cream. From the list of main courses: coq au vin, filled pasta with Gorgonzola cream, and a platter of cured salmon, crab, prawns, avocado and duck terrine. Dinner could be peppered loin of venison with game sauce, or wild mushroom risotto with Parmesan biscuits. One-price desserts include glazed lemon tart, mango cheesecake, sticky toffee pudding with ice cream and selected farmhouse cheeses. The attractive rear garden is popular for summer drinking, and peaceful overnight accommodation is available in four comfortable en suite bedrooms.

CHURCH HANBOROUGH — Map 11 SP41

Pick of the Pubs

The Hand & Shears 🐾 ♀
OX29 8AB ☎ 01993 883337 📠 01993 883060
e-mail: handandshears@t-f-h.co.uk
Dir: *From A40 Eynsham rdbt follow signs for The Hanboroughs. Turn L at sign for Church Hanborough follow road through village, pub is on R opposite church.*

Stylish pub-restaurant situated opposite the 11th-century church and the village green, just 10 minutes' from Blenheim Palace. There's a good choice of ales and wine by the glass, and discerning folk travel miles for the innovative brasserie-type food served in an informal pub atmosphere. Favourite dishes include seafood rendezvous in Champagne cream sauce, local sausages with creamy mash and ale gravy, and corn-fed chicken wrapped in Parma ham with rich sherry jus. Regular live jazz Sunday lunches with Jamie Cullum are a feature (reputed to be like a young Harry Connick Junior), plus monthly live electronic blues nights with 'King B' and a Tex-Mex menu. The pub is also a great base for circular walks and the local cycle route, and is particularly popular with admirers of the bluebells in Pinsley Woods.

OPEN: 11-3 6-11 (open all day Easter-end Summer) Sunday Closed for food **BAR MEALS:** L served all week 12-3 D served all week 6.30-10 Av main course £8.95 **RESTAURANT:** L served all week 12-3 D served all week 6.30-10 Av 3 course à la carte £17 **BREWERY/COMPANY:** 🛢 Hook Norton Best Bitter, Hobgoblin, Fiddlers Elbow, Adnams. ♀: 10 **FACILITIES:** Children welcome Benches opposite village green Dogs allowed Water **NOTES:** Parking 40

CLIFTON — Map 11 SP43

Duke of Cumberland's Head
OX15 0PE ☎ 01869 338534 📠 01869 338643
Dir: *A4260 from Banbury, then B4031 from Deddington*
Stone and thatch pub situated in the hamlet of Clifton, between the historic villages of Deddington and Aynho. It was built in 1645, originally as cottages, and is named after Prince Rupert who led the king's troops at the battle of Edge Hill. A good range of food is offered, from sandwiches and deep-fried haddock to substantial dishes of rabbit in cream and bacon sauce, and boeuf bourguignon.

OPEN: 12-2.30 (w/end 12-3) 6.30-11 Closed: Dec 25 Sun eve **BAR MEALS:** L served all week 12-2 D served Mon-Sat 6-9 Av main course £8.50 **RESTAURANT:** L served Wed-Sun 12-2 D served Wed-Sat 7-9.30 Av 3 course à la carte £18 Av 2 course fixed price £15 **BREWERY/COMPANY:** 🛢 Hook Norton, Adnams, Wadworth 6X, Jennings. **FACILITIES:** Children welcome Garden: beer garden, outdoor eating, BBQ Dogs allowed **NOTES:** Parking 20

CLIFTON HAMPDEN — Map 05 SU59

Pick of the Pubs

The Plough Hotel & Restaurant ♀
Abingdon Rd OX14 3EG ☎ 01865 407811 📠 01865 407136
e-mail: admin@ploughinn.co.uk
A pretty thatched and beamed 17th-century inn with inglenook fireplaces and oodles of charm. Set close to the River Thames with its peaceful riverside walks, it is owned and run along traditional lines by Yuksel Bektas, a Turk

whose tail-coated presence guarantees the inn's hallmark of courteous hospitality. This delightful country pub has a cosy, heavily-beamed main bar (watch your head when entering), and a smart dining room featuring check tiled floor and polished wooden tables. Good food is guaranteed in both rooms, with interesting menus: from the carte expect starters like smoked duck breast salad, avocado and William pear, and warm baby brioche filled with wild mushroom and whisky ragout, followed perhaps by roast fillet of venison, escalopes of pork fillet, and supreme of chicken.

OPEN: Open all day **BAR MEALS:** L served all week 11 D served all week 11 **RESTAURANT:** L served all week D served all week **BREWERY/COMPANY:** 🛢 Scottish Courage John Smith's, Courage Best & Directors. **FACILITIES:** Children welcome Garden: **NOTES:** Parking 35

CUMNOR — Map 05 SP40

Pick of the Pubs

Bear & Ragged Staff ♀
28 Appleton Rd OX2 9QH ☎ 01865 862329 📠 01865 865947
Dir: *A420 from Oxford, R to Cumnor on B4017*

A 700-year-old pub dating back to Cromwell's days, and allegedly haunted by the mistress of the Earl of Warwick. Cromwell's brother Richard is believed to have chiselled out the royal crest from above one of the fireplaces. The wooden décor, including beams and floors, and two of the original massive fireplaces add to the atmosphere, and the appeal is enhanced by soft furnishings and warm colours. The pub caters for a wide cross section of locals as well as being a popular destination for lovers of good food. Freshly-prepared meals with full service might produce starters like smoked duck breast on a mixed leaf salad, or timbale of salmon, crab and prawns, followed by monkfish in smoked bacon with saffron sauce, or Thai

continued

continued

CUMNOR continued

chicken curry, and perhaps profiteroles with Chantilly cream and a rich chocolate sauce. A good range of Havana cigars, ports and brandies.
OPEN: 12-11 (Sun 12-10.30) **BAR MEALS:** L served all week 12-3 D served all week 6-9.30 Av main course £11.50
RESTAURANT: L served all week 12-3 D served all week 6-10 Av 3 course à la carte £20 **BREWERY/COMPANY:** Morrells
🍺: IPA, Old Speckled Hen, Abbot Ale, Old Hooky.
FACILITIES: Children welcome Garden: Food served outdoors, patio, BBQ Dogs allowed Water, toys **NOTES:** Parking 60

The Vine Inn 🍴
11 Abingdon Rd OX2 9QN ☎ 01865 862567 🖷 01865 862567
Dir: *A420 from Oxford, R onto B4017*
An old village pub whose name, when you see the frontage, needs no explanation. A typical menu here could include lamb shank with a red wine and mint sauce, pan-fried fillet steak with brandy and mushroom sauce, and the day's fresh fish. There's also a good range of snacks. Children love the huge garden. In 1560, the suspicious death of an earl's wife in Cumnor Place first had people asking 'Did she fall, or was she pushed?'
OPEN: 11-3 6-11 (Sat 11-11) (Sun 12-10.30) **BAR MEALS:** L served all week 12.30-2.15 D served Mon-Sat 6.30-9.15 Av main course £4.50
RESTAURANT: L served all week 12.30-2.15 D served Mon-Sat 6.30-9.15 Av 3 course à la carte £19.50 **BREWERY/COMPANY:** Punch Taverns
🍺: Adnams Bitter, Carlsberg-Tetely Tetely Bitter, Wadworth 6X + guest beers. **FACILITIES:** Children welcome Garden: Fenced with tables and chairs & lawn area Dogs allowed Water **NOTES:** Parking 45

DEDDINGTON
Map 11 SP43

Pick of the Pubs

Deddington Arms ★★★ ◎ 🍴 ♀
Horsefair OX15 0SH ☎ 01869 338364 🖷 01869 337010
e-mail: deddarms@aol.com
Dir: *A43 to Northampton, B4100 to Aynho, B4031 to Deddington. M40 J11 to Banbury. Follow signs for hospital, then towards Adderbury & Deddington, on A4260.*
The Deddington Arms has provided some of the finest hospitality in North Oxfordshire for 400 years. From the lively, timbered bar, with open fires blazing away whenever the weather demands, there's a good view of the village. You can eat in the bar, choosing from the blackboard's tasty selection, or from a carte menu in the smart air-conditioned restaurant. It goes without saying that all food is fresh, and of top quality. Two examples help to convey the kitchen's approach: the first is grilled fillet of beef on sautéed oyster mushrooms, with silver-skin onions, salsify and a mustard and black pepper crust on potato rosti with port jus; the second is crisp-skin sea bass on chorizo, fennel, aubergine caviar and basil with tomato syrup. The wine list features labels from all around the world. The spacious en suite bedrooms have been completely modernised without any loss of charm or character.
OPEN: 11-11 **BAR MEALS:** L served all week 12-2 D served all week 6.30-9 Av main course £9 **RESTAURANT:** L served all week 12-2 D served all week 6.30-10.00 Av 3 course à la carte £23
BREWERY/COMPANY: Free House 🍺: Carlsberg-Tetleys Tetleys Bitter, Green King IPA. ♀: 8 **FACILITIES:** Children welcome **NOTES:** Parking 36 **ROOMS:** 27 bedrooms 27 en suite 3 family rooms s£75 d£85

DORCHESTER (ON THAMES)
Map 05 SU59

Pick of the Pubs

The George ★★★ ◎ ♀
25 High St OX10 7HH ☎ 01865 340404 🖷 01865 341620
e-mail: thegeorgehotel@fsmail.net
Dir: *From M40 J7 take A329 S to A4074 at Shillingford. Follow signs to Dorchester. From M4 J13 take A34 to Abingdon then A415 E to Dorchester*

Historic features throughout this 15th-century hostelry – the centrepiece of the village – include the inglenook fireplaces of Potboys Bar and a fine vaulted ceiling in the hotel restaurant. Bar menus change daily with a weather eye to high quality fresh produce from near and far. Starters might include roast plum tomato soup, and rabbit confit with mustard sauce, followed by boar and apple sausages with chive mash, wild mushroom and basil tagliatelle, and grilled salmon fillet with sauce vierge. Dinner menus offer chargrilled scallops with pancetta, roast peppered saddle of lamb, home-made blueberry ice cream and commendable British farmhouse cheeses.
OPEN: 11.30-11 (Sun 12-10.30) Closed: X-mas to New Year
BAR MEALS: L served all week 12-2.15 D served all week 7-9.45 Av main course £7.50 **RESTAURANT:** L served all week 12-2.15 D served all week 7-9.45 Av 3 course à la carte £24
BREWERY/COMPANY: 🍺: Brakspear. ♀: 10
FACILITIES: Garden: **NOTES:** Parking 150 **ROOMS:** 18 bedrooms 18 en suite s£65 d£85 no children overnight

Pick of the Pubs

The White Hart ★★★ ◎ ♀
High St OX10 7HN ☎ 01865 340074 🖷 01865 341082
e-mail: whitehartdorch@aol.com
Dir: *A4074 Oxford to Reading, 5M J7 M40 A329 to Wallingford*
Service is the keynote at this privately-owned hotel, situated in the heart of one of Oxfordshire's most famous villages. With its ancient beams and 24 comfortably furnished en suite bedrooms, the White Hart offers a perfect base for exploring the Cotswolds and the Chilterns. Dorchester's Roman ramparts may be only faintly visible, but the gatehouse adjoining the 12th-century abbey is now a museum. Take a cruise on the Thames or, for a unique experience visit the exquisitely-modelled historic landscapes at Pendon museum in nearby Long Wittenham. As an alternative to bar meals, Hartes restaurant offers a select range of fine wines and delicious cooking. Polish up your palate with roasted red pepper mousse, or home-smoked duck with fennel and mango salad, before moving on to sea bass and seared

continued

scallop with black noodles, rack of lamb with pomme fondant, or twice-baked goats' cheese and basil soufflé with roasted ratatouille.
OPEN: 11-11 **BAR MEALS:** L served all week 12-2.30 D served all week 6.30-9.30 Av main course £16 **RESTAURANT:** L served all week 12-2.30 D served all week 6.30-9.30 Av 3 course à la carte £26 **BREWERY/COMPANY:** Free House 🍺: Greene King, Marstons Pedigree,. ♀: 12 **FACILITIES:** Children welcome **NOTES:** Parking 28 **ROOMS:** 24 bedrooms 24 en suite 4 family rooms s£75 d£95

DUNS TEW
Map 11 SP42

The White Horse Inn 🐾 ♀
OX25 6JS ☎ 01869 340272 🖷 01869 347732
e-mail: whitehorse@dunstew.fsbusiness.co.uk
Dir: M40 J11, A4260, follow signs to Deddington and then onto Duns Tew
A change of hands has added an exciting new menu to this inn's many charms. Log fires, oak panelling and flagstone floors create a cosy atmosphere appropriate for a 17th-century coaching inn. The food now ranges from baguettes and salads (spinach, bacon and Parmesan; crevettes and hot potatoes) through to main courses such as slow-cooked lamb in rosemary and red wine gravy, or salmon en croute with a lobster sauce.
OPEN: 12-11 (Sun 12-10.30) **BAR MEALS:** L served all week 12-2.45 D served all week 6-9.45 Av main course £10 **RESTAURANT:** L served all week 12-2.45 D served all week 6-9.45 Av 3 course à la carte £19 **BREWERY/COMPANY:** Old English Inns 🍺: Greene King IPA, Batemans XXXX, Ruddles County, Abbot Ale. ♀: 10
FACILITIES: Children welcome Garden: Patio area enclosed by bushes Dogs allowed Water **NOTES:** Parking 25

EAST HANNEY
Map 05 SU49

The Black Horse ♀
Main St OX12 0JE ☎ 01235 868212 🖷 01235 868989
e-mail: bhhoxon@onetel.net.uk
Bavarian home-cooked specialities reflect the origin of this traditional pub's chef/proprietor, whose schnitzels come in various guises. Lighter eclectic selections include chicken korma, fish 'n' chips, and lasagne grande, as well as baguettes, ploughman's and salads. Main courses include peppered pork steak, duck in a port wine sauce, pork in Madeira sauce, and poached salmon "Parisienne". German apfelküchen to finish.
OPEN: 12-2.30 6-11 **BAR MEALS:** L served Tue-Sun 12-2 D served Tue-Sun 6-9 **RESTAURANT:** L served Tue-Sun 12-2 D served Tue-Sun 6-9 **BREWERY/COMPANY:** Free House 🍺: Hook Norton, Brakspear, Vale Brewery-Wychert, Fuller's London Pride.
FACILITIES: Children welcome Garden: **NOTES:** Parking 10

EAST HENDRED
Map 05 SU48

The Wheatsheaf
Chapel Square OX12 8JN ☎ 01235 833229
Dir: 2m from the A34 Milton interchange
Two miles from the Ridgeway path in a pretty village of thatched properties, this 16th-century beamed coaching inn was formerly used as the magistrates' court. Freshly-prepared food includes steak-and-kidney pie and home-made puds, and specials such as home-smoked local trout and English beef steaks. Sunday lunch.
OPEN: 12-3 6-11 (All day Sat, Sun, BHs) **BAR MEALS:** L served all week 12-2 D served Mon-Sat 6.30-9 Av main course £5.50

continued

BREWERY/COMPANY: Greene King 🍺: Greene King Abbot Ale, IPA, plus guest ales. **FACILITIES:** Children welcome Garden: Dogs allowed Water **NOTES:** Parking 12

FARINGDON
Map 05 SU29

The Lamb at Buckland ⊛ 🐾 ♀
Lamb Ln, Buckland SN7 8QN ☎ 01367 870484 🖷 01367 870675
Dir: Just off A420 3m E of Faringdon
A civilised little 18th-century inn standing on the very edge of the Cotswolds, with spectacular views across the Thames flood plain. Inside the charming stone building, the tastefully-furnished bar is warmed in winter by a log fire, while the restaurant boasts a large inglenook fireplace and exposed beams. Peta and Paul Barnard have earned an enviable reputation for their real ales, restaurant quality food and decent wine list. The varied and imaginative menu makes good use of the finest quality local ingredients, with the likes of lemon sole fillets with chive butter sauce, monkfish and prawn ragout, and sea bass with a light Pernod sauce to satisfy fish lovers, and oxtail casserole or roast rack of lamb for heartier appetites. Lighter meals include ploughman's lunches and Welsh rarebit, and there are tasty puddings too, like baked bananas with rum, and dark chocolate mousse.
OPEN: 10.30-3 5.30-11 Closed: 25-26 Dec **BAR MEALS:** L served Tue-Sun 12-2 D served Tue-Sat 6.30-9.30 **RESTAURANT:** L served Tue-Sun 12-2 D served Tue-Sat 6.30-9.30 Av 3 course à la carte £25 **BREWERY/COMPANY:** Free House 🍺: Hook Norton, Adnams Broadside, Arkells 3Bs. ♀: 12 **FACILITIES:** Children welcome Garden: Food served outside. Dogs allowed In the garden only **NOTES:** Parking 50

Pick of the Pubs

The Trout at Tadpole Bridge ♀
Buckland Marsh SN7 8RF ☎ 01367 870382
e-mail: info@trout-inn.co.uk
Dir: Halfway between Oxford & Swindon on the A420, take rd signed Bampton, pub is approx 2m down it.
A 17th-century inn that has been tastefully refurbished into a light, modern and airy hostelry with polished wooden tables, oak beams and a roaring log fire in winter. Originally a coal storage house, the building was converted into cottages, and then into an inn towards the end of the 19th century. Its pretty riverside garden on the banks of the River Thames makes it ideal for summer drinking, and a very popular dining destination. Above average pub food, cooked with style using fresh local produce, is the key to the success of the Trout. Such delights as pan-fried scallops with chilli jam, coriander and spring onion salad, and wild mushroom risotto with flaked Parmesan might be followed by roast loin of venison with sautéed greens and fig tart, or roast rack of lamb with roasted parsnips and haggis sauce.
OPEN: 11.30-3 6-11 Closed: 25, 31 Dec, 1 Jan, 1st wk in Feb **BAR MEALS:** L served all week 12-2 D served Mon-Sat 7-9 Av main course £12.95 **RESTAURANT:** L served all week 12-2 D served Mon-Sat 7-9 Av 3 course à la carte £25 **BREWERY/COMPANY:** Free House 🍺: Archers Village Bitter & Golden Bitter, Youngs PA Bitter, Butts Barbis. ♀: 10 **FACILITIES:** Children welcome Garden: Garden next to the River Thames Dogs allowed Water **NOTES:** Parking 70 **ROOMS:** 6 bedrooms 6 en suite s£55 d£80 (♦♦♦♦)

England

FIFIELD
Map 10 SP21

Merrymouth Inn
Stow Rd OX7 6HR ☎ 01993 831652 🖷 01993 830840
e-mail: alan.flaherty@btclick.com
Dir: *Situated on the A424 between Burford (3M) and Stow on the Wold (4M)*

A 13th-century inn, hunting lodge and farm have been combined to form the bar and restaurant at the Merrymouth. Formerly owned by the monks of Bruern Abbey, the inn takes its name from the Murimuth family who acquired the village of Fifield six centuries ago. A typical menu includes jugged hare, bobotie (a South African dish made with beef, wine and spices), roast loin of pork, Merrymouth chicken, grilled gilt head sea bream, and pheasant casserole.
OPEN: 12-2.30 6-10.30 (Closed Sun eve in winter) 25 & 26 Dec Closed eve **BAR MEALS:** L served all week 12-2 D served all week 6.30-9 Av main course £8.50 **RESTAURANT:** L served all week 12-2 D served all week 6.30-9 Av 3 course à la carte £16
BREWERY/COMPANY: Free House ◀: Hook Norton Best Bitter, Wychwood Hobgoblin. **FACILITIES:** Children welcome Garden: Small patio & enclosed garden at pubs front Dogs allowed **NOTES:** Parking 70

FRINGFORD
Map 11 SP62

The Butchers Arms
OX27 8EB ☎ 01869 277363
Boasting a mention in Flora Thompson's novel 'Lark Rise to Candleford', this traditional village pub has a wide range of ales on offer. From the patio you can watch cricket matches in progress during the summer.
OPEN: 12-3 6-11 (Sun 12-10.30) **BAR MEALS:** L served Tue-Sat 12-2 D served Mon-Sat 7-10 Av main course £7.95 **RESTAURANT:** L served Tue-Sat 12-2 D served Tue-Sat 7-10 Av 3 course à la carte £14
BREWERY/COMPANY: Pubmaster ◀: Youngs Bitter, Jennings Cumberland, Adnams Broadside. **FACILITIES:** Children welcome Dogs allowed **NOTES:** No credit cards

FYFIELD
Map 05 SU49

The White Hart
Main Rd OX13 5LW ☎ 01865 390585 🖷 01865 390671
Dir: *Just off A420, 8m SW of Oxford*
A wonderful old chantry house erected in 1442 to house five people engaged to pray for the soul of the lord of Fyfield manor. It has retained many original features, but now offers succour of a different kind. Food ranges from seared escalopes of salmon or pan-fried swordfish to aubergine stuffed with grilled Mediterranean vegetables or breast of duck with orange and fennel sauce. The extensive gardens include a children's play area.

continued

OPEN: 11-3 6-11 **BAR MEALS:** L served all week 12-2 D served all week 7-10 Av main course £9 **RESTAURANT:** L served all week 12-2 D served all week 7-10 Av 3 course à la carte £16
BREWERY/COMPANY: Free House ◀: Hook Norton, Wadworth 6X, Scottish Courage Theakstons Old Peculier, Fuller's London Pride. **FACILITIES:** Children welcome Garden: Lrg, ample tables Dogs allowed Water provided **NOTES:** Parking 40

GORING
Map 05 SU68

Miller of Mansfield
High St RG8 9AW ☎ 01491 872829 🖷 01491 874200
Dir: *From Pangbourne A329 to Streatley, then R on B4009, 0.5m to Goring*

Historic ivy-clad pub in a sprawling riverside village, set between the Chilterns and the Berkshire Downs. The pub is close to the River Thames and handy for both the Ridgeway national trail and the Thames Path. Snacks are served in the oak-beamed bar, and there is a full restaurant menu. Typical dishes include grilled duck breast with orange sauce, pork tenderloin with Calvados, apple and cream, and pan-fried sea bass with butter sauce.
OPEN: 11-11 (Sun 12-10.30) **BAR MEALS:** L served all week 12-2 D served all week 6.30-10 Av main course £9.50 **RESTAURANT:** L served all week 12-2 D served all week 7-10 Av 3 course à la carte £17
BREWERY/COMPANY: Free House ◀: Greene King Old Speckled Hen, Brakspear Bitter, Adnams Best. **FACILITIES:** Children welcome Dogs allowed Water **NOTES:** Parking 8 **ROOMS:** 10 bedrooms 10 en suite s£65 d£49.50 (♦♦♦)

GREAT TEW
Map 11 SP42

Pick of the Pubs

The Falkland Arms
OX7 4DB ☎ 01608 683653 🖷 01608 683656
e-mail: sjcourage@btconnect.com
Dir: *Off A361 1.25m, signposted Great Tew*
This 500-year-old inn takes its name from Lucius Carey, 2nd Viscount Falkland, who inherited the manor of Great Tew in 1629. Nestling at the end of a charming row of

continued

Cotswold stone cottages, the Falkland Arms is a classic: flagstone floors, high-backed settles and an inglenook fireplace characterise the intimate bar, where a huge collection of beer and cider mugs hangs from the ceiling. Home-made specials such as beef and ale pie or salmon and broccoli fishcakes supplement the basic lunchtime menu, served in the bar or the pub garden. In the evening, booking is essential for dinner in the small, non-smoking dining room. Expect parsnip soup or grilled goats' cheese salad, followed by chicken breast with bacon and mushrooms in shallot sauce; salmon and prawns with lemon and dill sauce; or mushroom and herb Stroganoff. **OPEN:** 11.30-2.30 6-11 (Sat 11.30-3, Sun 12-3, 7-10.30) Rest:25/26 Dec & 1 Jan Closed eve **BAR MEALS:** L served all week 12-2 D served Mon-Sat Av main course £6.50 **RESTAURANT:** L served all week 12-2 D served Mon-Sat 7-8 Av 3 course à la carte £18 **BREWERY/COMPANY:** Wadworth 🍺: Wadworth 6X & Henry's IPA. ⚱: 23 **FACILITIES:** Garden: Landscaped garden. Food served at lunchtime Dogs allowed on lead, water

---

HAILEY   Map 11 SP31

Pick of the Pubs

Bird in Hand 🛏 ⚱
Whiteoak Green OX29 9XP
☎ 01993 868321 📠 01993 868702
Dir: Leave A40 for Witney town centre, onto B4022, through Hailey, inn 1m N

Expect a warm welcome at this 17th-century Cotswold stone inn where the heavily-beamed bars have an ageless charm. The focal point of the oldest room is a huge inglenook fireplace where logs blaze on winter days. In the summer the garden is a pleasant place to sit, and the splendid modern English food can be served here or anywhere else in the pub, including the stylish, subtly-lit restaurant. Renowned for good quality cooking of fresh ingredients, it offers a choice of bar meals like creamy seafood pasta, wild boar and apple sausages, and hot baguettes. Blackboard specials might include rack of lamb with garlic mash, and Cajun chicken breast, and from the menu the likes of sautéed chicken livers followed by Banbury duck breast. **OPEN:** 11-11 **BAR MEALS:** L served all week 12-2.30 D served all week 7-9.30 Av main course £12.95 **RESTAURANT:** L served all week 12-2.30 D served all week 7-9.30 Av 3 course à la carte £20 **BREWERY/COMPANY:** Heavitree 🍺: Worthingtons, Brakspear, Adnams, Fullers London Pride. **FACILITIES:** Children welcome Garden: Food served outside. Patio & lawn areas Dogs allowed In the garden only **NOTES:** Parking 100

HENLEY-ON-THAMES   Map 05 SU78

Pick of the Pubs

The Five Horseshoes 🛏 ⚱
Maidensgrove RG9 6EX ☎ 01491 641282 📠 01491 641086
Dir: A4130 from Henley, onto B480
A 17th-century vine-covered inn located high above Henley with breathtaking views over the valley below. Red kites regularly soar overhead and deer from nearby Stonor Park can be spotted from the garden, yet this idyllic spot is only 10 minutes' drive along a twisty road from Henley-on-Thames. There is a fascinating collection of curios on display in the low-beamed bar, from old tools and banknotes to firearms and brasses. The interior exudes old-world charm, with its wood-burning stove and rustic stripped tables – just the place to relax over a pint of Brakspear Special and a plate of superior food. The regularly-changing menu offers the likes of crab cakes, mussel ravioli, Stonor venison pie topped with cheesy creamed potatoes, and lamb's liver on mustard mash with rich onion gravy. Favourite finishes include home-made banoffee pie or spotted dick and custard. **OPEN:** 11-3 6-11 **BAR MEALS:** L served all week 12-2 D served all week 6.30-9.30 Av main course £8 **RESTAURANT:** L served all week 12-2 D served all week 6.30-9.30 Av 3 course à la carte £18 Av 3 course fixed price £14.95 **BREWERY/COMPANY:** Brakspear 🍺: Brakspear Ordinary & Special. ⚱: 10 **FACILITIES:** Children welcome Garden: 2 gardens lovely views, 1 with a BBQ Dogs allowed Water **NOTES:** Parking 85

The Golden Ball
Lower Assendon RG9 6AH ☎ 01491 574157 📠 01491 576653
e-mail: Golden.Ball@theseed.net
Dir: A4130, R onto B480, pub 300yds on L
Dick Turpin hid in the priest hole at this 400-year-old building tucked away in the Stonor Valley close to Henley. It has a traditional pub atmosphere with well-used furnishings, open fire, exposed timbers, brasses and a collection of old bottled ales. Well-kept beer and home-cooked food are served, and there's a south-facing garden with plenty of garden furniture and undercover accommodation. Favourite fare includes sausage and mash, fish pie and lasagne. **OPEN:** 11-3 6-11 **BAR MEALS:** L served all week 12-2.15 D served all week 7-9.30 Av main course £5.95 **BREWERY/COMPANY:** Brakspear 🍺: Brakspear Bitter & Special. **FACILITIES:** Children welcome Garden: Large south facing garden Dogs allowed on lead only **NOTES:** Parking 50

The White Hart Hotel 🏨 ⚛⚛⚛ 🛏 ⚱
High St, Nettlebed RG9 5DD ☎ 01491 642145 📠 01491 649018
e-mail: Info@whitehartnettlebed.com
Dir: On the A4130 between Henley-on-Thames and Wallingford
Beautifully-restored brick and flint building dating from 17th century, with a stylish bar containing many cosy nooks and crannies for a quiet drink, and a quality restaurant called The Nettlebed. Chris Barber, former private chef to the Prince of Wales, serves his own version of classic pub cooking at affordable prices. A typical menu may include fishcakes with creamed spinach and chive sauce, roast saddle of Stonor venison with parsnip purée, or pan-fried seabass fillet on potato rösti. Pub and restaurant have separate menus. **OPEN:** 11-11 **BAR MEALS:** L served all week 12-2.30 D served all week 6-10 Av main course £12 **RESTAURANT:** L served Tue-Sat 12-2 D served Tue-Sat 7-9 Av 3 course à la carte £45 Av 3 course fixed price £25 🍺: Brakspear. ⚱: 10 **FACILITIES:** Children welcome **NOTES:** Parking 50 **ROOMS:** 12 bedrooms 12 en suite 3 family rooms s£105 d£105

HOOK NORTON

Map 11 SP33

The Gate Hangs High

Whichford Rd OX15 5DF ☎ 01608 737387
Dir: *Off A361 SW of Banbury*
Originally a toll house, this charming country pub is well worth tracking down. Its name refers to the toll gate which was hung high so that chickens and ducks could go under but large animals had to stop. It's close to the Rollright stones and just down the lane from the famous Hook Norton Brewery from where the pub sources its tip-top ales. Imaginative menus could include salmon and prawn pie or half a roast duck with leeks and mango.
OPEN: 12-3 6-11 (Sun 12-4, 7-10.30) **BAR MEALS:** L served all week 12-2.30 D served all week 6-10 Av main course £7.50 **RESTAURANT:** L served all week 12-2.30 D served all week 6-10 Av 3 course à la carte £17 Av 3 course fixed price £11.95 **BREWERY/COMPANY:** Hook Norton ◀: Hook Norton - Best, Old Hooky, Haymaker & Generation.
FACILITIES: Children welcome Garden: Wonderful views overlooking fields Dogs allowed Water **NOTES:** Parking 30

Sun Inn ♀

High St OX15 5NH ☎ 01608 737570 🖹 01608 730717
e-mail: enquiries@the-sun-inn.com
Traditional, extended pub in good walking country close to the Oxfordshire/Warwickshire border. Hook Norton is a sizeable village and close by is the famous, old-established Hook Norton Brewery. Festooned with hops, the candlelit bar has a cosy log fire and relaxed atmosphere. Fresh food is cooked to order and among the imaginative specials you may find whole baked lemon sole, calves' liver with black pudding, shank of English lamb on mustard mash, or Thai chicken curry. Appetising bar menu for those popping in for a pint and a light snack. Combine a visit with a tour of the brewery.
OPEN: 11.30-3 6-11.30 **BAR MEALS:** L served all week 12-2 D served all week 7-9.30 **RESTAURANT:** L served all week 12-2 D served all week 7-9.30 **BREWERY/COMPANY:** Hook Norton ◀: Hook Norton Best Bitter, Old Generation, Mild & Double Stout. **FACILITIES:** Children welcome Garden: Patio area, walled **NOTES:** Parking 20

KELMSCOT

Map 05 SU29

The Plough Inn 🐦

GL7 3HG ☎ 01367 253543 🖹 01367 252514
e-mail: plough@kelmscottgl7.fsnet.co.uk
Dir: *From M4 onto A419 then A361 to Lechlade & A416 to Faringdon, pick up signs to Kelmscot*

Peacefully situated in an unspoilt village close to Kelmscot Manor and the Thames, a 17th-century inn favoured as a refreshment stop among the walking and boating fraternity. Sympathetically restored inside, it has grassed and patio areas for outdoor eating. Look out for spiced lamb meatballs, traditional beef stew and treacle tart with custard for lunch,

with more ambitious evening choices including roast veal sweetbreads, and grilled red mullet with pan-fried scallops.
OPEN: 11-3 7-11 (Sun 12-3, 7-10.30) Closed: 6-20 Jan
BAR MEALS: L served all week 12-2.30 D served all week 7-9 Av main course £6.50 **RESTAURANT:** L served Tue-sun 12-2.30 D served Tue-Sun 7-9 Av 3 course à la carte £22
BREWERY/COMPANY: Free House ◀: Fullers London Pride, Hook Norton, Guest beers. **FACILITIES:** Garden: Grassed area with patio Dogs allowed Water provided **NOTES:** Parking 4

KINGSTON LISLE

Map 05 SU38

The Blowing Stone Inn

OX12 9QL ☎ 01367 820288 🖹 01367 821102
e-mail: luke@theblowingstoneinn.com
Dir: *B4507 from Wantage toward Ashbury/Swindon, after 6m R to Kingston Lisle*

The inn's name comes from a legend that King Alfred used a nearby stone pierced with holes to make a trumpet sound to summon his troops. Situated in a pretty village in the Berkshire Downs, the inn's open fires and warm hospitality make this a great place to relax and it is popular with many in the horse racing fraternity. Menu choices include lamb, rosemary and redcurrant pie; salmon and tarragon fishcakes; and wild boar and apple sausages with mustard mash.
OPEN: 12-2.30 6-11 **BAR MEALS:** L served Tue-Sun 12-2.30 D served Tue-Sat 7-9.30 Av main course £5.50 **RESTAURANT:** L served Tue-Sun 12-2.30 D served Tue-Sat 7-9.30 Av 3 course à la carte £19
BREWERY/COMPANY: Free House ◀: Courage Best, Fuller's London Pride & Guest Beers. **FACILITIES:** Children welcome Garden: Large with pond and fountain Dogs allowed Water **NOTES:** Parking 30

LEWKNOR

Map 05 SU79

The Leathern Bottel ♀

1 High St OX9 5TW ☎ 01844 351482

Run by the same family for 25 years, this 16th-century coaching inn is set in the foothills of the Chilterns. Walkers with dogs,

continued

continued

families with children, parties for meals or punters for a quick pint are all made equally welcome. In winter there's a wood-burning stove, a good drop of Brakespears ale, nourishing specials and a quiz on Sunday. Summer is the time for outdoor eating, the children's play area, Pimm's and Morris dancers.
OPEN: 10.30-3 6-11 **BAR MEALS:** L served all week 12-2 D served all week 7-9.30 Av main course £6.95
BREWERY/COMPANY: Brakspear ◀: Brakspear Ordinary, Special. ♀: 12 **FACILITIES:** Children welcome Garden: Large garden enclosed with hedge Dogs allowed Water **NOTES:** Parking 35

LOWER SHIPLAKE — Map 05 SU77

The Baskerville Arms ♀ NEW
Station Rd RG9 3NY ☎ 0118 940 3332 📠 0118 940 7235
e-mail: thebaskervillearms@hotmail.com
Situated in the lovely village of Shiplake, near Henley-on-Thames, this attractive brick-built pub stands close to the river and a short walk from the railway station. It has beautiful gardens and a good restaurant. Starters (also available as snacks) might include soup of the day, bacon and Stilton salad or nachos. Typical main courses include beef and Guinness pie, slow-roasted lamb shank, curry, and sausages and mash.
OPEN: 11.30-2.30 6-11 (Fri 11.30-2.30, 5.30-11.30) (Sun 11.30-2.30, 5.30-11) **BAR MEALS:** L served all week 12-2 D served all week 7-9.30 Av main course £9 **RESTAURANT:** L served Mon-Sun 12-2 D served Mon-Sat ◀: Fullers London Pride, Brakspear. ♀: 8
FACILITIES: Children welcome Garden: Spacious garden with play area & BBQ Dogs allowed **NOTES:** Parking 12

LOWER WOLVERCOTE — Map 05 SP40

The Trout Inn ♀
195 Godstow Rd OX2 8PN ☎ 01865 302071
Dir: From A40 at Wolvercote rdbt (N of Oxford) follow signs for Wolvercote

A riverside inn which has associations with Matthew Arnold, Lewis Carroll and Colin Dexter's Inspector Morse. Constructed in the 17th century from the ruins of Godstow Abbey, its rich history includes being torched by Parliamentarian troops. A good choice of food offers baked whole trout with garlic mushrooms and cheddar mash, lemon chicken, beef, mushroom and Bass pie, or Cumberland sausage wrapped in Yorkshire pudding, with liver and bacon.
OPEN: 11-11 **BAR MEALS:** L served all week D served all week
BREWERY/COMPANY: Vintage Inns ◀: Interbrew Bass, Fuller's London Pride. **FACILITIES:** Garden: **NOTES:** Parking 100

MARSTON — Map 05 SP50

Victoria Arms
Mill Ln OX3 0PZ ☎ 01865 241382
Dir: From A40 follow signs to Old Marston, sharp R into Mill Lane, pub lane 500yrds on L
Friendly country pub situated on the banks of the River Cherwell, occupying the site of the old Marston Ferry that connected the

north and south of the city. The old ferryman's bell is still behind the bar. Popular destinations for punters, and fans of TV sleuth Inspector Morse, as the last episode used it as a location. Typical menu includes lamb cobbler, steak and Guinness pie, spicy pasta bake, battered haddock, and ham off the bone.
OPEN: 11.30-11 **BAR MEALS:** L served all week 12-9 Av main course £5.50 **BREWERY/COMPANY:** Wadworth ◀: Wadworth 6X, Henrys IPA, Badger, Wadworth JCB. **FACILITIES:** Children welcome Garden: Food served in patio & lawn area Dogs allowed **NOTES:** Parking 70

MIDDLETON STONEY — Map 11 SP52

Pick of the Pubs

The Jersey Arms ♀
OX25 8AD ☎ 01869 343234 📠 01869 343565
e-mail: jerseyarms@bestwestern.co.uk
Charming family-run hotel, formerly a coaching inn. Cosy bar offering good range of popular bar food with the extensive menu supplemented by daily blackboard specials, including soups, pâtés, pasta dishes and traditional main courses like steak and kidney pie. Beamed and panelled Livingston's restaurant with Mediterranean terracotta decor and cosmopolitan brasserie-style menu.
OPEN: 12-11 **BAR MEALS:** L served all week 12-2.15 D served all week 6.30-9.30 Av main course £10 **RESTAURANT:** L served all week 12-2.15 D served all week 6.30-9.30 Av 3 course à la carte £21 **BREWERY/COMPANY:** Free House ◀: Interbrew Flower, Boddingtons. **FACILITIES:** Children welcome Garden: Courtyard garden **NOTES:** Parking 50

MURCOTT — Map 11 SP51

The Nut Tree 🏠
Main St OX5 2RE ☎ 01865 331253 📠 01865 331977
Dir: Off B4027 NE of Oxford via Islip & Charlton-on-Moor
14th-century thatched country inn, dating back to 1360. Set in a country idyll (six acres of gardens, a duck pond, donkeys, geese, peacocks and chickens) its interior delivers all the hoped-for rustic charm, with bare beams, inglenooks with wood-burning stoves, real ales and home-cooked meals. Expect traditional dishes with a modern twist: perhaps panaché, of fish with potatoes and vegetables, rib-eye steak with pepper sauce, or cod with mash and cherry tomato compote.
OPEN: 12-3 6-11 (Sun 12-5) **BAR MEALS:** L served Tue-Sun 12-2 D served Tue-Sat 6.30-9.30 Av main course £12 **RESTAURANT:** L served Tue-Sun 12-2 D served Tue-Sat 6.30-9.30 Av 3 course à la carte £22 Av 2 course fixed price £9.95 **BREWERY/COMPANY:** Free House ◀: Hook Norton, Timothy Taylor, Breakspears, West Berkshire Brewery. **FACILITIES:** Children welcome Children's licence Garden: Fenced and hedged with trees and lawns Dogs allowed Kennel **NOTES:** Parking 40

NORTH MORETON — Map 05 SU58

The Bear 🏠 ♀
High St OX11 9AT ☎ 01235 813236
Dir: Off A4130 between Didcot & Wallingford
15th-century inn on the village green, with exposed beams, open fireplaces and a cosy, relaxed atmosphere. Hook Norton ales.
OPEN: 12-3 6.30-11 **BAR MEALS:** L served Tue-Sun 12-2.30 D served Tue-Sun 7-9 **RESTAURANT:** L served Tue-Sun 12-2.30 D served Tue-Sat 7-9 **BREWERY/COMPANY:** Free House ◀: Hook Norton Best Bitter, Interbrew Bass & Hancocks HB.
FACILITIES: Children welcome Garden: Beer garden, food served outdoors, patio Dogs allowed garden only **NOTES:** Parking 50

continued

NUFFIELD　　　　　　　　　　　　Map 05 SU68

The Crown at Nuffield
RG9 5SJ ☎ 01491 641335 📠 01491 641335
e-mail: simon@supanet.com
Dir: Follow Henley signs, then Wallingford rd on L past turning for village
Heavily beamed 17th-century pub, originally a waggoners' inn. Located in the wooded country of the Chilterns, on the route of the Ridgeway long-distance trail. Now under new management, the Crown has re-opened with a bistro-style restaurant that combines contemporary decor with "tradition still visible". Readers comments are welcomed.
OPEN: 11.30-2.30 6.30-11 (open all day-Summer, Wkds) (Sun 12-3) **BAR MEALS:** L served all week 12-2 D served all week 6.30-9.30 Av main course £8.50 **RESTAURANT:** L served all week 12-2 D served all week 6.30-9.30 Av 3 course à la carte £16
BREWERY/COMPANY: Brakspear **☎:** Brakspear, Brakspears Bitter, Special. **FACILITIES:** Children welcome Garden: Dogs allowed **NOTES:** Parking 40

OXFORD　　　　　　　　　　　　　Map 05 SP50

The Anchor ♀
2 Hayfield Rd, Walton Manor OX2 6TT ☎ 01865 510282
Dir: A34 Oxford Ring Road(N), exit Peartree Roundabout, 1.5m then R at Polstead Rd, follow rd to bottom, pub on R
Local resident T E Lawrence (of Arabia) once frequented this friendly 1930s pub. Nowadays you'll find a relaxed atmosphere, and good food and drink. The wide-ranging menu offers pub favourites such as steak and ale pie, sausage and mash, and fish and chips.

OPEN: 12 -11 (Mon-Sat 12-11, Sun 12-10.30) Dec 25 Closed eve **BAR MEALS:** L served all week 12-2.30 D served all week 6-9 Av main course £5 **BREWERY/COMPANY:** Wadworth **☎:** Wadworth 6X, Henrys IPA, JCB. **FACILITIES:** Garden: Patio at front and rear of pub Dogs allowed Water, on leads **NOTES:** Parking 15

Turf Tavern ♀
4 Bath Place, off Holywell St OX1 3SU
☎ 01865 243235 📠 01865 243838
e-mail: turftavern.oxford@laurelpubco.com
Situated in the heart of Oxford, approached through hidden alleyways and winding passages, this famous pub lies in the shadow of the city wall and the colleges. It is especially popular in the summer when customers can relax in the sheltered courtyards. Eleven real ales are served daily, from a choice of around 500 over a year, along with some typical pub fare. The pub has been featured in TV's 'Inspector Morse', and was frequented by JRR Tolkien.
OPEN: 11-11 (Sun 12-10.30) **BAR MEALS:** L served all week 12-8 D served all week **RESTAURANT:** L served all week D served Sun (Roast) **BREWERY/COMPANY:** **☎:** Traditional Ales, changing daily. **FACILITIES:** Garden: Patio area with lights and heaters

The White House
2 Botley Rd OX2 0AB ☎ 01865 242823 📠 01865 793331
e-mail: thewhitehouseoxford@btinternet.com
Dir: 2 minutes walk from rail station
Set back from a busy road, this pub was once a tollhouse where people crossed the river to enter Oxford. The menu may include roast fillet of salmon with roast peppers and fresh herbs, sautéed calves' liver with onion sauce, pork cutlets cooked in beer with cabbage and bacon, or wild mushroom ravioli.
OPEN: 11-11 Closed: Dec 25 **BAR MEALS:** L served all week 12-2.30 D served all week 6.30-9.30 Av main course £6 **RESTAURANT:** L served all week 12-2.30 D served all week 6-9.30 Av 3 course à la carte £25
BREWERY/COMPANY: Punch Taverns **☎:** Wadworth 6X, Greene King Abbot Ale, Fullers London Pride, Hook Norton. **FACILITIES:** Children welcome Garden: Dogs allowed **NOTES:** Parking 15

PISHILL　　　　　　　　　　　　Map 05 SU78

Pick of the Pubs

The Crown Inn 🐾 ♀
RG9 6HH ☎ 01491 638364 📠 01491 638364
e-mail: robin@crownpishill.fsnet.co.uk
Dir: On B480 off A4130, NW of Henley-on-Thames
A long-standing favourite, close to the magnificent parkland of Stonor House, this 15th-century brick and flint coaching inn has origins that may well date back to the 11th century. At the top of a steep climb for horse-drawn carriages from Henley to the Chilterns and on to Oxford, ostlers once watered the horses while everyone else refreshed themselves. Its 400-year-old thatched barn (infamous in the 1960s as a club venue where Dusty Springfield, George Harrison and Ringo Starr all played) has been renovated to cater for private functions and weddings. Typical options from the fixed-price lunch menu include half a roast pheasant in peach sauce and darne of salmon with celeriac fondant and lime and coriander mayonnaise, whilst regular menus range from familiar pub dishes (shepherd's pie, Thai curry, sirloin steak) to mouthwatering creations such as venison casserole with crispy herb dumplings, and breast of Gressingham duck roasted in honey and spices, served on a stirfry of pak choi, noodles and beansprouts.

OPEN: 11.30-2.30 6-11 (Sun 12-3, 7-10.30) Closed: 25-26 Dec, 1 Jan **BAR MEALS:** L served all week 12-2 D served all week 7-9.30 Av main course £8 **RESTAURANT:** L served all week 12-2 D served all week 7-9.30 Av 3 course à la carte £22
BREWERY/COMPANY: Free House **☎:** Fuller's, Hook Norton, Marstons Pedigree. ♀: 8 **FACILITIES:** Children welcome Garden: Extensive gardens overlooking the valley
NOTES: Parking 60

RAMSDEN
Map 11 SP31

The Royal Oak ♀
High St OX7 3AU ☎ 01993 868213 ▤ 01993 868864
Dir: From Witney take B4022 toward Charlbury, then turn R before Hailey, and go through Poffley End.

The Royal Oak was originally built as a coaching inn, so it seems appropriate that there are still nosebags available for hungry passing horses. Human diners are catered for even more impressively with dishes ranging from chicken liver parfait to pot-roasted pheasant or even Royal Oak smokies cooked in whisky and cream. Bar meals and Sunday luncheons are appreciated by those walking in the Wychwood forest or visiting Blenheim palace.
OPEN: 11.30-3 6.30-11 Closed: Dec 25 **BAR MEALS:** L served all week 12-2 D served all week 7-10 **RESTAURANT:** L served all week 12-2 D served all week 7-10 **BREWERY/COMPANY:** Free House
🍺: Hook Norton Old Hooky, Best, Fuller's ESB, Adnams Broadside.
FACILITIES: Garden: Dogs allowed Water **NOTES:** Parking 20

ROKE
Map 05 SU69

Home Sweet Home 🏠
OX10 6JD ☎ 01491 838249
Dir: Just off the B4009 from Benson to Watlington, signed posted on B4009
Long ago converted from adjoining cottages by a local brewer, this pretty 15th-century inn stands in a tiny hamlet surrounded by lovely countryside. A wealth of oak beams and the large inglenook fireplace dominate a friendly bar with an old-fashioned feel. There is a friendly home-from-home menu with reasonably-priced traditional pub food and a pint of top-class ale. Steak and kidney pudding, fresh cod in a light beer batter, calves' liver with crispy bacon, beef fillet strips in a cream brandy and mushroom sauce, and warm fresh Cornish crab tart are typical choices.
OPEN: 11-3 6-11 (Sun 12-3, closed Sun eve) Closed: Dec 25-26
BAR MEALS: L served all week 12-2 D served Mon-Sat 6-9 Av main course £7.95 **RESTAURANT:** L served Mon-Sun 12-2 D served Mon-Sat 7-9 Av 3 course à la carte £15 **BREWERY/COMPANY:** Free House 🍺: Wadworth Henry's Original IPA. **FACILITIES:** Children welcome Garden: Dogs allowed Water **NOTES:** Parking 60

ROTHERFIELD PEPPARD
Map 05 SU78

The Greyhound 🏠
Gallowstree Rd RG9 5HT ☎ 0118 9722227 ▤ 0118 9722227
e-mail: kwhitehouse@thegreyhound-peppard.com
Dir: 4 miles from Henley on Thames
A picture-postcard, 400-year-old village inn with a splendid front garden with tables and parasols. Owned since mid-2002 by a Savoy Hotel-trained chef, it offers French/English-style meals in both the beamed, candle-lit bar, with woodblock floor, and open brick fireplace, and in the restaurant. This is in the adjacent, and impressive, converted timber barn and a

continued

typical option might be fillet steak, with chestnut, mushroom and brandy cream sauce. Prawn stirfry is a typical bar meal.
OPEN: 11-3 6-11 (Sat till 12, Sun till 8) **BAR MEALS:** L served all week 12-2.30 D served all week 7-9.30 **RESTAURANT:** L served Mon 12-2.30 D served Mon 7-9.30 Av 3 course à la carte £18.50
BREWERY/COMPANY: Free House 🍺: Brakspear, Fuller's London Pride, San Miguel. **FACILITIES:** Children welcome Garden: Dogs allowed **NOTES:** Parking 40

SHENINGTON
Map 11 SP34

The Bell 🏠
OX15 6NQ ☎ 01295 670274
e-mail: thebell@shenington.freeserve.co.uk
Dir: M40 J11 take A422 towards Stratford. Village is signposted 3m N of Wroxton
Nestling amid mellow stone houses, a classic village green and a church with an impressive Tudor tower, the comfortable and welcoming 300-year-old Bell has an open log fire burning in winter, and tables outside in the summer. The pub promises home-cooked food prepared with fresh local ingredients. Expect duck in port and black cherries, braised beef with Madeira and medley of mushrooms, pork loin in apple cider and pineapple, plus soups and devilled sausages on toast.

OPEN: 12-2.30 7-11 **BAR MEALS:** L served all week 12-2 D served all week 7-11 Av main course £9 **RESTAURANT:** L served all week 12-2 D served all week 7-11 Av 3 course à la carte £12.50
BREWERY/COMPANY: Free House 🍺: Hook Norton, Flowers.
FACILITIES: Children welcome Garden: Beer garden, outdoor eating, Dogs allowed Water

SHIPTON-UNDER-WYCHWOOD
Map 10 SP21

The Lamb Inn 🏠 ♀
High St OX7 6DQ ☎ 01993 830465 ▤ 01993 832025
e-mail: info@thelambinn.net
Dir: 4m N of Burford on the A361
'You just don't know who you're going to bump into', says the Lamb's manager - even minor royals, apparently. It's probably not surprising, given that this beautiful pale gold-stone inn is in one of the Cotswolds' most picturesque villages. The rustic beamed bar with its stone walls, wooden floor and sturdy furniture makes a fine setting for eating crab, avocado and tomato tian, then roast quail, foie gras, crispy pancetta and Albufera sauce, and hazelnut soufflé with Bailey's parfait.
OPEN: 11-11 (Sun 12-10.30) (Winter 12-3, 5.30-11), (Summer 11-11)
Closed: 7-14 Jan **BAR MEALS:** L served all week 12-2 D served all week 7-9.30 Av main course £10.95 **RESTAURANT:** L served all week 12-2 D served all week 7-9.30 Av 3 course à la carte £22.50
BREWERY/COMPANY: Old English Inns 🍺: IPA, Hook Norton Old Hooky. ♀: 9 **FACILITIES:** Garden: Landscaped formal garden Dogs allowed Water **NOTES:** Parking 20 **ROOMS:** 5 bedrooms 5 en suite 2 family rooms s£90 d£129 (♦♦♦♦♦) no children overnight

England

Pick of the Pubs

The Shaven Crown Hotel 🐾 ♀
High St OX7 6BA ☎ 01993 830330 📠 01993 832136
Dir: On A361, halfway between Burford and Chipping Norton opposite village green and church
Built around 1300 by the monks of neighbouring Bruern Monastery as a resting place for travellers and pilgrims, it is one of the ten oldest hostelries in the country. After the Dissolution of the Monasteries, Queen Elizabeth I used it as a hunting lodge, before giving it to the village in 1580, when it became the Crown Inn. In 1930, a whimsically-minded brewery changed the name to reflect monkish hairdos. Constructed of local honey-coloured stone around an attractive central courtyard garden, it retains its original gateway, a medieval hall (now the residents' lounge), stone-flagged floors, and mullioned windows. There is also a tree-filled beer garden. The extensive menu includes lamb shank with rosemary and garlic, and venison sausages with juniper berries and celeriac mash. From the fish section come salmon in filo pastry, with dill and tomato sauce, peppered monkfish and red pepper coulis, and deep-fried plaice. Specials include jugged hare and pheasant casserole.
OPEN: 11.30-2.30 5-11 **BAR MEALS:** L served all week 12-2 D served all week 5.30-9.30 Av main course £8.95
RESTAURANT: L served Sun 12-2 D served all week 7-9 Av 3 course fixed price £22.50 **BREWERY/COMPANY:** Free House 🍺: Hook Norton Best, Greene King Abbot Ale, Fuller's London Pride. ♀: 8 **FACILITIES:** Children welcome Garden: Enclosed courtyard, lawned with trees Dogs allowed Water
NOTES: Parking 15

The Crown Inn 🐾 ♀
High St OX11 9AG ☎ 01235 812262
Dir: From Didcot take A4130 towards Wallingford. Village on R
This friendly pub runs a regular fun quiz on Monday nights. The building dates from around 1870, and features antique furnishings to complement the rustic cottage-style decor. Expect steak, kidney and Stilton pie, fresh beer-battered haddock, chicken Elizabeth with cream and mushrooms, chicken Kiev, and fresh salmon fishcakes.
OPEN: 11-3 5.30-11 (Sun 12-3, 7-10.30) Closed: Dec 25-26
BAR MEALS: L served all week 12-2 D served all week 7-9.30 Av main course £9 **RESTAURANT:** L served all week 12-2 D served all week 7-9.30 Av 3 course à la carte £14.50
BREWERY/COMPANY: Wadworth 🍺: Badger Tanglefoot, Adnams Best, Wadworth 6X & Henrys IPA. ♀: 8 **FACILITIES:** Children welcome Garden: 2 areas with bench style seating Dogs allowed Water **NOTES:** Parking 30

**Room prices show the minimum double and single rates charged.
Room rates in hotels and B&Bs often vary depending on the facilities, so be sure to check prices with the establishment before booking.**

The Perch and Pike
RG8 0JS ☎ 01491 872415 📠 01491 875852
e-mail: helpdesk@perchandpike.com
Dir: Between Goring and Wallingford just off B4009
Beautifully-located 17th-century inn near the River Thames and right beside The Ridgeway. The brick and flint building has been refurbished recently, but still has bags of atmosphere and warming open fires. New owners are continuing to serve interesting food in the rebuilt barn restaurant, like baked mussel provençale with shellfish bisque, glazed pork belly, and tagliatelle with a Thai cream sauce, with pineapple Bavarois to finish. Feedback welcome.

OPEN: 11-3 6-11 (Closed Sun night) **BAR MEALS:** L served all week 12-2.30 D served Mon-Sat 7-9.45 Av main course £12
RESTAURANT: L served all week 12-2.30 D served Mon-Sat 7-9.45 Av 3 course à la carte £25 Av 3 course fixed price £25
BREWERY/COMPANY: Brakspear 🍺: Brakspear Bitter, Special & Seasonal. **FACILITIES:** Children welcome Children's licence Garden: Split on 2 levels Dogs allowed **NOTES:** Parking 30

Pick of the Pubs

The Crazy Bear Hotel 🐾 ♀
Bear Ln OX44 7UR ☎ 01865 890714 📠 01865 400481
e-mail: sales@crazybearhotel.co.uk
Dir: M40 J7 L on A329
Just 15 minutes drive from Oxford is an unusual small hotel full of eccentric and amusing surprises. A flamboyant refurbishment has resulted in this rural 16th-century property having two separate dining rooms, one embracing fine English dining, and the other offering a Thai-style brasserie. Menus from both restaurants are also available in the bar along with open Swiss sandwiches and exotic salads. The choice of food is extensive, and can be sampled in the likes of dry-roasted tournedos of monkfish, lobster and prawn risotto, and grilled fillet of cod, plus starters like king sea scallops, and marinated duckling. Nearly 50 Thai dishes best tasted from good-value set menus. No Thai desserts, but classic English offerings might include chocolate marquise, or the ubiquitous sticky toffee pudding. The garden has palm trees, and a large pond.
OPEN: 12-11 **BAR MEALS:** L served all week 12-10 D served all week **RESTAURANT:** L served all week 12-3 D served all week 7-10 **BREWERY/COMPANY:** Free House 🍺: Greene King IPA, Ruddles County & Abbot Ale. **FACILITIES:** Garden: Patio, pond **NOTES:** Parking 30

STANTON ST JOHN — Map 05 SP50

Star Inn ♀
Middle Rd OX33 1EX ☎ 01865 351277 📠 01865 351006
Dir: At A40/Oxford ring road rdbt take Stanton exit, follow rd to T junct, R to Stanton, 3rd L, pub on L 50yds

Although the Star is only fifteen minutes drive from the centre of Oxford, it still retains a distinctly 'village' feel. The oldest part of the pub dates from the early 17th century, and in the past, the building has been used as a butcher's shop and an abattoir. The garden is peaceful and secluded. A varied menu features cheddar and broccoli quiche, lasagne verdi, herb-crusted cod, steak and Guinness pie, seafood pasta marinara, and Mexican bean pot. Also available are a range of sandwiches, soups and jacket potatoes.
OPEN: 11-2.30 6.30-11 **BAR MEALS:** L served all week 12-2 D served all week 6.30-9.30 Av main course £7
BREWERY/COMPANY: Wadworth ◖ Wadworth 6X, Henrys IPA & JCB. ♀: 7 **FACILITIES:** Children welcome Garden: Large secure garden Dogs allowed Water bowls **NOTES:** Parking 50

Pick of the Pubs

The Talk House 🛏
Wheatley Rd OX33 1EX ☎ 01865 351648 📠 01865 351085
e-mail: talkhouse@t-f-h.co.uk
Dir: Stanton-St-John signed from the Oxford ring road
The Talk House is a cleverly converted 17th-century inn located within easy reach of Oxford and the A40 and well worth seeking out. It comprises three bar and dining areas, all with a Gothic look and a welcoming atmosphere. Business, wedding and function bookings are catered for, and The Snug is ideal for private parties of eight to fifteen, with its own fireplace and private bar. The menu offers chargrilled sirloin steak, roast loin of pork with honey and mustard sauce, Pedro's game and sherry pie, beef bourguignon, and chargrilled Scotch salmon with a lemon and dill hollandaise. Bed and breakfast accommodation is also offered in four chalet-style rooms situated around the attractive rear courtyard.
OPEN: 12-3 5.30-11 (Open all day in Summer May-Oct)
BAR MEALS: L served all week 12-2 D served all week 7-10 Av main course £10 **RESTAURANT:** L served all week 12-2 D served all week 7-10 Av 3 course à la carte £20
BREWERY/COMPANY: Free House ◖ Hook Norton Best Bitter, Interbrew Bass, Fuller's London Pride, Wadworth 6X.
FACILITIES: Children welcome Garden: Courtyard garden
NOTES: Parking 60 **ROOMS:** 4 bedrooms 4 en suite s£40 d£60 (♦♦♦)

STEEPLE ASTON — Map 11 SP42

Red Lion
South Side OX25 4RY ☎ 01869 340225
Dir: Off A4260 between Oxford & Banbury
The art of conversation and the enjoyment of fresh food is positively encouraged at this traditional pub. The 17th-century building comprises a bar, separate dining room, library and floral terrace. Typical dishes include Arbroath smokies en cocotte, jugged hare with forcemeat balls, and a soufflé of fresh lime.
OPEN: 11-3 6-11 (Sun 12-3, 7-10.30) **BAR MEALS:** L served Mon-Sat 12-2 Av main course £4.80 **RESTAURANT:** D served Tue-Sat 7.30-9.15 Av 3 course à la carte £23.50 **BREWERY/COMPANY:** Free House ◖ Hook Norton. **FACILITIES:** Garden: Floral terrace Dogs allowed **NOTES:** Parking 15

STOKE ROW — Map 05 SU68

Pick of the Pubs

Crooked Billet 🐷 ♀
RG9 5PU ☎ 01491 681048 📠 01491 682231
See Pick of the Pubs on page 382

STRATTON AUDLEY — Map 11 SP62

The Red Lion 🐷 ♀
Church St OX27 9AG ☎ 01869 277225 📠 01869 277225
Dir: 2 Miles N of Bicester, just off the Buckingham Road
A charming thatched country pub with a warm and friendly atmosphere and cosy interior brightened by open fires. Low beams, stone walls and antique posters create a congenial setting for a pint or two of Hook Norton or a meal from wide-ranging menus. 'Bob's ballistic baltis' and a dozen 'giant gourmet burgers' share space with barbecue rack of ribs, vegetarian sausages with colcannon and seafood gumbo. The fillet steak with mushrooms is a full half-pound cut.
OPEN: 12-3 6-11 (all Sat-Sun) **BAR MEALS:** L served all week 12-2 D served Mon-Sat 6.30-9 Av main course £8.95
BREWERY/COMPANY: ◖ Hook Norton Best, Greene King Ruddles Best, Adnams Broadside. ♀: 7 **FACILITIES:** Garden: 60 seater paved terrace Dogs allowed Water

Open: 12-11 (Sun 12-10.30).
Bar Meals: L served all week 12-2.30, D served all week 7-10. Av cost main course £12.95.
RESTAURANT: L served all week 12-2.30, D served all week 7-10.
BREWERY/COMPANY: Brakspear
🍺: Brakspear Bitter
FACILITIES: Children welcome, Garden - Beautiful, rustic, over-looking farmland.
NOTES: Parking 50

Crooked Billet

A rustic country inn hidden away down a single-track lane in deepest Oxfordshire, still retaining all the original charm of a true country pub.

 ♀

Stoke Row, nr Henley-on-Thames, RG9 5PU
☎ 01491 681048 📠 01491 682231
Dir: From Henley to Oxford A4130. Turn L at Nettlebed for Stoke Row.

It dates back to 1642, and was once the haunt of the notorious highwayman Dick Turpin who used to lie low here when the forces of the law were after him, and who courted the landlord's daughter Bess. Many of its best features are unchanged, including the low beams, tiled floors and open fires that are so integral to its character. Nowadays this old inn is very much food-driven, and it attracts many local celebrities, including several introduced to it by the late George Harrison. Kate Winslet famously held her wedding reception here, and from the lowbrow (cast of Eastenders) to the highbrow (Jeremy Paxman) it continues to draw the well heeled and well known. Extensive, carefully thought-out menus are created by award-winning chef/proprietor Paul Clerehugh, with local produce and organic fare being the mainstay of the kitchen. Expect sautéed partridge and wild mushroom fricassée; pan-fried bass, with baby squid, roast Mediterranean vegetables and salsa verde; and pink-carved venison with haggis, baby spinach, roast figs, and a port, redcurrant and juniper sauce.

Grilled turbot with buttered spinach, seared scallops, and prawn, champagne and chive sauce is one of the seafood specials, along with sea bream tagliatelle with confit tomatoes, olives and gremolina. A separate vegetarian choice lists the likes of Moroccan vegetable tagine with Marrakech mint and coriander couscous and spicy harissa dipping pot. Puddings include Bakewell tart and custard sauce, passion fruit mousse charlotte, with vanilla ice cream, strawberry and raspberry coulis, and champagne and fresh raspberry trifle. A global list of over 80 wines, and Brakspear Bitter.

SUTTON COURTENAY   Map 05 SU59

Pick of the Pubs

The Fish 🐾 ♀
4 Appleford Rd OX14 4NQ ☎ 01235 848242 ▤ 01235 848014
e-mail: mike@thefish.uk.com
Dir: From A415 in Abingdon take B4017 then L onto B4016 to village
Unassuming late 19th-century brick-built pub located a
short stroll from the Thames in the heart of this beautiful
and historic village - Asquith and George Orwell are buried
here. Very much a dining pub-restaurant although drinkers
are welcome at the bar. Good value bistro lunches are
served in the front bar-cum-dining area and outside in the
attractive garden when the weather's fine. Expect modern
versions of classic French and English dishes with a strong
emphasis on fresh seafood. Choices change frequently to
reflect season and availability, and might include moules
marinière, Cornish hen crab with herb mayonnaise and
new potatoes, fillet of venison with port wine and forest
fruit sauce, or provençale vegetable tart with new potatoes
and pesto salad. Leave room for desserts such as
marmalade bread and butter pudding or toffee and
banana pancake. Set-price and à la carte dinners.

OPEN: 12-3.30 6-11 Closed: 2 days between Xmas & New Year
BAR MEALS: L served all week 12-2 D served all week
RESTAURANT: L served all week 12-2 D served all week 7-9.30
Av 3 course à la carte £25 Av 3 course fixed price £21.95
BREWERY/COMPANY: Greene King 🍺 Greeen King IPA.
♀: 10 **FACILITIES:** Garden: Large enclosed lawn with flower
beds Dogs allowed Water **NOTES:** Parking 30

SWALCLIFFE   Map 11 SP33

Stag's Head 🐾 ♀
OX15 5EJ ☎ 01295 780232 ▤ 01295 788977
e-mail: stagsheadswalcliffe@dial.pipex.com
Dir: 6M W of Banbury on the B4035
Believed to have been built during the reign of Henry VIII, this
thatched pub originally housed builders working on the nearby
church. It enjoys picture postcard looks and a pretty village
setting, and as a result attracts a broad range of customers. An
apple tree in the garden was reputedly grown from a pip
brought back from the Crimean War, and its fruit is still used in
home-made puddings. Among the better dining pubs in
Oxfordshire, this ancient inn offers an eclectic range of dishes,
from traditional 'surf & turf', and steak with a Stilton and
mushroom sauce, to the more exotic lime and chilli chicken,
black tiger prawns, and gnocchi potato pasta with chorizo.
Vegetarian options might include stuffed pepper with Mozzarella,
tomatoes and olives on a potato cake. The landscaped garden is
the ideal setting for dining or enjoying a decent pint.

continued

OPEN: 12-2.30 6.30-11 Sun Closed eve **BAR MEALS:** L served
Tues-Sun 12-2.15 D served Tues-Sat 7-9.30 Av main course £9.95
RESTAURANT: L served Tues-Sun 12-2.15 D served Tues-Sat 7-9.30
BREWERY/COMPANY: Free House 🍺 Brakspears PA, Wychwood
Seasonal, Spinning Dog Brewery, Rebellion. ♀: 7
FACILITIES: Children welcome Garden: Beautiful terraced garden
with play area Dogs allowed Water, biscuits

SWERFORD   Map 11 SP33

Pick of the Pubs

The Mason's Arms 🐾
OX7 4AP ☎ 01608 683212 ▤ 01608 683105
e-mail: themasonsarms@tablesir.com
Dir: Between Banbury and Chipping Norton A361
Set in 3 acres overlooking the Swere Valley on the edge of
the Cotswolds, the Masons is a lovely, 300-year-old stone
pub that has been stylishly redesigned throughout in
country-farmhouse style to provide a modern dining
venue without destroying the traditional charm of a village
inn. In addition to wonderful views and a relaxed,
informal atmosphere, fresh produce is sourced locally to
create the imaginative, modern pub dishes listed on the
eclectic menu available in the bar. From starters like South
Coast mussels, or Thai fishcakes with seasonal leaves and
sweet chilli sauce, main course options range from pub
favourites - pork and chive sausages with creamy mash,
traditional steak and kidney pudding - given a modern
makeover, to chicken supreme with lime and coriander
salsa, roasted pepper, caramelised red onion and Brie
tartlet, or fillet of salmon topped with a herb crust. Hook
Norton Best on tap, a select list of wines, and popular
themed evenings.
OPEN: 12-3 7-11 **BAR MEALS:** L served Tue-Sun 12-2.30 D
served Tue-Sat 7-9 Av main course £12 **RESTAURANT:** L served
all week 12-2.30 D served all week 7-10 Av 3 course à la carte £19
BREWERY/COMPANY: Free House 🍺 Hook Norton Best,
IPA Smoothflow. **FACILITIES:** Children welcome Garden: Food
served outside Dogs allowed Water provided **NOTES:** Parking
50

SWINBROOK   Map 10 SP21

The Swan Inn
OX18 4DY ☎ 01993 822165
*Dir: Take the A40 towards Burford & Cheltenham at the end of the dual
carriageway is a rdbt, straight over the turn R for Swinbrook the pub can
be found over the bridge on the left side*
With its flagstone floors, antique furnishings and open fires,
the 400-year-old Swan is full of charm and character and sits
next to the River Windrush, a setting that cannot fail to

continued

SWINBROOK continued

impress. Plenty of scenic walks and popular tourist attractions close by. Choose cottage pie, spaghetti bolognese or deep-fried whitebait with horseradish from the snack menu, followed perhaps by sirloin steak, Norfolk chicken cooked with tarragon or pan-fried trout with dried fruits.
OPEN: 11.30-3 6.30-11 Closed: Dec 25 **BAR MEALS:** L served all week 12-2 D served Mon-Sat 7-9 **RESTAURANT:** L served all week 12-2 D served Mon-Sat 7-9 **BREWERY/COMPANY:** Free House ◖: Greene King IPA, Old Speckled Hen, Wadworth 6X, Archers.
FACILITIES: Children welcome Garden: Large garden with Cotswold stone walls Dogs allowed Water provided **NOTES:** Parking 10

TADMARTON   Map 11 SP33

The Lampet Arms ♦♦♦ 🐾 ♀
Main St OX15 5TB ☎ 01295 780070 🖷 01295 788066
e-mail: mike@lampet.co.uk
Dir: take the B4035 from Banbury to Tadmarton for 5m
Victorian-style building named after Captain Lampet, the local landowner who built it. The captain mistakenly believed he could persuade the council to have the local railway line directed through the village, thereby increasing trade. Typical menu choices include the likes of salmon in lime and coriander, casserole, vegetable lasagne, salmon steak and fish pie.
OPEN: 11.30-3 5-11 (Sun 12-4, 7-10.30) **BAR MEALS:** L served all week 12-2.30 D served all week 6.30-9.30 Av main course £5.50
RESTAURANT: L served all week 12-2 D served all week 6.30-9.30 **BREWERY/COMPANY:** Free House ◖: Interbrew Flowers IPA & Boddingtons, Marston's Pedigree, Fuller's London Pride.
FACILITIES: Children welcome Garden: Dogs allowed
NOTES: Parking 18 **ROOMS:** 4 bedrooms 4 en suite s£43 d£60

THAME   Map 05 SP70

The Swan Hotel 🐾 ♀
9 Upper Hight St OX9 3ER ☎ 01844 261211 🖷 01844 261954
e-mail: swanthame@hotmail.com
Dir: Telephone for directions

Former coaching inn dating from the 16th century, overlooking the market square at Thame. The Tudor-painted ceiling is a feature of the upstairs restaurant, while downstairs in the cosy bar there is an open fire. Typical dishes served here include steak sandwich with mustard, onions, salad, cheese and chips, smoked salmon and creamed cheese omelette, lazy-aged rump steak, and cottage pie. Several real ales are always on tap.
OPEN: 11-11 Closed: 25-26 Dec **BAR MEALS:** L served all week 12-2.30 D served all week 7-9 Av main course £6.95
RESTAURANT: L served Wed-Sun 12-2 D served Tues-Sat 7-9.30 Av

3 course à la carte £25 **BREWERY/COMPANY:** Free House
◖: Hook Norton, Timothy Taylor Landlord, Brakspears, Shepherd Neame Spitfire. ♀: 9 **FACILITIES:** Dogs allowed Water
NOTES: Parking 200

WANTAGE   Map 05 SU38

The Hare ♀
Reading Rd, West Hendred OX12 8RH
☎ 01235 833249 🖷 01235 833268
Dir: Situated at West Hendred on A417 between Wantage (3 m W)and Didcot (5 m E)
A late 19th-century inn mid-way between Wantage and Didcot, modernised in the 1930s by local brewers, Morland, and featuring a colonial-style verandah and colonnade. Inside it retains the more original wooden floors, beams and open fire. A brasserie-style menu delivers fillets of salmon, chumps of lamb and chargrilled rib-eye steaks. More serious diners might try bouillabaisse terrine, pan-seared venison black cherry rösti and French yellow-plum tart or home-made ice creams.
OPEN: 11.30-2.30 5.30-11 (Fri-Sun 11.30-11) Closed: 1 Jan
BAR MEALS: L served all week 12-2 D served all week 7-9 Av main course £10 **RESTAURANT:** L served all week 12-2 D served all week 7-9 Av 3 course à la carte £20.25 Av 2 course fixed price £15
BREWERY/COMPANY: Greene King ◖: Greene King Abbot Ale, IPA, Morland Original. **FACILITIES:** Children welcome Garden: Food served outside Dogs allowed Water, during the day
NOTES: Parking 37

The Star Inn
Watery Ln, Sparsholt OX12 9PL
☎ 01235 751539 & 751001 🖷 01235 751539
Dir: Sparsholt is 4m west of Wantage, take the B4507 Wantage to Ashbury road and turn off R to the village; the Star Inn is signposted
Four miles out of town in downland country close to The Ridgeway, this 300-year-old village pub is popular with the local horseracing fraternity. Log fires, attractive prints and daily papers lend the pub special character. Fresh fish is often highlighted on the specials board. Look otherwise for prawn platter, home-cooked ham and eggs, chicken creole and grilled steaks, culminating in a gargantuan mixed grill with fresh, hand-cut chips.
OPEN: 12-3 6-11 (Sat 12-11, Sun 12-10.30) **BAR MEALS:** L served all week 12-3 D served all week 7-9 Av main course £6.95
RESTAURANT: L served Tue-Sun 12-2 D served Mon-Sat 7-9
BREWERY/COMPANY: Free House ◖: Hook Norton, Timothy Taylor Landlord, Adnams , Spitfire. **FACILITIES:** Children welcome Garden: Food served outside Dogs allowed **NOTES:** Parking 20

WESTCOTT BARTON   Map 11 SP42

The Fox Inn
Enstone Rd OX7 7BL ☎ 01869 340338
Original flagstone floors, oak beams and a roaring fire in the ancient inglenook are among the attractions at this welcoming 17th-century Cotswold village pub. A changing variety of dishes including cold platters, salads and traditional bar snacks is served, and there's a separate restaurant menu. Typical dishes here include medallions of venison and chargrilled steak with pepper and cognac sauce.
OPEN: 12-2.30 5-11 (Sun 12-10.30) **BAR MEALS:** L served all week 12-2 D served all week 7-9 **RESTAURANT:** L served all week D served Mon-Sat 7-9 **BREWERY/COMPANY:** Enterprise Inns
◖: Hook Norton Best, Greene King, Pedigree. **FACILITIES:** Children welcome Garden: Food served outside Dogs allowed Water (dogs on leash) **NOTES:** Parking 20

continued

WESTON-ON-THE-GREEN   Map 11 SP51

The Chequers 🍽 ♀
Northampton Rd OX25 3QH ☎ 01869 350319 🖷 01869 350024
e-mail: rchequers@aol.com
Dir: 2m from M40 J9
17th-century Cotswold stone coaching inn with a serious
approach to food. An English bar menu with everything from
lamb shank and grilled steak to hot seafood platter and
sandwiches is matched by a restaurant devoted to Thai food.
Sizzling lamb stirfry with ginger, mushrooms and pepper, and
roast duck marinated in honey served with a choice of spicy
sauces are among the many options.
OPEN: 11.30-3 6-11 **BAR MEALS:** L served all week 12-2.30 D
served all week 7-10.30 Av main course £7.50 **RESTAURANT:** L
served all week 12-2.30 D served all week 7-10.30 Av 3 course à la
carte £13.95 Av fixed price £11.95 **BREWERY/COMPANY:** Fullers
🍺: Fullers London Pride, Fullers ESB. **FACILITIES:** Children
welcome Garden: Dogs allowed Water provided **NOTES:** Parking
45

WHEATLEY   Map 05 SP50

Bat & Ball Inn ♦♦♦ 🍽
28 High St OX44 9HJ ☎ 01865 874379 🖷 01865 873363
*Dir: Pass thru Wheatley towards Garsington, take only L turn, signed
Cuddesdon*
As you might have guessed from its name, this former
coaching inn has a cricketing theme. The bar is absolutely
packed with cricketing memorabilia and the seven letting
rooms are named after famous cricketers. A good choice of
hand-pulled ales is served, and there's a comprehensive menu
supplemented by daily specials. Expect the likes of smoked
salmon fishcakes, smothered chicken breast with bacon,
onions and mushrooms, and braised half shoulder of lamb.
OPEN: 11-11 **BAR MEALS:** L served all week 12-2.45 D served all
week 6.30-9.45 **RESTAURANT:** L served all week 12-2.45 D served
all week 6.30-9.45 **BREWERY/COMPANY:** Marstons 🍺: Marston's
Pedigree & Original. **FACILITIES:** Children welcome Garden: Dogs
allowed **NOTES:** Parking 15 **ROOMS:** 7 bedrooms 7 en suite

WITNEY   Map 05 SP31

The Bell Inn 🍽 ♀
Standlake Rd, Ducklington OX29 7UP
☎ 01993 702514 🖷 01993 706822
*Dir: One mile south of Witney in Ducklington village off
A415 Abingdon road.*
Erected in 1315 as a hostel for builders of the adjacent church,
this popular village local has been extended over the years
and now includes the former William Shepheards brewery
which closed in 1886. Many original features - and a collection
of some 500 bells - add to the pub's strongly traditional
character. Home-made pies are a speciality, and there's a pig
roast on Boxing Day.
OPEN: 12-3 5-11 (Fri-Sun 12-11) 25 Dec closed eve
BAR MEALS: L served all week 12-2 D served Mon-Sat 6-9 Av main
course £10 **RESTAURANT:** L served all week 12-2 D served Mon-Sat
6-9 Av 3 course à la carte £17 🍺: Greene King, IPA & Old Speckled
Hen, Morland Original. **FACILITIES:** Children welcome Garden:
Terrace at front and rear of pub **NOTES:** Parking 12

★ **Pubs with Red Stars are part of the
AA's Top 200 Hotels in Britain & Ireland**

WOODSTOCK   Map 11 SP41

Pick of the Pubs

Kings Head Inn ♦♦♦♦ ◉ 🍽 ♀
Chapel Hill, Wootton OX20 1DX ☎ 01993 811340
e-mail: t.fay@kings-head.co.uk
*Dir: On A44 2m N of Woodstock then R to Wootton. Inn near church
on Chapel Hill*
A traditional country inn with a warm atmosphere, built in
the 17th century from mellow Cotswold stone and
sensitively modernised in recent years. The beamed bar
offers a civilised mix of wooden tables, old settles and soft
seating, adding to the relaxed, informal mood. Winter
brings cosy log fires, and in summer you can enjoy
peaceful meals in the garden. Comfortable bedrooms
offer well-equipped accommodation for those who decide
to stay over and explore the Cotswolds and Oxfordshire.
Imaginative meals are served in both the non-smoking
restaurant and the bar, based on modern British ideas
with some Mediterranean and New World influences.
Starters like Gressingham duck salad, toasted goats'
cheese or Szechuan pigeon breast might be followed by
wild mushroom risotto, tower of Orkney fillet steak with
potato rösti or chargrilled pork medallions with red onion
marmalade and juniper berry sauce.
OPEN: 11-2 6.30-11 Closed: Dec 25 **BAR MEALS:** L served
Tue-Sun 12-2 D served Mon-Sat 7-9 Av main course £10.95
RESTAURANT: L served all week 12-2 D served Mon-Sat 7-9 Av
3 course à la carte £21 **BREWERY/COMPANY:** Free House
🍺: Wadworth 6X, Greene King Triumph, Ruddles Country. ♀: 7
FACILITIES: Garden: Beer garden, food served outdoors
NOTES: Parking 8 **ROOMS:** 3 bedrooms 3 en suite s£60 d£75
no children overnight

WOOLSTONE   Map 05 SU28

The White Horse ♦♦♦♦ ♀
SN7 7QL ☎ 01367 820726 🖷 01367 820566
e-mail: raybatty@aol.com
Attractive beamed and thatched 16th-century village inn, just
five minutes' walk from the Uffington White Horse and
Ancient Monument. Bar food includes salads, ploughman's
lunches and freshly-cooked cod and chips. In the restaurant
expect calves' liver, rack of lamb, steaks, and baked
swordfish.
OPEN: 11-3 6-11 (Sun 12-3 7-10.30) **BAR MEALS:** L served all
week 11-3 D served all week 6-9.30 Av main course £6
RESTAURANT: 12-3 6-10 Av 3 course à la carte £20
BREWERY/COMPANY: Free House 🍺: Arkells, Hook Norton Best,
Moonlight. **FACILITIES:** Children welcome Garden:
NOTES: Parking 80 **ROOMS:** 6 bedrooms 6 en suite s£50 d£65

WOOTTON   Map 11 SP41

The Killingworth Castle Inn ♀
Glympton Rd OX20 1EJ ☎ 01993 811401 🖷 01993 811401
e-mail: wiggiscastle@aol.com
Dir: Exit A34 onto B4027, cross over A4260, pub on N edge of Wootton
Built in 1637 as a coaching inn on the former Worcester to
London 'highway'. At the popular end, bar food strays little
from beef and ale pie and toad-in-the-hole backed up by
burgers, baguettes and baked potatoes. A dining menu more
adventurously adds tortellini al pesto, chicken Dijonaise and
Thai green curry with spinach. The live music scene flourishes

continued

WOOTTON continued

here, with folk every Friday, and jazz and Irish music alternating on Wednesdays.

OPEN: 12-2.30 6.30-11 (Sun 12-3, 7-10.30) **BAR MEALS:** L served all week 12-2 D served all week 7-9 Av main course £10 **RESTAURANT:** L served all week 12-2 D served all week 7-9 Av 3 course à la carte £16 **BREWERY/COMPANY:** Greene King **🍺:** Greene King Morland Original, Ruddles Best, IPA. **♀:** 8 **FACILITIES:** Garden: Patio area and large grass area with plants Dogs allowed Water **NOTES:** Parking 80

WYTHAM   Map 05 SP40

White Hart

OX2 8QA ☎ 01865 244372 e-mail: dapeev@aol.com
Dir: Just off A34 NW of Oxford
An attractive, creeper-covered gastropub with flagstone floors and open fires, set in the pretty, thatched village of Wytham which is owned by Oxford University. An Italian/modern English menu features dishes like seared scallops with a basil dressing, and roast venison with fondant potatoes and blackcurrant jus. Outside, a Mediterranean-style terrace is a delightful spot in summer, and the pub has frequently been used in the television series 'Inspector Morse'.
OPEN: 12-3 6-11 (Summer-Sat 12-11, Sun 12-10.30)
BAR MEALS: L served all week 12-3 D served Mon-Sat 7-10 Av main course £11 **RESTAURANT:** L served Mon-Sun 12-3 D served Mon-Sat 7-10 Av 3 course à la carte £22
BREWERY/COMPANY: **🍺:** Old Speckled Hen, Hook Norton.
FACILITIES: Children welcome Garden: Mediterranean Terrace
NOTES: Parking 80

RUTLAND

BARROWDEN   Map 11 SK90

Exeter Arms 🍽 ♀

LE15 8EQ ☎ 01572 747247 e-mail: info@exeterarms.com
Once a smithy, then the village dairy, the Exeter Arms was also a coaching inn before it became the village pub. Nestling in the picturesque Welland Valley overlooking the village green and duck pond, this 17th-century inn now offers cosy, character bars where the home-brewed family of 'Boys' beers is served. Tours of the Blencowe Brewing Company, housed in a nearby stone barn, can be arranged by appointment. A good reputation has been built up locally around the food. Specialities include fish and game when seasonally available, and a choice of traditional roast dishes on Sundays. Nearby is the Cecil family seat of Burghley House at Stamford, whose heraldry appears on the inn sign. Ideally placed for walking in Rockingham Forest, and visiting Rutland Water.

continued

OPEN: 12-2 6-11 (Sun & BHs 7-10.30) **BAR MEALS:** L served Tue-Sun 12-2 D served Tue-Sat 7-9 Av main course £8.50
RESTAURANT: L served Tue-Sun 12-2 D served Tue-Sat 7-9 Av 3 course à la carte £17 **BREWERY/COMPANY:** **🍺:** Beach Boys, Bevin Boys, Farmers Boy, Golden Boy. **FACILITIES:** Garden: 1/2 acre. Over-looks Welland Valley Dogs allowed Water **NOTES:** Parking 15

CLIPSHAM   Map 11 SK91

Pick of the Pubs

The Olive Branch ⊛⊛ 🍽 ♀

Main St LE15 7SH ☎ 01780 410355 🖷 01780 410000
e-mail: olive@work.gb.com
Dir: 2 miles off A1 at Ram Jam Inn junction, 10 miles north of Stamford
There's an inspirational story behind the success of this traditional village pub. A few years back it was faced with closure but was saved by three young men, with the support of families, friends and locals, who shared a passion for the institution. Since then the pub has flourished, building a reputation for its fine food. An attractive front garden and terrace, and an interior full of locally-made furniture and artists' works (all for sale) set the scene. For atmosphere, add log fires, mulled wine and chestnuts in winter, and barbecues, Pimm's cocktails and garden skittles in summer. Local produce governs the menus, from the sandwiches made from Rearsby bread to dishes of game casserole with wholegrain mustard and herb dumplings, or chargrilled halibut with champ mash and crispy pancetta. Drinks include a wide choice of wines by the glass and real ales from Oakham's Grainstore brewery.
OPEN: 12-3.30 6-11 (Sun 12-6 only) Closed: 26 Dec 1 Jan
BAR MEALS: L served all week 12-2 D served Mon-Sat 7-9.30 Av main course £10.95 **RESTAURANT:** L served all week 12-2 D served Mon-Sat 7-9.30 Av 3 course à la carte £20 Av 3 course fixed price £10.50 **BREWERY/COMPANY:** Free House **🍺:** Grainstore 1050 & Olive Oil, Fenland, Brewster's. **♀:** 15
FACILITIES: Children welcome Garden: Gravelled area with picnic tables Dogs allowed **NOTES:** Parking 15

COTTESMORE   Map 11 SK91

The Sun Inn 🍽

25 Main St LE15 7DH ☎ 01572 812321
Dating back to 1647, this whitewashed pub has recently been re-thatched in its original style. Stone and quarry tiled floors, oak beams and a cosy fire in the bar add to the charm. Handy for visiting Rutland Water and historic Oakham. Expect traditional fish and chips, steak and venison pie, seared scallops and black pudding on colcannon, or rack of lamb with redcurrant and port sauce, among many popular dishes on the varied menu. Brave drinkers may wish to attend "Bucket Night", on the last Sunday before Christmas.
OPEN: 11-2.30 6.30-11 **BAR MEALS:** L served Tue-Sun 12-2 D served Tue-Sat 7-9 Av main course £8.95 **RESTAURANT:** L served Tue-Sun 12-2 D served Tue-Sat 7-9 Av 3 course à la carte £16.50
BREWERY/COMPANY: Everards Brewery **🍺:** Adnams Bitter, Everards Tiger, Marston's Pedigree, Scottish Courage Courage Directors. **FACILITIES:** Garden: Patio area with water feature Dogs allowed **NOTES:** Parking 15

Pubs offering a good choice of fish on their menu

EMPINGHAM
Map 11 SK90

White Horse Inn ★★ 🛏️
Main St LE15 8PS ☎ 01780 460221 🖨 01780 460521
e-mail: info@whitehorserutland.co.uk
Dir: From A1 take A606 signed Oakham & Rutland Water
This stone-built 17th-century former farmhouse is in a lovely village alongside Europe's largest man-made lake, Rutland Water, the source of the wild trout often featured on the menu. Other choices might include home-baked ham with fresh pineapple and sunblush tomato cream sauce; lemon sole with cherry tomato, spring onion and herb butter; and 'bangers and mash' featuring locally-made sausages in onion and red wine gravy. Home-made sweets are on offer from 'Auntie June's kitchen'. Bedrooms include a honeymoon suite with four-poster bed.
OPEN: 8-11 **BAR MEALS:** L served all week 12-2.15 D served all week 7-9.45 Av main course £8.95 **RESTAURANT:** L served all week 12-2.15 D served all week 7.15-10
BREWERY/COMPANY: 🍺: Scottish Courage Courage Directors & John Smith's, Greene King Old Speckled Hen & Ruddles County, Marston's Pedigree. **FACILITIES:** Children welcome Garden: Small sheltered garden, seating **NOTES:** Parking 60 **ROOMS:** 13 bedrooms 13 en suite 3 family rooms s£50 d£65

EXTON
Map 11 SK91

Fox & Hounds 🛏️ 🍷
LE15 8AP ☎ 01572 812403 🖨 01572 812403
Fine old 1840-vintage coaching inn, under friendly new ownership since August 2002. A strong Italian influence puts traditional antipasti, pasta and pizzas alongside home-made steak and kidney pudding, venison sausages, Rutland trout and Sunday roasts. Peroni beer shares the bar with the smallest county's own Grainstore real ales. Large walled garden and patio area. The village and pub featured extensively in the 1936 Freddy Bartholomew film classic Little Lord Fauntleroy.
OPEN: 11-3 6-11 **BAR MEALS:** L served all week 11-2 D served all week 6.30-9 Av main course £7.50 **RESTAURANT:** L served all week 12-2 D served all week 6.30-9 Av 3 course à la carte £15
BREWERY/COMPANY: Free House 🍺: Greene King IPA, Grainstore Real Ales, John Smiths Smooth. 🍷: 8
FACILITIES: Children welcome Garden: Large walled garden & patio area Dogs allowed Water **NOTES:** Parking 20

LYDDINGTON
Map 11 SP89

Pick of the Pubs

Old White Hart 🍷
51 Main St LE15 9LR ☎ 01572 821703 🖨 01572 821965
Dir: On A6003 between Uppingham and Corby, take B672
Honey-coloured 17th-century stone pub standing by the green in an attractive village high above the Welland Valley, close to good walks and Rutland Water. Interesting, freshly-prepared food is served in the cosy main bar, with its heavy beams, dried flower arrangements, traditional furnishings and splendid log fire, and in the adjoining dining areas. Good blackboard specials may include warm salad of smoked bacon, black pudding and cherry tomatoes topped with grilled Slipcote cheese and balsamic dressing, and grilled sardines with garlic toast for starters, followed by deep-fried Grimsby haddock, whole Dover sole, herb-crusted cod with pesto dressing, wild mushroom and asparagus risotto, home-made Gloucester Old Spot sausages, and confit neck of lamb on mash. Ambitious evening carte. Good selection of real ales and wines by the glass. Flower-filled rear garden with 10 pétanque pitches.

continued

OPEN: 12-3 6.30-11 Closed: 25 Dec **BAR MEALS:** L served all week 12-2 D served Mon-Sat 6.30-9 Av main course £18 **RESTAURANT:** L served all week 12-2 D served Mon-Sat 6.30-9 Av 3 course à la carte £18 Av 3 course fixed price £12.95
BREWERY/COMPANY: Free House 🍺: Greene King IPA & Abbot Ale, Timothy Taylor Landlord. **FACILITIES:** Garden: Beer garden, patio, outside eating Children welcome, Dogs allowed **NOTES:** Parking 25

MARKET OVERTON
Map 11 SK81

Black Bull 🛏️
2 Teigh Rd LE15 7PW ☎ 01572 767677 🖨 01572 767291
e-mail: vowenbull@aol.com
Since the 15th century, this thatched and beamed pub has stood opposite the stocks on the green of the picture-postcard village where the young Isaac Newton once played. Starters from the long-serving chef include smoked haddock and peeled prawn pancake, and black pudding roulade. Main courses might be roasted venison marinated in gin and juniper berries, or Stilton lamb. Look under the blackboard for the daily fish selection.
OPEN: 11.30-2.30 6-11 (Sun 12-3.00, 7-10.30) **BAR MEALS:** L served all week 12-1.45 D served all week 6.30-9.45 Av main course £9.70 **RESTAURANT:** L served all week 12-1.45 D served all week 6.30-9.45 **BREWERY/COMPANY:** Free House 🍺: Hook Norton, Scottish CourageTheakston, Greene King IPA, Wells Bombardier. **FACILITIES:** Dogs allowed Water **NOTES:** Parking 20

OAKHAM
Map 11 SK80

Barnsdale Lodge Hotel ★★★ 🏵️ 🛏️ 🍷
The Avenue, Rutland Water, North Shore LE15 8AH
☎ 01572 724678 🖨 01572 724961
e-mail: barnsdale.lodge@btconnect.com
An Edwardian-style hotel overlooking Rutland Water in the heart of this picturesque little county. Its rural connections go back to its 17th-century origins as a farmhouse, but nowadays the Barnsdale Lodge offers modern comforts and hospitality. Real ales including local brews are served in the bar, with dishes such as escalope of springbok, and cannon of lamb from the gourmet menu, and typically posh fish and chips, or steak and kidney pie amongst house specialities.
OPEN: 7-11 **BAR MEALS:** L served all week 12.15-2.15 D served all week 7-9.45 Av main course £9.95 **RESTAURANT:** L served all week 12.15-2.15 D served all week 7-9.45 Av 3 course à la carte £37.50
BREWERY/COMPANY: Free House 🍺: Rutland Grainstore, Marstons Pedigree, Scottish Courage Courage Directors, Theakston Best Bitter. 🍷: 11 **FACILITIES:** Children welcome Garden: Courtyard, established garden with lawns Dogs allowed Water **NOTES:** Parking 280 **ROOMS:** 45 bedrooms 45 en suite 4 family rooms s£75 d£95

The Blue Ball 🍷
6 Cedar St, Braunston-in-Rutland LE15 8QS ☎ 01572 722135
Dir: From A1 take A606 to Oakham.Village SW of Oakham
Thatched and beamed village inn, formerly called The Globe, dating from the 1600s, and reputedly Rutland's oldest pub. A warm and friendly welcome and traditional pub food awaits from new licensees.
OPEN: 12-3 6-10 (Sun 12-5) **BAR MEALS:** L served all week 12-2 D served all week 6-9.30 Av main course £7.95 **RESTAURANT:** L served all week 12-3 D served all week 6-10 Av 3 course à la carte £12
BREWERY/COMPANY: Old English Pub Co 🍺: Fullers London Pride, Greene King IPA, John Smiths, Morland Old Speckled Hen. 🍷: 10 **FACILITIES:** Children welcome Garden: Patio, beer garden, food served outside Dogs allowed garden only **NOTES:** Parking 8

Pick of the Pubs

The Finch's Arms ♀
Oakham Rd, Hambleton LE15 8TL
☎ 01572 756575 📠 01572 771142
See Pick of the Pubs on opposite page

The Grainstore Brewery
Station Approach LE15 6RE ☎ 01572 770065 📠 01572 770068
e-mail: grainstorebry@aol.com
Founded in 1995, Davis's Brewing Company is housed in the three-storey Victorian grain store next to Oakham railway station; rustic wooden floors and furniture that attract walkers by the score. Finest quality ingredients and hops are used to make the beers that can be sampled in the pub's Tap Room. Filled baguettes and Stilton and pork pie ploughman's are of secondary importance, but very tasty all the same. Go for the brewery tours and blind tastings
OPEN: 11-3 5-11 **BAR MEALS:** L served all week 11-2.15
BREWERY/COMPANY: Free House ⬤: Grainstore Cooking Bitter, Triple B, Ten Fifty, Steaming Billy Bitter. **FACILITIES:** Dogs allowed Water, biscuit **NOTES:** Parking 8

Pick of the Pubs

The Old Plough 🍴 ♀
2 Church St, Braunston LE15 8QY
☎ 01572 722714 📠 01572 770382
e-mail: info@oldplough.co.uk
An old coaching inn that has kept its traditional identity despite being tastefully modernised. This genteel and very popular country pub dates back to 1783, and its village location makes it handy for visiting the lovely Georgian town of Oakham, as well as touring the rest of the old county of Rutland. Owners Claire and David host lots of speciality evenings and various weekend entertainments, and their enthusiasm for good food extends to candlelit dinners in the picturesque conservatory, as well as light lunches on the terrace. Expect favourites like liver, bacon and onions, and Cajun chicken, as well as steak and kidney pudding, Braunston chicken stuffed with creamy cheese, trio of sausages with mustard mash and Calvados sauce, mushroom Stroganoff, salmon en croûte, and beer-battered cod fillet. Regular guest ales are always available.
OPEN: 11-3 6-11 (Fri-Sun 11-11) **BAR MEALS:** L served all week 12-2.30 D served all week 6-9.30 Av main course £6
RESTAURANT: L served all week 12-2.30 D served all week 6-9.30 Av 3 course à la carte £18 **BREWERY/COMPANY:** Free House ⬤: Boddingtons, Bass Cask, Greene King IPA, plus 2 guests. **FACILITIES:** Children welcome Garden: Food served outside, garden terrace Dogs allowed (not overnight in bedrooms) **NOTES:** Parking 30

Stars or Diamonds after the ROOMS information at the end of an entry denotes accommodation that has been inspected by an organisation other than the AA, eg the RAC, VisitBritain, VisitScotland or WTB.

Pick of the Pubs

Ram Jam Inn ★★ ◉ 🍴 ♀
The Great North Rd LE15 7QX
☎ 01780 410776 📠 01780 410361 e-mail: rji@rutnet.co.uk
Dir: On A1 northbound carriageway past B1668 turn off, through service station into hotel car park

This inn is something of a legend: it acquired its present name in the 18th century when the landlord's sign advertised "Fine Ram Jam". No one is quite sure what this was, but the odds are on it being a drink of some kind. Today, the informal café-bar and bistro exudes warmth, and bright, spacious en suite bedrooms make this a popular overnight stop. All-day menus offer everything from sandwiches and clotted cream teas through to appealing three-course meals - with everything home made. Goat's cheese and red onion tartlet served with fresh figs and salad, Rutland black pudding on a bed of warm shallot, apple and pickled walnut compote, seafood ravioli, game casserole, spicy tomato and pepperoni pasta, renowned Rutland sausages, or good old fish and chips are all options. Tempting puddings often include rum, chocolate and cream torte with a crunchy Amaretto topping. Delicious!
OPEN: 7am-11pm Closed: 25 Dec **BAR MEALS:** L served all week 12-9.30 D served all week Av main course £8.95
RESTAURANT: L served all week 12-9.30 D served all week **BREWERY/COMPANY:** Free House ⬤: Fuller's London Pride, Scottish Courage John Smith's. ♀: 11 **FACILITIES:** Children welcome Garden: Dogs allowed **NOTES:** Parking 64
ROOMS: 7 bedrooms 7 en suite 1 family rooms s£47 d£57

Noel Arms Inn
Main St LE15 8BW ☎ 01780 460334 📠 01780 460531
Dir: From A1 take A606 to Oakham
Country pub near Rutland Water with a cosy lounge in the original thatched building and a more modern bar. Dishes range from bangers and mash at lunchtime, to roast monkfish with sauté potatoes, spinach and braised leek, and rack of English lamb with Mediterranean vegetables.
OPEN: 11-11 (Breakfast 7.30-9.30) **BAR MEALS:** L served all week 12-9.30 D served all week Av main course £8.50 **RESTAURANT:** L served all week 12-9.30 D served all week Av 3 course à la carte £18 **BREWERY/COMPANY:** Free House ⬤: Marstons Pedigree, Adnams Broadside, Old Speckled Hen and John Smiths. **FACILITIES:** Children welcome Garden: BBQ Dogs allowed **NOTES:** Parking 60

Open: 10.30-3, 6-10.30
Bar Meals: L served all week 12-2.30,
D served all week 7-9.30.
Av cost main course £8.50
RESTAURANT: L served all week 12-2.30,
D served all week 7-9.30.
Av cost 3 course £16
BREWERY/COMPANY:
Free House.
🍺: Greene King Abbot Ale, Scottish
Courage Theakston Best, Timothy Taylor
Landlord.
FACILITIES: Children welcome, Garden -
Large garden overlooks Rutland Water.
NOTES: Parking 40

The Finch's Arms

Set in a sleepy village on a narrow strip of land jutting into Rutland Water, this stone-built 17th-century inn offers tasty food in a relaxed atmosphere.

♈

Oakham Road, Hambleton,
Oakham, LE15 8TL
☎ 01572 756575 📠 1572 771142

Once the pub would have looked out over a valley and the little village of Lower Hambleton, but these days it has stunning views over Rutland Water, Europe's largest man-made lake. During the time they have been here, Colin and Celia Crawford have tastefully refurbished the pub. The comfortable bar area has stripped pine, wooden floors and open fires, while the furnishings in the stylish Garden Room restaurant - which leads out to the pleasant summer patio - are cane. From inside and out, diners can enjoy the vista across the water while tucking into bar snacks such as corned beef hash with fried eggs; smoked chicken and bacon penne pasta; sun-dried tomato and mozzarella tart with basil pesto; and crisp Thai fishcakes on sesame noodles. There's often a set two- or three-course menu of the day offering interesting dishes as well as good value. In the Garden Room, dishes are more ambitious: choose from starters such as duck liver, pancetta and truffle slice with cranberry chutney, or baked goats' cheese and figs wrapped in Parma ham with rosemary and tomato oil. Main event selections might include roast breast of goose with sage and onion rösti and cinnamon braised pear with a rich port wine sauce; tagine of vegetables with lemon and date couscous, spinach, fennel and orange salad with mint and yoghurt sauce; or medallions of pork on caramelised apple mash with parsnip crisps and honey and clove sauce. To accompany it all, there's a selection of well-kept cask ales, well-chosen wines and decent coffee.

OPEN: 12-3, 6-11
BAR MEALS: L served all week 12-2,
D served all week 6.30-9.
Av main course £8
RESTAURANT: L served all week 12-2,
D served all week 6.30-9.
Av cost 3 courses £20
BREWERY/COMPANY:
Free House.
🍺: Grainstore, Oakham Ales, Fenland.
FACILITIES: Children welcome, Garden
NOTES: Parking 25.
ROOMS: 8 en suite from s£40 d£50

King's Arms

A traditional, family-run inn built from local stone and Collyweston roofing slates. Wing is a quaint village just two miles from Rutland Water, and an ideal point from which to tour England's smallest county.

♦♦♦♦ ♀

Top Street, Wing, LE15 8SE

☎ 01572 737634 📠 01572 737255

📧 enquiries@thekingsarms-
  wing.co.uk

Dir: 1m off A6003 between Uppingham & Oakham

The Kings Bar, dating back to 1649, with flagstone floors, low beams, nooks and crannies, and winter fires, is the oldest part of the building. Oakham's Grainstore brewery is well represented among the cask ales, including guests, served here. Bar meals are supplemented by an à la carte menu, and daily specials, among which cider and apple sausages on herb-mashed potato with red wine gravy, home made steak and kidney pie, or deep-fried fresh haddock in beer batter with mushy peas and chunky chips, feature. The snack menu might include a three-cheese ploughman's board, or fresh spaghetti with a cream, chive and smoked salmon sauce. Head chef Simon Richards is renowned for creating mouthwatering meals from fresh ingredients. Restaurant starters include gravadlax with king prawns and dill crème fraîche, home made soup of the day, or the less frequently encountered strips of crocodile in a tangy plum sauce on salad leaves. Of the main courses, halibut fillet on Parmesan mash with oriental spring onions, roast partridge on caramelised red cabbage with port and cranberry sauce, or roasted artichoke and wild mushroom risotto served on house salad, are typical. Half of the cottage-style en suite bedrooms are built in the old village bakery, and the largest room contains the original bread ovens. In summer the large garden comes into its own, with scattered tables and chairs as well as a children's play area. The garden also makes an ideal venue for weddings and private parties, held in a marquee on the lawn.

England

WING
Map 11 SK80

The Cuckoo Inn
3 Top St LE15 8SE ☎ 01572 737340
Dir: A6003 from Oakham, turn R then L
Four miles from Rutland Water, a part-thatched 17th-century coaching inn noted for unusual guest ales from micro-breweries: the pub has a rose garden and barbecue. Home-cooked food is notably good value: steak and kidney pie and lamb casserole, supplemented by some authentic Indian dishes such as chicken Madras and lamb rogan josh.
OPEN: 11.30-2.30 6.30-11 (Sun 12-4, 7-10.30) (closed Tue lunch)
BAR MEALS: L served Wed-Mon 11.30-2.30 D served all week 7-10 Av main course £5.50 **BREWERY/COMPANY:** Free House
🍺: Marston's Pedigree. **FACILITIES:** Children welcome Garden: BBQ, outdoor eating, floral display Dogs allowed **NOTES:** Parking 20 **NOTES:** No credit cards

Pick of the Pubs

Kings Arms ♦♦♦♦ ♀
Top St LE15 8SE ☎ 01572 737634 ▤ 01572 737255
e-mail: enquiries@thekingsarms-wing.co.uk
See Pick of the Pubs on opposite page

SHROPSHIRE

ALBRIGHTON
Map 15 SJ41

The Horns of Boningale
WV7 3DA ☎ 01902 372347 ▤ 01902 372970
e-mail: horns@boningale.freeserve.co.uk
Dir: From Wolverton, follow the A41 to Oaken, turn L at traffic lights onto the Holyhead Road towards Shifnal. The Horns is on the L, 2 miles from Oaken.
This 300-year-old free house was formerly popular as a 'ham and eggery' with Shropshire cattlemen, and the dish is still available. Now completely refurbished as a civilised dining pub, the main bar is divided into three cosy rooms. There's also a large formal restaurant, leading out to landscaped gardens and an ornamental fishpond. Expect steak and ale pie, Thai curry, savoury bean tartlet, and halibut mornay.
OPEN: 12-3 6-11 **BAR MEALS:** L served all week D served all week 6-9.30 Av main course £7 **RESTAURANT:** L served all week 12-2 D served Mon-Sat 6-9.30 Av 3 course à la carte £15 Av 3 course fixed price £6.50 🍺: Hook Norton Old Hooky, Enville Ale, Boddingtons, plus guest. **FACILITIES:** Children welcome Garden: Food served outside **NOTES:** Parking 50

BISHOP'S CASTLE
Map 15 SO38

Boars Head ♦♦♦ 🐱 ♀
Church St SY9 5AE ☎ 01588 638521 ▤ 01588 630126
e-mail: sales@boarsheadhotel.co.uk
Granted its first licence in 1642, this old coaching inn was once the centre of one of England's most Rotten Boroughs; its former stable block - known as 'The Curly Tail' - now accommodating overnighters in considerable comfort. Inside, look for the priest hole in one of the chimneys and settle in the popular beamed bar, a focus of village life, where food, accurately described as traditional, takes in trout with almonds, sausages, and steaks in various guises.
OPEN: 11.30-2.30 6.30-11 **BAR MEALS:** L served all week 12-2 D served all week 6-9.30 Av main course £7 **RESTAURANT:** L

continued

served all week 12-2 D served all week 6.30-9.30 Av 3 course à la carte £18 **BREWERY/COMPANY:** Free House 🍺: Scottish Courage Courage Best & Courage Directors & Theakstons Best. ♀: 8 **FACILITIES:** Children welcome Children's licence Dogs allowed **NOTES:** Parking 20 **ROOMS:** 4 bedrooms 4 en suite s£35 d£55

The Three Tuns Inn ♀
Salop St SY9 5BW ☎ 01588 638797 ▤ 01588 638081
e-mail: info@thethreetunsinn.co.uk
Dir: 22m SW of Shrewsbury

Late 16th-century timber-framed pub in the centre of the village serving tip-top ales brewed across the courtyard, and home-cooked food prepared from fresh local produce. Expect specialities like warm French onion tart, potted shrimps, rabbit casserole and game pie in season, and lemon tart, plus sandwiches and other snacks at lunchtime. An added attraction is a small brewing museum.
OPEN: 12-11 (Sun 12-10.30) **BAR MEALS:** L served all week 12-2.30 D served all week 7-9.30 Av main course £8
BREWERY/COMPANY: Free House 🍺: Tuns Offa's Ale, & Tuns XXX. **FACILITIES:** Children welcome Garden: Beer garden, patio, outdoor eating Dogs allowed **NOTES:** Parking 6

WHICH IS THE OLDEST PUB?
The question has no sure answer. Records are fragmentary and a building, or part of it, may be far older than its use as a drinking house. The Old Ferry Boat Inn at Holywell in the Cambridgeshire fens is claimed to go back to the 6th century as a monastic ferry station and the Olde Fighting Cocks in St Albans to the 8th century as an abbey fishing lodge by the River Ver. A more believable contender is the Bingley Arms at Bardsey, West Yorkshire, recorded as the 'priest's inn' in 905, but it was completely rebuilt in 1738. The Ostrich at Colnbrook, Buckinghamshire, is apparently on the site of a monastic hospice recorded in 1106 (and its odd name is a pun on 'hospice'). Others claiming a 12th-century origin include the wonderfully named Olde Trip to Jerusalem in Nottingham, the Cromwell-linked Royal Oak at Whatcote in Warwickshire, the venerable Oxenham Arms at South Zeal in Devon, the half-timbered Pandy Inn at Dorstone, Herefordshire, the Olde House Inn at Llangynwyd in South Wales and the Oldes Boar's Head at Middleton, Greater Manchester. All of them, of course, have been repeatedly rebuilt and altered over the centuries.

The Sun Inn

Explore a delightful corner of Shropshire on this classic country walk which offers superb views of the lovely Clee Hills.

Walk to the crossroads and take the lane opposite the Sun leading to Lower Corfton, following it as far as Karray Cottage on the left. Just beyond it are a finger-post and two kissing gates. Pass through them and go half left across the field to a stile and fence in the far hedge.

Cross the stile and the stream beyond it, bearing slightly left to a further stile and fence. Once over, follow the path to a metal gate in the far right-hand corner. Pass through it and continue ahead for a short distance to a metal gate. Go through the gate and continue ahead across parkland, crossing the drive to Delbury Hall and then making for a small wood on the right.

The path crosses two stiles to the left of the trees and then runs downhill to a footbridge. Cross it and follow the stream into Diddlebury, keeping the church on the right. Turn left through the village, following the B4368. Turn left and then right up the lane to an area of farmland and woodland known as Pinstones, climbing for about 1 mile/1.6km.

From here there are impressive views over the Clee Hills. On reaching Pinstones, keep ahead through a gate, veer left at the fork and, after passing through a second gate, turn left along a grassy track to reach a waymark. Turn sharp right here, down to Goosefoot. At the bottom turn sharp left and follow the path down Corfton Bache. On reaching the lane, continue ahead and return to the inn.

THE SUN INN, CRAVEN ARMS
Corfton SY7 9DF
☎ 01584 861239

Dir: On the B4368 7m N of Ludlow
Friendly family-owned pub serving (and selling by the glass from the barrel) home-made beer. Beer festivals are regularly held, and the pub is welcoming to all comers.
Open: 12-2.30 6-11
Bar Meals: 12-2 6-9.30
Notes: Children welcome (swing, high chairs, play area) & dogs (water). Garden benches/tables & pretty views. Parking.
(See page 394 for full entry)

DISTANCE: 3 miles/4.8km
MAP: OS Explorer 217
TERRAIN: Farmland, woodland, gentle hills
PATHS: Paths, tracks and bridleways
GRADIENT: Gentle climbing

Walk submitted and checked by Sharon Walters

BRIDGNORTH — Map 10 SO79

The Bear ♀
Northgate WV16 4ET ☎ 01746 763250
e-mail: thebearinn@aol.com
Dir: *From High Street (Bridgnorth) go through Northgate (sandstone archway) and the pub is on the L*

Traditional Grade II listed hostelry in one of the loveliest of the Severn-side towns. The way it clings to the top of a high sandstone cliff gives it an almost continental flavour. A former coaching inn, the award-winning Bear boasts two carpeted bars which are characterised by whisky-water jugs, gas-type wall lamps and wheelback chairs. Good quality, appetising menu offers the likes of ham, egg and chips, braised lamb shank, wild mushroom and spinach risotto, and salmon and herb fishcakes. Daily-changing real ales and a choice of seven malts.
OPEN: 11-3 5-11 (Sun 7-10.30) **BAR MEALS:** L served all week 12-2 Av main course £5.50 **BREWERY/COMPANY:** Free House
◀: Changing guest ales. **FACILITIES:** Children welcome Garden: Food served outside Dogs allowed **NOTES:** Parking 18 No credit cards

The Lion O'Morfe ♀
Upper Farmcote WV15 5PS ☎ 01746 710678 🖷 01746 710678
Dir: *Off A458 (Bridgnorth/Stourbridge) 2.5m from Bridgnorth follow signs for Claverley on L, 0.5m up hill on L*
Friendly pub dating from the early 1850s when the owner took advantage of the Duke of Wellington's Beer House Act of 1830, and paid two guineas to Excise for change of use from a Georgian farmhouse to an inn. The name 'Morfe' is derived from the Welsh for 'marsh'. A sample evening menu offers traditional pub food dishes such as steak and kidney pie, battercrisp cod, chicken curry, tuna salad, and gammon steak.
OPEN: 12-2.30 7-11 **BAR MEALS:** L served all week 12-2 D served Mon-Sat 7-9 **RESTAURANT:** L served all week 12-2 D served Mon-Sat 7-10 Av 3 course à la carte £10 **BREWERY/COMPANY:** Free House
◀: Banks, Bass, Woods, Wye Valley. ♀: 30 **FACILITIES:** Children welcome Garden: Food served outside. Orchard & play area Dogs allowed Water provided **NOTES:** Parking 40

BURLTON — Map 15 SJ42

Pick of the Pubs

The Burlton Inn ♀
SY4 5TB ☎ 01939 270284 🖷 01939 270204
e-mail: bean@burltoninn.co.uk
Dir: *8m N of Shrewsbury on A528 towards Ellesmere*
Following last year's restructuring, this classy 18th-century free house now has a larger dining area, and a new soft-furnished relaxing section. Just the place, then, for a pint of Proud Salopian, or one of the many guest beers, especially for those who dislike pubs with music and amusement machines. Every ingredient is carefully selected, whether for mushroom and spinach filo parcels with tomato and garlic sauce, wholegrain mustard and parsley butter, or seafood pie (fresh and smoked fish and prawns in wine and lemon cream sauce, with rösti potato topping). Among the specials are noisettes of lamb with sautéed apricots, celeriac, and redcurrant and red wine sauce, and fresh ravioli filled with Mozzarella, black olives and goats' cheese. Light meals, which can also serve as starters, include tapas, baked mushrooms with ricotta and fresh basil pesto, and skewered sesame chicken with garlic, tomato and red pepper dip.

OPEN: 11-3 6-11 (Sun 12-3 7-10.30) Closed: Dec 25-26 Jan 1, Mon Close at lunch time **BAR MEALS:** L served all week 12-2 D served all week 6.30-9.45 Av main course £10.50
RESTAURANT: L served all week 12-2 D served all week 6.30-9.45 Av 3 course à la carte £20 **BREWERY/COMPANY:** Free House ◀: Banks, Greene King Abbot Ale, Wye Valley Bitter, Salopian Brewing. ♀: 7 **FACILITIES:** Garden: South facing patio and grass area with tables Dogs allowed at discretion of landlord **NOTES:** Parking 40

CHURCH STRETTON — Map 15 SO49

The Royal Oak
Cardington SY6 7JZ ☎ 01694 771266
Reputedly the oldest pub in Shropshire, dating from 1462, this Grade II listed pub is all atmosphere and character. Nestling in the out-of-the-way village of Cardington, the pub, with its low beams, massive walls and striking inglenook, is a great place to seek out on cold winter days. In the summer it is equally delightful with its peaceful garden and patio. The proprietors provide packed lunches on request and a free walkers' guide.
OPEN: 12-2 7-11 (Sun 12-3, 7-10.30) **BAR MEALS:** L served Tue-Sun 12-2 D served Tue-Sun 7-9 Av main course £7.50
RESTAURANT: L served Tue-Sun 12-2 D served Tue-Sun 7.30-9 Av 3 course à la carte £15 **BREWERY/COMPANY:** Free House
◀: Hobsons Best Bitter, Duck and Dive, Golden Arrow, Timothy Taylor Landlord. **FACILITIES:** Children welcome Garden: Patio, food served outdoors **NOTES:** Parking 30

CLEOBURY MORTIMER — Map 10 SO67

Pick of the Pubs

The Crown at Hopton ◆◆◆◆◆ ◉
Hopton Wafers DY14 0NB ☎ 01299 270372 ▤ 01299 271127
Dir: *On A4117 8m west of Ludlow, 2m east of Cleobury Mortimer*

Located in a sleepy hollow, this former coaching inn is surrounded by immaculate gardens and has its own duck pond. The 16th-century free house was once owned by a nearby estate, and the informal Rent Room bar recalls the days when rents were collected here from the local tenants. The inn, which has been lovingly restored to a high standard, boasts two inglenook fireplaces, exposed timbers and an elegant dining room. Bedrooms are individually furnished to maximum guest comfort and, in addition to occasional period furniture, all offer en suite facilities. Altogether a perfect base for exploring this magnificent area. The chef, Barry Price, creates imaginative dishes using fresh seasonal ingredients. Roast avocado with garlic and bacon, or grilled Feta cheese with prosciutto might precede beef Wellington, loin of lamb, chicken en croûte, or roast monkfish wrapped in bacon. Leave room for the pastry chef's home-made desserts.
OPEN: 12-3 6-11 **BAR MEALS:** L served all week 12-2.30 D served all week 6-9.30 Av main course £9.95 **RESTAURANT:** L served Sun 12-3 D served Tue-Sat 7-9.30 Av 3 course à la carte £21.95 **BREWERY/COMPANY:** Free House ◖: Timothy Taylor Landlord, Hobsons Best. **FACILITIES:** Children welcome Garden: Patio area, Food served outside **NOTES:** Parking 40 **ROOMS:** 7 bedrooms 7 en suite s£47.50 d£75

The Kings Arms Hotel 🐾 ⅄
DY14 8BS ☎ 01299 270252 ▤ 01299 271968
Dir: *take A456 from Kidderminster the A4117 to Cleobury Mortimer*

Simple victuals have given way to steak and kidney pie, and braised duck breast in Grand Marnier, and the home-brewed

ales are nowadays from Youngs and Greene King as this 18th-century inn has moved with the times. The oak floors, exposed beams and fine inglenook fireplace remain a pleasant setting for popular choices of food that might also include fish pie, battered haddock, and various home-made pâtés.
OPEN: 11.30-11 (Sun 12-10.30) **BAR MEALS:** L served all week 11.30-3.30 D served Mon-Wed, Fri-Sat 6.30-9 Av main course £6.75 **RESTAURANT:** L served all week 12-3 D served Mon-Wed, Fri-Sat 7-9 ◖: Hobsons Best, Youngs Special, Greene King Abbot Ale. **FACILITIES:** Children welcome Garden: Food served outside. Dogs allowed **NOTES:** Parking 4

CRAVEN ARMS — Map 09 SO48

The Plough ⅄
Wistanstow SY7 8DG ☎ 01588 673251 ▤ 01588 672419
e-mail: plough@bartender.net
Dir: *Telephone for directions*
Brewery tap to the Wood Brewery alongside, and its only tied house, this country pub is well worth the short diversion off the A49. Sample a pint of Special, Parish or Shropshire Lad in the welcoming, simply-furnished bar. The seasonal menu leans towards English cooking, offering the likes of venison sausages with root vegetable mash and mulled wine sauce, loin of cod with a mustard crust, served on ratatouille, and various home-made puddings.
OPEN: 11.30-2.30 6.30-11 **BAR MEALS:** L served all week 12-2 D served Tue-Sat 6.30-9 Av main course £8.50 **RESTAURANT:** L served Tue-Sun 12.00-2 D served Tue-Sun 6.30-9 Av 3 course à la carte £13.75 **BREWERY/COMPANY:** ◖: Wood Parish Special, Shropshire Lad, Guest Beer. **FACILITIES:** Dogs allowed **NOTES:** Parking 50

The Sun Inn 🐾 ⅄
Corfton SY7 9DF ☎ 01584 861239 & 861503
e-mail: normanspride@aol.com
Dir: *on the B4368 7m N of Ludlow*
In beautiful Corvedale, a friendly, family-owned pub, first licensed in 1613, that puts on small beer festivals during Easter and August bank holidays. The landlord brews his own Corvedale beers, using local borehole water, and sells them bottled and from the barrel. Typical home-prepared dishes include beer-flavoured, locally made sausages, Shrewsbury lamb, chicken Madras, fried cod, salmon and dill lasagne, and broccoli and cream cheese bake. Very friendly for children and people with disabilities.
OPEN: 12-2.30 6-11 **BAR MEALS:** L served all week 12-2 D served all week 6-9.30 Av main course £6.95 **RESTAURANT:** L served all week 12-2 D served all week 6-9.30 Av 3 course à la carte £10 **BREWERY/COMPANY:** Free House ◖: Corvedale Normans Pride, Secret Hop, Dark & Delicious, Julie's Ale. ⅄: 14 **FACILITIES:** Children welcome Children's licence Garden: 4 benches with tables, pretty views Dogs allowed Water **NOTES:** Parking 30
See Pub Walk on page 392

CRESSAGE — Map 10 SJ50

Pick of the Pubs

The Cholmondeley Riverside Inn ⅄
Connd SY5 6AF ☎ 01952 510900 ▤ 01952 510980
Dir: *On A458 Shrewsbury-Bridgnorth rd*
In three acres of garden alongside the River Severn, this extensively-refurbished coaching inn offers river-view dining both outdoors and in a modern conservatory. The single menu serves both dining areas and spacious bar, the latter furnished and decorated in haphazard country style.

continued

continued

Traditional pub dishes include hot crab pâté and mushrooms with Shropshire blue cheese, followed by local lamb noisettes with parsnip chips, or salmon fishcakes with hollandaise. Exotic alternatives follow the lines of Peking duck pancakes with hoisin sauce, "Pee-kai" chicken breasts with satay sauce, and spinach, sorrel and Mozzarella parcels. **OPEN:** 11.30-3 6-11 **BAR MEALS:** L served all week 12-2.30 D served all week 7-9.30 Av main course £7.50 **RESTAURANT:** L served all week 12-2.30 D served all week 7-9.30 Av 3 course à la carte £22 **BREWERY/COMPANY:** Free House ☎: Riverside Ale, guest beers. **FACILITIES:** Children welcome Garden: beer garden, patio, outdoor eating Dogs allowed **NOTES:** Parking 100

HODNET   Map 15 SJ62

The Bear Hotel ★★ 🐝
TF9 3NH ☎ 01630 685214 🗎 01630 685787
e-mail: info@bearhotel.org.uk
Dir: Junction A53 & A442 on sharp corner in middle of small village
An illuminated cellar garden, once a priest hole, is one of the more unusual attractions at this 16th-century coaching inn. There was also a bear pit in the car park until 1970. Hodnet Hall Gardens are close by. An extensive menu includes bar snacks and restaurant meals, with dishes like large home-made steak and mushroom Yorkshire pudding, and grilled pork loin steak with apple sauce and sage and apricot stuffing. **OPEN:** 10.30-11 (Sun 12-10.30) **BAR MEALS:** L served all week 12-2 D served all week Av main course £8 **BREWERY/COMPANY:** Free House ☎: Theakston, John Smiths, Courage Directors. **FACILITIES:** Children welcome Garden: Large lawn area, shrubs and hedges Dogs allowed In the garden only **NOTES:** Parking 70 **ROOMS:** 8 bedrooms 8 en suite 2 family rooms s£42.50 d£60

IRONBRIDGE   Map 10 SJ60

The Grove Inn ♦♦♦
10 Wellington Rd, Coalbrookdale TF8 7DX
☎ 01952 433269 🗎 01952 433269
e-mail: frog@fat-frog.co.uk
Dir: Telephone for directions
Pure France in the Ironbridge Gorge, in a former coaching inn next to Coalbrookdale Museum. Johnny, the French proprietor, prepares 'Frog Food' (his words) for both the Grove and the Fat Frog Restaurant. Le patron himself is depicted on one of the many murals, and frogs are everywhere. The menu includes moules marinière, mignons of pork tenderloin with cider and Dijon mustard sauce, and monkfish Thermidor. A separate fish and seafood wine bar has daily specials. **OPEN:** 12-2.30 5.30-11 (Sun 12-5.30) 25 Dec Closed eve **BAR MEALS:** L served all week 12.30-2 D served Mon-Sat 6.30-8.30 Av main course £7.95 **RESTAURANT:** L served all week 12.30-2 D served Mon-Sat 7-9.30 Av 3 course à la carte £19.50 Av 3 course fixed price £19.50 **BREWERY/COMPANY:** Free House ☎: Banks Original, Traditional, Marston's Pedigree. **FACILITIES:** Children welcome Garden: Large lawned flowered garden Dogs allowed Water, food if required **NOTES:** Parking 12 **ROOMS:** 5 bedrooms 5 en suite 2 family rooms s£30 d£45

Pick of the Pubs

The Malthouse ♦♦♦♦ ♀
The Wharfage TF8 7NH ☎ 01952 433712 🗎 01952 433298
e-mail: enquiries@malthousepubs.co.uk
Dir: Telephone for directions
The Malthouse is situated on the banks of the River Severn in Ironbridge, a village renowned for its spectacular natural beauty and award-winning museums, and now a designated UNESCO World Heritage Site. It has been an inn since the turn of the 20th century, and before that a malthouse. The building has been extensively refurbished; to one side there is a bar with its own menu and kitchen - a popular music and dining venue - and on the other a restaurant, the two styles of food and decor completely different. Fresh fish is a speciality, and while the bar offers cod in beer batter with fries, the restaurant has tempura-battered monkfish with curried chickpeas, spinach and coriander dressing. A popular concept is Art at the Malthouse, launched to provide free space for artists. The only condition is that the owners like the work and the artist helps hang the exhibition. **OPEN:** 11-11 (Sun 12-3 6-10.30) Closed: 25-26 Dec **BAR MEALS:** L served all week 12-2.30 D served all week 6-9.30 **RESTAURANT:** L served all week 12-2 D served all week 6.30-9.45 **BREWERY/COMPANY:** Inn Partnership ☎: Flowers Original, Boddingtons, Tetley. **FACILITIES:** Children welcome Garden: **NOTES:** Parking 15 **ROOMS:** 6 bedrooms 6 en suite

---

LLANFAIR WATERDINE   Map 09 SO27

Pick of the Pubs

The Waterdine ♦♦♦♦♦
LD7 1TU ☎ 01547 528214 🗎 01547 529992
See Pick of the Pubs on page 396

LUDLOW   Map 10 SO57

The Charlton Arms ♦♦♦ 🐝 ♀
SY8 1PJ ☎ 01584 872813 🗎 01584 879120
Dir: Situated on Ludford Bridge on the Hereford road, South exit Ludlow town centre
In a spectacular riverside setting beside the medieval pack-horse bridge over the River Teme, here is a family-run free house that features six local real ales, and home cooking that relies on fresh seasonal produce. Main courses are created from fresh fish and organic beef, lamb and pork from local suppliers - the high points of the ever-popular Sunday lunches. **OPEN:** 11-11 **BAR MEALS:** L served all week 12-2 D served all week 7-9 Av main course £8 **BREWERY/COMPANY:** Free House ☎: Hobsons Best Bitter, Wye Valley Butty Bach, Woods Shropshire Lad. **FACILITIES:** Garden: Riverside Patio Dogs allowed Water **NOTES:** Parking 40 **ROOMS:** 6 bedrooms 6 en suite no children overnight

See Pub Walk on page 398

Open: 12-3, 7-11
Closed: Mon
Bar Meals: L served Tue-Sun 12-2,
D served Tue-Sat 7-9.
Av cost main course £13
RESTAURANT: L served Tue-Sun 12-1.45,
D served Tue-Sat 7-9.
Av cost 3 course £24
BREWERY/COMPANY:
Free House.
🍺: Woodhampton Jack Snipe, Wood
Shropshire Legends, Parish Bitter &
Shropshire Lad.
FACILITIES: Garden - quiet walled
garden with good views.
NOTES: Parking 12
ROOMS: 3 en suite from s£50 d£80

The Waterdine

An original Welsh longhouse built in the second half of the 16th century as a drovers' inn. In lovely mature gardens, it is surrounded by the typically peaceful, beautiful countryside which nearby Offa's Dyke Path follows for most of its 182-mile course from Prestatyn to Chepstow.

Llanfair Waterdine, LD7 1TU
☎ 01547 528214 📠 01547 529992
Dir: 4m NW of Knighton, just off the Newtown road, turn R in Lloyney, over bridge, follow road to village, last on left opposite church.

The views from the garden are superb, and at its foot runs - literally - the England-Wales border in liquid form, the River Teme. It was in the lounge bar of what was then called the Red Lion that Col John (later Lord) Hunt, a village resident, planned a mountaineering milestone, the first ascent of Everest in 1953. He would have been familiar with the heavy ceiling beams, and the three large inglenooks, but not today's wood-burning stoves that are fired up whenever necessary. In the summer, the south-facing building enjoys the sun all day. Owner and internationally renowned chef, Ken Adams, is the inspiration behind the food, much of which he sources from the inn's own highly-productive gardens. Meals are served in the two dining rooms, one a bright conservatory with breathtaking views. Typical meals might include herb risotto with sherry-roasted vegetables, or parsnip and Monkland cheese soufflé, followed by fillet of sea bass, braised leeks and a light butter sauce, or roast saddle of Mortimer Forest roe deer with braised red cabbage, spiced pears, fondant potato and bitter chocolate sauce. Bar meals are substantial too, as roasted monkfish on provençale vegetables with spiced couscous, and fillet of Black Hall beef with shallot and port sauce demonstrate. Desserts include crisp lemon curd tart, and brandysnap filled with rich rice pudding and fruit compôte. Good drinking can be had in the pint-glass shape of Wood's Shropshire Legends, Parish Bitter and Shropshire Lad, from Craven Arms. Individually-designed bedrooms are well furnished and decorated.

LUDLOW continued

The Church Inn ◆◆◆ ♀
Buttercross SY8 1AW ☎ 01584 872174 🗎 01584 877146
Dir: Town centre
Down the ages this inn has been occupied by a blacksmith, saddler, druggist and barber-surgeon, and since being an inn its name has changed several times. It sits on one of the oldest sites in Ludlow, where nowadays it enjoys a good reputation for traditional pub food and good beer including Hobsons Town Crier and Hook Norton. Expect the likes of lasagne, scampi, chilli, and gammon.
OPEN: 11-11 **BAR MEALS:** L served all week 12-2 D served all week 6.30-9 Av main course £5.95 **RESTAURANT:** L served all week 12-2 D served all week 6.30-9 Av 3 course à la carte £11
BREWERY/COMPANY: Free House 🍺: Hobsons Town Crier, Brains Bitter, Hook Norton Old Hooky, Weetwood. ♀: 14
FACILITIES: Children welcome Dogs allowed **ROOMS:** 8 bedrooms 8 en suite 1 family rooms s£30 d£50

See Pub Walk on page 398

The Cookhouse ⊚⊚ ♀
Bromfield SY8 2JR ☎ 01584 856565 & 856665 🗎 01584 856661
e-mail: info@thecookhouse.org.uk
Dir: Telephone for directions
Once a farmhouse occupied by the soldier and colonial ruler 'Clive of India', the Cookhouse now offers something for everyone. Clive's coat of arms can still be seen in the lounge bar, which now serves local ales, a large selection of wines or even tea, coffee and snacks. In the Café bar in the evening diners are invited to draw on the brown paper tablecloths with pens provided. The restaurant offers more formal, award-winning dinners. A variety of dishes could include bangers and mash, tagliatelle with salmon and broccoli, sweet and sour chicken, venison and rich port pie, halibut fillet on a bed of spinach, or root vegetable pavé with tomato and red wine sauce.

OPEN: 11-11 (Sunday 12-10.30) 25 Dec Closed eve
BAR MEALS: L served all week 12-3 D served all week 6-10 Av main course £8.95 **RESTAURANT:** L served all week 12-3 D served all week 6-10 Av 3 course à la carte £25 **BREWERY/COMPANY:** Free House 🍺: Hobsons Best Bitter & Town Crier, Interbrew Worthington Cream Flow. ♀: 8 **FACILITIES:** Children welcome Garden: Courtyard and beer lawn **NOTES:** Parking 100

Pick of the Pubs

The Roebuck Inn ◆◆◆◆ ⊚⊚ 🐶 ♀
Brimfield SY8 4NE ☎ 01584 711230 🗎 01584 711654
e-mail: dave@roebuckinn.demon.co.uk
Dir: Just off the A49 between Ludlow & Leominster
A classy country inn offering comfortable bedrooms, a brightly-coloured and airy dining room, and traditional bars with inglenooks and wood panelling. The snug bar is popular with locals who relax in here over a pint and a game of crib or dominoes. Imaginative and interesting food uses locally-sourced quality ingredients and a daily, home-baked selection of breads, with everything prepared by the Roebuck's team of young chefs. Starters and light meals might include grilled goats' cheese salad, spring rolls of beef fillet, and coarse country paté, while main courses range from roast rump of lamb and tenderloin of pork to fillet of fresh Cornish brill and oven-baked fish pie. The British cheese board, served with home-made fruit bread and oatcakes and garnished with the pub's own chutney, grapes and celery, is recommended.
OPEN: 11.30-3 6.30-11 (Sun 12-3, 7-10.30) **BAR MEALS:** L served all week 12-2.30 D served all week 7-9.30 Av main course £12.50 **RESTAURANT:** L served all week 12-2.30 D served all week 7-9.30 Av 3 course à la carte £22.50
BREWERY/COMPANY: Free House 🍺: Carlsberg-Tetley Tetley, Woods, Wadworth 6X. **FACILITIES:** Children welcome
NOTES: Parking 24 **ROOMS:** 3 bedrooms 3 en suite s£45 d£70

Pick of the Pubs

Unicorn Inn 🐶 ♀
Corve St SY8 1DU ☎ 01584 873555
Dir: A49 to Ludlow
With a typical Shropshire black and white façade, this traditional inn dating from 1635 stands on the edge of town, beside the River Corve. One of Ludlow's many acclaimed restaurants, the Unicorn's home-cooked food offers high quality. Different elements contribute to its friendly atmosphere, not least the log fires in winter and the sunny riverside terrace on which to bask in summer. Then there's the candlelit dining room, where sample starters include warmed goats' cheese, seafood and hot cheesy crab pot, and home-made soup of the day. For a main course try roast half duck with perry and ginger wine sauce, caramelised honey and mustard salmon fillet, farmhouse grill, or push the boat right out with a seafood medley for two. Bar food is also memorable: typically, spicy jerk pork with stirfry vegetables and noodles, and home-made faggots with mustard mash and onion gravy.
OPEN: 12-3 6-11 (Sun 12-3.30, 7-10.30) Closed: Dec 25
BAR MEALS: L served all week 12-2.15 D served all week 6-9.15 Av main course £7.25 **RESTAURANT:** L served all week 12-2.15 D served all week 6-9.15 Av 3 course à la carte £20
BREWERY/COMPANY: Free House 🍺: Interbrew Bass, Hancocks HB, Guest Ale. **FACILITIES:** Garden: Patio garden over-looks river Dogs allowed Water **NOTES:** Parking 3

MADELEY   Map 10 SJ60

The New Inn
Blists Hill Victorian Town, Legges Way TF7 5DU
☎ 01952 588892 🗎 01952 243447
e-mail: rhamundy@btinternet.com
Dir: Between Telford & Broseley
In the Victorian town of Ironbridge Gorge Open Air Museum, this pub was re-located brick by brick from the Black Country but remains basically as it was in 1890. Customers buy old currency at the bank, then exchange it for traditionally-brewed beer at five-pence farthing per pint - equal to about £2.10 today. Mostly traditional food options include home-made steak and ale casserole with Yorkshire pudding and chicken

continued

continued

The Charlton Arms or The Church Inn

Enjoy this pleasant walk in the fields and pastures below the hilltop town of Ludlow.

From the pub make for the castle entrance in the town centre, keep right of it and follow the Mortimer Trail down to Dinham Bridge over the River Teme. Cross over and follow the road round to the right. Pass a row of stone cottages and then take the lane signposted Priors Halton.

Swing right just before Cliffe Hotel and go diagonally right in the field towards woodland. Descend steeply to a stile in the field corner, cross a footbridge and a second stile and keep right in the next field. Make for the next stile and keep ahead for some time until you draw level with a farm over to the left.

Turn left to a waymark, footbridge and stile in the boundary and then head slightly right. Cross into the next field, maintain the same direction and join a grassy track in the corner. Turn right after a few paces and follow a firm track towards Bromfield.

On reaching the A49 turn right, re-cross the Teme and pass the Cookhouse pub. Follow the A49, turning right just beyond the Bromfield village sign to follow a bridleway running parallel to the road. Keep on the grassy track to a bridleway sign by a road junction and turn right. Follow the Shropshire Way south, pass under power lines and swing left at the next waymark.

Keep Ludlow church tower ahead in the distance and pass to the right of some farm outbuildings. Join a track and continue to the next farm buildings. Cross an intersection, make for a gate and waymark and pass a school. The track graduates to a tarmac lane before reaching the road. Turn right towards Ludlow town centre.

Turn right at a bus stop and head diagonally left across the field, in line with the Castle.

♦♦♦
THE CHARLTON ARMS, LUDLOW
SY8 1PJ
☎ 01584 872813

Directions: On Ludford Bridge on the Hereford Rd, S exit town centre
Open: 11-11
Bar Meals: 12-2 7-9
Notes: Children & dogs welcome. Riverside patio. Parking.
(see page 395 for full entry)

♦♦♦
THE CHURCH INN, LUDLOW
Buttercross SY8 1AW
☎ 01584 872174

Directions: Town centre
Open: 11-11
Bar Meals: 12-2 6.30-9
Notes: Children & dogs welcome.
(See page 397 for full entry)

Go through a kissing gate into the next pasture and cross a footbridge. Make for the next gate and footbridge and walk along to the road.

Go straight ahead and when the road curves right, keep ahead. Climb some steps, turn left into Upper Linney, then right to the parish church. From St Laurence make for the town centre and return to the pub.

DISTANCE: 6 miles/9.7km
MAP: OS Explorer 203
TERRAIN: Fields and pasture
PATHS: Field paths, tracks and bridleways
GRADIENT: Mainly flat

Walk submitted and checked by Nick Channer

MADELEY continued

sauced with white wine and cream: but what would our forbears have made of the lasagne and creamily-sauced vegetable pancakes?
OPEN: 11-4 Closed: Dec 24-25 Nov-Mar Closed Thurs-Fri
BAR MEALS: L served all week 12-2.30 Av main course £4
RESTAURANT: L served all week 12-2.30 Av 3 course fixed price £8.25 **BREWERY/COMPANY:** 🍺: Banks Bitter.
FACILITIES: Children welcome Garden: Food served outside
NOTES: Parking 300

MARKET DRAYTON
Map 15 SJ63

The Hinds Head 🛏️
Norton in Hales TF9 4AT ☎ 01630 653014 🖹 01630 653014
Dir: *Norton in Hales is about 3m NE of Market Drayton*
An 18th-century coaching inn located by the parish church. It has been much extended, with a conservatory built out over the old courtyard, but the bars retain their original atmosphere. The pub is now under new management with a new menu offering British fare freshly prepared from local produce. Dishes include lamb Shrewsbury, traditional fish and chips, and home-made puddings. Vegetarians and vegans are also catered for.
OPEN: 12-2 6.30-11 **BAR MEALS:** L served Tue-Sun 12-2 D served Tue-Sun 6.30-9 **RESTAURANT:** L served Tue-Sun 12-2 D served Tue-Sun 6.30-9 Av 3 course à la carte £19 **BREWERY/COMPANY:** Free House 🍺: Wells Bombadier Premium, Scottish Courage Theakstons Best & John Smith's. **NOTES:** Parking 15

MINSTERLEY
Map 15 SJ30

The Stables Inn
Drury Ln, Hopesgate SY5 0EP ☎ 01743 891344
Dir: *From Shrewsbury A488 turn L at rdbt in Minsterely. At Plox Green x-roads turn R. Pub approx 3m.*
In a peaceful hamlet of just eight houses, the Stables was built in 1680 to serve the drovers travelling between Montgomery and Shrewsbury markets. Overlooking scenic pastureland, its beamed bar warmed by an open fire is the place to settle over a beer and contemplate a traditional menu that majors in steaks and home-made casseroles. Fresh daily soups precede chicken curry, chilli con carne, vegetable korma and sausages with mash and onion gravy.
OPEN: 7-11 (Sat-Sun open 12-3pm) Closed: 1 Jan 25 Dec closed evening **BAR MEALS:** L served Sat-Sun 12-1.45 D served Tue-sun 7-9.30 Av main course £8 **RESTAURANT:** D served Tue-Sun 7-9.30 Av 3 course à la carte £13.50 **BREWERY/COMPANY:** Free House 🍺: Interbrew Worthington Bitter, Youngs, Hancocks HB, Wells Bombardier. **FACILITIES:** Garden: Picturesque views, peaceful **NOTES:** Parking 40 **NOTES:** No credit cards

---

MORVILLE
Map 10 SO69

Acton Arms
WV16 4RJ ☎ 01746 714209 🖹 01746 714102
e-mail: acton-arms@madfish.com **Dir:** *On A458, 3m W of Bridgnorth*
Successive landlords have all frequently seen the apparition making this one of Britain's most haunted pubs. Described as 'like a sheet flicking from one door to another', the spectre may be a former abbot of Shrewsbury who lived in the village in the 16th century. There's nothing spectral about the food, though, with completely worldly dishes such as natural smoked haddock with cream cheese sauce, lamb shank in red wine sauce, steak and ale pie, and broccoli and Brie rösti.
OPEN: 11.30-2.30 6-11 (all day during Summer) **BAR MEALS:** L served all week 12-2 D served all week 6-9 **RESTAURANT:** L served
continued

---

all week 12-2.30 D served all week 7-9.30
BREWERY/COMPANY: W'hampton & Dudley 🍺: Bank's Hanson's Mild & Banks Bitter. **FACILITIES:** Children welcome Garden: Large area with benches & seats Dogs allowed Water **NOTES:** Parking 40

MUCH WENLOCK
Map 10 SO69

The George & Dragon
2 High St TF13 6AA ☎ 01952 727312
Dir: *On A458 halfway between Shrewsbury & Bridgnorth*
There's a remarkable collection of brewery memorabilia, including over 500 water jugs hanging from the ceiling, in this historic Grade II listed building. Adjacent to the market square, Guildhall and ruined priory, the inn's cosy and inviting atmosphere makes this an obvious choice for locals and visitors alike. Expect a good range of popular dishes, including perhaps sirloin steak; rack of lamb; duck; pheasant and mackerel.
OPEN: 12-3 6-11 (Wknds & summer June-Sep all day)
BAR MEALS: L served Mon-Sun 12-2.00 D served Mon-Tue, Thur-Sat 6-9.00 Av main course £7.95 **RESTAURANT:** L served Mon-Sun 12-2.00 D served Mon-Tue, Thur-Sat 6.30-9.00 Av 3 course à la carte £16.95 **BREWERY/COMPANY:** 🍺: Greene King Abbot Ale, Old Speckled Hen & IPA, Adnams Broadside, Hobsons Town Crier.
FACILITIES: Children welcome

Longville Arms 🛏️
Longville in the Dale TF13 6DT ☎ 01694 771206 🖹 01694 771742
e-mail: longvillearms@aol.com
Dir: *From Shrewsbury take A49 to Church Stretton, then B4371 to Longville*
Prettily situated in a scenic corner of Shropshire, ideally placed for walking and touring, this welcoming country inn has been carefully restored and now includes a 60-seat dining room. Solid elm or cast-iron-framed tables, oak panelling and wood-burning stoves are among the features which help to generate a warm, friendly ambience inside. Favourite main courses on the wide-ranging bar menu and specials board include steak and ale pie, chicken wrapped in bacon and stuffed with paté, monkfish thermidor, or a range of steaks.
OPEN: 12-3 7-11 (Sat-Sun 12-3 6-11) Dec 25 No food
BAR MEALS: L served all week 12-2.30 D served all week 7-9.30
RESTAURANT: L served all week 12-2.30 D served all week 7-9.30
BREWERY/COMPANY: Free House 🍺: Scottish Courage Courage Directors, John Smith's & Courage Best, Theakstons Best, Wells Bombardier. **FACILITIES:** Children welcome Garden: Dogs allowed Not in garden **NOTES:** Parking 40

The Talbot Inn 🛏️ 🍷
High St TF13 6AA ☎ 01952 727077 🖹 01952 728436
e-mail: maggie@talbotinn.idps.co.uk

Dating from 1360, the Talbot was a hostel for travellers and a centre for alms giving. The delightful courtyard was used in the 1949 Powell and Pressburger film 'Gone to Earth'. Daily specials
continued

MUCH WENLOCK continued

highlight the varied menu, which may include steak and kidney pie, baked seabass, Shropshire pie and cod mornay.
OPEN: 11-3 6.15-11 (Sun 12-3, 7-10.30) (Summer, Sat-Sun 11-11) Closed: 25 Dec **BAR MEALS:** L served all week 12-2.30 D served all week 7-9.30 **RESTAURANT:** L served all week 12-2.30 D served all week 7-9.30 Av 3 course à la carte £20 Av 4 course fixed price £15.95
BREWERY/COMPANY: Free House ◗: Bass. ♀: 7
FACILITIES: Children welcome Garden: Paved courtyard
NOTES: Parking 5

Pick of the Pubs

Wenlock Edge Inn
Hilltop, Wenlock Edge TF13 6DJ
☎ 01746 785678 ▤ 01746 785285
e-mail: info@wenlockedgeinn.co.uk
Dir: 4.5m from Much Wenlock on B4371

Originally a row of 17th-century quarrymen's cottages, the inn is located on a country road at one of the highest points of Wenlock Edge's dramatic wooded ridge. It is a popular pub with a convivial atmosphere and has recently changed hands. Inside there is a small country-style dining room and a choice of cosy bars, one with a wood-burning stove. Outside a furnished patio takes full advantage of the views, which stretch across Apedale to Caer Caradoc and the Long Mynd. Favourite dishes like Bradon Rost (smoked fillet of salmon) or fillet of beef on the Edge (prime steak served on a croûte with a layer of chicken liver pâté and a wild mushroom and brandy cream sauce) are supplemented by weekly specials such as Shropshire-reared venison pie or rack of local lamb in a redcurrant and rosemary jus.
OPEN: 12-2.30 6.30-11 (Winter-Closed Mon) Closed: 24-26 Dec
BAR MEALS: L served all week 12-2 D served all week 7-9 Av main course £7.50 **RESTAURANT:** L served all week 12-2 D served all week 7-9 Av 3 course à la carte £15
BREWERY/COMPANY: Free House ◗: Hobsons Best & Town Crier. **FACILITIES:** Children welcome Garden: Patio area with furniture, stunning views Dogs allowed Water, toys
NOTES: Parking 50

MUNSLOW
Map 10 SO58

The Crown Country Inn ♦♦♦♦ 🍴
SY7 9ET ☎ 01584 841205 ▤ 01584 841255
e-mail: info@crowncountryinn.co.uk
Dir: On B4368 between Craven Arms & Much Wenlock

A Shropshire Hundred House dating back to Tudor times, where Judge Jeffries is said to have presided, the inn has massive oak beams, inglenook fireplaces and flagstone floors. A warm welcome and seriously good food are today's hallmarks. Evening menus invite you to try roast loin of Ludlow venison, pavé of local beef sirloin, medallion of fresh Porbeagle shark, breast of Gressingham duck, or spiced vegetable samosas.
OPEN: 12-2.00 7-11 **BAR MEALS:** L served Tues-Sun 12-2 D served Tues-Sat 7-9 Av main course £12 **RESTAURANT:** L served Tues-Sun 12-2 D served Tues- Sat 7-9 Av 3 course à la carte £18
BREWERY/COMPANY: Free House ◗: Holden's Black Country Bitter, Black Country Mild, Golden Glow & Special Bitter.
FACILITIES: Children welcome Children's licence Garden: Dogs allowed Water **NOTES:** Parking 20 **ROOMS:** 3 bedrooms 3 en suite 1 family rooms s£35 d£55

NESSCLIFFE
Map 15 SJ31

The Old Three Pigeons Inn 🍴 ♀
SY4 1DB ☎ 01743 741279 ▤ 01743 741259
Dir: On A5 London road, 8 m W of Shrewsbury

A 600-year-old inn built of ship's timbers, sandstone, and wattle and daub, set in two acres of land looking towards Snowdonia and the Bretton Hills. There is a strong emphasis on fish, with a choice of many seasonal dishes, and it is a venue for gourmet club and lobster evenings. Characteristic dishes include seafood platter, duck and cranberry, braised oxtails, liver and bacon, chicken Merango, and oak-smoked haddock.
OPEN: 11.30-3 7-11 (closed Mon) **BAR MEALS:** L served Tue-Sun 11.30-3 D served Tue-Sun 6-9.30 Av main course £7
RESTAURANT: L served Tue-Sun 11.30-3 D served Tue-Sun 7-9 Av 3 course à la carte £18 **BREWERY/COMPANY:** Free House ◗: Scottish Courage John Smith's, Moles Best Bitter, Matston's Pedigree, Interbrew Flowers Original. ♀: 10 **FACILITIES:** Children welcome Garden: Lawn, lake, excellent views Dogs allowed
NOTES: Parking 50

NEWPORT
Map 15 SJ71

The Swan at Forton ♀
TF10 8BY ☎ 01952 812169 ▤ 01952 812722
e-mail: mailtheswan@forton.co.uk
Dir: Telephone for directions

On the border between Shropshire and Staffordshire, a family-run free house with an extensive menu served throughout the two large, comfortable bars and non-smoking restaurant. Regular evenings featuring home-made pies or curries are a great success, while other popular dishes include a steak and kidney pies, poacher's chicken and treacle tart. At the weekends a sumptuous four-course carvery is the focal point.
OPEN: 12-3 6-11 (Sun 12-10.30) **BAR MEALS:** L served all week 12-2.30 D served all week 6-10 Av main course £5.95
RESTAURANT: L served all week 12-2 D served all week 6-10
BREWERY/COMPANY: ◗: Interbrew Bass, Flowers IPA & Boddingtons Bitter, Greene King Abbot Ale, Charles Wells Bombardier.
FACILITIES: Children welcome Garden **NOTES:** Parking 67

NORTON
Map 10 SJ70

Pick of the Pubs

Hundred House Hotel ★★ ◉◉ 🍴 ♀
Bridgnorth Rd TF11 9EE
☎ 01952 730353 & 0845 6446 100 ▤ 01952 730355
e-mail: hundredhouse@lineone.net
See Pick of the Pubs on page 401

continued

Open: 11.30-3, 6-11 (Sun 11-10.30)
Bar Meals: L served all week 12-2.30, D served all week 6-10.
Av cost main course £8.95
RESTAURANT: L served all week 12-2.30, D served Mon-Sat 6-10.
Av cost 3 course £25
BREWERY/COMPANY:
Free House.
🍺: Phillips Heritage, Higate Saddlers & Old Ale, Everards Tiger, Robinsons Bitter, Phillips Mild.
FACILITIES: Children welcome, Garden - Large water garden, with herb and rose gardens.
NOTES: Parking 40
ROOMS: 10 en suite from s£75 d£99

The Hundred House Hotel

"Excellent people, rooms, food. Epitomises hospitality" is the sort of guest comment that this very special hotel has come to expect.

★★ ◎ ◎ 🥄 ♀
Bridgnorth Road, Norton, nr Shifnal, TF11 9EE
☎ 01952 730353 📠 01952 730355
✉ hundredhouse@lineone.net
Dir: On A442 6m N of Bridgnorth, 5 mile south of Telford Centre.

Lovingly run by the Phillips family, the creeper-clad building may appear predictably traditional, but inside it offers a unique experience that's received much praise from the press in recent years. Everything - staff, décor, accommodation and food - reflects the tremendous human as well as economic investment that has gone into the place. The oldest part of the hotel dates from the 14th century, but the main building is Georgian with many additions made over the past few centuries. The atmosphere is intimate, friendly and relaxed. Bedrooms are decorated in a unique interpretation of country-house style - romantic, luxurious and slightly eccentric, with an upholstered swing hanging from the beams in most rooms. The bars and restaurant are filled with fresh flowers, and herbs drying from the rafters; both are the products of the lovely gardens, through which guests are invited to wander. Home-grown herbs are used extensively in the cooking, and are placed in a bowl on the table so that guests can add what they like to their meals. This clear commitment to well-sourced ingredients is evident throughout the menus: the specials board might offer Carlingford loch oysters, locally-farmed steak and kidney pie, or Loch Fyne salmon with mussel and chive mousse and a saffron tomato cream sauce. If you're after something really special opt for the carte - perhaps confit of Hereford duck legs with rocket, tomato and chorizo salad and white bean purée followed by roasted rack of Shropshire spring lamb with tapenade, aubergine tian and gratin dauphinoise.

England

OSWESTRY
Map 15 SJ22

Pick of the Pubs

The Bradford Arms ♦♦♦♦ 🛏 ♀
Llanymynech SY22 6EJ ☎ 01691 830582 🖷 01691 830728
e-mail: info@bradfordarmshotel.com
Dir: On A483 in village centre

A former coaching inn Victorianised in 1901 when it was
part of the Earl of Bradford's estate, this carefully-upgraded
property is located close to the Welsh border. Meals can be
enjoyed in the spacious conservatory, the more formal
dining room, or the inviting bar, the same menu serving all.
The lounge is the perfect place for a pre- or after- dinner
drink, its soft lighting and open fire providing a relaxed and
intimate. Everything except ice cream is made on the
premises, and the inn offers an enterprising modern
English and European menu. Typical dishes are roast
salmon and smoked salmon roulade with capers and
cream cheese, monkfish provençale with saffron rice, and
loin of lamb on wilted spinach with a sauce of redcurrants,
garlic, rosemary and red wine. Attractive accommodation is
available in five en suite bedrooms.
OPEN: 12-2 7-11 Closed: 2wks Sept, 25-26 Dec, 2 wks Jan
BAR MEALS: L served Tues-Sun 12-2 D served Tues-Sun 7-10 Av main
course £9.95 **RESTAURANT:** L served Tues-Sun 12-2 D served Tues-
Sun 7-10 Av 3 course à la carte £20 **BREWERY/COMPANY:** Free
House 🍺: Greene King Abbot Ale, Shepherd Neame Bishops Finger.
♀: 7 **NOTES:** Parking 20 **ROOMS:** 5 bedrooms 5 en suite 1 family
rooms s£35 d£55 no children overnight

Pick of the Pubs

The Old Mill Inn
Candy SY10 9AZ ☎ 01691 657058 🖷 01691 680918
e-mail: theoldmill.inn@virgin.net
Dir: from B4579 turn L after bridge, follow signs for Trefonen, through
traffic lights, turn R towards Llansilin, then first R
Not easily found but well worth seeking out, The Old Mill is
peacefully situated in a rural valley not far from Oswestry.
Offa's Dyke Path - one of Britain's most popular national
trails - is just a few strides from the door and the River
Morda runs beside the inn. The pub's cosy interior is the
place to be on winter days, with a spacious conservatory
overlooking extensive gardens, a warming log fire and a
welcoming ambience. Constantly-changing blackboard
menu includes bar meals, vegetarian dishes and pub
classics. Starters may include baked salmon ring, Thai-style
breaded king prawns, and a trio of chicken kebabs with
lemon sauce. Among main courses, look out for lamb
Henry with raspberry and minted gravy; game pie; chicken
and cashew nut stirfry; and lemon sole 'Helsinki style'.
Tempting sweets often include sticky toffee pudding with
whipped Devon cream, toffee sauce and vanilla ice cream.

OPEN: 12-3 7-11 (Sun 12-3, 7-10.30) (Fri-Sat 12-3, 6-11)
BAR MEALS: L served Wed-Sun 12-2 D served Wed-Sun 7-9 Av
main course £6.95 **RESTAURANT:** L served Wed-Sun 12-2.30 D
served Wed-Sun 6-9.30 Av 3 course à la carte £11
BREWERY/COMPANY: Free House 🍺: Greene King Old
Speckled Hen, Carlsberg-Tetley Tetleys Bitter.
FACILITIES: Children welcome Garden: Natural wooded area
Dogs allowed Water **NOTES:** Parking 200

PICKLESCOTT
Map 15 SO49

Bottle & Glass Inn
SY6 6NR ☎ 01694 751345
Dir: Turn off A49 at Dorrington between Shrewsbury & Church Stretton
This traditional country inn serves all kinds of people but locals
always come first. It is situated in beautiful countryside on the
slopes of the Longmynd in the heart of South Shropshire hill
country. The emphasis is on local ales and local produce.
Straightforward dishes including steaks, cod, and gammon off
the bone, and there is a popular Sunday carvery.
OPEN: 12-2 7-11 Seasonal opening times vary **BAR MEALS:** L
served Sat & Sun 12-2 D served Mon-Sat 7-8.45 Av main course £6.25
RESTAURANT: L served Sun 12-2 D served Fri-Sat 7-8.45 Av 3
course à la carte £14 **BREWERY/COMPANY:** Free House
🍺: Woods Parish, Shropshire Gold Salopians, guest ale.
FACILITIES: Children welcome Garden: patio Dogs allowed bar
only, Water **NOTES:** Parking 20

SHIFNAL
Map 10 SJ70

Odfellows Wine Bar ♀
Market Place TF11 9AU ☎ 01952 461517 🖷 01952 463855
e-mail: matt@odley.co.uk
Dir: 3rd exit from Mway rdbt, at next rdbt take 3rd exit, past petrol station,
round bend under railway bridge, bar on L
Originally a private house, dating from the time of Queen Anne,
this is a single room wine bar with high ceilings and an elevated
dining area leading into an attractive conservatory. There's a
good choice of wines from around the globe, including 12 by the
glass, and speciality dishes include salmon with a herb and
mustard crust served with roasted fennel, rump steak with
chestnut and horseradish mash, and duck in plum and brandy
sauce.
OPEN: 12-2.30 5.30-11 (Sun & Fri open all day) Closed: Dec 25-26,
Jan 1 **BAR MEALS:** L served all week 12-2 D served all week 7-10
Av main course £10.95 **RESTAURANT:** L served all week 12-2 D
served all week 7-10 **BREWERY/COMPANY:** Free House
🍺: Bathams, Timothy Taylor Landlord, Enville, Holdens. ♀: 12
NOTES: Parking 35

SHREWSBURY
Map 15 SJ41

Pick of the Pubs

The Armoury 🛏 ♀
Victoria Quay, Victoria Av SY1 1HH
☎ 01743 340525 🖷 01743 340526
e-mail: armoury@brunningandprice.co.uk
The Armoury has had a chequered history; the building
itself - originally an armoury, of course - is late 18th
century, but is not on its original site. The whole building
was moved in 1922, from the Armoury Gardens, due to
the shortage of building materials at the time. It has
served various purposes, most recently as a bakery, but
its riverside location and large warehouse windows make

continued

continued

it a marvellous pub. Its current life began in 1996, and all-day opening, regular guest ales and modern food prove as popular as ever. If you find yourself there on your own, pick up a book from the ceiling high bookcase. Samples from a typical menu include salmon and tarragon fishcake with yoghurt and mayonnaise raita, pan-fried rib eye steak, wild mushroom lasagne, black olive, goats' cheese and sun-dried tomato ravioli, or pan-fried chicken on blue cheese and leek potato cake.
OPEN: 12-11 (Mon-Sat 12-11, Sun 12-10.30) Closed: 25-26 Dec **BAR MEALS:** L served all week 12-2.30 D served all week 6-9 Av main course £8.25 **RESTAURANT:** L served all week D served all week **BREWERY/COMPANY:** 🍺: Wood Shropshire Lad, Wadworth 6X, Interbrew Boddingtons, Guest Ales. 🍷: 16 **FACILITIES:** Tables by river Severn

The Plume of Feathers
Harley SY5 6LP ☎ 01952 727360 📠 01952 728542
Many original features still survive at this historic inn which started life as a pair of cottages around 1620. The name of the inn was recorded in 1842. Open fires, antique furniture and old beams give the interior a cosy, inviting atmosphere.
OPEN: 12-3 6-11 (Sat, Sun and summer 12-11) **BAR MEALS:** L served all week 12-2 D served Mon-Sat 7-9 Av main course £6 **RESTAURANT:** L served all week 12-3 D served Mon-Sat 7-9 A 3 course à la carte £20 **BREWERY/COMPANY:** Free House 🍺: Worthingtons, guest beers. **FACILITIES:** Children welcome **NOTES:** No credit cards

White Horse Inn 🍴
Pulverbatch SY5 8DS ☎ 01743 718247
Dir: 7m past the Nuffield Hospital
Some 8 miles south of Shrewsbury off the A49, a cruck-structured building houses this fine old inn which was mentioned in the Domesday Book. Up to 40 main dishes are on offer every day, ranging from salmon, plaice and haddock in various guises to home-made steak and ale pie, whole lamb shanks and half a dozen speciality curries. Grills include chicken, gammon and various cuts of steak: a daily special might be beef bourguignon.
OPEN: 12-2.30 7-11 (Summer open till 4pm weekends) **BAR MEALS:** L served all week 12-2 D served all week 7-9.30 Av main course £7.50 **RESTAURANT:** L served all week 12-2 D served all week 7-9.30 Av 3 course à la carte £15.95 **BREWERY/COMPANY:** Enterprise Inns 🍺: Guest Ale. **FACILITIES:** Children welcome Garden: patio area, seats 12 Dogs allowed Water **NOTES:** Parking 50

WENTNOR   Map 15 SO39

The Crown Inn
SY9 5EE ☎ 01588 650613 📠 01588 650436
e-mail: crowninn@wentnor.com
Dir: From Shrewsbury A49 to Church Stretton, follow signs over Long Mynd to Asterton, R to Wentnor
Standing in the shadow of the famous Long Mynd, in an area with vast potential for walking and other outdoor pursuits, the Crown is a traditional, unspoilt 17th-century coaching inn with log fires, beams and horse brasses. Sophisticated meals are served in the bar and non-smoking restaurant: pork tenderloin filled with marinated fruits, pan-fried breast of duck with a burnt orange sauce, and grilled sea bass with couscous are typical of the choices.

continued

OPEN: 12-3 7-11 (Sat 12-3 6-11) (Summer: Sat 12-11, Sun 12-10.30) Closed: Dec 25 **BAR MEALS:** L served all week 12-2 D served all week 7-9 **BREWERY/COMPANY:** Free House 🍺: Hobsons, Greene King Old Speckled Hen, Salopian Shropshire Gold. **FACILITIES:** Children welcome Garden: **NOTES:** Parking 20

WESTON HEATH   Map 10 SJ71

Pick of the Pubs

The Countess's Arms 🍷
TF11 8RY ☎ 01952 691123 📠 01952 691660
In the owners' own words, 'a large contemporary eatery in a refurbished traditional pub', very popular particularly for jazz night on Fridays. Customers in the spacious gallery bar can look down on the blue glass mosaic-tiled bar below. The Earl of Bradford owns it - the family seat is Weston Park down the road. A stylish, modern approach mixes old favourites such as faggots, mushy peas and mash, with monkfish and salmon kebab, chickpea and spinach curry, and Cajun-spiced chicken salad.
OPEN: 11-11 (Sun 12-10.30) Closed: 25 Dec **BAR MEALS:** L served all week 12-2.30 D served all week 6-9.45 Av main course £9 **RESTAURANT:** L served all week 12-2.30 D served all week 6-9.45 Av 3 course à la carte £20 **BREWERY/COMPANY:** Free House 🍺: Banks's, Boddingtons, Flowers Original. 🍷: 8 **FACILITIES:** Children welcome Garden: Large grassed area **NOTES:** Parking 100

WHITCHURCH   Map 15 SJ54

The Horse & Jockey 🍴
Church St SY13 1LB ☎ 01948 664902 📠 01948 664902
e-mail: andy.thelwell@onmail.co.uk
Dir: In town centre next to church

This coaching inn was built on Roman ruins and extended between the 17th and 19th centuries. Inside you'll find

continued

England

WHITCHURCH continued

exposed beams, an open fire and a menu that runs to over 40 home-cooked dishes. Choices range from snacks, sandwiches and pizzas to traditional dishes with chips and an eclectic selection of main courses: cannelloni, curry, paella, Mexican chicken casserole and roasted rack of lamb with port and rosemary sauce are just a few.
OPEN: 11.30-2.30 6-11 **BAR MEALS:** L served Tues-Sun 11.30-2.30 D served Tues-Sun 6-10 Av main course £4.95 **RESTAURANT:** L served Tues-Sun 11.30-2.30 D served Tues-Sun 6-10 Av 3 course à la carte £16.45 **BREWERY/COMPANY:** Pubmaster 🍺: Interbrew Worthington, Scottish Courage John Smith's. **FACILITIES:** Children welcome Garden: Patio and grassed area, with wooden benches **NOTES:** Parking 10

Willey Moor Lock Tavern ♀
Tarporley Rd SY13 4HF ☎ 01948 663274
Dir: 2m N of Whitchurch on A49 (Warrington/Tarporley)
A former lock keeper's cottage idyllically situated beside the Llangollen Canal. Mrs Elsie Gilkes has been licensee here for some 25 years. Low-beamed rooms are hung with a novel teapot collection, there are open log fires and a range of real ales. Deep-fried fish and a choice of grills rub shoulders with traditional steak pie, chicken curry and vegetable chilli. Other options include salad platters, children's choices and gold rush pie for dessert.
OPEN: 12-2.30 6-11 (Sun 12-2.30 7-10.30) Closed: 25 Dec
BAR MEALS: L served all week 12-2 D served all week 6-9 Av main course £5.50 **RESTAURANT:** L served all week 12-2 D served all week 7-9.30 **BREWERY/COMPANY:** Free House 🍺: Guest Ales, Abbeydale, Moonshine, Westwood. **FACILITIES:** Children welcome Garden: Beside canal, enclosed play area **NOTES:** Parking 50 **NOTES:** No credit cards

WOORE   Map 15 SJ74

Swan at Woore 🍴 ♀
Nantwich Rd CW3 9SA ☎ 01630 647220
Dir: A51 Stone to Nantwich road 10 miles from Nantwich in the village of Woore which is between Stone and Nantwich

Refurbished 19th-century dining inn by the A51 near Stapley Water Gardens. Four separate eating areas lead off from a central servery. Daily specials boards supplement the menu, which might include crispy confit of duck, slow roast knuckle of lamb, roasted salmon on vegetable linguine, or red onion and garlic 'tarte Tatin'. There's a separate fish menu - grilled red mullet fillets, perhaps, or seared tuna on roasted sweet peppers.
OPEN: 12-3 5-11 **BAR MEALS:** L served all week 12-2.15 D served all week 7-9.15 Av main course £8 **RESTAURANT:** L served all week 12-2.15 D served all week 6.30-9.15 Av 3 course à la carte £14.50

continued

BREWERY/COMPANY: Inn Partnership 🍺: Marston's Pedigree, Boddingtons, John Smiths. **FACILITIES:** Children welcome Garden: Food served outside, Small lawn Dogs allowed **NOTES:** Parking 40

WORFIELD   Map 10 SO79

The Dog Inn & Davenport Arms 🍴
Main St WV15 5LF ☎ 01746 716020 📠 01746 716050
e-mail: thedog@tinyworld.co.uk
Dir: On the Wolverhampton road turn L opposite the Wheel pub over the bridge and turn R in to the village of Worfield. The Dog is on the L. Tourist signs on the A454 & A442
The Dog is an ancient pub nestling in a picturesque village of handsome houses close to the River Worfe. The list of licensees near the entrance dates back to 1820. Spick-and-span with a tiled floor and light pine furnishings inside, it offers tip-top Butcher's Ales (brewed at the Munslow Arms) and a short menu listing home-cooked dishes. Choose from a varied menu that offers dishes such as pasta da casa, country vegetable and mixed bean casserole, lamb chops, baby squid in Mediterranean tomato, classic lobster thermidor, or oven-roasted chicken breast.
OPEN: 12-2.30 7-11 **BAR MEALS:** L served all week 12-2 D served all week 7-9.30 **RESTAURANT:** L served all week 12-2 D served all week 7-9.30 **BREWERY/COMPANY:** Free House 🍺: Courage Directors, Wells Bombardier, Highgate Mild, Courage Best.
FACILITIES: Children welcome Children's licence Garden: Dogs allowed **NOTES:** Parking 8

SOMERSET

APPLEY   Map 03 ST02

Pick of the Pubs

The Globe Inn 🍴
TA21 0HJ ☎ 01823 672327
Dir: From M5 J6 take A38 towards Exeter. Village signposted in 5m
Despite being a bit off the beaten track down tortuous lanes, this one's well worth a visit. The rambling 500-year-old slate-and-cob-built pub stands in glorious countryside criss-crossed with signed footpaths. Its four rooms are warmed by inglenook fires, making it the perfect place to finish an energetic walk (or just a drive!). Each room has its own themed memorabilia: Corgi and Dinky cars, for example, or Titanic memorabilia. The extensive choice of food includes blackboard specials (perhaps grilled tuna with lime or lamb stew in Yorkshire pudding) and a menu that offers plenty of options for vegetarians, children and fish lovers as well as traditional pub food such as steak and chips or steak and kidney pie. Look out for novel desserts such as Terry's Chocolate Orange crêpe with ice cream, washed down perhaps with a pint of Cotleigh ale.
OPEN: 11-3 6.30-11 (closed Mon) **BAR MEALS:** L served Tue-Sun 12-2 D served Tue-Sun 7-10 Av main course £9
RESTAURANT: L served Tue-Sun D served Tue-Sun 7-10 Av 3 course à la carte £25 **BREWERY/COMPANY:** Free House 🍺: Cotleigh Tawny, Palmers IPA, Palmers 200 & other Cotleigh Ales. **FACILITIES:** Children welcome Garden: Large garden overlooking countryside Dogs allowed Garden only **NOTES:** Parking 30

◆ **Diamond rating for inspected guest accommodation**

The Fountain Inn

Explore the magnificent Mendips on this glorious country walk.

From the pub turn into Vicar's Close and make for a narrow alleyway and some steps at the top. Turn right at the road and then left into College Road. Follow it to the A39.

Turn right and swing left into Walcombe Lane, passing Walcombe Farmhouse. Keep right at the fork and then turn right at the next junction. Take the bridleway on the right, further up the hill. Follow the sunken woodland path and turn sharp right at a junction, following the path along the grassy slopes and round to the right by a footpath sign. Keep to the hedgerow on the right and head for an intersection of tracks further down.

Turn left, pass Pen Hill Farm and continue ahead on the tarmac track. Pass a house called Gollege and continue to a T junction. Turn left and walk along to the A39. Cross over by a cottage, turn right and follow the path down the field boundary to a gate. Keep ahead along the woodland edge with a stream on the right. Cross a footbridge and follow the path just outside the trees. Re-enter the woodland and ascend the grassy slope to a seat.

Turn right here and keep a house on the left. Follow the grassy path to a stile. Cross the field, keeping to the left perimeter. Avoid the first stile and cross the second. Turn right and skirt the field to a kissing gate. Follow stone steps down through trees to a stream and cross a stone bridge.

Go over the junction and uphill, signposted Hawkers Lane. On reaching the field

THE FOUNTAIN INN, WELLS
1 St Thomas Street BA5 2UU
☎ 01749 672317
Directions: City centre, at junc of A371 & B3139
Close to the cathedral, an inn with a good reputation for food and wine, as well as locally-brewed and other ales. Unpretentious ground floor bar with fires, and an upstairs restaurant where a more sophisticated menu is served.
Open: 10.30-2.30 6-11 (Sun 12-3 7-10.30)
Bar Meals: 12-2.30 6-10
Notes: Children welcome. Parking. (See page 426 for full entry)

edge, keep left to a stile and cut through trees and alongside a fence. Pass through a wrought iron kissing gate and continue ahead in the field. Pass a gate on the right and follow the path as it curves left in line with the boundary. Walk down towards some houses and reach the road. Turn left and cut through the housing estate to the B3139. Turn right here and return to the centre of Wells.

DISTANCE: 6 miles/9.7km
MAP: OS Explorer 141
TERRAIN: Rolling Mendip country – rolling hills and wooded combes
PATHS: Roads, bridleways and paths
GRADIENT: Some moderate climbing

Walk submitted and checked by Nick Channer

ASHCOTT
Map 04 ST43

Ashcott Inn ♀
50 Bath Rd TA7 9QQ ☎ 01458 210282 ▤ 01458 210282
Dir: M5 J23 follow signs for A39 to Glastonbury
Dating back to the 16th century, this former coaching inn has an attractive bar with beams and stripped stone walls, as well as quaint old seats and an assortment of oak and elm tables. Outside is a popular terrace and a delightful walled garden. A straighforward menu offers 'Home Favourites' such as Cumberland sausages, pasta carbonara, Spanish omelette and steak baguette, while poultry and seafood choices include chicken provençale, tuna steak with salad, or chicken tikka masala. Vegetarians may enjoy mushroom Stroganoff with gherkins and capers, or Stilton and walnut salad.
OPEN: 11-11 **BAR MEALS:** L served all week 12-2.45 D served all week 5.30-9.30 Av main course £5 **RESTAURANT:** L served all week 12-2.45 D served all week 5.30-9.30
BREWERY/COMPANY: Heavitree ◀: Otter. ♀: 12
FACILITIES: Children welcome Garden: Large seclude area, shaded with large trees **NOTES:** Parking 50

Ring O Bells 🐑 ♀
High St TA7 9PZ ☎ 01458 210232 ▤ 01458 210880
e-mail: info@ringobells.com
Dir: From M5 follow signs A39 & Glastonbury, turn north off A39 at post office, follow signs to church and village hall
Traditional village pub, recipient of many awards for its quality ales, good food, and friendly service. A pleasant blend of original 18th-century building and modern function room and skittle alley. Fresh local ingredients go into typical blackboard specials like Yorkshire pudding filled with steak and kidney, and Mexican tortilla stuffed with spicy vegetables in peanut sauce. An interesting collection of old bells and horse brasses. Brave drinkers may care to sample Somerset Rough cider.
OPEN: 12-3 7-11 (Sun 7-10.30) Closed: 25 Dec **BAR MEALS:** L served all week 12-2.30 D served all week 7-10 Av main course £6 **RESTAURANT:** L served all week 12-2.30 D served all week 7-10 Av 3 course à la carte £12 **BREWERY/COMPANY:** Free House
◀: Regular & Variety Guest Ales & Beers. ♀: 7
FACILITIES: Children welcome Garden: Large, safe, enclosed garden, grass, patio **NOTES:** Parking 25

ASHILL
Map 04 ST31

Square & Compass 🐑
Windmill Hill TA19 9NX ☎ 01823 480467
Dir: Turn off A358 at Stewley Cross service station (Ashill). 1m along Wood Road, behind service station
Beautifully located overlooking the Blackdown Hills in the heart of rural Somerset, a traditional country pub with a warm, friendly atmosphere. Lovely gardens make the most of the views, and the refurbished bar area features hand-made settles and tables. Very extensive choice of food includes pasta, steaks, fish such as breaded plaice, battered cod, and seafood crêpes, and specials like tenderloin of pork with an apple and cider sauce, or cauliflower cheese topped with mushrooms or bacon. A good range of West Country ales. As the pub is often busy, booking a table is recommended.
OPEN: 12-2.30 6.30-11 (Sun 7-11) Tues-Thur Closed lunchtime **BAR MEALS:** L served all week 12-2.30 D served all week 7-10 Av main course £9.50 **BREWERY/COMPANY:** Free House
◀: Exmoor Ale & Gold Moor Withy Cutter, Wadworth 6X, Branscombe Bitter. **FACILITIES:** Children welcome Garden: patio area, amazing views Dogs allowed **NOTES:** Parking 30

AXBRIDGE
Map 04 ST45

Lamb Inn 🐑
The Square BS26 2AP ☎ 01934 732253 ▤ 01934 733821
Rambling, 15th-century town-centre inn, once the guildhall and licensed only since 1830. On the other side of the square where it stands is King John's hunting lodge. Comfortable bars have log fires, and there's a skittle alley and large terraced garden. On the menu are beef and Butcombe pie, lamb shank, smoked haddock and trout, salmon, scampi, plaice, Aberdeen Angus burger, and local award-winning sausages and mash. Good range of Butcombe and guest ales, and farm ciders.
OPEN: 11.30-11 (Mon-Wed, 11.30-3, 6-11) **BAR MEALS:** L served all week 12-2.30 D served Sun-Fri 6.30-9.30 Av main course £6.50
BREWERY/COMPANY: ◀: Butcombe, Butcombe Gold, Guest Beers. **FACILITIES:** Garden: Patio at front of pub, landscaped garden Dogs allowed **ROOMS:** 2 bedrooms 2 en suite s£30 d£40 (♦♦♦) no children overnight

The Oak House ♀
The Square BS26 2AP ☎ 01934 732444 ▤ 01934 733112
Dir: From M5 J22, take A38 to Bristol. Turn onto A371 to Cheddar/Wells, then L at Axbridge. Town centre
Parts of the house date back to the 11th century, with exposed beams, massive inglenook fireplaces and an ancient well linked to the Cheddar Caverns. The bar is small and intimate, while in the bistro food is served in an informal atmosphere. Sirloin and gammon steaks, Cumberland sausages and Cajun chicken share the menu with 'family favourites' comprising fisherman's pie, pork and cider casserole, leek and potato bake and specials on the chalkboard.
OPEN: 12-3 6.30-11 **BAR MEALS:** L served all week 12-2.30 D served all week 6.30-9.30 Av main course £7.95 **RESTAURANT:** 12-3 7-9 Av 3 course à la carte £10.95
BREWERY/COMPANY: ◀: Fullers London Pride, Bombadier, Bass.
FACILITIES: Children welcome

BATH
Map 04 ST76

The Old Green Tree ♀
12 Green St BA1 2JZ ☎ 01225 448259
Dir: Town centre
18th-century, three-roomed, oak-panelled pub, loved for its faded splendour, dim and atmospheric interior and a front room decorated with World War II Spitfires. Menus include basic pub fare - soup, bangers and mash ('probably the best sausages in Bath'), rolls and salads, steak and ale pie, and the more exotic roasted vegetable risotto with melted Brie. Often six or seven local real ales are served, along with German lager, local cider, and an array of malts, wines and good coffee.
OPEN: 11-11 (Sun 12-10.30) Closed: 25-26 Dec, 1 Jan
BAR MEALS: L served Mon-Sun 12-2.45 Av main course £5.50
BREWERY/COMPANY: Phoenix Inns ◀: Bench Mark, Brand Oak Bitter, Pitchfork, Mr Perrretts Stout. **FACILITIES:** Dogs allowed (manager's discretion only) **NOTES:** No credit cards

Pack Horse Inn 🐑
Hods Hill, South Stoke BA2 7DU
☎ 01225 832060 ▤ 01225 830075
Dir: 2.5m from Bath city centre, via the A367(A37). Turn onto B3110 towards Frome. South Stoke turning on R.
The pub, dating from 1489, was built by monks to provide shelter for pilgrims and travellers, and still has the original bar and inglenook. It is known locally for its traditional ciders and good choice of food - 33 main courses, half a dozen of them vegetarian. Favourites are pork and cider, beef and ale, and

continued

sherry chicken. Views from the garden take in rolling Somerset countryside, and there are some lovely local walks.
OPEN: 11.30-2.30 6-11 (Sun all day) **BAR MEALS:** L served all week 12-2 D served Tues-Sat 6-9 Av main course £7.95
BREWERY/COMPANY: Ushers Best, Scottish Courage Courage Best, Wadworth 6X. **FACILITIES:** Children welcome Children's licence Garden: Country garden overlooking countryside Dogs allowed Water

Richmond Arms
7 Richmond Place BA1 5PZ ☎ 01225 316725
e-mail: cunifletch@aol.com
A mile from the city centre in a long Georgian terrace with a south-facing garden, the pub has been sympathetically refurbished. The light interior has varnished wood floors, yellow walls, a zinc-topped bar, and Asian artefacts. Attention turns rapidly to inventive food with a mix of Asian and Mediterranean influences: spicy Indonesian style king prawns, Thai pork red curry, roast guinea fowl with Puy lentils, tagliatelle with smoked salmon and rocket, and warm squid salad.
OPEN: 12-3 6-11 **BAR MEALS:** L served Tue-Sat 12-2 D served Tue-Sat 6-8.30 Av main course £10.50
BREWERY/COMPANY: Interbrew Bass, Butcombe, Scottish Courage Courage Best. 10 **FACILITIES:** Garden: Peaceful, seats around 30 Dogs allowed Only on Mon & Sun when no food
NOTES: No credit cards

BECKINGTON   Map 04 ST85

Pick of the Pubs

Woolpack Inn
BA11 6SP ☎ 01373 831244 🖹 01373 831223
Dir: Just off A36 near junction with A361
Relaxing 16th-century coaching inn featuring an attractive, flagstoned bar and various cosy dining areas. Noted locally for good food, the wide range of freshly-prepared dishes may include pan-fried calamari with almonds and saffron, crab cakes with red Thai curry sauce, sea bass on squid with Parma ham, pan-fried pork fillet with roast baby sweet potatoes and Drambuie reduction, and caramelised pear mille feuille with coffee and caramel sauce.
OPEN: 11-11 (Sun 12-10.30) **BAR MEALS:** L served all week 12-2.30 Av main course £7 **RESTAURANT:** L served all week 12-2.30 D served all week 6.30-9.30
BREWERY/COMPANY: Old English Inns Greene King IPA, Old Speckled Hen, Abbots Ale & Guest. **FACILITIES:** Dogs allowed

BLAGDON   Map 04 ST55

The New Inn
Church St BS40 7SB ☎ 01761 462475 🖹 01761 463523
e-mail: the.new-inn@virgin.net
Dir: From Bristol take A38 S then A368 towards Bath
Open fires, traditional home-cooked food, and magnificent views across fields to Blagdon Lake are among the attractions at this welcoming 17th-century inn, tucked away near the church. A hearty pub food menu offers lamb chops, Mexican chilli, battered cod and chips, grilled rainbow trout, chicken curry, and a selection of filled rolls, jacket potatoes, ploughman's and basket meals.
OPEN: 11.30-2.30 7-10.30 (times vary, contact for details)
BAR MEALS: L served all week 12-2 D served all week 7-9 Av main course £7.25 **BREWERY/COMPANY:** Wadworth Wadworth 6X, Henry's IPA & Butcombe Best. **FACILITIES:** Children welcome Garden: Food served outside. Picnic benches Dogs allowed In the garden only **NOTES:** Parking 40

BRADFORD-ON-TONE   Map 04 ST12

White Horse Inn
TA4 1HF ☎ 01823 461239 🖹 01823 461872
Dir: N of A38 between Taunton & Wellington
A stone-built country pub, the White Horse is situated in the centre of the village opposite the church. Expect a friendly welcome and good value food, including bar snacks, a restaurant menu (also available in the bar) and daily specials from the blackboard. Favourites are salmon fishcakes, half shoulder of lamb with redcurrant jus, chicken stuffed with smoked cheese, and venison with port and redcurrant.
OPEN: 11.30-3.00 5.30-11 (Summer Sat-Sun open all day)
BAR MEALS: L served all week 12-2 D served Mon-Sun 6.30-9.30 Av main course £9 **RESTAURANT:** L served all week 12-2 D served all week 6.30-9.30 Av 3 course à la carte £18
BREWERY/COMPANY: Enterprise Inns Butcombe Bitter, Marston's Pedigree, Cotleigh Tawney, Scottish Courage John Smith's. **FACILITIES:** Garden: Large, neat garden Dogs allowed **NOTES:** Parking 20

BRUTON   Map 04 ST63

The Claire De Lune
2-4 High St BA10 0AA ☎ 01749 813395 🖹 01749 813395
e-mail: drew.beard@virgin.net
Dir: 6 miles off the A303 on the B3081, situated on the eastern end of Bruton High St
A press feature on the filming of 'Chocolat' rated this 500-year-old, double-fronted bar, bistro and restaurant with rooms as 'the' place to stay in the locality. From a sample, daily-revised dinner menu comes panaché of lobster tail and shrimp with garlic and lime butter glaze, Moroccan-style chicken with spicy soup and couscous, and Swiss raclette on new potatoes, with tomato and red onion salad. Among the desserts, apple cobbler with Calvados custard.
OPEN: 11-2 7-11 Closed: 1 Jan-31 Jan **BAR MEALS:** L served Fri 12-2 D served Tue-Sat 7-9 **RESTAURANT:** L served Tue-Sun 12-2 D served Tue-Sat 7-9 Av 3 course fixed price £19.95
BREWERY/COMPANY: Free House **FACILITIES:** Garden: Roof garden. Views of Dovecote etc **ROOMS:** 3 bedrooms 3 en suite s£35 d£55 no children overnight

> **The Rosette is the AA award for food. Look out for it next to a pub's name.**

England

BUTLEIGH
Map 04 ST53

The Rose & Portcullis
Sub Rd BA6 8TQ ☎ 01458 850287 ▤ 01458 850120
Dir: Telephone for directions

A 16th-century free house, drawing its name from the local lord of the manor's coat of arms. Thatched bars and an inglenook fireplace are prominent features of the cosy interior. Large bar and dining room menus are on offer daily. Typical hot food choices include omelettes, burgers, fish, curry, steaks, hot baguettes, jacket potatoes, ploughman's, salads, and vegetarian choices.
OPEN: 12-3 6-11 **BAR MEALS:** 12-2 7-9 **RESTAURANT:** 12-2 7-9 **BREWERY/COMPANY:** Free House ◀: Interbrew Flowers IPA, Butcombe Bitter, Wadworth 6X. **FACILITIES:** Children welcome Garden: Dogs allowed **NOTES:** Parking 50

CASTLE CARY
Map 04 ST63

The George Hotel ★★ ⏑
Market Place BA7 7AH ☎ 01963 350761 ▤ 01963 350035
e-mail: sarslou@aol.com
Dir: From A303 take A371 at Wincanton, then N to Castle Cary

Built of stone and thatch, this lovely 16th-century inn blends perfectly into this pretty, historic market town. It offers spacious bedrooms and cosy bars. An imaginative range of dishes is available, making good use of fresh local produce, and may include Hunter's chicken, poached swordfish steak, prawn and cream cheese cannelloni, and sirloin steak.
OPEN: 11-11 **BAR MEALS:** L served all week 12-10 D served all week 5.30-10 **RESTAURANT:** L served all week 12-5.30 D served all week 5.30-10.00 Av 3 course à la carte £15
BREWERY/COMPANY: Old English Inns ◀: Greene King IPA, Ruddles County & Abbot Ales. ⏑: 10 **FACILITIES:** Children welcome Dogs allowed **NOTES:** Parking 10 **ROOMS:** 14 bedrooms 14 en suite 2 family rooms s£40 d£60

Horse Pond Inn ♦♦♦
The Triangle BA7 7BD ☎ 01963 350318 ▤ 01963 351764
e-mail: horsepondinn@aol.com

Modernised and extended 16th-century inn, with en suite motel-style accommodation, situated in the historic country town of Castle Cary. Comfortable bar offering a range of real ales and an extensive menu of traditional pub food. For a lighter meal choose from omelettes, salads, jacket potatoes, or sandwiches. More substantial main courses include chicken Kiev, sweet and sour pork in batter with noodles and onions, sole filled with scallops and crabmeat, Thai vegetable curry, and a variety of pies.
OPEN: 10.30-11.00pm (Sun 12-3, 7-10.30) **BAR MEALS:** L served all week 12-2 D served Tue-Sun 7-9 Av main course £5.50
RESTAURANT: L served D served all week 7-9 Av 3 course à la carte £12 **BREWERY/COMPANY:** Free House ◀: Scottish Courage Courage Best, Directors, John Smiths, Greene King Ruddles Best. **FACILITIES:** Children welcome Garden: Lawn, wishing well, seating area Dogs allowed Water **NOTES:** Parking 28 **ROOMS:** 5 bedrooms 5 en suite 2 family rooms s£35 d£50

CHEW MAGNA
Map 04 ST56

Pony & Trap ⏑
Newtown BS40 8TQ ☎ 01275 332627
Refurbished 200-year-old rural pub enjoying a peaceful hillside location with beautiful views across the Chew Valley from the rear garden. Good informal pubby atmosphere, a warm welcome and traditional home-cooked food await in the bar. Typical dishes range from beef casserole, fish pie, and chicken and mushroom pie, to salmon in white wine sauce, and fillet steak.
OPEN: 11-3 7-11 **BAR MEALS:** L served all week 12-2 D served all week 7-9.30 Av main course £8.50 **RESTAURANT:** L served all week 12-2 D served all week 7-9.30 **BREWERY/COMPANY:** Ushers ◀: Ushers Best, Butcombe Bitter. **FACILITIES:** Children welcome Garden: Terraced area overlooking garden and valley Dogs allowed **NOTES:** Parking 50

CHURCHINFORD
Map 04 ST21

The York Inn 🍴
Honiton Rd TA3 7RF ☎ 01823 601333
Dir: Exit M5 J26, towards Wellington for 0.5m, 1st L at rdbt. 1m L onto Ford St, 2m at top of hill 2m phone box, R to Inn
Traditional inn with beams and an inglenook fireplace, dating from around 1600 and located in an Area of Outstanding Natural Beauty. There is a lively locals' bar and a separate dining room, but the same menu is served throughout. Options include mussels, steak and ale pie, sausage and mash, and bubble and squeak. New management plan to continue the York Inn's high standards of traditional village hostelry.

continued

OPEN: 12-3 5-11 Mon Closed Morning **BAR MEALS:** L served all week 12-3 D served Mon-Sat 6-9.30 Av main course £8.75 **RESTAURANT:** L served all week 12-3 D served Mon-Sat 6-11 Av 3 course à la carte £20 **BREWERY/COMPANY:** Enterprise Inns ◀: Otter Bitter, Guest Ales. **FACILITIES:** Children welcome Garden: Outside patio Dogs allowed **NOTES:** Parking 12

CLAPTON-IN-GORDANO   Map 04 ST47

The Black Horse
Clevedon Ln BS20 7RH ☎ 01275 842105

Built in the 14th century, a genuinely unspoilt, traditional country inn with flagstone floors, wooden settles and a large open fireplace. For a while it housed village miscreants, and one window still has prison bars on it. Simple bar food includes various ploughman's, hot filled baguettes, chilli and homemade soups. There is a large beer garden with a children's play area. From the cask come Smiles Best, Fuller's London Pride, Courage Best and ciders.
OPEN: 11-3 5-11 (All day Fri-Sat) **BAR MEALS:** L served Mon-Sat 12-2 Av main course £4.50 **BREWERY/COMPANY:** ◀: Scottish Courage Courage Best, Smiles Best, Interbrew Bass, Fuller's London Pride. **FACILITIES:** Children welcome Garden: Lrg garden, patio Dogs allowed **NOTES:** Parking 40 **NOTES:** No credit cards

---

CLUTTON   Map 04 ST65

The Hunters Rest ◆◆◆◆ 🕭 ♀
King Ln, Clutton Hill BS39 5QL ☎ 01761 452303 ▤ 01761 453308
e-mail: info@huntersrest.co.uk
Dir: Follow signs for Wells A37 go through village of Pensford until large rdbt turn L towards Bath after 100 meters turn R into country lane pub 1m up hill

This inn, built as a hunting lodge for the Earl of Warwick around 1750, later became a smallholding and tavern for the local north Somerset coal-mining community. The coal is long gone and the new clientele can now expect starters of breaded Somerset Brie, Hunter's Smoky, or Norwegian prawn

continued

cocktail, progress to Hunters 'Oggies' (giant filled pasties), grills and Somerset faggots. Comfortable en suite bedrooms are on the pub's upper floor.
OPEN: 11.30-3 6.30-11 (All day Sun) **BAR MEALS:** L served all week 12-2 D served all week 6.30-9.45 Av main course £8 **RESTAURANT:** L served all week D served all week Av 3 course à la carte £20 **BREWERY/COMPANY:** Free House ◀: Interbrew Bass, Smiles Best, Exmoor Ale, Wadworth 6X. ♀: 10 **FACILITIES:** Children welcome Garden: Lrg landscaped areas with country views Dogs allowed Water **NOTES:** Parking 80 **ROOMS:** 4 bedrooms 4 en suite s£60 d£80

COMBE HAY   Map 04 ST75

Pick of the Pubs

The Wheatsheaf ◆◆◆◆ 🕭
BA2 7EG ☎ 01225 833504 ▤ 01225 833504
e-mail: jakica@btclick.com
Dir: Take A369 Exeter rd from Bath to Odd Down, turn L at park towards Combe Hay. Follow lane for approx 2m to thatched cottage & turn L
Nestling on a hillside overlooking a peaceful valley, 2 miles south of Bath off the A367, the 17th-century Wheatsheaf is a pretty black and white timbered pub, adorned with flowers in summer, and featuring an attractively-landscaped terraced garden, an ideal spot for summer imbibing. The unspoilt character of the rambling bar has been maintained, with massive solid wooden tables, sporting prints and open log fire. Food on the varied carte features home-cooked dishes, notably local game in season and fresh fish. Typical choices may include ploughman's lunches, terrines, and locally-caught trout, in addition to roast rack of lamb, breast of pheasant stuffed with cream cheese, mushrooms and garlic, and chicken filled with crab and prawns and wrapped in bacon. Comfortable overnight accommodation in a converted stable block.
OPEN: 11-2.30 6-10.30 (Sun 12-3, 7-10.30) Closed: 25-26 Dec, Jan 1 **BAR MEALS:** L served all week 12-2.30 D served all week 6.30-9.30 **RESTAURANT:** L served all week 12-2 D served all week 6.30-9.30 **BREWERY/COMPANY:** Free House ◀: Courage Best, John Smith, Old Speckled Hen. **FACILITIES:** Children welcome Garden: Dogs allowed on leads **NOTES:** Parking 100 **ROOMS:** 3 bedrooms 3 en suite 1 family rooms s£55 d£80

COMPTON MARTIN   Map 04 ST55

Ring of Bells
Main St BS40 6JE ☎ 01761 221284
e-mail: roger@ring47.freeserve.co.uk
Village pub with views of the Mendip Hills and the coast, with rugs on flagstone floors, and inglenook seats beside the log fire. Family-friendly landlord and staff, serving good ales (Butcombe) along with bar food and daily specials using local produce.
OPEN: 11.30-3 6.30-11 **BAR MEALS:** L served all week 12.30-2 D served all week 7-9 Av main course £4 ◀: Butcombe Bitter, Abbot Ale, plus guest beers. **FACILITIES:** Children welcome Dogs allowed **NOTES:** No credit cards

---

◆ **Diamond rating for inspected guest accommodation**

CRANMORE

Map 04 ST64

Strode Arms ♀
BA4 4QJ ☎ 01749 880450 ▤ 01749 880823
Dir: *S of A361, 3.5m E of Shepton Mallet, 7.5m W of Frome*
Rambling, mostly 15th-century building, formerly a farmhouse and coaching inn, with a splendid front terrace overlooking the village duck pond. Spacious bar areas are neatly laid-out with comfortable country furnishings and warmed by open log fires. Both the varied printed menu and daily specials draw local diners and visitors to the nearby East Somerset Railway. From the board order, perhaps, smoked haddock and cod fishcakes, peppered rib of beef with a shallot and red wine sauce, braised lambs' heart with lemon and lime stuffing and, for pudding, a home-made coconut and orange tart.
OPEN: 11.30-2.30 6-11.30 (Sun 12-3, 7-10.30) Oct-Mar closed Sun evening **BAR MEALS:** L served all week 12-2 D served Mon-Sat 7-9.30 Av main course £8 **RESTAURANT:** L served all week 12-2 D served Mon-Sat 7-9.30 Av 3 course à la carte £13.50
BREWERY/COMPANY: Wadworth ■: Henry's IPA, Wadworth 6X, JCB. **FACILITIES:** Children welcome Garden: Beer garden, patio, outdoor eating Dogs allowed **NOTES:** Parking 24

CREWKERNE

Map 04 ST40

The Manor Arms ♦♦♦ 🐾 ♀
North Perrott TA18 7SG ☎ 01460 72901 ▤ 01460 72901
Dir: *From A30 (Yeovil/Honiton rd) take A3066 towards Bridport, N Perrott 1.5m further on*

On the Dorset-Somerset border, this 16th-century Grade II listed pub and its neighbouring hamstone cottages overlook the village green. The popular River Parrett trail runs by the door. The inn has been lovingly restored and an inglenook fireplace, flagstone floors and oak beams are among the charming features inside. Bar food includes fillet steak medallions, pan-fried whole plaice, shank of lamb, and chicken supreme. Most of the bedrooms are located in a converted coach house.
OPEN: 11.30-2.30 6.45-11.00 (Sun 12-2.30 7-10.30) **BAR MEALS:** L served all week 12-1.45 D served all week 7-9 Av main course £5.50 **RESTAURANT:** L served all week 12-1.45 D served all week 7-9 Av 3 course à la carte £16 **BREWERY/COMPANY:** Free House ■: Butcombe, Otter. ♀: 7 **FACILITIES:** Children welcome Garden: Secluded, lawn, Lrg wooden tables **NOTES:** Parking 20 **ROOMS:** 8 bedrooms 8 en suite 1 family rooms s£42 d£54

CROSCOMBE

Map 04 ST54

The Bull Terrier ♦♦♦ 🐾
Long St BA5 3QJ ☎ 01749 343658
e-mail: barry.vidler@bullterrierpub.co.uk
Dir: *half way between Wells & Shepton Mallet on the A371*
One of Somerset's oldest pubs, formerly the Rose & Crown, first licensed in 1612. The building dates from the late 15th century, though the fireplace and ceiling in the inglenook bar were added in the 16th century. One menu is offered throughout, including steak and kidney pie, fresh trout and almonds, mushroom and cashew pasta, and English lamb steak.
OPEN: 12-2.30 7-11 (Sun 12-2.30, 7-10.30) Oct 1-31 March Closed Mon **BAR MEALS:** L served all week 12-2 D served all week 7-9 Av main course £6.25 **RESTAURANT:** L served all week 12-2 D served all week 7-9 Av 3 course à la carte £11.75
BREWERY/COMPANY: Free House ■: Butcombe, Courage Directors, Marston's Pedigree, Greene King Old Speckled Hen. **FACILITIES:** Garden: Patio, walled garden Dogs allowed Water bowls **NOTES:** Parking 3 **ROOMS:** 2 bedrooms 2 en suite s£30 d£50 no children overnight

CROWCOMBE

Map 03 ST13

Carew Arms 🐾 NEW
TA4 4AD ☎ 01984 618631
Dir: *Village is 10 miles form both Taunton and Minehead*
Changes are afoot at this free house to make it even more appealing. Local beers, including Exmoor and Otter Ales, accompany hearty meals such as tender belly pork with mashed potatoes, pan-fried lambs' liver and kidneys with grilled bacon, ruby red fillet mignon, and chicken Dolcelatte. Fresh fish choices usually include mussels, king scallops and sea bass. Eat inside or enjoy the views from the garden in summer.
OPEN: 11-3 6-11 **BAR MEALS:** L served all week 12-2.30 D served Mon-Sat 6.30-10 Av main course £10 **RESTAURANT:** L served all week 11 D served Mon-Sat 11 Av 3 course à la carte £18
BREWERY/COMPANY: Free House ■: Exmoor Ale, Otter Ale, Bishops Tipple, Worthington. **FACILITIES:** Children welcome Garden: Beautiful garden with countryside views Dogs allowed **NOTES:** Parking 30

DINNINGTON

Map 04 ST41

Dinnington Docks
TA17 8SX ☎ 01460 52397 ▤ 01460 52397
e-mail: hilary@dinningtondocks.co.uk
Dir: *A303 between South Petherton And Ilminster*
Formerly the Rose & Crown, and licensed for over 250 years, this traditional village pub is situated on the old Fosse Way, and has a very relaxed atmosphere and friendly locals. Rail or maritime enthusiasts will enjoy the large collection of memorabilia, and it's an ideal location for cycling and walking. Roast lunch available every day, along with local beers . Channel 4's Time Team used the pub as its base while filming a programme on mosaics found in a nearby field.
OPEN: 11.30-3.30 6-11 **BAR MEALS:** L served all week 12-2.30 D served all week 6-9.30 Av main course £6 **RESTAURANT:** L served all week 12-2.30 D served all week 6-9.30 Av 3 course à la carte £11.50
BREWERY/COMPANY: Free House ■: Butcombe Bitter, Wadworth 6X, Guest Ales. **FACILITIES:** Children welcome Garden: Lrg, children's play area Dogs allowed Water provided **NOTES:** Parking 30

> 🐾 **Pubs offering a good choice of fish on their menu**

DITCHEAT
Map 04 ST63

The Manor House Inn ◆◆◆◆ ♀
BA4 6RB ☎ 01749 860276
e-mail: manorhouseinn@onetel.net.uk
Dir: from Shepton Mallet take the Castle Cary road, after 3m R to Ditcheat

Over the years since its first appearance as The White Hart, this red-brick pub has had a number of names, but the current owners chose to subtitle it "The Heart of Somerset Hospitality." There are flagstone floors, en suite bedrooms in a nearby cottage, and a menu that offers the likes of lamb and mint sausages, grilled calves liver with bacon on bubble and squeak cake, wild mushroom and brandy risotto, and individual aubergine charlotte with spicy vegetable filling. There are also light luncheons, ciabattas, and specials.
OPEN: 12-2.30 6.30-11 (Sun 7-10.30) **BAR MEALS:** L served all week 12-2 D served all week 7-9.30 **RESTAURANT:** L served all week 12-2 D served all week 7-9.30 **BREWERY/COMPANY:** Free House 🍺: Butcombe, Scottish Courage John Smith's & Guest Ales.
FACILITIES: Garden: Dogs allowed Water, toys **NOTES:** Parking 25 **ROOMS:** 3 bedrooms 3 en suite 1 family rooms s£45 d£65 no children overnight

EAST COKER
Map 04 ST51

The Helyar Arms ◆◆◆◆ ♀
Moor Ln BA22 9JR ☎ 01935 862332 🖷 01935 864129
e-mail: info@helyar-arms.co.uk
Dir: from Yeovil, take A30 or A37, follow signs for East Coker

Named after Archdeacon Helyar, a chaplain to Queen Elizabeth I, this Grade II listed country inn and restaurant dates back in part to 1460. Log fires warm the old world bar, while the separate restaurant was restored from an original apple loft. Meals are prepared from fresh market produce covering a wide range of local specialities. En suite bedrooms are furnished to a high standard with period appeal.
OPEN: 11-3 6-11 (Sun 12-3, 6-10.30) **BAR MEALS:** L served all week 12-2 D served all week 7-9 Av main course £7.95

continued

RESTAURANT: L served all week 12-2.30 D served all week 6.30-9.30 Av 3 course à la carte £15 **BREWERY/COMPANY:** Pubmaster 🍺: Bass, Flowers Original, Fullers London Pride. ♀: 20 **FACILITIES:** Children welcome Garden: Grassed area seats 40, BBQ in the summer Dogs allowed **NOTES:** Parking 40 **ROOMS:** 6 bedrooms 6 en suite 3 family rooms s£59 d£70

EXFORD
Map 03 SS83

Pick of the Pubs

The Crown Inn ★★★ 🏨🏨 🐾 ♀
TA24 7PP ☎ 01643 831554 🖷 01643 831665
e-mail: info@crownhotelexmoor.co.uk
Dir: From M5 J25 follow signs for Taunton. Take A358 then B3224 via Wheddon Cross to Exford

R D Blackmore wrote part of Lorna Doone in this charming 16th-century coaching inn in the heart of Exmoor National Park. The book's hero, John Ridd, often 'drank' here. Facing Exford's village green, it has a spacious, mature water and terrace garden at the rear, and there are super views from many of the comfortable, well-equipped bedrooms. The cosy bar, and a smart dining-room set with crisp white table linen, both have imaginative menus drawing fully on local produce. On offer in the bar at lunch or in the evening might be salmon and coriander fishcake, stir-fried duck and egg noodles, and pan-seared salmon, while gourmet meals in the dining room include carpaccio of Exmoor beef, roast breast of guinea fowl with a lime jus, smoked salmon salad, and a selection of cheeses with aged port. More basic dishes, such as sausage and mash, and ham, egg and chips, are available too.
OPEN: 11-3 6-11 **BAR MEALS:** L served all week 12-2 D served all week 6.30-9.30 Av main course £7.50 **RESTAURANT:** L served Sun 12-2 D served all week 7-9 Av 3 course à la carte £25 Av 4 course fixed price £25 **BREWERY/COMPANY:** Free House 🍺: Exmoor Ale, Gold & Stag, Cotleigh Tawny, Guest ales. ♀: 8 **FACILITIES:** Children welcome Garden: Beer garden, next to stream Dogs allowed Water **NOTES:** Parking 20 **ROOMS:** 17 bedrooms 17 en suite 1 family rooms s£55 d£47.50

**Do you have a favourite pub
that we have overlooked?
Please use the Reader's Report form at
the back of this guide to tell us all about it.**

FAULKLAND — Map 04 ST75

The Faulkland Inn
BA3 5UH ☎ 01373 834312
e-mail: enquiries@faulkland-inn.co.uk
Dir: *On the A366 between Radstock and Trowbridge, 17m from Bristol & the M4/M5*

Family-run coaching inn set in a village complete with a green, stocks, standing stones and pond. The style of cooking is unique to the area, with a modern international approach, utilising local fish, game and cheese. Weekly menus range through various platters, pasta, curry and chargrilled steaks in the bar, and restaurant dishes such as noisettes of wild boar, haggis and red onion tart with brandy and peppercorn sauce.
OPEN: 12-3 6-11 (Sun 12-4, 6-10.30) **BAR MEALS:** L served Tue-Sat 12-2 D served Tue-Sat 7-10 Av main course £6 **RESTAURANT:** L served Tue-Sun 12-2 D served Tue-Sat 7-9.30 Av 3 course à la carte £22 **BREWERY/COMPANY:** Free House **🍺:** Bass & guest ales.
FACILITIES: Children welcome Garden: Food served outside
NOTES: Parking 30

Tuckers Grave
Faulkland BA3 5XF ☎ 01373 834230
Tapped ales and farm cider are served at Somerset's smallest pub, a tiny atmospheric bar with old settles. Lunchtime sandwiches and ploughman's lunches are available, and a large lawn with flower borders makes an attractive outdoor seating area.
OPEN: 11-3 **🍺:** Interbrew Bass, Butcombe Bitter.
FACILITIES: Garden: Large lawns with flower borders Dogs allowed Water

FITZHEAD — Map 03 ST12

Fitzhead Inn ♦♦♦ 🛏
TA4 3JP ☎ 01823 400667
Expect a relaxed atmosphere, good real ales - including local varieties - and appetising home-cooked food at this 250-year-old pub hidden away in the Vale of Taunton. One can expect to encounter daily specials such as fillet steak stuffed with Stilton wrapped in smoked bacon, duck breast with confit of roasted shallots, English cod fillet with Cajun spices on a cherry tomato salsa, or fresh Cornish fish mix on a lemon-minted chiffonade. The four bedrooms are all en suite, but note that credit cards are not taken.
OPEN: 12-3 7-11 (Closed Mon-Fri Lunch) Closed: 25-26 Dec
BAR MEALS: L served Sat, Sun 12-2 D served all week 7-9.45 Av main course £9.50 **RESTAURANT:** L served Sat, Sun 12-2 D served all week 7-9.45 Av 3 course à la carte £18
BREWERY/COMPANY: Free House **🍺:** Cotleigh Tawny, Fuller's London Pride, Juwards Ales, Interbrew Bass. **FACILITIES:** Children welcome Garden Dogs allowed **ROOMS:** 4 bedrooms 4 en suite
NOTES: No credit cards

FRESHFORD — Map 04 ST76

The Inn at Freshford 🐑 ♀
BA3 6EG ☎ 01225 722250 📠 01225 723887
e-mail: dwill60632@aol.com
Dir: *1m from A36 between Beckington & Limpley Stoke*
Traditional 17th-century inn with log fires, located in the Limpley Valley. The area is ideal walking country, especially down by the Kennet & Avon Canal, and has extensive gardens. A typical menu includes fresh local trout, salmon with herb crust and cracked black pepper, venison, beef, or pork.
OPEN: 11-3 6-11 **BAR MEALS:** L served all week 12-2 D served all week 6-9 Av main course £9 **RESTAURANT:** L served all week 12-2 D served all week 6-9 **BREWERY/COMPANY:** Latona Leisure
🍺: Wadworth 6X, Marston's Pedigree, Interbrew Bass, Scottish Courage Courage Best. **FACILITIES:** Children welcome Garden: Lrg terraced garden Dogs allowed Water **NOTES:** Parking 60

FROME — Map 04 ST74

Pick of the Pubs

The Horse & Groom 🐑 ♀
East Woodlands BA11 5LY ☎ 01373 462802 📠 01373 462802
e-mail: horse.and.groom@care4free.net
Dir: *Just off Frome by-pass (A361 Shepton Mallet/Devizes rd)*

At the end of a narrow lane, the Jockey, as its regulars know it, began life in the 17th century as a smallholding with pigs and a small dairy. Its familiar name recalls an earlier title - the Horse and Jockey. Customers and staff have had paranormal experiences and all strongly suspect ghosts. Inside, you'll find stone flags, two inglenook fireplaces, stripped pine furniture and a charming conservatory-style restaurant. A huge range of food is served from the bar menu, the restaurant carte and daily specials. Bar snacks and meals include filled baguettes, roasted vegetable tart with Mozzarella, and Yorkshire pudding with roast beef or sausages in onion gravy. A typical meal in the restaurant might be chicken satay with peanut soy dip, Calvados pork fillet with prunes, and hot Scotch pancakes with banana and maple syrup.
OPEN: 11.30-2.30 6.30-11 (Sun 12-3, 7-10) **BAR MEALS:** L served Tue-Sun 12-2 D served Tue-Sat 6.30-9 Av main course £7
RESTAURANT: L served Tue-Sun 12-2 D served Tue-Sat 6.30-9 Av 3 course à la carte £17
BREWERY/COMPANY: **🍺:** Wadworth 6X, Butcombe Bitter, Branscombe Branoc, Brakspear Bitter. **♀:** 7
FACILITIES: Garden: Large garden with fruit trees and 7 tables Dogs allowed Water **NOTES:** Parking 20

England

Pick of the Pubs

The Talbot Inn ◆◆◆◆
Selwood St, Mells BA11 3PN
☎ 01373 812254 📠 01373 813599
e-mail: roger@talbotinn.com

See Pick of the Pubs on page 414

The White Hart
Trudoxhill BA11 5DP ☎ 01373 836324 📠 01373 836566
Dating back to 1623, this popular pub once served as the village hall and during World War II was a dance venue for American GIs based here. Today it attracts locals and visitors alike with good beers and a wide-ranging menu, including chicken and wild mushroom pâté with apple cider marmalade; home-made chicken, bacon and mushroom pie; steamed steak and kidney suet pudding; roast cod on spicy chick peas with crème fraîche; and vegetarian wild rice, spinach and honey roast.
OPEN: 12-3 5.30-11 **BAR MEALS:** L served all week 12-2.30 D served all week 6.30-9.30 **RESTAURANT:** L served all week 12-2.30 6.30-9.30 **BREWERY/COMPANY:** Free House ◀: Butcombe, Hewish IPA, Wadworth 6X. **FACILITIES:** Children welcome Garden: Secluded with play area **NOTES:** Parking 40

GLASTONBURY — Map 04 ST53

The Who'd a Thought It Inn ♀
17 Northload St BA6 9JJ ☎ 01458 834460 📠 01458 831039
e-mail: restaurant@whodathoughtit.co.uk
Dir: Bottom of High St, 100yds from Abbey ruins
A feature of this 18th-century building is its abundant collection of interesting artefacts, memorabilia and local prints. One of the town's ancient wells is situated in the Well Room, with the original hand pump by the front door. There is a good choice of sandwiches, snacks and specials, such as Thai fish cakes, sirloin steak, aubergine bake and lots of popular home-made stews and pies. Outside there is a large patio accommodating 30 people.
OPEN: 11-11 (Sun 12-10.30) Closed: 25 Dec **BAR MEALS:** L served all week 12-2.15 D served all week 5-9.15 Av main course £7.50 **RESTAURANT:** L served all week 12-2.15 D served all week 5.45-9.15 **BREWERY/COMPANY:** Palmers Brewery ◀: Palmers IPA & 200 Premium Ale, Dorset Gold. ♀: 14 **FACILITIES:** Children welcome Garden: Paved patio area with seating for around 30 Dogs allowed Water **NOTES:** Parking 15

HASELBURY PLUCKNETT — Map 04 ST41

Pick of the Pubs

The Haselbury Inn ♀
North St TA18 7RJ ☎ 01460 72488 📠 01460 72488
e-mail: howard@haseleburyinn.fsnet.co.uk
Dir: Just off A30 between Crewkerne & Yeovil on B3066
This extended village inn started life as a rope factory. It now boasts a comfortable bar with exposed stone and brickwork and open fires, and a separate dining room. Circular pub walks details are available from the bar. Food includes great value set lunches, an excellent fresh fish board and main courses that range from steaks and grills to specialities such as thyme baked trio of lamb cutlets with caramelised oranges and lemons. Great British roasts on Sunday are another highlight.

OPEN: 11.45-2.30 6-11 (closed Mon) **BAR MEALS:** L served Tue-Sun 12-2 D served Tue-Sun 6.30-9.30 Av main course £8.95 **RESTAURANT:** L served Tue-Sun 12-2 D served Tue-Sun 6.30-9.30 Av 3 course à la carte £17 Av 2 course fixed price £6.95 **BREWERY/COMPANY:** Free House ◀: Palmers IPA, Otter Ale. ♀: 12 **FACILITIES:** Garden: Picnic tables, cottage garden style **NOTES:** Parking 50

HINTON BLEWETT — Map 04 ST55

Ring O'Bells ♀
BS39 5AN ☎ 01761 452239
e-mail: jonboy2ringer@aol.com
Dir: 11 miles S of Bristol on A37 toward Wells, small road signed in Clutton & Temple Cloud
A 200-year-old pub with a traditional log fire in winter months, and a cosy, warming atmosphere. The pub, which sits on the edge of the Mendips and has good views of the Chew Valley, boasts several sports teams, including cricket, rugby, golf and shove ha'penny. It serves a wide choice of real ales, and concentrates on good value food. Typical dishes include beef in Guinness served in a giant Yorkshire pudding, chicken stuffed with Stilton, and Persian chicken curry.
OPEN: 11-3.30 5-11 (Sat 11-4, 6-11 Sun 12-4, 7-10.30) **BAR MEALS:** L served all week 12-2 D served all week 6.30-10 Av main course £7 **BREWERY/COMPANY:** Free House ◀: Abbey Ales Bellringer, Wadworth 6X, Fuller's London Pride, Wickwar BOB. **FACILITIES:** Children welcome Garden: Enclosed garden with lovely views Dogs allowed Water **NOTES:** Parking 20

HINTON ST GEORGE — Map 04 ST41

The Lord Poulett Arms ◆◆◆◆ ♀
High St TA17 8SE ☎ 01460 73149
Dir: 2m N of Crewkerne, 1.5m S of A303
New owners Michelle Paynton and Stephen Hill are progressively restoring the 17th-century, thatched Ham-stone inn with its pretty garden featuring fruit trees full of mistletoe. Real ales are served from the barrel, and the monthly-changing menu places a strong emphasis on local fresh, seasonal and often organic produce. Choices might include luxury fish pie with a caper rösti topping; venison, port and chestnut casserole; pan-fried trout with bacon, hazelnuts and rocket; and spicy parsnip-topped shepherd's pie.
OPEN: 12-2.30 6.30-11 (Mon 7-10.30) (Sun 12-3.30, 7-10.30) **BAR MEALS:** L served Tue-Sun 12-2 D served Tue-Sat 7-9 **RESTAURANT:** L served Tue-Sun 12-2 D served Tue-Sun 7-9 **BREWERY/COMPANY:** Free House ◀: Butcombe Bitter, Palmers IPA + Changing Guest Beers. ♀: 9 **FACILITIES:** Children welcome Garden: Garden with fruit trees and Poleta wall Dogs allowed Water tap **NOTES:** Parking 10 **ROOMS:** 4 bedrooms 4 en suite 1 family rooms s£28 d£45

continued

OPEN: 12-2.30, 6-11
CLOSED: 25-26 Dec
BAR MEALS: L served all week 12-2.30, D served all week 7-12. Av main course £7.50
RESTAURANT: L served all week 12-2, D served all week 7-9.30. Av cost 3 courses £21
BREWERY/COMPANY: Free House.
🍺: Butcombe Bitter, Fuller's London Pride, Scottish Courage Best Bitter, Smiles, Adnams, Palmers.
FACILITIES: Dogs welcome, Children welcome, Cottage garden.
NOTES: Parking 10.
ROOMS: 8 en suite from s£55 d£75

The Talbot 15th-Century Coaching Inn

According to legend, Little Jack Horner, aka the steward to the Abbot of Glastonbury Abbey, lived next door to this rambling coaching inn. Dating from the 15th-century, it sits at the heart of a timeless feudal village noted for a magnificent manor house, splendid church and several unspoilt cottages made from traditional stone. Built from the same materials, the friendly inn has loads of character and a pleasant, buzzy atmosphere.

◆◆◆◆

Selwood Street, Mells, Frome, BA11 3PN
☎ 01373 812254 🖷 01373 813599
✉ roger@talbotinn.com
Dir: From A36(T), R onto A361 to Frome, then A362 towards Radstock, 0.5m then L to Mells 2.5m

Lots of little stone-flagged and beamed bars and eating areas are charmingly decorated with terracotta-painted walls and country prints. These make a delightful setting for some excellent real ales, and well-planned menus offering reliable home-cooked food. For lunch there are Mediterranean sandwiches made from regional breads and different daily fillings from the blackboard, plus curry of the day with basmati rice and all the trimmings, and various ploughman's (ham, Stilton, Cheddar or pâté). The evening menu picks up the pace with starters like hot individual tomato and mozzarella tartlet, toasted goats' cheese ciabatta drizzled with pesto, and Talbot's fine chicken liver pâté. The main courses are also full of interest, with perhaps fillet of pork on a bed of braised red cabbage, roast best end of lamb with ratatouille and basil sauce, and roast breast of chicken with wild mushrooms and watercress sauce. Fish specials delivered daily from Brixham include roasted cod fillet with a mussel, saffron and chive sauce, and poached skate wing with nut-brown butter. From the chargrill comes a selection of steaks with choice of sauce. For those who want the evening to go on and on, there is well-furnished and comfortable accommodation.

ILCHESTER
Map 04 ST52

Ilchester Arms 🛏 ♀
The Square BA22 8LN ☎ 01935 840220 📠 01935 841353
e-mail: enquiries@ilchesterarms.co.uk
Dir: *From A303 take A37 to Ilchester/Yeovil, L towards Ilchester at 2nd sign marked Ilchester. Hotel 100yds on R*
Dominating the old town square, this elegant Georgian building still sports flagstone floors and open fires. Dine in the bar or the more formal restaurant from a classically-based menu. Dishes (prepared by the landlord himself) could include seared calves' liver with onions, bacon and a grain mustard sauce, baked fillet of salmon with buttered spinach, chervil cream and new potatoes, or medallions of pork fillet with braised lentils and a cider sauce.
OPEN: 11-11 Closed: 26 Dec **BAR MEALS:** L served all week 12-2.30 D served Mon-Sat 7-9.30 Av main course £7 **RESTAURANT:** L served all week 12-2.30 D served Mon-Sat 7-9.30 Av 3 course à la carte £18.50 Av 3 course fixed price £15.50
BREWERY/COMPANY: Free House 🍺: Buttcombe, Flowers IPA & regularly changing ales from local breweries. **FACILITIES:** Children welcome Garden: Enclosed, walled English garden **NOTES:** Parking 15

ILMINSTER
Map 04 ST31

New Inn
Dowlish Wake TA19 0NZ ☎ 01460 52413
Dir: *From Ilminster follow signs for Kingstone then Dowlish Wake*
A 350-year-old stone-built pub tucked away in a quiet village close to Perry's thatched cider mill. There are two bars with woodburning stoves, bar billiards and a skittle alley. The menu features local produce and West Country specialities, including fish, steaks and home-made pies.
OPEN: 11-3 6-11 (Sun 12-3, 7-10.30) 25 Dec Closed eve **BAR MEALS:** L served all week 12-2.30 D served Mon-Sat 7-9.30 Av main course £6.50 **BREWERY/COMPANY:** Free House
🍺: Butcombe Bitter + guest beers. **FACILITIES:** Children welcome Garden: Beer garden, Food served outdoors Dogs allowed **NOTES:** Parking 50

KILVE
Map 03 ST14

The Hood Arms ♦♦♦♦ 🛏
TA5 1EA ☎ 01278 741210 📠 01278 741477
e-mail: bheason1942@aol.com
Dir: *Off A39 between Bridgwater & Minehead*
Traditional 17th-century coaching inn, set among the Quantock Hills, and a popular watering hole for walkers. Kilve Beach is within a short walking distance, past an old priory thought to have been the haunt of smugglers, and is famous for its strange 'moonscape' landscape and fossils. A typical menu includes steak and ale pie, salmon on spinach and tarragon mash, mussels with sweet chilli sauce, and trout with apple and almond butter. Accommodation includes two-self-catering cottages.
OPEN: 11-3 6-11 **BAR MEALS:** L served all week 12-2.30 D served all week 6.15-9.30 Av main course £7 **RESTAURANT:** L served all week 12-2.30 D served all week 7-9 Av 3 course à la carte £16
BREWERY/COMPANY: Free House 🍺: Wadworth 6X, Otter Ale, Exmoor Fox, Cotleigh Tawney Ale. **FACILITIES:** Children welcome Garden: Walled garden with patios and play area Dogs allowed Some areas, Water **NOTES:** Parking 40 **ROOMS:** 6 bedrooms 6 en suite 2 family rooms s£38 d£60

KINGSDON
Map 04 ST52

Kingsdon Inn 🛏 ♀
TA11 7LG ☎ 01935 840543
See Pick of the Pubs on page 416

LANGLEY MARSH
Map 03 ST02

The Three Horseshoes 🛏
TA4 2UL ☎ 01984 623763 📠 01984 623763
Dir: *M5 J25 take B3227 to Wiveliscombe. From square follow signs for Langley Marsh. 1m*
A handsome, 17th-century red sandstone village inn on the edge of Exmoor, with a friendly poltergeist. It proudly boasts 'no fancy chefs, silly prices, chips, fruit machines or juke boxes, just good old locals, good beer straight from the cask, and genuinely home-cooked food'. Local suppliers are loyally supported, and fruit and veg comes from the garden, 'slugs and weather permitting'. Usual pub favourites, plus duck in pork and honey, lamb's liver in milk and wine, and cheesy leek pancakes.
OPEN: 12-2.30 7-11 (closed Mon Oct-Mar) **BAR MEALS:** L served all week 12-2 D served all week 7-9.30 Av main course £7.50 **RESTAURANT:** L served all week 12-2 D served all week 7-9.30 Av 3 course à la carte £15 **BREWERY/COMPANY:** Free House
🍺: Palmer IPA, Otter Ale, Fuller's London Pride, Adnams Southwold. **FACILITIES:** Garden: Enclosed garden **NOTES:** Parking 6

LANGPORT
Map 04 ST42

Rose & Crown
Huish Episcopi TA10 9QT ☎ 01458 250494
Dir: *Telephone for directions*
Boasting an 80-year old licensee who was born on the premises, this charming thatched pub is probably better known in the area as 'Eli's' - the name of the owner's father who ran the Rose & Crown for 55 years. In the same family for 130 years, few changes have taken place here and the pub still has flagstones and a wide selection of old pub games. Local farm cider and cider brandy accompany dishes such as steak and ale pie, spinach lasagne, pork and cider cobbler, chicken and mushroom pie, chicken curry, and various ploughman's lunches.
OPEN: 11.30-2.30 5.30-11 (Fri-Sat 11.30-11, Sun 12-10.30) 25 Dec closed eve **BAR MEALS:** L served all week 12-2 D served all week 6-8 Av main course £6.25 **BREWERY/COMPANY:** Free House
🍺: Teignworthy Reel Ale, Mystery Tour, Hop Back Summer Lightning, Butcombe Bitter. **FACILITIES:** Children welcome Garden: Mainly lawns, seating, play area Dogs allowed Water **NOTES:** Parking 50 **NOTES:** No credit cards

Open: 11-3, 6-11
Bar Meals: L served all week 12-2,
D served all week 7-10.
Av cost main course £9.20
BREWERY/COMPANY:
Free House.
🍺: Cotleigh Barn Owl, Otter Bitter,
Cottage Golden Arrow, Butcombe Best.
FACILITIES: Children welcome,
Garden - Front lawn with picnic
benches.
NOTES: Parking 18

Kingsdon Inn

A delightful 300-year-old thatched cottage at the end of a flower-edged path. Located just off the A303 in an attractive village, it is an ideal staging post on those long journeys to and from the West Country.

Kingsdon, nr Somerton, TA11 7LG
☎ 01935 840543
Dir: From A303 take A372 towards
Langport then B3151 toward Street,
1st R and R again.

Peaceful pastoral views make the front garden, with plenty of wooden seating, a pleasant spot in summer, while the rambling bars create a charming ambience all year round. The warmly decorated original front rooms have low beamed ceilings, scrubbed pine and stripped tables and chairs, and a huge stone inglenook, sadly only decorative, although on cooler days there is a blazing log fire on a raised hearth in the lower bar. All told, a welcoming, convivial atmosphere in which to linger over a good home-cooked lunch or supper complemented by a pint or so of Cotleigh Barn Owl and Cottage Golden Arrow bitters from Somerset, Otter from Devon or Butcombe from Bristol. Food is presented on separate lunchtime and evening menus, with daily-changing choices featuring fresh fish and game in season. Good value dishes include roasted, free-range half duck in scrumpy sauce, chicken breast stuffed with Stilton, and braised oxtail in Guinness. Fish dishes include trio of cod, haddock and salmon in wholegrain mustard sauce, and king prawns in lime and ginger. In the evening expect kidneys in Madeira sauce, crab and prawn mornay, and Mediterranean vegetable parcels followed by wild rabbit in Dijon mustard sauce, and roast whole shank of pork. Desserts not to be missed: lemon brioche pudding, banana fudge pie, and chocolate truffle torte.

LEIGH UPON MENDIP
Map 04 ST64

The Bell Inn ♀
BA3 5QQ ☎ 01373 812316 📠 01373 812163
Dir: head for Bath, then twrds Radstock following the Frome Rd, turn twrds Mells and then Leigh-upon-Mendip

Situated on the old pilgrims' route to Glastonbury, this historic inn has a fireplace dating back to 1687, built by the same stonemasons who constructed the church. Traditional pub grub includes steak and kidney pie, pork, leek and cider sausages, chicken, ham and leek pie, and scampi with salad. More adventurous dishes include lamb shanks, Normandy pork, osso bucco of lamb, wild rice risotto with woodland mushrooms, oven-roast chicken supreme with port and raisin sauce, and various fish choices.

OPEN: 12-3 6.30-11 **BAR MEALS:** L served all week 12-2 D served all week 6.30-9.30 Av main course £8.50 **RESTAURANT:** L served all week 12-2 D served all week 6.30-9
BREWERY/COMPANY: Wadworth 🍺: Wadworth 6X, Butcombe Bitter, Wadworths JCB, Henrys IPA. ♀: 12 **FACILITIES:** Children welcome Garden: Patio area, grassed area with flower borders
NOTES: Parking 20

LITTON
Map 04 ST55

The Kings Arms
BA3 4PW ☎ 01761 241301

Full of nooks and crannies, this 15th-century local at the heart of the Mendips has a large garden with a stream running through it, and boasts a separate children's play area and outdoor eating. Menus offer smoked haddock fish pie, home made chilli, and steak, mushroom and Guinness pie. Kings Arms Platters include Pigman's Platter - jumbo pork Lincolnshire sausage with eggs and chips.

OPEN: 11-2.30 6-11 **BAR MEALS:** L served all week 12-2.30 D served all week 6.30-10 Av main course £8
BREWERY/COMPANY: Free House 🍺: Bass, Butcombe, Wadworth 6X, Flowers. **FACILITIES:** Children welcome Garden
NOTES: Parking 50

LOWER VOBSTER
Map 04 ST74

Vobster Inn 🛏
BA3 5RJ ☎ 01373 812920
e-mail: vobsterinn@bt.com

Set in four acres of rolling countryside, the Vobster Inn is a 17th-century Mendip stone building with a large garden including a popular summer barbecue and established boules pitch. In addition to salmon and trout fishcakes, pork, leek and herb sausages on mash, and steak sandwich on ciabatta, the interesting menu may list steak, ale and Stilton pie, Thai green chicken curry, Parma ham, and pan-fried crispy duck

breast. Puddings might include lemon cheesecake, caramel apple pie, and treacle and walnut tart and custard.
OPEN: 12-3 7-11 **BAR MEALS:** L served all week 12-2 D served all week 7-10 Av main course £7.25 **RESTAURANT:** L served all week 12-2 D served all week 7-11 Av 3 course à la carte £20
BREWERY/COMPANY: Free House 🍺: Butcombe, Scottish Courage Courage Best, Wadworth 6X, Fullers London Pride.
FACILITIES: Children welcome Garden: Boule court, 10 tables Dogs allowed Water **NOTES:** Parking 45

LUXBOROUGH
Map 03 SS93

Pick of the Pubs

Royal Oak Inn 🛏
TA23 0SH ☎ 01984 640319 📠 01984 641561
e-mail: royaloakof.luxborough@virgin.net
Dir: From A38 (Taunton/Minehead) at Washford take minor road S through Roadwater

The Royal Oak is a 14th-century inn at the heart of the local community and farming life in the small Exmoor hamlet of Luxborough. In previous incarnations it has been an abattoir, a butcher's and a tailor's, and the Blazing Stump bar refers to a parsimonious landlord who fed the fire only one log at a time. Renovation has left the rustic character intact, with a large open fireplace, low beams and slate floor in the main bar, and tastefully-decorated dining areas. The fine food and well-kept ales deserve their reputation. Dishes are freshly cooked to order, the regular menu supplemented by a daily specials board in the bar. Game (pies and casseroles) and fresh fish feature strongly, with options like whole sea bream stuffed with fresh thyme and lemon, or seared loin of tuna with sweet chilli sauce and crème fraîche.
OPEN: 12-2.30 6-11 (Mon-Wed 6-10.30, Sun 7-10.30)
BAR MEALS: L served all week 12-2 D served all week 7-9 Av main course £9.45 **RESTAURANT:** L served all week 12-2 D served all week 6-9 Av 3 course à la carte £22.50
BREWERY/COMPANY: Free House 🍺: Tawney, Palmer 200, Exmoor Gold, Palmer Dorset Gold. **FACILITIES:** Children welcome Garden: Courtyard garden Dogs allowed Water provided **NOTES:** Parking 18 **ROOMS:** 12 bedrooms 11 en suite s£55 d£65 (♦♦♦)

> **Pick of the Pubs** have that extra special quality that makes them stand out from the crowd. Their entries are highlighted, and may be a full page.

continued

LYNG
Map 04 ST32

Rose & Crown 🛏 NEW
East Lyng TA3 5AU ☎ 01823 698235
e-mail: derek.mason@btinternet.com
Set among the Somerset Levels, this 13th-century coaching inn serves a range of real ales, and offers a relaxed atmosphere. The menu includes a variety of ploughman's, omelettes and salads, as well as vegetarian dishes such as country style vegetable Kiev and vegetable curry. Meat-based main dishes include roast duckling with orange sauce, T-bone steak, and pork chop with mustard sauce.
OPEN: 11-2.30 6.30-11 **BAR MEALS:** L served all week 12-2 D served all week 7-9.15 Av main course £6.50 **RESTAURANT:** L served all week 12-2 D served all week 7-9.15
BREWERY/COMPANY: Free House 🍺 Butcombe Bitter & Gold, Palmer 200 Premium Ale. **FACILITIES:** Garden: Lrg garden, approx 8 tables **NOTES:** Parking 40

MARSTON MAGNA
Map 04 ST52

The Marston Inn NEW
BA22 8BX ☎ 01935 850365 📠 01935 850397
Dir: Telephone for directions

Grade II listed building close to Yeovilton Air Museum, and handy for the link road to the West Country. The oldest parts of the inn are reputed to be haunted, and there's a skittle alley for the energetic. The menu offers rump steak with Stilton sauce, chicken breast grilled with mushrooms, seafood fettuccine, and ham and eggs, washed down with seasonal guest ales.
OPEN: 12-2.30 6-11 Jun-Sep open 3pm Open all day Sat, Sun 12-10.30 **BAR MEALS:** L served all week 12-2 D served Mon-Sat 6-9.30 Av main course £5.95 **RESTAURANT:** L served all week 12-2 D served Mon-Sat 6-9.30 Av 3 course à la carte £15
BREWERY/COMPANY: 🍺 Banks Bitter, Worthington Cream Flow, Seasonal Guest Ale. **FACILITIES:** Children welcome Garden: Walled patio area, secure play area Dogs allowed Water & Toys
NOTES: Parking 16

MARTOCK
Map 04 ST41

The Nag's Head Inn NEW
East St TA12 6NF
Dir: Telephone for directions
A 200-year-old former cider house set in a picturesque village in rural south Somerset. Al fresco eating and drinking is encouraged in the landscaped garden and a huge orchard area, with the home-made food being much sought after locally. Lamb shanks, venison casserole, various Thai and other oriental dishes, and delicious steaks are also available in the bar and restaurant.

continued

OPEN: 12-2.30 6-11 **BAR MEALS:** L served Tue-Sun 12-2 D served all week 6-9 Av main course £10 **RESTAURANT:** L served Tue-Sun 12-2 D served all week 6-9 Av 3 course à la carte £17.50 🍺 Otter Bitter, Worthington. **FACILITIES:** Children welcome Garden: Landscaped garden with flower beds Dogs allowed Water, Biscuits
NOTES: Parking 25

MIDFORD
Map 04 ST76

Hope & Anchor 🛏 ♀
BA2 7DD ☎ 01225 832296 📠 01225 832296
Dir: A367 from Bath to Radstock, L onto B3110 to Frome/Midford. Pub on bottom of hill under railway bridge

Busy food pub, dating from the mid 18th-century and extended in the 19th, in the village of Midford at the heart of the Cam Valley, three miles south of Bath. The comfortably-furnished bar and dining area, with bare boards, open stone fireplace and warm decor, is the setting for some enjoyable pub food. The tapas selection is a feature, alongside salmon fish cakes with tarragon mayonnaise, or venison with blueberries and redcurrants.
OPEN: 11.30-2.30 6.30-11 Closed: Dec 25-26 **BAR MEALS:** L served all week 12-2 D served all week 6.30-9.30 Av main course £6
RESTAURANT: L served all week 12-2 D served all week 6.30-9.30 Av 3 course à la carte £20 **BREWERY/COMPANY:** Free House 🍺 Deuchars IPA, Bass, Butcombe, Fullers London Pride. ♀: 10
FACILITIES: Garden: Terraced garden well planted, 10 tables Dogs allowed In the garden only **NOTES:** Parking 30

MIDSOMER NORTON
Map 04 ST65

Old Station
Wells Rd, Hallatrow, nr Paulton BS39 6EN ☎ 01761 452228
Eccentric pub full of bric-a-brac and curios, including appropriate railway relics - the biggest of which is the railway carriage that now houses the restaurant. A good range of West Country ales is on offer, and in the summer the garden is popular with its five-a-side football pitch and swings for the children. Menu choices include fillet of beef en croûte, pan-fried duck breast with fruit kebabs, and chicken breast wrapped in bacon and stuffed with apricot and brandy mousse.
OPEN: 12-3 5-11 (Open all day Sat-Sun) **BAR MEALS:** L served all week 12-2 D served all week 6-9.30 Av main course £8
RESTAURANT: Av 3 course à la carte £15 🍺 Brains S.A, Rev James, Draught Bass, Butcombe. **FACILITIES:** Children welcome Garden: Large well maintained garden, 20 benches **NOTES:** Parking 40

♀ 7 **Number of wines by the glass**

MONKSILVER   Map 03 ST03

Pick of the Pubs

The Notley Arms ♀
TA4 4JB ☎ 01984 656217
Dir: Telephone for directions

Situated on the edge of Exmoor in a small hamlet where
barely 90 people live. Their winter trade contributes
largely to the success of the coach-house skittle alley that
graces the pub car park. It is the second pub in the village,
the other being the thatched cottage opposite. They are
connected with Old Cleeve Abbey, and started out, as did
many village pubs, as a 'resting place' for visiting monks.
The daily blackboard menu offers a good choice of home-
made fare: coarse country-style pâté, soup and smoked
mackerel, and special dishes such as cheesy potato cakes
with leek and mustard sauce; pork braised with wild
mushrooms, cream and sherry; braised bacon, leek and
cider pudding; aubergine tagine with dates, almonds and
couscous; and Mediterranean-style red mullet fillets with
orange and capers. Old-fashioned puddings may include
hazelnut and apple cake, treacle tart with clotted cream,
and home-made brown bread ice cream.
OPEN: 11.30-2.30 6.30-11 Closed: Last wk Jan first wk Feb
BAR MEALS: L served all week 12-2 D served all week 7-9.30
BREWERY/COMPANY: Unique Pub Co 🍺: Exmoor Ale,
Wadworth 6X, Smiles Best. ♀: 8 **FACILITIES:** Children
welcome Garden: Dogs allowed On lead, water provided
NOTES: Parking 26

MONTACUTE   Map 04 ST41

Kings Arms Inn 🛏 ♀
TA15 6UU ☎ 01935 822513 📠 01935 826549
e-mail: dearsley@supanet.com
Dir: Turn off A303 at A3088 roundabout signposted Montacute. Hotel by
church in village centre

Picturesquely located near the National Trust's Montacute
House, the location of the 1995 film 'Sense and Sensibility',
this delightful 17th-century hamstone inn offers a relaxed,
country house atmosphere. Freshly-cooked food can be
enjoyed in the restaurant or bar, with a variety of lunchtime
snacks, and meals typically including smoked duck breast,
grilled pork loin with wholegrain mustard sauce, and rum and
chocolate parfait.
OPEN: 11-11 (Sun 12-10.30) **BAR MEALS:** L served all week 12-
2.30 D served all week 7-9 Av main course £9.50 **RESTAURANT:** L
served all week 12-2.30 D served all week 7-9 Av 3 course à la carte
£27.50 Av 3 course fixed price £19.95 🍺: Greene King Abbot & IPA.
♀: 15 **FACILITIES:** Children welcome Garden: Large lawn, orchard
Dogs allowed Water **NOTES:** Parking 12

The Phelips Arms 🛏 ♀
The Borough TA15 6XB ☎ 01935 822557
e-mail: thephelipsarms@aol.com
Dir: From Cartgate roundabout on A303 follow signs for Montacute

A 17th-century listed hamstone building overlooking the
village square and close to historic Montacute House (NT)
features a secluded rear garden and comfortable bars. The
pub was a location for the recent film version of 'Sense and
Sensibility'. Freshly-prepared ingredients, using local produce
wherever possible, supplement baguettes and jacket potatoes
at lunchtime with queen scallops in garlic butter, local ham,
egg and chips and a selection of delicious home-made pies.

OPEN: 11.30-2.30 6-11 Closed: 25 Dec **BAR MEALS:** L served all
week 12-2 D served all week 6-9 Av main course £7
RESTAURANT: L served all week 12-2 D served all week 6-9
BREWERY/COMPANY: Palmers 🍺: Palmers IPA & 200 Premium
Ale. ♀: 7 **FACILITIES:** Garden: Secluded and sheltered walled
garden Dogs allowed Water **NOTES:** Parking 40 **ROOMS:** 4
bedrooms 4 en suite s£35 d£60 (♦♦♦) no children overnight

NETHER STOWEY   Map 04 ST13

The Cottage Inn 🛏
Keenthorne TA5 1HZ ☎ 01278 732355
Dir: M5 J23 follow A39 signs for Cannington/Minehead. Inn on A39

Dating from the 16th century, the Cottage is an old coaching
inn and traditional cider house where cider was made until
about 15 years ago. The walls of the bar are original cob-
stone and wattle around one metre thick at its base. Hearty
eating options include a carvery with four roasts and five veg,
cottage pies, curries, steaks, and Thai green curry.
OPEN: 11-11 (Sun 12-10.30) **BAR MEALS:** L served all week 12-
2.30 D served all week 6-9 **RESTAURANT:** L served all week 12-2.30
D served Tue-Sun 6-9.30 Av 3 course à la carte £13
BREWERY/COMPANY: Free House 🍺: Bass, Butcombe Bitter,.
FACILITIES: Children welcome Garden: Food served outside. Patio
area Dogs allowed In the garden only **NOTES:** Parking 60

NORTH CURRY   Map 04 ST32

The Bird in Hand
1 Queen Square TA3 6LT ☎ 01823 490248
Dir: 6m from Taunton off the A358

A friendly 300-year-old village inn with large stone inglenook
fireplaces, flagstone floors, exposed beams and studwork.
Cheerful staff make you feel at home. Blackboard specials
concentrate on local produce.
OPEN: 12-3 7-11 25 Dec Closed eve **BAR MEALS:** L served Tues-
Sun 12-2 D served Tues-Sun 7-9.30 Av main course £5
RESTAURANT: L served Tue-Sun 12-2 D served Tue-Sun 7-9.30 Av 3
course à la carte £20 **BREWERY/COMPANY:** Free House
🍺: Otter Ale, plus guest. **FACILITIES:** Children welcome Dogs
allowed **NOTES:** Parking 20

Stars or Diamonds after the ROOMS
information at the end of an entry denotes
accommodation that has been inspected
by an organisation other than the AA,
eg the RAC, VisitBritain, VisitScotland or WTB.

continued

England

NORTON ST PHILIP
Map 04 ST75

Pick of the Pubs

George Inn ♀
High St BA3 6LH ☎ 01373 834224 🖷 01373 834861
e-mail: info@thegeorgeinn-nsp.co.uk
Dir: From A36 take A366 on R to Radstock, village 1m
This handsome old inn has been lovingly restored by
Wadworth. Built in the late 14th century as a monastic
guest house, the stone and timber-framed building is
among the finest surviving medieval inns in the land. The
George has featured in movies and TV series including
'Moll Flanders' and 'The Remains of the Day'. With its
galleried courtyard, soaring timber roofs and 15th-century
stair tower, it merits a daytime detour. Well-kept real ales
and a decent wine list complement lunchtime snacks and a
full carte. Bar food includes ham, egg, and chips, mussels
in white wine and cream, and chilli con carne. Barbary
duck breast with wild berry sauce, and pork tenderloin with
Calvados and apple on the carte.

George Inn

OPEN: 11-2.30 5.30-11 **BAR MEALS:** L served all week 12-
2.30 D served all week 7-9.30 Av main course £6.95
RESTAURANT: L served all week 12-2.30 D served all week 7-
9.30 Av 3 course à la carte £17.95
BREWERY/COMPANY: Wadworth ◖: Wadworth 6X, Henrys
IPA, Wadworth, J.C.B. **FACILITIES:** Garden: Terrace garden
overlooking village green Dogs allowed Allowed in some rooms
NOTES: Parking 26

NUNNEY
Map 04 ST74

The George at Nunney ★★ 🖼
Church St BA11 4LW ☎ 01373 836458 🖷 01373 836565
Dir: 0.5m N off A361, Frome/Shepton Mallet
The garden was used in the Middle Ages as a place of
execution, and the pub is reputedly haunted, but this rambling
old coaching inn is deservedly popular. Set in a historic
conservation village opposite a romantic, ruined 13th-century
castle, it serves a wide choice of food. Big steaks, mixed grill,
steak and ale pie, and double chicken breasts with choice of
sauces, plus a separate fish menu including sea bass, hake,
bream and fresh dressed crabs.
OPEN: 12-3 5-11 **BAR MEALS:** L served all week 12-2 D served all
week 7-9 Av main course £8 **RESTAURANT:** L served all week 12-2
D served all week 7-9 Av 3 course à la carte £20
BREWERY/COMPANY: Free House ◖: Highgate Brewery Saddlers
Best Bitter, Wadworth 6X, Interbrew Bass. **FACILITIES:** Children
welcome Garden: Walled cottage type **NOTES:** Parking 30
ROOMS: 9 bedrooms 8 en suite 2 family rooms s£45 d£62

OVER STRATTON
Map 04 ST41

The Royal Oak
TA13 5LQ ☎ 01460 240906 🖷 01460 242421
e-mail: chris&jill@the-royal-oak.net
Dir: A3088 from Yeovil, L onto A303, Over Stratton on R after S Petherton
A welcoming old thatched inn built from warm Ham stone, full
of blackened beams, flagstones, log fires, pews and settles -
with the added attraction of a garden, children's play area and
barbecue. Real ales, including Tanglefoot, from the Badger
brewery in Blandford Forum, and world-wide selections of
wines supplement traditional menus of fish pie, salmon with
saffron hollandaise, and game cobblers.
OPEN: 11-3 6-11 (wkds all day) **BAR MEALS:** L served all week
12-2.30 D served all week 6.30-9.30 Av main course £6.95
RESTAURANT: L served all week 12-2.30 D served all week 6.30-
9.30 **BREWERY/COMPANY:** Woodhouse Inns ◖: Badger Best,
Tanglefoot. **FACILITIES:** Children welcome Garden: Dogs allowed
Water **NOTES:** Parking 70

PITNEY
Map 04 ST42

Pick of the Pubs

The Halfway House
TA10 9AB ☎ 01458 252513
Dir: on B3153 between Langport and Somerton
This is a pub largely dedicated to the promotion of real
ale as produced by the many excellent micro-breweries in
Somerset, Devon and Wiltshire. There are always six to
ten real ales available in tip-top condition. There is also an
excellent choice of bottled Continental beers. This
delightfully old-fashioned rural pub draws customers from
a huge area. Three homely rooms boast open fires, books
and games, but no music or electronic games. Home-
cooked meals (except Sundays when it is too busy with
drinkers) include soups, local sausages, sandwiches and a
good selection of curries in the evening.
OPEN: 11.30-3 5.30-11 (Sun 12-3, 7-10.30) Closed: 25 Dec
BAR MEALS: L served Mon-Sat 12-2 D served Mon-Sat 7-9.30
BREWERY/COMPANY: Free House ◖: Butcombe Bitter,
Teignworthy, Otter Ale, Cotleigh Tawny Ale.
FACILITIES: Children welcome Garden Dogs allowed Water
NOTES: Parking 30

PORLOCK
Map 03 SS84

The Ship Inn 🖼 ♀
High St TA24 8QD ☎ 01643 862507 🖷 01643 863224
e-mail: mail@shipinnporlock.co.uk

Dir: A358 to Williton, then A39 to Porlock

continued

This 13th-century inn has welcomed many travellers, including Wordsworth, Coleridge and even Nelson's press gang. Nestling at the foot of Porlock's notorious hill, where Exmoor tumbles into the sea, its thatched roof and traditional interior provide an evocative setting for a meal, drink or overnight stay. Food-wise, most tastes are catered for: menus include light bites (from sandwiches to mussels cooked in cider), children's meals and specials such as steak and ale pie, fish and chips or wild mushroom risotto.
OPEN: 11-11 (Sun 12-11) **BAR MEALS:** L served all week 12-2 D served all week 6.30-9.00 **RESTAURANT:** L served Sun 12-2 D served all week 7-9 **BREWERY/COMPANY:** Free House
🍺: Cotleigh Barn Owl, Bass, Courage Best, Regular Guest Ales.
FACILITIES: Children welcome Garden: Dogs allowed Water provided **NOTES:** Parking 40

PRIDDY   Map 04 ST55

New Inn 🛏 🍷
Priddy Green BA5 3BB ☎ 01749 676465
Dir: From M4 J18 take A39 R to Priddy 3m before Wells. From J19 through Bristol onto A39. From M5 J21 take A371 to Cheddar, then B3371
Overlooking the village green high up in the Mendip Hills, this old former farmhouse is popular with walkers, riders and cavers, and once served beer to the local lead miners. A typical dinner menu features liver and bacon, chargrilled steaks, Brixham plaice, and fillet of pork with braised red cabbage. Plus New Inn pies, including a vegetarian version, various jacket potatoes, omelettes and toasties. Skittle alley. Priddy hosts the 'friendliest folk festival in England' every July.
OPEN: 11.30-2.30 7-11 (Sun & Mon 12-2.30) **BAR MEALS:** L served all week 12-2 D served all week 7-9.30 Av main course £5.25 **RESTAURANT:** L served all week 12-2 D served all week 7-9.30 Av 3 course à la carte £15 **BREWERY/COMPANY:** Free House
🍺: Interbrew Bass, Fuller's London Pride, Wadworth 6X, New Inn Priddy. **FACILITIES:** Children welcome Garden: Lrg garden Dogs allowed Water **NOTES:** Parking 30

RUDGE   Map 04 ST85

The Full Moon at Rudge 🛏 🍷
BA11 2QF ☎ 01373 830936 📠 01373 831366
e-mail: enquiries@thefullmoon.co.uk
Dir: From A36 (Bath/Warminster rd) follow signs for Rudge
Standing at the crossroads of old drovers' routes, there's been a coaching inn or hostelry on this site since the early 1700s. The inn retains its small rooms, scrubbed tables and stone floors. Daily-changing fish board offers the likes of fillet of brill with seared oranges and spring onions, and king prawns and scallops with grilled black pudding. Other options might include shoulder of lamb, fillet steak and leek and asparagus tart. Great views of Westbury White Horse.
OPEN: 11-11 **BAR MEALS:** L served all week 12-3 D served all week 6.30-9.30 Av main course £9.95 **RESTAURANT:** L served all week 12-3 D served all week 6.30-9.30 Av 3 course à la carte £19 **BREWERY/COMPANY:** Free House 🍺: Butcombe Bitter, Interbrew Worthington Bitter, Wadworth 6X. 🍷: 7 **FACILITIES:** Garden: rear of pub with wall and fence Dogs allowed **NOTES:** Parking 50

SHEPTON MALLET   Map 04 ST64

Pick of the Pubs

The Three Horseshoes 🛏 🍷
Batcombe BA4 6HE ☎ 01749 850359 📠 01749 850615
See Pick of the Pubs on page 422

Pick of the Pubs

The Waggon and Horses 🛏 🍷
Frome Rd, Doulting Beacon BA4 4LA
☎ 01749 880302 📠 01749 880602
e-mail: fcardona@onetel.com
Dir: 1.5m N of Shepton Mallet at crossroads with Wells-Frome road

An 18th-century coaching inn which is at the heart of artistic life in this community, hosting regular art exhibitions, an impressive classical music concert programme and regular jazz nights. It's all the result of the enthusiasm of its widely-travelled owner and landlord, Francisco Cardona, who also has a passion for horses - he has bred an Olympic competitor. The pub, with its walled garden, is set in a small village - but customers travel quite a distance to enjoy the food, ale and Somerset cider brandy whether or not entertainment is on offer. Meal choices range from sandwiches and baguettes through to cosmopolitan dishes including roast haunch of wild boar in Tuscan wine; Mediterranean-style fish stew; spaghetti in a mushroom and truffle salsa with flaked Parmesan; and pot-roasted wild goose in a Seville orange and Grand Marnier sauce. Desserts include steamed ginger and lemon pudding and sticky toffee pudding with pecan nut sauce.
OPEN: 11-3 6-11.20 (Sun 12-3, 7-11) 25 Dec Only open for lunchtime drinks **BAR MEALS:** L served all week 12-2 D served all week 6.30-9.30 Av main course £9.90 **RESTAURANT:** L served all week 12-2 D served all week 6.30-9.30 Av 3 course à la carte £20 **BREWERY/COMPANY:** Ushers 🍺: Thomas Hardy Ushers Best & Founders. 🍷: 7 **FACILITIES:** Garden: Beer garden, very nice Dogs allowed on lead please **NOTES:** Parking 40

SHEPTON MONTAGUE   Map 04 ST63

The Montague Inn
Shepton Montague BA9 8JW ☎ 01749 813213 📠 01749 813213
Dir: R off A371 between Wincanton & Castle Cary toward Shepton Montague
This comfortably-refurbished, stone-built village inn nestles in rolling unspoilt Somerset countryside on the edge of sleepy Shepton Montague. Tastefully decorated throughout, with the homely bar featuring old dark pine and an open log fire; cosy, yellow-painted dining room. Menu choices include bacon and Brie ciabatta, seafood gratin, venison steak, and organic lamb. Attractive summer terrace with rural views for summer sipping.
OPEN: 11-2.30 6-11 **BAR MEALS:** L served Tue-Sun 11-2 D served Tue-Sat 7-9 Av main course £8 **RESTAURANT:** L served Tue-Sun 11-2 D served Tue-Sat 7-9 Av 3 course à la carte £17 **BREWERY/COMPANY:** Free House 🍺: Greene King IPA & Guest Beer. **FACILITIES:** Children welcome Garden: Large raised area overlooking countryside **NOTES:** Parking 30

Open: 12-3, 6.30-11
Closed: 25-26 Dec
Bar Meals: L served all week 12-2,
D served all week 7-9.30.
Av cost main course £9
RESTAURANT: L served all week 12-2,
D served all week 7-9.30.
Av cost 3 courses £16
BREWERY/COMPANY:
Free House.
: Butcombe Bitter, Mine Beer &
Golden Spring. Both brewed locally.
FACILITIES: Children and dogs
welcome, Garden.
NOTES: Parking 25

The Three Horseshoes

A honey-coloured stone, 16th-century coaching inn tucked away in a pretty village in the heart of the very rural Batcombe Vale.

Batcombe, Shepton Mallet, BA4 6HE
☎ 01749 850359 📄 01749 850615
Dir: Take A359 from Frome to
Bruton. Batcombe signed on R

Terracotta painted walls, exposed stripped beams and a fine stone inglenook with log fire characterise the long and low-ceilinged main bar. A separate restaurant made from stone and with similar low beams is relaxed and homely, with comfortable seating and welcoming atmosphere. There is a good range of real ales and the menu offers a wide range of interesting home-cooked dishes that attract discerning diners from far and wide. A typical sample includes tian of fresh Cornish crab and prawns with dill crème fraiche, and spiced smoked sausage sautéed in paprika sauce with sweet pepper to start, followed by rich casserole of marinated venison and smoked bacon in red wine with creamed potatoes; pot roast half shoulder of lamb with white wine herb gravy and gratin potatoes; and pan-fried wild boar steak with butter potato cake and a cider and celery jus. Steaks are also on offer, and puddings range from orange, lemon and blueberry martello cheesecake to galliano and brioche bread and butter pudding with peaches, plums and ice cream. There is a lovely rear garden and views of the parish church. Expect a warm welcome and good hospitality from proprietors David and Liz Benson.

SOMERTON

Map 04 ST42

The Globe

Market Square TA11 7LX ☎ 01458 272474 🖹 01458 274789

Dir: *4m from A303*

Fresh fish at weekends and hearty English cooking draw local diners to this 17th-century former coaching inn in the market square.

OPEN: 11-2.30 5.30-11 Closed: 25 Dec **BAR MEALS:** L served all week 12-2 D served all week 7-9.30 Av main course £1.80 **RESTAURANT:** L served all week 12-2 D served all week 7-9.30 **BREWERY/COMPANY:** Punch Taverns ◗: Interbrew Bass & Boddingtons, Butcombe Bitter. **FACILITIES:** Children welcome Garden Dogs allowed **NOTES:** Parking 8

SPARKFORD

Map 04 ST62

The Sparkford Inn

High St BA22 7JH ☎ 01963 440218 🖹 01963 440358

e-mail: sparkfordinn@sparkford.fsbusiness.co.uk

Dir: *just off A303, 400yds from rdbt at Sparkford*

A picturesque 15th-century former coaching inn characterised by its popular garden, beamed bars and fascinating old prints and photographs. Nearby are the Haynes Motor Museum and the Yeovilton Fleet Air Arm Museum. A varied menu offers a selection of traditional meals and home-cooked favourites, including salmon and spinach pie, deep-fried breaded plaice, jumbo sausages, spinach and ricotta cannelloni, cottage pie with cheese topping, and a good lunchtime carvery.

OPEN: 11-11 **BAR MEALS:** L served all week 12-2 D served all week 7-9.30 **RESTAURANT:** L served all week 12-2 D served all week 7-9.30 **BREWERY/COMPANY:** Free House ◗: Interbrew Bass, Otter Ale, Butcombe Bitter, Greene King Abbot. **FACILITIES:** Children welcome Garden Dogs allowed **NOTES:** Parking 50

STANTON WICK

Map 04 ST66

Pick of the Pubs

The Carpenters Arms 🐾 ⌾

BS39 4BX ☎ 01761 490202 🖹 01761 490763

e-mail: carpenters@buccaneer.co.uk

Dir: *From A37(Bristol to Wells rd) take A368 towards Weston-Super-Mare, take 1st R*

A converted row of honey-stoned former miners' cottages in a tiny hamlet overlooking the Chew Valley. Beyond the pretty façade with its climbing roses and colourful flower tubs is a comfortable stone-walled bar with low beams, warming open fire and a chatty, music-free atmosphere. Comfortable, cottage-style bedrooms are a particular draw for harassed business types and weekenders. The

Cooper's Parlour, with an extensive daily chalkboard, is the focus of imaginative snacks and bar food. Starters include slices of smoked duck on herb salad and quenelles on chicken liver and mushroom paté. Main offerings include dishes like roast cod fillet on baby spinach with orange butter sauce, and The Carpenters traditional steak and Butcombe Ale pie. Lighter options include salads and sandwiches.

OPEN: 11-11 Closed: 25/26 Dec **BAR MEALS:** L served all week 12-2 D served all week 7-10 Av main course £11 **RESTAURANT:** L served Sun 12-2 D served Mon-Sat 7-10 Av 3 course à la carte £22.50 **BREWERY/COMPANY:** Buccaneer Holdings ◗: Interbrew Bass, Butcombe Bitter, Scottish Courage Courage Best, Wadworth 6X. ⌾: 12 **FACILITIES:** Children welcome Garden: Landscaped. Patio area, pond, heaters Dogs allowed Water **NOTES:** Parking 200 **ROOMS:** 12 bedrooms 12 en suite 1 family rooms s£62 d£84.50 (♦♦♦♦)

STAPLE FITZPANE

Map 04 ST21

The Greyhound Inn ♦♦♦♦ 🐾 ⌾

TA3 5SP ☎ 01823 480227 🖹 01823 481117

e-mail: ivor-lucy@the-greyhoundinn.com

Dir: *From M5, take A358 E, signed Yeovil, after 4m follow sign to R, signed Staple Fitzpaine*

Nestling in a picturesque village, this 16th-century coaching inn takes its name from the men on horseback who dispatched news before the days of the Royal Mail. The surrounding garden guarantees sun at any time of day (British weather permitting). Alternatively, take refuge in rambling rooms characterised by flagstone floors, old timbers and natural stone walls. A good selection of traditional ales and seasonal, freshly-prepared dishes awaits: perhaps breast of chicken with tagiatelle and tarragon cream, or baked wild rainbow trout with toasted almonds and lemon juice.

OPEN: 12-3 6-11 (Summer open all day) **BAR MEALS:** L served all week 12-2 D served all week 7-9.30 Av main course £6.50 **RESTAURANT:** D served Thur-Sat 7-9 Av 3 course à la carte £32.50 **BREWERY/COMPANY:** Free House ◗: Otter, Exmoor, Fullers London Pride, Castle Eden. **FACILITIES:** Children welcome Garden: Split level, all round the Inn Dogs allowed On leads. Water/Food provided **NOTES:** Parking 60 **ROOMS:** 4 bedrooms 4 en suite s£49.95 d£66

STOGUMBER

Map 03 ST03

The White Horse

High St TA4 3TA ☎ 01984 656277 🖹 01984 656277

Dir: *Opposite the church in the centre of the village*

Tucked away in gentle folds between the Quantock and Brendon Hills, this part 18th-century freehouse incorporates the village's old Market Hall. Like other local pubs, it once brewed Stogumber ale, allegedly 'able to cure anything from leprosy to flatulence'. It specialises in home-cooked pub grub, including locally-sourced steaks, gammon, and pork. Local guest beers are a speciality. A mile down a pretty country lane is the West Somerset Railway's Stogumber station.

OPEN: 11.30-2.30 6.30-11 (open all day Thu-Sun) Wed in winter Closed lunch **BAR MEALS:** L served all week 12-2 D served all week 7-9.30 Av main course £5 **RESTAURANT:** L served all week 12-2 D served all week 7-9.30 **BREWERY/COMPANY:** Free House ◗: Cotleigh Tawny Bitter, Marstons Pedigree, Greene King, Abbot Ale. **FACILITIES:** Garden: Enclosed patio Dogs allowed Water, in bedrooms by arrangement **NOTES:** Parking 5

continued

STOKE ST GREGORY — Map 04 ST32

Rose & Crown 🐾 ♀
Woodhill TA3 6EW ☎ 01823 490296 📠 01823 490996
e-mail: ron.browning@virgin.net
Dir: *M5 J25, A358/A378 then 1st L through North Curry to Stoke St Gregory church on R. Pub 0.5m on L*
Close to the famous Somerset Levels and handy for Wells and Glastonbury, this 17th-century picturesque cottage-style pub includes a 60-ft well and an attractive dining room recently converted from the inn's old skittle alley. Fresh local produce and fish from Brixham are used, and there is a good selection of real ales and guest beers. Grilled skate wings, mixed grill and lamb cutlets are popular in the bar, and restaurant dishes might include grilled pork valentine with apple sauce, scrumpy chicken and local trout.
OPEN: 11-3 7-11 Dec 25 Closed eve **BAR MEALS:** L served all week 12.30-2 D served all week 7-9.30 Av main course £7.50
RESTAURANT: L served all week 12.30-2 D served all week 7-10
BREWERY/COMPANY: Free House 🍺: Exmoor Fox, & Stag, Guest Ales. **FACILITIES:** Children welcome Garden: Pretty patio area with tables **NOTES:** Parking 20

TAUNTON — Map 04 ST22

Queens Arms 🐾
Pitminster TA3 7AZ ☎ 01823 421529 📠 01823 451529
In 1086 the Domesday Book recorded this ancient building as a mill, which for nearly 800 years it remained before becoming a pub. Local (ie Somerset, Bristol and Devon) real ales are available, as well as an extremely varied menu. Almost everything is home made with locally, purchased ingredients. Starters include medley of tempura vegetables and chicken satay, and to follow could come vegetable, Brie and cranberry crumble, black-fin shark steak in creamy peppercorn sauce, or chicken curry.
OPEN: 11-11 (Sun 12-10.30) **BAR MEALS:** L served all week 12-2 D served all week 6.30-9 Av main course £7
BREWERY/COMPANY: Enterprise Inns 🍺: Butcombe Bitter, Butcombe Gold, Cotleigh Tawny, Otter Bitter. **FACILITIES:** Children welcome Garden: South facing terrace and lawned area Dogs allowed Water bowl in bar **NOTES:** Parking 20

TRISCOMBE — Map 04 ST13

Pick of the Pubs

AA Pub of the Year for England 2004

The Blue Ball ♀
TA4 3HE ☎ 01984 618242 📠 01984 618371
Dir: *9M from Taunton on the Minehead A358 road, turn L signposted Triscombe the pub is 1m along this road*
Unspoilt 18th-century thatched pub hidden away along a narrow lane amid the Quantock Hills, offering imaginative pub food, Somerset ales, decent wines and an informal dining atmosphere to a well heeled and discerning clientele. Carpeted main bar with rustic, country-style furnishings, sporting prints, and daily-changing blackboard menus above the huge inglenook fireplace. Locally-sourced produce features in tea-smoked Quantock duck breast with port and redcurrant sauce, pheasant with Calvados and caramelised apples, lamb loin stuffed with apricots and pistachio nuts, and Dunster Beach codling with Puy lentils and salsa verde. Starters may include spicy carrot, coconut and coriander soup and terrine of ham and foie gras, while for pudding try the prune and Armagnac tart or a plate of West Country cheeses. Impressive list of 400 wines; any under £20 available by the glass. Super terraced garden with view over the Vale of Taunton. Footpaths lead into the Quantocks and miles of breezy walks.
OPEN: 12-3 7-11 25 Dec, closed am 26 Dec closed pm
BAR MEALS: L served all week 12-1.45 7-9.30 Av main course £7.50 **RESTAURANT:** L served all week 12-1.45 D served all week 7-9.30 Av 3 course à la carte £21.50 **BREWERY/COMPANY:** Free House 🍺: Cotleigh Tawny, Youngs Special, Hop Back Summer Lightning, plus guests. ♀: 400+ **FACILITIES:** Children welcome Garden: Food served outside Dogs allowed Water **NOTES:** Parking 20 **NOTES:** No credit cards

WAMBROOK — Map 04 ST20

The Cotley Inn
TA20 3EN ☎ 01460 62348 📠 01460 68833
Located in an area renowned for good walks, the interior walls of this traditional stone-built inn are lined with works by local artists. The cosy bar and adjoining dining room offer a choice of full meals or lighter snacks. Among the starters expect lamb kidneys with port and cream, and mushroom fritters with garlic mayonnaise. Main courses include three lamb chops with rosemary and garlic, gammon steak with egg, and trout fillets stuffed with apple and celery.
OPEN: 11-3 7-11 **BAR MEALS:** L served all week 12-3 D served all week 7-11 **RESTAURANT:** L served all week 12-3 D served all week 7-11 **BREWERY/COMPANY:** Free House 🍺: Otter Ale, Interbrew Boddingtons Bitter. **FACILITIES:** Children welcome Garden: Patio area, tables & chairs available Dogs allowed **NOTES:** Parking 40

WASHFORD — Map 03 ST04

The Washford Inn ♀
TA23 0PP ☎ 01984 640256
Located beside the Washford Steam Railway Station through which trains run between Minehead and Bishop's Lydeard near Taunton, a pleasant family inn. Well situated for many enjoyable walking routes, it offers home-cooked, locally-produced food. Expect lasagne, Stilton bake, chilli rabbit pie, and steak and kidney pie among the appetising dishes. New managers Spring 2003.
OPEN: 12-11 (Winter 11-3, 5-11) **BAR MEALS:** L served all week 12-9 D served all week 12-9 Av main course £5.95 **RESTAURANT:** L served all week 12-2.30 D served all week 5-9
BREWERY/COMPANY: Scottish & Newcastle 🍺: Butcombe Gold, Courage Directors, Wadworth 6X, Bass. **FACILITIES:** Children welcome Garden: Dogs allowed Bedroom by request only **NOTES:** Parking 40

WATERROW — Map 03 ST02

The Rock Inn ◆◆◆
TA4 2AX ☎ 01984 623293 📠 01984 623293
Dir: *From Taunton take B3227. Waterrow approx 14m W*
400-year-old former smithy and coaching inn built into the rock face, in a lovely green valley beside the River Tone. Sit in the peaceful bar, with winter log fire and traditional furnishings, and sample the appetising menu including steaks and various home-made dishes. Heather & George Shillitto are its friendly managers.

continued

continued

OPEN: 11.30-3 6-11 Closed: 25-26 Dec **BAR MEALS:** L served all week 11-2.30 D served all week 7-9.30 Av main course £9
RESTAURANT: L served all week 11-2.30 D served all week 7-9.30
BREWERY/COMPANY: Free House ◼: Cotleigh Tawny, Exmoor Gold, monthly guest ales. **FACILITIES:** Children welcome
NOTES: Parking 20 **ROOMS:** 7 bedrooms 7 en suite 1 family rooms s£24 d£48

WELLS   Map 04 ST54

Pick of the Pub

The Fountain Inn/Boxers Restaurant 🍴 ♀
1 St Thomas St BA5 2UU ☎ 01749 672317 🖳 01749 670825
e-mail: reservations@fountaininn.co.uk
See Pick of the Pubs on page 426
See Pub Walk on page 405

The Pheasant Inn 🍴
Worth, Wookey BA5 1LQ ☎ 01749 672355
Dir: W of Wells on the B3139
Set at the foot of the Mendips, with impressive views, this popular country pub has a traditional public bar where walkers can enjoy a pint of real ale beside a welcoming log fire. There is a bar snack menu and a carte with a distinctly Italian flavour, offering a good choice of home-made pasta dishes, including a vegetarian choice. Scampi alla Pietro is a house speciality, and other favourites are home-made minestrone, veal rustica, chicken cacciatore, and tiramisù.
OPEN: 11-3 6-11 (Sun 12-3, 7-11) Closed: Dec 26, Jan 1
BAR MEALS: L served all week 12-2 D served all week 6.30-9.30 Av main course £7.95 **RESTAURANT:** L served all week 12-2 D served all week 6.30-9.30 Av 3 course à la carte £15.50
BREWERY/COMPANY: Free House ◼: Butcombe, Greene King Old Speckled Hen, Castle Rock Elsie Mo, St Austell HSD.
FACILITIES: Children welcome Children's licence Garden: Garden with tables and umbrellas Dogs allowed **NOTES:** Parking 28

WEST CAMEL   Map 04 ST52

The Walnut Tree 🍴
Fore St BA22 7QW ☎ 01935 851292 🖳 01935 851292
Dir: Off A303 between Sparkford & Yeovilton Air Base
Close to the border between Dorset and Somerset, this well-kept inn is in a quiet village. The famous Leyland Trail that passes close by brings plenty of walkers to the area. The cosily-carpeted lounge bar and a choice of restaurant and bistro entice the hungry with prominently displayed blackboards. Fresh fish from Poole like monkfish medallions in a sweet pepper and tomato sauce, and the likes of beef Wellington with Madeira sauce are served along with snacks.
OPEN: 11-3 6.30-11.30 (Closed Sun eve, Mon lunch) Closed: 25-26

continued

Dec **BAR MEALS:** L served Tue-Sun 12-2 D served Mon-Sat 7-9.30
RESTAURANT: L served Tue-Sun 12-2 D served Mon-Sat 7-9.30
BREWERY/COMPANY: Free House ◼: Butcombe Bitter, St Austell Dartmoor Best. **FACILITIES:** Garden: Tranquil **NOTES:** Parking 40

WEST HUNTSPILL   Map 04 ST34

Crossways Inn 🍴 ♀
Withy Rd TA9 3RA ☎ 01278 783756 🖳 01278 781899
e-mail: crossways.inn@virgin.net
Dir: On A38 3.5m from M5 J22/23
A relaxing atmosphere pervades this 17th-century coaching inn on the old Taunton to Bristol route. Sash windows and part-panelled walls with a large fireplace in the central bar set the tone. Bar meals that include Singapore prawn curry, Greek lamb and apricots and Thai fish cakes add an eclectic touch to the more usual beef and Guinness pie, liver and bacon casserole and stuffed chicken breast with tarragon cream sauce. There is a family room and safe rear garden.
OPEN: 12-3 5.30-11 Closed: 25 Dec **BAR MEALS:** L served all week 12-2 D served all week 6.30-9 Av main course £5.50
RESTAURANT: L served all week 12-2 D served all week 6.30-9.00 Av 3 course à la carte £10.50 **BREWERY/COMPANY:** Free House
◼: Interbrew Bass, Flowers Original & Flowers IPA, Fuller's London Pride, Greene King Abbot Ale. **FACILITIES:** Children welcome Garden: Seating, food served outside Dogs allowed **NOTES:** Parking 60

WHEDDON CROSS   Map 03 SS93

The Rest and Be Thankful Inn ♦♦♦♦ 🍴 ♀
TA24 7DR ☎ 01643 841222 🖳 01643 841813
e-mail: enquiries@restandbethankful.co.uk
Dir: 5m S of Dunster

Wonderful views of the moors can be enjoyed from this old coaching inn, located in the highest village on Exmoor. Old world charm blends with friendly hospitality in the cosy bar and spacious restaurant, where both traditional and contemporary food is served. Bar snacks from ploughman's to pies join vegetable lasagne, macaroni cheese, duckling à l'orange, scampi and rump steak, with perhaps profiteroles or apple and blackberry pie to round off.
OPEN: 9.30-3 6.30-11 (Winter 7pm Opening) **BAR MEALS:** L served all week 12-2 D served all week 7-9.30 Av main course £10
RESTAURANT: L served all week 12-2 D served all week 7-10 Av 3 course à la carte £15 **BREWERY/COMPANY:** Free House
◼: Exmoor Ale, Interbrew Bass & Worthington Bitter, Abbott Ale.
♀: 7 **FACILITIES:** Children welcome Garden: Paved Patio
NOTES: Parking 50 **ROOMS:** 5 bedrooms 5 en suite s£27.50 d£58

♀ 7   **Number of wines by the glass**

Open: 10.30-2.30, 6-11
(Sun 12-3, 7-10.30)
Bar Meals: L served all week 12-2.30,
D served all week 6-10.
Av cost main course £6.50
RESTAURANT: L served all week 12-2.30,
D served all week from 6.
Av cost 3 course £18.50
BREWERY/COMPANY: INNSPIRED
🍺: Butcombe Bitter, Interbrew Bass,
Scottish Courage Courage Best.
FACILITIES: Children welcome.
NOTES: Parking 24

The Fountain Inn

This popular pub restaurant stands close by the cathedral as you enter the city from the east, and takes its name from the spring that feeds the roadside conduits lapping the city centre pavements.

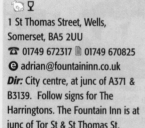

1 St Thomas Street, Wells,
Somerset, BA5 2UU
☎ 01749 672317 📠 01749 670825
📧 adrian@fountaininn.co.uk
Dir: City centre, at junc of A371 &
B3139. Follow signs for The
Harringtons. The Fountain Inn is at
junc of Tor St & St Thomas St.

The 16th-century Fountain has long been a favourite haunt of the cathedral choir - hardly surprising, since it's just around the corner from Vicars Close, a street of medieval houses built specially for the Vicars Choral. Although the pub is reputed to have housed the cathedral builders, this is probably a reference to maintenance staff, since the great church was substantially complete by the year 1465. Nowadays the pub's popularity rests firmly on the shoulders of Adrian and Sarah Lawrence, who fell in love with the city on a bright spring day in 1981 and have been here ever since. Locally-brewed Butcombe bitter is amongst the beers offered in the unpretentious ground floor bar with its roaring winter fires. The bar menu begins with varied and substantial choices for brunch, but also features roasts, specials and home-made cream teas! In Boxer's upstairs restaurant, choices include starters like chilled melon with raspberry coulis; deep-fried Brie with tomato and garlic sauce; or smoked salmon roses with a lemon vinaigrette. Main course options such as fruity chicken curry; beef, ale and mushroom pie; or speciality sausages with seasoned mash and red wine gravy are complemented by a deep-filled leek, sweet potato, Stilton and chestnut pie. Finish off with rum and raisin torte; dark chocolate and Bailey's terrine; or treacle sponge and custard.

WINCANTON
Map 04 ST72

Bull Inn 🕮 ♀
Hardway, nr Bruton BA10 0LN ☎ 01749 812200

A regular in this 17th-century free house is enjoying free beer for life after betting landlord Martin Smith that he could promote the pub on TV during England's World Cup matches in Korea and Japan. Luckily, says Martin, he's not a big drinker. Meals in the bar or restaurant include sirloin, rump and fillet steaks, ostrich steak, curries, home-made pies, chicken supreme, sea bass, red mullet, smoked haddock, and salmon and cod fish cakes. A gentle stream runs alongside the suntrap beer garden.

OPEN: 11.30-2.30 6-11 **BAR MEALS:** L served all week 12-2 D served Mon-Sat 6-10 Av main course £8 **RESTAURANT:** L served all week 12-2 D served Mon-Sat 7-9.30 **BREWERY/COMPANY:** Free House ◀: Butcombe Bitter, Greene King IPA & Old Speckled Hen, Shepherd Neame- Spitfire, Bass. **FACILITIES:** Children welcome Garden: Beer garden with tables and chairs Dogs allowed Water tap outside **NOTES:** Parking 30

WITHYPOOL
Map 03 SS83

Pick of the Pubs

Royal Oak Inn ★★ ◉
TA24 7QP ☎ 01643 831506 🖷 01643 831659
e-mail: enquiries@royaloakwithypool.co.uk
Dir: *From M5 through Taunton on B3224, then B3223 to Withypool*

With an ever-growing reputation as a sporting hotel for its hunting, shooting, walking and activity holidays in the Exmoor National Park, this old inn has a long and colourful history - R D Blackmore stayed here whilst writing the classic 'Lorna Doone' and the hotel was once owned by spymaster Maxwell Knight. The Rod Room is chock-full of fishing memorabilia and in both beamed bars, warmed by open fires, a wealth of good food created from local produce, accompanies real Exmoor ales and guest beers. Starters could include duck liver parfait with warm onion bread, crispy salmon fishcakes with dill and lime mayonnaise, or home-made blinis with wild mushroom and tarragon fricassée. Main courses range from old favourites (grilled plaice, sirloin steak, ham, egg and chips) to imaginative dishes such as loin of wild boar with caramelised apple sauce, Savoy cabbage, bacon and fried onion potatoes.

OPEN: 11-2.30 6-11 **BAR MEALS:** L served all week 12-2 D served all week 6.30-9.30 Av main course £10 **RESTAURANT:** L served Sun 12-2 D served all week 7-9 Av 3 course à la carte £23 Av 3 course fixed price £25 **BREWERY/COMPANY:** Free House ◀: Exmoor Ale & Exmoor. **FACILITIES:** Children welcome Dogs allowed Kennels if needed **NOTES:** Parking 20 **ROOMS:** 8 bedrooms 7 en suite s£60 d£90

WOOKEY
Map 04 ST54

The Burcott Inn 🕮 ♀
Wells Rd BA5 1NJ ☎ 01749 673874

A convenient stop for visitors to Wells or the Mendip Hills, this stone-built roadside inn sits opposite a working water mill, and is characterised by beams, open fires, pine tables and settles. Freshly-prepared food is available in the bars, restaurant or large garden. The menu includes such dishes as leek and Stilton chicken goujons, fresh grilled salmon steak, steak and ale pie, battered cod fillet, vegetable and cashew nut bake, or roast topside of beef. French sticks, sandwiches and salads are also available. Try your hand at the traditional pub games.

OPEN: 11.30-2.30 6-11 Closed: 25/26 Dec, 1 Jan **BAR MEALS:** L served all week 12-2.30 D served Tue-Sat 6.30-9.30 Av main course £8 **RESTAURANT:** L served all week 12-2.30 D served Tue-Sat 6.30-9.30 Av 3 course à la carte £15 **BREWERY/COMPANY:** Free House ◀: Teignworthy Old Moggie, Greene King Abbot Ale, Cotleigh Barn Owl Bitter, RCH Pitchfork. **FACILITIES:** Children welcome Garden: Lrg garden, beautiful views **NOTES:** Parking 30

WOOLVERTON
Map 04 ST75

Red Lion 🕮 ♀
Bath Rd BA2 7QS ☎ 01373 830350 🖷 01373 831050
Dir: *On the A36 between Bath & Warminster*

Once a court room, with possible connections to Hanging Judge Jeffries, this 400-year-old building has lovely slate floors and an open fire. It is decorated in Elizabethan style and is an ideal place to enjoy real ales, country wines and good home cooking. Look out for steak and 6X ale pie, roasted lamb shoulder, ocean lasagne, smoked haddock and asparagus tart, butterflied chicken fillet, and a selection of hot rolls, jacket potatoes and sandwiches.

OPEN: 11.30-11 (Sun 12-10.30) **BAR MEALS:** L served all week 12-2.30 D served all week 6-9 Av main course £6.75 **BREWERY/COMPANY:** Wadworth ◀: Wadworth 6X, Henry's IPA, Wadworth JCB & Seasonal, Guest Beers. ♀: 30 **FACILITIES:** Children welcome Garden: Large garden, benches Dogs allowed Water **NOTES:** Parking 40

YARLINGTON
Map 04 ST62

The Stags Head Inn NEW
BA9 8DG ☎ 01963 440393 🖷 01963 441015
e-mail: steveculverhouse@compuserve.com
Dir: *Telephone for directions*

A completely unspoilt country inn with flagstones, real fires and no electronic intrusions. In the summer, a pretty garden with fruit trees and a stream comes into its own. An appealing blackboard menu lists such daily choices as pan-fried chicken livers flamed in Madeira, skate wing with black butter and capers, and sticky apple tart, while a guest beer supplements the Greene King and Bass regulars.

OPEN: 12-2.30 6-11 Close 3pm on Sat-Sun Closed: 25 Dec **BAR MEALS:** L served Tue-Sun 12-2 D served Tue-Sun 7-9 Av main course £6.50 ◀: Greene King, IPA, Bass, Guest Beer (Changes Weekly). **FACILITIES:** Garden: Heated patio, stream, fruit trees Dogs allowed Water **NOTES:** Parking 20

Most of the pubs in this guide book pride themselves on the quality of their food. This may take a little time to prepare.

England

STAFFORDSHIRE

ALREWAS
Map 10 SK11

The Old Boat 🐕 ♀
DE13 7DB ☎ 01283 791468 🖷 01283 792886

Situated on the Trent and Mersey Canal, the pub was originally a watering hole for canal construction workers, and later for bargemen. The snug at the far end of the bar used to be the cellar; casks of ale were rolled off the barges into the room and kept cool in up to two feet of water. Typical dishes are corn-fed chicken breast with wild mushroom risotto, baked sea bass with sun-blushed tomatoes, John Dory in red wine sauce, or shank of Welsh lamb in a rosemary sauce. Good wine list.
OPEN: 11.30-3.30 6.30-11.30 **BAR MEALS:** L served all week 12-2.30 D served all week 7-10 Av main course £8 **RESTAURANT:** L served all week 12-2.30 D served all week 7-10 Av 3 course fixed price £13.95 **BREWERY/COMPANY:** 🍺: Thomas Hardy Ushers Bitter & Founders Ale, Marston's Pedigree. ♀: 8 **FACILITIES:** Children welcome Garden: Large lawn **NOTES:** Parking 40

ALTON
Map 10 SK04

Bulls Head Inn ♦♦♦
High St ST10 4AQ ☎ 01538 702307 🖷 01538 702065
e-mail: janet@alton.freeserve.co.uk
Traditional beers, home cooking and well-equipped accommodation are provided in the heart of Alton, less than a mile from Alton Towers theme park. Oak beams and an inglenook fireplace set the scene for the old world bar, the cosy snug (where children can sit) and the country-style restaurant. Menus offer the likes of sirloin steak, deep-fried breaded plaice, lasagne verdi, steak, ale and mushroom pie, and hunters chicken.
BAR MEALS: L served Mon-Fri 12-2 D served all week 6.30-9.30 **RESTAURANT:** D served all week 6.30-9.30 **BREWERY/COMPANY:** Free House 🍺: Interbrew Bass, Coors Worthington's, Fuller's London Pride. **FACILITIES:** Children welcome **NOTES:** Parking 15 **ROOMS:** 6 bedrooms 6 en suite

ANSLOW
Map 10 SK22

The Burnt Gate Inn 🐕 ♀ NEW
Hopley Rd DE13 9PY ☎ 01283 563664
e-mail: theburntgateinn@aol.com
Dir: *From Burton take B5017 towards Abbots Bromley. At top of Henhurst Hill turn right, Inn on Hopely Road, 2 miles from town centre*
The Burnt Gate, so called because many years ago a tollgate opposite was destroyed by fire, is Britain's only pub with this name. Owner Marie Stevens has refurbished, working hard to retain its original character. Plaudits from many sources for its home-made food, which includes steaks, gammon, chicken, game

(in season), fresh fish, and vegetarian and gluten-free options. Specials change every six weeks. The Jacob Flyn restaurant links Marie's grandfather's name with Flyn, her pet name for her father.
OPEN: 11.30-3 6-11 (Sun 12-3, 6.30-10.30) **BAR MEALS:** L served all week 11.30-2.15 D served Mon-Sat Av main course £5.95 **RESTAURANT:** L served all week 11.30-2.15 D served Mon-Sat 6-9 Av 3 course à la carte £18 Av 3 course fixed price £10 🍺: Bass, Pedigree (Cask ales). ♀: 8 **FACILITIES:** Dogs allowed Water **NOTES:** Parking 26

BURTON UPON TRENT
Map 10 SK22

Burton Bridge Inn ♀
24 Bridge St DE14 1SY ☎ 01283 536596
Dir: *Telephone for directions*
With its own brewery at the back, this is one of the oldest pubs in the area. The unspoilt old-fashioned interior has oak panelling, feature fireplaces, and a distinct lack of electronic entertainment. A full range of Burton Bridge ales is on tap, and the menu includes straightforward meals like roast pork or beef cobs, as well as traditional filled Yorkshire puddings.
OPEN: 11.30-2.30 (Sun 12-2.30, 7-10.30) 5-11 **BAR MEALS:** L served Mon-Sat 11.30-2 Av main course £3.50
BREWERY/COMPANY: 🍺: Burton Bridge Gold Medal Ale, Burton Bridge Festival Ale, Burton Bridge Golden Delicious & Bridge Bitter. ♀: 15 **FACILITIES:** Garden Dogs allowed Water **NOTES:** No credit cards

BUTTERTON
Map 16 SK05

The Black Lion Inn ♀
ST13 7SP ☎ 01538 304232
Dir: *From A52 (between Leek & Ashbourne) take B5053*

This charming, 18th-century village inn lies on the edge of the Manifold valley, in the heart of the Peak District's walking and cycling country. Winter fires add to the pleasure of a well-kept pint. The popular bar menu includes pies and steaks, as well as lamb casserole, spinach and ricotta cannelloni, and plenty of interesting fish dishes. A comfortable base from which to explore the National Park.
OPEN: 12-3 7-11 **BAR MEALS:** L served Tues-Sun 12-2 D served all week 7-9 **RESTAURANT:** L served Tues-Sun 12-2 D served all week 7-9.30 **BREWERY/COMPANY:** Free House 🍺: Scottish Courage Theakston Best, Interbrew Bass, Everards Tiger Best, Timothy Taylor. ♀: 10 **FACILITIES:** Children welcome Garden **NOTES:** Parking 30 **ROOMS:** 3 bedrooms 3 en suite 1 family rooms s£45 d£55 (♦♦♦)

> We endeavour to be as accurate as possible but changes to times and other information can occur after the guide has gone to press

continued

Ye Olde Royal Oak Inn

This short yet fairly challenging ramble explores the Manifold Valley, a spectacular limestone gorge, its steep, wooded slopes around Thor's Cave and upland farmland. Wildlife abounds and the Peak District views are magnificent.

Turn left out of the pub car park and follow signs for Wetton Mill, bearing left and on past the church. Ignore the road for Grindon and take the next left down a rough track, signed to Thor's Cave. In approximately 3/4 mile (1.2km), cross the stile on your right and head across the field towards the rocky outcrop. Cross a stile and take the right-hand path which leads to the mouth of the cave. Take care as the path can be slippery. Excavations of the cave have revealed flint arrowheads, bronze bracelets, pottery and animal bones, indicating that man once lived here thousands of years ago.

Opposite the cave entrance, take the stepping stone path and steeply descend into the Manifold Valley. At the bottom, cross the river and turn right along the broad pathway, fomerly the trackbed of the Manifold Light Railway and now a walk/cycle track. Cross the Wetton to Butterton road and continue until you reach Wetton Mill (National Trust café). Take the waymarked path to the rear of the café between cottages, signed to Wetton.

Climb steeply at first, then follow the well worn path through woodland and into a broad grassy glen between steep-sided hills. Walk through the valley until you reach a restored stone house (Pepper Inn). Go through the gateway and turn right through a squeeze-stile, signposted to Wetton. Head uphill to a stile and go over Wetton Hill, the path leading to a disused small quarry. Go through another squeeze-stile and follow the track to a road. Descend into Wetton, following it back to the inn.

YE OLDE ROYAL OAK INN, LEEK
DE6 2AF.
☎ 01335 310287

Directions: off Hulme End to Alstonefield road, between B5054 and A515
In an area much favoured by walkers and handy for the Peak District, this 17th-century stone-built inn is well furnished and offers an excellent choice of real ales. Traditional bar food; good Sunday lunches. Moorland garden.
Open: 12-3 7-11.
Bar Meals: 12-2 7-9.
Notes: Children welcome. Garden/patio. Parking.
(See page 431 for full entry)

DISTANCE: 4 miles (6.4km)
MAP: OS Landranger 119
TERRAIN: National Trust farmland, river valley and wooded hillsides
PATHS: Field and woodland paths, old railway track
GRADIENT: Some steep ascents and descents (can be muddy)

Walk submitted by Ye Olde Royal Oak

CAULDON

Map 16 SK04

Yew Tree Inn
ST10 3EJ ☎ 01538 308348 🖹 01782 212064

300-year-old pub with plenty of character and lots of fascinating artefacts, including pianolas, grandfather clocks, a crank handle telephone, a pub lantern and an award-winning landlord who's been here for over forty years! Interesting and varied snack menu consists of locally-made, hand-raised pork pies, sandwiches, rolls and quiche. Banana split and home-made fruit crumble feature among the sweets.
OPEN: 10-2.30 6-11 (Sun 12-3, 7-10.30) **BAR MEALS:** Snacks available during opening hours **BREWERY/COMPANY:** Free House 🍺: Burton Bridge, Titanic Mild, Interbrew Bass.
FACILITIES: Children welcome Dogs allowed Water
NOTES: Parking 50 **NOTES:** No credit cards

CHEADLE

Map 10 SK04

The Queens At Freehay 🍴
Counslow Rd, Freehay ST10 1RF
☎ 01538 722383 🖹 01538 722383
Dir: *Two miles from Alton Towers*
Located just 3.5 miles from Alton Towers, The Queens was transformed a few years ago from a run-down pub into a popular, award-winning eating house. The freshly-cooked meals include fish and game in season, along with traditional chargrilled steaks, and home-made beef and Guinness pie, and imaginative options like Moroccan lamb tagine, stir-fried duck with noodles, and Rumplestiltskin (rump steak with herby onions and melted Stilton).
OPEN: 12-2.30 6-11 Closed: 25-26 Dec, 31 Dec (eve), 1 Jan (eve) **BAR MEALS:** L served all week 12-2 D served all week 6-9.30 Av main course £7.95 **RESTAURANT:** L served all week 12-2 D served all week 6-9.30 **BREWERY/COMPANY:** Free House 🍺: Draught Bass, Draught Worthington Bitter. **FACILITIES:** Children welcome Garden: Small garden with four benches Dogs allowed Guide dogs only **NOTES:** Parking 30

CRESSWELL

Map 10 SJ93

Izaak Walton Inn 🍴 ♀
Cresswell Ln ST11 9RE ☎ 01782 392265 🖹 01782 392265
Dir: *Just off A50 SE of Stoke-on-Trent*

Named after the renowned author of 'The Compleat Angler', it is said that Isaak himself used to break his journey here to fish the River Blythe. Believed to date back to the mid-17th century, refurbishment in 1999 has recaptured its roots. Surrounded by wood panelling, in front of open fires, diners can choose chicken with ginger and apricot, sea bass with prawn and lobster sauce, beef in brandy mushroom sauce, or steak pie. There are super salads and grills with optional special sauces.

continued

OPEN: 12-11 (Sun 12-10.30) Closed: 25 Dec **BAR MEALS:** L served all week 12-10 D served all week **RESTAURANT:** L served all week 12-10 D served all week Av 3 course à la carte £15
BREWERY/COMPANY: Free House 🍺: Bass.
FACILITIES: Garden **NOTES:** Parking 80

ECCLESHALL

Map 15 SJ82

The George 🍴 ♀
Castle St ST21 6DF ☎ 01785 850300 🖹 01785 851452
e-mail: information@thegeorgeinn.freeserve.co.uk

A family-run, 16th-century former coaching inn with its own micro-brewery, where the owners' son produces award-winning Slater's ales. A new chef was expected at the time of preparing this report, but - as a guide - his predecessor's restaurant/bistro menu included medallions of beef fillet on a pâté croûton with Madeira sauce, mussels poached in garlic with cream and herb liquor (optional chilli), Staffordshire leg of lamb with black cherry sauce, and nutty creamed mushroom crumble.
OPEN: 11-11 (12-10.30 Sun) Closed: 25 Dec **BAR MEALS:** L served all week 12-9.30 D served all week 6-9.45 Av main course £9.95 **RESTAURANT:** L served all week 12-2.30 D served all week 6-9.45 Av 3 course à la carte £20 **BREWERY/COMPANY:** Free House 🍺: Slaters Ales. **FACILITIES:** Children welcome Dogs allowed **NOTES:** Parking 30

HIMLEY

Map 10 SO89

Crooked House
Coppice Mill DY3 4DA ☎ 01384 238583 🖹 01384 214911
Dir: *Telephone for directions*
Just three miles from the Black Country museum, this remarkable pub was built as a farmhouse in 1765. Mine shafts beneath the building collapsed in the late 19th century, leaving it leaning alarmingly. Optical illusions such as the wonky grandfather's clock, and bottles that roll uphill, are unsettling after a few pints! Traditional guest ales accompany grills, salads, and hot dishes like liver, bacon and onions; crusted trout; or leek and Gruyère crown.
OPEN: 11.30-2.30 5-11 Open all day Mar-Oct **BAR MEALS:** L served Mon-Sun 12-2 D served Mon-Sun 6-9 Av main course £5.50 **RESTAURANT:** L served Mon-Sun 12-2 D served Mon-Sun 6-9 **BREWERY/COMPANY:** 🍺: Pedigree, Camerons.
FACILITIES: Children welcome Children's licence Garden: Patio area with 10-12 tables Dogs allowed Water **NOTES:** Parking 40

★ **Star rating for inspected hotel accommodation**

LEEK
Map 16 SJ95

Abbey Inn ◐ ♀
Abbey Green Rd ST13 8SA ☎ 01538 382865 ▤ 01538 398604
e-mail: martin@abbeyinn.co.uk
Dir: Telephone for directions
Set in beautiful countryside on the Staffordshire moorlands, this 17th-century inn is on the outskirts of Leek, and handy for the potteries of Stoke-on-Trent. It is also conveniently close to Alton Towers and Tittesworth Reservoir, and with its spacious bars and restaurant, and large terrace, it is an ideal destination for a meal or a drink.
OPEN: 11-2.30 6.30-11 **BAR MEALS:** L served all week 11-2 D served all week 6.30-9 Av main course £4
BREWERY/COMPANY: Free House ◀: Interbrew Bass. ♀: 8
FACILITIES: Children welcome Children's licence Garden
NOTES: Parking 30

Ye Olde Royal Oak ◐
Wetton DE6 2AF ☎ 01335 310287 ▤ 01335 310336
e-mail: royaloakwetton@aol.com
Dir: A515 twrds Buxton, L after 4 miles to Manifold Valley-Alstonfield, follow signs to Wetton village,
Formerly part of the Chatsworth estate, this stone-built inn dates back over 400 years and has wooden beams recovered from oak ships at Liverpool Docks. It is now home to the World Annual Toe Wrestling Championships in June. The Tissington walking and cycling trail is close by, and the pub's moorland garden includes a camper's croft. Sample the landlord's collection of over 40 single malts, then tuck into steak and Guinness pie or filled Staffordshire oatcakes.
OPEN: 12-3 7-11 **BAR MEALS:** L served Thur-Tue 12-2 D served Thur-Tue 7-9 Av main course £7 **RESTAURANT:** L served Thur-Tue 12-2 D served Thur-Tue 7-9 Av 3 course à la carte £11.50
BREWERY/COMPANY: Free House ◀: Greene King Ruddles County, Jennings Cumberland, Black Sheep Special.
FACILITIES: Children welcome Garden: Grassed area with seating Dogs allowed Water, exercize area **NOTES:** Parking 20
See Pub Walk on page 429

Three Horseshoes Inn ★★ ◉ ♀
Buxton Rd, Blackshaw Moor ST13 8TW
☎ 01538 300296 ▤ 01538 300320
Dir: Telephone for directions
A sprawling creeper-covered inn geared to catering for visitors and locals in three smart eating outlets. Choose from the traditional décor and food of the bar carvery, the relaxed atmosphere of the brasserie, or the more formal restaurant. In both of these, the award-winning menu offers dishes ranging from traditional (tournedos Rossini; bangers and mash) to international steamed monkfish in banana leaf or Thai duck curry.
OPEN: 12-3 6-11 **BAR MEALS:** L served all week 12-2 D served all week 6.30-9 Av main course £6.95 **RESTAURANT:** L served Sun 12.30-1.30 D served Sun-Fri 6.30-9 Av 3 course à la carte £21
BREWERY/COMPANY: Free House **FACILITIES:** Children welcome Garden **NOTES:** Parking 100 **ROOMS:** 7 bedrooms 7 en suite s£45 d£60

NEWCASTLE-UNDER-LYME
Map 10 SJ84

Mainwaring Arms ♀
Whitmore ST5 5HR ☎ 01782 680851 ▤ 01782 680224
e-mail: info@mannersrestaurant.co.uk

A welcoming old creeper-clad inn on the Mainwaring family estate. Crackling log fires set the scene at this very traditional country retreat, where daily blackboard specials support the popular bar menu. Expect freshly-made sandwiches, home-made steak and kidney pie, pork and leek sausages with chive mash, grilled plaice with mustard sauce, or battered cod with chips and mushy peas.
OPEN: 12-11 (Sun 12-10.30) **BAR MEALS:** L served all week 12-2.30 D served all week 6-8.30 Av main course £5
BREWERY/COMPANY: Free House ◀: Boddingtons, Marstons Pedigree, Carling, Bombardier. **FACILITIES:** Children welcome Garden: Patio seats 25-30, food served outside Dogs allowed only when food service is over **NOTES:** Parking 60

NORBURY JUNCTION
Map 15 SJ72

The Junction Inn ◐
ST20 0PN ☎ 01785 284288 ▤ 01785 284288
Dir: From M6 take road for Eccleshall, L at Gt Bridgeford & head for Woodseaves, L there & head for Newport, L for Norb Junct
Not a railway junction, but a beautiful stretch of waterway where the Shropshire Union Canal meets the disused Newport arm. The inn offers fabulous views and a great stop-off point for canal walkers. Food ranges through baguettes, burgers and basket meals through grills and home-made pies. Popular options are sizzling chicken fajitas, giant battered cod and a gargantuan mixed grill. Caravans are welcome and canal boat hire is available.
OPEN: 11-11 (12-10.30 Sun) **BAR MEALS:** L served all week 11-9 D served all week 11-9 Av main course £4.95 **RESTAURANT:** L served all week 12-9 D served all week 12-9 Av 3 course à la carte £10 Av 4 course fixed price £10 **BREWERY/COMPANY:** Free House ◀: Banks Mild, Banks Bitter, Junction Ale and Guest ales.
FACILITIES: Children welcome Garden: Scenic garden with fabulous views Dogs allowed Water provided
NOTES: Parking 100

ONECOTE
Map 16 SK05

Jervis Arms ◐
ST13 7RU ☎ 01538 304206
Convenient for visitors from Leek or Ashbourne, this 17th-century inn set in the Peak National Park has a large streamside garden kitted out with swings and slides. Some 500 guest ales have featured over the past five years to accompany home-cooked steak and ale pie, salmon hollandaise, battered cod, popular roasts and T-bone steak

continued

ONECOTE continued

weighing in - uncooked - at 20oz. Additional menu items to satisfy vegetarians and children. Two annual beer festivals.
OPEN: 12-3 7-11 (Open from 6 in Summer) **BAR MEALS:** L served all week 12-2 D served all week 7-10 Av main course £5.50
BREWERY/COMPANY: Free House ◀: Interbrew Bass, Marston's Pedigree, Titanic Premium, Sarah Hughes Dark Ruby Mild.
FACILITIES: Children welcome Garden: Large beer garden, river, seats approx 60 Dogs allowed Water **NOTES:** Parking 50

ONNELEY   Map 15 SJ74

The Wheatsheaf Inn 🐾 ⊻
Barhill Rd CW3 9QF ☎ 01782 751581 ▤ 01782 751499
e-mail: thewheatsheaf.inn@virgin.net
Dir: *On the A525 between Madeley & Woore, 6.5m W of Newcastle Under Lyme*

Overlooking the local golf course and village cricket ground, this renovated wayside inn has been a hostelry since 1769. Solid oak beams, roaring log fires and distinctive furnishings are a smart setting for some fine dining. Specials include Chateaubriand roast, steamed halibut steak on buttered spinach, pan-fried kangaroo, and chicken breast in smoked bacon with creamy grape and cheese sauce. Bar meals are also available.
OPEN: 12-2.30 6-11 **BAR MEALS:** L served all week 12-2.30 D served all week 6-9.30 Av main course £6 **RESTAURANT:** D served all week 6.30-9.30 Av 3 course à la carte £15
BREWERY/COMPANY: Free House ◀: Bass, Worthington, Guest Ales. **FACILITIES:** Children welcome Garden: Food served outside Dogs allowed In the garden only **NOTES:** Parking 60

STAFFORD   Map 10 SJ92

Pick of the Pubs

The Hollybush Inn ⊻
Salt ST18 0BX ☎ 01889 508234 ▤ 01889 508058
e-mail: geoff@hollybushinn.co.uk
Dir: *Telephone for directions*
In the Domesday Book the village of Salt was recorded as Selte, which in Old English meant a salt pit. There's no written evidence of workings within the parish, but some existed not far away. In open countryside close to the Trent & Mersey Canal, the thatched Holly Bush became, during Charles II's time, only the second Staffordshire pub to be licensed, although the building may well date from the 12th century. Carved heavy beams, open fires, attractive prints and cosy alcoves characterise the comfortably old-fashioned interior. Lunchtime offerings include triple-decker sandwiches, jacket potatoes and toasties, while the main menu proposes Greek lamb, pot-roast venison,

home-made steak and kidney pudding, Holly Bush mixed grill, poached fillet of plaice and chargrilled steaks. Appearing as specials might be braised ham hock with horseradish sauce, hand-made pork, leek and Stilton sausages with fried eggs and chips, and slow-roast lamb shank with redcurrant gravy. Seafood dishes include blackened Cajun tuna loin with caramelised capsicums and red onions, and chargrilled red snapper with Jamaican spiced tomato chutney. You'll also find vegetarian options and a full range of desserts. A list of house wines by the glass supplements the cask ales. The pub regularly wins awards for its summer flower displays - all grown and planted by the landlady. In summer the large secluded beer garden plays host to jazz concerts and hog roasts. It won the Pub Website of the Year award in 2003.
OPEN: 12-2.30 6-11 (open all day Sat-Sun) **BAR MEALS:** L served all week 12-2 D served all week 6-9.30 Av main course £7.95 **BREWERY/COMPANY:** Free House ◀: Boddingtons, Pedigree, Bass. ⊻: 12 **FACILITIES:** Children welcome Garden: Large lawned garden with seatings Dogs allowed Water provided **NOTES:** Parking 25

Pick of the Pubs

The Moat House ★★★★ ◎◎ 🐾 ⊻
Lower Penkridge Rd, Acton Trussell ST17 0RJ
☎ 01785 712217 ▤ 01785 715344
e-mail: info@moathouse.co.uk
Dir: *M6 J13 towards Stafford, 1st R to Acton Trussell*

Grade II listed mansion dating back to the 15th century and situated behind its original moat. Quality bedrooms, conference facilities and corporate events are big attractions, and with four honeymoon suites, the Moat House is a popular venue for weddings. Inside are oak beams and an inglenook fireplace, and the bar and food trade brings in both the hungry and the curious who like to savour the charm and atmosphere of the place. Among the more popular dishes are chicken kebabs on a bed of mixed leaves with sweet chilli jam, Barnsley chop with mint mash, glazed vegetables and a red wine jus, Mediterranean vegetable strudel, tagliatelle carbonnara, and steak and ale pie. If there's room afterwards, try lemon steamed sponge, apple and banana crumble or banoffee pie in a caramel sauce. Up-market dining in the canal-side conservatory.
OPEN: 12-11 Closed: Dec 25-26 **BAR MEALS:** L served Mon-Sat 12-2.15 D served Sun-Fri 6-9.30 Av main course £10.50 **RESTAURANT:** L served all week 12-2 D served all week 7-10 Av 3 course à la carte £34 Av 3 course fixed price £27.95
BREWERY/COMPANY: Free House ◀: Bank's Bitter, Marston's Pedigree, Greene King Old Speckled Hen. ⊻: 8

continued

continued

England

FACILITIES: Children welcome Children's licence Garden: Adjoining the Moated Manor, overlooks moat **NOTES:** Parking 150 **ROOMS:** 32 bedrooms 32 en suite s£70 d£100

TATENHILL   Map 10 SK22

Horseshoe Inn ♀

Main St DE13 9SD ☎ 01283 564913 ▤ 01283 511314
Dir: *From A38 at Branston follow signs for Tatenhill*
Probably five to six hundred years old, this historic pub retains much original character, including evidence of a priest's hiding hole. In winter, log fires warm the bar and family area. In addition to home-made snacks like chilli con carne, and Horseshoe brunch, there are sizzling rumps and sirloins, chicken curry, moussaka, battered cod with chips and mushy peas, and a pasta dish of the week. And specials too - beef bourguignon, or steak and kidney pudding, for instance.
OPEN: 11-11 **BAR MEALS:** L served all week 2-9.30 D served all week 12-9.30 Av main course £6.50 **RESTAURANT:** L served all week 12-9.30 D served all week 12-9.30
BREWERY/COMPANY: W'hampton & Dudley ◖: Marstons Pedigree, Banks Original. ♀: 9 **FACILITIES:** Children welcome Garden: Small enclosed garden with fish pond Dogs allowed Water **NOTES:** Parking 70

TUTBURY   Map 10 SK22

Pick of the Pubs

Ye Olde Dog & Partridge Inn ★★ 🐾 ♀

High St DE13 9LS ☎ 01283 813030 ▤ 01283 813178
e-mail: info@dogandpartridge.net
Dir: *On A50 NW of Burton upon Trent (signposted from A50 & A511)*
A beautiful period building resplendent in its timbers and whitewashed walls, with abundant flower displays beneath the windows. The inn has stood in this charming village since the 15th century when Henry IV was on the throne. Its connection with the village sport of bull-running brought it into prominence, and it remains a focus of local activity including the nearby hunt. During the 18th century it became a coaching inn on the route to London. Five hundred years of offering hospitality has resulted in a well-deserved reputation for good food, comfortable accommodation and restful public areas. Bedrooms, including four posters and half testers, are individually furnished and charmingly decorated, and filled with modern luxuries. Two smart eating outlets ensure that all tastes are catered for. In the Carvery, a grand piano plays while diners choose from an extensive menu; start with a selection from the buffet, or go for fisherman's platter, or woodman's mushrooms, and follow on with a plate of roast meat, or perhaps steak and kidney pie, or ratatouille bake. In the brasserie, with its leather chairs and bare wooden tables, the fixed-price menu may lists fallen Dovedale blue cheese soufflé, or terrine of tame and wild duck, followed by chargrilled swordfish loin with mango and chilli salsa, or breast of guinea fowl. Time and space should be found for mouthwatering desserts like chocolate truffle torte, and pear and almond tart.
OPEN: 11.45-2 6-11 25-26 Dec Closed eve **RESTAURANT:** L served Tues-Sun 11.45-2 D served Tues-Sat 6-9.45 Av 3 course à la carte £19.95 **BREWERY/COMPANY:** Free House ◖: Marston's Pedigree, plus guest. **FACILITIES:** Children welcome Garden: Food served outside **NOTES:** Parking 100 **ROOMS:** 20 bedrooms 20 en suite s£75 d£95

WATERHOUSES   Map 16 SK05

Ye Olde Crown ♦♦ 🐾

Leek Rd ST10 3HL ☎ 01538 308204

A traditional village local, Ye Olde Crown dates from around 1648 when it was built as a coaching inn. Sitting on the bank of the River Hamps, it's also on the edge of the Peak District National Park and the Staffordshire moorlands. Inside are original stonework and interior beams, and open fires are lit in cooler weather. Sample menu includes roast beef, steak and kidney pie, chicken tikka masala, battered cod, and tuna pasta bake. Homely accommodation includes an adjacent cottage.
OPEN: 11.30-3 6.30-11 (Sun 12-3, 6.30-11) Closed: Dec 25 Sunday closed eve in Jan-Feb **BAR MEALS:** L served all week 12-2 D served all week 7-9.30 Av main course £7 **BREWERY/COMPANY:** Free House ◖: Carlsberg-Tetley Tetley Bitter, Burton Ale.
FACILITIES: Children welcome Dogs allowed except overnight by arrangement **NOTES:** Parking 30 **ROOMS:** 7 bedrooms 6 en suite s£22.50 d£45

WRINEHILL   Map 15 SJ74

The Crown Inn 🐾

Den Ln CW3 9BT ☎ 01270 820472 ▤ 01270 820472
e-mail: mark_condliffe@hotmail.com
Dir: *Telephone for directions*

A long-standing family-run pub that serves food, not a restaurant that serves beer. Food, nevertheless, plays an important part and the Crown is locally renowned for consistent good quality and generous portions. Some lunch or dinner ideas from the varied monthly-changing menu are its famous Crown steaks, fish specials, such as crayfish with a creamy tomato and tequila sauce, and oven-baked garlic chicken with herb mayonnaise. Vegetarians are well catered for, and vegans can be accommodated. Always five real ales.

continued

continued

England

WRINEHILL continued

OPEN: 12-3 6-1 (Sun 12-4 6-10.30) **BAR MEALS:** L served Tue-Sun 12-2 D served all week 6.30-9.30 Av main course £7.45
🍺: Marstons Pedigree, Marstons Bitter, Adnams Bitter, Banci Original & Guest Beers. **FACILITIES:** Garden: Secluded lawn area with benches **NOTES:** Parking 36

YOXALL   Map 10 SK11

The Crown
Main St DE13 8NQ ☎ 01543 472551
Dir: On A515 N of Lichfield
In a picturesque village, this pub is reputedly over 250 years old, its name possibly deriving from its former use as the local courthouse. Within easy reach of Uttoxeter racecourse and Alton Towers, it's a great spot to enjoy locally-sourced, home-cooked food prepared by the landlord. Expect on the regularly-changing menu such lunchtime bites as a breakfast brunch and hot filled baguettes, whilst evening options such as steak and Guinness pie are supplemented by offerings posted on the chalkboard.
OPEN: 11.30-3 5.30-11 (Sat-Sun & BHs open all day)
BAR MEALS: L served all week 12-2 D served Mon-Sat 6.30-9 Av main course £6.50 **BREWERY/COMPANY:** Marstons
🍺: Marston's Pedigree. **FACILITIES:** Children welcome Garden Dogs allowed **NOTES:** Parking 20

SUFFOLK

ALDEBURGH   Map 13 TM45

The Mill Inn
Market Cross Place IP15 5BJ ☎ 01728 452563 ▤ 01728 452028
e-mail: tedmillinn@btinternet.com
Dir: Follow Aldeburgh signs from A12 on A1094. Pub last building on L before sea

Occupying a seafront position, this genuine traditional fisherman's inn is frequented by the local lifeboat crew, those visiting the North Warren bird reserve, or walkers from Thorpness and Orford. Opposite is the 17th-century Moot Hall. Good value food ranges from baguettes, crab salads and sandwiches to seafood lasagne and a choice of steaks. The emphasis is very much on locally-caught fish.
OPEN: 11-3 6-11 (11-11 summer) **BAR MEALS:** L served all week 12-2 D served Fri-Wed 7-9 Av main course £7 **RESTAURANT:** L served all week 12-2 D served Fri-Wed 7-9 Av 3 course à la carte £14 **BREWERY/COMPANY:** Adnams 🍺: Adnams Bitter, Broadside, Regatta & Fisherman. **FACILITIES:** Dogs allowed Water

♀ 7   **Number of wines by the glass**

ALDRINGHAM   Map 13 TM46

The Parrot and Punchbowl Inn & Restaurant
Aldringham Ln IP16 4PY ☎ 01728 830221
e-mail: paul@parrotandpunchbowl.fsnet.co.uk

Just a mile from the Suffolk Heritage Coast, this 16th-century pub was once the centre of local smuggling activities. Inside you can expect plenty of beams, brasses and good ales on tap. The wide-ranging bar menu features good seafood options - pan-roasted salmon on buttered spinach, grilled thick end of cod, or Dover sole. Other options include peppered rump of lamb, slow honey-roasted belly of pork, tournedos Rossini, or wild mushroom risotto. Outside there's a family garden with children's adventure playground.
OPEN: 11.30-3 5.30-11 (Sun 12-3, 7-10.30) **BAR MEALS:** L served Everyday 12-2.30 D served Everyday 6.30-9.30 Av main course £8.50 **RESTAURANT:** L served Everyday 12-2.30 D served Everyday 6.30-9.30 Av 3 course à la carte £20 Av 2 course fixed price £9.75 **BREWERY/COMPANY:** Enterprise Inns 🍺: Adnams, Greene King, Guest beer. ♀: 10 **FACILITIES:** Garden: Family garden, walled shaded garden **NOTES:** Parking 60

BARNBY   Map 13 TM49

Pick of the Pubs

The Swan Inn
Swan Ln NR34 7QF ☎ 01502 476646 ▤ 01502 562513
Dir: Just off the A146 between Lowestoft and Beccles
Arguably one of Suffolk's foremost fish restaurants - the menu lists up to 80 different seafood dishes - the Swan still looks on itself as a traditional village pub with a strong local following. The distinctive pink-painted property dates from 1690, and can be found in the picturesque village of Barnby, which nestles in its rural surroundings. Owned by a family of Lowestoft fish wholesalers, it comprises a village bar that is at the centre of local activities, and the rustic Fisherman's Cove restaurant, with its low beams and nautical memorabilia. The menu is a fish-lovers delight: starters include smoked sprats, smoked trout pâté and Italian seafood salad, while main dishes range from monkfish tails in garlic butter, to crab gratin and whole grilled turbot. Meat lovers are not left out: various steaks are offered along with home-cooked gammon salad.
OPEN: 11-3 6-12 **BAR MEALS:** L served all week 12-2 D served all week 7-9.30 Av main course £8 **RESTAURANT:** L served all week 12-2 D served all week 7-9.30 Av 3 course à la carte £15 **BREWERY/COMPANY:** Free House 🍺: Interbrew Bass, Adnams Best, Broadside, Greene King Abbot Ale.
FACILITIES: Children welcome Garden: Food served outside **NOTES:** Parking 30

The Angel

Combine a fascinating stroll around England's best preserved medieval town, where some 300 listed buildings line its quaint streets, with an excursion into the peaceful countryside to the north of the town.

From the Angel, walk ahead through the Market Square and take the narrow street (Market Lane) in the right-hand corner to reach the High Street. Turn right and walk along the pavement for around 300 yards (274m) to the old railway bridge. Just before the bridge, take the signed path left for the railway walk. Turn left onto the railway cutting at the bottom and follow the old track bed. Cross a road via gates and continue along the course of the old railway.

Pass beneath a bridge and walk up the ramp onto the road. Turn right over the bridge, then take the footpath left in the direction of Lavenham church. Follow this path until you reach Park Road to the rear of the church and turn left.

Bear right at the road junction and look for a footpath on your right by a gap in the wall. Go through a gate, cross a bridge and walk past The Hall. Enter the churchyard via a gate, visit the impressive church with its great square-buttressed flint tower rising to more than 140ft (40m), and exit onto the main road. Turn left downhill into the town.

At The Swan Hotel, turn right along Water Street and then left into Lady Street, opposite Lavenham Priory. Enter Market Place and walk back to the inn. If you wish to explore and learn more about this prosperous medieval wool town, why not hire the audio tour of the town from the pharmacy next to the Swan Hotel.

★★ ⊚
THE ANGEL, LAVENHAM
Market Place CO10 9QZ.
☎ 01787 247388

Directions: village on A1141 E of A134 between Sudbury & Bury St Edmunds Delightful early 15th-century inn overlooking the medieval marketplace and the magnificent timbered guildhall. Expect a friendly welcome, East Anglian ales and freshly prepared food in the traditionally furnished bar. Bedrooms.
Open: 11-11 (Sun 12-10.30).
Bar Meals: 12-2.15 6.45-9.15.
Notes: Children welcome. Garden, front patio. Parking.
(See page 444 for full entry)

DISTANCE: 3 miles (4.8km)
MAP: OS Landranger 155
TERRAIN: Town streets and farmland
PATHS: Field paths, disused railway, pavements
GRADIENT: General level

Walk submitted by The Angel Inn

England

BILDESTON
Map 13 TL94

The Crown Hotel
High St IP7 7EB ☎ 01449 740510 ▤ 01449 740510
Dir: *On B1115 between Hadleigh & Stowmarket*
A beautiful 15th-century half-timbered former coaching inn with oak-beamed bars and lounge. There is also a formal restaurant, and two acres of garden. Originally a wool merchants', it lays claim to being one of the most-haunted pubs in Britain; only the brave, it's said, will stay in Room 6! A typical menu includes oven-baked cod with garlic and thyme, steak and kidney pie, vegetable lasagne, and chicken stuffed with wild mushrooms and apricots.
OPEN: 11-2.30 6-11 **BAR MEALS:** L served all week 12-2 D served all week 6.30-9.30 **RESTAURANT:** L served all week 12-2 D served all week 6.30-9.30 **BREWERY/COMPANY:** Free House
🍺: Adnams, Broadside. **FACILITIES:** Children welcome Garden Dogs allowed **NOTES:** Parking 30

BLYFORD
Map 13 TM47

Queens Head Inn
Southwold Rd IP19 9JY ☎ 01502 478404
Dir: *From A12 after Blythburgh take A145, fork L towards Halesworth, Pub on L opp church*
Once used by smugglers, with a secret underground passage linking the inn with the nearby church, this 14th-century thatched building is supposedly haunted by the ghosts of seven smugglers shot in the tunnel by excise men.
BAR MEALS: L served Mon-Sun & BH 12-2.30 D served Mon-Sun & BH 7-9.30 **BREWERY/COMPANY:** Adnams 🍺: Adnams - Bitter, Broadside. **FACILITIES:** Garden: Large grassed area leading to large field **NOTES:** Parking 50

BRANDESTON
Map 13 TM26

The Queens Head
The Street IP13 7AD ☎ 01728 685307
Dir: *From A14 take A1120 to Earl Soham, then S to Brandeston*
A village pub dating back 400 years, with wooden panelling, quarry tile floors and open fires. The extensive gardens and play tree are ideal for children, and camping and caravanning facilities are available, with electric hook up, shower and toilet facilities. Adnams ales are served, and a comprehensive menu taking in sandwiches, jacket potatoes, pizza, curries, seafood casserole, and steak and kidney pudding. Every Monday there's an offer of two main meals for the price of one.
OPEN: 11.30-3 6-11 (Sun 12-3, 7-10.30) **BAR MEALS:** L served all week 12-2 D served all week 6.30-9 **RESTAURANT:** L served all week D served all week **BREWERY/COMPANY:** Adnams
🍺: Adnams Broadside, & Bitter seasonal ale. **FACILITIES:** Garden: Dogs allowed **NOTES:** Parking 30

We only include details of accommodation that has been inspected by the AA (big Stars or Diamonds at the top of an entry), or the RAC, VisitBritain, VisitScotland or WTB (small Stars or Diamonds at the end of an entry).

BROCKLEY GREEN
Map 12 TL74

The Plough Inn 🛏 ⚲
CO10 8DT ☎ 01440 786789 ▤ 01440 786710
e-mail: ploughdave@aol.com
Dir: *Take B1061 from A143, approx 1.5m beyond Kedington*
Quality and service are the hallmark of this delightfully-situated free house, which has been run by the same family since 1957. The traditional interior retains its oak beams and soft red brickwork, whilst major extensions have added a restaurant and eight comfortable bedrooms. The distinctive bar menu includes hunky lamb shank, venison steak and daily specials, whilst restaurant diners can expect honey-glazed duck, chargrilled tuna loin, or vegetable stirfry with wild rice.
OPEN: 12-2.30 5-11 **BAR MEALS:** L served all week 12-2 D served all week 7-9.30 Av main course £8.50 **RESTAURANT:** L served all week 12-2 D served all week 7-9.30 Av 3 course à la carte £22.50
BREWERY/COMPANY: Free House 🍺: Greene King IPA, Adnams Best, Fuller's London Pride, Woodforde's Wherry Best Bitter. ⚲: 12
FACILITIES: Children welcome Garden: Large lawn bordered by shrubs Dogs allowed Water bowls **NOTES:** Parking 50

BROME
Map 13 TM17

Pick of the Pubs

Cornwallis Arms ★★★ ◎ 🛏 ⚲
IP23 8AJ ☎ 01379 870326 ▤ 01379 870051
e-mail: info@cornwallis.com
Dir: *Just off A140 at Brome, follow B1077 to Eye.*
Pub is 30 metres on the left
An avenue of limes, some impressive yew topiary and a pretty water garden provide a fine backdrop to Brome Hall's former Dower House. Set in 20 acres, the building dates back to 1561, and many of the original beams, panels and oak and mahogany settles remain from those far-off days. In the log-fired Tudor Bar there's a 60-foot well. Chef and his team make everything from fresh, mostly locally-supplied ingredients. Ham and eggs here is not that simple, because what you actually get is roulade of smoked ham, fried quails' eggs and truffled crisps. Even the ploughman's sets itself apart from its plebeian cousins - mature cheddar and spring onion in a fried sandwich with pickled beetroot and shallots. Steak and kidney pudding is made with beef suet and Adnam's ale, baked hake comes with a purée of celeriac, crispy ham and red chard, and supreme of chicken with harissa, firecracker rice and pickled mouli.
OPEN: 11-11 **BAR MEALS:** L served all week 12-10 D served all week Av main course £9 **RESTAURANT:** L served all week 12-2.30 D served all week 6.30-9.45 Av 3 course fixed price £24 **BREWERY/COMPANY:** Free House 🍺: Adnams, Broadside, St Peters Best. ⚲: 30 **FACILITIES:** Children welcome Garden: 21 acres of gardens, pond with ducks Dogs allowed Water **NOTES:** Parking 400 **ROOMS:** 16 bedrooms 16 en suite 3 family rooms s£90.50 d£112.50

BURY ST EDMUNDS
Map 13 TL86

The Linden Tree 🛏
7 Out Northgate IP33 1JQ ☎ 01284 754600
Dir: *Opposite railway station*
A former Victorian station hotel with a charming garden and conservatory. It has a bustling, cheery atmosphere in its

continued

stripped pine bar and family dining area with something for everyone on the menu. Family favourites include home-made sausage casserole, chicken curry, or steak and mushroom pies and lamb, duck, turkey and beef in various guises from the grill. Linden burgers, leek and mushroom lasagne, assorted salads and children's dishes complete a large repertoire that lives up to its promise.
OPEN: 11-3 5-11 Closed: Xmas for 3 days **BAR MEALS:** L served all week 12-2 D served all week 6-9.30 Av main course £8
RESTAURANT: L served all week 12-2 D served all week 6-9.30
BREWERY/COMPANY: Greene King ◀: Greene King, IPA, Abbot Ale, Ruddles County & Old Speckled Hen. **FACILITIES:** Children welcome Garden: Large, picnic tables, play area

The Nutshell
17 The Traverse IP33 1BJ ☎ 01284 764867
Only a few customers can drink in this diminutive three-storey pub at any one time, although 102 people and a dog were shoehorned in 20 years ago. Measuring just 15' x 7' 6", it's acknowledged by Guinness World Records as Britain's smallest pub, requiring its three resident ghosts to forever walk through each other. A 400-year-old cat hangs from the ceiling. No food, although the pub jokes about its dining area for parties of two or fewer.
OPEN: 12-11pm (closed Sun) **BREWERY/COMPANY:** Greene King ◀: Greene King IPA & Abbot Ale, Guest Ales.
FACILITIES: Dogs allowed **NOTES:** No credit cards

The Six Bells at Bardwell ♦♦♦♦ 🐾 ♀
The Green, Bardwell IP31 1AW
☎ 01359 250820 ▤ 01359 250820
e-mail: sixbellsbardwell@aol.com
Dir: From A143 take turning marked Six Bells & Bardwell Windmill, premises 1m on L just before village green
This low-beamed 16th-century inn was immortalised in the classic comedy series Dad's Army. The name refers to the number of bells in the village church, which were rung at the impending arrival of a coach. Notable features inside are the inglenook fireplace and old Suffolk range. The daily dinner menu offers dishes like Suffolk loin of pork steaks topped with Parma-style ham, Mozzarella, tomato and a herb crust, and breast of Barbary duck with an orange and ginger sauce. Cottage-style accommodation is available in a converted barn.
OPEN: 6.30-10.30 (Fri-Sat 6-11) Closed: 25-26 Dec
BAR MEALS: D served all week 6.15-9 Av main course £10.95
RESTAURANT: D served all week 6.45-8.30 Av 3 course fixed price £17.50 **BREWERY/COMPANY:** Free House ◀: Boddingtons, Batemans, Greene King IPA. ♀: 7 **FACILITIES:** Garden: Courtyard area with seating **NOTES:** Parking 40 **ROOMS:** 10 bedrooms 10 en suite 1 family rooms s£45 d£60 no children overnight

The Three Kings ♦♦♦♦ 🐾 NEW
Hengrave Rd, Fornham All Saints IP28 6LA
☎ 01284 766979 ▤ 01284 723308
e-mail: enquiries@the-three-kings.com
A pretty pub with lots of converted Grade II listed outbuildings providing comfortable bedrooms. Plenty of exposed wood and interesting artefacts create a traditional pub atmosphere, and food is served in the bar, conservatory and restaurant, as well as the courtyard. Specials range from steak and ale pie to toad in the hole, and there are steaks, ploughman's, and vegetarian dishes.
OPEN: 11-3 5.30-11 (Sun 12-10.30) **BAR MEALS:** L served all week 11.30-2.30 D served all week 5.30-9.30 Av main course £6
RESTAURANT: L served Tue-Sun 12-2 D served Tue-Sat 7-8.30
BREWERY/COMPANY: Greene King ◀: Greene King IPA & Abbot.

FACILITIES: Children welcome Children's licence Garden: Patio area, benches **NOTES:** Parking 28 **ROOMS:** 9 bedrooms 9 en suite 2 family rooms s£55 d£75

CAVENDISH   Map 13 TL84

Bull Inn ♀
High St CO10 8AX ☎ 01787 280245
Dir: A134 Bury St Edmunds to Long Melford, then R at green, pub 5m on R
A Victorian pub set in one of Suffolk's most beautiful villages, with an unassuming façade hiding a splendid 15th-century beamed interior. Expect a good atmosphere and decent food, with the daily-changing blackboard menu listing perhaps curries, shank of lamb, fresh fish and shellfish, and a roast on Sundays. Outside there's a pleasant terraced garden.
OPEN: 11-3 6-11 (Sun 12-10.30) **BAR MEALS:** L served Tue-Sun 12-2 D served Tue-Sun 6.30-9 Av main course £7.95
RESTAURANT: L served Tue-Sun 12-2 D served Tue-Sun 6.30-9 Av 3 course à la carte £18 **BREWERY/COMPANY:** Adnams ◀: Adnams Bitter & Broadside. **FACILITIES:** Children welcome Garden: Terraced Garden Dogs allowed **NOTES:** Parking 30

CHELMONDISTON   Map 13 TM23

Butt & Oyster ♀
Pin Mill Ln IP9 1JW ☎ 01473 780764 ▤ 01473 780764
The role of this 16th-century pub on the eerie Suffolk coast has always been to provide sustenance for the local bargees and rivermen whose thirst for beer is near legendary. Today, with its character still thankfully intact, the Butt & Oyster is a favourite haunt of locals, tourists and yachting types. A mixture of seafood and traditional dishes characterises the menu, including toad in the hole, steak and kidney pie and scampi and chips.
OPEN: 11-11 (Sun 12-10.30) Dec 25-26 Dec 31 Closed eve
BAR MEALS: L served all week 12-2.30 D served all week 6.30-9.30 Av main course £8 **BREWERY/COMPANY:** Pubmaster ◀: Tolly Cobbold, IPA, Adnams, Flowers Original. **FACILITIES:** Children welcome Garden: outdoor eating, riverside Dogs allowed Garden only, Water **NOTES:** Parking 40

CHILLESFORD   Map 13 TM35

The Froize Inn 🐾
The Street IP12 3PU ☎ 01394 450282 ▤ 01394 459174
e-mail: dine@froize.co.uk
Dir: From the A12 (toward Lowestoft) take B1084, Chillesford 5m
Built on the site of Chillesford Friary, this distinctive red-brick building dates back to around 1490 and stands on today's popular Suffolk Coastal Path. Since summer 2002, the Froize has been owned by local Chef David Grimwood whose blend of rustic British and continental food offers varied menus in a traditional English pub with a modern dining room. Food options may include honey-roast lamb shanks, venison, ale and mushroom pie, or oven-baked salmon with pistachio crust.
OPEN: 11.30-2.30 6.30-11 Closed Mon **BAR MEALS:** L served Tues-Sun D served Tues-Sun 6.30 **RESTAURANT:** L served Tue-Sun 12-2 D served Thu-Sat 6.30 Av 3 course à la carte £23 Av 2 course fixed price £9 **BREWERY/COMPANY:** Free House ◀: Adnams.
FACILITIES: Children welcome Garden: Large fenced area with outside seating **NOTES:** Parking 70

♦ **Pubs with Red Diamonds are the top places in the AA's three, four and five diamond ratings**

continued

COCKFIELD — Map 13 TL95

Three Horseshoes 🛏 ♀
Stow's Hill IP30 0JB ☎ 01284 828177 🖷 01284 828177
e-mail: john@threehorseshoespub.co.uk
Dir: A134 towards Sudbury, then L onto A1141 towards Lavenham

Built as a thatched long hall around 1350, the oak kingpost supporting its massive beams and vaulted ceilings is one of the oldest in Suffolk. No doubt Lovejoy, TV's dodgy antique dealer, spotted it while filming here. Eat in the restaurant, bar or conservatory, with its views over rolling countryside. A good selection of starters precedes steaks, grills, fish, pies, curries and vegetarian dishes. Specialities include cod poached in brandy and lobster sauce.
OPEN: 11-3 6-11 Sun 10.30 Closed: 1st 2 wks in Jan **BAR MEALS:** L served Wed-Mon 12-2 D served Wed-Mon 6-9.30 Av main course £7.95 **RESTAURANT:** L served Wed-Mon 12-2 D served Wed-Mon 6-9.30 Av 3 course fixed price £12.95 **BREWERY/COMPANY:** Free House ◖: Greene King IPA, Adnams, Horseshoes Bitter, Mauldons. ♀: 9 **FACILITIES:** Children welcome Garden: Enclosed with gazebo and water feature Dogs allowed Water **NOTES:** Parking 90

COTTON — Map 13 TM06

Pick of the Pubs

The Trowel & Hammer Inn 🛏
Mill Rd IP14 4QL ☎ 01449 781234 🖷 01449 781765
Dir: From A14 follow signs to Haughley, then Bacton, then turn left for Cotton.

A little hidden away - find Scuffin's Lane and you're warm - this thatched, wisteria-covered pub dates back some 550 years. Merchants and cotton traders heading inland from the coast used to pull in here, and Milton drank in the bar when he lived in Stowmarket. The relaxed atmosphere owes much to a decorative style that stays traditional without the need for any twee bits of nonsense - old oak timbers, red carpets, and various lighting levels do the job nicely. Daily-changing menus offer unfussy, freshly-cooked food, with nine or ten starters ranging from farmhouse vegetable and chicken soup, to goujons of plaice, whitebait and squid rings. Among some 14 main courses are Chinese duck stirfry with pak choi and noodles, sirloin steak with peppercorn sauce, and whole trout and tiger prawn salad. Real ales come from Suffolk's Adnams, Mauldens and Nethergate breweries, and there's a good wine list with several half bottles.
OPEN: 12-3 6-11 (Sat/Sun all day) **BAR MEALS:** L served all week 12-2 D served all week 6-9.30 **RESTAURANT:** L served all week 12-2 D served Mon-Sat 6-9.30 **BREWERY/COMPANY:** Free House ◖: Adnams Bitter, Greene King IPA & Abbot Ale, Nethergate, Mauldons. **FACILITIES:** Garden: Large garden with swimming pool Dogs allowed Water, biscuits **NOTES:** Parking 50

DUNWICH — Map 13 TM47

Pick of the Pubs

The Ship Inn 🛏
St James St IP17 3DT ☎ 01728 648219 🖷 01728 648675
Dir: N on A12 from Ipswich thru Yoxford, R signed Dunwich
Dunwich, famous for being one of England's premier ports in the Middle Ages, is now just a small, but appealing, seaside village with a ruined friary. Its long decline began with a devastating storm in 1326, and continues even today as the sea erodes Suffolk's soft cliffs. Whoever built the Ship had the foresight to do so inland. Once the haunt of smugglers and seafarers, it is now a popular dining pub using the best and freshest local produce, especially fish. At lunchtime, cod and chips, salads and ploughman's are usually available. Starters at dinner include whitebait, bacon and walnut salad, and black pudding, with apple cider and wholegrain mustard sauce. Main courses include steak and ale casserole, pork in peach and Madeira sauce, and several salads. Vegetarians could opt for spinach flan and there is a small selection of children's dishes. Real ales from Suffolk's own Adnams and Mauldons.
OPEN: 11-11 **BAR MEALS:** L served all week 12-2 D served all week 7-9.00 Av main course £7.95 **RESTAURANT:** L served all week 12-2 D served all week 7-9.00 Av 3 course à la carte £16 **BREWERY/COMPANY:** Free House ◖: Adnams, Mauldons. **FACILITIES:** Children welcome Garden: Dogs allowed **NOTES:** Parking 10

EARL SOHAM — Map 13 TM26

Victoria 🛏
The Street IP13 7RL ☎ 01728 685758
Dir: From the A14 at Stowmarket, Earl Soham is on the A1120
Backing on to the village green, this friendly, down-to-earth pub has its own brewery attached to the rear of the building. Traditional pub fare is on offer, like home-made chilli, baked gammon, various meat and game casseroles, and smoked salmon salad, along with such light lunches as macaroni cheese, filled jacket potatoes, toasted sandwiches and various ploughman's. Home-made desserts include sponge pudding and treacle, and walnut tart.
OPEN: 11.30-3 6-11 (Sun 12-3, 7-10.30) **BAR MEALS:** L served all week 11.30-2 D served all week 6-10 Av main course £6.95 **BREWERY/COMPANY:** Free House ◖: Earl Soham-Victoria Bitter, Albert Ale, & Gannet Mild (all brewed on site). Earl Soham Porter, Edward Ale. **FACILITIES:** Children welcome Garden: Benches at front and rear of pub Dogs allowed garden only **NOTES:** Parking 25

EASTBRIDGE — Map 13 TM46

The Eels Foot Inn 🐑
IP16 4SN ☎ 01728 830154 e-mail: corinnewebber@aol.com
Dir: *From A12 at Yoxford take B1122 (signed Leiston/Sizewell). Turn L at Theberton*
An ale house since at least 1533, part of today's pub was a cobbler's cottage: he used a metal 'eel' to help shape the ankle-piece on a lady's boot. Right on the river, it has in its time been a smugglers' pub and a regular stop for journeymen and drovers. Straightforward menus offer egg and chips, liver and bacon, salmon, cod and smoked eels. Regular folk music nights since the 1800s, and it's handy for visitors to Minsmere Bird Reserve.
OPEN: 12-3 6-11 Mon, Wed Closed eve **BAR MEALS:** L served all week 12-2.30 D served all week 7-9.30 Av main course £7 **RESTAURANT:** L served all week 12-2.30 D served all week 7-9.30 **BREWERY/COMPANY:** Adnams 🍺: Timothy Taylor Landlord, Adnams Regatta, Pedigree. **FACILITIES:** Children welcome Garden: Food served outside Dogs allowed water bowls **NOTES:** Parking 200 No credit cards

ERWARTON — Map 13 TM23

The Queens Head 🐑
The Street IP9 1LN ☎ 01473 787550
Dir: *From Ipswich take B1456 to Shotley*
Fine views of the coast and countryside can be enjoyed from this handsome 16th-century building in traditional Suffolk style. Low oak-beamed ceilings, exposed timbers and first class meals make this a worthwhile destination. In the conservatory restaurant overlooking the River Stowe enjoy chestnut casserole, vegetable stew with herb dumpling, pan-fried Cajun-style chicken breast, duck with black cherry and brandy sauce, and steak and kidney pie. Good pudding dishes, like chocolate lumpy bumpy.
OPEN: 11-3 6.30-11 (Sun 12-3, 7-10.30) Closed: 25 Dec **BAR MEALS:** L served all week 12-2.45 D served all week 7-9.30 Av main course £7.95 **RESTAURANT:** L served all week 12-2.45 D served all week 7-9.30 **BREWERY/COMPANY:** Free House 🍺: Adnams Bitter & Broadside, Greene King IPA. **FACILITIES:** Children welcome Garden **NOTES:** Parking 30

EYE — Map 13 TM17

The White Horse Inn ◆◆◆◆ 🐑 NEW
Stoke Ash IP23 7ET ☎ 01379 678222 ▤ 01379 678557
e-mail: whitehorse@stokeash.fsbusiness.co.uk
Dir: *On the main A140 between Ipswich & Norwich*
A 17th-century coaching inn set amid lovely Suffolk countryside. The heavily-timbered interior, comprising two bars and a restaurant, features an inglenook fireplace, and outside there is a patio with a grassy area secluded from the main road. An extensive menu is supplemented by lunchtime snacks and daily specials from the blackboard. Dishes include seafood tagliatelle, and fillet of beef Wellington with bitter onions and wholegrain mustard. Spacious motel accommodation is available in the grounds.
OPEN: 11-11 (Sun 11-10.30) **BAR MEALS:** L served all week 11-9.30 D served all week 11-9.30 Av main course £8 **RESTAURANT:** L served all week 11-9.30 D served all week 11-9.30 Av 3 course à la carte £14.50 **BREWERY/COMPANY:** Free House 🍺: Adnams, Greene King Abbot. **FACILITIES:** Children welcome Children's licence Garden: Patio & grass area **NOTES:** Parking 60 **ROOMS:** 7 bedrooms 7 en suite 1 family rooms s£39.95 d£54.95

FRAMLINGHAM — Map 13 TM26

The Station Hotel 🐑 ♀
Station Rd IP13 9EE ☎ 01728 723455
Dir: *Bypass Ipswich heading toward Lowestoft on the A12*
Since trains stopped coming to Framlingham in 1962, the buildings of the former station hotel have been put to good use. One is a vintage motorcycle repair shop, while another is an antique bed showroom. The hotel has established itself as a popular destination, with a good reputation for seafood and locally-brewed beers. Check out the menu for roll-mop herrings, seafood platter, Loch Fyne oysters, smoked trout salad, greenlip mussels and corn beef hash with a cheese topping.
OPEN: 12-2.30 5-11 **BAR MEALS:** L served all week 12-2 D served all week 7-9.30 Av main course £6.95 **RESTAURANT:** L served all week 12-2 D served all week 7-9.30 Av 3 course à la carte £11 **BREWERY/COMPANY:** Free House 🍺: Earl Soham Victoria, Albert & Mild. **FACILITIES:** Children welcome Garden: Pond, patio, food served outdoors Dogs allowed Water, Biscuits **NOTES:** Parking 20

FRAMSDEN — Map 13 TM15

The Dobermann Inn 🐑
The Street IP14 6HG ☎ 01473 890461
Dir: *S off A1120 (Stowmarket/Yoxford)*
Previously The Greyhound, the pub was renamed by its current proprietor, a prominent breeder and judge of Dobermanns. The thatched roofing, gnarled beams, open fire and assorted furniture reflect its 16th-century origins. Food ranges from sandwiches and salads to main courses such as game pie, liver and bacon casserole or favourites such as Dover sole or sirloin steak. Vegetarians could feast on mushroom Stroganoff or spicy nut loaf. Indulge yourself with the legendary banana split!
OPEN: 12-3 7-11 **BAR MEALS:** L served all week 12-2 D served all week 7-10 Av main course £7 **RESTAURANT:** L served all week 12-2 D served all week 7-10 **BREWERY/COMPANY:** Free House 🍺: Adnams Bitter & Broadside, Greene King Abbot Ale, Mauldons Moletrap Bitter. **FACILITIES:** Garden: Small beer garden, BBQ, shrubs, stream Dogs allowed Water **NOTES:** Parking 27 No credit cards

GREAT GLEMHAM — Map 13 TM36

The Crown Inn
IP17 2DA ☎ 01728 663693
Dir: *A12 Ipswich to Lowestoft, in Stratford-St-Andrew L at Shell garage. Crown 1.5m*
Cosy 17th-century village pub overlooking the Great Glemham Estate and within easy reach of the Suffolk Heritage Coast. You can eat in the extensively-renovated bars and large flower-filled garden, where moussaka, carbonnade of beef, Somerset lamb casserole, roasted vegetables with pasta, and spinach and Feta cheese tart from the specials menu might be followed by fresh fruit Pavlova or traditional sherry trifle.
OPEN: 11.30-2.30 6.30-11 (closed Mon) **BAR MEALS:** L served Tue-Sun 11.30-2.30 D served Tue-Sun 6.30-10 Av main course £7.95 **BREWERY/COMPANY:** Free House 🍺: Greene King Old Speckled Hen & IPA. **FACILITIES:** Children welcome Garden: Large lawn, flower border, picnic table Dogs allowed **NOTES:** Parking 20

◆ **Pubs with Red Diamonds are the top places in the AA's three, four and five diamond ratings**

England

HADLEIGH — Map 13 TM04

The Marquis of Cornwallis ♀
Upper St, Layham IP7 5JZ ☎ 01473 822051 🖷 01473 822051
e-mail: marquislayham@aol.com
Dir: *From Colchester take A12 then B1070 towards Hadleigh. Layham signed on L, last village before Hadleigh*

This late 16th-century inn is named after a British military commander who was defeated in the American War of Independence, and the candlelit building is situated in two acres of gardens overlooking the Brett Valley. Dishes are cooked to order from local Suffolk produce, and traditional bar snacks and home-made pies are supplemented by a menu that includes whole baked trout, leek and cheese quiche, Scotch rump steak, or lamb and coconut curry.
OPEN: 12-3 6-11 (Sun 7-10.30) (Whit-Aug Sat 12-11, Sun 12-10.30)
BAR MEALS: L served all week 12-2.30 D served all week 7-9.30 Av main course £6.75 **RESTAURANT:** L served all week 12-2.30 D served all week 7-9.30 Av 3 course à la carte £15 **BREWERY/COMPANY:** Free House ◫: Adnams & Broadside, Greene King IPA & Abbot Ale. ♀: 9
FACILITIES: Children welcome Garden: 2 acres, river, overlooks valley Dogs allowed Water **NOTES:** Parking 30

HALESWORTH — Map 13 TM37

Pick of the Pubs

The Queen's Head 🛏 ♀
The Street, Bramfield IP19 9HT
☎ 01986 784214 🖷 01986 784797 e-mail: qhbfield@aol.com
Dir: *2m from A12 on the A144 towards Halesworth*
The emphasis is very much on dining at this traditional pub, with its scrubbed pine tables, exposed beams, vaulted ceiling and huge fireplaces. Most of the ingredients are sourced from small local suppliers and organic farms - always identified on the menu - and virtually all the dishes are home made, even the ice cream. Not far from the Suffolk heritage coast, the pub has a beautiful rear garden overlooked by the thatched village church with its unusual round bell tower. Typical of daily-changing meals are Northend Farm pork steaks with blackcurrant sauce; River Farm Smokery salmon; roast rack of Stonehouse Farm lamb; Denham Estate venison steak with redcurrant, port and orange sauce; and Larchfield Cottage leek and bacon crumble. There are tempting puddings, too: rich chocolate and brandy pot, apple crumble with custard, Pavlova with banana, coconut and mango sauce, or perhaps tarte au citron with Village Farm Jersey cream.
OPEN: 11.45-2.30 6.30-11 (Sun 12-3, 7-10.30) Closed: 26 Dec
BAR MEALS: L served all week 12-2 D served all week 6.30-10 Av main course £8.95 **BREWERY/COMPANY:** Adnams

◫: Adnams Bitter & Broadside. **FACILITIES:** Children welcome Garden: Enclosed garden with seating, willow dome Dogs allowed Water **NOTES:** Parking 15

HOLBROOK — Map 13 TM13

The Compasses 🛏
Ipswich Rd IP9 2QR ☎ 01473 328332 🖷 01473 327403
Dir: *From A137 S of Ipswich, take B1456/B1080*
Holbrook is bordered by the Orwell and the Stour rivers, and the traditional country pub, dating back to the 17th century, is on the Shotley peninsula. For several decades the inn was a staging post on the road between London and Ipswich, and the area is still popular with visitors. The appetising, varied menu includes stuffed mushrooms, local sausages, kleftico, grilled salmon, seafood lasagne, and changing specials.
OPEN: 11-2.30 6-11 Closed: 25-26 Dec, 1 Jan **BAR MEALS:** L served all week 11.30-2.15 D served all week 6-9.15 Av main course £7.95 **RESTAURANT:** L served all week 11.30-2.15 D served all week 6-9.15 **BREWERY/COMPANY:** Pubmaster ◫: Carlsberg, Greene King IPA, Adnams Bitter, Scottish Courage John Smith's & Guest Ales.
FACILITIES: Children welcome Garden: Six picnic benches, childrens play area **NOTES:** Parking 30

HONEY TYE — Map 13 TL93

The Lion 🛏 ♀
CO6 4NX ☎ 01206 263434 🖷 01206 263434
Dir: *On A134 between Colchester & Sudbury*
Low-beamed ceilings and an open log fire are charming features of this traditional country dining pub on the Essex/Suffolk border. An extensive menu offers lots of interesting choices, including grilled whole plaice with Cajun potato wedges, baked chicken breast stuffed with Mozzarella and green pesto, or sweet pepper and cheese sacchetini. Sunday lunch may comprise of poached salmon supreme with fresh chive and white wine sauce, roast topside of beef with Yorkshire pudding, or roast turkey served with all the trimmings.
OPEN: 11-3 5.45-11 (Sun 12-10.30) **BAR MEALS:** L served all week 12-2 D served all week 6-9.30 Av main course £8.50
RESTAURANT: L served all week 12-2 D served all week 6-9.30
BREWERY/COMPANY: Free House ◫: Greene King IPA, Adnams Bitter. **FACILITIES:** Children welcome Garden: Patio with tables and umbrellas Dogs allowed **NOTES:** Parking 40

HORRINGER — Map 13 TL86

Pick of the Pubs

Beehive ♀
The Street IP29 5SN ☎ 01284 735260
Dir: *From A14, 1st turning for Bury St Edmunds, sign for Westley & Ickworth Park*
Buzzing (what else?) with activity, the Beehive is a converted Victorian flint and stone cottage, close to the National Trust's Ickworth House. Its succession of cosy dining areas is furnished with antique pine tables and chairs. In season, visitors head for the tables on the patio and the picnic benches in the walled beer garden. The proprietors respond to changing customer appetites with seasonal produce and daily-changing menus. With these factors in mind therefore they may, for instance, offer starters of salmon and crayfish tail terrine with lemon dressing, or twice-baked cheese soufflé with marinated

continued   continued

artichokes. And for main courses there could well be seared liver with balsamic jus, home-made pork apple and leek sausages on creamy mash, or sea bass on sun-ripened tomatoes and pesto potatoes. If it's just a tasty snack you want, try warm three cheeses and broccoli tart with salad, and round off with fruit and vanilla cream roulade.

OPEN: 11.30-2.30 7-11 Closed: Dec 25-26 **BAR MEALS:** L served all week 12-2 D served Mon-Sat 7-9.45 Av main course £7.95 **RESTAURANT:** L served all week 12-2 D served 6.5 days a week 7-9.45 Av 3 course à la carte £19
BREWERY/COMPANY: Greene King 🍺: Greene King IPA & Abbot Ale, Guest beers. **FACILITIES:** Children welcome Garden: Patio, picnic benches, walled garden
NOTES: Parking 30

HOXNE
Map 13 TM17

The Swan 🛏
Low St IP21 5AS ☎ 01379 668275
e-mail: hoxneswan@supanet.com
The grounds of this 15th-century Grade II listed building run down to the river, and its interior is packed with original features. Food ranges from lunchtime snacks (salads, sandwiches, soups) to main meals including steaks, fish and chips, and local sausages and mash. There's a good children's menu, and vegetarians are well catered for with dishes such as stuffed tomatoes or baked field mushrooms. Good real ales. Ask at the bar for the circular pub walk.

OPEN: 11.30-3 6-11 (Sun 12-10.30) **BAR MEALS:** L served all week 12-2.30 D served all week 7-9 Av main course £6.95
RESTAURANT: L served all week 12-2.30 D served all week 7-9.30
BREWERY/COMPANY: Enterprise Inns 🍺: Adnams Broadside, Adnams Broadside, Greene King IPA, Bass. **FACILITIES:** Garden: River at rear of pub Dogs allowed Water **NOTES:** Parking 30

ICKLINGHAM
Map 13 TL77

Pick of the Pubs

The Red Lion 🛏 ♟
The Street IP28 6PS ☎ 01638 717802 🖷 01638 515702
e-mail: lizard2020@supernet.com
See Pick of the Pubs on page 442

IXWORTH
Map 13 TL97

Pykkerell Inn 🛏 ♟
38 High St IP31 2HH ☎ 01359 230398
Dir: A14 trunk rd/jct Bury St Edmunds central to A143, towards Diss
Attractive 16th-century coaching inn with original beams, inglenook fireplace, wood-panelled library room, and 14th-century barn enclosing a patio with barbecue. Menu boards highlight fresh fish, such as sea bass on basil mash with herb dressing, alongside steak and ale pie, venison with red wine and mushroom sauce, and lamb chops.

OPEN: 12-3 5.30-11 **BAR MEALS:** L served all week 12-2.30 D served all week 7-10 Av main course £9.95 **RESTAURANT:** L served all week 12-2.30 D served all week 6-9.30 Av 3 course à la carte £20 Av 3 course fixed price £15 **BREWERY/COMPANY:** Greene King 🍺: Greene King IPA & Abbot Ale. **FACILITIES:** Children welcome Garden: Food served outside. Courtyard Dogs allowed
NOTES: Parking 30

KERSEY
Map 13 TM04

The Bell Inn 🛏
The Street IP7 6DY ☎ 01473 823229
Dir: Follow A1171 from Bury St Edmunds thru Lavenham
Surrounded by thatched cottages, the 14th-century Bell stands next to a ford that crosses the main street of this picturesque Suffolk village. Largely beamed within, the grand winter log fire is a focal point. Home-made fare includes warming soups in winter, and pies such as steak and Guinness, fisherman's, and chicken and mushroom. Well-kept cask ales and a warm family-friendly atmosphere.

OPEN: 12-3 7-11 Sun-Mon Closed eve **BAR MEALS:** L served all week 12-2 D served all week 7-9 Av main course £8
RESTAURANT: L served all week 12-2 D served all week 7-9
BREWERY/COMPANY: Enterprise Inns 🍺: Adnams Bitter & Broadside. **FACILITIES:** Children welcome Garden: Double patio, food served outside **NOTES:** Parking 15

KETTLEBURGH
Map 13 TM26

The Chequers Inn
IP13 7JT ☎ 01728 723760 & 724369 🖷 01728 723760
e-mail: info@thechequers.net
Dir: From Ipswich A12 onto B1116, L onto B1078 then R through Easton
The Chequers is set in beautiful countryside on the banks of the River Deben. The landlord serves a wide range of cask ales endorsed by the Cask Marque. In addition to snack and restaurant meals, there is a £3 menu in the bar including local sausages and ham with home-produced free-range eggs.

OPEN: 12-2.30 6-11 **BAR MEALS:** L served all week 12-2 D served all week 7-9.30 Av main course £4 **RESTAURANT:** L served all week 12-2 D served all week 7-9.30 Av 3 course à la carte £16
BREWERY/COMPANY: Free House 🍺: Greene King IPA, Adnams Southwold, plus two guest ales. **FACILITIES:** Children welcome Garden: beer garden, outdoor eating, patio Dogs allowed
NOTES: Parking 40

LAVENHAM
Map 13 TL94

Pick of the Pubs

Angel Hotel ★★ ⊛ ♟
Market Place CO10 9QZ ☎ 01787 247388 🖷 01787 248344
e-mail: angellav@aol.com
See Pub Walk on page 435
See Pick of the Pubs on page 444

LAXFIELD
Map 13 TM27

Pick of the Pubs

The Kings Head
Gorams Mill Ln IP13 8DW ☎ 01986 798395
Virtually unchanged since Victorian times, this charming inn is known locally as The Low House. Beer is served from the tap room. There is no bar and customers sit on original high-backed settles and enjoy traditional Suffolk music on Tuesday lunchtimes. Home-cooked fare includes game duck and steak and kidney pie.

OPEN: 12-3 7-11 **BAR MEALS:** L served all week 12-2 D served all week 7-9 Av main course £10
BREWERY/COMPANY: Adnams 🍺: Adnams Best & Broadside & Guest ale. **FACILITIES:** Garden: Large lawned area Dogs allowed **NOTES:** Parking 30 **NOTES:** No credit cards

Open: 12-3, 6-11
Bar Meals: L served all week 12-2.30,
D served all week 6-10.
Av cost main course £9.95
RESTAURANT: L served all week 12-2.30,
D served all week 6-10.
BREWERY/COMPANY:
Greene King
🍺: Greene King Abbot Ale & IPA.
FACILITIES: Children welcome, Garden
- Large lawned area with picnic tables.
NOTES: Parking 50

The Red Lion

A sympathetically-restored 16th-century thatched inn, set back from the road beyond its neat front lawn. A raised rear terrace overlooks the river Lark and open fields.

The Street, Icklingham, Bury St
Edmunds, IP28 6PS
☎ 01638 717802 📠 01638 515702
✉ lizard2020@supernet.com
Dir: On A1101 between Mildenhall &
Bury St Edmunds.

Full of exposed beams, log fires, rugs on wooden floors, and antique furniture, and glowing with mellow candlelight in the evenings, the Red Lion is a popular place, particularly well known for fish, seafood and game. With daily deliveries of fish and seafood from the reasonably-near port of Lowestoft, the kitchen is able to maintain a choice of 15 to 20 dishes. If a 'puny', 'average' or 'stupendous' portion of fresh

Brancaster mussels in a cream, garlic, celery and white wine sauce appeals, this is the right place to eat. A typical selection could continue with fresh oysters, whole Lowestoft plaice, fresh skate wing with caramelised onion and bacon, and fillets of smoked Finnan haddock with tomato and cheese. The game menu is available all week - in season, that is - but for the widest selection go at the weekend. Typically available might be succulent pheasant breasts with port and blackcurrant sauce, wild boar fillet steak with red onion and garlic butter, and game grill. Moving on to the carte, expect Norfolk chicken

breast with a mild curry, mango sauce and rice timbale, rack of English lamb with a Burgundy and mushroom jus, or roasted hock of ham with a parsley sauce and champ potato. Finally, from the bar menu, there's Norfolk crayfish cocktail, home-made soups and patés, Excalibur sausages with mash and onion gravy, prime pork chops with apple and cider sauce, and gammon steak with wholegrain mustard sauce. Follow with home-made puddings. At the bar, choose from well-kept Greene King ales, a good range of wines, including country fruit varieties, and fruit pressés.

LEVINGTON
Map 13 TM23

The Ship Inn 🛏 ⚲
Church Ln IP10 0LQ ☎ 01473 659573
Dir: off the A14 towards Felixstowe. Nr Levington Marina
This charming 14th-century thatched pub overlooks the River Orwell, and there are pleasant walks in the surrounding countryside. The Ship is already popular with birdwatchers and yachting folk, and the new owners are establishing a reputation for fresh, home-made dishes. Fish and seafood both feature strongly; mussels have their own speciality menu, with crevettes, lobster, crab, haddock, tuna and monkfish all making an appearance when available. The main menu changes twice daily.
OPEN: 11.30-3 6.30-11 **BAR MEALS:** L served all week 12-2 D served all week 6.30-9.30 Av main course £8.50 **RESTAURANT:** L served all week 12-2 D served all week 6.30-9.30 Av 3 course à la carte £20 **BREWERY/COMPANY:** Pubmaster 🍺 Greene King IPA, Adnams Best & Broadside. ⚲: 8 **FACILITIES:** Children welcome Garden: Patio area front and back Dogs allowed Water
NOTES: Parking 70

LIDGATE
Map 12 TL75

Pick of the Pubs

Star Inn 🛏
The Street CB8 9PP ☎ 01638 500275 ▤ 01638 500275
e-mail: tereaxon@aol.com
Dir: From Newmarket, clocktower in High St, follow signs toward Clare on B1063. Lidgate 7m from Newmarket

A warm, cosy country inn, a unique blend of typical English pub and Spanish eating house. The Catalan landlady has made her mark on the menu with Spanish, imaginative international and British choices. The pretty pink-painted Elizabethan building is made up of two cottages with gardens front and rear, and indoors, two traditionally-furnished bars with heavy oak and pine furniture lead into a fairly simple dining room. Popular with trainers on Newmarket race days, and with dealers and agents from all over the world during bloodstock sales. Look out for scampi provençale, scallops Santiago, and paella Valenciana, along with home-grown choices like lamb steaks in blackcurrant, monkfish marinière, wild boar in cranberry sauce, sirloin steak in Stilton sauce and lambs' kidneys in sherry.
OPEN: 11-3 5-11 Closed: 25-26 Dec, 1 Jan **BAR MEALS:** L served all week 12-2 D served Mon-Sat 7-10 **RESTAURANT:** L served all week 12-2 D served Mon-Sat 7-10 Av 3 course à la carte £21 Av 2 course fixed price £10.50 **BREWERY/COMPANY:** Greene King 🍺 Greene King IPA, Old Speckled Hen & Abbot Ale.
FACILITIES: Children welcome Garden **NOTES:** Parking 12

LONG MELFORD
Map 13 TL84

The Crown Hotel 🛏 ⚲
Hall St CO10 9JL ☎ 01787 377666 ▤ 01787 379005
e-mail: quincy@crownmelford.fsnet.co.uk
Dir: from Sudbury take A134 to Bury St Edmunds, at 1st rndbt take 1st L to Long Melford

At the heart of Constable country, Long Melford's pub was built in 1610 yet retains a Tudor cellar and oak beams. In 1885, the Crown was the last place to hear the Riot Act read in West Suffolk. A hearty bar menu includes salads, ploughman's, jacket potatoes, sandwiches, mixed grill, poached salmon, aubergine and mushroom bake, steak and mushroom pie, and fish and chips.
OPEN: 11.30-11 (Sun 12-10.30) **BAR MEALS:** L served all week 12-2.30 D served all week 7-9.30 Av main course £8.50
RESTAURANT: L served all week 12-2.30 D served all week 7-9.30 Av 3 course à la carte £16 **BREWERY/COMPANY:** Free House 🍺 Greene King Old Speckled Hen, IPA. ⚲: 12
FACILITIES: Children welcome Garden: large umbrellas, patio area **NOTES:** Parking 6

MARKET WESTON
Map 13 TL97

The Mill Inn 🛏 ⚲
Bury Rd IP22 2PD ☎ 01359 221018
e-mail: andrew@leacy3.freeserve.co.uk
Dir: A14 Bury St Edmunds, follow A143 to Great Barton & Stanton, L on B1111 thru Barningham, next village M Weston
Old Chimneys ales from the nearby micro-brewery boost the choice of beers at this Victorian manor house situated at the centre of the local Windmill Trail. Local produce features in a varied menu that may include New England bean and vegetable casserole, grilled salmon fillet with herb and caper butter, pan-fried duck breast with orange and gooseberry sauce, steak and stout pie, guinea fowl calvados, and chicken breast stuffed with crab. Variety of grills also available.
OPEN: 12-3 5-11 (Mon-Fri 5-11, Sat-Sun 7-11pm) **BAR MEALS:** L served all week 12-2 D served all week 7-9.30 Av main course £7 **RESTAURANT:** 12-2 D served Tue-Sun 7 Av 3 course à la carte £12.50 **BREWERY/COMPANY:** Free House 🍺 Greene King, Adnams Best, Old Chimneys Great Raft & Military Mild.
FACILITIES: Children welcome Garden: Patio, lawn **NOTES:** Parking 30

> ⭐ **Pubs with Red Stars are part of the AA's Top 200 Hotels in Britain & Ireland**

Open: 11-11 (Sun 12-10.30)
Bar Meals: L served all week 12-2.15,
D served all week 6.45-9.15.
Av cost main course £9
RESTAURANT: L served all week 12-
2.15, D served all week 6.45-9.15.
Av cost 3 courses £17
BREWERY/COMPANY:
Free House.
🍺: Adnams Bitter, Nethergate, Greene
King IPA & Greene King Abbott.
FACILITIES: Children welcome,
Garden - Lawn and patio area with
tables and seating.
NOTES: Parking 105
ROOMS: 8 en suite from s£50 d£75

Angel Hotel

This fine historic inn, which was originally licensed in 1420, stands amid some 300 listed buildings in England's best-preserved medieval wool town.

★★ ⊛ ♀
Market Place, Lavenham, CO10 9QZ
☎ 01787 247388 📠 01787 248344
✉ angellav@aol.com
Dir: From A14 take Bury East/Sudbury turn off A143, after 4m take A1141 to Lavenham, Angel is off the High Street.

The building retains many original features such as exposed timbers, an Elizabethan shuttered shop window and a fully pargetted ceiling in the residents' sitting room. Furnishings are comfortable and traditional in the public rooms, and eight excellent en suite bedrooms have recently all had their bathrooms upgraded to a very high standard. The Angel is a bustling pub with a warm and friendly atmosphere, helped by the open plan layout which blurs the line between the bar and restaurant areas. Customers can sit and eat wherever they feel most comfortable, either in the formal or informal areas, choosing dishes from the same menu. In summer, food is also served outside on the front terrace, which overlooks the market place, and in the rear lawned garden with its herb collection. The food style is British with continental influences, using local suppliers for game, meat, vegetables and bread. Fresh fish is delivered daily. Lunchtime menus (except Sundays) feature a number of lighter meals such as home-made salmon fishcakes, local sausages and mash, and tomato, basil and Brie tart with salad. Home-made pickles and chutneys accompany home-made pork pies in summer. On Sundays throughout the year, traditional roast lunches are served. Main courses at other times might typically include pork and paprika casserole, red bream fillet with sun-dried tomato risotto, steak and ale pie, roast loin of lamb, grilled lemon sole, and aubergine, black olive and spinach lasagne. Chocolate raspberry tartlet and apricot and passion fruit syllabub may be among the dessert choices, along with a selection of local cheeses. Local real ales, an extensive wine list and a good selection of malt whiskies are on offer.

MELTON
Map 13 TM25

Wilford Bridge
Wilford Bridge Rd IP12 2PA ☎ 01394 386141
Dir: *Head to the coast from the A12, follow signs to Bawdsey & Orford, cross railway lines, next pub on L*

Chargrills are a speciality on the menu at this pub, which is just a short way from the famous Saxon burial ship at Sutton Hoo. Chargilled chicken Dijonnaise served with salad and sautéed potatoes is a favourite, with chargilled lamb and steak dishes also popular. Other menu choices include wild mushroom and tomato lasagne, home made steak and kidney pudding, and vegetable and Stilton pie. Sweets include year-round Christmas pudding with advocaat cream, and toffee apple and pecan pie with ice cream.
OPEN: 11-3 6.30-11 food served all day Sat-Sun Closed: 25-26 Dec
BAR MEALS: L served all week 11.30-2 D served all week 6.30-9.30 Av main course £8.95 **RESTAURANT:** L served all week 11.30-2 D served all week 6.30-9.30 Av 3 course à la carte £16
BREWERY/COMPANY: Free House ◀: Adnams Best, Broadside, Scottish Courage John Smith's Guest ales. **FACILITIES:** Children welcome Garden: Patio, seats up to 30 people Dogs allowed Water available **NOTES:** Parking 40

MONKS ELEIGH
Map 13 TL94

Pick of the Pubs

The Swan Inn ♀
The Street IP7 7AU ☎ 01449 741391 ▤ 01449 741391
Dir: *On the B1115 between Sudbury & Hadleigh*
Just across the street from the village green, pub dates partly from the 14th century. Wattle and daub panels were discovered in one room during renovations, and the dining room boasts a magnificent beamed ceiling and open fire. The kitchen uses seasonal local produce to create menus that change almost daily. Game features heavily during the winter months, while lobsters, fish and asparagus take pride of place during summer. An example menu includes roast red pepper filled with goats' cheese and pesto, crispy Peking duck salad with spring onions, cucumber and hoi sin sauce, slowly-braised lamb knuckle with garlic and rosemary, and roast partridge and honey glazed parsnips. All this is complemented by a good pudding selection.
OPEN: 12-3 7-11 **BAR MEALS:** L served Wed-Sun 12-2 D served Wed-Sun 7-9.30 **RESTAURANT:** L served Wed-Sun 12-2 D served Wed-Sun 7-9.30 Av 3 course à la carte £20
BREWERY/COMPANY: Free House ◀: Greene King IPA, Adnams Bitter & Broadside. **FACILITIES:** Children welcome Garden **NOTES:** Parking 10

ORFORD
Map 13 TM45

Jolly Sailor Inn
Quay St IP12 2NU ☎ 01394 450243 ▤ 0870 128 7874
e-mail: jacquie@jollysailor.f9.co.uk
Dir: *On B1084 E of Woodbridge*
Until the 16th century Orford was a bustling coastal port, and this ancient, timber-framed smugglers' inn stood on the quayside. But, as Orford Ness grew longer, the harbour silted up and fell out of use. Nevertheless, the pub still serves visiting yachtsman, and local fishermen supply the fresh fish and crabs that feature prominently on the menu. Other dishes might include lasagne, sweet and sour pork, mixed grill, and chicken and mushroom pie.
OPEN: 11.30-2.30 7-11 **BAR MEALS:** L served all week 12-2 D served all week 7.15-8.45 Av main course £5.50
BREWERY/COMPANY: Adnams ◀: Adnams Bitter & Broadside. **FACILITIES:** Garden: Food served outside Dogs allowed on lead only **NOTES:** No credit cards

King's Head
Front St IP12 2LW ☎ 01394 450271
e-mail: ian_thornton@talk21.com
Dir: *From Woodbridge follow signs for Orford Castle along the B1084 through Butley and Chillesford onto Orford*
Atmospheric 13th-century inn with a smuggling history, located a short walk from the quay. The interior includes a beamed bar serving Adnams ales, and a wood-floored restaurant offering plenty of local produce. Typical starters include locally-smoked mackerel with a salad garnish, and deep-fried Brie with a Cumberland sauce, followed perhaps by 'boozy beef' (made with steak and Adnams ale), or Orford-made salmon fish cakes. Bar snacks include sandwiches, burgers and things with chips.
OPEN: 11.30-3 6-11 **BAR MEALS:** L served all week 12-2 D served all week 6-9 Av main course £7.50 **RESTAURANT:** L served all week 12-2 D served all week 6-9 Av 3 course à la carte £15
BREWERY/COMPANY: Adnams ◀: Adnams Bitter, Adnams Broadside, Adnams Regatta, Adnams Fisherman.
FACILITIES: Children welcome Garden: Large grassed area with flower border Dogs allowed Water **NOTES:** Parking 20

POLSTEAD
Map 13 TL93

Pick of the Pubs

The Cock Inn
The Green CO6 5AL ☎ 01206 263150 ▤ 01206 263150
e-mail: enquiries@the-cock-inn-polstead.fsbusiness.co.uk
Dir: *Colchester/A134 towards Sudbury then R, follow signs to Polstead*

continued

England

POLSTEAD continued

A 17th-century pub with a Victorian restaurant extension, the Cock is situated overlooking the village green in a lovely village at the heart of Constable country. With some of Suffolk's prettiest landscapes right on the doorstep, not surprisingly the pub attracts many cyclists and ramblers. Originally a farmhouse, the building is characterised by oak beams, quarry-tiled floors and plain painted walls. The wide-ranging menu changes frequently and all the food is home made using fresh local ingredients. Typical dishes range from Suffolk huffers (to eat in or takeaway), salmon fishcakes and steak and kidney pudding to marmalade-marinated duck breast with spaghetti vegetables and sauté potatoes. Senior citizens' lunches provide good value from Tuesday to Friday. Families are especially welcome - there's a children's menu and an award-winning garden with a water feature and hanging baskets - a great attraction on a fine summer's day.
OPEN: 11-3 6-11 (Open Mon during X-mas, Easter) (Sun-BHS 12-3, 6-10.30) **BAR MEALS:** L served Tues-Sun 11.30-2.30 D served Tues-Sun 6.30-9.30 Av main course £8
RESTAURANT: L served Tue-Sun 11.30-2.30 D served Tues-Sun 6.30-9.30 Av 3 course à la carte £17.50
BREWERY/COMPANY: Free House **:** Greene King IPA, Scottish Courage John Smiths, Adnams. **FACILITIES:** Children welcome Garden: Picnic tables, pretty garden, water feature Dogs allowed Water **NOTES:** Parking 20

RAMSHOLT   Map 13 TM34

Pick of the Pubs

Ramsholt Arms
Dock Rd IP12 3AB ☎ 01394 411229
Dir: End of lane on beach at Ramsholt, signed off B1083 Woodbridge to Bawdsey

Enjoying a glorious, unrivalled postion on a tidal beach overlooking the River Deben, this 18th-century, pink-washed former farmhouse, ferryman's cottage and smugglers' inn is the perfect summer evening destination for a pint on the terrace to watch the sunset over the river. Expect a civilised atmosphere, picture windows, Adnams ales, and good home-cooked food, in particular fish and seafood in summer and local game in winter. Blackboard dishes could include cod and chips, local lobster, Cromer crab, whole Dover sole, roast partridge and decent pies. Comfortable bedrooms make the most of the view; rewarding riverside walks.

OPEN: 11.30-11 **BAR MEALS:** L served all week 12-3 D served all week 6.30-9 Av main course £7.50 **RESTAURANT:** L served all week 12-3 D served all week 6.30-9
BREWERY/COMPANY: Free House **:** Adnams, Greene King, Nethergates. **FACILITIES:** Children welcome Garden: Food served outside. Large garden, estuary Dogs allowed Water provided **NOTES:** Parking 60

RATTLESDEN   Map 13 TL95

Brewers Arms
Lower Rd IP30 0RJ ☎ 01449 736377 737057 ▤ 01449 736377
e-mail: rocksue@lineone.net
Dir: From A14 take A1088 toward Woolpit, Rattlesden 2.8m from Woolpit
Enjoy a decent pint of Abbot Ale at this solid 16th-century village pub, situated a short drive from Bury St Edmunds. The dining area was originally the public bar, and the lounge bar has book-lined walls and memorabilia from its American Air Force connections. Open fires and an old bread oven add to the charm. A comprehensive menu takes in snacks and robust country fare like poacher's pot or good gamekeeper's pie.
OPEN: 11.30-2.30 6.00-11 **BAR MEALS:** L served all week 11.30-2 D served all week 6-9 Av main course £7 **RESTAURANT:** L served all week 11.30-2 D served all week 6-9 Av fixed price £15
BREWERY/COMPANY: Greene King **:** Greene King IPA, Abbot Ale & Old Speckled Hen. **FACILITIES:** Children welcome Garden: Walled garden Dogs allowed Water **NOTES:** Parking 20

REDE   Map 13 TL85

The Plough
IP29 4BE ☎ 01284 789208
Dir: on the A143 between Bury St Edmunds and Haverhill
Picture-postcard thatched 16th-century pub set beside a pond on the village green. Worth the effort in finding for the freshly-prepared food served in rambling low-beamed bars. Blackboard-listed dishes may include linguine with clams, monkfish creole, hock of venison in a wild mushroom sauce, citrus lamb shank, grilled salmon with sauce vierge, or seared calves' liver.
OPEN: 11-3 6.30-11 **BAR MEALS:** L served all week 12-2 D served Mon-Sat 7-9 **RESTAURANT:** L served all week 12-2 D served Mon-Sat 7-9 **BREWERY/COMPANY:** Greene King **:** Greene King IPA & Abbot Ale & Ruddles County. **FACILITIES:** Children welcome Garden **NOTES:** Parking 60

RISBY   Map 13 TL86

The White Horse Inn ♀
Newmarket Rd IP28 6RD ☎ 01284 810686
Dir: A14 from Bury St Edmunds
Former coaching inn with a colourful history - as a communications centre in World War II in case of invasion, and for the ghostly spectre of a murdered hanging judge occasionally reflected in the restaurant mirror. The pub is otherwise known for its real ales - up to 15 each week - its extensive carte and freshly-produced bar food.
OPEN: 12-2.30 6-11 (Fri-Sun all day) **BAR MEALS:** L served all week 12-2.30 D served all week 6.30-9.30 Av main course £5
RESTAURANT: L served all week 12-2.30 D served all week 6.30-9.30 Av 3 course à la carte £22 **BREWERY/COMPANY:** Free House **:** Fullers London Pride, Shepherd Neame Spitfire, Tetleys. **FACILITIES:** Children welcome Garden: Food served outside **NOTES:** Parking 100

continued

England

ST PETER SOUTH ELMHAM   Map 13 TM38

Pick of the Pubs

St Peter's Hall ◉ ♀
NR35 1NQ ☎ 01986 782322 🖷 01986 782505
e-mail: beers@stpetersbrewery.co.uk
Dir: From A143/A144 follow brown and white signs to St Peter's Brewery

A magnificent moated, former monastery dominating the surrounding farmland. Built in 1280, it was extended in 1539 using stones salvaged from nearby Flixton Priory, a victim of the Dissolution of the Monasteries. Look for the chapel above the porch, the carvings on the front façade, and the tombstone in the entrance, and then take in the stone floors, lofty ceilings, and 17th- and 18th-century furnishings. Open only from Friday to Sunday, there's a new menu every week. Starters may include sweet potato tart with sage, red onion marmalade and rocket, and potted shrimps with rye sourdough toast. There are usually six main courses, among which may be chilli pork with lemongrass and steamed rice, wild mushroom linguine, aromatic herbs and Parmesan, and roast peppered skate wing, caper butter and new potatoes. Take the opportunity to tour the adjacent St Peter's Brewery, whose huge range of beers carries ABVs from 3.7 to 6.5.
OPEN: 11-11 (Sun 11-7) **BAR MEALS:** L served Fri-Sun 12.30-2 D served Fri-Sat 7-9 Av main course £10.95
RESTAURANT: L served Fri-Sun 12.30-2 D served Fri-Sat 7-9 Av 3 course à la carte £22 Av 3 course fixed price £17.95
BREWERY/COMPANY: St Peters Brewery ◀: Golden Ale, Organic Ale, Grapefruit Beer, Cream Stout. ♀: 7
FACILITIES: Garden: Attractive garden overlooking medieval moat **NOTES:** Parking 150

SNAPE   Map 13 TM35

Pick of the Pubs

The Crown Inn 🐾 ♀
Bridge Rd IP17 1SL ☎ 01728 688324
Dir: A12 N to Lowestoft, R to Aldeburgh, then R again in Snape at crossroads by church, pub at bottom hill
Old beams, brick floors and open fires are characteristic of this 15th-century smugglers' inn, as well as the 'codgers' - old Suffolk settles clustered around the inglenook fireplace. Lying close to the River Alde with its timeless scenery and tranquil coastal bird reserves, the pub and its sheltered garden provides a refuge from the clamour of gaming machines and piped music. (You'll

continued

find all the entertainment you need at the nearby Snape Maltings concert venue.) The selection of Adnams beers is supported by an interesting wine list, and the dining room offers a changing menu with the emphasis on local produce. Seafood is a speciality, particularly in summer, with the likes of Dover sole, lobster thermidor, and moules à la marinière. Other options are venison casserole with juniper and red wine, and calves' liver mash with onion marmalade and rack of lamb. The sticky toffee pudding remains a firm favourite to finish.
OPEN: 12-3 6-11 (Sunday 7-10.30) Closed: Dec 25, 26 Dec (evening) **BAR MEALS:** L served all week 12-2 D served all week 7-9 Av main course £10 **RESTAURANT:** L served all week 12-2 D served all week 7-9 **BREWERY/COMPANY:** Adnams
◀: Adnams Best & Broadside. ♀: 11 **FACILITIES:** Garden: Large area, 5 benches, umbrellas **NOTES:** Parking 40

The Golden Key 🐾 ♀
Priory Ln IP17 1SQ ☎ 01728 688510 🖷 01728 688784
A pub since around 1480 when it was known as The Cock, this extended, cottage-style building is located in the centre of the village, about 400 yards from the famous Snape Maltings concert hall. Not surprisingly seafood figures prominently, including crab and lobster, and dishes such as cullen skink. Other popular choices are smoked haddock, sausage, egg and onion pie, and game in season. There are two large patio areas for use in fine weather.
OPEN: 12-3 6-11 Closed: 25 Dec **BAR MEALS:** L served all week 12-2.15 D served all week 6-9.30 Av main course £8.95
RESTAURANT: L served all week 12-2.15 D served all week 6-9.30 Av 3 course à la carte £16 **BREWERY/COMPANY:** Adnams
◀: Adnams Best, Broadside & Regatta, Tally Ho, Oyster Ale. ♀: 12
FACILITIES: Garden: Dogs allowed **NOTES:** Parking 20

Plough & Sail ♀
Snape Maltings IP17 1SR ☎ 01728 688413 🖷 01728 688930
e-mail: enquiries@snapemaltings.co.uk

Part of the Snape Maltings Riverside Centre, incorporating the famous Concert Hall, art gallery and shops, the bustling Plough and Sail is justifiably popular with pre-concert goers. The rambling interior includes a bar and restaurant, and a large terrace provides seating in summer. A typical meal might be warm salad of black pudding, crispy bacon and spiced sausage, then medallions of monkfish with saffron shallot sauce, and chocolate and pecan tartlet with pistachio ice cream.
OPEN: 11-3 5.30-11 (summer 11-11) **BAR MEALS:** L served all week 12-2.30 D served all week 7-9 Av main course £11.50
RESTAURANT: L served all week 12-2.30 D served all week 7-9
BREWERY/COMPANY: Free House ◀: Adnams Broadside, Woodfordes, Adnams Bitter, Regatta. ♀: 10 **FACILITIES:** Children welcome Garden Dogs allowed **NOTES:** Parking 100

SOUTHWOLD   Map 13 TM57

Pick of the Pubs

Crown Hotel ★★ @@
The High St IP18 6DP ☎ 01502 722275 ▤ 01502 727263
Dir: *off A12 take A1094 to Southwold, stay on main road into town centre, hotel on L in High St*
Posting inn, dating from 1750, fulfilling the purposes of pub, wine bar, restaurant and small hotel. As flagship for Adnams brewery, it offers excellent ales and wines, and good food in both the bar and restaurant. Typical imaginative dishes in the bar might be smoked haddock and mussel chowder, deep-fried Feta wrapped in Parma ham, pan-fried skate with gremolata butter, and braised lamb shank with pease pudding. In the restaurant look for pork fillet with rosemary polenta and marinated vegetables, and glazed lemon tart with chocolate mousse to finish. Bedrooms are attractively decorated with co-ordinated soft furnishings and well equipped.
OPEN: 11-11 **BAR MEALS:** L served all week 12-10 D served all week Av main course £11 **RESTAURANT:** L served all week 12-1.30 D served all week 7.30-9.30 Av 3 course à la carte £29 Av 3 course fixed price £27.50 **BREWERY/COMPANY:** Adnams
◖: Adnams. **FACILITIES:** Children welcome **NOTES:** Parking 18
ROOMS: 13 bedrooms 12 en suite s£75 d£110

STANTON   Map 13 TL97

The Rose & Crown 🐑
Bury Rd IP31 2BZ ☎ 01359 250236
Dir: *A14 to Bury St E, then A143. or A140 to Diss, then A143 to Bury St E*
The original 17th-century thatched pub has been carefully extended into an old flint barn, to provide a main restaurant, conservatory restaurant, large bar and separate function room. An extensive garden with children's play equipment, including two bouncy castles, is popular for summer use. The main menu is supported by up to ten daily specials - maybe monkfish with lime and crème fraîche, Stilton-stuffed steak with whisky sauce, and porcini ravioli with fresh tomato and basil.
OPEN: 12-11 **BAR MEALS:** L served all week 12-2.15 D served all week 6-9 Av main course £5 **RESTAURANT:** L served all week 12-9 **BREWERY/COMPANY:** Pubmaster ◖: Tetley, Greene King Abbot Ale, Adnams Broad Side. **FACILITIES:** Children welcome Garden: Food served outside Dogs allowed **NOTES:** Parking 100

STOKE-BY-NAYLAND   Map 13 TL93

Pick of the Pubs

The Angel Inn ♦♦♦♦ @ 🐑 ☲
CO6 4SA ☎ 01206 263245 ▤ 01206 263373
Dir: *From A12 take Colchester R turn, then A134, 5m to Nayland. From A12 S take B1068*
Set in a landscape immortalised by the paintings of local artist, John Constable, the Angel is a 16th-century inn with beamed bars, log fires and a long tradition of hospitality. In a more modern vein, the pub also has an air-conditioned conservatory, patio and sun terrace. Tables for lunch and dinner may be reserved in The Well Room which has a high ceiling open to the rafters, a gallery leading to the pub's accommodation, rough brick and timber-studded walls, and the well itself, fully 52 feet deep. Eating in the bar, by comparison, is on a strictly first-come, first-served basis. The chalkboard menus change daily,

with first-class fish options and generous portions of salad or fresh vegetables. Look out for dishes such as baked tenderloin of pork Wellington, deep-fried haddock in Adnams beer batter, baked salmon fillet with parsley pesto and griddled fennel, roast venison with dauphinoise potatoes, spinach and ricotta cannelloni, or chargrilled Suffolk black bacon with apple mashed potato.

OPEN: 11-2.30 6-11 (Sun Dinner 5:30, 9:30) Closed: Dec 25-26, Jan 1 **BAR MEALS:** L served all week 12-2 D served all week 6.30-9 Av main course £9.95 **RESTAURANT:** L served all week 12-2 D served all week 6.30-9 Av 3 course à la carte £22
BREWERY/COMPANY: Free House ◖: Greene King IPA & Abbot Ale, Adnams Best. ☲: 9 **FACILITIES:** Garden: Patio area seating 20 Dogs allowed Water **NOTES:** Parking 25 **ROOMS:** 6 bedrooms 6 en suite 1 family rooms s£54.50 d£69.50 no children overnight

---

STOWMARKET   Map 13 TM05

The Buxhall Crown 🐑
Mill Rd, Buxhall IP14 3BW ☎ 01449 736521 ▤ 01449 736528
e-mail: trevor@buxhallcrown.fsnet.co.uk
Original beams in hidden 15th-century dining pub, offering a warm welcome to families, Greene King ales and pleasant garden. Choose from whole sea bass stuffed with fresh herbs, sautéed lambs' liver on a bed of braised pak choi, winter vegetable stew with dumplings or pan-fried calves' liver, followed by bread and butter pudding or lemon mousse.
OPEN: 12-3 6.30-11 **BAR MEALS:** L served all week 12-2 D served Mon-Sat 6.30-9.30 Av main course £9 **RESTAURANT:** L served all week 12-2 D served Mon-Sat 6.30-9.30 Av 3 course à la carte £18
BREWERY/COMPANY: Greene King ◖: Greene King IPA, Woodforde's Wherry, Old Chimneys Mild, Abbot Ale.
FACILITIES: Children welcome Garden: Patio, food served outside Dogs allowed Water **NOTES:** Parking 25

SWILLAND   Map 13 TM15

Moon & Mushroom Inn ☲
High Rd IP6 9LR ☎ 01473 785320 ▤ 01473 785320
Dir: *6 miles north of Ipswich taking the Westerfield Rd*
A row of former 16th-century village cottages and a pub since 1721; its current name the result of a locals' competition 250 years later. Real ale is sold by gravity only, and home cooking prevails. Venison with haggis, beef with dumplings and haddock mornay are ladelled from tureens with self-served vegetables.
OPEN: 11-2.30 6-11 (Mon 6-11 only) **BAR MEALS:** L served Tue-Sat 12-2 D served Tue-Sat 6.30-8.15 Av main course £7.95
RESTAURANT: L served Tue-Sat 12-2 D served Tue-Sat 6.30-8.15 **BREWERY/COMPANY:** Free House ◖: Nethergate Umbel, Wolfs Coyote, Wolf Ale, Woodfords Wherry. **FACILITIES:** Garden: Vine surrounded patio Dogs allowed **NOTES:** Parking 47

continued

THORNHAM MAGNA   Map 13 TM17

The Four Horseshoes ♀
Wickham Rd IP23 8HD ☎ 01379 678777 ▤ 01379 678134
Dir: From Diss on A140 turn R and follow signs for Finningham, 0.5m turn R for Thornham Magna

Thornham Magna is a delightful, unspoilt village close to Thornham Country Park and the interesting thatched church at Thornham Parva. This fine 12th-century inn is also thatched, and has timber-framed walls and a well in the bar. Varied bar food includes home-made steak and ale pie, chicken Kiev, Dover sole, mussels or roasts.
OPEN: 11.30-11 **BAR MEALS:** L served all week 12.00-3.00 D served all week 6-9.30 Av main course £6.95 **RESTAURANT:** L served all week 12.00-2.30 D served all week 6-9
BREWERY/COMPANY: Greene King ◖: Greene King IPA, Abbot & Old Speckled Hen. **FACILITIES:** Children welcome Garden Dogs allowed **NOTES:** Parking 80

TOSTOCK   Map 13 TL96

Gardeners Arms
IP30 9PA ☎ 01359 270460
Dir: From A14 follow signs to Tostock (0.5m)
Parts of this charming pub, at the end of the village green, near the horse chestnut tree, date back 600 years. The basic bar menu - salads, grills, ploughman's, sandwiches, toasties, etc - is supplemented by specials boards that offer six starters and 12 main courses in the evening. Look out for lamb balti, Thai king prawn green curry, steak and kidney pie, or chicken and Stilton roulade. Large grassy garden.
OPEN: 11.30-2.30 7-11 **BAR MEALS:** L served Mon- Sat 12-2 D served Wed-Sun 7-9 Av main course £8 **RESTAURANT:** L served Mon-Sat 12-2 D served Wed-Sun 7.15-9.30 Av 3 course à la carte £13
BREWERY/COMPANY: Greene King ◖: Greene King IPA, Greene King Abbot, Greene King seasonal beers. **FACILITIES:** Children welcome Garden: Food served outside, large grass area Dogs allowed **NOTES:** Parking 20

WALBERSWICK   Map 13 TM47

Pick of the Pubs

Bell Inn 🛏 ♀
Ferry Rd IP18 6TN ☎ 01502 723109 ▤ 01502 722728
e-mail: bellinn@btinternet.com
Dir: From A12 take B1387 to Walberswick

Reputedly 600 years old, the Bell is situated at the heart of Walberswick, close to the village green and a stone's throw from the beach and the ancient fishing harbour on the River Blyth. The artists Charles Rennie Macintosh and Philip Wilson Steer would have stayed at the Bell, the latter

also lodging at Valley Farm next door. To the north, across the River Blyth, is delightful Southwold, a classic seaside town with a highly-individual, old-fashioned air. Reach it either by foot or seasonal ferry. Inside the inn, the Bell's low beams, open fires, flagged floors and high wooden settles create a warm, homely welcome. Traditional English pub fare and a seasonal menu are the Bell's hallmarks, and among the perennial favourites are whole grilled plaice, traditional beef stew and dumplings, mushroom Stroganoff and chicken supreme. There is a good range of vegetarian dishes and sandwiches too, all to be washed down with well-kept Adnams ales or a selection of wines.
OPEN: 11-3 6-11 (Summer open all day) (Sun 12-10, Sat 11-11)
BAR MEALS: L served all week 12-2 D served all week 6-9 Av main course £7.25 **RESTAURANT:** D served Fri-Sat 6-9 Av 3 course à la carte £16 Av 3 course fixed price £15
BREWERY/COMPANY: Adnams ◖: Adnams Best, Broadside, Mayday Regatta. **FACILITIES:** Children welcome Garden: Food served outside Dogs allowed on leads only **NOTES:** Parking 10

WANGFORD   Map 13 TM47

The Angel Inn 🛏
High St NR34 8RL ☎ 01502 578636 ▤ 01502 578535
e-mail: enquiries@angelinn.freeserve.co.uk

A traditional green-and-cream-painted inn with a handsome Georgian façade, set in the heart of the pretty village of Wangford. Dating back to the 16th century, and complete with resident ghost, its cosy bar and restaurant are characterised by exposed beams and roaring log fires in winter. Home-made dishes include fresh fish (grilled sea bass steak with citrus butter; baby crayfish tails sautéed in garlic butter), hearty favourites such as steaks, pies and sausages, and good vegetarian options.
OPEN: 12-3 6-11 **BAR MEALS:** L served Tues-Sun 12-2 D served Tues-Sun 6.30-9 Av main course £8 **RESTAURANT:** L served Tues-Sun 12-2 D served Tues-Sun 6.30-9 Av 3 course à la carte £15
BREWERY/COMPANY: Free House ◖: Adnams Best, Spitfire, Greene King Abbot Ale, Brakspear Bitter. **FACILITIES:** Children welcome Garden: Large walled garden with benches Dogs allowed One bedroom available **NOTES:** Parking 20

> **Pick of the Pubs have that extra special quality that makes them stand out from the crowd. Their entries are highlighted, and may be a full page.**

continued

England

WESTLETON

Map 13 TM46

The Crown at Westleton ★★ ◉◉
IP17 3AD ☎ 0800 328 6001 🖷 01728 648239
e-mail: reception@westletoncrown.com
Dir: Off the A12 N just past Yoxford, follow tourist signs for 2 miles

Bustling old coaching inn nestling in a quiet village close to the coast and bird reserves. Well established and offering genuine hospitality in a relaxed atmosphere, it also features sound home cooking and good wines and whiskies. Menu choices range from interesting salads and ploughman's to roasted rump of lamb with bubble and squeak or slow-roasted pork belly.
OPEN: 11-3 6-11 (Sun 7-10.30) **CLOSED:** Dec 25-26
BAR MEALS: L served all week 12-2.15 D served all week 7-9.30 Av main course £6.95 **RESTAURANT:** L served all week 12-2.15 D served all week 7-9.30 Av 3 course à la carte £20
BREWERY/COMPANY: Free House 🍺: Adnams, Greene King IPA.
FACILITIES: Children welcome Garden Dogs allowed **ROOMS:** 19 bedrooms 19 en suite s£59.50 d£69.50

WINGFIELD

Map 13 TM27

Pick of the Pubs

De la Pole Arms 🐑 ♀
Church Rd IP21 5RA ☎ 01379 384545 🖷 01379 384377
Dir: Opposite Wingfield College and Wingfield Church
Well worth finding, as many motorists, cyclists and ramblers do, the De la Pole Arms is hidden away down narrow country lanes opposite the village church and Wingfield College. This exquisite 16th-century country pub and restaurant has two lovingly-restored bars with stripped wooden tables, quarry-tiled floors and wood-burning stoves. Bungay-based St Peter's Brewery owns the pub, and their classic range of draught and bottled ales is sold here. The quality and breadth of local produce is reflected in house specialities such as fish pie, monkfish kebabs, Welsh rarebit on haddock, wild rabbit casserole, turkey, leek and pancetta pie, peppered chicken breast and roast vegetable cassoulet. For something lighter there are wraps - sweet chilli beef tortilla, and chunky vegetable - toasties, baguettes and sandwiches. Desserts include zuccotto, a creamy, chocolatey Italian concoction that will tug at the most committed dieter's resolve.
OPEN: 11-3 6-11 (Winter Tue-Thur 11-3, 6.30-11) 1 Oct-31 Mar Closed Mon **BAR MEALS:** L served all week 12-2 D served all week 7-9 Av main course £8.50 **RESTAURANT:** L served Tue-Sun 12-2 D served Tue-Sat 7-9 Av 3 course à la carte £20
BREWERY/COMPANY: St Peters Brewery 🍺: St Peters Best, Strong Ale, Fruit Beer, Golden Ale and Wheat beer. ♀: 7
FACILITIES: Patio, tables and chairs **NOTES:** Parking 20

SURREY

ABINGER

Map 06 TQ14

The Volunteer 🐑 ♀
Water Ln, Sutton RH5 6PR ☎ 01306 730798 🖷 01306 731621
Dir: Between Guildford & Dorking, 1m S of A25

Enjoying a delightful rural setting with views over the River Mole, this popular village pub was originally farm cottages and first licensed about 1870. An ideal watering hole for walkers who want to relax over a pint in the attractive pub garden. Typical fish dishes include lobster thermidor, Mediterranean squid pasta and fillet of sea bass, while Thai coconut chicken, partridge with red wine and junipers and fillet of braised beef on fennel feature among the meat dishes.
OPEN: 11.30-3 6-11 (All day Sat & Sun) **BAR MEALS:** L served all week 12-2.30 D served all week 7-9.30 Av main course £10
BREWERY/COMPANY: Woodhouse Inns 🍺: Badger Tanglefoot, King & Barns Sussex, plus guest ales. **FACILITIES:** Children welcome Garden: Terrace, food served outside Dogs allowed Water, biscuits **NOTES:** Parking 30

ALBURY

Map 06 TQ04

The Drummond Arms Inn ♦♦♦
The Street GU5 9AG ☎ 01483 202039 🖷 01483 205361
Situated in the pretty village of Albury below the North Downs, this charming old inn has an attractive garden overlooking the River Tillingbourne and offers comfortable en suite accommodation. A varied menu of pub food, served in the panelled bars, ranges from sandwiches and light bites (burgers, baked potatoes and ploughman's lunches) through to specials such as home-made steak and kidney pie, or cod and queen scallops provençale.
OPEN: 11-3 6-11 **BAR MEALS:** L served all week 12-2 D served Mon-Sat 7-9 Av main course £9 **RESTAURANT:** L served all week 12-2 D served Mon-Sat 7-9 Av 3 course à la carte £20
BREWERY/COMPANY: Merlin Inns 🍺: Scottish Courage Courage Best, Gales HSB, Breakspear Bitter. **FACILITIES:** Garden: Large garden seats 120 Dogs allowed Water **NOTES:** Parking 40 **ROOMS:** 11 bedrooms 11 en suite 2 family rooms s£50 d£65 no children overnight

---

Do you have a favourite pub that we have overlooked?
Please use the Reader's Report form at the back of this guide to tell us all about it.

The Wheatsheaf Hotel

The spectacular ornamental lake and lush country park at Virginia Water form the backdrop to this very pleasant walk at the southern end of Windsor Great Park. The route is perfect in any season.

Fringed by trees, Virginia Water covers about 160 acres and is a little over 2 miles/3.2km in length. The lake was developed in the middle of the 18th century for the Duke of Cumberland after his victory at Culloden. Before it was created, Virginia Water was nothing more than a large swamp. George VI ordered that a scaled-down frigate be built for the lake, which was still in existence during Queen Victoria's reign.

From the car park by the Wheatsheaf make for the lakeside path and turn left. Head south until you reach a triangular junction. There is a sign here advising that paddling and bathing are not permitted.

Leave the lakeside path at this point and follow the road down towards the A30. Keep to it as it swings right and heads down between the trees to a bridge over the Virginia Stream. After heavy rain the scene here is very spectacular, with water cascading down over the rocks.

Go up the slope and when you break cover from the trees, you get a splendid view of the lake. On the left now are the remains of the colonnade of ancient stone pillars erected here in 1818 and brought from the Roman city of Leptis Magna in Libya. Follow the path all the way round the lake to the classical bridge, cross it and continue ahead to some

★★
THE WHEATSHEAF HOTEL, VIRGINIA WATER
London Road GU25 4QF
☎ 01344 842057

Directions: M25 Jct 13, head towards A30 Bracknell
Overlooking Virginia Waters on the edge of Windsor Great Park. A chalk-board menu gives plenty of choice.
Open: 11-11
Bar Meals: 12-10
Notes: Children welcome. Beer garden & patio.
(See page 460 for full entry)

railings. Swing right here and keep the lake to your right.

Pass several signs for the 450-acre Valley Gardens and continue on the path to the Totem Pole, commemorating the centenary of British Columbia in 1958. Keep the lake on the right and return to the Wheatsheaf.

DISTANCE: 4 miles/6.4km
MAP: OS Explorer 160
TERRAIN: Ornamental parkland
PATHS: Well-defined lakeside paths and drives
GRADIENT: Level ground

Walk submitted and checked by Nick Channer

ALBURY continued

William IV
Little London GU5 9DG ☎ 01483 202685
Dir: just off the A25 between Guildford & Dorking

This quaint country pub is only a stone's throw from Guildford, yet deep in the heart of the Surrey countryside. The area is great for hiking and the pub is popular with walkers, partly due to its attractive garden, which is ideal for post-ramble relaxation. A choice of real ales and a blackboard menu that changes daily is also part of the attraction. Expect steak and kidney pie, pot-roast lamb shank, battered cod and chips, and Sunday roasts.
OPEN: 11-3 5.30-11 (Sun 12-3, 7-10.30) Closed: 25 Dec
BAR MEALS: L served all week 12-2 D served Tue-Sat 7-9 Av main course £6.50 **RESTAURANT:** L served Sun 12-2 D served Fri-Sat 7-9 Av 3 course à la carte £18 **BREWERY/COMPANY:** Free House
🍺: Interbrew Flowers IPA, Hogs Back, Greene King Abbot Ale, Interbrew Bass. **FACILITIES:** Garden: Seating area, grass, patio in front of pub Dogs allowed Water **NOTES:** Parking 15

BETCHWORTH
Map 06 TQ25

The Dolphin Inn 🛏 🍷
The Street RH3 7DW ☎ 01737 842288
Dir: Between Reigate and Dorking, off A25
This 400-year-old inn stands opposite one of the churches that appeared in Four Weddings and a Funeral. Inside, the pub is the epitome of country charm, with three open fires and bare flagstones in the public bar. The menu features equally-traditional dishes such as double jumbo sausage and chips, gammon, rump and sirloin steaks, and deep-fried calamari and chips (yes, even that's traditional now). Specials include ratatouille in potato skins topped with cheese, and spaghetti Bolognese.
OPEN: 11-3 5.30-11 (open all day Sat-Sun) **BAR MEALS:** L served all week 12-3 D served all week 7-10 Av main course £6.50
BREWERY/COMPANY: Youngs **🍺:** Young's PA, Special, Winter Warmer & Waggle Dance. **🍷:** 10 **FACILITIES:** Garden: Small garden and patio area Dogs allowed Water **NOTES:** Parking 25

> **For a list of pubs with AA Inspected Accommodation Awards**
> ◆ **see pages 646-651** ★

The Red Lion 🛏
Old Reigate Rd RH3 7DS ☎ 01737 843336 🗎 01737 845242

Set in 18 acres with a cricket ground and rolling countryside views, this award-winning, 200-year-old pub offers an extensive menu. Beyond baguettes and ploughman's lunches the choice includes sole and smoked salmon, Barbary duck breast, aubergine and broccoli fritters, deep-fried plaice and chips, Toulouse sausage and mash, and steak and ale pie.
OPEN: 11-11 (Sun 12-10.30) **BAR MEALS:** L served all week 12-3 D served all week 6-10 **RESTAURANT:** L served all week 12-3 D served all week 6-10 **BREWERY/COMPANY:** Punch Taverns
🍺: Fullers London Pride, Greene King, IPA, Adnams Broadside.
FACILITIES: Children welcome Garden **NOTES:** Parking 50

BLACKBROOK
Map 06 TQ14

The Plough at Blackbrook 🛏 🍷
RH5 4DS ☎ 01306 886603
Dir: A24 to Dorking, then toward Horsham, 0.75m from Deepdene rdbt, L to Blackbrook
Originally a coaching inn and a popular haunt of highwaymen, this popular pub is known in the area for its striking views and delightful cottage garden. Extensive specials board offers the likes of calves' liver, chicken curry, deep-fried cod fillets, and roast half duckling with a Calvados jus served on red cabbage. The snack menu includes a range of filled jacket potatoes, ploughman's lunches and toasted deli bagels.
OPEN: 11-2.30 6-11 (Sat 12-3) (Sun 12-3, 7-10.30) Closed: 25-26 Dec, 1 Jan **BAR MEALS:** L served all week 12-2 D served Tue-Sun 7-9 **BREWERY/COMPANY:** Hall & Woodhouse **🍺:** Badger King & Barnes Sussex, Tanglefoot, Badger Best. **🍷:** 18
FACILITIES: Garden: Secluded cottage garden Dogs allowed Water **NOTES:** Parking 22

BRAMLEY
Map 06 TQ04

Jolly Farmer Inn 🛏 🍷
High St GU5 0HB ☎ 01483 893355 🗎 01483 890484
e-mail: accom@jollyfarmer.co.uk
Dir: Onto A3, then A281, Bramley 3m S of Guildford
Originally a coaching inn, this family-run free house has been in existence for over 400 years and still offers home-cooked food and a wide choice of ales and lagers to both travellers and locals. Seafood dishes on the specials board might include pan-fried king scallops in coriander and pine nut butter, and baked bass with red wine gravy. Other options are Scottish beef, game, and exotics like alligator tail.

continued

OPEN: 11-3 6-11 (Sun 12-3, 7-10.30) **BAR MEALS:** L served all week 12-2 D served all week 6.30-10 Av main course £11 **BREWERY/COMPANY:** Free House 🍺: Hogs Back TEA, Badger Best, Timothy Taylor Landlord, Hopback Summer Lightning. 🍷: 15 **FACILITIES:** Children welcome Garden: Large patio at front and rear **NOTES:** Parking 22

CHIDDINGFOLD   Map 06 SU93

Pick of the Pubs

The Crown Inn
The Green GU8 4TX ☎ 01428 682255 📠 01428 685736
Dir: On A283 between Milford & Petworth

Historic inn dating back over 700 years, with lots of charming features, including ancient panelling, open fires, distinctive carvings and huge beams. Comfortably refurbished by owning brewery Hall and Woodhouse, this striking inn offers individually-styled bedrooms, some with four-poster beds, in a unique setting making it an excellent choice for a relaxing weekend break, especially with Petworth, the famous Devil's Punch Bowl and miles of walking on the scenic South Downs nearby. Reliable food ranges from sausage and mash with onion gravy, chicken tagliatelle, freshly-battered fish and chips, and decent sandwiches, warm salads and ploughman's at lunchtime, to Torbay sole, monkfish and tiger prawns pan-fried with ginger and lime cream sauce and served on tagliatelle, and roast duck with sweet plum sauce on the evening menu.
OPEN: 10-11 **BAR MEALS:** L served all week 12-2.30 D served Mon-Sat 6.30-9.30 Av main course £9.95
BREWERY/COMPANY: Hall & Woodhouse 🍺: Badger Tanglefoot, King & Barnes Sussex Ale. **FACILITIES:** Garden: beer garden, outdoor eating, patio, BBQ Dogs allowed

The Swan Inn & Restaurant 🍷
Petworth Rd GU8 4TY ☎ 01428 682073 📠 01428 683259
A lovely 14th century village pub whose sympathetic refurbishment has included bare floors, wooden furniture and big leather sofas. The chef makes impressive use of seafood, fish and local game. A meal could include pan-fried sardines with lime salsa and herb salad, followed by roasted guinea fowl with confit of leg, served with stir-fried vegetables, puréed potatoes and a herb cream sauce. Bar snacks are also available.
OPEN: 11-3 5.30-11 (Sun 12-4, 7-10.30) Closed: First week in Jan
BAR MEALS: L served all week 12-2.30 D served all week 6.30-10
RESTAURANT: L served all week 12-2.30 D served all week 6.30-10
BREWERY/COMPANY: Free House 🍺: Hogs Back TEA, Ringwood Best, Timothy Taylor Landlord, Fuller's London Pride.
FACILITIES: Children welcome Garden: Dogs allowed Water
NOTES: Parking 25

CLAYGATE   Map 06 TQ16

Swan Inn & Lodge 🍷
Hare Ln KT10 9BT ☎ 01372 462582 📠 01372 467089
e-mail: info@theswanlodge.co.uk
Only 15 miles from London, yet this pub overlooks a village green and cricket pitch. Rebuilt in 1905, its Edwardian interior features an attractive, colonial-style bar. Hearty bar food includes all the regulars, such as chilli and rice, potato wedges with sour cream, ploughman's, and chargrilled hamburger and chips. The Swan is particularly proud of its Thai restaurant, where dinner can be selected from a long list of starters, soups, spicy salads, curries, stirfries, seafood and vegetarian dishes.
OPEN: 11-11 **BAR MEALS:** L served all week 12-2.30 D served Mon-Sat 6-10.30 Av main course £5.50 **RESTAURANT:** L served Sun 12-4 D served Mon-Sat 6 Av 3 course à la carte £20 Av 3 course fixed price £16 **BREWERY/COMPANY:** Wellington Pub Co 🍺: Fullers London Pride, Adnams. 🍷: 8 **FACILITIES:** Garden
NOTES: Parking 12

COBHAM   Map 06 TQ16

The Cricketers 🐾 🍷
Downside KT11 3NX ☎ 01932 862105 📠 01932 868186
e-mail: jamesclifton@msn.com
Dir: From A3 take A245 towards Cobham, 2nd r'about turn R, then 1st R opp Waitrose. Pub 1.5m
It must be rare for a pub to contain the original wattle and daub walls of a former abattoir, but this one, dating back to the mid-1500s, does just that. It offers a good hot lunch selection and nearly thirty different salads. Dinner main courses include duo of baked salmon and sole, beef entrecôte with artichokes, mushrooms and béarnaise sauce, and Thai vegetable and nut pancakes. In summer, enjoy a drink or meal in the garden overlooking Downside Common.
OPEN: 11-2.30 6-11 Winter Sun (12-5) Closed: 25 Dec
BAR MEALS: L served all week 12-2 D served all week 6.30-10 Av main course £7.50 **RESTAURANT:** L served Tue-Sun 12.15-1.45 D served Tue-Sat 7.15-9.30 Av 3 course à la carte £25 Av 3 course fixed price £16.95 **BREWERY/COMPANY:** Unique Pub Co
🍺: Wadworth 6X, Young's Bitter, Greene King Old Speckled Hen.
🍷: 10 **FACILITIES:** Garden: Large open garden over looking village Dogs allowed Water **NOTES:** Parking 80

COLDHARBOUR

Map 06 TQ14

Pick of the Pubs

The Plough Inn 🕲 ♀

Coldharbour Ln RH5 6HD ☎ 01306 711793 📠 01306 710055
e-mail: ploughinn@btinternet.com
Dir: M25 J9 - A24 to Dorking. A25 towards Guildford. Coldharbour
signposted from the one-way system

A 363-year-old pub, 25 minutes walk from the top of Leith
Hill, southern England's highest point. A well-worn
smugglers' route from the coast to London once passed
its door, which probably explains why the resident ghost
is a matelot. The only time owners Anna and Rick saw this
gentleman, they were in bed, and they haven't seen him
since! The surrounding hills are the North Downs, so this
is great walking country, and while many customers arrive
on foot, horseriders and cyclists pitch up too. Major draws
include Leith Hill Brewery's Crooked Furrow and
Tallywhacker ales, available only here. Fish dishes, such as
seared fresh salmon and poached haddock, are always
plentiful, and so are good pub stalwarts like duck breast
with orange and port sauce, prime Scotch fillet steak and
peppercorn sauce, and calves' liver and bacon on creamy
mash, to name merely three. Don't leave without
sampling Anna's home-made puddings.
OPEN: 11.30-3 6-11 (Sat-Sun 11.30-11) Closed: 25 Dec
BAR MEALS: L served all week 12-2.30 D served all week
7-9.30 Av main course £8.75 **RESTAURANT:** L served all
week 12-2.30 D served all week 7-9.30 Av 3 course à la
carte £20 **BREWERY/COMPANY:** Free House ◑: Crooked
Furrow, Leith Hill Tallywhacker, Ringwood Old Thumper,
Timothy Taylor Landlord. ♀: 8 **FACILITIES:** Garden:
shrubs and picnic benches Dogs allowed

COMPTON

Map 06 SU94

The Harrow Inn 🕲 ♀

The Street GU3 1EG ☎ 01483 810379 📠 01483 813854
Dir: 3m S of Guildford on A3 then B3000 towards Godalming.
Compton on R

Some parts of this beamed pub date back 500 years, so some
of the floors and doors are quaintly sloping. In an attractive
village, the Harrow Inn has a friendly atmosphere, and is a
handy refreshment stop for those travelling on the A3. A
varied menu may include fillet of beef Stroganoff, lamb
kidneys and baby sausages in sherry and mustard sauce or
seared tuna steak on sun-dried tomato risotto.
OPEN: 8-11 (Sun 10-6) **BAR MEALS:** L served all week 12-3 D
served all week 6-10 **RESTAURANT:** L served all week 12-3 D
served Mon-Sat 6-10 **BREWERY/COMPANY:** Punch Taverns
◑: Greene King IPA, Hogs Back TEA, Marston's Pedigree.
FACILITIES: Children welcome Garden: Food served outside Dogs
allowed **NOTES:** Parking 50

The Withies Inn ♀

Withies Ln GU3 1JA ☎ 01483 421158 📠 01483 425904
Dir: Telephone for directions
The splendid garden is one of the pub's chief attractions, filled
with overhanging weeping willows, apple trees and dazzling
flower borders. Inside, the atmosphere is friendly and
welcoming, with low beams, 17th-century carved panels and
an art nouveau settle, while log fires crackle away in the huge
inglenook fireplace. Expect a good choice of bar snacks, filled
jacket potatoes and sandwiches, while the restaurant menu

offers dishes such as beef Wellington, tournedos Rossini, steak
diane flambée, chicken kiev, or poached halibut with prawns
and brandy sauce.
OPEN: 11-3 6-11 (Sun 12-3) **BAR MEALS:** L served all week 12-
2.30 D served all week 7-10 Av main course £4.75 **RESTAURANT:** L
served all week 12-2.30 D served Mon-Sat 7-10 Av 3 course à la carte
£28.30 **BREWERY/COMPANY:** Free House ◑: Greene King IPA,
Tea, Fullers London Pride, Sussex. ♀: 8 **FACILITIES:** Garden Dogs
allowed garden only **NOTES:** Parking 70

DORKING

Map 06 TQ14

Abinger Hatch 🕲

Abinger Ln, Abinger Common RH5 6HZ ☎ 01306 730737
Dir: A25 from Guildford, L to Abinger Common

Flagged floors, beamed ceilings and open fires are features of
this 18th-century coaching inn, classically located opposite the
church and duck pond. It's a free house serving Harveys,
Fullers London Pride, Badger Tanglefoot, Youngs, Adnams and
Chiswick beers, and home-cooked food prepared by the
landlord. Options range from hot and kickin' chicken with
BBQ dressing to double-baked loin of lamb with rosemary
and red wine sauce.
OPEN: 11-11 **BAR MEALS:** L served all week 11.30-2.30 D served
Mon-Sat 6.30-9.30 Av main course £5 **BREWERY/COMPANY:** Free
House ◑: Ringwood Best, Old Thumper, Old Forester, 49er. Fullers
London Pride. **NOTES:** Parking 35, Dogs allowed.

Pick of the Pubs

The Stephan Langton ♀

Friday St, Abinger Common RH5 6JR ☎ 01306 730775
Dir: Between Dorking & Guildford leave A25 at Hollow Lane, W of
Wootton. Go S for 1.5m then L into Friday Street

A lovely brick and timber inn named after the 13th-
century archbishop of Canterbury and local boy who was
instrumental in drawing up the Magna Carta. Although it
looks much older, and was built on the site of another

continued

continued

inn, this secluded hostelry only dates back to 1930. Some of Surrey's loveliest walks are found nearby, including the challenging Leith Hill, and walkers find this a perfect place to recover. The pub is being gradually refurbished to match Jonathan Coomb's upmarket food. The bar choice includes duck confit with Puy lentils and spring greens, and Moroccan-style braised lamb, while the dinner menu offers a short but well-balanced choice: chargrilled squid with chilli and rocket, seared marlin niçoise, and buttermilk pudding with poached rhubarb is a typically appealing meal.
OPEN: 11-3 5-11 Open all day at the weekend in summer **BAR MEALS:** L served Tues-Sun 12.30-2.30 D served Tues-Sun 7-10 Av main course £10 **RESTAURANT:** 12.30-3 D served Tues-Sat 7-10 Av 3 course à la carte £19
BREWERY/COMPANY: Free House ◖: Fuller's London Pride, Adnams. **FACILITIES:** Children welcome Garden: Food served outside Dogs allowed Water provided **NOTES:** Parking 20

DUNSFOLD
Map 06 TQ03

The Sun Inn ♀
The Common GU8 4LE ☎ 01483 200242 ▤ 01483 201141
Dir: A281 thru Shalford & Bramley, take B2130 to Godalming. Dunsfold on L after 2 miles
Pretty timbered coaching inn, opposite the cricket green in a village that boasts no fewer than seven ponds. It's a family-run affair, offering a warm welcome, blazing fires and a broad selection of food. Typical starters include nachos with salsa, paté, with melba toast, or chargrilled vegetables with goats' cheese. Follow with a choice of popular favourites such as curry, steaks, bangers and mash, and fish and chips.
OPEN: 11-11 (Sun 12-10.30) Closed 3-5 Mon-Wed (Jan-Mar)
BAR MEALS: L served all week 12-2.15 D served all week 7-9.15 Av main course £7.95 **RESTAURANT:** L served all week 12-2.15 D served all week 7-9.15 **BREWERY/COMPANY:** Punch Taverns ◖: Knight Barnes Sussex, Ansells Best, Bass, Adnams Broadside.
♀: 10 **FACILITIES:** Children welcome Garden: Large patio garden to side Dogs allowed Water **NOTES:** Parking 40

EFFINGHAM
Map 06 TQ15

The Plough ♀
Orestan Ln KT24 5SW ☎ 01372 458121 ▤ 01372 458121
Dir: Between Guildford & Leatherhead on A246
A modern pub with a traditional feel, The Plough provides a peaceful retreat in a rural setting close to Polesden Lacy National Trust House. Home-cooked British dishes include the likes of wild boar with mushroom sauce, bangers with spring onion mash and gravy, rib-eye steak, and bacon and avocado salad. Once owned by Jimmy Hanley and used in the 1960s TV series 'Jim's Inn', it also boasts a popular beer garden.
OPEN: 11-3 5.30-11 (Sun 12-3, 7-10.30) Closed: 25, 26 Dec, 1 Jan (Eve) **BAR MEALS:** L served all week 12-2.30 D served all week 7-10 Av main course £8.95 **RESTAURANT:** L served all week 12-2.30 D served all week 7-10 Av 3 course à la carte £18
BREWERY/COMPANY: Young & Co ◖: Youngs IPA, Special, Winter Warmer. ♀: 12 **FACILITIES:** Garden: Beer garden with willow tree **NOTES:** Parking 40

◆ **Pubs with Red Diamonds are the top places in the AA's three, four and five diamond ratings**

EGHAM
Map 06 TQ07

The Fox and Hounds ♀
Bishopgate Rd, Englefield Green TW20 0XU
☎ 01784 433098 ▤ 01784 438775
e-mail: thefoxandhounds@4cinns.co.uk
Dir: From village green turn L into Castle Hill Rd, then R into Bishops Gate Rd

The Surrey border once ran through the centre of this good English pub, which is on the edge of Windsor Great Park, convenient for walkers and riders. Features include a large garden, handsome conservatory and weekly jazz nights. Menus offer a range of daily-changing fish specials as well as dishes like orange and sesame chicken fillets on coriander and lime noodles, or roast pork with grain mustard glaze and Parmesan crisps.
OPEN: 11-11 (Sun 12-10.30) **BAR MEALS:** L served all week 12-2.30 D served all week 6.30-9.30 Av main course £13.50
RESTAURANT: L served all week 12-2.30 D served all week 6.30-10 Av 3 course à la carte £25 Av fixed price £21.95 ◖: Fullers London Pride, Fosters, IPA, Courage Best. ♀: 8 **FACILITIES:** Children welcome Garden Dogs allowed **NOTES:** Parking 60

ELSTEAD
Map 06 SU94

Pick of the Pubs

The Woolpack 🐑 ♀
The Green GU6 6HD ☎ 01252 703106 ▤ 01252 703497
See Pick of the Pubs on page 456

EPSOM
Map 06 TQ26

Derby Arms ♀ NEW
KT18 5LE
Dir: Exit the M25 at J8, take the A217 towards Sutton. Turn left towards Epsom Downs. The Derby Arms is opposite the Queen's stand of the racecourse
Dating back to the 18th century, the Derby Arms is situated opposite Epsom's famous and historic racecourse. Long popular with jockeys and trainers, the pub includes a popular garden with colourful floral displays and a patio area. Expect baked red onion and potato tart, chicken breast, and hake topped with breadcrumbs among a choice of popular and imaginative dishes.
OPEN: 12 -11 (Sun 12-10.30) **RESTAURANT:** L served all week D served all week Av 3 course à la carte £16.70
BREWERY/COMPANY: ◖: Carlsberg Export, Tetley Bitter, Cask Bass. ♀: 16 **FACILITIES:** Garden: Outdoor furniture and floral display

OPEN: 11-3, 5.30-11 (Sat-Sun 11-11)
CLOSED: 26 Dec
BAR MEALS: L served all week 12-2, D served all week 7-9.45. Av main course £8.50
RESTAURANT: L served all week 12-2, D served all week 7-9.45
BREWERY/COMPANY: Punch Taverns.
🍺: Greene King Abbot Ale, Shepherd Neame Best Bitter.
FACILITIES: Dogs welcome. Children welcome. Walled garden at rear.
NOTES: Parking 15.

The Woolpack

There's plenty of atmosphere in this busy and attractive tile-hung pub overlooking the village green, where drovers used to stop and rest their sheep on their way to the markets at Godalming and Farnham. Nearby, the River Wey flows beneath the ancient Elstead Bridge, and there are many good walks in the area.

The Green, Elstead, nr Godalming, GU8 6HD
☎ 01252 703106 📠 01252 703497
Dir: Milford exit off A3. Take the B3001 towards Farnham. Pub is on the village green in Elstead, about 3m from the A3

The building was originally constructed as a store for woollen bales, but over the years it has also served as a bicycle repair shop, a band practice hall, a butcher's shop and the local Co-op. Remnants of the wool industry, including weaving shuttles and cones of wool, decorate the bar which also features low beams, open log fires and high-backed settles, window seats and spindle-backed chairs. You'll find good cask-conditioned ales and large blackboard menus that are regularly changed. The pub has a reputation for its generously-portioned 'old English and colonial' food. As well as a good selection of salads and ploughman's lunches, look out for starters such as mustard-breaded turkey strips with port and cranberry sauce; New Zealand green lip mussels in herb and garlic butter; and mushrooms in creamy Stilton and port sauce with rice and salad. Mains include spicy lamb curry; venison steak with blackcurrant, port, tarragon, mushroom and cream sauce; a trio of locally-made sausages with garlic mash; duck in plum, soy, sherry and coriander sauce; and a selection of home-made pies, including prawn and egg, chicken and ham, steak and kidney, and smoked cod. A large selection of fresh, home-made desserts is always on offer, usually including Yorkshire curd tart, mango and lychee brûlée, grape and mandarin Pavlova, spiced plum crumble, and trifle with apricot and brandy.

England

EWHURST
Map 06 TQ04

The Windmill Inn ♀
Pitch Hill GU6 7NN ☎ 01483 277566 ▤ 01483 277566
Dir: *From Cranleigh take B2127, through Ewhurst. At mini rndbt take Shere road. Pub 1.5m on R*
This welcoming inn was originally the haunt of 18th-century smugglers. Its tempting menu is best enjoyed in the conservatory restaurant, which makes the most of the pub's panoramic downland views. Typical meals include duck breast with apple and honey sauce, chicken breast with parsnip mash and cream sauce, and baked smoked haddock with mash and cream of leek sauce. The beautiful country setting means you can always walk it off later.
OPEN: 12-11 (Sun 12-10.30) **BAR MEALS:** L served all week 12-2.15 D served Tue-Sat 7-9.30 Av main course £8.50 **RESTAURANT:** L served all week 12-2.15 D served Tue-Sat 7-9.30 Av 3 course à la carte £17.50 **BREWERY/COMPANY:** Free House ◀: Hogs Back TEA, Old Speckled Hen, Fuller's London Pride, Greene King, IPA. ♀: 7 **FACILITIES:** Children welcome Garden: Terrace leads to large pond, BBQ area Dogs allowed Water **NOTES:** Parking 30

GUILDFORD
Map 06 SU94

Red Lion 🐾 ♀
Shamley Green GU5 0UB ☎ 01483 892202 ▤ 01483 894055
Attractive old village pub with large front and rear gardens, ideal for whiling away summer afternoons watching the local cricket team play on the green opposite. In the cosy bar or large comfortable restaurant, peruse no fewer than four varied menus on which everything listed is home prepared including roast half duck with black cherry sauce, vegetable tartlet with Mornay sauce, fresh fish pie, and another four or more fish/seafood dishes. Young's and Adnam's in the bar.
OPEN: 7.30 -11.30 **BAR MEALS:** L served all week 12-3 D served all week 7-10 Av main course £10.95 **RESTAURANT:** L served all week 12-3 D served all week 7-10 Av 3 course à la carte £22.50 **BREWERY/COMPANY:** Pubmaster ◀: Youngs Pedigree, Adnams Broadside. ♀: 6 **FACILITIES:** Children welcome Children's licence Garden: Large front and rear garden **NOTES:** Parking 20

HASCOMBE
Map 06 TQ03

The White Horse 🐾
The Street GU8 4JA ☎ 01483 208258 ▤ 01483 208200
Dir: *from Godalming take B2130. Pub on L 0.5m after Hascombe*
A friendly 16th-century pub situated in picturesque countryside that is good for walking. The pub is particularly noted in summer for its colourful garden, with hanging baskets and flowers. Restaurant menu and extensive blackboard specials in the bar may offer Thai-style salmon and prawn fishcakes, home-made steak burger, pies, and calves' liver and bacon. Fresh fish is delivered daily.
OPEN: 10-3 5.30-11 (Sat 10-11, Sun 12-10.30) **BAR MEALS:** L served all week 12-2.20 D served all week 7-10 Av main course £9 **RESTAURANT:** L served all week 12-2 D served Mon-Sat 7-10 Av 3 course à la carte £25 **BREWERY/COMPANY:** Punch Taverns ◀: Adnams, Fullers London Pride, Harveys Flowers. **FACILITIES:** Children welcome Garden: outdoor eating, patio Dogs allowed **NOTES:** Parking 55

Most of the pubs in this guide book pride themselves on the quality of their food. This may take a little time to prepare.

HASLEMERE
Map 06 SU93

The Wheatsheaf Inn ♦♦♦ 🐾 ♀
Grayswood Rd, Grayswood GU27 2DE
☎ 01428 644440 ▤ 01428 641285
Dir: *Leave A3 at Milford, A286 to Haslemere. Grayswood approx 1.5m N*

Edwardian village inn at the heart of the county with one of Surrey's loveliest walks right on its doorstep. Nearby is the magnificent viewpoint at Black Down where Alfred, Lord Tennyson lived for 24 years. Extensive menu ranging from snacks and sandwiches through traditional roasts and steaks to dishes such as venison with summer fruit sauce; aubergine and pepper bruschetta with goats' cheese and basil oil; and skate en papillote with lime ginger butter.
OPEN: 11-3 6-11 **BAR MEALS:** L served all week 12-2 D served all week 7-10 Av main course £9.95 **RESTAURANT:** L served all week 12-2 D served all week 7-10 Av 3 course à la carte £18.50 **BREWERY/COMPANY:** Free House ◀: Fullers London Pride, Timothy Taylor Landlord, Ringwood Best. ♀: 8 **FACILITIES:** Garden: Patio area, pergola terrace **NOTES:** Parking 20 **ROOMS:** 7 bedrooms 7 en suite no children overnight

HINDHEAD
Map 06 SU83

Devil's Punchbowl Inn ♀
London Rd GU26 6AG ☎ 01428 606565 ▤ 01428 605713
Dir: *from M25 take A3 to Guildford, from there head toward Portsmouth*
The hotel, which dates from the early 1800s, stands 900ft above sea level with wonderful views as far as London on a clear day. The 'punchbowl' is a large natural bowl in the ground across the road. The kitchen specialises in steaks. Recent change of hands - readers' comments welcome.
OPEN: 7-11 **BAR MEALS:** L served all week 12-3 D served all week 6-10 Av main course £7.95 **RESTAURANT:** L served all week 12-3 D served all week 6-10 **BREWERY/COMPANY:** Eldridge Pope ◀: Bass, 6 X, Tetleys. ♀: 10 **FACILITIES:** Children welcome Children's licence Garden: Lawn area with benches patio area, seating Dogs allowed **NOTES:** Parking 65

LEIGH
Map 06 TQ24

The Plough ♀
Church Rd, LEIGH RH2 8NJ ☎ 01306 611348 ▤ 01306 611299
Dir: *Telephone for directions*
A welcoming country pub overlooking the village green and situated opposite St Bartholomew's Church. Varied clientele, good atmosphere and quaint low beams which are conveniently padded! A hearty bar menu offers steak sandwiches, burgers, melts, salads, ploughman's and jacket potatoes, while the restaurant-area menu features tomato and

continued

LEIGH continued

artichoke pasta, smoked haddock fillet mornay, or Mexican style tortilla wraps.

OPEN: 11-11 (Sun 12-10.30) **BAR MEALS:** L served all week 12-3 D served all week 7-10 Av main course £8 **RESTAURANT:** L served all week 12-3 D served all week 7-10 Av 3 course à la carte £15 **BREWERY/COMPANY:** Hall & Woodhouse ◑: Badger Best , Tanglefoot, Sussex Bitter. ♀: 15 **FACILITIES:** Children welcome Garden: Patio/Paved surrounded by climbing roses Dogs allowed Water **NOTES:** Parking 6

MICKLEHAM   Map 06 TQ15

Pick of the Pubs

King William IV 🐑
Byttom Hill RH5 6EL ☎ 01372 372590
Dir: Just off A24 (Leatherhead-Dorking), by partly green-painted restaurant, just N of B2289

Formerly an ale house for Lord Beaverbrook's staff at his nearby Cherkley estate, this popular, family-run free house has steadily built up a reputation for its good food and well-kept real ales. With a dedicated proprietor at the helm, this has resulted in the introduction of popular monthly cookery demonstrations in the winter months, balanced in summer by a special events calendar for the numerous walkers and cyclists. Selections from recent menus include daily specials such as pan-fried calves' liver with sage and garlic butter, chicken breast with a black pepper and thyme crumble, and Mediterranean stirfry, with vegetarian alternatives like Brie and leek in filo pastry. There are Sunday roasts, too, and summer barbecues in the attractive terraced garden. The building itself dates from 1790 with some Victorian additions, displayed to effect in the panelled snug and the larger back bar with its open fire, cast iron tables and grandfather clock.

OPEN: 11-3 6-11 (Sun 12-3, 7-10.30) Closed: 25 Dec, 31 Dec Closed eve **BAR MEALS:** L served all week 12-2 D served all week 7-9.30 Av main course £9.50

BREWERY/COMPANY: Free House ◑: Hogs Back TEA & Hop Garden Gold, Badger Best, Adnams Best, Monthly Guest Beers. **FACILITIES:** Garden: Terraced garden with picturesque views

The Running Horses 🐾 ♀
Old London Rd RH5 6DU ☎ 01372 372279 🖶 01372 363004
e-mail: info@therunninghorses.co.uk
Dir: Off A24 between Leatherhead & Dorking

Attracting travellers for more than 400 years, this inn is only half a mile from famous Box Hill. The bar features a

highwayman's hideaway and an inglenook fireplace. Chunky sandwiches, croque monsieur and grilled sardines are available in the bar. On the menu in both bar and restaurant, look for peppered medallion of venison, cream and mustard poached smoked haddock, or baby vegetable ratatouille tart.

OPEN: 11.30-3 5.30-11 (Sun 12-3.30, 7-10.30) Dec 25, Jan 1 Closed eve **BAR MEALS:** L served all week 12-2.30 D served Mon-Sat 7-9.30 Av main course £13.50 **RESTAURANT:** L served all week 12-2.30 D served Mon-Sat 7-9.30 Av 3 course à la carte £250 **BREWERY/COMPANY:** Punch Taverns ◑: Fuller's London Pride, Young's Bitter, Greene King, Adnams Bitter. ♀: 7 **FACILITIES:** Garden: Patio area Dogs allowed Water

NEWDIGATE   Map 06 TQ14

The Six Bells
Village St RH5 5DH ☎ 01306 631276 🖶 01306 631793
Dir: 5m S of Dorking (A24), L at Beare Green rdbt, R at T-jct in village

Picturesque timber-framed pub in a quiet village location and reputedly once a smugglers' haunt. Light meals and bar snacks might include the Six Bells club sandwich and a range of baguettes and filled jacket potatoes. Daily-changing blackboard menu may offer rack of lamb and poached salmon.

OPEN: 11-3 6-11 (Sun 12-10.30) **BAR MEALS:** L served all week 12-3 D served all week 6-9 Av main course £6.50 **RESTAURANT:** L served all week 12-3 D served all week 7-9.30 Av 3 course à la carte £20 Av 3 course fixed price £13.90 **BREWERY/COMPANY:** Free House ◑: Badger Tanglefoot & Sussex Ale, Carlsberg-Tetley Tetleys Smooth, Fursty Ferret. **FACILITIES:** Children welcome Garden: patio/terrace, food served outdoors Dogs allowed Water **NOTES:** Parking 40

The Surrey Oaks
Parkgate Rd RH5 5DZ ☎ 01306 631200 🖶 01306 631200
Dir: turn off either A24 or A25 and follow signs to Newdigate, The Surrey Oaks is 1m E of Newdigate Village on the road towards Leigh/Charwood

Parts of this country pub date from 1570, the Georgian bar has been converted into a restaurant, and there are two

continued

continued

small beamed bars, one with an inglenook fireplace and stone-flagged floor. It is a renowned real ale pub, and a regular CAMRA award-winner. Restaurant and bar menus offer a good range of dishes plus a daily choice from the blackboard - maybe steak and kidney pudding, guinea fowl, sea bass, calves' liver, or ham, egg and chips. Big annual beer festival over August Bank Holiday, with live music and pig roasts.

OPEN: 11.30-2.30 5.30-11 (Sat 11.30-3, 6-11) (Sun 12-3, 7-10.30) **BAR MEALS:** L served all week 12-2 D served Tue-Sat 7-9.00 Av main course £6.50 **RESTAURANT:** L served all week 12-2 D served Tue-Sat 7.00-9.00 Av 3 course à la carte £15 **BREWERY/COMPANY:** Punch Taverns ◀: Adnams, Fuller's London Pride, Wells Bombardier Premium Bitter. **FACILITIES:** Children welcome Garden: Child area, pond, aviary, goat paddock Dogs allowed Water **NOTES:** Parking 75

OCKLEY Map 06 TQ14

Pick of the Pubs

Bryce's at The Old School House ◉ ◯ ♀
RH5 5TH ☎ 01306 627430 ▤ 01306 628274
e-mail: bryces.fish@virgin.net
Dir: *8m S of Dorking on A29*

Bill Bryce acquired this former boys' boarding school in 1982, converting the 17th-century building into a spacious bar and restaurant, the latter located in the old school gym. Fresh fish is the speciality of the house - usually grilled, steamed or poached. The range offered is limited only by market availability, and Bill prides himself both on its freshness and the simplicity of its presentation. Bar meals include platters, open sandwiches, fresh pasta, and dishes from cullen skink to chilli salt skate fillets. In the restaurant expect the likes of steamed Scottish halibut with prawn and chilli beignet and saffron vanilla sauce, or seared king scallop feuillantine with mild garlic and red pepper risotto. Non-fish alternatives are also listed: maybe ham hock and parsley sauce, steak, and confit duck leg. There's also a good wine list including special cellar vintages and 14 wines available by the glass.

OPEN: 11-3 6-11 (Closed Sun pm Nov, Jan, Feb) Closed: 25 Dec, 1 Jan **BAR MEALS:** L served all week 12-2.30 D served Mon-Sat 6.30-9.30 Av main course £8.50 **RESTAURANT:** L served all week 12-2.30 D served Mon-Sat 7-9.30 Av 3 course fixed price £25 **BREWERY/COMPANY:** Free House ◀: Gales HSB, GB & Butser, Scottish Courage John Smith's Smooth. ♀: 14 **FACILITIES:** Children welcome Garden: Terrace area Dogs allowed Water **NOTES:** Parking 25

The Kings Arms Inn ◠
Stane St RH5 5TS ☎ 01306 711224 ▤ 01306 711224
Dir: *From M25 J9 take A24 through Dorking towards Horsham, A29 to Ockley*

Charming heavily-beamed 16th-century village inn in the picturesque Ockley village, overlooked by the tower of Leith Hill. Welcoming log fires, a priest hole, a friendly ghost, an award-winning garden and six recently refurbished bedrooms are all features. Home-made food is offered in both restaurant and bar, with dishes such as pheasant breast wrapped in bacon and stuffed with Stilton; home-made game pie; fresh Whitstable oysters; rack of lamb cooked in molasses; and a range of chargrilled steaks.

OPEN: 11-2.30 6-11 (Sun 12-3, 7-10.30) **BAR MEALS:** L served all week 12-2 D served all week 7-9 Av main course £8.50 **RESTAURANT:** L served Tue-Sun 12-2 D served Tue-Sat 7-9 Av 3 course à la carte £17.50 **BREWERY/COMPANY:** Free House ◀: Interbrew Flowers Original, Boddingtons, Greene King Old Speckled Hen, Wadworth 6X. **FACILITIES:** Garden: Landscaped garden, with patio BBQ **NOTES:** Parking 40 **ROOMS:** 6 bedrooms 6 en suite s£50 d£70 (♦♦♦♦) no children overnight

---

OXTED Map 06 TQ35

George Inn ♀
High St RH8 9LP ☎ 01883 713453
Dir: *Telephone for directions*

A 500-year-old pub and restaurant with a friendly family atmosphere, warmed by log fires under the original oak beams. Home-made steak and kidney pudding, braised shank of lamb, sardines and salmon fillets from its seasonal menus epitomise the range of carefully-sourced and well-cooked fare that is available on any day. There are decent wines to accompany the food, with Badger beers as alternative supping. A committed team let their quality of service speak for itself.

OPEN: 11-11 (Sun 12-10.30) **BAR MEALS:** L served all week 12-9.30 D served all week Av main course £6.50 **RESTAURANT:** L served all week 12-2.30 D served all week 6-9.30 **BREWERY/COMPANY:** Woodhouse Inns ◀: Badger Tanglefoot, Badger Best, King & Barnes, Sussex. **FACILITIES:** Children welcome Garden: Patio Area Dogs allowed **NOTES:** Parking 25

PIRBRIGHT Map 06 SU95

The Royal Oak ♀
Aldershot Rd GU24 0DQ ☎ 01483 232466
Dir: *M3 J3 take A322 towards Guildford, then A324 towards Aldershot*

A genuine old world pub specialising in real ales (up to nine at any time), and well known for its glorious prize-winning garden. The Tudor cottage pub has an oak church door, stained glass windows and pew seating, and in winter there

continued

continued

England

PIRBRIGHT continued

are welcoming log fires in the rambling bars. The menu may include smoked salmon and pesto, braised lamb shoulder, steak and ale pie, and penne pasta Alfredo, along with various specials.

OPEN: 11-11 (Sun 12-10.30) **BAR MEALS:** L served all week 12-2 D served all week 6.30-9.00 Av main course £7
BREWERY/COMPANY: 🍺 Flowers IPA, Hogsback Traditional English Ale, Bass Ringwood Ale. 🍷: 17 **FACILITIES:** Garden
NOTES: Parking 50

REDHILL   Map 06 TQ25

William IV Country Pub 🛏
Little Cotton Ln, Bletchingly RH1 4QF ☎ 01883 743278
Dir: from M25 J6 take A25 towards Redhill. Turn R at top of Bletchingly High Street
An early Victorian hostelry comprising a traditional snug, lounge and dining-room. Located down a leafy lane past a terraced row of cottages, it is very close to the Pilgrims' Way, which traverses the North Downs. Home-made specials dot the lunchtime menu, with accomplished special dishes including pork fillet with mushrooms, beef and onion patties, and seafood pancakes. Alfresco eating in the peaceful garden is an additional summer bonus.

OPEN: 12-3 6-11 (Sun noon until 10.30) 25 Dec Closed eve
BAR MEALS: L served all week 12-2.15 D served all week 6.45-9.30 Av main course £7.50 **RESTAURANT:** L served all week 12-2.15 D served all week 6.45-9.30 Av 3 course à la carte £18
BREWERY/COMPANY: Punch Taverns 🍺 Adnams Bitter, Young's Bitter, Harveys Sussex Best, Fullers London Pride.
FACILITIES: Garden: Large 2 tier garden, enclosed fence & gates Dogs allowed **NOTES:** Parking 10

SOUTH GODSTONE   Map 06 TQ34

Fox & Hounds 🛏 🍷 NEW
Tilbarstow Hill Rd RH9 8LY
Old fashioned in an attractive way, with a cosy low-beamed bar, antique high-backed settles, and a wood-burning stove. Pleasant country views can be enjoyed from the garden. Typical pub favourites go down well here - steak and kidney pudding, sausage and mash etc - but expect too tournados Rossini, calves' liver with onion gravy, and pan-fried scallops in garlic butter.

BAR MEALS: L served all week 12-2.30 D served all week 7-9.30 Av main course £8 **RESTAURANT:** L served all week 12-2.30 D served all week 7-9.30 Av 3 course à la carte £15 🍺 All Greene King. 🍷: 7
FACILITIES: Children welcome Garden: Large garden Dogs allowed
NOTES: Parking 20

STAINES   Map 06 TQ07

The Swan Hotel 🛏 🍷
The Hythe TW18 3JB ☎ 01784 452494 ▤ 01784 461593
e-mail: swan.hotel@fullers.co.uk
Dir: Just off A308, S of Staines Bridge. Minutes from M25, M4 & M3. 5m from Heathrow
Once used by bargemen, this 18th-century hotel on the south bank of the Thames is just down river from Runnymede. Today it has two bars serving Fuller's ales from the nearby Chiswick brewery, and a riverside restaurant. The menu offers traditional English fare - from ploughman's and sandwiches to fish and chips with beer batter or chicken and field mushroom pie - along with some favourites from around the world.

continued

OPEN: 11-11 **BAR MEALS:** L served all week 12-6 D served all week 6-9.30 **RESTAURANT:** L served all week 12-6 D served all week 6-9.30 **BREWERY/COMPANY:** Fullers 🍺 Fuller's London Pride, ESB. 🍷: 10 **FACILITIES:** Children welcome Garden: Patio with seating. Overlooks River Thames Dogs allowed

---

VIRGINIA WATER   Map 06 TQ06

The Wheatsheaf Hotel ★★ 🍷
London Rd GU25 4QF ☎ 01344 842057 ▤ 01344 842932
e-mail: sales@wheatsheafhotel.com
Dir: M25 Jct 13, head towards A30 Bracknell
The Wheatsheaf dates back to the second half of the 18th century and is beautifully situated overlooking Virginia Water on the edge of Windsor Great Park. Chalkboard menus offer a good range of freshly-prepared dishes with fresh fish as a speciality. Popular options are beer-battered cod and chips, roast queen fish with pesto crust, and braised lamb shank on mustard mash.

OPEN: 11-11 **BAR MEALS:** L served all week 12-10 D served all week Av main course £8 **RESTAURANT:** L served all week 12-10 D served all week Av 3 course à la carte £16
BREWERY/COMPANY: 🍺 Guest Ales. **FACILITIES:** Children welcome Garden: beer garden, patio, outdoor eating
NOTES: Parking 90 **ROOMS:** 17 bedrooms 17 en suite s£90 d£95
See Pub Walk on page 451

WALLISWOOD   Map 06 TQ13

The Scarlett Arms
RH5 5RD ☎ 01306 627243
Dir: S on A29 from Dorking, thru Ockley, R for Walliswood/Oakwood Hill
Oak beams, a stone floor and a fine open fireplace give a homely feel to this unspoilt, 400-year-old rural pub. Simple country cooking is the perfect complement to the excellent King & Barnes ales on offer.

OPEN: 11-3.30 5-11 **BAR MEALS:** L served all week 12-3 D served all week 6-10 Av main course £6.25 **BREWERY/COMPANY:** Hall & Woodhouse 🍺 King & Barnes Sussex, Mild & Broadwood.
FACILITIES: Garden Dogs allowed Children allowed
NOTES: Parking 30

WARLINGHAM   Map 06 TQ35

The White Lion
CR6 9EG ☎ 01883 629011
Listed 15th-century inn with low ceilings and oak beams. The main bar area has a popular inglenook fireplace. Traditional pub grub menu.

OPEN: 12-11 (Sun 12-10.30) **BAR MEALS:** L served all week 12-8 D served all week Av main course £5 **BREWERY/COMPANY:** Bass 🍺 Fullers London Pride, plus Guest beers. **FACILITIES:** Children welcome Dogs allowed **NOTES:** No credit cards

WEST CLANDON
Map 06 TQ05

Onslow Arms ♀
The Street GU4 7TE ☎ 01483 222447 🖹 01483 211126
e-mail: onslowarms@massivepub.com
Dir: A3 then A247

Though it dates from 1623 and retains some charming
historical features, including an inglenook fireplace and
traditional roasting spit, this pub certainly moves with the
times by providing its own helipad for customers'
convenience. It's handy, too, for both Gatwick and Heathrow
airports. The Cromwell Bar, popular with locals, has a good
choice of real ales, and food is available in the French
restaurant, L'Auberge, or La Rotisserie, which serves soups,
salads, omelettes and baguettes.
OPEN: 11-11 (Sun 12-10.30) **BAR MEALS:** L served all week 12-
2.30 D served all week 7-10 Av main course £8 **RESTAURANT:** L
served all week 12.30-2.30 D served all week 7-10 Av 3 course à la
carte £30 **BREWERY/COMPANY:** Free House 🍺: Scottish
Courage Courage Best & Directors, Young's Bitter, Badger King &
Barnes & Sussex, Fuller's London Pride. ♀: 11 **FACILITIES:** Children
welcome Garden: Patio, garden, alcove seating Dogs allowed
NOTES: Parking 200

WEST END
Map 06 SU96

Pick of the Pubs

The Inn @ West End 🐑 ♀
42 Guildford Rd GU24 9PW
☎ 01276 858652 🖹 01276 485842
e-mail: greatfood@the-inn.co.uk
Dir: On the A322 towards Guildford 3M from J3 of the M3

Stylish pub-restaurant, refurbished and renamed for
contemporary appeal. The pub's sign depicts a scene from
Othello, where the English are praised for being good
drinkers. Light and airy throughout, it attracts both locals
and travellers for first class food and decent wines -
proprietors Gerry and Ann Price also run a small wine-
importing business. Wine tastings, quiz nights and themed
dinners are regular features. At lunchtime there is a
choice of snacks or a fixed-price meal, while the main
menu might offer baked pheasant with parsnip crisps and
apple brandy, or pan-fried calves' liver with mash, red
onion marmalade and sage fritters. Fish is bought from
the boats in Portsmouth so a very fresh variety appears
on the menu: maybe moules à la crème, pan-fried sea
bass with salsa verde, or gilt head bream with basil oil
and sunblush tomatoes.
OPEN: 12-3 5-11 **BAR MEALS:** L served all week 12-2.30 D
served all week 6-9.30 Av main course £13.50 **RESTAURANT:** L
served all week 12-2.30 D served all week 6-9.30 Av 3 course à la

continued

carte £22.50 Av 2 course fixed price £9.95
BREWERY/COMPANY: Free House 🍺: Scottish Courage
Courage Best, Fuller's London Pride. **FACILITIES:** Garden:
Dining patio, pergola, boules pitch Dogs allowed
NOTES: Parking 35

WITLEY
Map 06 SU93

The White Hart ♀
Petworth Rd GU8 5PH ☎ 01428 683695 🖹 01428 682554
Dir: From A3 follow signs to Milford, then A283 towards Petworth.
Pub 2m on L

16th-century coaching inn with illustrious connections. Richard
II used to pub as a hunting lodge and George Eliot based
characters in her novel Middlemarch on the clientele.
Shepherd Neame beers are a feature.
OPEN: 11.30-3.00 (summer 11-11) 5.30-11 (Sun 7.00 -10.30)
BAR MEALS: L served all week 12-2.30 D served Tue-Sat 7-9.30 Av
main course £7 **RESTAURANT:** L served all week 12-2.30 D served
Tue-Sat 7-9.30 Av 3 course à la carte £14.50
BREWERY/COMPANY: Shepherd Neame 🍺: Shepherd Neame
Master Brew, Spitfire & Best. ♀: 7 **FACILITIES:** Children welcome
Garden: Patio, large grassed area Dogs allowed Water & Chews
NOTES: Parking 20

SUSSEX, EAST

ALCISTON
Map 06 TQ50

Pick of the Pubs

Rose Cottage Inn 🐑 ♀
BN26 6UW ☎ 01323 870377 🖹 01323 871440
e-mail: ian@alciston.freeserve.co.uk
Dir: Off A27 between Eastbourne & Lewes

Wisteria and roses climb up the front of this traditional
Sussex country pub. Ancient Alciston has many thatched
houses and a tithe barn with 50,000 roof tiles. Beyond,
the South Downs rise steeply, so the narrow road from
the A27 is both way in and way out. The inn, owned by
the same family for over 40 years, is renowned for good
home-cooked food, including locally-supplied fish and
game. Walkers flock to it, and locals are more than happy
to drink in one of its rambling bars, or in the small front
garden (with heaters). Bar menus list ploughman's,
salads, scampi, sausage and chips, and steaks. In the
restaurant, maybe sliced loin of pork with sherry cream
and green peppercorn sauce, or half a roast duckling with
passion fruit and Marsala sauce. Specials might be
chicken balti, home-made steak and ale shortcrust pastry
pie, and vegetarian spinach pancakes. No children under
10, though.
OPEN: 11.30-3 6.30-11 (Sun 12-3, 7-10.30) Closed: 25-26 Dec
BAR MEALS: L served all week 12-2 D served all week 7-9.30
RESTAURANT: D served Mon-Sat 7-9
BREWERY/COMPANY: Free House 🍺: Harveys Best. ♀: 9
FACILITIES: Garden: Patio area Dogs allowed Water provided
NOTES: Parking 25

◆ **Pubs with Red Diamonds are the top places in
the AA's three, four and five diamond ratings**

The Ram Inn

Climb high above a sprawling country estate and look towards distant horizons on this superb downland walk.

At the centre of Firle lies Firle Place, home to the Gage family for more than 500 years and now open to the public. The 18th-century house is magnificent and a tour of it reveals some fascinating treasures, many of which were brought back from America by Sir Thomas Gage. The paintings include an important collection of Old Masters with works by Van Dyck, Reynolds, Gainsborough and Rubens.

From the Ram turn left and follow the road round to the right, through Firle. Walk along to the village stores and a footpath to Charleston. Pass the turning to Firle's Church of St Peter, which contains a window by John Piper, and continue heading southwards, out of the village.

Turn right at a junction of concrete tracks and make for the road. Turn left, head for the downland escarpment and begin the long climb, steep in places. On reaching the car park at the top, swing left to a gate and join the South Downs Way.

Head eastwards on the long-distance trail and as you approach a kissing gate and adjoining gate, turn sharp left. Follow the path in a north-westerly direction, down the steep slope of the escarpment. On reaching a wooden post, where the path forks, take the lower grassy path and follow it as it descends in a wide sweep. Drop down to a gate and walk ahead, keeping a fence on the left. Skirt around Firle Plantation and follow the track all the way to the junction.

THE RAM INN, FIRLE
BN8 6NS
☎ 01273 858222

Directions: R off A27, 3m E of Lewes The oldest part of this inn dates from 1542, with many later additions that have done nothing to spoil the atmosphere. Part of the Firle Estate, owned by the Gage family for over 500 years. Traditional pub food.
Open: 11.30-11 (Sun 12-10.30)
Bar Meals: 12-9
Notes: Children welcome (high chairs, changing room, play equip) & dogs (water). Two gardens, picnic benches & orchard. Parking. (See page 466 for full entry)

Turn left and walk along the track, keeping the dramatic escarpment on the left. As you approach the village of Firle, the track curves to the right towards the buildings of Place Farm. Cross over the junction of concrete tracks and return to the pub.

DISTANCE: 4 1/2 miles/7.2km
MAP: OS Explorer 123
TERRAIN: Downland and farmland
PATHS: Quiet roads, tracks and paths
GRADIENT: One steep climb to the South Downs followed by a dramatic descent

Walk submitted and checked by Nick Channer

ALFRISTON
Map 06 TQ50

George Inn ♀
High St BN26 5SY ☎ 01323 870319 ▤ 01323 871384
e-mail: george_inn@hotmail.com
Dir: Telephone for directions
A splendid flint and half-timbered building with 13th-century foundations and a network of smugglers' tunnels leading from its cellars. The Grade II listed inn is set in one of the area's loveliest villages, and boasts an interior featuring heavy oak beams and an ancient inglenook fireplace. The menus change regularly, with fresh ingredients going into escalope of veal filled with Parma ham and shrimp, Szechwan style trout, chicken, leek and bacon pie, and beer-battered salmon and chips. Good choice of desserts.
OPEN: 11-11 Closed: Dec 25 **BAR MEALS:** L served all week 12-2.30 D served all week 7-9 **RESTAURANT:** L served all week 12-2.30 D served all week 7-9 **BREWERY/COMPANY:** Greene King ◖: Greene King Old Speckled Hen, Abbot Ale, Ruddles Country. **FACILITIES:** Children welcome Garden Dogs allowed

The Sussex Ox ♀
Milton St BN26 5RL ☎ 01323 870840 ▤ 01323 870715
e-mail: sussexox@aol.com
Dir: Off the A27 between Polegate and Lewes, signed to Milton Street

Idyllically-situated pub, tucked away down a meandering country lane. There are two restaurants here, The Sty family room leading out to the garden, and the peaceful Front Room restaurant with candlelit tables and soft background music. Favourite food includes Sussex Ox burger, poussin with fruity nut stuffing, chargrilled tuna steak, chicken, leek and ham pie, and game in season. There are also fresh pasta dishes, curries, and loin of lamb in white onion sauce. Look out for regularly-changing specials.
OPEN: 11-3 6-11 (Sun 12-3, 6-10.30) 25 Dec Closed eve **BAR MEALS:** L served all week 12-2.30 D served all week 6-9 **RESTAURANT:** L served all week 12-2.30 D served all week 6-9 **BREWERY/COMPANY:** Free House ◖: Hop Back Summer Lightning, Harveys Best, Youngs Bitter. **FACILITIES:** Children welcome Garden Dogs allowed Water **NOTES:** Parking 60

ARLINGTON
Map 06 TQ50

Old Oak Inn 🛏
BN26 6SJ ☎ 01323 482072 ▤ 01323 895454
Dir: N of A27 between Polegate & Lewes
Originally the village almshouse, dating from 1733, which became a pub in the early 1900s. Opposite Abbots Wood, an ideal area for walking. Typical bar dishes include filled baguettes and ploughman's, as well as pasta and curries. In the restaurant expect the likes of roast duck, fresh grilled seabass, lamb steaks in rosemary, duck with citrus and ginger,

rabbit pie, fresh salmon and crab salad, and home-made steak and kidney pudding.
OPEN: 11-3 6-11 **BAR MEALS:** L served all week 12-3 D served all week 6.30-9.30 Av main course £7 **RESTAURANT:** L served all week 12-3 D served all week 6.30-9.30 Av 3 course à la carte £10 **BREWERY/COMPANY:** Free House ◖: Harveys, Badger, Adnams Broadside & Guest ales. **FACILITIES:** Children welcome Garden: Grassed and hedged with tables Dogs allowed Water provided. To be kept on lead **NOTES:** Parking 40

ASHBURNHAM PLACE
Map 06 TQ61

Ash Tree Inn 🛏
Brownbread St TN33 9NX ☎ 01424 892104
The Ash Tree is a friendly old pub with three open fires, plenty of exposed beams and a traditional local atmosphere. Bar food includes ploughman's, salads and sandwiches, while the restaurant may be serving steaks, local lamb, steak and ale pie, or salmon in a variety of sauces.
OPEN: 12-3 7-11 (Summer 6.30-11) **BAR MEALS:** L served all week 12-2 D served all week 7-9 Av main course £7 **RESTAURANT:** L served all week 12-2 D served Tue-Sun 7-9 **BREWERY/COMPANY:** Free House ◖: Harveys Best, Greene King Old Speckled Hen, Brakspear Bitter + Guest ales. **FACILITIES:** Garden: Grass with picnic tables **NOTES:** Parking 20

BARCOMBE
Map 06 TQ41

The Anchor Inn ♀
Anchor Ln BN8 5BS ☎ 01273 400414 ▤ 01273 401029
Dir: From A26 (Lewes to Uckfield road)

In an unspoiled part of rural Sussex on the banks of the River Ouse, the Anchor started life in 1790, catering for bargees who travelled from Newhaven to Slaugham; the last commercial barge moored here in 1861. Two bars have been added using oak from a French priory. A typical meal may start with roasted Italian artichokes, or vegetarian terrine, continue with Dover sole with lime butter, sirloin steak with a peppercorn sauce, or medallions of lamb with rosemary and redcurrant sauce, and finish up with a tasty dessert from the daily blackboard. Boats are available for customers to hire.
OPEN: 11-11 (Sun 12-10.30) Closed: 25 & 31 Dec **BAR MEALS:** L served all week 12-3 D served all week 6-9 **RESTAURANT:** L served all week 12-3 D served all week 6-9 **BREWERY/COMPANY:** Free House ◖: Harvey Best, Badger & Tanglefoot. **FACILITIES:** Children welcome Garden **NOTES:** Parking 300 **ROOMS:** 3 bedrooms 1 en suite s£45 d£55 (♦♦♦)

> ♦ **Diamond rating for inspected guest accommodation**

continued

England

Pick of the Pubs

The Cricketers Arms 🍽 ♀

BN26 6SP ☎ 01323 870469 📠 01323 871411

Dir: Off A27 between Polegate & Lewes (follow signs for Church)

A traditional flint-stoned cottage, originally one of a terrace, dating back 500 years although it has been an ale house for a mere 200 of them. The unspoilt old building, just off the A27, is a handy watering hole for walkers on the South Downs Way. Delightfully unpretentious inside, its three charming rooms sport half-panelled walls, open fires, scrubbed tables and a nice chatty atmosphere free from background music, fruit machines and pool tables. Harvey's ales tapped straight from the cask are part of the appeal; another is the short menu listing home-made, traditional choices of starters and light bites like smoked salmon pâté, and butterfly prawns, such local favourites as home-baked ham with egg and chips, and scampi and chips, and a main choice of steaks, local cod in batter, and fresh local dressed crab are sought after by locals and visitors alike. A stunning cottage garden for summer use.
OPEN: 11-3 6-11 (May-mid Sep open everyday 11-11) Closed: 25 Dec **BAR MEALS:** L served all week 12-2.15 D served all week 6.30-9.00 Av main course £6 **BREWERY/COMPANY:** Harveys of Lewes 🍺: Harveys Sussex Best & Sussex Pale Ale, Seasonal Ales. **FACILITIES:** Garden: Traditional cottage style garden Dogs allowed Water, long walks **NOTES:** Parking 25

BLACKBOYS   Map 06 TQ52

The Blackboys Inn 🍽 ♀

Lewes Rd TN22 5LG ☎ 01825 890283
Dir: On B2192 between Halland and Heathfield
Rambling, black-weatherboarded, 14th-century inn set in large gardens overlooking an iris- and lily-covered pond. It has a splendid beamed interior, complete with resident ghost. A wide range of fresh home-cooked dishes is served from the bar snack menu, restaurant carte and blackboard specials. Expect the likes of lamb fillet wrapped in Parma ham, linguine pesto, whole grilled seabass, classic Spanish paella, saltimbocca, or stuffed chicken breast.
OPEN: 11-3 5-11 (Sat 11-3, 6-11, Sun 12-3, 7-10.30) Closed: Jan 1 **BAR MEALS:** L served all week 12-2.00 D served Mon-Sat 6.30-10.00 Av main course £12.50 **RESTAURANT:** L served all week 12-1.45 D served Mon-Sat 7-10 Av 3 course à la carte £20 Av fixed price £30 **BREWERY/COMPANY:** Harveys of Lewes 🍺: Harveys Sussex Best Bitter, Sussex Pale Ale, Sussex XXXX Old Ale. ♀: 8
FACILITIES: Children welcome Garden: Large front and side gardens with pond Dogs allowed water **NOTES:** Parking 40

The Basketmakers Arms NEW

12 Gloucester Rd BN1 4AD ☎ 01273 689006
Dir: First left out of Brighton station main entrance (Gloucester Rd). Pub is on right at the bottom of the hill
Traditional back-street local appealing to a real mix of people, with wooden floors and a vast array of memorabilia on display. The emphasis is on good drink (Gales BBB and HSB, and over 80 malt whiskies to choose from) and quality food. Fish and chips is a typical Friday special, with home-made burgers, steak and Guinness pie, fish pie with a crispy potato topping, and various salads proving very popular.
OPEN: 11-11 (Sun 12-10.30) **BAR MEALS:** L served all week 12-3 D served Mon-Fri 5.30-8.30 Av main course £4
BREWERY/COMPANY: Gales 🍺: HSB, Buster Bitter, GB, Festival Mild & Seasonal Beers. **FACILITIES:** Children welcome Dogs allowed Dogs on lead

The Greys

105 Southover St BN2 9UA ☎ 01273 680734 606475
e-mail: mike@greyspub.com
Laid-back pub with a Bohemian feel which has long been a popular live music venue - a reputation new landlord Christopher Taylor plans to continue. Typical dishes include grilled salmon steak with prawns and sautéed cucumber; game pie; hake fillet in a tomato, herb and garlic sauce with black olives; and tomatoes stuffed with spiced lentils served with tagliatelle and shaved Parmesan. Sweets include Irish whiskey ice cream, and fried milk with almond and honey syrup.
OPEN: 11-3 5.30-11 (Sat-Sun 11-11) **BAR MEALS:** L served Tue-Sun 12-2 D served Tue-Sat 7-9.30 Av main course £10
RESTAURANT: L served Tue-Sun 12-2 D served Tue-Thur, Sat 7-9.30 Av 3 course à la carte £18.50 Av 3 course fixed price £17 **BREWERY/COMPANY:** Enterprise Inns 🍺: Timothy Taylor Landlord, Itchen Valley Godfathers, Harveys. **FACILITIES:** Dogs allowed on leads **NOTES:** Parking 16 No credit cards

The Market Inn ♦ ♦ ♦ NEW

1 Market St BN1 1HH ☎ 01273 329483 📠 01273 777227
e-mail: ac.tull@reallondonpubs.com
Dir: In Brighton's Lanes area. 50 metres from junc of North St and East St
Located in the heart of Brighton's historic Lanes, this classic south coast pub is within easy reach of the Royal Pavilion and seafront. The building was formerly used by George IV for liaisons with his lady friends, and now features two tastefully-furnished en suite bedrooms. Daily blackboard specials supplement the traditional pub menu, which includes popular dishes like sausage and mash, steak and kidney pudding, and home-cooked curry.
OPEN: 11-11 12-10.30 (Mon-Sat 11-11, Sun 12-10.30)
BAR MEALS: L served all week 11.30-6 D served Sat-Sun 6-8.30 Av main course £5 **BREWERY/COMPANY:** Scottish Courage 🍺: Harveys, Wells Bombardier Premium. **FACILITIES:** Dogs allowed **ROOMS:** 2 bedrooms 2 en suite s£45 d£50 no children overnight

> **Pick of the Pubs** have that extra special quality that makes them stand out from the crowd. Their entries are highlighted, and may be a full page.

CHIDDINGLY
Map 06 TQ51

The Six Bells ♀
BN8 6HE ☎ 01825 872227

Dir: E of A22 between Hailsham & Uckfield turn opp Golden Cross PH

Inglenook fireplaces and plenty of bric-a-brac are to be found at this large characterful free house which is where various veteran car and motorbike enthusiasts meet on club nights. The jury in the famous onion pie murder trial sat and deliberated in the bar before finding the defendant guilty. Live music at weekends. Exceptionally good value bar food includes such dishes as shepherds pie, steak and kidney pie, tuna pasta bake, buttered crab with salad and chicken curry with rice.

OPEN: 11-3 6-11 **BAR MEALS:** L served all week 11-2.30 D served all week 6-10.30 Av main course £4 **BREWERY/COMPANY:** Free House ◀: Courage Directors, John Smiths, Harveys Best.
FACILITIES: Children welcome Garden Dogs allowed
NOTES: Parking 60

COWBEECH
Map 06 TQ61

Merrie Harriers ♀
BN27 4JQ ☎ 01323 833108 📠 01323 833108
e-mail: rmcotton@btopenworld.com

Dir: Off A271, between Hailsham & Herstmonceux

A traditional clapboarded coaching inn, dating from the 17th century, within easy reach of Pevensey Levels and the fascinating Herstmonceux Castle. Inside the pub are low-beamed ceilings, open fires and fresh flowers on every table. New owners Roger Cotton and Lesley Day have introduced a changing menu using much local produce, and also host themed gourmet nights. Popular dishes include Portobello mushrooms stuffed with spinach and Stilton; pan-fried sea bass served on roasted Mediterranean vegetables; and steak, mushroom and kidney pie.

OPEN: 11.30-3.00 6-11 Sun eve open for food Mar-31 Dec
BAR MEALS: L served all week 12-2 D served all week 7-9 Av main course £10 **RESTAURANT:** L served all week 12-2 D served all week 7-9 Av 3 course à la carte £20 **BREWERY/COMPANY:** Free House ◀: Harveys Best, Horsham Best, London Pride. ♀: 8
FACILITIES: Garden: Large sloping garden, water feature Dogs allowed **NOTES:** Parking 20

DANEHILL
Map 06 TQ42

Pick of the Pubs

The Coach and Horses 🐾 ♀
RH17 7JF ☎ 01825 740369

Dir: From E Grinstead travel S through Forest Row on A22 to junc with A275 Lewes Road turn R on A275 for 2m until Danehill turn L on school lane 1/2m pub is on the L

A 19th-century cottagey pub built of local sandstone with former stables forming part of the restaurant. Homely winter fires and neatly-tended gardens add plenty of character and colour to the picturesque surroundings, and half-panelled walls, highly-polished wooden floorboards and vaulted beamed ceilings give the place a charming, timeless feel. In an age when the traditional village local is coming under increasing threat, the Coach and Horses proves that some classic hostelries can still survive. Food plays a key role in the pub's success, with a good selection of lunchtime snacks and a constantly-changing evening menu. Expect the likes of smoked haddock with poached egg, buttered spinach and new potatoes, pork

leek sausages, chargrilled organic veal escalope with wild mushrooms and crème fraîche, or goats' cheese and red pepper ravioli with a herb cream. Leave room for a dessert, which might be sticky toffee pudding, treacle tart with vanilla ice cream, or pannacotta with mixed berry compote.

OPEN: 11.30-3 6-11 **BAR MEALS:** L served all week 12-2 D served all week 7-9 Av main course £9 **RESTAURANT:** L served all week 12-2 D served all week 7-9 Av 3 course à la carte £19.50 **BREWERY/COMPANY:** Free House ◀: Harveys Best & Old Ale, Hook Norton, Badger IPA, Archers Golden. ♀: 7
FACILITIES: Garden: Beautifully kept, tables, good views Dogs allowed Water **NOTES:** Parking 30

EAST CHILTINGTON
Map 06 TQ31

Pick of the Pubs

The Jolly Sportsman 🐾 ♀
Chapel Ln BN7 3BA ☎ 01273 890400 📠 01273 890400
e-mail: thejollysportsman@mistral.co.uk

Dir: From Lewes take Offham/Chailey rd A275, L at Offham onto B2166 towards Plumpton, take Novington Ln, after approx 1m L into Chapel Ln

An isolated pub with a lovely garden set on a quiet no-through road looking out to the South Downs. The small atmospheric bar, with its stripped wooden floor and mix of comfortable furniture, has been sympathetically upgraded to a character Victorian-style dining inn by respected restaurateur Bruce Wass from Thackerays in Tunbridge Wells. Well-sourced food features on the daily-changing menus, served throughout the bar and smart, yet informal restaurant. The vegetarian choice embraces blue cheese and squash risotto, and potato gnocchi with piquillo peppers and capers, while a fixed-price lunch might feature mussel, cockle and saffron linguini, pork goulash and basmati rice, and chocolate mousse or steamed lemon pudding. Otherwise expect peppered Barbary duck breast, baked whole red mullet, and spiced pear and almond tart, or a plate of ripe cheeses. The nearby Rectory Brewery (run by the vicar) supplies some of the beers drawn from the cask.

OPEN: 12-2.30 6-11 (Sun 12-4) Closed: 25/26 Dec
BAR MEALS: L served Tue-Sun 12.30-2.30 D served Tue-Sat 7-9 Av main course £12 **RESTAURANT:** L served Tue-Sun 12.30-2.30 D served Tue-Sat 7-9 Av 3 course à la carte £25 Av 3 course fixed price £14.75 **BREWERY/COMPANY:** Free House ◀: Changing guest beers. ♀: 8 **FACILITIES:** Children welcome Children's licence Garden: quiet, secluded, view of South Downs Dogs allowed Water **NOTES:** Parking 30

continued

England

EAST DEAN   Map 06 TV59

Pick of the Pubs

The Tiger Inn ♀
BN20 0DA ☎ 01323 423209 ▤ 01323 423209
Dir: Signed from A259 heading to the coast
Rose-covered flint-built pub on the village green, popular
with walkers for its real ales and home-cooked food -
from steak and ale pie to whole lobster. Candlelit in the
evenings, offering an intimate and cosy environment.
Quality wines are offered from a blackboard, as many as
ten by the glass. In summer you can choose from 20
different ploughman's, featuring 13 English cheeses.
Bookings are not taken and it can get very busy.
OPEN: 11-3 6-11 (Sat 11-11, Sun 12-10.30) **BAR MEALS:** L
served all week 12-2 D served all week 6.30-9 Av main course £6
BREWERY/COMPANY: Free House ◀: Harvey Best, Adnams
Best. Brakspear **FACILITIES:** Dogs allowed **NOTES:** No credit
cards

EXCEAT   Map 06 TV59

The Golden Galleon 🐾 ♀
Exceat Bridge BN25 4AB ☎ 01323 892247 ▤ 01323 892555
e-mail: info@goldengalleon.co.uk
Dir: On A259, 1.5m E of Seaford
Not only do the Cuckmere Haven real ales on tap here come
from the pub's own micro-brewery, but the hops grow in its
garden. Once just a shepherd's bothy, it has grown enough to
comfortably accommodate TV crews making an episode of
Eastenders, a Gary Rhodes commercial, and a Dickens
costume drama. A wide-ranging menu includes pizzas, steak
and stout pie, vegetable curry with rice, penne al funghi, and
fresh sea bass.
OPEN: 10.30-11 (closed Sun evening Winter) **BAR MEALS:** L
served all week 12-2 D served Mon-Sat, Sun in Summer 6-9 Av main
course £7.50 **RESTAURANT:** L served all week 12-2.30 D served
Mon-Sat, Sun in Summer 6-9.30 Av 3 course à la carte £15.50
BREWERY/COMPANY: Free House ◀: Cuckmere Haven Golden
Peace & Downland Bitter, Harveys Armada Ale, King Red River Ale.
♀: 16 **FACILITIES:** Children welcome Garden: Terraces and
intimate gardens near pub. Dogs allowed **NOTES:** Parking 100

FIRLE   Map 06 TQ40

The Ram Inn ♀
BN8 6NS ☎ 01273 858222
e-mail: nikwooller@raminnfirle.net
Dir: R off A27 3m E of Lewes
The oldest part of the Ram dates from 1542, and though
added to many times - it has 14 staircases - it has changed
little in recent years. Situated at the foot of the South Downs,
the inn is part of the Firle Estate, seat of the Gage family. Its
flint-walled garden includes picnic tables and children's play
equipment. Menu choices range through burgers, pastas and
six varieties of ploughman's to fish and chips and rack of pork
loin ribs.
OPEN: 11.30-11 (Sun 12-10.30) Dec 25 Open 12-2 **BAR MEALS:** L
served all week 12-9 D served all week
BREWERY/COMPANY: Free House ◀: Harveys Best plus regular
changing ales. ♀: 8 **FACILITIES:** Children welcome Children's
licence Garden: Two gardens 1 with picnic benches, 1 orchard Dogs
allowed Water **NOTES:** Parking 10
See Pub Walk on page 462

FLETCHING   Map 06 TQ42

Pick of the Pubs

The Griffin Inn 🐾 ♀
TN22 3SS ☎ 01825 722890 ▤ 01825 722810
e-mail: thegriffininn@hotmail.com
*Dir: M23 J10 to East Grinstead then A22 then A275. Village signed on
L. 10m from M23*

In an unspoilt village three miles from Ashdown Forest,
and overlooking the Ouse Valley, this fine pub is reputedly
the county's oldest licensed building. Its two-acre, west-
facing garden has a particularly fine view. Old beams,
wainscoting, open fires and a collection of old pews and
wheel-back chairs characterise the main bar. Both the bar
and restaurant menus change daily, with food sourced
locally as much as possible. A bar meal might be organic
veal meatballs with fresh tomato salsa on tagliatelle, or
roasted, locally-caught mackerel with fennel and cider
sauce. In the restaurant, there could be Thai red vegetable
and sweet potato curry with cardamom rice, or grilled
fillet of beef, field mushrooms, gratin potatoes and sauce
béarnaise. Traditional Sunday lunch is followed by home-
produced puddings. More than a dozen wines from its
extensive list are served by the glass. Real ales include
Harvey's Sussex, brewed locally at Lewes.
OPEN: 12-3 6-11 Closed: 25 Dec **BAR MEALS:** L served all
week 12-2.30 D served all week 7-9.30 Av main course £9.50
RESTAURANT: L served all week 12.15-2.30 D served Mon-Sat
7.15-9.30 Av 3 course à la carte £24 Av 3 course fixed price £19.50
BREWERY/COMPANY: Free House ◀: Harvey Best, Badger
Tanglefoot, Thomas Hardy Hardy Country. ♀: 12
FACILITIES: Children welcome Garden: 2 large lawns, beautiful
views Dogs allowed Water **NOTES:** Parking 20 **ROOMS:** 8
bedrooms 8 en suite (♦♦♦♦)

GUN HILL   Map 06 TQ51

The Gun Inn 🐾
TN21 0JU ☎ 01825 872361 ▤ 01825 873081
*Dir: From A22 London-Eastbourne, Golden Cross (3m N of Hailsham) L
past Esso station, 1.5m down lane on L*
Originally a 15th-century farmhouse, the Gun Inn is situated
in a tiny hamlet amid rolling Sussex countryside. It got its
name from the cannon foundries that were located at Gun
Hill. The pub also served as the courthouse for hearings in
the 'Onion Pie Murder', a local crime of passion. Resplendent
in summer with its pretty gardens and flower-adorned
façade, it offers fresh grilled plaice, steak and kidney pie,
smoked haddock in cheese and mustard sauce, and seafood
platter.

continued

OPEN: 11.30-3 6-11 (Sun Close 10:30) Closed: Dec 25-26
BAR MEALS: L served all week 12-2 D served all week 6-9.30 Av main course £7 **BREWERY/COMPANY:** Free House
🍺: Wadworth 6X, Adnams Best, Harvey Best. **FACILITIES:** Children welcome Garden: Food served outside Dogs allowed Water provided **NOTES:** Parking 55

HARTFIELD   Map 06 TQ43

Anchor Inn
Church St TN7 4AG ☎ 01892 770424
Dir: On B2110
On the edge of Ashdown Forest, at the heart of 'Winnie the Pooh' country, stands this old inn dating back to the 14th century, complete with stone floors and a large inglenook. Sandwiches, ploughman's, and baked potatoes are among the bar snacks, or try Tandoori spare ribs, and prawn and mango curry for a starter or snack, and main dishes such as venison steak with port and redcurrant sauce.
OPEN: 11-11 **BAR MEALS:** L served all week 12-2 D served all week 6-10 **RESTAURANT:** L served all week 12-2.00 D served Tue-Sat 7-9.30 Av 3 course à la carte £20 Av 3 course fixed price £20
BREWERY/COMPANY: Free House 🍺: Fuller's London Pride, Harveys Sussex Best Bitter, Interbrew Flowers IPA, Flowers Original Bitter & Bass. **FACILITIES:** Children welcome Garden Dogs allowed Water **NOTES:** Parking 30

Pick of the Pubs

The Hatch Inn 🍴 ♀
Coleman's Hatch TN7 4ET
☎ 01342 822363 📠 01342 822363
e-mail: Nickad@bigfoot.com
Dir: A22 14 miles, L at Forest Row rdbt, follow for 3 miles until Colemans Hatch and turn R

Classic 15th-century inn that was originally a row of three cottages reputed to date back to 1430, and thought to have been built to house workers at the local water-driven hammer mill. Previously known as the Cock Inn, the

Hatch takes its name from the original coalman's gate leading on to Ashdown Forest. It is frequently seen on television in various dramas and adverts, and was a possible haunt of smugglers at one time. The inn is only minutes away from the famous, restored Pooh Bridge, immortalised in A.A. Milne's 'Winnie the Pooh' stories. Good quality food is served at lunchtime, from sandwiches, jacket potatoes and ploughman's to sizzling chicken fajitas, and the more elaborate lamb Stroganoff with brandy and cream. In the evening (booking essential) there might be wild mushroom salad, roast lamb chump with Shrewsbury sauce, and hot cherry Bakewell tart.
OPEN: 11.30-3.00 5.30-11.00 Open all day Sat May-Sept Open all day Sun Closed: Dec 25 **BAR MEALS:** L served all week 12.00-2.30 D served Tue-Sun 7-9.15 Av main course £11.50
RESTAURANT: L served all week 12.00-2.30 D served Tue-Sun 7-9.15 Av 3 course à la carte £26 **BREWERY/COMPANY:** Free House 🍺: Harveys, Fuller's London Pride, Larkins. ♀: 10
FACILITIES: Garden: Two large beer gardens, One with forest view Dogs allowed Water

---

HOLTYE   Map 06 TQ43

The White Horse Inn 🍴 ♀ NEW
TN8 7ED ☎ 01342 850640 📠 01342 850032
Dir: Situated in the A264, 4 miles E of East Grinstead and 8 miles W of Tunbridge Wells
A very old coaching inn where prisoners for Lewes Assizes used to be held overnight. The menu has been revamped to include Vietnamese prawns, meatballs in cheese sauce, fillet steak Marilyn Monroe (with cream, garlic, lemon juice, brandy, mushrooms, onions and Worcestershire sauce), plaice Florentine, satay chicken and a larger than average vegetarian selection. Larkins Chiddingstone is on tap. The large paddock overlooks Ashdown Forest, and the bridge where A A Milne's ursine hero played Pooh sticks is nearby.
OPEN: 11-3 5.30-11 **BAR MEALS:** L served all week 12-2.30 D served all week 6-9.30 Av main course £10 **RESTAURANT:** L served all week 12-2.30 D served all week 6-9.30 Av 3 course à la carte £20 🍺: Old Speckled Hen, IPA, Larkins Chiddingstone, Abbott. ♀: 8
FACILITIES: Children welcome Garden: Large grassed paddock Dogs allowed **NOTES:** Parking 50

ICKLESHAM   Map 07 TQ81

Pick of the Pubs

The Queen's Head 🍴 ♀
Parsonage Ln TN36 4BL ☎ 01424 814552 📠 01424 814766
e-mail: ianhick@hotmail.com
Dir: Between Hastings & Rye on A259
There's always a warm welcome beneath the high beamed ceilings of this distinctive, tile-hung pub, renowned for its hearty home-cooked meals and good selection of well-kept ales. The 17th-century building has been licensed since 1831 and enjoys spectacular views across the Brede Valley to the historic town of Rye. Large inglenook fireplaces, church pews and a clutter of old farm implements all add to the relaxed character of this bustling, independent free house. A full menu is served all day at weekends and the printed selection is supplemented by fresh fish and daily specials listed on the blackboard. Meals range from ploughman's to fillet steak, and there is a popular daily curry. Typical dishes include

continued

continued

England

ICKLESHAM continued

smoked salmon, deep-fried Brie, or steak in French bread as starters or snacks, and main courses of pork chops with apple sauce, lamb and mint pie or ham, egg and chips.
OPEN: 11-11 (Sun 12-10.30) **BAR MEALS:** L served all week 12-2.45 D served all week 6.15-9.45 Av main course £7.50
RESTAURANT: L served all week D served all week
BREWERY/COMPANY: Free House 🍺: Rother Valley Level Best, Greene King Abbot Ale, Ringwood Old Thumper, Woodforde Wherry. **FACILITIES:** Children welcome Garden: Seating for 60, boules pitch **NOTES:** Parking 50

KINGSTON (NEAR LEWES)   Map 06 TQ30

The Juggs ♀
The Street BN7 3NT ☎ 01273 472523 📄 01273 483274
Dir: *E of Brighton on A27*
Named after the women who walked from Brighton with baskets of fish for sale, this rambling, tile-hung 15th-century cottage, tucked beneath the South Downs, offers an interesting selection of freshly-cooked food.
OPEN: 11-11 **BAR MEALS:** L served all week 12-2.30 D served all week 6-9 Av main course £8 **RESTAURANT:** L served all week 12-2 D served all week 6-9.30 Av 3 course à la carte £15
BREWERY/COMPANY: Shepherd Neame 🍺: Shepherd Neame Spitfire. **FACILITIES:** Children welcome Garden: patio, beer garden, food served outdoors Dogs allowed on lead **NOTES:** Parking 30

LEWES   Map 06 TQ41

The Snowdrop ♀
South St BN7 2BU ☎ 01273 471018

In 1836 this was the site of the UK's biggest avalanche. Hence the pub's deceptively-gentle name. Proudly vegetarian for over ten years, the menu offers constantly-changing specials, including Sunday roasts. Entertainment is a big feature here, from jazz on a Monday evening, or bands on a Saturday night, to the annual 'Alternative Miss Snowdrop' contest.
OPEN: 11-11 (Sun 12-10.30) **BAR MEALS:** L served all week 12-3 D served all week 6-9 Av main course £5.95
BREWERY/COMPANY: Free House 🍺: Harveys Best, plus Guests.
FACILITIES: Children welcome Dogs allowed **NOTES:** No credit cards

★ **Star rating for inspected hotel accommodation**

LITLINGTON   Map 06 TQ50

Plough & Harrow
BN26 5RE ☎ 01323 870632 📄 01323 870632
Dir: *S of A27 between Lewes & Polegate*
Gloriously situated on the edge of the South Downs, this Grade II listed thatched building lies in a small village on the scenic Cuckmere Haven. Only minutes from historic Alfriston and the Sussex coast. Good, wholesome pub fare includes ploughman's, home-made pie, fresh cod, quiche, Litlington beef, steak and swordfish.
OPEN: 11-3 6.30-11 (Sun 12-3, 7-10.30) **BAR MEALS:** L served all week 12-2 D served all week 7-9 Av main course £9.95
RESTAURANT: L served all week 12-2.30 D served all week 6.30-9.30 Av 3 course à la carte £18 **BREWERY/COMPANY:** Free House 🍺: Harveys Best, Badger Best & Tanglefoot, Youngs Double Chocolate. **FACILITIES:** Children welcome Garden: beer garden, outdoor eating Dogs allowed not in restaurant **NOTES:** Parking 50

MAYFIELD   Map 06 TQ52

Pick of the Pubs

The Middle House 🏨 ♀
High St TN20 6AB ☎ 01435 872146 📄 01435 873423
Dir: *E of A267, S of Tunbridge Wells*

So much history is associated with this elegant old Grade I property - 'one of the finest timber framed buildings in Sussex' - that deciding what to leave out is hard. It was built in 1575 for Sir Thomas Gresham, Elizabeth I's Keeper of the Privy Purse, and founder of the London Stock Exchange. A private residence until the 1920s, it retains a fireplace by master carver Grinling Gibbons, wattle and daub infill, and a magnificent oak-panelled restaurant, still incorporating a private chapel. You may dine in the relaxing bar, where the inglenook houses a weekly spit roast, or in the restaurant, from where there's a super view south over the terraced garden and lawns to the Vale of Heathfield. The menu includes roast duck with plum and Cognac sauce, Moroccan lamb casserole with pepper, butter beans and rice, beef Stroganoff, and seared salmon fillet on roasted vegetables with balsamic and sesame glaze.
OPEN: 11-11 **BAR MEALS:** L served all week 12-2.30 D served all week 7-9.30 Av main course £9 **RESTAURANT:** L served all week 12-2 D served all week 7-9.30 Av 3 course à la carte £25 Av 3 course fixed price £19.95
BREWERY/COMPANY: Free House 🍺: Harvey Best, Greene King Abbott Ale, Black Sheep Best, Theakston Best.
FACILITIES: Children welcome Garden: Terraced area with flower beds, good views **NOTES:** Parking 25

Rose & Crown Inn 🛏️

Fletching St TN20 6TE ☎ 01435 872200 📠 01435 872200
Attractive and friendly, this 16th-century, typical Sussex pub
has a splendid front patio and a rambling interior with low
beams and open fires. The blackboard lists the day's selection
of fresh fish - probably trout, monkfish, sole and scallops -
and other choices, such as home-made beef and Guinness
pie, or steak and kidney pie. Lighter meals include Sussex
Smokie, and Italian ciabatta sandwiches, for example. Lewes-
based Harveys beers in the bar.
OPEN: 11-3 5.30-11 (Sun 12-10.30) **BAR MEALS:** L served all
week 12-2.30 D served Mon-Sat 6-9.30 Av main course £8
RESTAURANT: L served all week 12-2.30 D served Mon-Sat 6-9.30
Av 3 course à la carte £20 🍺: Harveys, Adnams.
FACILITIES: Children welcome Garden: Front of house with tables
Dogs allowed **NOTES:** Parking 15

OFFHAM   Map 06 TQ41

The Blacksmith's Arms 🛏️

London Rd BN7 3QD ☎ 01273 472971
A busy 200-year-old roadside pub with a reputation for good
local produce freshly cooked by its chefs. Pan-fried chicken
breast filled with shallot and pork forcemeat on a cranberry
lyonnaise; Sussex smokie; roast salmon fillet on garlic and
rosemary braised flageolet; steak and kidney shortcrust pastry
pie; and roasted sea bass demonstrate the versatility of the
kitchen. Bar snacks and tempting dessert menu.
OPEN: 12-3 6.30-11 Closed: Dec 25-26 **BAR MEALS:** L served all
week 12-2.30 D served Mon-Sat 7-9 **RESTAURANT:** L served all
week 12-2 D served Mon-Sat 7-9 **BREWERY/COMPANY:** Free
House 🍺: Harveys Ales. **FACILITIES:** Garden: Patio area Dogs
allowed **NOTES:** Parking 22

OLD HEATHFIELD   Map 06 TQ52

Pick of the Pubs

Star Inn 🛏️ 🍷

Church St TN21 9AH ☎ 01435 863570 📠 01435 862020
Dir: *Take A21 from M25 towards Hawkhurst, R towards Broadoak, L
to Battle (B267), R into Heathfield*
Built as an inn for the stonemasons who constructed the
church in the 14th century, this creeper-clad building has
a wonderful, award-winning summer garden. It abounds
with colourful flowers and unusual picnic benches, and
affords impressive views across the High Weald. Equally
appealing is the atmospheric, low-beamed main bar with
its huge inglenook fireplace and cosy dining ambience.
Good bar food focuses on fresh fish from Billingsgate or
direct from boats in Hastings, like cod and chips, red
mullet served with squid ink linguinie, large cock crabs,
and bouillabaisse. For those favouring meat, you will find
home-made steak and kidney pie, marinated duck breast,
Highland steaks and local venison on menu. Generous
ploughman's lunches and excellent Harveys and Shepherd
Neame brews on handpump.
OPEN: 11.30-3 5.30-11 **BAR MEALS:** L served all week 12-
2.15 D served all week 7-9.30 Av main course £9
RESTAURANT: L served all week 12-2.15 D served all week 7-
9.30 **BREWERY/COMPANY:** Free House 🍺: Harvey Best,
Shepherds Neame, Master Brew, Bishops Finger.
FACILITIES: Children welcome Garden: 15 Oak tables,
umbrellas, fountain, flowers Dogs allowed **NOTES:** Parking 20

POYNINGS   Map 06 TQ21

Royal Oak Inn 🛏️ 🍷

The Street BN45 7AQ ☎ 01273 857389 📠 01273 857202
Dir: *N on the A23 just outside Brighton, take the A281 (signed for Henfield
& Poynings), then follow signs into Poynings village*

Nestling at the foot of the South Downs, close to the famous
Devil's Dyke, this white-painted village pub is popular on
summer weekends for its excellent barbecue facilities. Also
very popular with walkers, it offers good ales and a varied
menu, including oven-roasted rack of lamb, prime beef
burger, swordfish steak, fillet of cod, and home-roast ham.
OPEN: 11-11 (Sun 12-10.30) **BAR MEALS:** L served all week 12-
2.30 D served all week 6-9.30 Av main course £7.50
BREWERY/COMPANY: Free House 🍺: Harveys Sussex, Courage
Directors, Greene King Morland Old Speckled Hen. 🍷: 10
FACILITIES: Garden: Large garden with BBQ facilities & nice views
Dogs allowed **NOTES:** Parking 35

RINGMER   Map 06 TQ41

The Cock 🛏️ 🍷

Uckfield Rd BN8 5RX ☎ 01273 812040 📠 01273 812040
Dir: *On A26 approx 2m N of Lewes (not in Ringmer village)*

This atmospheric old inn takes its name from the cock horse,
the extra four-legged power needed to haul coaches up steep
hills. Its unspoilt, no-smoking bar has original oak beams, a
flagstone floor and an inglenook fireplace. The bar/restaurant
(also no-smoking) menu caters for all tastes, with main dishes
such as tiger prawns in créole sauce, swordfish provençale,
and the more prosaic sausage, beans and chips. A good range
of straightforward desserts. Popular with musicians from
nearby Glyndebourne.
OPEN: 11-3 6-11 (Sun open 12-3, 7-11pm) Closed: Dec 25 Dec 26
BAR MEALS: L served all week 12-2 D served all week 6.30-9.30 Av
main course £8 **RESTAURANT:** L served all week 12-2 D served all
week 6.30-9.30 Av 3 course à la carte £16.50
BREWERY/COMPANY: Free House 🍺: Harveys Sussex Best Bitter,

continued

RINGMER continued

Sussex XXXX Old Ale & Sussex XX Mild Ale, Fuller's London Pride, Interbrew Flowers Original Bitter. ♀: 7 **FACILITIES:** Children welcome Garden: Over 30 tables on paved terraces and grass Dogs allowed Dog chews **NOTES:** Parking 20

RUSHLAKE GREEN   Map 06 TQ61

Horse & Groom ⌂ ♀

TN21 9QE ☎ 01435 830320 ▤ 01435 830320
e-mail: chappellhatpeg@aol.com
Grade II listed building on the village green with pleasant views from the well-cultivated gardens. Dishes are offered from blackboard menus in the cosy bars: steak, kidney and Guinness pudding, and rabbit in cider are favourites, along with the excellent fresh fish choice - perhaps baby squid with fresh crab couscous or smoked salmon with home-made tagliatelle.
OPEN: 11.30-3 5.30-11 **BAR MEALS:** L served all week 12-2.30 D served all week 7-9.30 **RESTAURANT:** L served all week 12-2.30 D served all week 7-9.30 **BREWERY/COMPANY:** Free House
🍺: Harveys Master Brew, Shepherd Neame Spitfire. ♀: 7
FACILITIES: Children welcome Garden Dogs allowed
NOTES: Parking 20

RYE   Map 07 TQ92

Mermaid Inn ★★★ ◉ ⌂ ♀

Mermaid St TN31 7EY ☎ 01797 223065 ▤ 01797 225069
e-mail: mermaidinnrye@btclick.com
Destroyed by the French in 1377 and rebuilt in 1420, this famous smugglers' inn is steeped in history. Beams hewn from ancient ships' timbers, secret passageways and log fires are all part of the enchantment, and the Giant's Fireplace Bar has a priest hole as well as its enormous inglenook. Both traditional bar food and restaurant fare are offered, favourites including pan-fried crab cakes, seafood platter, cannon of venison and steak and kidney pudding.
OPEN: 11-11 (Sun 12-11) **BAR MEALS:** L served all week 12-2.15 D served Sun-Fri 7-9.15 Av main course £8.50 **RESTAURANT:** L served all week 12-2.15 D served all week 7-9.15 Av 3 course à la carte £35 Av 3 course fixed price £19.50 **BREWERY/COMPANY:** Free House 🍺: Greene King Old Speckled Hen, Scottish Courage Courage Best. **FACILITIES:** Children welcome Garden: Paved patio Dogs allowed Water **NOTES:** Parking 26 **ROOMS:** 31 bedrooms 31 en suite 6 family rooms s£75 d£140

Pick of the Pubs

The Ypres Castle Inn ⌂ ♀

Gun Garden TN31 7HH ☎ 01797 223248
e-mail: tomandmichael@hotmail.com
In a superb location, next to the 13th-century Ypres Tower and Gun Gardens with views to the coast and marshes, this attractive weather-boarded building dates from 1640. It is named after Sir John Ypres and was once something of a smuggling centre. The large garden includes a boules pitch, while inside there are traditional pub games like shove ha'penny. Live music nights on Fridays provide a showcase for local professional musicians. Four good cask-conditioned ales are usually offered, and a comprehensive wine list with at least 12 wines by the glass. Seafood is well represented on the menu, with grilled Rye Bay plaice, seared Rye king scallops, and roast cod wrapped in prosciutto with gremolata. Other options are rack of salt marsh lamb with mint and redcurrant glaze, or Gloucester Old Spot pork steak with apple and cider sauce. A full bar menu is available at lunchtime.
OPEN: 11.30-11 (seasonal times vary) **BAR MEALS:** L served all week 12-2.30 D served Mon-Sat 6-9 Av main course £6
RESTAURANT: L served all week 12-2.30 D served Mon-Sat 6.30-9 Av 3 course à la carte £22 **BREWERY/COMPANY:** Free House 🍺: Harveys Best, Youngs, Adnams Broadside, Interbrew Bass. ♀: 12 **FACILITIES:** Children welcome Garden: Lawn, views of river & castle Dogs allowed Water

THREE LEG CROSS   Map 06 TQ63

The Bull

Dunster Mill Ln TN5 7HH ☎ 01580 200586 ▤ 01580 201289
Dir: From M5 exit at Sevenoaks toward Hastings, R at x-rds onto B2087, R onto B2099 through Ticehurst, R for Three Legged Cross

In a peaceful hamlet setting, the Bull is a real country pub, with oak beams and large open fires, based around a Wealden hall house built between 1385 and 1425. The garden features a duck pond, a pétanque court and a children's play area. A typical menu might include strips of chicken breast pan-fried with bacon, tagine of lamb, Barbury duck, smoked haddock Florentine or mushroom tortellini Raphael. The Bull has recently come under new management.
OPEN: 11-11 Closed: Dec 25, 26 (evening) **BAR MEALS:** L served all week 12-2.30 D served all week 6.30-9.30 Av main course £6 **RESTAURANT:** L served all week 12-2.30 D served all week 6.30-9.30 **BREWERY/COMPANY:** Free House 🍺: Harveys, Interbrew Bass, Speckled Hen. **FACILITIES:** Children welcome Children's licence Garden Dogs allowed **NOTES:** Parking 80 **ROOMS:** 4 bedrooms 4 en suite s£35 d£60 (♦♦♦)

Open: 11.30-3, 6-11
Bar Meals: L served all week 12-2, D served Tue-Sat 7.30-9.30. Av cost main course £6.95
RESTAURANT: L served all week 12-2, D served Tue-Sat 7.30-9.30.
BREWERY/COMPANY:
Harveys of Lewes
🍺: Harveys Sussex Best and seasonal beers.
FACILITIES: Dogs allowed, Garden.
NOTES: Parking 20

The Dorset Arms

On the borders of Kent and Sussex close to Ashdown Forest and Royal Tunbridge Wells, a historic, white, weather-boarded 15th-century inn with many original features intact.

Withyham, nr Hartfield, TN7 4BD
☎ 01892 770278 📠 01892 770195
✉ jep@dorset-arms.co.uk
Dir: 4M W of Tunbridge Wells on B2110 between Groombridge and Hartfield.

The name comes from the arms of the Sackville family from nearby Buckhurst Park, although the building itself dates from around the reigns of Henry VI and Edward IV. Records show that it became an inn by the turn of the 18th century, prior to which it would have been an open-halled farmhouse with soot-covered rafters and an earthen floor. Many interesting Tudor and later period features remain, such as the ice cave buried in the hillside behind the pub, the bar with Sussex oak floor and magnificent open log fire, and the massive wall and ceiling beams in the restaurant. In these splendid surroundings it would be natural to expect some decent food, and the pub kitchen does not disappoint. From the tempting blackboard specials to the wide-ranging bar menu, fixed-price dining room menu, and another one for Sunday lunch, there's plenty of choice. You can eat in style with starters like Thai crab cakes with sweet and sour sauce, or tempura-battered vegetables, then move on to grilled fillets of sea bass with hollandaise sauce, crispy roast half duckling with Morello cherry sauce, or pan-fried pork fillet. Specials such as monkfish and prawns in a rich tomato, herb and white wine sauce, and creamy chicken and mushroom pie might entice diners away from light meals like smoked salmon and prawn salad, jumbo sausage, chips and beans. The home-made desserts are quite irresistible: meringues with pears and chocolate sauce, steamed raisin and apple pudding, and luxury bread and butter pudding offer the same good value as the rest of the food. Locally-brewed real ales of quality from Harveys Brewery in Lewes are always available.

England

UPPER DICKER
Map 06 TQ50

The Plough 🛏️ 🍷
Coldharbour Rd BN27 3QJ ☎ 01323 844859
Dir: *Off A22, W of Hailsham*
17th-century former farmhouse which has been a pub for over
200 years, and now comprises two bars and two restaurants.
Excellent wheelchair facilities, a large beer garden and a
children's play area add to the appeal, and the Plough is also
a handy stop for walkers. Expect such fish dishes as Sussex
smokie or prawn, Brie and broccoli bake, while other options
include duck breast in spicy plum sauce, veal in lemon cream,
or lamb cutlets in redcurrant and rosemary sauce.
OPEN: 11-3 6-11 (Sun 12-3, 7-10.30, Summer wknd 11-11)
BAR MEALS: L served all week 12-2.30 D served all week 6.30-9.30
Av main course £7.50 **RESTAURANT:** L served all week 12-2.30 D
served all week 6.30-9.30 Av 3 course à la carte £15
BREWERY/COMPANY: Shepherd Neame 🍺: Shepherd Neame
Spitfire Premium Ale, Best & Bishop's Finger. 🍷: 21
FACILITIES: Children welcome Garden: Large open 1 acre, boules,
horseshoe toss Dogs allowed **NOTES:** Parking 40

WARBLETON
Map 06 TQ61

The Warbill in Tun Inn 🛏️
Church Hill TN21 9BD ☎ 01435 830636 🖨 01435 830636
e-mail: warbillintun@ic24.net
An old smugglers' haunt, at least 400 years old. The Beatles
used to drink here in the '60s when visiting their manager,
Brian Epstein, who lived half a mile away. Old locals still recall
meeting Lennon and McCartney, as well as the resident ghost.
Representative dishes include steaks, duck breast, lamb shank,
Barnsley chops, lemon sole and poached salmon. Beers
include Harvey's Sussex Best, Crown Inn Ironmaster,
Warbleton's Winter Ale and guests.
OPEN: 12-3 7-11 **BAR MEALS:** L served all week 12-1.45 D served
all week 7-9.30 **RESTAURANT:** L served all week 12-1.45 D served
all week 7-9.30 **BREWERY/COMPANY:** Free House 🍺: Harveys
Best, Crown Inn Ironmaster, Warbleton Winter Ale.
FACILITIES: Children welcome Garden: Small, table seating, good
views Dogs allowed Water **NOTES:** Parking 20

WINCHELSEA
Map 07 TQ91

The New Inn 🛏️
German St TN36 4EN ☎ 01797 226252
e-mail: newinnchelsea.co.uk
Rambling, characterful 18th-century inn on a street corner in
this dignified small town, one of the seven former Cinque
Ports. Although there are home-made specials, the main
restaurant and bar menu is by no means adventurous, but the
opportunity to eat the likes of simple steak and chips, grilled
loin of pork, battered wholetail scampi, or breaded goujons of
lemon sole is why so many people dine in pubs, especially in
a cosy restaurant like the New Inn's.
OPEN: 11.30-3 6-11 (Open all Day May-Oct) (Open all Day Sun)
BAR MEALS: L served all week 12-3 D served all week 6.30-9.30 Av
main course £7.50 **RESTAURANT:** L served all week D served all
week Av 3 course à la carte £15 **BREWERY/COMPANY:** Greene
King 🍺: Morlands Original, Abbots Ale, Greene King IPA.
FACILITIES: Children welcome Garden: Traditional Old English
NOTES: Parking 20

WITHYHAM
Map 06 TQ43

SUSSEX, WEST

AMBERLEY
Map 06 TQ01

Black Horse
High St BN18 9NL ☎ 01798 831552
A traditional tavern with a lively atmosphere, in a beautiful
South Downs village. There is a display of sheep bells
donated by the last shepherd to have a flock on the local
hills. Good food served in the large restaurant and bar,
including extensive vegetarian choice and children's menu.
Expect rack of lamb, beef Wellington, and salmon steak with
a lime and hollandaise sauce. Lovely gardens, and good local
walks.
OPEN: 11-11 (Sun 12-10.30) **BAR MEALS:** L served all week 12-3
D served all week 6-9 🍺: Greene King Old Speckled Hen,
Carlsberg-Tetley Friary Meux Bitter. **FACILITIES:** Garden: Food
served outdoors
See Pub Walk on opposite page

The Bridge Inn 🛏️
Houghton Bridge BN18 9LR ☎ 01798 831619
Dir: *5m N of Arundel on B2139*
The Bridge Inn dates from 1650, and has a Grade II listing.
It is very popular with cyclists and walkers, and is only a
two minute walk from the Amberley chalk pits and
museum. Special features are the open fires and display of
original oil and watercolour paintings. Campers can
arrange pitches in the garden. The menu offers a
comprehensive fish choice plus dishes such as braised
lamb shank, rack of pork ribs, leek and Stilton crêpes, and
Lincolnshire sausage.
OPEN: 11-11 (Sun 12-10.30) **BAR MEALS:** L served all week 12-3
D served all week 6-9 Av main course £9 **RESTAURANT:** L served
12-3 D served 7-9 Av 3 course à la carte £17
BREWERY/COMPANY: Free House 🍺: Harveys Sussex, Fullers
London Pride, Youngs, Bass. **FACILITIES:** Children welcome
Garden: Food served outside. Well kept garden Dogs allowed Water
provided **NOTES:** Parking 20

The Black Horse

Climb into remote downland country above the Arun on this scenic walk.

Turn left out of the pub and walk through the village to the B2139. Cross over at the junction and take the road opposite. Turn right into High Titten and follow the road between trees and hedgerows.

On reaching the road junction, turn right and follow the tarmac path parallel to the road. Turn left at the South Downs Way sign and follow the concrete track over the railway line to a galvanised gate. Turn left here and follow the bridleway to the bank of the River Arun. Swing left, veering slightly away from the riverbank, to join a drive.

On reaching the road near the railway bridge, turn right. Begin to cross the road bridge spanning the Arun and then turn left at the footpath sign to a stile by a galvanised gate. Once over it, cross the water-meadows to the next stile and a few paces beyond it you reach a footpath sign. Turn left here.

Follow the path between trees, turn right on reaching a lane and pass Sloe Cottage.

Turn left just beyond a caravan site to join a bridleway. Follow the path as it runs above the camping ground and make for a gate and bridleway sign. Cross the track here and join a rough lane. Stay on it as it climbs gradually, providing views of the River Arun. Pass some ruined outbuildings and keep ahead, the lane dwindling to a track now. Veer left at the fork and follow the right of way. Make for a signposted crossroads and take the left-hand bridleway.

Walk down the chalk track, pass through the gate and continue the steep descent. Look for two gates down below, some distance apart. Cross to the right-hand gate and a bridleway sign is seen here. Follow the bridleway as it bends left, climbing steeply towards Downs Farm. Keep a

THE BLACK HORSE, AMBERLEY
High Street BN18 9NL
☎ 01798 831552

Lively tavern in beautiful South Downs village, with lovely garden. Good food includes extensive vegetarian choice.
Open: 11-11 (Sun 12-10.30)
Bar Meals: 12-3 6-9
Notes: Food served outdoors. (See opposite page for full entry)

fence on the left and follow the right of way as it merges with a wide track.

Keep left at the next junction and follow the South Downs Way towards the entrance to Downs Farm. Veer to the right of the gateway and join a narrow path which begins a steep descent. Turn right on reaching a tarmac lane, keep right at the fork and retrace your steps to the Black Horse.

DISTANCE: 7 miles/11.3km
MAP: OS Explorer 121
TERRAIN: Downland and valley
PATHS: Paths, bridleways and roads
GRADIENT: Some climbing and several steep descents

Walk submitted and checked by Nick Channer

ARDINGLY Map 06 TQ32

The Gardeners Arms
Selsfield Rd RH17 6TJ ☎ 01444 892328 📠 01444 892331
Dir: On B2028 between Haywards Heath and Turners Hill, follow signs to Wakehurst Place

Reputedly the home of a former magistrate who often conducted hangings on the front lawn, this pub dates back over 400 years. No such grisly scenes today in the inviting interior with its open fires, oak beams and panelling, antique furniture, and charming nooks and crannies. Straightforward bar food, grills and blackboard specials produce steak, mushroom and ale pie, Sussex smokies, wild mushroom and chestnut filo parcel, tuna and sweetcorn pasta, poached salmon salad, hearty bread and butter pudding, and rhubarb and apple crumble.
OPEN: 11.30-3 6-11 **BAR MEALS:** L served all week 12-2 D served all week 6.30-9.30 **RESTAURANT:** L served all week 12-2 D served all week 6.30-9.30 **BREWERY/COMPANY:** Woodhouse Inns
🍺: Badger Best, Tanglefoot & Champion Ale, King & Barnes Sussex Bitter. **FACILITIES:** Garden: Patio with pergola. Lawn area Dogs allowed Water **NOTES:** Parking 60

ASHURST Map 06 TQ11

The Fountain Inn
BN44 3AP ☎ 01403 710219 📠 01403 710219
Dir: On B2135 N of Steyning
A 16th-century free house located in a peaceful village. Local resident Laurence Olivier frequented the pub and Paul McCartney made the video for 'White Christmas' in the bar. A typical meal may include Sussex smoked haddock and prawns in cheese sauce, lasagne verde, steak, mushroom and ale pie, chargrilled chicken breast and bacon salad, or beefburgers and steaks from the chargrill. Good selection of puddings.
OPEN: 11.30-2.30 6-11 (Sun 12-3, 7-10.30) Dec 25 & 26, Jan 1 Closed in evening **BAR MEALS:** L served all week 11.30-2 D served Tue-Sat 6-9.30 Av main course £8 **BREWERY/COMPANY:** Free House
🍺: Harveys Sussex, Shepherd Neame Master Brew, Fuller's London Pride, Adnams Best, Black Sheep Best. **FACILITIES:** Children welcome Garden Dogs allowed Water provided **NOTES:** Parking 50 **NOTES:** No credit cards

BARNHAM Map 06 SU90

The Murrell Arms NEW
Yapton Rd PO22 0AS ☎ 01243 553320
Dir: Telephone for directions
Attractive white-painted inn distinguished by lavish window boxes and hanging baskets that add a wonderful splash of colour in summer. Built in 1750 as a farmhouse, it became a pub shortly after the railway station opened over 100 years

later. A straightforward menu offers bacon hock, curries, belly pork with parsley sauce, bacon and onion suet pudding, and liver and bacon casserole. Various Gale's ales on tap.
OPEN: 11-2.30 6-11 (Sat 11-11, Sun 12-10.30) **BAR MEALS:** L served all week 12-2 D served Fri-Wed 6-9 Av main course £3.50
🍺: Butser Best. 🍷: 28 **FACILITIES:** Garden: Grass area, tarmac area, grape vines Dogs allowed Water **NOTES:** Parking 14 **NOTES:** No credit cards

BILLINGSHURST Map 06 TQ02

The Blue Ship
The Haven RH14 9BS ☎ 01403 822709
Victorian brick and tile-hung rural cottage with 15th-century interior, hidden down a country lane off the A29. The games room features bar billiards, darts and shove ha'penny. Newfoundland dogs are particularly welcome as the owners have many of their own. Home-made pub grub includes ham, egg and chips, steak and onion pie and cottage pie.
OPEN: 11-3 6-11 **BAR MEALS:** L served all week 12-2 D served Tues-Sat 7-9.15 Av main course £5.50 **RESTAURANT:** L served all week D served Tue-Fri **BREWERY/COMPANY:** Hall & Woodhouse
🍺: Badger King & Barnes Sussex Bitter, Badger Best.
FACILITIES: Children welcome Garden: Large garden with play area Dogs allowed Water **NOTES:** Parking 9 **NOTES:** No credit cards

Cricketers Arms
Loxwood Rd, Wisborough Green RH14 0DG
☎ 01403 700369 📠 01403 700398
Dir: Telephone for directions
A traditional village pub dating from the 16th century with oak beams, wooden floors and open fires. Idyllic location overlooking the village green with views of cricket matches and hot-air-balloon rides. Fans of extreme sports will appreciate the fact that the Cricketers is the home of lawn mower racing. A full bar menu is served, ranging from snacks to three course meals and Sunday roasts, and there is a large selection of specials. Typical dishes include steak pie, sea bass in a prawn and oyster sauce, game dishes in season, and 'mega' salads.
OPEN: 11.00-2.30 5.30-11 All day Sat & Sun **BAR MEALS:** L served Mon-Sun 12-2 D served Mon-Sat 6.30-9.30 Av main course £7 **RESTAURANT:** L served Mon-Sun 12-2 D served Mon-Sat 6.30-9.30 **BREWERY/COMPANY:** Enterprise Inns 🍺: Fuller's London Pride, Greene King, IPA, Youngs Original. 🍷: 7 **FACILITIES:** Children welcome Garden: Grass area with benches Dogs allowed Water **NOTES:** Parking 20

Ye Olde Six Bells
76 High St RH14 9QS ☎ 01403 782124 📠 01403 780520
Dir: On the A29 between London & Bognor, 17m from Bognor
This attractive timbered pub dates from 1436 and features flagstone floors and an inglenook fireplace. Legend has it that a curse will fall on anyone who moves the old fireback, made from a re-used pattern of an iron grave slab. There is also reputed to be a smugglers' tunnel leading to the nearby church. Home-cooked food is served and the pastry is a highlight. The pub has a pretty roadside garden and is part of a Badger Ale Trail.
OPEN: 11-11 (Sun 12-10.30) 25 Dec closed eve **BAR MEALS:** L served all week 12-2 D served Mon-Sat 7-9 Av main course £6.50 **RESTAURANT:** L served Mon-Sat 12-2 7-9
BREWERY/COMPANY: Hall & Woodhouse 🍺: Badger Tanglefoot, Best and Sussex Ale. 🍷: 8 **FACILITIES:** Children welcome Garden: Large garden, rose archway, lawned area Dogs allowed on a lead **NOTES:** Parking 15

continued

BURPHAM
Map 06 TQ00

Pick of the Pubs

George & Dragon ⓖ
BN18 9RR ☎ 01903 883131

Dir: Off A27 1m E of Arundel, signed Burpham, 2.5m pub on L

An old smuggling inn located in a peaceful village at the foot of the South Downs, perfect for lovely walks alongside the nearby River Arun. The interior features beamed ceilings and walls hung with a variety of modern prints. It's very much a dining pub, with informal but attentive service, and attracts a sociable local clientele. Snacks (available at lunch and supper) include ploughman's platters, filled potatoes and warm filled baguettes. The main menu evolves with the seasons. Starters could include avocado and seafood timbale with Selsey crab, prawns, brown bread and butter, or warm smoked duck and bacon salad. Follow with the likes of local trout with orange and thyme stuffing, breast of guinea fowl stuffed with Brie in a tomato and basil sauce or (in season) half a local pheasant with juniper and red wine sauce.

OPEN: 11-2.30 6-11 (Oct-Apr, closed Sun eve) Closed: 25 Dec **BAR MEALS:** L served all week 12-2 D served Mon-Sat 7-9.30 Av main course £8.95 **RESTAURANT:** D served Mon-Sat 7-9.30 Av 3 course à la carte £30 Av 3 course fixed price £24.95 **BREWERY/COMPANY:** Free House 🍺: Harvey Best, Brewery-on-Sea Spinnaker Bitter, Fuller's London Pride. **NOTES:** Parking 40

CHILGROVE
Map 05 SU81

The White Horse at Chilgrove ♦♦♦♦♦ ⓐⓑ ⓒ ♈
High St PO18 9HX ☎ 01243 535219 🖷 01243 535301

Dir: On B2141 between Chichester & Petersfield

Picturesque South Downs hostelry, dating from 1756, with a team of French chefs and a celebrated wine list - in essence a gastronomic inn, offering a fusion of French cuisine and English hospitality. Bar lunches do give way to the restaurant's greater clout, yet the selection will still impress, with favourites like dressed Selsey crab and plenty of game in season.

OPEN: 11-3 6-11 (Closed Mon Winter) **BAR MEALS:** L served all week 11-3 D served all week 6-11 Av main course £10.50 **BREWERY/COMPANY:** Free House 🍺: Ballard's. **FACILITIES:** Children welcome Garden Dogs allowed **NOTES:** Parking 100

COMPTON
Map 05 SU71

Coach & Horses ⓒ
The Square PO18 9HA ☎ 02392 631228

Dir: On B2146 S of Petersfield

The pub stands beside the square of this prettiest of downland villages. The original timber-framed 16th-century dining room and the pine-clad Victorian extension create an evocative ambience enjoyed by villagers and visitors alike. Well known locally for its rib-eye steaks with multifarious sauces, the menu also includes a good fresh fish selection. Also expect dishes such as chicken, mushroom and tarragon pie, pot-roasted lamb shank with mash, and bacon hock with mustard mash. Hearty bar snacks can accompany a good choice of real ales. There is also a skittle alley and sheltered rear garden.

OPEN: 12-3 6-11 **BAR MEALS:** L served all week 12-2 D served all week 6-9 **RESTAURANT:** L served Tues-Sun 12-2 D served Tue-Sat

continued

6-9 **BREWERY/COMPANY:** Free House 🍺: Fuller's ESB, Ballard's Best, Cheriton Diggers Gold, Dark Star Golden Gate. **FACILITIES:** Children welcome Garden: Dogs allowed **NOTES:**

COPTHORNE
Map 06 TQ33

Hunters Moon Inn ⓒ
Copthorne Bank RH10 3JF ☎ 01342 713309 🖷 01342 714399 e-mail: enquiries@huntersmooninn.co.uk

Dir: M23, J10 Copthorne Way to roundabout, 1st L, then R into Copthorne Bank

Once associated with poachers and smugglers, this village pub has comfortable lounges, open log fireplace and a walled patio garden. A varied menu offers seared salmon with yellow and green courgettes, faggots with onion gravy and mashed potatoes, half shoulder of lamb, duck breast with walnut and pomegranate sauce, and pan-fried fillet of monkfish with seared oranges and spring onions. Good wine list.

OPEN: 12-11 Closed: Dec 26 **BAR MEALS:** L served Mon-Sun 12-2 D served Mon-Sun 6-9.30 Av main course £11 **RESTAURANT:** L served Mon-Sun 12-2 D served all week 7-9.30 **BREWERY/COMPANY:** Free House 🍺: Fuller's London Pride, Abbot Ale, Greene King, IPA. **FACILITIES:** Garden: Walled patio, with BBQ seating Dogs allowed **NOTES:** Parking 100

DUNCTON
Map 06 SU91

The Cricketers ⓒ ♈
GU28 0LB ☎ 01798 342473 🖷 01799 344753 e-mail: info@thecricketersinn.co.uk

Attractive white-painted pub situated in spectacular walking country at the western end of the South Downs. Delightful and very popular garden with extensive deck seating and weekend barbecues. Rumoured to be haunted, the inn has changed little over the years. Full range of meat, fish and salad dishes, with main courses including half shoulder of lamb, bangers and mash, and Cornish scallops.

OPEN: 11-3.00 6-11 Sun Closed eve **BAR MEALS:** L served all week 12-2.30 D served Mon -Sat 7-9.30 Av main course £8.50 **RESTAURANT:** L served all week 12-3 D served Mon-Sat 7-9.30 Av 3 course à la carte £20 **BREWERY/COMPANY:** Free House 🍺: Youngs Bitter, Archers Golden, Harvey Sussex, Ballards. **FACILITIES:** Garden: Food served outside Dogs allowed Must be on lead. Water provided **NOTES:** Parking 30

> **Do you have a favourite pub that we have overlooked?**
> **Please use the Reader's Report form at the back of this guide to tell us all about it.**

EARTHAM — Map 06 SU90

The George Inn

PO18 0LT ☎ 01243 814340 📠 01243 814725
e-mail: thegeorgeinn@hotmail.com
Dir: *From A27 at Tangmere r'about follow signs for Crockerhill/Eartham*
Built in the 18th century as an ale house for local estate workers, the pub has a village bar with a flagstone floor (walkers and dogs welcome), and a cosy lounge with an open fire and patio doors leading to a delightful garden. Exposed ships' timbers are a feature of the candlelit restaurant, where the regularly-changing blackboard menu might offer braised lamb shank, seared salmon with cucumber salsa, and duck breast with chilli lime dressing, along with typical bar favourites.
OPEN: 11 -11 **BAR MEALS:** L served all week 12-3 D served all week 6-9.30 Av main course £9 **RESTAURANT:** L served all week 12-2 D served all week 6-9 Av 3 course à la carte £16
BREWERY/COMPANY: Free House 🍺: Greene King Abbot Ale and guest beers. **FACILITIES:** Children welcome Garden: Patio & large grassed area with picnic tables Dogs allowed Water & Treats
NOTES: Parking 30

ELSTED — Map 05 SU81

Pick of the Pubs

The Three Horseshoes

GU29 0JY ☎ 01730 825746
Dir: *A272 from Midhurst to Petersfield, after 2m L to Harting & Elsted, after 3m pub on L*
Tucked below the steep scarp slope of the South Downs is the peaceful village of Elsted and this 16th-century former drovers' ale house. It's one of those quintessential English country pubs that Sussex specialises in, full of rustic charm, with unspoilt cottagey bars, worn tiled floors, low beams, latch doors, a vast inglenook, and a motley mix of furniture. On fine days the extensive rear garden, with roaming chickens and stunning southerly views, is hugely popular. Tip-top real ales, including Cheriton Pots from across the Hampshire border, are drawn from the cask, and a daily-changing blackboard menu offers good old country cooking. Starters may include avocado with Stilton and mushroom sauce with spinach, and prawn mayonnaise wrapped in smoked salmon. Main courses are likely to include steak, kidney and Murphy's pie, pheasant breast in cider with shallot and prune sauce and, in summer, crab and lobster. Excellent ploughman's are served with unusual cheeses. Puddings include treacle tart, and raspberry and hazelnut meringue.
OPEN: 11-2.30 6-11 (Sun 12-3, 7-10.30) **BAR MEALS:** L served all week 12-2 D served all week 7-9.00 **RESTAURANT:** L served all week 12-2 D served all week 7-9.00
BREWERY/COMPANY: Free House 🍺: Cheriton Pots Ale, Ballard's Best, Fuller's London Pride, Timothy Taylors Landlord. **FACILITIES:** Garden: Dogs allowed **NOTES:** Parking 30

Restaurant and Bar Meal times indicate the times when food is available. Last orders may be approximately 30 minutes before the times stated.

FERNHURST — Map 06 SU82

Pick of the Pubs

The King's Arms 🍴 ♀

Midhurst Rd GU27 3HA ☎ 01428 652005 📠 01428 658970
Dir: *On A286 between Haslemere and Midhurst, 1m S of Fernhurst*

A 17th-century, Sussex stone-built freehouse and restaurant with a large pretty garden, set amid rolling farmland. The L-shaped bar and restaurant, with their beams, lowish ceilings and large inglenook fireplace are cosy. Owners Annabel and Michael Hirst long ago twigged what makes a good dining pub. Not least, everything here is home made, from salad dressings to sorbets. The cooking style combines modern and traditional British, as is evident from monthly-changing menus ranging from classic pub food such as corned beef hash with fried egg, to roasted monkfish with basil ratatouille, roasted garlic and red wine jus. Michael visits the coast frequently to buy fish for specials such as pan-fried turbot with spaghetti Nero, courgettes and sweet pepper and chive sauce. A long wine list has enough by the glass for most tastes. One of the real ales is brewed for the pub by the Ventnor Brewery. Late-August beer and music festival.
OPEN: 11.30-3 5.30-11 Closed: 25 Dec **BAR MEALS:** L served all week 12-2.30 D served Mon-Sat 7-10 Av main course £7.70 **RESTAURANT:** L served all week 12-2.30 D served Mon-Sat 7-10 Av 3 course à la carte £24 **BREWERY/COMPANY:** Free House 🍺: Kings Arms Best Bitter, Ringwood Brewery Best Bitter, Arundel Brewrey Gold, Grainstore Triple. **FACILITIES:** Children welcome Garden: Large garden with trees overlooking fields Dogs allowed Water **NOTES:** Parking 45

The Red Lion ♀

The Green GU27 3HY ☎ 01428 643112 & 653304 📠 01428 64393●
e-mail: michaelgcameron@aol.com
Dir: *From A3 at Hindhead take A287 to Haslemere, then A286 to Fernhurst*
This 500-year-old building, reputedly the oldest pub in the village, overlooks the village green and has a striking sandstone exterior, old oak beams and open fires. Freshly-cooked food from an interesting, varied and constantly-changing menu.
OPEN: 12-3.20 5-11.20 Open all day during summer
BAR MEALS: L served all week 12-2.30 D served Tue-Sat 6.30-9.30 Av main course £7 **RESTAURANT:** L served all week 12-2.30 D served Tue-Sat 6.00-9.30 Av 3 course à la carte £20
BREWERY/COMPANY: Fullers 🍺: Fuller's ESB, Chiswick, London Pride, and Seasonal Guest. ♀: 8 **FACILITIES:** Garden: Dogs allowed Water **NOTES:** Parking 50

HALNAKER
Map 06 SU90

Anglesey Arms 🐷
PO18 0NQ ☎ 01243 773474
Dir: *4m E from centre of Chichester on A285 (Petworth Road)*

A change of hands here, but things are looking good: the new landlord also runs the cellar at the annual Chichester real ale and jazz festival. The pub is close to 'Glorious Goodwood', the Downs and Chichester Harbour, and the village itself is famous for its windmill, immortalised in a poem by Hilaire Belloc. The menu includes steaks, grills, fresh seafood and home-made pies.
OPEN: 11-3 5.30-11 (Open all day Sat-Sun) Closed: 25 Dec
BAR MEALS: L served all week 12-2.30 D served all week 7-10 Av main course £7.50 **RESTAURANT:** L served all week 12-2 D served all week 7.30-10 Av 3 course à la carte £16.50
BREWERY/COMPANY: Pubmaster 🍺: Burton Ale, Young's Bitter, Adnams Bitter. **FACILITIES:** Children welcome Garden: Two gardens, one courtyard for dining Dogs allowed Water **NOTES:** Parking 50

HAMMERPOT
Map 06 TQ00

The Woodman Arms 🐷
BN16 4EU ☎ 01903 871240 📠 01903 871240
e-mail: landlord@thewoodmanarms.co.uk
Dir: *E of Arundel, off the A27*
A thatched pub with low beams and an award-winning garden, popular for its consistently-good food and friendly service. Beside the South Downs, it is ideally placed for spectacular downland rambles (maps provided free of charge). In addition to lunchtime soup and sandwiches, evening menus include a daily curry, fresh cod in beer batter, steak and kidney pie, grilled whole plaice, and salmon en croûte.
OPEN: 11-3 6-11 (Sun 12-3, 7-10.30) **BAR MEALS:** L served all week 12-2.15 D served Mon-Sat 6.45-9 **RESTAURANT:** L served all week 12-2.15 D served Mon-Sat 6.45-9
BREWERY/COMPANY: Gales 🍺: Gales HSB, Gales Butser, Gales GB. **FACILITIES:** Children welcome Garden: Award winning rose garden Dogs allowed **NOTES:** Parking 30

HASSOCKS
Map 06 TQ31

Pilgrim Goose 🍷 NEW
London Rd BN6 9NA
Just before the road begins its climb over the South Downs to the sea, lies this former coaching inn. A continuity of sorts exists today because it's now a popular vantage point for watching the London to Brighton Veteran Car Run. Typical dishes are gammon steak, chicken, leek and ham pie, beef and ale pie, sea bass and hot chicken salad with raspberry vinaigrette.
OPEN: 12 -11 (Sun 12-10.30) **RESTAURANT:** L served all week D served all week Av 3 course à la carte £16
BREWERY/COMPANY: 🍺: Tetley Bitter, Cask Bass, Budvar. 🍷: 16
FACILITIES: Garden: Patio, floral display and garden furniture
NOTES: Parking 255

HAYWARDS HEATH
Map 06 TQ32

The Sloop 🐷 🍷
Sloop Ln, Scaynes Hill RH17 7NP ☎ 01444 831219
e-mail: nigel.cannon@lineone.net

Located next to the tranquil River Ouse and taking its name from the vessels which once worked the adjacent Ouse Canal, the Sloop is surrounded by beautiful countryside. The older part of the building, originally two lock-keepers cottages, dates back over several centuries and records indicate it has been trading since 1815. Inside, the pub has undergone major changes in the last year, with additional dining areas and a new dining/meeting room among many new features. A varied and imaginative menu offers the likes of Sussex sausages, duck breast, grilled salmon and chicken curry.
OPEN: 12-3 6-11 Sun 12-10.30 **BAR MEALS:** L served all week 12-2.30 D served Tue-Sat 6.30-9.30 Av main course £9
RESTAURANT: L served all week 12-2.30 D served all week 6.30-9.30 Av 3 course à la carte £16 **BREWERY/COMPANY:** Greene King 🍺: Greene King IPA, Abbot Ale, Ruddles county, XX Dark Mild & Guest beers. 🍷: 8 **FACILITIES:** Children welcome Garden: Two secluded gardens, parkland Dogs allowed Water
NOTES: Parking 75

HORSHAM
Map 06 TQ13

The Black Jug 🐷 🍷
31 North St RH12 1RJ ☎ 01403 253526 📠 01403 217821
e-mail: black.jug@brunningandprice.co.uk
Dir: *100yrds from Horsham railway station, opp Horsham Art Centre*
Relaxed, light and airy town pub with stripped wood floors, darkwood furnishings, and a spacious rear conservatory. An interesting menu includes spiced seafood chowder, Black Jug steak and ale pie, braised lamb shank on colcannon, lamb lasagne with roasted red peppers, Moroccan chicken on vegetable couscous, pan-fried snapper on lentils and chorizo sausage.
OPEN: 11-11 (Sun 12-10.30) Closed: 26 Dec **BAR MEALS:** L served all week 12-10 D served all week 12-10 Av main course £8.95
RESTAURANT: L served all week 12-10 D served all week Av 3 course à la carte £18 **BREWERY/COMPANY:** 🍺: Courage Directors, Marstons Pedigree, Wadworth 6X, Harveys Best. 🍷: 23
FACILITIES: Children welcome Garden: Flower filled, 10 tables, Seating for 40 Dogs allowed **NOTES:** Parking 9

KIRDFORD
Map 06 TQ02

Pick of the Pubs

The Half Moon Inn 🐷
RH14 0LT ☎ 01403 820223 📠 01403 820224
e-mail: halfmooninn.kirdford@virgin.net
See Pick of the Pubs on page 478

Open: 11-3, 6-11
Closed: Mon
Bar Meals: L served Tue-Sun 12-2,
D served Tue-Sat 7-9.
Av cost main course £10
RESTAURANT: L served Tue-Sun 12-2,
D served Tue-Sat 7-9.
Av cost 3 course £22.50
BREWERY/COMPANY:
LAUREL PUB PARTNERSHIPS
☎: Fuller's London Pride,
Young's Special.
FACILITIES: Children welcome,
Garden - 3 separate gardens for
families and dining.
NOTES: Parking 12

The Half Moon Inn

Officially one of the prettiest pubs in Southern England, this red-tiled 16th-century village inn is covered in climbing rose bushes, and sits directly opposite the church in this unspoilt Sussex village near the River Arun.

Kirdford, nr Billingshurst, RH14 0LT
☎ 01403 820223 📠 01403 820224
✉ halfmooninn.kirdford@virgin.net
Dir: Off A272 between Billingshurst &
Petworth. At Wisborough Green
follow signs 'Kirdford'.

Although drinkers are welcome, the Half Moon is mainly a dining pub. Barrister Francesca Burfield and her husband Patrick, a former TV commercial maker, abandoned their careers a few years ago to take over the pub. Since then it has grown in popularity, while the interior, with its low beams and log fires, has been fully redecorated. Well-presented cask ales and lagers are on offer, as well as a varied wine list featuring four house choices available by the glass. A talented young team specialises in 'British food with a twist', and there is plenty of variety. Lunch choices from the bistro menu might include starters of garlic langoustine with coriander rice, shards of black pudding with beetroot chutney, and Spanish omelette, followed by mains such as beef Bourguignon with mashed potatoes, salmon and cod fishcake with a beurre blanc, or Madras lamb curry. Vegetarians are well catered for with at least two starters and two main choices always available (perhaps pancetta, leek and Cheddar cheese tart on a bed of leaves, wild mushroom bread and butter pudding with a garlic sauce, or roasted butternut squash risotto). Home-made desserts take in the likes of plum and frangipane tart, rhubarb and ginger crumble, or trio of chocolate, while the cheeseboard is impressive. At dinner, the menu is broadly similar, although the atmosphere changes, with candlelight, tablecloths and polished glassware. Well-tended gardens, a small children's play area and a boules pitch are an added draw in the summer, while for the more energetic, a pamphlet featuring local country walks is available.

LICKFOLD
Map 06 SU92

Pick of the Pubs

Lickfold Inn 🍸 ◉ ♀
GU28 9EY ☎ 01798 861285 🖷 01798 861342
Dir: *From A3 take A283, through Chiddingfold, 2m on R signed 'Lurgashall Winery', pub in 1m*

Lickfold is a tiny hamlet with no shop or post office. But it does have this pub, dating back to 1460, which the community's own website describes as 'excellent'. It's popular with ramblers and handy for anyone visiting the National Trust's magnificent Petworth House a few miles away. The interior is characterised by Georgian settles, oak beams, moulded panelling and an enormous inglenook with a spit. Food is always freshly prepared, and a serious approach to cooking is displayed by the carte, which offers five choices per course. Thus, visitors could encounter starters of foie gras boudin with lentil and rocket salad, or home-cured salmon; possible main courses of pan-fried grey mullet with couscous, or Mediterranean-style pasta with courgettes, aubergines, peppers and garlic; and home-made apple tart or banoffee crumble for pudding. There are also chef's specials, and roast dinners for tables of eight or more.
OPEN: 11-3.30 6-11.30 Closed: 25 Dec **BAR MEALS:** L served all week 12-2.30 D served all week 7-9.30 **RESTAURANT:** L served all week 12-2.30 D served all week 7-9.30
BREWERY/COMPANY: Free House 🍺: Ballard Best, Summer Lightning, Youngs, 49er. **FACILITIES:** Children welcome Garden: Large patio with traditional garden area Dogs allowed Water bowl **NOTES:** Parking 50

LODSWORTH
Map 06 SU92

Pick of the Pubs

The Halfway Bridge Inn
Halfway Bridge GU28 9BP ☎ 01798 861281 🖷 01798 861878
e-mail: mail@thesussexpub.co.uk
Dir: *On A272*
Attractive brick-and-flint Sussex coaching inn, steeped in history and standing in lovely countryside mid-way between Midhurst and Petworth. Locally popular, especially with the polo set from nearby Cowdray Park, the pub has no fewer than five open fires to provide a warm winter welcome; in summer the sheltered patio and lawn come into their own. An interesting variety of fresh food features on the menu and daily-changing specials, with local produce used where possible. Lunch and evening starters such as risotto fish cakes with spicy

continued

dipping sauce, and rocket and spinach Caesar salad might be followed by an enormous roast half shoulder of lamb, or pheasant breast Rossini with home-made duck liver paté. Puddings involve scrumptious-sounding baked chocolate and orange cheesecake, and banana toffee pie. Upmarket bedroom accommodation meets 21st-century expectations in a converted Sussex barn.
OPEN: 11-3 6-11 (Sun 12-3, 7-10.30) Closed: 25 Dec
BAR MEALS: L served all week 12-2 D served all week 7-10 Av main course £8.95 **RESTAURANT:** L served all week 12-2 D served all week 7-10 **BREWERY/COMPANY:** Free House 🍺: Gales HSB, Cheriton Pots Ale, Fuller's London Pride, Harveys Best. **FACILITIES:** Garden: Dogs allowed Water **NOTES:** Parking 30 **ROOMS:** 8 bedrooms 8 en suite s£45 d£75 (♦♦♦♦) no children overnight

LOWER BEEDING
Map 06 TQ22

The Crabtree Inn 🍸 ♀
Brighton Rd RH13 6PT ☎ 01403 891273
Dir: *On A281, 4m SE of Horsham. 0.5m south of Leonardslee Gardens*
Writer Hilaire Belloc enjoyed drinking in this pub, which was once used by smugglers on their way from the coast to London. It is said to be linked by tunnels to a nearby monastery. The owners have built a strong following with good beers and their broad traditional-cum-modern dishes. Start with gingered crab cakes or chicken and ham beignets, before moving on to saltimbocca, fresh fish of the day, or vegetable terrine.
OPEN: 11-3 6-11 **BAR MEALS:** L served all week 12-2 D served all week 7-9.30 Av main course £5 **RESTAURANT:** L served all week 12-2 D served all week 7-9.30 Av 3 course à la carte £20 **BREWERY/COMPANY:** Hall & Woodhouse 🍺: King & Barnes Sussex, Hall & Woodhouse Badger Best, Stowford Press. ♀: 10 **FACILITIES:** Children welcome Garden: Food served outside. Large garden Dogs allowed **NOTES:** Parking 30

LURGASHALL
Map 06 SU92

The Noah's Ark 🍸
The Green GU28 9ET ☎ 01428 707346 🖷 01428 707742
e-mail: bernard@noahsarkinn.co.uk
Dir: *Off A283 N of Petworth*
This charming 16th-century inn is the perfect grandstand for cricket on the village green. When the nights draw in, settle down by the log fire for a game of cribbage or dominoes. The snack menu includes hot wraps and jacket potatoes, but for more substantial fare try chargrilled lamb steak, roast pheasant with caramelised apples, collops of venison with apricot and red wine sauce, or seared tuna with lime and avocado salsa.
OPEN: 11-3 6-11 Closed: Dec 25 **BAR MEALS:** L served all week 12-2.30 D served Mon-Sat 7-10 Av main course £8 **RESTAURANT:** L served all week 12-2.00 D served Mon-Sat 7-10.00 Av 3 course à la carte £20 Av 3 course fixed price £20 **BREWERY/COMPANY:** Greene King 🍺: Greene King IPA ,Old Speckled Hen & Abbot. **FACILITIES:** Children welcome Garden: Lrg garden, seats over 60 people **NOTES:** Parking 20

> **We endeavour to be as accurate as possible but changes to times and other information can occur after the guide has gone to press**

MIDHURST
Map 06 SU82

The Angel Hotel ★★★ ⊛ ℉
North St GU29 9DN ☎ 01730 812421 ▤ 01730 815928
An elegant Georgian façade disguises the history of this much-extended coaching inn, which actually dates from the 16th century. It is located in the centre of Midhurst, with the front of the hotel overlooking the town, while at the rear attractive gardens give way to meadowland and the ruins of Cowdray Castle. Options from the brasserie menu include roast monkfish with a herb risotto and deep-fried leeks, and honey-roast duck breast with cabbage, bacon and blackcurrant jus.
OPEN: 11-11 **BAR MEALS:** L served all week 12-2.30 D served all week 6-9.30 Av main course £10 **RESTAURANT:** L served all week 12-2.30 D served all week 6.30-9.30 Av 3 course à la carte £23 Av 3 course fixed price £16 **BREWERY/COMPANY:** Free House
🍺: Gale's HSB & Best. ℉: 12 **FACILITIES:** Children welcome Garden: walled garden, pond, views of Cowdrey Ruins Dogs allowed **NOTES:** Parking 42 **ROOMS:** 28 bedrooms 28 en suite 18 family rooms s£80 d£110

NUTHURST
Map 06 TQ12

Pick of the Pubs

Black Horse Inn ℉
Nuthurst St RH13 6LH ☎ 01403 891272 ▤ 01403 892656
e-mail: cliveh@henwood.fsbusiness.co.uk
See Pick of the Pubs on opposite page

OVING
Map 06 SU90

The Gribble Inn 🐶 ℉
PO20 2BP ☎ 01243 786893 ▤ 01243 788841
e-mail: brianelderfield@hotmail.com
Dir: From A27 take A259. After 1m L at roundabout, 1st R to Oving, 1st L in village
A fine thatched 16th-century building that became a pub as recently as 1980. It has a secluded garden, two enormous log fires, low wooden beams, settle seating in the character main bar and a skittle alley. Seven beers are brewed at the on-site micro-brewery. Menu choices include home-made steamed steak and kidney pudding, sausage and mustard mash, smoked haddock and salmon fishcakes, and chicken breast wrapped in bacon on a bed of apples and mushrooms with a cider cheese sauce.
OPEN: 11-3 5.30-11 (Sun 12-4, 7-10.30) **BAR MEALS:** L served all week 12-2.30 D served all week 6-9.30 Av main course £7
RESTAURANT: L served all week 12-2.30 D served all week 6-9.30
BREWERY/COMPANY: Woodhouse Inns 🍺: Gribble Ale, Reg's Tipple, Badger Tanglefoot, Plucking Pheasant. ℉: 8
FACILITIES: Children welcome Garden: Large shaded garden with seating for over 100 Dogs allowed Toys & water provided
NOTES: Parking 40

Stars or Diamonds after the ROOMS
information at the end of an entry denotes
accommodation that has been inspected
by an organisation other than the AA,
eg the RAC, VisitBritain, VisitScotland or WTB.

PETWORTH
Map 06 SU92

Badgers 🍴
Station Rd GU28 0JF ☎ 01798 342651 ▤ 01798 343649
Dir: On A285 1.5 miles outside of Petworth, just over bridge on L
A country dining pub once the Railway Tavern, serving Petworth's old station. It has plenty of charm, with open fires inside and a pretty courtyard area outside, overlooking the small garden, carp pond and stream. The menu specialises in fish during the summer and game during the winter: typical options are pasta with scallops and tiger prawns, lambs' liver with bacon, onions, peas and coriander, and steak and kidney pudding.
OPEN: 11-3 5.30-11 (Sat 11-3, 6.30-11) (Sun 12-3, 7-10.30) Closed: Bank holidays **BAR MEALS:** L served all week 12-2 D served all week 7-9 Av main course £9.50 **RESTAURANT:** L served all week 12-2 D served all week 7-9 **BREWERY/COMPANY:** Free House
🍺: Badgers, Sussex. **FACILITIES:** Children welcome Garden
NOTES: Parking 20

The Black Horse 🐶
Byworth GU28 0HL ☎ 01798 342424 ▤ 01798 342868
e-mail: blackhorsebyworth@btopenworld.com

An unspoilt pub built on the site of an old priory in a beautiful garden. The three-storey Georgian frontage hides a much older interior dating back to the 14th century. Wooden floors, half-panelled walls and open fires characterise the three rustic rooms. Good ales and traditional home-cooked food includes pheasant Calvados, Cajun chicken, lasagne verdi, crab cakes, and steak and kidney pudding. Under new management.
OPEN: 11 -11 (Sun 12-10.30) **BAR MEALS:** L served all week 12-3 D served all week 7-9 Av main course £8.50 **RESTAURANT:** L served all week 12-3 D served all week 7-9 Av 3 course à la carte £20
🍺: Arundel Gold, Cheriton Pots Ale, Hogs Back Brew, Itchen Valley.
FACILITIES: Garden: Country garden, views of Shimmings Valley Dogs allowed Water, on leads **NOTES:** Parking 24

Welldiggers Arms 🐶 ℉
Polborough Rd GU28 0HG ☎ 01798 342287
Dir: 1m E of Petworth on the A283
Welldiggers once occupied this rustic, 300-year-old roadside pub, which boasts low-beamed bars with open log fires and huge oak tables. Handy for racing at Goodwood and Fontwell, and Sir Edward Elgar's cottage. Dishes may include English steaks, butchered on the premises, fresh scallops, lobster and crab and cod with home-made chips.
OPEN: 11-3 6.30-10 Closed: Dec 25 Sun-Mon Closed pm
BAR MEALS: L served all week 12-2 D served Thu-Sat 6.30-9.30 Av main course £8.50 **RESTAURANT:** L served all week 12-2 D served Thu-Sat 6.30-9.30 Av 3 course à la carte £13.50
BREWERY/COMPANY: Free House 🍺: Youngs.
FACILITIES: Children welcome Garden: Large lawn & patio, food served outside Dogs allowed **NOTES:** Parking 35

Open: 12-3, 6-11
(Sat-Sun, BHs open all day)
Bar Meals: L served all week 12-2.30,
D served all week 6.30-9.30.
Av cost main course £6.25
RESTAURANT: L served all week 12-2.30,
D served all week 6.30-9.30.
Av cost main course £16.75
BREWERY/COMPANY:
Free House.
🍺: Harveys Sussex, W J King, Weltons,
Fullers London Pride, T.T. Landlord,
Youngs Bitter and guest ales.
FACILITIES: Dogs allowed, Children
welcome, Garden - Front & rear patio
area, garden with stream.
NOTES: Parking 28

Black Horse Inn

True to its history as a smuggler's hideout, this lovely pub is still hidden away in a quiet backwater, half masked by its impressive window boxes.

🍷
Nuthurst Street, Nuthurst, Horsham,
RH13 6LH
☎ 01403 891272 📠 01403 892656
🌐 cliveh@henwood.fsbusiness.co.uk
Dir: 4m S of Horsham, between the
A281, A24 and the A272.

Built of clay tiles and mellow brick, it originally formed a row of cottages with a forge in the adjoining barn. Plenty of its history remains: inside you'll find stone-flagged floors, an inglenook spit roast fireplace and an exposed wattle and daub wall. The place is spotlessly clean, with smoke-free areas and a warm and cosy atmosphere perfect for dining or just enjoying a drink. The pub has a reputation for good ales, including Harvey's of Sussex and numerous guest beers. On sunny days, guests can sit out on the patio, or venture over the stone bridge that leads to a delightful garden with its babbling brook. There are plenty of good walks in the vicinity, including a four-mile circular walk based around the pub. It's a good opportunity to explore the beautiful woodland and rolling downland of West Sussex, as well as a way to work up an appetite before a pub meal. Food is readily available, all freshly prepared and cooked under the supervision of the resident chef. There are menus for lunchtimes, evenings and bar snacks. The aim is to appeal to all appetites, and the menus specify dishes that are gluten free or suitable for vegetarians. Expect traditional and imaginative cooking, including Sunday roasts and some very tempting desserts. Children are well catered for too.

ROWHOOK
Map 06 TQ13

The Chequers Inn ⊛ 🍴
RH12 3PY ☎ 01403 790480 📠 01403 790480
e-mail: thechequers1@aol.com
Dir: Off A29 NW of Horsham

A 15th-century Grade II listed building of great character with original beams, Horsham flagstones and open fires. The landlord is a member of the Master Chefs of Great Britain and the emphasis is on fresh, seasonal produce. Options range from a bowl of marinated olives in the bar to restaurant dishes like sauté loin of venison on truffled Savoy cabbage. From the specials board come local pheasant, pan-fried calves' liver and chicken and cep risotto.
OPEN: 11.30-3.30 6-11.30 **BAR MEALS:** L served all week 12-2 D served Mon-Sat 7-9.30 **RESTAURANT:** L served all week 12-2 D served Mon-Sat 7-9.30 Av 3 course à la carte £25 Av 3 course fixed price £15 **BREWERY/COMPANY:** Punch Taverns 🍺: Harvey's Sussex Ale, Young's Special, Fuller's London Pride.
FACILITIES: Garden: Spacious, peaceful Dogs allowed Water **NOTES:** Parking 40

RUDGWICK
Map 06 TQ03

The Fox Inn 🍴 ♀
Guildford Rd, Bucks Green RH12 3JP
☎ 01403 822386 📠 01403 823950
e-mail: seafood@foxinn.co.uk
Dir: situated on A281 midway between Horsham and Guildford
'Famous for Fish!' is the claim of this attractive 16th-century inn, a message borne out by the extensive menu. Long food hours take in all-day breakfast and afternoon tea, while the bar menu focuses on seafood. Whole grilled sea bass with sesame and chilli dressing, smoked haddock on buttered spinach, Thai fish curry, and seafood platter are some of the choices, along with sausage and mash, chicken supreme, and sizzling beef stirfry.
OPEN: 11-11 (Sun 12-10.30) **BAR MEALS:** L served all week 12-10 D served all week Av main course £12.50 **RESTAURANT:** 12-10 Av 3 course à la carte £22.50 **BREWERY/COMPANY:** Hall & Woodhouse 🍺: King & Barnes Sussex, Badger Tanglefoot, Best.
FACILITIES: Children welcome Garden: Food served outdoors Dogs allowed Water **NOTES:** Parking 30

SHIPLEY
Map 06 TQ12

George & Dragon
Dragons Green RH13 7JE ☎ 01403 741320
Dir: Signposted off A272 between Coolham and A24
A 16th-century, tile-hung cottage that provides welcome peace and quiet, especially on balmy summer evenings when the peaceful garden is a welcome retreat. Its interior is all head-

continued

banging beams and character inglenook fireplaces where a pint of Badger or Tanglefoot will not come amiss. The food is home made using fresh vegetables and 'real' chips, and offer dishes such as roasts of lamb and crispy-coated chicken brea with sweet-and-sour sauce. Shipley is famous for its smock mill.
OPEN: 11-3 6-11 (Sun & BHs open all day) **BAR MEALS:** L serve all week 12-2 D served all week 6.45-9.30 Av main course £6.50
RESTAURANT: L served all week 12-2 D served all week 6.45-9 Av course à la carte £11.50 Av 3 course fixed price £10
BREWERY/COMPANY: Hall & Woodhouse 🍺: Badger Best, Tanglefoot & Sussex Best. **FACILITIES:** Children welcome Garden: Beer garden, food served outdoors, BBQ Dogs allowed **NOTES:** Parking 20 **NOTES:** No credit cards

SIDLESHAM
Map 05 SZ8⬥

Crab & Lobster ♀
Mill Ln PO20 7NB ☎ 01243 641233
Dir: Off B2145 between Chichester & Selsey
Well-kept pub situated close to the shores of Pagham Harbour, a noted nature reserve. Popular with walkers and twitchers who fill the cosy bars in winter, and the pretty rear garden with mudflat views in summer.
OPEN: 11-3 6-11 (Closed Dec 25-26 eve) **BAR MEALS:** L served all week 12-2.30 D served Tue-Sat 7-9.45 Av main course £6.50
RESTAURANT: L served all week 12 D served Tue-Sat 7
BREWERY/COMPANY: Free House 🍺: Timothy Taylor Landlord, Itchin Valley Fagins, Cheriton Pots Ale. **FACILITIES:** Garden: Dogs allowed Water Provided **NOTES:** Parking 12

SINGLETON
Map 05 SU8

The Fox and Hounds 🍴 .
PO18 0EY ☎ 01243 811251 📠 01243 811792
Dir: Telephone for directions

The building probably dates from the 16th century, when it would have been part of a huge hunting park owned by the Fitzalan family, Earls of Arundel. Today, it is popular with walkers enjoying the rolling Sussex countryside and visitors to Goodwood for motor and horse-racing. A menu of typical pul fare includes liver and bacon, steak and ale pie, Goodwood gammon, salmon fishcakes, and home-made puddings.
OPEN: 11.30-3 6-11 **BAR MEALS:** L served all week 12-2 D served all week 6.30-9 Av main course £8 **RESTAURANT:** L served all wee 12-2 D served all week 6.30-9 **BREWERY/COMPANY:** Enterprise Inns 🍺: Hancocks HB, Greene King IPA, Fullers London Pride, Ringwood Best Bitter. **FACILITIES:** Garden Dogs allowed Water **NOTES:** Parking 40

> ♀ 7   **Number of wines by the glass**

Pick of the Pubs

The Fox Goes Free 🐾 ⅄
Charlton PO18 0HU ☎ 01243 811461 🖷 01243 811461
e-mail: thefoxgoesfree@hotmail.com
Dir: A286 6m from Chichester, towards Midhurst 1m from Goodwood racecourse

Built in 1588, the pub was a favoured hunting lodge of William III; more recently, it also hosted the first Women's Institute meeting in 1915. The lovely old brick and flint building still nestles in unspoilt countryside, and is handy for the Weald and Downland Museum and nearby Goodwood races. With its two huge fireplaces, old pews and brick floors, the pub simply exudes charm and character. But this is an inn for all seasons as the outdoor bar and barbecue make good use of the lovely flint-walled herb garden and apple trees. The menu marries traditional and modern styles: typical dishes include duck breast in honey and ginger jus; steak and kidney pie; red mullet with red onion, peppers and pesto; or tuna steak with pepper and tomato compote.

OPEN: 11-3 6-11 (Sat-Sun all day in summer) **BAR MEALS:** L served all week 12-2.30 D served all week 6.30-10.30
RESTAURANT: L served all week 12-2.30 D served all week 6-10.30 Av 3 course à la carte £18 **BREWERY/COMPANY:** Free House 🍺: Ringwood Best, Ballard's Best, Fox Bitter, Interbrew Bass. ⅄: 8 **FACILITIES:** Garden: Lrg, with patio & lawn. Seats approx 90 Dogs allowed Water **NOTES:** Parking 8

SOUTHBOURNE
Map 05 SU70

The Old House at Home 🐾 ⅄
Cot Ln, Chidham, nr Southbourne PO18 8SU
☎ 01243 572477 🖷 01243 574978
e-mail: thebar@theoldhouseathome.com

Sleepy Chidham and its 17th-century pub lie on a low peninsula jutting out into Chichester Harbour. Wonderful scenic walks and wildlife-rich marshes entice ramblers and birdwatchers in particular, while more universally appreciated perhaps are the warm, music-free welcome, traditional ales, wines from its own vineyards, and good food. In addition to lunchtime snacks, there are heartier dishes like lamb's liver and bacon, fillet of beef Wellington, pan-fried monkfish and specials. Guest beers change weekly.

OPEN: 11.30-2.30 6-11 (Summer Sun 12-10.30) **BAR MEALS:** L served all week 12-2 D served all week 6.30-9.30 Av main course £7.25
RESTAURANT: L served all week 12-2 D served all week 6.30-9.30
BREWERY/COMPANY: Carlsberg Tetley 🍺: Greene King Abbot Ale, Fuller's London Pride, two guest beers changed weekly.
FACILITIES: Garden: Patio at front & grass area at rear. Seating Dogs allowed Water **NOTES:** Parking 30

SOUTH HARTING
Map 05 SU71

The Ship Inn 🐾
GU31 5PZ ☎ 01730 825302
Dir: From Petersfield take B2146 towards Chichester

17th-century inn made from a ship's timbers, hence the name. Home-made pies are a feature, and other popular dishes include fresh sea bass, fish pie, calves' liver, rack of lamb, ham and asparagus mornay, and hot beef Hungarian goulash. A range of vegetarian dishes and bar snacks is also available.
OPEN: 11-11 (Oct-Mar 12-3, 6-11) **BAR MEALS:** 12-2.30 D served Mon-Sat 7-9 Av main course £7 **RESTAURANT:** L served all week 12-2.30 7-9.30 Av 3 course à la carte £25
BREWERY/COMPANY: Free House 🍺: Palmer IPA, Cheriton Pots Ale. **FACILITIES:** Garden: Food served outdoors Dogs allowed Water **NOTES:** Parking 5

STEDHAM
Map 05 SU82

Hamilton Arms/Nava Thai Restaurant 🐾
Hamilton Arms School Ln GU29 0NZ
☎ 01730 812555 🖷 01730 817459
e-mail: hamiltonarms@hotmail.com
Dir: Off A272 between Midhurst & Petersfield

Renowned for its traditional Thai cuisine, friendly ambience and impressive display of floral hanging baskets, the Hamilton Arms is named after Emma Hamilton, Admiral Lord Nelson's mistress, who lived nearby. Good walking in the South Downs. Large range of English and Thai bar meals, including the popular mixed titbits sampler, and almost 100 choices from the main restaurant menu including curried chicken with red chilli paste, bamboo shoots and coconut milk; and stir-fried prawns with hot basil leaves, baby aubergines and fresh chillies.

OPEN: 11-3 6-11 (Sun 12-3, 7-10.30) Closed: 1 Week Jan
BAR MEALS: L served Tues-Sun 12-2.30 D served Tues-Sun 6-10.30 Av main course £7 **RESTAURANT:** L served Tues-Sun 12-2.30 D served Tues-Sun 6-10.30 Av 3 course à la carte £16 Av 4 course fixed price £19.50 **BREWERY/COMPANY:** Free House 🍺: Ballard's Best, Fuller's London Pride, Everards Tiger Best, Gales HSB.
FACILITIES: Children welcome Garden: Lawn with benches and umbrellas Dogs allowed Water **NOTES:** Parking 40

> **Pick of the Pubs** have that extra special quality that makes them stand out from the crowd. Their entries are highlighted, and may be a full page.

SUTTON

Map 06 SU91

Pick of the Pubs

White Horse Inn
The Street RH20 1PS ☎ 01798 869221 📠 01798 869291
Dir: *Turn off A29 at foot of Bury Hill. After 2m pass Roman Villa on R. 1m to Sutton*

Pretty Georgian inn tucked away in a sleepy village at the base of the South Downs. In the neat bars and dining room expect imaginative food, the daily-changing choice featuring perhaps Stilton and broccoli soup, baked sea bass with lemon basil and tomato, confit of duck, lamb shank with tomatoes and red wine, and French lemon tart. Now under new management.
OPEN: 11-3 6-11 **BAR MEALS:** L served all week 12-2 D served all week 6-9 Av main course £6.50 **RESTAURANT:** L served all week 12-2 D served all week 7-9 Av 3 course à la carte £30 **BREWERY/COMPANY:** Free House 🍺: Shepherd Neame Spitfire, Courage Best, plus guests. **FACILITIES:** Children welcome Garden Dogs allowed **NOTES:** Parking 10

TILLINGTON

Map 06 SU92

Pick of the Pubs

The Horse Guards Inn ♀
GU28 9AF ☎ 01798 342332 📠 01798 344351
e-mail: mail@horseguardsinn.co.uk
Dir: *On A272 1m W of Petworth. Inn next to church*

Once a regular watering hole for the horse guards who travelled from London to Portsmouth transporting gold bullion or dealing with smugglers, this 18th-century inn nestles on a hillside on the edge of Petworth Park. Converted from three cottages, its rambling series of tastefully-refurbished rooms feature stripped beams, open fires, pine panelling and antique furnishings. The restaurant, with its emphasis on quality local produce,

enjoys views across the Rother valley to the South Downs. Menus continue to offer imaginative home-cooked food. Lighter lunchtime meals could include Parma ham and Dolcelatte cheese with home-made foccacia and soft herb salad, whilst the evening à la carte offers meals such as cider-cured salmon with gribeche potatoes followed by roast rump of lamb with roasted Mediterranean vegetables and garlic mash. Wash it all down with quality wines.
OPEN: 11-3 6-11 (open all day in the summer) **BAR MEALS:** L served all week 12-2 D served all week 7-9 **RESTAURANT:** L served all week 12-2 D served all week 7-9
BREWERY/COMPANY: Free House 🍺: Fullers London Pride, Fullers IPA. ♀: 7 **FACILITIES:** Children welcome Garden: Garden at rear of pub, terrace at front Dogs allowed Water
NOTES: Parking 5

WALBERTON

Map 06 SU90

Oaks Bar 🍴 ♀
Yapton Ln BN18 0LS ☎ 01243 552865 📠 01243 553862
e-mail: info@oaksbrasserie.com
Dir: *on A27 between Arundel & Fontwell*

This fine 18th-century coaching inn, which has served the needs of many generations of travellers, has been fully renovated in a light contemporary style. It's an award-winning pub, serving good food in a relaxed atmosphere. Dishes are based on fresh local produce - maybe crispy oriental duck on a wild roquette and crisp vegetable salad with chilli jam, pan-seared Scottish king scallops with creamed leeks, or fillet of venison served on a fondant potato with braised red cabbage.
OPEN: 11.30-3 6-11 Closed: 26-29 Dec **BAR MEALS:** L served all week 12-3 D served all week 6-10 Av main course £8
RESTAURANT: L served all week 12-3 D served Mon-Sat 6-10 Av 3 course à la carte £23 Av 3 course fixed price £17
BREWERY/COMPANY: Free House 🍺: Old Speckled Hen, Fullers London Pride, Youngs Special, John Smiths. ♀: 8
FACILITIES: Children welcome Garden: Terrace overlooking Avisford Park Golf Course **NOTES:** Parking 30

WALDERTON

Map 05 SU71

The Barley Mow 🍴 NEW
PO18 9ED ☎ 023 9263 1321 📠 023 9263 1403
e-mail: mowbarley@aol.co.uk
Dir: *North Chichester B2146. From Havant B2147. Turn R signed Walderton the Barley Mow is 100 yds on L*
Ivy-clad with hanging baskets, this pretty pub is comfortably set beside the rolling Sussex Downs, and is a magnet for walkers, cyclists and riders with a special tethering pole for horses. Famous locally for its skittle alley, it also has a reputation for good home-made pub food: steak and ale pie,

continued

continued

lasagne, chargrilled steaks, and deep-fried cod and chips, with Old Thumper and Forty-Niner on tap.
OPEN: 11-3 6-11.30 **BAR MEALS:** L served all week 12-2.15 D served all week 6-9.30 Av main course £5 **RESTAURANT:** L served all week 12-2.15 D served all week 6-9.30 Av fixed price £5
BREWERY/COMPANY: Free House ◖: Ringwood Old Thumper & Fortyniner, Fuller's London Pride, Itchen Valley Godfathers, Scottish Courage John Smith's. **FACILITIES:** Children welcome Garden: Mature garden, tables, seats, stream Dogs allowed **NOTES:** Parking 50

WARNHAM
Map 06 TQ13

The Greets Inn 🐾 ♀
47 Friday St RH12 3QY ☎ 01403 265047 📄 01403 265047
Dir: Off A24 N of Horsham
A fine Sussex hall house dating from about 1350 and built for Elias Greet, a local merchant. Magnificent inglenook fireplace and head-crackingly low beams in the flagstone-floored bar. There is a rambling series of dining areas where specialities such as lemon sole with lemon and dill butter, sea bass with red wine and rosemary, and calves' liver with bacon are served. There is also traditional pub food and in summer weekend barbecues.
OPEN: 11-2.30 6-11 (Sun 12-2, 7-10.30) **BAR MEALS:** L served all week 12-2 D served all week 7-9 Av main course £8
RESTAURANT: L served all week 12-2 D served all week 7-9 Av 3 course à la carte £20 **BREWERY/COMPANY:** ◖: Interbrew Flowers Original, Fuller's London Pride, Harvey's Sussex.
FACILITIES: Children welcome Garden: Large, food served outside Dogs allowed Water **NOTES:** Parking 30

WEST HOATHLY
Map 06 TQ33

The Cat Inn 🐾 ♀
Queen's Square RH19 4PP ☎ 01342 810369
An oasis of calm only twenty minutes from Gatwick. In order to preserve the peace, children are not allowed, and if you're after pool, darts or music, it's better to look elsewhere. This is a place for quiet relaxation - perhaps on the sunny terrace opposite an historic 11th-century church or beside an inglenook fire. Try the duck in angel sauce, lemon sole or venison steak perhaps from the wholesome restaurant menu. Bar meals are also available.
OPEN: 12-2.30 6-11 **BAR MEALS:** L served all week 12-2 D served all week 7-9.15 Av main course £10 **RESTAURANT:** L served all week 12-2 D served all week 7-9.15 Av 3 course à la carte £20
BREWERY/COMPANY: Free House ◖: Harveys Best, Adnams, Southwold. ♀: 7 **FACILITIES:** Patio **NOTES:** Parking 30

WINEHAM
Map 06 TQ22

The Royal Oak
BN5 9AY ☎ 01444 881252 📄 01444 881530

continued

This delightful 14th-century, black and white timbered cottage has been dispensing ale for over 200 years and continues to maintain its traditional, unspoilt character. A true ale house, so expect head-cracking low beams, a huge inglenook with winter log fire, wooden and flagged floors, rustic furnishings and real ale straight from the cask. Extensive summer gardens and a limited menu of decent sandwiches, home-made soup and ploughman's.
OPEN: 11-2.30 5.30-11 (Sun 12-3, 7-10.30) **BAR MEALS:** L served all week 11-2.30 5.30-11 **BREWERY/COMPANY:** Inn Business ◖: Harveys Sussex Best Bitter, Marston's Pedigree, Fuller's London Pride, Wadworth 6X. **FACILITIES:** Garden: Lrg lawn with seating Dogs allowed Water **NOTES:** Parking 40 **NOTES:** No credit cards

---

TYNE & WEAR

NEWCASTLE UPON TYNE
Map 21 NZ26

Shiremoor House Farm
Middle Engine Ln, New York NE29 8DZ ☎ 0191 257 6302

Located in what were once derelict farm buildings, this pub offers large bars, plenty of ale choice, and tables in the courtyard. Pub grub. Children welcome.
NOTES: No credit cards

WHITLEY BAY
Map 21 NZ37

The Waterford Arms ♀
Collywell Bay Rd, Seaton Sluice NE26 4QZ
☎ 0191 237 0450 & 0191 296 5287
Dir: From A1 N of Newcastle take A19 at Seaton Burn then follow signs for A190 to Seaton Sluice
The building dates back to 1899 and is situated close to the small local fishing harbour, overlooking the North Sea. Splendid beaches and sand dunes are within easy reach, and the pub is very popular with walkers. Seafood dishes are the speciality, including a whale-sized cod or haddock and chips, seafood feast, and salmon.
OPEN: 12-11 (Sun 12-10.30) **BAR MEALS:** L served all week 12-9 D served all week Av main course £3 **RESTAURANT:** L served all week 12-9 D served all week Av 3 course à la carte £8.50
BREWERY/COMPANY: Pubmaster ◖: Tetleys & guest.
FACILITIES: Children welcome Food served outside
NOTES: Parking 90

> Pick of the Pubs have that extra special quality that makes them stand out from the crowd. Their entries are highlighted, and may be a full page.

England

WARWICKSHIRE

ALDERMINSTER   Map 10 SP24

Pick of the Pubs

The Bell ♦♦♦♦ 🐑 ♀
CV37 8NY ☎ 01789 450414 📠 01789 450998
e-mail: thebellald@aol.com
Dir: *On A3400 3.5m S of Stratford-upon-Avon*

The Bell is widely recognised for its high food standards, friendly atmosphere and attentive service. Once a busy coaching inn catering for passing travellers, nowadays it is noted for its many food-themed events, like the Belgian food festival which features dishes like coquilles Oostendaises and carbonnade flamandes. The bars are friendly and welcoming, and the spacious Conservatory restaurant looks out over a delightful old courtyard towards the rolling Stour Valley. Nothing is frozen, everything is freshly prepared, and the menus are forever changing. A good starter could be baked spinach and avocado soufflé with Parmesan before, say, crispy-topped lamb in cider, or garlicky prawn platter with mussels and salad, followed by home-made chilled lemon tart and cream. There are daily blackboard specials too. The pub is well placed for the Cotswolds, and offers accommodation in seven individually furnished rooms.
OPEN: 12-2.30 7-11 **BAR MEALS:** L served all week 12-2 D served all week 7-9.30 Av main course £8 **RESTAURANT:** L served all week 12-2 D served all week 7-9.30 Av 3 course à la carte £18.95 Av 3 course fixed price £10.50
BREWERY/COMPANY: Free House 🍺: Greene King IPA & Ruddles County. ♀: 11 **FACILITIES:** Children welcome Garden: Conservatory, overlooks countryside & hills Dogs allowed Water **NOTES:** Parking 70 **ROOMS:** 6 bedrooms 4 en suite s£30 d£45

ARDENS GRAFTON   Map 10 SP15

Pick of the Pubs

The Golden Cross 🐑 ♀
B50 4LG ☎ 01789 772420 📠 01789 773697
Nestling in the heart of Shakespeare country west of Stratford, with views across a rolling Warwickshire landscape, the Golden Cross is a stylishly-refurbished rural inn offering imaginative, freshly-prepared food in an informal pub atmosphere. Relax with a pint in the beamed bar, with its rug-strewn stone floor mellow decor and scrubbed pine tables, or dine in style in the light and airy, high-ceilinged dining-room. Extensive menus successfully

blend traditional pub favourites (given a modern twist) with more inventive dishes. Start with confit duck leg with ginger and vanilla-scented rice, cream of roast tomato and rosemary soup or chicken liver parfait with orange and lime confit. To follow, choices include braised lamb shank with celeriac mash and redcurrant sauce, steak, ale and root vegetable pie, and spiced chicken breast with ratatouille couscous and red pepper jus. At lunch accompany a pint of Hook Norton with an avocado and smoked bacon ciabatta or marmalade-glazed ham, egg and chips. Home-made puddings.

OPEN: 11-3 5-11 (all day Sat-Sun) **BAR MEALS:** L served all week 12-2.30 D served all week 6-9 Av main course £7 **RESTAURANT:** L served all week 12-2.30 D served all week 7-9.30 Av 3 course à la carte £20 🍺: Hook Norton, Bass, Guest ales. **FACILITIES:** Children welcome Garden: Food served outside Dogs allowed In the garden only **NOTES:** Parking 80

ASTON CANTLOW   Map 10 SP16

Pick of the Pubs

King's Head 🐑 ♀
21 Bearley Rd B95 6HY ☎ 01789 488242 📠 01789 488137
Shakespeare's parents were married in the ancient village of Aston Cantlow and had their wedding breakfast at the King's Head. It is a pretty black and white Tudor pub flanked by a huge spreading chestnut tree, with a hedged beer garden and an attractive terrace for summer use. The interior is tastefully rustic with huge polished flagstones, exposed beams, scrubbed pine tables, open log fires and scatter cushions on pew benches and antique settles. The atmosphere is very relaxed - you can sit where you want and eat what you like from a diverse menu with dishes from around the world, though the famous King's Head duck suppers are among the most popular options. Enjoy the piped jazz; sup one of the first-rate real ales and sample Thai spiced monkfish fillet with mango and ginger salsa, or daube of beef with button onions, mushrooms, lardons and olive oil mash.
OPEN: 11-3 5.30-11 (Summer open all day) 25 Dec open 12-2 only **BAR MEALS:** L served all week 12-2.30 D served all week 7-10 Av main course £10 **RESTAURANT:** L served all week 12-2.30 D served all week 7-10 Av 3 course à la carte £16 Av 3 course fixed price £21.95 **BREWERY/COMPANY:** Furlong 🍺: Greene King Abbot Ale, Fuller's London Pride, Black Sheep. ♀: 8 **FACILITIES:** Children welcome Garden: Large hedged beer garden, food in summer Dogs allowed Water **NOTES:** Parking 60

continued

The Castle Inn

Enjoy fine views over a Civil War battleground on this spectacular walk in the heart of England.

From the pub turn left to a right-hand path running between Cavalier Cottage and Rupert House. Make for a stile, turn left at the road and walk along to Ratley. When the road bends left by a copper beech tree, turn right to a fork. Veer right and follow the High Street down and round to the left. Pass the church and keep left at the triangular junction.

With the Rose and Crown over to your right, follow Chapel Lane and when it bends left, go straight ahead up some steps to a stile. Keep the fence on the left initially before striking out across the field to a stone stile in the boundary hedge. Turn right and follow the Centenary Way across the field to a line of trees.

Swing left and now skirt the field to a gap in the corner. Follow the path down to a galvanised kissing gate, cut across the field to a footbridge and then head up the slope to a gap in the field boundary. Turn left and follow the road past some bungalows. Pass Battle Lodge and make for the junction.

Cross over and join a woodland path running along the top of the escarpment. On reaching some steps on the left, turn right and descend steeply via a staircase known as Jacobs Ladder. Drop down to a gate and then follow the path straight down the field to a stile at the bottom. Go through a kissing gate beyond it and alongside a garden to reach a drive. Follow it to the road and turn left for Radway.

Walk through the village to the church, veer left into West End and pass alongside The Grange.

THE CASTLE INN, EDGEHILL
OX15 6DJ
☎ 01295 670255

Directions: M40 then A422 for 6m to Upton ouse, R in 1.5m
Unusual pub built as a copy of Warwick Castle to commemorate the Battle of Edgehill. Licensed since 1822, it stands high up on a beech-clad ridge. Serves traditional pub food.
Open: 11.15-2.30 6.15-11 (summer w/e open all day)
Bar Meals: 12-2 6.30-9
Notes: Dogs welcome. Large garden with good views. Parking.
(See page 488 for full entry)

Curve left by a pond and go through a kissing gate into a pasture. Cross a stile and keep ahead across the fields towards a wooded escarpment. Enter the wood via a stile, cross over the junction and follow the Macmillan Way up to the road. The inn is on the right.

DISTANCE: 3 1/2 miles/5.7km
MAP: OS Explorer 206
TERRAIN: Farmland and wooded escarpment
PATHS: Field and woodland paths, country roads
GRADIENT: Dramatic descent followed by a steep climb at the end

Walk submitted and checked by Nick Channer

BROOM

Map 10 SP05

Broom Tavern

High St B50 4HL ☎ 01789 773656 📠 01789 772983
e-mail: richard@distinctivepubs.freeserve.co.uk
Dir: *N of B439 W of Stratford-upon-Avon*

Charming brick-and-timber 16th-century inn, reputedly haunted by a cavalier killed on the cellar steps. The same menu is offered in the bar and restaurant. 'Tavern Favourites' include home-made steak and kidney pie and the Tavern crispy duck supper, while 'Your Local Butcher' may offer fillet or sirloin steak, rack of lamb, calves' liver, or Sunday roast. Legend has it that William Shakespeare and friends fell asleep under a tree outside the Broom, after losing a drinking contest nearby.
OPEN: 11.30-2.30 5.30-11 **BAR MEALS:** L served all week 12-2 D served all week 6.30-9 Av main course £8.50 **RESTAURANT:** L served all week 12-2 D served all week 6.30-9 Av 3 course à la carte £15 **BREWERY/COMPANY:** Greene King 🍺: Green King IPA, Adnams Bitter, Rotation Ale. 🍷: 7 **FACILITIES:** Children welcome Garden: Front lawn with picnic tables **NOTES:** Parking 30

DUNCHURCH

Map 11 SP47

Dun Cow 🍷 NEW

The Green CV22 6NJ ☎ 01788 810305
Dir: *Exit the M1 J17 (filters on to the M45) take the first exit onto the B4429 takes you to Dunchurch. The Dun Cow is at the crossroads in the village*
Dating back to 1560, this former coaching inn has several strong literary associations. The poet Longfellow is said to have written his Smithy poem here, while Robert Louis Stevenson and his father reputedly dined here. A varied and imaginative menu offers the likes of whole baked sea bass finished with a lemon and parsley butter, baked red onion and potato tart, 8oz grilled sirloin, and large ribbon pasta in a spinach, tomato and ricotta sauce.
OPEN: 12-11 (Sun 12-10.30) **BAR MEALS:** D served all week. Available all day **RESTAURANT:** D served all week L served all day Av cost 3 course £16.70 **BREWERY/COMPANY:** Vintage Inns 🍺: Carlsberg Export, Tetley Bitter, Cask Bass. 🍷: 16 **FACILITIES:** Garden Floral display and outdoor furniture **NOTES:** Parking 80

EDGEHILL

Map 11 SP34

The Castle Inn 🍷

OX15 6DJ ☎ 01295 670255 📠 01295 670521
e-mail: castleedgehill@btopenworld.com
Dir: *M40 then A422. 6m until Upton House, then turn next R 1.5m*
Standing on the summit of a beech-clad ridge, this is one of the most unusual pubs in the country. Built as a copy of Warwick Castle to commemorate the Battle of Edgehill, it was first licensed in 1822 and opened on the anniversary of

Cromwell's death. Traditional, home-cooked dishes such as mixed grills, goujons of lemon sole, and liver and bacon casserole appear on the menu along with ploughman's lunches and snacks in a basket.

OPEN: 11.15-2.30 6.15-11 Summer weekends open all day
BAR MEALS: L served all week 12-2 D served all week 6.30-9 Av main course £6 **BREWERY/COMPANY:** Hook Norton 🍺: Hook Norton Best, Old Hooky & Generation, Guest Ales.
FACILITIES: Garden: Large garden area good views Dogs allowed
NOTES: Parking 40

See Pub Walk on page 487

ETTINGTON

Map 10 SP24

The Houndshill ♦♦♦

Banbury Rd CV37 7NS ☎ 01789 740267 📠 01789 740075
Dir: *On A422 SE of Stratford-upon-Avon*

Attractive traditional family-run inn set at the Heart of England, making it the ideal base for visits to Stratford-upon-Avon and the Cotswolds. The Houndshill has a pleasant tree-lined garden and is very popular with families. Typical dishes include grilled sirloin steak, seared swordfish, pan-fried fillet of salmon, lamb cutlets and haddock Kiev. Lots of light bites.
OPEN: 12-3 7-11 (Sun 12-3, 7-10.30) Closed: Dec 25-28
BAR MEALS: L served all week 12-2 D served all week 7-9.30
RESTAURANT: 12-2 7-9.30 **BREWERY/COMPANY:** Free House 🍺: Hook Norton Best, Marston's Pedigree. **FACILITIES:** Children welcome Garden Dogs allowed **NOTES:** Parking 50 **ROOMS:** 8 bedrooms 8 en suite

GREAT WOLFORD

Map 10 SP23

Pick of the Pubs

Fox & Hounds Inn ♦♦♦♦

CV36 5NQ ☎ 01608 674220 📠 01608 684871
e-mail: info@thefoxandhoundsinn.com
See Pick of the Pubs on opposite page

continued

OPEN: 12-2.30, 6-11 (Sun 12-3)
CLOSED: Mon
BAR MEALS: L served Tue-Sun 12-2, D served Tue-Sat 6-9. Av main course £10.50
RESTAURANT: L served Tue-Sun 12-2, D served Tue-Sat 7-9. Av cost 3 courses £21
BREWERY/COMPANY: Free House.
🍺: Hook Norton Best, Adnams Broadside, North Cotswold Genesis, Wye Valley Dorothy Goodbody, Frankton Bagby Old Chestnut.
FACILITIES: Dogs allowed. Children welcome. Garden - Terrace with seating
NOTES: Parking 15.
ROOMS: 3 en suite from s£40 d£60

Fox & Hounds Inn

A honey-coloured stone inn where pints were first poured in 1540, and the atmosphere has not changed too much since. An ideal base for exploring the glorious Cotswolds, the Fox & Hounds exudes plenty of character and old-world charm.

♦♦♦♦ 🛏

Great Wolford, Nr Shipston-on-Stour, CV36 5NQ

☎ 01608 674220 📠 01608 684871

📧 info@thefoxandhoundsinn.com

Dir: Off A44 NE of Moreton-in-Marsh

Good food, good beer and exceptional whiskies are all on offer, along with an inviting ambience enhanced by old settles, Tudor inglenook fireplaces and solid ceiling beams adorned with jugs or festooned with hops. Fascinating features recall the history of this Cotswold stone building down the years - for example, the bar entrance is a double-hinged 'coffin door' which allowed coffins to be brought in and laid out prior to the funeral service. Supposedly, a secret tunnel, along which bodies were sometimes carried, linked the cellar with the nearby church, and the inn abounds with colourful tales of poltergeists and ghostly sightings. The Warwickshire Hunt meets at the inn and, appropriately, the highly-amusing, though somewhat controversial, pub sign depicts Tony Blair confronting a pack of hounds with several foxes behind him blowing raspberries. In addition to a range of traditional ales, the bar also offers a staggering selection of almost 200 fine whiskies. The bar menu is characterised by interesting light bites like creamy garlic field mushrooms, and crispy-fried whitebait, along with traditional favourites including soup, sandwiches and baguettes. The well-planned specials board is imaginative and impressive. Expect to start with pheasant, apricot and pecan terrine with spiced kumquat chutney and toasted brioche, or Thai-style fishcakes, move on to lamb's liver and smoked bacon with mashed potato, or pan-seared monkfish, bream and salmon, and wind up deliciously with chocolate brownies and clotted cream.

ILMINGTON   Map 10 SP24

Pick of the Pubs

Howard Arms 🅱 🅰 ♈
Lower Green CV36 4LT ☎ 01608 682226 ▤ 01608 682226
e-mail: info@howardarms.com
Dir: Off A429 or A3400

Occupying an idyllic spot on the village green, this mellow Cotswold stone inn has been welcoming travellers and local customers for over 400 years. Three comfortable, non-smoking upstairs bedrooms encourage visitors to stay longer, while the excellent food and good real ales provide more delightful temptations. Robert and Gill Greenstock have successfully created a civilised dining pub where the varied weekly-changing menus offer freshly-prepared dishes cooked to a high standard. Against a backdrop of period charm and character including stone floors, open fires and heavy timbers, enjoy starters like oak-smoked salmon, twice-baked goat's cheese and thyme soufflé, or spicy crabcake. Main choices range from blackened salmon with wilted spinach, or seared scallops, to chargrilled lamb cutlets with herbed lentils, or braised venison sausages. Home-made puddings follow the same interesting trend, as in warm pear and Amaretti tart, or apple and prune flapjack crumble.
OPEN: 11-3 6-11 (Sun 7-10.30) Closed: 25 Dec **BAR MEALS:** L served all week 12-2 D served all week 7-9 Av main course £11 **RESTAURANT:** L served all week 12-2 D served all week 7-9 Av 3 course à la carte £20 **BREWERY/COMPANY:** Free House 🍺: Everards Tiger Best, North Cotswold Genesis, Greene King Old Speckled Hen, Timothy Taylor landlord. ♈: 15
FACILITIES: Garden: 1/3 acre, bordered by a stream, terrace area **NOTES:** Parking 25 **ROOMS:** 3 bedrooms 3 en suite s£52 d£84 (♦♦♦♦♦) no children overnight
See Pub Walk on opposite page

KENILWORTH   Map 10 SP27

Clarendon House ★★ 🅱
High St CV8 1LZ ☎ 01926 857668 ▤ 01926 850669
e-mail: info@clarendonhousehotel.com
Dir: From A452 pass castle, turn L into Castle Hill and continue into High Street
The original (1430) timber-framed Castle Tavern is incorporated within the hotel, still supported by the oak tree around which it was built. Big, comfortable sofas indoors and a heated patio outside. From the brasserie menu: Thai chicken curry and rice, salad of pigeon and pancetta, honey and lemon dressing, and kedgeree fishcakes, light curry sauce and quails' eggs. The specials board might feature pan-fried wild boar steak with crushed parsnips, roasted baby onions and cranberry and thyme jus.

continued

OPEN: 11-11 (Sun 12-10.30) Closed: 25-26 Dec, 1 Jan
BAR MEALS: L served all week 12-10 D served all week 12-10 Av main course £9.50 **RESTAURANT:** L served all week 12-10 D served all week 12-10 Av 3 course à la carte £18 **BREWERY/COMPANY:** Free House 🍺: Greene King Abbot Ale, IPA, Hook Norton Best.
FACILITIES: Children welcome Garden: Patio garden seats about 100. Outdoor heating Dogs allowed **NOTES:** Parking 35 **ROOMS:** 22 bedrooms 22 en suite 2 family rooms s£57.50 d£79.50

LAPWORTH   Map 10 SP17

Pick of the Pubs

The Boot Inn 🅱 ♈
Old Warwick Rd B94 6JU ☎ 01564 782464 ▤ 01564 784989
Within easy travelling distance from the M42 (J4), Birmingham, Solihull and Warwick, is a country pub and restaurant that exudes a lively and convivial atmosphere. Standing beside the Grand Union Canal in the unspoilt village of Lapworth, this 16th-century former coaching inn is well worth seeking out. Apart from its smartly refurbished interior, it is the modern brasserie-style food and interesting global wine list that draw the most attention. Wide-ranging menus promise - and deliver - home-produced dishes in a delightful, modern style. This might include 'first plates' of mixed seafood cannelloni with Newburg sauce and goats' cheese or chargrilled fennel with Parma ham and Greek yoghurt, followed by 'seconds' typified by calves' liver with black pudding and leek mash, teriyaki salmon on cucumber noodles or spaghetti with broccoli, Parmesan and basil. Side orders offer frites, olive oil mash and mixed leaf salads, while the 'Puds and Stickies' list a chocolate and Mocha slice, washed down, perhaps, with Beaumes de Venise sold by the glass from the extensive wine list.
OPEN: 12-11 Closed: Dec 25 **BAR MEALS:** L served all week 12-2.30 D served all week 7-10 Av main course £10
RESTAURANT: L served all week 12-2.30 D served all week 7-10 Av 3 course à la carte £18.95 Av 4 course fixed price £21.95
BREWERY/COMPANY: Enterprise Inns 🍺: Greene King Old Speckled Hen, Wadworth 6X, Scottish Courage John Smith's.
FACILITIES: Children welcome Garden: Food served outside Dogs allowed Water **NOTES:** Parking 200

LOWER BRAILES   Map 10 SP33

The George Hotel ♈
High St OX15 5HN ☎ 01608 685223 ▤ 01608 685916
e-mail: thegeorgehotel@speed-e-mail.com
Dir: B4035 toward Shipston on Stour
Reputedly built as lodgings for the monks constructing the 12th-century village church, the George later served its time as a coaching inn. Appropriately, the original outhouses have been rebuilt to provide stabling. The parish has 25 miles of footpaths, several of which require climbing a flight of 99 steps - ideal for working up an appetite, a thirst, or both. Typical dishes would be rib-eye steaks, fish and chips, spicy sausages and mash, and 'walking' and 'flying' game pies.
OPEN: 11-11 (Sun 12-10.30) **BAR MEALS:** L served all week 12-2 D served all week 7-9.30 Av main course £9.65 **RESTAURANT:** L served all week 12-2 D served all week 7-9.30 Av 3 course à la carte £19 **BREWERY/COMPANY:** Hook Norton 🍺: Hook Norton - Generation, Mild, Hooky Best, Old Hooky & Seasonal Beers.
FACILITIES: Garden: Large open plan Dogs allowed Water
NOTES: Parking 60

Howard Arms

From the charming village of Ilmington, set on the northern scarp of the Cotswold Hills, this beautiful walk takes in Foxcote House, an old drovers' road, and magnificent views from the highest point in Warwickshire.

Turn right from the pub and take the waymarked footpath to the left of Vine Cottage. Follow the path to the lane and turn left. Just before the school, go through the kissing-gate and follow the fenced path to a stile. Proceed with the footpath arrows through three meadows via stiles. At the far end of the third meadow, cross the stile close to the right-hand corner and head left up the bank to cross a stile near a pool.

Continue along the left-hand field edge, drop downhill to cross a stile and bear left over a brook. Keep to the path across a further brook and climb the stile into a field. Turn left around the field edge to join a drive. Pass through a gate to Drover's Road and turn left. Ascend to TV masts.

Turn left, opposite the masts, alongside the wall and proceed through the gate in the field corner. Walk to the left of the oak tree to reach a gate and a lane. Turn left, then immediately right along a farm road to reach a lane (views of Foxcote House). Turn left, then in 250 yards (228m) take the arrowed path left. Cross the field to a stile into old quarry meadow and head down the gully to a gate in the far right corner.

Walk down the hedged track, which becomes Grump Street, to reach the village. Proceed downhill to Lower Green and the inn

HOWARD ARMS, ILMINGTON
Lower Green CV36 4LT.

☎ 01608 682226

Directions: off A4300 or A429 S of Stratford-upon-Avon
Rambling, 17th-century Cotswold stone inn overlooking the village green. Full of period charm and character with stone floors, heavy timbers, open fires and civilised decor. Innovative modern menu, good ales and comfortable accommodation.
Open: 11-3 6-11
Bar Meals: 12-2 7-9 (9.30 Fri & Sat).
Notes: No dogs inside. Garden & patio. Parking.
(See opposite page for full entry)

DISTANCE: 4 miles (6.4km)
MAP: OS Landranger 151
TERRAIN: Downland and farmland
PATHS: Field paths and farm tracks
GRADIENT: Undulating with some short steep climbs

Walk submitted by Richard Shurey

LOWSONFORD
Map 10 SP16

Fleur De Lys ♀
Lapworth St B95 5HJ ☎ 01564 782431 🗎 01564 782431
e-mail: Fleurdelys.solihull@laurelpubco.com
Dir: A34 (Birmingham to Stratford)

Converted from three cottages and a mortuary and located alongside the Stratford-upon-Avon Canal, this 17th-century pub boasts a galleried dining room and atmospheric bars with low beams and real log fires. Fleur de Lys pies were originally made here. The style is casual dining with steak and Guinness pie, free-range sausages with bubble and squeak and traditional fish and chips among the wholesome dishes. The large canalside garden is the ideal place to enjoy a drink or meal.
OPEN: 9-11 (Sun 12-10.30) **BAR MEALS:** L served all week 12-2.30 D served all week 6-9.30 Av main course £10
BREWERY/COMPANY: 🍺: Interbrew Flowers Original & IPA, Wadworth 6X, Guest Ale. ♀: 16 **FACILITIES:** Children welcome Garden: Lrg canalside Dogs allowed Water **NOTES:** Parking 150

MONKS KIRBY
Map 11 SP48

The Bell Inn 🍴
Bell Ln CV23 0QY ☎ 01788 832352 🗎 01788 832352
e-mail: belindagb@aol.com
Dir: Off The Fosseway junction with B4455

The Spanish owners of this quaint timbered inn, originally a priory gatehouse and brewhouse cottage, describe it as 'a corner of Spain in the heart of England'. Not surprisingly, there's a strong emphasis on Mediterranean cuisine and an extensive tapas menu. Sample paella Valencia, chicken with chorizo or Chateaubriand Spanish style, or perhaps choose from the wide-ranging selection of seafood dishes - fresh hake in garlic and herb butter, sea bass in a white wine and shellfish sauce, whole lobster, and paella marinara among them.
OPEN: 12-2.30 7-11 Closed: 26 Dec, 1 Jan **BAR MEALS:** L served Tue-Sun 12-2.30 D served all week 7-11 **RESTAURANT:** L served Tue-Sun 12-2.30 D served all week 7-11
BREWERY/COMPANY: Free House 🍺: Interbrew Flowers IPA & Boddingtons. **FACILITIES:** Children welcome Garden

PRESTON BAGOT
Map 10 SP16

The Crabmill 🍴 ♀
B95 5EE ☎ 01926 843342 🗎 01926 843989
e-mail: thecrabmill@amserve.net
Dir: Telephone for directions
Crab apple cider was once made at this 15th-century hostelry, which is set in beautiful rural surroundings. Restored to create an upmarket venue, the pub has a light, open feel with a range of themed dining rooms, including a 'rude' room with risqué caricatures. An Italian influence is evident in both the decor and menu, with dishes such as Sicilian mutton pie, swordfish with herb and lemon polenta, and pappardelle with spinach, rocket and Somerset Brie.
OPEN: 11-11 **BAR MEALS:** L served all week 12-2.30 D served Mon-Sat 6.30-9.30 **RESTAURANT:** L served all week 12-2.30 D served Mon-Sat 6.30-9.30 🍺: Wadworth 6X, Tetleys, Old Speckled Hen. **FACILITIES:** Garden: Beautiful landscaped rolling gardens Dogs allowed Water provided

PRINCETHORPE
Map 11 SP47

The Three Horseshoes ♀
Southam Rd CV23 9PR ☎ 01926 632345
Dir: On A423 at X of B4455 & B4453
Traditional coaching inn, built about 1856, on the Fosse Way. It has a large garden with a range of children's play equipment overlooking open countryside. Beams, horse brasses and log fires characterise the bar, where a blackboard menu of home-cooked food is available.
OPEN: 11.30-2.30 6-11 (Sun 12-10:30) Closed: 25 Dec **BAR MEALS:** L served all week 12-2 D served all week 6-9.30 **RESTAURANT:** L served all week 12-2 D served all week 6-11 **BREWERY/COMPANY:** Free House 🍺: Ruddles Best, John Smiths, Bombadier, Pedigree.
FACILITIES: Children welcome Garden: Large eating area, patio **NOTES:** Parking 50 **ROOMS:** 4 bedrooms 4 en suite s£20 d£40 (♦♦♦) no children overnight

RATLEY
Map 11 SP34

The Rose and Crown
OX15 6DS ☎ 01295 678148
Dir: Follow Edgehill signs, 7m N of Banbury or 13m SE of Stratford-On-Avon on A422.
Following the Battle of Edgehill in 1642, a Roundhead was discovered in the chimney of this 11th (or 12th)-century pub and beheaded in the hearth. His ghost reputedly haunts the building. Enjoy the peaceful village location and the traditional pub food, perhaps including beef and ale pie, scampi and chips, chicken curry and the Sunday roast.
OPEN: 12-2.30 6.30-11 Sun (12-3.30, 7-11) **BAR MEALS:** L served all week 12-2 D served all week 7-9 **RESTAURANT:** D served Thu-Sat 7-9.30 **BREWERY/COMPANY:** Free House 🍺: Wells Bombardier & Eagle IPA, Greene King Old Speckled Hen.
FACILITIES: Children welcome Garden: Garden with wooden benches Dogs allowed Water **NOTES:** Parking 4

RUGBY
Map 11 SP57

Golden Lion Inn ★★ 🍴 ♀
Easenhall CV23 0JA ☎ 01788 832265 🗎 01788 832878
e-mail: goldenlioninn@aol.com
Dir: from Rugby Town Centre take A426, follow signs for Nuneaton
Three generations of the Austin family have run this 16th-century village inn since 1931, the current owners alone for 33 years. Beams, narrow doorways and exposed wattle and daub walls

continued

testify to its great age. Home-cooked food in the bar and candlelit restaurant always includes four or more fish and seafood main courses, alongside others such as pan-fried venison, slow-braised lamb shoulder, stir-fried pork, and Thai green chicken curry. Large landscaped garden with fine countryside views.
OPEN: 11-11 **BAR MEALS:** L served all week 12-2 D served all week 6-9.45 Av main course £6.30 **RESTAURANT:** L served Tue-Sun 12-2 D served Mon-Sun 6-9.45 Av 3 course à la carte £24 Av 2 course fixed price £18.75 **BREWERY/COMPANY:** Free House ⚫: Greene King Abbot Ale, Ruddles Best Bitter, IPA. **FACILITIES:** Children welcome Garden: Large landscaped garden, good views
NOTES: Parking 80 **ROOMS:** 12 bedrooms 12 en suite d£65

SHIPSTON ON STOUR   Map 10 SP24

The Red Lion ◆◆◆◆ ♀

Main St, Long Compton CV36 5JS
☎ 01608 684221 📠 01608 684221
e-mail: redlionhot@aol.com
Dir: On A3400 between Shipston on Stour & Chipping Norton
A Grade II listed stone-built coaching inn dating from 1748, located in an area of outstanding natural beauty. Inside are stone walls, sturdy beams and log fires. The menu includes a good selection of sandwiches, snacks and grills, old favourites (cod and chips, steak and kidney pie) and chalkboard specials such as pork tenderloin with cream, apple and Calvados sauce. An ideal base for exploring and touring the area and visiting Stratford, Blenheim Palace and Warwick Castle.
OPEN: 11-2.30 6-11 (Sun 12-3, 7-10.30) **BAR MEALS:** L served all week 12-2 D served all week 7-9 Av main course £7.25
RESTAURANT: L served all week 12-2 D served all week 7-9 Av 3 course à la carte £15 **BREWERY/COMPANY:** Free House
⚫: Hook Norton Best, Websters Bitter, Theakston Best, Adnams.
FACILITIES: Children welcome Garden: Large garden with views of surrounding hills Dogs allowed **NOTES:** Parking 60 **ROOMS:** 5 bedrooms 5 en suite 1 family room s£30 d£50

White Bear Hotel ♀

High St CV36 4AJ ☎ 01608 661558 📠 01608 662612
e-mail: whitebearhot@hotmail.com

This former coaching inn, parts of which date from the 16th century, has a Georgian façade overlooking the market place. The Bear, as it is known to locals, is a lively pub serving good food and fine ales, and the two beamed bars are full of character. A typical menu might include halibut on sweet potato mash with tomato and capers, and slow-roasted oxtail casserole on mustard mash.
OPEN: 11-11 (Sun 12-10.30) **BAR MEALS:** 12-2 6.30-9.30
RESTAURANT: 12-2 6.30-9.30 **BREWERY/COMPANY:** Punch Taverns ⚫: Marstons Pedigree, Interbrew Bass & Guest Ales.
FACILITIES: Children welcome Garden: Patio, food served outside Dogs allowed Water **NOTES:** Parking 20 **ROOMS:** s£30 d£50
(★★)

STRATFORD-UPON-AVON   Map 10 SP25

The Dirty Duck

Waterside CV37 6BA ☎ 01789 297312 📠 01789 293441
Frequented by members of the Royal Shakespeare Company from the nearby theatre, this traditional, partly-Elizabethan inn has a splendid front terrace with peaceful views across the River Avon.
OPEN: 11-11 (Sun 12-10.30) **BAR MEALS:** L served all week 12-3 D served all week 5.30-11 Av main course £6 **RESTAURANT:** L served all week 12-2 D served Mon-Sat 5.30 Av 3 course à la carte £15 **BREWERY/COMPANY:** Whitbread ⚫: Flowers Original, Greene King Old Speckled Hen, Wadworth 6X. **FACILITIES:** Children welcome Garden: raised terrace overlooking theatre garden and river Dogs allowed manager's discretion

Pick of the Pubs

The Fox and Goose Inn ◆◆◆◆ ◎ 🐾 ♀
CV37 8DD ☎ 01608 682293 📠 01608 682293

Stylish pub/restaurant-with-rooms that has been transformed by local entrepreneur Sue Gray. To find it, look for Armscote close to the River Stour mid-way between Stratford and Shipston. Two old cottages and a former blacksmith's forge have been converted to create a buzzy, cosmopolitan atmosphere. The deep red-walled bar and brightly-painted dining room, along with slightly-eccentric, luxury en suite bedrooms have proven an instant hit since their opening just two years ago. Matching the decor and ambience is a daily-changing menu from a team of young chefs whose overall talent belies their years. Seared scallops on wilted pak choi with sweet chilli dressing, home-made tagliatelle with roast peppers, goats' cheese and pepper essence, and calves' liver and bacon on bubble and squeak with red wine gravy are followed perhaps by dark chocolate torte. Regular monthly fish nights and summer barbecues on a decked terrace in the pretty country garden are popular.
OPEN: 11-3 6-11 Closed: 25-26 Dec **BAR MEALS:** L served all week 12-2.30 D served all week 7-9.30 Av main course £10
RESTAURANT: L served all week 12-2.30 D served all week 7-9.30 Av 3 course à la carte £18 **BREWERY/COMPANY:** Free House ⚫: Hook Norton Old Hooky, Greene King Old Speckled Hen, Wells Bombardier, Fuller's London Pride. ♀: 8
FACILITIES: Garden: Wooden deck coverd by pergola
NOTES: Parking 20 **ROOMS:** 4 bedrooms 4 en suite s£40 d£80 no children overnight

 Pubs offering a good choice of fish on their menu

England

TEMPLE GRAFTON
Map 10 SP15

The Blue Boar ♦♦♦ 🛏 ♀
B49 6NR ☎ 01789 750010 📠 01789 750635
e-mail: blueboar@covlink.co.uk
Dir: Take left turn to Temple Grafton off A46 (from Stratford to Alcester). Pub at 1st x-roads

An inn since the early 1600s, it now features a glass-covered well from which water was formerly drawn for brewing. Not long before it first opened for business, William Shakespeare married Ann Hathaway in the village church. Dishes on offer include pan-fried monkfish noisettes served with a tomato and orange coulis; chicken supreme wrapped in smoked bacon and filled with cheese and chives; and Greenland halibut with caper and anchovy sauce. Open fires in winter, and good views of the Cotswolds from the patio garden year-round.
OPEN: 7-12 **BAR MEALS:** L served all week 12-3 D served all week 6-10 Av main course £8.50 **RESTAURANT:** L served all week 12-3 D served all week 6-10 Av 3 course à la carte £20 Av 4 course fixed price £13.95 **BREWERY/COMPANY:** Free House ⬛: Greene King Old Speckled Hen, Scottish Courage Theakston XB & Best. ♀: 9 **FACILITIES:** Children welcome Children's licence Garden: Terraced patio area, tables, benches **NOTES:** Parking 50 **ROOMS:** 15 bedrooms 15 en suite s£45 d£65

WARWICK
Map 10 SP26

Pick of the Pubs

The Tilted Wig 🛏
11 Market Place CV34 4SA
☎ 01926 410466 & 411534 📠 01926 495740
e-mail: freemanshome@hotmail.com
Dir: From M40 J15 follow A429 into Warwick, after 1.5m L into Brook St on into Market Place

Overlooking the market square, this attractive pine-furnished hostelry combines the atmosphere of a brasserie,

wine bar and restaurant all rolled into one. Originally a coaching inn and now a Grade II listed building. The name stems from its proximity to the Crown Court. A wide range of cask-conditioned ales and a good menu offering quality, home-cooked dishes, which might include cottage pie, tuna steak, whole-tailed scampi, Barnsley chop, chilli con carne, liver, bacon and onions, and tagliatelle.
OPEN: 11-11 (Sun 12-10.30) Closed: Dec 25 **BAR MEALS:** L served all week 12-3 D served Mon-Sat 6-9 Av main course £7 **BREWERY/COMPANY:** Punch Taverns ⬛: Carlsberg-Tetley Tetely Bitter, Adnams Broadside. **FACILITIES:** Children welcome Garden: **NOTES:** Parking 6 **ROOMS:** 4 bedrooms 4 en suite s£58 d£58 (♦♦♦♦)

WHATCOTE
Map 10 SP24

Royal Oak 🛏 ♀
CV36 5EF ☎ 01295 680319
Dir: 11m from Stratford-on-Avon. 11m from Banbury. Just off A422, signed Whatcote

Historic 12th-century inn built for workers building churches in the area. Cromwell reputedly stopped here for a drink after the Battle of Edge Hill. Sample menu includes sausage and chips, lasagne verdi, cottage pie, Mongolian lamb with ginger, chicken and cheese with mushrooms, and hot and spicy chicken goujons. A choice of vegetarian meals is also available.
OPEN: 12-3 5.30-11 **BAR MEALS:** L served Tue-Sun 12-2 D served all week 6-9.30 Av main course £6 **RESTAURANT:** L served Tue-Sun 12-2 D served all week 6-9.30 Av 3 course à la carte £13 **BREWERY/COMPANY:** Hook Norton ⬛: Hook Norton, Scottish Courage Theakston & John Smith's, Stowford Press. ♀: 15 **FACILITIES:** Children welcome Garden: Small garden to the side and front of pub Dogs allowed On a lead. Water provided **NOTES:** Parking 25

WITHYBROOK
Map 11 SP48

The Pheasant 🛏 ♀
Main St CV7 9LT ☎ 01455 220480 📠 01455 220633
Dir: Off B4112 NE of Coventry

Charming 17th-century coaching inn once known as the Half Moon, located next to the brook from which the village takes its name. The interior is characterised by an inglenook fireplace, farm implements and horse racing photographs. A wide choice of food encompasses crab and prawn cocktail, and ravioli Niçoise to start, venison pie, chicken Kiev, and fisherman's pie plus blackboard specials to follow, and desserts like lemon meringue with cream. Cold meats, cheeses and sandwiches or rolls also feature.
OPEN: 12-3 6-11 (Sun 12-10.30) Closed: 25-26 Dec

continued

continued

BAR MEALS: L served all week 12-2 D served all week 6.30-10
BREWERY/COMPANY: Free House ◀: Courage Directors,
Theakstons Best. ♀: 9 **FACILITIES:** Children welcome Garden:
Tables alongside a Brook with grassy banks **NOTES:** Parking 55

WOOTTON WAWEN   Map 10 SP16

The Bulls Head
Stratford Rd B95 6BD ☎ 01564 792511
Dir: On A3400
There is plenty of atmosphere at this picturesque inn,
originally two large cottages. Low beams, flagstones and old
pews can be found inside. A variety of dishes is available and
the blackboard changes daily. Fillet of plaice on a chive and
cheese crust, or Indian spicy lamb and roast aubergine may
be on the menu.
OPEN: 12-3 6-11 **BAR MEALS:** 12-2.30 7-10 **RESTAURANT:** 12-
2.30 7-10 **BREWERY/COMPANY:** Whampton & Dudley
◀: Marston's Pedigree, Banks Bitter plus Guest ales.
FACILITIES: Children welcome Garden: **NOTES:** Parking 30

WEST MIDLANDS

BARSTON   Map 10 SP27

Pick of the Pubs

The Malt Shovel ⊛ ☺ ♀
Barston Ln B92 0JP ☎ 01675 443223 ▤ 01675 443223
Bustling, award-winning country pub and restaurant
converted from an early 20th-century mill where malt was
ground. Inside is a welcoming bar and relaxed
atmosphere, with a popular barn for more formal eating.
The latter features light green wooden panelling, peach
coloured walls and original timbers. Cask-conditioned
ales, imported beers and good wines are on offer along
with a well-planned, imaginative menu using plenty of
fresh fish. A good choice of starters, including duck spring
roll with mango salsa, or crab and spring onion risotto.
Main courses include grilled fillet steak with a fondant
potato, Stilton butter and crispy onions, roast venison on
parsnip purée, pancetta and wild mushrooms, or confit of
duck with cassoulet of borlotti beans glazed with honeyed
dijon. Try glazed lime tart with ginger ice cream or a plate
of Stilton, mature Cheddar and baby goats' cheese,
grapes, celery and apple chutney to follow.
OPEN: 12-3 5.30-11 (Sun 12-10.30) Dec 25-26 closed evenings
BAR MEALS: L served all week 12-2.30 D served Mon-Sat 6.30-
9.45 Av main course £12.95 **RESTAURANT:** L served Fri-Sun
12-2.30 D served Mon-Sat 7-9.45 Av 3 course à la carte £29
BREWERY/COMPANY: Free House ◀: Greene King Old
Speckled Hen, Interbrew Bass, Brew VI. ♀: 8
FACILITIES: Children's licence Garden: Square with patio,
grassed back, wooded area **NOTES:** Parking 30

BIRMINGHAM   Map 10 SP08

The Peacock ☺
Icknield St, Forhill, nr King's Norton B38 0EH
☎ 01564 823232 ▤ 01564 829593
Despite its out of the way location, at Forhill just outside
Birmingham, the Peacock keeps very busy serving nine
traditional ales and a varied menu, (booking essential). Expect
the likes of minted half shoulder of lamb with roasted

parsnips and mint and redcurrant jus, or monkfish wrapped in
pancetta on a bed of asparagus. Several friendly ghosts are in
residence, and one of their tricks is to disconnect the taps
from the barrels.
OPEN: 12-11 (Sun 12-10.30) **BAR MEALS:** L served all week 12-10
D served all week Av main course £7.95 **RESTAURANT:** L served all
week 12-10 D served all week 6.30-9.30
BREWERY/COMPANY: Scottish & Newcastle ◀: Hobsons Best
Bitter, Theakstons Old Peculier, Enville Ale. **FACILITIES:** Children
welcome Garden: Patio at front, food served outside Dogs allowed
Water **NOTES:** Parking 100

COVENTRY   Map 10 SP37

The Rose and Castle
Ansty CV7 9HZ ☎ 024 76612822
*Dir: From junct of M6 & M69 at Walsgrave follow signs for Ansty.
0.75m to pub*
Small family-friendly pub with a canal running through the
garden. Inside, exposed beams and a varied menu that
includes smoked haddock in a creamy sauce with cheese and
mashed potato topping, garden pancake, chicken curry, a
variety of grills and steaks, and filled giant Yorkshire puddings.
The Burger Collection includes such oddly-named items as
The Godiva Burger, The Great Dane and The Italian Job.
OPEN: 12-3 6-11 (BHs 12-11) **BAR MEALS:** L served all week 12-3
D served all week 6-11 **BREWERY/COMPANY:** Free House
◀: Interbrew Bass, Hook Norton, Brew XI, Worthington.
FACILITIES: Children welcome Garden: **NOTES:** Parking 50

OLDBURY   Map 10 SO98

Waggon & Horses
17a Church St B69 3AD ☎ 0121 5525467
Dir: Telephone for directions
A listed back bar, copper ceiling and original tilework are
among the character features to be found at this real ale pub
in the town centre. Traditional pub food includes filled
baguettes, toasties, jacket potatoes, and main meals such as
fish and chips, and faggots and mash with mushy peas and
gravy.
OPEN: 12 -11 (Sun 12-5) **BAR MEALS:** L served Mon-Sat 12-3
D served Wed-Fri 5.30-7.30 Av main course £4.25
BREWERY/COMPANY: ◀: Marston's Pedigree, Enville White,
Holden Special, Brains Bitter. **FACILITIES:** Children welcome
NOTES: Parking 3

SEDGLEY   Map 10 SO99

Beacon Hotel
129 Bilston St DY3 1JE ☎ 01902 883380 ▤ 01902 883381
This traditional brewery tap retains its Victorian atmosphere,
with its rare tiny snob-screened island bar serving a taproom,
snug, large smoke-room and veranda. Proprietor John Hughes
reopened the brewery in 1987, 30 years after it had closed and
66 years after his grandmother became the licencee. The only
food is cheese and onion cobs at lunchtime. Flagship beer is
Dark Ruby Mild, with Sedgeley Surprise, Pale Amber and guest
bitters also available. Brewery open days are held weekly.
OPEN: 12-2.30 5.30-10.45 (Sat 12.3, 6-11 Sun 12-3, 7-10.30)
BREWERY/COMPANY: ◀: Sarah Hughes Dark Ruby, Surprise &
Pale Amber, Selection of Guest Beers and seasonal products.
FACILITIES: Children welcome Garden: Beer garden with benches
and tables Dogs allowed Water **NOTES:** Parking 50 **NOTES:** No
credit cards

continued

England

WEST BROMWICH
Map 10 SP09

The Vine ♀
Roebuck St B70 6RD ☎ 0121 5532866 ▤ 0121 5255450
e-mail: bharat@sukis.co.uk
Dir: *Telephone for directions*

In the surroundings of a typically Victorian ale house, today's clientele congregates in the front bar to appreciate the quality and range of Suki Patel's eclectic cooking which has been gracing these tables for 25 years. Traditional English cooking of ham, eggs, chips and peas rubs shoulders with Indian dishes. Real ale or the local mild go down well with vegetable balti, chicken bhuna, lamb rogan josh, or sag paneer cooked before your eyes in the bright and cheerful verandah restaurant. Additionally there's a barbecue menu served throughout the day at weekends.
OPEN: 11.30-2.30 5-11 (Fri-Sun all day) **BAR MEALS:** L served all week 12-2 D served all week 5-10.30 **RESTAURANT:** D served all week 5-10.30 **BREWERY/COMPANY:** Free House ◨: Banks, Brew XI. ♀: 6 **FACILITIES:** Children welcome Garden: Large beer garden, play area

WIGHT, ISLE OF

ARRETON
Map 05 SZ58

Hare and Hounds 🛏
Downend Rd PO30 2NU ☎ 01983 523446 ▤ 01983 523378
Next to Robin Hill Country Park with fine downland views, an old historic thatched pub with a long, colourful history that has been much extended and opened up in recent years. Day-long menus cater for a variety of tastes, and the pub is very family friendly. Good walking area. Greene King.
OPEN: 11-11 (Sun 12-10.30) **BAR MEALS:** L served all week 12-9 D served all week 3-9.30 Av main course £6.95 **RESTAURANT:** L served all week 12-3 D served all week 3-9.30 Av 3 course à la carte £13 **BREWERY/COMPANY:** Greene King ◨: Greene King, Local guests. **FACILITIES:** Children welcome Garden: Food served outside, patio Dogs allowed Water **NOTES:** Parking 60

The White Lion 🛏
PO30 3AA ☎ 01983 528479
e-mail: cthewhitelion@aol.com
A 300-year-old former coaching inn with oak beams, polished brass, open fires and added summer attractions in the children's playground and aviary. Popular locally for its cosy atmosphere, well-priced bar food and the starting point for the Isle of Wight ghost hunt. Curious visitors can stoke up on hearty vegetable lasagne, steak and kidney pie, pork escalope, a variety of steaks, half roasted chicken, or ratatouille cheesy

suet pastry pudding. The kitchen's proudest (and largest) offering is the seafood fan's delight: 'Shell Shocked' - A whole lobster on a bed of mussels served with calamari rings, scampi, fish goujons and tiger prawns.

OPEN: 11-12 (Sun 11-10.30) **BAR MEALS:** L served all week 12-9 D served all week 12-9 Av main course £8
BREWERY/COMPANY: ◨: Badger Best, Fuller's London Pride, Interbrew Flowers IPA. **FACILITIES:** Children welcome Garden: Patio area in pleasant old village location Dogs allowed Water
NOTES: Parking 6

BEMBRIDGE
Map 05 SZ68

The Crab & Lobster Inn 🛏 ♀
32 Foreland Fields Rd PO35 5TR
☎ 01983 872244 ▤ 01983 873495
e-mail: allancrab@aol.com
Dir: *Telephone for directions*

Clifftop inn with a large patio area affording magnificent views across the Solent and English Channel. Locals and tourists alike seek out the friendly atmosphere in the nautically-themed bars, and walkers find the cliffs particularly rewarding. As the name suggests, local seafood is the speciality, with warm hors d'oeuvre of lobster, scallops, shrimps, mussels, prawns and crab, and locally-caught lobster served grilled, thermidor or with salad.
OPEN: 11-3 6-11 (Wknds & summer all day) **BAR MEALS:** L served all week 12-2.30 D served all week 6.30-9.30 Av main course £7.50 **RESTAURANT:** L served all week 12-2.30 D served all week 7-10 **BREWERY/COMPANY:** Enterprise Inns ◨: Interbrew Flowers Original, Goddards Fuggle-Dee-Dum. **FACILITIES:** Children welcome Garden: Patio overlooking the beach Dogs allowed Water
NOTES: Parking 40

⭐ **Pubs with Red Stars are part of the AA's Top 200 Hotels in Britain & Ireland**

continued

BONCHURCH

Map 05 SZ57

The Bonchurch Inn

Bonchurch Shute PO38 1NU ☎ 01983 852611 ▤ 01983 856657
e-mail: gillian@bonchurch-inn.co.uk
Dir: *South coast of the Island*
17th-century coaching inn with cobbled courtyard, located in a
picturesque village where Charles Dickens wrote part of David
Copperfield. Owner Aline Besozzi's menu features many
Italian dishes including seafood spaghetti, risotto Milanese
and a range of pizzas. Also on offer are various sandwiches,
ploughman's and chicken, fish and steak selections.
'Bonchurch sauce', created with mushrooms, onions, pâté,
mustard, cream and brandy, is popular with fillet steak.
OPEN: 11-3.30 6.30-11 Closed: 25 Dec **BAR MEALS:** L served all
week 11-2.15 D served all week 6.30-9 Av main course £7.50
RESTAURANT: D served all week 6.30-9.30
BREWERY/COMPANY: Free House ◖: Scottish Courage Courage
Directors & Courage Best. **FACILITIES:** Children welcome Garden:
Courtyard, patio Dogs allowed Water **NOTES:** Parking 7

CHALE

Map 05 SZ47

Wight Mouse Inn ♀

PO38 2HA ☎ 01983 730431 ▤ 01983 730431
e-mail: info@wightmouseinns.co.uk
Dir: *On B3399 next to St Andrews church, Chale*
This 17th-century coaching inn overlooks West Wight's superb
coastline and is handy for Blackgang Chine and lovely sandy
beaches. Families will find this inn particularly welcoming as it has
an indoor play area with a fun pond, as well as slides and swings.
Selections from the menu may include steak and Tanglefoot pie,
chicken and bacon salad, rib-eye steak, and steak and kidney pie.
OPEN: 11-midnight (Sun 12-10.30) **BAR MEALS:** L served all week
12-10 D served all week Av main course £4.95
BREWERY/COMPANY: Woodhouse ◖: Six real ales including
Badger Best Bitter. ♀: 12 **FACILITIES:** Children welcome Garden
Dogs allowed **NOTES:** Parking 200

COWES

Map 05 SZ49

The Folly ♀

Folly Ln PO32 6NB ☎ 01983 297171 ▤ 01983 297444
Dir: *A3054*
Reached by both land and water and very popular with the
Solent's boating fraternity, the Folly is one of the island's more
unusual pubs. Timber from an old sea-going French barge was
used in the construction and wood from the hull can be found in
the nautical theme of the bar. Extensive specials board menu
ranging from 'Crewpot' casserole - beef goulash, lamb and
vegetable or spicy sausage - to plaice, mackerel trout and salmon.
OPEN: 9-11 BHs & Cowes Week late opening **BAR MEALS:** L
served all week 12-9.30 D served all week Av main course £7
◖: Interbrew Flowers Original, Bass, Goddards Best Bitter.
FACILITIES: Children welcome Garden: Food served outside Dogs
allowed Water **NOTES:** Parking 30

FRESHWATER

Map 05 SZ38

Pick of the Pubs

The Red Lion ♀

Church Place PO40 9BP ☎ 01983 754925 ▤ 01983 754925
Dir: *In Freshwater follow signs for parish church*
Husband and wife-run pub in a picturesque setting just a
short stroll from the tidal River Yar, which is popular with

the sailing set from nearby Yarmouth. The Red Lion's
origins date from the 11th century, though the current red
brick building is much newer. The open-plan bar is
comfortably furnished with country kitchen-style tables
and chairs, plus relaxing sofas and antique pine. In
addition to the pub's four real ales, including the island's
Goddard Best, and a good wine selection with 16 by the
glass, the pub is renowned for its daily blackboard menu
of interesting food. You are advised to order early to
secure your chosen dish as demand soon exceeds supply.
Everything is freshly made from tried and tested recipes
using good quality meat, fish and vegetables. Typical
dishes are whole crab salad, braised half shoulder of lamb
with minted gravy, and apple pie with custard.

OPEN: 11.30-3 (Sun 12-3, 7-10.30) 5.30-11 **BAR MEALS:** L
served all week 12-2 D served all week 6.30-9 Av main course
£8.50 **BREWERY/COMPANY:** Enterprise Inns ◖: Interbrew
Flowers Original, Fuller's London Pride, Goddards. ♀: 16
FACILITIES: Garden: Dogs allowed **NOTES:** Parking 20

NITON

Map 05 SZ57

Buddle Inn ♀

St Catherines Rd PO38 2NE ☎ 01983 730243
e-mail: buddleinn@aol.com
Dir: *Take A3055 from Ventnor. In Niton take 1st L signed 'to the lighthouse'*
One of the island's oldest hostelries, a cliff-top farmhouse in
the 16th century, which abounds with local history and tales
of smuggling and derring-do. Popular with hikers and
ramblers (dogs and muddy boots welcome), the interior is
characterised by stone flags, oak beams and a large open fire.
Specialising in real ale, wines and good company, home-
cooked food includes local crab and lobster, daily pies and
curries, ploughman's and steaks.
OPEN: 11-11 (Sun 12-10.30) 25-26 Dec Closed eve **BAR MEALS:** L
served all week 11.30-2.45 D served all week 6-9.30 Av main course
£10 ◖: Interbrew Flowers Original & Bass, Greene King Abbot Ale,
Adnams best. ♀: 12 **FACILITIES:** Garden: Food served outside
Dogs allowed Water **NOTES:** Parking 50

ROOKLEY

Map 05 SZ58

The Chequers

Niton Rd PO38 3NZ ☎ 01983 840314 ▤ 01983 840820
Horses in the neighbouring riding school keep a watchful eye
on comings and goings at this old, family-friendly country
freehouse. Surrounded by farms, much as it probably was
when first mentioned in 17th-century parish records, today it
is a meeting place for walkers. Simple but hearty meals
include pork medallions, rack of lamb, T-bone steak, salmon
escalope, mussels and plaice. Parents will find plenty for

continued

continued

ROOKLEY continued

children to do here - maybe even hire a pony from next door.
OPEN: 11-11 **BAR MEALS:** L served all week 12-10 D served all week 12-10 Av main course £8.50 **RESTAURANT:** L served all week 12-10 D served all week Av fixed price £8.50
BREWERY/COMPANY: Free House ◧: Gale's HSB, Greene King Old Speckled Hen, Scottish Courage John Smiths, Courage Directors. **FACILITIES:** Children welcome Children's licence Garden: Large garden and patio with seating Dogs allowed Water **NOTES:** Parking 70

SEAVIEW
Map 05 SZ69

Pick of the Pubs

Seaview Hotel & Restaurant ♀
High St PO34 5EX ☎ 01983 612711 ▤ 01983 613729
e-mail: reception@seaviewhotel.co.uk
Dir: B3330 (Ryde-Seaview rd), turn L via Puckpool along seafront road, hotel on left adjacent to sea
Seaview's picturesque sailing village is one of the island's best-loved spots, and the jewel in its crown has to be this pub-cum-restaurant. Built in 1795, there are stunning views across the sea to Portsmouth naval dockyard. Both navies - merchant and royal - are commemorated in the fascinating collection of artefacts displayed throughout the pub and the different restaurants, including classic ship models, letters from the Titanic, and bills from the Queen Mary. In amongst this homage to the sea is another tribute, this time to the fish and seafood freshly caught and brought to the table by local fishermen. Skate wing with lemon and caper noisette, fillet of brill, and monkfish tail are likely to appear on the restaurant menu, along with loin of island pork, and breast of corn-fed chicken stuffed with wild mushrooms and spinach. From the bar menu expect hot crab ramekin, smoked duck breast salad, and braised lamb shank.
OPEN: 11-2.30 6-11 Closed: Dec 24-27 **BAR MEALS:** L served all week 12-2 D served all week 7-9.30 Av main course £8.95
RESTAURANT: L served all week 12-1.30 7.30-9.30 Av 3 course à la carte £25 **BREWERY/COMPANY:** Free House
◧: Goddards, Greene King Abbot Ale. **FACILITIES:** Children welcome Garden: Courtyard/patio, Food served outside Dogs allowed **NOTES:** Parking 12

SHALFLEET
Map 05 SZ48

Pick of the Pubs

The New Inn 🛏 ♀
Mill Ln PO30 4NS ☎ 01983 531314 ▤ 01983 531314
e-mail: martin.bullock@virgin.net
In his booklet (available in the bar), local historian Ian Broad explains how the New Inn was built in 1744, on the ashes of its predecessor. The interior tells of its long past, with beamed ceilings, open fireplaces and flagstone floors. Today it is one of the island's best-known eating pubs, partly thanks to its location on Newtown Estuary, which makes it attractive to the yachting fraternity. For good measure, the 65-mile coast path runs past its door. Fish dishes are its speciality, and expectations of sea bass, lobster and crab salads, moules marinière, tandoori baked cod, Thai-style swordfish, and mackerel in mustard sauce, are rewarded. Not all the dishes are fish, of course, and lamb shank

with garlic mash, and chicken breast with Dolcelatte are representative of others. Also on offer is probably the most extensive wine selection of any Wight pub. Local brew Ventnor Golden is always among the four real ales.

OPEN: 11-3 6-11 (Jul-Aug all day) **BAR MEALS:** L served all week 12-2.30 D served all week 6-10 Av main course £10
RESTAURANT: L served all week 12-2.30 D served all week 6-10 Av 3 course à la carte £20 **BREWERY/COMPANY:** ◧: Interbrew Bass, Flowers Bitter, Greene King IPA, Marston's Pedigree. ♀: 6
FACILITIES: Garden: Raised lawned garden, sells seafood in summer Dogs allowed Water **NOTES:** Parking 20

SHANKLIN
Map 05 SZ58

Fisherman's Cottage ♀
Shanklin Chine PO37 6BN ☎ 01983 863882 ▤ 01983 874215
Situated right on Appley beach, this unusual thatched cottage was built in 1817 by Shanklin's first operator of covered 'bathing machines'. Inside the low-beamed bar, the pub's history is recorded in the period pictures that line the walls. The simple menu includes sandwiches, salads, jacket potatoes and popular favourites like steak pie, battered cod and jumbo sausages. The pub is closed from November to February.
OPEN: 11-3 7-11 (Mar-Oct all day every day) Closed: Nov-Feb
BAR MEALS: L served all week 11-2 D served all week 7-9
BREWERY/COMPANY: Free House ◧: Scottish Courage Courage Directors & John Smiths Smooth. **FACILITIES:** Children welcome Garden: Terrace leading to beach Dogs allowed Water **NOTES:** No credit cards

---

SHORWELL
Map 05 SZ48

The Crown Inn 🛏
Walkers Ln PO30 3JZ ☎ 01983 740293 ▤ 01983 740293
Dir: From Newport to Carisbrooke High St, then L at rdbt at top of hill, take B3323 to Shorwell

Lots of spirits here, and not all of them behind the bar. The resident ghost apparently dislikes any card games. Still, you

continued

continued

can bet on the quality of the food, drink and welcome. Pub favourites, sandwiches and jacket potatoes are offered from a bar menu and the specials board includes such trump cards as fillet of bream with a fresh crab sauce or braised crown of pheasant with chestnuts and red wine.
OPEN: 10.30-3.00 6-11 (Sun 12-3, 6-10.30) **BAR MEALS:** L served all week 12-2.30 D served all week 6-9.30 Av main course £6.95
BREWERY/COMPANY: Whitbread ◆: Interbrew Boddingtons, Flowers Original, Badger Tanglefoot, Wadworth 6X.
FACILITIES: Children welcome Garden: Large, sheltered, flower beds, stream Dogs allowed must be on lead **NOTES:** Parking 60

VENTNOR
Map 05 SZ57

The Spyglass Inn ◌ ♀
The Esplanade PO38 1JX ☎ 01983 855338 🖹 01983 855220

The huge collection of seafaring memorabilia fascinates visitors to this popular 19th-century pub at the western end of Ventnor Esplanade. An extensive terrace overlooking the sea is ideal for summer drinks and meals. Seafood is the speciality, including Ventnor Bay lobsters and crabs. Daily specials board may offer seafood chowder, chicken curry, chicken supreme, lamb chops, or steak and ale pie. Live music is provided most evenings - country, folk or jazz.
OPEN: 10.30-3 6.30-11 (May-Oct 10.30-11) **BAR MEALS:** L served all week 12-9.30 D served all week 12-9.30 **RESTAURANT:** L served all week 12-9.30 D served all week 12-9.30
BREWERY/COMPANY: Free House ◆: Badger Dorset Best & Tanglefoot, Ventnor Golden, Goddards Fuggle-Dee-Dum, Yates Undercliff Experience. ♀: 8 **FACILITIES:** Children welcome Garden: Terraces over looking sea Dogs allowed Water **NOTES:** Parking 10

WILTSHIRE

ALDERBURY
Map 05 SU12

The Green Dragon ♀
Old Rd SP5 3AR ☎ 01722 710263
Dir: 1m off A36 (Southampton/Salisbury rd)
There are fine views of Salisbury Cathedral from this 14th-century pub. Dickens wrote Martin Chuzzlewit here, and called the pub the Blue Dragon. An interesting and daily-changing menu features home-made meat and vegetarian dishes using locally-sourced produce.
OPEN: 11.30-2.30 6-11 (Sun 12-3, 7-10.30) **BAR MEALS:** L served all week 12-2 D served Tue-Sat 7-9 Av main course £5 **RESTAURANT:** D served all week 7-9 Av 3 course à la carte £16 **BREWERY/COMPANY:** Hall & Woodhouse ◆: Badger Dorset Best & Tanglefoot, King & Barnes. ♀: 12
FACILITIES: Children welcome Garden: BBQ, beer garden, outdoor eating Dogs allowed outside on lead **NOTES:** Parking 10

ALVEDISTON
Map 04 ST92

Pick of the Pubs

The Crown ◌
SP5 5JY ☎ 01722 780335 🖹 01722 780836
See Pick of the Pubs on page 500

AXFORD
Map 05 SU27

Red Lion Inn ◌ ♀
SN8 2HA ☎ 01672 520271 🖹 01672 520271
e-mail: info@redlionaxford.com
Dir: M4 J15, A246 Marlborough centre. Follow signs for Ramsbury. Inn 3m

A 17th-century brick and flint inn set in the beautiful Kennet valley with views across the river to Savernake Forest. Fresh fish and game (in season) feature strongly on the regularly-changing menu. Typical dishes include venison, woodland mushroom and chestnut casserole with red onion and potato mash, portabella mushroom Stroganoff with rice, and baked fillets of sea bass on a bed of Pernod-infused fennel.
OPEN: 12-3 6.30-11 **BAR MEALS:** L served all week 12-2 D served all week 7-9 **RESTAURANT:** L served all week 12-2 D served all week 7-9 Av 3 course à la carte £20 **BREWERY/COMPANY:** Free House ◆: Hook Norton Best, Wadworth 6X plus guest beers. ♀: 14
FACILITIES: Children welcome Garden: rear of pub, patio area at front **NOTES:** Parking 30

BARFORD ST MARTIN
Map 05 SU03

Barford Inn ♀
SP3 4AB ☎ 01722 742242 🖹 01722 743606
e-mail: ido@barfordinn.co.uk
Dir: on A30 5m W of Salisbury
A welcoming lounge, lower bar area and intimate snug greet visitors to this 16th-century former coaching inn, just five miles from Salisbury. During World War II the Wiltshire Yeomanry dedicated a tank to the pub, then known as The Green Dragon. The varied menu includes freshly-cut ciabattas, chargrilled medallions of beef, seafood linguine, or vegetarian stuffed aubergine, and there's an Israeli barbecue on Friday nights.
OPEN: 11-11 Closed: Dec 25 **BAR MEALS:** L served all week 12-2.30 D served all week 7-9.30 Av main course £9 **RESTAURANT:** L served all week 12-2.30 D served all week 7-9.30 Av 3 course à la carte £16 **BREWERY/COMPANY:** Hall & Woodhouse ◆: Badger Dorset Best & Tanglefoot. ♀: 12 **FACILITIES:** Children welcome Garden: **NOTES:** Parking 40

◆ Pubs with Red Diamonds are the top places in the AA's three, four and five diamond ratings

Open: 11.30-3, 6-11
(Sun 12-3, 7-10.30, 25 Dec 12-2 only)
Bar Meals: L served all week 12-2,
D served all week 6.30-9.
Av cost main course £5
RESTAURANT: L served all week 12-2,
D served all week 6.30-9.30.
Av cost 3 courses £19
BREWERY/COMPANY:
Free House.
🍺: Ringwood Best, Wadworth 6X.
FACILITIES: Children and dogs welcome,
Garden.
NOTES: Parking 40

The Crown

Tucked away in the Ebble Valley between Salisbury and Shaftesbury, the Crown is a well-known landmark with its pink-washed walls, thatched roof, clinging creepers and colourful window boxes.

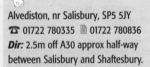

Alvediston, nr Salisbury, SP5 5JY
☎ 01722 780335 📠 01722 780836
Dir: 2.5m off A30 approx half-way between Salisbury and Shaftesbury.

Its old world setting is characterised by head-cracking low beams, two inglenook fireplaces that burn invitingly on cooler days, and comfortable furnishings. The inn serves entirely home-made food, with particular emphasis on fresh local produce whenever possible. The cosy bar sets the scene for food that can range from a simple sandwich to fresh fish and rib-eye steaks - a steal on Tuesday nights for just under £6. Listed daily on chalkboards, expect to find salmon fillet with home-made tartare sauce, chargrilled red snapper with stir-fried vegetables, lambs' liver with smoked bacon and pork fillet in Dijon mustard sauce. The pub makes a handy stopover for splendid local walks and visits to Salisbury Cathedral and Stonehenge. New owner in February 2003, Leslie Finch, is a friendly host.

England

BECKHAMPTON Map 05 SU06

Waggon & Horses

SN8 1QJ ☎ 01672 539418

Dir: *Telephone for directions*

Located close to Avebury's stone circle, this is a beautiful thatched inn dating back some 400 years. Charles Dickens stayed at the pub and is said to have written part of 'The Pickwick Papers' here. The menu includes a range of home-made beef dishes, including beef and Stilton pie, beef lasagne, beef in ale casserole and chilli con carne. Other choices are spicy Thai crab cake, chicken Kiev with garlic, and home-cooked ham with egg and chips.

OPEN: 11-3 5.30-11 **BAR MEALS:** L served all week 12-1.45 D served Mon-Sat 7-8.45 Av main course £6.95
BREWERY/COMPANY: Wadworth **:** Wadworth Henry's IPA, 6X, JCB. **:** 14 **FACILITIES:** Children welcome Garden: Dogs allowed
NOTES: Parking 50

BERWICK ST JAMES Map 05 SU03

Pick of the Pubs

The Boot Inn

High St SP3 4TN ☎ 01722 790243 01722 790243

Dir: *Telephone for directions*

Half of this attractive, 16th-century stone and flint inn was once a cobblers - hence the name. Tucked away in picturesque countryside, the ivy-covered building is surrounded by award-winning gardens, complete with a summer house, colourful borders and hanging baskets. The interior is traditional in style, and the atmosphere warm and friendly. Real ales are served - Wadworth 6X, Bass and Henrys IPA - and an award-winning menu of good quality home-cooked food. Fresh local produce, including herbs and vegetables from the garden, appear in daily-changing dishes such as beef, mushroom, red wine and Stilton stew, green Thai chicken curry, and venison sausages with mash and onion gravy. Game is offered in season, and fresh fish according to availability, with dishes like baked sea bass stuffed with spring onion and ginger, and warm salad of scallops with crispy bacon.

OPEN: 12-3 6-11 **BAR MEALS:** L served Tues-Sun 12-2.30 D served Tues-Sun 6.30-9.30 Av main course £8.95
BREWERY/COMPANY: Wadworth **:** Wadsworth 6x, Bass, Henrys IPA. **FACILITIES:** Garden: Large award winning garden Dogs allowed Water **NOTES:** Parking 18

Pubs offering a good choice of fish on their menu

BOX Map 04 ST86

The Quarrymans Arms

Box Hill SN13 8HN ☎ 01225 743569

e-mail: John@quarrymans-arms.co.uk

Dir: *Please phone the pub for accurate directions*

A 300-year-old miners' pub tucked away up a narrow hillside lane. Really splendid views over the Colerne Valley - great for walkers, cavers, potholers and cyclists as it is on the Macmillan Way, a long distance footpath. The interior is packed with mining memorabilia, and you can hear and feel the trains taking trips down the stone mines. Popular dishes are Stilton and asparagus pancake, steak and ale pie, poached salmon, and lamb shank with mint and rosemary sauce.

OPEN: 11-3.30 6-11 (all day Fri-Sun) **BAR MEALS:** L served all week 11-3 D served all week 6.30-10.30 Av main course £9
RESTAURANT: L served all week 11-3 D served all week 6.30-10.30 Av 3 course à la carte £16 **BREWERY/COMPANY:** Free House **:** Butcombe Bitter, Wadworth 6X, Moles. **:** 8
FACILITIES: Children welcome Garden Dogs allowed
NOTES: Parking 25

BRADFORD-ON-AVON Map 04 ST86

The Cross Guns Freehouse Restaurant NEW

Avoncliff BA15 2HB ☎ 01225 862335 & 867613

e-mail: enquiries@crossedguns.com

A beautiful 16th-century inn nestling between the canal and the river. Exposed stone walls, low-beamed ceilings and inglenook fires deliver bags of rustic charm, whilst the idyllic riverside terraces provide a perfect location to enjoy a sunny day. Don't forget to sample the acclaimed food: typical dishes include steak and ale pie, chicken stuffed with Stilton and wrapped in bacon, and salmon and monkfish lattice with white wine and cucumber sauce.

OPEN: 10 -11 **BAR MEALS:** L served all week 12-9 D served all week 12-9 Av main course £10 **RESTAURANT:** L served all week 12-2 D served all week 6.30-9 **:** Millworkers, Token Ale, Worthington, Bass. **:** 12 **FACILITIES:** Children welcome Garden: Seats 300 people, external heaters Dogs allowed
NOTES: Parking 16

The Dandy Lion

35 Market St BA15 1LL ☎ 01225 863433 01225 869169

A 17th-century town centre pub that was once a traditional grocery. Internally, the décor reflects Bradford-on-Avon's flourishing antique trade. Lunch is mostly a selection of snacks and light meals such as sausage and mash, pastas, vegetarian options and daily specials. In the evening, main courses include mussels, pan-fried sardines, kleftiko, beef Stroganoff and, if you feel like rolling up your sleeves, steaks

continued

BRADFORD-ON-AVON continued

or chicken and duck breasts to cook on hot stones at your table. **OPEN:** 10.30-3 6-11 (Sun 11.30-3, 7-10.30) **BAR MEALS:** L served all week 12-2.15 D served all week 7-9.30 Av main course £9.25 **RESTAURANT:** L served Sun 12-2.15 D served all week 7-9.30 Av 3 course à la carte £18 **BREWERY/COMPANY:** Wadworth ⬤: Butcombe, Wadworth 6X, Henrys IPA, Wadworth Seasonal Ales. ♀: 8 **FACILITIES:** Children welcome

Pick of the Pubs

The Kings Arms ♀
Monkton Farleigh BA15 2QH
☎ 01225 858705 ▤ 01225 858999
e-mail: enquiries@kingsarms-bath.org.uk
See Pick of the Pubs on opposite page

BRINKWORTH   Map 04 SU08

Pick of the Pubs

The Three Crowns 🐷 ♀
SN15 5AF ☎ 01666 510366 ▤ 01666 510303
Dir: A3102 to Wootton Bassett, then B4042, 5m to Brinkworth
The owner's research tells him that his pub acquired its name in 1801, but did it have an earlier name? The search continues. It stands on the village green by the church and, although deceptively small from the outside, opens up in a way Dr Who would have appreciated into a large, bright conservatory, a garden room and then out to a heated patio. In winter, an open log fire heats the traditional bars. All menus are written on large blackboards where, among the chicken supreme, rack of lamb, Somerset wild boar and home-made seafood pie, are crocodile and Taste of the Wild - marinated slices of kangaroo, venison and ostrich, served with a brandy-based sauce. Other main meals include various pies, and a satisfying number of fish dishes. Lunchtime snacks such as ploughman's, filled rolls and jacket potatoes, are generously proportioned.
OPEN: 11-3 6-11 Closed: 25-26 Dec **BAR MEALS:** L served all week 12-2 6-9.30 Av main course £15 **RESTAURANT:** L served all week 12-2 D served all week 6.15-9.30
BREWERY/COMPANY: Enterprise Inns ⬤: Wadworth 6X, Boddingtons, Castle Eden, Fullers London Pride. ♀: 15
FACILITIES: Children welcome Garden: Sheltered patio with heaters, well maintained Dogs allowed **NOTES:** Parking 40

BROAD CHALKE   Map 05 SU02

The Queens Head Inn 🐷 ♀
1 North St SP5 5EN ☎ 01722 780344 ▤ 01722 780344
Dir: Take A354 from Salisbury toward Blandford Forum, at Coombe Bissett turn R toward Bishopstone, follow rd for 4m
Attractive 15th-century inn with friendly atmosphere and low-beamed bars, once the village bakehouse. On sunny days, enjoy the flower-bordered courtyard, whilst in colder weather the wood burner in the bar provides a cosy refuge. Menus include light snacks such as sandwiches, ploughman's lunches and home-made soups, as well as more substantial main courses: perhaps grilled trout with almonds, sirloin steak with a choice of vegetables, or wild game casserole.

OPEN: 11-3 6-11 (Sun 12-3, 7-10.30) **BAR MEALS:** L served all week 12-2 D served all week 7-9 Av main course £8.50 **RESTAURANT:** L served all week 12-2 D served all week 7-9 **BREWERY/COMPANY:** Free House ⬤: Greene King IPA & Old Speckled Hen, Wadworth 6X. ♀: 7 **FACILITIES:** Children welcome Garden: Paved courtyard with flower borders **NOTES:** Parking 30 **ROOMS:** 4 bedrooms 4 en suite 2 family rooms s£35 d£60 (♦♦♦♦)

BURTON   Map 04 ST87

The Old House at Home 🐷 ♀
SN14 7LT ☎ 01454 218227 ▤ 01454 218227
Dir: On B4039 NW of Chippenham
A soft stone, ivy-clad pub with beautiful landscaped gardens and a waterfall. Inside there are low beams and an open fire. Overseen by the same landlord for nearly twenty years, the crew here are serious about food. The kitchen offers a good fish choice, vegetarian and pasta dishes, and traditional pub meals. Favourites include lamb cutlets with champ, salmon and crab cakes, woodland duck breast with stuffing, butterfly red mullet, and king scallops in Cointreau.
OPEN: 11.30-2.30 7-11 (w/end 11.30-3, Sun 7-10.30)
BAR MEALS: L served Mon-Sun 12-2 D served Mon-Sun 7-10 Av main course £12 **BREWERY/COMPANY:** Free House ⬤: Wadworth 6X, Interbrew Bass. ♀: 20 **FACILITIES:** Children welcome Garden: 3 tiered, landscaped **NOTES:** Parking 25

CALNE   Map 04 ST97

Lansdowne Arms ♀
Derry Hill SN11 9NS ☎ 01249 812422
e-mail: thelansdownearms@supanet.com

Coaching house dating from 1843, with scenic views along the Avon Valley and close to Bowood House. An interesting menu includes grills such as Scrumpy pork, minted lamb béarnaise, and honey glazed gammon. Specials may include seared tuna with Thai sauce, lamb's liver with onions and bacon, spinach, mushroom and pepper parcel, and old favourites like steak and kidney pie, breaded plaice fillet, broccoli and Swiss cheese quiche. 'Sandwedges', jacket potatoes, and ploughmans' also available.
OPEN: 11.30-2.30 6-11 (Sun 12-3, 7-10.30) **BAR MEALS:** L served all week 12-2 D served Mon-Sat 7-9
BREWERY/COMPANY: Wadworth ⬤: Wadworth 6X, IPA, Summersault & JCB, Butcombe Best Bitter. **FACILITIES:** Children welcome Garden Dogs allowed **NOTES:** Parking 50

> ♦ **Diamond rating for inspected**
> **guest accommodation**

continued

Open: 12-3, 5.30-11
(Sat 12-1, Sun 12-10.30)
Bar Meals: L served all week 12-3,
D served all week 6-9.30.
Av cost main course £6.25.
RESTAURANT: L served all week 12-3,
D served all week 6-9.30.
Av cost 3 courses £19.00
BREWERY/COMPANY: INNSPIRED
🍺: Greene King Old Speckled Hen,
Wadworth 6X, Buttcombe Bitter.
FACILITIES: Dogs allowed, Children
welcome, Garden - Garden has aviaries
and overlooks countryside.
NOTES: Parking 45

The Kings Arms

Dating back to the 11th century, this historic Bath stone building is situated in a most attractive village five minutes' drive from Bradford-on-Avon. It was originally a monks' retreat attached to the nearby and now ruined monastery, and one former monk is said to be among several ghosts at the pub.

♀

Monkton Farleigh,
Bradford-on-Avon, BA15 2QH
☎ 01225 858705 📠 01225 858999
✉ enquiries@kingsarms-bath.org.uk
Dir: Follow A4 from Bath to Bradford.
At Bathford join A363, turn L to
Monkton Farleigh.

In the 17th century the building was converted into a public house, but many original features remain, including mullion windows, flagged floors and a vast inglenook - said to be the biggest in the county - in the medieval-style Chancel Restaurant, which is hung with tapestries and pewter plates. Approached by way of an arboreal courtyard, the pub leads through to an enclosed garden with parasol-shaded tables and two aviaries - home to golden pheasants, lovebirds and 'Spook', the resident long-eared eagle owl. Beers and wines are supplemented by a range of around 20 malt whiskies plus a good selection of Cognacs, Armagnacs and ports. In the bar at lunchtime, the menu choices are mainly traditional - fish and chips, sausages and mash, jacket potatoes and the like - supplemented by a good selection of vegetarian dishes and some tasty baguettes such as Camembert with apple, cider and brandy chutney, and smoked bacon and avocado. The restaurant menu (lunchtime and evenings) is more adventurous. Starters may include deep-fried duck dim sums with hoi sin noodles, home-made fishcakes with lemon and chive mayonnaise, or grilled sardines with Greek salad. Mains often feature the chef's speciality chicken Kiev with Dolcelatte cheese on a bed of creamed spinach; whole red gurnard with chicory and orange compote; venison casserole with sage dumplings; and pork loin stuffed with wild mushrooms served with a pink peppercorn sauce. There is always a selection of special desserts, but the regular offerings are tempting enough, from white chocolate and hazelnut pie through to banoffee crème brûlée.

England

CALNE
Map 04 ST97

White Horse Inn ◆◆◆◆
Compton Bassett SN11 8RG ☎ 01249 813118 📠 01249 811595
Beneath its impressive, stone-tiled roof, the White Horse Inn has been welcoming visitors since 1850. Now this stylish village inn with its cosy bar, attractive restaurant and seven en suite bedrooms makes an ideal base for exploring the Wiltshire countryside. Lunchtime brings cold snacks or a selection from the set menu. In the restaurant, Cumberland sausages and mash rub shoulders with smoked haddock Florentine, rib-eye steak, and garlic-roasted vegetarian stuffed peppers.
OPEN: 11-3 5-11 Closed: 25 Dec **BAR MEALS:** L served all week 12-2 D served all week 7-9.00 **RESTAURANT:** L served all week 12-2 D served all week 7-9.00 **BREWERY/COMPANY:** ☜: Wadworth 6X, Greene King Abbot Ale, Adnams Broadside, Scottish Courage Couarge Directors. **FACILITIES:** Garden: Dogs allowed
NOTES: Parking 75 **ROOMS:** 7 bedrooms 7 en suite 2 family rooms s£65 d£65 no children overnight

CASTLE COMBE
Map 04 ST87

The White Hart ♀
SN14 7HS ☎ 01249 782295
Dir: *Centre of village*
Historic, part-timbered 14th-century pub in a classic village which film fans will recognise as Puddleby-on-the-Marsh in the movie version of Doctor Doolittle. Many charming features inside the inn, including low ceilings, beams and a cosy log fire. Pleasant patio gardens, sunny conservatory and sheltered courtyard also attract customers. An extensive menu offers the likes of cod and chips, mixed grill and steak and ale pie.
OPEN: 11-11 (Sun 11-10.30) **BAR MEALS:** L served all week 12-2.45 D served all week 6.30-9 Av main course £5.95 **RESTAURANT:** L served all week 12-2.45 D served all week 6.30-9 Av 3 course à la carte £12 **BREWERY/COMPANY:** Wadworth ☜: Wadworth 6X, Henry's Original IPA, plus Guest ales. **FACILITIES:** Children welcome Garden: beer garden, outdoor eating Dogs allowed

CHILMARK
Map 04 ST93

Pick of the Pubs

The Black Dog ♀
SP3 5AH ☎ 01722 716344 📠 01722 716124
e-mail: blackdogwessexinns@freeserve.com
Set beside the B3089 west of Salisbury in the pretty village of Chilmark, the 15th-century stone-built Black Dog is a great country pub. First and foremost, it is the village local, yet successfully combines its unspoilt historic charm with an appealing modern décor, tip-top local ales, a warm, friendly welcome, and offers excellent contemporary pub food. Classic main bar with red and black tiled floor, a huge table topped with unusual dried flower arrangements, and a chatty atmosphere; adjoining beamed and cosy dining areas. Good, popular food ranges from Black Dog burger, imaginatively-filled baguettes and venison in red wine casserole at lunchtime, to modern, well-presented evening dishes listed on the interesting carte. For starters, try lime and basil-marinated salmon with hollandaise or smoked chicken and asparagus Caesar salad with Parmesan shaving, followed by grilled Torbay sole, roast monkfish on lightly-curried mussels with cream, coconut and lime, or a prime fillet steak with cracked black pepper, Dijon mustard, brandy and cream. Huge rear garden for summer imbibing.

continued

OPEN: 11-3 6-11 Closed: Dec 25 **BAR MEALS:** L served all week 12-2 D served all week 7-9 Av main course £7 **RESTAURANT:** L served all week 12-2.30 D served all week 6-9.30 Av 3 course à la carte £20 ☜: Bass, Wadworth 6X. **FACILITIES:** Children welcome Garden: Food served outside Dogs allowed **NOTES:** Parking 30

CHRISTIAN MALFORD
Map 04 ST97

The Rising Sun ♀
Station Rd SN15 4BL ☎ 01249 721571 📠 01249 721571
e-mail: risingsun@tesco.net
Dir: *From M4 J 17 take B4122 towards Sutton Benger, turn L on to the B4069, pass through Sutton Benger after 1m you come into Christian Malford, turn R into the village (station road) the pub is the last building on the L*
The essence of a convivial, unspoilt country inn has been preserved by the Hutchens family, who have also brought a refreshing approach to pub food. Wherever possible all dishes are cooked with local ingredients and organic produce. Particularly popular are the slow-cooked braised steaks and casseroles, and dinner specials such as pheasant or venison in the winter months, while peppered steak with mustard mash or rabbit in white wine with bubble-and-squeak will tease the taste buds at any time.
OPEN: 12-2.30 6.30-11 **BAR MEALS:** L served Tues- Sun 12-2 served Tues-Sun 6.30-10 Av main course £7 **RESTAURANT:** L served Tues-Sun 12-2 D served Tues-Sun 6.30-10 Av 3 course à la carte £18 **BREWERY/COMPANY:** Free House ☜: RCH Hewish IPA & Two guest beers. ♀: 9 **FACILITIES:** Garden: Food served outside, lawn Dogs allowed Water & Treats **NOTES:** Parking 15

COLLINGBOURNE DUCIS
Map 05 SU25

The Shears Inn & Country Hotel 🛏 ♀
The Cadley Rd SN8 3ED ☎ 01264 850304 📠 01264 850220
Dir: *On A338 NW of Andover & Ludgershall*

A thatched 16th-century building that used to function as a shearing shed for market-bound sheep. Now a thriving country inn, it owes some of its popularity to fresh seafood specials, including roast monkfish in Parma ham, seared tuna with quails' eggs and fresh anchovies, and gâteau of lobster, sole and salmon with basil and tomato dressing. Venison, rack of lamb, and various steaks, all with a delicious sauce or jus, are among other contributory factors.
OPEN: 11-3 5.30-11 **BAR MEALS:** L served all week 12-2.30 D served all week 6.30-9.30 Av main course £6.95 **RESTAURANT:** L served all week 12-2.30 D served all week 6.30-9.30 Av 3 course à la carte £20 **BREWERY/COMPANY:** Free House ☜: Theakstons Best, Wadworth 6X, Otter Ale, Bass. ♀: 10 **FACILITIES:** Children welcome Garden: Small area with 10 picnic tables Dogs allowed **NOTES:** Parking 50

CORSHAM   Map 04 ST87

Methuen Arms Hotel 🐑 ♀
2 High St SN13 0HB ☎ 01249 714867 🖷 01249 712004
e-mail: methuenarms@lineone.net
Dir: *Town centre, on A4 between Bath & Chippenham*
Locally called 'The Met', it started out in the 14th century as a
nunnery. More recently, the Georgians added the fine
Cotswold stone façade, behind which lies a welcoming lounge,
public bar, and the candlelit Winter's Court Restaurant. Snacks
and appetising meals, such as breast of marinated spicy Cajun
chicken, and steaks are served in the bar, while dinner choices
in the restaurant include Caribbean tenderloin of pork, grilled
fillet of plaice, and vegetable spaghetti.
OPEN: 11-11 (Sun 12-3, 7-10.30) **BAR MEALS:** L served all week
12-2.15 D served all week 6.30-9.15 Av main course £6.95
RESTAURANT: L served all week 12-2 D served Mon-Sat 7-9.45 Av 3
course à la carte £21 Av 3 course fixed price £16.95
BREWERY/COMPANY: Latona Leisure 🍺: Wadworth 6X,
Interbrew Boddingtons Bitter & Bass, Scottish Courage Courage Best.
♀: 12 **FACILITIES:** Children welcome Garden: Lrg grassy area
Dogs allowed **NOTES:** Parking 60

CORTON   Map 04 ST94

Pick of the Pubs

The Dove Inn ♦♦♦♦ 🐑 ♀
BA12 0SZ ☎ 01985 850109 🖷 01985 851041
e-mail: info@thedove.co.uk
Dir: *Between Salisbury & Warminster on minor rd (parallel to A36)*
A thriving, traditional pub tucked away in a beautiful
Wiltshire village close to the River Wylye. A dramatic
central fireplace is a feature of the refurbished bar, and the
large garden is the site of summer barbecues, and ideal for
a drink on warm days. The award-winning food is based
firmly on West Country produce, with many ingredients
coming from within just a few miles. Popular lunchtime bar
snacks give way to a full evening carte, featuring starters
like Thai crab cakes, duck confit, and smoked halibut,
followed by calves' liver, pheasant risotto, and braised
lamb. A good range of well-kept real ales includes Oakhill,
Wadworth, Fullers and Hopback. Five en suite bedrooms
built around a courtyard make The Dove an ideal touring
base, with Bath and Salisbury within easy range.
OPEN: 12-3.30 6.30-11 **BAR MEALS:** L served all week 12-
2.30 D served all week 7-9.30 Av main course £6.50
RESTAURANT: L served all week 12-3 D served all week 7-9.30
Av 3 course à la carte £20 **BREWERY/COMPANY:** Free House
🍺: Wadworth 6X, Fuller's London Pride & Butcombe.
FACILITIES: Children welcome Garden: Beer garden, patio,
food served outdoors Dogs allowed Water **NOTES:** Parking 24
ROOMS: 5 bedrooms 5 en suite s£49.50 d£70

DEVIZES   Map 04 SU06

The Bear Hotel ★★★ ♀
The Market Place SN10 1HS ☎ 01380 722444 🖷 01380 722450
e-mail: info@thebearhotel.net
A quintessential coaching inn dating from at least 1559, listing
Judge Jeffreys, George III, and Harold Macmillan among many
notable guests. You'll find old beams, log fires and fresh
flowers throughout the comfortable lounges and bars. The
restaurant offers dishes such as crab brûlée, chargrilled steak
with Welsh rarebit and peppercorn sauce, and rack of lamb.

There's also an extensive choice of grills, omelettes, baguettes
and sandwiches. Devizes is home to Wadworth's, so the 6X
has merely yards to travel.
OPEN: 9.30-11 Closed: 25-26 Dec **BAR MEALS:** L served all week
11.30-2.30 D served all week 7-9.30 Av main course £3.95
RESTAURANT: L served Sun-Fri 12.15-1.45 D served Mon-Sat 7-9.30
Av 3 course à la carte £26 Av 3 course fixed price £13.95
BREWERY/COMPANY: Wadworth 🍺: Wadworth 6X, Wadworth
IPA, Wadworth JCB, Old Timer. ♀: 18 **FACILITIES:** Children
welcome Courtyard Dogs allowed **ROOMS:** 25 bedrooms 25 en
suite 3 family rooms s£50 d£75

The Raven Inn ♀
Poulshot Rd SN10 1RW ☎ 01380 828271 🖷 01380 828271
e-mail: pjh@raveninn.co.uk
Dir: *Take A361 out of Devizes towards Trowbridge, turn L at sign for
Poulshot*
A traditional part-timbered, 18th-century inn situated just
beyond the northern edge of the expansive village green.
From here you can enjoy classic Kennet and Avon Canal
towpath walking beside the famous Caen Hill locks. Speciality
dishes include lamb and apricots, pork Madras, chicken
Parmesan, entrecôte au poivre, and home-made chicken pie.
Home-made soups, pâté and puddings are also an attraction.
OPEN: 11-2.30 6.30-11 (Sun, 12-3, 7-10.30) **BAR MEALS:** L served
Tue-Sun 12-2 D served Tue-Sun 7-9.30 Av main course £8
RESTAURANT: L served Tue-Sun 12-2 D served Tue-Sun 7-9.30 Av 3
course à la carte £13 **BREWERY/COMPANY:** Wadworth
🍺: Wadworth 6X, Wadworth IPA, Summersault, Wadworth Jeb.
FACILITIES: Garden: Walled with gate **NOTES:** Parking 20

DONHEAD ST ANDREW   Map 04 ST92

The Forester Inn 🐑 ♀ NEW
Lower St SP7 9EE ☎ 01747 828038
Dir: *Near Shaftesbury, 4.5 miles on A30 to Salisbury*

An attractive 14th-century thatched inn, under new ownership
and recently refurbished to add a modern feel to its rustic
charm. The interior still includes an inglenook fireplace and
traditional wooden furnishings, and the pub retains a good
local trade. There's an increased emphasis on home-cooked
food such as grilled steaks, smoked haddock fishcakes or
roast salmon on crushed new potatoes with orange
cardamom sauce. Other charms include a good wine list, an
attractive garden and lunchtime bar snacks such as ciabattas
and ploughman's platters.
OPEN: 12-3 6.30-11 **BAR MEALS:** L served all week 12-2 D served
all week 7-9.30 Av main course £9.95 **RESTAURANT:** 12-2 7-9.30 Av
3 course à la carte £20 🍺: 6X, Adnams, Bass, Ringwood. ♀: 10
FACILITIES: Children welcome Children's licence Garden: Large
patio area and garden Dogs allowed **NOTES:** Parking 30

continued

EAST KNOYLE
Map 04 ST83

The Fox and Hounds
The Green SP3 6BN ☎ 01747 830573 📠 01747 830865
Dir: *Off A303 onto A350 for 200yds, then R. Pub 0.5m on L*
Originally three cottages, dating from the late 15th century, this thatched pub overlooks the Blackmore Vale with fine views for up to 20 miles. East Knoyle is the birthplace of Sir Christopher Wren, and was also home to Lady Jayne Seymour.
OPEN: 11-2.30 6-11 **BAR MEALS:** L served all week 12-2.30 D served all week 7-10 🍴: Fullers London Pride, Smiles Golden, Butts Barbus Barbus. **FACILITIES:** Children welcome Garden: Dogs allowed **NOTES:** Parking 10

EBBESBOURNE WAKE
Map 04 ST92

Pick of the Pubs

The Horseshoe
Handley St SP5 5JF ☎ 01722 780474
Reflecting the rural charm of the village in which it stands, the 17th-century Horseshoe Inn nestles into the folds of the Wiltshire Downs, close to the meandering River Ebble. The small building was originally the stables for the old stagecoach road that ran along the ridge not more than two miles away. These days it is a homely and traditional local, adorned with climbing roses. Outside there is a pretty, flower-filled garden and inside is a central servery dispensing ale from the barrel to two rooms, both filled with simple furniture, old farming implements and country bygones. Good value bar food is freshly prepared from local produce and meals are accompanied by plenty of vegetables. Hearty dishes include pheasant and cranberry or steak and kidney pies, fresh fish bake, honey-roasted duckling, and lambs' liver and bacon casserole.
OPEN: 12-3 6.30-11 **BAR MEALS:** L served Tue-Sun 12-2 D served Tue-Sat 7-9.30 Av main course £8.95 **RESTAURANT:** L served Tue-Sun 12-2 D served Tue-Sat 7-9.30 Av 3 course à la carte £20 **BREWERY/COMPANY:** Free House 🍴: Wadworth 6X, Ringwood Best Bitter, Adnams Broadside, Butcombe Best. **FACILITIES:** Garden: Dogs allowed Water **NOTES:** Parking 20

FONTHILL GIFFORD
Map 04 ST93

Pick of the Pubs

Beckford Arms
SP3 6PX ☎ 01747 870385 📠 01747 870385
e-mail: beck.ford@ukonline.co.uk
See Pick of the Pubs on opposite page

FORD
Map 04 ST87

Pick of the Pubs

The White Hart 🛏 ♀
SN14 8RP ☎ 01249 782213 📠 01249 783075
Dir: *From M4 J17 take A429 then A420 to Ford*
In a sleepy village deep in the Bybrook Valley, this rambling 15th-century coaching inn stands by a babbling trout stream. Within, it has a traditional bar with tub armchairs and good real ales, as well as an intimate beamed dining-room with wooden tables candlelit by night. Most of the bedrooms are in converted stables and hayloft across the lane, well fitted with modern

appointments with a peaceful night's rest promised. The pleasant atmosphere is decidedly country inn and suitably informal. The usual menu features warmed Barbary duck, Hunters chicken, Cumberland sausage ring, and Mediterranean pasta, while a sample of the specials board may include liver and bacon casserole with creamed potatoes, Spanish-style chicken, scallops of pork in Dijonaise sauce, fillet of beef Rossini with Madeira sauce, or spinach and red pepper lasagne. The White Hart recently underwent a change of hands and brewery, so readers' reports are welcome.

OPEN: 11-11 Dec 25 Closed eve **BAR MEALS:** L served all week 12-2 D served all week 9.15 Av main course £9.95 **RESTAURANT:** L served all week 12-2.15 D served all week 7-9.15 Av 3 course à la carte £14 **BREWERY/COMPANY:** Eldridge Pope 🍴: Wadsworth 6X, Interbrew Bass, Carlsberg-Tetley Tetley Imperial. ♀: 12 **FACILITIES:** Children welcome Garden: Terrace & grassy area along stream Dogs allowed by arrangement **NOTES:** Parking 80 **ROOMS:** 11 bedrooms 11 en suite 2 family rooms s£64 d£79 (♦♦♦♦)

GREAT HINTON
Map 04 ST95

Pick of the Pubs

The Linnet 🛏 ♀
BA14 6BU ☎ 01380 870354 📠 01380 870354
Dir: *Just off the A361 Devizes to Trowbridge rd*
Chef/landlord Jonathan Furby has transformed this quiet village local into a pub restaurant with a great reputation for its freshly-prepared food. Everything is home made, including the range of breads, the pasta and the ice cream. Fresh ingredients, locally produced wherever possible, are reflected in menus that are kept to a sensible length and supplemented daily by whatever is available at market. The set lunch menu might offer haddock and prawn fishcake with spiced tomato compote, venison sausages on honey-roasted celeriac, and pear and Calvados crème brûlée. While dishes from the more extensive carte include marinated Thai-style salmon, and braised lamb shank with haricot bean and mint casserole. Tables are comfortably spaced, presentation is top-class, and the service is pleasantly relaxed and informal. In the summer months there are seats in the large patio area in front of the pub.
OPEN: 11-2.30 6.30-11 (Sun 12-3, 7-10.30) Closed: 1 Jan **BAR MEALS:** L served Tue-Sun 12-2 D served Tue-Sun 6.30-9.30 Av main course £8 **RESTAURANT:** L served Tue-Sun 12-2 D served Tue-Sun 6.30-9.30 Av 3 course à la carte £22 Av 3 course fixed price £20 **BREWERY/COMPANY:** Wadworth 🍴: Wadworth 6X & Henrys IPA. ♀: 8 **FACILITIES:** Garden: large patio area in front of pub Dogs allowed Water **NOTES:** Parking 45

continued

Open: 12-11 (Sun 12-10.30)
Closed: 25 Dec
Bar Meals: L served all week 12-2,
D served all week 7-9.30.
Av cost main course £8.95
RESTAURANT: L served all week 12-2,
D served all week 7-9.30.
Av cost 3 courses £18.95
BREWERY/COMPANY:
Free House.
◖: Hop Back Best, Timothy Taylor
Landlord, Abbot, Hopback Summer
Lightning, Old Speckled Hen.
FACILITIES: Children and dogs
welcome, Garden.
NOTES: Parking 40

The Beckford Arms

Substantial 18th-century stone-built inn peacefully situated opposite the Fonthill Estate and providing a good base from which to explore the unspoilt Nadder Valley. Eddie and Karen Costello have transformed this rural retreat since arriving here a few years ago.

Fonthill Gifford, nr Tisbury,
Salisbury, SP3 6PX
☎ 01747 870385 📠 01747 870385
✉ beck.ford@ukonline.co.uk
Dir: 2m from A303 (Fonthill Bishop turning) halfway between Hindon & Tisbury at crossroads next to Beckford Estate.

Beyond the basic locals' bar you will find a rambling main bar, adjoining dining area and an airy garden room all decorated in a tastefully-rustic style, complete with scrubbed plank tables topped with huge candles, and warm terracotta-painted walls. Expect a roaring log fire in winter, a relaxed, laid-back atmosphere, and interesting modern pub menus. From petit pain baguettes, hearty soups, salads, Asian-style fishcakes with sweet chilli dip, or a Thai curry at lunchtime, the choice of well-presented dishes extends, perhaps, to rack of lamb with tomatoes, wine and Italian herbs, sautéed medallions of Wiltshire pork with caramelised apple, Calvados and cider, and salmon with Vermouth glaze in the evening. Generous bowls of fresh vegetables, colourful plates and friendly service all add to the dining experience here. Sun-trap patio and a delightful garden - perfect for summer sipping.

GRITTLETON Map 04 ST88

The Neeld Arms ♀
The Street SN14 6AP ☎ 01249 782470 🖃 01249 782168
e-mail: neeldarms@zeronet.co.uk
Dir: *Telephone for directions*

Just 5 minutes' drive from the M4 (J 17) this 17th-century
Cotswold stone pub stands at the centre of a pretty village in
lush Wiltshire countryside. Quality real ales and freshly-
prepared food are an equal draw to diners who will eagerly
tuck in to lamb shanks, pheasant casserole, steak and kidney
pie or local venison when available. Children are welcome
and the small garden is especially popular for alfresco eating
in fine weather.
OPEN: 12-3 5.30-11 **BAR MEALS:** L served all week 12-2 D served
all week 7-9.30 Av main course £10 **BREWERY/COMPANY:** Free
House **🍺:** Wadworth 6X, Buckleys Best, Brakspear Bitter.
FACILITIES: Children welcome Garden: Patio Dogs allowed
NOTES: Parking 12

HANNINGTON Map 05 SU19

The Jolly Tar ♦♦♦♦ ♀ NEW
Queens Rd SN6 7RP ☎ 01793 762245 🖃 01793 762247
e-mail: thejollytar@btopenworld.com
Old timbers and a log fire create a warm atmosphere in this
old farmhouse that has been an inn for 150 years. Locally-
brewed Arkells real ale and decent wines make an ideal
accompaniment to the conservatory restaurant menu: expect
oriental crab cakes with a sweet chilli dressing, Cajun chicken
with creamy garlic mayonnaise, and chocolate brownie with
warm chocolate sauce. The converted skittles alley offers
tasteful bedrooms.
OPEN: 12-3 6.30-11 **BAR MEALS:** L served all week 12-2 D served
all week 6.30-9 Av main course £8.50 **RESTAURANT:** L served all
week 12-2 D served all week 6.30-9 Av 3 course à la carte £16
BREWERY/COMPANY: **🍺:** Arkells 3B, 2B, JRA & Summer Ale.
♀: 9 **FACILITIES:** Garden: Sun terrace patio, grass play area
NOTES: Parking 30 **ROOMS:** 4 bedrooms 4 en suite 1 family
rooms s£50 d£65 no children overnight

> 🐟 **Pubs offering a good choice of
> fish on their menu**

HEYTESBURY Map 04 ST94

Pick of the Pubs

The Angel Inn ♦♦♦♦
High St BA12 0ED ☎ 01985 840330 🖃 01985 840931
e-mail: Angelheytesbury@aol.com
Dir: *From A303 take A36 toward Bath, 8m, Heytesbury on L*
With all the charm and character of a traditional coaching
inn, the Angel is a dining pub in the modern idiom. This
charming free house is tucked away in a tiny village in the
lovely Wylye Valley, close to the edge of Salisbury Plain.
Heytesbury was a parliamentary borough for several
hundred years until 1831, and the Angel was used as a
polling station. Now, eight stylishly-furnished en-suite
bedrooms make this an excellent base for exploring Bath,
Salisbury and the nearby Longleat Estate. The pub has a
reassuringly-civilised atmosphere, with relaxed and
friendly service that makes for a pleasurable dining
experience. The beamed bar features scrubbed pine
tables, warmly-decorated walls and an attractive fireplace
with a wood-burning stove. In summer, guests spill out
into the secluded courtyard garden, which is furnished
with hardwood tables and cotton parasols. Good quality
local ingredients feature strongly in a range of seasonal
menus that combine modern flavours with the best of
traditional cuisine. The lighter menu includes glazed goats'
cheese on a toasted croûton and salad leaves, baked
stuffed field mushroom, and smoked salmon roulade with
lemon and dill dressing. Follow through with roasted
Wylye valley trout, sautéed new potatoes and fennel
salad; rack of lamb with pimento peppers, sautéed garlic
potatoes and thyme jus; or pan-fried guinea fowl with
crisp potato rösti, wilted pousse and cherry tomatoes.
Sumptuous desserts include cappuchino crème brûlée;
pineapple sorbet served in half a baby pineapple; and
chocolate and orange pudding with a hot chocolate and
Cointreau sauce. After eating, diners may take coffee by
the open fire in the sitting room, with its comfortable
sofas and easy chairs.
OPEN: 11.30-3 6.30-11 (Sun 12-10.30) **BAR MEALS:** L served
all week 12-2.30 D served all week 7-9.30 Av main course £9.95
RESTAURANT: L served all week 12-2.30 D served all week 7-
9.30 Av 3 course à la carte £20 **BREWERY/COMPANY:** Free
House **🍺:** Ringwood Best, Marstons Pedigree, Old Hooky,
Ringwood Boondoogle. **FACILITIES:** Children welcome
Children's licence Dogs allowed Water **NOTES:** Parking 12
ROOMS: 8 bedrooms 8 en suite 1 family rooms s£50 d£65

HINDON Map 04 ST93

Pick of the Pubs

Angel Inn ★★ 🏵🏵 🐾 ♀
SP3 6DJ ☎ 01747 820696 🖃 01747 820869
e-mail: eat@theangelhindon.fslife.co.uk
See Pick of the Pubs on opposite page

Open: 10.30-3, 6-11 (Sun eve-closed)
Bar Meals: L served all week 12-2,
D served Mon-Sat 7-9.
Av cost main course £11
RESTAURANT: L served all week 12-2,
D served Mon-Sat 7-9.
Av cost 3 course £18.50
BREWERY/COMPANY:
Free House.
🍺: Wadworth 6X, Bass, Wadworth
Henry's Original IPA.
FACILITIES: Dogs allowed, Children
welcome, Garden - Paved courtyard
with garden furniture.
NOTES: Parking 20
ROOMS: 7 en suite from s£55 d£65

Angel Inn

A handsome coaching inn standing opposite the parish church in Hindon, a particularly attractive and unspoilt Georgian village in the most rural part of Wiltshire. Enthusiastic owners are proud of their good food and ales.

Hindon, Salisbury, SP3 6DJ
☎ 01747 820696 📠 01747 820869
✉ eat@the-angel-inn.co.uk
Dir: 1.5m from A303, on B3089 towards Salisbury.

From its medieval origins the pub was named the Angel, and when the current Georgian building was erected on the ruins of the original inn its name was changed to the Grosvenor Arms. Now back to its original name, the Angel has benefited from an extensive and sympathetic refurbishment. The interior is a warm red, with open fires, old beams and flagstone flooring gracing the three bars and stylish sitting room. Coir flooring and fresh flowers bring an open feel to the airy restaurant, which was created from the former stable block. Totally-fresh produce, much of it organic, forms the basis of the modern cooking, and the owners are enthusiastic about their wines and ales. The versatile starters menu allows plenty of choice for those wanting just a light bite: pan-fried crab cake, terrine of ham hock and parsley, and Cajun-spiced yellowfin tuna with black bean salsa stand on their own, or might be followed by oriental crispy salmon with pickled cabbage and a spicy sauce, roast chump of lamb with baby fennel and aubergine pureé, or poached halibut fillet with a fricassée of mussels, clams and scallops. Desserts are deliciously tempting, with compote of Victoria plums with Breton shortcake, and hot chocolate brownie with lemon and parsley sorbet among the unusual choices. Fish from Brixham, meats from Aubrey Allen and cheeses from Neal's Yard underpin the kitchen's credentials. The wine list is carefully selected and offers 14 wines by the glass. The inn is approached though a pleasant tree-filled courtyard which buzzes with life in the summer months when it is prettily lit, and food is served outside.

HINDON continued

Pick of the Pubs

The Lamb at Hindon ♀
High St SP3 6DP ☎ 01747 820573 ▤ 01747 820605
e-mail: the-lamb@demon.co.uk
Dir: 1m from A303 & B3089, in village centre

Situated in picturesque Hindon, this 17th-century posting inn is a handy refreshment stop for A303 travellers. A weekly market was held here until 1862, with business transactions conducted in the bar. A relaxing restaurant serves local produce, including game in season, while bar food may feature hearty ploughman's lunches, venison and mushroom casserole, and whole Dover sole. Cold food is served in the bar until 12.30, and tea and scones are served throughout the afternoon too.
OPEN: 11-11 (Sun 12-11) **BAR MEALS:** L served all week 12-2.30 D served all week 7-10 Av main course £7.50
RESTAURANT: L served all week 12-1.45 D served all week 7-9.30 Av 3 course à la carte £19.95 Av 3 course fixed price £19.95
BREWERY/COMPANY: Free House ◖: Youngs. ♀: 17
FACILITIES: Children welcome Garden: outdoor eating, patio, beer garden Dogs allowed **NOTES:** Parking 25

HOLT   Map 04 ST86

Pick of the Pubs

The Tollgate Inn ♦♦♦♦ ◎◎ 🐾 ♀
BA14 6PX ☎ 01225 782326 ▤ 01225 782805
e-mail: alison@tollgateholt.co.uk
See Pick of the Pubs on opposite page

HORNINGSHAM   Map 04 ST84

The Bath Arms ♀
BA12 7LY ☎ 01985 844308 ▤ 01985 844150
Dir: Off B3092 S of Frome
An impressive, creeper-clad stone inn occupying a prime position at one of the entrances to Longleat Estate. Purchased from Glastonbury Abbey and converted into a pub in 1763, the Bath Arms has been comfortably refurbished and features a fine beamed bar with settles and old wooden tables, and a terracotta-painted dining-room with open fire. Menus offer traditional fish and chips, tuna with mango salsa and herb oil, poussin with bacon and braised Savoy cabbage, rib-eye steak with red wine jus, and snacks like Longleat ploughman's. Rear terrace.
OPEN: 12-3 6-11 **BAR MEALS:** L served all week 12-2.30 D served Mon-Sat 7-9.30 Av main course £7 **RESTAURANT:** L served all week 12-2.30 D served Mon-Sat 7-9.30 Av 3 course à la carte £13.95
BREWERY/COMPANY: Young & Co ◖: Youngs Bitter, Special, Triple AAA. ♀: 15 **FACILITIES:** Children welcome Garden: Food served outside Dogs allowed **NOTES:** Parking 15

HORTON   Map 05 SU06

The Bridge Inn 🐾 ♀
Horton Rd SN10 2JS ☎ 01380 860273 ▤ 01380 860273
e-mail: manager@thebridgeinn.freeserve.co.uk
Dir: A361 from Devizes, R at 3rd roundabout
Spacious renovated pub, with well-furnished bars, log fires, and a large garden with barbecue and pétanque pitch. Standing next to the Kennet and Avon Canal, it was once a farm and later a flour mill and bakery. As well as snacks, sandwiches, various ploughman's lunches and vegetarian options, the menu also features a wide range of filling offerings such as half a shoulder of oven-roasted lamb, and Stincotta - a 21oz slow-roasted shank of pork on the bone.
OPEN: 12-3 6.30-11 **BAR MEALS:** L served all week 12-2.15 D served all week 7-9.15 Av main course £4.95 **RESTAURANT:** L served all week 12-2.15 D served all week 7-9.15
BREWERY/COMPANY: Wadworth ◖: Wadworth Henry's original IPA, 6X. ♀: 8 **FACILITIES:** Children welcome Garden: Lrg garden, on canal-side Dogs allowed Water **NOTES:** Parking 50

KILMINGTON   Map 04 ST73

The Red Lion Inn
BA12 6RP ☎ 01985 844263
Dir: B3092 off A303 N towards Frome. Pub 2.5m from A303 on R on B3092 just after turning to Stourhead Gardens
A 14th-century coaching inn that once regularly provided two spare horses to assist coaches in the climb up nearby White Sheet Hill. The interior, unchanged over decades, features flagstone floors, oak beams, antique settles and two blazing log fires. As well as being a champion of real ale, the long-standing landlord supervises his kitchen to ensure that all produce - much of it local - is served in prime condition. A typical menu includes meat or vegetable lasagne, creamy fish pie, and lamb and apricot pie, as well as a wide selection of pasties, baked potatoes, toasted sandwiches and salads.
OPEN: 11.30-2.30 6.30-11 (Sun 12-3, 7-10.30) **BAR MEALS:** L served all week 12-1.50 Av main course £4.65
BREWERY/COMPANY: Free House ◖: Butcombe Bitter, Jester, Guest Ale. **FACILITIES:** Children welcome Garden: Large with picnic tables Dogs allowed **NOTES:** Parking 25 **NOTES:** No credit cards

OPEN: 11.30-2.30, 5-11 (Sun closed eve)

CLOSED: 1st week Jan

BAR MEALS: L served Tue-Sun 12-2, D served Mon-Sat 7-9.30. Av main course £12.50

RESTAURANT: L served Tue-Sun 12-2, D served Mon-Sat 7-9.30. Av cost 3 courses £20.50

BREWERY/COMPANY: Free House.

◀: Timothy Taylor Landlord, Exmoor Gold, West Berkshire Mr Chubbs, Glastonbury Ales Mystery Tor, York Ales, Yorkshire Terrier.

FACILITIES: Assistance Dogs only. Established garden with wooden furniture

NOTES: Parking 40.

ROOMS: 4 en suite from d£65

The Tollgate

In the 16th century, this was a weaving shed, while the restaurant, upstairs in an adjoining building, was a Baptist chapel for the weavers, and still has the original windows and stone steps. Also upstairs are four en suite bedrooms with private dining facilities.

◆◆◆◆ ◉◉ 🐄 ♀

BA14 6PX

☎ 01225 782326   🖷 01225 782805

℮ alison@tollgateholt.co.uk

Dir: On B 3105 between Bradford on Avon and Melksham M4 J18, A46 towards Bath, then A363 to Bradford on Avon then B3105 Melksham, pub on the R hand side

From the terrace the Westbury White Horse, carved on the chalk hillside, is visible beyond the River Avon, and sheep, goats and chickens wander in the pub's own paddock. The welcoming bars include daily papers, glossy magazines and deep, comfortable sofas, around a log fire. The Tollgate always has plenty of customers, attracted not just by the quality of the cooking, but also by the knowledge that local farms supply the meat, game, poultry, fruit and vegetables, and a specialist in Bradford-on-Avon its English cheeses. Only the fish comes from farther afield - Brixham, in fact, where it is line-caught when possible - and delivered fresh daily. Even the pickles, chutneys, pastas, breads and ice creams are home made. The cooking style is modern English with Mediterranean undertones, and might include sea bass en papillote with herbs and lemon grass, roasted pheasant breast on a herb and olive potato cake, with apple and cider sauce, or black bream cooked in Cajun spices with a crab and cream bisque-flavoured brandy sauce. The daily-changing blackboard specials might include salad of confit of duck with roasted pumpkin and ginger sauce, or calves' liver with bacon, creamed potatoes, onion and red wine sauce. To finish, apart from all those local cheeses, there could be orange posset, apple crumble, or strawberry and cream iced parfait. The wine list runs to more than 40, including several desserts and a fair sprinkling of halves.

LACOCK

Map 04 ST96

The George Inn 🐾 ⛄

4 West St SN15 2LH ☎ 01249 730263
Dir: M4 J17 take A350 S

Steeped in history and much used as a film and television location, this beautiful National Trust village includes an atmospheric inn. The George dates from 1361 and boasts a medieval fireplace, a low-beamed ceiling, mullioned windows, flagstone floors and an old treadwheel by which a dog would drive the spit. Selection of tasty pies, and favourites like chicken and wild mushrooms in red wine, and pork fillet medallions with a Stilton and port sauce.

OPEN: 10-2.30 5-11 **BAR MEALS:** L served all week 12-2 D served all week 6-9.30 Av main course £7.50 **RESTAURANT:** L served all week 12-2 D served all week 6-9.30 Av 3 course à la carte £20 Av 3 course fixed price £13.95 **BREWERY/COMPANY:** Wadworth
◾: Wadworth 6X, Henrys IPA, J.C.B & Farmers Glory. ⛄: 13
FACILITIES: Children welcome Garden: Large patio, Grass area, Swings, See-Saw Dogs allowed **NOTES:** Parking 40

Red Lion Inn 🐾 ⛄

1 High St SN15 2LQ ☎ 01249 730456 📠 01249 730766
Dir: just off A350 between Chippenham & Melksham

Set in a National Trust village immortalised in many a TV and film recording, the Red Lion dates from the 1700s. The older part of the building has exposed timbers and a large open fire. The same menu is offered throughout, and the bestselling dishes are the home-made pies, casseroles and vegetarian items. Fishy dishes include whole tail scampi, breaded cod, red snapper and fisherman's platter.

OPEN: 11.30-3 6-11 (all day weekends) **BAR MEALS:** L served all week 12-2.30 D served all week 6-9 Av main course £6.95
RESTAURANT: L served all week 12-2.30 D served all week 6-9 Av 3 course à la carte £15 **BREWERY/COMPANY:** Wadworth
◾: Wadworth Henry's IPA & 6X, JCB, plus guests. **FACILITIES:** Children welcome Garden: Patio, food served outdoors Dogs allowed
NOTES: Parking 70 **ROOMS:** 6 bedrooms 6 en suite s£55 d£75

The Rising Sun ⛄

32 Bowden Hill SN15 2PP ☎ 01249 730363
The pub is located close to the National Trust village of Lacock, on a steep hill, providing spectacular views over Wiltshire from the large garden. Live music and quiz nights are a regular feature, and games and reading material are provided in the bar. Thai curries and stirfries are popular options, alongside traditional liver, bacon and onions.

OPEN: 12-3 6-11 (Sun 12-5, 7-10.30) **BAR MEALS:** L served all week 12-2 D served Wed-Sat 7-9 ◾: Moles Best, Moles Molennium, Molecatcher, Tap Bitter. **FACILITIES:** Children welcome Garden Dogs allowed Water **NOTES:** Parking 25

LIMPLEY STOKE

Map 04 ST76

The Hop Pole Inn 🐾

Woods Hill, Lower Limpley Stoke BA3 6HS
☎ 01225 723134 📠 01225 723199
e-mail: latonahop@aol.com
Dir: Off A36 (Bath to Warminster road)

The Hop Pole is set in the beautiful Limpley Stoke valley and dates from 1580, the name coming from the hop plant that still grows outside the pub. Eagle-eyed film fans may recognise it as the pub in the 1992 film 'Remains of the Day'. A hearty menu includes home-made pies, fresh local trout, and home-made specials such as Thai chicken, liver and bacon casserole, and whole plaice meunière. Giant filled baps and other light bites are available.

continued

OPEN: 11-2.30 6-11 (Sun 12-3, 7-10.30) Closed: 25 Dec
BAR MEALS: L served all week 12-2.15 D served all week 6.30-9.15 Av main course £7.95 **RESTAURANT:** L served all week 12-2.15 D served all week 6.30-9.15 Av 3 course à la carte £15.50
BREWERY/COMPANY: Free House ◾: Scottish Courage Courage Best, Butcombe Bitter, Interbrew Bass, Guest Beers.
FACILITIES: Children welcome Garden: Large garden, patio, 15 benches Dogs allowed **NOTES:** Parking 20

LITTLE CHEVERELL

Map 04 ST95

The Owl 🐾 ⛄

Low Rd SN10 4JS ☎ 01380 812263
e-mail: jamie@theowl.info
Dir: A344 from Stonehenge, then A360, after 10m L onto B3098, R after 0.5m, Owl signposted

Recently refurbished 19th-century local situated well off-the-beaten-track in a tiny hamlet surrounded by farmland, with views of Salisbury Plain and plenty of good walks. The pretty split-level garden runs down to the Cheverell Brook. Home-cooked food might include tournedos Rossini, game pie, Thai chicken curry or sea bass with lemon and parsley stuffing. In April and August the pub hosts a beer festival (21 ales, 21 wines, live music and a barbecue).

OPEN: 11-3 6.30-11 (Sat 11-11) **BAR MEALS:** L served all week 12-3 D served all week 7-10 Av main course £7.95 **RESTAURANT:** L served all week 12-3 D served all week 7-10 Av 3 course à la carte £18 **BREWERY/COMPANY:** Free House ◾: Wadworth 6X, Hook Norton Best, Cotleigh Tawney Owl, Scottish Courage Courage Directors. ⛄: 23 **FACILITIES:** Children welcome Children's licence Garden: Decked area, brook, benches Dogs allowed Water **NOTES:** Parking 20

LOWER CHICKSGROVE

Map 04 ST92

Pick of the Pubs

Compasses Inn 🐾 ⛄

SP3 6NB ☎ 01722 714318 📠 01722 714318
e-mail: thecompasses@aol.com
Dir: A30 W from Salisbury, after 10m R signed Chicksgrove

Genuine 14th-century thatched inn set in the beautiful Nadder Valley, which despite its remote rural location attracts customers from quite some distance. These discerning folk happily negotiate the narrow lanes and old cobbled pathway leading to the inn's latched door, for the sake of the local real ales and imaginative food. Inside, the long, low-beamed bar has stone walls, worn flagstone floors and a large inglenook fireplace with a wood-burning stove. Here an ever-changing blackboard menu might feature pork tenderloin with cider, Vinny and apple sauce; lamb shoulder with soy and molasses, or pigeon with wild mushrooms in Madeira sauce. Lunchtime snacks are offered and some good desserts - maybe brioche bread and butter pudding with banana and rum. The garden has a cobbled area for outside eating affording stunning country views.

OPEN: 12-3 6-11 Closed: Tue after BH Mon **BAR MEALS:** L served Tue-Sun 12-2 D served Tue-Sat 7-9 Av main course £11 **RESTAURANT:** L served Tues-Sun 12-2 D served Tues-Sat 7-9 Av 3 course à la carte £20 **BREWERY/COMPANY:** Free House ◾: Interbrew Bass, Wadworth 6X, Ringwood Best, Chicksgrove Churl. ⛄: 7 **FACILITIES:** Children welcome Garden: Large grass area with nice views, seats 20 Dogs allowed Water **NOTES:** Parking 30

OWER WOODFORD Map 05 SU13

he Wheatsheaf 🛏 ♀
P4 6NQ ☎ 01722 782203
ir: Take A360 N of Salisbury. Village signposted 1st R
nce a farm and brewhouse, now a thriving country pub in
e Avon Valley. A rustic décor gives the interior a
ontemporary twist. Expect dishes like seared tuna steak with
mon and coriander butter, salmon and dill fishcakes, and
aditional cod and chips. Steak and Tanglefoot ale pie,
umberland sausage and mash, and slow-roasted lamb shank
hould also be available.
PEN: 11-11 (sun 12.10.30) **BAR MEALS:** L served all week 12-
.30 D served all week Av main course £7.50 **RESTAURANT:** L
rved all week 12-2.30 D served all week 7-9.30
BREWERY/COMPANY: Hall & Woodhouse 🍺: Badger Dorset Best
Tanglefoot, plus guest ales. **FACILITIES:** Children welcome
arden: Food served outside. Enclosed garden Dogs allowed In the
arden only **NOTES:** Parking 50

UDWELL Map 04 ST92

Grove Arms Inn 🛏
P7 9ND ☎ 01747 828328 📠 01747 828960
ir: On main A30 Shaftesbury to Salisbury Rd 3 M from Shaftesbury
rade II listed thatched inn, completely refurbished. Home-
ooked pub food includes steaks (up to 40oz!), smoked
addock in creamy sauce, cod in batter, steak and kidney
udding, and chicken curry, all cooked "just like mum does".
he owners pride themselves on their Sunday roast, and
elicious desserts like spotted Dick, sherry trifle, apple pie,
nd peach melba.
PEN: 12-11 **BAR MEALS:** L served all week 12-2.30 D served all
eek Av main course £6 **RESTAURANT:** L served all week 12-2.30
serve all week 6-9.30 Av 3 course à la carte £15
BREWERY/COMPANY: Free House 🍺: Ringwood Best & 49er,
reene King IPA. **FACILITIES:** Children welcome **NOTES:** Parking
0

MALMESBURY Map 04 ST98

Pick of the Pubs

Horse & Groom ♦♦♦♦♦ 🏵 ♀
The Street, Charlton SN16 9DL
☎ 01666 823904 📠 01666 823390
Dir: from M4 head toward Malmesbury, 2nd rdbt go R towards
Cricklade on B4040, premises through the village on the left

A 16th-century coaching inn set amid lovely Cotswold
countryside, with its own pleasant garden complete with
duck-pond. Sympathetic conversion has brought the three

bedrooms, two bars and the dining room up to modern
expectations without any detriment to the inn's inherent
character. Log fires burn in winter, and drinks and snacks
are served outdoors in fine weather. The well-chosen real
ales attract a loyal local following, and the menus have
wide appeal. Options range from light bites in the
Charlton Bar - paninis, sandwiches, burgers and pub
favourites like ham, egg and chips, chilli con carne and
even a chip butty - to more substantial meals in the
restaurant. The latter might offer smoked kedgeree of smoked
haddock and salmon, seasonal game casserole with herb
dumplings and game chips, and blueberry spotted dick on
blueberry compôte.
OPEN: 12-3 7-11 (all day Wknds) Closed: 25-26 Dec
BAR MEALS: L served all week 12-2 D served all week 7-10 Av
main course £4 **RESTAURANT:** L served all week 12-2 D served
all week 7-10 Av 3 course à la carte £22
BREWERY/COMPANY: Free House 🍺: Wadworth 6X, Archers
Village, Smiles Best, Uley Old Spot. ♀: 10 **FACILITIES:** Garden:
Seating available on grass and at front Dogs allowed Water,
biscuits **NOTES:** Parking 40 **ROOMS:** 3 bedrooms 3 en suite
s£60 d£80 no children overnight

The Smoking Dog ♀
62 The High St SN16 9AT ☎ 01666 825823 📠 01666 8296273
Log fires, solid wooden floors and a relaxed atmosphere
greet visitors to this refined 18th-century stone-built pub, right
in the heart of Malmesbury. There's an expanding range of
real ales that features continually-changing guest beers, and
the pub has a good reputation for interesting, freshly-cooked
food. Expect a daily choice of home-made soup and hot-pot,
plus cod brochettes, smoked salmon and home-made
burgers.
OPEN: 11.30-11 (Sun 12-10.30) **BAR MEALS:** L served all week 12-
2 D served all week 7-9.30 Av main course £9.50 **RESTAURANT:** L
served all week 12-2 D served all week 7-9.30 Av 3 course à la carte
£18.95 **BREWERY/COMPANY:** 🍺: Wadworth 6X, Archers Best,
Brains Bitter, SA & Reverend James plus guest. **FACILITIES:** Children
welcome Garden: Dogs allowed Water, Biscuits

Pick of the Pubs

The Vine Tree 🛏 ♀
Foxley Rd, Norton SN16 0JP
☎ 01666 837654 📠 01666 838003
See Pick of the Pubs on page 514

MELKSHAM Map 04 ST96

Kings Arms Hotel
Market Place SN12 6EX ☎ 01225 707272 📠 01225 792986
Dir: In the town centre opposite Lloyds Bank
Once an important coaching house on the London to Bath
route, warmth and hospitality are offered by this traditional
market place inn.
OPEN: 11-2.30 6-11 **BAR MEALS:** L served all week 12-2 D served
all week 7-9.30 Av main course £6 **RESTAURANT:** L served all week
12-2 D served all week 7-9 Av 3 course à la carte £12
BREWERY/COMPANY: Wadworth 🍺: Wadworth 6X, Wadworth
Henrys Original IPA, John Smiths, plus guest. **FACILITIES:** Children
welcome Dogs allowed **NOTES:** Parking 30

continued

Open: 12-2.30, 6.30-11 (Sun 12-10.30)
Closed: 25 Dec
Bar Meals: L served all week 12-2,
D served all week 6-9.30.
RESTAURANT: L served all week 12-2,
D served all week 6-9.30.
BREWERY/COMPANY:
Free House.
🍺: Youngs P.A.,
Wychwood Fiddlers Elbow.
FACILITIES: Children welcome, Dogs
allowed, Garden: Terrace with fountain.
NOTES: Parking 100

The Vine Tree

The Vine Tree is a converted 16th-century mill house in the heart of the Wiltshire countryside, close to the famous Westonbirt Arboretum, and well worth seeking out for its interesting modern pub food and memorable outdoor summer dining.

Foxley Road, Norton,
Malmesbury, SN16 0JP
☎ 01666 837654 📠 01666 838003
Dir: 5 minutes from J17 off the M4
on the Wiltshire/Gloucestershire
border.

The tranquil sun-trap terrace includes a fountain, lavender hedge, pagodas, trailing vines and a barbecue. There's also a two-acre garden with a play area to keep the kids entertained, and two boules pitches - a useful addition in a village that hosts the biggest boules competition in England. If the weather isn't up to it, be consoled by the log fire in the main bar, with its old oak beams and flagstone floors. The drinks selection extends to a regular range of real ales, a glass of wine from the carefully selected list (up to 30 available by the glass), or decent cappuccino and espresso coffee. Cooking is modern British in style, and meals are served in the pine-furnished dining areas. The menu changes daily and follows the seasons closely, using local produce wherever possible. A good variety of dishes includes light bites and vegetarian options, and a particularly popular choice is moules marinère made with white wine, garlic, shallots, cream and leeks, and accompanied by home made mini loaves. Other dishes might include a trio of local award-winning sausages, with bubble and squeak and a grain mustard and heather honey sauce, or pan-fried monkfish cheeks with Parma ham, roasted Mediterranean peppers and cherry tomatoes. Imaginative puddings are well represented by 'Wardens in Comfort', a William pear poached in spiced mulled claret, served with home-made shortbread and rosemary-scented chocolate sauce.

MERE   Map 04 ST83

The George Inn ♦♦♦ 🛏
The Square BA12 6DR ☎ 01747 860427 📠 01747 861978
Dir: follow signs from A303 into village
Following extensive but careful refurbishment, the former
Talbot Hotel has been reborn as the George. It was built about
1580 and, in 1651, Charles II dined here en route to exile in
France. Today's diners, however, are unlikely to be looking
over their shoulders as they enjoy home-made soups and
gratin dishes, Scottish sirloin, steak and ale pie, succulent local
pork, lamb, poultry and game, traditional Sunday roasts and
West Country cheeses.
OPEN: 11-11 (Mon-Tue 11-3, 6-11 Sun 12-3, 7-10.30)
BAR MEALS: L served all week 12-2.30 D served all week 6.30-9 Av
main course £6.50 **RESTAURANT:** L served all week 12-2 D served
all week 6.30-9 Av 3 course à la carte £16
BREWERY/COMPANY: Hall & Woodhouse 🍺: Champion Ale,
Badger IPA, Tanglefoot, Badger Best. **FACILITIES:** Children welcome
Garden: Patio area **NOTES:** Parking 20 **ROOMS:** 7 bedrooms 7 en
suite s£32.50 d£50

NEWTON TONEY   Map 05 SU24

The Mallet Arms 🍷
SP4 0HF ☎ 01980 629279 📠 01980 629459
e-mail: Malet@doghouse.co.uk
Dir: 8 miles NE of Salisbury on A338, 5 miles SW of A303
Built around 350 years ago, the Mallet stands on the banks of
the River Bourne, originally the bake house for a long gone
Elizabethan manor. It's a village pub with a lively bar scene,
an enthusiastic cricket team, and a 'Flying Mallet' facility
providing outside catering and beer tents for local events.
Food is all home made - beef burgers, fish, curries and lots of
game in season, and special culinary evenings are a regular
occurrence.
OPEN: 11-3 6-11 Closed: 26 Dec, 1 Jan **BAR MEALS:** L served all
week 12-2.30 D served all week 6.30-10 Av main course £7.50
RESTAURANT: L served all week 12-2.30 D served all week 6.30-10 Av
3 course à la carte £20 **BREWERY/COMPANY:** Free House
🍺: Wadworth 6X, Stonehenge Heelstone, Butts Barbus Barbus & local
guest ales. **FACILITIES:** Children welcome Garden: paved with
seating area, large paddock Dogs allowed Water **NOTES:** Parking 30

NUNTON   Map 05 SU12

The Radnor Arms 🛏 🍷
SP5 4HS ☎ 01722 329722
*Dir: From Salisbury ring road take A338 to Ringwood. Nunton signposted
on R*

A popular pub in the centre of the village dating from around
1750. In 1855 it was owned by the local multi-talented

brewer/baker/grocer then bought by Lord Radnor in 1919. Bar
snacks are supplemented by an extensive fish choice and daily
specials, which might include braised lamb shank, wild
mushroom risotto, turbot with spinach or Scotch rib-eye fillet,
all freshly prepared. Fine summer garden with rural views.
Hosts an annual local pumpkin competition.
OPEN: 11-3 6-11 (Sun 12-3, Sun 7-10.30) **BAR MEALS:** L served
all week 12-2.30 D served Mon-Sat 7-9.30 **RESTAURANT:** L served
all week 12-2.30 D served Mon-Sat 7-9.30 Av 3 course à la carte
£19.25 **BREWERY/COMPANY:** Hall & Woodhouse 🍺: Badger
Tanglefoot, Best & Golden Champion. **FACILITIES:** Children
welcome Garden: Food served outside Dogs allowed
NOTES: Parking 40

PEWSEY   Map 05 SU16

The French Horn 🛏 🍷
Marlborough Rd SN9 5NT ☎ 01672 562443 📠 01672 562785
e-mail: info@french-horn-pewsey.co.uk
Dir: A338 thru Hungerford, at Burbage take B3087 to Pewsey
Popular local pub set beside historic Pewsey Wharf on the
Kennet & Avon Canal, busy with walkers and cyclists.
Napoleonic prisoners of war working on the canal were
summoned to the inn for meals by the sound of a French
horn. Quality food is served in the restaurant - confit of
Barbary duck leg, smoked haddock rarebit, pan-fried rib-eye
steak, and the bar - vegetable quiche, beef stew and
dumplings, ploughman's platter.
OPEN: 11-2.30 6.30-11 25 Dec Closed: evening **BAR MEALS:** L
served all week 12-2 D served all week 6.30-9 Av main course £4.95
RESTAURANT: L served all week 12-2 D served all week 7-9 Av 3
course à la carte £20 **BREWERY/COMPANY:** Wadworth
🍺: Wadworth 6X, Henry's Original IPA, JCB. **FACILITIES:** Children
welcome Garden: Beer garden, food served outdoors Dogs allowed
Water **NOTES:** Parking 20

Pick of the Pubs

The Seven Stars 🛏 🍷
Bottlesford SN9 6LU ☎ 01672 851325 📠 01672 851583
e-mail: sevenstars@dialin.net
Dir: Off A345
Well worth seeking out for its splendid seven-acre garden
alone, is this thatched, creeper-clad 16th-century pub.
Appropriately, it's tucked away in the hamlet of Bottlesford
in the heart of the Vale of Pewsey. The front door opens
straight on to the low-beamed, black oak-panelled bar,
with dining areas to the left and right. Chef and co-owner
Philippe Cheminade's Gallic origins show through in
dishes such as Brittany seafood platter, fillet of pork with
plums and Armagnac, and smoked salmon Niçoise. But
forget national labels: if they happen to be on the menu,
just enjoy grilled strawberry grouper with herbs and roast
vegetables, jugged hare, whole crab with mayonnaise and
salad, or confit of duck with sauté potatoes. Snacks include
decent sandwiches, filled baguettes and ploughman's. An
unusual conversation piece is Lily, the giant elephant
dropping from Botswana, which 'entered this world' in
November 2002 and now sits in a glass case.
OPEN: 12-3 6-11 (closed Sun eve & all Mon) **BAR MEALS:** L
served Tue-Sun 12-2 D served Tue-Sat 7-9.30 Av main course
£10.75 **RESTAURANT:** L served Tue-Sun 12-2 D served Tue-Sat
7-9.30 Av 3 course à la carte £20 Av 3 course fixed price £16
BREWERY/COMPANY: Free House 🍺: Wadworth 6X, Badger
Dorset Best, Fullers London Pride. 🍷: 9 **FACILITIES:** Garden:
Lawned with terrace at front of pub **NOTES:** Parking 50

continued

PEWSEY continued

The Woodbridge Inn

North Newton SN9 6JZ ☎ 01980 630266 ▤ 01980 630457
e-mail: woodbridgeinn@btconnect.com

Dir: 2m SW on A345

Variously a toll house, bakery and brewhouse, this Grade II-listed, 16th-century building stands in over four acres of beautiful grounds by the Wiltshire/Hampshire Avon. Dishes range from pub traditional to sizzling stirfries, by way of Mexican, grilled chicken and pork, hot open ciabatta melts and big open sandwiches. An interesting main course is lamb, pork or duck stincotto, an Italian treatment in which the leg is gently cooked until meltingly tender and then served with an appropriate sauce.

OPEN: 12-11.30 (Sun 12-10.30) Closed: Jan 1 **BAR MEALS:** L served all week 12-10 D served all week 12-10 Av main course £6.95 **RESTAURANT:** L served all week 12-10 D served all week 12-10 Av 3 course à la carte £17.50 **BREWERY/COMPANY:** Wadworth ◀: Wadworth 6X, Henrys IPA, Summersault & Old Timer. **FACILITIES:** Children welcome Garden: Large grassed with flower beds Dogs allowed Water **NOTES:** Parking 60

PITTON   Map 05 SU23

Pick of the Pubs

The Silver Plough 🐾 Ÿ

White Hill SP5 1DU ☎ 01722 712266 ▤ 01722 712266

Dir: From Salisbury take A30 towards Andover, Pitton signposted (approx 3m)

Surrounded by rolling countryside and with a peaceful garden, this popular pub is at the heart of a village full of thatched houses. Converted from a farmstead around 60 years ago, inside you will find beams strung with antique glass rolling pins - said to bring good luck - along with bootwarmers, toby jugs and various other artefacts. It also features a skittle alley adjacent to the snug bar and there are darts and board games available. It is within easy reach of many lovely downland and woodland walks. Hughen and Joyce Riley took over as hosts at The Silver Plough in late 2002 and offer a range of dishes at both lunchtime and evening, including children's meals. House specialities include half a roast shoulder of lamb with mint and garlic gravy, and red bream fillet with caramelised onions, prosciutto and pesto sauce. We welcome further feedback from readers.

OPEN: 11-3 6-11 (Sun 12-3, 6-10.30) **BAR MEALS:** L served all week 12-2.30 D served all week 7-9.30 Av main course £8 **RESTAURANT:** L served all week 12-2.30 D served all week 7-9.30 Av 3 course à la carte £18 **BREWERY/COMPANY:** Hall & Woodhouse ◀: Badger Tanglefoot, Dorset Best, IPA & King & Barnes Sussex. **FACILITIES:** Children welcome Garden: Lots of bench tables Dogs allowed Water, biscuits **NOTES:** Parking 50

RAMSBURY   Map 05 SU27

Pick of the Pubs

The Bell 🐾 Ÿ

The Square SN8 2PE ☎ 01672 520230

Refurbished in a light and contemporary style, The Bell is in the centre of Ramsbury and has a pretty garden to the rear. The chef provides a fresh and innovative menu,

continued

described as "northern with a southern twist", producing strong flavours and imaginative combinations using local produce. Desserts are also a speciality. The well-kept cellar offers good real ales, while the constantly-changing wine list offers a colourful journey around the world's vineyards.

OPEN: 12-3 6-11 **BAR MEALS:** L served Tue-Sun 12-2 D served Tue-Sat 7-9 Av main course £9 **RESTAURANT:** L served all week 12-2 D served Mon-Sat 7-9 Av 3 course à la carte £18 **BREWERY/COMPANY:** Free House ◀: Butts, Wadworth 6X & Henry's Original IPA, West Berkshire, Arkells. Ÿ: 15 **FACILITIES:** Children welcome Garden: Country garden Dogs allowed Water bowls **NOTES:** Parking 20

ROWDE   Map 04 ST96

Pick of the Pubs

The George and Dragon ◉ 🐾 Ÿ

High St SN10 2PN ☎ 01380 723053 ▤ 0871 242 2964
e-mail: gdrowde@tiscali.co.uk

Fascinating features of this 17th-century hostelry include a tunnel linking the building to the old vicarage in the village, which is not far from the Caen Hill flight of locks on the Kennet and Avon Canal. The pub, which dates back to 1675, has panelled bars and a dining room seasonally warmed by log fires. Tim Withers' daily-changed menus have shown real consistency over the years, with fresh fish from Cornwall the highlight. Among the starters, provençale fish soup with rouille, Gruyère and garlic croutons is a favourite alongside tasty fishcakes with hollandaise. There are good meat dishes, but the breadth of the fish menu is often just too tempting. Steamed sea bass with ginger, soy and spring onion; Thai curry of lobster, monkfish and squid; or beer-battered cod with coriander chutney may well be on offer. There's an appealing selection of bottled beers and wines by the glass as well as good ales on tap.

continued

OPEN: 12-3 7-11 (Closed Mon morning) Closed: 25 Dec, 1 Jan
BAR MEALS: L served Tues-Sat 12-2 D served Tues-Sat 7-10 Av
main course £15 RESTAURANT: L served Tues-Sat 12-2 D
served Tues-Sat 7-10 Av 3 course à la carte £25 Av 3 course fixed
price £12.50 BREWERY/COMPANY: Free House ⬛: Hop
Back Summer Lightning, Butcombe Bitter, Milk Street Brewery,
Bath Ales. ♀: 9 FACILITIES: Children welcome Garden: Lawn
area Dogs allowed Water NOTES: Parking 10

SALISBURY   Map 05 SU12

The Coach & Horses 🛏️
Winchester St SP1 1HG ☎ 01722 414319 📠 01722 414319
Many changes have taken place in its 500-year history, but the
black and white timbered facade of Salisbury's oldest inn
remains. Slate-floored bar and cobbled courtyard.
OPEN: 11.30-11 (Sun 12-10.30) BAR MEALS: L served Mon-Sat D
served Mon-Sat 11.30-9.30 RESTAURANT: L served Sat D served Sat
Av 3 course à la carte £17 BREWERY/COMPANY: Scottish &
Newcastle FACILITIES: Children welcome Garden: Dogs allowed

The Old Mill Hotel ♀
Town Path, West Harnham SP2 8EU
☎ 01722 327517 📠 01722 333367
e-mail: oldmill@ingoodcompany.co.uk
Dir: near city centre, on River Avon
Listed building which became Wiltshire's first papermaking
mill in 1550. Tranquil meadow setting with classic views of
Salisbury Cathedral. Crystal clear water diverted from the
River Nadder cascades through the restaurant.
OPEN: 11-11 BAR MEALS: L served all week 12-2.30 D served all
week 7-9 Av main course £4.95 RESTAURANT: L served all week
12-2 D served all week 7-9 Av 3 course à la carte £18
BREWERY/COMPANY: Eldridge Pope ⬛: Greene King IPA, Old
Speckled Hen & Ruddles Smooth. FACILITIES: Children welcome
Garden: Food served outside Dogs allowed NOTES: Parking 10

SEEND   Map 04 ST96

The Barge Inn 🛏️ ♀
Seend Cleeve SN12 6QB ☎ 01380 828230 📠 01380 828972
Dir: Off A365 between Melksham & Devizes

Delightfully-situated Victorian barge-style pub, converted from
a wharf house, on the Kennet and Avon Canal between Bath
and Devizes. Note the delicately-painted Victorian flowers
adorning the ceilings and upper walls. Once upon a time it
was home to 8'2" Fred Kempster, the 'Wiltshire Giant'. In
addition to the lunchtime menu of snacks and hot dishes
(wharfman's purse and navvie's pie, for example), there's a
seasonal carte supported by blackboard specials with daily
vegetarian, meat and fish options.

OPEN: 11-3 6-11 BAR MEALS: L served all week 12-2 D served all
week 7-9.30 Av main course £9 RESTAURANT: L served all week
12-2 D served all week 7-9.30 BREWERY/COMPANY: Wadworth
⬛: Wadworth 6X & Henry's IPA, Badger Tanglefoot, Butcombe Bitter.
FACILITIES: Children welcome Garden: Large canal side garden
Dogs allowed Water NOTES: Parking 50

Bell Inn 🛏️
Bell Hill SN12 6SA ☎ 01380 828338
e-mail: Bellseend@aol.com
Local tradition has it that Oliver Cromwell and his troops
breakfasted at this inn on 18 September 1645, when
advancing from Trowbridge to attack Devizes Castle. The pub
has been extended to include the old brewhouse, a two-floor
restaurant with wonderful views over the valley. House
specialities include Thai green chicken, beef and Stilton pie,
chicken cacciatore, and spinach and ricotta cannelloni. A good
choice of fish dishes is also offered.
OPEN: 11-3 5.30-11 Jan-May, Oct-Nov Closed Tues BAR MEALS: L
served all week 11.45-2.15 D served all week 6.15-9.30 Av main course
£6.75 RESTAURANT: 11.45-2.15 6.15-9.30
BREWERY/COMPANY: Wadworth ⬛: Wadworth 6X, Henry's IPA
& Henrys Smooth. FACILITIES: Children welcome Garden: Lrg,
seating for 60 people, beautiful views Dogs allowed Water
NOTES: Parking 30

SHERSTON   Map 04 ST88

Carpenters Arms 🛏️ ♀ NEW
SN16 0LS ☎ 01666 840665
Dir: On the B4040 W of Malmesbury
A locals' pub of whitewashed Cotswold stone dating from the
17th century. It has four interconnecting rooms, with low,
beamed ceilings, a wood-burner and a cosy old-world
atmosphere. The sunny conservatory restaurant overlooks the
garden - a gardener's delight with its large variety of shrubs,
climbers, specimen roses, acers and herbaceous perennials.
Seasonal fish dishes are served alongside pies, venison
sausages, smoked salmon crêpes, and mushroom and paprika
parcels.
OPEN: 12-2.30 5-11 (Sat 10-2.30, Sun 7-10.30) BAR MEALS: L
served all week 12-2 D served Mon-Sat 7-9 Av main course £7.50
RESTAURANT: L served all week 12-2 D served Mon-Sat 7-9 Av 3
course à la carte £15 BREWERY/COMPANY: Enterprise Inns
⬛: Interbrew Flowers IPA & Whitbread Best, Guest Ales. ♀: 7
FACILITIES: Children welcome Garden: Plantsmans garden, array of
plants NOTES: Parking 12

The Rattlebone Inn ♀
Church St SN16 0LR ☎ 01666 840871 📠 01666 840871
Dir: M4 J18 take A46 towards Stroud, then R onto B4040 through Acton
Turville & onto Sherston. Or N from M4 J17 & follow signs
A 16th-century village inn standing where, according to
legend, local hero John Rattlebone died of his wounds after
the Battle of Sherston in 1016. The rambling series of beamed
rooms have kept their existing character, and the inn offers a
good choice of imaginative dishes: expect perhaps Welsh
lamb noisettes, stuffed chicken breasts, and chargrilled
swordfish steak.
OPEN: 12-11 BAR MEALS: L served all week 12-2 D served all
week 7-9 Av main course £8.95 RESTAURANT: L served all week
12-2 D served all week 7-9 Av 3 course à la carte £17.50
BREWERY/COMPANY: Young & Co ⬛: Youngs Special, Bitter,
Smiles Best, Youngs Triple A. FACILITIES: Children welcome
Garden: Food served outside

continued

STOFORD
Map 05 SU03

The Swan Inn ♦♦♦ 🕙 NEW
SP2 0PR ☎ 01722 790236 📠 01722 790115
e-mail: info@theswanatstoford.co.uk
Picturesque views of the Wylye Valley can be enjoyed from
the riverside garden and bar of this former coaching inn.
Dating back over 300 years, the family-owned inn has been
extended and renovated over the years, and is now well
known locally for its good food. A typical meal starts with
pan-fried mushrooms in a Stilton and port sauce, moves on to
honey-marinated shoulder of lamb, and ends with apple pie
with maple syrup.
OPEN: 11-3 6-11 **BAR MEALS:** L served all week 12-2 D served all
week 6.30-9 Av main course £9 **RESTAURANT:** L served all week
12-2 D served all week 6.30-9 Av 3 course à la carte £15 Av 3 course
fixed price £9.75 🍺: Ringwood Best, Greene King Old Speckled Hen,
Swan Inn Best, Fuller's London Pride. **FACILITIES:** Garden: 1 garden
by river, landscaped garden at rear **NOTES:** Parking 100
ROOMS: 9 bedrooms 9 en suite 2 family rooms s£35 d£45 no
children overnight

STOURHEAD
Map 04 ST73

Spread Eagle Inn 🕙 ♀
BA12 6QE ☎ 01747 840587 📠 01747 840954
e-mail: thespreadeagle@aol.com
Dir: N of A303 off B3092
Fine 18th-century brick inn peacefully located in the heart of
Stourhead Estate (NT), just yards from the magnificent
landscaped gardens, enchanting lakes and woodland walks.
Popular all day with visitors seeking refreshment, it offers
traditional pub food, including lasagne, steak and kidney pie
and sandwiches.
BAR MEALS: L served all week 12-3 D served all week 6-9 Av main
course £5.50 **RESTAURANT:** D served all week 6-9 Av 3 course à la
carte £19 **BREWERY/COMPANY:** Free House 🍺: Courage Best,
Wadworth 6X. **FACILITIES:** Children welcome Garden:
NOTES: Parking 200

SWINDON
Map 05 SU18

The Sun Inn 🕙 ♀
Lydiard Millicent SN5 3LU ☎ 01793 770425 📠 01793 778287
e-mail: bleninns@clara.net
Dir: 3 miles to the W of Swindon, 1.5 miles from Junct 16 of M4

Two restaurants have been created from old ground-level
cellars at this 18th-century pub in the conservation area of
Lydiard Millicent. Completely restored in recent years, the
inn has exposed beams, open fires and antique furnishings
throughout. The gardens include a large grassed area with
picnic tables and barbecue. Snacks, full meals and some

adventurous daily specials are all offered. Popular choices
include rack of lamb with leek and herb mash, and
faggots, black pudding and onions with mash and onion
gravy.
OPEN: 11.30-2.30 5.30-11 **BAR MEALS:** L served all week 12-2.30
D served all week 6.30-9.30 Av main course £8.50 **RESTAURANT:** L
served all week 12-2.30 D served all week 6.30-9.30 Av 3 course à la
carte £17 **BREWERY/COMPANY:** Free House 🍺: Hook Norton
Best, Fuller's London Pride, Interbrew Flowers original, Wadsworth 6X.
♀: 8 **FACILITIES:** Children welcome Garden: Large garden for BBQ
Dogs allowed Water **NOTES:** Parking 50

TOLLARD ROYAL
Map 04 ST91

King John Inn 🕙
SP5 5PS ☎ 01725 516207
Dir: On B3081 (7m E of Shaftesbury)
A Victorian building, opened in 1859, the King John is a
friendly and relaxing place. Nearby is a 13th-century church,
and it is also a good area for walkers. Typical menu offers
casseroled rump and kidney, lamb with cranberry and
orange, plaice goujons, garlic king prawns, and beer-battered
cod.
OPEN: 12-2.30 6.30-11 (Sun 12-10.30) **BAR MEALS:** L served all
week 12-2 D served all week 7-9 Av main course £4.95
RESTAURANT: L served all week 12-2 D served all week 7-9 Av 3
course à la carte £12 **BREWERY/COMPANY:** Free House
🍺: Courage Best, John Smith's, Wadworth 6X, Ringwood.
FACILITIES: Garden: Terrace, food served outside Dogs allowed
Water **NOTES:** Parking 18

UPPER CHUTE
Map 05 SU25

The Cross Keys 🕙 ♀
SP11 9ER ☎ 01264 730295 📠 01264 730679
Dir: Near Andover
Located in a walkers' paradise on top of the North Wessex
Downs, this free house adjoins a village shop and post office
and boasts commanding views from its south-facing terrace
and garden. People flock here by foot, bike and car to enjoy
the views, the welcome and of course good home-cooked
food: perhaps cottage pie, Irish stew, Sunday roast or cod and
chips.
OPEN: 11-3 6-11 (Sun 12-4, 7-10.30) **BAR MEALS:** L served all
week 12-2 D served all week 6-9 Av main course £7.50
RESTAURANT: L served all week 12-2 D served all week 6-9 Av 3
course à la carte £15 **BREWERY/COMPANY:** Free House
🍺: Fuller's London Pride, Hampshire Strong's Best, Greene King IPA,
Ringwood Best. ♀: 10 **FACILITIES:** Children welcome Children's
licence Garden: picnic tables, patio area, chairs Dogs allowed Water,
doggie treats **NOTES:** Parking 40

UPTON LOVELL
Map 04 ST94

Prince Leopold 🕙 ♀
BA12 0JP ☎ 01985 850460 📠 01985 850737
e-mail: Princeleopold@Lineone.net
Dir: S of A36 between Warminster & Salisbury
Built in 1887 as a general store and post office, the inn is
named after Queen Victoria's youngest son, who was a
frequent visitor to the inn when he lived at nearby Boyton.
The River Wylye runs through the garden and there are some
fine views across the meadows to the Great Ridge. Specialities
include a range of authentic balti dishes, bouillabaisse, seared
salmon cured with dill and black pepper, and slow-cooked leg
of lamb.

continued

continued

OPEN: 12-3 7-11 (Not open Sun night) **BAR MEALS:** L served Tue-Sun 12-2.30 D served Tue-Sun 7-10 Av main course £6.30 **RESTAURANT:** L served Tue-Sun 12-2.30 D served Tue-Sun 7-10 Av 3 course à la carte £16.50 **BREWERY/COMPANY:** Free House **:** Ringwood Best, Scottish Courage John Smith's. **:** 8 **FACILITIES:** Children welcome Garden: Riverside garden, spectacular views **NOTES:** Parking 20

WARMINSTER · Map 04 ST84

Pick of the Pubs

The Angel Inn ♦♦♦♦ ⊚ 📷 ⏛
Upton Scudamore BA12 0AG
☎ 01985 213225 📠 01985 218182
e-mail: theangelinn.uptonscudamore@btopenworld.com
A relaxed and unpretentious old inn in a small village with a name Agatha Christie might have made up. Freshly-prepared lunch could be Cumberland sausage with horseradish mash and blackcurrant sauce, or game casserole with juniper berries and bacon dumplings. Dinner candidates include honey-glazed breast of duck with cumin and sweet potato pancake and pineapple sauce, or bacon-wrapped gilthead fillet of sea bream with saffron mash, roasted almonds and red curry sauce. Walled terrace garden.
OPEN: 12-3 6-11 Closed: 25-26 Dec, 1 Jan **BAR MEALS:** L served all week 12-2 D served all week 7-9.30 Av main course £13 **RESTAURANT:** L served all week 12-2 D served all week 7-9.30 Av 3 course à la carte £20 **BREWERY/COMPANY:** Free House **:** Wadworth 6X, Butcombe, Scottish Courage John Smith's Smooth, Guest Ales. **:** 8 **FACILITIES:** Children welcome Garden: Walled terrace Dogs allowed Water provided **NOTES:** Parking 30 **ROOMS:** 10 bedrooms 10 en suite 3 family rooms s£60 d£75

The Bath Arms 📷 ⏛ NEW
Clay St, Crockerton BA12 8AJ ☎ 01985 212262 📠 01985 218670
A new entry to the Guide after a decade or so of neglect. Chef/proprietor Dean Carr took over in late 2002, bringing

with him the experience gained from stints at London's Langan's Brasserie, The Ivy and The Avenue. Among his offerings are sticky beef with braised red cabbage, saddle of rabbit with Denhay ham, white beans and leeks, fishcake with Cornish crab and broad beans, River Wylye trout with capers and anchovies, grills, snacks and baguettes.
OPEN: 11-3 6-11 (open all day in Summer) **BAR MEALS:** L served all week 12-2.30 D served all week 6-9.30 Av main course £8.75 **RESTAURANT:** L served all week 12-2.30 D served all week 6-9.30 Av 3 course à la carte £16.25 **:** Butcombe Courage, Crockerton Classic, Burlington Bertie, Blackrat. **:** 10 **FACILITIES:** Children welcome Garden: Stone walled, lawned garden, 19 tables & BBQ Dogs allowed Water bowls **NOTES:** Parking 45

The George Inn ♦♦♦♦
BA12 7DG ☎ 01985 840396 📠 01985 841333

The hub of local activity in the small village of Longbridge Devrill, the George is a picturesque 200-year-old inn in two acres of engaging riverside setting. The ten bedrooms have recently had a makeover to meet modern-day expectations. Bar snacks feature home-made pâté, steak and ale pie, and lasagne plus daily specials, while the restaurant promises the likes of medallions of beef fillet and shanks of lamb supplied by the village butcher. There's a patio and beer garden, and a separate function suite.
OPEN: 11-11 25 Dec Closed eve **BAR MEALS:** L served all week 12-2.30 D served all week 6.30-9.30 Av main course £8.95 **RESTAURANT:** L served all week 12-2.30 D served all week 6.30-9.30 Av 3 course à la carte £16.95 **BREWERY/COMPANY:** Free House **:** Scottish Courage John Smith's, Wadworth 6X, Interbrew Bass. **FACILITIES:** Garden: Lrg riverside setting **NOTES:** Parking 50 **ROOMS:** 10 bedrooms 10 en suite 1 family rooms s£40 d£60 no children overnight

WESTBURY · Map 04 ST85

The Duke at Bratton 📷 ⏛
Melbourne St, Bratton BA13 4RW
☎ 01380 830242 📠 01380 831239
Dir: from Westbury follow B3098

continued

continued

England

WESTBURY continued

A "Country Inn with Rooms and Restaurant" fairly describes this pub in the centre of a picturesque village beneath the famous White Horse. Built up from virtually nothing by its current licensees, its reputation continues to grow (it holds awards not only for its wonderful Sunday dinners, but also for the standard of its loos!). Seasonal menus include plenty of salads, vegetarian dishes and traditional favourites like Wiltshire ham with egg and chips or local chicken breast poached in white wine.
OPEN: 11.30-3 7-11 **BAR MEALS:** L served all week 12-2 D served Mon-Sat 7-9 Av main course £6.50 **RESTAURANT:** L served Tues-Sun 12-2 D served Tues-Sat 7-9 Av 3 course à la carte £15
BREWERY/COMPANY: Free House ▪: Moles Best, Scottish Courage Courage Best, Interbrew Bass, John Smiths Bitter. **FACILITIES:** Garden: Large beer garden at rear Dogs allowed Water **NOTES:** Parking 30

WHITLEY
Map 04 ST86

Pick of the Pubs

The Pear Tree Inn ◉ ⌂ ♀
Top Ln SN12 8QX ☎ 01225 709131 ▤ 01225 702276
Dir: A365 from Melksham toward Bath, at Shaw R on B3353 into Whitley, 1st L in lane, pub is at end of lane.

The Pear Tree is a pub/restaurant in a rural setting, surrounded by parkland studded with great oak trees. The gardens are well planted and there is an extensive patio area with solid teak furniture and cream parasols. At the front there's a large boules piste, and the inn annually fields a team for the Bath Boules Competition. The original part of the pub dates back to 1750 when it was a farmstead, and the bar is a comfortable domain for locals with at least four real ales on hand pump. For those who want to eat, a high standard of food is produced from as much locally-sourced produce as possible. A selection of breads is baked from locally-milled stoneground flour, and ice creams and sorbets are made daily on site. Example dishes are roast hake fillet with olive crushed potatoes, sugar snap peas and chive oil, tagliatelle with blue cheese, broccoli and toasted almonds, and pan-fried fillets of seabass with leek mash and creamed spinach.
OPEN: 11-3 6-11 Closed: 25/26 Dec, 1 Jan **BAR MEALS:** L served all week 12-2 D served all week 6.30-9.30 Av main course £11.07
RESTAURANT: L served all week 12-2 D served all week 6.30-9.30 Av 3 course à la carte £24 Av 3 course fixed price £14
BREWERY/COMPANY: Free House ▪: Wadworth 6X, Oakhill Best, Bath Ales Gem, Smiles Best. ♀: 10 **FACILITIES:** Children welcome Garden: Cottage garden with views over parkland **NOTES:** Parking 60

WINTERBOURNE BASSETT
Map 05 SU07

The White Horse Inn ⌂ ♀
SN4 9QB ☎ 01793 731257 ▤ 01793 731257
e-mail: ckstone@btinternet.com

Atmospheric village pub on the Marlborough Downs, two miles north of the legendary Avebury stone circle. Food is served in both the bar and conservatory restaurant, where budget lunches and snacks give way to a full evening menu. Warm chicken and bacon salad, Peking prawns in filo pastry, or lamb Marrakesh, and steamed chocolate sponge make up a typical meal, with a specials board to extend the choice.
OPEN: 11-3 7-11 **BAR MEALS:** L served all week 12-2.30 D served all week 7-10 Av main course £8.50 **RESTAURANT:** L served all week 12-2.30 D served all week 7-10 Av 3 course à la carte £15 Av 2 course fixed price £4.95 **BREWERY/COMPANY:** Wadworth ▪: Wadworth 6X, IPA, Hophouse Brews. ♀: 9
FACILITIES: Garden: Safe lawned area with wooden benches **NOTES:** Parking 25

WOODFALLS
Map 05 SU12

The Woodfalls Inn ♦♦♦♦ ⌂ ♀
The Ridge SP5 2LN ☎ 01725 513222 ▤ 01725 513220
e-mail: woodfallsi@aol.com
Dir: B3080 to Woodfalls
Built in 1868 as an ale house and coaching inn on the northern edge of the New Forest, this attractively-refurbished inn offers well-equipped bedrooms and a good range of food from the bar menu and restaurant à la carte. Typical examples include pan-fried chicken with bacon topped with cheese, steak and ale pie, swordfish steak in Thai sauce, and salmon steak.
OPEN: 11-11 **BAR MEALS:** L served all week 12-2.15 D served all week 6.30-9.30 Av main course £6.95 **RESTAURANT:** L served all week 12-2.15 D served all week 6.30-9 **BREWERY/COMPANY:** Free House ▪: Courage Directors & Best, HSB, Hopback's GFB, John Smiths. ♀: 9 **FACILITIES:** Children welcome Garden: Dogs allowed Toys & water provided **NOTES:** Parking 40 **ROOMS:** 10 bedrooms 10 en suite 1 family rooms s£49.95 d£77.90

WOOTTON RIVERS
Map 05 SU16

Royal Oak ⌂ ♀
SN8 4NQ ☎ 01672 810322 ▤ 01672 811168
e-mail: royaloak35@hotmail.com
Dir: 3m S from Marlborough
Set in one of Wiltshire's prettiest villages, a thatched and timbered 16th-century inn just 100 yards from the Kennet and Avon Canal, and close to Savernake Forest - a wonderful area for canal and forest walks. Menus are flexible, with light basket meals, ploughman's and sandwiches, and specials like

continued

partridge with game sauce, rich beef and Burgundy casserole, and medallions of pork and leek with a pine nut stuffing.

OPEN: 10.30-3.30 6-11 **BAR MEALS:** L served all week 11.30-2.30 D served all week 6-9.30 Av main course £10 **RESTAURANT:** L served all week 11.30-2.30 D served all week 6-9.30 Av 3 course à la carte £20 Av 3 course fixed price £12.50
BREWERY/COMPANY: Free House 🍺: Wadworth 6X + guest ales.
🍷: 8 **FACILITIES:** Children welcome Garden: Lrg lawn area. Raised terrace with seating Dogs allowed **NOTES:** Parking 20

WYLYE
Map 04 SU03

The Bell Inn ◆◆◆ 🍷
High St, Wylye BA12 0QP ☎ 01985 248338
e-mail: lk.thebell@wylye2.freeserve.co.uk

There's a wealth of old oak beams, log fires and an inglenook fireplace at this 14th-century coaching inn, situated in the pretty Wylye Valley. If that's not enough to satisfy the traditionalist, an equally-authentic home-cooked menu should fit the bill. Not that it's restrictive: alongside British classics (local partridge; braised lamb shank; Gressingham duck) you may encounter smoked trout with haloumi cheese or stuffed peppers with tagliatelle. Quick meals include freshly-cut sandwiches and jacket potatoes.
OPEN: 11.30-2.30 6-11 (Sun 12-3, 7-10.30) **BAR MEALS:** L served all week 12-2 D served all week 6-9.30 Av main course £7.95
RESTAURANT: L served all week 12-2 D served all week 6-9.30 Av 3 course à la carte £25 **BREWERY/COMPANY:** Free House 🍺: Hop Back GFB & Summer Lightning, Ringwood, Stonehenge, Hampshire.
🍷: 7 **FACILITIES:** Children's licence Garden: Walled garden Dogs allowed Water **NOTES:** Parking 20 **ROOMS:** 3 bedrooms 3 en suite 1 family rooms s£35 d£50 no children overnight

We endeavour to be as accurate as possible but changes to times and other information can occur after the guide has gone to press

WORCESTERSHIRE

ABBERLEY
Map 10 SO76

Manor Arms Country Inn 🍷
WR6 6BN ☎ 01299 896507 📠 01299 896723
e-mail: themanorarms@btconnect.com

Set just across the lane from the Norman church of St Michael, the interior of this 300-year-old inn is enhanced by original oak beams and a log-burning fire. Expect a wide choice of grills and roasts, plus alternatives such as poached haddock with a poached egg and chive and butter sauce, or cheese and lentil terrine on smooth tomato coulis.
OPEN: 12-3 6-11 (closed Mon lunchtime in winter)
BAR MEALS: L served all week 12-2.00 D served all week 7-9.00 Av main course £6.50 **RESTAURANT:** D served all week 7-9.30 Av 3 course fixed price £14 **BREWERY/COMPANY:** Enterprise Inns
🍺: Fuller's London Pride, Scottish Courage John Smith's, Courage Directors & Theakstons Best Bitter. **FACILITIES:** Garden: Patio/terrace, food served outdoors **NOTES:** Parking 25

BEWDLEY
Map 10 SO77

Pick of the Pubs

Horse & Jockey 🐴 🍷
Far Forest DY14 9DX ☎ 01299 266239 📠 01299 266227
e-mail: info@horseandjockey-farforest.co.uk
Serving fresh food sourced from local farms and cooked with imagination, this peaceful country pub is dedicated to maintaining traditional practices of hospitality - and thanks to the owners' enthusiasm and dedication, it is now a deservedly-successful dining destination. The family owners, Richard and Suzanne Smith, bought the Horse and Jockey as a declining business and have put new life in to it. The pub was first licensed in 1838 to serve cider to farm workers on the local estate; restoration of the premises some years ago uncovered oak beams, floorboards and an inglenook fireplace. The much-extended original building incorporates a glass-covered well which locals recall being in the garden. Today's garden, with its children's play area and seating for customers of all ages, overlooks the Lem valley and Wyre Forest. Regularly-changing menus incorporate a selection of beef and lamb from the local Detton Farm, typically roast topside of beef with a dark shallot and chestnut sauce or slow-roasted lamb shank glazed with honey and rosemary jus. A good selection of fresh fish is delivered every Friday, so expect some adventurous as well as traditional dishes at the weekend. For example, whole baby sea bass is oven baked wrapped in banana leaves and then served with a fruity chilli sauce; while silver

continued

England

BEWDLEY continued

dorado fillets are pan fried and served on a capsicum and bulgar wheat timbale garnished with chargrilled walnut-scented scallions. The accomplished pace is maintained with desserts like coffee and orange torte, spiced pear tarte Tatin, and an irresistible 'chocolate celebration' assiette. More traditional pub food is also on offer - but at the same high quality - in dishes such as home-baked ham and eggs, and beef pie cooked in Hobson's ale.
OPEN: 12-3 6-11 (Sun 12-10.30) **BAR MEALS:** L served all week 12-2.30 D served all week 6-9.30 Av main course £8.40 **RESTAURANT:** L served Sun 12-4 D served all week 6-9.30 Av 3 course à la carte £20 **BREWERY/COMPANY:** Free House ◀: Hobsons Original & Town Crier, Wood Shropshire Lad, Enville Ale. ♀: 11 **FACILITIES:** Children welcome Children's licence Garden: Large lawn, play area, seating, good views Dogs allowed Garden only **NOTES:** Parking 50

Little Pack Horse 🕯♀
31 High St DY12 2DH ☎ 01299 403762 ▤ 01299 403762
e-mail: littlepackhorse@aol.com
Historic timber-framed inn with low beams and an elm timber bar, located in one of the Severn Valley's prettiest towns. The interior is warmed by a cosy wood-burning stove and candle-lit at night, and its full of eccentricities and oddities. Expect beer-battered cod and chips, potato and onion omelette, half roast duckling with orange and brandy sauce, pink trout with lemon nut brown butter, minted lamb and tattie pie, or chicken and mushroom balti on the menu.
OPEN: 12-3 6-11 (Sat-Sun 12-11) **BAR MEALS:** L served all week 12-2.15 D served all week 6.30-9.30
BREWERY/COMPANY: ◀: Thomas Hardy Ushers Best & Four Seasons, Burton Ale. **FACILITIES:** Children welcome Garden Dogs allowed

BRANSFORD
Map 10 SO75

The Bear & Ragged Staff 🕯♀
Station Rd WR6 5JH ☎ 01886 833399 ▤ 01886 833106
e-mail: bearragged@aol.com
Dir: 3m from centre of Worcester off the A4103 (Hereford Rd). Or 3m from the centre of Malvern off A449, turning L just before Powick Village. Signpost for Bransford.

Mid-way between Worcester and the Malvern Hills, this smart dining pub has an enviable reputation for its imaginative menus and fresh Cornish fish. The name comes from the family crest of the Earl of Warwickshire. Lunchtime bar meals include brunch rolls, Cajun-spiced salmon, and five cheese tortellini. It's wise to book for the restaurant at weekends, when starters like avocado, crab and tomato pancake might

precede rib-eye steak with shallots and red wine sauce, roast cod on butter bean mash, or fillet of venison on purée of aubergine and rich redcurrant sauce flavoured with chocolate.
OPEN: 12-2.30 6.30-10.30 **BAR MEALS:** L served all week 12-2.00 D served Sun-Sat 6.30-8 Av main course £6 **RESTAURANT:** L served all week 12-2 D served all week 7-9 Av 3 course à la carte £20 **BREWERY/COMPANY:** Free House ◀: Bass, Highgate Special Bitter, Worthington. **FACILITIES:** Garden: Food served outside Dogs allowed In the garden only. Water provided **NOTES:** Parking 40

BREDON
Map 10 SO93

Fox & Hounds Inn & Restaurant 🕯♀
Church St GL20 7LA ☎ 01684 772377 ▤ 01684 772377
Dir: M5 J9 into Tewkesbury take B4080 towards Pershore. Bredon 3m
Resplendent with colourful, over-flowing hanging baskets in summer, this pretty 16th-century thatched pub is located close to the River Avon. Food is served in the bar areas and dining lounge, including blackboard specials, lunchtime bar snacks and the main menu. Favourite dishes include chicken Caribbean, pork tenderloin, pasta carbonara, and the daily fresh fish selection, as well as filled hot and cold baguettes, and various tasty ploughman's.
OPEN: 11.30-3 6-11 (Sun 12-3, 6.30-10.30) 25/26 Dec closed eve **BAR MEALS:** L served all week 12-2 D served all week 6.30-9.30 Av main course £7 **RESTAURANT:** L served all week 12-2 D served all week 6.30-9.30 Av 3 course à la carte £15 **BREWERY/COMPANY:** Whitbread ◀: Banks, Marstons Pedigree, Greene King Old Speckled Hen. **FACILITIES:** Children welcome Garden: Small shaded garden with BBQ area Dogs allowed guide dogs only **NOTES:** Parking 35

BRETFORTON
Map 10 SP04

Pick of the Pubs

The Fleece Inn 🕯♀
The Cross WR11 7JE ☎ 01386 831173
e-mail: nigel@thefleeceinn.co.uk
Dir: B4035 from Evesham

An extraordinary slice of history, this 17th-century inn stayed in the same family until Lola Taplin bequeathed it to the National Trust in 1977. It has remained largely unchanged over the centuries, providing the contemporary customer with an extraordinary experience. The pub's pewter room is a notable example, where a fine collection of pewter has been displayed for over 300 years. Local tradition has it that Lola still watches over the pub, which was her home for 77 years, in the form of an owl perched on the thatched roof of the barn next door. Cask ale and honest home-cooked food are served. Local produce is featured, and options range from snacks to

continued

continued

main meals. Home-made pies and farmhouse hot pots are house specialities, there's daily fresh fish according to availability and traditional puddings and gateaux. Children's meals are offered and vegetarian options include a popular cheese, leek and potato bake.
OPEN: 11-3 6-11 (open all day summer) **BAR MEALS:** L served all week 12-2.30 D served all week 6.30-9 Av main course £5.95 **RESTAURANT:** L served all week 12-2 D served all week 6.30-9 Av 3 course à la carte £5.50
BREWERY/COMPANY: Free House ◀: Uley Beer, Hook Norton Best, Woods, Pigs Ear. **FACILITIES:** Children welcome Garden: Food served outside, large Dogs allowed

---

CLENT — Map 10 SO97

The Bell & Cross 🍴 NEW
Holy Cross DY9 9QL ☎ 01562 730319 📠 01562 730733
Dir: Telephone for directions
Carefully-preserved old pub with various small rooms including one that used to be the butcher's shop, with meat hooks still in place. The emphasis is on satisfying modern food, cooked by owner Roger Narbets who is also chef to the England football team, and has plenty of memorabilia from world cup matches on display. Expect seared calves' liver and bacon, glazed pork belly, baked polenta, and pot-roasted saddle of lamb.
OPEN: 12-3 6-11 Closed: Dec 25 & Jan 2 **BAR MEALS:** L served all week 12-2 D served Mon-Sat 6.30-9.15 Av main course £10.50
RESTAURANT: L served all week 12-2 D served Mon-Sat 6.30-9.15
BREWERY/COMPANY: Enterprise Inns ◀: Pedigree, Mud, Bitter & Guest Beers. **FACILITIES:** Children welcome Children's licence Garden: Raised terrace, oval shaped landscaped garden Dogs allowed Water **NOTES:** Parking 26

DROITWICH — Map 10 SO86

The Chequers 🍴
Cutnall Green WR9 0PJ ☎ 01299 851292 📠 01299 851744
Dir: Telephone for directions
This charming country pub is decorated in traditional style, with an open fire, timbered bar and richly-coloured furnishings. The effect is cosy and welcoming - a good place to linger over numerous real ales, fine wines and perhaps a meal from the all-encompassing menu. Dishes range from lunch light bites (imaginative sandwiches, soups and platters) through to dinner dishes such as slow-roasted shoulder of lamb with caper and mint jus and garlic mash or fillet of salmon with prawn, garlic and tomato stew.
OPEN: 12-3 6-11 Closed: Xmas/New Year **BAR MEALS:** L served all week 12-2 D served all week 6.30-9.15 Av main course £9.75
RESTAURANT: L served all week 12-2 D served all week 6.30-9.15 Av 3 course à la carte £19.95 Av 3 course fixed price £14.95
BREWERY/COMPANY: Enterprise Inns ◀: Timothy Taylors, Banks Pedigree, Banks Bitter, Banks Mild. **FACILITIES:** Children welcome Garden: Large garden with benches, flower borders Dogs allowed **NOTES:** Parking 75

Old Cock Inn 🍴
Friar St WR9 8EQ ☎ 01905 774233
This charming old pub has three stained-glass windows rescued from the local church after it was destroyed during the Civil War The stone carving above the front entrance is believed to be of Judge Jeffreys who presided over the local magistrates' court. Various snacks and light meals feature on the menu, while more substantial fare includes rump steak,

continued

---

steak and Guinness pie, grilled cod with Stilton and mushroom, and fillet of lamb with artichoke, wild mushrooms, mint, peppercorns and wine sauce.
OPEN: 11.30-3.00 5.30-11 Closed: Sun evening **BAR MEALS:** L served Everyday 12.00-2.30 D served 6 days 5.30-9.30 Av main course £8 **RESTAURANT:** L served all week 12-2.30 D served Mon-Sat & Sun 5.30-9.30 Av 3 course à la carte £25 Av fixed price £18.90
BREWERY/COMPANY: ◀: Marston's Pedigree & Bitter, Guest.
FACILITIES: Garden: Small beer garden

FLADBURY — Map 10 SO94

Chequers Inn
Chequers Ln WR10 2PZ ☎ 01386 860276 📠 01386 861286
Dir: Off A4538 between Evesham and Pershore
The Chequers is a 14th-century inn with plenty of beams and an open fire, tucked away in a pretty village with views of the glorious Bredon Hills. Local produce from the Vale of Evesham provides the basis for home-cooked dishes offered from the monthly-changing menu, plus a choice of daily specials. A lawned garden overlooks open fields.
OPEN: 11-3 6-11 **BAR MEALS:** L served all week 12-2 D served Mon-Sat 6.30-10 **RESTAURANT:** L served all week 12-2 D served Mon-Sat 6.30-10 **BREWERY/COMPANY:** Free House ◀: Hook Norton Best, Scottish Courage Directors, Fuller's London Pride, Wyre Piddle Piddle In The Wind. **FACILITIES:** Children welcome Garden: Lawned garden with open field views **NOTES:** Parking 28

FLYFORD FLAVELL — Map 10 SO95

The Boot Inn ◆◆◆◆ 🍴 ♀
Radford Rd WR7 4BS ☎ 01386 462658 📠 01386 462547
Dir: Take Evesham rd, L at 2nd rdbt onto A422, Flyford Flavell signed after 3m
Family-run inn, dating from circa 1350, situated in a lovely village on the Wychavon Way, well placed for the Cotswolds and Malvern Hills. There are gardens front and back, with a heated patio and quality wooden furniture. Home-cooked food, from an extensive carte and specials board, includes monkfish goujons with basil and garlic dressing, whole grilled lemon sole, and seared tuna on pineapple with chilli sauce. Award-winning accommodation is provided in the converted coach house.
OPEN: 11-2.30 6.30-11 **BAR MEALS:** L served all week 12-2 D served all week 6.30-10 Av main course £8.50 **RESTAURANT:** L served all week 12-2 D served all week 6.30-10 Av 3 course à la carte £18 **BREWERY/COMPANY:** Free House ◀: Wadworth 6X, Greene King Old Speckled Hen, Worthingtons, Green King IPA. ♀: 7
FACILITIES: Children welcome Garden: Patio with wooden furniture Dogs allowed **NOTES:** Parking 30 **ROOMS:** 5 bedrooms 5 en suite s£50 d£60

HONEYBOURNE — Map 10 SP14

The Thatched Tavern 🍴 ♀
WR11 5PQ ☎ 01386 830454 📠 01386 833842
e-mail: timandjane@thethatchedtavern.co.uk
Dir: 6 miles from Chipping Campden
This charming 13th-century tavern is indeed thatched, and with its flagstone floors, open fires and cheerful atmosphere, possesses all the expected attributes of a textbook village pub. Well-kept ales, including Adnams Broadside, accompany good-value meals that range from brunch, pizzas and bar snacks to the long list that makes up Fanny's à la carte menu, with aubergine and two-cheese melt, spinach and red

continued

England

HONEYBOURNE continued

pepper lasagne, beef Stroganoff with rice, and salmon with dill.
OPEN: 11-3 5.30-11 **BAR MEALS:** L served all week 12-2.30 D served all week 7-10 Av main course £10 **RESTAURANT:** L served all week 12-2.30 D served all week 7-10 Av 3 course à la carte £22.50 **BREWERY/COMPANY:** Punch Taverns 🍺: Adnams Broadside, Interbrew Bass, Fuller's London Pride, Marston's Pedigree.
FACILITIES: Garden: Secluded garden, seats 100
NOTES: Parking 25

KEMPSEY   Map 10 SO84

Pick of the Pubs

Walter de Cantelupe Inn ♦♦♦ 🛏️ ♀
Main Rd WR5 3NA ☎ 01905 820572 📠 01905 820572
e-mail: walter.depub@fsbdial.co.uk
See Pick of the Pubs on opposite page

KNIGHTWICK   Map 10 SO75

Pick of the Pubs

The Talbot at Knightwick ♀
WR6 5PH ☎ 01886 821235 📠 01886 821060
e-mail: admin@the-talbot.co.uk
Dir: A44 through Worcester, 8m W turn onto B4197

The business rule KISS - Keep It Simple, Stupid - definitely applies in the bar of this 15th-century coaching inn. Real ales called This, That, Wot and T'other are all brewed on the premises from hops grown in the parish. In fact, everything bar the fresh fish, which comes from Wales and Cornwall, is made here from local ingredients, or from produce grown in the 'chemical free' garden. And that includes preserves, breads and black pudding. At lunchtime, have a ploughman's by all means, but why not try fresh crab blinis and garlic mayonnaise, pheasant breast with tarragon sauce, and treacle hollygog (should ring a bell with Cambridge graduates)? A truly different dinner selection would be fried bread spread with garlicky pesto topped with preserved turkey bits, then a main course such as parsnip roulade, roast pig's cheek or wild rabbit stew, and finally a gooseberry crumble or spotted dick. The beamed lounge bar leads to an arboured patio and riverside lawn. Beer festival October 8th-10th.
OPEN: 11-11 (Sun 12-10.30) Dec 25 Closed eve
BAR MEALS: L served all week 12-2 D served all week 6.30-9.30 Av main course £13.95 **RESTAURANT:** L served all week

12-2 D served all week 6.30-9.30 Av 3 course à la carte £26 Av 3 course fixed price £22.95 **BREWERY/COMPANY:** Free House 🍺: Teme Valley This, That , T'Other, City of Cambridge Hobsons Choice. **FACILITIES:** Children welcome Garden: Riverside grass area Dogs allowed **NOTES:** Parking 50 **ROOMS:** 11 bedrooms 11 en suite 3 family rooms s£38 d£69.50 (★★)

MALVERN   Map 10 SO74

Farmers Arms
Birts St, Birtsmorton WR13 6AP ☎ 01684 833308
e-mail: farmersarmsbirtsmorton@yahoo.co.uk
Dir: On B4208 S of Great Malvern
Expect a friendly welcome at this 15th-century black and white timbered pub, in a quiet parish close to the Malvern Hills. It serves decent ales and homely bar food in its low-beamed rooms, including cottage pie, macaroni cheese, Hereford pie and a variety of jacket potatoes, Vienna rolls and sandwiches.
OPEN: 11-2.30 6-11 (Sun 12-2.30, 7-11) **BAR MEALS:** L served all week 11-2 D served all week 6-9.30 **BREWERY/COMPANY:** Free House 🍺: Hook Norton Best & Old Hooky. **FACILITIES:** Children welcome Garden: Dogs allowed Water **NOTES:** Parking 30 No credit cards

MARTLEY   Map 10 SO76

Admiral Rodney Inn ♦♦♦♦ 🛏️
Berrow Green WR6 6PL ☎ 01886 821375 📠 01886 821375
e-mail: rodney@admiral.fslife.co.uk
Dir: From M5 Junc 7, take A44 signed Bromyard & Leominster. After approx 7m at Knightwick turn R onto B4197, Inn 1.5m on L at Berrow Green

Early 17th-century farmhouse-cum-alehouse, named after the man who taught Nelson all he knew. Its lofty position gives it great views of Worcester and the Malvern Hills. New owners Kenneth and Gillian say they have been made very welcome - a good sign. Plenty of good pub grub. Lunch choices are legion, while in the evening meals include chicken roulade, Barbary duck breasts in oyster sauce, and various fish specials. Enjoy a pint of Wye Valley or other guest beers.
OPEN: 11-3 5-11 (Mon open 5-11, open all day Sat, Sun)
BAR MEALS: L served Tues-Sun 12-2.30 D served all week 6.30-9 Av main course £6.50 **RESTAURANT:** L served Sun D served Mon-Sun 7-9 Av 3 course à la carte £20
BREWERY/COMPANY: Free House 🍺: Wye Valley Bitter, Greene King IPA, Guest Beers. **FACILITIES:** Children welcome Children's licence Garden: Beautiful views, seating, grass area, terrace Dogs allowed Water **NOTES:** Parking 40 **ROOMS:** 3 bedrooms 3 en suite s£45 d£55

continued

OPEN: 12-2, 6-11
CLOSED: Dec 25-26 & Mon except BHs
BAR MEALS: L served Tue-Sat 12-2, D served Tue-Sun 6.30-9.30. Av main course £6.75
RESTAURANT: L served Tue-Sun 12-2, D served Tue-Sat 7-9. Av cost 3 courses £17
BREWERY/COMPANY: Free House.
🍺: Timothy Talyor Landlord, Canon Royalls, Everards Beacon Bitter, Kings Shilling.
FACILITIES: Dogs allowed. Walled paved garden
NOTES: Parking 24.
ROOMS: 3 en suite from s£35 d£45

Walter de Cantelupe

The pub's name is taken from the mid-13th-century Bishop of Worcester, who had a residence in the village. He was in cahoots with Baron Simon de Montfort, who was killed at the Battle of Evesham, and the bishop was later excommunicated as a result of his association with de Montfort. Walter de Cantelupe was strongly against the brewing and selling of ales, which his parishioners undertook as a way of raising church funds.

◆◆◆ 🐾 ♀

Main Road, Kempsey, nr Worcester, WR5 3NA

☎ 01905 820572   🖷 01905 820572

📧 walter.depub@fsbdial.co.uk

Dir: 4m S of Worcester City centre, on A38 in the centre of village

The pub was formed out of a row of cottages three centuries later, and its naming is presumably ironic! This small village inn is full of genuine character, and its whitewashed walls bedecked with flowers is a magnet for passing motorists and locals alike. Outside, a walled and paved garden has been fragrantly planted with clematis, roses and honeysuckle, and its south-facing position is a sun-trap on hot days. A gas heater has extended its use into the cooler months. The food is written up each day on a blackboard, with plenty of appetising choice both at lunchtime and in the evening. Prawn, red grape and cream cheese filo parcels on a bed of mixed leaves, and smooth chicken liver pâté spiked with brandy might kick off a typical meal. Perhaps followed by wild mushroom and spinach lasagne, slow-roasted spiced lamb shank in a tomato and root vegetable sauce, and roast Gressingham duck breast with honey and thyme sauce. Whiskey bread and butter pudding with custard, and strawberry Pavlova, make desirable desserts. Well-kept Timothy Taylor bitter. Recently introduced en suite accommodation is popular with visitors to historic Worcester, the Malvern Hills and Severn Vale.

England

OMBERSLEY
Map 10 SO86

Pick of the Pubs

Crown & Sandys Arms
Main Rd WR9 0EW ☎ 01905 620252 📠 01905 620769
e-mail: richardeverton@crownandsandys.co.uk
Dir: Telephone for directions

Old and new rub shoulders in this well-established inn, where original beams and fireplaces are teamed with leopard skin prints and modern furniture. Local wine merchant Richard Everton has transformed a rather drab and dated village pub into a classy bistro-style affair. The building, which belongs to Lord Sandys' estate, now sports a trendy open-plan bar and bistro, together with an up-to-date restaurant sponsored by a well-known champagne house. Regular 'wine dinners' and theme evenings add to the appeal for regulars, and dishes are changed every week. Lunchtime brings freshly-made sandwiches and baguettes, as well as hot dishes: steak and kidney with red wine and mushrooms is typical. In the evening, the wide choice of fresh market fish might include swordfish, sea bass or red bream. A pan-fried medley of local game on honey-roast parsnips; or winter vegetable casserole with butter beans and Mozzerella are amongst the other alternatives.
OPEN: 11-2.30 5-11 **BAR MEALS:** L served all week 11.30-2.30 D served all week 6-10 Av main course £8.95
RESTAURANT: L served all week 11.30-2.30 D served all week 6-10 Av 3 course à la carte £20
BREWERY/COMPANY: Free House 🍺: Marston's Pedigree, Sam Powell, Woods Parish Bitter, IPA Shropshire Lad plus guest beers. ♀: 10 **FACILITIES:** Children welcome Garden: Large beer garden, Japanese style terrace **NOTES:** Parking 100

Pick of the Pubs

The Kings Arms
Main Rd WR9 0EW ☎ 01905 620142 📠 01905 620142
e-mail: kaombersley@btconnect.com
Dir: Just off A449
Reputedly King Charles II's first stop after fleeing the Battle of Worcester in 1651, this wonderful black and white timbered inn is steeped in history, dating all the way from 1411. The inviting, dimly lit interior welcomes visitors with intimate nooks and crannies, flagstone floors, and three blazing fires in winter. On warmer days, customers spill out into the pretty walled garden to eat at tables set amid the summer flowers. A tempting array of

modern pub food is available, with a daily blackboard selection of fresh fish. Seafood platter is a popular choice, typically including whole lobster, crab, oysters, king prawns, langoustines and smoked salmon served cold on ice. Other options are pot roast pheasant with shallots and caramelised apples, fresh local rabbit with cream and mustard, and a variety of local sausages served with mash and onion gravy.
OPEN: 11-3 5.30-11 (Sun all day) Closed: 25 Dec **BAR MEALS:** L served all week 12-2.15 D served all week 6-10 Av main course £10.95 **RESTAURANT:** L served all week 12-2.15 D served all week 6-10 Av 3 course à la carte £15 **BREWERY/COMPANY:** Free House 🍺: Banks's Bitter, Marston's Pedigree, Cannon Royall Arrowhead, Morrells Varsity. **FACILITIES:** Children welcome Garden: Walled garden **NOTES:** Parking 60

PENSAX
Map 10 SO76

The Bell Inn ♀
WR6 6AE ☎ 01299 896677
Dir: From Kidderminster A456 to Clows Top, B4202 towards Abberley, pub 2m on L

Friendly rural local offering five real ales by the jug at weekends to extend the choice available. There's also a beer festival held at the end of June. Home-made dishes are prepared from seasonal local produce - steaks, liver and onions, and home-cooked ham with free-range eggs. Superb views are enjoyed from the garden, and great local walks. Walkers and cyclists are welcome, and there's a registered caravan/campsite opposite. Look out for the new bargain lunchtime menu.
OPEN: 12-2.30 5-11 (Sun 12-11) **BAR MEALS:** L served Tues-Sun 12-2 D served all week 6-9 Av main course £6.50 **RESTAURANT:** L served Tue-Sun 12-2 D served all week 6-9
BREWERY/COMPANY: Free House 🍺: Timothy Taylor Best Bitter, Hobsons Best, Hook Norton Best, Cannon Royall.
FACILITIES: Children welcome Garden: Food served outside Dogs allowed **NOTES:** Parking 20

POWICK
Map 10 SO85

The Halfway House Inn
Bastonford WR2 4SL ☎ 01905 831098
Dir: From A15 J7 take A4440 then A449
Situated on the A449 between Worcester and Malvern, this delightful family-run pub is just a few minutes' drive from the picturesque spa town of Malvern, a popular centre for exploring the Malvern Hills. The menu choice ranges from Herefordshire fillet steak or roasted Gressingham duck breast to baked fillet of Scottish salmon and spinach, ricotta and beef tomato lasagne. Other options might include pasta dishes,

continued

continued

fresh filled rolls, and jacket potatoes. At the time of going to press extension plans were under way for the restaurant.
OPEN: 12-3 6-11 **BAR MEALS:** L served Mon-Sun 12-2.00 D served Mon-Sun 6-9 Av main course £9 **RESTAURANT:** L served Mon-Sun 12-2.00 D served Mon-Sun 6-9 Av 3 course à la carte £20 **BREWERY/COMPANY:** Free House ◀: Marston's Pedigree, St Georges Bitter, Fuller's London Pride, Timothy Taylor.
FACILITIES: Garden: Lawn area **NOTES:** Parking 30

SHATTERFORD
Map 10 SO78

The Bellmans Cross Inn 🔊 ♀
Bridgnorth Rd DY12 1RN ☎ 01299 861322 📠 01299 861047
Dir: on A442 5m outside Kidderminster

The Bellman's Cross Inn dates back to the mid 1800's and changed hands in 1919 for the princely sum of £675. Nowadays the bar menu offers traditional dishes such as pork and leek sausages or home-made steak and kidney pie while the restaurant serves up delights like pan-fried guinea fowl, or rack of lamb with garlic potatoes and goats' cheese. A pleasant, friendly environment.
OPEN: 11-3 6-11 (Open all day on Sat & BHs) Dec 25 Closed eve **BAR MEALS:** L served all week 12-2.15 D served all week 6-9.30 Av main course £10 **RESTAURANT:** L served all week 12-2.15 D served all week 6-9.30 Av 3 course à la carte £22.50
BREWERY/COMPANY: Free House ◀: Interbrew Bass, Greene King Old Speckled Hen, Worthington, Carlsberg-Tetley Tetley Bitter.
FACILITIES: Children welcome Garden: Patio area with tables and umbrellas Dogs allowed Guide dogs only **NOTES:** Parking 30

Red Lion Inn 🔊 ♀
Bridgnorth Rd DY12 1SU ☎ 01299 861221
Dir: N from Kidderminster on the A442
This largely 'non-smoking' free house enjoys panoramic views towards the Clee Hills and Severn Valley. You're as welcome to drop in for a pint from the fine selection of real ales and a sandwich as you are for a bottle of Chablis and rack of lamb. Popular hot and cold bar meals provide a simpler alternative to the restaurant menu, which includes duck breast with orange and Cointreau, fresh trout with capers and white wine, as well as a selection of grills.
OPEN: 11.30-2.30 6.30-11 (Sun 12-3, 7-10.30) Closed: Dec 25 **BAR MEALS:** L served all week 11.30-2 D served all week 6.30-9.30 Av main course £8 **RESTAURANT:** L served all week 11.30-2 D served all week 6.30-9.30 Av 3 course à la carte £15
BREWERY/COMPANY: Free House ◀: Bathams, Banks' Mild & Bitter, Shropshire Lad, Wye Valley Butty Bach. ♀: 9
FACILITIES: Children welcome Garden: Small garden
NOTES: Parking 50

◆ **Pubs with Red Diamonds are the top places in the AA's three, four and five diamond ratings**

TENBURY WELLS
Map 10 SO56

Pick of the Pubs

The Fountain Inn 🔊 ♀
Oldwood, St Michaels WR15 8TB
☎ 01584 810701 📠 01584 819030
e-mail: miamifountain@aol.com
Dir: 1m out of Tenbury Wells on the A4112 Leominster Road

Few pubs can offer live sharks as part of their décor, and the Fountain must surely be the only such establishment whose chef found fame through being bitten by one of them. The shark tank nestles incongruously by the roaring log fire, and the nearest table to it is definitely the most popular for bookings. The rest of the interior is more traditional - what you might expect from a 19th-century beer and cider house. Hand-pulled guest beers and the exclusive Fountain ale are offered alongside a short snack menu and an extensive selection of daily specials. Seafood is well represented, and favourite dishes include sea bass roulade, 18oz jumbo cod, and the award-winning beef and Fountain ale pie. The pub has a large, secluded garden including an organic herb garden, a children's play area and a heated patio for outdoor dining.
OPEN: 9-11 **BAR MEALS:** L served all week 9-9 D served all week 9-9 **RESTAURANT:** L served all week 12.00-10pm D served all week 12-10pm Av 3 course à la carte £16 Av 3 course fixed price £12.95 **BREWERY/COMPANY:** Free House ◀: Black Sheep Best, Shepherd Neame Spitfire, Fuller's London Pride, Adnams Broadside. **FACILITIES:** Children welcome Children's licence Garden: Lrg, secluded. Patio area with heaters Dogs allowed Guide dogs only **NOTES:** Parking 60
See advertisement under Preliminary Section

Pick of the Pubs

Peacock Inn 🏠 ◎ 🔊 ♀
WR15 8LL ☎ 01584 810506 📠 01584 811236
e-mail: jvidler@fsbdial.co.uk
Dir: A456 from Worcester then A443 to Tenbury Wells. Inn is 1.25m E of Tenbury Wells
Nestling in the Teme Valley, famous for its orchards and hopyards, and with impressive views across the river, this 14th-century coaching inn has been sympathetically extended and a wealth of pretty shrubs, ivy and colourful hanging baskets help create a splendidly welcoming exterior. Oak beams and open log fires enhance the relaxing bars and oak-panelled restaurant. Local market produce plays a key role in the Peacock's menus, and dishes range from traditional steak and wild mushroom pie in a rich gravy to green Thai prawn and chicken curry.

continued

England

TENBURY WELLS continued

Other options might include chicken supreme with black and white pudding, tagliatelle with Mediterranean vegetables, seared tuna steak on a bed of noodles, home-made pizzas, or cannelloni of spinach and wild mushrooms with Feta cheese and tomato sauce. Quality overnight accommodation in spacious, well-equipped and attractive bedrooms; two with four-poster beds.

Peacock Inn

OPEN: 12.30-3 6-11 **BAR MEALS:** L served all week 12-2.15 D served all week 6.30-9.30 Av main course £8 **RESTAURANT:** L served all week 12-2.15 D served all week 7-9.30 Av 3 course à la carte £18 **BREWERY/COMPANY:** Free House ◖: Hobsons Best Bitter, Adnams Bitter, Old Hooky. ♀: 10 **FACILITIES:** Children welcome Garden: Overlooks River Teme Dogs allowed
NOTES: Parking 30 **ROOMS:** 3 bedrooms 3 en suite s£45 d£60

WYRE PIDDLE   Map 10 SO94

The Anchor Inn ♀
Main St WR10 2JB ☎ 01386 552799 ▤ 01386 552799
e-mail: ngreen32@btinternet.com
Dir: From M5 J6 take A4538 S towards Evesham

An impressive half-timbered inn on the banks of the Avon, standing in gardens that overlook the pleasure craft moored by the water's edge. Old world in style, the 400-year-old building features a cosy lounge with original low-timbered ceiling, old coaching prints around the walls and an inglenook fireplace decorated with horse brasses. The dining room enjoys a panoramic view out over the river and countryside. The asparagus supper is very popular when in season, as is local game.
OPEN: 12-3 6-11 (Sat 12-3, Sun 12-3, 7-10.30) **BAR MEALS:** L served all week 12-2 D served all week 7-9 Av main course £7.50 **RESTAURANT:** L served all week 12-2 D served all week 7-9 Av 3 course à la carte £15 **BREWERY/COMPANY:** Enterprise Inns

continued

◖: Interbrew Flowers Original & Boddingtons Bitter, Marston's Pedigree, Piddle Ale, Guest Ale. ♀: 8 **FACILITIES:** Garden: River Avon at bottom, wonderful views **NOTES:** Parking 10

YORKSHIRE, EAST RIDING OF

BEVERLEY   Map 17 TA03

White Horse Inn 🐾
22 Hengate HU17 8BN ☎ 01482 861973 ▤ 01482 861973
e-mail: anname@talk21.com
Dir: A1079 from York to Beverley
A classic 14th-century local with atmospheric little rooms arranged around the central bar. Gas lighting, open fires, antique cartoons and high-backed settles add to the charm. John Wesley preached in the back yard in the mid-18th century. Traditional bar food includes many popular dishes - among them pasta and mushrooms, fresh jumbo haddock, bangers and mash, and steak and ale pie. Toasted and plain sandwiches and daily specials also feature. Under new management.
OPEN: 11-11 (Sun 12-10.30) **BAR MEALS:** L served all week 11-4.45 D served all week 5-6.45 Av main course £4.50
BREWERY/COMPANY: Samuel Smith ◖: Samuel Smith Old Brewery Bitter & Sovereiegn Bitter. **FACILITIES:** Children welcome Garden: Dogs allowed on leads only, Water **NOTES:** Parking 30 No credit cards

BRANDESBURTON   Map 17 TA14

The Dacre Arms ♀
Main St YO25 8RL ☎ 01964 542392 ▤ 01964 542392
This popular village inn is the home of the Franklin Dead Brief. The society was started in 1844 and currently has 300 members. Each one pays 20p on the death of a member and the landlord is always the treasurer. An extensive range of quality pub food includes large filled Yorkshire puddings, steak and ale pie, lasagne and curries.
OPEN: 11.30-2.30 6-11 (open all day wknds) Closed: 25 Dec
BAR MEALS: L served all week 12-2 D served all week 6-10
RESTAURANT: D served all week 7-9 **BREWERY/COMPANY:** Free House ◖: Black Sheep Best, Scottish Courage John Smith's & Theakston's Old Peculiar. **FACILITIES:** Garden: **NOTES:** Parking 60

CONISTON   Map 17 TA13

Gardeners Country Inn 🐾 ♀
Hull Rd HU11 5AE ☎ 01964 562625 ▤ 01964 564079
e-mail: gardeners@mgrleisure.com
There's clearly been a lot of investment in this lovely country inn: the interior (log fires, low beams and exposed brickwork) is old world without looking worn out, and bedroom accommodation is amazingly stylish. Food is taken seriously, and most needs are catered for, from light bites (soup, nachos, mussels) through to traditional main courses and spicy international dishes such as oriental duck wraps, Thai green curry or beef fajitas.
OPEN: 12 -11 (Sun 12-10.30) **BAR MEALS:** L served all week 12-2.30 D served all week 5-9 Av main course £8 ◖: Theakstons, John Smith, Guest Ales. ♀: 24 **FACILITIES:** Children welcome Garden: Well kept grass area next to conservatory **NOTES:** Parking 55 **ROOMS:** 11 bedrooms 11 en suite 6 family rooms s£60 d£50 (♦♦♦)

> ★ **Star rating for inspected hotel accommodation**

DRIFFIELD — Map 17 TA05

The Bell ★★★

46 Market Place YO25 6AN ☎ 01377 256661 ▤ 01377 253228
e-mail: bell@bestwestern.co.uk
Dir: Enter town from A164, turn R at traffic lights. Car park 50yrds on L behind black railings

A delightful 18th-century coaching inn furnished with antiques, with an oak-panelled bar serving cask beers and 300 whiskies. Food ranges from grilled salmon steak with hollandaise sauce, and poached halibut with white wine and spring onions, to strips of chicken cooked with honey, mustard and cream served with rice, and breast of duckling served on a lake of plum sauce. Snooker, swimming and squash are available.

OPEN: 10-2.30 6-11 Closed: Dec 25 **BAR MEALS:** L served all week 12-1.30 D served all week 7-9.30 **RESTAURANT:** L served all week 12-1.30 D served Mon-Sat 7-9.30
BREWERY/COMPANY: Free House ◖: Daleside Old Leg Over, Hambleton Stud, Stallion. **NOTES:** Parking 18 **ROOMS:** 16 bedrooms 16 en suite no children overnight

FLAMBOROUGH — Map 17 TA27

The Seabirds Inn 🐑 ♀

Tower St YO15 1PD ☎ 01262 850242 ▤ 01262 850242
Dir: On B1255 E of Bridlington

Just down the road from the RSPB's spectacular Bempton Cliffs bird sanctuary and the stunning cliffs at Flamborough Head. This aptly-named pub has a reputation for fresh fish dishes, including paupiettes of plaice filled with salmon and prawn mousse, smoked haddock and broccoli pie, and poached cod Florentine. Other options include beef Wellington, and pork and Stilton sausages on a bed of apple mash with redcurrant and red onion gravy.

OPEN: 11-3 7-11 (Sat 6.30-11) Mon Closed eve in winter
BAR MEALS: L served all week 12-2 D served Mon-Sat 7-9 Av main course £8.50 **RESTAURANT:** L served all week 12-2 D served Mon-Sat 7-9 Av 3 course à la carte £12 **BREWERY/COMPANY:** Free House ◖: Scottish Courage John Smith's, Interbrew Boddingtons Bitter. ♀: 9 **FACILITIES:** Garden: Lrg grassed area, picnic tables Dogs allowed water **NOTES:** Parking 20

HOLME UPON SPALDING MOOR — Map 17 SE83

Ye Olde Red Lion Hotel 🐑 ♀

Old Rd YO43 4AD ☎ 01430 860220 ▤ 01430 861471
Dir: off A1079 (York/Hull road). At Market Weighton take A614

A historic 17th-century coaching inn that once provided hospitality for weary travellers who were helped across the marshes by monks. It's still a great refuge, with a friendly atmosphere, oak beams and a cosy fire. The inspiring menu could include oven-

baked duck breast with start anise sauce, corn-fed chicken coq-au-vin or pan-seared sea bass with wilted greens and vierge sauce.
OPEN: 11.30-2.30 6-11 (Sun 12-3, 7-10.30) **BAR MEALS:** L served all week 12-2 D served all week 6.45-9.30 Av main course £8.50 **RESTAURANT:** L served all week 12-2 D served all week 7-9.30 Av 3 course à la carte £19.50 **BREWERY/COMPANY:** Free House ◖: Carlsberg-Tetley, Tetley Bitter, Interbrew Bass & Blacksheep.
♀: 13 **FACILITIES:** Children welcome Garden: Patio area with water feature, flowers **NOTES:** Parking 60

HUGGATE — Map 19 SE85

The Wolds Inn ♦♦♦ 🐑

YO42 1YH ☎ 01377 288217
e-mail: huggate@woldsinn.freeserve.co.uk
Dir: S of A166 between York & Driffield

Probably the highest inn on the Yorkshire Wolds, this venerable village local, close to the parish church, also claims 16th-century origins. Beneath a huddle of tiled roofs and white-painted chimneys, it sports an interior of wood panelling, gleaming brassware and open fires. Baguettes and sandwiches and bar main dishes of gammon and egg, Whitby seafood and a Sunday roast. Restaurant specials move on to salmon goujons, steak pie, loin of pork, rack of lamb, and roast duckling with orange sauce.

OPEN: 12-2 6.30-11 (May-Sept open Sun at 6pm) (Oct-May closed Fri lunch) **BAR MEALS:** L served Tues-Sun 12-2 D served Tues-Sun 6.30-9.30 Av main course £5.50 **RESTAURANT:** L served Tues-Sun 12-2.30 D served Tues-Sun 6.30-9.30 **BREWERY/COMPANY:** Free House ◖: Carlsberg-Tetley Tetley Bitter, Timothy Taylor Landlord, Black Sheep. **FACILITIES:** Children welcome Garden: Lrg & contained **NOTES:** Parking 50 **ROOMS:** 3 bedrooms 3 en suite s£24.50 d£35

KILHAM — Map 17 TA06

The Old Star

Church St YO25 4RG ☎ 01262 420619 ▤ 01262 420712
e-mail: oldstarkilham@ntlbusiness.com

A sympathetically restored 17th-century inn retaining its essential character whilst providing comfortable, modern facilities. Standing opposite Kilham's parish church, it remains the hub of the local community. Seasonal produce from local suppliers, interesting guest ales and house wines all indicate an interest in the customer. Extensive and well priced menus include everything from sandwiches to home-made pies, steaks and daily fish dishes. If you're spoilt for choice at dessert, plump for mini portions of any three.

OPEN: 11-2 6-11 (Sat 11-11, Sun 11-10.30) **BAR MEALS:** L served all week 12-2 D served Wed-Sat 7-9.30 Av main course £7.50 **RESTAURANT:** L served all week 12-2 D served Wed-Sat 7-9.30 **BREWERY/COMPANY:** Free House ◖: Scottish Courage John Smiths Cask, Theakstons XB & Mild. **FACILITIES:** Children welcome Garden: Lrg patio area, 1/2 acre of lawn Dogs allowed **NOTES:** Parking 5

continued

England

KINGSTON UPON HULL — Map 17 TA02

The Minerva Hotel
Nelson St, Victoria Pier HU1 1XE
☎ 01482 326909 🖹 01482 326909
Dir: M62 onto A63, then Castle St, turn R at signpost for Fruit Market into Queens St at the top of Queenes St on R hand side of the pier

Famous in the area for its nautical memorabilia, this handsome riverside pub with old-fashioned rooms and cosy snugs dates from 1831. Within walking distance are fifteen more pubs on the Hull Ale Trail. In addition to the pub's annual beer festivals, there is always a good choice of ales. Simple yet appetising bar food includes meat and potato pie, lasagne, beef cobbler, gammon steak, and various filled baguettes and baked potatoes. Alfresco eating in summer.
OPEN: 11-11 (Sun 12-10.30) Closed: Dec 25 **BAR MEALS:** L served all week 11.30-2.30 D served Mon-Thu 6-9 Av main course £4.85 **RESTAURANT:** L served Mon-Fri 11.30-2.30 D served Mon-Thu 6-9 **BREWERY/COMPANY:** 🍺: Carlsberg-Tetley Tetley Bitter, Roosters, Orkney, Boat. **FACILITIES:** Children welcome Garden: Eight fixed benches for eating Dogs allowed Water

LUND — Map 17 SE94

Pick of the Pubs

Wellington Inn ♀
19 The Green YO25 9TE ☎ 01377 217294 🖹 01377 217192
Dir: On B1284 NE of Beverley
Opposite the picture-postcard village green, the Wellington is a focal point: completely renovated by the present owners, its clientele come from far afield for decent bar lunches and à la carte dining. Traditional soups and sandwiches supplement a frequently-changed lunch menu featuring the likes of smoked haddock fishcakes with mild curried apple sauce followed by braised lamb shank with roasted root vegetables. At dinner expect imaginative but classically-influenced cooking: among the starters, perhaps red onion and shallot tarte Tatin with toasted goats' cheese or smoked duck, Mozzarella, tomato and basil salad. Typical main courses include pan-fried calves' liver, Toulouse sausage and crispy pancetta with sage and onion mash or venison loin with parsnip and pear rösti, red wine and white chocolate reduction. Good list of wines with useful tasting notes.
OPEN: 12-3 6.30-11 **BAR MEALS:** L served Tue-Sun 12-2 D served Tue-Thu 6.30-9 Av main course £9.50 **RESTAURANT:** D served Tue-Sat 7-9.30 Av 3 course à la carte £22
BREWERY/COMPANY: Free House 🍺: Timothy Taylor Landlord, Dark Mild, Black Sheep Best, John Smiths. ♀: 8
FACILITIES: Children welcome Garden: Courtyard
NOTES: Parking 40

SLEDMERE — Map 17 SE96

The Triton Inn ♦♦♦ ♀
YO25 3XQ ☎ 01377 236644
e-mail: thetritoninn@sledmere.fsbusiness.co.uk
Dir: Leave A166 at Garton on the Wolds, take B1252 to Sledmere
Still licensed to post horses, this 18th-century coaching inn is set in the shadow of historic Sledmere House, halfway between York and the coast on the scenic route to Bridlington. It makes an ideal base for touring the wolds, moors and coast. A log fire burns in the oak-panelled bar and home-made food is freshly prepared to order. Options range from sandwiches

and baked potatoes to Thai prawns in batter, lemon chicken, and brandy peppered steak.
OPEN: 11.30-2.30 7-11 Closed: Mon 1 Oct-31 Mar **BAR MEALS:** L served Tues-Sun 12-2 D served Wed-Sun 7-9 Av main course £6.50 **RESTAURANT:** L served Sun 12-2 D served Wed-Sun 7-9 Av 3 course à la carte £16
BREWERY/COMPANY: Free House 🍺: Carlsberg-Tetley Tetley Bitter, Scottish Courage John Smith's & Theakston's Best.
FACILITIES: Children welcome Garden: Rear terrace with patio tables & chairs **NOTES:** Parking 35 **ROOMS:** 5 bedrooms 2 en suite 1 family rooms s£24 d£44

SOUTH CAVE — Map 17 SE93

The Fox and Coney Inn ♦♦♦♦ 🍴 ♀ NEW
52 Market Place HU15 2AT ☎ 01430 422275 🖹 01430 421552
e-mail: foxandconey@aol.com
Dir: 4 miles E of M62 on A63. 4 miles N of Brough mainline railway
Standing in the centre of South Cave, this traditional stone building dates from 1739. Thought to be the only Fox & Coney in Britain, the pub was simply known as The Fox until its second owner, William Goodlad, added the Coney (rabbit) in 1788. The pub is handy for walkers on the nearby Wolds Way. Baguettes, salads and jacket potatoes supplement a varied menu that includes an honest selection of British, European and Indian dishes.
OPEN: 11.30-11 **BAR MEALS:** L served all week 11.30-2 D served all week 5.30-9.30 Av main course £5 **RESTAURANT:** L served all week 11.30-2 D served all week 5.30-9.30 Av 3 course à la carte £20
BREWERY/COMPANY: Enterprise Inns 🍺: Timothy Taylors Landlord, Scottish Courage John Smith's & Theakston Cool Cask, Rooster's Yankee, Guest Beers. ♀: 15 **FACILITIES:** Children welcome Garden: Seats approx 30 Dogs allowed Water
NOTES: Parking 22 **ROOMS:** 12 bedrooms 12 en suite 2 family rooms s£42 d£55

SUTTON UPON DERWENT — Map 17 SE74

Sutton Arms ♦♦♦♦ 🍴 ♀ NEW
Main St YO41 4BT ☎ 01904 608477 🖹 01904 607585
e-mail: enquiries@suttonarms.co.uk
Dir: From the A64, take the Hull exit (A1079) and the immediate right on to Elvington (B1228) and then on to Sutton Derwent. The Sutton Arms is situated on the right past the school

Modern pub built on the site of a much older one which got too small for the village, and dedicated to the 1940s with its wind-up gramophone, valve radios, sheet music and other memorabilia from this period. There are plenty of eating areas, including the smart Mediterranean-style restaurant and a heated courtyard. Expect chargrilled beef, moussaka, steak and ale pie, and chicken stirfry.
OPEN: 5.30 -11 (Sat-Sun, 12-11) **BAR MEALS:** L served Sat-Sun & BH's 12-2.45 D served Tue-Sun & BH's 6-9.15 Av main course £6

continued

continued

RESTAURANT: L served Sun 12-2.45 D served Tue-Sun & BH's 6-9.15 Av 3 course à la carte £12 Av 3 course fixed price £6.75 🍺: John Smiths Bitter, Black Sheep Bitter, Kronenbourg, Old Legover Bitter. 🍷: 8 **FACILITIES:** Garden: Paved area with three tables **NOTES:** Parking 30 **ROOMS:** 3 bedrooms 3 en suite 1 family rooms s£28 d£48 no children overnight

YORKSHIRE, NORTH

ACASTER MALBIS
Map 16 SE54

The Ship Inn 🍷
Moor End YO23 2UH ☎ 01904 703888 📠 01904 705971
Dir: From York take A1036 south, after Dringhouses follow signs for Bishopthorpe and then Acaster Malbis

A 17th-century coaching house in a village on the outskirts of York. The Romans built a fort here, presumably to guard the River Ouse on which today, from the pub's delightful beer garden, you can watch pleasure craft and barges cruising slowly by. Traditional bar food is available in the evenings, including steak and ale pie, cod in beer batter, steak, gammon, pizzas and vegetarian lasagne.
OPEN: 11-11 (Sun 12-10.30) **BAR MEALS:** L served all week 12-2.30 D served all week 4.30-8pm Av main course £5.50
RESTAURANT: D served Thu-Sat 7-9 Av 3 course à la carte £19 Av 3 course fixed price £15 **BREWERY/COMPANY:** Enterprise Inns 🍺: Marston's Pedigree, Theakstons Best, John Smiths Cask, Tetley. 🍷: 12 **FACILITIES:** Children welcome Garden: Large garden with benches and tables Dogs allowed Water **NOTES:** Parking 60

AKEBAR
Map 19 SE19

The Friar's Head 🏠 🍷
Akebar Park DL8 5LY ☎ 01677 450201 📠 01677 450046
Dir: Take A684 from Leeming Bar Motel (on A1). W towards Leyburn for 7m. Friar's Head is in Akebar Park

Originally a farm and adjoining cottages, this is a typical stone-built Yorkshire Dales pub in Lower Wensleydale at the entrance to the National Park. The well-stocked bar, hand-pulled Yorkshire ales and blazing log fire make it perfect for relaxing after an invigorating walk in the hills. Freshly-cooked lunch might be sausages, mustard mash and onion gravy, or various snacks, with seafood bake, halibut steak, and medallions of pork in the evening.
OPEN: 10-2.30 6-11.30 (Sun 7-10.30) **BAR MEALS:** L served all week 12-2.30 D served all week 6-11 Av main course £8
RESTAURANT: L served all week 12-2.30 D served all week 6-10 Av 3 course à la carte £16 **BREWERY/COMPANY:** Free House 🍺: Scottish Courage John Smith's & Theakston Best Bitter, Black Sheep Best. 🍷: 16 **FACILITIES:** Children welcome Garden: Terrace overlooks green, next to golf course **NOTES:** Parking 60

APPLETREEWICK
Map 19 SE06

The Craven Arms
BD23 6DA ☎ 01756 720270
e-mail: cravenapple@aol.com
Dir: From Skipton take A59 towards Harrogate, B6160 N. Village signed on R. (Pub just outside village)

Old world Dales pub with beams, a Yorkshire range and log fires, and spectacular views of the River Wharfe and Simon's Seat. Old artefacts and notes are displayed on the bar ceiling. Steak and kidney pie, Yorkshire puddings, local pork sausages, deep-fried battered haddock, and lentil and potato pie are among the traditional dishes.

continued

OPEN: 11.30-3 6.30-11 (Sun 12-3,7-10.30) **BAR MEALS:** L served all week 11.30-2.30 D served all week 6.30-9 Av main course £5.50
BREWERY/COMPANY: Free House 🍺: Black Sheep, Tetley, Old Bear Original, Old Bear Hibernator. **FACILITIES:** Children welcome Garden: Walled grass beer garden, hill views **NOTES:** Parking 35

ASENBY
Map 19 SE37

Crab & Lobster 🍴🍴 🏠 🍷
YO7 3QL ☎ 01845 577286 📠 01845 577109
e-mail: reservations@crabandlobster.co.uk
Dir: From A1(M) take A168 towards Thirsk

Amid seven acres of garden, lake and streams stands this unique 17th-century thatched pub and adjacent small hotel that have been the consuming passion of owners David and Jackie Barnard for all of a decade. At the Crab & Lobster, an Aladdin's Cave of themed bric-à-brac and antiques, low beams, ledges and window sills in both the cosy bar and brasserie dining-room is covered with pots, pans, parasols and puppets and old fishing nets housing mock crabs. Equally well known for excellent food, notably their innovative fish dishes, menus are rather less cluttered but just as inventive, embracing culinary influences from France and Italy, with a nod towards Asia thrown in for good measure. From the famous fish club sandwich (lunch only) through an array of chunky fish soup, hand carved Craster salmon and lobster, asparagus and Brie spring rolls feature among starters alone. Typical main dishes feature brill fillet with crab and wilted spinach, posh fish and chips with minted mushy peas and salmon, clams, scallops and mussels in tarragon butter sauce. All is not lost for carnivores, who can tuck into oriental beef pancakes followed by braised lamb shank and crispy confit duck with toffee apples and oranges. Alfresco eating and summer barbecues, good real ales and extensive wine list - and a pavilion open all day for food, drinks, coffees and relaxing. The adjacent Crab Manor is delightfully eccentric, standing apart from the pub in well-manicured gardens, with opulent, individually-furnished bedrooms, including three in a thatched tropical beach house, named after famous hotels world-wide.
OPEN: 11.30-3 6.30-11 **BAR MEALS:** L served all week 12-2.15 D served all week 7-9.45 Av main course £11.50
RESTAURANT: L served all week 12-2.15 D served all week 7-9.45 Av 3 course à la carte £28 Av 3 course fixed price £27.50
BREWERY/COMPANY: Free House 🍺: John Smiths, Theakstons XB, Directors. **FACILITIES:** Children welcome Garden: 7 acre mature gardens, food served outdoors Dogs allowed **NOTES:** Parking 50

The Blue Lion

From the attractive estate village of East Witton, this varied walk climbs steadily to open moorland where you are rewarded with fine views across the Ure Valley to Jervaulx Abbey, and into the Yorkshire Dales.

From the front of the inn, cross the road and turn right, then left along the road past the telephone box. In 200 yards (182m), where the road turns sharp left, fork right up the fell road. Ascend steeply to the top of the hill, then follow the track round to the right to reach a gate on to the moor. Turn left through the gate and walk down to Sowden Beck farmhouse, crossing the beck by the ford or bridge.

Pass in front of the house, and keep to the track up the field to a gate and track. Turn left and pass a small plantation to the entrance to house called Moorcote. Go through the gate beside the cattle grid, walk up the drive, following the waymarker round the buildings to a track. Turn left, cross a bridge to reach a gate and field. Turn half-right and go through a gate into woodland.

Proceed downhill to Hammer Farm. Cross the farm road and take the footpath behind farm buildings. Proceed through two fields, then in a steep field, turn left and follow a sunken path down to a gate. Turn right to a further gate onto a road and bridge over a beck. Pass Thirsting Castle Lodge and continue through Waterloo Farm and past the old churchyard and the former rectory. Shortly, rejoin your outward route, following the road back to the inn.

THE BLUE LION, EAST WITTON
DL8 4SN.
☎ 01969 624273

Directions: on A6108 between Leyburn and Ripon
Civilised 18th-century coaching inn overlooking the village green and classic estate village, close to Jervaulx Abbey and beautiful Dales scenery. Delightful interior, excellent Black Sheep ales, upmarket pub food.
Open: 11-11 (Sun 12-10.30).
Bar Meals: 12-2 7-9.
Notes: Children and dogs welcome. Garden and patio. Parking.
(See page 540 for full entry)

DISTANCE: 4 1/2 miles (7.2km)
MAP: OS Landranger 99
TERRAIN: Farmland, moorland, country lanes
PATHS: Field and woodland paths, tracks and fell roads
GRADIENT: Undulating; uphill first 1 1/2miles (2km)

Walk submitted by The Blue Lion

ASKRIGG
Map 18 SD99

Kings Arms
Market Place DL8 3HQ ☎ 01969 650817 ▤ 01969 650856
e-mail: kingsarms@askrigg.fsnet.co.uk
Dir: N off A684 between Hawes & Leyburn

At the heart of the Yorkshire Dales, Askrigg is surrounded by stunning scenery against a backdrop of Pennine hills: its pub, built in 1762 as racing stables, was converted to an inn in 1860. Bar and bistro specialities include traditional Yorkshire country cooking as well as oriental dishes. Try fillet of sea bass with a pesto and black olive crust, braised lamb shank with mash and leek gravy, or whole baby chicken with peppers and chorizo.
OPEN: 11-3 6-11 (Sat 11-11, Sun 12-10.30) **BAR MEALS:** L served all week 12-2 D served all week 6.30-9 Av main course £9.50
RESTAURANT: D served Fri-Sat 7-9 Av 3 course à la carte £17 Av 3 course fixed price £15.95 **BREWERY/COMPANY:** Free House
🍺: Scottish Courage John Smiths & Theakston Cool Cask, Black Sheep, Guest Ales. **FACILITIES:** Children welcome Garden Dogs allowed Water provided

AUSTWICK
Map 18 SD76

The Game Cock Inn
The Green LA2 8BB ☎ 015242 51226 ▤ 015242 51028
In the Three Peaks area north of Settle in a pretty limestone village, a cosy family-run pub popular with locals - always a good sign. Everything is freshly prepared and cooked on the premises. From the printed menu come rabbit fricassée, tandoori lamb and fillet of halibut, while there are daily specials too. In winter, warm up by the open log fire; in summer bask in the large rear garden with play area and aviary.
OPEN: 11.30-3 6-11 (All day Sun) **BAR MEALS:** L served all week 11.30-2 D served all week 6-9 Av main course £8
RESTAURANT: L served all week 11.30-2 D served all week 6-9
BREWERY/COMPANY: 🍺: Thwaites Best Bitter & Smooth.
FACILITIES: Children welcome Garden: large beer garden
NOTES: Parking 6

AYSGARTH
Map 19 SE08

The George & Dragon Inn ★★
DL8 3AD ☎ 01969 663358 ▤ 01969 663773
Dir: On the A68 in the centre or the village of Aysgarth, midway between Leyburn and Hawes
Beautifully situated near Aysgarth Falls in the heart of Herriot country, the owners of this attractive 17th century free house continue the long tradition of Yorkshire hospitality. Beamed ceilings and open fires set the scene for freshly-cooked courses like roasted leg of Dales lamb with Yorkshire pudding;

peppered steak; fresh egg fettuccine; Chinese pancake; tiger prawn steak; blue cheese and red onion steak; fillet of battered haddock; chicken schnitzel; or steamed monkfish tail.

OPEN: 11-11 **BAR MEALS:** L served all week 12-2 D served all week 6-9 Av main course £10 **RESTAURANT:** L served all week 12-2 D served all week 6-9 Av 3 course à la carte £20 Av 3 course fixed price £12.95 **BREWERY/COMPANY:** Free House 🍺: Black Sheep Best, Scottish Courage John Smith's Cask, Smooth & Theakstons Bitter. 🍷: 10 **FACILITIES:** Children welcome Garden: Large paved area, benches and tables Dogs allowed Water **NOTES:** Parking 35 **ROOMS:** 7 bedrooms 7 en suite 2 family rooms s£36 d£62

BAINBRIDGE
Map 18 SD99

Rose & Crown Hotel ★★
DL8 3EE ☎ 01969 650225 ▤ 01969 650735
e-mail: stay@theprideofwensleydale.co.uk
Dir: On A684 in centre of village

A 500-year-old coaching inn surrounded by spectacular scenery, whose cosy interior is home to the forest horn. Blown each evening from Holy Rood (September 27th) to Shrovetide, it would guide travellers safely to the village. The award-winning chef offers such delights as salmon and dill dumplings with caviar sauce, while a main course from the specials menu might consist of whole black bream baked in a sea salt crust and served in with mint hollandaise. Other dishes could include haunch of rabbit studded with garlic or breast of chicken filled with crayfish.
OPEN: 11-11 (Sun 12-10.30) **BAR MEALS:** L served all week 12-2.15 D served all week 6-9.30 Av main course £9.50
RESTAURANT: L served Sun 12-2.15 D served all week 7-9.30 Av 3 course à la carte £20 **BREWERY/COMPANY:** Free House
🍺: Websters Bitter, Black Sheep Best, Scottish Courage John Smith's, Old Peculiar. **FACILITIES:** Children welcome Garden: Raised patio area Dogs allowed **NOTES:** Parking 65 **ROOMS:** 11 bedrooms 11 en suite s£26 d£64

continued

England

BILBROUGH — Map 16 SE54

Pick of the Pubs

The Three Hares Inn & Restaurant 🏅🏅 ♀
Main St YO23 3PH ☎ 01937 832128 📠 01937 834626
e-mail: info@thethreehares.co.uk
See Pick of the Pubs on opposite page

BOROUGHBRIDGE — Map 19 SE36

Pick of the Pubs

The Black Bull Inn 🐑 ♀
6 St James Square YO51 9AR
☎ 01423 322413 £ 📠 01423 323915
Dir: *From A1(M) J48 take B6265 E for 1m*
Grade II listed building, 800 years old in parts and reputedly haunted, which has always been an inn. A stroll through the wide-ranging menu finds pan-fried venison with parsnip purée, smoked chicken, red onion and spinach omelette, noisettes of lamb with colcanon mash, Chinese mushroom and pepper stirfry, and sirloin steak from the chargrill.
OPEN: 11-11 (Sun 12-10.30) **BAR MEALS:** L served all week 12-2 D served all week 6-9.30 Av main course £9
RESTAURANT: L served all week 12-2 D served all week 6-9.30 Av 3 course à la carte £16 **BREWERY/COMPANY:** Free House 🍺: Black Sheep, Scottish Courage John Smiths, Timothy Taylor Landlord, Cottage Brewing. ♀: 10 **FACILITIES:** Children welcome Dogs allowed Water, Toys **NOTES:** Parking 4

BREARTON — Map 19 SE36

Pick of the Pubs

Malt Shovel Inn 🐑 ♀
HG3 3BX ☎ 01423 862929
Dir: *From A61 (Ripon/Harrogate) take B6165 towards Knaresborough. Turn at Brearton - 1.5m.*
The oldest building in a very old village, The Malt Shovel has been at the heart of this small farming community - which has some good examples of ancient strip farming - since 1525. The setting is very rural, surrounded by rolling farmland yet only 15 minutes from Harrogate and in easy reach of Knaresborough and Ripon. A collection of beer mugs, horse brasses and hunting scenes decorates the heavily-beamed rooms leading off the carved oak bar, and you can enjoy a quiet game of dominoes or shove ha'penny without any electronic intrusions. The blackboard menu has something for everyone, with the likes of seafood gratin, or Cajun haddock for fish lovers, as well as lamb shank, liver and bacon with black pudding, and ham and blue Wensleydale tart. Everything is home made, including puddings like banana cheesecake with toffee sauce, rum and raisin bread and butter pudding, and treacle tart.
OPEN: 12-2.30 6.45-11 (Sun 12-2.30, 7-10.30) **BAR MEALS:** L served Tue-Sun 12-2 D served Tue-Sat 7-9 Av main course £6.50
BREWERY/COMPANY: Free House 🍺: Daleside Nightjar, Durham Magus, Black Sheep Best, Theakston Masham.
FACILITIES: Children welcome **NOTES:** Parking 20
NOTES: No credit cards

BROUGHTON — Map 18 SD95

The Bull ♀
BD23 3AE ☎ 01756 792065
e-mail: janeneil@thebullatbroughton.co.uk
Dir: *On A59 4m from Skipton coming from M6*
Like the village itself, the pub is part of the 3,000-acre Broughton Hall estate, owned by the Tempest family for 900 years. The chef-cum-manager was enticed from his much acclaimed former establishment to achieve similar if not higher standards here. His compact, thoughtful menu offers slow-roasted ham shank glazed with orange and honey, crab and lobster risotto, and chargrilled chicken breast with herby cream cheese. Locally brewed Bull Bitter and guest ales.
OPEN: 12-3 5-11 **BAR MEALS:** L served all week 12-2 D served Mon-Sat 6-9 **RESTAURANT:** 12-2 5.30-9 Av 3 course fixed price £14.95 **BREWERY/COMPANY:** Jennings 🍺: Scottish Courage John Smith's Smooth, Bull Bitter (Local), Guest Ales.
FACILITIES: Children welcome Garden **NOTES:** Parking 60

BUCKDEN — Map 18 SD97

Pick of the Pubs

The Buck Inn ★★ 🏅🏅 🐑 ♀
BD23 5JA ☎ 01756 760228 📠 01756 760227
e-mail: info@thebuckinn.com
Dir: *From Skipton take B6265, then B6160*

Set at the foot of Buckden Pike which rises to a dramatic 2,300 feet, this Georgian inn faces south across the village green where it is surrounded by picturesque stone cottages, and affords panoramic views of this beautiful part of the Dales. The cosy bar, where real ales are hand pulled and a stock of over 25 malts is kept, has lots of old world charm and character. Bar meals might include a trio of local sausages with champ potatoes, or venison and cranberry burger with fries. Imaginative dishes are also served in the pretty restaurant, where the carte menu offers a daily-changing choice based on Dales meat, fresh fish and local vegetables. A typical selection might be breaded fish cake with home-made tartare sauce and deep-fried leeks; confit of roast lamb shank with olive mash, redcurrant and mint gravy, and warm treacle tart with ginger ice cream.
OPEN: 8-11 **BAR MEALS:** L served all week 12-5 D served all week 6.30-9 Av main course £8.50 **RESTAURANT:** D served all week 6.30-9 Av 3 course à la carte £23.95 Av 4 course fixed price £23.95 **BREWERY/COMPANY:** Free House 🍺: Theakston Best, Black Bull, & Old Peculiar, Scottish Courage John Smith's.
FACILITIES: Children welcome Dogs allowed **NOTES:** Parking 40 **ROOMS:** 14 bedrooms 14 en suite s£36 d£72

Open: 12-3, 7-11.
Closed: Mon
Bar Meals: L served 12-2,
D served 7-9.15.
RESTAURANT: L served Tue-Sun 12-2,
D served Tue-Sat 7-9.15.
BREWERY/COMPANY:
Free House.
🍺: Timothy Taylors Landlord, Black Sheep, Guest ales each week.
FACILITIES: Dogs allowed, Garden.
NOTES: Parking

The Three Hares Inn & Restaurant

A stylishly-presented 18th-century inn, the Three Hares is peacefully located in a village near York, providing a particularly appealing bolthole from the city.

Main Street, Bilbrough, YO23 3PH
☎ 01937 832128 🖨 01937 834626
e info@thethreehares.co.uk
Dir: Off A64, SW of York.

It is a renowned dining pub with an interesting restaurant incorporating the old village forge. The bar with its old beams and flagstone floor is the engaging setting for hand-pulled, cask-conditioned ales, including a new guest beer each week, and a good list of wines by the glass. An imaginative choice of bar food is listed on immaculately written blackboards, changing regularly according to market availability. Well-made soups, such as Chinese vegetable or chicken and ham broth kick off the starters, which might also offer home-made corned beef terrine with pickled onions and Three Hares salsa, or salmon and spinach fish cake with avocado, tomato and red pepper relish. Sauté potatoes and mixed salad are offered as optional side orders. Mains encompass spinach and three cheese pudding with tomato salad and confit of onions; cassoulet of seafood with a pastry crust and creamy rouille, and slow-cooked Moroccan lamb shank with spicy couscous. To finish, there's maybe bread and butter pudding with warm sauce Anglais, or a selection of Yorkshire cheeses. The restaurant, adorned with some striking modern art, provides an equally-attractive environment for some seriously good food. All main courses are plated with vegetables designed to complement the dish: roast rump of lamb with confit of sweet potato and aubergine, and a pepper and pine nut jus, or pan-seared scallops with crushed potato and rocket layered between leaves of puff pastry, served with a chilli dressing.

BURNSALL   Map 19 SE06

Pick of the Pubs

The Red Lion ★★ 🌐 🐕 ♀
By the Bridge BD23 6BU ☎ 01756 720204 🖷 01756 720292
e-mail: redlion@dalenet.co.uk
*Dir: From Skipton take A59 east, take B6160 towards Bolton Abbey,
Burnsall 7m*

Set in a picture postcard village, this 16th-century
ferryman's inn stands on the banks of the River Wharfe
with grounds running down to the water (fishing
available). The old-world charm continues inside, with
cosy armchairs, sofas and wood-burning stoves. Pride is
taken in the seasonal menus based on fresh local
produce. The extensive range of food includes light
lunches (speciality salads and sandwiches), familiar
favourites such as steak and kidney pie or grills, and
plenty of traditional and classically-based specials. Expect
braised Wharfedale beef with horseradish mash and
onions or duckling breast with red onion marmalade and
bubble and squeak. Evening menus might include hot pot
of local lamb with parsnip purée and crispy leeks or roast
Wharfedale pheasant with leg confit, orange and sage
seasoning and caramelised apple. Desserts range from
jam roly poly to Yorkshire curd tart with Swaledale
cheese.
OPEN: 08.00-11.30 (Sun closes 10.30) **BAR MEALS:** L served
all week 12-2.30 D served all week 6-9.30 Av main course £11.50
RESTAURANT: L served all week 12-3.00 D served all week 7-
9.30 Av 3 course à la carte £27 Av 3 course fixed price £27.95
BREWERY/COMPANY: Free House 🍺: Theakston Black Bull,
Greene King Old Speckled Hen,Timothy Taylor Landlord, Scottish
Courage John Smith's. ♀: 14 **FACILITIES:** Children welcome
Garden: Large garden, bordering the river Wharf Dogs allowed
NOTES: Parking 70 **ROOMS:** 11 bedrooms 11 en suite 2 family
rooms s£57 d£112

BYLAND ABBEY   Map 19 SE57

Pick of the Pubs

Abbey Inn 🐕 ♀
YO61 4BD ☎ 01347 868204 🖷 01347 868678
e-mail: jane@nordli.freeserve.co.uk
See Pick of the Pubs on opposite page

CARLTON   Map 19 SE08

Foresters Arms 🐕 ♀
DL8 4BB ☎ 01969 640272 🖷 01969 640467
e-mail: gpsurtees@aol.com
Dir: S of Leyburn off A684 or A6108

There has been a change of hands at the Foresters Arms, an
early 17th-century, Grade II listed building located in a
picturesque Dales village convenient for Middleham Castle,
Aysgarth Falls and Bolton Castle. The bars have been carefully
refurbished to retain their historic atmosphere with fine open
fireplaces and beamed ceilings. A good choice of ales is
offered, alongside dishes of moules marinière, monkfish in
garlic butter, and medallions of pork in apple and cider sauce.
OPEN: 12-3 6.30-11 Closed: 2nd 2 weeks of Jan **BAR MEALS:** L
served Wed-Sun 12-2 D served Tues-Sat 7-9 Av main course £9.50
RESTAURANT: L served Wed-Sun 12-2 D served Tue-Sat 7-9.30 Av 3
course à la carte £17 **BREWERY/COMPANY:** Free House
🍺: Scottish Courage John Smith's, Black Sheep Best & Special,
Greene King Ruddles County. **FACILITIES:** Children welcome Dogs
allowed Water **NOTES:** Parking 15

SHADES & GRADES OF BEER

A distinction between beer and ale used to be drawn centuries ago. Ale was the old British brew made without
hops. Not until the 15th century did the use of hops spread to Britain from the Continent and the suspect, newfangled,
bitterer drink was called beer. Ale is no longer made and the two words are now used indiscriminately. Bottled beer is
distinguished from draught beer from a cask, keg or tank, but a more useful dividing line may be the one between real ale,
which matures in the cask, and keg or bottled beer that does not.
Bitter is the classic British draught beer, brewed with plenty of hops. Mild, less heavily hopped and less sharp in taste, is most
often found in the Midlands and the North West of England. Old ale usually means stronger mild, matured longer. Light ale
or pale ale is bottled beer of a lightish colour Lager is lighter and blander still, in a bottle or on draught. Brown ale
is a darker, richer bottled beer, and porter is richer still. Stout is the blackest and richest of all.Strong ale or
barley wine has a higher alcohol content than the others, or should have.

Open: 11.30-3, 6.30-11
Bar Meals: L served Tue-Sun 12-2,
D served Mon-Sat 6.30-9.
Av cost main course £7.50
RESTAURANT: L served Tue-Sun 12-2,
D served Mon-Sat 6.30-9.
Av cost 3 courses £20
BREWERY/COMPANY:
Free House.
🍺: Black Sheep Best, Carlsberg-Tetley Bitter.
FACILITIES: Children welcome, Garden.
NOTES: Parking 30

Abbey Inn

Like so many other monasteries, Byland Abbey became a ruin thanks to Henry VIII. But the thing about ruins is that they can be hauntingly beautiful - and Byland's, in whose shadows the Abbey Inn lies, certainly are.

 🍷
Byland Abbey, Coxwold, YO61 4BD
☎ 01347 868204 📠 01347 868678
📧 jane@nordli.freeserve.co.uk
Dir: From A19 Thirk/York follow signs to Byland Abbey/Coxwold.

Cistercian monks built the abbey over a thousand years ago and it was again monks - Benedictines this time - who, three hundred years after the Dissolution, built the inn. Do seek out this isolated rural pub - it's worth it for the modern British-based food it serves and, if you're looking for somewhere to stay, its superior accommodation. A well-proportioned, creeper-clad façade conceals a highly

distinctive interior with four splendid dining areas with, variously, bare boards, rug-strewn flagstones, open fireplaces, huge settles with scatter cushions, Jacobean-style chairs, and oak and stripped deal tables topped with large, Gothic candlesticks. Fine tapestries, stuffed birds, dried flowers and unusual objets d'art complete the picture. The food comes from a frequently-changing menu and daily specials board. At lunchtime your meal could comprise white onion soup, crèpes filled with chicken in a cream and Byland blue cheese sauce, and raspberry marshmallow meringue. The

evening menu may list main courses such as roast breast of duck with orange and cherry sauce, oriental stirfry in oyster sauce with egg noodles, or pan-fried sirloin steak with either peppercorn or Stilton sauce. Seafood is always well represented on the specials board. A commendable list of Old and New World wines includes a dozen or so by the glass. The abbey ruins are floodlit at night.

England

CARTHORPE
Map 19 SE38

Pick of the Pubs

The Fox & Hounds
DL8 2LG ☎ 01845 567433 📠 01845 567155
Dir: Off A1, signposted on both northbound & southbound carriageways

Tucked away just off the A1, in considerably quieter surroundings, this neat 200-year-old free house, run by the Fitzgerald family for 20 years, was once the village smithy. In fact, the old anvil and other tools of the trade can still be seen in the dining room. The midweek set-price lunch and dinner menu offers grilled honey and mustard sausages with parsley mash and onion gravy, baked haddock with a crispy crumb topping, and penne pasta with mushroom and white wine sauce. From the blackboard come steamed game pudding, breast of corn-fed chicken with chargrilled vegetables, and whole freshly-dressed Whitby crab with salad. Sunday lunch includes all the usual roasts, home-made steak and kidney pie, and poached Scottish salmon with hollandaise sauce. For pudding, try apple and cinnamon flan with cream, or one of the range of ice creams - also home-made. All wines are available by the glass.
OPEN: 12-2.30 7-11 Closed: 1st wk Jan **BAR MEALS:** L served Tue-Sun 12-2 D served Tue-Sun 7-10 Av main course £9.50
RESTAURANT: L served Tue-Sun 12-2 D served Tue-sun 7-9.30 Av 3 course à la carte £18 Av 3 course fixed price £12.95
BREWERY/COMPANY: Free House 🍺 Black Sheep Best, Coors Worthington's Bitter. **FACILITIES:** Children welcome
NOTES: Parking 22

CLAPHAM
Map 18 SD76

New Inn
LA2 8HH ☎ 015242 51203 📠 015242 51496
e-mail: info@newinn-clapham.co.uk
Dir: On A65 in Yorkshire Dales National Park

Family-run 18th-century coaching inn located in a peaceful Dales village beneath Ingleborough, one of Yorkshire's most

continued

famous summits. There are plenty of good walks from the pub, including one to Ingleborough Show Cave, open to the public at weekends and on Bank Holidays throughout the year. Honest, wholesome food includes Thai-style chicken and noodles, game casserole, slow-roast lamb shank, and Sunday roasts.
OPEN: 11-11 (Winter open 11-3, 6.30-11) **BAR MEALS:** L served all week 12-2 D served all week 6.30-8.30 Av main course £7.95
RESTAURANT: L served all week 12-2 D served all week 6.30-8.30 Av 3 course à la carte £22.50 Av 4 course fixed price £18.50
BREWERY/COMPANY: Free House 🍺 Black Sheep Best, Carlsberg-Tetley Tetley Bitter, Daleside Bitter, Guests. ♀ 18
FACILITIES: Children welcome Garden: Riverside seats, beer garden Dogs allowed Water **NOTES:** Parking 35 **ROOMS:** 19 bedrooms 19 en suite s£29 d£58 (★★)

COLTON
Map 16 SE54

Ye Old Sun Inn ♀ NEW
Main St LS24 8EP ☎ 01904 744261 📠 01904 744261
Dir: 15 minutes from York on A64 towards Leeds, signposted to Appleton, Roebuck and Colton, 0.75 mile off A64
Lovely little 18th-century inn on the old main road into York, where roaring fires and candlelight enhance the cosy atmosphere. The pub grows its own herbs and interesting vegetables that are otherwise difficult to source, and makes its own ice creams - from vanilla to liquorice flavour. Imaginative menus include brill and trout strudel on braised red cabbage, and basil and honey-marinated pork loin on saffron risotto with chargrilled red peppers.
OPEN: 12-2.30 6-11 Closed: 1-26 Jan **BAR MEALS:** L served Tue-Sun 12-2 D served Tue-Sun 6.30-9.30 Av main course £11.50
BREWERY/COMPANY: Enterprise Inns 🍺 John Smith, Directors, Tetleys, Guest Ale (changing weekly). ♀ 16 **FACILITIES:** Garden: Lawn with tables and chairs **NOTES:** Parking 48

COXWOLD
Map 19 SE57

Pick of the Pubs

The Fauconberg Arms
Main St YO61 4AD ☎ 01347 868214 📠 01347 868172
e-mail: fanconbergarms@aol.co.uk
Dir: Take A19 S from Thirsk, 2m turn L, signposted alternative route for caravans/heavy vehicles. 5m to village
Named after a peer who married Oliver Cromwell's daughter Mary, this family-run pub surveys a broad, flowertub-lined village street. The food - there are separate bar and restaurant menus - is prepared with fresh local produce, and it's good. Restaurant menu starters may include roasted pigeon in a light broth, and grilled kidneys with mustard sauce. Sample main courses include lamb's liver with black pudding and pancetta with red wine jus, monkfish wrapped in Mozzarella and bacon with tomato dressing, and baked cabbage with nut and mushroom stuffing and sweet pepper coulis.
OPEN: 11-2.30 6.30-11 (Summer all day) **BAR MEALS:** L served all week 12-2.30 D served all week 6.30-9
RESTAURANT: L served Sun 12-4 D served Wed-Sat 6.30-9.30 Av 3 course à la carte £25 Av 3 course fixed price £17
BREWERY/COMPANY: Free House 🍺 Theakston Best, Carlsberg-Tetley Tetley Bitter, Scottish Courage, John Smith's.
NOTES: Parking 25

 Pubs offering a good choice of fish on their menu

CRAY — Map 18 SD97

The White Lion Inn ♀
Cray BD23 5JB ☎ 01756 760262 ▤ 761024
e-mail: admin.whitelion@btinternet.com

Renowned as a 'tiny oasis' of hospitality, this traditional Dales inn nestles beneath Buckden Pike, and is the highest pub in Wharfedale. The tastefully-restored former drovers' hostelry remains faithful to its origins with old beams, log fires and stone-flagged floors. Hand-pulled ales and home-cooked food complete the picture: try whole rack of barbecued ribs, mild lamb curry, or pan-fried chicken breast, along with various lighter bites at lunchtime.
OPEN: 11-11 Closed: 25 Dec **BAR MEALS:** L served all week 12-2.15 D served all week 5.45-8.45 Av main course £8.50
BREWERY/COMPANY: Free House ◀: Daleside Blonde, Moorhouse Pendle witches Brew, Premier Bitter, Timothy Taylor Landlord. ♀: 12 **FACILITIES:** Children welcome Garden: Beer garden with 10 trestle tables Dogs allowed Water **NOTES:** Parking 20 **ROOMS:** 8 bedrooms 8 en suite s£37.50 d£55 (♦♦♦)

CROPTON — Map 19 SE78

The New Inn ☜ ♀
YO18 8HH ☎ 01751 417330 ▤ 01751 417582
e-mail: newinn@cropton.fsbusiness.co.uk

With the award-winning Cropton micro-brewery in its own grounds, this family-run free house on the edge of the North York Moors National Park is popular with locals and visitors alike. Meals are served in the restored village bar, and in the elegant Victorian restaurant: black pudding and peppercorn, prawn and paw-paw salad, pork fillet stuffed with mango, and breast of chicken stuffed with Cashell Blue cheese perhaps, along with various sandwiches.
OPEN: 11-11 **BAR MEALS:** L served all week 12-2 D served all week 6-9.30 **RESTAURANT:** L served all week 12-2 D served all week 6-9.30 **BREWERY/COMPANY:** Free House ◀: Cropton Two Pints, Monkmans Slaughter & Backwoods, Thwaites Best Bitter.
FACILITIES: Children welcome Garden **NOTES:** Parking 50

DACRE BANKS — Map 19 SE16

The Royal Oak Inn ☜
Oak Ln HG3 4EN ☎ 01423 780200
e-mail: enquiries@theroyaloak.uk.com
Dir: From A59 (Harrogate/Skipton) take B6451 towards Pateley Bridge

In the heart of Nidderdale, this family-run free house was built in 1752. With its open fires and timbered beams, the Royal Oak offers fine Yorkshire ales and home-cooked meals. There's also an attractive rear garden, and three en suite bedrooms. The snack menu includes hot baguettes and jacket potatoes, whilst serious diners can expect roast rib of local beef, Nidderdale sausage and mash, marlin steak in white wine, tomato and orange sauce and Savoy cabbage roulade.
OPEN: 11.30-3 5-11 (Sun 12-3, 7-10.30) Rest: Dec 25 Closed eve **BAR MEALS:** L served all week 11.30-2 D served all week 6.30-9 Av main course £7 **RESTAURANT:** L served all week 11.30-2 D served all week 6.30-9 Av 3 course à la carte £18.50 Av 3 course fixed price £12.95 **BREWERY/COMPANY:** Free House ◀: Rudgate Yorkshire Dales & Special, Black Sheep Best, Royal Oak Dacre Ale, Carlsberg-Tetley Tetley's Mild. **FACILITIES:** Children welcome Garden: Tables, garden at rear overlooks river **NOTES:** Parking 15 **ROOMS:** 3 bedrooms 3 en suite s£30 d£50 (♦♦♦♦)

DANBY — Map 19 NZ70

Duke of Wellington Inn ☜
YO21 2LY ☎ 01287 660351
e-mail: landlord@dukeofwellington.freeserve.co.uk
Dir: From A171 between Guisborough & Whitby take rd signed 'Danby & Moors Centre'

An attractive, ivy-clad inn overlooking the village green. It was a recruiting post during Napoleon's threatened invasion of England - thus the name - and Wellington's cast-iron plaque, exposed during renovations, is above the fireplace. The diminutive Corsican never even crossed the Channel, let alone reach North Yorkshire, but today's visitors arrive from far and wide. Standard pub fare at lunchtime, with a wider choice in

continued

England

DANBY continued

the evening, including beef and mushrooms in Guinness, deep-fried cod fillet in beer batter, and poached haggis.
OPEN: 11-3 7-11 **BAR MEALS:** L served all week 12-2 D served all week 7-9 Av main course £7.25 **RESTAURANT:** 12-2 7-9
BREWERY/COMPANY: Free House **:** Scottish Courage John Smith's, Cameron's Strongarm **FACILITIES:** Children welcome Garden Dogs allowed Water **NOTES:** Parking 12 **ROOMS:** 9 bedrooms 9 en suite s£33 d£60 (♦♦♦♦)

EAST WITTON   Map 19 SE18

Pick of the Pubs

The Blue Lion 🐾 ♀
DL8 4SN ☎ 01969 624273 📠 01969 624189
e-mail: bluelion@breathemail.net

From the end of the 18th century onwards, coach travellers and drovers journeying through Wensleydale could refuel at the Blue Lion. Probably largely unchanged since then, its stone façades have featured in the sixties-based TV series 'Heartbeat'. Depending on one's preference, the bar with its open fire and flagstone floor, and the restaurant, candlelit in the evening, are both perfect settings. Beer drinkers will appreciate the traditional hand-pulled beers, including Black Sheep's fruity Riggwelter. Restaurant diners could well mull over the menu choices for ages before settling on, say, Roquefort and cos salad garnished with croûtons, followed by roast fillet of cod with pesto parsley crust and roast fennel, and then home-made melon sorbet with vanilla syrup. The bar menu is no slouch either in the choice department: starters include crispy prawn and ginger spring roll with sweet and sour dressing, and warm onion and blue Wensleydale cheese tart with tomato chutney, with home-made spaghetti carbonara, or roast fillet of cod with brown shrimps and lemon butter, to follow.
OPEN: 11-11 **BAR MEALS:** L served all week 12-2 D served all week 7-9 Av main course £12 **RESTAURANT:** L served Sun 12-2 D served all week 7-9 Av 3 course à la carte £25
BREWERY/COMPANY: Free House **:** Black Sheep Riggwelter, Scottish Courage Theakston Old Peculier. ♀: 12
FACILITIES: Children welcome Garden: Large lawn, beautiful views Dogs allowed **NOTES:** Parking 30

See Pub Walk on page 532

♀ 7   **Number of wines by the glass**

EGTON BRIDGE   Map 19 NZ80

Horseshoe Hotel ♀
YO21 1XE ☎ 01947 895245
Dir: From Whitby take A171 towards Middlesborough Village signed in 5m

Right on the banks of the River Esk, its large garden with picnic tables a draw to the local ducks and geese, a residential 18th-century country inn with fishing rights. Inside the bar is a welcoming open fire, oak settles and tables, and local artists' paintings adorning the walls. Bar food includes such delights as lamb shank on minted mash with rosemary and red wine sauce, fish pie, vegetable lasagne, sirloin of beef, chicken breast with red wine, mushroom and bacon sauce, and scampi with home-made tartare sauce.
OPEN: 11.30-3 6.30-11 (All day Sat & Sun in Summer) Closed: 25 Dec **BAR MEALS:** L served all week 12-2 D served all week 7-9 Av main course £8 **RESTAURANT:** L served all week 12-2 D served all week 7-9 Av 3 course à la carte £8 **BREWERY/COMPANY:** Free House **:** Scottish Courage & John Smiths, Durham, Whitby. ♀: 7 **FACILITIES:** Children welcome Garden: Beautiful garden on banks of River Esk Dogs allowed Water Provided **NOTES:** Parking 25

ELSLACK   Map 18 SD94

The Tempest Arms ♀
BD23 3AY ☎ 01282 842450 📠 01282 843331
Dir: From Skipton take A59 towards Gisburn. Elslack signed on L on A56
Peaceful Dales countryside surrounds this essentially English pub, traditionally built from stone and named after a local landowner. The same quality food is served in both the cosy bar with its wing chairs and log fires, and the candle-lit dining room. From an inviting and intriguing menu expect such delights as Lamb Thingy Me Bob, Eastern Spice Pot, steak melt, and lamb's liver and 'It'; the 'It' being an award-winning black pudding. Cool sandwiches, hot sandwiches and fresh fish and vegetarian options are also available.
OPEN: 7-11 **BAR MEALS:** L served all week 12-2.30 D served all week 6-9 Av main course £9 **RESTAURANT:** L served all week 12-2.30 D served all week 6-9 **BREWERY/COMPANY:** Free House **:** Timothy Taylor Best & Landlord, Black Sheep Best, Scottish Courage Theakston Best. ♀: 8 **FACILITIES:** Garden **NOTES:** Parking 120

ESCRICK   Map 16 SE64

Black Bull Inn ♦♦♦ 🐾 ♀
Main St YO19 6JP ☎ 01904 728245 📠 01904 728154
e-mail: blackbullhotel@btconnect.com
Dir: From York follow the A19 for 5m, enter Escrick, take second L up main street, premises located on the L
Situated in the heart of a quiet village, this 19th-century pub is within easy reach of York racecourse and the historic city

continued

centre. A typical menu may include Moroccan chicken, haddock mornay, steak and ale pie, oriental salmon, fillet steak rossini, or chicken and vegetable pie.

OPEN: 12-3 5-11 (Sun all day) **BAR MEALS:** L served all week 12-2.30 D served all week 6-9.30 Av main course £6 **RESTAURANT:** L served all week 12-2.30 D served all week 6-9.30 Av 3 course à la carte £12 ❦: John Smiths, Tetleys, Carlsberg, Stella. ♉: 7 **FACILITIES:** Children welcome Dogs allowed Guide dogs only **NOTES:** Parking 10 **ROOMS:** 10 bedrooms 10 en suite 2 family rooms s£42 d£65

FADMORE   Map 19 SE68

Pick of the Pubs

The Plough Inn ♉
Main St YO62 7HY ☎ 01751 431515 ▤ 431515
Dir: *1m N of Kirkbymoorside on the A170 Thirsk to Scarborough Rd*

A well-established restaurant and country inn located on the edge of the North Yorkshire Moors National Park. From its position overlooking the tranquil village green, the genuinely-hospitable Plough enjoys views towards the Vale of Pickering and the Wolds. Snug little rooms and open fires draw local people to this stylishly-refurbished pub, and the imaginative food is another attraction. A good selection of home-cooked dishes includes plenty of fresh fish and seafood, and most of the kitchen produce is locally sourced. Starters might include home-made farmhouse terrine, steamed Shetland mussels or paupiette of lemon sole stuffed with smoked salmon mousse. Main courses include firm favourites such as griddled rump steak or roasted lamb shank, and a good range of seafood such as pan-fried medallions of monkfish with curried mussels, king prawns and saffron egg noodles or seared smoked haddock fillet with a creamy white wine and parsley sauce. Well-chosen wines and real Yorkshire ales go down well with bar snacks too.
OPEN: 12-2.30 6.30-11 Closed: 25-26th Dec, 1st Jan

continued

BAR MEALS: L served Mon-Sun 12-2 D served Mon-Sun 6.30-8.45 Av main course £10 **RESTAURANT:** L served Mon-Sun 12-2 D served Mon-Sun 6.30-8.45 Av 3 course à la carte £17 **BREWERY/COMPANY:** Free House ❦: Black Sheep Best, Scottish Courage John Smith's + Guest beers. ♉: 6 **FACILITIES:** Children welcome Garden: Raised patio area overlooking garden **NOTES:** Parking 20

GIGGLESWICK   Map 18 SD86

Black Horse Hotel ◆◆◆
32 Church St BD24 0BE ☎ 01729 822506
The Black Horse is set in the middle of an attractive village, next to the church and behind the market cross. A good choice of home-cooked meals is served either in the bar or dining room, perhaps lamb hotpot, lasagne (meat or vegetarian), poached salmon, and a selection of pizzas. There are three comfortable en suite bedrooms.
OPEN: 12-2.30 5.30-11 (Sat-Sun all day) **BAR MEALS:** L served Tue-Sun 12-1.45 D served all week 7-8.45 Av main course £6.50
RESTAURANT: L served Tue-Sun 12-1.45 D served all week 7-8.45 Av 3 course à la carte £13 **BREWERY/COMPANY:** Free House ❦: Carlsberg-Tetley Bitter, Timothy Taylor Landlord, Scottish Courage John Smiths. **FACILITIES:** Garden **NOTES:** Parking 16 **ROOMS:** 3 bedrooms 3 en suite s£38 d£52 no children overnight

GOATHLAND   Map 19 NZ80

Birch Hall Inn
Beckhole YO22 5LE ☎ 01947 896245
e-mail: birchhallinn@beckhole.freeserve.co.uk
Dir: *Telephone for directions*

Remotely situated between the North York Moors steam railway and the Grosmont Rail Trail walk, this extraordinary little free house comprises two very small rooms separated by a confectionary shop. There's an open fire in the main bar and a tiny family room that leads out into a large garden. Well-kept ales wash down home-baked pies, Beckhole butty sandwiches, home-made scones and buttered beer cake. Operated by the same owners for over twenty years.
OPEN: 11-3 7.30-11 (Sun 12-3, 7.30-10.30) (Summer 11-11, Sun 12-10.30) Rest: 25 Dec, Mondays (Sep-May) Closed eve
BAR MEALS: L served all week 11-3 D served all week 7.30-11
BREWERY/COMPANY: Free House ❦: Black Sheep Best, Theakstons Black Bull, Cropton Yorkshire Moors Bitter & Honey Gold.
FACILITIES: Garden: Terraced area Dogs allowed on leads, Water & dog treat **NOTES:** No credit cards

---

★ **Star rating for inspected hotel accommodation**

England

GREAT AYTON
Map 19 NZ51

The Royal Oak Hotel ♦♦♦ ♀
123 High St TS9 6BW ☎ 01642 722361 📠 01642 724047
e-mail: derekmonaghan@aol.co.uk

Real fires and a relaxed, smokey atmosphere are all part of
the attraction at this traditional corner pub. Behind the
Georgian façade the decor is basic but welcoming, and the
place positively hums with people eagerly seeking out the
highly-reputable food. A range of simple, robust dishes might
include starters like pigeon, duck and foie gras terrine,
Anglesea charcuterie platter, or butternut squash and goats'
curd risotto. Among main courses could be slow-cooked belly
of pork, Brittany 'Cotriade' fish stew, pot-roast stuffed saddle
of lamb, and toasted sea bass with saffron potatoes. Puddings
are also exemplary: expect poached pear, brandy snap and
pear sorbet, chocolate, pecan and hazelnut 'brownie' cake
with vanilla ice cream, or perhaps buttermilk pudding with
pineapple and almond biscotti. A savoury alternative might be
Cornish yarm with chutney and water biscuits.
OPEN: 11-11 (Sun 12-10.30) Closed: Dec 25 **BAR MEALS:** L
served all week 11-6 D served all week 6.30-9.30 Av main course
£8.95 **RESTAURANT:** L served all week 12-2 D served all week 7-
9.30 Av 3 course à la carte £15.75 Av 3 course fixed price £17.75
BREWERY/COMPANY: 🍺: Theakstons, J Smiths Smooth,
Directors. ♀: 10 **FACILITIES:** Children welcome Children's licence
ROOMS: 5 bedrooms 4 en suite s£40 d£60

GREAT OUSEBURN
Map 19 SE46

Pick of the Pubs

The Crown Inn 🐾 ♀
Main St YO26 9RF ☎ 01423 330430 📠 01423 331095
The Crown is proud of its history. Here, Ambrose Tiller
founded his world-renowned troupe of dancing 'Tiller
Girls', while another regular, Norman Barrett, went on to
become ringmaster at Blackpool's Tower Circus. The
original brew-house is now the dining room, and the
pub's wrought iron tables have been in constant use for at
least seventy years. Between the wars, you could dine on
steak, chips and peas, followed by home-made apple pie
and cream - all for one shilling and sixpence, or the
equivalent of seven and a half new pence! Prices may
have changed, but two-course bar lunches remain good
value. In the dining room, a Greek salad or freshly-made
fishcakes might precede rack of lamb, duck with port and
blackberries, haddock and prawns au gratin, or parsnip,
Stilton and chestnut bake. Puddings include treacle tart,
banoffee meringue, and fruit platter.
OPEN: 12-2 5-11 (All day BHS) (Sat 11-11 Sun 12-10.30) Rest:
Mon-Fri Closed lunch **BAR MEALS:** L served Sat-Sun D

served all week 5-9.30 Av main course £6 **RESTAURANT:** L
served Sat-Sun D served all week 5-9.30 Av 3 course à la carte
£22 **BREWERY/COMPANY:** Free House 🍺: Black Sheep
Best, Scottish Courage John Smith's, Timothy Taylor Landlord,
Carlsberg-Tetley Tetley's Cask. ♀: 10 **FACILITIES:** Children
welcome Garden: Paved, walled area **NOTES:** Parking 60

GREEN HAMMERTON
Map 19 SE4

The Bay Horse Inn
York Rd YO26 8BN ☎ 01423 330338 331113 📠 01423 331279
e-mail: thebayhorseinn@aol.com

An old coaching inn with bags of character located in a small
village between the North Yorkshire Moors and Yorkshire
Dales National Park, eight miles from either Harrogate or
York. It offers traditional bars with log fires, a cosy restaurant
and en suite accommodation. Food is served in both the bar
and restaurant, and popular options include sirloin au poivre,
Bayhorse chicken, roast beef, surf 'n' turf, salmon hollandaise,
steak and kidney pie, lasagne, and Maderia pork.
OPEN: 11.30-2.30 6.30-11 **BAR MEALS:** L served all week 12-2 D
served all week 6.30-9.15 Av main course £6.50 **RESTAURANT:** L
served all week D served all week 6.30-9.15 Av 3 course à la carte
£15.75 **BREWERY/COMPANY:** Free House 🍺: Daleside,
Carlsberg-Tetley Tetley's. **FACILITIES:** Children welcome Garden
Dogs allowed Water **NOTES:** Parking 40 **ROOMS:** 10 bedrooms
10 en suite 2 family rooms s£40 d£60 (♦♦♦)

HAROME
Map 19 SE6

Pick of the Pubs

The Star Inn ⚬⚬ 🐾 ♀
YO62 5JE ☎ 01439 770397 📠 01439 771833
Dir: From Helmsley take A170 towards Kirkbymoorside. 0.5m turn R
for Harome
A cruck-framed longhouse containing cow byres and an
old dormitory once used by travelling monks, are two of
the fascinating features of this picturesque 14th-century
inn. Nowadays the dormitory houses a distinctive coffee
loft, while the byres have been converted into a stylish
and reputable restaurant. The part-thatched inn also has a
separate bar full of the hand-carved furniture of 'Mousey'
Thompson, and where fine real ales and carefully-selected
house wines by the glass are served. Home-grown herbs
from a fragrant, lovingly-tended garden, and seasonal
exotica chosen from local suppliers all feature in the
cooking. The lunch menu lists braised faggot of local
game, and risotto of Dalby Forest mushrooms with baby
spinach leaves, available as a small or large dish. In the
evening expect roast pork fillet with black pudding risotto,

continued

continued

and seared yellow fin tuna with anchovy salad.
OPEN: 11.30-3 6.30-11 Closed: 2 wks Jan, 1 wk Nov
BAR MEALS: L served Tue-Sun 11.30-2 D served Tue-Sun 6.30-10 Av main course £13 **RESTAURANT:** L served Tue-Sun 11.30-2 D served Tue-Sun 6.30-10 Av 3 course à la carte £27
BREWERY/COMPANY: Free House ◄: Black Sheep Special, Scottish Courage John Smiths & Theakston Best. ♀: 8
FACILITIES: Children welcome Garden: Approx 10 tables with umbrellas Dogs allowed Water **NOTES:** Parking 40

HARROGATE
Map 19 SE35

Pick of the Pubs

The Boars Head Hotel ★★★ @@ ☜ ♀
Ripley Castle Estate HG3 3AY
☎ 01423 771888 ▤ 01423 771509
e-mail: reservations@boarsheadripley.co.uk
Dir: On the A61 Harrogate/Ripon road, the Hotel is in the centre of Ripley village

The Boars Head is an old coaching inn on the Ripley Castle Estate, luxuriously refurbished by Sir Thomas and Lady Ingilby. Guests never tire of the selection of locally-brewed guest beers and fine choice of malt whiskies, and the resident chef/patron offers creative cooking in both the restaurant and bistro from an ever-changing menu. Starter dishes, which can also be taken as mains in a larger portion, include warm salad of Spanish chorizo sausage, plum tomatoes and linguini, or venison and goats' cheese terrine with a warm horseradish dressing. The eponymous wild boar turns up in sausages with Parmesan creamed potatoes and red wine gravy, and a favourite pudding comprises a dark chocolate cone filled with white chocolate mousse. The walled courtyard situated to the rear of the hotel is wonderful in summer when guests can dine outside. Children and well-behaved dogs are welcome.
OPEN: 11-11 (Winter Mon-Sat 11-3, 5-11) Sun 12-10.30 (Winter Sun 12-3, 5-10.30) **BAR MEALS:** L served all week 12-2.30 D served all week 6.30-10 Av main course £8.95 **RESTAURANT:** L served all week 12-2 D served all week 7-9.30
BREWERY/COMPANY: Free House ◄: Scottish Courage Theakston Best & Old Peculier, Daleside Crackshot, Hambleton White Boar, Jennings Cumberland. ♀: 7 **FACILITIES:** Children welcome Garden: Courtyard area Dogs allowed Overnight in bedrooms only **NOTES:** Parking 45 **ROOMS:** 25 bedrooms 25 en suite

---

◆ **Diamond rating for inspected guest accommodation**

HAWES
Map 18 SD88

Board Hotel ◆◆◆ ♀
Market Place DL8 3RD ☎ 01969 667223 ▤ 01969 667970
Dir: M6 J37 - A684 E to Hawes. Down hill & 1st pub on L opp market hall

Majestic views of Wensleydale can be relished from this typical Dales pub in the highest market town in Britain. Directly opposite the pub is the famous Wensleydale cheese factory and close by are numerous stunning walks. In addition, there is plenty of opportunity for cycling, fishing and hang-gliding. Expect a friendly welcome and good, hearty pub food like gammon and pineapple, 'hungry shepherd', mushroom Stroganoff, and choice of omelettes among the well-established favourites.
OPEN: 11-11 **BAR MEALS:** L served all week 12 D served all week 8.30 Av main course £5.25 **RESTAURANT:** 12 8.30
BREWERY/COMPANY: Free House ◄: Carlsberg-Tetley Tetley Bitter, Black Sheep Best, Theakston Bitter, Marston's Pedigree. ♀: 8
FACILITIES: Children welcome Garden: 6 tables outside
NOTES: Parking 10 **ROOMS:** 3 bedrooms 3 en suite d£25

HELMSLEY
Map 19 SE68

The Feathers Hotel
YO62 5BH ☎ 01439 770275 ▤ 01439 771101
e-mail: feathers@destination-england.co.uk
Dir: From A1(M) Jct 168 to Thirsk, then A170 for 14M to Hemsley
This traditional country inn overlooking the market place was once the home of the local doctor and is one of Helmsley's oldest houses. The beamed Pickwick Bar is popular with locals, and freshly-cooked food is served in the Feversham dining room and bar with its Mouseman of Kilburn furniture. Home-made pie and quiche, sausages, mash and onion gravy, mixed grill and 8oz (225gm) hamburger are among the popular dishes.
OPEN: 10.30-11 **BAR MEALS:** 12-2.30 6-9 **RESTAURANT:** 12-2.30 6-9 **BREWERY/COMPANY:** Free House
FACILITIES: Children welcome Garden Dogs allowed
NOTES: Parking 24

Pick of the Pubs

The Feversham Arms Hotel ★★★ @ ♀
High St YO62 5AG ☎ 01439 770766 ▤ 01439 770346
e-mail: fevershamarmshotel@msn.com
Dir: from the A1(M) jct A168 to Thirsk, then A170 for 14m to Helmsley
Built in 1855, this stylish little hotel has been completely transformed by its owners, who have created an intimate dining room, lounge and bar area. Look, too, for the 'Brasserie at the Fev' which aims for adventurous contemporary cooking in a relaxed atmosphere. The menu starts with seafood pancake, filo-wrapped goats'

continued

England

HELMSLEY continued

cheese or eggs Benedict with air-dried ham. Main courses include pan-seared salmon steak on linguine noodles with a chilli and basil dressing, rich home-made Bolognese sauce on a bed of fresh spaghetti with Parmesan flakes, and rack of lamb on minted potato with rosemary-infused jus. Extensive international wine list and good choice of lunchtime light bites. The accommodation offers seven suites, and 17 upmarket en suite bedrooms. Guests can also avail themselves of the poolside terrace and corner garden, state-of-the-art gym, sauna, heated outdoor pool and tennis court.

OPEN: 10-11 **BAR MEALS:** L served all week 12-2
BREWERY/COMPANY: Free House 🍺 Landlord & Tetley.
FACILITIES: Children welcome Garden: Food served outside
NOTES: Parking 50 **ROOMS:** 17 bedrooms 17 en suite s£80 d£100

HETTON
Map 18 SD95

Pick of the Pubs

The Angel 🏵🏵 🛏 ⵠ
BD23 6LT ☎ 01756 730263 📠 01756 730363
e-mail: info@angelhetton.co.uk
Dir: From A59 take B6265 towards Grassington/Skipton

The Angel has a legendary reputation: genuinely unspoilt, it is a traditional 400-year-old Dales pub with lots of nooks and crannies, oak beams and roaring log fires in winter. It is everything a British pub should be, with real ales, 20 wines by the glass and 50 types of whisky including its own label 30-year single malt. Whether you choose a pint of Black Sheep and a bowl of soup or a three-course meal, the intention is to make your visit memorable. The emphasis is on thoroughly good food prepared from the freshest ingredients. Seafood is a speciality, and dishes from the blackboard might feature queen scallops baked in garlic butter and Gruyère, pan-fried silver mullet with tagliolini pasta, spinach caponata and Parmesan shavings, or chargrilled free range 'Spotwood' pork chop with Tuscan grilled vegetables. Meals can also be enjoyed on the terrace with views of Rylestone Fell.

OPEN: 12-3 6-10.30 Closed: Dec 25 **BAR MEALS:** L served all week 12-2 D served all week 6-9 Av main course £8.50
RESTAURANT: L served Sun 12-2 D served Mon-Sat 6-9 Av 3 course à la carte £25 Av 3 course fixed price £18.50
BREWERY/COMPANY: Free House 🍺 Blacksheep Bitter, Taylor Landlord, Worthington Best. ⵠ: 20
FACILITIES: Children welcome Garden: Terrace in front of Pub
NOTES: Parking 56

HOVINGHAM
Map 19 SE67

The Malt Shovel 🛏
Main St YO62 4LF ☎ 01653 628264 📠 01653 628264
Dir: 18 miles NE of York, 5 miles from Castle Howard
The Malt Shovel is a stone-built pub set in a pretty Ryedale village close to Castle Howard. It offers a friendly and traditional atmosphere with good-value food. Popular options are fresh Whitby haddock with the house's own tartare sauce, or home-made steak and mushroom pie. Game is speciality, including pheasant casserole served with Yorkshire pudding, or plump local partridge breasts with Irish mashed potatoes.
OPEN: 12-2.30 7-11 **BAR MEALS:** L served all week 12-2 D served all week 6-9 Av main course £6 **RESTAURANT:** L served all week 12-2 D served all week 6-9 Av 3 course à la carte £20
BREWERY/COMPANY: Pubmaster 🍺: Carlsberg-Tetleys Tetley's, Greene King IPA. **FACILITIES:** Children welcome Garden
NOTES: Parking 50

Pick of the Pubs

The Worsley Arms Hotel ★★★ 🏵🏵 ⵠ
Main St YO62 4LA ☎ 01653 628234 📠 01653 628130
e-mail: worsleyarms@aol.com
See Pick of the Pubs on opposite page

HUBBERHOLME
Map 18 SD97

The George Inn
BD23 5JE ☎ 01756 760223 📠 01756 760808
e-mail: visit@thegeorge-inn.co.uk
Dir: At Buckden on B6160 take turn for Hubberholme
The highest road in Yorkshire runs through the village of Hubberholme, rising to 1,934 feet. Writer J B Priestley regarded the village's 18th-century George Inn as his favourite pub - a traditional Dales inn with flagstone floors, mullioned windows and an open fire. Home-cooked meals are prepared from local produce, with filled rolls, Yorkshire puddings and steak and chips at lunchtime, and Black sheep casserole, Dales lamb chops and Wensleydale pork on the dinner menu.
OPEN: 11.30-3 6.30-11 (Summer 11.30-11) Closed: Middle 2 wks in Jan
BAR MEALS: L served all week 12-2 D served all week 6.30-8.45 Av main course £7.95 **BREWERY/COMPANY:** Free House 🍺 Black Sheep Best, Carlsberg-Tetley, Tetley Bitter. **FACILITIES:** Garden Dogs allowed Water, Biscuits **NOTES:** Parking 20

HUNTON
Map 19 SE19

The Countryman's Inn ♦♦♦♦ 🛏 NEW
DL8 1PY ☎ 01677 450554 📠 01677 450570
e-mail: contactus@thecountrymansinn.co.uk
Outside it's all light, mellow stone attractively renovated with large picture windows, while inside you will find an atmospheric bar with beamed ceilings and an open fireplace, plus various cosy alcoves. The menu extends to the smart restaurant, including the likes of baked Brie with apple and blackberry chutney, pan-fried pheasant breast with Theakston and mushroom sauce, and chocolate mousse with raspberry purée.
OPEN: 12-3 6-11 (Sun 7-11) **BAR MEALS:** L served all week 12-1.45 D served all week 6-9 Av main course £9 **RESTAURANT:** L served all week 12-1.45 D served all week 6-9 Av 3 course à la carte £15 **BREWERY/COMPANY:** Free House 🍺: Scottish Courage Theakston Black Bull, Bitter & John Smith's Extra Smooth, Black Sheep.
FACILITIES: Children welcome Garden: Patio, grass areas Dogs allowed **NOTES:** Parking 16 **ROOMS:** 5 bedrooms 5 en suite 1 family rooms s£40 d£60

Open: 12-2.30, 7-11
Bar Meals: L served all week 12-2,
D served all week 7-10.
Av cost main course £10
RESTAURANT: L served Sun 12-2,
D served all week 7-10.
Av cost 3 course £30
BREWERY/COMPANY:
Free House.
🍺: Scottish Courage John Smith's,
Hambleton Stallion.
FACILITIES: Dogs allowed, Children
welcome, Garden - Formal and open
gardens, mahogany furniture.
NOTES: Parking 30
ROOMS: 19 en suite from s£70 d£95

The Worsley Arms Hotel

Built in the 18th century as a spa hotel to rival Bath and set the village on the map, the attempt failed but the hotel and inn have happily survived.

★★★ ◉◉ ♈

Main Street, Hovingham, YO62 4LA
☎ 01653 628234 📠 01653 628130
📧 worsleyarms@aol.com
Dir: From A1 take A64 towards
Malton, L onto B1257 signed Slingsby
& Hovingham. 2m to Hovingham.

Located opposite Hovingham Hall, birthplace of the Duchess of Kent, this place is some 20 minutes' drive north of York, and worth the trip to admire the many family portraits that hang throughout. Set in the centre of the village opposite the Hall, it is now a country house hotel with a separate pub where good food, beer and wine can be enjoyed. The bar is of great interest to cricket lovers with its 150-year-long history of matches played on the village green. The Cricketers' Bar menu supplements a wide-ranging sandwich selection with glazed Swaledale goats' cheese with honey and walnut dressing or steamed mussels with shallots, garlic and cream in regular or large portions, and a rib-eye beef steak with green peppercorn sauce and chips for those with healthy appetites. In the Worsley Arms Restaurant, the menus are more sophisticated, with half a dozen award-winning choices at each course. Typical starters might include ballontine of ham hock wrapped in Savoy cabbage with apple and vanilla chutney, and grilled sardines with rocket, black olives and home-dried tomato salad. Delicious main dishes like steamed local rabbit, fennel and tarragon suet pudding with curly kale and cream sauce, and creamed fillet of Yorkshire beef, wild mushrooms, buttered spaghetti and baby spinach show plenty of imagination and good use of fresh local produce. A range of memorable desserts includes lemon posset with fresh raspberries, and banana sticky toffee pudding with butterscotch sauce and rum and raisin ice cream. Tastefully modernised and comfortable lounges, smart bedrooms and a private garden make this an attractive destination.

INGLETON   Map 18 SD67

Marton Arms Hotel ♦♦♦♦ 🛏 ♀ NEW
Thornton-in-Lonsdale LA6 3PB
☎ 01524 241281 📠 01524 242579
e-mail: mail@martonarms.co.uk
Dir: *At junction A65/A687, take the road opposite the A687, take the first or second left. The Marton Arms is situated opposite the Church of St Oswald.*
Dating back to the 13th century, the Marton Arms used to count Sir Arthur Conan Doyle among its patrons. In 1953 it doubled as a gun shop for a film. In the bar is a line-up of sixteen hand-pulled, constantly-changing real ales, bottled beers from around the globe and a selection of over 200 malts. An extensive menu of hearty food includes home-made specials and pizzas (eight listed but more available), steaks, chicken, curries, fish, and burgers.
OPEN: 11-11 (Sun 12-10.30) **BAR MEALS:** L served all week 12-2 D served all week 6-9 Av main course £3 🍺: Timothy Taylor Golden Best, Black Sheep Bitter, Sharps Doom Bar, Jennings Cumberland.
♀: 8 **FACILITIES:** Children welcome Garden: Lawned garden with tables and shrubs **NOTES:** Parking 40 **ROOMS:** 12 bedrooms 12 en suite 1 family rooms s£32 d£64

KELD   Map 18 NY80

Tan Hill Inn
☎ 01833 628246
Dir: *Telephone for directions*
In an isolated position on the Pennine Way, this hospitable 16th-century inn is the highest in England, at 1,732 feet above sea level. Once at a major trading crossroads, the Tan Hill Inn is now popular with walkers and motorists enjoying the austere beauty of the Pennines. The beamed, flag-stoned bar with its roaring fires sets the scene for hand-pulled beers and hearty bar food, featuring the spicy Tan Hill sausage, filled Yorkshire puddings, soups and sandwiches.
OPEN: 11-11 **BAR MEALS:** 12-2.30 7-9
BREWERY/COMPANY: Free House 🍺: Theakstons Best, XB, Old Peculier. **FACILITIES:** Children welcome **NOTES:** No credit cards

---

KILBURN   Map 19 SE57

The Forresters Arms Hotel ♦♦♦ 🛏 NEW
YO61 4AH ☎ 01347 868386 & 868550 📠 01347 868386
e-mail: paulcussons@forrestersarms.fsnet.co.uk
Sturdy stone former-coaching inn still offering ten comfortable rooms for travellers passing close by the famous White Horse of Kilburn on the North York Moors. The cosy lower bar has some of the earliest oak furniture by Robert Thompson, with his distinctive mouse symbol on every piece. Evidence of the inn's former stables can be seen in the upper bar. Steak and ale pie, pheasant casserole, home-made lasagne and lamb chops are popular dishes.
OPEN: 11-11 **BAR MEALS:** L served all week 12-2.30 D served all week 6.30-9 Av main course £6.95 **RESTAURANT:** L served all week 12-2.30 D served all week 6.30-9 **BREWERY/COMPANY:** Free House 🍺: Scottish Courage John Smiths, Carlsberg-Tetley Tetley's, Hambleton. **FACILITIES:** Children welcome Dogs allowed Dog bowl, biscuits **NOTES:** Parking 40 **ROOMS:** 10 bedrooms 10 en suite 2 family rooms s£38 d£48

> **Do you have a favourite pub
> that we have overlooked?
> Please use the Reader's Report form at
> the back of this guide to tell us all about it.**

KIRBY HILL   Map 19 NZ10

The Shoulder of Mutton Inn 🛏 ♀
DL11 7JH ☎ 01748 822772 📠 01325 718936
e-mail: info@shoulderofmutton.net
Dir: *4m N of Richmond, 6m from A1 A66 J at Scotch Corner*
A 200-year-old traditional inn in an elevated position overlooking Holmedale. Log fires burn in the bar areas, while the separate Stable restaurant retains its original beams. Choose whether to eat here or in the bar from a menu that takes in Kirby Hill half shoulder of lamb, chicken bonne femme and fresh salmon steak hollandaise. Of less classical origin are the steaks, salads and jacket potatoes that complete the picture.
OPEN: 12-3 6-11 (Sat-Sun) 12-3 **BAR MEALS:** L served Sat-Sun 12-2 D served all week 7-9.30 Av main course £8 **RESTAURANT:** L served Sat-Sun 12-2 6-9.30 **BREWERY/COMPANY:** Free House 🍺: Scottish Courage John Smiths, Jennings Cumberland Ale, Black Sheep Best.
FACILITIES: Children welcome Garden: Paved Dogs allowed
NOTES: Parking 28 **ROOMS:** 5 bedrooms 5 en suite 1 family rooms s£35 d£44 (♦♦♦)

KIRKBYMOORSIDE   Map 19 SE68

Pick of the Pubs

George & Dragon Hotel ★★ 🛏 ♀
17 Market Place YO62 6AA ☎ 01751 433334 📠 01751 432933
e-mail: georgeatkirkby@aol.com
Dir: *Just off A170 between Scarborough & Thirsk in centre of the Market Town*

Maintaining a long tradition of hospitality, this 17th-century former coaching inn provides a haven of warmth, refreshment and rest to the weary in the heart of Kirkbymoorside - a great base from which to explore North Yorkshire and its moors and dales. Sports enthusiasts will appreciate the collection of rugby and cricket memorabilia in the bar, including photographs, autographs, prints and other paraphernalia. In these beamed surroundings, by the log fire in winter, visitors can sample hand-pulled real ales, 10 wines by the glass and a choice of over 30 malt whiskies. A good variety of food is offered from snacks and blackboard specials in the bar to candlelit dinners in Knights' Restaurant or the bistro. Examples of daily specials include steamed venison pudding with thyme gravy, oven-roasted sea bass with sweet peppers and sorrel butter, and wild mushroom ravioli with haricot beans.
OPEN: 10-11 **BAR MEALS:** L served all week 12-2.15 D served all week 6.30-9.15 Av main course £6.50 **RESTAURANT:** L served all week 12-2.15 D served all week 6.30-9.15 Av 3 course à la carte £16 **BREWERY/COMPANY:** Free House 🍺: Black Sheep Best, Tetley and Changing Guest Beers. ♀: 10 **FACILITIES:** Children welcome Garden: Walled garden, Herb Garden Dogs allowed
NOTES: Parking 15 **ROOMS:** 18 bedrooms 18 en suite s£49 d£79

England

The Lion Inn

Blakey Ridge YO62 7LQ ☎ 01751 417320 ▤ 01751 417717
e-mail: info@lionblakey.co.uk
Dir: From A170 follow signs 'Hutton le Hole/Castleton'. 6m N of Hutton le Hole.

The Lion stands 470m above sea level, the fourth highest inn in England, with breathtaking views over the beautiful North York Moors National Park. The cosy interior with original beamed ceilings, 4ft-thick stone walls and blazing fires in the bars makes up for the isolated location. Typical chef's specials are beef Wellington, Blakey mixed grill, and breast of roast duckling, with other choices like wild mushroom and brandy sauce parcel, chicken Kiev, and Old Peculier casserole.
OPEN: 10-11 **BAR MEALS:** all week 12-10 Av main course £6.75
RESTAURANT: L served Sun only 12-7 D served all week 7-10 Av 3 course à la carte £19.50 Av 3 course fixed price £10.95
BREWERY/COMPANY: Free House ◀: Scottish Courage Theakston Blackbull, XB & Old Peculier, Scottish Courage John Smith's Bitter, Greene King Old Speckled Hen. ♀: 9 **FACILITIES:** Children welcome Garden: Large garden, picnic benches, well Dogs allowed
NOTES: Parking 200 **ROOMS:** 10 bedrooms 8 en suite 3 family rooms s£17.50 d£50 (♦♦♦)

KIRKHAM   Map 19 SE76

Pick of the Pubs

Stone Trough Inn

Kirkham Abbey YO60 7JS ☎ 01653 618713 ▤ 01653 618819
e-mail: info@stonetroughinn.co.uk
Dir: 1 1/2m off A64, between York & Malton

Stone-built country inn high above Kirkham Abbey and the River Derwent, offering impressive modern pub menus. Roast chunk of cod on pea purée with warm cockle butter is a typical bar dish, while in the restaurant you might sample whole boned roast partridge with lemon thyme and jumbo raisin stuffing and sloe gin and peppercorn sauce. Desserts are a particular strength - from syrup sponge pudding to chocolate 'opera' gateau.
OPEN: 12-2.30 6-11 (Sun 11.45-10.30) Closed: Dec 25
BAR MEALS: L served Tues-Sun 12-2 D served Tues-Sun 6.30-8.30 Av main course £8.95 **RESTAURANT:** L served Sun 12-2.15 D served Tue-Sat 6.45-9.30 Av 3 course à la carte £24
BREWERY/COMPANY: Free House ◀: Carlsberg-Tetley Tetley Bitter, Timothy Taylor Landlord, Black Sheep Best, Malton Golden Chance. ♀: 9 **FACILITIES:** Children welcome Garden Dogs allowed Water **NOTES:** Parking 100

KNARESBOROUGH   Map 19 SE35

Pick of the Pubs

The General Tarleton Inn ★★★

Boroughbridge Rd, Ferrensby HG5 0PZ
☎ 01423 340284 ▤ 01423 340288
e-mail: gti@generaltarleton.co.uk
Dir: On A6055, on crossroads in Ferrensby

Traditional 18th-century coaching inn conveniently close to the A1 and many of Yorkshire's top attractions. Named after Sir Banastre Tarleton, a distinguished 18th-century war hero and politician. It is thought the inn was opened by a member of the General's platoon and named in his honour. Tastefully refurbished, the General Tarleton offers a rambling, low-beamed bar with open fires and a popular covered courtyard where you may like to eat. The menu is impressive and wide ranging: roast loin of Yorkshire Dales lamb with garlic mash, roccola and a tomato and basil jus, pan-seared gilt-head sea bream with a cep risotto, petit salad and a warm truffle and tarragon vinaigrette, or breast of cornfed chicken wrapped in Parma ham and savoy leaves with tarragon sauce. Impressive wine list and fourteen tastefully decorated bedrooms.
OPEN: 12-3 6-11 **BAR MEALS:** L served all week 12-2.15 D served all week 6-9.30 Av main course £9.25 **RESTAURANT:** L served Sun 12-1.30 D served Tue-Sat 7-9.30 Av 3 course à la carte £34.50 Av 3 course fixed price £29.50
BREWERY/COMPANY: Free House ◀: Black Sheep Best, Timothy Taylors Landlord, Worthingtons Creamflow. ♀: 20
FACILITIES: Children welcome Garden Dogs allowed but not in bar **NOTES:** Parking 60 **ROOMS:** 14 bedrooms 14 en suite s£71.95 d£84.90

LASTINGHAM   Map 19 SE79

Blacksmiths Arms

YO62 6TL ☎ 01751 417247
e-mail: blacksmithslastingham@hotmail.com
A stone-built inn dating from 1693 and unspoilt by progress, situated in a beautiful village that is part of a conservation area within the National Park. Furnishings are in keeping with the pub's great age, while its ambience is provided by a rich cross-section of folk engaged in lively conversation at the bar. Lamb and mint pie, roast duck, seafood platter, cod in beer batter, steak and ale pie.

continued

LASTINGHAM continued

Blacksmith's Arms

OPEN: 12-3.30 (Winter 12-3, 7-11) 6.30-11 **BAR MEALS:** L served all week 12-2.15 D served all week 7-9 Av main course £7.95 **RESTAURANT:** L served all week 12-2 D served all week 7-9.15 Av 3 course à la carte £14.75 **BREWERY/COMPANY:** Free House 🍺: Theakstons Best Bitter, Marston's Pedigree, Black Bull Bitter. **FACILITIES:** Children welcome Garden: Cottage garden seating 32, decking seats 20 Dogs allowed Water and food

---

LEYBURN   Map 19 SE19

The Old Horn Inn ♦♦♦ NEW
Spennithorne DL8 5PR ☎ 01969 622370
e-mail: desmond@furlong1706.fsbusiness.co.uk
Dir: From Leyburn approx 1.5 miles heading E along A684. Take R turn signposted Spennithorne. From Bedale & A1 approx 9 miles heading W along A684. Take L turn signposted Spennithorne.

Traditional Dales pub dating back to the 17th century, once a farmhouse but an alehouse for at least the past 100 years. Visitors and locals are encouraged to feel at home in the informal atmosphere enhanced by low beams and open log fires, and enjoy good food in the bistro-style restaurant. Steak and kidney pie, braised lamb shank, and roast cod wrapped in Parma ham all feature on the menu and specials board.
OPEN: 12-3 7-11 (Open all day Fri-Sat during Jul-Aug)
BAR MEALS: L served Tue-Sun 12-2 D served Tue-Sun 7-9.30 Av main course £7.50 **RESTAURANT:** L served Tue-Sun 12-2 D served Tue-Sun 7-9.30 🍺: Blacksheep Bitter & Special, Scottish Courage John Smith's Cask, Coors Worthington's Cream Flow. **FACILITIES:** Garden: Small seating area with wooden benches Dogs allowed Water, toys, kennel **NOTES:** Parking 12 No credit cards **ROOMS:** 2 bedrooms 2 en suite d£43 no children overnight

♦ **Pubs with Red Diamonds are the top places in the AA's three, four and five diamond ratings**

Pick of the Pubs

Sandpiper Inn ♀
Market Place DL8 5AT ☎ 01969 622206 📠 01969 625367
e-mail: hsandpiper@aol.com
Dir: From A1 take A684 to Leyburn

The oldest building in Leyburn, dating back to around 1640, has been a pub for just 30 years and an outstanding one since its purchase some years ago by the Harrison family. With a beautiful summer garden, a bar, snug and dining room within, it is traditional in style yet thoroughly sensible in approach to food. In addition to the safer options such as fish and chips in real ale batter, and Yorkshire ham with eggs and fried potatoes that proliferate on the bar lunch menu, expect a good choice of starters: apple-smoked black pudding with a celeriac mash and a port wine jus, traditional fish cakes, and warm goats' cheese salad. Crispy duck leg with plum and orange sauce might follow, or loin fillet of lamb, pot-roast rabbit with lemon and thyme, grilled swordfish with sweet potatoes and red onion, and stuffed aubergine topped with a herb crust. To finish off, sample raspberry and almond tart with clotted cream, or sticky toffee pudding and a butterscotch sauce.
OPEN: 11.30-3 6.30-11 (Sun 12-3, 6.30-10.30) **BAR MEALS:** L served all week 12-2.30 D served all week 6.30-9 Av main course £9.95 **RESTAURANT:** L served all week 12-2.30 D served all week 6.30-9 Av 3 course à la carte £21
BREWERY/COMPANY: Free House 🍺: Black Sheep Best, Black Sheep Special, Daleside, Theakstons Hogshead. ♀: 8
FACILITIES: Children welcome Garden Dogs allowed
NOTES: Parking 6

Wyvill Arms 🐑 ♀
Constable-Burton DL8 5LH ☎ 01677 450581

Situated on the edge of the Yorkshire Dales, this popular inn offers welcoming bars with open fires, beams and flagstones.

continue

It takes its name from a local family who converted what was a 1920s farmstead into a pub. Pan-fried breast of chicken with smoked bacon and Stilton sauce, lamb shank with mushy peas, roast Gressingham duck with orange and peppercorn sauce, steak and onion pie, and a wide choice of steaks feature on the appetising menu.
OPEN: 11-3 5.30-11 **BAR MEALS:** L served all week 11.30-2.15 D served all week 5.30-9.30 Av main course £11 **RESTAURANT:** L served all week 12-2.15 D served all week 5.30-9.30 Av 3 course à la carte £21 **BREWERY/COMPANY:** Free House 🍺: Scottish Courage Theakston & John Smiths, Blacksheep.
FACILITIES: Children welcome Garden: 3 lawn areas Dogs allowed **NOTES:** Parking 40

LINTON
Map 19 SD96

The Fountaine Inn
BD23 5HJ ☎ 01756 752210 📠 01756 752210
Dir: From Skipton take B6162 8m turn R for Linton
Located within the magnificent Yorkshire Dales National Park, in a sleepy hamlet beside the River Beck, this 16th-century inn takes its name from a local man who made his fortune in the Great Plague of London in 1665 - burying the bodies! On a more cheerful note, the new management offer a regularly changing menu and specials. The pub features in the opening credits of the soap, 'Emmerdale'.
OPEN: 11-11 (11-3, 5.30-11 in winter) **BAR MEALS:** L served all week 12-5.30 D served all week 5.30-9 Av main course £6.50
RESTAURANT: L served Mon-Sun 12-5.30 D served Mon-Sun 5.30-9 Av 3 course à la carte £17 **BREWERY/COMPANY:** Free House
🍺: Black Sheep Best, Carlsberg-Tetley Tetley Bitter, Scottish Courage John Smith's. **FACILITIES:** Children welcome Garden: Village green Dogs allowed **NOTES:** Parking 20

LITTON
Map 18 SD97

Queens Arms
BD23 5QJ ☎ 01756 770208
e-mail: queensarmslitton@mserve.net
Dir: Skipton: Northvale Road, follow for 15 miles. Signposted
Early 16th-century inn located in a remote corner of the Yorkshire Dales, a perfect base for walking and touring. Low ceilings, beams and coal fires give the place a traditional, timeless feel. A good range of food incorporates local produce and international flavours. There's plenty of fish, including fresh halibut with seafood sauce, vegetarian dishes, home-made pies and a generous mixed grill.
OPEN: 12-3 7-11 (July-Aug Sat-Sun open all day) Closed: 3 Jan-1Feb **BAR MEALS:** L served Tue-Sun 12-2 D served Tue-Sun 7-9 Av main course £6.50 **RESTAURANT:** L served Tue-Sun 12-2 D served Tue-Sun 7-9 Av 3 course à la carte £15 **BREWERY/COMPANY:** Free House 🍺: Litton Ale, Teltleys, plus Guest ales.
FACILITIES: Children welcome Garden: beer garden, outdoor eating, patio Dogs allowed **NOTES:** Parking 10

LONG PRESTON
Map 18 SD85

Maypole Inn 🏠 ♀
Maypole Green BD23 4PH ☎ 01729 840219 📠 01729 840456
e-mail: landlord@maypole.co.uk
Dir: On A65 between Settle and Skipton
The Maypole has been plying its trade since 1695: 300 years on it still thrives, offering comfortable bedrooms, Yorkshire ales and traditional home cooking. At the edge of the Yorkshire Dales National Park, this is a good base for walking and cycling. Relax in the beamed dining room or cosy bar

continued

over a pint and a simple snack, sandwich, steak or salad - or try a special like cod and fennel bake, stir-fry vegetable pancakes or Murphy rich beef stew.
OPEN: 11-3 6-11 (Sun 12-10.30) (Sat 11-11) **BAR MEALS:** L served all week 12-2 D served all week 6.30-9 Av main course £6.50
RESTAURANT: L served all week 12-2 D served all week 6.30-9 Av 3 course à la carte £12 **BREWERY/COMPANY:** Enterprise Inns
🍺: Timothy Taylor Landlord, Castle Eden, Moorhouses Premier, Tetley & Guest. ♀: 10 **FACILITIES:** Children welcome Garden: Patio Dogs allowed Water **NOTES:** Parking 30 **ROOMS:** 6 bedrooms 6 en suite 3 family rooms s£29 d£49 (♦♦♦)

MARTON
Map 19 SE78

The Appletree Country Inn 🏠 ♀
YO62 6RD ☎ 01751 431457 📠 01751 430190
e-mail: appletreeinn@supanet.com
Dir: From Kirkby Moorside on A170 turn right after one mile, follow road for two miles to Marton

A village dining pub where, says the chef, the food is influenced by cuisines from Europe to the Far East, sometimes with a twist. Everything is fresh, locally sourced where possible, with herbs from the pub garden and fruit from its own orchard for home-made breads, ice creams, chocolates, chutneys and dressings. Typical dishes are crab cheesecake with tomato salsa and Parmesan crisp, lamb rump with tapenade in puff pastry, and venison on dauphinois potato with red wine and chocolate sauce.
OPEN: 12-2.30 6.30-11 (Open all day in summer) Closed: 2 weeks Jan, 2 weeks Oct **BAR MEALS:** L served Wed-Mon 12-2 D served Wed-Mon 6.30-9 Av main course £8.50 **RESTAURANT:** L served Wed-Mon 12-2 D served Wed-Mon 6.30-10 Av 3 course à la carte £22 **BREWERY/COMPANY:** Free House 🍺: Scottish Courage John Smiths Cask, Malton, York, Daleside, Guest ales. ♀: 12
FACILITIES: Children welcome Garden: Patio, seats 16, adjoining orchard **NOTES:** Parking 30

MASHAM
Map 19 SE28

The Black Sheep Brewery
HG4 4EN ☎ 01765 689227 680100 📠 01765 689746
e-mail: helen.broadley@blacksheep.co.uk
Dir: Off the A6108 between Ribon & Leyburn, follow brown tourist signs
Schoolboy humour is on the menu at this popular brewery complex on the edge of the Yorkshire Dales. Besides the 'shepherded' brewery tours, 'ewe' can simply call in to eat and drink in the stylish bistro and 'baa...r'. In just ten years, Black Sheep ales have achieved a national reputation, and dishes like lamb shank in Square Ale sauce, and Riggwelter casserole make the most of them. Also lunchtime sandwiches, roast local pheasant, poached salmon, or provençale vegetable tartlet.

continued

England

MASHAM continued

The Black Sheep Brewery

OPEN: 11-5.30 7-11 **BAR MEALS:** L served all week 12-2.30 D served Wed-Sat 7-9.30 Av main course £6.95 **RESTAURANT:** L served all week 12-2.30 D served all week 7-9.30 **BREWERY/COMPANY:** Black Sheep beers. **FACILITIES:** Children welcome Garden **NOTES:** Parking 25

Kings Head Hotel ★★ 🏠 ♀
Market Place HG4 4EF ☎ 01765 689295 🗎 01765 689070 e-mail: masham.kingshead@snr.co.uk
Overlooking Masham's spacious market square with its cross and maypole, this 18th-century, three-storey former posting house and excise office is a perfect base for touring the Yorkshire Dales. Grilled whole sea bass, venison and pesto mash, chicken, bacon and cheese melt, penne with rocket pesto, and warm and cold salads will all be found on the menu, along with specials. Theakston's Best Bitter, Old Peculier and guest ales are on tap. Bedrooms are well decorated and comfortable.
OPEN: 11-11 **BAR MEALS:** L served all week 12-3 D served all week 6-10 Av main course £8 **RESTAURANT:** L served all week 12-3 D served all week 6-10 **BREWERY/COMPANY:** Scottish Courage Theakstons Best Bitter, Black Bull & Old Peculier, Guest Ales. ♀: 14 **FACILITIES:** Children welcome Garden: Georgian patio style Dogs allowed Water **ROOMS:** 10 bedrooms 10 en suite s£50 d£65

MIDDLEHAM   Map 19 SE18

Black Swan Hotel 🏠
Market Place DL8 4NP ☎ 01969 622221 🗎 01969 622221 e-mail: blackswanmiddleham@breathe.com
Dominated by Middleham Castle, the home of Richard III, this welcoming Grade II listed inn dates back to 1670. Exposed beams and wooden panelling lend character to the stone-built property, which can be found in the centre of this famous horse-training area. Traditional country cooking results in dishes like 'tipsy' casseroles, local steaks, and game in season. Many circular walks of varying lengths can begin here.
OPEN: 11-3.30 6-11 (open all day Sat-Sun summer) **BAR MEALS:** L served all week 12-2 D served all week 6.30-9 Av main course £6 **RESTAURANT:** L served all week 12-2 D served all week 6.30-9 Av 3 course à la carte £17 **BREWERY/COMPANY:** Free House ⚫: Scottish Courage John Smiths, Theakstons Best Bitter, Black Bull, Old Peculier & Guest Beers. **FACILITIES:** Children welcome Garden: Patio and lawn with benches, tables Dogs allowed by appointment

---

★ **Pubs with Red Stars are part of the AA's Top 200 Hotels in Britain & Ireland**

The White Swan Hotel 🏠 ♀
Market Place DL8 4PE ☎ 01969 622093 🗎 01969 624551 e-mail: whiteswan@easynet.co.uk
Dir: *From A1, take A684 toward Leyburn then A6108 to Ripon, 1.5m to Middleton*
Traditional Dales coaching inn located on the market square, with beams, flagstone floors and open fires. An ideal place to sit and watch the racehorses riding out in the morning. The emphasis is on quality accommodation and good food. The bar menu offers baked cod in a rarebit sauce, sausage and bubble and squeak with onion gravy, and fillet of salmon on wilted spinach with a tomato and tarragon sauce.
OPEN: 12-11 **BAR MEALS:** L served all week 12-2.15 D served all week 6.30-9.15 Av main course £8 **RESTAURANT:** L served all week 12-2.15 D served all week 6.30-9.15 Av 3 course à la carte £17 **BREWERY/COMPANY:** Free House ⚫: Black Sheep Best, Riggwelter, Scottish Courage John Smith's. **FACILITIES:** Children welcome Garden: Food served outside Dogs allowed

MIDDLESMOOR   Map 19 SE07

Crown Hotel ♀
HG3 5ST ☎ 01423 755204
Dir: *Telephone for directions*
The original building dates back to the 17th century; today it offers the chance to enjoy a good pint of local beer by a cosy, roaring log fire, or in a sunny pub garden. Stands on a breezy 900ft hilltop with good views towards Gouthwaite Reservoir. Ideal for those potholing or following the popular Nidderdale Way. Under new management - readers' comments welcome.
OPEN: 12-2.30 7-11 **BAR MEALS:** L served Mon-Sun 12-2.30 D served Mon-Sat 7-8.30 Av main course £5.50 **RESTAURANT:** L served all week 12-2.30 D served all week 7-9 **BREWERY/COMPANY:** Free House ⚫: Black Sheep Best, Scottish Courage John Smith's, Theakstons Bitter. ♀: 10 **FACILITIES:** Children welcome Garden Dogs allowed Water **NOTES:** Parking 20 **NOTES:** No credit cards

MOULTON   Map 19 NZ20

Pick of the Pubs

Black Bull Inn 🏠
DL10 6QJ ☎ 01325 377289 🗎 01325 377422 e-mail: sarah@blackbullinn.demon.co.uk
Dir: *1m S of Scotch Corner off A1*
The Pagendam family has been serving discerning diners at the Black Bull for some forty years. Just one mile south of Scotch Corner, this well-established free house is also well placed for motorists seeking a civilised retreat from the A1. Hot and cold lunchtime snacks are served in the relaxing bar, with its roaring winter fire. In the evening, the dining focus shifts to the fish bar and conservatory, as well as to The Brighton Belle - one of the original 1932 Pullman carriages that operated premier express services between London and Brighton. The seasonally changing menu lists light snacks such as Welsh rarebit and bacon, and barbecued spare ribs. In the evenings, seafood takes centre stage. Start with oysters or smoked salmon, then choose from lobster with hazelnut and coriander butter; grilled Dover sole; or poached turbot. Other dishes include pan-fried duck breast; roast venison cutlet; and lamb loin with flageolet beans.
OPEN: 12-2.30 6-10.30 Closed: 24-26 Dec **BAR MEALS:** L served Mon-Fri 12-2 D served Mon-Sat Av main course £5.50 **RESTAURANT:** L served Mon-Fri 12-2 D served Mon-Sat 6.45-10.15 Av 3 course à la carte £27.50 Av 3 course fixed price £16.50

continued

England

BREWERY/COMPANY: Free House **:** Theakstons Best, John Smiths Smooth. **FACILITIES:** Garden: Patio area with seating **NOTES:** Parking 80

MUKER
Map 18 SD99

The Farmers Arms
DL11 6QG ☎ 01748 886297
Dir: *From Richmond take A6108 towards Leyburn, turn R onto B6270*
This traditional village local at the head of beautiful Swaledale is popular with walkers on the Pennine Way and the Coast-to-Coast route. Take a seat by the fire in the simply-furnished main bar and enjoy a pint of Theakstons with a decent bar meal. Try tandoori chicken masala, lamb hot pot, wild mushroom lasagne or a steak. In summer you can sit outside in a cobbled area amid flowerbeds and planters.
OPEN: 11-3 7-11 Sun (12-3 7-10.30) **BAR MEALS:** L served all week 12-2.30 D served all week 7-8.50 Av main course £7.50
BREWERY/COMPANY: Free House **:** Theakston Best & Old Peculier, John Smith's, Nimmo's XXXX. **FACILITIES:** Children welcome Garden: Cobbled area with flower beds Dogs allowed Water Provided **NOTES:** Parking 6 No credit cards

---

NUNNINGTON
Map 19 SE67

The Royal Oak Inn ♀
Church St YO62 5US ☎ 01439 748271 ⬛ 01439 748271
Dir: *Close to church at the opposite end of the village to Nunnington hall (National Trust)*
A solid stone pub in this sleepy rural backwater in the Howardian Hills, a short drive from the North Yorkshire Moors. The immaculate open-plan bar is furnished with scrubbed pine and decorated with farming memorabilia, just the place for a pint of Theakstons and a bite to eat. An extensive range of filling bar food plus specials like pork medallion in a cream, white wine and Pernod sauce, and goats' cheese and leek tart.
OPEN: 12-2.30 6.30-11 **BAR MEALS:** L served Tue-Sun 12-2 D served Tue-Sun 6.30-9.50 **RESTAURANT:** L served Tue-Sun 12-2 D served Tue-Sun 6.30-9 **BREWERY/COMPANY:** Free House **:** Scottish Courage Theakston Best & Old Peculier, Carlsberg-Tetley Tetley Bitter. **NOTES:** Parking 18

OSMOTHERLEY
Map 19 SE49

Queen Catherine Hotel ♦♦ 🦌 NEW
7 West End DL6 3AG ☎ 01609 883209
e-mail: info@queencatherinehotel.co.uk
Named after Henry VIII's wife, Catherine of Aragon, who left her horse and carriage here while sheltering from her husband with nearby monks. There is no sense of menace around this friendly hotel nowadays, believed to be the only one in Britain bearing its name, and visitors can enjoy a well-cooked meal: steak and onion pie, Cajun poached cod fillet, seafood crumble, and duck breast in hoi-sin sauce are all on the menu.
OPEN: 12-3 6-11 (open all day Sat-Sun) **BAR MEALS:** L served all week 12-2 D served all week 6-9 Av main course £7.50
RESTAURANT: L served all week 12-2 D served all week 6-9 **:** Hambleton Ales-Stud, Stallion, Bitter, Goldfield. John Smiths Bitter. **FACILITIES:** Children welcome Dogs allowed Water **ROOMS:** 5 bedrooms 5 en suite s£25 d£50

> ♦ Pubs with Red Diamonds are the top places in the AA's three, four and five diamond ratings

---

Three Tuns Inn 🏠 ◉ 🦌 ♀
South End DL6 3BN ☎ 01609 883301 ⬛ 01609 883301
Dir: *Off A19*

Osmotherley is the starting point for the Lyke Wake Walk, a forty-mile trail across the North Yorkshire Moors to the coast. Completion in 24 hours qualifies for membership of the Lyke Wake Club. The pub stands among 17th-century stone cottages, its hanging baskets brightening up the exterior in summer, and the views of the Cleveland Hills providing a grand sight from its rear garden all year round. The stylish interior has attracted a lot of interest, but it's the quality of the food that has ensured its success since reopening in 2001. There are usually four or more seafood/fish dishes on offer, examples being roast fillet of monkfish with mascarpone and herb risotto in red wine sauce, and whole grilled sea bass. Meat options include pan-fried fillet of beef with braised oxtail and baby onions, and confit duck leg with Toulouse sausage, fricassée of cabbage, bacon and a redcurrant reduction. All rooms have good views of the hills.
OPEN: 12-3 6-11 **BAR MEALS:** L served all week 12-2.30 D served all week 6-10.30 Av main course £11 **RESTAURANT:** L served all week 12-2.30 D served all week 6-9.30 Av 3 course à la carte £23.50
BREWERY/COMPANY: Free House **:** Caffreys, John Smiths Smooth. **FACILITIES:** Children welcome Garden: Decorative, paved with ornamental features **NOTES:** Parking 4 **ROOMS:** 7 bedrooms 7 en suite 1 family rooms s£49 d£65

PATELEY BRIDGE
Map 19 SE16

Pick of the Pubs

The Sportmans Arms Hotel 🦌 ♀
Wath-in-Nidderdale HG3 5PP
☎ 01423 711306 ⬛ 01423 712524
Dir: *A39/B6451, restaurant 2m N of Pateley Bridge*
Beloved of sports people from far and wide, this special pub and small hotel stands in a conservation village in one of the most beautiful areas of the Yorkshire Dales. Inside you'll find immaculate traditional décor, real fires and comfy chairs. A custom-built kitchen, run by chef/patron Ray Carter for nearly a quarter of a century (now assisted by his son) lies at the heart of the operation. True to the best pub traditions, real ales and fine wines accompany blackboard dishes served in an informal bar and daily restaurant menus that tempt all-comers. Fresh Whitby fish dominates in dishes such as ling with a garlic and mustard crust, monkfish provençale, and roasted seabass on tomato mash with beurre blanc. Other delights include rack of venison with wild mushrooms and beetroot in red wine and garlic cream, prime sirloin with béarnaise sauce, and seared and roasted breast of Gressingham duckling with sun dried fruits and nuts. Finish in style with double chocolate

continued

England

PATELEY BRIDGE continued

roulade, hot banana macaroons, or the ever-popular Sportsman's summer pudding.
OPEN: 12-2.30 7-11 Closed: 25 Dec **BAR MEALS:** L served all week 12-2 D served all week 7-9 Av main course £10.50
RESTAURANT: L served all week 12-2 D served all week 7-9.30 Av 3 course à la carte £25 **BREWERY/COMPANY:** Free House
◖: Younger, Theakston, John Smiths. **♀:** 12
FACILITIES: Children welcome Garden: Country garden with large lawns, good views **NOTES:** Parking 30 **ROOMS:** 13 bedrooms 12 en suite s£60 d£85 (★★)

PICKERING — Map 19 SE78

Pick of the Pubs

Fox & Hounds Country Inn 🏚 ⊚ 🐾
Sinnington YO62 6SQ ☎ 01751 431577 🗎 01751 432791
e-mail: foxhoundsinn@easynet.co.uk
Dir: 3m W of town, off A170

Sinnington is one of Yorkshire's loveliest villages, with a little river running through its centre, banks of daffodils in the spring, and a maypole on the village green. It makes an entirely appropriate setting for this handsome 18th-century coaching inn with its oak-beamed ceilings, old wood panelling and open fires. Imaginative modern cooking is served in the well-appointed dining room. Fish dishes are a strength, including grilled skate wing on Mozzarella and black olive ravioli with pomegranate, chilli and chive butter, or seared halibut fillet with sautéed king prawns and fig and pine kernel salsa. Alternatively, a list of chef's specials offers pan-fried pig's liver, confit of corn-fed chicken or twice-baked goats' cheese soufflé. Pleasant accommodation is provided in en suite bedrooms, and there is a great 7.5-mile circular walk starting from the village.
OPEN: 12-2 6-11 Sun-bar closes at 10.30 **BAR MEALS:** L served all week 12-2 D served all week 6.30-9 Av main course £8.45 **RESTAURANT:** L served all week 12-2 D served all week 6.30-9 **BREWERY/COMPANY:** Free House **◖:** Camerons Bitter, Black Sheep Special, Caffereys. **FACILITIES:** Children welcome Garden: Lawn with tree feature, herb garden Dogs allowed **NOTES:** Parking 30 **ROOMS:** 10 bedrooms 10 en suite 1 family rooms s£44 d£60

Do you have a favourite pub that we have overlooked?
Please use the Reader's Report form at the back of this guide to tell us all about it.

Horseshoe Inn
Main St, Levisham YO18 7NL ☎ 01751 460240 🗎 01751 460240
e-mail: horseshoeinn@levisham.com
Dir: Telephone for directions
16th-century family-run inn with spacious lounge bar and inviting atmosphere. Situated in a peaceful village, this is an ideal base for walking and touring in the beautiful North York Moors National Park. Very handy also for the nearby steam railway which features in the 'Heartbeat' television series. Extensive menu of traditional dishes offers home made steak and kidney pie, poached salmon, Whitby haddock and a good vegetarian selection.
OPEN: 11-3 6-11 Closed: 25 Dec **BAR MEALS:** L served all week 12-2 D served all week 6.30-9 Av main course £7.50
RESTAURANT: L served all week 12-2 D served all week 6.30-9 **BREWERY/COMPANY:** Free House **◖:** Theakstons Best Bitter, Scottish Courage John Smiths, Old Peculier. **FACILITIES:** Children welcome Garden Dogs allowed **NOTES:** Parking 50 **ROOMS:** 6 bedrooms 3 en suite 1 family rooms s£28 d£56 (♦♦♦)

Pick of the Pubs

The White Swan ★★ ⊚ 🐾 ♀
Market Place YO18 7AA ☎ 01751 472288 🗎 01751 475554
e-mail: welcome@white-swan.co.uk
Dir: In Market Place between church & steam railway station
The White Swan was originally built as a four-room cottage in 1532, after which it was extended as a coaching inn for the York to Whitby stagecoach. It also figured in the smuggling of salt via Saltersgate. It is a handsome building in the centre of Pickering, the largest of Ryedale's four market towns, and an ideal base for exploring nearby Dalby Forest, the glorious North York Moors and the spectacular heritage coastline. Seafood is well represented with dishes like grilled sea bass fillets with spinach and aïoli, king scallops with Gruyère and garlic, or posh fish and chips with home-made mushy peas and tartare sauce or ketchup. Alternatives are green Thai curry with basmati rice, or chargrilled fillet of beef with field mushrooms and béarnaise sauce. Food and drink can also be enjoyed outside on the beautifully planted terrace.
OPEN: 10-3 6-11 **BAR MEALS:** L served all week 12-2 D served all week 7-9 Av main course £10.95 **RESTAURANT:** L served all week 12-2 D served all week 7.00-9 Av 3 course à la carte £25
BREWERY/COMPANY: Free House **◖:** Black Sheep Best & Special. **♀:** 8 **FACILITIES:** Children welcome Garden: Beautifully planted terrace Dogs allowed **NOTES:** Parking 35 **ROOMS:** 12 bedrooms 12 en suite s£70 d£110

PICKHILL — Map 19 SE38

Pick of the Pubs

Nags Head Country Inn ★★ 🐾 ♀
YO7 4JG ☎ 01845 567391 🗎 01845 567212
e-mail: enquiries@nagsheadpickhill.freeserve.co.uk
Dir: 1 E of A1(4m N of A1/A61 junction). W of Thirsk
Beamed ceilings, stone-flagged floors and crackling log fires welcome visitors to this cosy free house. The 16th-century building is located in the heart of Herriot Country, and was formerly a blacksmith's shop and coaching inn. The tiny village of Pickhill is a handy base for touring the area, and the inn offers seventeen modern ensuite bedrooms. Bar and restaurant meals are chosen from a single menu that changes with the seasons to make the most of available produce. Starters range from broccoli

continue

and Stilton soup, or marinated squid and mussel salad, to Parma ham with galia melon, or crusty garlic bread. There's a wide choice of main courses, from straightforward dishes like fish, chips and mushy peas, or hot chilli and rice, to more adventurous offerings such as stuffed pork with apricots and celeriac, or tagliatelle with mixed salami, sun-dried red peppers and tomato sauce.

OPEN: 11-11 All day **BAR MEALS:** L served all week 12-2 D served all week 6-9.30 Av main course £11.95 **RESTAURANT:** L served all week 12-2 D served all week 7-9.30 Av 3 course à la carte £22 **BREWERY/COMPANY:** Free House 🍺 Hambleton Bitter & Goldfield, Black Sheep Best & Special, John Smiths Cask. **FACILITIES:** Children welcome Garden: Secluded wall area with seating area Dogs allowed Water and toys **NOTES:** Parking 40 **ROOMS:** 17 bedrooms 17 en suite s£40 d£60

RAMSGILL
Map 19 SE17

Pick of the Pubs

The Yorke Arms 🏨 😊😊😊 🐕 ♀
HG3 5RL ☎ 01423 755243 📠 01423 755330
e-mail: enquiries@yorke-arms.co.uk
Dir: Turn off at Pateley Bridge at the Nidderdale filling station on Low Wath rd. Signed to Ramsgill, continue for 3⁄4m
The Yorke's foundations date back to the 11th century when it was part of a small monastic settlement producing cheese. This striking building is now more a civilised inn and restaurant than archetypal village pub. All are welcome to relax in the stone-floored bar and lounge with easy chairs and open fires, prior to dining in the bistro or neatly appointed restaurant, to which an alfresco dining area was recently added. It is a comfortable environment in which to enjoy creative modern English cooking, based on best local produce and majoring increasingly in fine fresh fish. A starter might be roasted wood pigeon with pineapple relish and foie gras or leek tart with celeriac pannacotta, followed by roast brill, gratin of artichoke, langoustine and shrimps. Fillet of beef, anchovy and parsley butter, bacon rösti and field mushrooms is similarly accomplished, with cherry tart and vanilla ice cream to finish. Fine British cheeses and a wine list of notable pedigree.
OPEN: 11-3 6-11 (Sun 12-3, 6-10.30) **BAR MEALS:** L served all week 12-2 D served Mon-Sat 7-9 Av main course £12.50 **RESTAURANT:** L served all week 12-2 D served all week 7-9 Av 3 course à la carte £30 **BREWERY/COMPANY:** Free House 🍺 Black Sheep Special, Scottish Courage Theakstons Best & John Smith's. ♀: 12 **FACILITIES:** Garden: Semi-covered area at rear Dogs allowed **NOTES:** Parking 20 **ROOMS:** 13 bedrooms 13 en suite 3 family rooms s£80 d£160 no children overnight

---

REETH
Map 19 SE09

Pick of the Pubs

Charles Bathurst Inn ♦♦♦♦ 🍴
Arkengarthdale DL11 6EN
☎ 01748 884567 & 884265 📠 01748 884599
e-mail: info@cbinn.co.uk

Located in glorious Arkengarthdale, the most northerly of the Yorkshire Dales, this 18th-century inn is ideal for walkers, being close to the mid point of the Coast-to-Coast Walk. A popular hostelry, it is known throughout the area as the 'CB Inn', named after the son of Oliver Cromwell's physician who once owned lead mines in the area. The bar was originally a hay barn and stable for guests' horses, though it looks very different today with its antique pine furniture and welcoming open fires. Excellent fresh fish, Swaledale lamb, and locally-produced fruit and vegetables form the basis of the ever-changing menu. Typical of the dishes offered are five-fish fishcake, shank of lamb on lentil potato cake with juniper jus, and (in season) roast grouse with ham and horseradish sauce. Accommodation is available in individually-designed, en suite bedrooms with some stunning views.
OPEN: 11-11 **BAR MEALS:** L served all week 12-2 D served all week 6.30-9 **RESTAURANT:** L served all week 12-2 D served all week 6.30-9 **BREWERY/COMPANY:** Free House 🍺: Scottish Courage Theakstons, John Smiths Bitter & John Smiths Smooth, Black Sheep Best & Riggwelter.
FACILITIES: Children welcome Garden: Dogs allowed **NOTES:** Parking 50 **ROOMS:** 18 bedrooms 18 en suite s£45 d£65

ROBIN HOOD'S BAY
Map 19 NZ90

Laurel Inn
New Rd YO22 4SE ☎ 01947 880400
Picturesque Robin Hood's Bay is the setting for this small, traditional pub which retains lots of character features, including beams and an open fire. The bar is decorated with old photographs, and an international collection of lager bottles. This coastal fishing village was once the haunt of smugglers who used a network of underground tunnels and secret passages to bring the booty ashore. Straightforward simple menu offers wholesome sandwiches and soups.
OPEN: 12-11 (Sun 12-10.30) **BREWERY/COMPANY:** Free House 🍺: Scottish Courage John Smiths, Scottish Courage Theakston's Black Bull & Old Peculier. **FACILITIES:** Children welcome Dogs allowed **NOTES:** No credit cards

ROSEDALE ABBEY — Map 19 SE79

Pick of the Pubs

The Milburn Arms Hotel ★★ ◉ ♥
YO18 8RA ☎ 01751 417312 📠 01751 417541
e-mail: info@millburnarms.co.uk
Dir: A170 W from Pickering 3m, R at sign to Rosedale then 7m N

A charming country house hotel that acts as a perfect retreat from the hustle and bustle of the modern world. Hidden deep in the folds of the spectacular North York Moors National Park, and dating back to 1776, the family-run Milburn Arms Hotel offers eleven beautifully furnished en suite bedrooms, with a welcoming bar and log fires in the public rooms. Rosedale, once a centre for ironstone mining, is great for walking and you can quite literally begin a local hike at the front door of the hotel. Also close by are some of Yorkshire's best-loved attractions, including Castle Howard, Rievaulx Abbey and the region's famous steam railway. The Priory Restaurant is known for its quality cuisine. Pan-fried ducks' livers and medley of seafood sharpen the palate for local roast pheasant, grilled halibut steak and roast rack of Yorkshire lamb. Steamed date pudding or strawberry brûlée complete what should be a very enjoyable occasion.

OPEN: 11.30-3 6.30-11 Closed: 25 Dec **BAR MEALS:** L served all week 12-2.15 D served all week 6.30-9 **RESTAURANT:** L served Sun 12-2.30 D served all week 7-9
BREWERY/COMPANY: Free House 🍺 Black Sheep Best, Carlsberg-Tetley Tetely Bitter, Scottish Courage John Smith's.
FACILITIES: Children welcome Garden: Large grassed lawn area to side and front **NOTES:** Parking 60 **ROOMS:** 11 bedrooms 11 en suite 3 family rooms s£37.50 d£30

Pick of the Pubs

White Horse Farm Inn ★★ 🛏 ♥
YO18 8SE ☎ 01751 417239 📠 01751 417781
e-mail: sales@whitehorsefarmhotel.co.uk
Dir: Turn off A170, follow signs to Rosedale for approx 7m, hotel sign points up steep hill out of village, hotel 300yds on left
Part of this former farm overlooking Rosedale Abbey was granted its first licence in 1702 so that thirsty ironstone miners could sink a few pints on their way home. Despite recent improvements, its warm charisma remains unsullied. This is prime walking and riding country and the far-reaching views are worth the effort, if only for a refreshing Black Sheep Bitter or Timothy Taylor Landlord in the beer garden. The stonewalled interior with open fires, farming memorabilia and easy atmosphere provides the setting for generous, good pub food. There's a

comprehensive bar menu, while for dinner in the restaurant (for which booking is advised) there may be supreme of strawberry-filled chicken with chive sauce, pork fillet sautéed with green peppercorn and white wine sauce, and smoked haddock with mash topped with cheese and crispy bacon, and vegetarian dish of the day. Bedrooms, some in a rear annexe, all have a share of the views.
OPEN: 12-2.30 5.30-11 (Fri-Sun open all day) **BAR MEALS:** L served all week 12-2.30 D served all week 6.30-9 Av main course £4.95 **RESTAURANT:** L served all week 12-2 D served all week 7-9 **BREWERY/COMPANY:** Free House 🍺 Blacksheep Bitter, Special & Riggwelter, Scottish Courage John Smith's, Timothy Taylor Landlord. **FACILITIES:** Children welcome Garden: Grassed area with picnic benches Dog friendly **NOTES:** Parking 100 **ROOMS:** 13 bedrooms 13 en suite 2 family rooms s£32.50 d£50

See Pub Walk on opposite page

SAWLEY — Map 19 SE26

The Sawley Arms 🛏 ♥
HG4 3EQ ☎ 01765 620642
Dir: A1-Knaresborough-Ripley, or A1-Ripon B6265-Pateley Bridge

Guaranteeing old-fashioned courtesy, manners and service, June Hawes has run this delightfully old-fashioned, 200-year-old pub since 1969. Veterinary author James Herriot was a regular, and it's a favourite of former cricketer Fred Trueman. Just down the road is Fountains Abbey, a World Heritage Site. Mrs Hawes, who makes everything herself, offers a four-main course menu which could include deep-fried king scampi, sautéed corn-fed chicken with mushroom and herb sauce, steak pie with buttercrust pastry, and roast half duckling with curaçao sauce.
OPEN: 11.30-3 6.30-10.30 Closed: 25 Dec **BAR MEALS:** L served all week 12-2.30 D served Tue-Sat 6.30-9 Av main course £8 **RESTAURANT:** L served all week 12-2.30 D served Tue-Sat 6.30-9 **BREWERY/COMPANY:** Free House 🍺 Theakston Best, Scottish Courage John Smith's. ♥: 8 **FACILITIES:** Garden: Award winning garden **NOTES:** Parking 50 **ROOMS:** 2 bedrooms 2 en suite (★★★★) no children overnight

continued

White Horse Farm Hotel

Explore Rosedale's 19th-century mining industry and savour magnificent moorland and valley views on this invigorating ramble in the North Yorkshire Moors

From the car park, cross the main road and follow the delightful Daleside road to the hamlet of Thorgill. Keep to this quiet country lane, pass some holiday cottages and continue to a track on your left, near an old chapel. Follow this track through a gate and begin climbing past the ruin of Gill Bank Farm. Continue uphill to a stile in a wall, and keep to the footpath to another stile. You are now on the moor that leads up to Sheriff's Pit and ahead of you you can see your destination, the former pit manager's house.

Keep to the path uphill to Sheriff's Pit. Note the 280-ft open shaft beyond the wire fence, pause to savour the memorable views, and then set off along the cinder track of the old ironstone railway in a south-south-easterly direction. Enjoy the lovely views of Rosedale Abbey nestling in the valley below, and look out for the many moorland birds and wildlife that thrive here. Continue along the former trackbed, passing old mine workings, to Chimney Bank Terminus. Walk to the road, turn left and steeply descend off the moor back to the inn.

★★
WHITE HORSE FARM HOTEL, ROSEDALE ABBEY
YO18 8SE.
☎ 01751 417239

Directions: village 7m off A170, signed 3m NW of Pickering Former farmhouse situated high up in Rosedale overlooking the moors and village, with spectacular views from the front terrace. Convivial stone-walled bar, hearty Yorkshire cooking and beers from Black Sheep and Timothy Taylor Landlord. Accommodation.
Open: 12-2.30 6.30-11. Closed Mon & Tue lunch Nov-Feb.
(Fri-Sun open all day).
Bar Meals: 12.30-2 6.30-9
(Sun 12-2 only).
Notes: Children and dogs welcome. Garden & terrace. Parking.
(See page 554 for full entry)

DISTANCE: 5 miles (8km)
MAP: OS Landranger 94
TERRAIN: Moorland, country lanes
PATHS: Old railway trackbed and metalled lanes
GRADIENT: Undulating; one fairly steep climb and one steep descent

Walk submitted by Robert Horseman

SCAWTON   Map 19 SE58

Pick of the Pubs

The Hare Inn 🐕 ♀
YO7 2HG ☎ 01845 597289 📠 01845 597158
e-mail: rowanhall@thehareinn.co.uk

Mentioned in the Domesday Book, and once frequented by the abbots and monks of Rievaulx Abbey. In the 17th century ale was brewed here for local iron workers. Inside, as you might expect, low-beamed ceilings and flagstone floors, walls and shelves lined with bric-a-brac, a wood-burning stove providing a warm welcome in the bar, and an old-fashioned kitchen range in the dining area. At lunch, the daily-changing menus might list curried chicken and rice, smoked duck salad with bacon lardons, or leek and garlic sausages, beetroot mash and red onion gravy. At dinner, venison Wellington, salmon steak with tomato and basil sauce on a bed of spinach, suckling pig with cider gravy, or roast duck breast with black pudding and cherry sauce. Vegetarian main courses include spicy bean casserole with cheddar mash, and mushroom, garlic and basil risotto. Among the beers, award-winning Timothy Taylor's Landlord. Outside is a herb garden and dovecote.
OPEN: 12-3 6.30-11 (Sun 12-3.30, 6.30-11) **BAR MEALS:** L served Tue-Sun 12-2.30 D served Tue-Sun 6.30-9.30 Av main course £9.95 **RESTAURANT:** L served Tue-Sun 12-2.30 D served Tue-Sun 6.30-9.30 Av 3 course à la carte £22 **BREWERY/COMPANY:** Free House 🍺: Timothy Taylor Landlord, Black Sheep, Scottish Courage John Smiths, Guest Beers. ♀: 9 **FACILITIES:** Children welcome Garden: Small area at front, at back large seated area Dogs allowed in the garden, water **NOTES:** Parking 18

SETTLE   Map 18 SD86

Golden Lion Hotel ♦♦♦♦ 🐕 ♀
Duke St BD24 9DU ☎ 01729 822203 📠 01729 824103
e-mail: info@goldenlion.yorks.net
Dir: in the town centre opposite Barclays bank
Built around 1640, this former coaching inn stands in the heart of Settle's 17th-century market place. Its cosy, fire-warmed bar and comfy bedrooms make it a good overnight stop for travellers on the spectacular Settle-Carlisle railway line. Large blackboards display daily menus - perhaps chicken with goat's cheese and cranberry sauce or seafood salad - whilst the à la carte might feature pepper-crusted rack of lamb with port, rosemary and redcurrant, or crispy Norfolk duckling with Cassis and forest fruit.
OPEN: 11-11 **BAR MEALS:** L served all week 12-2.30 D served all

week 6-10 Av main course £7.50 **RESTAURANT:** L served all week 12-2.30 D served all week 6-10 Av 3 course à la carte £17 **BREWERY/COMPANY:** Thwaites 🍺: Thwaites Bitter, Bomber, Thoroughbred, Smooth & Guest beers. ♀: 8 **FACILITIES:** Children welcome Patio with picnic benches & umbrellas Dogs allowed Water **NOTES:** Parking 14 **ROOMS:** 12 bedrooms 10 en suite 2 family rooms s£27 d£64

SKIPTON   Map 18 SD95

Devonshire Arms 🐕 ♀
Grassington Rd, Cracoe BD23 6LA
☎ 01756 730237 📠 01756 730142
e-mail: theded.cracoe@totalise.co.uk

The Rhylstone Ladies WI calendar originated at this pub, a convivial 17th-century inn convenient for the Three Peaks. There are also excellent views of Rhylstone Fell. A wide range of cask ales plus extensive wine list will wash down a menu that includes steak and mushroom pie cooked in Jennings Snecklifter ale, lamb Jennings, chicken Diane, and haddock and chips.
OPEN: 11.30-3 (Sat 11.30-11, Sun 12-10.30) 6-11 **BAR MEALS:** L served all week 11.30-2 D served all week 6.30-9 Av main course £7 **RESTAURANT:** L served all week 12-2.30 D served all week 6.30-9.30 Av 3 course à la carte £16 **BREWERY/COMPANY:** Jennings 🍺: Jennings, Jennings Cumberland, Theakstons.
FACILITIES: Children welcome Garden: Food served outside Dogs allowed in the garden only **NOTES:** Parking 80

Herriots ♦♦♦ ♀ NEW
Broughton Rd BD23 1RT ☎ 01756 792781 📠 01756 793967
e-mail: herriots@mgrleisure.com
Herriots is located in the heart of the historic market town of Skipton and backs onto the Liverpool-Leeds Canal. The pale orange bar with flagstones and potted plants is traditional yet modern. The cooking reflects this with a bar and restaurant menu providing dishes that range from chilli with cheese nachos or Cumberland sausage with onion gravy to breast of duck in blueberry and balsamic dressing or grilled salmon and tiger prawns with red pepper coulis.
BAR MEALS: L served all week 12-2.30 D served Mon-Sat 7-9.30 Av main course £8.10 **RESTAURANT:** D served Mon-Sat 7-9.30 Av 3 course à la carte £15 🍺: Tetleys Cask, Theakstons Cask, John Smiths Smooths. ♀: 16 **NOTES:** Parking 44 **ROOMS:** 14 bedrooms 14 en suite 3 family rooms s£50 d£60 no children overnight

---

STARBOTTON   Map 18 SD97

Fox & Hounds Inn ♀
BD23 5HY ☎ 01756 760369 📠 01756 760867
Dir: On B6160 N of Kettlewell
Situated in a picturesque limestone village in Upper Wharfedale, this ancient pub was originally built as a private

continued

continued

house. Much of its trade comes from the summer influx of tourists and those tackling the long-distance Dales Way nearby. Make for the cosy bar, with its solid furnishings and flagstones, and sample a pint of Black Sheep or Boddington ales while you peruse the extensive blackboard menu which offers interesting main courses and good vegetarian meals. Expect minty lamb casserole, Somerset pork, steak and ale pie, or Stilton and broccoli quiche. Now under new ownership.
OPEN: 11.30-3 (Open all day Sat-Sun) 5.30-10.30 (BHs open lunch only) **BAR MEALS:** L served all week 12-2.30 D served all week 5.30-9 Av main course £6.95 **BREWERY/COMPANY:** Free House ◀: Black Sheep, Timothy Taylor Landlord, Tetleys, Boddingtons & Guest Beers. **FACILITIES:** Children welcome Garden: Patio with 10 tables Dogs allowed **NOTES:** Parking 15

TERRINGTON
Map 19 SE67

Bay Horse Inn 🍴
YO60 6PP ☎ 01653 648416
Homely 400-year old village pub with a good food trade. Part of the pub used to be a tailor's shop. Game pie, fresh fish and locally produced steaks and roasts are features of the menu, supported by blackboard specials such as pork chop with Madeira and mushrooms, pheasant in red wine, and salmon with capers and prawns.
OPEN: 12-3 6.30-11 (Sun 12-3, 6.30-10.30) **BAR MEALS:** L served all week 12-2 D served all week 7-9 Av main course £6 **RESTAURANT:** L served all week 12-2 D served all week 7-9 **BREWERY/COMPANY:** Free House ◀: John Smiths, Theakstons, Timothy Taylor Landlord & Guest Beers. **FACILITIES:** Children welcome Garden: Very quiet, well kept, secluded garden **NOTES:** Parking 30

THIRSK
Map 19 SE48

Pick of the Pubs

The Carpenters Arms 🍴 ♀
YO7 2DP ☎ 01845 537369 📠 01845 537889
e-mail: karen@karenlouise.fsnet.co.uk
Dir: *2M outside Thirsk on the A170*
An 18th-century inn standing on the site of a former carpenters' and blacksmiths' premises, in a delightfully quiet rural setting. The bar's low beams are adorned with old tradesmen's tools that reinforce the rustic pastoral atmosphere. An imaginative kitchen brigade produces a comprehensive choice, listed on an appetising lunch menu and an evening carte. On the former you might encounter spiced teriyaki beef with noodles, warm salad of duck confit, chorizo and pancetta, or chunky fish soup as starters. Follow up with fisherman's pie, home-made Carpenter's casserole with herb dumplings, or queen scallop, prawn and crispy bacon tagliatelle, and perhaps bread and butter pudding with whisky sauce. The same dishes appear at dinner, along with vegetarian risotto of cherry tomatoes and red chillies, with a list of daily specials, and a wonderful selection of English and French cheeses.
OPEN: 11.30-3 6.30-11 Closed: 25 Dec, 1 Jan (eve)
BAR MEALS: L served all week 12-2 D served all week 7-9 Av main course £12 **RESTAURANT:** L served Mon-Sun 12-2 D served Mon-Sun 7-9 Av 3 course à la carte £20 Av 2 course fixed price £11.50 **BREWERY/COMPANY:** Free House ◀: Carlsberg-Tetley Tetley Bitter, Timothy Taylor Landlord, Greene King Old Speckled Hen. **FACILITIES:** Children welcome **NOTES:** Parking 50

THORGANBY
Map 17 SE64

The Jefferson Arms
Main St YO19 6DA ☎ 01904 448316 📠 01904 449670
Dir: *Telephone for directions*

In picturesque surroundings, a beautiful public house dating from 1730. It is lavishly decorated in Gothic style reminiscent of an old manor house, and overlooking a patio beer garden with fishpond, fountain and waterfall. Lengthy menus list house specialities such as goats' cheese with Cumberland sauce, salmon en croûte with prawns and a choice of steaks with optional sauces.
OPEN: 12-2 6-11 **BAR MEALS:** L served Tue-Sun 12-2 D served all week 6-9 **RESTAURANT:** L served all week 12-2 D served all week 6-9 **BREWERY/COMPANY:** Free House ◀: Scottish Courage John Smiths, Black Sheep Best, Theakston Cool Cask, Black Bull. **FACILITIES:** Children welcome Garden: Side of pub with fish pond and fountain **NOTES:** Parking 55

THORNTON LE DALE
Map 19 SE88

The New Inn 🍴
Maltongate YO18 7LF ☎ 01751 474226 📠 01751 477715

A Georgian coaching inn in the centre of a picturesque village complete with beck running beside the main street, and village stocks and market cross. Like the village, the inn retains its old world charm, with its log fires and hand-pulled ales. Freshly-cooked food is one of its attractions, with many tempting choices on the menu and specials board: medallions of beef fillet, pan-fried chicken supreme, grilled halibut steak, seven bone rack of lamb, and salmon fillet with baby cucumber show the range.
OPEN: 12-2.30 5-11 (open all day-Summer) **BAR MEALS:** L served all week 12-2 D served all week 6-9 Av main course £7.95 **RESTAURANT:** L served all week 12-2 D served all week 6-9 Av 3 course à la carte £12 **BREWERY/COMPANY:** Scottish & Newcastle ◀: Theakston Black Bull, John Smith's, Cask old Speckled Hen. **FACILITIES:** Garden: Enclosed floral courtyard **NOTES:** Parking 15 **ROOMS:** 6 bedrooms 6 en suite s£38 d£56 (♦♦♦♦) no children overnight

England

THORNTON WATLASS   Map 19 SE28

Pick of the Pubs

The Buck Inn ★ 🛏️
HG4 4AH ☎ 01677 422461 📠 01677 422447
e-mail: buckwatlass@btconnect.com
*Dir: From A1 at Leeming Bar take A684 to Bedale, then B6268.
Village 2m on R, hotel by cricket green*

After many years of running the Buck, Margaret and
Michael Fox still strive to maintain the warm welcome and
relaxed atmosphere that keeps people coming back. The
inn overlooks the village green and cricket pitch (the pub
is the boundary), facing the old stone cottages of the
village in a peaceful part of Wensleydale, yet is only five
minutes' drive from the A1. Cricket isn't the only sport
associated with the pub, as quoits are played in the back
garden. Live traditional jazz is also a feature on at least
two Sundays a month. Five real ales are served, most of
them from local independent breweries, and English
cooking, freshly prepared on the premises. Specialities are
Masham rarebit (Wensleydale cheese with local ale on
toast, topped with ham and bacon), deep-fried fresh
Whitby cod, and breast of chicken stir fried in black bean
sauce.
OPEN: 11-11 (Sun 12-10.30) **BAR MEALS:** L served all week
12-2 D served all week 6-9.30 Av main course £10
RESTAURANT: L served all week 12-2 D served all week 6.30-
9.30 Av 3 course à la carte £16.50 **BREWERY/COMPANY:** Free
House 🍺: Theakston Best, Black Sheep Best, John Smith's &
Guest beers. **FACILITIES:** Children welcome Garden: Food
served outside Dogs allowed Water **NOTES:** Parking 40
ROOMS: 7 bedrooms 5 en suite s£45 d£65

WASS   Map 19 SE57

Wombwell Arms 🛏️ 🍷
YO61 4BE ☎ 01347 868280 📠 01347 868039
e-mail: thewombwellarms@aol.com
*Dir: From A1 take A168 to A19 junct. Take York exit, then L after 2.5m, L at
Coxwold to Ampleforth. Wass 2m*
The building was constructed in 1620 as a granary, probably
using stone from nearby Byland Abbey, and it became an ale
house in about 1640. A series of stylishly decorated rooms
provide the setting for bistro-style cooking. Local suppliers
have been established for all the produce used; at least three
vegetarian dishes are offered daily and a good choice of fresh
fish, including Whitby cod. Popular options are steak,
Guinness and mushroom pie, and game casserole.
OPEN: 12-2.30 7-11 (closed Sun eve in winter & all Mon)
BAR MEALS: L served all week 12-2 D served all week 7-9

RESTAURANT: L served all week 12-2 D served all week 7-9
BREWERY/COMPANY: Free House 🍺: Black Sheep Best, Timothy
Taylor Landlord, Cropton Two Pints. **FACILITIES:** Children welcome
Garden: Gravel beer garden, seats approx 25 **NOTES:** Parking 15

WEAVERTHORPE   Map 17 SE97

Pick of the Pubs

The Star Country Inn 🛏️
YO17 8EY ☎ 01944 738273 📠 01944 738273
e-mail: info@starinn.net
*Dir: 12 m E of Malton to Sherborn Village, traffic lights on A64, turn R
at the lights, Weaverthorpe 4 m Star inn on the Junct facing*

This brightly-shining Star has expanded over the years to
incorporate adjoining cottages that house an extended
dining area and comfortable accommodation for
overnight guests. The inn is set in the midst of the
Yorkshire Wolds and is handy for visiting Castle Howard,
Sledmere House and Nunnington Hall. The rustic facilities
of bar and dining room, with large open fires and a
convivial atmosphere, complement food cooked to
traditional family recipes using fresh local produce.
Favourite starters include Brompton sausages and sautéed
onions in ale, Wold mushrooms with walnuts and Stilton
sauce, and Yorkshire pudding with a savoury medley.
Traditional main courses include slow-roasted mini lamb
joint; wild boar with black pudding, brandy and apple
cream sauce; jugged Yorkshire hare; and local game
casserole. There are always seafood and vegetarian
choices, too, like mixed fish and prawn lattice, and
asparagus and spinach pancakes with three cheeses.
OPEN: 12-3 7-11 Rest:Mon-Tues Closed Lunch **BAR MEALS:** L
served Wed-Sun 12-2 D served Wed-Sun 7-9.30
RESTAURANT: L served Wed-Sun 12-2 D served Wed-Sun 7-
9.30 **BREWERY/COMPANY:** Free House 🍺: Carlsberg-Tetely
Tetely Bitter, Scottish Courage John Smith's, Durham Ales.
FACILITIES: Garden: Patio, Tables/Chairs, Shrubberies
NOTES: Parking 30

continued

England

WEST BURTON
Map 19 SE08

Fox & Hounds
DL8 4JY ☎ 01969 663111 ▤ 01969 663279
Dir: A468

Close to the heart of beautiful Wensleydale, this 17th-century coaching inn is attractively located by the pretty green in a totally unspoilt village. Traditional pub food and bedrooms.

OPEN: 11-11 **BAR MEALS:** L served all week 12-2 D served all week 6-9 Av main course £5.95 **RESTAURANT:** L served all week 12-2 D served all week 6.30-9 Av 3 course à la carte £15
BREWERY/COMPANY: Free House 🍺: Black Sheep, Old Peculier, John Smiths, Tetleys. **FACILITIES:** Children welcome Dogs allowed **NOTES:** Parking 7 **ROOMS:** 7 bedrooms 7 en suite s£35 d£56 (★★★)

WEST TANFIELD
Map 19 SE27

Pick of the Pubs

The Bruce Arms ♦♦♦♦ ◎ ☜ ♀
Main St HG4 5JJ ☎ 01677 470325 ▤ 01677 470796
e-mail: iwanttostay@brucearms.com
Dir: On A6108 Ripon/Masham rd, close to A1

Just a few miles' drive north of Ripon, this ivy-clad, stone-built free house is situated in close proximity to the River Ure. Expect to find a well-run and informal inn whose exposed beams, log fires and candle-topped tables complement the traditional décor. Cosy, comfortable bedrooms provide an excellent base for touring the Yorkshire Dales, Jervaulx Abbey, Aysgarth Falls and the Hawes Wensleydale cheese centre. Built in 1820, the premises now run as a "bistro with bedrooms" following extensive alterations in 1998. A good wine list underlines the pubs bistro atmosphere, with a regularly changing blackboard menu that displays a healthy interest in the sourcing of seasonal produce. Twice-baked cheese soufflé or smoked haddock with spinach, poached egg and hollandaise as openers may be followed by Dover sole with asparagus and east coast crab in filo pastry or a rack of Dales lamb and fresh tarragon. A choice of home-made desserts or local Yorkshire cheeses promises to round off a memorable meal.
OPEN: 12-2 6.30-11 Closed: 1 Wk Feb **BAR MEALS:** L served Sat-Sun. No weekday lunch Dec-Apr 12-2 D served Tues-Sat 6.30-9.30 Av main course £12.50 **RESTAURANT:** L served Sat-Sun. No weekday lunch Dec-Apr 12-2 D served Tues-Sat 6.30-9.30 Av 3 course à la carte £25 **BREWERY/COMPANY:** Free House 🍺: Black Sheep Best. ♀: 10 **FACILITIES:** Children welcome Garden: Terrace **NOTES:** Parking 15 **ROOMS:** 3 bedrooms 3 en suite 1 family rooms s£40 d£60

WEST WITTON
Map 19 SE08

Pick of the Pubs

The Wensleydale Heifer Inn ★★ ☜ ♀
DL8 4LS ☎ 01969 622322 ▤ 01969 624183
e-mail: info@wensleydaleheifer.co.uk
Dir: A684, at west end of village.

A welcoming whitewashed roadside inn with roaring open fires, exposed stonework and beams, and cosy snugs. Set in the heart of Wensleydale and the Yorkshire Dales National Park, and ideally placed for walking and exploring the exploring the countryside, it dates back to 1631 when it served as a traditional coaching inn. The heart of this old inn is the kitchen, where the owners oversee preparation of a wide range of dishes. Game comes from the moors, fish from Scotland and the East Coast, beef and lamb from the Dales - all supplemented by local vegetables and fresh garden herbs, with puddings and bread baked daily. Despite its inland location, seafood features prominently on the menu, in the form of haddock with rarebit, Dover and lemon sole, king prawns in filo pastry, and lobster cooked in various ways.

OPEN: 11-9 **BAR MEALS:** L served all week 12-2 D served all week 6-9 Av main course £8.50 **RESTAURANT:** L served all week 12-2 D served all week 6.30-9 Av 3 course à la carte £22 **BREWERY/COMPANY:** Free House 🍺: Theakston Best Bitter, Scottish Courage John Smith's, Black Sheep Best. ♀: 7 **FACILITIES:** Children welcome Garden: Lawned, with bench seats and tables Dogs allowed **NOTES:** Parking 30 **ROOMS:** 9 bedrooms 9 en suite 2 family rooms s£60 d£72

England

WHITBY
Map 19 NZ81

The Magpie Cafe 🍴 🍷
14 Pier Rd YO21 3PU ☎ 01947 602058 ▤ 01947 601801
e-mail: ian@magpiecafe.co.uk

More a licensed restaurant than a pub, the award-winning Magpie has been the home of North Yorkshire's best-ever fish and chips since the late 1930s when it moved to its present site in Pier Road. The dining rooms command excellent views of the harbour, the Abbey and St Mary's Church. Fresh Whitby fish and shellfish, with up to 10 daily choices, feature on the menu, as well as an extensive range of salads and over 20 home-made puddings.
OPEN: 11.30-9 Closed: 5 Jan-6 Feb **BAR MEALS:** L served all week 11.30-9 D served all week Av main course £6 **RESTAURANT:** L served all week 11.30-9 D served all week **BREWERY/COMPANY:** Free House 🍺: Crompton, Scoresby Bitter, Carlsberg-Tetley Tetley Bitter.. 🍷: 9 **FACILITIES:** Children welcome

WIGGLESWORTH
Map 18 SD85

The Plough Inn
BD23 4RJ ☎ 01729 840243 ▤ 01729 840638
e-mail: Sue@ploughinn.info
Dir: *From A65 between Skipton & Long Preston take B6478 to Wigglesworth*

A traditional 18th-century country inn ideally placed for exploring the bustling market towns and pretty villages of the Dales. The imaginative menu draws inspiration from English, European and Oriental sources, and the quality and presentation of the food here attracts custom from far and wide. Expect grilled shark steak in Cajun crumb with lime butter, chicken balti, and baked salted cod on crab mash, plus a traditional bar menu.
OPEN: 11-2.30 6.30-11 **BAR MEALS:** L served all week 12-2 D served all week 7-9 Av main course £7.50 **RESTAURANT:** L served all week 12-2 D served all week 7-9 Av 3 course à la carte £18 Av 2 course fixed price £6.50 **BREWERY/COMPANY:** Free House 🍺: Carlsberg-Tetley Tetley Bitter, Black Sheep Best.

FACILITIES: Children welcome Garden: Large area with views over Yorkshire Dales Dogs allowed Water **NOTES:** Parking 70 **ROOMS:** 12 bedrooms 12 en suite 3 family rooms s£42.50 d£61 (★★)

YORKSHIRE, SOUTH

BRADFIELD
Map 16 SK29

The Strines Inn 🍴
Bradfield Dale S6 6JE ☎ 0114 2851247
Dir: *off A57 between Sheffield toward Manchester*
The inn is set amid the grouse moors of the Peak District National Park, overlooking the Strines Reservoir. Originally a manor house, it was built in 1275, though most of the present building dates from the 1550s. It has been an inn since 1771. Real fires burn in all three rooms and home-made food is served. Pies are popular, and giant Yorkshire pudding with prime roast beef. Speciality coffees are also a feature.
OPEN: 10.30-3 (all day Mar-Sep) 6.30-11 (Wkds open all day) Closed: Dec 25 **BAR MEALS:** L served all week 12-2.30 D served all week 6.30-9 **BREWERY/COMPANY:** Free House 🍺: Marston's Pedigree, Kelham Island. **FACILITIES:** Children welcome Garden: Large garden. Roaming peacocks Dogs allowed Water **NOTES:** Parking 50

DONCASTER
Map 16 SE50

Waterfront Inn 🍴
Canal Ln, West Stockwith DN10 4ET ☎ 01427 891223
Built in the 1830s overlooking the Trent Canal basin and the canal towpath, and near a marina, the pub is now popular with walkers. Real ales and good value food that includes pasta with home-made ratatouille, broccoli and cheese bake, deep fried scampi, half honey-roasted chicken, and home-made lasagne are served. On Sundays there's a carvery as well and there's a children's menu. Serves over 40 real ales and ciders at its annual May Bank Holiday beer festival.
OPEN: 11-11 **BAR MEALS:** L served all week 12-2.30 D served all week 5.30-8.30 **RESTAURANT:** L served all week 12-2.30 D served all week 5.30-8.30 **BREWERY/COMPANY:** Enterprise Inns 🍺: Scottish Courage John Smith Cask, Black Sheep, Timothy Taylors, Charles Wells Bombardier Premium Bitter. **FACILITIES:** Children welcome Garden Dogs allowed Water provided **NOTES:** Parking 30

INGBIRCHWORTH
Map 16 SE20

The Fountain Inn 🍴 🍷 NEW
Wellthorne Ln S36 7GJ ☎ 01226 763125 ▤ 01226 761336
e-mail: reservations@fountain-inn.co.uk
Dir: *Exit M1 Junction 37. Take A628 to Manchester then take A629 to Huddersfield*
Busy but friendly and informal country inn with stylish, cosy interior. Famous for the local choir which gathers here every Christmas and brings a countrywide following, it is also next door to 'Summer Wine' country. Favourite bar meals include ale-braised steak, shoulder of lamb, Fountain grill, and bean fajitas, with a good fish choice ranging around buttered haddock, crab linguini, and salmon and prawn fishcakes.
OPEN: 11.45-2.30 5-11 Closed: 25 Dec **BAR MEALS:** L served all week 12-2 D served all week 5-9.30 Av main course £9.50 🍺: Tetleys Cask, Theakstons Best, Black Sheep, John Smith Smooth. 🍷: 9 **FACILITIES:** Children welcome Garden: Enclosed patio, only drinks served **NOTES:** Parking 45 **ROOMS:** 10 bedrooms 10 en suite s£50 d£60 (♦♦♦♦)

continued

PENISTONE
Map 16 SE20

Cubley Hall 🏠 ♀
Mortimer Rd, Cubley S36 9DF ☎ 01226 766086 📠 01226 767335
e-mail: cubley.hall@ukonline.co.uk
Dir: Telephone for directions

Cloaked in history, Cubley Hall has evolved through the
centuries from moorland farm on the Pennine packhorse
route of the 1700s to gentleman's residence and children's
home. Many original features have been retained, including
the renowned restaurant converted from an oak-beamed
barn. The menu offers a choice of pizzas, pastas, fish,
chargrills and salads, notably herbed baked salmon, tuna and
mixed bean salad, and bread and butter pudding.
OPEN: 11-11 (Sun 12-10.30) **BAR MEALS:** L served all week 12-
9.30 D served all week 12-9.30 Av main course £7.50
RESTAURANT: L served Sun 12-9.30 D served Wknds Av 3 course à
la carte £16 **BREWERY/COMPANY:** Free House 🍺: Carlsberg-
Tetley Tetley Bitter, Burton Ale, Greene King Abbot Ale, Young's
Special. ♀: 7 **FACILITIES:** Children welcome Garden: Large lawns,
seating areas and tables **NOTES:** Parking 100 **ROOMS:** 12
bedrooms 12 en suite s£57 (♦♦♦♦)

SHEFFIELD
Map 16 SK38

Pick of the Pubs

The Fat Cat
23 Alma St S3 8SA ☎ 0114 249 4801 📠 0114 249 4803
e-mail: enquiries@thefatcat.co.uk
Dir: Telephone for directions
So unique is the Fat Cat, dating back to 1855 and now a listed
building, that it defies the opposition of the larger chain pubs
that surround it. The Fat Cat's aims are to provide a wide
range of micro-brewery ales, to be a place of quiet(ish)
relaxation free from music and amusement machines and to
provide good home-cooked food. The well-kept hand-
pumped beers, usually as many as ten, include some from
their own popular brewery, plus guest beers and a range of
bottled beers from Britain and the continent. The keenly
priced food always includes a variety of vegetarian and
gluten-free fare as well as daily specials to appease its many
regular carnivores. The menu changes weekly, but a typical
selection includes braised beef and black peppers, tikka
mushrooms with rice and nutty parsnip pie, followed by fruit
crumble and jam roly-poly. Consistently one of the top-rated
urban pubs in Britain for many years - and deservedly so.
OPEN: 12-3 5.30-11 (Sun 7-10.30) Closed: Dec 25-26
BAR MEALS: L served all week 12-2.30 D served Mon-Fri 6-7.30
Av main course £3 **BREWERY/COMPANY:** Free House
🍺: Timothy Taylor Landlord, Kelham Island Bitter, Pale Rider,
Pride of Sheffield. **FACILITIES:** Children welcome Garden: Hard
surface walled area Dogs allowed **NOTES:** No credit cards

WENTWORTH
Map 16 SK39

Rockingham Arms
8 Main St S62 7TL ☎ 01226 742075 📠 01226 361099
Dir: M1 J36 to Hoyland Common then B6090

Attractive ivy-clad village pub on the Wentworth estate with a
large orchard beer garden overlooking the bowling green. Folk
music is a feature on a Friday night and quizzes on a Tuesday or
Sunday. Dishes on offer include Wexford steaks, steak and ale
pie, salmon and prawn salad, beer-battered cod, and game pie.
OPEN: 11-11 (Sun 12-10.30) **BAR MEALS:** L served all week 12 D
served Mon-Sun 9 **RESTAURANT:** L served all week 12-9 Av 3 course à
la carte £7.95 **BREWERY/COMPANY:** 🍺: Theakston XB, Old Peculier, &
Best, Old Speckled Hen. **FACILITIES:** Garden: Large orchard garden,
large bowling green Dogs allowed very dog friendly **NOTES:** Parking 30

YORKSHIRE, WEST

BRADFORD
Map 19 SE13

New Beehive Inn
171 Westgate BD1 3AA ☎ 01274 721784 📠 01274 735092
e-mail: newbeehiveinn@talk21.com

Classic Edwardian inn, dating from 1901 and retaining its
period atmosphere with separate bars and gas lighting.
Outside, with a complete change of mood, you can relax in
the Mediterranean-style courtyard. The pub offers a good
range of unusual real ales and a selection of over 100 malt
whiskies, served alongside some simple bar snacks.
Accommodation is available in 13 antique-furnished rooms,
including eight with en suite facilities.
OPEN: 12-11 **BAR MEALS:** L served Mon-Sat 12-2
BREWERY/COMPANY: Free House 🍺: Timothy Taylor Landlord,
Kelham Island Bitter, Hop Back Summer Lightning, Abbeydale
Moonshine. **FACILITIES:** Garden: Mediterranean style courtyard
NOTES: Parking 20 **ROOMS:** 13 bedrooms 8 en suite 2 family
rooms s£22 d£32 (♦♦♦) no children overnight

CLIFTON
Map 16 SE12

Black Horse Inn 🛏 ♀
HD6 4HJ ☎ 01484 713862 📠 01484 400582
e-mail: mail@blackhorseclifton.co.uk
Dir: N of Brighouse
A 16th-century coaching inn with oak-beamed rooms, open coal fires and an interesting history. It was once used as a meeting place for the loom-wrecking Luddites, and later as a variety club playing host to Roy Orbison, Showaddywaddy and Shirley Bassey. Good home-cooked food has been served here for over 50 years, the likes of chargrilled halibut steak with capers, and roast sirloin of beef with chicken parfait, redcurrant jelly and rich red wine jus.
OPEN: 11-11 **BAR MEALS:** L served all week 12-5.30 D served all week 5.30-9.30 Av main course £9 **RESTAURANT:** L served all week 12-5.30 D served all week 5.30-9.30 Av 3 course à la carte £20 **BREWERY/COMPANY:** Enterprise Inns 🍺: Black Sheep, Timothy Taylor Landlord, Old Speckled Hen, Tetleys. ♀: 10 **FACILITIES:** Children welcome Garden: Courtyard on two levels, hanging baskets Dogs allowed **NOTES:** Parking 50

DEWSBURY
Map 16 SE22

West Riding Licensed Refreshment Rooms
Dewsbury Railway Station, Wellington Rd WF13 1HF ☎ 01924 459193 📠 01924 507444

Trains regularly pass this converted Grade II listed railway station built in 1848 and located on the Trans-Pennine route between Leeds and Manchester. The pub supports northern micro-breweries and is linked to an Anglo Dutch brewery in Dewsbury. A daily-changing menu offers such dishes as ham and cottage cheese flan and salad, carrot cakes stuffed in cabbage served with sweet pepper sauce, mushroom and parsnip crumble and chicken tikka in pitta bread served with rice, salad and raita.
OPEN: 11-11 Closed: 25 Dec **BAR MEALS:** L served Mon-Fri 12-3 D served Tues-Wed 6-9 **BREWERY/COMPANY:** Free House 🍺: Timothy Taylor Dark Mild & Landlord, Black Sheep Best. **FACILITIES:** Children welcome Garden: Food served outside Dogs allowed **NOTES:** Parking 600 No credit cards

EAST KESWICK
Map 16 SE34

The Travellers Rest
Harewood Rd, East Keswick LS17 9HL ☎ 01937 572766 572766
Dir: 2m from Harewood House on the A659, 4m from the A1/M1
Mid-way between Harewood House and Collingham, an old hostelry dating from 1641 - once the pack-horse route from York to Skipton and beyond. With spectacular views over the Wharfe Valley, it is equally popular with hikers and riders for home-cooked food from local suppliers. The pub is only two miles from Harewood House and the set of TV soap 'Emmerdale Farm'. Recent change in management.
OPEN: 12-11 (Sunday 12-10.30) **BAR MEALS:** L served all week 12-2 D served all week 5.30-9 Av main course £5.95 **RESTAURANT:** L served all week 12-6 D served all week 6-9 Av 3 course fixed price £10 **BREWERY/COMPANY:** Punch Taverns 🍺: Tetleys Bitter, Black Sheep, Stella Artois, Murphys. **FACILITIES:** Children welcome Garden: Patio area **NOTES:** Parking 90

HALIFAX
Map 19 SE02

Pick of the Pubs

Shibden Mill Inn ♦♦♦♦ ◎◎ 🛏 ♀
Shibden Mill Fold HX3 7UL
☎ 01422 365840 📠 01422 362971
e-mail: shibdenmillinn@zoom.co.uk
Nestling in the fold of the Shibden Valley, this low, whitewashed 17th-century inn retains much of its original charm and character. A cosy friendly bar and an intimate candlelit restaurant attract plenty of drinkers and diners and chef Neil Butterworth, having gained experience in some of London's top restaurants, offers a wide and varied selection of dishes to accommodate individual tastes. Grilled red mullet, goats' cheese savoury muffin, smoked chicken salad and melon slices feature among the interesting starters. For main courses there may be grilled calves' liver with a wholegrain mustard sauce, seared salmon fillet with a cider sauce and braised shin of beef with celeriac mash and herb dumpling - among other dishes. Lighter fare includes scrambled eggs with smoked salmon and baby capers, honey roast ham bloomer with home-made salad cream and poached egg and glazed buck rarebit on sun-dried tomato bread. Tasteful en suite bedrooms are thoughtfully equipped.
OPEN: 12-2.30 5.30-11 **BAR MEALS:** L served all week 12-2 D served all week 6-9.30 **RESTAURANT:** L served all week 12-2 D served all week 6-9.30 **BREWERY/COMPANY:** Free House 🍺: John Smiths, Theakston XB, Shibden Mill, Stella Artios. ♀: 12 **FACILITIES:** Children welcome Garden: Walled garden with heated patio Dogs allowed In garden only **NOTES:** Parking 200 **ROOMS:** 12 bedrooms 12 en suite

HAREWOOD
Map 19 SE34

Harewood Arms Hotel ♀
Harrogate Rd LS17 9LH ☎ 0113 2886566 📠 0113 2886064
e-mail: unwind@the-harewood-arms-hotel.co.uk
Dir: On A61 S of Harrogate
Built in 1815 this former coaching inn is close to Harewood House, home of the Earl and Countess of Harewood. A smart and comfortable location for those visiting Harrogate, Leeds, York and the Dales. In the bar traditional local ale is hand pulled from wooden casks and bar snacks are available throughout the day. The elegant restaurant serves lunch and dinner menus. Typical dishes include roast rack of lamb, escalope of pork Holstein, bouchée of seafood or vegetarian stir-fry.
OPEN: 11-11 **BAR MEALS:** L served all week 12-3 D served all week 5-10 **RESTAURANT:** L served all week 12-2 D served all week 7-10 Av 3 course fixed price £22.95 **BREWERY/COMPANY:** Samuel Smith 🍺: Samuel Smith OBB & Sovereign. **FACILITIES:** Garden Dogs allowed **NOTES:** Parking 90

continued

HAWORTH
Map 19 SE03

The Old White Lion Hotel ★★ 👑
Main St BD22 8DU ☎ 01535 642313 📠 01535 646222
e-mail: enquiries@oldwhitelionhotel.com
Dir: Turn off A629 onto B6142, hotel 0.5m past Haworth Station

300-year-old former coaching inn located at the top of a cobbled street, close to the Brontë Museum and Parsonage. Traditionally furnished bars offer a welcome respite from the tourist trail. Theakston ales, and a wide range of generously served snacks and meals. A carte features chicken Italia, champagne halibut, scampi Mediterranean, chicken Rockafella, pork fillet Calvados, fillet steak of Old England, and crepe Italiana among others. Jacket potatoes, giant Yorkshire puddings and specials also available. Comfortable bedrooms.
OPEN: 11-3 6-11 **BAR MEALS:** L served all week 11.30-2.30 D served all week 5.30-9.30 Av main course £6 **RESTAURANT:** L served Sun 12-2.30 D served all week 7-9.30 Av 3 course à la carte £22 Av 3 course fixed price £13.25 **BREWERY/COMPANY:** Free House 🍺: Theakstons Best & Black Bull, Carlsberg-Tetley Tetley Bitter, Scottish Courage John Smith's. **FACILITIES:** Children welcome **NOTES:** Parking 9 **ROOMS:** 14 bedrooms 14 en suite 2 family rooms s£47 d£65

HORBURY
Map 16 SE21

Quarry Inn & Cottages
70 Quarry Hill WF4 5NF ☎ 01924 272523
Dir: On the A642 approx 2.5m from Wakefield
Located in the hollow of a disused quarry, a creeper-clad stone pub with original features like stone walls and beams. Harry Secombe, Roy Castle and members of Wakefield Trinity have visited this traditional pub over the years. Good range of appetising dishes in the bar and restaurant, and good ales: Camerons Creamy, Banks Original, Mansfield Smooth. New owners.
OPEN: 11.30-11 (Sun 12-4,7-10.30) **BAR MEALS:** L served all week 12-2 D served Mon-Sat 5.30-8.30 Av main course £4
RESTAURANT: L served all week 12-2 D served Mon-Sat 5.30-8.30 Av 3 course fixed price £5 **BREWERY/COMPANY:** Marstons 🍺: Marston's Pedigree, Camerons Creamy, Banks Original, Mansfield Smooth. **FACILITIES:** Dogs allowed Food, water, shelter **NOTES:** Parking 36

LEDSHAM
Map 16 SE42

The Chequers Inn
Claypit Ln LS25 5LP ☎ 01977 683135 📠 01977 680791
Dir: Between A1 & A656 above Castleford
Quaint creeper-covered inn located in an old estate village in the countryside to the east of Leeds. Unusually, the pub is closed on Sunday because the one-time lady of the manor

was offended by drunken farm workers on her way to church more than 160 years ago. Inside are low beams and wooden settles, giving the pub the feel of a traditional village establishment.
OPEN: 11-3 5-11 (Sat 11-11) **BAR MEALS:** L served Mon-Sat 12-2.15 D served Mon-Sat 5.30-9.45 Av main course £9.45
BREWERY/COMPANY: Free House 🍺: Theakston Best, John Smiths, Brown Cow, Timothy Taylor Landlord. **FACILITIES:** Children welcome Garden: outdoor eating, patio Dogs allowed
NOTES: Parking 35

LEEDS
Map 19 SE23

Whitelocks 🍷
Turks Head Yard, Briggate LS1 6HB
☎ 0113 2453950 📠 0113 2423368
Dir: Next to Marks & Spencer in Briggate
Leeds' oldest pub, first licensed in 1715, was originally the Turks Head. The current name comes from the family who owned it for 90 years up till 1944. Classic features include a long bar with polychrome tiles, stained-glass windows and advertising mirrors. Look out for the Dickensian-style bar at the end of the yard. There are four guest ales in addition to the regulars and popular pub food like steak pie and Yorkshire puddings.
OPEN: 11-11 (Sun 12-10.30) Closed: 25-26 Dec, 1 Jan
BAR MEALS: L served all week 11-5 D served all week Av main course £3.95 **RESTAURANT:** L served all week 12-2.30 D served all week 5.30-7 **BREWERY/COMPANY:** 🍺: Scottish Courage Theakston Best, Old Peculier & John Smiths, Greene King Ruddles Best, Guest Ales every week. 🍷: 9 **FACILITIES:** Garden: Beer garden, sun trap Dogs allowed Water

LINTON
Map 16 SE34

The Windmill Inn 👑 🍷
Main St LS22 4HT ☎ 01937 582209 📠 01937 587518
Dir: from A1 exit at Tadcaster/Otley junction and follow Otley signs. In Collingham follow signs for Linton
A coaching inn since the 18th century, the building actually dates back to the 14th century, and originally housed the owner of the long-disappeared windmill. Stone walls, antique settles, log fires, oak beams and lots of brass set the scene in which to enjoy good bar food prepared by enthusiastic licensees. Expect the likes of steak and Theakston pie, chicken stuffed with haggis, halibut on pasta with basil sauce, and tuna on stir-fried vegetables. While you're there, ask to take a look at the local history scrapbook.
OPEN: 11.30-3 5-11 (Summer, Sat, Sun open all day)
BAR MEALS: L served all week 12-2.30 D served Mon-Sat 5.30-9 Av main course £7.50 **RESTAURANT:** L served all week 12-2 D served Mon-Sat 5.30-9 Av 3 course à la carte £15
BREWERY/COMPANY: Scottish Courage 🍺: Scottish Courage John Smith's & Theakston Best, Daleside, Greene King Ruddles County. **FACILITIES:** Children welcome Garden: Quiet secluded garden with beautiful view Dogs allowed Water **NOTES:** Parking 60

MYTHOLMROYD
Map 19 SE02

Shoulder of Mutton 🍷
New Rd HX7 5DZ ☎ 01422 883165
Dir: A646 Halifax to Todmorden, in Mytholmroyd on B6138, opp train station
A typical Pennines pub, next to a trout stream, well situated for local walks and the popular Calderdale Way. It was associated with the infamous Crag Coiners, 18th-century

continued

continued

England

MYTHOLMROYD continued

forgers. The pub's reputation for good ales and food remains undimmed after nearly 30 years of current ownership. A menu of home-cooked dishes from fresh ingredients includes beef and ale pie, fish and chips and a daily carvery of pork, lamb, beef and turkey.
OPEN: 11.30-3 7-11 (Sat 11.30-11, 12-10.30) **BAR MEALS:** L served all week 12-2 D served Wed-Mon 7-8 Av main course £3.99
RESTAURANT: L served all week 11.30-2 D served Wed-Mon 7-8.30 Av 3 course fixed price £3.99 🍺: Black Sheep, Boddingtons, Flowers, Taylor Landlord. 🍷: 10 **FACILITIES:** Children welcome Garden: Riverside garden with floral display, seating Dogs allowed Water, Treats **NOTES:** Parking 25 **NOTES:** No credit cards

NEWALL
Map 19 SE14

The Spite 🍴
LS21 2EY ☎ 01943 463063
'There's nowt but malice and spite at these pubs', said a local who one day did the unthinkable - drank in both village hostelries, renowned for their feuding landlords. The Traveller's Rest, which became The Malice, is long closed, but the Roebuck has survived as The Spite. Salmon mornay, haddock, scampi, steak and ale pie, ostrich fillet and speciality sausages are likely to be on offer.
OPEN: 11.30-3 (Thurs- Sun 11.30-11) 6-11 **BAR MEALS:** L served all week 12-2 D served Tue-Sat 6-8.30 Av main course £5.50
RESTAURANT: L served all week 11.30-2 D served Tue-Sat 6-9
BREWERY/COMPANY: Unique Pub Co 🍺: John Smiths, Tetleys, Bombardier, Worthington Creamflow. **FACILITIES:** Children welcome Garden: Food served outside. Lawned area Dogs allowed Water provided **NOTES:** Parking 50

RIPPONDEN
Map 16 SE01

Old Bridge Inn 🍷
Priest Ln HX6 4DF ☎ 01422 822595
Dir: 5m from Halifax in village centre by church

Just beside a cobbled packhorse bridge this friendly 14th-century hostelry is in a picturesque conservation village. Inside are thick stone walls, gnarled beams and antique oak tables, whilst in summer the window boxes outside are delightful. The mid-week cold buffet and vegetarian options are popular. In the evening, an imaginative menu may suggest smoked haddock and spinach pancakes, mushroom, lentil and Stilton lasagne, or rabbit and tarragon sausages, followed by gooseberry crème brûlée or maple syrup and whiskey tart.
OPEN: 12-3 5.30-11 **BAR MEALS:** L served Mon-Fri 12-2 D served Mon-Fri 6.30-9.30 Av main course £6.25
BREWERY/COMPANY: Free House 🍺: Timothy Taylor Landlord, Golden Best, & Best Bitter, Black Sheep Best. 🍷: 12

FACILITIES: Children welcome Garden: Riverside terrace.
NOTES: Parking 40

SHELF
Map 19 SE12

Duke of York 🍷
West St, Stone Chair HX3 7LN ☎ 01422 202056 🖷 01422 206618
e-mail: kathrynwepworth@lunet.ak.uk
Dir: M62 J25 to Brighouse. Take A644 N. Inn 500yds on R after Stone Chair r'about
A vast array of brassware and bric-a-brac adorns this 17th-century former coaching inn located between Bradford and Halifax, and the atmosphere is lively and friendly. Expect classic dishes such as beef bourguignon, grilled fillet steak with peppercorn sauce, and braised lamb Henry with orange mashed potatoes and rosemary broth. The pub carries a wide range of cask ales.
OPEN: 11.30-11.30 (Sun 12-10.30) **BAR MEALS:** L served all week 12-2.30 D served all week 5-9.30 **RESTAURANT:** L served all week 12-2.30 D served all week 5-9.30 Av 3 course fixed price £11.95
BREWERY/COMPANY: Whitbread 🍺: Landlord, Landlady, J.W Lees, Tetleys & Guest beer. 🍷: 15 **FACILITIES:** Children welcome Garden: Patio at front with chairs **NOTES:** Parking 30

SHELLEY
Map 16 SE21

Pick of the Pubs

The Three Acres Inn 🍴 🍷
HD8 8LR ☎ 01484 602606 🖷 01484 608411
e-mail: 3acres@globalnet.co.uk
Dir: From Huddersfield take A629 then B6116, take L turn for village

With its commanding views over the Pennines, reputation for quality food and welcoming atmosphere, this charming inn is a longstanding favourite. Located just ten minutes from the M1 (J38), it has been in the same hands for over thirty years. Warmly lit outside by night, and cosy and inviting at all times, it is a beacon of hospitality above the rolling green countryside around the Pennines - the sort of place that's hard to leave. Dine in the bar or the restaurant, a charming and elaborately decorated room featuring bare beams, ornamental plates and a corner filled with antique books. An exhaustive selection of dishes ranging from traditional to oriental, all freshly prepared to order, can be sampled from the menus. Bar choices can be as light as sandwiches filled with an elaborate selection like steak on toasted onion bread with rocket, caramelised onions and blue cheese. Starters might be devilled king prawns with chilli on a warm noodle and pak choi salad, and flash-fried Loch Fyne queenies. Main courses are also varied: expect Whitby

continued

continued on p. 566

The Millbank at Millbank

The spectacular Pennine hills surrounding the village of Mill Bank form the backdrop to this fascinating walk, which follows ancient backhorse routes, tracks and valley paths. The route coincides with part of the Calderdale Way, a popular long-distance trail that explores the rugged Calder Valley. Along the way are wooded cloughs, several Pennine smallholdings and some fine examples of 16th-century architecture.

From the pub turn left and after about 100yds (91m) turn left down Lower Mill Bank Road, following it through the village of Mill Bank and down to a stream. Turn left immediately beyond the bridge, by a converted watermill, and follow the waterside path. The path soon swings right and heads up a slope through Fiddle Wood, gradually ascending the hillside. Make for a series of stone steps that lead up to a stony and grass track known as Clapgate Lane. Turn right and after about 100yds (91m) veer left at the fork, following High Field Lane. The cobbled track climbs steeply to High Field Farm and then on to Top O' Th' Town Farm in the hamlet of Soyland. Turn right at the next road and follow it as it swings left to become Lane Head Road. Continue for 600yds before bearing right at the staggered crossroads onto Cross-Wells Road. This descends fairly steeply to a small bridge over Severhills Clough stream. Keep ahead for about 500yds (457m), passing Clay House to reach a track on the right known as Gough Lane. Here, you

have a choice. To follow the shorter route back to the Millbank, turn right down Gough Lane. On reaching a wood look for a footpath on the left, climb the stile and cut between fir trees to reach the bridge at the bottom of Lower Mill Bank Road. Retrace your steps up the road to the pub.

To extend the walk by about 2 miles (3.2km), avoid the lane and continue along what is now Lighthazels Road. Turn right down Clay Pits Lane, pass the Alma pub and cross the bridge at Salt Drake. Climb the hill to Cottonstones Church and, 50yds (46m) beyond it, look for a sharp right-hand turn. Follow the track for about 1/4 mile (400m), to the hamlet of Helm,

THE MILLBANK AT MILLBANK, SOWERBY BRIDGE
HX6 3DY
☎ 01422 825588

Directions: A58 from Sowerby Bridge to Ripponden, R at Triange Stone-built pub with a growing reputation for food. There's a wine bar ambience in the main bar, plus a cosy tap room and a dining room. Fresh local produce including seafood and robust meat dishes. Stunning views from garden.
Open: 12-3 6-11 (Closed Mon, & 1st 2 wks Oct)
Bar Meals: 12-2 (no lunch Tues) (Sun 12.30-3.30) 6-10
Notes: Children & dogs welcome. Garden & decking.
(See page 566 for full entry)

look for a gate and turn right along Helm Lane. Go straight over at the T junction to Spout Field Farm, follow the waymarked path across several fields and down a long flight of stone steps. The Millbank pub is a short distance to the right, along Millbank Road.

DISTANCE: 4 miles/6.4km (including extension)
MAP: OS Explorer OL 21
TERRAIN: Scenic valley, woodland and farmland
PATHS: Paths, tracks and roads
GRADIENT: Steep in places

Walk submitted by The Millbank at Mill Bank

SHELLEY continued

lobster cooked in several ways, and seared steak of calves' liver with blue cheese dumplings. There's a similar choice in the restaurant, and the pudding list is shared: whisky and orange jelly with Drambuie sauce, green apple and grape Bavarois, and almond and cherry Pithiviers with Kirsch ice cream make the choice agonising. On summer days, the front terrace makes the most of the Pennine views. Guests are invited to sample the delights of 'The Grocer', Truelove and Orme's much-acclaimed delicatessen, which sells the very best British regional produce and many of the delightful ingredients used in the restaurant.
OPEN: 12-3 7-11 (Sat 7-11 only) Closed: 25 Dec
BAR MEALS: L served all week 12-2 D served all week 7-9.45 Av main course £11.95 **RESTAURANT:** L served Sun-Fri 12-2 D served all week 7-9.45 Av 3 course à la carte £22.50
BREWERY/COMPANY: Free House 🍺: Timothy Taylor Landlord, Adnams Bitter, Marston's Pedigree, Banks's Mansfield Smooth. ♀: 9 **FACILITIES:** Children welcome Garden: Covered terrace **NOTES:** Parking 100

SOWERBY BRIDGE   Map 16 SE02

Pick of the Pubs

The Millbank at Millbank ♀
HX6 3DY ☎ 01422 825588 📠 01422 822080
e-mail: millbankph@ukonline.co.uk
Dir: *A58 from Sowerby Bridge to Ripponden turn R at Triangle*
Traditional stone-built pub and restaurant in a delightful village setting, with contemporary interior design and a growing reputation for its food. The cosy Tap Room has stone-flagged floors and serves a range of real ales, while the main wooden-floored bar has more of a wine bar ambience. The dining room, furnished with ex-mill workers' and chapel-goers' seats, complete with prayer-book racks as dining chairs, has French windows opening on to a raised terrace with stunning views of the gardens and valley beyond. Menus emphasise fresh local produce cooked to maximise flavour. Seafood dishes include roast scallops with celeriac purée, smoked chicken and bacon salad, or ravioli of Holy Island lobster with lobster cream. Alternatives are robust dishes of roast suckling pig with buttered cabbage and shitake mushrooms, or oxtail pie with red wine, tarragon mash and root vegetables. There is also a good choice of regional cheeses.
OPEN: 12-3 6-11 Closed: First 2 weeks in Oct **BAR MEALS:** L served Wed-Sun 12-2 D served Tues-Sat 6-10 Av main course £10.90 **RESTAURANT:** L served Wed-Sun 12-2 D served Tues-Sun 6-10 **BREWERY/COMPANY:** Free House 🍺: Timothy Taylor Landlord, Carlsberg-Tetley Tetley Bitter. ♀: 11 **FACILITIES:** Children welcome Garden: Decking, stunning views, seating, heating Dogs allowed
See Pub Walk on page 565

THORNTON   Map 19 SE03

Pick of the Pubs

Ring O'Bells 🐑 ♀
212 Hilltop Rd BD13 3QL ☎ 01274 832296 📠 01274 831707
e-mail: ringobells@btinternet.com
See Pick of the Pubs on opposite page

TODMORDEN   Map 18 SD92

Staff of Life ♦♦♦ 🐑
550 Burnley Rd OL14 8JF ☎ 01706 812929 📠 01706 813773
e-mail: staffoflife@btconnect.com
Dir: *on A646 between Halifax & Burnley*

Once at the heart of a thriving mill community, this quaint stone-built 1838 inn is surrounded by the spectacular countryside of the South Pennines. Its wide range of pies, steaks and grills is augmented by - and we're trying to do justice here to a long, long list - Mozzarella chicken, salmon en papillotte, macaroni bake, Spanish, Mexican and Indian menus, and daily specials. A free house served real ales. The large rear garden blends into the wild, natural surroundings.
OPEN: 12-4 7-11 (Sat 12-11, Sun 12-4, 7-10.30) Closed: 25 Dec
BAR MEALS: L served Sat-Sun 12-2.30 D served Tue-Sun 7-9.30 Av main course £6.95 **BREWERY/COMPANY:** Free House 🍺: Taylor Landlord, Golden Best, Best Bitter, Ram Tam. **FACILITIES:** Garden: Large residents garden at rear, patio at front Dogs allowed Water provided **NOTES:** Parking 26 **ROOMS:** 3 bedrooms 3 en suite 1 family rooms s£26 d£38 no children overnight

---

WAKEFIELD   Map 16 SE32

Pick of the Pubs

Kaye Arms Inn & Brasserie 🐑 ♀
29 Wakefield Rd, Grange Moor WF4 4BG
☎ 01924 848385 📠 01924 848977
e-mail: niccola@kayearms.fsbusiness.co.uk
Dir: *from M1 follow signs for mining museum, 3m further on (A642)*
A family-run dining pub with a refreshing attitude towards food that is matched by good cooking skills. Located within easy reach of the popular National Coal Mining Museum, this long established inn has been run by Brenda and Stuart Coldwell for 30 years, and for most of that time the kitchen has been in the capable hands of their son-in-law Adrian. The imaginative bar menu runs to the likes of cheese soufflé, steak sandwich, and charcuterie plate. While those looking for something more substantial could try the set lunch - perhaps smoked salmon risotto and marinated chicken breast - or from the menu, grilled fillet of sea bass, salmon and prawn fishcake, wild boar and black sheep sausages, and loin of lamb. There's an impressive pudding list: caramelised rice pudding, or treacle and lemon tart, and a serious wine list.
OPEN: 11.30-3 7-11 Closed: Dec 25- Jan 2, **BAR MEALS:** L served Tue-Sun 12-2 D served Tue-Sun 7.15-9.30 Av main course £12 **RESTAURANT:** L served Tue-Sun 12-2 D served Tue-Sun 7.15-9.30 Av 3 course à la carte £19 **BREWERY/COMPANY:** Free House 🍺: Scottish Courage John Smiths, Theakstons Best.
NOTES: Parking 50

Open: 11.30-3.30, 5.30-11
(Sun 12-4.30, 6.30-10.30)
Bar Meals: L served all week 12-2,
D served all week 5.30-9.30.
RESTAURANT: L served all week 12-2,
D served all week 7-9.30.
Av cost 3 courses £14.
BREWERY/COMPANY:
Free House.
🍺: Scottish Courage John Smiths &
Courage Directors, Black Sheep & Black
Sheep Special.
FACILITIES: Children welcome, Garden.
NOTES: Parking 25

Ring O'Bells

The Ring O'Bells has stunning views across the Yorkshire Pennines, stretching up to 30 miles on a clear day. This pub and restaurant was created from a 19th-century Wesleyan chapel and two adjoining mill-workers cottages.

212 Hilltop Road, Thornton,
Bradford, BD13 3QL
☎ 01274 832296 📠 01274 831707
📧 ringobells@btinternet.com
Dir: From M62 take A58 for 5m, R at
crossroads onto A644, after 4.5m
follow signs for Denholme, on to
Well Head Rd into Hilltop Rd.

The unusual interior retains many original features and it is said that the ghost of a former minister is still in residence. The pub is convenient for visiting Haworth, the village celebrated as the home of the novelist Brontë sisters, who were actually born in Thornton when their father was curate there. Both the bar and Brontë Restaurant have a good reputation for their food,

offering a range of both traditional and imaginative cooking with both British and European influences. Imagination has also gone in to the naming of the carte dishes, which include Billy's Blush (tian of goat's cheese and sunblushed tomato mousse between Parmesan discs), Highland Fling (baked salmon fillet in puff pastry with dill, white wine and cream sauce) and Pauline's Treasures (a tempting plate of chocolate puddings). There is always a choice of daily special pies, sausages and pastas. Look out for slow-roasted half duckling glazed with honey, haggis and bacon potato cakes, or maybe pork and black pudding with wholegrain mustard mash. Fish

is also a strength: try smoked haddock and spring onion fishcakes or chargrilled Cajun swordfish steak with fresh mango and pineapple salsa - or jumbo deep-fried haddock. From the daily specials expect pan-fried turbot, and braised brisket stuffed with mushrooms and haggis, finished with a whisky jus. Filling puddings are likely to bring back happy memories - like 'School pud' (steamed roly-poly and custard) and 'O'Rafferty's tipple' (warm date and sticky toffee pudding with butterscotch sauce and Bailey's ice cream), but there are lighter choices, too, and a selection of Yorkshire Dales cheeses.

England

WIDDOP — Map 18 SD93

Pack Horse Inn
HX7 7AT ☎ 01422 842803 ▨ 01422 842803
Dir: Off A646 & A6033
A converted laithe farmhouse dating from the 1600s, 300 yards from the Pennine Way and popular with walkers. The isolated pub promises warm winter fires and well-kept ales, plus 130 single malts.
OPEN: 12-3 7-11 **BAR MEALS:** L served all week 12-2 D served Tue-Sun 7-10 Av main course £6.95 **RESTAURANT:** D served Sat 7-9.30 **BREWERY/COMPANY:** Free House ◀: Thwaites, Theakston XB, Morland Old Speckled Hen, Blacksheep Bitter.
FACILITIES: Children welcome Dogs allowed **NOTES:** Parking 40

CHANNEL ISLANDS

GUERNSEY

CATEL — Map 24

Hotel Hougue du Pommier ★★ ◎ 🍴 ⵁ
Hougue Du Pommier Rd GY5 7FQ
☎ 01481 256531 ▨ 01481 256260
e-mail: hotel@houguedupommier.guernsey.net
Translated as 'Apple Tree Hill,' this lovely inn dates back to 1712 and stands amid ten acres of orchards from which cider was once produced. The Tudor Bar used to be the stables of a farmhouse. Expect a varied choice of dishes, including, perhaps, caramelised sea bass on lemon and cracked pepper risotto, and roast lobster with champagne, Cognac and English mustard gratin.
OPEN: 11 -11.45 **BAR MEALS:** L served all week 12-1.45 D served all week 6.30-8.45 Av main course £5.95 **RESTAURANT:** D served all week 6.30-9 Av 3 course à la carte £20 4 course fixed price £17.25 ◀: John Smith's, Extra Smooth, Guernsy Best. ⵁ: 8
FACILITIES: Children welcome Garden: Ten acres of land, pitch & putt course, BBQ **NOTES:** Parking 60 **ROOMS:** 43 bedrooms 43 en suite 5 family rooms s£35 d£70

JERSEY

GOREY — Map 24

Castle Green Pub and Bistro 🍴 NEW
La Route de la Cote JE3 6DR ☎ 01534 853103 ▨ 01534 853103
e-mail: castlegreenpub@hotmail.com
A superbly located pub overlooking Gorey harbour and, in turn, overlooked by dramatic Mont Orgueil Castle. What may rank as Jersey's most famous setting can be enjoyed from the terrace, during the summer at least, while dining on the pan-Pacific-style dishes produced by Australian chef/manager Stephen Mills. Examples include marinated duck breast with cumin-scented vegetable spaghetti and passion fruit sauce, aromatic herb-poached mahi mahi with warm salad, and open lasagne with roasted organic vegetables and spiced plum tomato sauce.
OPEN: 11 -11 **BAR MEALS:** L served all week 12-2.30 D served all week 6-9 Av main course £12 **RESTAURANT:** L served all week 12-2.30 D served all week 6-9 Av 3 course à la carte £25 ◀: Stella, Directors, Fosters, John Smith Extra Smooth. **FACILITIES:** Children welcome

ST AUBIN — Map 24

Old Court House Inn 🍴
St Aubin's Harbour JE3 8AB ☎ 01534 746433 ▨ 745103
e-mail: ochstaubins@jerseymail.co.uk
Dir: Telephone for directions
Steeped in history is this combination of 15th-century courthouse and 17th-century merchant's harbourside home, tastefully converted and restored to 21st-century standards. Fresh seafood like pan-steamed moules, duo of stir-fried king prawns and crab claws, and baked sea bass with lemon hollandaise feature in the bistro and restaurant, along with pan-fried calves' liver, and grilled chicken breast on sautéed risotto. There are sunny, sheltered terraces and courtyard for alfresco dining.
OPEN: 11-11.30 **BAR MEALS:** L served Mon-Sun 12.30-2.30 D served Mon-Sun 7.30-10 Av main course £6 **RESTAURANT:** L served all week 12.30-2.30 D served all week 7.30-10 Av 3 course à la carte £18.20 Av 3 course fixed price £14 **BREWERY/COMPANY:** Free House ◀: Directors.

ST BRELADE — Map 24

La Pulente Hotel 🍴 ⵁ
La Route de la Pulente JE3 8HG
☎ 01534 744487 ▨ 01534 498846
Dir: West side of the Island, along the 5 mile road.

Amazing sea views, open fires on chilly days and a welcoming atmosphere at all times are promised at this friendly pub. The artistic bar and rustic restaurant are complemented in summer by a balcony and terrace where freshly-caught fish can be enjoyed along with choices from the specials menu: seafood platter, crab salad, fruits de mer, and perhaps garlic and herb chicken on cracked-pepper mash, green vegetable stew, and Caesar salad. Live music on Sunday afternoons in summer.
OPEN: 11-11 **BAR MEALS:** L served all week 12-2.20 D served Mon-Sat 6-8.20 Av main course £6.50 **RESTAURANT:** L served all week 12-2.20 D served Mon-Sat 6-8.20 Av 3 course à la carte £12 **BREWERY/COMPANY:** ◀: Interbrew Bass Bitter, Scottish Courage Theakstons Best, Stella, Kronenbourg 1664. ⵁ: 11
FACILITIES: Children welcome **NOTES:** Parking 30

> **Restaurant and Bar Meal times indicate the times when food is available. Last orders may be approximately 30 minutes before the times stated.**

PEEL
Map 24 SC28

The Creek Inn 🏠 ⚲ NEW

Station Place IM5 1AT ☎ 01624 842216 ▤ 01624 817103
Family-run free house in a quayside setting, overlooking the
harbour at Peel, on the picturesque west coast of the island. A
good choice of food ranges through filled baguettes, children's
favourites, vegetarian dishes and three-course dinners. Look
out for Manx queenies and locally-smoked cod, kippers or
finnan haddie. Other delicacies are freshly-dressed crab salad
and the local seafood platter.

OPEN: 10am-12am 10am-1am (Sun-Thu 10-12, Fri-Sat 10-1)
BAR MEALS: L served all week 10am-9.30 D served all week Av
main course £5.50 **BREWERY/COMPANY:** Free House ◀: Okells
Bitter, Scottish Courage John Smith's. ⚲: 8 **FACILITIES:** Children
welcome Children's licence Outside seating for up to 150
NOTES: Parking 8

PORT ERIN
Map 24 SC26

Falcon's Nest Hotel ★★ 🏠 NEW

The Promenade, Station Rd IM9 6AF
☎ 01624 834077 ▤ 01624 835370
e-mail: falconsnest@enterprise.net
Dir: Telephone for directions
Overlooking Port Erin's pretty harbour, the Falcon's Nest is a
popular 35-bedroom hotel. Lounge and saloon bars are both
open to non-residents and the local real ales and over 150
whiskys are a real draw. Meals and snacks are served in both
bars and there is a carte menu in the hotel restaurant. Try
tenderloin fillet of Manx pork in sherry sauce with apples and
peaches, or locally-caught queenies pan-fried with garlic in a
bacon and white wine sauce.

OPEN: 11-11 Nightclub (winter) 10-2 Fri-Sat (11-12)
BAR MEALS: L served Mon-Sun 12-2 D served Mon-Sat 6-9.30 Av
main course £5.50 **RESTAURANT:** L served Mon-Sun 12-2 D served
Mon-Sat 6-9.30 Av 3 course à la carte £15 Av 4 course fixed price
£13.50 **BREWERY/COMPANY:** Free House ◀: Okells, Bushbys,
Bass, Old Speckled Hen. **FACILITIES:** Children welcome Children's
licence Garden: Benches on Verranda Dogs allowed Blankets, water
NOTES: Parking 20 **ROOMS:** 35 bedrooms 35 en suite 8 family
rooms s£39.50 d£39.50

AA Pub Of The Year for Scotland

The Plockton Hotel, Plockton, Highland

SCOTLAND

SCOTLAND

ABERDEEN CITY

ABERDEEN   Map 23 NJ90

Old Blackfriars
52 Castle Gate AB11 5BB ☎ 01224 581922 🖹 01224 582153

Traditional city centre pub with many fascinating features,
including stone and wooden interior and original stained glass
window display. Built on the site of property owned by
Blackfriars Dominican monks. Battered haddock, home-made
beefburgers and mixed grills feature among the popular bar
meals. Breakfasts, toasted sandwiches and freshly-prepared
daily specials.
OPEN: 11-12 (Sun 12.30-11) Closed: Dec 25 & Jan 1
BAR MEALS: L served all week 11-9 D served all week
BREWERY/COMPANY: Belhaven 🍺: Belhaven 80/-, Belhaven St
Andrews, Caledonian IPA, Caledonian 80/-. **FACILITIES:** Children
welcome Children's licence

Prince of Wales ♈
7 St Nicholas Ln AB10 1HF ☎ 01224 640597
Dir: city centre

Historic city centre pub, dating back to 1850 and boasting the
longest bar in Aberdeen, extending to 60 feet. Originally
known as the Café Royal, the pub was renamed in 1856. Wide
range of real ales, a selection of freshly-made soups, filled
baguettes and baked potatoes, and home-cooked food that
might include breaded haddock, chicken pie, baked potatoes,
roast pork with apricot stuffing and local turbot.
OPEN: 10-12 (Sunday 12-11) Closed: Dec 25 + Jan 1
BAR MEALS: L served all week 11.30-2.30 Av main course £4.70
BREWERY/COMPANY: Free House 🍺: Theakstons Old Peculier,
Caledonian 80/-, Courage Directors, & Guest beers.

> **Pubs offering a good choice of
> fish on their menu**

ABERDEENSHIRE

MARYCULTER   Map 23 NO8

Old Mill Inn
South Deeside Rd AB12 5FX ☎ 01224 733212 🖹 01224 732884
e-mail: Info@oldmillinn.co.uk
Dir: 5m W of Aberdeen on B9077
A 200-year-old country inn on the edge of the River Dee, just
10 minutes' from Aberdeen city centre. Fresh local produce is
a feature of the menu, with interesting dishes such as sirloin
steak chasseur, supreme of chicken Rob Roy, king prawn
jambolaya, or leek and cheese parcels.
OPEN: 11-11 **BAR MEALS:** L served all week 12-2 D served all
week 5.30-9.30 Av main course £5.50 **RESTAURANT:** L served all
week 12-2 D served all week 5.30-9.30 Av 3 course à la carte £15.50
Av 2 course fixed price £5 **BREWERY/COMPANY:** Free House
🍺: Interbrew Bass, Caledonian Deuchers IPA. **FACILITIES:** Children
welcome Garden: Food served outdoors, patio **NOTES:** Parking 10

NETHERLEY   Map 23 NO8

Pick of the Pubs

Lairhillock Inn and Restaurant 🍽 ♈
AB39 3QS ☎ 01569 730001 🖹 01569 731175
e-mail: lairhillock@breathemail.net
Dir: From Aberdeen take A90 turn R at Durris turning

For over 200 years the Lairhillock has offered traditional
hospitality right in the heart of magnificent countryside,
yet nowadays it is only a 15 minute drive south from
Aberdeen. The landscape has changed little over the
centuries, and there are many opportunities for walking
and sightseeing. Enjoy breathtaking views from the pub's
recently added conservatory, which is already a favourite
with families. The Lairhillock boasts a good choice of well-
kept real ales and malt whiskies, and the central log fire is
a popular feature in the lounge. Freshly prepared food is
served in both bars, with menus based on local produce.
Lunchtime brings filled baguettes, salads and ciabatta
steak sandwiches, whilst the hungry might enjoy venison
and wood pigeon platter or braised lamb shank. Starters
from the dinner menu include grilled mussels, home-
made soup and wood pigeon salad. Follow with the likes
of venison medallions with polenta, wild mushrooms and
smoked bacon or prime Angus steaks from the grill.
OPEN: 11-2.30 5-11 (Sat 11-12, Sun 12-11) Closed: 25-26 Dec, 1-
2 Jan **BAR MEALS:** L served all week 12-2 D served all week 6-
9.30 Av main course £8.95 **RESTAURANT:** L served Sun 12-2 D
served Wed-Mon 7-11 **BREWERY/COMPANY:** Free House
🍺: Timothy Taylor Landlord,Courage Directors, Isle of Skye
Brews. ♈: 7 **FACILITIES:** Children welcome Garden: Small
patio in garden Dogs allowed **NOTES:** Parking 100

OLDMELDRUM   Map 23 NJ82

The Redgarth ♀
Kirk Brae AB51 0DJ ☎ 01651 872353
Dir: On A947

The Redgarth is a granite-built property, originally a house, with an attractive garden offering magnificent views of Bennachie and the surrounding countryside. Cask-conditioned ales and fine wines are served along with dishes prepared on the premises using fresh local produce. Fish features as the 'catch of the day', and other options are chicken Maryland, beef bourguignon and duck breast with Sanguinello, kumquats and dates.
OPEN: 11-2.30 5-11 (Fri-Sat 12pm) (Fri-Sat close 11:45) Closed: Dec 25-26 Jan 1-3 **BAR MEALS:** L served all week 12-2 D served all week 5-9 Av main course £5.25 **RESTAURANT:** L served all week 12-2 D served all week 5-9 Av 3 course à la carte £15
BREWERY/COMPANY: Free House ◀: Inveralmond Thrappledouser, Caledonian Deuchers IPA, Taylor Landlord, Redsmiddy. ♀: 8 **FACILITIES:** Children welcome Children's licence Garden: Beer garden, Outdoor eating Dogs allowed Water **NOTES:** Parking 60 **ROOMS:** 3 bedrooms 3 en suite s£45 d£60 (VisitScotland) no children overnight

STONEHAVEN   Map 23 NO88

Marine Hotel ◎ ♀
9/10 Shorehead AB39 2JY ☎ 01569 762155 ▤ 01569 766691
Dir: 15m south of Aberdeen on A90

Ironically, this harbour-side bar was built, from the remains of Dunnottar Castle as a temperance hotel in the 19th century. A number of 500-year-old gargoyles are visible on the front. A choice of six real ales is offered - 800 different brews over the years - including Dunnottar Ale especially brewed for the establishment. There are also around a hundred malts at the bar. Seasonal dishes feature game, seafood and fish, maybe venison rump with mustard mash, dressed crab with coriander cream, and herring in oatmeal.
OPEN: 11-12 Closed: 25 Dec, 1 Jan **BAR MEALS:** L served all week 12-2 D served all week 5-9 Av main course £8
RESTAURANT: L served all week 12-2 D served all week 5-9
BREWERY/COMPANY: Free House ◀: Timothy Taylor Landlord, Caledonian Deuchars IPA, Fuller's London Pride, Moorhouses Black Cat. ♀: 16 **FACILITIES:** Children welcome Dogs allowed

---

**Do you have a favourite pub
that we have overlooked?
Please use the Reader's Report form at
the back of this guide to tell us all about it.**

GLENISLA   Map 23 NO26

Pick of the Pubs

The Glenisla Hotel ◎
PH11 8PH ☎ 01575 582223 ▤ 01575 582203
e-mail: glenislahotel@btinternet.com
Dir: On B954

Fine Scottish hospitality is a feature of this lovely whitewashed 17th-century coaching inn. The hotel stands in a magnificent glen on the former route from Perth to Braemar, where the nearby River Isla flows down towards the falls at Reekie Linn. Visitors mingle with locals around a roaring log fire in the convivial, oak-beamed bar where Inveralmond Ales and hearty meals are served to guests at plain wooden tables or in the elegantly furnished dining room. Shooting parties are particularly popular in season, complementing the fresh local produce - venison, pheasant, trout and hill-farmed lamb - that are mainstays of the dining room's adventurous menus. Aberdeen Angus steaks are a permanent feature alongside salmon fishcakes, herb-roasted cod with queenie scallops, game casserole and free-range duck breast with garlic, ginger and soy sauce.
OPEN: 11-11 (Mon-Fri 7 Sun 11-Midnight, Sat 11-1am) Closed: Dec 25-26 **BAR MEALS:** L served all week 12-2.30 D served all week 6-9 Av main course £11 **RESTAURANT:** L served all week 12-2.30 D served all week 6-9.30 Av 3 course à la carte £18 Av 3 course fixed price £15 **BREWERY/COMPANY:** Free House ◀: Inveralmond Independence, Thrappledouser & Lia Fail.
FACILITIES: Children welcome Garden: Barbeque, food served outside Dogs allowed Outside kennels available if required **NOTES:** Parking 20

ARDENTINNY   Map 20 NS18

Ardentinny Hotel
Loch Long PA23 8TR ☎ 01369 810209
One of the West Coast of Scotland's most enchanting old droving inns, dating back to the early 1700s. Local produce is sourced from the surrounding hills and lochs.
OPEN: 11-11 (Fri-Sat open til 2) **BAR MEALS:** L served all week 12-8 D served all week Av main course £6.25 **RESTAURANT:** D served all week 7-9 Av 3 course fixed price £22.50
BREWERY/COMPANY: Free House ◀: Tennants.
FACILITIES: Garden: barbecue Dogs allowed **NOTES:** Parking 40

Scotland

Scotland

ARDFERN   Map 20 NM80

Pick of the Pubs

The Gallery of Lorne Inn 🛏
PA31 8QN ☎ 01852 500284 🖹 01852 500284
e-mail: Galleyoflorne@aol.com
Dir: 25 S of Oban. A816 then B8002

Just a few minutes' walk from the local marina will bring
you to the Galley of Lorne, right on the shores of Loch
Craignish and with lovely coastal views towards Jura.
Originally an 18th-century drovers' inn, the hotel and
restaurant have now expanded into a more modern
extension. The blackboard, bar and restaurant menus
offer plenty of choice, including pan-fried duck breast with
orange and lime sauce, game ragout, fresh Loch Etive
salmon, pan-fried Islay scallops, Thai green vegetable
curry, roast rack of lamb, and the 'Angus Claymore' - a
rib-eye steak marinated in mixed garden herbs,
chargrilled, and served with a baked potato and salad dip.
OPEN: 12-3 5-12 (April-Sept 12-12) Closed: Dec 25
BAR MEALS: L served Sometimes 12-2.30 D served all week 6-
8.30 Av main course £9 **RESTAURANT:** D served all week 6.30-
9.15 Av 3 course à la carte £25 **BREWERY/COMPANY:** Free
House 🍺: Caledonian Deuchars IPA, guest ale from Fyne Ales or
Houston. **FACILITIES:** Children welcome Garden: Picnic tables,
sun terrace, Loch views Dogs allowed Water **NOTES:** Parking
50 **ROOMS:** 7 bedrooms 7 en suite s£45 d£70 (VisitScotland)

ARDUAINE   Map 20 NM71

Pick of the Pubs

Loch Melfort Hotel ★★★ 🌟🌟 🛏
PA34 4XG ☎ 01852 200233 🖹 01852 200214
e-mail: reception@lochmelfort.co.uk
Dir: on the A816 20m south of Oban
A long-standing favourite of visitors to the West Coast, the
hotel has a stunning loch-side location with views across
Asknish Bay and the Sound of Jura, with a panorama of
mountains in the background. Formerly a private
residence, the property is set in 26 acres of grounds with
moorings on the loch and the National Trust's Arduaine
Gardens just next door. The Skerry Bar/Bistro specialises
in local seafood, including hand-dived Mull scallops and
lobsters from Luing - check out the daily specials board.
Alternatives range from sandwiches and kids' fare to
Highland beef burgers, Aberdeen Angus steaks and
Speyside lamb cutlets grilled with rosemary. As well as its
choice of beers, the bar stocks a good range of malt

whiskies. Accommodation is provided in comfortable en
suite rooms, most with views across the bay to the islands
of Jura, Shuna and Scarba.

OPEN: 10.30-10.30 Fri & Sat (10.30-11) **BAR MEALS:** L served
all week 12-2.30 D served all week 6-9 Av main course £7.50
RESTAURANT: D served all week 7-9 Av 5 course fixed price
£29 **BREWERY/COMPANY:** Free House 🍺: 80/-, Theakstons,
Miller, Kronenburg. **FACILITIES:** Children welcome Garden:
Overlooking the Loch, spectacular views Dogs allowed Water
NOTES: Parking 50 **ROOMS:** 26 bedrooms 26 en suite 2
family rooms s£49 d£78

CLACHAN-SEIL   Map 20 NM71

Pick of the Pubs

Tigh an Truish Inn 🛏
PA34 4QZ ☎ 01852 300242
*Dir: 14m S of Oban, take A816, 12m turn off B844 toward Atlantic
Bridge*
Loosely translated, Tigh an Truish is Gaelic for 'house of
trousers'. After the Battle of Culloden in 1746, kilts were
outlawed and anyone caught wearing one was executed.
In defiance of this edict the islanders wore their kilts at
home. However, if they went to the mainland, they would
stop en route at the Tigh an Truish and change into the
hated trews before continuing their journey. Handy for
good walks and lovely gardens, and particularly popular
with tourists and members of the yachting fraternity, the
Tigh an Truish offers a good appetising menu based on
the best local produce. Home-made seafood pie, moules
marinière, salmon steaks, and mussels in garlic cream
sauce feature among the fish dishes, while other options
might include meat or vegetable lasagne, beef or nut
burgers, steak and ale pie, venison in a pepper cream and
Drambuie sauce, and chicken curry. Round off your meal
by sampling syrup sponge, apple crumble or chocolate
puddle pudding.
OPEN: 11-3 (May-Sept all day) 5-11 Closed: 25 Dec & Jan 1
BAR MEALS: L served all week 12-2 D served all week 6-8.30
Av main course £5.95 **RESTAURANT:** L served all week 12-2 D
served all week 6-8.30 **BREWERY/COMPANY:** Free House
🍺: McEwans 80/- plus guest beers. **FACILITIES:** Children
welcome Garden: Tables beside the sea in garden with lawn
Dogs allowed **NOTES:** Parking 35 No credit cards

┌─────────────────────────────────────┐
│   ★ Star rating for inspected   │
│   hotel accommodation   │
└─────────────────────────────────────┘

continued

Pick of the Pubs

Crinan Hotel
PA31 8SR ☎ 01546 830261 📠 01546 830292
e-mail: nryan@crinanhotel.com
200-year-old Scottish baronial hotel built at the time the
Crinan Canal, which connects Loch Fyne to the Atlantic,
was being constructed by James Watt. Puffers are still
moored outside. Part of the James Bond classic movie
'From Russia with Love' was filmed locally. From the
harbour there are magnificent views across Loch Fyne to
the hills beyond. A varied and imaginative menu offers
such dishes as grilled Perthshire pork chop, wild salmon
and scallop fishcake, pan-fried Aberdeen Angus rib-eye
steak, hand-made pork and leek sausages, braised
shorthorn of Buccleuch beef and Loch Etive mussels.
Interesting and unusual wine list, with good red and white
listings, pudding wines and at least one vintage port
available by the glass.
OPEN: 11 -11 Closed: Xmas & New Year **BAR MEALS:** L
served all week 12.30-2.30 D served all week 6.30-8.30 Av main
course £12 **RESTAURANT:** D served all week 7-9 Av 5 course
fixed price £42.50 **BREWERY/COMPANY:** Free House
🍺: Belhaven, Interbrew Worthington Bitter, Tenants Velvet.
FACILITIES: Children welcome Children's licence Garden: Patio
available Dogs allowed Water **NOTES:** Parking 30
ROOMS: 20 bedrooms 20 en suite s£130 d£180 (VisitScotland)

Coylet Inn
Loch Eck PA23 8SG ☎ 01369 840426 📠 01369 840426
e-mail: coylet@btinternet.com

Comfortable 17th-century coaching inn with much character,
located on the shores of Loch Eck at the heart of the Argyll
Forest Park. The inn was used as a location in the BBC ghost
film 'Blue Boy' starring Emma Thompson. Local produce
forms a major part of a hearty menu that may include whole
sea bream en papillote, pan-seared Loch Fyne scallops with a
langoustine, wild mushroom and vanilla risotto, and pan-fried
pork fillet.
OPEN: 11-2.30 5-12 Closed: 25 Dec **BAR MEALS:** L served all
week 12-2 D served all week 5-7 Av main course £10
RESTAURANT: L served all week 12-2 D served all week 7.30-9:30
Av 3 course à la carte £22.50 **BREWERY/COMPANY:** Free House
🍺: Scottish Courage McEwans 80/-, Caledonian Deuchars IPA.
FACILITIES: Garden: Overlooking Loch Eck **NOTES:** Parking 40

Pick of the Pubs

Kilberry Inn
PA29 6YD ☎ 01880 770223 📠 01880 770223
e-mail: relax@kilberryinn.com
Dir: From Lochgilphead take A83 south. Take B8024 signposted
Kilberry
A traditional Highland building way off the beaten track,
on a scenic single-track road with breathtaking views
across Loch Coalisport to Gigha and the Paps of Jura.
Dating from the 18th and 19th centuries, it was converted
from a 'but 'n' ben' cottage with quarried walls, beams
and log fires. Today it is renowned for its fine food, which
is special enough to encourage travellers to make the long
journey. The dining room is warmly welcoming and family
friendly, and everything served here, including bread and
cakes, preserves and chutneys, is home made. Menu
favourites include honey-roast ham with cauliflower
cheese, medallions of pork in a prune and Armagnac
sauce, and duck with wild bramble and red onion confit.
A range of Scottish bottled beer, and over 30 malt
whiskies make the bar a popular place. Three bedrooms
offer full en suite facilities.
OPEN: 11-3 6.30-10.30 Closed: Nov-Easter **BAR MEALS:** L
served Tue-Sun 12.30-2 D served Tue-Sat 7-8.30 Av main course
£7 **RESTAURANT:** L served Tue-Sun 12.30-2 D served Tue-Sat
6.30-8.30 Av 3 course à la carte £18
BREWERY/COMPANY: Free House 🍺: Arran Blonde, Arran
Darke, Fynne Alles Maverick, Tennents Velvet/Amber.
FACILITIES: Children welcome Dogs allowed Water
NOTES: Parking 8 **ROOMS:** 3 bedrooms 3 en suite s£37.50
d£75 (VisitScotland)

Kilfinan Hotel Bar
PA21 2EP ☎ 01700 821201 📠 01700 821205
e-mail: hotel@fsbdial.co.uk
Dir: Near Loch Fyne
Expect a warm Scottish welcome and good, wholesome food
at this old coaching inn. You can dine in the bistro or bar, on
fresh lamb, salmon, steak, pheasant and duck. Popular
ceilidhs are regularly held, and a relaxing drink can be
enjoyed in the small beer garden that offers a good view of
the loch.
OPEN: 11-11 **BAR MEALS:** L served Wed-Sun 12-2 D served Wed-
Sun 6.30-7.30 Av main course £6 **RESTAURANT:** L served Wed-Sun
12-2 D served Wed-Sun 7-8.30 Av 3 course à la carte £30
BREWERY/COMPANY: Free House **FACILITIES:** Garden: Small
beer garden, view of loch Dogs allowed 2 kennels **NOTES:** Parking
40

Pick of the Pubs

Cairnbaan Hotel & Restaurant ★★★ 🌐 🛏 ♀
Cairnbaan PA31 8SJ ☎ 01546 603668 📠 01546 606045
e-mail: cairnbaan.hotel@virgin.net
See Pick of the Pubs on page 576

Open: 11-11
Bar Meals: L served all week 12-2.30,
D served all week 6-9.30.
Av cost main course £9
RESTAURANT: D served all week 6-9.30.
Av cost 3 courses £28
BREWERY/COMPANY:
Free House.
🍺: Bass.
FACILITIES: Garden.
NOTES: Parking 50
ROOMS: 12 en suite from s£69.50 d£88

Cairnbaan Hotel & Restaurant

Built in the late 18th century as a coaching inn to serve fishermen and puffers trading on the Crinan Canal, this hotel now offers smart accommodation and high standards of hospitality.

★★★
Cairnbaan, Lochgilphead, PA31 8SJ
☎ 01546 603668 📠 01546 606045
📧 cairnbaan.hotel@virgin.net
Dir: 2m N, take A816 from
Lochgilphead, hotel off B841.

The eleven bedrooms are all furnished and decorated to individual designs, and provide the ideal opportunity to stay in this lovely area and visit the many local places of interest. From nearby Oban there are sailings to Mull, Tiree and Colonsay among other islands and Inveraray Castle is well worth a visit, as is Dunadd Fort where the ancient kings of Scotland were crowned. Visitors need not roam away from the hotel to seek their pleasure, however. You can watch the world go by on the canal, or enjoy a meal in the serene restaurant, where the carte specialises in the use of fresh local produce, notably scallops, langoustines and game. Loch Etive mussels are likely to appear on the starter menu, along with Ford smoked salmon and smoked trout pâté, while mains like pan-fried breast of pheasant on sautéed cabbage and bacon with plum and sage glaze, lobster served thermidor or cold with mayonnaise, and fillet of halibut with bay leaf, pink peppercorns and lemon hollandaise sauce are guaranteed to revitalise any jaded palate. The choice of daily specials might include loin of tuna with pesto sauce, wild mushroom Stroganoff, or tenderloin of pork in sweet ginger. For a lighter meal from the bistro-style menu served in the lounge bar and conservatory, try fish cakes, or grilled haloumi cheese to begin, then Cairnbaan fish pie, or perhaps chicken stuffed with haggis, followed by profiteroles drizzled with warm chocolate sauce.

Scotland

Pick of the Pubs

Pierhouse Hotel & Restaurant 🦴
PA38 4DE ☎ 01631 730302 📠 01631 730400
On A85 from Oban
By the edge of Loch Linnhe, looking out over Lismore Island towards Mull, the Pierhouse started life as the residence of the Pier Master, who oversaw the passenger and cargo traffic boarding steam boats that went up and down the Loch. The house came into private ownership after the steam trade disappeared, but the property was only granted a liquor licence around 15 years ago. Extensions were built and now the Pierhouse has a strong local reputation for good quality local lobsters, prawns, scallops and salmon caught by local fishermen within sight of the hotel. Lismore oysters, langoustine thermidor, scampi, and mussels extend the options, followed by seafood pasta, and a giant platter sufficient for two. Non-seafood alternatives include venison, pork or chicken stirfry, sirloin steak, beef Stroganoff and vegetable pasta. There is an extensive wine list.
OPEN: 11.30-11.30 (Sun 12-11) Closed: Dec 25 **BAR MEALS:** L served all week 12.30-2.30 D served all week 6.30-9.30 Av main course £13 **RESTAURANT:** L served all week 12.30-2.30 D served all week 6.30-9.30 Av 3 course à la carte £25 **BREWERY/COMPANY:** Free House 🍺: Calders Cream, Calders 70/-, Carlsberg-Tetley Tetley Bitter.
FACILITIES: Children welcome Garden: Food served outdoors, patio Dogs allowed **NOTES:** Parking 20

Pick of the Pubs

Creggans Inn ★★★ ◎ 🦴
PA27 8BX ☎ 01369 860279 📠 01369 860637
e-mail: info@creggans-inn.co.uk
Dir: A82 from Glasgow, at Tarbet take A83 to Cairndow, then A815 down coast to Strachur
A comfortable small hotel standing on the very lip of Loch Fyne, and a coaching inn since Mary Queen of Scots' day. Views from the hills above take in vistas across the Mull of Kintyre to the Western Isles beyond. It has 14 en suite bedrooms and facilities suitable for all the family including a safe garden and patio for alfresco summer eating. Use of local produce plays its full part in the preparation of seasonal menus likely to include Loch Fyne oysters and mussels, salmon, local wild game, venison and hill lamb. The brave might plump for a timbale of haggis, neeps and tatties with whisky chasseur sauce, whilst more conservative choices include fresh Tarbert cod in a light beer batter or locally farmed beef steaks with chips and perhaps a pepper sauce.
OPEN: 11-11 **BAR MEALS:** L served all week 12-3 D served all week 6-9 Av main course £7 **RESTAURANT:** D served all week 7-9 Av 3 course fixed price £26.50 **BREWERY/COMPANY:** Free House 🍺: Interbrew Flowers IPA, Coniston Bluebird Bitter, Fyne Ales Highlander, Marston's Pedigree. **FACILITIES:** Children welcome Garden: Formal, terraced, occasional seating **NOTES:** Parking 36
ROOMS: 14 bedrooms 14 en suite s£42.50 d£85

> **Pick of the Pubs have that extra special quality that makes them stand out from the crowd. Their entries are highlighted, and may be a full page.**

Victoria Hotel ♦♦♦ ◎ 🦴
Barmore Rd PA29 6TW ☎ 01880 820236 📠 01880 820638
e-mail: victoria.hotel@lineone.net

Centrally situated in a picturesque fishing village on the Kintyre peninsula, this 18th-century hotel is renowned for its restaurant, which enjoys romantic views over Loch Fyne. Bar and restaurant menus provide a good choice, featuring local game and seafood. Salt-crust salmon, poached halibut steak, roast haunch of venison and chicken breast stuffed with haggis are examples of the dishes on offer. The patio is great for barbecues and is often used for live music.
OPEN: 11-12 (Sun 12-12) (Closed 3-5.30 in winter) Closed: 25 Dec **BAR MEALS:** L served all week 12-2.30 D served all week 6-9.30 Av main course £6.95 **RESTAURANT:** L served all week 12-2.30 D served all week 6.30-9.30 Av 3 course à la carte £20
BREWERY/COMPANY: Free House 🍺: Scottish Courage John Smiths, 80 Shilling, Tartan Special. **FACILITIES:** Children welcome Children's licence Garden: Patio area Dogs allowed Water provided
ROOMS: 5 bedrooms 5 en suite 1 family rooms s£32 d£64

Polfearn Hotel ★★ 🦴 ♀
PA35 1JQ ☎ 01866 822251 📠 01866 822251
Dir: turn off A85, continue 1.5m through village down to loch shore

Close to the shores of Loch Etive, with stunning all-round views, this friendly family-run hotel sits at the foot of Ben Cruachan. Whether you're working, walking, cycling, riding, shooting or fishing in the area, the proprietors will store things, dry things, feed, water and warm you with little

continued

Scotland

TAYNUILT continued

formality. Dishes are cooked to order from fresh local produce, notably seafood, steak from the local butcher, and home-made pies.
OPEN: 12-2 5.30-11 Closed: 25-26 Dec **BAR MEALS:** L served all week 12-1.45 D served all week 5.30-8.45 Av main course £7
RESTAURANT: 12-1.45 D served all week 5.30-8.45 Av 3 course à la carte £25 **BREWERY/COMPANY:** Free House ◀: Weekly changing Guest ale. ♀: 15 **FACILITIES:** Children welcome Garden: Nice lawn, sea view & mountains Dogs allowed Water, Food
NOTES: Parking 50 **ROOMS:** 14 bedrooms 14 en suite 2 family rooms s£25 d£50

TAYVALLICH Map 20 NR78

Pick of the Pubs

Tayvallich Inn 🐾

PA31 8PL ☎ 01546 870282 📠 01546 870333
Dir: *From Lochgilphead take A816 then B841/B8025*
Converted from an old bus garage in 1971, this 'house in the pass' as it translates, stands by a natural harbour at the head of Loch Sween with stunning views over the anchorage, especially from the picnic tables that front the inn in summer. The cosy bar with a yachting theme and the more formal dining-room feature original works by local artists and large picture windows from which to gaze out over the village and across Tayvallich Bay. Those interested in the works of 19th-century engineer Thomas Telford will find plenty of bridges and piers in the area. Expect a lot of seafood choices, including pan-fried Sound of Jura scallops, Cajun salmon with black butter, or warm salad of smoked haddock with prawns. Meat choices include grilled prime Scottish sirloin steak, chicken curry and honey and mustard glazed rack of lamb. The truly hungry may try the Tayvallich Seafood Platter that combines prawns, mussels, oysters, smoked salmon, pickled herring and crab claws.
OPEN: 11-2.30 6-11.30 (Summer 11-12, 1am Fri-Sat) (Fri -Sat 5-1am, Sun 5-12) Closed: 25/26 Dec, 1-2 Jan **BAR MEALS:** L served all week 12-2 D served all week 6-8 Av main course £10
RESTAURANT: D served all week 7-9 Av 3 course à la carte £26.50 **BREWERY/COMPANY:** Free House ◀: Calders70/-, Calders 80/-,. **FACILITIES:** Children welcome Garden: Food served outside. Patio area Dogs allowed except meal times
NOTES: Parking 20

CITY OF EDINBURGH

EDINBURGH Map 21 NT27

Bennets Bar ♀

8 Leven St EH3 9LG ☎ 0131 229 5143
With its stained glass windows, hand-painted tiles and a traditional brass and wood look, this friendly pub is popular with the actors from the adjacent Kings Theatre. Established in 1839, Bennets keeps over 100 malt whiskies, has a well-kept cellar and serves straightforward home-made food at a reasonable price. Typical menu features roast, steak pie, breaded haddock fillet, macaroni cheese, salads and burgers.
OPEN: 11-12.30 (Sun 12.30-11.30) **BAR MEALS:** L served Mon-Sat 12-2 D served Mon-Sat 5-8.30 Av main course £4
BREWERY/COMPANY: Scottish & Newcastle ◀: Caledonian Deuchars IPA, McEwans 80/-. **FACILITIES:** Children welcome

The Bow Bar ♀

80 The West Bow EH1 2HH ☎ 0131 2267667
Dir: *Telephone for directions*
Located in the heart of Edinburgh's old town, the Bow Bar reflects the history and traditions of the area. Tables from decommissioned railway carriages and gantry from an old church used for the huge selection of whiskies create interest in the bar, where 140 malts are on tap, and eight cask ales are dispensed from antique equipment. Bar snacks only are served, and there are no gaming machines or music to distract from good conversation.
OPEN: 12-11.30 Mon-Sat 12.30-11 Sun Closed: 25-26 Dec, 1-2 Jan
BREWERY/COMPANY: Free House ◀: Deuchars IPA, Belhaven 80/-, Taylors Landlord, Harviestown Bitter & Twisted. ♀: 6
FACILITIES: Children's licence Dogs allowed Water provided

Doric Tavern ♀

15-16 Market St EH1 1DE ☎ 0131 225 1084 📠 0131 220 0894

Bustling bistro and pub close to the castle - haunt of the city's writers, artists and journalists. It was built in 1710 and over the next few hundred years developed into a convivial place to eat with a cheery pub downstairs. Options from a variety of menus range from bruschetta with Mozzarella, through classics like haggis, neeps and tatties, to whole seasonal fish, or shank of lamb, slowly braised with Old Jenny liqueur.
OPEN: 12-1am Closed: Dec 25-26, Jan 1 **BAR MEALS:** L served all week 12-7 D served all week 12-1am Av main course £4.50
RESTAURANT: L served all week 12-4 D served all week 5-11 Av 3 course à la carte £16 Av 3 course fixed price £19.95
BREWERY/COMPANY: Free House ◀: Caledonian Deuchars IPA & 80/-, Tennents. ♀: 16

The Ship on the Shore

24/26 The Shore, Leith EH6 6QN ☎ 0131 555 0409 📠 555 0409
Anyone who remembers only the old Leith will be astonished at today's trendy bars and restaurants. This is one of them - a popular, cosy bistro-bar decked out with shipping and nautical paraphernalia. As befits a port, seafood is a speciality and may include steamed West Coast mussels with creamy onion and tarragon sauce, or warm monkfish salad with bacon, chilli, ginger and coriander. There may also be quenelles of haggis with Drambuie sauce, Toulouse sausages, steaks and curries.
OPEN: 12-1 Closed: Dec 25-26, 1-2 Jan **BAR MEALS:** L served all week 12-2.30 D served Mon-Thur 6.30-9.30 Av main course £5.95
RESTAURANT: L served all week 12-2.30 D served Mon-Sat 6.30-9.30 Av 3 course fixed price £21.25 **BREWERY/COMPANY:** Free House ◀: Caledonian Deuchars IPA, 80/-, 70/-.

⭐ **Pubs with Red Stars are part of the AA's Top 200 Hotels in Britain & Ireland**

The Bridge Inn

An interesting and unusual walk providing a fascinating insight into the history and development of Edinburgh's Union Canal, which was built between 1818-22. Extending for 30 miles/48.2km, the canal meets the Forth and Clyde Canal at Falkirk. Various seats beside the towpath enable you to rest and savour the scene.

Begin the walk at the picnic site next to the canal bridge in Baird Road, noting the information board which tells you about the area. Turn left and follow the Union Canal towpath towards Edinburgh, passing rows of moored narrow boats. The land behind them represents the site of the old village gasworks - earmarked for development. Keep ahead to what is known as the 'betwixt and between stone' which marks the end of the fare stage for those travelling by barge from Edinburgh.

Look out for a dovecote over to your right. Constructed in 1713 for nearby Ratho House, the dovecote has boxes for more than a thousand birds. There is also an icehouse nearby, covered by thick undergrowth. Ratho House was rebuilt in the 1800s and rented by Corstorphine Golf Club in 1928. The club eventually acquired the house and later changed its name to Ratho Park Golf Club.

As the canal bends to the right, the rooftops of Edinburgh edge into view. Look out, too, for the castellated roof of Ashley House. Approaching the next bridge, you pass a milestone with 24/7 inscribed on it - this represents 24 miles to Falkirk and 7 miles to Edinburgh Canal Basin. Pass another milestone to reach Gogar Moor Bridge. At this point retrace your steps back to the car park, completing the walk.

THE BRIDGE INN, RATHO
27 Baird Road EX28 8RA
☎ 0131 3331320

Directions: From Newbridge B7030 junc, follow signs for Ratho. Former farmhouse on the Grand Union Canal, now at the heart of the city's Canal Centre. A thriving, award-winning family attraction, where imaginative food is the lure.
Open: 12-11 (Sat 11-12, Sun 12.30-11)
Bar Meals: 12-9
Notes: Parking. Children welcome - high chairs, baby-changing facilities, toys. Landscaped patio garden.
(See page 580 for full entry)

DISTANCE: 2 miles/3.2km
MAP: OS Explorer 350
TERRAIN: Semi residential
PATHS: Canal towpath
GRADIENT: Easy, level surface

Walk submitted and checked by the Bridge Inn, Ratho and Ron Day

Scotland

EDINBURGH continued

The Starbank Inn ♀
64 Laverockbank Rd EH5 3BZ
☎ 0131 552 4141 ▤ 0131 552 4141

Tastefully renovated stone pub situated on the waterfront of North Edinburgh, affording splendid views over the Firth of Forth to the Fife coast. The bar menu typically offers roast lamb with mint sauce, poached salmon, mince and tatties, a vegetarian dish of the day, and chicken with tarragon cream sauce. **OPEN:** 11-11 (Thu-Sat 11-12, Sun 12.30-11) **BAR MEALS:** L served all week 12-2.30 D served all week 6-9.30 Av main course £5 **RESTAURANT:** L served all week 12-2.30 D served all week 6-9.30 Av 3 course à la carte £10 **BREWERY/COMPANY:** Free House ◀: Belhaven 80/-, Belhaven Sandy Hunters Traditional, Belhaven St Andrews/Deuchars IPA, Timothy Taylor Landlord & guests. **FACILITIES:** Children welcome Food served outside. Patio area Dogs allowed (on leash)

RATHO   Map 21 NT17

Pick of the Pubs

The Bridge Inn 🛈
27 Baird Rd EH28 8RA ☎ 0131 3331320 ▤ 0131 333 3480
e-mail: info@bridgeinn.com
Dir: From Newbridge B7030 junction, follow signs for Ratho

Dating back to about 1750, the Bridge Inn began life as a farmhouse before becoming an important staging-post during the construction of the Union Canal, which opened in 1822. By the mid-1820s numerous canal travellers were stopping here for refreshment. However, in later years it fell into decay until the present owner restored and re-opened it in the early 1970s. It is now a thriving and award-winning family attraction at the heart of the city's Canal Centre, famous for its fleet of restaurant boats and sightseeing launches. Freshly prepared and served local

produce is the Bridge Inn's hallmark, which has also specialised in top quality Scottish meat for over 30 years. Typical dishes on the imaginative menu include venison casserole; pumpkin and pancetta risotto; stuffed roast pepper with lemon and mint couscous; grilled salmon fillet stuffed with haggis served with raspberry and bramble butter; and the ever-popular haddock in batter or breadcrumbs. **OPEN:** 12-11 (Sat 11-12, Sun 12.30-11) Closed: 26 Dec, 1 & 2 Jan **BAR MEALS:** L served all week 12-9 Av main course £6.95 **RESTAURANT:** L served all week 12-2 D served all week 6.30-9 Av 3 course à la carte £22 **BREWERY/COMPANY:** Free House ◀: Belhaven 80/- & Belhaven Best. **FACILITIES:** Children welcome Children's licence Garden: Landscaped, Patio, enclosed, ducks roaming **NOTES:** Parking 60
See Pub Walk on page 579

CITY OF GLASGOW

GLASGOW   Map 20 NS56

Auctioneers ♀
6 North Court, Vincent Place G1 2DP
☎ 0141 229 5851 ▤ 0141 229 5852
Once an auction room known as McTears, this city centre pub, 200 yards from George Square, retains its original valuation booths. It is decorated with plenty of eclectic memorabilia, including framed football shirts, old football programmes and newspaper cuttings, and is an ideal location for watching a big screen sporting event. Good pub grub includes home-made steak pie, mixed grill, fish and chips, burgers and baked potatoes. **OPEN:** 12-11 (Mon-Wed 12-11, Fri-Sat 11-12) 11-12 (Sun 12.30-11) Closed: 25 Dec & 1 Jan **BAR MEALS:** L served all week 12-8 D served all week 12-8 Av main course £5.50 **RESTAURANT:** L served all week 12-8 D served all week 12-8 **BREWERY/COMPANY:** ♀: 7 **FACILITIES:** Children's licence

Rab Ha's
83 Hutchieson St G1 1SH ☎ 0141 572 0400 ▤ 0141 572 0402
Dir: City centre
Victorian building housing a refurbished pub and restaurant. Expect a traditional pub atmosphere and some innovative cooking. Choices include fajitas, tempura, Thai curries and organic beef burger in the bar. The restaurant offers fusion cooking with dishes from the ocean, the earth and from home. **OPEN:** 11-12 Closed: Jan 1 **BAR MEALS:** L served all week 12-10 D served all week Av main course £5.90 **RESTAURANT:** D served all week 5.30-10 Av 3 course à la carte £16 **BREWERY/COMPANY:** Free House ◀: McEwans 70/- & 80/-, Theakstons. **FACILITIES:** Children welcome Dogs allowed

Pick of the Pubs

Ubiquitous Chip ⊛⊛ 🛈 ♀
12 Ashton Ln G12 8SJ ☎ 0141 334 5007 ▤ 0141 337 1302
e-mail: mail@ubiquitouschip.co.uk
Dir: In the west end of Glasgow, off Byres Road
Once a stable for Clydesdale horses, the 'Chip' centres on a traditional bar with an open coal fire and the original byres tastefully incorporated. It continues to buzz, as it has since 1971 when Ronnie Clydesdale opened up his restaurant. Traditional draught beers, selected malt whiskies and first class wines by the glass supplement a

continued   *continued*

menu that is full of refreshingly bright ideas. In a lofty covered courtyard the main dining area sports plenty of live greenery, and a smart choice of dishes. These may include pan-fried scallops on a roasted potato cake, roasted Perthshire wood partridge with a rich game sauce, and Caledonian oatmeal ice cream with fruit compote (Delia Smith asked for the recipe!). Upstairs is a brasserie-style eating area offering wholesome Scottish produce at more modest prices: brandied chicken liver parfait with sherry jelly, Ayrshire bacon chop with basil mash and Malmsey sauce, and white chocolate burnt cream are typical.
OPEN: 11-12 (Mon-Sat) 12.30-12 (Sun) Closed: 25 Dec, 1 Jan
BAR MEALS: L served all week 12-4 D served all week 4-11 Av main course £7.50 **RESTAURANT:** L served all week 12-2.30 D served all week 5.30-11 Av 3 course fixed price £32.50
BREWERY/COMPANY: Free House ◗: Caledonian 80/- & Deuchars IPA. ☥: 19 **FACILITIES:** Children welcome

DUMFRIES & GALLOWAY

AULDGIRTH
Map 21 NX98

Auldgirth Inn ☥
DG2 0XG ☎ 01387 740250 ▤ 01387 740694
e-mail: auldgirthinn@aol.com
Dir: 8m NE of Dumfries on A76 Kilmarnock Rd
This 500-year-old riverside inn with its prominent chimneystack featuring a distinctive cross was originally a stopping-off place for monks and pilgrims walking across Scotland. Later Robert Burns, who lived nearby, made it his local. David and Beverly Brown took over this free house in 2002. Their menu includes Celtic chicken breast stuffed with whisky-soaked haggis, salmon and asparagus crêpes, and traditional favourites such as steak and ale pie, liver and bacon, and fish and chips.
OPEN: 11.30-11 (Open all day everyday) **BAR MEALS:** L served all week 12-9 D served all week 12-9 Av main course £6
RESTAURANT: L served all week 12-9 D served all week 12-9
BREWERY/COMPANY: Free House ◗: Belhavens Best, Guest Ale.
☥: 12 **FACILITIES:** Children welcome Garden: Small grass area, picnic benches Dogs allowed Water, food if required
NOTES: Parking 30 **ROOMS:** 3 bedrooms 2 en suite 1 family rooms s£40 d£55 (VisitScotland)

CASTLE DOUGLAS
Map 21 NX76

Douglas Arms Hotel
206 King St DG7 1DB ☎ 01556 502231 ▤ 01556 504000
e-mail: doughot@aol.com
Modernised 18th-century coaching inn, one of the oldest buildings in town, where welcoming open fires are lit in the winter months. Chicken curry and fresh haddock in batter are typical bar dishes, while the restaurant might offer supreme of salmon, or medallions of beef in whisky and mustard sauce. Good choice of interesting real ales.
OPEN: 11-12 **BAR MEALS:** L served all week 12-2 D served all week 5-9 Av main course £7.50 **RESTAURANT:** D served all week 6-9 Av 3 course fixed price £19.50 **BREWERY/COMPANY:** Free House ◗: Black Calloway, Calloway Gold, Knockendoch, Wilhill.
FACILITIES: Children welcome Children's licence Dogs allowed
NOTES: Parking 18

DALBEATTIE
Map 21 NX86

Anchor Hotel
Main St, Kippford DG5 4LN ☎ 01556 620205 ▤ 01556 620205
Dir: A711 to Dalbeattie. follow Solway Coast sign to Kippford
Now under new management, this small hotel overlooks the Marina and Urr Water estuary, and its Seafarers' Bar is a sailor's haven. The area is also ideal for walkers and bird watchers. The menu includes such specialities as swordfish steaks, haddock and cod in butter, chicken tikka, game casserole, and Solway salmon. Most bedrooms are en suite, and some overlook the Marina.
OPEN: 11-3 5-12 (all day opening-peak season) Closed: 25 Dec
BAR MEALS: L served all week 12-2.30 D served all week 6-9.30 Av main course £7 **RESTAURANT:** L served all week 12-2.30 D served all week 6-9.30 Av 3 course à la carte £13
BREWERY/COMPANY: Free House ◗: Local Ales-Criffel Cuil Hill, Knockendoch, John Smiths McEwans 80. **FACILITIES:** Children welcome Dogs allowed Water Bowls **ROOMS:** 6 bedrooms 6 en suite s£40 d£65 (VisitScotland)

EAGLESFIELD
Map 21 NY27

The Courtyard Restaurant
DG11 3PQ ☎ 01461 500215
e-mail: mike@douglashouse.free-online.co.uk
Dir: 8m N of Gretna
Former draper's shop built of sandstone in 1913, and converted into a bar/restaurant in 1985, the Courtyard is an ideal stopping-off spot for travellers on their way to the Highlands. The cuisine is traditional Scottish with a French influence, and the kitchen prides itself on making good use of local produce. Try duck breast with cranberry sauce, loin of lamb with sherry sauce, or baked cod with a cheese and mustard topping.
OPEN: 12-2.30 6.30-12 **BAR MEALS:** L served all week 12-2 D served all week 6.30-9 Av main course £6 **RESTAURANT:** L served Sun 12-2 D served all week 7-9 **BREWERY/COMPANY:** Free House
◗: Belhaven Best, Tennents, Laser, McEwans '60.
FACILITIES: Children welcome Garden Dogs allowed Kennels
NOTES: Parking 20

ISLE OF WHITHORN
Map 20 NX43

The Steam Packet Inn ☺
Harbour Row DG8 8LL ☎ 01988 500334 ▤ 01988 500627
e-mail: steampacketinn@btconnect.com
Dir: From Newton Stewart take A714, then A746 to Whithorn, then Isle of Whithorn
There are spectacular harbour views from the picture windows in the attractively modernised bar of this 18th-century inn, and a new 40-seat conservatory dining area adds to the charm. The inn makes good use of seafood straight off the boats: blackboard specials change twice daily, with basic lunchtime dishes and a more extensive evening choice. Expect wild mallard breast with brandy sauce, pork loin medallions or pan-fried brill with beetroot compote.
OPEN: 11-11 (Winter open 11-3, 6-11) Closed: Dec 25
BAR MEALS: L served all week 12-2 D served all week 6.30-9 Av main course £5.50 **RESTAURANT:** L served all week 12-2 D served all week 6.30-9 **BREWERY/COMPANY:** Free House ◗: Scottish Courage Theakston XB, Caledonian Deuchars IPA, Black Sheep Best Bitter. **FACILITIES:** Children welcome Garden Dogs allowed
NOTES: Parking 4

Scotland

Scotland

Selkirk Arms Hotel ★★★ ◉◉ ♀
Old High St DG6 4JG ☎ 01557 330402 ▤ 01557 331639
A traditional white-painted pub on a street corner, with nice gardens to the rear. It has associations with the Scottish poet, Robert Burns, who reputedly penned *The Selkirk Grace* here in 1784. Traditional dishes using Scottish fare includes fresh fish and tasty desserts. Good choice of beers, including Solway Criffel and Youngers Tartan.
OPEN: 11 -12 ◖: Youngers Tartan, John Smiths Bitter, Solnath Criffel. ♀: 8 **NOTES:** No credit cards

Black Bull Hotel ◎ ♀
Churchgate DG10 9EG ☎ 01683 220206 ▤ 01683 220483
e-mail: hotel@blackbullmoffat.co.uk
The main building dates from the 16th century and was used by Graham of Claverhouse as his headquarters. Graham and his dragoons were sent to quell Scottish rebellion in the late 17th century. Scottish bard Robert Burns was a frequent visitor around 1790. The Railway Bar is the place for drinking and pub games, while the Burns Room or restaurant are for eating or relaxation. Traditional fare includes steak and ale pie, seafood platter, Galloway chicken sizzler, Eskdale venison sausage, and of course, haggis with neeps and tatties.
OPEN: 11-11 (Thu-Sat 11-12) **BAR MEALS:** L served all week 11.30-2.15 D served all week 6-9.15 **RESTAURANT:** L served all week 11.30-2.15 D served all week 6-9.15 **BREWERY/COMPANY:** Free House ◖: McEwans, Scottish Courage Theakston 80/-.
FACILITIES: Children welcome Dogs allowed **ROOMS:** 13 bedrooms 13 en suite 2 family rooms s£39 d£59 (VisitScotland)

Criffel Inn
2 The Square DG2 8BX ☎ 01387 850305 ▤ 01387 850305
Dir: M/A74 leave at Gretna, A75 to Dumfries, A710 S to New Abbey
A small, unassuming hotel set on the Solway Coast in a historic conservation village close to the ruins of the 13th-century Sweetheart Abbey. Some breathtaking walks nearby, including Criffel Hill, and an attractive garden for summer enjoyment. Unchanged for many years, it offers appetising dishes such as chicken St Andrews, steak Diane, and a good choice of fish including swordfish, breaded haddock, tuna and Solway salmon.
OPEN: 12-2.30 5-11 **BAR MEALS:** L served all week 12-2 D served all week 5-8 Av main course £7 **RESTAURANT:** L served all week 12-2 D served all week 5-8 Av 3 course à la carte £14
BREWERY/COMPANY: Free House ◖: Belhaven IPA, Caledonian Deuchars IPA, Interbrew Flowers Original, Timothy Taylor Landlord.
FACILITIES: Children welcome Garden: Garden overlooking historic Cornmill & Square Dogs allowed Water **NOTES:** Parking 8
ROOMS: 5 bedrooms 4 en suite 2 family rooms s£25 d£54 (VisitScotland)

Pick of the Pubs

Creebridge House Hotel ★★★ ◉ ◎ ♀
Minnigaff DG8 6NP ☎ 01671 402121 ▤ 01671 403258
e-mail: info@creebridge.co.uk
Dir: From A75 into Newton Stewart, turn right over river bridge, hotel 200yds on left.
A listed country house hotel dating from 1760, formerly the Earl of Galloway's shooting lodge and part of his estate. The River Cree runs nearby, and the hotel nestles in grounds at the foot of Kirroughtree Forest. The informal Bridge's bar and brasserie offers a fine selection of malts, and real ales from a local micro-brewery. Food from a daily-changing blackboard and a main menu includes chicken and field mushroom wholemeal pancake, mixed bean tortilla, and tandoori-style chicken. The Garden Restaurant overlooking the landscaped grounds offers fine dining in elegant surroundings. Modern Scottish cooking on a fixed-price menu might start with seared king scallops in a sage and cured-ham brioche, grilled breast of guinea fowl, and Blairgowry raspberry parfait and cracked honeycomb. The hotel is frequented by golfers, fishermen, shooters, walkers and families.
OPEN: 12-2.30 6-11 (Sun, all day) **BAR MEALS:** L served all week 12-2 D served all week 6-9.30 Av main course £9.50 **RESTAURANT:** D served all week 7-9 Av 3 course à la carte £25 Av 3 course fixed price £25 **BREWERY/COMPANY:** Free House ◖: Fuller's London Pride, Tenants. ♀: 8
FACILITIES: Children welcome Children's licence Garden: Garden with Rose Beds, Fish Pond and Lawns Dogs allowed Kennels, Water **NOTES:** Parking 40 **ROOMS:** 19 bedrooms 19 en suite s£60 d£98

Pick of the Pubs

Crown Hotel ◎ ♀
9 North Crescent DG9 8SX ☎ 01776 810261 ▤ 01776 810551
e-mail: crownhotel@supanet.com
Former fishermen's cottages converted into a bustling harbourside hotel, with fine views across the Irish Sea. There is a great atmosphere in the rambling old bar with its open fire and seafaring displays. Extensive menus are based on fresh local produce with an emphasis on seafood - whitebait, langoustine, herring, lobster, crab and mussels are among the options.

**Room prices show the minimum double and single rates charged.
Room rates in hotels and B&Bs often vary depending on the facilities, so be sure to check prices with the establishment before booking.**

continued

OPEN: 11-12 **BAR MEALS:** L served all week 12-9.30 D served all week **RESTAURANT:** L served all week 12-2.30 D served all week 6-9.30 Av 3 course à la carte £16.50
BREWERY/COMPANY: Free House 🍺: Scottish Courage John Smith's, McEwans 80/-. **FACILITIES:** Children welcome Garden Dogs allowed

DUNDEE CITY

BROUGHTY FERRY
Map 21 NO43

Fisherman's Tavern 🐾 ♀
10-16 Fort St DD5 2AD ☎ 01382 775941 📠 01382 477466
e-mail: bookings@fishermans-tavern-hotel.co.uk
Dir: *From Dundee city centre follow A930 to Broughty Ferry, R at sign for hotel*
This listed 17th-century fisherman's cottage, converted to a pub in 1827, combines a picturesque coastal setting with award-winning hospitality and acclaimed bar food. The inn also offers tastefully-decorated en suite bedrooms. The popular, well-planned menu ranges from light snacks to traditional wholesome fare and international favourites. After a stroll along the sands, try grilled fillet of salmon with parsley butter and fresh lemon, chicken curry, fisherman's seafood crêpes, vegetable lasagne, breaded Norwegian scampi, or a selection of seasonal salads.
OPEN: 11-12 11am-1am (Thu-Sat) **BAR MEALS:** L served all week 11.30-2.30 Av main course £6 **BREWERY/COMPANY:** Free House 🍺: Belhaven, Inveralmond Ossian's Ale, Caledonain Deuchers IPA,Timothy Taylor Landlord. ♀: 26 **FACILITIES:** Children welcome Garden: Dogs allowed Water, Biscuits **ROOMS:** 11 bedrooms 11 en suite 1 family rooms s£39 d£62 (VisitScotland)

The Royal Arch Bar 🐾 ♀
285 Brook St DD5 2DS ☎ 01382 779741
Originally named after the Masonic Arch, the present logo is based on the now-demolished monument commemorating Queen Victoria's visit to Dundee in 1863. With its traditional public bar and art deco lounge, the Royal Arch is renowned for its wide range of cask beers and malt whiskies. Meals are served in either bar; beef Highlander, and chicken and cashew nuts in oyster sauce among daily specials, plus several traditional favourites.
OPEN: 11-12 (Sun 12.30-12) Closed: 1 Jan **BAR MEALS:** L served all week 11.30-2.30 D served all week 5-8 Av main course £5 **RESTAURANT:** L served all week 11.30-2.30 D served all week 5-8 **BREWERY/COMPANY:** Free House 🍺: Scottish Courage McEwans80/-, Belhaven Best. ♀: 12 **FACILITIES:** Children welcome Children's licence Dogs allowed Water, treats

EAST AYRSHIRE

DALRYMPLE
Map 20 NS31

The Kirkton Inn ♦♦♦ 🐾 ♀
1 Main St KA6 6DF ☎ 01292 560241 📠 01292 560835
e-mail: kirkton@cqm.co.uk
Dir: *Between A77 & A713 approx 5m from Ayr signed from both roads*

Village centre inn situated a short stroll from the River Doon where the salmon leap. Well situated for a visit to the Burns Centre and Cottage, the beach at Ayr or Blairquhan Castle. Allegedly haunted by an old landlord who liked it so much he wouldn't leave. There was also the time when Hollywood musical star Howard Keel bought a round for the whole pub. Local produce is used in a variety of dishes including roast sirloin of beef and Yorkshire pudding, traditional steak pie, exotic pork with pineapple in a Malibu and cream sauce, lobster thermidor, haddock mornay, and roast pheasant Kirkton style.
OPEN: 11am-midnight **BAR MEALS:** L served all week 11-9 D served all week 11-9 Av main course £8.50 **RESTAURANT:** L served all week 11-9 D served all week 11-9 Av 3 course à la carte £16 Av 3 course fixed price £14.95 **BREWERY/COMPANY:** Free House 🍺: Belhaven Best & St Andrews. **FACILITIES:** Children welcome Garden: Red chipped area Dogs allowed Water provided
NOTES: Parking 50 **ROOMS:** 11 bedrooms 11 en suite s£26 d£46 (VisitScotland)

GATEHEAD
Map 20 NS33

The Cochrane Inn
45 Main Rd KA2 0AP ☎ 01563 570122
Dir: *from Glasgow A77 to Kilmarnock, then A759 to Gatehead*

The emphasis is on contemporary British food at this village centre pub, just a short drive from the Ayrshire coast, and with a friendly, bustling atmosphere inside. Good choice of starters may include soused herring and grilled goat's cheese, while main courses might feature stuffed pancake, pan-fried trio of seafood with tiger prawns, or smoked haddock risotto.

continued

Scotland

GATEHEAD continued

OPEN: 1-11 Closed: 1 Jan **BAR MEALS:** L served all week 12-2 D served all week 6-9 Av main course £7.95 **RESTAURANT:** L served all week 12-2 D served all week 6-9 Av 3 course à la carte £15 **BREWERY/COMPANY:** Free House **●:** Theakstons Beamish. **FACILITIES:** Children welcome Garden Dogs allowed guide dogs only **NOTES:** Parking 30

EAST LOTHIAN

EAST LINTON   Map 21 NT57

Pick of the Pubs

Drovers Inn ♀
5 Bridge St EH40 3AG ☎ 01620 860298 ▤ 01620 860298
e-mail: thedroversinn@aol.co.uk
Dir: Off A1 5m past Haddington, follow rd under railway bridge, then L
Herdsmen used to stop here as they drove their livestock to market. Those passing through in the late-19th century would undoubtedly have been aware of the then landlord's son's liking for young Jessie Cowe, daughter of the appropriately-named local butcher. The church clock tower in the village square was named Jessie after her. Those old drovers are long gone but the bar, with wooden floors, beamed ceilings and half-panelled walls, retains an old-world charm. Upstairs, though, is more sumptuous with rich colours, low-beamed ceilings and antique furniture. Bistro menus offer Highland haggis with a creamy pepper sauce, shank of Borders lamb with vegetables, and crispy skinned codling on a basil and mustard mash. The chef's daily creations depend on seasonal local produce, while sizzling honey and ginger pie, chargrilled steaks and goats' cheese-filled pastry patties with slow-roasted plum tomatoes, are always popular.
OPEN: 11.30-11 11.30-1 Thu-Sat **BAR MEALS:** L served all week 11.30-2 D served Sun-Fri 6-9.30 Av main course £10 **RESTAURANT:** L served all week 11.30-2 D served all week 6-9.30 **BREWERY/COMPANY:** Free House **●:** Adnams Broadside, Deuchars IPA, Old Speckeled Hen, Burton Real Ale. ♀: 6 **FACILITIES:** Children welcome Garden Dogs allowed In the garden only

GIFFORD   Map 21 NT56

Goblin Ha' Hotel 🐾 ♀
EH41 4QH ☎ 01620 810244 ▤ 01620 810718
e-mail: douglasmuir@btconnect.com
Dir: On A846, 100yrds from main village square on shore side of the road

continued

Traditional hotel with a large patio for summer eating and a good garden with a play area and a dolls' house for children. Members of the Walt Disney company stayed here when they were filming scenes for Greyfriars Bobby in the hills to the south of the village. Malcolm Muggeridge was a regular visitor in the 1960s, and Joan Baez attracted some dedicated hippies when she had supper here one night. A varied range of home-cooked dishes includes breast of duck, fillet of salmon, chef's curry, shank of lamb and beer-battered haddock.
OPEN: 11-2.30 5-11 **BAR MEALS:** L served all week 12.30-2 D served all week 6.30-9 Av main course £7.50 **RESTAURANT:** L served all week 12.30-2 D served all week 6.30-9 Av 3 course à la carte £15 **BREWERY/COMPANY:** Free House **●:** Hop Back Summer lightning, Timothy Taylor Landlord, Caledonian Deuchers IPA, Fuller's ESB. ♀: 12 **FACILITIES:** Children welcome Children's licence Garden: Two acres of garden, seats 80 Dogs allowed **ROOMS:** 7 bedrooms 6 en suite 2 family rooms s£37.50 d£75 (VisitScotland)

GULLANE   Map 21 NT48

The Golf Inn ♀
Main St EH31 2AB ☎ 01620 843259 ▤ 01620 842066
e-mail: info@golfinn.co.uk
The inn has 12 golf courses in its vicinity, including the Muirfield Golf Course, which hosted the 2002 British Open Championship, which is just 500 yards away. Golf is the theme in the public bar with a full-length wall display of trophies and memorabilia. Fish features prominently, with dishes such as fish and chips with minted pea purée, crispy fillet of salmon, Parmesan-crusted sea bass with thyme courgettes, and saffron-baked cod with ragôut of peppers. There's also an impressive choice of single malt whiskies.
OPEN: 11-11 **BAR MEALS:** L served all week 12-2.30 D served all week 6.30-9.30 Av main course £7.50 **RESTAURANT:** L served all week 12-2.30 D served all week 6.30-9.30 Av 3 course à la carte £20 **BREWERY/COMPANY:** Free House **●:** McEwans 70/-, Belhaven Best. **FACILITIES:** Children welcome Garden: Food served outside Dogs allowed

FALKIRK

CASTLECARY   Map 21 NS77

Castlecary House Hotel ★★ 🐾 ♀
Castlecary Rd G68 0HD ☎ 01324 840233 ▤ 01324 841608
e-mail: enquiries@castlecaryhotel.com
Dir: Off A80 N of Cumbernauld
A friendly hotel complex on the watershed of Scotland's central belt and close to the historic Antonine Wall and Forth & Clyde Canal. 70 bedrooms created mainly in the form of cottages surround the main hotel building. Camerons Restaurant, seating 120, is the perfect meeting place for lunch. From traditional pub food and home-made burgers, the varied menus include collops of venison on a bed of caramelised red cabbage, baked Highland chicken en croûte with Drambuie sauce, or Cajun seared sea bass with couscous and pickled vegetables.
OPEN: 11-11 **BAR MEALS:** L served all week 12-2 D served all week 6-9 Av main course £6 **RESTAURANT:** L served Mon-Sat 12-2 D served Mon-Sat 7-10 Av 3 course à la carte £20 **BREWERY/COMPANY:** Free House **●:** Arran Blonde, Harviestoun Brooker's Bitter & Twisted, Inveralmond Ossian's Ale, Housten Peter's Well. ♀: 10 **FACILITIES:** Children welcome Children's licence Garden Dogs allowed **NOTES:** Parking 100 **ROOMS:** 70 bedrooms 65 en suite 2 family rooms s£54.50 d£54.50

FIFE

ANSTRUTHER
Map 21 NO50

The Dreel Tavern
16 High St West KY10 3DL ☎ 01333 310727 ▤ 01333 310577
e-mail: dreeltavern@aol.com
Complete with a local legend concerning an amorous
encounter between James V and a local gypsy woman, the
16th-century Dreel Tavern has plenty of atmosphere. Its oak
beams, open fire and stone walls retain much of the distant
past, while home-cooked food and cask-conditioned ales are
served to hungry visitors of the present. Expect to savour
steak pie, lamb in a red wine sauce, stuffed chicken parcels,
deep-fried haddock in batter, and smoked fish pie. Peaceful
gardens overlook Dreel Burn.
OPEN: 11-12 (Sun 12.30-12) **BAR MEALS:** L served all week 12-2
D served all week 5.30-9 Av main course £6.95 **RESTAURANT:** L
served all week 12-2 D served all week 5.30-9
BREWERY/COMPANY: Free House ◖: Orkney Dark Island,
Carlsberg-Tetley Tetley's Imperial, Harviestoun Bitter & Twisted, Greene
King IPA. **FACILITIES:** Children welcome Garden: Enclosed area,
seats approx 20, peaceful Dogs allowed Water, Biscuits
NOTES: Parking 3

AUCHTERMUCHTY
Map 21 NO21

Forest Hills Hotel
23 High St KY14 7AP ☎ 01337 828318 ▤ 01337 828318
e-mail: info@theforesthillshotel.com
Dir: *Telephone for directions*
Popular inn located in the village square, with an oak-beamed
bar, Flemish murals, and a cosy lounge. The town of
Auchtermuchty is well known as home to TV series Dr Finlay's
Casebook, acoustic duo The Proclaimers, and accordionist
extraordinare Jimmy Shand. A new restaurant planned for
2003 will boost the traditional pub food of baguettes and
open sandwiches.
OPEN: 11.30-2.30 5-10 **BAR MEALS:** L served all week 12-2 D
served all week 6-9 **RESTAURANT:** L served all week 12.30-2 D
served Mon-Thu 7-9 **BREWERY/COMPANY:** Free House
FACILITIES: Children welcome Dogs allowed

BURNTISLAND
Map 21 NT28

Burntisland Sands Hotel ♀
Lochie Rd KY3 9JX ☎ 01592 872230
Small, family-run hotel situated just yards from a sandy beach
with view across the bay. Popular with families. Good range of
traditional pub food.
OPEN: 11-12 **BAR MEALS:** L served all week 12-2.30 D served all
week 6-8.30 Av main course £4.95 **RESTAURANT:** L served all week
12-2.30 D served all week 6-8.30 Av 3 course à la carte £12
BREWERY/COMPANY: Free House ◖: Two changing guest ales.
FACILITIES: Children welcome Garden: patio/terrace, BBQ, rabbit
hutch Dogs allowed **NOTES:** Parking 20

CRAIL
Map 21 NO60

The Golf Hotel
4 High St KY10 3TD ☎ 01333 450206 ▤ 01333 450795
e-mail: enquiries@thegolfhotelcrail.com
Dir: *Telephone for directions*
Rooted in the 14th century, this is the site of one of Scotland's
oldest licensed inns, although the current building dates from
the early 18th century. The golfing connection comes from the
Crail Golfing Society, formed in 1786, at the heart of Scottish
golfing life. Local seafood is a speciality, including home-made
cullen skink, seafood platter, or baked haddock and crab en
croute with lobster sauce. Traditional high tea with home
baking is also served.
OPEN: 11-12 **BAR MEALS:** L served all week 12-7 D served all
week 7-9 Av main course £6 **RESTAURANT:** L served all week 12-7
D served all week 7-9 **BREWERY/COMPANY:** Free House
◖: Scottish Courage McEwans 80/-, 70/-, John Smith's, Tetleys.
FACILITIES: Children welcome Garden Dogs welcome
NOTES: Parking 10 **ROOMS:** 5 bedrooms 5 en suite 1 family
rooms s£23 d£25 (VisitScotland)

DUNFERMLINE
Map 21 NT08

The Hideaway Lodge & Restaurant ♀
Kingseat Rd, Halbeath KY12 0UB
☎ 01383 725474 ▤ 01383 622821
e-mail: enquiries@thehideaway.co.uk
Dir: *Telephone for directions*

Originally built in the 1930s as a miners' welfare institute,
this pleasant country inn enjoys a rural setting on the
outskirts of Dunfermline. Each room is named after a
Scottish loch, and the extensive menu makes good use of
fresh local produce. A typical meal may begin with grilled
goats' cheese salad or Oban mussels, then move on to
chargrilled tuna steak, Scottish seafood crumble or fillet of
Highland venison, and finish with summer fruit pudding or
steamed ginger pudding.
OPEN: 12-3 5-11 (Sun 12-10) **BAR MEALS:** L served all week 12-2 D
served all week 5-9.30 **RESTAURANT:** L served all week 12-2 D served
all week 5-9.30 **BREWERY/COMPANY:** Free House ◖: John Smith, 80
Special. **FACILITIES:** Children welcome Garden **NOTES:** Parking 35

Skittles

Skittles is a far older game than darts or dominoes, on record in London since the 15th century, when it was
banned. Henry VIII enjoyed it and had his own skittle alley, but governments kept vainly trying to stop ordinary
people playing, because they ought to have been practising their archery and because they gambled so heavily.
Even so, the game became popular enough to make 'beer and skittles' proverbial. Basically, three wooden balls
are propelled at nine pins to knock them down, but there are sharp variations in the rules between different areas
and pubs. Varieties include London or Old English Skittles, West Country Skittles, Long Alley and Aunt Sally, as
well as several types of table skittles.

Scotland

ELIE
Map 21 NO40

Pick of the Pubs

The Ship Inn 🐑 ♀
The Toft KY9 1DT ☎ 01333 330246 📠 01333 330864
e-mail: shipinnelie@aol.com
Dir: Follow A915 & A917 to Elie. Follow signs from High St to Watersport Centre to the Toft.

There's always something happening at this lively free house, located right on the waterfront at Elie Bay, just a stone's throw from one of Scotland's finest water-sports centres. The pub's own cricket team plays regularly on the beach, and the annual rugby match against Edinburgh Academicals attracts a huge crowd. A pub since 1838, it has been run for over 20 years by the Philip family whose enthusiasm remains undimmed. Fresh fish takes pride of place on the specials board to supplement the regular menu offering Bob the butcher's award-winning haggis with neeps, tatties and whisky sauce; chicken fillet with coriander and stem ginger, finished with white wine and cream, or finnan haddock, whole and boneless, locally smoked over oak chips and brushed with butter. There are plenty of children's choices, and summer barbecues in the beer garden.
OPEN: 11-11 (Sun 12.30-11) Closed: 25 Dec **BAR MEALS:** L served all week 12-2 D served all week 6-9 **RESTAURANT:** L served all week 12-2 D served all week 6-9
BREWERY/COMPANY: Free House 🍺: Caledonian Deuchars IPA, Belhaven Best, Tetleys Xtra Cold, Theakstons Best. ♀: 7
FACILITIES: Children welcome Garden: Beer garden, food served outdoors, patio, Dogs allowed Water, biscuits

KIRKCALDY
Map 21 NT29

Pick of the Pubs

The Old Rectory Inn 🐑 ♀
West Quality St, Dysart KY1 2TE
☎ 01592 651211 📠 01592 655221
Dir: From Edinburgh take A92 to Kirkcaldy, then A907, A955 to Dysart R at Nat Trust sign

A delightful Georgian inn with a splendid walled garden. Chocoholics might like the West Quality Street address, while just round the corner is Hot Pot Wynd. At various times as a gentleman's residence, rectory and laundry, this well-preserved old building near the harbour has been a pub only since the 1980s. Fife's good food lovers increasingly recognise its commitment to local produce. Should it be lunchtime, go maybe for a large Yorkshire pudding filled with chilli con carne, or hot Indiana

spaghetti - pasta with spicy chicken, red and green peppers and tomato sauce. From the carte come starters like duck and pork terrine, cebiche of salmon with red pepper and cucumber mayonnaise, and omelette rognons. Baked halibut fillet with stir-fry vegetables, and pork escalopes with green ginger wine sauce, buttered spinach and sweetcorn pancake, could follow. The supper menu offers, among others, fish stew, boiled brisket of beef with carrots, Scottish steaks, pasta and vegetarian dishes.
OPEN: 12-3 7-12 (Sun 12.30-3.30) Closed: 1wk Jan & 2wks mid-Oct, 1 wk early July **BAR MEALS:** L served Tue-Sun 12-2 D served Tue-Sat 7-9.30 Av main course £8.75 **RESTAURANT:** L served Tue-Sun 12-2 D served Tue-Sat 7-9.30 Av 3 course à la carte £22.65 **BREWERY/COMPANY:** Free House 🍺: Calders Cream Ale. **FACILITIES:** Garden: Large oval garden, sheltered by high stone wall **NOTES:** Parking 12

LOWER LARGO
Map 21 NO40

Crusoe Hotel
2 Main St KY8 6BT ☎ 01333 320759 📠 01333 320865
Dir: A92 to Kirkcaldy East, A915 to Lundin Links, then R to Lower Largo
This historic inn is located on the sea wall in Lower Largo, the birthplace of Alexander Selkirk, the real-life castaway immortalised by Daniel Defoe in his novel, Robinson Crusoe. In the past the area was also the heart of the once-thriving herring fishing industry. Today it is a charming bay ideal for a golfing break. A typical menu may include 'freshly shot' haggis, Pittenweem haddock and a variety of steaks.
OPEN: 11-12 (Fri 11-1am) **BAR MEALS:** L served all week 12-3 D served all week 6-9 Av main course £6 **RESTAURANT:** 12-3 D served all week 6.30-9 Av 3 course à la carte £22
BREWERY/COMPANY: Free House 🍺: Belhaven 80/- & Best.
FACILITIES: Children welcome Dogs allowed **NOTES:** Parking 30

MARKINCH
Map 21 NO20

Town House Hotel ◆◆◆◆
1 High St KY7 6DQ ☎ 01592 758459 📠 01592 755039
Dir: Off A92(Dundee/Kirkcaldy rd) Hotel opp. rail station
Family-run 17th-century coaching inn situated in the heart of town, and offering a fixed-price lunch menu of two or three courses, and a supper carte of imaginative dishes. Expect grilled Gressingham duck breast served with an orange and Cointreau sauce, pan-fried blackened Cajun salmon fillets and cheese or sun-dried tomato tortellini in a tomato and pesto sauce.
OPEN: 12-2 6-11 Closed: 25-26 Dec, 1-2 Jan **BAR MEALS:** L served Mon-Sat 12-2 D served all week 6-9 Av main course £8.95 **RESTAURANT:** L served Mon-Sat 12-2 D served all week 6-9 Av 3 course à la carte £16.95 **BREWERY/COMPANY:** Free House
FACILITIES: Children welcome **ROOMS:** 4 bedrooms 3 en suite 1 family rooms s£30 d£60

continued

Shieldaig Bar

A very varied walk exploring the old fishing village of Shieldaig and its Caledonian pine woods. One of the route's highlights is an easy traverse of Beinn Shieldaig that offers magnificent views of Loch Torridon, Skye and the Outer Hebrides.

★ ◉
SHIELDAIG BAR, SHIELDAIG
IV54 8XN
☎ 01520 755251

Lochside bar in a charming fishing village, with stunning views. A popular rendezvous throughout the day, serving tea and coffee with cakes, as well as drinks and meals.
Open: 11-11 (Sun 12.30-10)
Bar Meals: 12-2.30 6-8.30
Notes: Children welcome (highchairs). Dogs in garden only. Lochside courtyard with umbrellas. Parking.
(See page 594 for full entry)

From the pub turn right along the sea front where seals, herons and otters can be spotted. At low tide you can pick your way among the rock pools hunting for shells and crabs. Look out along the shore for the old post office, the customs house - more recently the registry for births, deaths and marriages - the manse and the local church with its distinctive millennium mosaic.

Continue ahead up the hill and turn left at the school to look at the remnants of the old preachers' wall on the right, where non-conformist ministers, having no church of their own, preached to hundreds of worshippers in the open air.

Return to the village lane, passing the war memorial on your left. On reaching the main road, cross over and begin ascending Beinn Shieldaig. There is no obvious path here, so pick a spot below the rocky crags before heading up the hillside to it. Various sheep tracks cutting across the grassy slopes make the going easier, though don't attempt to reach the summit via the rocks unless you are an experienced scrambler.

Traverse the hillside at an angle of 90 degrees and once past Shieldaig, visible below, turn down the slope and through one of Scotland's last surviving stands of Caledonian pines. Make for the main road as close to the coast road to Kenmore as you can and take a short detour along it

(200yds/183m) to visit the Shieldaig Sea Trout Project, which is open between April and October 9.30am-4.30pm (or by prior appointment). The project studies the lives of local sea trout and how they interact with other species.

Return to the main road and follow the shore to the village, the pier and the pub.

DISTANCE: 3 miles/4.8km
MAP: OS Landranger 24
TERRAIN: Coastal
PATHS: Roads and clear paths – undefined paths on the higher slopes of Beinn Shieldaig
GRADIENT: Moderate climbing

Walk submitted and checked by the Shieldaig Bar, Tigh an Eilean Hotel, Shieldaig

ST MONANS — Map 21 NO50

Pick of the Pubs

Seafood Bar & Restaurant 🏵🏵 🛏 ♀
16 West End KY10 2BX ☎ 01333 730327 📠 01333 730508
e-mail: info@theseafoodrestaurant.com
Dir: *Take A595 from St Andrews to Anstruther, then W on A917 through Pittenweem. At St Monans harbour turn R*

This little seafood bar and restaurant perched close to the harbour's edge, affords stunning views over St Monans Harbour, the Isle of May, Bass Rock and the Firth of Forth from its harbourside terrace. Below the terrace you can see fascinating examples of rock formations caused by plate movements, plus the resident heron. The bar is housed in a 400-year-old fisherman's dwelling with its own freshwater well. Now located in the adjoining Conservatory restaurant, the well dates back to the time of King David I, who was healed of an arrow wound by the miraculous powers of its water. Seafood specialities include seared scallops with mango and sweet chilli salsa, grilled turbot with red onion marmalade and mustard sauce, and carpaccio of albacore tuna with hoi sin dressing.
OPEN: 12-3 6-11 June-August open 7 days a week Closed: 25-26 Dec, 1-3 Jan **BAR MEALS:** L served Tue-Sun 12-3 D served Tue-Sat 7-9.30 Av main course £12 **RESTAURANT:** L served Tue-Sun 12-3 D served Tue-Sat 7-9.30 Av 3 course fixed price £20
BREWERY/COMPANY: Free House ◀ Belhaven Best, Belhaven Extra Cold. ♀ 14 **FACILITIES:** Garden: Overlooking Monans harbour, seats 32 **NOTES:** Parking 10

HIGHLAND

ACHILTIBUIE — Map 22 NC00

Summer Isles Hotel & Bar 🏵🏵 🛏
IV26 2YG ☎ 01854 622282 📠 01854 622251
Dir: *take A835 N from Ullapool for 10m, Achiltibuie signed on L, 15m to village, hotel 1m on L*
The only watering hole in the area for 150 years, this peaceful bar and hotel can be found at the end of a long and winding single track lane that skirts lochs Lurgain, Badagyle and Oscaig. The emphasis is on locally-caught and home-produced food, and there's a wide choice of malts and real ale. Seafood platter, spiny lobster, smoked salmon, and Cumberland sausages all feature on the menu, along with a casserole of the day, and various snacks.
OPEN: 12-11 (4-11 in winter) Closed: Mid Oct-Easter
BAR MEALS: L served all week D served all week Av main course £7.50 **RESTAURANT:** L served all week 12.30-2 D served all week 8 **BREWERY/COMPANY:** Free House ◀ Orkney Dark Island, Raven & Red Macgregor. **FACILITIES:** Children welcome Garden Dogs allowed **NOTES:** Parking 20

ALTNAHARRA — Map 23 NC53

Altnaharra Hotel 🛏
IV27 4UE ☎ 01549 411222 📠 01549 411222
e-mail: altnaharra@btinternet.com
Dir: *A9 to Bonar Bridge, A336 to Lairg & Tongue*
Traditional Highland hotel with a major focus on sea trout and salmon fishing, set amid fantastic scenery - perhaps Britain's last remaining wilderness. Lunch and dinner are available on pre-booking, the set-price menus featuring the best of Scottish produce. Options might include ragout of seafood with julienne vegetables, garlic and white wine sauce, braised local venison, Strathmore lamb and Aberdeen Angus beef.
OPEN: 12-2.30 5-11 **BAR MEALS:** L served all week 12-11 D served all week Av main course £6 **RESTAURANT:** D served all week 7.30-9.30 Av 5 course fixed price £30
BREWERY/COMPANY: Scottish & Newcastle ◀ No real ale.
FACILITIES: Children welcome Garden: Large lawn area, Loch views, seating Dogs allowed garden only **NOTES:** Parking 60

APPLECROSS — Map 22 NG74

Pick of the Pubs

Applecross Inn 🛏 ♀
Shore St IV54 8LR ☎ 01520 744262 📠 01520 744400
e-mail: applecrossinn@globalnet.co.uk
See Pick of the Pubs on opposite page

AVIEMORE — Map 23 NH81

The Old Bridge Inn 🛏 ♀
Dalfaber Rd PH22 1PU ☎ 01479 811137 📠 01479 810270
e-mail: highlandcatering@aol.com
Dir: *Exit A9 to Aviemore, 1st L to 'Ski road', then 1st L again - 200mtrs*
Cosy and friendly Highland pub overlooking the River Spey. Dine in the relaxing bars or in the attractive riverside garden. A tasty chargrill menu includes lamb chops in redcurrant jelly, Aberdeen Angus sirloin or rib-eye steaks, or butterflied breast of chicken marinated in yoghurt, lime and coriander. Seafood specials include monkfish panfried in chilli butter, mussels poached in white wine, and seafood crumble. Large selection of malt whiskies.
OPEN: 11-11 **BAR MEALS:** L served all week 12-2 D served all week 6-9 Av main course £5.90 **RESTAURANT:** L served all week 12-2 D served all week 6-9 **BREWERY/COMPANY:** Free House ◀ Caledonian 80/-, Cairngorm Highland IPA. ♀ 11
FACILITIES: Children welcome Children's licence Garden **NOTES:** Parking 24

> Most of the pubs in this guide book pride themselves on the quality of their food. This may take a little time to prepare.

Hops in Ale

The introduction of hops was stoutly resisted. Henry VIII would drink only hopless ale and the brewers were castigated for ruining the traditional drink. Beer brewed with hops kept better for longer, however, which stimulated the development of large-scale breweries and both inns and alehouses gradually gave up brewing their own.

Open: 11-11 (Sun 12.30-11)
Bar Meals: Food served all week 12-9.
Av cost main course £6.95
RESTAURANT: L served by appointment only,
D served all week 6-9.
Av cost 3 course £20
BREWERY/COMPANY:
Free House.
🍺: Scottish Courage John Smith's, Cask Ale, Red Cullin, Millers.
FACILITIES: Dogs allowed, Children welcome, Garden - Grassed area on beach.
NOTES: Parking 30

Applecross Inn

The drive to Judith Fish's door at Applecross Inn will take you through some of Scotland's most awe-inspiring scenery, for you must cross the Bealach Na Ba (pass of the cattle) rising to 2053 feet with triple hairpin bends before descending through forests into Applecross (An Comeraich, meaning sanctuary).

Shore Street, Applecross, Wester Ross, IV54 8LR
☎ 01520 744262 📠 01520 744400
✉ applecrossinn@globalnet.co.uk
Dir: From Lochcarron to Kishorn then L onto unclassifed rd to Applecross over 'Bealach Na Ba'.

Here is the site of the old monastery where St Maelrubha brought Christianity to Scotland in 632. The traditional white-painted inn is set on a sandy cove looking over to Skye and the Cuillins. The bar retains its Highland character, warmed by a wood burning stove, lively with convivial company (fishermen, locals, visitors) and occasional traditional music nights, and inspired by a choice of over 50 malt whiskies. The kitchen takes its pick of top quality local produce: locally-landed fish, and game from neighbouring estates. Seafood, of course, is a speciality, including marinated local squat lobsters in tempura batter with salad and red pesto, and hand-dived king scallops with crispy bacon and garlic butter served on a bed of rice. Alternatives are Applecross Estate venison casserole, with mustard and apple mash and braised red cabbage, or local lamb curried with spinach from the walled garden. Sandwiches, burgers and home-made soups are also available for a snack meal, and puddings are worth a look, including the regional raspberry Cranachan, or hot chocolate fudge cake and cream. The inn's beer garden comprises a grassed area on the beach surrounded by a fuchsia hedge. Those tempted to stay a while can book one of the romantic bedrooms with magnificent sea views.

CAWDOR
Map 23 NH85

Pick of the Pubs

Cawdor Tavern 🏮 🍷
The Lane IV12 5XP ☎ 01667 404777 🖷 01667 404777
e-mail: cawdortavern@btopenworld.com
Dir: *from A96 (Inverness-Aberdeen) take B9006 & follow signs for
Cawdor Castle. Tavern in village centre.*

Set in a picturesque conservation village alongside the
famous Cawdor Castle, this was formerly the joiners'
workshop for the estate. Oak panelling gifted from the
castle itself has been used to great effect in the
refurbished bar, which draws discerning diners from far
and wide. Roaring log fires keep the place cosy and warm
on long winter evenings, while the garden patio comes
into its own in summer. Plenty of choice from the lunch
carte, like fresh Mallaig mussels, or mini cold seafood
platter to start, then perhaps beefsteak casserole, pan-
seared lamb's liver with caramelised onions and bacon, or
vegetarian Thai green curry, plus light bites such as warm
crab, mascarpone and basil tart. The evening menu might
focus on haggis dumplings, roast fillet of Morayshire pork,
and warm Belgian chocolate tart. More than 100 malt
whiskies, and three Scottish ales including Dark Island
from Orkney.
OPEN: 11-3 5-11 (May-Oct 11-11) Closed: 25 Dec, 1 Jan
BAR MEALS: L served all week 12-2 D served all week 5.30-9
Av main course £7.95 **RESTAURANT:** L served all week 12-2 D
served all week 6.30-9 Av 3 course à la carte £15.95
BREWERY/COMPANY: Free House 🍺: Tennents 80/-,
Tomintoul Stag. 🍷: 8 **FACILITIES:** Children welcome
Children's licence Garden: Patio area at front of Tavern Dogs
allowed Water provided. **NOTES:** Parking 60

CONTIN
Map 23 NH45

Achilty Hotel ★★ 🏮 🍷
IV14 9EG ☎ 01997 421355 🖷 01997 421923
e-mail: info@achiltyhotel.co.uk
Dir: *On A835, at the northern edge of Contin*
Former drovers' inn, now a cosy, relaxed hotel with the
original stone walls and log fire showing its origins. Set on the
edge of the village near a fast-flowing mountain river, it serves
good Scottish food made from fresh local produce. The
bar/restaurant menu offers extensive choices, and has a
seafood slant: seafood pasta, scampi provençale, seafood
platter plus large selection of steaks and a good choice of
home-made desserts.
OPEN: 11-2.30 5-11 (Apr-31 Oct 11-11) **BAR MEALS:** L served all
week 12-5 D served all week 5-8.30 Av main course £10

RESTAURANT: L served all week 12-2.30 D served all week 5.30-9
Av 3 course à la carte £20 Av 3 course fixed price £9.95
BREWERY/COMPANY: Free House 🍺: Calders Cream, Calders
70/-. 🍷: 8 **FACILITIES:** Garden: Courtyard style **NOTES:** Parking
80 **ROOMS:** 12 bedrooms 12 en suite 1 family rooms s£36.75 d£57
no children overnight

DORNOCH
Map 23 NH78

Mallin House Hotel 🏮
Church St IV25 3LP ☎ 01862 810335 🖷 01862 810810
e-mail: mallin.house.hotel@zetnet.co.uk
Dir: *From Tain, on A9, take A836 to Bonar Bridge, then left onto A949
towards Dornoch (approx 10m)*

Mallin House is a modern hotel just 200 yards from the Royal
Dornoch Golf Course. The area is also ideal for angling, pony-
trekking and birdwatching. A single menu, strong on Scottish
cooking, is offered throughout, with an emphasis on fresh
seafood, including langoustines in hot garlic butter, and sea
bass with citrus and saffron sauce.
OPEN: 11-2.30 5-11 **BAR MEALS:** L served Sun 12.30-2 D served
all week 6.30-9 Av main course £6.95 **RESTAURANT:** L served Sun
12.30-2 D served all week 6.30-9 Av 3 course à la carte £26
BREWERY/COMPANY: Free House 🍺: Carlsberg-Tetley Tetley
Bitter, Caledonian 80/-. **FACILITIES:** Children welcome Garden
Dogs allowed **NOTES:** Parking 22 **ROOMS:** 10 bedrooms 10 en
suite 2 family rooms s£30 d£50 (VisitScotland)

DUNDONNELL
Map 22 NH08

Pick of the Pubs

Dundonnell Hotel ★★★ 🏮 🍷
IV23 2QR ☎ 01854 633204 🖷 01854 633366
e-mail: selbie@dundonnellhotel.co.uk
Dir: *From Inverness W on the A835, at Braemore junct take A832 for
Gairloch*
Sheltering beneath the massive Al Teallach mountain
range, with superb views down Little Loch Broom, this
much-extended former drovers' inn boasted just four
bedrooms when acquired by the Florence family some
forty years ago. Today, in one of Scotland's finest holiday
areas, their acclaimed hotel is a magnet for visitors to
Wester Ross. The Broom Beg ('little broom') bar and
bistro provide a casual atmosphere in which to relax after
a day exploring and enjoy good food, beers and an
extensive range of malt whiskies. It is a long way to the
shops, so local produce plays a full part on a menu
providing batter-crisp haddock fillets, with chips and
tartare sauce, local salmon with prawn, chervil and citrus
butter, chicken fillets and prime Angus steaks from their

continued

continued

own Aberdeenshire butcher. Lunchtime snacks can be as simple as Orkney Cheddar cheese and apple open sandwiches, beef- or veggie-burgers and local oak-smoked salmon with dill sauce and brown bread. Dinner in the spacious restaurant continues to be a key attraction for residents.
OPEN: 11-11 Reduced Hrs Jan-Feb please phone
BAR MEALS: L served all week 12-2 D served all week 6-8.30 Av main course £7.95 **RESTAURANT:** L served none D served all week 7-8.30 Av 3 course à la carte £27.50
BREWERY/COMPANY: Free House 🍺 John Smiths,.
FACILITIES: Children welcome Dogs allowed **NOTES:** Parking 60 **ROOMS:** 28 bedrooms 28 en suite s£40 d£45

FORT AUGUSTUS Map 23 NH30

Pick of the Pubs

The Lock Inn 🐷 ♈
Canalside PH32 4AU ☎ 01320 366302
Dir: On banks of Caledonian Canal in Fort Augustus
Built in 1820, this former bank and post office building, replete with flagstone floors and original beams, stands on the banks of the Caledonian Canal close to Loch Ness. The state-of-the-art kitchen has been recognised by the Scottish Beef Guild Society for its use of local produce. A thousand Celtic welcomes are extended to regulars and visitors who come to enjoy the regular Scottish folk music evenings when a special dinner features brandied seafood bisque and Loch an Ora whisky-flavoured game pâté, followed by seared calves' liver and Angus sirloin steaks. House specials include Roast Hebridean lamb, loin of Grampian pork fillet, and Monarch of the Glen venison casserole. Start perhaps with seafood chowder and round off with Loch Ness mud pie.
OPEN: 11-11 Closed: 25 Dec, 1 Jan **BAR MEALS:** L served all week 12-3 D served all week 6-9.30 Av main course £6
RESTAURANT: L served all week 12-3 D served all week 6-10 Av 3 course à la carte £20 **BREWERY/COMPANY:** Free House 🍺 Caledonian 80/-, Orkney Dark Island, Black Isle.
FACILITIES: Children welcome Garden: Food served outside Dogs allowed In the garden only

FORT WILLIAM Map 22 NN17

Pick of the Pubs

Moorings Hotel ★★★ ◉
Banavie PH33 7LY ☎ 01397 772797 🖷 01397 772441
e-mail: reservations@moorings-fortwilliam.co.uk
Dir: from A82 in Fort William follow signs for Mallaig, then L onto A830 for 1m. Cross canal bridge then 1st R signposted Banavie
Standing on the banks of the Caledonian Canal beside Neptune's Staircase - a historic monument comprising eight lock gates that raise boats by 64 feet. This striking modern hotel on the west side of town has panoramic views on clear days towards Ben Nevis and the surrounding mountains. Most bedrooms share this stunning outlook, including a new wing that mirrors the shape of the nearby Thomas Telford house. The Upper Deck lounge and popular Mariners' Bar share the nautical theme, and offer an appealing place for a drink or a meal. The daily-changing bar food has a strong inclination towards local fish such as West coast haddock, loch

salmon, Angus beef, Grampian chicken and, of course, haggis served with clapshot and Drambuie sauce. Herb roast rack of lamb, pan-seared scallops on wilted spinach, and gently-baked fillet of hake make up the numbers, along with bangers, burgers, and sandwiches.

OPEN: 12-11.45 Closed: Dec 25-6 **BAR MEALS:** L served all week 12-9.30 D served all week Av main course £7.95
RESTAURANT: D served all week 7-9.30 Av 4 course fixed price £26 **BREWERY/COMPANY:** Free House 🍺 Calders 70/- & Sport. **FACILITIES:** Children welcome Garden: Small patio, food served outdoors Dogs allowed Water **NOTES:** Parking 80 **ROOMS:** 28 bedrooms 28 en suite s£40 d£78

GAIRLOCH Map 22 NG87

Pick of the Pubs

The Old Inn ♦♦♦♦ 🐷 ♈
IV21 2BD ☎ 01445 712006 🖷 01445 712445
e-mail: nomadscot@lineone.net
Dir: just off main A832, near harbour at S end of village

What accolade next for the AA's Pub of the Year for Scotland 2003? At the foot of Flowerdale Glen, this is the oldest hotel in Gairloch, dating from around 1792. Two-foot stone walls, fireplaces and other original features revealed during renovations have been restored. The isles of Skye, Rona, Raasay and even the Outer Hebrides can be seen across the harbour where Loch Ewe scallops, Gairloch lobster, Minch langoustines, brown crab, mussels, skate and salmon are landed. Some of this delicious bounty goes into Mediterranean-style bouillabaisse and home-made seafood ravioli, while smoked haddock goes into that famous Scottish fish soup, cullen skink. Expect Highland game, home-made pies and succulent spit-roasts, such as whole rack of Hebridean lamb, baby ribs and suckling pig - a weekend special. Desserts include orange and banana pudding, and apricot

continued

continued

GAIRLOCH continued

and peach crumble. Among the real ales is Blind Piper which commemorates composer Iain Dallmackay, whose fine music is remembered at the annual Gairloch Piping Festival. **OPEN:** 11-12 **BAR MEALS:** L served all week 12-2.30 D served all week 6-9 Av main course £6.95 **RESTAURANT:** L served all week 12-2.30 D served all week 6-9 Av 3 course à la carte £15.50 **BREWERY/COMPANY:** Free House 🍺 Greene King Old Speckled Hen, Scottish Courage Courage Directors, Isle of Skye Red Cullin & Blind Piper, Belhaven St Andrews Ale. ♀: 8 **FACILITIES:** Children welcome Children's licence **Garden:** Large grassy area with picnic tables Dogs allowed Rugs, water bowls, baskets **NOTES:** Parking 20 **ROOMS:** 14 bedrooms 14 en suite 3 family rooms s£32 d£45

GARVE
Map 23 NH36

Inchbae Lodge Hotel 🏠
IV23 2PH ☎ 01997 455269 📠 01997 455207
e-mail: info@inchbae-lodge-hotel.co.uk
Dir: On A835, hotel 6m W of Garve

Originally a 19th-century hunting lodge, Inchbae Lodge is situated on the banks of the River Blackwater, with an elegant dining room offering panoramic views. An ideal base for those keen walkers wishing to take on Ben Wyvis and the Fannich Hills. On the menu alongside venison sausages, smoked salmon, or haggis, neeps and tatties, vegetarians will find vegetarian haggis and lasagne. There is also a coffee shop.
OPEN: 8-11 Closed: Nov & Dec **BAR MEALS:** L served all week 8-8.30 D served all week Av main course £7 **RESTAURANT:** L served Sun 12-2 D served all week 7-8 Av 3 course fixed price £19.95
BREWERY/COMPANY: Free House 🍺 Belhaven plus Guest ale.
FACILITIES: Children welcome **Garden:** Food served outdoors Dogs allowed **NOTES:** Parking 30

GLEN'COE
Map 22 NN15

Clachaig Inn
PH49 4HX ☎ 01855 811252 📠 01855 811679
e-mail: inn@clachaig.com
Dir: Just off the A82, 20m S of Fort William and 2m E of Glencoe village
Situated at the heart of Glencoe, this 300-year-old inn is hugely popular with mountaineers and stands a short forest walk from Signal Rock, where the sign was given for the infamous massacre of 1692. Scenes for the third Harry Potter film were shot just 200 yards from the doorstep. The pub is renowned for its real ales, 120 malt whiskies, and warming food such as steak and ale pie, venison casserole, and Tex-Mex dishes.
OPEN: 11-11 (Fri 11-12, Sat 11-11.30, Sun 12.30-11))
BAR MEALS: L served all week 12-9 D served all week 12-9 Av main

continued

course £8.50 **BREWERY/COMPANY:** Free House 🍺 Isle of Skye Red Cuillin, Orkney Dark Island, Fraoch Heather Ale, Houston Peter's Well. **FACILITIES:** Children welcome Garden **NOTES:** Parking 40 **ROOMS:** 20 bedrooms 17 en suite s£26 d£52 (VisitScotland)

GLENELG
Map 22 NG81

Pick of the Pubs

Glenelg Inn 🏠
IV40 8JR ☎ 01599 522273 📠 01599 522283
e-mail: christophermain@glenelg-inn.com
Dir: From Shiel Bridge (A87) take unclassified road to Glenelg
Very much a home from home, this village inn occupies a 200-year-old stable mews and commands stunning views across the Glenelg Bay from its splendid waterside garden. Folk singers and musicians are frequent visitors to the bar where at times a ceilidh atmosphere prevails. The menu offers traditional Scottish fare based on local produce, including mussels, oysters, prawns and wild salmon, white fish, hill-bred lamb, venison and seasonal vegetables. Options at lunchtime range from filled ciabatta or granary rolls to fish pie with cheddar crust, while at dinner you might expect seared red mullet with sweet red pepper on roasted greens or roast loin of pork on steamed curly kale. A choice of vegetarian dishes and home-baked puddings also feature.
OPEN: 12-11 (Bar closed lunchtimes during winter) Closed: End Oct-Etr (ex by arrangement) **BAR MEALS:** L served all week 12.30-2 D served Mon-Sat 6-9.30 **RESTAURANT:** 12.30-2 7.30-9
BREWERY/COMPANY: Free House **FACILITIES:** Children welcome **Garden:** Large garden going down to the sea Dogs allowed

INVERNESS
Map 23 NH64

Snow Goose ♀ NEW
Stoneyfield IV2 7PA
Dir: From the A9, take the Aberdeen/Nairn Road. The snow goose is near the retail park on the first stretch of the A96
Once the coach house for Signeyfield, the 'big hoose', the Snow Goose stands in beautiful gardens just outside Inverness. Built in 1780, it retains many original features, such as open log fires, exposed beams and plenty of nooks and crannies. Typical dishes are gammon steak, chicken, leek and ham pie, beef and ale pie, sea bass, hunter's chicken and hot chicken salad with raspberry vinaigrette. Bass on draught, Budvar in a bottle.
OPEN: 12 -11 (Sun 12-10.30) **RESTAURANT:** L served all week D served all week Av 3 course à la carte £16.70
BREWERY/COMPANY: Vintage Inns 🍺 Tetley Bitter, Cask Bass, Budvar. ♀: 16 **FACILITIES:** **Garden:** Large garden with floral display **NOTES:** Parking 120

KYLESKU
Map 22 NC23

Kylesku Hotel 🏠
IV27 4HW ☎ 01971 502231 📠 01971 502313
e-mail: kyleskuhotel@lycos.co.uk
Dir: 35m N of Ullapool on A838, turn into Kylesku, hotel at end of road at old ferry pier
Ideal for birdwatchers, wildlife enthusiasts, climbers and walkers, this coaching inn is located on the old ferry slipway between Loch Glencoul and Loch Glendhu in the Highlands of Sutherland. Both bar and restaurant menus specialise in locally caught seafood and venison in season. Dishes might include local prawns with Marie-Rose sauce, pan-fried fillets of

continued

Lochinver haddock with lemon butter, or venison casserole cooked in red wine with root vegetables and lardons of bacon.

OPEN: 11-11.30 (Mon-Thu, Sat 10-11.30) (Fri 10-12, Sun 12.30-11) Closed: 1 Nov-28 Feb **BAR MEALS:** L served all week 12-2.30 D served all week 6-9.30 **RESTAURANT:** D served all week 7-8.30 **BREWERY/COMPANY:** Free House 🍺: Caledonian 80/-. **FACILITIES:** Children welcome Garden Dogs allowed **NOTES:** Parking 50 **ROOMS:** 8 bedrooms 6 en suite 1 family rooms s£35 d£60 (VisitScotland)

LYBSTER
Map 23 ND23

The Portland Arms Hotel 🛏
KW3 6BS ☎ 01593 721721 📠 01593 721722
e-mail: info@portlandarms.co.uk
Dir: Beside A9. From Inverness to Wick, hotel on left, 200yds from sign for Lybster

Long a favoured stop-off point between Wick and Thurso, the Portland Arms was built in the 19th century. It's grown in size since then to become a large, well-maintained hotel whose bar and dining areas cater for every mood: dine in the informal Jo's Kitchen, whose Aga sets a relaxed, farmhouse tone; the Bistro Bar; or the more formal Library. Two menus operate in all three areas. From the all day menu choose perhaps local Orkney roll-mop herrings followed by Aga-roasted beef sirloin with Yorkshire pudding, rich gravy and skirlie tomatoes. On the evening dinner menu, are the likes of award-winning haggis filos on a light Drambuie cream or roast loin of Caithness venison on a garlic potato cake with apple and mustard sauce.
OPEN: 7.30-11 Closed: Dec 31-Jan 3 **BAR MEALS:** L served all week 12-3 D served all week 5-9 Av main course £9 **RESTAURANT:** L served all week 11.30-3 D served all week 5-9 Av 3 course à la carte £17.50 **BREWERY/COMPANY:** Free House 🍺: Tennent 70/-. **FACILITIES:** Children welcome Children's licence Food served outside **NOTES:** Parking 20 **ROOMS:** 22 bedrooms 22 en suite 4 family rooms s£50 d£75 (VisitScotland)

NORTH BALLACHULISH
Map 22 NN06

Loch Leven Hotel 🛏
Old Ferry Rd, Onich PH33 6SA
☎ 01855 821236 📠 01855 821550
e-mail: reception@lochlevenhotel.co.uk
Dir: off the main A82 at N of Ballachulish Bridge

Over 350 years old, this was a working farm up to 50 years ago, as well as accommodating travellers from the Ballachulish ferry. On the northern shore of Loch Leven by the original slipway, it is ideally placed for touring the Western Highlands. Local specialities typified by Tobermoray smoked trout, braised Highland lamb shank and chicken stuffed with

haggis underpin a menu of traditional seafood favourites and an imaginative Oriental selection.
OPEN: 11am-midnight (Thur-Sat 11-1am) **BAR MEALS:** L served all week 12-3 D served all week 6-9 Av main course £4.50 **RESTAURANT:** 12-3 6-9 Av 3 course à la carte £16 Av 3 course fixed price £12.50 **BREWERY/COMPANY:** Free House 🍺: Scottish Courage John Smiths, Fountain McEwan 80/-. **FACILITIES:** Children welcome Garden Dogs allowed Water **NOTES:** Parking 50

PLOCKTON
Map 22 NG83

Pick of the Pubs

AA Pub of the Year for Scotland 2004

The Plockton Hotel ★★ 🛏
Harbour St IV52 8TN ☎ 01599 544274 📠 01599 544475
e-mail: sales@plocktonhotel.co.uk
Dir: On A87 to Kyle of Lochalsh turn at Balmacara. Plockton 7m N.

A Scottish hotel whose logo features a palm tree? Well yes, when it stands on the shores of Gulf Stream-warmed Loch Carron. Fans of TV's 'Hamish Macbeth' will recognise it as one of a row of whitewashed Highland cottages overlooking the loch's deep blue waters. Its speciality is seafood. Spare a thought then for those in, say, London who must wait hours for prawns that you could be eating moments after being landed. Or there's the freshest pan-fried herring in oatmeal, monkfish and smoked bacon brochettes, and loch-caught salmon, poached with lime leaves, whole peppercorns and served with a fresh lime and crème fraîche dressing. To backtrack, you could have started with Plockton smokies, haggis and whisky, or Talisker whisky pâté. And there's more: succulent Highland steaks, casserole of Highland venison, slowly cooked with red wine, herbs, juniper berries and redcurrant jelly, or chicken stuffed with Argyll smoked ham and cheese, sun-dried tomato, garlic and basil sauce.
OPEN: 11-11.45 (Sun 12.30-11) **BAR MEALS:** L served all week 12-2.15 D served all week 6-9.15 Av main course £8.50 **RESTAURANT:** L served all week 12-2.15 D served all week 6-9.15 Av 3 course à la carte £22.50 **BREWERY/COMPANY:** Free House 🍺: Caledonian Deuchars IPA. **FACILITIES:** Children welcome Garden: Beer garden, summer house, amazing views Dogs allowed Water in garden **ROOMS:** 15 bedrooms 15 en suite 1 family rooms s£50 d£80

For a list of pubs with AA Inspected
Accommodation Awards
◆ see pages 646-651 ★

continued

Scotland

PLOCKTON continued

Pick of the Pubs

AA Seafood Pub of the Year for Scotland 2004

Plockton Inn & Seafood Restaurant
Innes St IV52 8TW ☎ 01599 544222 ▤ 01599 544487
e-mail: stay@plocktoninn.co.uk
Dir: On A87 to Kyle of Lochalsh turn at Balmacara. Plockton 7m N

This attractive, stone-built free house stands just 50 metres from the sea, at the heart of the picturesque fishing village that formed the setting for the 'Hamish Macbeth' TV series. Formerly a church manse, the Plockton Inn is now run by a local family. The atmosphere is relaxed and friendly, with winter fires in both bars, and the prettily decorated en suite bedrooms offering well-equipped comfort. Local produce takes pride of place on the menu, and locally caught fish and shellfish are prepared in the family's purpose-built smokehouse behind the hotel. Lunchtime sees a choice of freshly-made sandwiches, home-made soups and hot snacks ranging from jacket potatoes or mussels in white wine to local specialities like seafood platter from the smokery, haggis with clapshot, or Plockton prawns. In the evening the choice increases to take in skate wing and black butter, queen scallops with bacon, garlic and cream, and Moroccan lamb casserole.
OPEN: 11-1am (Sun 12.30-11pm) **BAR MEALS:** L served all week 12-2.30 D served all week 5.30-9.30 Av main course £9.50 **RESTAURANT:** L served all week 12-2.30 D served all week 5.30-9.30 Av 3 course à la carte £14
BREWERY/COMPANY: Free House ◀: Greene King Abbot Ale & Old Speckled Hen, Fuller's London Pride, Isle Of Skye Blaven, Caledonian 80/-. **FACILITIES:** Children welcome Children's licence Garden: sloping space at back of inn, grass, trees Dogs allowed **NOTES:** Parking 6 **ROOMS:** 7 bedrooms 6 en suite 2 family rooms s£30 d£55 (VisitScotland)

SHIELDAIG   Map 22 NG85

Pick of the Pubs

Shieldaig Bar ★ ◉ ⓣ ♀
IV54 8XN ☎ 01520 755251 ▤ 01520 755321
e-mail: tighaneileanhotel@shieldaig.fsnet.co.uk
Dir: 5m S of Torridon off A896 on to village road signposted Shieldaig, bar on Loch front
Located right on the loch front in a charming fishing village, this popular bar provides a friendly welcome and stunning views across Loch Torridon to the sea beyond. Visitors and locals mix happily together, and the bar is

often alive with the sound of local musicians, including the owner Chris Field who can play a pretty exotic selection of instruments. This is a popular rendezvous location throughout the day, so in addition to a full range of alcoholic beverages, visitors can order real espresso, coffee, tea and home-baked cakes whilst perusing a ready supply of newspapers and magazines. The pub has a fine reputation for its food: choose from bar snacks (scampi and chips, sandwiches, soup, haggis) or daily-changing specials such as steak and ale pie, Tuscan-style leek tart, or fresh crab bisque with home-made bread. It's the sort of place you'll want to linger, so take note that the Fields also own the neighbouring Tigh an Eilean hotel.

OPEN: 11-11 (Sun 12.30-10) Closed: Dec 25 & Jan 1
BAR MEALS: L served all week 12-2.30 D served all week 6-8.30 Av main course £6.50 **RESTAURANT:** D served all week 7-8.30 Av 3 course fixed price £32 **BREWERY/COMPANY:** Free House ◀: Black Isle Ales, Tenants Superior Ale. ♀: 8
FACILITIES: Children welcome Children's licence Open courtyard on Lochside with umbrellas Dogs allowed In the garden only. Water provided **ROOMS:** 11 bedrooms 11 en suite 1 family rooms s£52.50 d£115

See Pub Walk on page 587

ULLAPOOL   Map 22 NH19

The Argyll Hotel

Argyll St IV26 2UB ☎ 01854 612422 ▤ 01854 612522
e-mail: stay@theargyll.com
Traditional family-run hotel just a short stroll from the shores of Loch Broom. Timeless public bar and comfortable main bar, both with open fires and a good choice of malt whiskies to choose from. West Coast scallops and halibut, chicken supreme, venison medallions, and haggis, neeps and tatties feature on the varied menus.
OPEN: 11-11 (Sun 12-11) **BAR MEALS:** L served all week 12-2.30 D served all week 5.30-9 Av main course £7.50 **RESTAURANT:** D served all week 5.30-9 Av 3 course à la carte £13.50 **BREWERY/COMPANY:** Free House ◀: Calders 70/-, Scottish Guest ales. **FACILITIES:** Children welcome Dogs allowed **NOTES:** Parking 20

Pick of the Pubs

The Ceilidh Place

14 West Argyle St IV26 2TY
☎ 01854 612103 ▤ 01854 612886
e-mail: reception@ceilidh.demon.co.uk
Dir: On entering Ullapool, along Shore St, pass pier and take 1st R. Hotel is straight ahead at top of hill
An Ullapool institution for more than 30 years, the Ceilidh Place is set back from the port from where the ferry

continued

continued

crosses to Lewis. It is a unique venue comprising an all-day bar, informal dining area, bookshop and a comprehensive display of art for visitors to enjoy at their leisure, all under one roof. Expect a friendly welcome and range of real ales and malt whiskies. Locally-landed fish is always available in dishes like fillet of cod on garlic mash and rocket purée, or monkfish wrapped in bacon with sauerkraut and chorizo sausage. Regular favourites from the menu are local haddock, lamb casserole with Heather Ale, and a Mediterranean vegetable pie.

OPEN: 11-11 (Sun 12.30-11) Closed: 2nd Wk in Jan for 2 Wks
BAR MEALS: L served all week 12-6 6.30-9.30
RESTAURANT: D served all week 7-9.30
BREWERY/COMPANY: Free House ◖: Belhaven Best, Stella Artois. **FACILITIES:** Garden: Dogs allowed Garden only, water available on terrace **NOTES:** Parking 20

Morefield Hotel & Mariners Restaurant
North Rd IV26 2TQ ☎ 01854 612161 ▤ 01854 612171
Dir: On outskirts of town
Popular bar and seafood restaurant, also known for its large selection of malt whiskies and ports. Possible dishes include lobster royale, seafood thermidor, or Achiltibuie salmon and roast scallop terrine. If you're not feeling fishy try Aberdeen Angus prime sirloin, pork fillet Stilton, or something from the vegetarian menu.
OPEN: 11-2.30 5-11 (11-11 summer) **BAR MEALS:** L served all week 12-2 D served all week 5.30-9.30 Av main course £9
RESTAURANT: D served all week 6.30-9.30 Av 3 course à la carte £20 **BREWERY/COMPANY:** Free House ◖: Belhaven, Tennent, 2 Guest ales. **FACILITIES:** Children welcome Small beer garden Dogs allowed **NOTES:** Parking 50

MIDLOTHIAN

PENICUIK   Map 21 NT25

The Howgate Restaurant
Howgate EH26 8PY ☎ 01968 670000 ▤ 01968 670000
e-mail: Peter@howgate.f9.co.uk
Dir: On A6094, 3m SE of Penicuik
This restaurant and bistro has been a dairy, cattle shed, racehorse stable, and the original home of the Howgate cheeses it serves today. The atmosphere is warm and welcoming, with winter log fires in the bistro. The menu lists Scottish steaks, salmon with roasted red pepper and basil crust, smoked chicken Caesar salad with herb croûtons, and traditional Angus beef and mushroom pie with hand-cut chips. Long wine list, with plenty of by-the-glass options.

OPEN: 12-2.30 6-11 Closed: Dec 25-26, 1-2 Jan **BAR MEALS:** L served all week 12-2.30 D served all week 6-9.30 Av main course £9
RESTAURANT: L served all week 12-2.30 D served all week 6-9.30 Av 3 course à la carte £25 **BREWERY/COMPANY:** Free House ◖: Belhaven Best, Hoegaarden, Wheat Biere. ♀: 12
FACILITIES: Children welcome Garden: Patio and tables adjacent to Bistro **NOTES:** Parking 45

MORAY

FOCHABERS   Map 23 NJ35

Gordon Arms Hotel
80 High St IV32 7DH ☎ 01343 820508 ▤ 01343 820300
e-mail: info@gordonarmshotel.com
Former coaching inn dating back over 200 years and situated close to the River Spey. Very popular with salmon fishers, golfers and walkers and within easy reach of Speyside's whisky distilleries. The hotel's public rooms have been carefully refurbished, and it's an ideal stopover while discovering this scenic corner of Scotland. Tasty lunches and suppers are served in the bar, while the restaurant menus make good use of local seafood, game and poultry.
OPEN: 11-3 5-11 (Sun 12-3, 6-10.30) **BAR MEALS:** L served all week 12-2 D served all week 5-7 **RESTAURANT:** L served all week 12-2 D served all week 7-9 **BREWERY/COMPANY:** Free House ◖: Caledonian Deuchars IPA, Scottish Courage John Smith's Smooth, Marstons Pedigree. **FACILITIES:** Children welcome Children's licence Dogs allowed **NOTES:** Parking 40

PERTH & KINROSS

ABERFELDY   Map 23 NN84

Ailean Chraggan Hotel
Weem PH15 2LD ☎ 01887 820346 ▤ 01887 829009
Dir: A9 N to junct at Ballinluig then A827 onto Aberfeldy, R onto B846
A small, friendly hotel set in two acres of grounds, including a large garden and two terraces with views over the River Tay to the hills beyond. Quality local produce is a feature of the menus, notably salmon from the Tay, seafood, beef, and game in season. Daily specials include mussels marinière with garlic butter, Loch Etive prawn platter, and baked whole brill with shrimp and white wine sauce.
OPEN: 12-2 6.30-9.30 (8.30 in winter) Closed: 25-26 Dec, 1-2 Jan
BAR MEALS: L served all week 12-2 D served all week 6.30-9.30
RESTAURANT: L served all week 12-2 D served all week 6.30-9.30
BREWERY/COMPANY: Free House **FACILITIES:** Children welcome Garden: Patio's, lawn Dogs allowed **NOTES:** Parking 40
ROOMS: 5 bedrooms 5 en suite s£37.50 d£75 (VisitScotland)

ALMONDBANK   Map 21 NO02

Almondbank Inn
31 Main St PH1 3NJ ☎ 01738 583242 ▤ 01738 582471
Dir: From Perth take A85 towards Crieff. 3m to Almondbank
A family-run pub a little way out of Perth. From its neat rear garden the views are wonderful, including of the River Almond whose waters once powered the local textile industry, but which is now famous for its fishing. As well as snacks and high teas, there's a dinner menu featuring steaks, chicken, fish, pastas and Mexican dishes, and specials such as duck with wild berries. Owner Tommy Campbell, a retired Scottish

continued

continued

Scotland

ALMONDBANK continued

football manager, has decorated his bar with football strips bearing famous players' signatures.
OPEN: 11-3 5-11 (Thu-Sun 11-11.30) (Fri-Sat 11-12.30) Closed: Dec, Jan **BAR MEALS:** L served all week 12-2 D served Wed-Sun 5-10 Av main course £3 **RESTAURANT:** L served all week 12-2.30 D served Wed-Sun 5-10 Av 3 course à la carte £12
BREWERY/COMPANY: Free House ◀: 70/-, White Thistle, Stella Artois. **FACILITIES:** Children welcome Children's licence Garden: 6 Tables Water Fountain Dogs allowed Water, Biscuits

---

BURRELTON   Map 21 NO23

The Burrelton Park Inn
High St PH13 9NX ☎ 01828 670206 ▥ 01828 670676
Ideally situated for touring the highlands, this long roadside inn is characterised by its typical Scottish vernacular style. Spacious lounge bar and conservatory offering steamed mussels, braised lambs' liver and farmhouse mixed grill, and a well-appointed restaurant featuring stuffed supreme of chicken and venison fillet - among other more elaborate dishes. Fresh catch of the day and special high teas served.
OPEN: 12-2.30 5-11 (Sat-Sun 12-11) **BAR MEALS:** L served all week 12-8.30 D served all week 12-8.30 **RESTAURANT:** L served all week 12-8.30 D served all week 12-8.30
BREWERY/COMPANY: Free House ◀: Changing Guest ales Tennents "YO", Velvet and Lager, Guinness, Bellhaven Best. **FACILITIES:** Children welcome Dogs allowed **NOTES:** Parking 30

GLENDEVON   Map 21 NN90

Pick of the Pubs

Tormaukin Hotel 🐾 ♀
FK14 7JY ☎ 01259 781252 ▥ 01259 781526
e-mail: enquiries@tormaukin.co.uk
Dir: On A823 between M90 & A9
Surrounded by the Ochil Hills, this 18th-century former drovers' inn is an idyllic setting in the middle of the 'Hidden Glen', yet hill walks, loch and river fishing and golf courses are all within easy reach. Sympathetic refurbishment has retained many original features, including stone walls, exposed beams and natural timbers. Bar lunches and suppers, served in front of blazing log fires in the cosy lounge and bars, cover a range of snacks, children's choices and daily blackboard specials. Dishes could include fillet steak with sauté mushrooms and onions or pork and apple sausages with lamb loin. The main menu has an equally traditional appeal: expect the likes of pan-seared fillet of Scottish salmon on mash, topped with spring onion crackling or breast of cornfed chicken served on wild mushroom risotto with brandy cream sauce. Round with desserts such as iced Drambuie soufflé with marmalade sauce or peach Pavlova served on a pear coulis.
OPEN: 11-11 (Sun 12-11) Closed: 25 Dec **BAR MEALS:** L served all week 12-2.15 D served all week 5.30-9.30 **RESTAURANT:** D served all week 6.30-9.30
BREWERY/COMPANY: Free House ◀: Harviestoun Brooker's Bitter & Twisted, Timothy Taylor Landlord. ♀: 12
FACILITIES: Children welcome Garden: Patio area food served outside **NOTES:** Parking 50

GLENFARG   Map 21 NO11

The Bein Inn 🐾 ♀
PH2 9PY ☎ 01577 830216 ▥ 01577 830211
e-mail: enquiries@beininn.com

A real treat awaits classical rock, folk or blues fans at Scotland's Music Pub of the Year. Many famous musicians have performed in its lively Bistro Bar, and the memorabilia collection in the Basement Bar rivals anything to be seen in a Hard Rock Café. House specialities include noisettes of Scottish lamb, poached halibut steak, and vegetables Bonnie Prince Charlie, in which they are cooked in Drambuie and mushroom sauce, and served with rice and noodles.
OPEN: 11-2.30 5-11 **BAR MEALS:** L served all week 12-2 D served all week 5-9 **RESTAURANT:** L served all week 12-2 D served all week 7-9 **BREWERY/COMPANY:** Free House ◀: Belhaven Best. **FACILITIES:** Dogs allowed **NOTES:** Parking 30

KILLIECRANKIE   Map 23 NN96

Pick of the Pubs

Killiecrankie House Hotel ★★ 🍴🍴 🐾 ♀
PH16 5LG ☎ 01796 473220 ▥ 01796 472451
e-mail: enquiries@killiecrankiehotel.co.uk
Dir: Turn off A9 at Killiecrankie. Hotel 3m N on B8079 on R
A sprawling, Scottish country-house hotel with a welcoming bar and restaurant renowned for good food. Genuine hospitality and a high level of personal attention are the other hallmarks of this charming whitewashed building, set in mature gardens at the northern end of the National Trust's Killiecrankie Pass. The cosy well-stocked bar with an adjacent conservatory for informal eating features an excellent choice of both light and more filling dishes: broccoli, Brie and walnut crumble, fresh tagliatelle with salmon, mussels and prawns in a herb and cream sauce, and deep-fried haddock sit alongside various interesting salads, and a coronation chicken open sandwich. The sweet-toothed should enjoy chocolate fudge brownie with vanilla ice cream. An elegant dining room is a more special location for fixed-price dinners that allow similarly fine ingredients to speak for themselves. Bright airy bedrooms are furnished in pine and well equipped with a wide range of amenities.
OPEN: 12-2.30 6-11 Closed: All Jan, Mon-Tue in Feb, Mar, Nov & Dec **BAR MEALS:** L served all week 12.30-2 D served all week 6.30-8 Av main course £8.95 **RESTAURANT:** L served none D served all week 7-8.30 Av 4 course fixed price £33
BREWERY/COMPANY: Free House ◀: Calders Cream Ale. ♀: 8
FACILITIES: Children welcome Children's licence Garden: 1 acre of lawns, formal/vegetable garden Dogs allowed **NOTES:** Parking 20 **ROOMS:** 10 bedrooms 10 en suite 2 family rooms s£79 d£158

KINNESSWOOD
Map 21 NO10

Pick of the Pubs

Lomond Country Inn ★★ ◉ 🐾 ♀
KY13 9HN ☎ 01592 840253 📠 01592 840693
e-mail: enquiries@lomondcountryinn.com
Dir: M90 J5, follow signs for Glenrothes then Scotlandwell,
Kinnesswood next village

A small, privately owned hotel on the slopes of the
Lomond Hills that has been entertaining guests for more
than 100 years. It is the only hostelry in the area with
uninterrupted views over Loch Leven to the island on
which Mary Queen of Scots was imprisoned. All the en
suite bedrooms are furnished to a high standard, whilst
cosy public areas offer log fires, a friendly atmosphere,
real ales and a fine collection of single malts. Bar meals
make superb use of local produce such as Pitween
haddock, game casserole or fillet of Tay salmon with herb
and prawn butter. If you want to make the most of the
loch views, choose the charming restaurant, a relaxing
room freshly decorated in country house style. The menu
incorporates dishes available in the bar alongside daily-
changing specials such as pan-seared breast of pheasant
with onion marmalade and black pudding.
OPEN: 11-11 (Fri-Sat 11-12.45, Sun 12.30-11) Closed: Dec 25
BAR MEALS: L served all week 12.30-2 D served all week 6-9
Av main course £8 **RESTAURANT:** L served all week 12-2.30 D
served all week 6-9.30 Av 3 course à la carte £20
BREWERY/COMPANY: Free House 🍺: Deuchers IPA, Calders
Cream, Tetleys, Orkney Dark Island. **FACILITIES:** Children
welcome Garden: Food served outside. Lawn & landscaping
Dogs allowed Kennels **NOTES:** Parking 50 **ROOMS:** 10
bedrooms 10 en suite s£44 d£68

KINROSS
Map 21 NO10

The Muirs Inn Kinross ♦♦♦ 🐾
49 Muirs KY13 8AU ☎ 01577 862270 📠 01577 862270
e-mail: themuirsinn@aol.com
Dir: from M90 J6 take A922 to T-junction. Inn diagonally opposite on R
Originally a small farmhouse where the local blacksmith
attended to travellers' horses and carriages, this listed inn
takes its name from the old Scottish word for moorland. The
Mash Tun public bar features rare, hand-etched ornamental
glass and mirrors, as well as a custom-built gantry dating back
to 1909. There is a good selection of beers and malt whiskies
to accompany starters such as smoked haddock chowder and
local black pudding, or main dishes of Cajun chicken breast,
lamb cutlets or pan-seared chicken breast stuffed with duck
parfait.

OPEN: 12-11 **BAR MEALS:** L served all week 12-2.30 D served all
week 5-9 Av main course £7.95 **RESTAURANT:** L served all week 12-
2 D served all week 5-9.30 **BREWERY/COMPANY:** Free House
🍺: Belhaven 80/-, Orkney Dark Island. **FACILITIES:** Children
welcome Garden: Beer garden Dogs allowed Water
NOTES: Parking 8 **ROOMS:** 5 bedrooms 5 en suite 1 family rooms
s£45 d£35

PITLOCHRY
Map 23 NN95

Pick of the Pubs

Moulin Hotel ★★ ♀
11-13 Kirkmichael Rd, Moulin PH16 5EW
☎ 01796 472196 📠 01796 474098
e-mail: hotel@moulin.u-net.com
Dir: From A9 at Pitlochry take A923. Moulin 0.75m

Half a century before the Jacobite rebellion of 1745, the
Moulin Hotel was established at the foot of 2,757ft Ben
Vrackie, on the old drove road from Dunkeld to Kingussie.
The modern road runs through nearby Pitlochry, leaving
Moulin as an ideal base for walking and touring. The
large, white-painted pub with its summer courtyard
garden is popular with tourists and locals alike, while in
winter, two blazing log fires set the scene for a game of
cards, dominoes or bar billiards. Well-kept real ales come
from the pub's own micro-brewery, and there's plenty of
Gaelic fare on the big all-day menu. Start with potted
hough and oatcakes, or Skye mussels with garlic, before
moving on to venison Braveheart, haggis and neeps, or a
game casserole McDuff. There's haddock or salmon too,
and vegetarians can expect sautéed mushroom pancakes,
stuffed peppers, and vegetable goulash. Comfortable
bedrooms.
OPEN: 12-11 (Fri-Sat 12-11.45) **BAR MEALS:** L served all
week 12-9.30 D served all week Av main course £6.95
RESTAURANT: D served all week 6-9
BREWERY/COMPANY: Free House 🍺: Moulin Braveheart,
Old Remedial, Ale of Atholl & Moulin Light.
FACILITIES: Children welcome Garden Dogs allowed
NOTES: Parking 40 **ROOMS:** 15 bedrooms 15 en suite s£40
d£50

> **Stars or Diamonds after the ROOMS
> information at the end of an entry denotes
> accommodation that has been inspected
> by an organisation other than the AA,
> eg the RAC, VisitBritain, VisitScotland or WTB.**

continued

Scotland

Scotland

PITLOCHRY continued

The Old Mill Inn 🛏 ♀
Mill Ln PH16 5BH ☎ 01796 474020
e-mail: r@old-mill-inn.com
Dir: In the centre of Pitlochry, along Mill Lane. Behind the post office.

Set at the gateway to the Highlands, this converted old mill still boasts a working water wheel, now with a patio overlooking it. Visitors are assured of a good choice of real ales, malts and wine by the glass to accompany an eclectic cuisine: smoked haddock chowder, Stornaway black pudding, steamed mussels, salmon stirfry, plus burgers, bacon and Brie ciabatta, and smoked salmon bagel.
OPEN: 10-11 **BAR MEALS:** L served all week 10-10 D served all week Av main course £7.95 **RESTAURANT:** L served all week 10-10 D served all week Av 3 course à la carte £15
BREWERY/COMPANY: Free House 🍺: Carlsberg-Tetley Tetley Bitter, Orkney Dark Island Kettle Ale. **FACILITIES:** Children welcome Garden: Food served outside **NOTES:** Parking 10

POWMILL   Map 21 NT09

Gartwhinzean Hotel
FK14 7NW ☎ 01577 840595 ▨ 01577 840779
Dir: A977 to Kincardine Bridge road, for approx 7m to the vilage of Powmill, hotel at the end of village
Located between two of Scotland's finest cities, Edinburgh and Perth, and handy for exploring the nearby Ochil and Cleish Hills, this attractive hotel overlooks Perthshire's picturesque countryside. A large selection of malt whiskies and a cosy open fire add to the attractions. Traditional steak pie, lightly-grilled fillet of salmon, and noisettes of lamb feature among the dishes on the interesting, regularly changing menu.
OPEN: 11-11 (Sun 12.30-10.30) **BAR MEALS:** L served all week 12-1.45 D served all week 5-8.45 Av main course £8 **RESTAURANT:** L served all week 12-1.45 D served all week 5-8.45 Av 3 course à la carte £20 Av 3 course fixed price £17.50 **BREWERY/COMPANY:** Free House 🍺: Tetley Smoothflow, 70/-. **FACILITIES:** Children welcome Garden: Food served outside Dogs allowed **NOTES:** Parking 100 **ROOMS:** 23 bedrooms 23 en suite s£50 d£70 (VisitScotland)

RENFREWSHIRE

HOUSTON   Map 20 NS46

Fox & Hounds 🛏 ♀
South St PA6 7EN ☎ 01505 612448 612991 ▨ 01505 614133
e-mail: jonathan@foxandhoundshouston.co.uk
Dir: M8 - Glasgow Airport. A737- Houston
Regulars at this popular, well-kept 18th-century village inn have included ex-Rangers striker Ally McCoist, as well as

actors Richard Wilson and Robert Carlyle. The extensive bar menu lists mussel, onion and white wine stew, chargrilled loin of fresh tuna, home-made aubergine bake, and slow-cooked barbecued pork ribs. The weekly specials might well include a 'big' T-bone steak, or baked seafood with fresh herbs, wine and garlic. Beers are from the award-winning, on-site Houston Brewing Company.
OPEN: 11-12 (11-1am Fri-Sat, 12.30-12 Sun) **BAR MEALS:** L served all week 12-2.30 D served all week 5.30-10 Av main course £7.50 **RESTAURANT:** L served all week 12-2.30 D served all week 5.30-10 Av 3 course à la carte £20 **BREWERY/COMPANY:** Free House 🍺: St Peters Well, Killelan, Barochan, Texas & Jack Frost. ♀: 10 **FACILITIES:** Children welcome Children's licence Dogs allowed Water **NOTES:** Parking 40

SCOTTISH BORDERS

EDDLESTON   Map 21 NT24

Horse Shoe Inn
EH45 8QP ☎ 01721 730225 ▨ 01721 730268
e-mail: horseshoe@ladon.co.uk
Dir: On A703 S of Edinburgh. From M74 to Biggar, then A72 to Peebles & A703 N to Eddleston
In glorious Borders country just the Edinburgh side of historic Peebles, this former village smiddy (blacksmith's) stood on the old coach road south. This was not today's A703, which is only 100 years old, but one that ran where the patio now stands. A short but impressive menu offers roast rump of lamb with mint apple compôte, warm salad of wild mushrooms with artichokes, sundried tomatoes and red pesto dressing, and chargrilled pork medallions with black pudding mousseline.
OPEN: 11-3 5.30-12 **BAR MEALS:** L served Tues-Sun 12-2 D served Tues-Sat 6-9 Av main course £7.95 **RESTAURANT:** L served Tues-Sun 12-2 D served Tues-Sun 6-9 Av 3 course à la carte £24.95 **BREWERY/COMPANY:** Free House 🍺: McEwans 70/-, Scottish Courage John Smith's, Caledonian 80/-. **FACILITIES:** Children welcome Children's licence Garden **NOTES:** Parking 35

ETTRICK   Map 21 NT21

Tushielaw Inn 🛏
TD7 5HT ☎ 01750 62205 ▨ 01750 62205
e-mail: Gordon.Harrison@Virgin.net
Dir: At junction of B709 & B711(W of Hawick)
An 18th-century former coaching inn and drovers' halt on the banks of Ettrick Water, and surrounded by the Border hills. Residents can enjoy free trout fishing on Clearburn, and salmon fishing permits are available. The inn appeals to walkers and cyclists with its welcoming open fire and wholesome meals, including deep-fried lamb samosas, butterfly chicken breast in a lemon and tarragon sauce, and mushroom and nut fettuccini, with hot chocolate fudge cake to finish.
OPEN: 12-2.30 6-11 (Closed Mon-Wed from Nov-Mar) Closed: 25 Dec, 1 Jan **BAR MEALS:** L served Fri-Mon (everyday from Easter-Nov) 12-2 D served all week 7-9 Av main course £7.50 **RESTAURANT:** L served all week 12-2 D served all week 7-9 Av 3 course à la carte £14 **BREWERY/COMPANY:** Free House **FACILITIES:** Children welcome Garden: Patio with picnic tables Dogs allowed **NOTES:** Parking 8 **ROOMS:** 3 bedrooms 3 en suite 3 family rooms s£30 d£48 (VisitScotland)

continued

GALASHIELS
Map 21 NT43

Abbotsford Arms ★★ 🍴
63 Stirling St TD1 1BY ☎ 01896 752517 📠 01896 750744
Dir: *Turn off A7 down Ladhope Vale, turn L opposite the Bus Station*
Handy for salmon fishing in the nearby Tweed and visiting
Melrose Abbey, this family-run, stone-built 19th-century
coaching inn offers comfortable accommodation and
traditional bar food. The lunchtime choice runs from filled
croissants, salads and baked potatoes to chicken curry and
sirloin steak, bolstered in the evening by roast lamb shank,
duck and orange sausages, and quails in cranberry and port.
A function room holds up to 150, and there are plenty of good
local golf courses.
OPEN: 11.30-11 **BAR MEALS:** L served all week 2-6 D served all
week 6-9 Av main course £4.50 **RESTAURANT:** L served all week
12-6 D served all week 6-9 Av 3 course à la carte £14
BREWERY/COMPANY: 🍺: Scottish courage John Smith's, Miller,
McEwans 70, K1664. **FACILITIES:** Children welcome Garden: Paved
area with grass **NOTES:** Parking 10 **ROOMS:** 14 bedrooms 14 en
suite

Kingsknowles ★★★ 🍴
1 Selkirk Rd TD1 3HY ☎ 01896 758375 📠 01896 750377
e-mail: enquiries@kingsknowles.co.uk
Dir: *Off A7 at Galashiels/Selkirk rdbt*

Set in over three acres of grounds on the banks of the famous
River Tweed, a splendid Victorian baronial mansion with lovely
views of Eildon Hills and Abbotsford House. Interesting for
being Sir Walter Scott's ancestral home. Only fresh local
produce is used in typical dishes like sea bream, vegetarian
haggis in batter, scallops, shish kebab, shank of lamb, braised
oxtails, and smoked salmon. Large selection of malts.
OPEN: 12-12 **BAR MEALS:** L served all week 11.45-2 D served all
week 5.45-9.30 Av main course £7.50 **RESTAURANT:** L served all
week 11.45-2 D served all week 5.45-9.30 Av 5 course fixed price
£19.95 **BREWERY/COMPANY:** Free House 🍺: McEwans 80/-,
Scottish Courage John Smith's. **FACILITIES:** Children welcome
Garden: 3.5 acres, lawn, rockery Dogs allowed **NOTES:** Parking 60
ROOMS: 11 bedrooms 11 en suite 3 family rooms s£54 d£80

INNERLEITHEN
Map 21 NT33

Traquair Arms Hotel ◆◆◆ 🍴
Traquair Rd EH44 6PD ☎ 01896 830229
e-mail: traquair.arms@scotborders.com
Dir: *6m E of Peebles on A72. Hotel 100metres from junc with B709*
This traditional stone-built inn is in a village setting close to
the River Tweed, surrounded by lovely Borders countryside
and offering en suite bedrooms, a dining room and cosy bar.
Real ales include Traquair Ale from nearby Traquair House,
and the food has a distinctive Scottish flavour with dishes of

Finnan savoury, salmon with ginger and coriander, and fillet
of beef Traquair. Also a selection of omelettes, salads, and
baked potatoes is available.
OPEN: 11-12 (Sun 12-12) Closed: 25& 26 Dec, 1-3 Jan
BAR MEALS: L served all week 12-9 D served all week Av main
course £6.50 **RESTAURANT:** L served all week D served all week
12-9 Av 3 course à la carte £18 Av 4 course fixed price £20
BREWERY/COMPANY: Free House 🍺: Traquair Bear, Broughton
Greenmantle, plus seasonal guest. **FACILITIES:** Children welcome
Garden Dogs allowed **NOTES:** Parking 75 **ROOMS:** 15 bedrooms
15 en suite s£45 d£58

LAUDER
Map 21 NT54

Lauderdale Hotel ★★
1 Edinburgh Rd TD2 6TW ☎ 01578 722231 📠 01578 718642
e-mail: Enquiries@lauderdale-hotel.co.uk
Dir: *on the main A68 25m S of Edinburgh*
This imposing Edwardian building with a cheerful lounge bar
stands in extensive and newly-landscaped grounds, which are
planted with young shrubs and lots of spring-flowering bulbs.
The menu offers a good range of generously served meals in
the bar or restaurant, including a vegetarian menu. Steak and
onion pie, chicken Maryland and pork medallions with red
onion marmalade go down well, and there are additional
options from the regularly-changing specials board.
OPEN: 11-12 **BAR MEALS:** L served all week 12-3 D served all
week 5-9 Av main course £7.50 **RESTAURANT:** L served all week 12-
3 D served all week Av 3 course à la carte £15
BREWERY/COMPANY: Free House 🍺: Deuchars IPA.
FACILITIES: Children welcome Children's licence Garden:
Landscaped garden with shrubs **NOTES:** Parking 50 **ROOMS:** 10
bedrooms 10 en suite 1 family rooms s£42 d£70

MELROSE
Map 21 NT53

Pick of the Pubs

Burts Hotel ★★★ 🍴🍴 ♀
Market Square TD6 9PL ☎ 01896 822285 📠 01896 822870
e-mail: burtshotel@aol.com
Dir: *A6091, 2m from A68 3m South of Earlston*

A hunting and shooting theme extends through the busy
bars and restaurant of this family-run hotel. Built for a
local dignitary in 1722, Burts stands on the picturesque
market square of this historic Borders town, and has
twenty comfortably-furnished en suite bedrooms. Large
parasols and a pergola shade the peaceful hotel garden,
with its roses, clematis and lavender. In winter, there are
welcoming log fires in the elegantly decorated bistro and
cheerful lounge bar; here, you'll find cask-conditioned
ales, and a fine selection of over 80 malt whiskies. Lunch

continued

continued

MELROSE continued

and bar suppers change to reflect the availability of local produce, whilst the fixed-price restaurant lunch and dinner menus offer similar quality ingredients in more elaborate guises. Expect smoked salmon and haddock fishcakes; Borders lamb shank on garlic and rosemary mash; or seared John Dory fillets with stuffed pepper and beurre blanc.
OPEN: 11-2.30 5-11 **BAR MEALS:** L served all week 12-2 D served all week 6-9.30 Av main course £7 **RESTAURANT:** L served all week 12-2 D served all week 7-9 Av 3 course fixed price £25.75 **BREWERY/COMPANY:** Free House ◀: Caledonian 80/-, Deuchars IPA, Timothy Taylor Ladlord, Fullers London Pride. ♀: 6 **FACILITIES:** Children's licence Garden: Terrace and grass furnished Dogs allowed **NOTES:** Parking 40 **ROOMS:** 20 bedrooms 20 en suite 2 family rooms s£54 d£96 no children overnight

ST BOSWELLS   Map 21 NT53

Buccleuch Arms Hotel ★★
The Green TD6 0EW ☎ 01835 822243 🖹 01835 823965
e-mail: bucchotel@aol.com
Dir: On A68, 8m N of Jedburgh
Perfectly placed at the heart of the Scottish Borders, this 16th-century inn offers a country welcome in its spacious and comfortable modern bar. The varied supper menu includes Whitby scampi tails, steak and ale pie, sausage and mash, and roast saddle of lamb with honey mustard and thyme sauce. The bar lunch menu offers toasted ciabatta steak sandwich, penne pasta, deep-fried haddock fillet, and baguettes with salad. Afternoon tea, high tea and a snack menu are also available.
OPEN: 7.30-11 Closed: 25 Dec **BAR MEALS:** L served all week 12-2 D served all week 6-9 Av main course £8 **RESTAURANT:** L served all week 12-2 D served all week 6-9 **BREWERY/COMPANY:** Free House ◀: Calders70/-,80/- & Calders Cream Ale, Broughton Greenmantle Ale. **FACILITIES:** Children welcome Garden: Quiet, Spacious & Peaceful garden Dogs allowed £5.00 Supplement per night **NOTES:** Parking 80 **ROOMS:** 19 bedrooms 19 en suite 1 family rooms s£40 d£75

SWINTON   Map 21 NT84

Pick of the Pubs

Wheatsheaf Hotel 🏠 ◉◉ 🐾 ♀
Main St TD11 3JJ ☎ 01890 860257 🖹 01890 860688
e-mail: reception@wheatsheaf-swinton.co.uk
Dir: 6m N of Duns on A6112
Husband and wife team Alan and Judy Reid have owned and run the Wheatsheaf for 17 years. Alan, the chef, is passionate about his use of local produce and has gained many accolades for his food. Locally-reared meats, salmon from the Tweed, game from the Borders and seafood from the Berwickshire coast are used in classic combinations - grilled Eyemouth langoustines in garlic and parsley butter, fillet of salmon with toasted oatmeal crust, or medallion of Scotch beef fillet served with breast of wood pigeon and black pudding on a garlic and thyme scented sauce. Light lunches and snacks, washed down with fine wines or the best Scottish ale, are no less pivotal to their success. The hotel has been developed over recent years to allow more guests to stay over, and to accommodate shooting, fishing and golfing parties. The Reids have also added the delightful Fisherman's Snug.
OPEN: 11-2.30 6-11 (Closed Sun eve in winter)) Closed: Last 2 wks Jan, 1 Wk July **BAR MEALS:** L served Tue-Sun 11.45-2.15 D

served Tue-Sat 6.30-9.30 Av main course £10.50 **RESTAURANT:** L served Tue-Sun 11.45-2.15 D served Tue-Sat 6-9.30 Av 3 course à la carte £20.50 **BREWERY/COMPANY:** Free House ◀: Caledonian 80/- & Deuchers IPA, Broughton Greenmantle Ale. ♀: 8 **FACILITIES:** Children welcome Children's licence Garden: Patio & grass area Dogs allowed **NOTES:** Parking 8 **ROOMS:** 8 bedrooms 8 en suite s£58 d£90

TIBBIE SHIELS INN   Map 21 NT22

Pick of the Pubs

Tibbie Shiels Inn ♦♦♦
St Mary's Loch TD7 5LH ☎ 01750 42231 🖹 01750 42302
Dir: From Moffat take A708. Inn is 14m on R
Set by the scenic Southern Upland Way on the isthmus between St Mary's Loch and Loch of the Lowes, the inn is named after the fine lady who first opened it in 1826 and prospered there for fully 50 years. During her time the inn was expanded from a small cottage to a hostelry capable of sleeping around 35 people, many of them on the floor! Famous visitors frequented the place, amongst them James Hogg, Walter Scott and Thomas Carlyle. Its spirit remains unchanged: low-ceilinged, cosy bars full of character and old-world charm are frequented by ramblers and rodsmen - residents fish free of charge. Menus reflect the seasons, with winter game and fresh fish, as well as more exotic dishes. A typical menu includes Holy Mole chilli rice, cashew nut loaf with tomato and herb salad, Tibbies mixed grill, and local Yarrow trout with chips or peas. The comfortable bedrooms are all en suite.
OPEN: 11-11 (Sun 12.30-11) **BAR MEALS:** L served all week 12.30-8.15 D served all week 12.30-8.15 **RESTAURANT:** L served all week 12-8.15 D served all week 12.30-8.15 Av 3 course à la carte £11.25 **BREWERY/COMPANY:** Free House ◀: Broughton Greenmantle Ale, Belhaven 80/-.
FACILITIES: Children welcome Children's licence Garden: 6 acres of Lochside **NOTES:** Parking 50 **ROOMS:** 5 bedrooms 5 en suite s£30 d£52

TWEEDSMUIR   Map 21 NT12

The Crook Inn
ML12 6QN ☎ 01899 880272 🖹 01899 880294
e-mail: thecrookinn@btinternet.com

The oldest licensed inn in Scotland is 400-years-old this year! It was frequented by none other than Rabbie Burns, and has seen feuds, cattle rustling and kidnappings in its time. The area is now less dangerous but still

continued

continued

breathtaking, and popular with walkers tackling nearby Broad Law. The 1930s art deco interior provides a delightful setting for a good range of food from snacks and sandwiches to herb-crusted salmon or haggis with whisky cream sauce.
OPEN: 9-12 Closed: Dec 25, 3rd week in Jan **BAR MEALS:** L served all week 12-2.30 D served all week 5.30-8.30 Av main course £7 **RESTAURANT:** L served all week D served all week 7-9 Av 3 course à la carte £15 Av 4 course fixed price £19.50
BREWERY/COMPANY: Free House 🍺: Broughton Greenmantle & Best, Scottish Courage John Smith's. **FACILITIES:** Children welcome Garden Dogs allowed **NOTES:** Parking 60

SHETLAND

BRAE   Map 24 HU26

Busta House Hotel ★★★ 🛏
Busta ZE2 9QN ☎ 01806 522506 📠 01806 522588
e-mail: reservations@bustahouse.com
A 16th-century laird's residence, Busta House is Britain's most northerly country house hotel offering superb sea views and boasting some of Shetland's few trees in its garden. Home-cooked food specialising in fresh Shetland and Scottish produce is served in both the cosy beamed bar and the restaurant, with dishes such as smoked salmon, marinated herring, game terrine, and roast lamb with red wine and juniper berries.
OPEN: 11.30-11 12.30-11 (Mon-Sat 11.30-11, Sun 12.30-11)
BAR MEALS: L served all week 12-2.30 D served all week 6-9.30 Av main course £9 **RESTAURANT:** L served Sun 12.30-2 D served all week 7-9 Av 4 course fixed price £30 **BREWERY/COMPANY:** Free House 🍺: Valhalla Alud Rock, Simmer Dim & White Wife, Belhaven Best. **FACILITIES:** Children welcome Children's licence Garden: Private harbour **NOTES:** Parking 50 **ROOMS:** 20 bedrooms 20 en suite 1 family rooms s£70 d£95

SOUTH AYRSHIRE

SYMINGTON   Map 20 NS33

Wheatsheaf Inn 🛏
Main St KA1 5QB ☎ 01563 830307 📠 01563 830307
Dir: Telephone for directions

This 17th-century inn lies in a lovely village setting close to the Royal Troon Golf Course, and there has been a hostelry here since the 1500s. Log fires burn in every room and the work of local artists adorns the walls. Seafood highlights the menu - maybe pan-fried scallops in lemon and chives - and alternatives include honey-roasted lamb shank; haggis, tatties

and neeps in Drambuie and onion cream, and the renowned steak pie.
OPEN: 11-12 Closed: 25 Dec, 1 Jan **BAR MEALS:** L served all week 12-4 D served all week 4-9.30 Av main course £7
RESTAURANT: L served all week 12-9.30 D served all week Av 3 course à la carte £13 **BREWERY/COMPANY:** Belhaven 🍺: Belhaven Best, St Andrews Ale. **FACILITIES:** Children welcome Garden **NOTES:** Parking 20

STIRLING

BALQUHIDDER   Map 20 NN52

Monachyle Mhor ★★ 🏅🏅
FK19 8PQ ☎ 01877 384622 📠 01877 384305
e-mail: info@monachylemhor.com
Dir: On A84, 11 miles N of Callander, turn right at Kingshouse. Monachyle Mhor is 6 miles along this road situated between two lochs.

Romantically located farmhouse hotel with dramatic loch and mountain views not far from the burial place of Rob Roy. The interior includes open fires, antique furniture, sporting prints and country fabrics. Don't miss the excellent cooking, full of local and home-grown produce. Dishes could range from seared scallops with smoked haddock, wild rice kedgeree, steamed garden greens and wasabi to rack of local lamb and slow-roasted shoulder on crushed olive oil potatoes with shallot, sun blushed tomato and black olive emulsion.
OPEN: 12 Closed: Jan-14 Feb **BAR MEALS:** L served all week 12-3 D served all week 7-8.45 Av main course £8.95
RESTAURANT: L served all week 12-1.45 D served all week 7-8.45 Av 4 course fixed price £35 **BREWERY/COMPANY:** Free House 🍺: Belhaven Best, Angel Organic, Heather Ale.
FACILITIES: Garden: Overlooking 2 Lochs, weather permitting **ROOMS:** 10 bedrooms 10 en suite s£55 d£95 no children overnight

continued

Scotland

Scotland

CRIANLARICH
Map 20 NN32

Ben More Lodge Hotel ♦♦♦
FK20 8QS ☎ 01838 300210 📠 01838 300218
e-mail: info@ben-more.co.uk
Dir: From Glasgow take A82 to Crianlarich, turn R at T Junc in village in direction of stirling

Beautifully set hotel at the foot of Ben More next to the River Fillan, on the road to the North West Highlands. Timber-built lodges accommodate guests, and both bar and restaurant offer good food: from the latter expect chicken and bacon salad, and roast haunch of venison with redcurrant jelly, while bar dishes includes oven-baked Mallaig trout, steak pie, and various traditional snacks.
OPEN: 11-12 (Restricted hrs Nov-March) Closed: Dec 25, Mon-Fri in Nov-Mar **BAR MEALS:** L served all week 12-2.30 D served all week 6-8.45 Av main course £6 **RESTAURANT:** L served all week 12-2.30 D served all week 6-8.45 Av 3 course à la carte £12 Av 3 course fixed price £16 **BREWERY/COMPANY:** Free House 🍺: Tennents 80/-.
FACILITIES: Children welcome Garden: Spacious grounds, fields adjacent Dogs allowed **NOTES:** Parking 50 **ROOMS:** 11 bedrooms 11 en suite s£30 d£50

DRYMEN
Map 20 NS48

Clachan Inn
2 Main St G63 0BG ☎ 01360 660824
Quaint, white-painted cottage, believed to be the oldest licensed pub in Scotland, situated in a small village on the West Highland Way. Locate the appealing lounge bar for freshly-made food, the varied menu listing filled baked potatoes, salads, fresh haddock in crispy breadcrumbs, spicy Malaysian lamb casserole, vegetable lasagne, a variety of steaks, and good daily specials.
OPEN: 11-12 (sun 11.30-10.30) Closed: 25 Dec & 01 Jan
BAR MEALS: L served all week 12.30-4.30 D served all week 6-10 Av main course £5.50 **RESTAURANT:** L served all week 12-4 D served all week 6-10 **BREWERY/COMPANY:** Free House 🍺: Caledonian Deuchars IPA, Belhaven Best. **FACILITIES:** Children welcome **NOTES:** Parking 2

KILMAHOG
Map 20 NN60

The Lade Inn
FK17 8HD ☎ 01877 330152 📠 01877 331878
e-mail: steve@theladeinnscotland.freeserve.co.uk
Detached white-painted building set in its own grounds on the Leny Estate west of Callander, named after a mill lade - a stream created from the River Leny to power the mills at Kilmahog. Cosy bar with open fire and collection of brasses, and separate dining area offering real Scottish cooking. Expect haggis, neeps and tatties, Arbroath platter (dressed crab, mackerel fillet,

poached salmon and smoked mussels), game casserole and local trout, alongside sandwiches and traditional pub meals.
OPEN: 12-3 5.30-10.30 **BAR MEALS:** L served all week 12-2.30 D served all week 5.30-9 Av main course £6.50 **RESTAURANT:** L served all week 12-2.30 D served all week 5.30-9 Av 3 course à la carte £20 **BREWERY/COMPANY:** Free House 🍺: Broughton Greenmantle Ale, Caledonian 80/-, plus Guest ales.
FACILITIES: Children welcome Garden: Food served outside Dogs allowed **NOTES:** Parking 40

KIPPEN
Map 20 NS69

Cross Keys Hotel
Main St FK8 3DN ☎ 01786 870293 📠 01786 870293
e-mail: crosskeys@kippen70.fsnet.co.uk

The village of Kippen, situated in the Fintry Hills overlooking the Forth Valley, has strong associations with Rob Roy. The pub dates from 1703, retains its original stone walls, and enjoys real fires in winter. Nearby Burnside Wood is managed by a local community woodland group, and is perfect for walking and nature trails. Look out for hearty dishes such as beef steak and mushroom pie, hand-filleted haddock in fresh breadcrumbs, lasagne, smoked salmon platter, Stilton and broccoli quiche, and a variety of salads.
OPEN: 12-2.30 Phone for further details 5.30-12 (Fri-Sat 5.30-12 Sun 12.30-11) Closed: 1 Jan **BAR MEALS:** L served all week 12-2 D served all week 5.30-9 Av main course £7
BREWERY/COMPANY: Free House 🍺: Belhaven Best, IPA, 80/-, Harviestoun Bitter & Twisted. **FACILITIES:** Children welcome Garden: Small garden with water feature Dogs allowed Water, Biscuits **NOTES:** Parking 5

STRATHBLANE
Map 20 NS57

Kirkhouse Inn
Glasgow Rd G63 9AA ☎ 01360 771771 📠 01360 771711
e-mail: kirkhouse@cawleyhotels.com
Dir: A81 Aberfoyce rd from Glasgow city centre through Bearsden & Milngavie, Strathblane on junct with A891
17th-century coaching inn nestling beneath the jagged scarp of the Campsie Fells, a rolling patchwork of green volcanic hills and picturesque villages. Interesting menu offers international cuisine as well as traditional British dishes. A selection from the menu includes tournedos Rossini, roast Burkhill duck, sirloin steak Jacobean, and fillet of salmon Gartness.
OPEN: 10-midnight (Fri-Sat 10-1) Closed: Dec 25 **BAR MEALS:** L served all week 12-7 Av main course £5 **RESTAURANT:** L served all week 12-5 D served all week 5-10 Av 3 course à la carte £27.50 **BREWERY/COMPANY:** 🍺: Belhaven, Tennants 70/-.
FACILITIES: Children welcome **NOTES:** Parking 300 **ROOMS:** 16 bedrooms 16 en suite s£49.50 d£79 (VisitScotland)

continued

THORNHILL
Map 20 NN60

Lion & Unicorn
FK8 3PJ ☎ 01786 850204
Dir: On A873 Blair Drummond to Aberfoyle
An old droving inn dating from 1635, once the favourite haunt of Rob Roy MacGregor. These days it has a games room for whiling away a few hours, and a beer garden for alfresco eating and drinking. Home-cooked dishes range from sizzling steaks and baked potatoes in the bar, to venison steak with cranberry and claret glaze in the restaurant.
OPEN: 12-12 (Fri-Sat 12-1) **BAR MEALS:** L served all week D served all week Av main course £5.50 **RESTAURANT:** L served all week 12-9 D served all week Av 3 course à la carte £20
BREWERY/COMPANY: Free House **FACILITIES:** Children welcome Garden Dogs allowed **NOTES:** Parking 25

WEST LOTHIAN

LINLITHGOW
Map 21 NS97

Pick of the Pubs

Champany Inn ⊚⊛
Champany EH49 7LU ☎ 01506 834532 🗎 01506 834302
e-mail: reception@champany.com

If you wish to sample the delights of best Scottish beef, this is a place not to be missed. A collection of buildings dating from the 17th century house the Chop and Ale House and its superior sister, the main restaurant. Both are renowned for the sourcing, handling and cooking of prime Scottish beef, but also offer a range of other dishes. Warm colours in the walls and table linen, and a central chimney with a roaring fire make the Chop and Ale House a smart and welcoming spot. Here are burgers as they should be, made from the same meat as the steaks and cooked medium rare. Aberdeen Angus steaks weigh as much as 600gm a portion, so hearty appetites are called for. Scottish lamb chops, home made sausages, chargrilled chicken and cod and chips are among other choices, and for those who have room, the sweet menu includes pecan pie, chocolate marquise and hazelnut meringues.
OPEN: 12-2 6.30-11 (all day w/end) Closed: 25-26 Dec, 1-2 Jan **BAR MEALS:** L served all week 12-2 D served all week 6.30-11 Av main course £12.45 **RESTAURANT:** L served Mon-Fri 12.30-2 D served Mon-Sat 7-11 Av 3 course à la carte £40 Av 2 course fixed price £16.75 **BREWERY/COMPANY:** Free House
🍺: Belhaven. **FACILITIES:** Children welcome Garden: Courtyard, traditional garden **NOTES:** Parking 50

SCOTTISH ISLANDS

ISLAY, ISLE OF

BALLYGRANT
Map 20 NR36

Ballygrant Inn
PA45 7QR ☎ 01496 840277 🗎 01496 840277
e-mail: info@ballygrant-inn.co.uk
Dir: NE of Isle of Islay, 3m from ferry terminal at Port Askaig
Situated in two and a half acres of grounds, this converted farmhouse offers a warm welcome to tourists, walkers and fishermen alike. Local ales and malt whiskies are served in the bar, along with bar meals that include venison casserole, grilled local scallops, and sirloin steaks. The restaurant menu features crab, lamb cutlets, salmon and grilled trout among others. Many of the ingredients used are locally produced. Occasional folk or blues music.
OPEN: 11-11 (Wkds 11-1am) **BAR MEALS:** L served all week 12-3 D served all week 7-10 Av main course £8.50 **RESTAURANT:** L served all week 12-3 D served all week 7-10 Av 3 course à la carte £20
BREWERY/COMPANY: Free House **FACILITIES:** Children welcome Garden: outdoor eating, patio Dogs allowed
NOTES: Parking 35

BOWMORE
Map 20 NR35

Pick of the Pubs

The Harbour Inn ♦♦♦♦ ⊚⊛ 🐕 ♈
The Square PA43 7JR ☎ 01496 810330 🗎 01496 810990
e-mail: harbour@harbour-inn.com

A gem of an inn, wedged between the square and harbour of the island's capital. It has been completely refurbished and extended to provide seven en suite bedrooms and a restaurant looking out from the water's edge across Lochindaal to the peaks of Jura beyond. A full range of Islay single malt whiskies is served in the small bar, and the menu offered in the restaurant is constructed around shellfish, locally fished and collected from the quay to ensure freshness, and beef, lamb and game from Islay or Jura. The dinner carte might offer local crab sushi with avocado chilli and lime vinaigrette, and beef fillet with haggis and rolls of Bruichladdich smoked beef surrounded by whisky sauce.
OPEN: 11-1 **BAR MEALS:** L served Mon-Sat 12-2.30 D served all week 6-9 **RESTAURANT:** L served Mon-Sat 12-2.30 D served all week 6-9 **BREWERY/COMPANY:** Free House
FACILITIES: Garden: Dogs allowed **ROOMS:** 7 bedrooms 7 en suite no children overnight

NORTH UIST

CARINISH
Map 22 NF86

Carinish Inn
HS6 5EJ ☎ 01876 580673 ▤ 01876 580665
e-mail: carinishinn@btconnect.com
Modern-style refurbished inn at Carinish, North Uist,
convenient for the RSPB Balranald Nature Reserve and local
archaeological sites. Fish features prominently on the set-price
menu, including roast fillet of West Coast salmon, stuffed
monkfish tail wrapped in bacon with stewed tomatoes and
polenta, and seafood casserole in a creamy wine and herb
sauce. Local artists perform every Saturday night.
OPEN: 11-11 (Thu-Sat 11-1am, Sun-Wed 11-11) **BAR MEALS:** L
served all week 12-2.30 D served all week 6.30-9.30 Av main course
£6.50 **RESTAURANT:** L served all week 12-2.30 D served all week
6.30-9.30 Av 3 course à la carte £17 **BREWERY/COMPANY:** Free
House **FACILITIES:** Children welcome **NOTES:** Parking 50
ROOMS: 8 bedrooms 8 en suite s£50 d£70 (VisitScotland)

SKYE, ISLE OF

ARDVASAR
Map 22 NG60

Ardvasar Hotel ★★ ♀
IV45 8RS ☎ 01471 844223 ▤ 01471 844495
e-mail: richard@ardvasar-hotel.demon.co.uk
Dir: From ferry terminal, 50yds & turn L
The second oldest inn on Skye, this white-painted cottage-
style hotel offers a warm, friendly welcome and acts as an
ideal base for exploring the island, spotting the wildlife and
enjoying the stunning scenery. Overlooking the Sound of
Sleat, the Ardvasar is within walking distance of the Clan
Donald Centre and the ferry at Armadale. Popular menus
offers freshly-caught seafood, as well as baked venison in
peppers and port wine pie, lamb and leek potato hot pot and
savoury vegetable crumble. Straightforward basket meals are
a perennial favourite.
OPEN: 12-12 **BAR MEALS:** L served all week 12-2.30 D served all
week 5.30-9.30 **RESTAURANT:** D served all week 7.30-9
BREWERY/COMPANY: Free House **◀:** 80/-, Deuchars, IPA.
FACILITIES: Children welcome Children's licence Garden Dogs
allowed **NOTES:** Parking 30 **ROOMS:** 10 bedrooms 10 en suite

CARBOST
Map 22 NG33

The Old Inn 🏮
IV47 8SR ☎ 01478 640205 ▤ 01478 640450
e-mail: oldinn@carbost.f9.co.uk
Dir: Telephone for directions
Once a croft house, this Highland inn is a perfect base for hill
walkers and climbers. Rents used to be collected here and a
local dentist pulled teeth in one of the upstairs rooms! The
patio offers splendid views of Loch Harport and the Cuillins,
while inside is a charming mix of wooden floors and original
stone walls. Traditional bar food includes the likes of Scottish
sausage hotpot, pasta bake, 8oz sirloin steak garni, baked
salmon, and sole and prawns in Pernod sauce.
OPEN: 11-12 (hours change in winter, please ring) **BAR MEALS:** L
served all week 12-2 D served all week 6.30-10 Av main course £7
BREWERY/COMPANY: Free House **FACILITIES:** Children
welcome Children's licence Garden: Shoreside Patio Dogs allowed
NOTES: Parking 20 **ROOMS:** 6 bedrooms 6 en suite s£28 d£52
(VisitScotland)

ISLE ORNSAY
Map 22 NG71

Pick of the Pubs

Hotel Eilean Iarmain ★★ ◉◉
IV43 8QR ☎ 01471 833332 ▤ 01471 833275
e-mail: hotel@eilean-iarmain.co.uk
Dir: A851, A852 right to Isle Ornsay harbour front

A very special, 19th-century award-winning Hebridean
hotel overlooking Isle Ornsay harbour - well-known to
fans of Flora MacDonald - that enjoys spectacular sea
views. Poets and artists are drawn here by its unique
heritage and the Celtic hertiage typified by the Celtic-
speaking staff. Morag MacDonald claims that her guests
will leave with their lives enriched: they will undoubtedly
depart with well-satisfied appetites! Look first to the
specials board for the likes of brandied crab and lobster
bisque, roast monkfish tails with mushroom duxelle and
tomato salsa and tian of raspberry tuiles served on a wild
berry coulis. Bar meals can be as simple as peppered
mackerel with creamed horseradish, roast baby chicken
with red wine and onion jus and hot apple sponge
crumble with rum and raisin ice cream.
OPEN: 12-12 (Winter Mon-Sun12-2.30, 5-12) **BAR MEALS:** L served
all week 12.30-2 D served all week 6.30-9 Av main course £5.50
RESTAURANT: L served all week D served all week 7.30-9 Av 3 course
à la carte £25 Av 5 course fixed price £31 **BREWERY/COMPANY:** Free
House **◀:** McEwans 80/-. **FACILITIES:** Children welcome Garden:
Food served outside Dogs allowed **NOTES:** Parking 30 **ROOMS:** 12
bedrooms 12 en suite s£90 d£120

SOUTH UIST

LOCHBOISDALE
Map 22 NF7▮

Polochar Inn
polocharinn@btconnect.co.uk, Polochar HS8 5TT
☎ 01878 700215 ▤ 01878 700768
Dir: W from Lochboisdale & take B888. Hotel at end of road
Overlooking the sea towards the islands of Eriskay and Barra,
this superbly situated 18th-century inn enjoys beautiful
sunsets. The bar menu offers fresh seafood dishes and steaks
with various sauces, while restaurant fare includes venison,
fresh scallops or steak pie.
OPEN: 11-11 (Fri 11-1, Sat 11-11.30 Sun 12.30-11) **BAR MEALS:** L
served all week 12.30-2.30 D served all week 6-9 Av main course £8
RESTAURANT: L served all week 12-2.30 D served all week 6-9 Av 3▮
course à la carte £17 **BREWERY/COMPANY:** Free House **◀:** No
real ale. **FACILITIES:** Children welcome Garden: barbecue
NOTES: Parking 40

AA Pub Of The Year for Wales

Pendre Inn, Cilgerran, Pembrokeshire

WALES

WALES

BRIDGEND

KENFIG
Map 09 SS88

Prince of Wales Inn ♀
CF33 4PR ☎ 01656 740356
Dir: M4 J37 into North Cornelly & follow signs for nature reserve, Kenfig
Dating from 1440, this stone-built inn has been many things in its time including a school, guildhall and courtroom. Why not sup some real cask ale in the bar by an inviting log fire? Typical menu includes steak and onion pie, lasagne, chicken and mushroom pie, and a variety of fish dishes. Look out for today's specials on the blackboard.
OPEN: 11.30-4 6-11 (Sun 12-10.30) **BAR MEALS:** L served all week 12-2.30 D served Tue-Sat 7-9.30 Av main course £5.95
RESTAURANT: L served all week 12-2.30 D served Tue-Sat 7-9.30 Av 3 course à la carte £14 **BREWERY/COMPANY:** Free House ☜: Bass Triangle, Worthington Best,. **FACILITIES:** Children welcome Garden: Food served outside Dogs allowed Water, toys **NOTES:** Parking 30

MAESTEG
Map 09 SS89

Old House Inn 🐾 ♀
Llangynwyd CF34 9SB ☎ 01656 733310 🖹 01656 733339

Dating back to 1147, The Old House can lay claim to being one of the oldest in the country. It has huge gnarled beams and stone walls over three feet thick and lots of Welsh antiques and bric-a-brac. Blackboard specials change every day, majoring in fresh fish, including plaice, hake, salmon, and cod. Other menus include traditional pub food, from beef curry and jumbo sausage to chicken chasseur and all-day breakfast. In the 1970s, the Old House was a regular haunt of Liz Taylor and Richard Burton.
OPEN: 11-11 **BAR MEALS:** L served all week 11-2.30 D served all week 6-10 Av main course £5 **RESTAURANT:** L served everyday 11-2.30 D served everyday 6-10 **BREWERY/COMPANY:** Free House ☜: Interbrew Flowers Original & Flowers IPA, Brains Bitter.
FACILITIES: Children welcome Garden: 2.5 acres of play area, view of countryside **NOTES:** Parking 150

CARDIFF

CARDIFF
Map 09 ST17

Buff's Wine Bar & Restaurant
8 Mount Stuart Square CF10 5EE
☎ 029 20464628 🖹 029 20480715
Housed in a listed building at the heart of the former docklands - now being restored as Cardiff Bay's commercial

centre - business executives here lunch on game terrine with Cumberland sauce, deep-fried goats' cheese with onion marmalade, chicken in Barbados sauce, and fish cakes in mild curry sauce. A la carte lunches above and evening dinner parties by arrangement.

OPEN: 11-11 (Sat 12-11 Sun 12-10.30) Closed: BHs **BAR MEALS:** L served all week 11.30-3.30 D served Thu-Sat 5-7 Av main course £5
RESTAURANT: L served Mon-Fri, Sun 12-2.30 D served Thu-Sat 7-9.45 Av 3 course à la carte £21 **BREWERY/COMPANY:** Free House ☜: Carling, Brainsmooth, Strongbow, Stella Artois.
FACILITIES: Garden: Paved area

Cayo Arms
36 Cathedral Rd CF11 9HL ☎ 02920 391910
e-mail: celticinns@twpubs.co.uk
Dir: From Cardiff take Kingsway West turn R into Cathedral Road
Wales's newest brewery company has moved into Cardiff at this nationally-known bi-lingual pub on a leafy thoroughfare leading to the new stadium and city centre. In front is a large patio garden with umbrella-ed tables and patio heaters that add to the draw on Match Days of Tomos Watkins's ales. The same brew is used in a steak and ale pie and the batter for their celebrated fish and chips.
OPEN: 12-11 **BAR MEALS:** L served all week 12-3 D served all week 5-8 Av main course £5.95 ☜: Watkins Brewery Bitter, OSB, Whoosh, Merlin Stout. **FACILITIES:** Children welcome Garden: Food served outside Dogs allowed **NOTES:** Parking 30

CREIGIAU
Map 09 ST0■

Pick of the Pubs

AA Seafood Pub of the Year for Wales 2004

Caesars Arms ◉ 🐾 ♀
Cardiff Rd CF15 9NN ☎ 029 20890486 🖹 029 20892176
Dir: 1m from M4 J34

continued

continue■

Wales

Some ten miles out of Cardiff, yet easily accessible from the M4 (J34), a sprawling pub down winding lanes that attracts a well-heeled clientele to its heated patio and terrace looking over the gardens and surrounding countryside. Head chef Emma Ward bravely undertakes responsibility for the vast selection of fresh fish, seafoods, meat and game enticingly displayed in shaven-ice display cabinets. To begin are Bajan fish cakes, crispy laver balls, tiger prawns in garlic and scallops with leeks and bacon, followed by cuts of monkfish and crawfish tails priced by weight. Welsh beef steaks, honeyed crispy duck and roast rack of Welsh lamb satisfy the most ardent meat eaters: meanwhile help yourself from brimming bowls full of assorted salads. All in a friendly and relaxed atmosphere, draught ales are somewhat overshadowed by a massive wine list with many selections by the glass.

OPEN: 12-2.30 7-12 Closed: 25 Dec **BAR MEALS:** L served all week 12-2.30 D served all week 7-10.30 Av main course £11.95 **RESTAURANT:** L served all week 12-2.30 D served Mon-Sat 7-10.30 Av 3 course à la carte £19.95 **BREWERY/COMPANY:** Free House 🍺: Hancocks. **FACILITIES:** Children welcome Garden: Terraced area with large umbrellas **NOTES:** Parking 100

CARMARTHENSHIRE

ABERGORLECH
Map 08 SN53

The Black Lion 🛏
SA32 7SN ☎ 01558 685271
Dir: From Carmarthen take A40 eastwards, then B4310 signposted Brechfa & Abergorlech

A 17th-century coaching inn in the Brechfa Forest, with a beer garden overlooking the Cothi River and a stone, arched packhorse bridge. Flagstoned floors, settles and a grandfather clock grace the antique-furnished bar, while the modern dining room is welcoming in pink and white. Try home-made game pie, beef bourguignon, steak, ale and mushroom pie and various fish dishes. Miles of forest and riverside walks are easily reached from the pub.

OPEN: 12-3.30 7-11 (Sat 11-11) **BAR MEALS:** L served Tue-Sun 12-2.30 D served Tue-Sun 7-9.30 Av main course £5.50 **RESTAURANT:** L served Tue-Sun 12.30-2.30 D served Tue-Sun 7-9.30 Av 3 course à la carte £12 **BREWERY/COMPANY:** Free House 🍺: Brains Reverend James. **FACILITIES:** Children welcome Garden: Food served outdoors Dogs allowed Water **NOTES:** Parking 20

📖 Pubs offering a good choice of fish on their menu

BRECHFA
Map 08 SN53

Forest Arms
SA32 7RA ☎ 01267 202339 🖷 01267 202339
Dir: 12m from Carmarthen on A48, L onto B4310 at Nantgaredig
Grade II-listed, early 19th-century stone-built inn in a pretty village in the beautiful Cothi Valley. A mile or so away, its own stretch of river yields salmon, sea and brown trout, which sometimes feature on the specials menu. Battered cod and scampi, and home-made chicken curry, spaghetti Bolognese, chilli con carne, and steak and mushroom pie are usually available. Fly-fishing mementoes adorn the unspoilt, traditional bars. The rear garden is a registered helipad.

OPEN: 12-2 6.30-11 **BAR MEALS:** L served all week 12-2 D served Mon-Sat 6.30-9 Av main course £6.25 **RESTAURANT:** L served Mon-Sat 12-2 D served Mon-Sat 6-9 **BREWERY/COMPANY:** Free House 🍺: Dylan's, Brains Buckleys Best, Worthington Creamflow. **FACILITIES:** Children welcome Garden: Food served outdoors Parking 15 **NOTES:** No credit cards

---

LLANARTHNE
Map 08 SN52

Golden Grove Arms 🛏 ♀
SA32 8JU ☎ 01558 668551 🖷 01558 668069
Dir: From end M4 take A48 toward Carmarthen, turn L off A48 (sign-posted National Botanical Gardens), follow signs to Llanarthne
Visitors to the Towy Valley and Wales's National Botanic Gardens will find Llanarthne midway between Carmarthen and Llandeilo. Facilities in a natural setting draw the crowds to both bars and the restaurant for home-cooking. Extensive choices encompass minted lamb chops, chicken Odessa, nut Wellington, sirloin steaks, Reverend James Pie, and Brie and broccoli bake. Under new management.

OPEN: 11-11 12-10.30 (Sun 12-10.30) **BAR MEALS:** L served all week 11.30-2.30 D served all week 6-9 Av main course £6.73 **RESTAURANT:** L served all week 11.30-2.30 D served all week 6-9 **BREWERY/COMPANY:** 🍺: Brains Buckleys Best & Reverend James. ♀: 7 **FACILITIES:** Children welcome Garden **NOTES:** Parking 40

LLANDDAROG
Map 08 SN51

White Hart Thatched Inn & Brewery 🛏
SA32 8NT ☎ 01267 275395 🖷 01267 275395
Dir: 6m E of Carmarthen towards Swansea, just off A48 on B4310, signed Llanddarog

Built in 1371, this thatched, stone-built pub has walls four-foot thick, heavy beams and an open log fire, and is filled with antique furniture and relics. Cole's Family Brewery makes 'Cwrw Blasus', or 'tasty ale', using water from the pub's own deep-bore well. Good home cooking using fresh local produce

continued

Wales

LLANDDAROG continued

is offered from a wide-ranging menu including home-made pies, daily roasts, Welsh black beef steaks, sizzling fresh sea bass, and old-fashioned puddings.
OPEN: 11.30-3 6.30-11 (Sun 12-3, 7-10.30) Closed: Dec 25-26 **BAR MEALS:** L served all week 11.30-2 D served all week 6.30-10 Av main course £10.50 **RESTAURANT:** L served all week 11.30-2 D served all week 6.30-10 Av 3 course à la carte £17.50
BREWERY/COMPANY: Free House 🍺 Coles family brewery Cwrw Blasus, Black Stag, Roasted Barley Stout, To Gwellt.
FACILITIES: Children welcome Garden: Patio, terrace, grassed area, seating, tables **NOTES:** Parking 50

LLANDEILO
Map 08 SN62

The Angel Inn 🐑 ♀
Salem SA19 7LY ☎ 01558 823394 📠 01558 823371
Dir: A40 then B4302, turn L 1m after leaving A40 then turn R at T junct and travel 0.25m to Angel Inn. Located on the right hand side

Traditional village pub characterised by beamed ceilings and a large collection of fascinating artefacts. Popular bar food is served along with a children's menu, a list of vegetarian dishes, and daily local specials. In the restaurant a typical meal might be roast fillet of Welsh beef, warm salad of chicken supreme, charred breast of Gressingham Duck, or seared escalope of salmon, and home-made ice creams.
OPEN: 12-2.30 6-11 **BAR MEALS:** L served Wed-Sun 12-2 D served Tue-Sat 6.30-9 Av main course £8 **RESTAURANT:** L served Wed-Sun 12-2 D served Tue-Sat 7-9.00 Av 3 course à la carte £22
BREWERY/COMPANY: Free House 🍺 Worthington Highgate Dark Mild, Buckleys Best, Colins, Stella. **FACILITIES:** Garden **NOTES:** Parking 60

The Castle Brewery 🐑
113 Rhosmaen St SA19 6EN ☎ 01558 823446 📠 01558 824256
e-mail: castle@twpubs.co.uk
A 19th-century Edwardian-style hotel within easy reach of Dinefwr Castle and wonderful walks through classic parkland. A charming, tiled and partly green-painted back bar attracts plenty of locals, while the front bar and side area offer smart furnishings and the chance to relax in comfort over a drink. Good range of Tomas Watkins ales available and good quality bar and restaurant food prepared with the finest of fresh local ingredients. Expect hearty dishes such as steak and ale pie, boiled ham, lasagne, and lamb casserole, along with seafood dishes incorporating monkfish, trout, salmon, cod, plaice and scampi. Under new management.
OPEN: 12-11 (Sun 12-10.30) **BAR MEALS:** L served all week 12-2.30 D served all week 6.30-9 Av main course £6.50
RESTAURANT: L served all week 12-2.30 D served all week 6.30-9 **BREWERY/COMPANY:** 🍺 Tomos Watkin Best, OSB & Merlin Stout, Coors Worthington Draught, Guest Ale. **FACILITIES:** Children welcome Garden: Slabbed area inside internal buildings

The Cottage Inn 🐑
Pentrefelin SA19 6SD ☎ 01558 822890 📠 01558 823309
Dir: On main A40 between Brecon & Carmarthen, 1.5 miles W of Llandeilo
Formerly the Nags Head Inn, this timbered coaching inn is just 1.5 miles from Aberglasney Gardens and six miles from the National Botanical Gardens. Plenty of fresh fish on the menu. Recently taken over by Enterprise Inns.
OPEN: 12-3 6-11.30 **BAR MEALS:** L served all week 12-2.30 D served all week 6-9.30 Av main course £6.27 **RESTAURANT:** L served all week 12-2.30 D served all week 6-9.30 Av 3 course fixed price £9.95 **BREWERY/COMPANY:** Enterprise Inns 🍺 Wadworth 6X, Interbrew Bass & Flowers, Coors Worthington's.
FACILITIES: Children welcome Garden **NOTES:** Parking 60

LLANDOVERY
Map 09 SN73

Neuadd Fawr Arms 🐑 ♀
SA20 0ST ☎ 01550 721644 📠 01550 721644
Dir: On the A40 take the A483 Builth Wells Rd, after 300 meters turn L at the crossroads. Continue along this rd for 3m and take 2nd L over river Bridge, continue to Cilycwm and pub is on R
Traditional local peacefully located next to the church in a picturesque village, with character slate floors, quarry tiles and oak boards. It lies on the route of an old drovers' trail, and is handy for exploring the Cambrian Mountains and the Towy Valley. There's a good range of wines and real ales, and a varied menu. Choices run from roasts and pies through to fish and Mediterranean dishes.
OPEN: 11-3 (open all day Fri-Sun) 6-11 **BAR MEALS:** L served all week 12-2.30 D served all week 6.30-9 Av main course £7.95
RESTAURANT: L served all week 12-2.30 D served all week 6.30-9 Av 3 course à la carte £15 **BREWERY/COMPANY:** Free House 🍺 Tomos Watkin Whoosh, Brains Reverend James, H.S.B Hawcocks.
FACILITIES: Children welcome Garden: Over looking river and mountains **NOTES:** Parking 15 **ROOMS:** 3 bedrooms 3 en suite s£27.50 d£45 (WTB)

LLANDYBIE
Map 08 SN61

The Red Lion Inn
SA18 3JA ☎ 01269 851202
Almost 300 years old, this historic inn retains the atmosphere and feel of the original pub. Several fireplaces and other original features remain to generate a friendly, welcoming environment in which to relax and enjoy good food and well kept real ales. Dishes range from fillet of salmon with roast potato and spinach, to breast of chicken stuffed with Mozzarella and wrapped in Parma ham.
OPEN: 12-2 6-11 (Sun closed evening) **BAR MEALS:** L served all week 12-2 D served all week 6-9 Av main course £6
RESTAURANT: L served all week 12-2 D served all week 6-9 Av 3 course à la carte £22 **BREWERY/COMPANY:** 🍺 Worthington, Tomos Watkin. **FACILITIES:** Children welcome Garden: Food served outside **NOTES:** Parking 50

NANTGAREDIG
Map 08 SN42

Pick of the Pubs

The Salutation Inn 🐑
Pont-ar-Gothi SA32 7NH ☎ 01267 290336
Dir: On A40 between Carmarthen & Llandeilo. 5mins from National Botanical Gardens
The 'Sal', as it is affectionately known to the locals, has long been pulling them in from as far away as Swansea and Llanelli. Partly, this can be put down to the lure of the

continue

Towy Valley, with its excellent fishing, but the Salutation has long had a reputation for food that has strengthened under the stewardship of Richard and Sera Porter. It's a pub with character and a loyal following of colourful locals who congregate in the bar where Felinfoel Double Dragon is the preferred ale. Stripped floors, bare tables and candles are the defining features of both bar and restaurant areas where generous blackboards offer a selection of broadly modern British dishes. Among the starters are crispy crab cake with avocado salad and a mild curry dressing or Pembrokeshire fish pie with parsley and cheddar crust. Robust mains might include loin of pork stuffed with apples and apricots on bubble and squeak or halibut wrapped in Parma ham with sauce vierge **OPEN:** 12-3 6-11 Closed: Mon in winter **BAR MEALS:** L served all week 12-2 D served all week 6-9.30 Av main course £7.50 **RESTAURANT:** L served all week 12-2 D served all week 6-9.30 Av 3 course à la carte £20

BREWERY/COMPANY: Felinfoel ◖: Felinfoel - Double Dragon, Dragon Bitter, Dragon Dark. **FACILITIES:** Children welcome Garden: Food served outside **NOTES:** Parking 15

RHANDIRMWYN
Map 09 SN74

The Royal Oak Inn ◆◆◆
LA20 0NY ☎ 01550 760201 🖷 01550 760332
e-mail: royaloak@rhandirmwyn.com
Dir: A484 between Carmarthen and Cardigan
Attractive 17th-century hillside inn, formerly Earl Cawdor's hunting lodge, in the hamlet of Rhandirmwyn, due north of Llandovery, and famed for its fine views over the upper Towy Valley. The Dinas bird reserve is literally on the doorstep. Stone interiors warmed by log fires, half-a-dozen real ales, home-cooked bar meals and beer garden. A typical menu includes Welsh fillet steak, beef strips in pepper sauce, and leek and mushroom crumble. **OPEN:** 11.30-3 6-11 **BAR MEALS:** 12-2.30 6-9.30 **BREWERY/COMPANY:** Free House ◖: Greene King Abbot Ale, Wadworth 6X, Burtons. **FACILITIES:** Children welcome Garden: Lawn, food served outside Dogs allowed **NOTES:** Parking 20 **ROOMS:** 5 bedrooms 3 en suite s£22.50 d£28

RHOS
Map 08 SN33

Lamb of Rhos ♀
SA44 5EE ☎ 01559 370055
Country inn with flagstone floors, beamed ceilings and open fires - as well as its own jail and the 'seat to nowhere'. A menu of traditional pub fare includes steaks, chops, mixed grill, vegetarian and vegan dishes all cooked on the premises. **OPEN:** 12-11 **BAR MEALS:** L served all week 12-2.30 D served all week 6-9 Av main course £5.50 **RESTAURANT:** L served Sun 12-2.30 D served Fri-Sat 7-9 Av 3 course à la carte £16 **BREWERY/COMPANY:** Free House ◖: Worthington Cream Flow, Banks Original. **FACILITIES:** Children welcome Garden: beer garden, outdoor eating, patio Dogs allowed except during meals **NOTES:** Parking 50 **NOTES:** No credit cards **ROOMS:** 5 bedrooms 5 en suite £50 (WTB)

CEREDIGION

CARDIGAN
Map 08 SN14

Black Lion Hotel 🍸
High St SA43 1HJ ☎ 01239 612532
Dir: On the A487 through Cardigan, 20 miles north of Fishguard
Established as a one-room 'grogge shoppe' in 1105, the Black Lion lays claim to being one of Wales' oldest coaching inns.

continued

Today, this family-run hotel offers comfortable town centre hospitality in an evocative atmosphere opposite the historic castle. Tomas Watkin Welsh Ales accompany sandwiches, coachman's platters and hot dishes in the spacious lounge bar, whilst restaurant diners can expect Welsh lamb or pan-fried duck, backed up with grills, seafood and vegetarian dishes. **OPEN:** 10-11 **BAR MEALS:** L served all week 12-2.30 D served all week 6-9 Av main course £4.95 **RESTAURANT:** L served all week 12-2.30 D served all week 6-9 Av 3 course à la carte £15 Av 3 course fixed price £11.50 **BREWERY/COMPANY:** Tomos Watkin & Sons ◖: Tomos Watkins Woosh, OSB. **FACILITIES:** Children welcome **NOTES:** Parking 20

Webley Hotel
Poppit Sands SA43 3LN ☎ 01239 612085
Dir: A484 from Carmarthen to Cardigan, then to St Dogmaels, turn R in village centre to Poppit Sands
Located on the coastal path, and within walking distance of Poppit Sands, this hotel overlooks the Teifi Estuary and Cardigan Island. New owners have taken over the pub recently, so watch out for new developments. Readers' reports welcome. **OPEN:** 11.30-3 7-11.30 (winter) All day (summer) **BAR MEALS:** L served all week 11.30-2 D served all week 6.30-9 Av main course £6.50 **RESTAURANT:** L served all week D served all week Av cost 3 course à la carte £9 **BREWERY/COMPANY:** Free House ◖: Bass, Buckleys Bitter, Worthington **FACILITIES:** Children welcome Dogs in garden only Garden **NOTES:** Parking 60

LLWYNDAFYDD
Map 08 SN35

Crown Inn & Restaurant
SA44 6BU ☎ 01545 560396 🖷 01545 560857
Dir: Off A487 NE of Cardigan
Traditional 18th-century Welsh longhouse with original beams and open fireplaces, close to Cardigan Bay. The delightful, award-winning garden attracts many customers with its tree-sheltered setting, pond and colourful flowers, and it's an easy walk down the lane to a cove where there are caves and National Trust cliffs. Plenty of bar dishes including various grills, pizzas, and steak and kidney pie, or vegetarian omelette. The pretty restaurant offers crab tartlet, pork tenderloin, and chocolate meringue nest. **OPEN:** 12-3 6-11 Rest:Nov-Easter closed Sun eve (Oct-Easter) **BAR MEALS:** L served all week 12-2 D served all week 6-9 Av main course £6.50 **RESTAURANT:** L served By appointment only 12-2.30 D served all week 6.30-9 Av 3 course à la carte £21 **BREWERY/COMPANY:** Free House ◖: Interbrew Flowers Original & Flowers IPA , Tomos Watkins OSB, Greene King Old Speckled Hen. **FACILITIES:** Children welcome Garden: Large Terraces **NOTES:** Parking 80

CONWY

ABERGELE
Map 14 SH97

The Kinmel Arms 🏠 ♀
St George LL22 9BP ☎ 01745 832207 🖷 01745 822044
e-mail: lynn@watzat.co.uk
Dir: from Bodelwyddan towards Abergele take slip road at St George. Take 1st L and Kinmel Arms is on L at top of hill
There's a panoramic view over marshy Morfa Rhuddlan to the sea from this stunning 17th-century free house in the St George conservation area. The food's pretty good too, and it

continued

Wales

ABERGELE continued

would be a real grouch who could find nothing tempting among the open sandwiches, baguettes, salads, light meals, pastas, meat and fish specials, not to mention the array of desserts. Every Friday is traditional Fish Night, with a wide range on offer. Guest ales change fortnightly.

The Kinmel Arms

OPEN: 12-3 7-11 Closed: 25 Dec **BAR MEALS:** L served Tue-Sun 12-2 D served Tue-Sun 7-9.30 Av main course £7.95
RESTAURANT: L served Tue-Sun 12-2 D served Tue-Sun 7-9.30 Av 3 course à la carte £14 **BREWERY/COMPANY:** Free House
🍺: Castle Eden, Brain Rev'd James, Wychwoodshires, Black Cat.
🍷: 8 **FACILITIES:** Children welcome Garden: Patio area, wooden garden furniture Dogs allowed **NOTES:** Parking 60

BETWS-Y-COED
Map 14 SH75

Ty Gwyn Hotel ♦♦♦♦ 🛏️ 🍷
LL24 0SG ☎ 01690 710383 710787 📠 01690 710383
e-mail: mratcl1050@aol.com
Dir: At Juction of A5/A470, 100 yards S of Waterloo Bridge.

Former coaching inn with old world characteristics situated overlooking the River Conwy amid marvellous mountain scenery. Good home-cooked food includes grilled seabass steak with lobster and prawn sauce, wild mushroom and pine nuts Stroganoff, breast of chicken California, chargrilled rump steak, fresh Conway salmon with dill and Dubonnet butter sauce, and king prawns Adelphi wrapped in bacon, lobster and prawn velouté.
OPEN: 12-2 7-9.30 **BAR MEALS:** L served all week 12-2 D served all week 7-9 Av main course £10 **RESTAURANT:** L served all week 12-2 D served all week 7-9 Av 3 course à la carte £20
BREWERY/COMPANY: Free House 🍺: Wadworth 6X, Welsh Smooth, Tetley Smooth. **FACILITIES:** Children welcome
NOTES: Parking 12 **ROOMS:** 13 bedrooms 10 en suite 2 family rooms s£30 d£36 (WTB)

Cobdens Hotel ★★ 🛏️
LL24 0EE ☎ 01690 720243 📠 01690 720354
e-mail: info@cobdens.co.uk
Dir: On A5, 4m N of Betws-Y-Coed
Situated at the foot of Moel Siabod in the heart of Snowdonia, this 250-year-old inn is a popular centre for outdoor pursuits. The management are continuing the emphasis on wholesome food prepared from fresh local ingredients. Look out for tagliatelle verdi topped with field mushrooms, red pepper and sweet roasted shallots, grilled fillet of Welsh black steak, toad-in-the-hole, fillet and thigh of roasted guinea fowl, or pan-sealed pork tenderloin. Light bites and sandwiches also available. Comfortable en suite bedrooms, and the newly re-opened Mountain Bar.
OPEN: 11-11 (Sun 12-10.30) Closed: 6-26 Jan **BAR MEALS:** L served all week 12-2.30 D served all week 6-9 Av main course £8
RESTAURANT: L served all week 12-2 D served all week 6-9 Av 3 course à la carte £15 **BREWERY/COMPANY:** Free House
🍺: Greene King Old Speckled Hen, Brains Bitter, Rev James Tetleys, plus Guest beers. **FACILITIES:** Children welcome Garden: Part of Snowdonia National Park Dogs allowed **NOTES:** Parking 35
ROOMS: 16 bedrooms 16 en suite 3 family rooms s£34 d£68

CONWY
Map 14 SH7

The Groes Inn ★★★ 🍴 🛏️ 🍷
LL32 8TN ☎ 01492 650545 📠 01492 650855
Dir: Off A55 to Conwy, L at mini r'about by Conwy castle onto B5106, 2 1/2m inn on R
Reputedly the first licensed house in Wales, the Groes Inn was built around 500 years ago and gained its first licence in 1573. Here you'll find beamed ceilings, roaring fires in rambling old rooms, and flower-decked gardens. Fish dishes include home-made fishcakes, Conwy plaice or Anglesey oysters, with alternatives like Welsh black beef and walnut casserole, Conwy saltmarsh lamb, and roast aubergine provençale. Finish with Welsh cheese and biscuits, or pecan nut treacle tart.
OPEN: 12-3 6.30-11 **BAR MEALS:** L served all week 12-2.15 D served all week 6.30-9 Av main course £9 **RESTAURANT:** L served all week 12-2.15 D served all week 6.30-9 Av 3 course à la carte £14 A 4 course fixed price £25 **BREWERY/COMPANY:** Free House
🍺: Tetley, Burton Ale. 🍷: 6 **FACILITIES:** Garden: Overlooking the Conwy River/Snowdonia **NOTES:** Parking 90 **ROOMS:** 14 bedrooms 14 en suite 1 family rooms s£68 d£85 no children overnight

Lion Inn 🍷
LL22 8UU ☎ 01745 860244
Dir: 3m off A548 (Llanrwst/Abergale rd) on B5384
The original inn dates back some 300 years, but has been gradually extended over the last century. It is located in a historic village surrounded by beautiful countryside. Food ranges from snacks and beer-battered cod in the bar, to Anglesey eggs and fillet steak in the restaurant.
OPEN: 12-3 7-11 (Times may vary, ring for details) **BAR MEALS:** L served Tue-Sun 12-2 D served Tue-Sun 7-9 Av main course £6
RESTAURANT: L served Tue-Sun 12-2 D served Tue-Sun 7-9 Av 3 course à la carte £12 Av 3 course fixed price £12
BREWERY/COMPANY: Free House 🍺: Marstons Pedigree.
FACILITIES: Children welcome Garden: beer garden, patio, outdoor eating, Dogs allowed Dog basket, food, water, blankets
NOTES: Parking 15

Wales

LLANDUDNO JUNCTION Map 14 SH77

Pick of the Pubs

The Queens Head 🍷
Glanwydden LL31 9JP ☎ 01492 546570 📠 01492 546487
Dir: *Take A470 from A55 towards Llandudno, at 3rd rnbt R towards Penrhyn Bay, then 2nd R into Glanwydden, pub on L*

This celebrated pub, three miles outside Llandudno, is well worth seeking out for its range of good food that relies largely on local Welsh produce imaginatively served. The daily fish dishes featuring Conwy salmon, fresh local mussels and Manx scallops are among highlights of a lengthy menu that also includes choices such as roast rib of Welsh beef with Yorkshire pudding; local lamb cutlets with blackberry and port sauce; Conwy venison sausages and mash; and pot-roasted pheasant served with an orange and cranberry jus. Open 'tasty baps' and steak rolls with sautéed onions are a lunchtime feature, supplemented by pasta, salads and vegetarian dishes such as mushroom and chestnut vol-au-vent with watercress cream sauce. There's an excellent hot and cold sweet menu if you have room, including locally-made ice creams and cheeses, chocolate nut fudge pie, fresh fruit crumble and Bara Brith bread and butter pudding.
OPEN: 11-3 6-11 (Sun 11-10.30) Closed: 25 Dec
BAR MEALS: L served all week 12-2.15 D served all week 6-9 Av main course £7.95 **RESTAURANT:** L served all week 12-2.15 D served all week 6-9 **BREWERY/COMPANY:** Vanguard
🍺: Carlsberg-Tetley, Burton, Greene King Old Speckled Hen, Wrexham. **🍷:** 7 **NOTES:** Parking 20

LLANNEFYDD Map 14 SH97

The Hawk & Buckle Inn
LL16 5ED ☎ 01745 540249 📠 01745 540316
e-mail: hawkandbuckle@btinternet.com

continued

A 17th-century coaching inn 200m up in the hills, with wonderful views to the sea beyond. Menus offer a good choice of food based on local produce, including grilled plaice with parsley butter, poached salmon in tarragon sauce, roast shoulder of Welsh lamb, with mint and blackcurrant glaze, and roast loin of pork, stuffed with Cumberland sausage, served with wholegrain mustard sauce.
OPEN: 12-2 6-11 Closed: 25-26 Dec **BAR MEALS:** 12-2 6-9.30 **RESTAURANT:** 6-9.30 **BREWERY/COMPANY:** Free House
🍺: Brains Bitter, Interbrew Boddingtons Bitter. **NOTES:** Parking 20

LLANRWST Map 14 SH86

White Horse Inn ♦♦♦♦ 🍷
Capel Garmon LL26 0RW ☎ 01690 710271 📠 01690 710721
e-mail: whitehorse@supanet.com
Dir: *Telephone for directions*

Capel Garmon perches high up on an escarpment at the Betws-y-Coed end of the Conwy valley: if you're driving, approach from the B5113 south of Llanrwst. The trip is rewarded by a striking collection of Victorian pottery and china hanging from the beams of this cosy 400-year-old inn, worth seeking out for decent real ales and modest accommodation. Fresh local produce underpins a pleasing menu that offers dishes such as smoked haddock and Mozzarella fish cake followed by lamb shank in sweet mint and onion gravy.
OPEN: 11-3 6-11 Closed: 2 wks Jan **BAR MEALS:** L served Sat-Sun 12-2 D served all week 6.30-9.30 Av main course £7
RESTAURANT: L served Sat-Sun 12-2 D served all week 6.30-9.30 Av 3 course à la carte £20 **BREWERY/COMPANY:** Free House
🍺: Tetley Imperial, Tetley Smoothflow. **🍷:** 23
FACILITIES: Children welcome Dogs allowed Water
NOTES: Parking 30 **ROOMS:** 6 bedrooms 6 en suite s£35 d£58 no children overnight

DENBIGHSHIRE

BODFARI Map 15 SJ07

The Dinorben Arms 🍷
LL16 4DA ☎ 01745 710309 📠 01745 710580
e-mail: info@dinorbenarms.com
Dir: *Come off A55 onto B5122 through Caerwys, R onto A541, R after 2.5m in Bodfari. Pub 100yrds of B541 next to church*
Extensive rebuilding has revealed evidence, including a well (now glass-covered) in the bar that suggests much earlier origins than 1640, the date on the porch. Interesting to see hot and cold lunch served smörgåsbord style, as well as farmhouse buffets, a wide range of traditional pub dishes, and a weekend carvery. Salads, vegetarian options and smaller

continued on page 613

Wales

Open: 12-11
Bar Meals: L & D served all week 12-9.30.
RESTAURANT: L served all week 12-3, D served all week 6-10.
BREWERY/COMPANY: Free House.
🍺: Greene King Old Speckled Hen, Shepherd Neame Spitfire.
FACILITIES: Children welcome, Garden.
NOTES: Parking 200

The Plough Inn

Unparallelled in the country, the development of this 18th-century former coaching inn over the past few years has been remarkable, and it now comprises a real ale bar, up-market bistro, an Italian-themed art deco restaurant and a wine shop.

The Roe, St Asaph, LL17 0LU
☎ 01745 585080 📠 01745 585363
Dir: Rhyl/St Asaph turning from A55, L at rdbt, pub 200yds on L.

This excitingly-refurbished traditional inn is just a mile from the A55 expressway, and can be found on the outskirts of town on the original Holyhead-to-London road. It buzzes with activity throughout the day and has become a notable dining venue by night. Whether you want to make a brief stop for morning coffee, have a leisurely or speedy lunch, sit indulgently over afternoon tea, or linger over a fantastic choice of evening meals, this place takes some beating. Taking horseracing as its principal theme, the Paddock Bar displays a quick bite menu on a blackboard: burgers, nachos, salads and kebabs and enhanced by chargrilled Welsh steak with caramelised red onions on a baguette, sun-dried tomato pannini with bacon, Brie and cranberry, and curried coronation chicken are accompanied by beers principally from local micro-breweries; other notable choices include Greene King Old Speckled Hen, and Shepherds Neame Spitfire. The Racecourse Bistro, with its mural of Chester racecourse, features a fresh fish display, assorted steaks from the chargrill, and house specialities from cod in beer batter with real chips to braised shank of Welsh lamb with roasted vegetables and crushed garlic potatoes. An entirely separate menu in Graffiti Italiano offers pizzas and pasta in many guises, in addition to meat dishes like veal medallions with mushrooms, cream and herb risotto, lemon sole with parsley butter from the fish section, and a choice of risottos from four cheese to smoked salmon and dill. Great desserts are a feature of all three eating places.

ODFARI continued

ortions for junior members of the party. Portion control, says
he pub's website, is a thing of the past here.
OPEN: 12-3 6-11.30 (Sun 12-11) **BAR MEALS:** L served all week
2-3 D served all week 6-10.30 Av main course £8.50
RESTAURANT: L served all week 12-3 D served all week 6-10.30 Av
course à la carte £15 **BREWERY/COMPANY:** Free House
1: Carlsberg, Stella Artois, Marston Pedigree, Banks Original. **Ⴘ:** 8
ACILITIES: Children welcome Garden: Landscaped terraced patio
Dogs allowed in garden Only **NOTES:** Parking 120

LANYNYS   Map 15 SJ16

errigllwydion Arms
L16 4PA ☎ 01745 890247
Dir: A525 towards Denbigh, R after 1.5m, then L and 1m to pub
his venerable old inn was built in 1400 on land where the
arish stables once stood. It was originally for the churchgoers
f St Saeran's church. Comfortable dining areas and a garden
ooking out to the Clwydian Hills make it a popular spot.
Menus are traditional so expect steak, kidney and ale pie,
opular grills and perhaps salmon with prawn sauce as dining
ptions, with lighter snacks available in the bar.
OPEN: 12-2 7-11 (closed Mon) **BAR MEALS:** L served Wed-Sun
2-2 D served Wed-Sun 7-9 Av main course £6 **RESTAURANT:** L
erved Wed-Sun 12-2 D served Wed-Sun 7-9 Av 3 course à la carte
12 **BREWERY/COMPANY:** Free House **1:** Interbrew Bass &
Northington Bitter,. **FACILITIES:** Children welcome Garden: Food
erved outdoors **NOTES:** Parking 50

RUTHIN   Map 15 SJ15

Pick of the Pubs

Ye Olde Anchor Inn 🏠
Rhos St LL15 1DY ☎ 01824 702813 🖹 01824 703050
e-mail: hotel@anchorinn.co.uk
Dir: at jct of A525 and A494
Located in the historic market town of Ruthin, this famous
17th-century inn is festooned with award-winning window
boxes. An ideal base for exploring the Conwy coast,
Preseli hills, Chester, Shrewsbury and Snowdonia, Ye Olde
Anchor exudes a comfortable atmosphere in the bar and
restaurant whose food output is clearly home made.
Chicken satay, and mushrooms stuffed with spinach and
cream cheese are typical starters, followed by scallops
with black pudding, chicken breast in Boursin sauce, and
carpet-bag or Chateaubriand steaks. Daily specials might
include Cumberland sausage, cod and chips, and sea
bass.
OPEN: 12 **BAR MEALS:** L served all week 12-9.30 D served
all week 12-9.30 Av main course £7 **RESTAURANT:** L served all
week 12-9.30 D served all week 7-9.30 Av 3 course à la carte £13
BREWERY/COMPANY: Free House **1:** Bass,Timothy Taylor,
Worthington, Carling. **FACILITIES:** Children welcome Dogs
allowed **NOTES:** Parking 20

**We only include details of accommodation
that has been inspected by the AA (big Stars or
Diamonds at the top of an entry), or the RAC,
VisitBritain, VisitScotland or WTB (small Stars
or Diamonds at the end of an entry).**

Pick of the Pubs

White Horse Inn
Hendrerwydd LL16 4LL ☎ 01824 790218
A traditional 17th-century inn nestling in the foothills of
the Clwydian Range, and once a stopping place for
drovers. From the outside it is nothing special, but step
inside and experience the wonderful modern European
and Celtic cooking of Londoner Ruth Vintr, and the warm
welcome provided by husband Vit, a Czech emigré.
Snacks include lamb steak and chips, cod fillet, and a
tower of a breakfast; from the main menu choose
between banana wrapped in smoked bacon, or split
herring with salsa to start, followed by Chinese style trout,
witch sole with dry vermouth and litchis, or poussin
cooked with red wine. Puddings are adventurous - cherry
pancake with cherry brandy and spices, or old favourites
like baked rice pudding with strawberry jam.
OPEN: 12-2.30 6-11 **BAR MEALS:** L served all week 12-2.30 D
served all week 6-9.30 Av main course £9 **RESTAURANT:** L
served all week 12-2.30 D served all week 6-9.15 Av 3 course à la
carte £22 **1:** Regular changing Guest ales.
FACILITIES: Children welcome Garden: Food served outside
Dogs allowed Water **NOTES:** Parking 50

ST ASAPH   Map 15 SJ07

Pick of the Pubs

The Plough Inn Ⴘ
The Roe LL17 0LU ☎ 01745 585080 🖹 01745 585363
See Pick of the Pubs on opposite page

FLINTSHIRE

BABELL   Map 15 SJ17

Black Lion Inn 🏠
CH8 8PZ ☎ 01352 720239
Dir: From Holywell take B5121 towards A541 & 2nd R to Babell
Some 35 years in the same ownership, this Grade II listed, 13th-
century former farmhouse, once used as a drovers' retreat,
ploughs a constant furrow. A constantly changing dinner menu
attracts many returning visitors. A relaxed, yet fairly formal
choice of fresh sea bass and game in season, roast duckling
with peach and brandy sauce and beef fillet with Stilton cream.
OPEN: 7-11 **BAR MEALS:** L served 1st Sun of month D served Fri-
Sat 7.30-9.30 Av main course £8.50 **RESTAURANT:** L served first
sunday of each month 12-2 D served Fri-Sat 7.15-9.30 Av 3 course à la
carte £13 **BREWERY/COMPANY:** Free House **1:** Interbrew
Boddingtons Bitter. **FACILITIES:** Children welcome
NOTES: Parking 80

CILCAIN   Map 15 SJ16

White Horse Inn 🏠
CH7 5NN ☎ 01352 740142 🖹 01352 740142
e-mail: christine.jeory@btopenworld.com
Dir: From Mold take A541 towards Denbigh. After approx 6m turn L
Situated in a lovely hillside village, the inn is several hundred
years old and very popular with walkers, cyclists, horse-riders
and people out for a drive. The dishes are home-made using
only the best quality ingredients - local wherever possible -

continued

Wales

CILCAIN continued

including steak and kidney pie, ham and eggs, lamb tajine, battered cod and chips, omelettes, Welsh lamb pie, and various curries.
OPEN: 12-3 6.30-11 (Sat-Sun 12-11) **BAR MEALS:** L served all week 12-2 D served all week 7-9 **BREWERY/COMPANY:** Free House ◀: Marston's Pedigree, Bank's Bitter, Greene King Abbot Ale, Thomas Hardy Varsity. **FACILITIES:** Garden: Tables, seating Dogs allowed **NOTES:** Parking 12

HALKYN
Map 15 SJ27

Britannia Inn
Pentre Rd CH8 8BS ☎ 01352 780272
e-mail: sarah.pollitt@britanniainn.freeserve.co.uk
Dir: Off A55 on B5123
On the old coach route between Chester and Holyhead, a 500-year-old stone pub with lovely views over the Dee estuary and the Wirral. It features a family farm with chickens, ducks and donkeys, and the large patio is ideal for alfresco eating and drinking on warm days. Typical dishes range from rump steak sandwich to pork escalope in pepper sauce, chicken tikka masala, three bean bake, and stuffed salmon roast.
OPEN: 11-11 (Sun 12-10.30) **BAR MEALS:** L served all week 12-2.30 D served all week 6.30-9 Av main course £5.50
RESTAURANT: L served all week 12-2.30 D served all week 6.30-9 Av 3 course à la carte £9 **BREWERY/COMPANY:** J W Lees ◀: J W Lees Bitter, GB Mild, Golden Original. **FACILITIES:** Children welcome Garden: Large patio area **NOTES:** Parking 40

LIXWM
Map 15 SJ17

The Crown Inn
CH8 8NQ ☎ 01352 781112
Dir: Off the B5121 S of Holywell
An early 17th-century inn in a pretty village not far from the Clwydian mountain range and Offa's Dyke Path. Hot dishes include Welsh black beef and mushroom pie, jumbo cod, aubergine moussaka, Tuscan bean crunch, and chicken and cheese bacon parcel. Sirloins and rumps are served with mushrooms, onion rings, garden peas, salad garnish and chips. Curries and lite bites also available. Recent change of ownership.
OPEN: 5.30-11 (Sun 6-11) **BAR MEALS:** L served Sat, Sun 12-2.30 D served Mon-Sun 6.30-9 Av main course £5.95 **RESTAURANT:** L served Sun 12-2.30 D served Mon-Sun 5-8.30 **BREWERY/COMPANY:** ◀: Robinsons Bitter, Frederics & Seasonal Ales. **FACILITIES:** Children welcome Children's licence Dogs allowed **NOTES:** Parking 40

MOLD
Map 15 SJ26

The Druid Inn ♀
Ruthin Rd, Llanferres CH7 5SN ☎ 01352 810225
Dir: A494 from Mold. Pub 4.5m on R
At this 17th-century coaching inn, overlooking the Alyn Valley and the Craig Harris mountains, a daily blackboard menu features decent home-cooked food such as braised shoulder of lamb in red wine, salmon wrapped in bacon with hollandaise, steak, ale and mushroom pie, and imaginatively-filled granary baps.
OPEN: 12-3 5.30-11 (Sat, Sun & BH all day & food 12-10)
BAR MEALS: L served all week 12-3 D served all week 6-10 Av main course £8.95 **RESTAURANT:** L served all week 12-3 D served all week 6-10 Av 3 course à la carte £8.95
BREWERY/COMPANY: Burtonwood ◀: Burtonwood Best Bitter & changing Guest ale. ♀: 10 **FACILITIES:** Children welcome Garden Dogs allowed **NOTES:** Parking 40

NORTHOP
Map 15 SJ2

Pick of the Pubs

Stables Bar Restaurant ⌂ ♀
CH7 6AB ☎ 01352 840577 📠 01352 840382
e-mail: info@soughtonhall.co.uk
Dir: from A55, take A5119 through Northop village
Opened in 1997, this magnificent destination pub was made from the Grade I listed stables of Soughton Hall, the former Bishop of Chester's Palace. Superbly converted under massive oak beams, the building retains a horseracing theme; the original brick floor and some of the stalls have been retained, and tables are named after famous racecourses. The ground floor contains a real ale bar with an impressive menu, and upstairs diners will find an open-plan kitchen with an adjacent, fully-stocked wine shop. Choose your own fresh fish, seafood or steaks and watch them cooked to order, accompanied by fresh breads, hand-cut chips and a self-served salad. Other dishes include roast salmon and couscous, Mexican chicken stirfry, and chargrilled vegetable kebabs. Right next door, the Hall itself is a magnificent pile in a breathtaking setting.
OPEN: 11-3 6-11.30 **BAR MEALS:** L served all week 12-3 D served all week 7-10 Av main course £7.95 **RESTAURANT:** L served all week 12-3 D served all week 7-10 Av. 3 course à la carte £20 Av 3 course fixed price £25 **BREWERY/COMPANY:** Free House ◀: Shepherds Neame Spitfire, Shepherd Neame Bishops Finger, Coach House Honeypot,. **FACILITIES:** Children welcome Garden: Food served outdoors, patio, Dogs allowed Water **NOTES:** Parking 150

GWYNEDD

ABERDYFI
Map 14 SN6

Dovey Inn ★★ ⌂ ♀
Seaview Ter LL35 0EF ☎ 01654 767332 📠 01654 767996
e-mail: info@doveyinn.com

Historic inn on the estuary of the River Dovey, only 20 yards from the sea and the fine sandy beach. An extensive seafood menu includes Thai-spiced shark steak, fish pie, Bantry Bay mussels, chargrilled swordfish, and tuna steak with red wine fish gravy. Other options including sandwiches, light bites, vegetarian, meat dishes and pizza.
OPEN: 11-11 (Sun 12-10.30) **BAR MEALS:** L served all week 12-2.30 D served all week 6-9.30 Av main course £7.50
BREWERY/COMPANY: Free House ◀: Hancock HB, Bass, Carling Black Label. ♀: 14 **FACILITIES:** Children welcome Children's licence Garden: Patio area Dogs allowed **ROOMS:** 8 bedrooms 8 en suite s£70 d£60

Harp Inn

Easy and breezy, this flat and enjoyable peninsula walk explores the fine beach at Dinas Dinlle and Foryd Bay, noted for its birdlife. Panoramic views extend from the mountains of Snowdonia to the Lleyn Peninsula.

Turn left from the front of the inn and walk along the road for 1/2 mile (0.8km) to a T-junction. Turn right and follow the road down to Dinas Dinlle beach, a fine stretch of sand running the whole length of the peninsula. Turn right along the promenade and enjoy views across the Menai Straits to the Isle of Anglesey on your right.

At the end of the promenade, keep to the seaward side and follow the path through the dunes, or if the tide is out walk along the beach. On nearing Fort Belan, cut inland away from the sea and pick up the grassy bank (old railway line) to reach a bird hide. Pause here for a moment to watch the birdlife in Foryd Bay.

With the sea to your left, follow the path south beside Foryd Bay and soon pass Morfa Lodge Caravan Site. Continue for about 1/2 mile (0.8km) and cross the footbridge over the river. Follow what can be an overgrown path to the road, passing Chatham Farm on your left. Turn right along the road and follow it for nearly 1 1/4 miles (2km) back to the village and the pub.

HARP INN, LLANDWROG
Tyn'llan LL54 5SY.
☎ 01286 831071
Directions: A55 from Chester bypass, signed off A487 Pwllheli rd
Close to Dinas Dinlle beach and handy for Snowdonia, this family-run inn offers interesting menus and good real ale in its welcoming lounge bar. Cottagey bedrooms.
Open: 12-3 6-11 (Sat 12-11, Sun 12-3 7-10.30, closed Sun eve Oct-Etr & Mon lunch).
Bar Meals: 12-2 6.30-8.30 (no food all Mon).
Notes: Children welcome. Garden. Parking.
(See page 617 for full entry)

DISTANCE: 6 miles (10km)
MAP: OS Landranger 115
TERRAIN: Beach, dunes, estuary, farmland
PATHS: Promenade, tracks, coast and estuary path
GRADIENT: Mainly level

Walk submitted by The Harp Inn

ABERDYEL continued

Pick of the Pubs

Penhelig Arms Hotel & Restaurant ★★ ◎ ⬥ ♀
Terrace Rd LL35 0LT ☎ 01654 767215 ▤ 01654 767690
e-mail: info@penheligarms.com
Dir: On A493 (coastal rd) W of Machynlleth

Spectacular views over the tidal Dyfi estuary can be enjoyed from this relaxed, family-run hotel and restaurant on the spectacular coastline of mid-Wales. Guests experience a warm welcome in the bar with its central log-burning hearth and in fine weather can lounge on the sea wall opposite, awaiting delivery of ever-enticing food. Good ales and huge list of around 300 wines available. Fresh fish, crabs and lobsters arrive straight from the quay and a solid reliance on such local produce is evident in menus. Dishes might include salmon fillet seared with spring onions, chilli and ginger; plaice fillet grilled with prawns and cheese; pan-fried swordfish finished in a cardamom, ginger and lemon sauce; or simply a fresh crab sandwich. Tempting desserts often include dark chocolate, orange and Cointreau torte; apricot frangipane tart with crème fraîche; and bread and butter pudding.
OPEN: 11.30-3.30 5.30-11 (Sun 12-3.30, 6-10.30) Closed: Dec 25-26 **BAR MEALS:** L served all week 12-2.30 D served all week 6.30-9.30 Av main course £8.95 **RESTAURANT:** L served all week 12-2.30 D served all week 7-9.30 Av 3 course fixed price £25 **BREWERY/COMPANY:** Free House ◀: Carlsberg-Tetley Tetley Bitter, Greene King Abbot Ale, Adnams Broadside, Brains Reverend James & SA. ♀: 20 **FACILITIES:** Children welcome Children's licence Garden: Seating opposite hotel on sea wall Dogs allowed **NOTES:** Parking 12 **ROOMS:** 14 bedrooms 14 en suite 4 family rooms s£40 d£69

ABERSOCH
Map 14 SH32

St Tudwal's Inn ◎ ♀
High St LL53 7DS ☎ 01758 712539 ▤ 01758 713701
Dir: take A499 from Pwllheli, follow one way system, pub on R
A Victorian building, now converted to provide two bars and a restaurant, believed to be haunted by a Victorian lady. Steaks are a popular option, alongside dishes such as sea bass poached in sherry with julienne peppers, duck with port, cream and mushroom sauce, and lamb cutlets with wine gravy.
OPEN: 11-11 (Sun 12-10.30) **BAR MEALS:** L served all week 12-2.30 D served all week 6-9 Av main course £6.50 **RESTAURANT:** D served all week 6-9 **BREWERY/COMPANY:** ◀: Robinsons Best, Hatters Mild. **FACILITIES:** Children welcome Garden: Food served outside. Beer patio Dogs allowed In the garden only **NOTES:** Parking 20

BLAENAU FFESTINIOG
Map 14 SH74

The Miners Arms
Llechwedd Slate Caverns LL41 3NB
☎ 01766 830306 ▤ 01766 831260
e-mail: quarrytours@aol.com
Dir: Blaenau Ffestiniog is 25 miles from Llandudno on the N Wales coast, situated on the A470 to main N-S Trunk Rd
Slate floors, open fires and staff in Victorian costume emphasise the heritage theme of this welcoming pub nestling in the centre of a Welsh village. On the site of Llechwedd Slate Caverns, one of the country's leading tourist attractions, it caters for all comers and tastes: expect steak and ale casserole, pork pie and salad, various ploughman's lunches, and hot apple pie, as well as afternoon tea with scones and cream.
OPEN: 11-5.30 Closed: Nov-Easter **BAR MEALS:** L served all week 11-5 **BREWERY/COMPANY:** Free House **FACILITIES:** Children welcome Garden Dogs allowed **NOTES:** Parking 200

BONTDDU
Map 14 SH61

The Halfway House ◎
LL40 2UE ☎ 01341 430635
e-mail: jamesnoonan883@aol.com
Dir: On A436 between Dolgellau & Barmouth
Dating back to 1700, the Halfway House has mellow pine chapel pews and fireplaces, giving the place a welcoming, cosy atmosphere. Situated near the Mawddach estuary, much loved by Wordsworth, the pub is directly on the route of several popular local walks. Good range of cask conditioned ales, several of which are from local breweries. Typical menu includes steak, mushroom and ale pie, wild mushroom and herb capelletti, lamb jalfrezi, and seared salmon on a bed of crispy leeks with soy and ginger sauce.
OPEN: 11-11 (Sun 12-10.30) 6-11 (Winter 11-3, 6-11) Closed: Dec 25 **BAR MEALS:** L served all week 12-2.30 D served all week 6-9.30 Av main course £7 **RESTAURANT:** L served all week 12-2.30 D served all week 6-9.30 **BREWERY/COMPANY:** Free House ◀: Robinsons, Hartleys Cumbria Way. **FACILITIES:** Children welcome Garden: Patio, food served outside Dogs allowed Water **NOTES:** Parking 30

DOLGELLAU
Map 14 SH71

Pick of the Pubs

George III Hotel ★★ ◎
Penmaenpool LL40 1YD ☎ 01341 422525 ▤ 01341 423565
e-mail: reception@george-3rd.co.uk
Dir: 2m West of A493 beyond RSPB Centre
At the edge of the magnificent Mawddach Estuary with splendid views to the Snowdonia National Park, the hotel stands a mile or so out of town, in tranquil waterside meadows inhabited by swans, herons and otters. Part of the accommodation is housed in a former railway station. The Cellar Bar beside the water is ideal for families, cyclists and walkers, whilst for a more genteel atmosphere try the main dining rooms or the upper level Dresser Bar with its unusual bar counter. Noted for local salmon, sea trout, pheasant and wild duck in season, the menu (cooked by the landlord) caters for most eventualities. At one end of the scale are bar snacks including soups, sandwiches and basket meals, while the restaurant menu weighs in with starters such as crepe de crevettes, followed perhaps by poached cod loin on spinach with mornay sauce, or best end of Welsh lamb roasted and served with broad beans, silverskin onions and a red wine and rosemary sauce. Morning and afternoon teas are also available.

continued

OPEN: 11-11 **BAR MEALS:** L served all week 12-2.30 D served all week 6.30-9.30 Av main course £8 **RESTAURANT:** L served Sun 12-2 D served all week 7-9 Av 3 course à la carte £27.50 **BREWERY/COMPANY:** Free House ☏: Ruddles Best, John Smiths Cask, Guest Beers: Theakstons, Pedigree and Directors. **FACILITIES:** Children welcome Dogs allowed **NOTES:** Parking 40 **ROOMS:** 11 bedrooms 11 en suite s£45 d£80

LLANBEDR
Map 14 SH52

Victoria Inn ♦♦♦♦ NEW

LL45 2LD ☎ 01341 241213 📠 01341 241644
e-mail: junebarry@lineone.net
Dir: Telephone for directions

Heavily beamed and richly atmospheric, the Victoria is ideal for the pub enthusiast seeking authentic features like flagged floors, an ancient stove, and unusual circular wooden settle. Good food is served in the bars and restaurant, including tasty filled baguettes, and lamb shoulder shank, fish pie, steak and kidney pie, and Welsh dragon pie. A well-kept garden is inviting on warmer days.

OPEN: 11-11 **BAR MEALS:** L served all week 12-9 D served all week 6-9 Av main course £7 **RESTAURANT:** L served all week 12-3 D served all week 6-9 Av 3 course à la carte £12 **BREWERY/COMPANY:** ☏: Robinson's Best Bitter, Hartleys XB, Carling Black Label. **FACILITIES:** Children welcome Garden: Riverside Garden, pond, trees & plants Dogs allowed **NOTES:** Parking 50 **ROOMS:** 5 bedrooms 5 en suite 1 family rooms s£42.50 d£72.50

LLANDWROG
Map 14 SH45

The Harp Inn 🏠

Tyn'llan LL54 5SY ☎ 01286 831071 📠 01286 830239
e-mail: management@theharp.globalnet.co.uk
Dir: A55 from Chester bypass, signed off A487 Pwllheli rd

A long established haven for travellers, the inn is located in the historic home village of the nearby Glynllifon Estate, between the mountains of Snowdonia and the beautiful beaches of Dinas Dinlle. A proudly Welsh menu offers lob scouse with roll and red cabbage, Welsh mackerel rarebit on toast, trio of local bangers and mash, Welsh lamb steaks with a laverbread and citrus sauce, local sea bass with ginger and sesame seeds, and Glamorgan sausages with red onion marmalade. Welsh language menu supplied.

OPEN: 12-3 6-11 (Times vary, ring for details, Sat 12-11) Closed: Jan 1 **BAR MEALS:** L served Tue-Sun 12-2 D served Tue-Sun 6.30-8.30 Av main course £7.95 **RESTAURANT:** L served Tue-Sun 12-2 D served Tue-Sun 6.30-8.30 Av 3 course à la carte £15 Av 3 course fixed price £9.95 **BREWERY/COMPANY:** Free House ☏: Interbrew Bass, Black Sheep Best, Wyre Piddle Piddle in the Wind, Plassey Bitter. **FACILITIES:** Children welcome Garden: 6 tables Dogs allowed Water **NOTES:** Parking 20 **ROOMS:** 4 bedrooms 1 en suite 1 family rooms s£25 d£50 (WTB)

See Pub Walk on page 615

LLANENGAN
Map 14 SH22

The Sun Inn

LL53 7LG ☎ 01758 712660
Dir: From Pwllheli take A499 S to Abersoch, then 1.5m towards Hells Mouth Beach

Friendly and welcoming pub, reputedly haunted, with a wishing well in the garden, and where the locals are likely to burst into song. The changing menu of home-cooked dishes includes steaks, lasagne and chicken breast.

OPEN: 12-2.30 6-11 (open all day Sat) **BAR MEALS:** L served all week 12-3 D served all week 6-9 Av main course £6.95 **BREWERY/COMPANY:** ☏: Robinson Best, Old Stockport Bitter. **FACILITIES:** Children welcome Garden **NOTES:** Parking 70

MAENTWROG
Map 14 SH64

Pick of the Pubs

Grapes Hotel 🏠

LL41 4HN ☎ 01766 590365 & 590208 📠 01766 590654
e-mail: grapesmaen@aol.com
Dir: A5 thru Corwen to Bala, A487 to Maentwrog, onto A496, pub 100yrds in RH side

The management, advises the menu, reserves the right to experience certain hazards - blown fuses, burst pipes, unreliable suppliers...and earthquakes, adding wryly 'Don't laugh, we've had one'. Whatever its impact on the Richter scale, it thankfully left this Grade II-listed, 17th-century coaching inn unscathed. Today, we're in the Snowdonia National Park, but long before anyone thought of such a thing Lloyd George and Lily Langtry took tea here - allegedly on separate occasions. Exposed stone walls, and heavily carved wooden bars help to create a clyd (as the Welsh say), or cosy feeling, accentuated by roaring log fires on wintry days. Specials change weekly, but there's always a good choice, including vegetarian. On the regular menu are the 'famous' pork ribs ('one is sensible, two not for the faint-hearted'), wholetail scampi, gammon steaks, lamb chops, chilli (again not for wimps), pastas and curries. Oh, and a little old Victorian lady sometimes frightens the kitchen staff 'plumb rigid'.

OPEN: 11-11 (Sun 12-10.30) Closed: Dec 25 **BAR MEALS:** L served all week 12-2 D served all week 6-9 **BREWERY/COMPANY:** Free House ☏: Marstons Pedigree, Greene King Old Speckled Hen, IPA, Wye Valley Butty Bach. **FACILITIES:** Children welcome Children's licence Garden: Large garden with stone water feature Dogs allowed **NOTES:** Parking 36

 The Rosette is the AA award for food. Look out for it next to a pub's name.

NANTGWYNANT
Map 14 SH65

Pen-Y-Gwryd
LL55 4NT ☎ 01286 870211
Dir: 6m S of Llanberis at head of Gwryd river, close to junction of A4086 & A498. 4 miles from Capel Curig on A4086 on T-Junction with lake in front
In the magnificently rugged Snowdonia National Park, this cosy climber's pub and rescue post is the home of British mountaineering. The 1953 Everest team scrawled their signatures on the ceiling when they used it as a training base. Wholesome, inexpensive, daily-changing menu offerings might be roast leg of Welsh lamb, rich steak and mushroom pie, or red wine-cooked chicken with smoked bacon and mushrooms, followed by bread and butter pudding and various ice creams.
OPEN: 11-11 Closed: Nov to New Year, mid-week Jan-Feb Closed: 25 Dec **BAR MEALS:** L served all week 12-2 D served all week **RESTAURANT:** L served all week D served all week 7.30-8 Av 5 course fixed price £20 **BREWERY/COMPANY:** Free House ◗: Interbrew Bass & Boddingtons Bitter. **FACILITIES:** Children welcome Garden: Mountain garden with lake and sauna Dogs allowed **NOTES:** Parking 25 No credit cards

PORTHMADOG
Map 14 SH53

The Ship 🍽 ♀
Lombard St LL49 9AP ☎ 01766 512990
Dir: From A55 take A470 S toward the coast
The oldest pub still operating in Porthmadog, The Ship is located close to the harbour and is mentioned in many maritime books on the area. One menu serves all, with plenty of fresh fish - chargrilled tuna steak, breaded plaice fillet, salmon and spinach in a tarragon sauce, or moules marinière. Other options include Thai red vegetable curry, lamb chump, steak and kidney pudding, and chicken with wild mushrooms. Over 90 malt whiskies available.
OPEN: 11-11 (Sun 12-10.30) Closed: Dec 25 **BAR MEALS:** L served all week 12-3 Av main course £4 **RESTAURANT:** L served all week **BREWERY/COMPANY:** Punch Taverns ◗: Greene King Old Speckled Hen & IPA, Carlsberg-Tetley Tetley Bitter, Timothy Taylor Landlord, M&B Mild. **FACILITIES:** Children welcome Dogs allowed

TUDWEILIOG
Map 14 SH23

Lion Hotel 🍽
LL53 8ND ☎ 01758 770244 📠 01758 770244
Dir: A499 from Caernarfon, B4417 Tudweiliog
The Lee family have run this friendly, 300-year-old village inn on the Lleyn Peninsula for 30 years. The large garden and children's play area makes the pub especially popular with cyclists, walkers and families. There is a non-smoking family dining room but food is served throughout, from lunchtime baguettes to traditional favourites such as roast chicken and home-made vegetarian lasagne.
OPEN: 11.30-11 (Winter 12-2, 7-11 all day Sat) (Sun 12-2) **BAR MEALS:** L served all week 12-2 D served all week 6-9 Av main course £6 **RESTAURANT:** L served all week 12-2 D served all week 6-9 **BREWERY/COMPANY:** Free House ◗: Marston's Pedigree, Interbrew Boddingtons, Theakston. **FACILITIES:** Children welcome Garden: Food served outside Dogs water **NOTES:** Parking 40

> ★ **Pubs with Red Stars are part of the AA's Top 200 Hotels in Britain & Ireland**

BEAUMARIS
Map 14 SH67

The Liverpool Arms Hotel ♀
Castle St LL58 8BA ☎ 01248 810362 📠 01248 811135
e-mail: enquiries@liverpoolarms.co.uk
Dir: A5 across the Menai Straits, R onto A545 through Menai Bridge
Historic inn dating back to 1706 when there was a busy trade between Liverpool and Beaumaris - hence the name. Strong nautical theme with timbers from HMS Victory, Nelson's flagship. Popular, daily-changing blackboard menus and a summer salad bar. Expect a choice of fish dishes, as well as scrumpy pork hock in cider sauce, home made steak pie, or salmon and ricotta cannelloni.
OPEN: 11-11 **BAR MEALS:** L served all week 12-2 D served all week 6-9.30 Av main course £7 **BREWERY/COMPANY:** Punch ◗: Greene King Morland Old Speckled Hen, IPA Flowers. **FACILITIES:** Children welcome **NOTES:** Parking 12

Pick of the Pubs

Ye Olde Bulls Head Inn ★★ ◎◎ ♀
Castle St LL58 8AP ☎ 01248 810329 📠 01248 811294
e-mail: info@bullsheadinn.co.uk
Dir: From Brittannia road bridge follow A545
Just a stone's throw from Beaumaris Castle and the Menai Straits, a traditional watering hole dating back to 1472 whose famous past guests have included Samuel Johnson and Charles Dickens. The smartly-furnished first-floor restaurant offers a formal menu based around acclaimed seafood dishes and a wine connoisseur's ideal list. Sample Thai-style scallops with coconut milk, coriander and chilli, and escabeche of red mullet with cider and orange, followed perhaps by grilled local sea bass with Conwy mussel ravioli, steamed black bream fillet with crab chowder, and poached brill fillet with salmon sausage. Pepper caviar and lax sauce. It's not all fish though: lamb and pistachio nut terrine with red port and fig chutney, and main dish of Hereford duck breast, might be rounded off with a delectable caramelised nut tart with gin and rosemary ice cream. A newer brasserie, complete with harlequin tiles, ranges through pasta, boeuf bourguignon, rack of lamb, and chargrilled pork or lamb.
OPEN: 10.30-11 (Sun-12-10.30) Closed: 25 Dec **BAR MEALS:** L served all week 12-2 D served all week 6-9 Av main course £7.50 **RESTAURANT:** D served Mon-Sat 7.30-9.30 Av 3 course à la carte £30 **BREWERY/COMPANY:** Free House ◗: Bass, Hancocks, Worthington. **FACILITIES:** Children welcome **NOTES:** Parking 10 **ROOMS:** 13 bedrooms 13 en suite s£65 d£92

LLANFACHRAETH
Map 14 SH38

Holland Hotel ♀
LL65 4UH ☎ 01407 740252
A friendly 18th-century inn within easy reach of the Anglesey Heritage coastline and Holyhead ferry port. Also convenient for stunning scenery, safe sandy beaches, and a championship golf course. Local produce forms the mainstay of menus that include steak in stout, salads, Indian dishes, a vegetarian selection, dressed crab and seafood platter.
OPEN: 12-11 **BAR MEALS:** L served all week 12-9 D served all week Av main course £5.50 **RESTAURANT:** L served all week 12-9 D served all week Av 3 course à la carte £10 **BREWERY/COMPANY:** J W Lees ◗: J W Lees. **FACILITIES:** Children welcome Garden: outdoor eating **NOTES:** Parking 40

Wales

RED WHARF BAY   Map 14 SH58

Pick of the Pubs

The Ship Inn 🍴 ♀

LL75 8RJ ☎ 01248 852568 🖷 01248 851013

At low tide, the sands of Red Wharf Bay stretch for miles, attracting large numbers of waterfowl and wading birds. Before the age of steam, sailing ships arrived with cargoes from all over the world, and sailors drank in the then Quay Inn from six in the morning. Today, Conwy Bay fish and seafood are landed here, before making the short journey via the kitchen to the plates of diners in the bars and non-smoking restaurant. Possible starters include hot and sour fish fillets on marinated beansprouts and shiitake mushrooms, and chilli crab linguine with garlic ciabattas and salad leaves, while for a main course why not try baked half shoulder of Welsh lamb with redcurrant and rosemary, or Mediterranean style couscous with roasted vegetables and Mozzarella. Warm rice pudding with Amaretto crust and tamarillo sauce, or Welsh cheeses would round things off well. The waterside beer garden is a big attraction on warm days.

OPEN: 11-3.30 6.30-11 (Sat 11-11, Sun 12-10.30) **BAR MEALS:** L served all week 12-2.30 D served all week 6.30-9 Av main course £8 **RESTAURANT:** L served Sun 12-2.30 D served Fri-Sat 7-9.30 Av 3 course à la carte £20 **BREWERY/COMPANY:** Free House 🍺: Imperial, Adnams, Greene King, Burton Ale.

FACILITIES: Children welcome Garden: On water's edge Dogs allowed Water **NOTES:** Parking 45

ABERGAVENNY   Map 09 SO21

Pick of the Pubs

Clytha Arms 🍴 ♀

Clytha NP7 9BW ☎ 01873 840206 🖷 01873 840206

Dir: From A449/A40 junction (E of Abergavenny) follow signs for 'Old Road Abergavenny/Clytha'

A former dower house set in pretty gardens alongside the old Abergavenny road, the Clytha Arms is an award-winning pub with an excellent reputation for its food. The bar offers six real ales and a range of snacks, including leek and laverbread rissoles, home-made wild boar sausages with potato pancakes, and salmon burger with tarragon mayonnaise. Typical dishes in the popular restaurant are grilled red mullet with cockle risotto, rabbit and wild mushroom pie, and Caribbean fruit curry. The pub is a popular festival venue and the two acres of grounds take in a paddock, lawns, gardens, a fountain, ducks and a boules pitch. Raglan's famous 15th-century castle is just a few miles down the road, and Cardiff with all its big city attractions is a 40-minute drive away.

OPEN: 12-3 6-11 (Sat 12-11) Closed: 25 Dec **BAR MEALS:** L served Tue-Sat 12.30-2.15 D served Tues-Fri 7-9.30 Av main course £6.90 **RESTAURANT:** L served all week 12.30-2.30 D served Tue-Sun 7-9.30 Av 3 course à la carte £25 Av 3 course fixed price £17.95 **BREWERY/COMPANY:** Free House 🍺: Bass, Felinfoel Double Dragon, Hook Norton. ♀: 10 **FACILITIES:** Children welcome Garden: 2 acres with paddock, fountain & lawns **NOTES:** Parking 100

Pantrhiwgoch Hotel & Riverside Restaurant ★★ 🍴

Brecon Rd NP8 1EP ☎ 01873 810550 🖷 01873 811880

e-mail: info@pantrhiwgoch.co.uk

Dir: On A40 between Abergavenny & Crickhowell

Last year, the new owners of this part 16th-century inn and restaurant featured in Channel 4's No Turning Back about major lifestyle change. The views from its elevated position above the River Usk are splendid, as those who watched the programme may recall. The mostly locally-sourced, but all home-made, dishes are available throughout the two bars, conservatory, dining room and patio. Fish choices include salmon, hake, bream and gurnard, while among the meats are duck, lamb, and fillet and rib-eye steaks.

OPEN: 11-11 **BAR MEALS:** L served all week 12-2 D served Mon-Sat 6.30-9 Av main course £13 **RESTAURANT:** L served all week 12-2 D served Mon-Sat 6.30-9 Av 3 course à la carte £23.50 **BREWERY/COMPANY:** Free House 🍺: Felinfoel Double Dragon, Tetley Smoothflow. **FACILITIES:** Children welcome Garden: Patio area overlooking the River Usk **NOTES:** Parking 40 **ROOMS:** 18 bedrooms 18 en suite 2 family rooms s£63 d£73

The Skirrid Mountain Inn

Lanvihangel Crucorney NP7 8DH ☎ 01873 890258

e-mail: mistyspooks@aol.com

Dir: A465 4 Miles outside Abergavenny, well signposted

Ancient, mainly Tudor stone inn, reputedly the oldest inn in Wales and a courthouse between 1110 and the 17th century. Nearly 200 people were hanged here and a beam above the foot of the stairs served as a scaffold. Appetising bar and restaurant menu offers the likes of local lamb chops, Welsh Champion sausages and home-made vegetarian Skirrid loaf.

OPEN: 11-11 **BAR MEALS:** L served all week 12-2 D served Mon-Sat 7-9 Av main course £7.95 **RESTAURANT:** L served all week 12-2.30 D served Mon-Sat 7-9 Av 3 course à la carte £12 **BREWERY/COMPANY:** 🍺: Ushers Best, Ushers Founders, Ushers Four Seasons, Bass. **FACILITIES:** Children welcome Garden: patio/terrace, BBQ, floral displays Dogs allowed **NOTES:** Parking 20 No credit cards

Pick of the Pubs

Walnut Tree Inn 🍴🍴 ♀

Llandewi Skirrid NP7 8AW

☎ 01873 852797 🖷 01873 859764

Dir: 3m NE of Abergavenny on B4521

Country dining that needs no introduction, so famous has the Walnut Tree become over the past 40 or so years. From its humble origins as a pub that served something a bit more interesting than pie and chips, this Abergavenny landmark and brainchild of Italian chef Franco Taruschio has retained its authenticity through changes in ownership. The menu stays true to tradition whilst blazing a new trail in trendy directions, and it is still worth travelling miles for. From the seasonal menu comes sea bass with artichokes and barba di fratti, steamed halibut with mussels and saffron, grilled tuna with tomatoes and salsa verde, and roast cod with lentils, bacon and red wine sauce. Braised shoulder of lamb, and Lady Llanover's salt duck are also there, with peerless wines to match, and the kitchen's pacey imagination shows with hot chocolate fondant and marmalade ice cream. Not a pub for the casual passer by.

OPEN: 12-3 7-12 Closed: 1 wk Xmas **BAR MEALS:** L served Tues-Sun 12-2.45 D served Tues-Sun 7-9.30 Av main course £16 **RESTAURANT:** L served Tue-Sat 12-3 D served Tue-Sat 7-11 Av 3 course à la carte £19.50 **BREWERY/COMPANY:** Free House 🍺: No real ale. **FACILITIES:** Children welcome **NOTES:** Parking 50

Wales

The Woodland Restaurant & Bar

A delightful country walk exploring the countryside to the north of Llanvair Discoed – meaning 'church under the wood.'

On leaving the restaurant and bar, take Well Lane, the narrow road to the left, and follow it uphill. Look out for the village well in the right boundary. Just beyond it, on the left, are the renovated buildings of a farm. New farm barns have also been built on the right-hand side of the lane.

Continue to where Well Lane terminates and you will see Slade's Cottage, which has been enlarged over the years from what was once a small dwelling. Look for a stile and gate just beyond the cottage. Cross over and turn immediately right, passing over a stream. Keep ahead up the field, with the fence and trees to your right.

As you begin to approach the top right-hand corner of the field, head towards a large tree near a gap in the stone wall. Pass through the gap, cross the stile and follow the path, keeping a thatched cottage to your right.

Just beyond the cottage, which was recently renovated as part of a medieval village restoration programme, you reach a junction of paths. Turn left here and follow a pleasant woodland path. Cross a stile and continue ahead until you reach a junction with a bridleway skirting the bottom of Gray Hill.

THE WOODLAND RESTAURANT & BAR, LLANVAIR DISCOED
NP16 6LX

☎ 01633 400313

Directions: Telephone for directions Extended old inn close to the Roman fortress town of Caerwent. At heart a friendly village local, serving a good range of beers, and a varied menu of fresh food.
Open: 11-3 6-11 (Sun 12-3 7-10.30)
Bar Meals: 12-2 (rest only Sun) 6.30-10
Notes: Children welcome (swings, slide). Dogs welcome (water). Garden, bench seating. Parking. (See opposite page for full entry)

Turn left here and head down the metalled road towards Llanvair Discoed. Turn left at the next junction and walk downhill to The Woodlands. Along here you can see the remains of Llanvair Castle located within the grounds of a private house. Below lies the local church, which is worth closer inspection.

DISTANCE: 2 1/4 miles/3.6km
MAP: OS Explorer OL 14
TERRAIN: Rolling hills and farmland
PATHS: Footpaths, bridleways and country roads
GRADIENT: Some steep climbs

Walk submitted and checked by the Woodlands Restaurant and Bar

BETTWS-NEWYDD   Map 09 SO30

Pick of the Pubs

Black Bear Inn
NP15 1JN ☎ 01873 880701 880701
Dir: *Off B4598 N of Usk*

Set in a tiny hamlet surrounded by rolling Monmouthshire countryside, the Black Bear is a study in black-and-white. The bar's oak beams, flagstone floor and open fire have been left as original as possible. A combination of good beers and spontaneous cooking by chef Stephen Molyneux is a winning formula. Local produce is used almost entirely in the dining-rooms: salmon and brown trout are landed from the River Usk less than a quarter mile away and farmed venison, lamb, beef and seasonal game are in plentiful supply. The blackboard menu changes daily or choose 'whatever comes from the kitchen' - that could be warm salad of crispy duck; terrine of local pheasant; fresh local salmon with tomato and basil sauce; turbot with white wine, mushrooms and cream; or one of many other surprise offerings. Also often available are tasty home-made fishcakes; beef medallions in Madeira sauce; and chocolate and orange terrine, all served with minimal formality.
OPEN: 12-2 6-12 **BAR MEALS:** L served Tue-Sun 12-2 D served Mon-Sat 6-10 Av main course £14 **RESTAURANT:** L served Tue-Sun 12-2 D served Mon-Sat 6-10 Av 3 course fixed price £23 **BREWERY/COMPANY:** Free House ◀: Fuller's London Pride, Timothy Taylor Landlord, Interbrew Bass, Greene King Old Speckled Hen. **FACILITIES:** Children welcome Garden: Shrubs, fruit trees, hen house, seating Dogs allowed Water tap **NOTES:** Parking 20 No credit cards

---

CHEPSTOW   Map 04 ST59

Pick of the Pubs

The Boat Inn
The Back NP16 5HH ☎ 01291 628192 ◻ 01291 628193
See Pick of the Pubs on page 622

Castle View Hotel
16 Bridge St NP16 5EZ ☎ 01291 620349 ◻ 01291 627397
e-mail: dave@castview.demon.co.uk
Dir: *Opposite Chepstow Castle*
Built as a private house some 300 years ago, its solid walls up to five feet thick in places, this hotel is situated opposite the castle, alongside the River Wye. The regularly-changing menu might offer steaks, breast of chicken stuffed with Stilton, Welsh lamb, and cod in beer batter.
OPEN: 12-2.30 6-11 **BAR MEALS:** L served all week 12-2 D served Mon-Sat 6.30-9.30 **RESTAURANT:** L served Sun D served Mon-Sat 6.30-9.30 **BREWERY/COMPANY:** Free House ◀: Wye Valley Real Ale, Coors Worthington's. **FACILITIES:** Children welcome Garden: Small secluded Dogs allowed **NOTES:** Parking 200

> **Restaurant and Bar Meal times indicate the times when food is available. Last orders may be approximately 30 minutes before the times stated.**

LLANTRISANT   Map 09 ST39

Greyhound Inn 🛏 ♀
NP15 1LE ☎ 01291 672505 & 673447 ◻ 01291 673255
e-mail: enquiry@greyhound-inn.com
Dir: *From M4 take A449 towards Monmouth, 1st jct to Usk, L into Usk Sq. Take 2nd L signed Llantrisant. 2.5m to inn*

Established as a country inn in 1845, the Greyhound was originally a 17th-century Welsh longhouse. Now, this charming free house features award-winning gardens, open log fires and ten comfortable en suite bedrooms in the converted stone stable block. There's a good range of home-cooked dishes and tempting daily specials that includes Welsh lamb shank with red wine; local River Usk salmon; stuffed broccoli and mushroom pancakes; and Abergavenny pheasant.
OPEN: 11-11 (Sun 12-4, 7-11) Closed: 25 Dec **BAR MEALS:** L served all week 12-2.15 D served Mon-Sat 6-10.30 Av main course £7.50 **RESTAURANT:** L served all week 12-2.15 D served Mon-Sat 6-10.30 **BREWERY/COMPANY:** Free House ◀: Interbrew Flowers Original & Bass, Marston's Pedigree, Greene King Abbot Ale. ♀: 10 **FACILITIES:** Children welcome Garden: Pond with fountain, delightful garden Dogs allowed Water **NOTES:** Parking 60 **ROOMS:** 10 bedrooms 10 en suite s£49 d£68 (WTB)

LLANVAIR DISCOED   Map 09 ST49

Pick of the Pubs

The Woodland Restaurant & Bar 🛏 ♀
NP16 6LX ☎ 01633 400313 ◻ 01633 400313
Dir: *Telephone for directions*
An old inn extended to accommodate a growing number of diners, the Woodland is located close to the Roman fortress town of Caerwent and Wentworth's forest and reservoir. It remains at heart a friendly village local, serving a good range of beers. A varied menu of freshly prepared dishes caters for all tastes from ciabatta bread with various toppings to Welsh lamb loin wrapped in spinach and filo pastry on a bed of wild mushroom and rosemary risotto. Meat is sourced from a local butcher, who slaughters all his own meat, and the fish is mostly from Cornwall, like sea bass cooked in rock salt and lemon. Outside there's a large, well-equipped garden with plenty of bench seating.
OPEN: 11-3 6-11 (Sun 12-3, 7-10.30) **BAR MEALS:** L served all week 12-2 D served Mon-Sat 6.30-10 Av main course £11.25 **RESTAURANT:** L served all week 12-2 D served Mon-Sat 6.30-9.30 Av 3 course à la carte £23 **BREWERY/COMPANY:** Free House ◀: Buckleys Best, Reverend James, Somerset & Dorset, H.B. **FACILITIES:** Children welcome Garden: Plenty of bench seating, play area Dogs allowed Water **NOTES:** Parking 30
See Pub Walk on opposite page

Wales

Open: 11-11 (Sun 12-10.30)
Bar Meals: L served all week 12-3,
D served all week 6.30-10.
RESTAURANT: L served all week 12-3,
D served all week 6.30-10.
BREWERY/COMPANY:
UNIQUE PUB CO LTD
🍺: Interbrew Bass, Smiles,
Wadworth 6X.
FACILITIES: Children welcome, Garden.
NOTES: Parking 20

The Boat Inn

Standing on the banks of the River Wye, The Boat Inn's front terrace is a perfect place to relax on a summer's day and watch the ever-changing scenery.

The Back, Chepstow, NP16 5HH
☎ 01291 628192 📠 01291 628193

This is a pub which manages to effortlessly combine the virtues of a popular local with an honest approach to providing good bar and restaurant food. Salmon fisheries were once sited virtually next door: the boats would moor in the tide with deep nets stretching across the tidal flow below Brunel's tubular bridge. Today's revitalised pub is an attractive whitewashed building brightened by hanging baskets of flowers. The well-furnished terrace includes decent seats and a barbecue for the summer, but the views can be enjoyed equally well from the first floor restaurant, a romantic setting (candlelit in the evenings) with a large bay window overlooking the river. The ground floor comprises a selection of traditionally furnished rooms decorated with boating memorabilia, and there is a real fire to warm yourself by in the winter months. For those who want something special to eat, the main menu, supplemented by a specials board, has plenty to recommend: starters like deep-fried Brie in a redcurrant coulis, smoked duck breast with red onion marmalade, grilled goats' cheese with a honeycomb dressing, and warm salad of chorizo and black pudding with vine tomato dressing, and such main dishes as grilled fillet of sea bass on wilted spinach with a lemon and dill beurre blanc, pork tenderloin on creamy mash with a Welsh honey and wholegrain mustard sauce, and Thai green curry with long grain rice. Lunch is an uncomplicated affair, with fresh soup and filled baguettes available alongside a full-length menu that can be chosen throughout the day. Other simple options include lasagne, curry, steak and jacket potatoes.

PENALLT
Map 04 SO51

The Boat Inn
Lone Ln NP25 4AJ ☎ 01600 712615 ▤ 01600 719120
Dir: From Monmouth take A466. In Redbrook the pub car park is
signposted. Park & walk across rail bridge over R Wye
Dating back over 360 years, this riverside pub has served as
a hostelry for quarry, mill, paper and tin mine workers, and
even had a landlord operating a ferry across the Wye at
shift times. The unspoilt slate floor is testament to the age of
the place. The excellent selection of real ales complement
the menu well, with choices ranging from various
ploughman's to lamb steffados or the charmingly-named
pan haggerty.
OPEN: 12-10.30 (Sun 12-10.30) **BAR MEALS:** L served all week
12-2.30 D served all week 6-9 **BREWERY/COMPANY:** Free House
🍺: Theakston Old Peculier, Freeminer Bitter, Wadworth 6X, Greene
King IPA. **FACILITIES:** Children welcome Garden: Rustic tables and
benches with waterfalls Dogs allowed Water **NOTES:** Parking 20

SHIRENEWTON
Map 09 ST49

The Carpenters Arms
Usk Rd NP16 6BU ☎ 01291 641231
Dir: M48 J2 take A48 to Chepstow then A4661, B4235. Village 3m on L

A 400-year-old hostelry, formerly a smithy and carpenter's
shop, with flagstone floors, open fires and a pleasant wooded
valley location near the Wye and Usk valleys. It is now
furnished with antiques, and offers straightforward bar food.
A typical menu includes steak and mushroom pie, guinea fowl
in orange sauce, pheasant casserole, and chicken in leek and
Stilton sauce.
OPEN: 11-2.30 6-11 **BAR MEALS:** 12-2 7-9.30
BREWERY/COMPANY: Free House 🍺: Fuller's London Pride,
Wadworth 6X, Marston's Pedigree, Theakston Old Peculier.
FACILITIES: Dogs allowed **NOTES:** Parking 20 No credit cards

SKENFRITH
Map 09 SO42

Pick of the Pubs

The Bell at Skenfrith 🏠 ⊛⊛ 🐾 ♀
NP7 8UH ☎ 01600 750235 ▤ 01600 750525
e-mail: enquiries@skenfrith.com
2003 AA Pub of the Year and AA Wine Award winner for
Wales, this recently-restored 17th-century coaching inn
stands on the banks of the Monnow - a tributary of the
River Wye. An oak bar, flagstones, and old settles provide
plenty of character, and there are eight well-equipped
bedrooms, some with four-poster beds. Opposite is
Skenfrith Castle, and nearby is the historic arched bridge
that once carried a main route from England to South

continued

Wales. Locally-sourced and mainly organic ingredients are
evident in many dishes. Try Usk Valley cannon of lamb
with smoked goat's cheese mash; Bigbury Bay moules
and fennel marinière with almonds; or red Thai fillet of
beef curry with steamed jasmine rice and basil. Dessert
choices often include the wicked pain au chocolat bread
and butter pudding along with Welsh cheeses and locally-
made ice creams. Real ales, hand-pumped local Broome
Farm cider and a good selection of wines by the glass are
served.

OPEN: Open all day Closed: 1st 2 wks of Feb **BAR MEALS:** L
served all week 12-2.30 D served all week 7-9.30 Av main course
£13 **RESTAURANT:** L served Sun, or by arrangement 12-2.30 D
served Fri-Sat 7-9.30 Av 3 course à la carte £28 Av 3 course fixed
price £17.50 **BREWERY/COMPANY:** Free House 🍺: Freeminer
Best Bitter, Hook Norton Best Bitter, Guest Ales. ♀: 10
FACILITIES: Children welcome Garden: Lawn, terrace, tables &
chairs Dogs allowed **NOTES:** Parking 30 **ROOMS:** 8 bedrooms
8 en suite s£65 d£85

TINTERN PARVA
Map 04 SO50

Fountain Inn ◆◆◆ 🐾 NEW
Trellech Grange NP16 6QW ☎ 01291 689303 ▤ 01291 689303
e-mail: dmaachi@aol.com
Dir: J2, M48 (8 miles)
A fire nearly destroyed this fine old inn, but the thick 17th-
century walls survived the flames, and its character remains
unspoilt. It enjoys open views of the Wye Valley, and is close
to Tintern Abbey. Food in the bar ranges from sandwiches and
pies to Hungarian goulash, grills and steaks, and asparagus
lasagne, with specials like beef Stroganoff, and duck à
l'orange. A couple of well-kept ales are always on tap, plus a
good selection of lagers.
OPEN: 12-3 6-10.30 **BAR MEALS:** L served all week 12-2 D served
all week 7-10 Av main course £6.95 **RESTAURANT:** L served all
week 12-2 D served all week 7-10 Av 3 course fixed price £15
BREWERY/COMPANY: Free House 🍺: Wye Valley Butter Bach,
Wadworth 6X, Interbrew Flowers. **FACILITIES:** Garden: Open views
of Wye Valley countryside Dogs allowed Water, open fields for walks
NOTES: Parking 30 **ROOMS:** 5 bedrooms 2 en suite s£30 d£40 no
children overnight

TREDUNNOCK
Map 09 ST39

Pick of the Pubs

The Newbridge Inn ⊛ 🐾 ♀
NP15 1LY ☎ 01633 451000 ▤ 01633 541001
e-mail: thenewbridge@tinyonline.co.uk
See Pick of the Pubs on page 624

Open: 12-2.30, 6-9.45
(Sat 7-9.45, Sun 12-4)
Bar Meals: L Mon-Sat,
D Mon-Sat.
Av cost main course £10.50.
RESTAURANT: L served all week
12-2.30,
D served all week 6-9.45.
Av cost 3 courses £22.
BREWERY/COMPANY:
Free House.
🍺: Interbrew Bass, Coor's
Hancock's HB, Brains Rev James,
Fullers London Pride.
FACILITIES: Garden - Patio area with
tables, overlooking the River Usk.
NOTES: Parking 65

The Newbridge Inn

This is a gastro-pub re-creation of a classic establishment, set on the southern bank of the River Usk by the 'new' 17th-century bridge. Under its high rafters, the whole place shimmering in candlelight is reflected in the river, creating a romantic setting for a top-class dinner.

Tredunnock, NP15 1LY
☎ 01633 451000 📠 01633 541001
📧 thenewbridge@tinyonline.co.uk
Dir: M4 J24 or J26, take Caerleon road to usk Road, follow lane opposite Cwrt Bleddyn Hotel. Through village to river.

The striking interiors are warm and welcoming with wooden floors, subtle lighting and comfy sofas; the walls are hung with fine art by contemporary Irish artist and sculptor Graham Knuttel; and regular special events are promoted on hand-decorated blackboards. Modern jazz creates the mood for informal eating on three levels, with a spiral staircase leading to the top-most floor. Expect modern British cooking with a touch of the Mediterranean, the chef's daily specials reflecting a passion for quality produce. Flexible menus allow for a choice from appealing club sandwiches, salads and pastas or alternatively a two- or three-course lunchtime fixed-price selection features dishes such as black bean soup with chilli sofrito, home-made salmon fishcakes and chocolate brownie with vanilla ice cream. A full carte menu is offered on Sunday lunchtimes. As well as daily specials - particularly fish from Cornwall delivered fresh each morning - the dinner menu features choices like carpaccio of yellowfin tuna, with radish, coriander and sesame; chargrilled Welsh rib-eye steak with roasted cherry tomatoes, straw potatoes and a herb and shallot butter; roasted rump of Welsh lamb with chargrilled vegetables, garlic and basil mash and a basil jus; and pinto bean, aubergine and tahini moussaka with rocket and Parmesan. Finish off with sweets like coconut tart with passion fruit Mascarpone; rhubarb and spiced pear trifle; or whisky and marmalade bread and butter pudding with clotted cream. Calorie counters beware!

TRELLECK
Map 04 SO50

The Lion Inn
NP25 4PA ☎ 01600 860322 📠 01600 860060
e-mail: lion@web-fanatics.co.uk
Dir: From A40 just south of Monmouth take B4293 and follow signs for Trelleck

This former brew and coach house stands opposite the church and is said to be haunted. Twice winners of the South Wales Argus pub restaurant of the year award, the menu ranges from traditional pub favourites like jacket potatoes or sausage and chips to an innovative selection of home-made vegetarian dishes and Hungarian specials. Rakott Krumpli, turkey Budapest, peppered sirloin steak and Nagy Mama's stuffed peppers are popular choices.
OPEN: 12-3 6-11 (Mon 7-11; closed Sun eve) **BAR MEALS:** L served all week 12-2 D served Mon-Sat 6-9.30 Av main course £9.25 **RESTAURANT:** L served all week 12-2 D served Mon-Sat 6-9.30 Av 3 course à la carte £17.50 Av 3 course fixed price £15.95
BREWERY/COMPANY: Free House 🍺: Bath Ales, Wadworth 6X, Fuller's London Pride, Wye Valley Butty Bach. **FACILITIES:** Children welcome Garden: Overlooks fields, stream. Large aviary Dogs allowed Water, biscuits **NOTES:** Parking 40

USK
Map 09 SO30

Pick of the Pubs

The Nags Head Inn ♀
Twyn Square NP15 1BH ☎ 01291 672820 📠 01291 672720
Dir: On A472
Flower-adorned 15th-century inn overlooking the town square, just a short stroll from the River Usk. The village itself has won Wales in Bloom for the last 17 years, and the same family have run the inn for over thirty years. The old coaching inn has a traditional bar with polished tables and chairs, and lots of horse brasses, farming tools and lanterns hanging from exposed oak beams. Local game in season includes pheasant cooked in port, while wild Usk salmon is a speciality on the menu, along with half a duck in Cointreau sauce, and wild boar steaks. Regular dishes include rabbit pie, pheasant in port, whole stuffed partridge, and chicken in red wine, and there are vegetarian options like Glamorgan sausage, and vegetable pancakes. Finish a meal with a home-made puddings, perhaps treacle and walnut tart, or hot chocolate fudge cake.
OPEN: 10-3 5.30-11 Closed: Dec 25 **BAR MEALS:** L served all week 10-2 D served all week 5.30-10.30 **RESTAURANT:** L served all week 11.30-2 D served all week 5.30-10.30
BREWERY/COMPANY: Free House 🍺: Brains Bitter, Dark, Buckleys Best & Reverend James. ♀: 8 **FACILITIES:** Children welcome

---

AMROTH
Map 08 SN10

The New Inn
SA67 8NW ☎ 01834 812368
Dir: A48 to Carmarthen, A40 to St Clears, A477 to Llanteg then L
A 400-year-old inn, originally a farmhouse, belonging to Amroth Castle Estate. It has old world charm with beamed ceilings, a Flemish chimney, a flagstone floor and an inglenook fireplace. It is close to the beach, and local lobster and crab are a feature, along with a popular choice of home-made dishes including steak and kidney pie, soup and curry.
OPEN: 11.30-3 5.30-11 (closed Nov-Mar) Closed: Nov-Mar
BAR MEALS: L served all week 12-2 D served all week 6-9
RESTAURANT: L served all week 12-2 D served all week 6-9
BREWERY/COMPANY: Free House 🍺: Burton, Carlsberg-Tetley Tetley Bitter. **FACILITIES:** Children welcome Garden Dogs allowed
NOTES: Parking 100 **NOTES:** No credit cards

CAREW
Map 08 SN00

Carew Inn
SA70 8SL ☎ 01646 651267 📠 01646 650126
e-mail: mandy@carewinn.co.uk
Dir: From A477 take A4075. Inn 400yds opp castle & Celtic cross
A traditional stone-built country inn situated opposite the Carew Celtic cross and Norman castle, which is a regular venue for activities by The Sealed Knot. Enjoy the one-mile circular walk around the castle and millpond before settling in the pub. Typical meals include chicken, leek and mushroom pie, pork tenderloin in mustard sauce or chicken in white wine and mustard sauce. Live music every Thursday night under the marquee.
OPEN: 11.30-2.30 4.30-11 (Summer & wknd 11-11) Closed: Dec 25
BAR MEALS: L served all week 11.30-2 D served all week 6-9
RESTAURANT: L served all week 12-2 D served all week 6-9 Av 3 course à la carte £14 Av 2 course fixed price £6.95
BREWERY/COMPANY: Free House 🍺: Worthington Best, SA Brains Reverend James. **FACILITIES:** Children welcome Garden: Overlooks Carew Castle Dogs allowed Water provided **NOTES:** Parking 20

CILGERRAN
Map 08 SN14

Pick of the Pubs

AA Pub of the Year for Wales 2004
Pendre Inn
Pendre SA43 2SL ☎ 01239 614223
e-mail: warmak@pendre.fsnet.co.uk
Dir: Off A478 south of Cardigan
Dating back to the 14th century, this is a pub full of memorabilia and featuring exposed interior walls, old beams, slate floors and an inglenook fireplace. An ancient ash tree grows through the pavement in front of the white stone, thick-walled building. Excellent value, freshly-made meals are on offer, ranging from lighter bites - omelettes, bagels, sandwiches, quiches and home-made pizza buns - alongside more adventurous choices. These typically include roast chicken with lemon curd and red apple sauce; medallions of turkey with coconut milk, mango, ginger, garlic and lime; peppers baked with spinach and a trio of cheeses on a tomato and basil sauce. Other offerings may be strips of liver, bacon and spiced sausage in creamy Stroganoff sauce, and duet of pork with spiced cabbage and onions with a mild mustard sauce. Follow on

continued

Wales

CILGERRAN continued

with one of the home-made puddings or ice cream if you have room.
OPEN: 12-3 6-11 **BAR MEALS:** L served Mon-Sat 12-2 D served Mon-Sat 6-8 Av main course £4.50 **RESTAURANT:** L served Mon-Sat 12-2 D served Mon-Sat 6-8 Av 3 course fixed price £9.50 **BREWERY/COMPANY:** Free House 🍺: Thomas Watkins. **FACILITIES:** Children welcome Garden: Lawn/patio with large trees and water feature Dogs allowed Enclosed kenneling, water, toys **NOTES:** Parking 6 No credit cards

---

HAVERFORDWEST
Map 08 SM91

Pick of the Pubs

The George's Restaurant/Café Bar 🐑 ♀
24 Market St SA61 1NH ☎ 01437 766683 🖷 01437 779090
e-mail: llewis6140@aol.com
See Pick of the Pubs on opposite page

LAMPHEY
Map 08 SN00

Pick of the Pubs

The Dial Inn 🐑 ♀
Ridgeway Rd SA71 5NU ☎ 01646 672426 🖷 01646 672426
Dir: *Just off A4139 (Tenby to Pembroke rd)*

The Dial started life around 1830 as the Dower House for nearby Lamphey Court, and was converted into a pub in 1966. It immediately established itself as a popular village local, and in recent years the owners have extended the dining areas. Food is a real strength, and you can choose from traditional bar, a daily blackboard or the imaginative dining room menu. Every effort is made to use as much fresh local produce as possible. Look out for specials such as beef olive carbonnade stuffed with walnuts and horseradish, smoked bacon, chicken and pepper roulade with potato rösti and spring onion sauce, and canon of Welsh lamb with cranberry and orange compôte. Fish dishes focus around shallow-fried cod with mashed potato and cockle sauce, and mixed shellfish remulata with home-made noodles and stem ginger. There's a family room, with darts, pool and other pub games.
OPEN: 11-3 6-12 **BAR MEALS:** L served all week 12-3 D served all week 6.30-10 Av main course £10.50 **RESTAURANT:** L served all week 12-3 D served all week 6.30-10 Av 3 course à la carte £25 **BREWERY/COMPANY:** Free House 🍺: Hancocks, Interbrew Bass, Worthington. ♀: 8 **FACILITIES:** Children welcome Children's licence Garden **NOTES:** Parking 50

LANDSHIPPING
Map 08 SN01

The Stanley Arms 🐑 ♀
SA67 8BE ☎ 01834 891227
Dir: *Off A40 at Canaston Bridge onto A4075, R at Cross Hands, next to Canaston Bowls*

Built as a farmhouse around 1765, first licensed in 1875, the pub has its own mooring on the Cleddau Estuary and is popular with sailors. There's an attractive garden with fine views across the water to Picton Castle, and the area is good for walking. Freshly-cooked pub food includes marinated chicken breast, gammon with egg or pineapple, grilled Milford plaice, Welsh dragon sausage in mustard sauce, home-made curries and Welsh steaks, as well as salads and a children's menu.
OPEN: 12-3 6-11 (Sun 7-10.30) **BAR MEALS:** L served all week 12-2.30 D served all week 6-9.30 Av main course £7 **RESTAURANT:** L served all week 12-2.30 D served all week 6-9.30
BREWERY/COMPANY: Free House 🍺: Worthington, Fuller's London Pride, Everards Tiger, Hancocks HB. ♀: 7
FACILITIES: Children welcome Children's licence Garden: Large garden with swings annd sandpit Dogs allowed Water
NOTES: Parking 20

LETTERSTON
Map 08 SM92

The Harp Inn
31 Haverfordwest Rd SA62 5UA
☎ 01348 840061 🖷 01348 840812
Dir: *Located on main A40*
Famous 15th-century country inn that has undergone plenty of extension and refurbishment, but retains period features such as the lovely inglenook fireplace in the restaurant. Until the turn of the century it was also a working farm, the site of a weekly market and a centre of mail distribution. The extensive bar menu ranges from jacket potatoes through to main meals such as grilled sirloin or home-made curry. Restaurant food could include pork fillet sweet and sour, or crispy roast duckling.
OPEN: 11-3 6-11 **BAR MEALS:** L served all week 12-2.30 D served all week 6-9.30 Av main course £9.50 **RESTAURANT:** L served all week 12-2.30 D served all week 6.30-9.30 Av 3 course à la carte £20 **BREWERY/COMPANY:** Free House 🍺: Tetleys, Greene King, Abbot Ale, Stella Artois. **FACILITIES:** Children welcome Garden **NOTES:** Parking 50

All AA rated accommodation can also be found on the AA's internet site
www.theAA.com

Open: 10.30-5.30 (Fri-Sat 10.30-11)
Closed: Sun
Bar Meals: L served Mon-Sat 12-5.30,
D served Fri-Sat 6-9.45.
Av cost main course £6.50
RESTAURANT: L served Mon-Sat 12-2.30,
D served Fri-Sat 6-9.30.
Av cost 3 courses £22.50
BREWERY/COMPANY:
Free House.
🍺: Marston's Pedigree, Wye Valley
Bitter, Adnams Broadside.
FACILITIES: Garden - Walled garden,
terrace, outdoor heaters.

The George's Restaurant/Café Bar

Built on the site of the former George's Brewery, this remarkable 18th-century building incorporates many original features in its restored vaulted wine cellar and eating areas.

 ♀

24 Market Street, Haverfordwest,
SA61 1NH
☎ 01437 766683 📠 01437 779090
✉ llewis6140@aol.com
Dir: On the A40

Its delightful, award-winning walled garden, with spectacular views over the ruins of 12th-century Haverfordwest Castle, has outdoor heating for chillier days and evenings. Genuine local character is a feature of the all-day café bar and cellar bistro, where freshly prepared food and sheer enthusiasm sets it apart from the norm. You'll find Wye Valley Bitter and a frequently changing guest ale on tap, plus a short, global list of wines and monthly wine specials. An extensive list of home-made dishes is served all day in the Celtic-themed, part non-smoking restaurant. Given the proximity of the sea, be prepared for plenty of fish dishes, including Cornish fish pie, crab crêpes and salmon linguine, as well as daily specials incorporating either plaice, halibut, sea bass or other locally-caught species. Meats and vegetables are also locally-sourced, and fresh herbs are harvested from the garden. Daily specials might include smoked honey-glazed duck breast salad, Welsh lamb stew topped with crispy potatoes, and George's turkey, gammon, leek and wild mushroom pie. Among possibly a dozen vegetarian options are cheese-topped nut and seed roast in filo pastry, wild mushroom pasta and a hot-and-spicy spinach dhal. Desserts include crêpes Suzette, chocolate nut Pavlova, old-fashioned treacle tart and luxury Belgian ice cream sundaes. Speciality teas, coffees and cakes are available all day in the café bar, while the Celtic gift shop sells a huge array of natural crystals, fossils and gifts.

NEVERN   Map 08 SN04

Trewern Arms ★★
SA42 0NB ☎ 01239 820395 ▤ 01239 820173
Dir: *On the A487 between Cardigan and Fishguard*

Ivy-clad 16th-century inn set in attractive grounds astride the River Nevern. The Brew House bar is a popular local, with flagstone floors and old settles. Dishes might include broccoli cream cheese, breaded cod, pork Normandy, lemon sole with Penclawdd cockles, roast pheasant marinated in port, or Preseli lamb in redcurrant and rosemary sauce.
OPEN: 11-3 (Sun 12-3 7-10.30) 6-11 **BAR MEALS:** L served all week 12-2 D served all week 6-9 Av main course £7.50 **RESTAURANT:** D served Thu-Sat 7-9 Av 3 course à la carte £18.50
BREWERY/COMPANY: Free House ◀: Interbrew Flowers Original, Castle Eden Ale, Wadworth 6X. **FACILITIES:** Children welcome Garden: Lawn/Patio Dogs allowed Dogs on leads **NOTES:** Parking 80 **ROOMS:** 10 bedrooms 10 en suite s£30 d£50

PEMBROKE DOCK   Map 08 SM90

Ferry Inn
Pembroke Ferry SA72 6UD ☎ 01646 682947
e-mail: williamsferryinn@aol.com
Dir: *A477, off A48, R at garage, signs for Cleddau Bridge, L at roundabout*
Once the haunt of smugglers, this 16th-century inn is situated on the banks of the Cleddau River, with fine views across the estuary from the nautical-themed bar and waterside terrace. Fresh local fish is a speciality - bass, lemon sole, plaice, sea bream, or fillet of cod in home-made crumb. Spaghetti marinara is a popular option, along with sirloin steak, lamb kebabs and vegetable korma.
OPEN: 11.30-2.45 7-11 Closed: 25-26 Dec **BAR MEALS:** L served all week 12-2 D served all week 7-10 Av main course £6.95
RESTAURANT: L served all week 12-2 D served all week 7-10 Av 3 course à la carte £15 **BREWERY/COMPANY:** Free House
◀: Interbrew Hancocks HB & Bass, Felinfoel Double Dragon, Weekly Guest Ale. **FACILITIES:** Children welcome Garden: Beer terrace on edge of river, amazing views Dogs allowed Water **NOTES:** Parking 12

Pick of the Pubs

PORTHGAIN   Map 08 SM83

The Sloop Inn
SA62 5BN ☎ 01348 831449 ▤ 01348 831388
e-mail: matthew@sloop-inn.freeserve.co.uk
Many a landlord would covet the Sloop's harbourside location in a fishing village in the Pembrokeshire Coast National Park. From the outside it looks small, but appearances can be deceptive, as entry quickly proves. Prominent on the right is the large stove, on a winter's day chucking out plenty of cheering heat. In the old bar, photos show what Porthgain was like before quarrying ceased in 1931. Clutter collected over the years includes a name plaque from the Carolina, wrecked in 1859. The Sloop is definitely a family pub; it holds a children's licence and caters for them on the menu. The main lunch and supper menu runs all year round, and specials are updated twice daily. At busy times there's an all-you-can-eat salad servery, and during the summer there's a sandwich bar where customers can choose their own fillings. Its south-facing patio makes an ideal spot for drinks or lunch in fine weather.
OPEN: 11-11 (Sun 12-4, 5.30-10.30) **BAR MEALS:** L served all week 12-2.30 D served all week 6-9.30 Av main course £6.90
RESTAURANT: L served all week 12-2.30 D served all week 6-9.30 **BREWERY/COMPANY:** Free House ◀: Interbrew Worthington Bitter, Felinfoel, Wadsworth 6X, Brains Reverend James. **FACILITIES:** Children welcome Children's licence Garden: Raised patio area, sun trap, safe Dogs allowed Outside water drinker **NOTES:** Parking 50

SOLVA   Map 08 SM82

The Cambrian Inn
Main St SA62 6UU ☎ 01437 721210
Dir: *13m from Haverfordwest on the St David's Rd*
Something of an institution in this pretty fishing village (but park down by the estuary) is a white-painted Grade II listed 17th-century inn that attracts local and returning visitors alike. Under new management, a sample restaurant menu offers diners the likes of roast cod with seafood white wine sauce, mushroom Stroganoff, fillet of pork in a honey and mustard sauce, Welsh black sirloin steak, and half local fresh duckling with Grand Marnier sauce. Lunchtime bar snacks include jacket potatoes, sandwiches and salads.
OPEN: 12-3 6.30-11 (Winter 12-2:30, 7-11) Closed: Dec 25-26 **BAR MEALS:** L served all week 12-2 D served all week 7-9.30 Av main course £5.50 **RESTAURANT:** L served all week 12-2 D served all week 7-9.30 Av 3 course à la carte £17.50
BREWERY/COMPANY: Free House ◀: Reverend James, Brains SA. **FACILITIES:** Children welcome Garden: patio, beer garden, outdoor eating Dogs allowed garden only **NOTES:** Parking 12 **NOTES:** No credit cards

---

Top of the Tree
Pubs called the Royal Oak were originally named in loyal remembrance of the day in 1651 when the youthful King Charles II hid in an oak tree at Boscobel in Shropshire, while Roundhead soldiers unsuccessfully searched the woods for him. The Royal Oak sign often shows simply the oak tree, or the king is shown perched among the branches - in plain view from all directions, but conventionally accepted as invisible to the purblind Parliamentarian troops. Sometimes, more subtly, the tree has a large crown among the foliage. Rarer variants include the king holding an oak spray with acorns, or acorns below a crown.

STACKPOLE   Map 08 SR99

Pick of the Pubs

The Stackpole Inn 🐾 ♀
SA71 5DF ☎ 01646 672324 🖹 01646 67216
e-mail: stackpoleinn@aol.com
Dir: From Pembroke take B4319 & follow signs for Stackpole
The inn is set in lovely landscaped gardens at the heart of
the National Trust's Stackpole Estate, close to the
Pembrokeshire coastal path. It was originally two 17th-
century stone cottages, one of which subsequently
became a post office, and the old King George post box is
still set in the wall. The bar is made of Welsh slate, and
the beams are all ash which was grown on the estate.
Warmth is provided by a wood-burning stove set within
the stone fireplace. Local produce plays its full part in the
menu, with options like rump of Welsh lamb with a garlic
and herb crust, or rib-eye of Welsh beef. An extensive
fresh fish choice is offered from the daily specials board:
maybe fillets of sea bass with spiced rice, or pan-fried cod
fillet with goats' cheese and basil mash, and white wine
and shallot sauce.

OPEN: 11-3 6-11 (winter 7-11) **BAR MEALS:** L served all week
12-2 D served all week 7-9 Av main course £10
RESTAURANT: L served all week 12-2 D served all week 7-9
BREWERY/COMPANY: Free House 🍺 Brains Reverend
James, Felinfoel, Double Dragon, Worthington Draught.
FACILITIES: Children welcome Garden: Landscaped garden,
picturesque Dogs allowed Water **NOTES:** Parking 25

WOLF'S CASTLE   Map 08 SM92

Pick of the Pubs

The Wolfe Inn ♦♦♦♦ 🐾 ♀
SA62 5LS ☎ 01437 741662 🖹 01437 741676
e-mail: eat@the-wolfe.co.uk
*Dir: On A40 between Haverfordwest and Fishguard, 7 miles
equidistant from both towns*
The Wolfe is an oak-beamed, stone-built property in a
lovely village setting. The inn offers a bar-brasserie and a
restaurant made up of three interconnecting but distinctly
different rooms: Victoria's Parlour, Hunters' Lodge and a
conservatory complete with grapevines. A proud holder of
the Pembrokeshire Product Mark, the inn uses mainly
local produce in the home-cooked food. Features of the
menu are a large selection of fish and game in season,
table-ready cheeses and fabulous desserts. Example
dishes are St Brides Bay seafood pancakes, steamed fillets
of brill with cockle and laver bread cream, pot-roasted

pheasant with root vegetables, port and redcurrant, and
Welsh lamb casserole with mint and leeks. Drinks options
include a monthly guest beer, a wide choice of coffees
(cappuccino, espresso, machiato, lungo, doppio and filter
coffees) and a range of teas. Self-catering and B&B
accommodation is also available.
OPEN: 11-3 6-11 **BAR MEALS:** L served all week 12-2 D
served all week 7-9 Av main course £8.50 **RESTAURANT:** L
served all week 12-2 D served all week 7-9 Av 3 course à la carte
£25 Av 3 course fixed price £14.95
BREWERY/COMPANY: Free House 🍺 Interbrew
Worthington Bitter, Monthly Guest Beer. ♀ 11
FACILITIES: Children welcome Garden: Enclosed garden,
secluded, patio area Dogs allowed **NOTES:** Parking 20
ROOMS: 3 bedrooms 2 en suite 2 family rooms s£40 d£60

POWYS

BERRIEW   Map 15 SJ10

Lion Hotel 🐾
SY21 8PQ ☎ 01686 640452 🖹 01686 640604
*Dir: 5m from Welshpool on A483, R to Berriew. Centre of village next to
church.*
Expect a friendly family welcome at this 17th-century inn,
which adjoins the churchyard in a pretty village setting. It is
a timbered black and white building, recently refurbished, with
oak beams and low ceilings throughout. Food options include
traditional bar snacks and a bistro menu supplemented by
daily fish options and chef's specials, maybe slow-roasted
shoulder of Welsh lamb, sea bass fillets, or Barbary duck
breast.
OPEN: 12-3 6-11 (Sun 7-10.30 Fri 5.30-11 Sat 7-11) Closed: Dec 25-26
BAR MEALS: L served all week 12-2 D served all week 7-9 Av main
course £9.95 **RESTAURANT:** L served all week 12-2 D served Mon-
Sat 7-9 Av 3 course à la carte £18 **BREWERY/COMPANY:** Free
House 🍺 Worthington Bitter, Woods Shropshire Lad, Brains
Reverend James, Woods Wonderful. **FACILITIES:** Children welcome
Children's licence Garden: Patio area surrounded by plants Dogs
allowed Water **NOTES:** Parking 6 **ROOMS:** 7 bedrooms 7 en suite
1 family rooms s£55 d£70 (WTB)

BRECON   Map 09 SO02

The Felin Fach Griffin ⊛⊛ ♀
Felin Fach LD3 0UB ☎ 01874 620111 🖹 01874 620120
e-mail: enquiries@eatdrinksleep.ltd.uk
Dir: 4.5m N of Brecon on the A470 (Brecon to Hay-on-Wye road)
Delightful country inn offering memorable food in an
unpretentious atmosphere. Located between the Black
Mountains and the Brecon Beacons, it specialises in local
produce cooked with distinction. A sample lunch menu
includes butternut squash and red onion risotto, minute steak
of Welsh black beef, oak roast salmon and crushed new
potatoes with spinach, or pan-fried calves' liver with mash and
bacon.
OPEN: 12-3 6-11 (Sunday 12-11) Closed: Last week Jan & First week
Feb **BAR MEALS:** L served Tue-Sun 12.30-2.30 D served Mon-Sun
7-9.30 Av main course £10.40 **RESTAURANT:** L served Tue-Sun
12.30-2.30 D served Mon-Sun 7-9.30 Av 3 course à la carte £20
BREWERY/COMPANY: Free House 🍺 Tomos Watkin OSB,
Scottish Courage John Smith's. ♀ 8 **FACILITIES:** Garden: Tables
and Chairs, Landscaping in progress Dogs allowed water
NOTES: Parking 60

continued

Wales

Cain Valley Hotel

A short walk across farmland and through John Adams Wood, with fine views of the Berwyn Mountains.

From the front of the hotel, cross the High Street and walk up Market Street. At the top, turn left at Moriah Chapel, then immediately right into New Road. At the end of Bronygaer housing estate on your right, turn left with the footpath sign and cross the bridge to a stile on the right. Cross the field, making for the gate in the corner by woodland.

Follow the well defined path through John Adams Woods. Head across the field to the mid-point of the hedge opposite and continue to a gate in the next field. Maintain direction across the next field to a stile in the hedge, with excellent views of the Berwyn Mountains to your right.

Turn right along Bachie Road, following it left to a fork with a farm road. Bear left along the farm road, pass through a gate, then climb an old gate on your left into a field. Follow the left-hand boundary to the bottom of the field and go over the wooden fence. Pass through the gateway immediately on your left and continue downhill with the hedge on your right to a gate. Turn left along the road for nearly a mile (1.6km) and turn left back into the town centre for the inn.

★★
CAIN VALLEY HOTEL, LLANFYLLIN
High Street SY22 5AQ.
☎ 01691 648366

Directions: From Shrewsbury & Oswestry follow signs for Lake Vyrnwy & onto A490 to Llanfyllin. Hotel on R.
17th-century coaching inn set in green hills with breathtaking views and great walks. Full bar menu lunch and evenings, and real ales. Heavily-beamed restaurant.
Open: 11.30-11 Sun 12-10.30
Bar Meals: 12-2 7-9
Notes: Children welcome (cot, high chair) & dogs. Parking.
(See page 636 for full entry)

DISTANCE: 3 1/2 miles (5.6km)
MAP: OS Landranger 125
TERRAIN: Farmland, woodland, country lanes
PATHS: Field and woodland paths, tracks, metalled lanes
GRADIENT: Gently undulating; no steep climbs

Walk submitted by The Cain Valley Hotel

BRECON continued

Pick of the Pubs

The Usk Inn ◆◆◆◆ ⊚ 🐾 ♀
Talybont-on-Usk LD3 7JE ☎ 01874 676251 🖹 01874 676392
e-mail: stay@uskinn.co.uk
Dir: *6m E of Brecon, just off the A40 towards Abergavenny & Crickhowell, if coming through Talybont turn onto Station Rd alongside the railway bridge and inn 500 yds on the R*

This refurbished free house has long been welcoming weary travellers with a good range of real ales. Today, visitors arrive on foot from the nearby Taff Trail, as well as on horseback, mountain bike or canal boat. The traditional open fire and flagstone floors remain, but now the inn offers just a little more style. There's a civilised restaurant, with crisp white napery and candlelit tables, and cheerful en suite guest bedrooms featuring locally-made pine furniture and patchwork quilts. Food is taken seriously, with imaginative menus that make good use of fresh local produce. Expect breast of duck with plum sauce and noodles; Welsh rib-eye steak with Stilton and Madeira sauce; fillet of salmon with Welsh rarebit topping or a tart of leek, apple, beetroot, cherry tomato, red onion and chilli. An equally exciting range of sandwiches could include smoked salmon and cream cheese, ham and mango or BLT.
OPEN: 8-11 Closed: Dec 25-26 **BAR MEALS:** L served all week 12-3 D served all week 6.30-10 **RESTAURANT:** L served all week 12-3 D served all week 7-9.30
BREWERY/COMPANY: Free House 🍺: Reverend James & Buckleys Best, Felinfoel Double Dragon, Hancocks HB, Buckleys IPA. ♀: 8 **FACILITIES:** Children welcome Garden: Lawned area with mature planting Dogs allowed Water
NOTES: Parking 35 **ROOMS:** 11 bedrooms 11 en suite 1 family rooms s£45 d£70

Pick of the Pubs

White Swan Inn ⊚ ♀
Llanfrynach LD3 7BZ ☎ 01874 665276
See Pick of the Pubs on page 632

Stars or Diamonds after the ROOMS information at the end of an entry denotes accommodation that has been inspected by an organisation other than the AA, eg the RAC, VisitBritain, VisitScotland or WTB.

CAERSWS   Map 15 SO09

Pick of the Pubs

The Talkhouse ◆◆◆◆◆ ⊚⊚ ♀
Pontdolgoch SY17 5JE ☎ 01686 688919 🖹 01686 689134
e-mail: info@talkhouse.co.uk
Dir: *From Newtown A487 about 5m towards Machynlleth & Dolgellau, turn R onto A470 just before level crossing into Caersws, and carry on about 1 m on A470; inn on the L*
If you're hungry or need a break, don't drive past this unassuming stone pub, set hard on the A470. Why? Because refurbishments by Colin and Melanie Dawson have created a beautifully furnished lounge area, complete with soft sofas, and a relaxing bar with a blazing log fire, wooden settles and relaxing music. The adjoining dining room features a good mix of tables topped with candles and an ever-changing blackboard menu listing an imaginative range of freshly-prepared dishes. Impressive use is made of local ingredients - some from as nearby as the garden. Typical dishes include chargrilled rib of Welsh black beef with horseradish mash and beetroot fondants, local venison sausages with Puy lentils, vegetables, roasted parsnip purée and home-made quince jelly, or seared fillet of cod with black pudding, bacon and oven dried cherry tomato rösti.
OPEN: 12-3 6-11 **BAR MEALS:** L served Mon-Sat 12-2 D served Mon-Sat 7-9 Av main course £10 **RESTAURANT:** L served Tue-Sat 12-1.30 D served Tue-Sat 6-9 Av 3 course à la carte £26 **BREWERY/COMPANY:** Free House 🍺: Worthingtons.
FACILITIES: Garden: Food served outside **NOTES:** Parking 30
ROOMS: 3 bedrooms 3 en suite s£70 d£80 no children overnight

CARNO   Map 14 SN99

Aleppo Merchant Inn 🐾
SY17 5LL ☎ 01686 420210 🖹 01686 420296
e-mail: reception@thealeppo.co.uk
Dir: *From Newtown, A489 and A470*
Established in 1632 as a coaching house, and named after a ship called 'The Aleppo' by the ship's captain who retired here, this stone-built inn is situated in majestic Welsh countryside between the Snowdonia and Brecon Beacons National Parks. The fashion designer Laura Ashley is buried nearby. The menu offers battered cod fillet, beef casserole, roasted vegetable lasagne, and Welsh lamb chops.
OPEN: 12-2.30 7-11 (Sat-Sun 12-11) **BAR MEALS:** L served all week 12-2 D served all week 7-9 Av main course £6.95
RESTAURANT: L served all week 12-2 D served all week 7-9
BREWERY/COMPANY: Free House 🍺: Interbrew Boddingtons, Castlemaine XXXX, Welsh Smooth, Boddingtons Smooth.
FACILITIES: Children welcome Garden: Private enclosed lawned garden **NOTES:** Parking 50

Use the AA Hotel Booking Service on
0870 5050505
to book at AA recognised hotels and B&B's in the UK and Ireland or through our internet site at
www.theAA.com

Open: 11-2, 6.30-11
Closed: Mon-Tue
Bar Meals: L served Wed-Sun 12-2,
D served Wed-Sun 7-9.30.
Av cost main course £7.95.
RESTAURANT: L served Wed-Sun 12-2,
D served Wed-Sun 7-9.30.
Av cost 3 course £20
BREWERY/COMPANY:
Free House.
◖: Worthington Cream Flow, Brains
Bitter, Worthington Cask, Brains
Reverend James.
FACILITIES: Children welcome, Garden
- Flagged terrace with vine.
NOTES: Parking 35

White Swan Inn

An impressive makeover has brought a sparkle to this unassuming inn, where polished floors, exposed oak beams and a vast inglenook fireplace provide armfuls of character. The long, low, white-painted stone frontage of the White Swan overlooks Llanfrynach churchyard in the heart of the Brecon Beacons National Park.

Llanfrynach, Brecon, LD3 7BZ
☎ 01874 665276
Dir: 3m E of Brecon off the A40, take the B4558 and follow signs to Llanfrynach.

Tucked safely away from the A40, it makes an ideal escape from the frenetic pace of Brecon's Jazz Festival week. It has been long renowned as an upmarket local, and is particularly popular with walkers and cyclists. Trout fishing is available on the nearby River Usk, and the Monmouthshire and Brecon canal is close by. The well-kept real ales are served in the comfortably furnished and attractively decorated bar, and log fires make it a cosy haunt in winter. The lounge and restaurant are equally inviting, while the secluded rear garden and attractive patio, with their stone-topped tables under a plant-swathed trellis, come into their own in warmer months. Menus are an innovative blend of traditional and modern recipes that make the most of well-chosen, locally produced ingredients. At lunchtime snacks might include open steak sandwich with caramelised onions and flat mushrooms, or leek, Stilton and red onion tart. At dinner, the menu moves up a notch with home-made soup, pheasant terrine with foie gras, pistachio nuts and caramelised apples, and perhaps spiced strips of beef with salsa and a yogurt and mint dressing. A fine wine list has something for every main dish: braised shank of Welsh lamb, chargrilled sirloin with chive and bacon mash and a wild mushroom sauce, or courgette and chilli polenta. The chalkboard lists a daily selection of fish dishes like chargrilled marlin with mango, ginger and lime salsa, and seared cod fillet with garlic sautéed seafood.

COEDWAY

Map 15 SJ31

Ye Old Hand and Diamond
SY5 9AR ☎ 01743 884379 ▤ 01743 884267

Close to the Shropshire border and the River Severn, this 19th-century inn still retains much of its original character. Large open log fires burn in the winter and autumn. Typical menu includes chicken in mushroom and Stilton cream sauce, pork chops with cider and apple sauce, fresh sea bass, roast beef and Yorkshire pudding, and vegetable cannelloni.
OPEN: 11-11 **BAR MEALS:** L served all week 12-10 D served all week Av main course £6.95 **RESTAURANT:** L served all week 12-10 D served all week **BREWERY/COMPANY:** Free House ◖: Bass, Worthington, Shropshire Lad + Guest beers. **FACILITIES:** Children welcome Garden: Food served outside Guide Dogs Only **NOTES:** Parking 90

CRICKHOWELL

Map 09 SO21

Pick of the Pubs

The Bear ★★★ ◎ ☜ ♀
Brecon Rd NP8 1BW ☎ 01873 810408 ▤ 01873 811696
e-mail: bearhotel@aol.com
See Pick of the Pubs on page 634

Pick of the Pubs

Gliffaes Country House Hotel ★★★ ◎ ♀
NP8 1RH ☎ 01874 730371 ▤ 01874 730463
e-mail: calls@gliffaeshotel.com
Dir: *1m off the A40, 2.5m W of Crickhowell*
A listed 19th-century Italianate building standing in 33 acres of gardens and wooded parkland overlooking the River Usk, which the owners claim offers some of the best private fishing in the UK. Family run for over 50 years, Gliffaes is now in the hands of a third generation, with standards remaining consistently high. Popular bar lunches feature interesting sandwiches, light meals such as minute steak baguette or bouillabaisse-style fish stew, and daily changing specials: seared fillet of pork with sautéed potatoes, beef Stroganoff, and pan-fried Gressingham duck.
OPEN: 12-3 6-11 **BAR MEALS:** L served all week 12-2.30 Av main course £7.95 **RESTAURANT:** L served Sun 12.30-2 D served all week 7.30-9.15 Av 3 course fixed price £28
BREWERY/COMPANY: Free House ◖: Felinfoel Double Dragon Ale, Greene King Old Speckled Hen. ♀: 10
FACILITIES: Children welcome Garden: Formal gardens, 33 acres Dogs allowed Kennels, Water **NOTES:** Parking 30
ROOMS: 22 bedrooms 22 en suite s£60 d£69

Pick of the Pubs

Nantyffin Cider Mill ◎ ☜ ♀
Brecon Rd NP8 1SG ☎ 01873 810775 ▤ 01873 812127
e-mail: info@cidermill.co.uk
Dir: *At junction of A40 & A479, 1.5m west of Crickhowell*
A genuine all-rounder, this quality pub and restaurant stands in a picturesque garden just across the road from the river Usk. The original cider mill, fully working until the 1960s, has been tastefully incorporated into the main dining room, while the bars are full of character and offer a wide range of real ales and interesting, mainly New World wines. In the kitchen, chef/partner Sean Gerrard continues to cook as passionately as when he started 13 years ago. His imaginative seasonal menus are fed by produce from the inn's own farm, currently in organic conversion, along with plenty of quality local produce including fine market-fresh fish. Kick off with the likes of Black Mountain smoked salmon, home-made soup or fresh open ravioli of goats' cheese. Main courses could include roast supreme of free-range duck with pear and apricot chutney, grilled fillets of red mullet with saffron, potato and leek casserole, or chargrilled sirloin of beef with Portabello mushrooms, Stilton pâté and Burgundy wine sauce.
OPEN: 12-2.30 6-9.30 Closed: 1wk Jan **BAR MEALS:** L served Wed-Tue 12-2.30 D served Wed-Tue 6.30-9.30 Av main course £12
RESTAURANT: L served Wed-Mon 12-2.30 D served Wed-Mon 7-9.30 Av 3 course à la carte £22 Av 2 course fixed price £10
BREWERY/COMPANY: Free House ◖: Uleys Old Spot, Felinfoel Best Bitter, Marston's Pedigree, Hancocks HB. ♀: 8
FACILITIES: Children welcome Garden: Overlooking Usk River **NOTES:** Parking 40

DOWN ON THE FARM

Cider has been drunk in Britain since before Roman times and was originally made of fermented crab apple juice. Farmers made their own, especially in the West Country, and by the 17th century about 350 varieties of cider apple tree were cultivated, with names like Redstreak and Kingston Black, Sweet Coppin and Handsome Maud.

The basic process of cider-making is to crush apples in a press, run off the juice and leave it to ferment naturally in casks for four months or so. The Industrial Revolution, however, transferred cider from the farm to the factory and by the 1960s the major producers were following the same path as the brewers and efficiently turning out a standardised product - weak, sweet and fizzy - that had only a distant resemblance to the powerful ' rough cider' or 'scrumpy' of earlier days. Fortunately, a draught cider renaissance has followed in the wake of the real ale revival, and one of the Campaign for Real Ale's aim is to prevent the disappearance of rough cider and perry.

Wales

Open: 10-3, 6-11
Bar Meals: L served all week 12-2,
D served all week 6-10.
Av main course £8.95
RESTAURANT: L served all week 12-2,
D Mon-Sat 7-9.30.
Av cost 3 courses £25
BREWERY/COMPANY:
Free House.
🍺: Interbrew Bass, Greene King Old
Speckled Hen, Hancocks HB, Brains
Reverand James.
FACILITIES: Garden - Small pretty
garden, pergola, seating.
NOTES: Parking 50
ROOMS: 35 en suite from s£54 d£70

The Bear

The heart of this comfortable free house is a rambling old coaching inn dating back to 1432. The same family has run the hotel for a quarter of a century, and over the years it has been restored and maintained to a high standard.

★★★ ◎ 🐾 ♀

Brecon Road, Crickhowell, NP8 1BW
☎ 01873 810408 📠 01873 811696
📧 bearhotel@aol.com
Dir: On A40 between Abergavenny
& Brecon.

The owners regard the hotel as their own home, treating guests with genuine hospitality and obvious enthusiasm. Besides the 35 tastefully furnished en suite bedrooms, every available nook and cranny has been put to good use as bar, bistro or restaurant space. Out of doors, guests can enjoy the attractive little garden with its pergola and comfortable seating area. The cooking is essentially modern English, using ingredients from the local farmer's markets to produce a good selection of wholesome, old-fashioned recipes supported by a range of popular dishes from other countries. The bar menu begins simply with soup, sandwiches and baguettes, but dishes like steamed white fish pudding with red pepper coulis, goats' cheese and fried onion pie with baked ratatouille and garlic bread, or Welsh black beef steaks with red wine sauce could prove hard to resist. Dining room menus might start with risotto of smoked haddock and chargrilled Mediterranean vegetables or a terrine of confit duck served with celeriac remoulade and home-made walnut bread. Main courses include smoked Welsh venison, roasted salmon with horseradish and crushed new potatoes, or aubergine and Gruyere torte on roasted provençale vegetables with fresh tomato coulis. Leave room for a mouthwatering range of home-made desserts like apple and whinberry pie with spiced mulled wine jelly with a poached pear. Crickhowell itself is a charming, well-kept little market town in the heart of the Brecon Beacons National Park, and the hotel is ideally located for a whole range of outdoor pursuits.

CWMDU — Map 09 SO12

Pick of the Pubs

The Farmers Arms
NP8 1RU ☎ 01874 730464 📠 01874 730988
e-mail: cwmdu@aol.com
Dir: From A40 take A479 signed Builth Wells, Cwmdu is 3m along this road

A welcoming pub tucked away in a tiny hamlet, itself idyllically set in a typically quiet valley of great natural beauty in the Brecon Beacons National Park. The Farmers Arms sits just on the edge of the Black Mountains, and is an increasingly popular inn offering a warm welcome, and plenty of good food. The building dates back to the 18th century, and its sympathetic owners have been careful to ensure that it is not spoilt by tasteless modern conversions. Inside, the emphasis is on traditional charm, and the unspoilt stone-flagged bar area tempts visitors to linger over good beer, friendly chatter and a game of cards or dominoes, warmed by the cast-iron log burning stove. In the dining room, there's a break from tradition in order to offer a modern, wide-ranging selection of dishes. The best possible local ingredients are used, and most dietary requirements can be catered for on request. Among the starters expect specialities such as smoked haddock and Welsh onion fishcakes, duck liver, apricot and brandy paté, and baked field mushrooms. Quality fresh ingredients also go into main courses like grilled supreme of chicken with sautéed wild mushrooms, roast leg and pan-fried breast of duckling with soy-scented noodles, and an elderflower, ginger and blackcurrant sauce, and roast rack of Brecon lamb topped with a herb crust and served with Cumberland sauce. Fish is also well represented, with perhaps poached tranche of Usk salmon, and there are good vegetarian choices too, like puff pastry pillows of leeks. Desserts range from sticky toffee fudge Pavlova, to dark chocolate and hazelnut roulade, and baked light lemon cheesecake, and there's also a commendable selection of real ales.
OPEN: 12-2.30 6.30-11 (Mon 6.30-11, open BH Mon all day) Closed: Two weeks in Nov **BAR MEALS:** L served Tue-Sun 12-2.15 D served Tue-Sun 7-9.30 Av main course £8 **RESTAURANT:** L served Tue-Sun 12-2.15 D served Tue-Sun 7-9.30 Av 3 course à la carte £20 Av 3 course fixed price £17.50 **BREWERY/COMPANY:** Free House 🍺: Uley Old Spot Prize Ale, Tomos Watkin OSB, Greene King Old Speckled Hen, Shepherd Neame Spitfire Premium Ale. **FACILITIES:** Children welcome Garden: Views over the Brecon Beacons Dogs allowed Water, food, secured penned area
NOTES: Parking 30

DYLIFE — Map 14 SN89

Star Inn ♦♦♦
SY19 7BW ☎ 01650 521345 📠 01650 521345
Dir: Between Llanidloes & Machynlleth on mountain rd
Situated at 1300 feet in some of Wales' most breathtaking countryside, the inn traces its roots back to the 17th century. The area was a favourite haunt of Dylan Thomas and Wynford Vaughan Thomas; red kites swoop overhead, and the magnificent Clywedog reservoir is close by. Varied choice of wholesome pub fare includes cottage pie, big banger and chips, jumbo cod, sirloin steak, chicken in

mushroom cream sauce, and gammon with egg or pineapple. Specials include broccoli and leek bake, loin of pork in cider and cream, and aubergine and mushroom nut bake.

OPEN: 12-2.30 7-11 Ring for opening details during Winter
BAR MEALS: L served all week 12-2.30 D served all week 7-11 Av main course £5.95 **RESTAURANT:** 12-2 7-10
BREWERY/COMPANY: Free House 🍺: Tetley Smooth, Marston Pedigree. **FACILITIES:** Children welcome Children's licence Garden: Dogs allowed on lead at all times **NOTES:** Parking 40
ROOMS: 6 bedrooms 2 en suite 1 family rooms s£18 d£38

ELAN VILLAGE — Map 09 SN96

Elan Valley Hotel
LD6 5HN ☎ 01597 810448 📠 01597 810448
e-mail: info@elanvalleyhotel.co.uk
Dir: A44 to Rhayader then B4518 for 2m
Situated below the last of the four reservoirs in the Elan Valley, this rejuvenated hotel, formerly a Victorian fishing lodge, stands in the heart of stunning mid-Wales scenery and is justifiably a popular refreshment stop among visitors to the area. From snacks like hot toasted baguettes and aromatic coriander and mixed bean curry in the bar, to grilled Pencerrig goats' cheese with apple chutney, fillet of Welsh beef teryaki, or poached halibut with sautéed oyster mushrooms in the restaurant, perhaps followed by fresh cream raspberry meringue roulade.
OPEN: 6-11 (weekends 12-2.30, 6-11.30) Mon-Sun 11-3
BAR MEALS: L served Sat-Sun(winter), Mon-Sun(summer only) 12-2.30 D served all week 7-9 Av main course £5.50 **RESTAURANT:** D served Thurs-Sat (winter) all (summer) 7-9
BREWERY/COMPANY: Free House 🍺: Interbrew Hancocks HB, Brains Buckley Best & Reverand James, Wood Shropshire Lad, Timothy Taylor Landlord. **FACILITIES:** Children welcome Garden Dogs allowed **NOTES:** Parking 30

continued

Wales

HAY-ON-WYE Map 09 SO24

Kilverts Inn
The Bullring HR3 5AG ☎ 01497 821042 ▤ 01497 821580
e-mail: info@kilverts.co.uk
Dir: *From A50 take A49, then L onto B4348 into Hay-on-Wye. In town centre near Butter Market*

At the heart of Wales's 'bookshop capital' near the Butter Market - though access and parking can be a little tricky - the hotel derives its name from a noted 19th-century cleric well commemorated in the town. A core menu uses local produce, while the bar menu features pizzas, pasta and other pub favourites. Restaurant dinners show rather more imagination: lightly spiced parsnip and sweet potato roulade, served with cream cheese and mint, pork baton stuffed with peaches, pistachio and sage served with green ginger wine sauce, or braised hock of Welsh lamb.
OPEN: 9-11 (Sun 12-10.30) Closed: 25 Dec **BAR MEALS:** L served all week 12-2 D served all week 7-9.30 Av main course £9
RESTAURANT: L served all week 12-2 D served all week 7-9.30 Av 3 course à la carte £19.95 **BREWERY/COMPANY:** Free House
◀: Wye Valley Butty Bach, Coors Worthington Cream Flow & Hancock's HB. **FACILITIES:** Children welcome Garden: Large lawns, pond area Dogs allowed before 7pm, water **NOTES:** Parking 13
ROOMS: 11 bedrooms 11 en suite 1 family rooms s£40 d£70 (WTB)

Pick of the Pubs

The Old Black Lion ★★ ⊛
HR3 5AD ☎ 01497 820841 ▤ 01497 822960
e-mail: info@oldblacklion.co.uk
See Pick of the Pubs on opposite page

LLANDINAM Map 15 SO08

The Lion Hotel
SY17 5BY ☎ 01686 688233 ▤ 01686 689124
Dir: *on the A470 midway between Newton and Llanidloes*
Llandinam is perhaps best known as the home of the first electric light in Wales. The Lion has an attractive riverside setting and offers a warm welcome to visitors enjoying the splendour of the Upper Severn Valley. The restaurant's menu features hearty casseroles of Welsh lamb and registered Welsh Black beef. Other dishes include traditional steaks and grills, and here is always a range of home-made sweets and puddings.
OPEN: 11.30-3 6.30-11 (Sun 7-10.30) **BAR MEALS:** L served all week 12-2.15 6.45-9.15 **RESTAURANT:** D served all week 6.45-9.15 **BREWERY/COMPANY:** Free House ◀: Greene King Old Speckled Hen, Carlsberg-Tetley Tetley Cask Bitter. **FACILITIES:** Children welcome Children's licence Garden **NOTES:** Parking 50
ROOMS: 4 bedrooms 4 en suite 1 family rooms (WTB)

LLANDRINDOD WELLS Map 09 SO06

The Bell Country Inn
Llanyre LD1 6DY ☎ 01597 823959 ▤ 01597 825899
e-mail: dgj.jones@virgin.net
Dir: *1 1/2m NW of Llandrindod Wells on the A4081*
Set in the hills above Llandrindod Wells, this former drovers' inn offers a varied menu in the dining room, lounge bar and Stables Restaurant. Seafood from the specials board includes jumbo cod, squid and pan-fried fillet of skate, while favourite alternatives are half a roasted duckling or prime 10oz sirloin steak. There's the courtyard for outdoor seating, and a play area for children is provided.
OPEN: 11-11 all week **BAR MEALS:** L served all week 12-2 D served all week 6.30-9.30 Av main course £6.35 **RESTAURANT:** L served all week 12-2 D served 6.30-9.30 Av 3 course à la carte £18.95 **BREWERY/COMPANY:** Free House ◀: Worthington, Bass Hancock's HB. **FACILITIES:** Children welcome Garden: Food served outside. Patio area Dogs allowed In the garden only. Water provided **NOTES:** Parking 20 **ROOMS:** 9 bedrooms 9 en suite £39.50 (WTB)

LLANFYLLIN Map 15 SJ11

Cain Valley Hotel ★★
High St SY22 5AQ ☎ 01691 648366 ▤ 01691 648307
e-mail: info@cainvalleyhotel.co.uk
Dir: *from Shrewsbury & Oswestry follow signs for Lake Vyrnwy & onto A490 to Llanfyllin. Hotel on R*

Family-run coaching inn dating from the 17th century, with a stunning Jacobean staircase, oak-panelled lounge bar and a heavily beamed restaurant, where the walls have been exposed to show off the hand-made bricks. A full bar menu is available at lunchtime and in the evening, alongside a choice of real ales. Home-made soup, mixed seafood, Welsh lamb, steaks and curries are offered. Llanfyllin is amid green hills, offering wonderful walks and breathtaking views.
OPEN: 11.30-11 (Sun 12-10.30) Closed: 25 Dec **BAR MEALS:** L served all week 12-2 D served all week 7-9 **RESTAURANT:** D served all week 7-9 **BREWERY/COMPANY:** Free House ◀: Carlsberg-Tetley Ansells Best Bitter, Interbrew Bass & Worthingtons.
FACILITIES: Children welcome Dogs allowed **NOTES:** Parking 12
ROOMS: 13 bedrooms 13 en suite 3 family rooms s£42 d£62
See Pub Walk on page 630

> We only include details of accommodation
> that has been inspected by the AA (big Stars or
> Diamonds at the top of an entry), or the RAC,
> VisitBritain, VisitScotland or WTB (small Stars
> or Diamonds at the end of an entry).

Wales

Open: 11-11 (Sun 12-10.30)
Bar Meals: L served all week 12-2.30, D served all week 6.30-9.30. Av cost main course £9.50
RESTAURANT: D served all week 6.30-9.30. Av cost 3 course £24
BREWERY/COMPANY: Free House.
🍺: Old Black Lion Ale, Wye Valley, & Guest Ales.
FACILITIES: Garden - Patio garden with flowers and herbs. .
NOTES: Parking 20.
ROOMS: 10 en suite from £42.50 to £110

The Old Black Lion

This colourful 17th-century inn, parts of which have been traced back to the 1300s, is close to where the Lion Gate, one of the original entrances to the old walled town of Hay-on-Wye, used to stand.

Hay-on-Wye, HR3 5AD
☎ 01497 820841 📄 01497 822960
📧 info@oldblacklion.co.uk
Dir: Town centre.

Now renowned as the world's largest second-hand book centre - there's even one in the castle courtyard - Hay attractively climbs up from the River Wye, which separates it from England. Each year the town invites distinguished guest speakers - even ex-President Clinton has been - to its annual literary festival. Book-searching is thirsty work, so time for a pint of the pub's eponymous real ale, or a Wye Valley bitter,

in the comfortable King Richard bar, should be allowed for. Informal meals are served on scrubbed pine tables, there's a log-burning fire, and exposed oak beams that would have witnessed Oliver Cromwell's presence if, as is reputed, he lodged here during the siege of Hay Castle. The friendly owner, Vanessa King, has acquired a reputation for providing excellent food. She changes her menus frequently, making sure she uses only the best of British produce whenever possible, including locally reared meat (some organic), fresh seafood from Cornwall, seasonal vegetables,

and herbs from her abundantly stocked garden. The bar menu includes freshly-made sandwiches and salads, as well as a more substantial sausage and mash, sirloin steak, and fish pie. Other main courses include wild boar steak with cider and seed mustard sauce; herb-crusted rack of Welsh lamb; fillet of wild sea bass with marsh samphire, sweet pepper and lime salsa; and wild mushroom and leek crêpes. There are ten bedrooms, many of whose occupants are likely to be visiting the Brecon Beacons, canoeing, whitewater-rafting, or walking the Offa's Dyke Path.

LLANFYLLIN continued

The Stumble Inn
Bwlch-y-Cibau SY22 5LL ☎ 01691 648860 🖹 01691 648955
Dir: A458 to Welshpool, B4393 to Four Crosses and Llansantffraid, A495 Melford, A490 to Bwlch-y-Cibau
Standing opposite the church in a rural farming hamlet in unspoilt mid-Wales countryside close to Lake Vyrnwy, this popular stone-built inn offers a traditional pub atmosphere and food. The menu changes monthly and might feature Thai monkfish, beef goulash, Welsh lamb steak and hake fillet with saffron and prawn cream sauce.
OPEN: 12-3 6-12 Closed Sun nights Dec-Mar Closed: 2 Wks Jan
BAR MEALS: L served Sun 12-2 D served Wed-Sat 6-9 Av main course £7 **RESTAURANT:** L served Sun 12-2 D served Wed-Sat 6-10 Av 3 course à la carte £15 **BREWERY/COMPANY:** Free House ◀: Coors Worthington's, Changing Ales. **FACILITIES:** Children welcome Garden **NOTES:** Parking 40

LLANGATTOCK   Map 09 SO21

The Vine Tree Inn
The Legar NP8 1HG ☎ 01873 810514 🖹 01873 811299
e-mail: s.lennox@virgin.net
Dir: Take A40 W from Abergavenny then A4077 from Crickhowell
A pretty pink pub located on the banks of the River Usk, at the edge of the National Park and within walking distance of Crickhowell. It is predominantly a dining pub serving a comprehensive menu from nut roast to 20oz rump steak. The additional lunch menu changes with the seasons offering locally-made spicy sausage, and local lambs' kidneys with a sweet sherry sauce. The large garden overlooks the river, bridge and Table Mountain.
OPEN: 12-3 6-11 (Sun 7-10.30) **BAR MEALS:** L served all week 12-3 D served all week 6-10 Av main course £8 **RESTAURANT:** L served all week 12-3 D served all week 6-10 Av 3 course à la carte £15 **BREWERY/COMPANY:** Free House ◀: Fuller's London Pride, Coors Worthington's, Cwmbran Crow Valley. **FACILITIES:** Children welcome Garden: Large private garden, stunning views **NOTES:** Parking 27

LLOWES   Map 09 SO14

The Radnor Arms
HR3 5JA ☎ 01497 847460 🖹 01497 847460
Dir: A438 Brecon-Hereford Rd between Glasbury & Clyro
The garden of this charming, 400 year-old whitewashed drovers' inn enjoys stunning views across the Wye Valley to the Black Mountains. Local Felinfoel bitter is amongst the superb range of beers served beside blazing winter fires in the cosy bar, and the extensive blackboard menus offer plenty of variety, with good vegetarian options. Expect ham, egg and chips, stir-fried chicken with walnuts, swordfish in white wine sauce, or vegetable and cheese Wellington.
OPEN: 11-2.30 6.30-10 (Sun 12-3) **BAR MEALS:** L served Tue-Sun 12-3 D served Tue-Sun 6.30-11 Av main course £7.50
RESTAURANT: L served Tue-Sun 12-3 D served Tue-Sun 6.30-11 **BREWERY/COMPANY:** Free House ◀: Felinfoel, Worthington, Carlsburg, Bitburger. **FACILITIES:** Children welcome Garden **NOTES:** Parking 50

> Most of the pubs in this guide book
> pride themselves on the quality of their food.
> This may take a little time to prepare.

LLYSWEN   Map 09 SO13

Pick of the Pubs

The Griffin Inn
LD3 0UR ☎ 01874 754241 🖹 01874 754592
e-mail: info@griffin-inn.freeserve.co.uk
Dir: On A470 (Brecon to Builth Wells rd)

Family-run favourite for nearly 20 years, this delightful ivy-covered inn offers a relaxed atmosphere and an assortment of traditional comforts. The Griffin is also an ideal base for touring the region and exploring the glorious upper Wye valley. In winter take refuge in one of the cosy public rooms, while in summer you can sit outside and watch the world go by. There is local Wye salmon, while lobster, sole and sea bass come direct from Cornwall. Desserts are all home made, and might include trifle or bread and butter pudding. Those who fancy a lighter lunch can opt for sandwiches, baguettes or a ploughman's.
OPEN: 10.30-3 6-11 (Summer 11-11) **BAR MEALS:** L served all week 12-2 D served all week 7-9 Av main course £6.95
RESTAURANT: L served all week 12-2 D served all week 7-9 Av 3 course à la carte £15 **BREWERY/COMPANY:** ◀: Brains Reverand James, SA, Arms Park, Buckleys Best & Smooth. ♀: 9 **FACILITIES:** Dogs allowed **NOTES:** Parking 20

MONTGOMERY   Map 15 SO2!

Pick of the Pubs

Dragon Hotel ★★
SY15 6PA ☎ 01686 668359 🖹 01686 668287
e-mail: reception@dragonhotel.com
Dir: A483 toward Welshpool, R onto B4386 then B4385, behind the town hall
Strikingly attractive coaching inn, with a black and white timbered frontage and historic interior, parts of which date from the mid-1600s. Beams in the bar, lounge and some of the bedrooms are believed to have come from the castle, which was destroyed by Oliver Cromwell, and outside an enclosed patio has been created from the former coach entrance. The bar snack menu features sandwiches, baked potatoes and jumbo Welsh rarebit specials with a variety of accompaniments, while the choice of freshly cooked main courses - based on best local produce - includes steaks, chicken Havana grilled with a spicy Cuban marinade, rich pork sausage with mash, and a platter of paella for a minimum of two people. It is a friendly, family-run establishment with wide-ranging facilities,

continue

Wales

including en suite bedrooms, an indoor swimming pool, sauna, and function room.

OPEN: 11-11 **BAR MEALS:** L served all week 12-2 D served all week 7-9 **RESTAURANT:** L served bookings only 12-2 D served bookings only 7-9 Av 3 course à la carte £25 Av 3 course fixed price £19.50 **BREWERY/COMPANY:** Free House
🍺: Wood Special, Interbrew Bass, Guest. **FACILITIES:** Children welcome Children's licence Garden: Patio area at the front **NOTES:** Parking 20 **ROOMS:** 20 bedrooms 20 en suite 5 family rooms

---

NEW RADNOR
Map 09 SO26

Red Lion Inn
Llanfihangel-nant-Melan LD8 2TN
☎ 01544 350220 📠 01544 350220
e-mail: enquiries@theredlioninn.net
Dir: A483 to Crossgates then R onto A44

Llanfihangel-nant-Melan may be a bit of a mouthful to the non-Welsh speaking, but it's easy to find being just three miles west of New Radnor. This 16th-century drovers' inn has recently had a new restaurant built to make sure the tradition of hospitality continues. A new Radnor Ale has also been brewed to wash down dishes such as Welsh beef fillet on egg noodles, wild mushroom Stroganoff in a tortilla basket, valentine of lamb glazed with redcurrant, or venison steak in cracked pepper and breadcrumbs.
OPEN: 12-2.30 6-11 **BAR MEALS:** L served Wed-Sun 12-2.15 D served Mon-Sun 6.30-9.45 Av main course £10 **RESTAURANT:** L served Wed-Sun 12-2.15 D served Mon-Sun 6.30-9.45 Av 3 course à la carte £15 **BREWERY/COMPANY:** Free House 🍺: Randor Ale, Chase My Tail, Real Ales. **FACILITIES:** Children welcome Garden: Country garden overlooking mid Wales Hills Dogs allowed
NOTES: Parking 30 **ROOMS:** 7 bedrooms 7 en suite s£35 d£45 (WTB)

OLD RADNOR
Map 09 SO25

Harp Inn 🐑
LD8 2RH ☎ 01544 350655 📠 01544 350655
Dir: A44 from Leominster to Gore, then L to Old Radnor
Although this 15th-century pub has been extensively renovated, great care has been taken to retain as much of its original period character as possible. The slate-flagged floor, exposed stone walls and ancient bread oven still remain, as do traditional standards of hospitality and good food. Charles I complained about the food here centuries ago, but he could scarcely do so today. A typical menu includes 10oz Herefordshire steaks, steak and mushroom pie, salmon steak in dill sauce, breast of chicken in Stilton sauce, and pork steak in mustard sauce. Vegetarian options always available.
OPEN: 12-2 6-11 (Sat-Sun 12-3, 6-10.30) **BAR MEALS:** L served Sat-Sun 12-2 D served Tue-Sun 6-9 Av main course £9
RESTAURANT: L served Sat-Sun 12-2 D served Tue-Sun 7-9 Av 3 course à la carte £16 **BREWERY/COMPANY:** Free House
🍺: Shepherd Neame, Six Bells Brewery, Bishops Castle, Big Neus.
FACILITIES: Children welcome Garden: Large lawn in front of Pub **NOTES:** Parking 18

PWLLGLOYW
Map 09 SO03

Pick of the Pubs

Seland Newydd ◎◎ 🛏 ♀
LD3 9PY ☎ 01874 690282 📠 690187
e-mail: sealand@newydd.fsbusiness.co.uk
Dir: 4m N of Brecon on B4520 to Builth Wells, 1m before Lower Chapel
The name of this 17th-century coaching inn is the Welsh translation of 'New Zealand' - it was changed from the former Camden Arms by previous owners. Enjoying a peaceful village setting in the Brecon Beacons National Park, it features a cosy bar and lounge area with a log fire and a separate rear restaurant. Half the building has always been an inn, but the other half was once the local blacksmith's - the large fireplace in the centre of the room is part of the old forge. A grassed area outside has picnic tables next to the pet goats. There's a changing menu, but well-prepared dishes often include creamed parsnip and smokey bacon soup; rosemary and garlic sausages with mustard mash, honey parsnips, shallots and onion gravy; creamy spinach tagliatelle served with roasted wild salmon, grilled mozzarella and pepper salsa; and monkfish wrapped in Parma ham with saffron risotto.
OPEN: 12-3 6-11 **BAR MEALS:** L served Wed-Sun 12-2 D served Tue-Sat 7-9 Av main course £10 **RESTAURANT:** L served Wed-Sun 12-2 D served Tue-Sat 7-9 Av 3 course à la carte £23
BREWERY/COMPANY: Free House 🍺: Brains Buckley's Best Bitter, Brains Dark & Rev James. ♀: 7 **FACILITIES:** Children welcome Garden: grassy area with picnic tables Dogs allowed Water **NOTES:** Parking 30

Pick of the Pubs have that extra special quality that makes them stand out from the crowd. Their entries are highlighted, and may be a full page.

TALGARTH
Map 09 SO13

Castle Inn ◆◆◆
Pengenffordd LD3 0EP ☎ 01874 711353 📠 01874 711353
e-mail: castlepen@aol.com
Dir: *4m S of Talgarth on the A479*
Formerly a hill farm and drovers' inn, the Castle is popular
with mountain walkers and outdoor enthusiasts tramping in
the Brecon Beacons. At just over 1,000 feet above sea level, it
takes its name from the nearby ancient hill-fort of Castell
Dinas. Substantial pub food includes cottage pie, tropical
curry, and vegetarian shepherd's pie, with treacle sponge
typically to follow. Bunkhouse accommodation is on offer in
the neighbouring converted barn.
OPEN: 12-3 7-11 (Mon 7-11, Sat 12-4, 7-11) Closed: Dec 25
BAR MEALS: L served Thur-Sun 12-2 D served all week 7-9
BREWERY/COMPANY: Free House 🍺: 2 or 3 regularly changing
ales. **FACILITIES:** Children welcome Garden: Small pond with
garden **NOTES:** Parking 60 **ROOMS:** 4 bedrooms 4 en suite 1
family rooms s£35 d£46

TALYBONT-ON-USK
Map 09 SO12

Star Inn 🍸
LD3 7YX ☎ 01874 676635
Dir: *Telephone for directions*
With its pretty riverside garden, this traditional 200-year-old
inn stands in a picturesque village within the Brecon Beacons
National Park. The pub has long been known for its constantly
changing range of well-kept real ales, and it's an excellent
centre for walking and outdoor pursuits. Quiz night on
Monday, live bands on Wednesday. Hearty bar food with
dishes such as chicken in leek and Stilton sauce, traditional
roasts, salmon fish cakes, and vegetarian chilli.
OPEN: 11-3 6.30-11 (Sat all day) **BAR MEALS:** L served Mon-Sun
12-2.15 D served Mon-Sun 6.30-9 Av main course £5.50
BREWERY/COMPANY: Free House 🍺: Felinfoel Double Dragon,
Theakston Old Peculier, Hancock's HB, Bullmastiff Best.
FACILITIES: Children welcome Garden: Shaded backed by canal
Dogs allowed

TRECASTLE
Map 09 SN82

Pick of the Pubs

Castle Coaching Inn 🍸
LD3 8UH ☎ 01874 636354 📠 01874 636457
e-mail: hotel.reservation@btinternet.com
Dir: *On A40 W of Brecon*

A Georgian coaching inn on the old London-Carmarthen
coaching route, now the main A40 trunk road. Family
owned and run, the hotel has been carefully restored in

recent years, and has lovely old fireplaces and a
remarkable bow-fronted bar window. Ten en suite
bedrooms are available and the inn also offers a peaceful
terrace and garden. Food is served in the bar or more
formally in the restaurant. Specialities include locally-
reared Welsh lamb chops served with rosemary and
redcurrant sauce and Welsh Black sirloin steaks topped
with fried onions and mushrooms and maybe a melting
smoked St David's cheese. There is also a good vegetarian
selection, including Stilton and pasta bake and bindi
vegetable curry. Complete your meal with a dessert such
as banana and amaretti cheesecake or summer pudding
with Cornish clotted cream - or perhaps sample the
selection of Welsh farmhouse cheeses.
OPEN: 12-3 6-11 **BAR MEALS:** L served Tues-Sun 12-2 D
served Mon-Sun 6.30-9.30 Av main course £7.95
RESTAURANT: L served Tues-Sun 12-2 D served Mon-Sun 7-9
Av 3 course à la carte £20 **BREWERY/COMPANY:** Free House
🍺: Fuller's London Pride, Shepherd Neame Spitfire, Young's
Special, Bragdy Ceredigion Red Kite. 🍸: 15
FACILITIES: Children welcome Children's licence Garden:
Paved sun terrace Dogs allowed Water, food **NOTES:** Parking
25 **ROOMS:** 10 bedrooms 10 en suite 2 family rooms s£45
d£60 (WTB)

UPPER CWMTWRCH
Map 09 SN71

George VI Inn 🍸
SA9 2XH ☎ 01639 830938 📠 01639 830932
e-mail: royjk@lineone.net
Dir: *2 M from Ystalyfera Rdbt at Upper Cwmtwrch is the George VI inn
next to the river*
A traditional family-owned pub and restaurant, which
occupies a scenic riverside location at the foot of the Black
Mountains. Relax by the cosy wood-burner on a cold winter's
day or, in summer, make use of the colourful garden and
patio for alfresco dining. The pub brews its own beers and
offers wholesome fare made from Welsh produce wherever
possible. Traditional roasts, sizzling bass in garlic, and Welsh
black beef feature on the extensive menu.
OPEN: 11-3 6-11 (Sun 12-3, 7-10.30) **BAR MEALS:** L served all
week 11.30-2.30 D served all week 6.30-10 Av main course £8.50
RESTAURANT: L served Wed-Mon 11.30-2.30 D served Wed-Mon
6.30-10 Av 3 course à la carte £15 **BREWERY/COMPANY:** Free
House 🍺: White Hart Brewery Cwrw Blasus, Cwrw Cwmtwrch, Brains
SA, Abbott Ale. **FACILITIES:** Children welcome Garden: Food served
outside **NOTES:** Parking 40

SWANSEA

LLANSAMLET
Map 09 SS69

Plough and Harrow
57 Church Rd SA7 9RL ☎ 01792 772263
Dir: *2 M from Junct 44 of M4, 5 m from the centre of Swansea near the
enterprise park*
Sitting in a quiet Swansea suburb next to a church, this Tomos
Watkin pub has a roaring log fire and some say, a resident
ghost. Cosy relaxed atmosphere with a good local reputation
for its food.
OPEN: 12-11 **BAR MEALS:** L served all week 12-2 D served all
week 6-9 Av main course £5 🍺: Watkins OSB, Merlins, Whoosh,
Worthington Best. **FACILITIES:** Children welcome Dogs allowed
NOTES: No credit cards

continued

PONTARDDULAIS

Map 08 SN50

The Fountain Inn

111 Bologoed Rd SA4 1JP ☎ 01792 882501 ▤ 01792 885340
e-mail: bookings@fountaininn.com
Dir: *A48 from M4 to Pontlliw then on to Pontarddulais, inn on R*
Memorabilia from Swansea's industrial past fill this carefully
modernised old free house. The chef uses fresh local
ingredients to produce an extensive and interesting range of
dishes. Expect cockle, bacon and laverbread crêpe; stuffed
Welsh saltmarsh lamb; cheese and leek crusted cod; or hake
and monkfish in prawn and watercress sauce. Round off your
meal with bara brith bread and butter pudding.
OPEN: 12-2 5.30-11.30 Closed: 25-26 Dec **BAR MEALS:** L served
all week 12-2 D served all week 5.30-9.30 Av main course £9.50
RESTAURANT: L served all week 12-2.30 D served all week 5.30-
9.30 **BREWERY/COMPANY:** Free House 🍺: Greene King Old
Speckled Hen, Fuller's London Pride, Batemans XXXX.
FACILITIES: Children welcome Garden **NOTES:** Parking 30

REYNOLDSTON

Map 08 SS48

King Arthur Hotel 🦜

Higher Green SA3 1AD ☎ 01792 390775 ▤ 01792 391075
e-mail: info@kingarthurhotel.co.uk
Dir: *Just N of A4118 SW of Swansea*
The Gower was Britain's first designated Area of Outstanding
Natural Beauty, and the King Arthur is a good base for a
peninsular tour. The varied regular menu offers locally-caught
fish and seafood, grills, meat dishes and salads. On the
specials board are likely to be cockles, laverbread and bacon
bites, all kinds of steaks, speciality pork and lamb dishes,
game sausages, faggots, peas and mash, and more fresh fish.
OPEN: 11-11 Closed: 25 Dec **BAR MEALS:** L served all week 12-
2.30 D served all week 6-9.30 Av main course £6 **RESTAURANT:** L
served all week 12-2.30 D served all week 6-9.30
BREWERY/COMPANY: Free House 🍺: Felinfoel Double Dragon,
Interbrew Worthington Bitter & Bass. **FACILITIES:** Children welcome
Garden Dogs allowed Water **NOTES:** Parking 80 **ROOMS:** 7
bedrooms 7 en suite 2 family rooms s£40 d£55 (WTB)

VALE OF GLAMORGAN

COWBRIDGE

Map 09 SS97

Victoria Inn

Sigingstone CF71 7LP ☎ 01446 773943 ▤ 01446 776446
Dir: *Off the B4270 in village of Sigingstone*

With an upstairs restaurant and a downstairs lounge, this
quiet village inn is decorated with old photographs and prints,
and a collection of antiques. It is also stocked with a selection

continued

of malt whiskies and Welsh ales. The kitchen offers home-
cooked bar meals and a comprehensive à la carte menu. The
specials board changes daily.
OPEN: 11-3 6-11 **BAR MEALS:** L served all week 11.45-2 D served
all week 6.30-9.30 Av main course £6.95 **RESTAURANT:** D served
Wed-Sat 6.30-9.30 Av 3 course à la carte £17.50 Av 3 course fixed price
£13.50 **BREWERY/COMPANY:** Free House 🍺: Tomas Watkins
Best Bitter, Whoosh, Worthington BB. **FACILITIES:** Children
welcome Garden **NOTES:** Parking 60

EAST ABERTHAW

Map 09 ST06

Pick of the Pubs

Blue Anchor Inn 🦜

CF62 3DD ☎ 01446 750329 ▤ 01446 750077
See Pick of the Pubs on page 642

See Pick of the Pubs on page 642

MONKNASH

Map 09 SS97

The Plough & Harrow ♀

CF71 7QQ ☎ 01656 890209
e-mail: pugs@publive.com
Dir: *Telephone for directions*
In a peaceful country setting, on the edge of a small village
with views across the fields to the Bristol Channel, this low,
state-roofed building was originally built as the chapter house
of a monastery, although it has been a pub for 500 of its 600-
year existence. Expect an atmospheric interior, open fires, an
excellent choice of real ale on tap, and home-cooked food
using fresh local ingredients.
OPEN: 12-12 **BAR MEALS:** L served all week 12-2 D served Mon-
Fri 6-9 **RESTAURANT:** D served Mon-Fri 6-9
BREWERY/COMPANY: Free House 🍺: Greene King Abbot,
Shepherds Neame Spitfire, Timothy Taylor Landlord, Bass.
FACILITIES: Garden **NOTES:** Parking 30

ST HILARY

Map 09 ST07

Pick of the Pubs

The Bush Inn 🦜

CF71 7DP ☎ 01446 772745
Dir: *S of A48, E of Cowbridge*
Picturesque village in the Vale of Glamorgan that is home
to a 16th-century thatched pub, a 12th-century church and
pretty thatched cottages. The Bush boasts a huge
inglenook fireplace, flagged floors, and an unusual spiral
staircase. In the restaurant you can sample spinach
pancake, beef Calvados, and poached salmon fillets, while
sandwiches and salads, and dishes like baked ham and
parsley sauce feature in the bar.
OPEN: 11.30-11 (Sun 12-10.30) **BAR MEALS:** L served all
week 12-2.30 D served all week 6.45-9.30 Av main course £6
RESTAURANT: L served all week 12-2.30 D served Mon-Sat,
6.45-9.30 Not Sun pm Av 3 course à la carte £15 Av 3 course
fixed price £12.95 **BREWERY/COMPANY:** Punch Taverns
🍺: Coors Hancock's HB, Greene King Old Speckled Hen,
Interbrew Worthington Bitter & Bass. **FACILITIES:** Children
welcome Garden: Bar tables on grass Dogs allowed Water
NOTES: Parking 60

★ **Pubs with Red Stars are part of the
AA's Top 200 Hotels in Britain & Ireland**

Wales

Open: 11-11 (Sun 12-10.30)
Bar Meals: L served Mon-Sat 12-2, D served Mon-Fri 6-8, Av cost main course £6.75
RESTAURANT: L served Sun 12-2.30, D served Mon-Sat 7-9.30.
BREWERY/COMPANY: Free House.
🍺: Brains Buckleys Best, Theakston Old Peculiar, Wadworth 6X, Interbrew Boddingtons Bitter, Marston's Bitter.
FACILITIES: Children welcome, Garden food served outside.
NOTES: Parking 70

Blue Anchor Inn

With a history dating from the 1380s, it is hardly surprising that this heavily-thatched inn has secrets. Among its many secrets is an underground passage down to the shore, where wreckers and smugglers formerly roamed the wild coastline that looks out across the Bristol Channel.

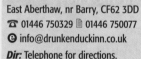
East Aberthaw, nr Barry, CF62 3DD
☎ 01446 750329 📠 01446 750077
📧 info@drunkenduckinn.co.uk
Dir: Telephone for directions.

Real ales and good food are also on hand for the lucky traveller. A thick thatch comes well down over the mellow ivy-covered stone walls, revealing tiny windows and low doors. Brightly coloured hanging baskets and flower-tubs grace the frontage in summer, and there are tables and benches on the courtyard and terrace. Inside is a warren of small rooms separated by

thick walls, and with low, beamed ceilings. A number of open fires and a large inglenook - built in the days when the warmest place to sit was in the fireplace - are still welcome today. A couple of guest ales are always available on the hand pumps, along with several regular real ales. The food varies between the bar and restaurant, with the latter divided between a carte and fixed-price menu. Starters like marinated chilli and garlic seafood, and game terrine wrapped in bacon, might be followed by baked pork

tenderloin, and pan-fried duck breast on a sweet potato and Stilton mash. In the bar choose from Welsh lamb and leek casserole, pot roast shank of lamb, and pan-fried breast of local pheasant, plus various snacks. A good way to round off a meal might be with traditional sherry trifle, or fresh strawberry flan. For those with the energy, there is a path that leads the short distance to the estuary.

Pick of the Pubs

HANMER
Map 15 SJ43

Hanmer Arms ★★ 🐾 ♀
SY13 3DE ☎ 01948 830532 📠 01948 830740
e-mail: enquiries@thehanmerarms.co.uk
Dir: Between Wrexham & Whitchurch on A539, off A525

Originally built in the 16th century, this comfortably furnished village hotel is centrally placed in the shadow of St Chad's church. The village bar serves a range of hand-drawn beers, whilst the first floor restaurant offers commanding views of the Berwyn Mountains and the Cheshire plain. A selection of dishes from a typical menu include stirfry chicken strips with sweet pepper, mango and beanshoots, sautéed cushions of venison with wild mushrooms, Gressingham duck breast with spicy plums, and vegetable tart with a basil pesto.
OPEN: 12 -11 **BAR MEALS:** L served all week 12-10 D served all week **RESTAURANT:** L served all week 12-9.30 D served all week **BREWERY/COMPANY:** Free House ◀: Interbrew Bass & Boddingtons, Castle Eden & Camerons. **FACILITIES:** Children welcome Garden: Large Dogs allowed **NOTES:** Parking 70 **ROOMS:** 26 bedrooms 26 en suite s£45 d£56.50

LLANARMON DYFFRYN CEIRIOG
Map 15 SJ13

The Hand Hotel 🐾
LL20 7LD ☎ 01691 600666 📠 01691 600262
e-mail: handllandc6@btopenworld.com
Tucked away in the Ceiriog valley, this inviting 16th-century hotel is characterised by darkened beams, open fireplaces and exposed stone walls - and glorious views from the beer garden. This is a popular base for walking and pony trekking. Traditional British tastes are reflected in the bar menu with steaks, home-made fish cakes and roasts, with a wider selection in the restaurant including poached salmon with fennel butter cream sauce and three-cheese pasta bake with broccoli spears.
OPEN: 8-12 **BAR MEALS:** L served Everyday 12-2.30 D served everyday 6.30-9 Av main course £7 **RESTAURANT:** L served everday 12-2.30 D served Everyday 6.30-9 Av 3 course à la carte £19 **BREWERY/COMPANY:** Free House ◀: Coors Worthington Cream Flow. **FACILITIES:** Garden: Patio style with flower borders Dogs allowed **NOTES:** Parking 18 **ROOMS:** 13 bedrooms 13 en suite 4 family rooms s£47.50 d£75 (WTB)

For a list of pubs with AA Inspected
Accommodation Awards
◆ see pages 646-651 ★

The West Arms Hotel ★★ ◉ 🐾
LL20 7LD ☎ 01691 600665 📠 01691 600622
e-mail: gowestarms@aol.com
Dir: Leave A483 at Chirk, follow signs for Ceiriog Valley B4500, hotel is 11m from Chirk
Sixteenth century in origin and a hotel since 1670, the West Arms is at the head of a long, winding valley in the Berwyn foothills. Cattle drovers heading for faraway markets would meet here, and shooting parties have been regulars for centuries. Very much a locals' bar, but visitors are still warmly welcomed, and warmth and character ooze from its undulating slate floors, ancient timberwork and vast inglenook fireplaces. Award-winning chef Grant Williams works to the highest standards; examples from his bar menu include pan-fried sirloin steak in garlic, and Ceiriog fishcake, a mix of spiced fresh fish with tarragon and cucumber dressing. In summer, light lunches are also served in the pretty riverside garden. On the short nightly dinner menu you might find leek and potato terrine with Mediterranean relish, fillet of Welsh beef with Welsh rarebit on a purée of celeriac, drizzled with port wine, and meringue roulade with toasted marshmallows and raspberry coulis.
OPEN: 8-11 **BAR MEALS:** L served all week 12-2 D served all week 7-9 Av main course £8.95 **RESTAURANT:** L served Sun 12-2 D served all week 7-9 **BREWERY/COMPANY:** Free House ◀: Interbrew Flowers IPA, Welsh Smooth, Trophy Real Ale. **FACILITIES:** Children welcome Garden: Large lawned area view of Berwyn Mountains Dogs allowed Water, 3 Kennels **NOTES:** Parking 30 **ROOMS:** 15 bedrooms 15 en suite 2 family rooms s£47.50 d£99

MARFORD
Map 15 SJ35

Trevor Arms Hotel 🐾 ♀
LL12 8TA ☎ 01244 570436 📠 01244 570273
e-mail: info@trevorarmsmarford.fsnet.co.uk
Dir: off A483 onto B5102 then R onto B5445 into Marford

Haunted 19th-century coaching inn that was once the scene of public hangings. It takes its name from Lord Trevor of Trevallin, who was killed in a duel. Grisly past notwithstanding, the Trevallin is a charming inn, offering a

continued

MARFORD continued

varied menu. Bar specials might include chicken curry, battered cod or a three course carvery, whilst the main menu takes in everything from steaks and burgers to oven-roasted duck breast with sautéed straw vegetables and a burnt orange sauce.
OPEN: 11-11 **BAR MEALS:** L served all week 11-11 D served all week Av main course £6.50 **RESTAURANT:** L served all week 11-11 D served all week Av 3 course à la carte £15 Av 3 course fixed price £7.95 **BREWERY/COMPANY:** Scottish Courage 🍺: Greenalls, Scottish Courage Theakston Old Peculier & John Smiths, Greene King Old Speckled Hen, Guest. ♀: 12 **FACILITIES:** Children welcome Garden: Large lawn area **NOTES:** Parking 70

All AA rated accommodation can also be found on the AA's internet site
www.theAA.com

WREXHAM

Map 15 SJ35

Pant-yr-Ochain ♀
Old Wrexham Rd, Gresford LL12 8TY
☎ 01978 853525 📠 01978 853505
e-mail: pant.yr.ochain@brunningandprice.co.uk
Dir: *A534 between Cresford and Wrexham*
The 'Hollow of Lamentation' is a singularly inappropriate name for this flourishing pub, comprising a 19th-century hall and much older farmhouse dating from the 16th-century. A wide-ranging menu encompasses sandwiches, ploughman's and dishes of Welsh black rump steak with creamed spinach, roast peppers, sauté potatoes and peppercorn sauce, or fillet of red bream with smoked haddock and spinach risotto. Interesting vegetarian options include chargrilled aubergine and roast parsnip timbale with creamy mushroom fricassée.
OPEN: 12-11 (Sun 12-10.30) Closed: 25-26 Dec **BAR MEALS:** L served all week 12-9.30 D served all week Av main course £8.95 🍺: Timothy Tailor Landlord, Interbrew Flowers Original, Boddingtons, Plassey Bitter. **FACILITIES:** Children welcome Garden: Food served outdoors **NOTES:** Parking 80

Wales

How can I get away without the hassle of finding a place to stay?

Booking a place to stay can be a time-consuming process. You choose a place you like, only to find it's fully booked. That means going back to the drawing board again. Why not ask us to find the place that best suits your needs? No fuss, no worries and no booking fee.

Whatever your preference, we have the place for you. From a rustic farm cottage to a smart city centre hotel - we have them all. Choose from around 8,000 quality rated hotels and B&Bs in Great Britain and Ireland.

Just AAsk.

Hotel Booking Service
www.theAA.com

You may contact us using a Textphone on 0870 243 2456.
Information is available in large print, audio and Braille on request

Index of Pub Walks

Pubs with AA Inspected Accommodation

This is a list of the pubs in this guide that have AA Diamond, AA Star or Restaurant with Rooms awards for accommodation. A full listing of AA B&B accommodation can be found in the *AA Bed & Breakfast Guide*, while Hotels are listed in our *AA Hotel Guide*. See page 8 for a full explanation of the AA's awards for accommodation.

Pubs with AA Inspected Accommodation

Pubs with AA Inspected Accommodation

How to Find a Pub in the Atlas Section

Pubs are located in the gazetteer under the name of the nearest town or village. If a pub is in a small village or rural area, it may appear under a town within fives miles of its actual location. The black dots and town names shown in the atlas refer to the gazetteer location in the guide. Please use the directions in the pub entry to find the pub on foot or by car. If directions are not given, or are not clear, please telephone the pub for details.

Key to County Map

The county map shown here will help you identify the counties within each country. You can look up each county in the guide using the county names at the top of each page. Towns featured in the guide use the atlas pages and index following this map.

England

1 Bedfordshire
2 Berkshire
3 Bristol
4 Buckinghamshire
5 Cambridgeshire
6 Greater Manchester
7 Herefordshire
8 Hertfordshire
9 Leicestershire
10 Northamptonshire
11 Nottinghamshire
12 Rutland
13 Staffordshire
14 Warwickshire
15 West Midlands
16 Worcestershire

Scotland

17 City of Glasgow
18 Clackmannanshire
19 East Ayrshire
20 East Dunbartonshire
21 East Renfrewshire
22 Perth & Kinross
23 Renfrewshire
24 South Lanarkshire
25 West Dunbartonshire

Wales

26 Blaenau Gwent
27 Bridgend
28 Caerphilly
29 Denbighshire
30 Flintshire
31 Merthyr Tydfil
32 Monmouthshire
33 Neath Port Talbot
34 Newport
35 Rhondda Cynon Taff
36 Torfaen
37 Vale of Glamorgan
38 Wrexham

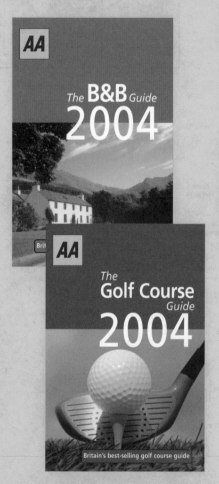
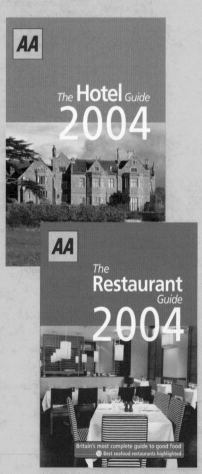

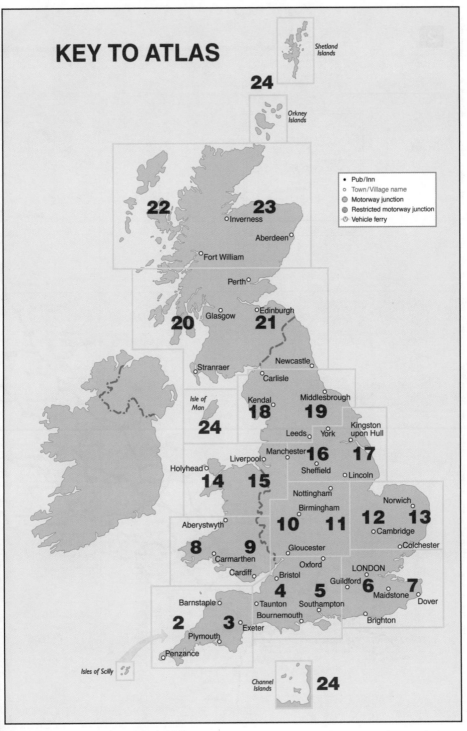

KEY TO ATLAS

Shetland Islands

24

Orkney Islands

- • Pub/Inn
- ○ Town/Village name
- ◎ Motorway junction
- ◉ Restricted motorway junction
- ⚓ Vehicle ferry

22

23

○ Inverness

Aberdeen ○

○ Fort William

Perth ○

○ Edinburgh

Glasgow ○

20

21

○ Stranraer

Newcastle ○

Carlisle ○

Isle of Man

Kendal ○

Middlesbrough ○

24

18

19

Leeds ○ York ○

Kingston upon Hull ○

Liverpool ○ Manchester ○

16

17

Holyhead ○

Sheffield ○

○ Lincoln

14

15

Nottingham ○

Norwich ○

Aberystwyth ○

Birmingham ○

10

11

12

13

○ Cambridge

8

9

Gloucester ○

○ Colchester

Carmarthen ○

Oxford ○

LONDON

Cardiff ○

Bristol ○

Guildford ○

6

7

Barnstaple ○

4

5

Maidstone ○

○ Dover

2

3

○ Taunton Southampton ○

Bournemouth ○

Brighton ○

Plymouth ○

Exeter ○

Penzance ○

Isles of Scilly

Channel Islands

24

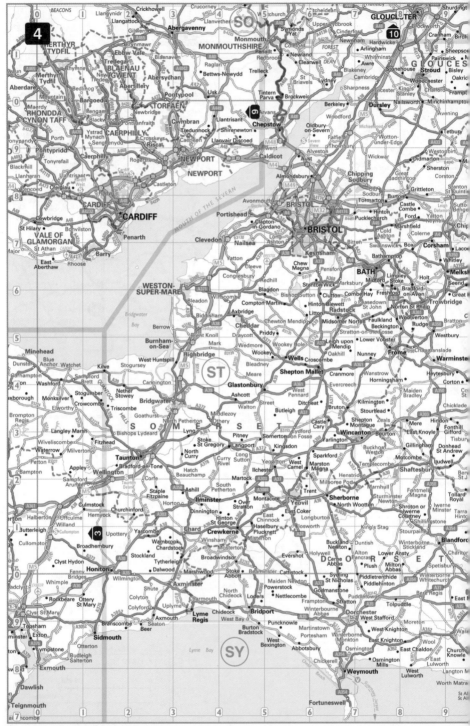

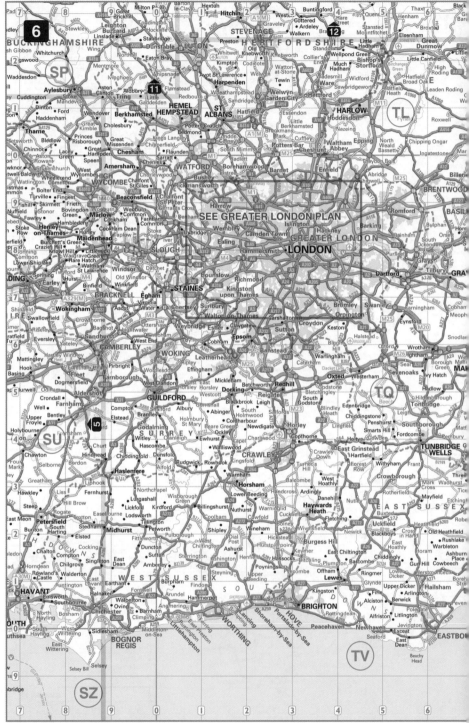

For continuation pages refer to numbered arrows

8

CARDIGAN BAY

Aberystwy

Llanfar

Llanrhystud
Llansantffraid

Aberarth   C

New
Quay   Aberaeron

Llwyndafydd

Llangranog   Temple
Aberporth   Bar

Tan-y-groes   Talgarreg
Blaenporth

St   Cardigan   Rhydowen
Dogmaels   Llechryd   Llanybydder

Nevern   Cilgerran   Llandysul

SN

Newport   Newcastle   Llangeler
Eglwyswrw   Emlyn

Fishguard   Rhos   Abergorle

Strumble Head   MYNYDD   PRESELI   Brechfa

Porthgain   Cynwyl
Letterston   Elfed

St David's   Wolf's   CARMARTHENSHI
Head   Castle
St David's   Solva   PEMBROKESHIRE   Nantgaredig

Llandissilio   Carmarthen   Llanarthne

Newgale   Roch   Llanddarog   L

St Brides   Robeston   Cross Hands
Bay   Wathen   Whitland   St
Broad   Clears   Llansteffan   Pontyberem
Haven   Haverfordwest   Narberth   Pontyates
Landshipping   Red   Laugharne   Kidwelly   Pont
Johnston   Roses   Pendine   Her
Marloes   Kilgetty   Amroth   Pwll
Milford   Penally   Pembrey   Burry
Broad Sound   Haven   Neyland   Carew   Saundersfoot   Port   Llanelli Gor
Dale   Pembroke   St   Carmarthen   Gower
Angle   Dock   Lampney   Florence   Bay
Pembroke   A4139   Llanrhidian   Dun
Castlemartin   Penally   SWANSEA
Bosherston   Manorbier   Llangennith
Stackpole   Rhossili   Reynoldston
Worms   Bisho
Head   Oxwich
Port
Einon

SR   SS

Pub/Inn
Town/Village name
0   10 miles
0   10   20 kilometres   Lundy   Ilfracombe
Mortehoe   Lee 5

For continuation pages refer to numbered arrows

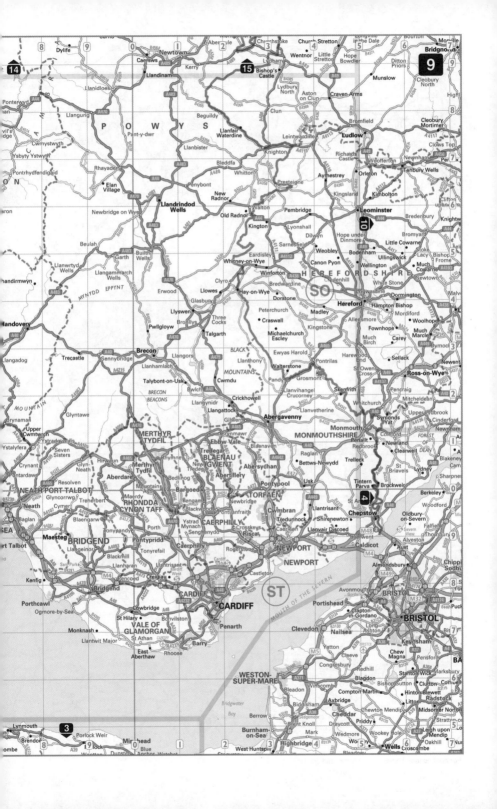

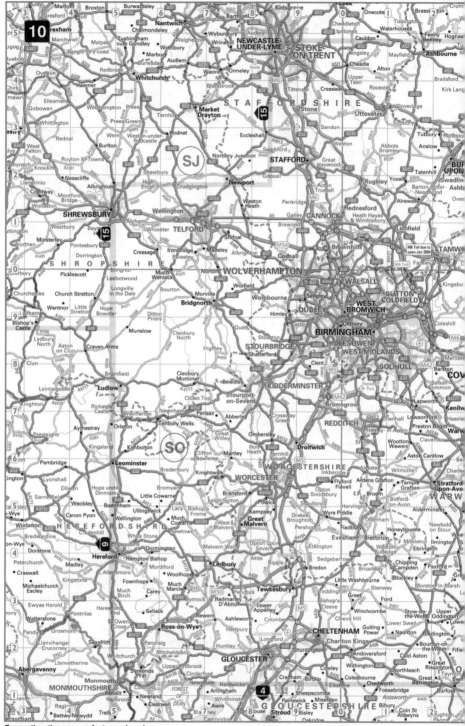

For continuation pages refer to numbered arrows

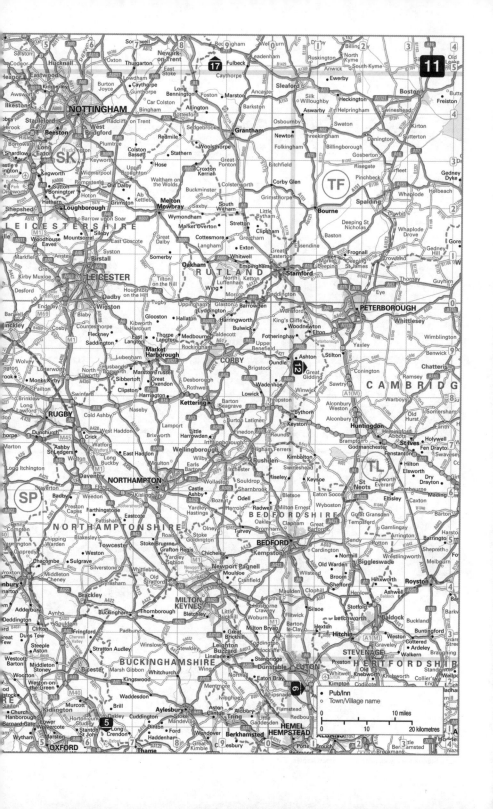

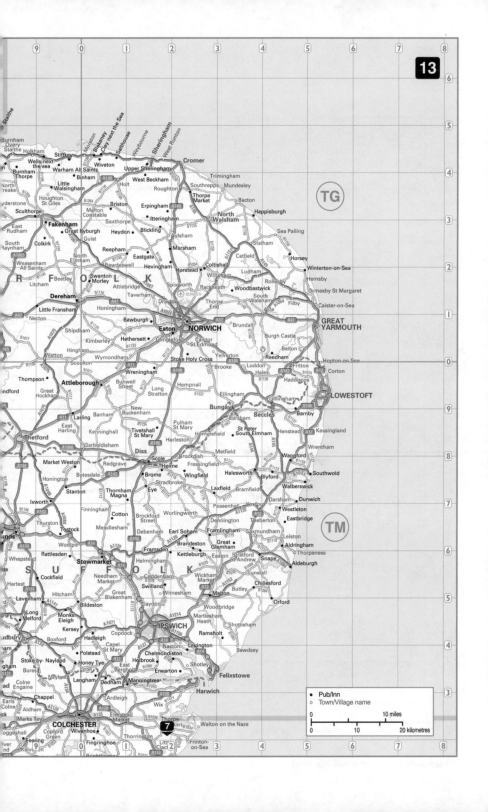

14

For continuation pages refer to numbered arrows

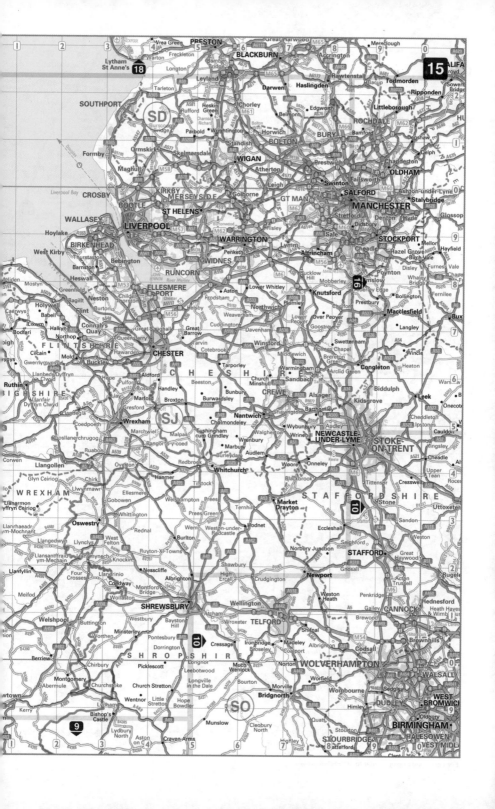

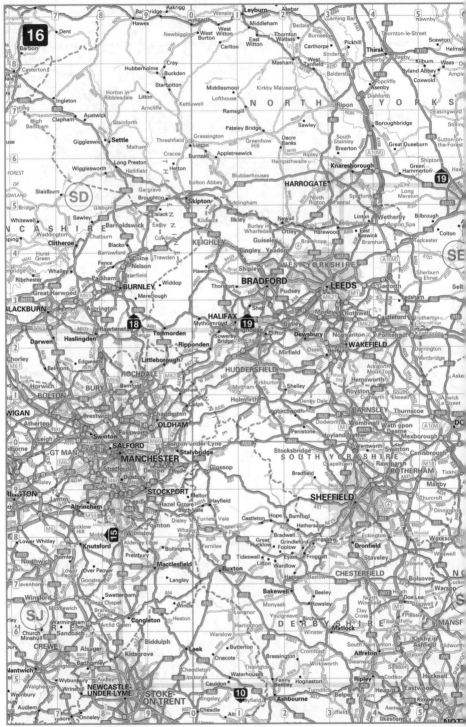

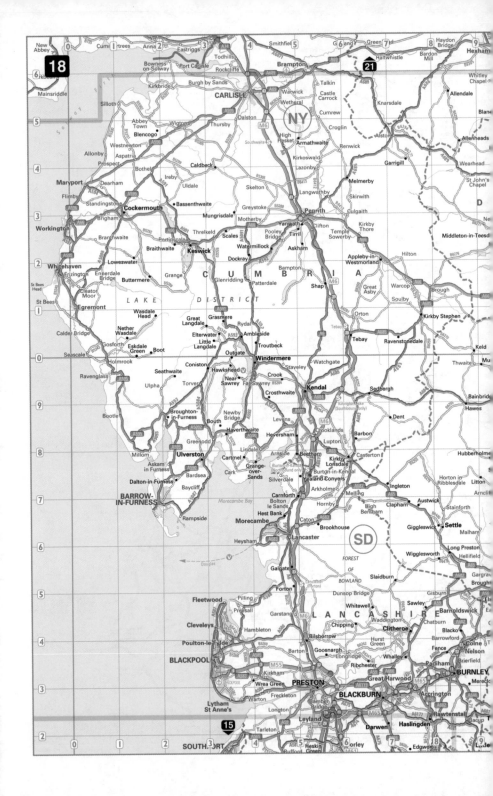

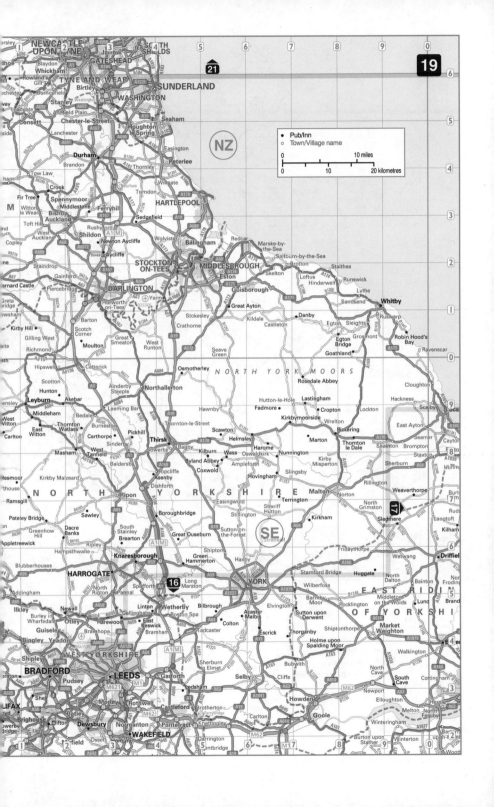

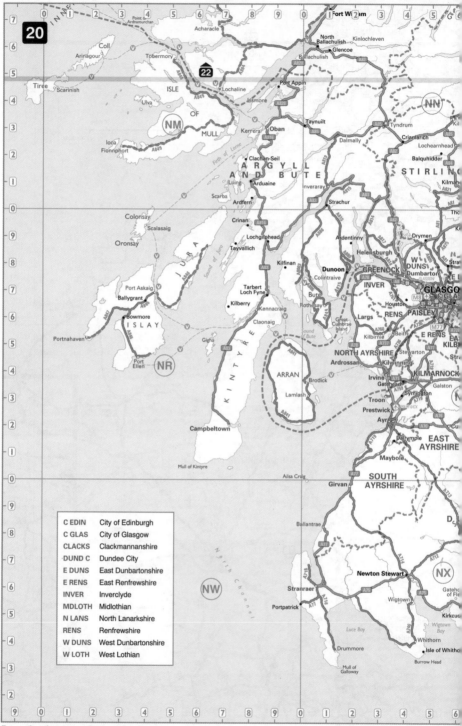

20

For continuation pages refer to numbered arrows

C EDIN	City of Edinburgh
C GLAS	City of Glasgow
CLACKS	Clackmannanshire
DUND C	Dundee City
E DUNS	East Dunbartonshire
E RENS	East Renfrewshire
INVER	Inverclyde
MDLOTH	Midlothian
N LANS	North Lanarkshire
RENS	Renfrewshire
W DUNS	West Dunbartonshire
W LOTH	West Lothian

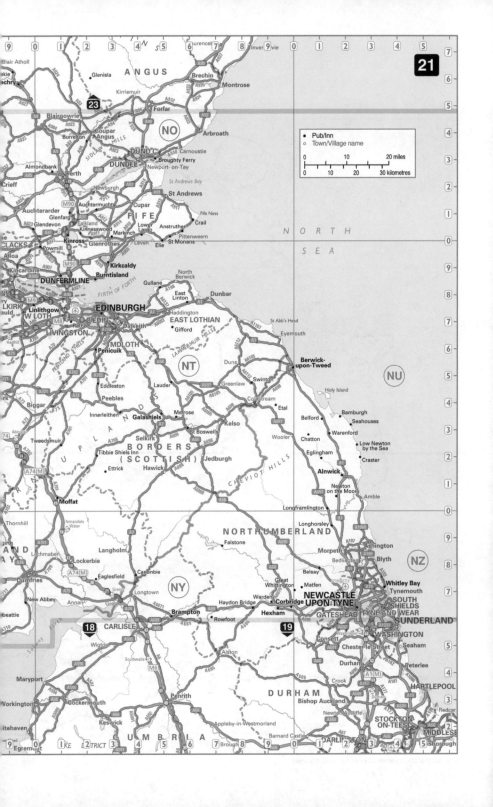

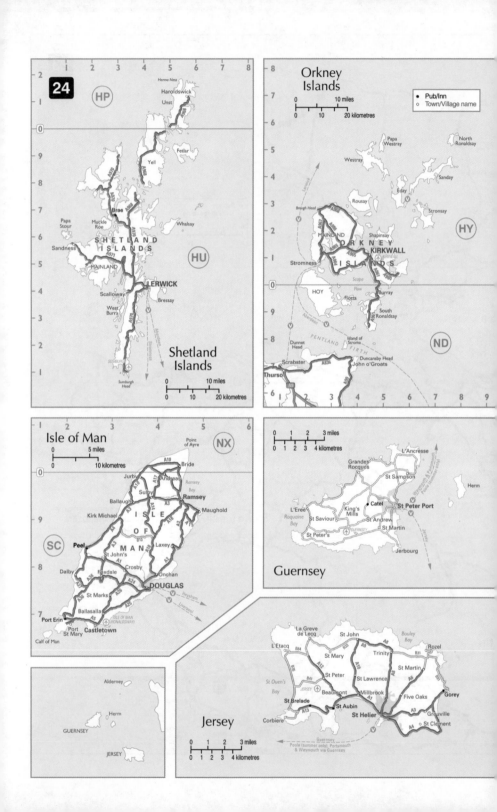

Central London

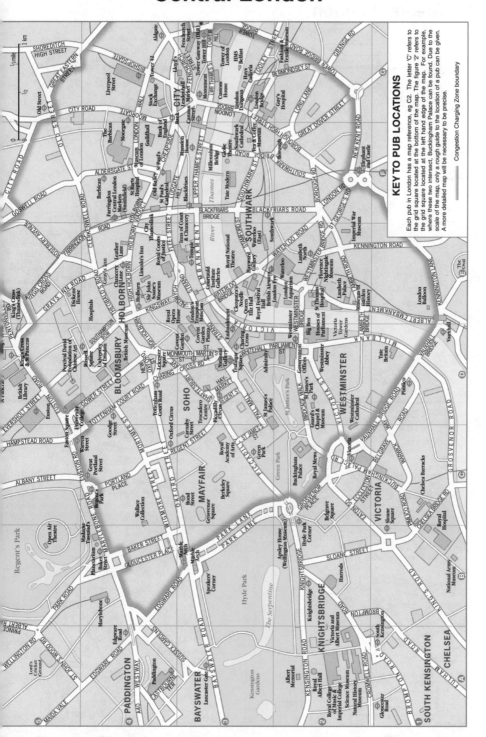

Index

F = Seafood Symbol

Index

Index

Index

Index

Index

Index

Index

Index

The Automobile Association would like to thank the following agencies and establishments for their assistance in the preparation of this book.

George III Hotel Dolgellau 1, 12; Nova Development Corp 2, 19t; Queen's Head, Hawkshead 3, 4; The King's Head, Masham 5, 8; The White Lion, Bourton 6, 9; Michael Joseph/Penguin Publicity Dept (copyright Harry Borden) 11; The Hoste Arms, Burnham Market 13t, 16b; Percy's Restaurant, Virginstowe 16t; The Plockton Inn, Plockton 17t; Caesars Arms, Creigiau 17b; The Boars Head, Ardington 360t; Yorkshire Bridge Inn, Bamford 117t; The Blewbury Inn, Blewbury 364t; The Catherine Wheel, Bibury 190t; The White Hart Inn, Bouth 91t; Castle Inn, Chiddingstone 259t; The Shireburn Arms, Clitheroe 277t; The Sun Inn, Craven Arms 392b; The Compasses Inn, Damerham 218t; The Blue Lion, East Witton 532t; The Castle Inn, Edgehill 487t; The Ram Inn, Firle 462t; The Falcon Inn, Fotheringhay 338t; The Royal Oak, Fritham 229b; The Halzephron Inn, Gunwalloe 73t; The Stag and Huntsman, Hambledon 41t; Dipton Mill Inn, Hexham 348t; The Swan, Hungerford 29b; Howard Arms, Ilminton 491b; The Angel, Lavenham 435b; Ye Olde Royal Oake Inn, Leek 429b; Harp Inn, Llandwrog 615t; Cain Valley Hotel, Llanfyllin 630t; The Seven Stars, London 298t, 298b; Masons Arms, Louth 295t; The Fox, Lower Oddington 203t; Dartmoor Inn, Lydford 144t; Rising Sun Inn, Lynmouth 146t; The Bridge Inn, Ratho 579t, 579b; Rose and Crown, Romaldkirk 174t; White Horse Farm Hotel, Rosedale Abbey 555t; The Bell at Sapperton, Sapperton 187t; Shieldaig Bar, Shieldaig 587b; The Boat Inn, Stoke Bruerne 345t; Saracens Head Inn, Symonds Yat 243t, 243b; Titchwell Manor, Titchwell 320t; The Fountain Inn, Wells 405t; The Ship Inn, Wincle 63t, 63b

The remaining photographs are held in the Association's own library (AA WORLD TRAVEL LIBRARY) with contributions from: AA Engraving 13b; Martyn Adelman 25t; Peter Baker 129t, 129b; Vic and Stewart Bates 29t; M Birkitt 290t, 295b, 338b, 343b, 345b; Derek Croucher 630b; Steve Day 187b, 190b, 203b, 364b; Robert Eames 532b; Derek Forss 35t, 35b, 160b, 218b, 259b, 451t; T Griffiths 227b; A J Hopkins 174b; Caroline Jones 41b, 146b, 398b, 105b; Andrew Lawson 73b; Cameron Lees 91b; Tom Mackie 320b; S & O Mathews 392t, 435t; John Millar 473t, 273b; Colin Molyneaux 343t; John Morrison 555b; Rich Newton 429t; Neil Ray 160t; Tony Souter 18bl, 19b, 229t; Forbes Stephenson 18t; Martin Trelawny 462b; Andrew Tryner 117b; Wyn Voysey 25b, 360t, 398t; Harry Williams 144b, 620t; Peter Wilson 565t; Stephen Whitehorne 587t; Jon Wyand 290b

Readers' Report Form

Please send this form to:
   Editor, The Pub Guide,
   Lifestyle Guides,
   The Automobile Association,
   Fanum House,
   Basingstoke RG21 4EA

Readers'
Report form

   or fax: 01256 491647
   or e-mail: lifestyleguides@theAA.com

Please use this form to tell us about any pub or inn you have visited, whether it is in the guide or not currently listed. We are interested in the quality of food, the selection of beers and the overall ambience of the establishment.

Feedback from readers helps us to keep our guide accurate and up to date. However, if you have a complaint to make during a visit, we do recommend that you discuss the matter with the pub management there and then, so that they have a chance to put things right before your visit is spoilt.

Please note that the AA does not undertake to arbitrate between you and the pub management, or to obtain compensation or engage in protracted correspondence.

Date: ....

Your name (block capitals) ....

Your address (block capitals) ....

....

....

.... Post Code.....................

e-mail address: ....

Name of pub: ....

Location ....

Comments ....

....

....

....

(please attach a separate sheet if necessary)

Readers' Report Form

	YES	NO
Have you bought this guide before?	☐	☐

Do you regularly use any other pub, accommodation or food guides?
If yes, which ones?

....

....

What do you find most useful about The AA Pub Guide?

....

....

....

....

Do you read the editorial features in the guide?..

Do you use the location atlas? ....

Have you tried any of the walks included in this guide?..............................

Is there any other information you would like to see added to this guide?

....

....

....

....

....

What are your main reasons for visiting pubs (tick all that apply)

food	☐	business	☐	accommodation	☐
beer	☐	celebrations	☐	entertainment	☐
atmosphere	☐	leisure	☐	other	....

How often do you visit a pub for a meal?

more than once a week	☐
one a week	☐
once a fortnight	☐
once a month	☐
once in six months	☐